The Cambridge Handbook of Spanish Linguistics

A state-of-the-art, in-depth survey of the topics, approaches, and theories in Spanish linguistics today, in which the language is researched from a number of different perspectives. This *Handbook* surveys the major advances and findings, with a special focus on recent achievements in the field. It provides an accurate and complete overview of research, as well as facilitating future directions. It encourages the reader to make connections between chapters and the parts into which they are organized, and promotes cross-theoretical dialogue. The contributions are by a wide range of specialists, writing on topics including corpus linguistics, phonology and phonetics, morphosyntax, pragmatics, the role of the speaker and speech context, language acquisition, and grammaticalization. This is a must-have volume for researchers looking to contextualize their own research and for students seeking a one-stop resource on Spanish linguistics.

KIMBERLY L. GEESLIN is Professor in the Department of Spanish and Portuguese at Indiana University.

CAMBRIDGE HANDBOOKS IN LANGUAGE AND LINGUISTICS

Genuinely broad in scope, each handbook in this series provides a complete state-of-the-field overview of a major sub-discipline within language study and research. Grouped into broad thematic areas, the chapters in each volume encompass the most important issues and topics within each subject, offering a coherent picture of the latest theories and findings. Together, the volumes will build into an integrated overview of the discipline in its entirety.

Published titles

The Cambridge Handbook of Phonology, edited by Paul de Lacy
The Cambridge Handbook of Linguistic Code-switching, edited by Barbara E. Bullock and Almeida Jacqueline Toribio
The Cambridge Handbook of Child Language, Second Edition, edited by Edith L. Bavin and Letitia Naigles
The Cambridge Handbook of Endangered Languages, edited by Peter K. Austin and Julia Sallabank
The Cambridge Handbook of Sociolinguistics, edited by Rajend Mesthrie
The Cambridge Handbook of Pragmatics, edited by Keith Allan and Kasia M. Jaszczolt
The Cambridge Handbook of Language Policy, edited by Bernard Spolsky
The Cambridge Handbook of Second Language Acquisition, edited by Julia Herschensohn and Martha Young-Scholten
The Cambridge Handbook of Biolinguistics, edited by Cedric Boeckx and Kleanthes K. Grohmann
The Cambridge Handbook of Generative Syntax, edited by Marcel den Dikken
The Cambridge Handbook of Communication Disorders, edited by Louise Cummings
The Cambridge Handbook of Stylistics, edited by Peter Stockwell and Sara Whiteley
The Cambridge Handbook of Linguistic Anthropology, edited by N. J. Enfield, Paul Kockelman and Jack Sidnell
The Cambridge Handbook of English Corpus Linguistics, edited by Douglas Biber and Randi Reppen
The Cambridge Handbook of Bilingual Processing, edited by John W. Schwieter
The Cambridge Handbook of Learner Corpus Research, edited by Sylviane Granger, Gaëtanelle Gilquin and Fanny Meunier
The Cambridge Handbook of Linguistic Multicompetence, edited by Li Wei and Vivian Cook
The Cambridge Handbook of English Historical Linguistics, edited by Merja Kytö and Päivi Pahta
The Cambridge Handbook of Formal Semantics, edited by Maria Aloni and Paul Dekker
The Cambridge Handbook of Morphology, edited by Andrew Hippisley and Greg Stump
The Cambridge Handbook of Historical Syntax, edited by Adam Ledgeway and Ian Roberts
The Cambridge Handbook of Linguistic Typology, edited by Alexandra Y. Aikhenvald and R. M. W. Dixon
The Cambridge Handbook of Areal Linguistics, edited by Raymond Hickey
The Cambridge Handbook of Cognitive Linguistics, edited by Barbara Dancygier
The Cambridge Handbook of Japanese Linguistics, edited by Yoko Hasegawa
The Cambridge Handbook of Spanish Linguistics, edited by Kimberly L. Geeslin

The Cambridge Handbook of Spanish Linguistics

Edited by
Kimberly L. Geeslin

Shaftesbury Road, Cambridge CB2 8EA, United Kingdom

One Liberty Plaza, 20th Floor, New York, NY 10006, USA

477 Williamstown Road, Port Melbourne, VIC 3207, Australia

314–321, 3rd Floor, Plot 3, Splendor Forum, Jasola District Centre, New Delhi – 110025, India

103 Penang Road, #05–06/07, Visioncrest Commercial, Singapore 238467

Cambridge University Press is part of Cambridge University Press & Assessment, a department of the University of Cambridge.

We share the University's mission to contribute to society through the pursuit of education, learning and research at the highest international levels of excellence.

www.cambridge.org
Information on this title: www.cambridge.org/9781316626764

DOI: 10.1017/9781316779194

© Cambridge University Press & Assessment 2018

This publication is in copyright. Subject to statutory exception and to the provisions of relevant collective licensing agreements, no reproduction of any part may take place without the written permission of Cambridge University Press & Assessment.

First published 2018
First paperback edition 2024

A catalogue record for this publication is available from the British Library

Library of Congress Cataloging-in-Publication data
Names: Geeslin, Kimberly L. editor.
Title: The Cambridge handbook of Spanish linguistics / edited by Kimberly L. Geeslin.
Description: Cambridge ; New York, NY : Cambridge University Press, 2018. | Series: Cambridge handbooks in language and linguistics | Includes bibliographical references and index.
Identifiers: LCCN 2017046826 | ISBN 9781107174825 (hardback)
Subjects: LCSH: Spanish language. | BISAC: FOREIGN LANGUAGE STUDY / General.
Classification: LCC PC4025 .C35 2018 | DDC 460–dc23
LC record available at https://lccn.loc.gov/2017046826

ISBN 978-1-107-17482-5 Hardback
ISBN 978-1-316-62676-4 Paperback

Cambridge University Press & Assessment has no responsibility for the persistence or accuracy of URLs for external or third-party internet websites referred to in this publication and does not guarantee that any content on such websites is, or will remain, accurate or appropriate.

To Patty, Kippy, Mom and Dad, for the constant love and support
To Logan and Hayden, for pushing me to learn new things and making me laugh
   and
To Sean, for your love, perspective and partnership

Contents

List of Figures	page ix
List of Tables	xiii
List of Contributors	xv
Acknowledgements	xxi
Abbreviations	xxv

Introduction *Kimberly L. Geeslin*	1
Part I Theories and Approaches to Spanish Linguistics	7
1 Generative Linguistics: Syntax *Paula Kempchinsky*	9
2 Optimality Theory and Spanish/Hispanic Linguistics *D. Eric Holt*	31
3 Usage-Based Approaches to Spanish Linguistics *Esther L. Brown*	52
4 Functional-Typological Approaches to Hispanic Linguistics *Rosa Vallejos*	72
5 Psycholinguistic Approaches to Hispanic Linguistics *Tania Leal and Christine Shea*	95
6 Corpus Approaches to the Study of Language, Variation, and Change *Manuel Díaz-Campos and Juan Escalona Torres*	121
Part II The Spanish Sound System	143
7 Vowels *Rebecca Ronquest*	145
8 Consonants *Rebeka Campos-Astorkiza*	165
9 The Syllable *Alfonso Morales-Front*	190
10 Prosody: Stress, Rhythm, and Intonation *Pilar Prieto and Paolo Roseano*	211
11 Speech Perception *Amanda Boomershine and Ji Young Kim*	237

Contents

Part III Spanish Morphosyntax and Meaning   259
12 Word Phenomena: Category Definition and Word
    Formation *Antonio Fábregas*   261
13 Properties of Pronominal Subjects *Pekka Posio*   286
14 Properties of the Verb Phrase: Argument Structure, Ellipsis,
    and Negation *Iván Ortega-Santos*   307
15 Properties of the Extended Verb Phrase: Agreement, the
    Structure of INFL, and Subjects *Julio Villa-García*   329
16 Properties of Nominal Expressions *M. Emma Ticio Quesada*   351
17 Information Structure *Laura Domínguez*   372
18 Syntax and its Interfaces *Timothy Gupton*   392
19 Lexis *Grant Armstrong*   415
20 Pragmatics *Maria Hasler-Barker*   437

Part IV Spanish in Social, Geographic, and Historical Contexts   457
21 Spanish in Contact with Other Languages and Bilingualism
    across the Spanish-Speaking World *Lotfi Sayahi*   459
22 Spanish as a Heritage Language in the US: Core Issues and
    Future Directions *Diego Pascual y Cabo*   478
23 Geographic Varieties of Spanish *Elena Fernández de
    Molina Ortés and Juan M. Hernández-Campoy*   496
24 Sociolinguistic Approaches to Dialectal, Sociolectal, and
    Idiolectal Variation in the Hispanophone World *Daniel Erker*   529
25 National and Diasporic Spanish Varieties as Evidence of Ethnic
    Affiliations *Almeida Jacqueline Toribio*   563
26 Current Perspectives on Historical Linguistics *Patrícia Amaral*   582
27 Grammaticalization *Chad Howe*   603

Part V The Acquisition of Spanish   625
28 Child Language Acquisition *Anna Gavarró*   627
29 Theories of Second Language Acquisition *Bill VanPatten*   649
30 The Acquisition of Second Language Spanish
    Sounds *Megan Solon*   668
31 The Acquisition of Second Language Spanish
    Morphosyntax *Jason Rothman, Jorge González Alonso,
    and David Miller*   689
32 Variation in Second Language Spanish *Matthew Kanwit*   716
33 Third Language Acquisition *Jennifer Cabrelli Amaro
    and Michael Iverson*   737

Index   758

Figures

1.1	The early Principles and Parameters framework	page 13
1.2	Minimalist Program (Chomsky 1993, 1995)	15
1.3	A simplified structure for the derivation of *Juan padece amnesia* 'John suffers from amnesia'	16
2.1	Strictness bands of NoCoda and Max following Hayes' (2000) model (from Cutillas Espinosa 2004)	38
3.1	Spanish ~ English bilingual lexicon	64
5.1	Cognitive processes involved in lexical access	97
7.1	Articulatory classification of Spanish vowels	146
7.2	Acoustic distribution of Spanish vowels: mean formant values of male speakers of Spanish	146
9.1	Depiction of prosodic hierarchy in Selkirk (1986)	191
9.2	Model of syllabic structure	192
9.3	Moraic view of the syllable	192
9.4	Moraic view of short and long vowels	193
9.5	Example representations of moraic structure	193
9.6	Structure of intermediate templates	193
9.7	Examples of sonority sequencing	195
9.8	Depiction of typical sonority scale	195
9.9	Maximum Onset Principle (Kahn 1976)	199
10.1	Prosodic features of the imperative question ¿*Callaréis?* 'Will you be quiet?' as uttered by a speaker of southern Peninsular Spanish	218
10.2	F0 contour, spectrogram, orthographic transcription, and prosodic annotation of the broad focus statement *Bebe una limonada* 'He/she's drinking a [his/her] lemonade' in Castilian Spanish	222
10.3	F0 contour, spectrogram, orthographic transcription, and prosodic annotation of the broad focus statement *Me encantó la película* 'I loved the film' as uttered by a speaker of Mexican Spanish	223

10.4 F0 contour, spectrogram, orthographic transcription, and prosodic annotation of the narrow focus statement *No, de LIMONES* 'No, [I want a kilo] of LEMONS' as uttered by a speaker of Castilian Spanish — 224

10.5 F0 contour, spectrogram, orthographic transcription, and prosodic annotation of the statement of the obvious *Sí, mujer, ¡de Guillermo!* '[It's] Guillermo's [of course]!' as uttered by a speaker of Castilian Spanish — 225

10.6 F0 contour, spectrogram, orthographic transcription, and prosodic annotation of the uncertainty statement *Puede que no le guste el regalo que le he comprado . . .* 'S/he may not like the gift I have bought him/her' as uttered by a speaker of Castilian Spanish — 226

10.7 F0 contour, spectrogram, orthographic transcription, and prosodic annotation of the information-seeking yes–no question *¿Tiene mermelada?* 'Do you have any jam?' as uttered by a speaker of Castilian Spanish — 227

10.8 F0 contour, spectrogram, orthographic transcription, and prosodic annotation of the information-seeking yes–no question *¿Hay reunión mañana?* 'Is there a meeting tomorrow?' as uttered by a speaker of Puerto Rican Spanish — 227

10.9 F0 contour, spectrogram, orthographic transcription, and prosodic annotation of the information-seeking yes–no question *¿Tienen mandarinas?* 'Do you have any tangerines?' as uttered by a speaker of Argentine Spanish — 228

10.10 F0 contour, spectrogram, orthographic transcription, and prosodic annotation of the confirmation question *¿Tienes frío?* 'Are you cold?' as uttered by a speaker of Castilian Spanish — 228

10.11 F0 contour, spectrogram, orthographic transcription, and prosodic annotation of the echo question *¿Las nueve?* 'Nine o'clock?' as uttered by a speaker of Castilian Spanish — 229

10.12 F0 contour, spectrogram, orthographic transcription, and prosodic annotation of the information-seeking *wh*-question *¿De dónde has llegado?* 'Where have you arrived from?' as uttered by a speaker of Castilian Spanish — 230

10.13 F0 contour, spectrogram, orthographic transcription, and prosodic annotation of the command *¡Ven!* 'Come here!' as uttered by a speaker of Castilian Spanish — 231

10.14 F0 contour, spectrogram, orthographic transcription, and prosodic annotation of the cajoling imperative request *Va, vente al cine, ¡hombre!* 'Come on, come to the cinema, man!' as uttered by a speaker of Castilian Spanish — 231

10.15	F0 contour, spectrogram, orthographic transcription, and prosodic annotation of the call ¡Marina! 'Marina!' uttered with the common calling contour	232
10.16	F0 contour, spectrogram, orthographic transcription, and prosodic annotation of the insistent call ¡¡Marina!! 'Marina!!'	232
15.1	V-to-T movement	331
15.2	Subjects in Spec,AgrSP/TP	341
15.3	Subjects in Spec,CP	342
16.1	Graphic illustration of Determiner Phrase	352
16.2	Structural positions for different quantifiers and determiners	363
18.1	VP assignation of Agent theta-role	394
18.2	Syntactic hierarchy with AspP between VP and TP	395
18.3	Mapping of theta-roles to arguments	396
18.4	Analysis of psychological predicates	397
18.5	Proposed hierarchy for the pronoun SE	398
18.6	"Big DP" proposal for languages with morphologically-rich verb agreement	400
18.7	Position of preverbal subjects as Ā constituents	400
18.8	Two morphology-related functional projections between the NP and the DP	401
18.9	Adjective–noun order in *un mero accidente* 'a mere accident'	402
18.10	Adjective–noun order in *la teoría sintáctica esa* 'that syntactic theory'	402
18.11	Corrective contrast constituents in Spec,FocP	405
18.12	[F] as a derived phrase marker	407
18.13	Simplified left-peripheral syntax model	408
23.1	Geographical distribution of Spanish in the world	497
23.2	Geographical distribution of *seseo* and *ceceo* in Andalusia	505
23.3	Southern European Spanish eight-vowel system	507
23.4	Tree model of Hispano-Romance varieties	511
23.5	Main dialect/**language** areas in Spain	512
23.6	European varieties of Spanish	512
23.7	Geographical varieties in Andalusian Spanish	513
23.8	Spanish-speaking areas in America	515
23.9	American varieties of Spanish	516
23.10	Asian and African varieties of Spanish	517
24.1a	Rates of referential use of *le* and *la* across three provinces in Castilla la Vieja	544
24.1b	Rates of referential use of *le* and *la* across three provinces in Castilla la Vieja: *intra*-provincial variation along lines of social class	544
24.2	Degrees of difference between females and males across the lifespan for word-final /s/ and intervocalic /d/	546
24.3	Boxplots showing voicing rates	549
24.4a	Subject pronoun rates of 140 speakers in New York City	551

24.4b	Subject pronoun rates of 140 speakers in New York City – Caribbeans and Mainlanders	552
24.5a	Duration and center of gravity of coda /s/ for 20 speakers in New York City	554
24.5b	Duration and center of gravity of coda /s/ for 20 speakers in New York City – *Newcomers* compared to *Longtime residents*	555

Tables

2.1	Illustration of Optimality Theory tableau	*page* 32
3.1	Syllable-initial /s/ reduction in New Mexican Spanish	63
4.1	Parameters of transitivity as adapted from Hopper and Thompson (1980)	81
6.1	Distribution of periphrastic future and morphological future across regions	133
6.2	Distribution of modal MF and temporal MF between regions	134
6.3	Contribution of linguistic and extralinguistic factors selected as significant predictor of PF across two data sets	135
8.1	Main Spanish consonant phonemes	166
8.2	Neutralization of stop voicing contrast in coda position	169
9.1	Complexity of the Spanish syllable	194
10.1	Schematic representation, Sp_ToBI labels, and phonetic descriptions of the most common pitch accents in Spanish	219
10.2	Schematic representation, Sp_ToBI labels, and phonetic descriptions of the most common boundary tones in Spanish	220
12.1	Word formation processes with category change (sample)	276
12.2	Word formation processes involving semantic change, but no category change (sample)	277
13.1	Variation in subject expression	287
13.2	Type of reference and subject expression in second-person singular	297
18.1	Nuclear pitch accent contours for Italian and German by topic type	409
23.1	Salient features in innovative and conservative varieties of Spanish spoken in Spain	502

23.2	Realization of intervocalic /ð/ in European and American Spanishes	504
23.3	Realization of postvocalic /s/ in European and American Spanishes	506
23.4	Examples of neutralization of distinction between liquid consonants	508
23.5	Examples of regressive assimilation in consonant clusters in word-medial position	509
23.6	Phonotactics of southern varieties of European Spanish in word-final position	509
23.7	Word-final /s/ in person marking	510
23.8	Usage rates (percent) of the subjunctive past perfect forms in Spanish	514
24.1	Pronoun rates (percent) for three generational groups in New York City	550
25.1	Characteristics of Hispanics with origins in Puerto Rico, Cuba, and the Dominican Republic	566
27.1	Development of the periphrastic and simple past in Romance Languages	607
27.2	Factor weights for temporal reference of present perfect across three centuries (Peninsular Spanish)	616

Contributors

Patrícia Amaral (Ph.D., The Ohio State University, 2007) is Assistant Professor of Hispanic Linguistics in the Department of Spanish and Portuguese at Indiana University. Her areas of research include syntactic and semantic change, Romance linguistics, and language contact.

Grant Armstrong is Assistant Professor in the Department of Spanish and Portuguese at the University of Wisconsin-Madison. His research focuses on the lexicon, morphology, and syntax of Spanish and Yucatec Maya.

Amanda Boomershine is Associate Professor of Spanish at the University of North Carolina, Wilmington, where she teaches courses in Hispanic linguistics, service-learning (community-based or community-engaged *learning*), and seminars on topics such as immigration and linguistic variation.

Esther L. Brown is Associate Professor of Hispanic Linguistics in the Department of Spanish and Portuguese at the University of Colorado, Boulder. Her research centers on usage-based approaches to phonological variation and change.

Jennifer Cabrelli Amaro is Assistant Professor of Spanish Linguistics at the University of Illinois at Chicago. Her research centers on adult phonological acquisition and attrition, and current work examines longitudinal phonological and morphosyntactic development in third language acquisition.

Rebeka Campos-Astorkiza is Associate Professor at The Ohio State University. She works on phonetics and phonology, both from a theoretical and an experimental perspective. Her work illustrates how phonetic data can help us develop theoretical models to explain sound patterns. In addition, she is interested in second language acquisition of phonology and sociophonetics.

Manuel Díaz-Campos is Full Professor of Hispanic Sociolinguistics at Indiana University. He has published on the acquisition of sociolinguistic variables in L1, sociolinguistics including phonological and morphosyntactic variation, acquisition of second language phonology, and topics in Spanish laboratory phonology.

Laura Domínguez is Associate Professor at the University of Southampton (UK). Her research interests lie in the areas of syntactic theory (syntax and its interfaces, information structure, Hispanic linguistics) and language development (first and second language acquisition, bilingualism, and language attrition). Her investigations have centered on the analysis of information structure and focus, in particular how word order in Spanish is affected by both prosodic and syntactic constraints. She is the co-director of the SPLLOC project (www.splloc.soton.ac.uk/) and her research has appeared in *Second Language Research, Lingua, Linguistic Approaches to Bilingualism, Bilingualism: Language and Cognition, The International Journal of Bilingualism*, and *Language Acquisition*.

Daniel Erker is Assistant Professor of Spanish and Linguistics at Boston University. His research focuses on language variation, contact, and change, especially in Spanish spoken in the United States. He is the director of the Spanish in Boston Project.

Juan Escalona Torres is currently a Ph.D. student of Spanish and Portuguese at Indiana University. He works with language variation and change with a special focus on the semantic and pragmatic factors that contribute to the evolution of language.

Antonio Fábregas (Ph.D. in linguistics, Universidad Autónoma de Madrid, 2005) is Full Professor of Hispanic Linguistics at UiT–Arctic University of Norway. His research concentrates on Spanish morphology and its syntactic analysis.

Elena Fernández de Molina Ortés is a Lecturer in Spanish sociolinguistics and dialectology at the University of Granada. She is a specialist in linguistic variation in the dialect of Extremadura and the presence of regional features in social networks.

Anna Gavarró obtained her doctorate at the University of Edinburgh and is Full Professor of Linguistics at the Universitat Autònoma de Barcelona. Her work has been published in several international journals, and she is also the author of a chapter in the authoritative grammar of contemporary Catalan.

Jorge González Alonso is a postdoctoral researcher in the LAVA group (Language Acquisition, Variation and Attrition) at UiT–Arctic University of Norway. His research interests include different types of bilingual and multilingual acquisition, with a particular focus on the acquisition and processing of morphology and morphosyntax by non-native speakers. He has worked with speakers of Spanish, Basque, English, Russian, and Polish, and is currently conducting research on the acquisition of Spanish as a third or further language. Recent studies have appeared in the journals *Second Language Research, International Journal of Bilingualism*, and *Frontiers in Psychology*.

Timothy Gupton is Associate Professor of Spanish Linguistics at the University of Georgia. His research focuses on the proposed model of elements that precede the verb in the speaker's mind among mono- and multilingual speakers of Western Iberian Romance.

Maria Hasler-Barker is Assistant Professor of Spanish at Sam Houston State University. Her work focuses primarily on interlanguage pragmatics and instruction of pragmatics. She also examines service encounters in public institutions.

Juan M. Hernández-Campoy is Professor in English Sociolinguistics at the University of Murcia. His books include *Sociolinguistic Styles* (2016), *Style-Shifting in Public* (with J. A. Cutillas-Espinosa, 2012), *The Handbook of Historical Sociolinguistics* (with J. C. Conde-Silvestre, 2012), *Diccionario de Sociolingüística* (with P. Trudgill, 2007), and *Metodología de la Investigación Sociolingüística* (with M. Almeida, 2005).

D. Eric Holt is Associate Professor of Spanish and Linguistics at the University of South Carolina. His scholarly work treats phonological theory, language variation and change, Hispanic sociolinguistics, and language acquisition. Among his publications is *Optimality Theory and Language Change* (Kluwer, 2003).

Chad Howe is Associate Professor of Hispanic Linguistics in the Department of Romance Languages at the University of Georgia. His primary areas of research include language variation and change and sociolinguistics, mainly from a grammaticalization perspective.

Michael Iverson is a Lecturer in Second Language Studies at Indiana University. His research investigates the knowledge of morphosyntax in bi- and multilingualism, with current work focusing on the acquisition and development of syntax and semantics in a third language.

Matthew Kanwit is Assistant Professor of Hispanic Linguistics in the Department of Linguistics at the University of Pittsburgh. He researches first and second language morphosyntactic variation and the effect of study abroad on the acquisition of variation. His research combines variationist and functional, concept-oriented approaches.

Paula Kempchinsky is on the faculty of the Department of Spanish and Portuguese and the Department of Linguistics at the University of Iowa. Her research program is focused on the syntactic analysis of Spanish and other Romance languages, with particular interest in subjunctive clauses, constructions with the reflexive clitic SE, and the clausal left periphery. She also collaborates on research projects on syntactic acquisition in second languages, from the perspective of generative linguistics.

Ji Young Kim is Assistant Professor in Spanish linguistics in the Department of Spanish and Portuguese at the University of California, Los Angeles. Her research focuses on how Spanish heritage speakers in the US perceive and produce speech sounds in Spanish.

Tania Leal is Assistant Professor at the University of Nevada, Reno, and she received her Ph.D. in Second Language Acquisition (specialization in linguistics) from the University of Iowa. She studies how L2 learners and heritage speakers acquire and process syntactic, pragmatic, and morphological phenomena. Her work has appeared in *Lingua, Studies in Second Language Acquisition, Language Acquisition, LAB,* and *Applied Linguistics.*

David Miller is a Ph.D. student at the University of Reading (UK) and a member of the University of Reading Psycholinguistics and Neurolinguistics Lab. His research interests are second language acquisition, bi- and multilingualism, as well as native language attrition. He has worked on Spanish, German, English, Catalan, and Turkish using electroencephalography/event-related potentials (EEG/ERP), eye-tracking, and self-paced reading methodologies. Currently, he is working on methodological approaches to testing scalar implicatures in native Spanish, as well as the psycholinguistic basis for native language attrition testing this same phenomenon. Recent studies have appeared in *Journal of Experimental Psychology: Learning, Memory and Cognition, International Journal of Bilingual Education and Bilingualism,* and *Linguistic Approaches to Bilingualism.*

Alfonso Morales-Front is Associate Professor in the Department of Spanish and Portuguese at Georgetown University. His research interests focus on prosodic aspects of Spanish phonology (syllable, stress, and intonation); on the acquisition of L1 and L2 phonology; and study abroad.

Iván Ortega-Santos is Associate Professor at the University of Memphis. He focuses on Spanish syntax with an emphasis on information structure, locality, and microvariation. His book *Focus-Related Operations at the Right Edge in Spanish: Subjects and Ellipsis* has been published by John Benjamins.

Diego Pascual y Cabo is Assistant Professor and Director of the Spanish Heritage Language Program at the University of Florida, where he teaches courses related to heritage speaker bilingualism. Diego's work on this topic on has appeared in journals such as *Foreign Language Annals, Applied Linguistics, Linguistic Approaches to Bilingualism,* and *Heritage Language Journal* (among others).

Pekka Posio is Associate Professor of Spanish at the University of Stockholm. His research interests include contrastive syntax and pragmatics, variable subject expression in Spanish and Portuguese, human impersonal constructions, and other ways of referring to human participants in spoken discourse.

Pilar Prieto is an ICREA (Catalan Institution for Research and Advanced Studies) Research Professor at the Department of Translation and Language Sciences at the Pompeu Fabra University in Barcelona. Her main research interests revolve around prosody, facial and manual gestures, and language acquisition.

Rebecca Ronquest is Assistant Professor of Spanish Linguistics at North Carolina State University. Her main research interests include the Spanish vowel system, the phonetic/phonological systems of heritage speakers of Spanish, and Spanish in the Southeastern United States.

Paolo Roseano is a linguist working at the University of Barcelona (Phonetics Laboratory and Department of Modern Languages and Literatures and of English Studies) and at the University of South Africa (Department of Linguistics and Modern Languages). His research interests include the prosody of Romance languages, language contact, and morphology.

Jason Rothman is Professor of Multilingualism and Language Development in the school of Psychology and Clinical Language Sciences at the University of Reading (UK) as well as a Professor II of Linguistics at UiT–Arctic University of Norway. His research program examines the acquisition and processing of (mainly) morphosyntax and semantics in various types of bilinguals (children and adults) and monolinguals. In addition to work on languages such as Turkish, Greek, Swedish, German, and more, he has carried out extensive research in the acquisition and processing of Spanish and Portuguese. He is editor of the journal *Linguistic Approaches to Bilingualism* as well as the long-running book series *Studies in Bilingualism (SiBIL)*. Recent studies have appeared in the journals *Language, Cognition and Neuroscience*, *Studies in Second Language Acquisition*, and *Bilingualism: Language and Cognition*.

Lotfi Sayahi is Professor of Linguistics in the Hispanic Studies Program in the Department of Languages, Literatures, and Cultures at the University at Albany, State University of New York. His research focuses on Spanish in contact with other languages.

Christine Shea is Assistant Professor of Spanish Linguistics in the Spanish and Portuguese Department at the University of Iowa. She researches speech perception and production, focusing on links between the development of a sound system and the lexicon. Dr. Shea's main area of research has been on the role of variability in the acquisition of a new phonological system. She conducts research with all types of bilingual Spanish speakers, native and non-native.

Megan Solon is Assistant Professor of Spanish Linguistics at the University at Albany, State University of New York. Her research focuses on second language Spanish and the acquisition of phonetics and phonology. Her publications have appeared in journals such as *Studies in Second Language Acquisition*, *Studies in Hispanic and Lusophone Linguistics*, and *Hispania*.

M. Emma Ticio Quesada is Associate Professor of Spanish and Linguistics at Syracuse University. Her theoretical research has focused on the syntactic properties of Romance languages, particularly Spanish. She has examined the structure of nominal expressions, the cliticization and ellipsis processes, the optionality of movement and its locality, and the argument/adjunct distinction. She has compiled Spanish–English longitudinal databases to support research on Spanish–English bilingualism, and she has conducted research on Bilingual First Language Acquisition.

Her research has appeared in several journals, edited volumes, and a research monograph.

Almeida Jacqueline Toribio is Professor of Linguistics in the Department of Spanish and Portuguese at the University of Texas. Her research program follows two lines of inquiry: One thread addresses the morphosyntactic and phonetic patterning of code-switching among diverse bilingual populations. A second line of study examines the speech of Dominicans in national and US diasporic settings, recording the incidence and dissemination of linguistic features that serve important functions as indices of ethnicity, race, and gender, among other variables. Dr. Toribio's investigations are informed by insights from disciplines in the humanities and social sciences and draw on diverse approaches in examining individuals' speech and representative datasets, to include field and laboratory as well as corpus linguistic methods.

Rosa Vallejos is Associate Professor of Linguistics at the University of New Mexico. Interested in language contact in Amazonia, she conducts documentary-fieldwork on Kukama-Kukamiria, Secoya, and Amazonian Spanish. Her publications include *A Grammar of Kukama-Kukamiria* (2016) and *Diccionario kukama-kukamiria/castellano* (2015).

Bill VanPatten is former Professor at Michigan State University and currently an independent scholar. He is widely known for his work on both second language acquisition and second language instruction from linguistic and psycholinguistic perspectives.

Julio Villa-García is a permanent Lecturer in Spanish Linguistics and Syntax at the University of Manchester (UK). His Ph.D. from the University of Connecticut (2012) concentrated on Spanish syntax and language acquisition. He is the author of a number of peer-reviewed publications.

Acknowledgements

More than most other projects, edited volumes require a team effort. The authors who contributed to this volume have been highly responsive, engaging, and good willed, and have produced amazing work in a short period of time. I am grateful for their collaboration, their questions, their suggestions and ultimately for the care and attention each paid to their individual contribution. There is some risk in identifying authors through their work, rather than through a prior personal connection but, in so doing, I believe the contents of this volume are a testament that the risk has paid off. The chapters are uniformly excellent and represent the leading edge of each sub-field included and, through the process of cross-referencing and planning, new collaborations have been established that will further enhance inquiry across fields. I wish to express my heartfelt thanks to each and every author who contributed to the *Handbook*.

Every volume begins with a dialogue between a handful of people, but the ultimate quality of the final product depends heavily on the input from many others. I am grateful to the anonymous reviewers of the original proposal, whose comments helped to delimit the scope of the volume even further. Additionally, I am indebted to the many colleagues who agreed to review individual chapters, providing helpful feedback for the authors along the way, often at a record pace. These reviewers are listed here in recognition of the important service they have provided:

Jessi Aaron
Patrícia Amaral
Mark Amengual
Meghan Armstrong-Abrami
Sonia Barnes
Silvina Bongiovanni

Melissa Bowles
María José Cabrera-Puche
José Camacho
María Cristina Cuervo
Lori Czerwionka
Justin Davidson
Gibran Delgado-Díaz
Manuel Delicado Cantero
Antonio Fábregas
Timothy Face
Carolina González
John Grinstead
Tim Gupton
Manuel Gutiérrez
Daniel Jung
Matt Kanwit
Tania Leal
Bret Linford
Luis López
Kelley Lowther Pereira
Cristóbal Lozano
Jim Michnowicz
Joan C. Mora
Neil Myler
Chiyo Nishida
Erin O'Rourke
Rafael Orozco
Ana Pérez-Leroux
María Elena Placencia
Jorge Porcel
Margaret Quesada
Katherine Rehner
Marcos Rohena-Madrazo
Francisco Salgado-Robles
Elena Schoonmaker-Gates
Sandro Sessarego
Christine Shea
Alexandra Spalek
Gabriela Terrazas Duarte
Ellen Thompson
Natasha Tokowicz
Rena Torres Cacoullos
Catherine Travis
Jorge Valdés Kroff

Julio Villa-García
Mark Waltermire
Caroline Wiltshire
Karen Zagona
Sara Zahler

I am grateful to Andrew Winnard, Executive Publisher at Cambridge University Press, for his guidance on this project from start to finish. From our first coffee meeting in Indiana to the present, he has been upbeat and has provided sound advice and valuable feedback. I am also thankful to Editorial Assistant Stephanie Taylor, Content Manager Adam Hooper, and Copy-editor Virginia Catmur, for their support and attention to detail. These individuals, and likely many others that I do not know, have been immensely helpful and have kept the volume moving forward. In developing the proposal and addressing helpful reviewer comments, I leaned heavily on colleagues across several fields for their insider knowledge. Most especially, I am thankful to Tania Leal for her assistance and her willingness to talk through some of the most vexing challenges with me. In order to manage the work of this particular project, I have relied on the help of several research assistants during this time period to help with other professional demands. Whether directly or indirectly involved in the *Handbook*, each has made this project possible. During the timeframe of this project Silvina Bongiovanni, Danielle Daidone, Megan DiBartolomeo, Juan Escalona Torres, Carly Henderson, Dylan Jarrett, Daniel Jung, Tess Kuntz, Sean McKinnon, Ian Michalski, and Sara Zahler have all been instrumental in keeping me afloat!

In addition to the many research assistants named above, there is one individual who has been dedicated to this project from the very beginning and has seen it through to today. My research assistant, Travis Evans-Sago, has been involved in every step of the production of this volume and I am especially grateful to him. He has helped manage records, correspondence, the review process, multiple versions of papers, marketing materials, and each editorial task along the way. What is more, he has done this with good humor and genuine interest in the process and quality of the volume. Working with him has made the *Handbook* project infinitely more engaging and enjoyable.

In writing this I reflected on the last chance I had the opportunity to individually and publicly acknowledge those who support my efforts to produce worthwhile scholarship and to balance those demands against other responsibilities, personal and professional. Although those demands have changed, I was struck by how fortunate I am to have a steady, continuous network of support. In the Department of Spanish and Portuguese, several colleagues continue to provide leadership, research and professional support, and an atmosphere of collegiality that makes a demanding profession enjoyable. Likewise, I am fortunate to belong to a program in Hispanic Linguistics that is energetic, hard-working and flexible enough to move forward in changing times. I am most especially grateful for the support of family and friends outside the office. Without each of them, the work–life balance would cease to exist.

Kimberly L. Geeslin

Abbreviations

When necessary, linguistic concepts, such as variables and operators (e.g. "Move") are written with upper-case initials to distinguish them from lexical items.

-	prosody: for edge tones, association with utterance-internal phrase boundaries
#	infelicitous; semantically anomalous
%	acceptable to some speakers as completely grammatical, while rejected by others; prosody: for edge tones, association with final edges of utterances
*	preceding: unattested, ungrammatical; following: recursive; in prosody: for pitch accent, association with stressed syllable
°	head in a tree projection
2L1	early simultaneous bilingual
∅	empty/nothing
ΣP	sigma phrase
θ role	thematic role
φ	phonological phrase
φ features	semantic features of person, number, and gender
A	attributive adjective; argument; agent
Ā	non-argument
ACC	accusative
ADVM	adverbial marker
Agr; AGR	agreement
AgrP	agreement phrase
AgrSP	agreement subject phrase
AH	at-home (environment)
AL	artificial language
ALL	artificial language learning

AM	adjective marker; autosegmental-metrical
A-movement	argument movement
AMPER-ESP	*Atlas Multimédia de la Prosodie de l'Espace Roman*, Spanish section
AP	adjectival phrase; adjective projection
ASALE	Asociación de Academias de la Lengua Española
Asp°	head of aspect
AspP	aspectual projection
ATU	attraction to the unmarked
BI	break index/indices
BIA+	Bilingual Interactive Activation Plus model
BP	Brazilian Portuguese
BT	boundary tone
C	consonant; complementizer
c-command	constituent command
CDA	constraint demotion algorithm
CEM	cumulative enhancement model
C-I	conceptual-intentional system
CL	clitic
CLI	cross-linguistic influence
CLLD, CLLDed	clitic left-dislocation, clitic-left dislocated
CLRD	clitic right-dislocation
CMC	computer-mediated communication
COG	center of gravity
CP	complementizer phrase; complementizer projection
CS	computational system
D	determiner; distance
D/PM	declarative/procedural model
D°	determiner head
DAT	dative
Deg; DegP	degree; degree phrase
DIM	diminutive
D-linked	discourse-linked
DMAs	direct modifier adjectives
DO	direct object
DOM	differential/direct object marking
DP	determiner phrase; determiner projection
DPBE	delay of Principle B effect
DRAE	*Diccionario de la lengua española* (Real Academia Española)
D-structure	deep structure
ECM	exceptional case marking
EEG	electroencephalography
EPP	extended projection principle
ERP	event-related potential
ESL	English second language

ESR	emphatic/contrastive stress rule
EVP	extended verb phrase
EXP	expression; experiencer
F	focus; functional head
F0, F1, F2	fundamental frequency; first, second formant
FF	focus fronted contrast
FIN	finite verb
FocP	focus projection
FP	functional projection
FPR	focus prominence rule
FRC	frequency of use in a reducing context
FTA	face-threatening act
FUT	future
GB/P&P	Government and Binding/Principles and Parameters
GLA	gradual learning algorithm
H	high
HL	heritage language
HPSG	Head-driven Phrase Structure Grammar
HS	heritage language speaker
HTLD	hanging-topic left-dislocation
i	index
IMAs	indirect modifier adjectives
IMP	imperative
IMPF	imperfect
IMPFV	imperfective
INF	infinitive
INFL	inflection; the functional head that deals with inflection
IO	indirect object
ip	intermediate phrase
IP	inflectional phrase; intonation(al) phrase
IP/TP-EPP	inflectional phrase/ tense phrase-extended projection principle
IS	information structure
L	low
L1, L2, L3, L4	first, second, third, fourth language
LAH	lexical aspect hypothesis
LCS	lexical-conceptual structures
LDG	Lexical Decomposition Grammar
$LD_{w/oRP}$	left-dislocation without a resumptive pronoun
LE	linking element
LF	logical form
LFG	Lexical Functional Grammar
LI	lexical item
LPM	linguistic proximity model
MASC	masculine

MF	morphological future
MLU	mean length of utterance
MSp.	medieval Spanish
N	noun
NEG	negation
NegP	negation phrase
NM	noun marker
NMS	New Mexican Spanish
Nom_{exp}	largest structure containing (explicit or implicitly) a noun
NP	noun phrase; noun projection
NPI	negative polarity item
NS	native speaker
NSP	null subject parameter
NSR	nuclear stress rule
NumP	number phrase; number projection
n-word	negative word
O; OBJ	object
OBL	oblique
OCP	obligatory contour principle
O-O	output-to-output
OP	optimal paradigms
OPC	overt pronoun constraint
OSp.	Old Spanish
OT	optimality theory
OVS	object–verb–subject
Q	quantifier
P	phrase; power; preposition
p.c.	personal communication
PA	pitch accent
PAM	perceptual assimilation model
PF	phonological/phonetic form; periphrastic future
PFCV	perfective
PFI	principle of full interpretation
phi features (also φ features)	semantic features of person, number, and gender
PL	plural
PLUS	percentage (of life) lived in US
p-movement	prosodically motivated movement
POS	poverty of the stimulus
PP	prepositional phrase; prepositional projection; periphrastic past; present perfect
PREP	preposition
PRET	preterit

PRESEEA	*Proyecto para el estudio sociolingüístico del español de España y de América*
pro	non-overt subject of finite sentences
pro$_{arb}$	arbitrary null pronominal
pro$_{expl}$	obligatorily null expletive
PS	phrase structure
PVS	preverbal subject
PW	prosodic word
RAE	Real Academia Española
RExp	dative experiencer
RHM	revised hierarchical model
RNSR	romance nuclear stress rule
RT	reading time
s	strong
S	subject; sentence
SA	study-abroad (context)
SBJV	subjunctive
SG	singular
SHL	Spanish as a heritage language
SI	scalar implicatures
SLM	speech learning model
SM	sensori-motor system
Sp_ToBI	Spanish tones and break indices labeling system
Spec	specifier position
SPP	subject personal pronoun
SPRLT	superlative
SSP	sonority sequencing principle
S-structure	surface structure
SUBJ	subject
SVO	subject–verb–object
T	tense
TETU	the emergence of the unmarked
theta role (also θ role)	thematic role
THV	thematic vowel
TMA	time, mood, and aspect
ToBI	tones and break indices
TopP	topic phrase; topic projection
TP	tense phrase; tense projection
TPM	typological primacy model
u	uninterpretable/unvalued
UB	usage-based
UG	Universal Grammar
uK	unvalued structural case feature
UTAH	Uniformity of Theta Assignment Hypothesis

v	a light verb that introduces a verbal argument
v, V	verb; vowel
V2	verb-second
VOS	verb–object–subject
VOT	voice onset time
VP	verb phrase; verb projection
V-to-I/T	verb-to-inflection/tense
V-to-T	verb-to-tense
w	weak
W	weight of imposition
WCT	written contextualized task
WMP	word marker projection
X°	minimal head
XP	variable value maximal projection

Introduction

Kimberly L. Geeslin

The field of Spanish linguistics (where "Spanish" is taken to refer to all varieties of that language spoken throughout the world) has a longstanding history, with an ever-increasing presence across multiple sub-fields of linguistic inquiry. This edited volume provides a state-of-the-art survey of the field of Spanish linguistics, striking a balance between depth of coverage in the most widely studied areas and breadth of coverage across sub-areas of this field. The *Handbook* aims to be accessible to a diverse audience, including those with less extensive knowledge of linguistics or Spanish. It is particularly well suited for advanced undergraduate students or beginning graduate students in the field of Spanish linguistics. Nevertheless, the current and critical accounts of the most important research developments in each sub-field contained in the *Handbook*, as well as the critical discussions of directions for future research, are also of interest to top scholars across sub-fields. The breadth of coverage and diversity of approaches contained in this volume further ensure that this collection serves readers working on Spanish linguistics as well as researchers and students in allied fields such as General Linguistics, Anthropology, Sociology, Cognitive Science, Psychology, and Language Education.

The current volume was designed to cover a diversity of topics and issues from distinct sub-domains of linguistics and language study. Additionally, it presents a wide range of approaches to language theory and research methodology. By incorporating chapters on Generative Theory, Optimality Theory, functional-typological approaches, and usage-based approaches, for example, the volume stands to foster cross-theoretic dialogue and to assist readers who seek to connect findings across theoretical approaches. Likewise, chapters on corpus and psycholinguistic approaches to Spanish linguistics provide an account of cutting-edge methods currently employed to test theoretical assumptions across approaches. This multi-theoretic approach provides tools for researchers seeking to understand the current trends outside their own theoretical framework and an introduction to students who have yet to adopt a single theoretical perspective. Moreover, this approach allows for a single issue or linguistic construct to be viewed through multiple lenses.

The authors of the individual chapters contained in this volume are the leaders in empirical research in their respective areas of study. While some are long-standing figures in the field, others represent up-and-coming scholars with exciting new contributions. These authors hail from many different countries and bring to their writing a range of research perspectives and traditions. Each author has worked hard to address the necessary tension between breadth and depth of coverage and the resulting work is an outstanding assessment of the priorities for research in the field. Likewise, the authors of individual chapters have collaborated with the editor and with each other to make connections across chapters, across domains of study, and across theoretical approaches. To this end, the volume contains critical accounts of cutting-edge research and the most pressing questions guiding investigation in each of the sub-fields covered, as well as multiple links between separate research programs that stand to contribute more broadly as a whole.

Overview of Contents

The *Cambridge Handbook of Spanish Linguistics* contains 33 chapters representing the range of sub-fields of investigation included in the field of Spanish linguistics. These chapters are organized into five parts based on their relationship to one another and the diversity of inquiry within those overarching areas. The first part covers a range of theories, approaches, and research methodologies employed in contemporary research on Spanish linguistics. As is likely anticipated, there is a chapter on Generative Theory (Paula Kempchinsky, Chapter 1), which represents the dominant paradigm in many of the sub-fields of research included in the *Handbook*. Additionally, chapters on Optimality Theory (D. Eric Holt, Chapter 2), usage-based approaches (Esther Brown, Chapter 3), and functional-typological approaches (Rosa Vallejos, Chapter 4) have been included to show how these theoretical approaches have made equally important contributions to our knowledge of Spanish linguistics. Each of these represents areas where important empirical and theoretical work is being conducted on Spanish. The first part ends with two chapters on approaches to research: psycholinguistic (Tania Leal and Christine Shea, Chapter 5) and corpus approaches (Manuel Díaz-Campos and Juan Escalona Torres, Chapter 6). From each approach we gain essential methodological tools that can be applied to data analysis across sub-disciplines and, in many cases, across theoretical approaches. This diversity of perspectives provides a critical review for those working within these frameworks as well as a suitable introduction for those who have made their mark primarily within a single theoretical framework or using a singular approach to data and analysis. Moreover, this opening part foreshadows the effort made throughout the volume to cover a range of approaches to each of the areas of Spanish linguistics covered.

The second part focuses on the Spanish sound system and addresses both segmental and suprasegmental issues. Chapters include critical reviews of empirical research and theoretical approaches to vowels (Rebecca Ronquest, Chapter 7), consonants (Rebeka Campos-Astorkiza, Chapter 8), syllables (Alfonso Morales-Front, Chapter 9), and stress and intonation (Pilar Prieto and Paolo Roseano, Chapter 10). In each case, authors have balanced issues of coverage and depth to arrive at a concise discussion of the most pressing issues in Spanish phonetics and phonology. Their work spans different Spanish-speaking populations and a variety of research methodologies, and is conducted within multiple theoretical frameworks. The final chapter in this part addresses research on speech perception (Amanda Boomershine and Ji Young Kim, Chapter 11), representing an even broader range of language phenomena and at the same time a more specific approach to language analysis and research. In these sub-fields, where research is characterized by rapidly growing analytical technologies, each chapter is a tremendous resource for current and future researchers who seek to expand our knowledge base by applying new tools to existing problems or by studying phenomena that are not yet well understood.

The third part covers topics in morphosyntax and meaning, building on the theoretical accounts described in Part I. Each chapter offers a critical review of cutting-edge research in these areas and identifies the questions that remain unanswered. Given the especially broad scope of research conducted across these sub-fields, this is one area where the tension between breadth and depth of coverage was especially acute. The result, however, is a collection of chapters that represents a clear view of priorities within certain sub-areas as well as some highly effective collaboration in making connections across chapters. Although it is likely that some important research areas have been omitted because of this approach, those that remain have the added benefit of being contextualized within a greater whole. Topics that are covered in this part include properties of the word (Antonio Fábregas, Chapter 12), pronominal subjects (Pekka Posio, Chapter 13), the verb phrase (Iván Ortega-Santos, Chapter 14), the extended verb phrase (Julio Villa-García, Chapter 15), and nominal expression (M. Emma Ticio Quesada, Chapter 16). Building on these chapters, the later contributions in this part address the issues of information structure (Laura Domínguez, Chapter 17) and syntax and its interfaces (Timothy Gupton, Chapter 18), as well as those related to meaning, such as lexis (Grant Armstrong, Chapter 19) and pragmatics (Maria Hasler-Barker, Chapter 20). Where space and expertise permitted, authors have taken care to include work from multiple theoretical perspectives and, in every case, the chapters contribute to larger theoretical discussions through critical accounts of the research in each author's own areas of expertise.

The fourth part in *The Cambridge Handbook of Spanish Linguistics* includes chapters devoted to the study of Spanish in its social, geographic, and historical contexts of use. The discussion includes topics such as language contact and bilingualism (Lotfi Sayahi, Chapter 21) and Heritage speakers of Spanish (Diego Pascual y Cabo, Chapter 22). Likewise, language variation is treated from synchronic and diachronic perspectives, featuring the role of geography, individual characteristics, and discourse context. To this end, Part IV includes chapters on geographic varieties of Spanish (Elena Fernández de Molina Ortés and Juan M. Hernández-Campoy, Chapter 23), individual variation (Daniel Erker, Chapter 24), national and diasporic Spanish varieties as evidence of ethnic affiliations (Almeida Jacqueline Toribio, Chapter 25), current perspectives on historical linguistics (Patrícia Amaral, Chapter 26), and grammaticalization (Chad Howe, Chapter 27). Although not unique, the inclusion of chapters on bilingual contexts and on Heritage speakers in particular demonstrates that this volume covers recent areas of interest in addition to long-standing fields of inquiry, such as historical linguistics. What is more, the organization of these topics into a single part allows the reader to appreciate that each is, in fact, a different perspective on the use of Spanish in context, where context itself may be defined diachronically, geographically, or socially. The chapters in this part are designed to be representative of the vast number of contexts in which Spanish is spoken, to be linguistically sophisticated in their accounts of patterns of use in these contexts, and to reflect the common patterns across these applied fields of linguistics.

The final part in the *Handbook* covers the acquisition of Spanish. This section includes a chapter on child language acquisition (Anna Gavarró, Chapter 28) to complement the other chapters, which focus primarily on adult language acquisition. Readers will anticipate chapters such as those on the acquisition of the Spanish sound system (Megan Solon, Chapter 30) and of Spanish morphosyntax (Jason Rothman, Jorge González Alonso, and David Miller, Chapter 31), and these will prove a good complement to the earlier chapters focusing on theoretical accounts of these issues. What is more, in the case of both these latter two chapters, the authors worked hard to balance breadth and depth, and to focus on recent research, signaling future directions for these sub-fields. In keeping with the goal of addressing multiple perspectives, a chapter on theories of second language acquisition (Bill VanPatten, Chapter 29) has been included in this part as well, with an eye to exploring theories specific to language learning and how these connect to research in first language contexts along with a chapter focused exclusively on the acquisition of variable structures in Spanish as a second language (Matthew Kanwit, Chapter 32). Finally, the chapter on third language acquisition (Jennifer

Cabrelli Amaro and Michael Iverson, Chapter 33) represents both a newer area of research with exciting empirical work and an important response to the many learning contexts in which monolingualism is not the norm. Taken together, the chapters in Part V contribute to our understanding of the development of language in multiple contexts and learning conditions across many areas of the Spanish language.

Concluding Remarks

These are genuinely exciting times to be working in the field of Spanish linguistics. The depth of inquiry across so many sub-fields is evidence that scholars of Spanish linguistics are active and are moving their respective fields forward at an astounding pace. The multiple approaches to research, to theory-building, and to examining language phenomena add to the interdisciplinary connections and collaborative discourse in these fields. It was most difficult to limit the number of chapters and scope of each, knowing full well that there are important areas of research that were thereby excluded. Nevertheless, this very tension is good evidence of how robust this field of research is. In every chapter the authors have made clear that researchers working on Spanish linguistics are making contributions well beyond the language of study or the sub-field of research. Most importantly, they have also provided a roadmap for the future of scholarship in Spanish linguistics and its allied fields of inquiry.

Part I

Theories and Approaches to Spanish Linguistics

1

Generative Linguistics: Syntax

Paula Kempchinsky

> You have to be operating within some kind of theoretical framework to ask any meaningful questions about language. Languages make sense, but only in terms of theories ... We learn to ask questions about individual languages on the basis of a theoretical framework, the two go side by side. The language is always influencing what the theory is going to say because they confront us with problems; that's how the field works. You have a theory, here are the facts. As soon as you look at the next language, you see something that is either going to force you to change the theory or, if you work hard enough, you'll see that not only does it turn out not to be an exception or something like that, but it actually proves the theory. They work together like that.   Ken Hale (1934–2001)[1]

1.1 Definition and Basic Assumptions

If linguistics is "the scientific study of language," as is often stated in introductory courses in the field, then Spanish linguistics is the scientific study of the Spanish language. Generative linguistics is one of the theoretical frameworks which poses the questions which are pursued by linguists working on Spanish. More precisely, in agreement with Suñer (2009), I would say that there does not exist a disciplinary entity which can be called "Spanish linguistics." There are disciplines within linguistics such as syntax, phonology, the study of acquisition, the study of language variation, and so on, and linguists who work in these disciplines typically

---

[1] The source of this quote is *Glot International*, 2: 9–10 (December 1996). A reviewer observes that the use of the word "proves" in the next to last sentence is infelicitous, in that proving a theory is not possible in a science such as linguistics. Nevertheless, the words are Ken Hale's.

do so within some particular theoretical framework. Thus, linguists who apply the basic assumptions, principles, and procedures of generative linguistics in the investigation of Spanish syntax (or morphology, or phonology, or semantics) are generative linguists who work on Spanish.

Paraphrasing Lorenzo (2016), to say that generative linguistics is a theoretical framework is to say that it conceives of its object of study in a certain way: it is a particular theory about the nature of language. For generative linguistics, the essential characteristic of language is the infinite capacity (in terms of the generation of possible expressions of a language) of a necessarily finite system of rules and linguistic objects (sounds, words): the property of discrete infinity. The object of study is, correspondingly, that finite system of knowledge in the mind/brain of the speaker.

As articulated by Chomsky (1986 and other works), the three basic questions that language as a human phenomenon presents us with are the following:

1 What constitutes knowledge of language? ("Humboldt's problem")
2 How is knowledge of language acquired? ("Plato's problem")
3 How is knowledge of language put to use? ("Descartes' problem")

Question (3) singles out the creative component of language, which lies not only in the potentially infinite number of the sentences/structures generated by the knowledge system, but also in the fact that speakers – even the "dullest of men," in Descartes' words – can produce "appropriately meaningful answer to whatever is said in [their] presence."[2] Crucially, however, linguistic responses to external stimuli are not determined by these stimuli: there is no one-to-one correlation between what a speaker says and the situation in which the speaker finds himself (Eguren and Fernández Soriano 2004). Question (2) is dubbed "Plato's problem" because a basic working assumption of generative linguistics is that the system of knowledge is underdetermined by the linguistic stimuli that the child hears during the process of acquisition, and hence exemplifies the broader question of how humans know so much given their limited experience. The basic research question of generative linguistics is question (1); the task is to discover the nature of the system of knowledge in the speaker's mind/brain and, to the extent possible, to explain it.

The term "generative linguistics" could, in principle, include any approach to linguistics which seeks to explain the linguistic capacity of speakers in terms of a system of rules or formal constructs which can generate all and only the grammatical sentences of the language, where to "generate" a sentence means to assign a well-formed structure to the sentence: a structure which does not violate any of the constraints in the system. All such approaches have as their point of origin Chomsky's 1957

---

[2] From Descartes, *Discours de la méthode* (1637); this translation is from Ben-Yami 2015: Ch. 5.

monograph, *Syntactic Structures*. In practice, the term is used to refer to research which continues to hold the basic assumptions introduced in that work: (i) the system of knowledge of the speaker – his/her grammar – is a distinct module of the mind/brain, (ii) the core of the grammar is the syntax, and (iii) part of this grammar is innate, i.e. ultimately part of our genetic endowment, given that it cannot be acquired on the basis of the linguistic evidence available to the child. In this use of the term, generative linguistics is distinct from, for example, the research grouped under the rubric of "cognitive linguistics," which rejects both the central role accorded to the syntax and the idea of language as a separate module of knowledge, seeing it as part of general human cognitive abilities. Nonetheless, in its focus on the internal system of knowledge hypothesized to underlie speakers' linguistic behavior, generative linguistics is a part of the wider research field of cognitive science: in Gardner's (1985) history of cognitive science to that date, he signals generative linguistics as one of the foundational disciplines.

With the publication of Chomsky (1981), the standard syntacticocentric use of the term "generative linguistics" is what comes to be known as the "Principles and Parameters" framework (see also Chapter 2, in this volume, for some discussion of syntax within Optimality Theory). For over two decades now, starting with Chomsky (1993), the particular turn that this research has taken is Minimalism, which Chomsky and others have emphasized is a programmatic set of assumptions, not a new overall theoretical framework. Rather, it can be seen as an evolution within Principles and Parameters, as will be discussed in Section 1.2. More importantly for the purposes of the present *Handbook*, a significant body of research on Spanish syntax and semantics has been produced by linguists working within generative linguistics, in its narrow definition.[3] Suñer (1989) in her review of research in Spanish syntax and semantics in the 1980s chose to focus on work within the Principles and Parameters framework.

1.2 Principles and Parameters: From the 1980s to Minimalism

As O'Grady (2012) points out, the descriptive challenge faced by linguistics (he does not limit himself here to generative linguistics) is to adequately describe "how individual languages employ form to express

---

[3] A reviewer notes, correctly, that the rubric term "Generative Linguistics" is not necessarily limited to Chomskyan approaches – what I have termed above its narrow definition. Alternative frameworks such as HPSG (Head-driven Phrase Structure Grammar) and LFG (Lexical Functional Grammar) are also generative, in the broad sense. Although some research on Spanish syntax within such frameworks, or others, has been conducted, the dominant theoretical paradigm within the field is Principles-and-Parameters/Minimalism. For this reason and because of space limitations, this chapter focuses on the narrow definition.

meaning," while the explanatory challenge is to explain why language has the properties that it does and, tightly related to this, how speakers' knowledge of their grammar arises in early childhood: the problems of language design and of language acquisition (Questions (1) and (2) above). The constant in generative linguistics has been to hypothesize that a significant part of the two explanatory problems is to be attributed to the language-specific module, although debate is ongoing as to exactly what the extent of the language-specific module is (see for example Chomsky 2005, touched upon below). The changes over time in the more specific hypotheses about the nature of that module stem directly from advances on the descriptive side of the ledger, as well as from the insights gained from psycholinguistic and neurolinguistic research.

1.2.1 Principles and Parameters before Minimalism

The Principles and Parameters framework of the 1980s, initially identified as "Government and Binding" (Chomsky 1981), was a strongly representational and modular view of syntax, in which each module accounted for some aspect of syntactic or syntacticosemantic properties of a sentence. Thus, for example, the first representational level, D (deep)-structure, was subject to X′ (X-bar)-theory as a template on the wellformedness of syntactic structures plus the Extended Projection Principle (EPP), which mandated that in the verb phrase headed by a given verb there be the necessary number of argument positions for that verb to assign its corresponding theta roles, plus a filler for the (external) subject position generated as the Specifier of the tense phrase (TP) – independently of whether that position was needed for the assignment of a theta role, as in the case of expletive (non-theta-role bearing) subjects (*it* seems that *it* will rain). The movement of constituents between the levels of D-structure and S (surface)-structure was allowed by the general rule "Move α," but subject to bounding constraints (subjacency theory) and motivated, in the case of A (argument)-movement, by the requirement that arguments be in a Case-marked position by S-structure, as dictated by Case theory. Movement to A′-positions, as for example with *wh*-movement, was motivated by operator theory, according to which at least by the level of Logical Form (LF), and for some languages by the level of S-structure, logical operators must be in a position to establish scope. Therefore, between the representational level of S-structure and the representational level of LF, further syntactic movement could occur, as for example with *wh* in-situ or with quantifier raising. At LF, furthermore, the binding theory conditions would apply, regulating the possible or necessary relations of coreference between arguments. Control theory, which determined the interpretation of the phonologically null subject of non-tensed clauses, also was relevant at LF. The formal model of the grammar in this framework is schematized in Figure 1.1.

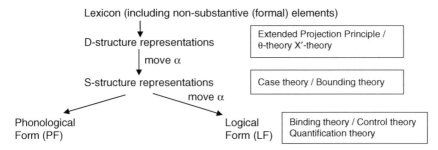

Figure 1.1 The early Principles and Parameters framework

Given that syntactic movement in this model is free, there are no constraints on the derivation per se, since even the subjacency constraints of the module most directly concerned with movement, bounding theory, could be stated in terms of conditions on movement chains at, for example, the level of S-structure. As an illustration, consider (1.1a) vs. (1.1b), with their associated S-structures:

(1.1)   a. Los estudiantes parecen entender esta teoría.
           the students seem.PRES.3PL understand.INF this theory
           'The students seem to understand this theory.'
           [[los estudiantes]$_i$ INFL$_{[+FIN]}$ parecen [$_{TP}$ t$_i$ INFL$_{[-FIN]}$ entender esta teoría]]
   b. *Los estudiantes parecen que entienden esta teoría.
           the students seem.PRES.3PL that understand.PRES.3PL this theory
           'The students seem that they understand this theory.'
           [[los estudiantes]$_i$ INFL$_{[+FIN]}$ parecen [$_{CP}$ que [$_{TP}$ t$_i$ INFL$_{[+FIN]}$ entienden esta teoría]]]

In the S-structure of (1.1a), the thematic subject of the infinitival clause[4] has moved to the subject position of the main clause – a position which, in accordance with the EPP, was already present at D-structure. In this position this subject can be assigned nominative Case by the tensed INFL, satisfying the S-structure requirement that all thematic noun phrases be assigned Case. Now consider (1.1b). If the non-thematic subject position of *parecen* does not have an expletive element inserted at D-structure, then once again the embedded subject can freely move there. But this noun phrase then ends up with nominative Case assigned twice, which is ruled out by Case theory. In addition, since the subordinate clause, as a finite clause, is now a complementizer phrase (CP) rather than a TP, movement of this noun phrase also violates the bounding conditions of subjacency theory: the trace in the embedded subject position is too far from its antecedent, separated by the "bounding nodes" TP and CP.

---

[4] For the purposes of this example I am following the earlier assumption in the Principles and Parameters model that external arguments are generated directly in clausal subject position, versus the now standard idea that subjects are first generated within an (extended) verb phrase (Sportiche 1988, Koopman and Sportiche 1991, and others.)

The fact that a sentence such as (1.1b) is doubly ruled out points to an undesirable redundancy in the theory. The modular Principles and Parameters framework, in which at least some principles were associated with parameters (that is, possible points of language variation expressed in terms of different values associated with the principle in question), greatly expanded the empirical coverage of the theory while avoiding a multiplicity of language-specific and construction-specific rules. Nonetheless, the explanatory cost was precisely the assumption of a language faculty with a number of module-specific principles.

1.2.2 Minimalism: A Research Program

The Minimalist Program, first articulated in Chomsky (1993), set as its goal the elimination or at least the paring down of specific syntactic principles. The building blocks of a sentence are the individual lexical items, which are themselves bundles of features: phonological, semantic, and formal (syntactic) features. The syntax assembles the lexical items into hierarchical structures, as dictated by the relations among these formal features, with the goal of delivering to the phonological interface and the semantic interface a structure which contains all and only the features which are needed by that interface. Syntax is accordingly strongly derivational, and proceeds in a bottom-up fashion, with the basic syntactic operations being Merge, Move, and Agree. The basic architecture of the grammar as thus conceived is illustrated in Figure 1.2.

As an illustration, consider the simple sentence *Juan padece amnesia* 'John suffers from amnesia.'[5] This sentence is constructed on the basis of the substantive lexical items *Juan, padece, amnesia* and the non-substantive or functional lexical items T and v (ignoring here the functional elements that may be at play within the noun phrases headed by *Juan* and *amnesia*; see also Chapter 16, this volume). These are the elements that compose the Numeration of the sentence. Suppose that categorial selection is expressed as an uninterpretable categorial feature on the selecting head.[6] The verb *padece* therefore has the interpretable feature [V] and the uninterpretable feature [uN] (or, assuming that the noun phrase is structurally a determiner phrase or DP, [uD]). The need to eliminate uninterpretable features is a driving force in the syntax, and in this instance Merge of the verb *padece* and the noun phrase *amnesia* – that is, the creation of a new complex LI, the verb phrase [padece amnesia] – will value and hence delete the [uN] feature on the verb. This new element is labeled as the verb – in other words, it is headed by the verb – because the operation of Merge was motivated by the uninterpretable feature on the verb.

---

[5] The purpose of the representation in Figure 1.2 is to illustrate the general architecture of the computational component, drawing principally on Chomsky (2000, 2001) and not on, for example, the earlier assumptions about derivational mechanisms as proposed in Chomsky (1993, 1995).

[6] Here for illustration I am following Adger (2003), but this is not an uncontroversial assumption.

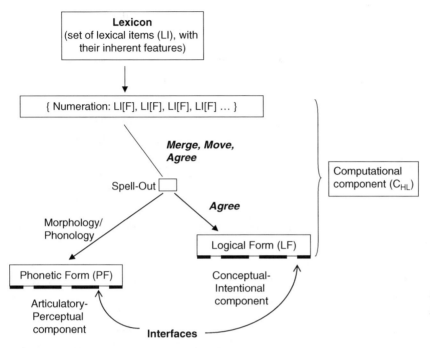

Figure 1.2 Minimalist Program (Chomsky 1993, 1995)

Continuing in the derivation, the functional element *v* now enters into the derivation, and via Merge creates a new hierarchical constituent, headed by the *v*. But *v*, like the lexical verb, also has a [*u*N] feature, motivating Merge with the noun phrase *Juan*. Further, the lexical verb *padece* must move to form a complex head with *v*, where the operation Move in Minimalism is a two-step operation of Copy and Merge, i.e. internal Merge of a lexical item already present in the derivation, not external Merge from the Numeration.[7] The final element to enter the derivation is the element T, which by Merge forms a new syntactic unit with the *v*P. Furthermore, T requires that a noun phrase (internally) merge with it – the EPP, recast in terms of an uninterpretable categorial feature on T.

Note that in the architecture of Figure 1.2 there are no representational syntactic levels; there are only two interfaces: the phonological form (PF) interface of the formal grammar with the grammar-external articulatory perceptual system and the LF interface with the grammar-external conceptual intentional system. The important implication of this is that grammar-internal principles have been eliminated in favor of principles whose sole purpose is to ensure that the syntactic derivation yields representations which are interpretable by the interface systems.[8]

---

[7] Note that one ongoing theoretical issue is the nature of head movement; concretely, whether it occurs in the "narrow" syntax or in PF (Chomsky 2000). For one narrow syntax approach, see Matushansky (2006).

[8] I thank one of the reviewers of this chapter for this observation.

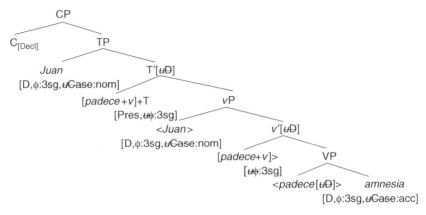

Figure 1.3 A simplified structure for the derivation of *Juan padece amnesia* 'John suffers from amnesia'

The operation of Merge eliminates uninterpretable categorial features, while the operation of Agree eliminates uninterpretable phi (φ) features (person, number, gender) on "agreeing" heads such as T and uninterpretable Case features on noun phrases.[9] "Subject–verb agreement," for instance, is an Agree relation established between T and the subject noun phrase in Spec,*v*P (specifier position of *v*P) by which the noun phrase values the uninterpretable phi features on T – a necessary precondition to deletion – and T values the uninterpretable Case feature on the subject (for more detail on the mechanics of these Agree relations, as well as a discussion of the important empirical and conceptual issues surrounding the workings of the EPP in Spanish, see also Chapter 15, this volume). A simplified structure for the derivation of *Juan padece amnesia* is given in Figure 1.3, where by convention valued and deleted features are indicated with strikeout and non-pronounced copies are indicated in angled brackets. Because Figure 1.3 is a static representation of the derivation, it does not transparently show the relevant syntactic operations. For example, Figure 1.3 assumes that there is an Agree relation established between *v* and the object *amnesia* (a DP), which has the effect of valuing the [*u*φ] features on *v* as [3SG], and of valuing the [*u*Case] feature on the DP as [accusative]. The same type of Agree relation, as already noted above, holds between T and the subject *Juan*, but this subject then undergoes Move to T because of the uninterpretable categorial feature on T, which hence is deleted as a result of Merge, not Agree.

In the schematic model in Figure 1.2 there appears a point in the derivation denoted as "Spell-Out," where the derivation branches and the structure which has been built to that point is sent to the

---

[9] The phi feature of [GENDER] does not enter into subject–verb agreement in languages like Spanish, but does in a variety of other languages (e.g. Hindi, Kannada, Russian, among many others), at least when the subject is valued with nominative case.

Morphophonological Component. However, the computation continues, at least insofar as the operation of Agree is concerned. As an illustration, consider the multiple *wh*-construction of (1.2a), with the simplified derivation shown in (1.2b):[10]

(1.2)   a. ¿Quién crees que enseña qué clase?
'Who do you think teaches what class?'
b. [$_{CP}$ [quién] C$_{[uwh]}$ [$_{TP}$ crees [$_{CP}$ que [$_{TP}$ <quién> enseña [qué clase]]]]]
Structure before Spell-Out
[$_{CP}$ [quién] C$_{[uwh]}$ [$_{TP}$ crees [$_{CP}$ que [$_{TP}$ <quién> enseña [qué clase]]]]]

Agree, post Spell-Out

The post Spell-Out Agree relation accounts for the fact that the two *wh*-phrases are interpreted together, yielding pair-list readings (I think that X teaches P and Y teaches Q).

Note that in an example such as (1.2a) in a language like Bulgarian, both of the *wh*-constituents move before Spell-Out. In other words, one way in which languages can differ is in terms of the point in the derivation at which Spell-Out is reached. More broadly, Minimalism carries over from the original conceptualization of the Principles and Parameters framework the notion that languages are parametrized in some way, and the locus of this parametrization must be in features themselves.

Given that the goal of the Minimalist Program is to eliminate as much language faculty-specific machinery as possible – in the ideal case, limiting it to the basic syntactic operations of Merge (external and internal) and Agree – the tension between empirical demands and theoretical desiderata is sharpened. Chomsky (2005) states the problem of determining the nature of the internal grammar of a language – i.e. internal language or I-language – in terms of the interplay of three factors: (i) the genetically determined language-specific module ("universal grammar"), (ii) experience – in other words, the particular external language (E-language) to which the speaker is exposed, and (iii) principles which are not specific to language, but perhaps related to general concerns of processability and economy, including principles of efficient computation. This appeal to the third factor has in turn brought renewed attention to an issue which has been present both in generative work itself and in criticisms of generative work, the question of data.

1.3 The Data Base of Generative Linguistics

As stated above, the goal of generative linguistics is to discover and propose a formal model of a speaker's system of knowledge. But of course the only access to this system is indirect: to discover the structure and the

---

[10] In particular, (1.2b) ignores phase theory (Chomsky 2001), according to which the two CPs (and their corresponding *v*Ps) constitute distinct phases for the purposes of sending the derivation to Spell-Out.

limits of the system of knowledge, linguists need to discover the limits of language use. This is Chomsky's famous dichotomy of competence and performance. But it is worth re-emphasizing yet once again. As is well known, the main type of data used in generative linguistics are what are somewhat misleadingly called grammaticality judgments: judgments solicited from speakers of the language under investigation of the acceptability or unacceptability of given sequences of words (for syntax) or given combinations of sounds (for phonology), or – in the case of semantics – of the possible interpretations of given sequences. In order to know what is not allowed by the mental grammar, it is necessarily the case that the linguist has to know that certain sequences or combinations are not possible, or that certain interpretations are not available. A typical example is an "island" violation in long-distance movement as in (1.3) below, where the bracketed instance of *cómo* represents the intended interpretation site:

(1.3)   a. ¿Cómo crees [que Ana prefiere [que hagan la reforma <cómo>]?]
           'How do you believe that Ana prefers that they do the remodel?'
    b. *¿Cómo crees [que Ana mantiene su preferencia de [que hagan la reforma <cómo>]?]
           'How do you believe that Ana maintains her preference that they do the remodel?'

The speaker-informant can indicate that (1.3b) is not an acceptable sentence, or that s/he cannot interpret (1.3b) as indicated, and this is then reported as a "grammaticality" judgment, with the accompanying asterisk. Strictly speaking, however, grammaticality is a property of the system under investigation, and the acceptability judgment on the part of the speaker is one piece of evidence to be used in investigating that system. More exactly, if a speaker indicates that (1.3b) is not acceptable, the linguist may hypothesize that this acceptability stems from the inability of the system to generate an appropriate structure for this sequence; i.e. its unacceptability is due to its ungrammaticality. Nevertheless, it is well recognized that a variety of factors enter into speakers' determinations of acceptability: lexical variation, (mis)perceptions of prescriptivism, stylistic and dialectal variation, and so on (Bosque and Gutiérrez-Rexach 2009).

The distinction between acceptability and grammaticality has long been discussed in generative syntax. (See Newmeyer 1983 for a review up to that point, and for later work see Schütze 1996; Phillips *et al.* 2011; Maynes 2012; among many others. For some earlier discussion with examples from Spanish, see Otero 1972, 1973.) I will continue to use in the remainder of this section the standard term of "grammaticality judgment," but with this background discussion as a caveat.

A long-standing criticism of generative linguistics has been its reliance on grammaticality judgments, which are seen as introspective rather than production data. But since both assigning judgments and producing/interpreting sentences are instances of linguistic performance, then in principle neither one nor the other has primacy. Further, as pointed out by Featherstone (2007:271), production data such as corpus data in and of itself is insufficient, because "neither occurrence nor frequency are identical with well-formedness." More crucially, superficial comparisons of possibly occurring sentences do not in and of themselves provide the necessary data for a structural analysis. As an example, we can consider the following examples of possible VOS sentences in Spanish and Italian:

(1.4)   a. Han comido las manzanas los niños.
        b. Hanno mangiato le mele i bambini.
           have eaten the apples the children
        'The children have eaten the apples.'

Gallego (2016), drawing on previous work by others, shows that in VOS sentences in Spanish (along with the other peripheral Romance languages, e.g. Portuguese and Romanian) the object shifts to a position above the subject (i.e. above vP); hence a quantified object can yield a bound variable interpretation on a pronoun within the subject. In contrast, in the central Romance languages, as exemplified by Italian, VOS order is derived by fronting of the entire VP (following Zubizarreta 1998, fronting of the TP after movement of the subject to FocusP); thus, the object within the fronted VP does not c-command the subject and cannot serve as an antecedent for an anaphor within the subject:

(1.5)   a. Recogió cada coche su dueño. (= Each car was picked up by its owner)
          picked.up each car its owner
          recogió [$_{vP}$ [cada coche]$_i$ [$_{v'}$ [su$_i$ dueño] <recogió + v> [$_{VP}$ <recogió> <cada coche>]]]
        b. *Hanno salutato Gianni i propri genitori.
           have greeted Gianni the own parents
          *[$_{TP}$ <i propri genitori> hanno salutato Gianni$_i$] [[$_{FocP}$ i propri$_i$ genitori] <TP>

For the purposes of this section, what is important to note here is that the necessary data to tease apart the different structural analyses of Spanish vs. Italian can only be obtained via elicitation of speaker judgments: in both cases, of possible or not possible interpretations.

   Of course, generative linguists working on diachronic syntax do not have access to speaker intuitions, and must make inferences on what structures are and are not possible in the language at a given earlier stage based on occurrence and frequency in the written corpora available. Leaving that particular case aside, the more basic claim (again, see Newmeyer 1983) is that the introspective judgments used are those of the linguist himself or herself. It is more accurate to say that the judgments reported are not based on some statistically relevant sampling of speakers. Den Dikken *et al.* (2007) explicitly refute the claim that some generative linguists have proposed analyses based solely on their own (admittedly self-interested) judgments, given that any claims are subjected to a review process which includes vetting of judgments with other native speakers.

Maynes (2012), who defends the necessity of introspective judgments in proposing and evaluating hypotheses about speakers' grammars, argues that such speaker intuitions need to be calibrated, whereby comparisons can be made across speakers or across judgments, as in data gathered using the technique of Magnitude Estimation (Sorace and Keller 2005). In fact, various researchers have employed psycholinguistic and neurolinguistic methodologies in the investigation of generative syntax, in particular in researching phenomena at the interface between syntax and discourse/information structure (see, for example, Gupton and Leal Méndez 2013 and Hoot 2016), and Marantz (2005) argues forcefully for the place of generative syntax in the general area of experimental cognitive neuroscience.[11] Although this "experimental turn" has become increasingly prominent in this decade, Goodall (2004) is an early study on the effect of memory and processing load on grammaticality judgments for Spanish *wh*-questions.

However, as den Dikken *et al.* (2007) argue forcefully, carefully gathered data from even one sole informant can be valid, given control of the linguistic/discourse context and comparison, when possible, of this informant's judgments on the particular construction being examined with his/her judgments on other constructions in the language for which data already exists. More importantly, they stress that the aim of generative grammar is, ultimately, the knowledge of an individual speaker (the I(nternal)-language). To the extent that some group of speakers of the same "language" (E(external)-language) have identical mental grammars, then their judgments will coincide. If, as is often the case, there are significant variations in the judgments in some experimental questionnaires, what this may reflect is differences in I-languages, and these differences themselves become a topic of investigation.

As Newmeyer (1983) already showed, and den Dikken *et al.* (2007) reiterate, the use of introspective judgments from often small groups of speakers (at times, with N = 1) has yielded an enormous amount of knowledge about the possibilities and the limits of the mental grammars of the speakers. Consider for example some of what we know about *wh*-movement in Spanish, with illustrating examples in (1.6):

---

[11] Marantz argues that generative linguistics has always been an integral part of cognitive neuroscience. Noting Gardner's (1985) identification of linguistics as a foundational component of cognitive science (see above), he states that "mainstream generative linguistics still operates at the nexus of computation, philosophy of language, and cognitive neuroscience. However, sometime in the 1970s it became legitimate for the study of language in psychology and computer science departments not to explore the ongoing discoveries of the generative linguistic tradition" (Marantz 2005:431).

1. *wh*-constituents in general must displace to the front of the clause (1.6a, b)
2. *wh*-constituents which do not appear at the front of the clause must be clause final (1.6c; see Uribe-Etxebarria 2002, Reglero 2005)
3. *wh*-fronting of simple *wh*-constituents triggers obligatory subject–verb "inversion" in both main and subordinate clauses (1.6d–g)[12]
4. *wh*-fronting of complex *wh*/D-linked *wh*-constituents does not trigger obligatory subject–verb "inversion" (1.6h; see Olarrea 1998, Martín 2003, Goodall 2004, among others; the lack of obligatory "inversion" with *por qué* 'why' was already noted earlier by Contreras 1991)
5. *wh*-movement shows the typical island effects noted in other languages (1.3b above), with the possibility of ameliorating *wh*-islands with resumptive pronouns (1.6i)
6. In multiple *wh*-constructions, only one *wh*-element moves overtly (1.2a above)

(1.6) a. ¿A quién le regaló Blanca unos aretes el Día de Reyes?
      'To whom did Blanca give earrings on Three Kings Day?'
   b. *¿Blanca le regaló unos aretes a quién el Día de Reyes?
   c. ¿Blanca le regaló unos aretes el Día de Reyes a quién?
   d. ¿Qué compró Juan para María?
      'What did Juan buy for Maria?'
   e. *¿Qué Juan compró para María?
   f. Me pregunto qué dirá el candidato sobre ese tema.
      'I wonder what the candidate will say about that topic.'
   g. *Me pregunto qué el candidato dirá sobre ese tema.
   h. ¿Qué disco de John Coltrane Juan compró para María?
                              Source: Olarrea (1998:92)
      'Which record by John Coltrane did Juan buy for Maria?'
   i. ¿A cuántos$_i$ de los niños no sabían a qué familia se los$_i$ había encomendado el director del orfanato?
                              Source: Suñer (1992:237)
      'How many of the children didn't they know to which family the director of the orphanage had entrusted them?'

Although some of the data patterns in (1.6) have been subjected to experimental studies, the original source for all of them were speaker judgments. Many of the recent studies on processing effects, impelled precisely by Chomsky's proposed third factor, have focused on *wh*-movement constructions, because their syntactic properties at this point are so well known (see the discussion in Phillips 2013), and the "experimental turn" is a significant current trend in generative linguistics. Nevertheless, to return to den Dikken *et al.* (2007) and Maynes (2012), introspective judgments will always be a necessary source of data in the field.

---

[12] I use quotes for "inversion" to indicate that the word is being used descriptively to indicate verb > subject order, and not to mean that the syntactic operation at play is necessarily one of inverting an already generated subject > verb order. Also note that the generalization here does not include the well-known cases of non-inversion in Puerto Rican Spanish such as *Qué tú haces?* 'What are you doing'; see Ordóñez and Olarrea (2006).

1.4 Topics of Research: How are they Determined?

This section does not pretend to give a comprehensive overview of current work in generative linguistic research on Spanish syntax, or even a comprehensive list of the theoretical issues involved – many of the chapters in this *Handbook* will be excellent sources. Rather, the intent is to illustrate the central idea of the quote at the beginning of this article: the interplay between the need to explain specific syntactic phenomena and the goal of furthering our understanding of the nature of Language – the theory of speakers' knowledge.

If one were to compare the list of research topics in Suñer's (1989) overview with, for example, the topics presented in recent conferences in the field such as the Hispanic Linguistics Symposium or the Linguistic Symposium on Romance Languages, one would see topics that consistently recur, while others come to prominence that were not as noticeable at earlier times. As an example of the former, we can take the topic of clitics, while a good example of the latter might be syntactic processes related to the periphery and information structure.

1.4.1 Clitics: The Language Confronts the Theory

Suñer (1989) observed that certain topics are constants "because of their intrinsic characteristics." This is certainly the case with clitics. In a nutshell, the essential property of clitics which must be accounted for is the relation between the clitic in its surface position adjacent to the verb (generally proclitic with finite verbs, although contact varieties of Spanish in the northwest of Spain can also show enclisis) with the postverbal position where the clitic is thematically interpreted. This of course is a classic diagnostic of syntactic displacement, and the earliest generative analyses of clitics in the Romance languages (e.g. Kayne 1975 for French) specifically proposed that the clitic moved from the thematic object position to its preverbal position. This analysis was immediately countered by the "base-generation" analysis of Strozer (1976), given the existence of clitic doubling in Spanish:

(1.7)   a. Ana ayudaba a su hijo.
           'Ana was helping her son.'
        b. Ana lo ayudaba. / *Ana ayudaba lo.
           'Ana was helping him.'
        c. Ana lo$_i$ ayudaba a él$_i$.

The movement vs. base-generation debate has been a constant over the years even as the tools of syntactic analysis have become more refined and the structures proposed more complex, precisely because the phenomenon of displacement is an essential property of human language that must be accounted for. As noted by Ormazabal and Romero (2013), this debate in its current guise poses the question of whether clitics are inflectional heads of a corresponding functional projection within the inflectional field of the clause (e.g. as proposed by Sportiche 1996, among others) or whether they are determiners which move from a DP in the canonical object position to their surface position (see Torrego 1995 and Uriagereka 1995, among others). Because generative syntax is necessarily strongly comparative, the working assumption has been that there should be one overarching analysis of clitics which accounts for their properties in, say, all the Romance languages (but see Ormazabal and Romero 2013 for a binary approach). But here again the empirical demands are considerable. Besides their basic displacement "flavor," and the possibility or impossibility of clitic doubling, depending on both the language in question and the nature of the doubled constituent, clitics pose a number of problems: the Person Case Constraint (Bonet 1991), illustrated in (1.8), the question of clitic ordering (1.9), the role of dative clitics in licensing benefactive arguments (1.10), "clitic climbing" (1.11), and others.[13]

(1.8) a. El   decano   me   lo   presentó.
         the   dean   DAT.1SG   ACC.3SG   introduce.PAST.3SG
         'The dean introduced him to me.'
      b. *El   decano   me   le   presentó.
         the   dean   ACC.1SG   DAT.3SG   introduce.PAST.3SG
         'The dean introduced me to him.'
      c. El decano me presentó a él.
         'The dean introduced me to him.'

(1.9) a. Te   me   recomendaron   para   el   trabajo.
         2SG   1SG   recommend.PRET.3PL   for   the   job
         'They recommended {you to me / me to you} for the job'
      b. *Me te recomendaron para el trabajo.

                                        Source: González López (2008:64)

(1.10) a. La madre hizo una sopa para Mafalda.
          'The mother made soup for Mafalda.'
       b. La   madre   le   hizo   una   sopa   a   Mafalda.
          the   mother   DAT.3SG   make.PRET.3SG   a   soup   to   Mafalda
          'The mother made soup for Mafalda.'
       c. ??La madre hizo una sopa a Mafalda.

(1.11) a. Ana   puede   denunciarlo   si   quiere.
          Ana   can   denounce.INF.ACC.3SG   if   want.PRES.3SG
          'Ana can denounce him if she wants.'
       b. Ana   lo   puede   denunciar   si   quiere.
          Ana   ACC.3SG   can   denounce.INF   if   want.PRES.3SG

---

[13] The literature on clitics is impossible to summarize, and each one of the clitic issues exemplified here has been studied by multiple linguists. For a recent overview, see Fernández Soriano (2016).

c. Ana puede no denunciarlo si (no) quiere
Ana can NEG denounce.INF.ACC.3SG if (NEG) want.PRES.3SG
'Ana can not denounce him if she wants/(doesn't) want.' (≠ 'Ana cannot denounce him ... ')

d. *Ana lo puede no denunciar si (no) quiere.
Ana ACC.3SG can NEG denounce.INF if (NEG) want.PRES.3SG

Each one of these issues is relevant for syntactic theory; in terms of the quote from Ken Hale at the head of this chapter, they confront the theory with facts. Clitics are in their essence bundles of formal features, and thus are a case study *par excellence* for minimalism, as a framework constructed on the basis of features. But because of their "intrinsic properties," they have always been a challenge for syntactic theory. Further, if we recall again Chomsky's three questions, while the object of study of generative linguists is the system of knowledge itself, this question is tightly intertwined with the question of how this system is acquired. The literature on children's acquisition of clitics in their first language seems to agree that they are acquired relatively late (Clark 1985 and various later studies; however, López Ornat (1990) claims an acquisition age of 3;0 for Spanish), but the fact is that they **are** acquired.[14] They will likely always be a continuing topic.[15]

1.4.2 The Left Periphery: The Theory Raises Questions about the Language

On the other side of the equation, the theory also presents questions. The change in the model of grammar from the modular pre-minimalist framework of Figure 1.1 to the minimalist framework of Figure 1.2 puts heightened focus on the interfaces between the syntax and other components. One beneficiary, as it were, of this new focus is attention to the interplay between syntax and information structure. The theoretical issue at play is the question of exactly what syntactic representation is needed at the syntax–information structure interface, more specifically, the exact syntactic structure of the left periphery of the clause. Consider the following examples, which illustrate (with the previous discourse context, as in López 2009), a fronted topic (1.12a), a fronted (corrective) focus (1.12b), and the combination of the two (1.2c, d):

---

[14] Grüter (2008) is an interesting attempt to use research findings on child L1 acquisition of clitics to tease apart competing theoretical analyses.

[15] A reviewer notes that without giving an example of progress made on these questions raised by clitic syntax, the possible conclusion is that researchers in the field are simply rehashing the same discussions over the same data sets. But the intent of this section of the chapter is merely to show how a given part of the grammar can raise research questions which then become pertinent to the theory, which in turn spurs the search for new data. Any good overview of research on Spanish clitics, and Romance clitics more generally, will show the significant gains in understanding that have been made since, e.g. Kayne (1975).

(1.12)   a. [Context: Ana gave a dog and a kitten to her children.]
El perro Ana se lo dio a su hija, y el gatito se lo dio a su hijo.
'The dog Ana gave to her daughter, and the kitten she gave to her son.'
b. [Context: Ana gave a kitten to her daughter.]
UN PERRO le dio Ana a su hija (no un gatito).
'A DOG Ana gave to her daughter (not a kitten).'
c. [Context: Ana gave pet animals to her children, and her son received a hamster.]
A su hijo UN GATITO le dio (no un hámster).
'To her son A KITTEN she gave (not a hamster).' (* in English)
d. *UN GATITO a su hijo le dio (no un hámster).

(1.12a–b) illustrate that fronted elements may integrate into the discourse context in different ways, and that this has phonological correlates (e.g. stress) and syntactic correlates (clitic doubling or lack thereof, obligatory subject–verb "inversion" or lack thereof).

The seminal work here is, of course, Rizzi (1997), a work which marked the initiation of what came to be known as the cartographic project. For Rizzi, the syntax provides the necessary information for the pragmatic component in the form of designated criterial heads in the left periphery which follow a certain (putatively universal) template; thus (1.12c) has the representation in (1.13), ignoring the derivational history of the TP itself:

(1.13)   [$_{ForceP}$ FORCE [$_{TopicP}$ a su hijo TOP [$_{FocusP}$ UN GATITO FOC [$_{FinP}$ FIN [$_{TP}$ le dio <un gatito> <a su hijo>]]]]]

In (1.13), besides the discourse-related heads of Topic and Focus, there appear the Force and Fin(ite) heads, representing the illocutionary force and finiteness value of the entire clause. Much of the research inspired by Rizzi's proposal has focused on developing an even finer-grained left peripheral structure, with multiple criterial heads. Again, this is both an empirical problem – how do we account for (1.12c) vs. (1.12d), how do we account for the apparent 'reduced' left periphery of English vs. the Romance languages? – and a theoretical issue. The theoretical issue can be stated in terms of the division of labor between the syntactic component and the pragmatic component: how much pragmatic information (e.g. topic vs. focus) is present already in the syntax? This theoretical issue has led to an "anti-cartographic" project, represented, for example, by López (2009). According to this analysis, all movement to the left periphery is to possibly multiple Specifiers of the Fin(ite) head, with the ordering of Topic > Focus due to interpretive constraints: the topicalized constituent, which is in discourse terms an anaphor (indicated in (1.14) with the diacritic [+a]), needs to be at the edge of the structure to find its discourse antecedent:

(1.14)   [$_{ForceP}$ FORCE [$_{FinP}$ [a su hijo]$_{+a}$ [$_{Fin'}$ [UN GATITO] FIN [$_{TP}$ le dio <un gatito> <a su hijo>]]]]

The exposition here ignores many important details of both classes of analyses (see also Chapters 17 and 18, this volume). The point again is to illustrate the role of the theory in bringing to the forefront problems of analysis which had previously been somewhat on the back burner.

1.4.3 Areas of Research

This chapter (like generative linguistics itself) is syntacticocentric. There are various gaps in this overview which it is crucial to mention.

First of all, as already noted by Suñer (1989), syntax and semantics cannot be separated, insofar as the units of interpretation, taking a Fregean view of semantics, are defined by the syntax. The inseparability of syntax and semantics has been most elegantly argued for by Gutiérrez-Rexach (2014) (also see Bosque and Gutiérrez-Rexach 2009), and this chapter has not been able to include any discussion of such work.

Secondly, although the discussion above in Sections 1.4.1 and 1.4.2 has focused on modern Spanish, generative linguistics also includes work on diachronic syntax (as well as phonology and morphology). Returning again to the quote from Ken Hale, the theory helps to "make sense" of changes in the language over time – lacking theory, we are limited to descriptions. This was already emphasized in earlier generative work (e.g. Kiparsky 1968 and, for Iberian Romance, Otero 1971, 1976) and continues to be an active field of endeavor.

Finally, generative linguistics has been the theoretical underpinning for a whole school of scholars working on language acquisition, both first and second (or third), as can be seen in a number of chapters in the last section of this *Handbook*.

In all of these areas, the interplay between theory and empirical data is crucial. Although for those outside of the field of generative linguistics it may seem that changes in the programmatic framework – for example, from the Revised Standard Theory of the late 1970s to "Government and Binding" in the early 1980s, or the introduction of Minimalism in the 1990s – are capricious,[16] the constant is the search for the object of study, the speaker's system of linguistic knowledge. The theory frames the questions that force us to look for the data, and the data in turn inform us in our process of hypothesizing about the nature of that system. As linguists we have learned an enormous amount of knowledge about language since the publication of *Syntactic Structures*, but this new knowledge only serves to deepen the quest, to try to get "beyond explanatory adequacy" (Chomsky 2004).

---

[16] As expressed by Eguren and Fernández Soriano (2004:15), there is "the impression of constantly witnessing sudden, even capricious, changes of direction" in the theoretical framework.

References

Adger, D. (2003). *Core Syntax*. Oxford: Oxford University Press.

Ben-Yami, H. (2015). *Descartes' Philosophical Revolution: A Reassessment*. Dordrecht: Springer.

Bonet, E. (1991). *Morphology After Syntax: Pronominal Clitics in Romance* (Doctoral dissertation). MIT.

Bosque, I. and Gutiérrez-Rexach, J. (2009). *Fundamentos de sintaxis formal*. Madrid: Akal.

Chomsky, N. (1957). *Syntactic Structures*. The Hague: Mouton.

Chomsky, N. (1981). *Lectures on Government and Binding*. Dordrecht: Foris.

Chomsky, N. (1986). *Knowledge of Language: Its Nature, Origin and Use*. New York: Praeger.

Chomsky, N. (1993). A Minimalist Program for Linguistic Theory. In K. Hale and S. J. Keyser (eds.), *The View from Building 20: Essays in Linguistics in Honor of Sylvain Bromberger*. Cambridge, MA: MIT Press, pp. 1–52.

Chomsky, N. (1995). *The Minimalist Program*. Cambridge, MA: MIT Press.

Chomsky, N. (2000). Minimalist Inquiries: The Framework. In R. Martin, D. Michaels, and J. Uriagereka (eds.), *Step by Step: Essays on Minimalist Syntax in Honor of Howard Lasnik*. Cambridge, MA: MIT Press, pp. 89–155.

Chomsky, N. (2001). Derivation by Phase. In M. Kenstowicz (ed.), *Ken Hale: A Life in Language*. Cambridge, MA: MIT Press, pp. 1–52.

Chomsky, N. (2004). Beyond Explanatory Adequacy. In A. Belletti (ed.), *The Cartography of Syntactic Structures, Vol. 3: Structures and Beyond*. Oxford: Oxford University Press, pp. 104–131.

Chomsky, N. (2005). Three Factors in Language Design. *Linguistic Inquiry*, 36, 1–22.

Clark, E. (1985). The Acquisition of Romance with Special Reference to French. In D. Slobin (ed.), *The Crosslinguistic Study of Language Acquisition*. Hillsdale, NJ: Erlbaum, pp. 688–782.

Contreras, H. (1991). On the Position of Subjects. In S. Rothstein (ed.), *Syntax and Semantics, Vol. 25: Perspectives on Phrase Structure*. San Diego, CA: Academic Press, pp. 63–79.

den Dikken, M., et al. (2007). Data and Grammar: Means and Individuals. *Theoretical Linguistics*, 33, 335–352.

Eguren, L. and Fernández Soriano, O. (2004). *Introducción a una sintaxis minimista*. Madrid: Gredos.

Featherstone, S. (2007). Data in Generative Grammar: The Stick and the Carrot. *Theoretical Linguistics*, 33, 269–318.

Fernández Soriano, O. (2016). Clíticos. In J. Gutiérrez-Rexach (ed.), *Enciclopedia de lingüística hispánica*. London: Routledge.

Gallego, A. (2016). Patterns of Object Agreement in Romance. *Paper given at 46th Linguistic Symposium on Romance Languages*, Stony Brook University, New York.

Gardner, H. (1985). *The Mind's New Science: A History of the Cognitive Revolution*. New York: Basic Books.

González López, V. (2008). *Spanish Clitic Climbing* (Doctoral dissertation). Pennsylvania State University.

Goodall, G. (2004). On the Syntax and Processing of *wh*-Questions in Spanish. In B. Schmeiser *et al.* (eds.), *Proceedings of the 23rd West Coast Conference on Formal Linguistics*. Somerville, MA: Cascadilla, pp. 101–114.

Grüter, T. (2008). When Learners Know More than Linguists: (French) Direct Object Clitics are not Objects. *Probus*, 20, 211–234.

Gupton, T. and Leal Méndez, T. (2013). Experimental Methodologies: Two Case Studies Investigating the Syntax–Discourse Interface. *Studies in Hispanic and Lusophone Linguistics*, 6, 139–164.

Gutiérrez-Rexach, J. (2014). *Interfaces and Domains of Quantification*. Columbus, OH: The Ohio State University Press.

Hoot, B. (2016). Narrow Presentational Focus in Mexican Spanish: Experimental Evidence. *Probus*, 28, 335–365.

Kayne, R. (1975). *French Syntax: The Transformational Cycle*. Cambridge, MA: MIT Press.

Kiparsky, P. (1968). Linguistic Universals and Linguistic Change. In E. Bach and R. T. Harms (eds.), *Universals in Linguistic Theory*. New York: Holt, Rinehart and Winston, pp. 171–202.

Koopman, H. and Sportiche, D. (1991). The Position of Subjects. *Lingua*, 85, 211–258.

López, L. (2009). *A Derivational Syntax for Information Structure*. Oxford: Oxford University Press.

López Ornat, S. (1990). La formación de la oración simple: Las omisiones sintácticas (S-V-O) en la adquisición del español. *Estudios de Psicología*, 11, 41–72.

Lorenzo, G. (2016). Gramática generativa. In J. Gutiérrez-Rexach (ed.), *Enciclopedia de lingüística hispánica*. London: Routledge, pp. 138–150.

Marantz, A. (2005). Generative Linguistics within the Cognitive Neuroscience of Language. *The Linguistic Review*, 22, 429–445.

Martín, J. (2003). Against a Uniform *wh*-Landing Site for Spanish. In P. Kempchinsky and C.-E. Piñeros (eds.), *Theory, Practice and Acquisition: Papers from the 6th Hispanic Linguistics Symposium*. Somerville, MA: Cascadilla, pp. 156–174.

Matushansky, O. (2006). Head Movement in Linguistic Theory. *Linguistic Inquiry*, 37, 69–109.

Maynes, J. (2012). Linguistic Intuition and Calibration. *Linguistics and Philosophy*, 35, 443–460.

Newmeyer, F. (1983). *Grammatical Theory: Its Limits and Possibilities*. Chicago, IL: University of Chicago Press.

O'Grady, W. (2012). Three Factors in the Design and Acquisition of Language. *Wiley Interdisciplinary Reviews: Cognitive Science*, 3, 493–499.

Olarrea, A. (1998). On the Position of Subjects in Spanish. *Anuario del Seminario de Filología Vasca Julio de Urquijo* (Universidad del País Vasco), 32, 47–108.

Ordóñez, F. and Olarrea, A. (2006). Microvariation in Caribbean and Non-Caribbean Spanish Interrogatives. *Probus*, 18, 59–97.

Ormazabal, J. and Romero, J. (2013). Object Clitics, Agreement and Dialectal Variation. *Probus*, 25, 301–344.

Otero, C. P. (1971). *Evolución y revolución en romance*, Vol. 1. Barcelona: Seix Barral.

Otero, C. P. (1972). Acceptable Grammatical Sentences in Spanish. *Linguistic Inquiry*, 3, 233–242.

Otero, C. P. (1973). Agrammaticality in Performance. *Linguistic Inquiry*, 4, 551–562.

Otero, C. P. (1976). *Evolución y revolución en romance*, Vol. 2. Barcelona: Seix Barral.

Phillips, C. (2013). On the Nature of Island Constraints I: Language Processing and Reductionist Accounts. In J. Sprouse and N. Hornstein (eds.), *Experimental Syntax and Island Effects*. Cambridge: Cambridge University Press, pp. 65–108.

Phillips, C., *et al.* (2011). Grammatical Illusions and Selective Fallibility in Real Time Language Comprehension. In J. Runner (ed.), *Syntax and Semantics*, Vol. 37: *Experiments at the Interfaces*. Bingley: Emerald Publications, pp. 147–180.

Reglero, L. (2005). *Wh*-in-situ Constructions: Syntax and/or Phonology? In J. Alderete *et al.* (eds.), *Proceedings of the 24th West Coast Conference on Formal Linguistics*. Somerville, MA: Cascadilla, pp. 334–342.

Rizzi, L. (1997). The Fine Structure of the Left Periphery. In L. Haegeman (ed.), *Elements of Grammar*. Dordrecht: Kluwer, pp. 281–337.

Schütze, C. (1996). *The Empirical Base of Linguistics: Grammaticality Judgments and Linguistic Methodology*. Chicago, IL: The University of Chicago Press.

Sorace, A. and Keller, F. (2005). Gradience in Linguistic Data. *Lingua*, 115, 1497–1524.

Sportiche, D. (1988). A Theory of Floating Quantifiers and its Corollaries for Constituent Structure. *Linguistic Inquiry*, 19, 425–449.

Sportiche, D. (1996). Clitic Constructions. In J. Rooryck and L. Zaring (eds.), *Phrase Structure and the Lexicon*. Dordrecht: Kluwer, pp. 213–275.

Strozer, J. (1976). *Clitics in Spanish* (Doctoral dissertation). University of California–Los Angeles.

Suñer, M. (1989). Spanish Syntax and Semantics in the Eighties: The Principles-and-Parameters Approach. *Hispania*, 72, 832–847.

Suñer, M. (1992). Two Properties of Clitics in Clitic-Doubled Structures. In C.-T. J. Huang and R. May (eds.), *Logical Structure and Linguistic Structure*. Dordrecht: Kluwer, pp. 233–252.

Suñer, M. (2009). Formal Linguistics and the Syntax of Spanish: Past, Present and Future. In J. Collentine *et al.* (eds.), *Selected Proceedings of the 11th Hispanic Linguistics Symposium*. Somerville, MA: Cascadilla, pp. 9–26.

Torrego, E. (1995). On the Nature of Clitic Doubling. In H. Campos and P. Kempchinsky (eds.), *Evolution and Revolution in Linguistic Theory*. Washington, DC: Georgetown University Press, pp. 399–418.

Uriagereka, J. (1995). Aspects of the Syntax of Clitic Placement in Western Romance. *Linguistic Inquiry*, 26, 79–124.

Uribe-Etxebarria, M. (2002). In Situ Questions and Masked Movement. In P. Pica and J. Rooryck (eds.), *Linguistic Variation Yearbook*. Amsterdam: John Benjamins, pp. 259–303.

Zubizarreta, M.-L. (1998). *Prosody, Focus and Word Order*. Cambridge, MA: MIT Press.

2
Optimality Theory and Spanish/Hispanic Linguistics

D. Eric Holt

2.1 Introduction

In the early 1990s, Optimality Theory (OT; Prince and Smolensky 1993/2004) emerged and quickly became the dominant framework within which to carry out research in linguistic theory from a generative perspective, at least in terms of phonology, with extensions and applications to other domains of linguistics as well, like certain aspects of prosodic morphology (McCarthy and Prince 1994). (For a more in-depth introduction to the working of OT, the reader is referred to the foundational documents, as well as Archangeli and Langendoen 1997, Kager 1999, much work by McCarthy and Prince, and others.) A particular strength of this general framework is that it is addresses linguistic universals and is inherently comparative/typological, and optimality-theoretic approaches have provided effective analyses of many phenomena both generally, and more relevantly for the purposes of this *Handbook*, in Spanish, both in isolation and across space (diatopically, dialectology), as well as over time (diachrony), and in language learning (development).

2.2 How Optimality Theory Works

It is important to note that OT is an approach to grammar, rather than a fixed or rigid model. Its fundamental characteristic is that it is constraint-based (rather than rule-based, or otherwise), and that constraints are violable, rather than universal in a hard or absolute sense. The architecture posited includes the Generator (GEN), which takes an input form and produces a set of potential output forms (called *candidates*) whose

Table 2.1 *Illustration of Optimality Theory tableau*

Input (≈ underlying form)	Constraint 1	Constraint 2	Constraint 3
Output candidate (≈ possible surface form) 1	*!		
Output candidate 2		*!	
Output candidate 3 ☞			**

satisfaction of the constraints is determined in parallel (rather than serially/in a multi-step derivation) by the Evaluator (EVAL). Constraints belong to various families, principally these: *markedness* (relative ill-formedness or complexity along various linguistic dimensions), *faithfulness* (the degree of identity or correspondence of features and structures between underlying/input and surface/output forms), and *alignment* (coincidence of segmental, prosodic or morphosyntactic boundaries or edges).

The successful output form (*winning candidate*, conventionally indicated with a pointing hand, ☞) minimally violates the set of constraints and the hierarchical ranking of them that define a particular language's grammar, and is so considered *optimal*. Thus, an output form (roughly, the surface form) will not satisfy all the constraints of a language (and may in fact incur more violations), but is optimal or preferable to others because these violate higher-ranked constraints and are thus eliminated from consideration (conventionally indicated with the exclamation point, !, to signal to the reader the fatal or determining violation). The content of the constraints (e.g. the importance or place of phonetics, functionalist approaches, etc.), and other matters of implementation (e.g. single-step vs. level-ordered derivation, strict dominance of constraints vs. a stochastic/probabilistic evaluation,[1] cumulative/gang-up effects, etc.), are, strictly speaking, logically separable from the basic architectural model sketched here and illustrated in a tableau (a standard expositional device in OT) as Table 2.1, and researchers have adopted vastly different assumptions that may still be classified as OT approaches, as illustrated in Table 2.1.

2.3 Optimality Theory Approaches to Spanish and Hispanic Linguistics

There is considerable OT literature that treats issues of Spanish, and of Hispanic linguistics a bit more broadly. Just as for other languages, these

---

[1] Under Stochastic Optimality Theory (Boersma and Hayes 2001), constraints occupy a certain range of values on a continuous ranking scale, and, upon a given evaluation, specific values are determined and these selection points condition the position of constraints in the tableau. This allows for the modeling of frequency distribution of empirical data, as the degree of overlap of constraints varies and corresponds with the probability of ranking reversal; for a visualization, see the discussion of Cutillas Espinosa (2004) in "Sociolinguistic and Other Variation" in Section 2.3.3.

have been largely concerned with issues of phonology, but there are also applications to other domains, a sampling of all of which will be sketched out in the remainder of this chapter. (Cutillas Espinosa 2003 is an early comprehensive work that outlines OT as applied to segments, syllables, metrical theory and suprasegmentals, as well as the interaction between phonology and morphology, and to issues of learning. Additionally, Gutiérrez-Bravo and Herrera 2008 treat syntax and phonology. See also Gutiérrez-Bravo et al. 2015.) While many phenomena have been analyzed, as the theory evolves and new approaches emerge, further treatments will continue to be necessary to improve explanatory adequacy and to reach a more cohesive overall picture of Optimality Theory as a model of the language faculty.

2.3.1 Phonology

Given that phonology is the area in which OT was first developed, it will be no surprise that the great majority of work that treats Spanish is in this subfield. What follows are some comprehensive works as well as other studies that treat less-studied data.

Colina (2014) provides a thorough introduction to the underpinnings of the overall theory, as well as discussion of developments and extensions like the Correspondence Theory (McCarthy and Prince 1994) model of faithfulness, the more functionalist allied approach Dispersion Theory (which looks at systemic markedness; see, e.g., Flemming 2002), and Stratal OT (which is a version of a multi-level Lexical Phonology and Morphology; in original form, rule-based; see work by Bermúdez-Otero). Case studies include resyllabification (*las alas* > [la-sa-las], where ONSET ("No vowel-initial syllables"), NOCODA ("Syllables cannot end in a coda") and various ALIGNMENT constraints (between edges of syllables, consonants, and vowels) interact), and Chilean vocalization (/pobɾe/ > [pow.ɾe], where constraints on sonority and on spirantization come into play). Bradley (2014) likewise presents an overview of the workings of OT of some of the same phenomena as Colina, and includes a bibliography of works in OT about Spanish.

Other data treated are the stop ~ spirant alternation ([b,d,g] ~ [β,ð,ɣ]), the conspiracy of gliding and resyllabification in avoiding onsetless syllables (/mi amiga/ > [mja-mi-ɣa], *[mi-_a-mi-ɣa], where, when the two words are syllabified together, /i/ is realized as part of a diphthong, and the initial syllable of *amiga* comes to acquire an onset from preceding *mi*), matters of word stress, and other issues of articulatory or gestural phonology (e.g. intrusive vowels in consonant + ɾ clusters, e.g. /paɾte/ > [paɾ^{a}te]), and discussion of the phonetic grounding of markedness constraints. Colina (2009) offers an extended application of OT to the syllabic phonology of Spanish: syllable types, phonotactics, syllabification of C#V and V#V across words, interactions between the syllable and morphology (including /s/ aspiration, velarization of coda nasals, and the strengthening of onsets and of /r/), and various cases of epenthesis and of deletion that serve as repair mechanisms to improve syllable structure. Likewise, Martínez-Gil and Colina (2006) present a collection of 20 papers on all aspects of Spanish phonology (some of which are mentioned specifically in what follows).

Recent work that involves instrumental measurement by electropalatography (EPG) of place and stricture assimilation data of Buenos Aires Spanish is found in Kochetov and Colantoni (2011), who argue for modified gestural representations and gestural coordination constraints. Buckley (2014, 2016) treats secondary stress in Spanish, and distinguishes between alignment at the lexical and phrasal levels, with variability in speech style between rhetorical (e.g. gra(màti)(càli)(dád)) and colloquial (e.g. (gràma)ti(càli)(dád)) secondary stress placement still captured with categorical alignment, thus obviating the need for less restrictive gradient alignment. Buckley (2016:97) acknowledges that the role of pragmatics here remains a complex, open question.

2.3.2 Morphology and its Interface with Phonology

The formation of words via inflection or derivation (or otherwise) often interacts in nontrivial ways with phonology; that is, the selection of some morphological structure may be dependent on certain phonological sound patterns (locus of stress, presence of high or front vowels, would-be occurrence of certain clusters of consonants, etc.). These alternations of different forms of the same morpheme in related words can be characterized in optimality-theoretic terms in a number of ways. (See Colina 2011 for an overview of Spanish morphophonology that includes OT; Colina 2009 likewise includes treatment of many of these phenomena.)

Examples of alternations discussed in OT include coronal (t, d) and velar (k, g) softening (e.g. cant̠ar ~ canci̠ón, eléctri̠co ~ electrici̠dad, mago ~ magia), diphthongization (e.g. pensar ~ pienso, bondad ~ bueno), nasal depalatalization (e.g. doña ~ don, desdeñar ~ desdén), diminutive formation (e.g. -ito vs. -ico; the morphological level to/at which these suffixes are attached), the nature of word-final -e and of plural alternations -(e)s (e.g. pan ~ panes, café(s)), and others.

For hypocoristic truncations (e.g. colegio > cole, or nickname forms like Francisco > Paco, or Enrique as any of Enri (left-anchored form), Rique (stress-anchored form) or K-ike (reduplicative form), see much work by Piñeros (e.g. 2000a, 2000b) and Colina, as well as Roca and Felíu (2003), Gutiérrez (2009), Grau Sempere (2013), and Sanz (2015), who offers a transderivational approach.

For word-final -e and plural formation, Colina (2006) argues that the -es allomorph (e.g. sol-es) is an attempt to improve upon morphological structure in providing the consonant-final word (*sol*) with a terminal element (*-e*), rather than being motivated by phonotactics, since /ls/ is indeed allowed in words such as *solsticio* and *vals*. The presence of *-e* in the plurals is argued to be a case of the emergence of the unmarked (a "TETU" effect) and the result of *CODA ("No coda"), which may be violated in Spanish (as it is in *sol*), coming to be satisfied ([so-les]). See Bonet (2006) for a different OT approach that includes discussion of gender allomorphs and that invokes RESPECT ("respect idiosyncratic lexical specifications") and PRIORITY ("respect lexical priority of order of allomorphs," here {o > e, Ø}). (Bradley and Smith 2011 likewise adopt an analysis based on allomorph selection, lexical ordering, and subcategorization in their treatment of diminutive formation in Judeo Spanish, and Smith 2011 adopts a similar approach for diminutivization in Sonoran Spanish in Northern Mexico.)

For inflectional paradigms, see Morris (2005) and Saltarelli (2006), who both work within McCarthy's (2004) model of optimal paradigms (OP). Morris looks at various cases of leveling in Old Spanish verbal forms, including cases that would appear to show underapplication of phonological processes like diphthongization (OSp. *entriega* > MSp. *entrega*) and overapplication of metaphony/harmony in the presence of yod (OSp. *fugyo* (< Lat. FUGIO), which attracts other members of the paradigm, e.g. FUGIS > FOGES > *fuges*) and of velar softening (the palatalization and affrication of [k] when followed by a front vowel, e.g. *vençer* and related forms attracting *ven[k]o* > *venço*). Similar to TETU effects, Morris argues that these show "ATU," attraction to the unmarked (where paradigm members adopt structures of some other less-marked member, which acts as an attractor). Morris also indicates that the OP approach cannot account for crucial intermediate stages, just the final completed outcome, inviting further research on the issue.

Saltarelli (2006) offers an account of Spanish number inflection in which singular and plural forms are evaluated together (with REALIZE NUMBER interacting with other constraints), and operating with a hierarchy of morphological categories (e.g. lexical (number) and functional (case, gender, etc.)). Data treated include palatal/depalatal alternations ([ɲ/n, ʎ/l]), cases of stress shift (*régimen ~ regímenes, carácter ~ caracteres*), invariant forms (*lunes ~ lunes, bíceps ~ bíceps*) and stressed-vowel-final words (*café(s), bajá(s) ~ bajá(es)*). For depalatalization (e.g. /desdeɲ/ > *desdén ~ desdenes*, vs. *desdeñar*), see also Lloret and Mascaró (2006), who offer a different approach that employs positional faithfulness as well as output–output correspondence constraints (IDENTITY–BASE) that favor assimilated/neutralized place of articulation, with a strong interpretation of what may be considered a base. Within Stratal OT, Bermúdez-Otero (2006) also treats depalatalization, as well as diphthongization and other denominal derivation.

For a broader discussion of OT in morphology, see Xu (2016), who discusses various OT approaches to the morphology–phonology interface and presents in abbreviated form their differing mechanisms and assumptions. Xu states that the assumptions of conventional OT, designed originally for phonology, are inadequate and need to be extended to account for certain aspects of morphology, like phonologically-conditioned allomorph selection, syncretism, and blocking and extension of morphological exponence. Regarding the tenets of various OT approaches, there are differences in terms of whether morphosyntactic features may be changed, how a morph is introduced (via input, output candidate or constraint), the types of constraints employed, and the question of serial vs. parallel derivation, among others (Xu 2016, sec. 3). These approaches include Realization OT (Xu and Aronoff 2011a, 2011b, and advocated by Xu), Optimal Interleaving (Wolf 2008, building on OT with Candidate Chains, McCarthy 2007), Optimal Construction Morphology (Caballero and Inkelas 2013), and Distributed Optimality (Trommer 2001). Xu offers a sketch of an analysis of Spanish conjunction allomorphy (*o* ~ *u*, *i* ~ *e*) within Realization OT that is claimed to be superior to the conventional OT approach to this data given by Bonet and Harbour (2012). (Among several other cases studied, Xu also offers analyses of Romanian syncretic verb forms and Latin second declension forms.)

For other studies of Romance phonology and morphology (Spanish diphthongization and suffixation, definite article allomorphy in Galician and Italian, other phenomena in French, Catalan, and Romanian), including discussion of serial vs. parallel versions of OT, see Bonet and Lloret (2016). See also the works mentioned in the section on dialect variation by Holt (2000) and Wiltshire (2006), as well as by Elsman and Holt (2009), which includes discussion of issues of grammaticalization, where one type of linguistic form becomes another or takes on new functions, which under OT would be due to a change in the grammar/constraint ranking and/or structural reanalysis. (See also Kiparsky 2012, who, in an extended discussion of optimization and grammaticalization/degrammaticalization, mentions the upgrading of affixal *-mos* to clitic *=nos* in Spanish, but offers no formal treatment of it.)

2.3.3 Other Applications

OT is inherently comparative, given that the Evaluation function identifies the optimal output candidate from among a set of forms that compete along multiple dimensions. The application of such an approach is also naturally extended to analyze or model different varieties of a language, either over time (historical change) or space (dialectology) or situation (register/sociolects); and similarly for stages of development within a single language, either as a first (native, L1) or second (often foreign, L2) language.

Historical Change and Dialect Variation

OT approaches to historical change and dialect variation look at not only the interaction of faithfulness and markedness constraints, but also the role of listener-based, perceptual, cognitive, systemic, and external (foreign) influences on linguistic structure and change (by reranking or reanalysis of underlying forms) at all levels of grammatical analysis, though most commonly on the segmental inventory, syllable and prosodic structure, and intersecting points of morphology (Holt 2006:378).

Because OT is inherently comparative, much work in all linguistic fields compares the grammars of related dialects and languages. This means that treatments of Spanish are often not exclusive, instead also treating more than one variety of Spanish, or Spanish and some other variety of Romance (Portuguese, Galician, Leonese, Catalan, French, Italian) or even more cross-linguistically (especially when some structure or constraint is being analyzed from a typological perspective). One example of this is Piñeros (2006), who treats the phonology of nasal consonants in five dialects of Spanish, giving evidence of place assimilation, neutralization, velarization, and absorption. Piñeros argues that ALIGN-C(NASAL) is gradiently violable in its interactions with AGREE(PLACE) and the PLACE HIERARCHY; when grammars opt for unmarked coda segments, coronals surface, but when grammars prefer the least consonantal nasal, velarization obtains (2006:169). Another example is Wiltshire (2006), who analyzes the status of prefix boundaries in several varieties of Spanish and their importance for /s/ aspiration (Caribbean), /n/ velarization (Granadan), and the realization of [Ø] (Argentine); Wiltshire argues for an internal word boundary, with alignment constraints targeting both lexical and prosodic edges, and interacting with positional faithfulness and with WEAK|$_{PW}$, a cover term for markedness constraints that favor increasing sonority in word-final position. See also Holt (2000) for singular/plural nasal alternations in Galician, Mirandese, and Spanish, and Elsman and Holt (2009) for preposition+article contractions in two varieties of Old Leonese.

For an extended overview of OT and language change in Spanish, see Holt (2006), and the entries from its Appendix ("Bibliography on Optimality Theory and Language Variation and Change in Spanish"), and, for historical sound change in OT from a broader perspective, see Holt (2015).

Sociolinguistic and Other Variation

Since language use is inherently variable, it is natural for some branch of linguistic theory to be concerned with its formalization, and some practitioners of OT have endeavored to incorporate the insights of both (linguistic theory and sociolinguistics) in their analyses of variable data of various sorts.

Cutillas Espinosa (2004) offers an analysis of variable coda /-s/ realization in two different contexts of Murcian Spanish broadcasting. He offers

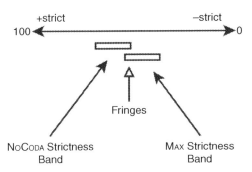

Figure 2.1 Strictness bands of NoCoda and Max following Hayes' (2000) model (from Cutillas Espinosa 2004)

a three-grammar model with continuous ranking values (that is, a stochastic/probabilistic approach). In this approach, there are two reference grammars, G_1 (that of the Peninsular standard, where /-s/ is retained, due to dominance of Max "no deletion") and G_3 (that of the local Murcian norm, where /-s/ is usually elided, due to dominance of NoCoda), with an intermediate G_2 whose variable output (here, [-s] ~ [Ø]) depends on social or other personal factors (2004:179). G_2 is instantiated by variable selection points of the two constraints under consideration, under conscious and meaningful control by the speaker who wishes to convey judgments or access the prestige associated with each variety. (See Figure 2.1, where the overlap of constraints that allows for variability is visualized.)

Holt (2004) treats sporadic sound changes in Old Spanish, not apparently sociolinguistically conditioned, where so-called bad syllable contact, either within word or at verb+clitic boundary, leads variably to metathesis, intrusive stop formation, palatalization, simplification or other resolution (Lat. CAT(E)NATU 'chained' > OSp. *cadnado* ~ *candado* ~ *cañado*; *dezid lo* 'say. PL.IMP it' > OSp. *dezidlo* ~ *dezildo*). This is modeled under a partially-ranked OT grammar with constraints on sonority sequencing and syllable contact, linearity, featural identity, and others. The results predicted by the combinatorics of these constraints match fairly closely with frequency of attested variable forms.

Finally, an example of the interaction of variation with acquisition comes from Díaz-Campos and Colina (2006), who look at the acquisition of phonological variation in first language speakers. (Additional discussion of acquisition follows in the section on acquisition.) Specifically, they analyze the school variety of Venezuelan Spanish, where younger lower-socioeconomic class children show lower retention of approximant [ð], but older children show increased retention that more closely resembles the academic variety norm (e.g. [pwe] vs. [pweðe]). Various constraints are employed that target segmental and contextual markedness, along with positional faithfulness, modeled in the stochastic approach to learning in OT, the

Gradual Learning Algorithm. (See also below in discussion of acquisition.) Under their approach, older children activate the constraint ranking of the more formal speech style upon exposure to the institutional setting, where retention of [ð̞] is favored (2006:444).

Acquisition

Regarding acquisition in OT, the learner must master both the lexicon and the grammatical system (and the interaction between these), and the interplay of markedness versus faithfulness as it develops over time. That is, it is a common assumption that children begin with markedness constraints dominating others, which is consistent with an immature articulatory system (in the case of segmental phonology) and with the notion that simpler structures are naturally more basic (less marked) and (therefore) easier to master (in the case of other areas of phonology, and other areas of grammar). Over time, with biological/articulatory and cognitive maturation, more complex structures emerge due to the demotion of more limiting constraints, with the concomitant emerging of faithfulness constraints that allow for a wider or fuller and adult-like range of expression.

Two prominent learning models are the Constraint Demotion Algorithm (CDA; Tesar and Smolensky 2000) and the Gradual Learning Algorithm (GLA; Boersma and Hayes 2001). The CDA, couched within standard OT, detects differences in constraint ranking between the current and target grammar, and iteratively applies a constraint demotion process, with each demotion corresponding to a stage in the interlanguage development of the learner. For learning in stochastic OT, the GLA is fed with data, relevant frequencies, and degree of constraint violations, and subsequently the necessary changes in the ranking values are made accordingly to more closely model actual usage.

Aspects of Spanish L1 acquisition that have been treated in OT include syllable structure and the role of frequency of input of various syllable types (Morales-Front 2006, arguing for the GLA and against the CDA), consonant clusters and the role of sonority (Barlow 2006, with universal ordering of sonority being incorporated into a fine-grained decomposed set of ONSET constraints that favors lower-sonority segments; see also Barlow 2003, 2005), word- and phrase-level stress, and the role of mastery of acoustic parameters (Lleó and Arias 2006, who argue that stress assignment is mastered early on in terms of footing, foot type, phrasal headedness, and alignment, but that proper production of phonetic parameters of amplitude, pitch, and duration emerges consistently only later).

For simultaneous bilingual L1 acquisition, Lleó (2002) looks at early child data from German–Spanish bilinguals, and analyzes the acquisition of prosodic word size and the truncation common in early learners' speech (e.g. Spanish: *mariposa* as [boza], later [pa'bɔta]; German: *Melone* as [jojo]), as they transition from producing a single metrical foot to larger prosodic units, success at which shows a slight delay (overcome by age 2;0) when compared to monolinguals. Metrical constraints on the alignment of metrical feet with prosodic words and on the parsing of syllables and the composition of feet are argued to be undominated in the initial stage of grammar, but come to be demoted. HEAD-MAX also plays a prominent role, in that the stressed syllable of the target word is retained in children's production. Lleó argues that considerations of markedness must be incorporated into the analysis to account for the prolonged use by bilinguals of truncated form, though this delay is short lived. (See also Lleó 2006 and Lleó and Arias 2009.)

For bilingual language processing, Goldrick *et al.* (2016) use the formalism of Gradient Symbolic Computation (Smolensky *et al.* 2014), an extension of OT, in offering a computational account of co-activation and code mixing in bilingual grammars. They model blend representations, where multiple elements are co-present within the linguistic representation (e.g. DOG and PERRO both in the (same) head of some noun phrase (NP)), not merely being simultaneously activated (2016:858).

For Spanish L2 acquisition that has been treated in OT, Cabrelli Amaro (2017) looks at the role of prosodic structure and of proficiency level in the acquisition by English-speaking learners of Spanish of this language's process of spirantization of voiced stops (/b d g/ > [β ð ɣ]). Since the approximant allophones are absent from English, they do pose a challenge to master in the path to acquisition, success at which is seen to depend on prosodic position (word-medially first, then also word-initially). Cabrelli Amaro adopts the GLA (Boersma and Hayes 2001) and implements her analysis in a stochastic version of OT, in which learners can converge on a target-like constraint ranking but still occasionally produce a non-target-like output in those cases where crucial constraints partially overlap and implementation yields a constraint reversal. Constraints employed include positional faithfulness constraints on the identity of the feature [continuant] in the onset (syllable, prosodic word, intonational phrase), and markedness constraints on the occurrence of stops and approximants post-vocalically, with the former being higher ranked in the L1 ranking and as the starting point for the interlanguage L2 Spanish grammar. Learners take in evidence for spirantized forms and gradually demote IDENTITY-INPUTOUTPUT(CONT) below the domain-based positional faithfulness constraints.

For a treatment of Spanish L2 vowels, Boersma and Escudero's (2008) account for how Dutch learners come to perceive a smaller L2 vowel inventory (12 vs. 5 vowels), some of which are easier to learn than others. They provide both an analysis couched within Stochastic OT that includes a separate perception grammar employing negative constraints on duration and spectral quality (first and second formats, F1, F2), and computational simulations. They argue that Dutch vowel categories are reused for Spanish vowels, with learning to properly map auditory continua to the five Spanish vowels. They argue that their account of perception (in a two-stage comprehension model) and its acquisition bridges the gap between phonological theory and the computational modeling of speech processing (2008:298).

For transfer and developmental effects of Spanish speakers learning English, Hancin-Bhatt and Bhatt (1997) offer an OT analysis of ESL syllable structure; they compare the differential learning paths of L1 speakers of Spanish and Japanese, whose different L1 phonotactics means a different initial state of the L2 grammar (constraint ranking), assuming a Full Transfer model of acquisition (see also Chapters 30 and 31, this volume). The authors employ constraints relating to sonority sequencing and minimal sonority distance, as well as other markedness (NoCODA, *COMPLEX (ONSET,CODA), CODACONDITION) and faithfulness (PARSE, FILL, now superseded in a Correspondence model)[2] constraints, their interaction models the effects for ESL clusters in terms of epenthesis, deletion, and eventual mastery of the wider and more complex range of English syllable margins.

Escudero and Boersma (2004) offer a stochastic OT treatment, together with the GLA, of Spanish-speaking learners' acquisition of the *ship–sheep* contrast in Scottish or Southern British English. They formulate negative constraints based on perceptual cues (here, relevant are height, tenseness, and duration) within a formal perceptual grammar, and claim that within this model (and replicated with computer simulations), the dialect-dependent and L2-specific facts provide evidence for the hypotheses of Full Transfer and Full Access (2004:583).

For Spanish acquisition that has been treated in OT in other subfields, some early work (LaFond 2001, 2003) looked at the syntax–pragmatics interface and the L2 learning by English speakers of null subjects (Ø *voy al cine*), subject–verb inversion (*vino Juan*), and *that*-trace effects (*¿Quién crees que ganará la carrera?* vs. 'Who do you think (*that) will win the race?'), phenomena often subsumed under a single 'pro-drop' parameter. LaFond offers a more nuanced analysis that accounts for the fact that these three properties are not acquired simultaneously, and argues that these effects obtain independently through the demotion of syntactic constraints in the English native grammar (SUBJECT, PARSE, TRACE-LEXICALLY-GOVERNED) such that they become dominated by constraints related to discourse function (DROPTOPIC, ALIGNFOCUS-RIGHT).[3] (This learning is modeled via Tesar and Smolensky's 2000 CDA.) (See also LaFond 2001, LaFond et al. 2001.)

---

[2] For those readers less familiar with these constraints, the NOCODA constraint prohibits codas, the *COMPLEX(ONSET, CODA) constraint prohibits consonant clusters in the syllable onset and coda, respectively, and the CODACONDITION constraint imposes specific constraints on the place features that are (or are not) allowed in the coda. Likewise, the PARSE constraint states that all elements in the input must be expressed in the output and the FILL constraint states that every element in the output must be present in the input.

[3] The SUBJECT constraint requires the highest A-specifier in an extended projection to be filled, DROPTOPIC states that arguments coreferent with the topic must be structurally unrealized, and ALIGNFOCUS-RIGHT requires that the left edge of focus constituents must align with the right edge of the maximal projection (LaFond 2003).

For a case of acquisition in the case of a syntax–morphology mismatch, Bermúdez-Otero (2007) looks at so-called Spanish pseudoplurals, arguing that phonological cues help guide their acquisition. He distinguishes singular forms like *Carlos* from *virus*, which are syntactically and phonologically the same (nouns ending in /-s/), but whose structural difference emerges only in derivational contexts (viz. *Carlote* vs. *virusote*). The emergence of the Spanish pseudoplural nouns shows that phonological properties of words can trigger syntax–morphology mismatches during language acquisition (2007:231). While mostly not really an OT analysis, Bermúdez-Otero does argue for certain "parsing preferences" that are violable and partially conflicting and that read very much like OT constraints (e.g. *Avoid masculine a-stems, Avoid pseudoplurals, Avoid athematic stems*, etc.; and that are presented in hierarchical form in his Ex. (40)). These, however, may "gang up," so are perhaps more akin to the constraints of Harmonic Grammar and Harmonic Serialism (e.g. McCarthy and Pater 2016), a more recent development of traditional OT, that allows for cumulative effects of the violation of lower-ranked constraints that overcome higher-ranked ones, not possible in standard OT. These and other notions are developed further in Bermúdez-Otero (forthcoming).

Syntax, Semantics, Discourse, and Pragmatics

As an overall approach to grammar via constraint ranking, OT is also applied to other areas of grammar which evidence their own types of universals, restrictions, and interactions both within and at the interface between modules. Syntax deals with the generation of grammatical sentences, with semantics and pragmatics dealing with interpretation, and there are abundant cases where these interact (e.g. scope relations, co-reference, control). A full discussion of these matters is beyond the scope of this chapter, and a sampling of issues and of treatments is given below. (The reader is referred to the chapters in Legendre *et al.* 2001, and other more recent works, e.g. Legendre 2016, Blutner 2000.)

A number of authors treat issues of word order in Spanish. For the ordering of clitic pronouns in Romance (including Spanish, and including spurious *se*), see Grimshaw (2001), where constraints on PERSON, NUMBER, and CASE interact with alignment and others. For clitic left-dislocation (CLLD) and the interaction of prosody and syntactic movement (e.g. (**A María**)$_{PrP1}$ (no *le* enviará ningún paquete)), see Feldhausen (2016), who employs ALIGN-TOPIC,R, ALIGN-CP,L, which both introduce boundaries, mitigated against by the structure-avoiding constraint MIN-N-PHRASES ("minimize the number of prosodic phrases"), and markedness constraints on the size of prosodic phrases, MIN-BIN and MAX-BIN$_{(IP\ HEAD)}$. (See also Feldhausen 2014a, 2014b.)

Additionally, for subject inversion in relative clauses (e.g. *el libro que __ escribió la maestra*), see Gutiérrez-Bravo (2005), who argues for conflict between syntactic (e.g. Extended Projection Principle, EPP) and intonational (e.g. TopicFirst, Weight-to-Prominence) requirements. (See also Gutiérrez-Bravo and Monforte 2008, as well as Bakovic 1998, who introduces a markedness subhierarchy for different types of argument operators in his analysis of *wh*-movement and inversion in matrix and subordinate clauses. For these and other issues relating to word order, see also Gutiérrez-Bravo 2007, 2008, 2010.)

And for further matters of focus and prosody, Gabriel (2010) treats word order in Argentine Spanish under a Minimalist OT framework. Other works on prosody and its interfaces include much work by Feldhausen and colleagues. For example, Feldhausen and Vanrell (2014) present comparative work with Catalan on strategies of focus (clefting, nuclear stress, prosodically-motivated movement) under a stochastic approach that employs the constraints StressFocus, Head-IP, Subject, FaithSyntax, *P-Movement, and FocusCleft.[4] (See also Patin *et al.* 2017.)

For matters of morphological case, Lestrade (2010) offers a functionally motivated account of the use of case (particularly when it indicates spatial relations) that combines insights from syntax, semantics, pragmatics, typology, and corpus research, with proposed constraints inspired by Grice's cooperative principle (1975). (Spanish is mentioned occasionally in discussions of typology.) Lestrade advocates for a bidirectional architecture where both speaker and hearer perspective are evaluated, and Case offers the optimal solution for the expression of a meaning. P. de Swart (2007, esp. ch. 3) likewise adopts a bidirectional account in his analysis of Direct Object Marking (DOM) and the use of so-called "personal" *a* as an aid to avoiding ambiguity and recovering grammatical relations when issues of animacy, definiteness, and specificity are at play.

For verbal aspect, Koontz-Garboden (2004) offers a stochastic OT analysis of contact-induced language change (which he also calls indirect transfer) of the expression of progressive aspect in Spanish under influence from English (synthetic *sale* vs. analytic *está saliendo*). He employs constraints *Progressive and *Habitual along with Max-λ ("All attribute/value pairs in the input f-structure are morpholexically represented in the output") and *Affix; results are further modeled under the GLA.

For matters of negation, there are several treatments. See de Swart (2010) for a typological treatment of the expression and interpretation of negation (negative quantifiers, negative words, uses as Negative Polarity Items, NPIs) in Spanish, Romance, and other languages. She distinguishes

---

[4] The StressFocus constraint requires that the focus be realized with main stress. Head-IP, on the other hand, demands that the main stress occur in the rightmost position in its intonational phrase; and FaithSyntax militates against syntactic material being added to the input. *P-Movement (see Zubizarreta 1998) prohibits prosodically-motivated movement such that non-focal material is moved to a non-final position as the result of prosodic demands; more formally, "phonetic material that does not belong to the verbal chain C-T-*v* is never realized below C, T, and *v*" (adapted from Gabriel's 2010 Stay-PhoneticForm). Finally, FocusCleft requires a focus element to be clefted (Feldhausen and Vanrell 2014, 2015).

strict negative concord from nonstrict depending on whether it obtains preverbally and postverbally, a distinction that falls out from the constraint ranking of *NEG, NEGFIRST, FOCUSLAST, and others. See Espinal *et al.* (2016) for double negation in Catalan and Spanish, where syntax and prosody (pitch accent, boundary tones) interact in a bidirectional model, in which forms and meanings converge in the interpretation of sentences like No ha llamado nadie, which shows nonstrict negative concord (*nonstrict*, because negative concord does not obtain in Spanish when the n-word appears preverbally, e.g. *Nadie ha llamado*).

For acquisition of issues of syntax and its intersection with discourse pragmatics, see the works previously cited by LaFond (2001, 2003) and LaFond *et al.* (2001), as well as Lleó (2001), who treats the interaction between prosody and emergence of the article in the early acquisition of Spanish and German.

2.4 Brief Concluding Remarks

In the past 25 years, OT has been a leading force in linguistic theory and a reevaluation of what constitutes the human language faculty. While a majority of early works treated issues of phonology, the scope of data treated and the interactions between modules of grammar has increased greatly, and many interesting analyses have been proposed in all areas, a selection of which is surveyed above, that both advance our understanding of Spanish as well as offer refinements to the theory itself. There continue to be many open questions, and readers are invited to continue in the exploration of OT and Spanish and Hispanic linguistics.

References

Archangeli, D. and Langendoen, T. (1997). *Optimality Theory: An Overview*. Malden, MA: Blackwell Publishers.

Bakovic, E. (1998). Optimality and Inversion in Spanish. In P. Barbosa, D. Fox, P. Hagstrom, M. McGinnis, and D. Pesetsky (eds.), *Is the Best Good Enough?* Cambridge, MA: MIT Press, pp. 35–58.

Barlow, J. (2003). Asymmetries in the Acquisition of Consonant Clusters in Spanish. *Canadian Journal of Linguistics*, 48 (3–4), 179–210.

Barlow, J. (2005). Sonority Effects in the Production of Consonant Clusters by Spanish Speaking Children. In D. Eddington (ed.), *Selected Proceedings of the 6th Conference on the Acquisition of Spanish and Portuguese as First and Second Languages*. Somerville, MA: Cascadilla, pp. 1–14.

Barlow, J. (2006). Constraint Conflict in the Acquisition of Clusters in Spanish. In F. Martínez-Gil and S. Colina (eds.), *Optimality Theoretic Studies in Spanish Phonology*. Amsterdam: John Benjamins, pp. 523–48.

Bermúdez-Otero, R. (2006). Morphological Structure and Phonological Domains in Spanish Denominal Derivation. In F. Martínez-Gil and S. Colina (eds.), *Optimality Theoretic Studies in Spanish Phonology*. Amsterdam: John Benjamins, pp. 278–311.

Bermúdez-Otero, R. (2007). Spanish Pseudoplurals: Phonological Cues in the Acquisition of a Syntax–Morphology Mismatch. In M. Baerman, G. Corbett, D. Brown, and A. Hippisley (eds.), *Deponency and Morphological Mismatches (Proceedings of the British Academy)*. Oxford: Oxford University Press, pp. 231–269.

Bermúdez-Otero, R. (forthcoming). *Stratal Optimality Theory*. Oxford: Oxford University Press.

Blutner, R. (2000). Some Aspects of Optimality in Natural Language Interpretation. *Journal of Semantics*, 17 (3), 189–216.

Boersma, P. and Escudero, P. (2008). Learning to Perceive a Smaller L2 Vowel Inventory: An Optimality Theory Account. In P. Avery, B. E. Dresher, and K. Rice (eds.), *Contrast in Phonology: Theory, Perception, Acquisition*. Berlin: De Gruyter, pp. 271–302.

Boersma, P. and Hayes, B. (2001). Empirical Tests of the Gradual Learning Algorithm. *Linguistic Inquiry*, 32 (1), 45–86.

Bonet, E. (2006). Gender Allomorphy and Epenthesis in Spanish. In F. Martínez-Gil and S. Colina (eds.), *Optimality Theoretic Studies in Spanish Phonology*. Amsterdam: John Benjamins, pp. 312–338.

Bonet, E. and Harbour, D. (2012). Contextual Allomorphy. In J. Trommer (ed.), *The Morphology and Phonology of Exponence*. Oxford: Oxford University Press, pp. 195–235.

Bonet, E. and Lloret, M.-R. (2016). Romance Phonology and Morphology in Optimality Theory. In S. Fischer and C. Gabriel (eds.), *Manual of Grammatical Interfaces in Romance*. Berlin and Boston, MA: De Gruyter, pp. 113–147.

Bradley, T. G. (2014). Optimality Theory and Spanish Phonology. *Language and Linguistics Compass*, 8, 65–88. doi: 10.1111/lnc3.12065.

Bradley, T. G. and Smith, J. (2011). The Phonology–Morphology Interface in Judeo-Spanish Diminutive Formation: A Lexical Ordering and Subcategorization Approach. *Studies in Hispanic and Lusophone Linguistics*, 4 (2), 247–300.

Buckley, E. (2014). Spanish Secondary Stress without Gradient Alignment. In H.-L. Huang, E. Poole, and A. Rysling (eds.), *Proceedings of the 43rd Annual Meeting of the North East Linguistic Society*. Amherst, MA: Graduate Linguistic Student Association, pp. 39–50.

Buckley, E. (2016). Foot Alignment in Spanish Secondary Stress. In J. Heinz, R. Goedemans, and H. van der Hulst (eds.), *Dimensions of Phonological Stress*. Cambridge: Cambridge University Press, pp. 79–100.

Caballero, G. and Inkelas, S. (2013). Word Construction: Tracing an Optimal Path through the Lexicon. *Morphology*, 23 (2), 103–143.

Cabrelli Amaro, J. (2017). The Role of Prosodic Structure in the L2 Acquisition of Spanish Stop Lenition. *Second Language Research*, 33 (2), 233–269.

Colina, S. (2006). Optimality-Theoretic Advances in our Understanding of Spanish Syllable Structure. In F. Martínez-Gil and S. Colina (eds.), *Optimality Theoretic Studies in Spanish Phonology*. Amsterdam: John Benjamins, pp. 172–204.

Colina, S. (2009). *Spanish Phonology: A Syllabic Perspective*. Washington, DC: Georgetown University Press.

Colina, S. (2011). Spanish Morphophonology. *Studies in Hispanic and Lusophone Linguistics*, 4 (1), 173–9.1

Colina, S. (2014). La teoría de la optimidad en la fonología del español. In Rafael Núñez Cedeño, Sonia Colina, and Travis G. Bradley (eds.), *Fonología generativa contemporánea de la lengua española* (2nd edn). Washington, DC: Georgetown University Press, pp. 291–317.

Cutillas Espinosa, J. A. (2003). *Teoría lingüística de la optimidad: fonología, morfología y aprendizaje*. Murcia: Universidad de Murcia.

Cutillas Espinosa, J. A. (2004). Meaningful Variability: A Sociolinguistically-Grounded Approach to Variation in Optimality Theory. *International Journal of English Studies*, 4 (2), 165–184.

de Swart, H. (2010). *Expression and Interpretation of Negation. An OT Typology*. Dordrecht: Springer.

de Swart, P. (2007). Cross-Linguistic Variation in Object Marking (Doctoral dissertation). Radboud University, Nijmegen.

Díaz-Campos, M. and Colina, S. (2006). The Interaction between Faithfulness Constraints and Sociolinguistic Variation: The Acquisition of Phonological Variation in First Language Speakers. In F. Martínez-Gil and S. Colina (eds.), *Optimality-Theoretic Studies in Spanish Phonology*. Amsterdam; Philadelphia, PA: John Benjamins, pp. 424–446.

Elsman, M. M. and Holt, D. E. (2009). When Small Words Collide: Morphological Reduction and Phonological Compensation in Old Leonese Contractions. In R. Leow, H. Campos, and D. Lardiere (eds.), *Little Words: Their History, Phonology, Syntax, Semantics, Pragmatics, and Acquisition*. Georgetown University Press, pp. 21–33.

Escudero, P. and Boersma, P. (2004). Bridging the Gap between L2 Speech Perception Research and Phonological Theory. *Studies in Second Language Acquisition*, 26 (4), 551–585.

Espinal, M. T., Tubau, S., Borràs-Comes, J., and Prieto, P. (2016). Double Negation in Catalan and Spanish: Interaction between Syntax and Prosody. In P. Larrivée and C. Lee (eds.), *Negation and Polarity: Experimental Perspectives, Language, Cognition, and Mind*. Berlin: Springer, pp. 145–176.

Feldhausen, I. (2014a). Modeling Individual Variation in Prosody: The Case of Spanish Clitic Left-Dislocations. In S. Fuchs, M. Grice, A. Hermes, L. Lancia, and M. Mücke (eds.), *Proceedings of the 10th International Seminar on Speech Production, 5–8 May 2014*. Cologne: University of Cologne, pp. 114–117.

Feldhausen, I. (2014b). The Intonation of Left-Dislocations in Spanish and Other Romance Languages – Experimental and Theoretical Studies on Prosodic Phrasing and Inter-Speaker Variation (Habilitation thesis). Goethe-Universität Frankfurt.

Feldhausen, I. (2016). Inter-Speaker Variation, OT, and the Prosody of CLLD in Spanish. *Probus*, 28 (2), 293–333.

Feldhausen, I. and Vanrell, M. (2014). Prosody, Focus and Word Order in Catalan and Spanish: An Optimality Theoretic Approach. In S. Fuchs, M. Grice, A. Hermes, L. Lancia, and M. Mücke (eds.), *Proceedings of the 10th International Seminar on Speech Production, 5–8 May 2014*. Cologne: University of Cologne, pp. 122–125.

Feldhausen, I. and Vanrell, M. (2015). Oraciones hendidas y otras estrategias de marcaje del foco en español: Una aproximación desde la Teoría de la Optimidad Estocástica. *Revista Internacional de Lingüística Iberoamericana*, 13 (2), 39–60.

Flemming, E. (2002). *Auditory Representations in Phonology*. New York: Garland.

Gabriel, C. (2010). On Focus, Prosody, and Word Order in Argentinean Spanish: A Minimalist OT Account. *Revista Virtual de Estudos da Linguagem*, 4, 183–222.

Goldrick, M., Putnam, M., and Schwarz, L. (2016). Coactivation in Bilingual Grammars: A Computational Account of Code Mixing. *Bilingualism: Language and Cognition*, 19 (5), 857–876.

Grau Sempere, A. (2013). Reconsidering Syllabic Minimality in Spanish Truncation. *Estudios de Lingüística Universidad de Alicante*, 27, 121–143.

Grice, P. (1975). Logic and Conversation. In P. Cole and J. Morgan (eds.), *Syntax and Semantics*, Vol. 3: *Speech Acts*. New York: Academic Press, pp. 41–58.

Grimshaw, J. (2001). Optimal Clitic Positions and the Lexicon in Romance Clitic Systems. In G. Legendre, J. Grimshaw, and S. Vikner (eds.), *Optimality Theoretic Syntax*. Cambridge, MA: MIT Press, pp. 205–240.

Gutiérrez, L. (2009). Procesos fonológicos utilizados en la formación de hipocorísticos: una aproximación desde la fonología no lineal (Doctoral dissertation). Universidad de Concepción, Chile.

Gutiérrez-Bravo, R. (2005). *Structural Markedness and Syntactic Structure*. New York: Routledge/Taylor and Francis.

Gutiérrez-Bravo, R. (2007). Prominence Scales and Unmarked Word Order in Spanish. *Natural Language and Linguistic Theory*, 25 (2), 235–271.

Gutiérrez-Bravo, R. (2008). Topicalization and Preverbal Subjects in Spanish *wh*-Interrogatives. In J. Bruhn de Garavito and E. Valenzuela (eds.), *Selected Proceedings of the 10th Hispanic Linguistics Symposium*. Somerville, MA: Cascadilla, pp. 225–236.

Gutiérrez-Bravo, R. (2010). Inputs and Faithfulness in OT Syntax: The Case of Subjects and Topics in Spanish Infinitival Clauses. *Revista Virtual de Estudos da Linguagem*, 8, 134–154.

Gutiérrez-Bravo, R., Arellanes Arellanes, F., and Chávez Peón, M. (eds.). (2015). *Nuevos estudios de teoría de la optimidad*. Mexico City: El Colegio de México.

Gutiérrez-Bravo, R. and Herrera, E. (eds.). (2008). *Teoría de optimidad: estudios de sintaxis y fonología*. Mexico City: El Colegio de México

Gutiérrez-Bravo, R. and Monforte, J. (2008). La alternancia sujeto inicial/verbo inicial y la Teoría de Optimidad. In R. Gutiérrez Bravo and E. Herrera (eds.), *Teoría de optimidad: estudios de sintaxis y fonología*. Mexico City: El Colegio de México, pp. 61–90.

Hancin-Bhatt, B. and Bhatt, R. (1997). Optimal L2 Syllables: Interactions of Transfer and Developmental Effects. *Studies in Second Language Acquisition*, 19 (3), 331–378.

Hayes, Bruce (2000). Gradient Well-Formedness in Optimality Theory. In J. Dekkers, F. van der Leeuw, and J. van de Weijer (eds.), *Optimality Theory: Phonology, Syntax and Acquisition*. Oxford: Oxford University Press, pp. 88–120.

Holt, D. E. (2000). Comparative Optimality-Theoretic Dialectology: Singular/Plural Nasal Alternations in Galician, Mirandese (Leonese) and Spanish. In H. Campos, E. Herburger, A. Morales-Front, and T. J. Walsh (eds.), *Hispanic Linguistics at the Turn of the Millennium: Papers from the Third Hispanic Linguistics Symposium*. Somerville, MA: Cascadilla, pp. 125–143.

Holt, D. E. (2003). The Emergence of Palatal Sonorants and Alternating Diphthongs in Hispano-Romance. In D. E. Holt (ed.), *Optimality Theory and Language Change*. Dordrecht: Springer, pp. 285–305.

Holt, D. E. (2004). Optimization of Syllable Contact in Old Spanish via the Sporadic Sound Change Metathesis. *Probus*, 16 (1), 43–61.

Holt, D. E. (2006). Optimality Theory and Language Change in Spanish. In F. Martínez-Gil and S. Colina (eds.), *Optimality-Theoretic Advances in Spanish Phonology*. Amsterdam: John Benjamins, pp. 378–396.

Holt, D. E. (2015). Historical Sound Change in Optimality Theory: Achievements and Challenges. In P. Honeybone and J. Salmons (eds.), *Handbook of Historical Phonology*. Oxford: Oxford University Press, pp. 545–562.

Kager, R. (1999). *Optimality Theory*. Cambridge: Cambridge University Press.

Kiparsky, P. (2012). Grammaticalization as Optimization. In D. Jonas, J. Whitman, and A. Garrett (eds.), *Grammatical Change: Origins, Nature, Outcomes*. Oxford: Oxford University Press, pp. 15–51.

Kochetov, A. and Colantoni, L. (2011). *Place vs. Stricture in Spanish Nasal Assimilation. West Coast Conference on Formal Linguistics 28*. Available from sites.google.com/site/wccfl28pro/kochetov-colantoni (last access October 9, 2017).

Koontz-Garboden, A. (2004). Language Contact and Spanish Aspectual Expression: A Formal Analysis. *Lingua*, 114 (9–10), 1291–1330.

LaFond, L. L. (2001). The Pro-Drop Parameter in Second Language Acquisition Revisited: A Developmental Account (Doctoral dissertation). University of South Carolina.

LaFond, L. L. (2003). Putting the Pieces Together: Second Language Learning of Null Subjects, Inversion, and *That-Trace*. In J. Liceras, H. Zobl, and H. Goodluck (eds.), *Proceedings of the 6th Generative Approaches to Second Language Acquisition Conference*. Somerville, MA: Cascadilla, pp. 168–175.

LaFond, L., Hayes, R., and Bhatt, R. (2001). Constraint Demotion and Null-Subjects in Spanish L2 Acquisition. In J. Camps and C. Wiltshire (eds.), *Romance Syntax, Semantics and L2 Acquisition: Selected Papers from the 30th Linguistic Symposium on Romance Languages*. Amsterdam: John Benjamins, pp. 121–135.

Legendre, G. (2016). *Optimality-Theoretic Syntax, Semantics, and Pragmatics. From Uni- to Bidirectional Optimization*. Oxford: Oxford University Press.

Legendre, G., Grimshaw, J., and Vikner, S. (eds.) (2001). *Optimality-Theoretic Syntax*. Cambridge: MIT Press.

Lestrade, S. (2010). The Space of Case (Doctoral dissertation). Radboud University, Nijmegen.

Lleó, C. (2001). The Interface of Phonology and Syntax: The Emergence of the Article in the Early Acquisition of Spanish and German. In J. Weissenborn and B. Höhle (eds.), *Approaches to Bootstrapping: Phonological, Lexical, Syntactic and Neurophysiological Aspects of Early Language Acquisition*. Amsterdam: John Benjamins, pp. 23–44.

Lleó, C. (2002). The Role of Markedness in the Acquisition of Complex Prosodic Structures by German–Spanish Bilinguals. *International Journal of Bilingualism*, 6 (3), 291–313.

Lleó, C. (2006). The Acquisition of Prosodic Word Structures in Spanish by Monolingual and Spanish–German Bilingual Children. *Language and Speech*, 49, 205–229.

Lleó, C. and Arias, J. (2006). Foot, Word and Phrase Constraints in First Language Acquisition of Spanish Stress. In F. Martínez-Gil and S. Colina (ed.), *Optimality-Theoretic Studies in Spanish Phonology*. Amsterdam: John Benjamins, pp. 472–496.

Lleó, C. and Arias, J. (2009). The Role of Weight-by-Position in the Prosodic Development of Spanish and German. In J. Grijzenhout and B. Kabak (eds.), *Phonological Domains: Universals and Deviations*. Amsterdam: John Benjamins, pp. 221–248.

Lloret, M.-R. and Mascaró, J. (2006). Depalatalization in Spanish Revised. In F. Martínez-Gil and S. Colina (eds.), *Optimality-Theoretic Studies in Spanish Phonology*. Amsterdam and Philadelphia, PA: John Benjamins, pp. 74–98.

Martínez-Gil, F. and Colina, S. (eds.) (2006). *Optimality-Theoretic Advances in Spanish Phonology*. Amsterdam and Philadelphia, PA: John Benjamins.

McCarthy, J. J. (2004). Optimal Paradigms. In L. J. Downing, T. A. Hall, and R. Raffelsiefen (eds.), *Paradigms in Phonological Theory*. Oxford: Oxford University Press, pp. 170–210.

McCarthy, J. J. (2007). *Hidden Generalizations: Phonological Opacity in Optimality Theory*. London: Equinox.

McCarthy, J. J. and Pater, J. (eds.) (2016). *Harmonic Grammar and Harmonic Serialism*. Sheffield: Equinox Publishing Limited.

McCarthy, J. and Prince, A. (1994). The Emergence of the Unmarked: Optimality in Prosodic Morphology. In M. González (ed.), *NELS 24: Proceedings of the North-East Linguistic Society*. Amherst, MA: Graduate Linguistic Student Association, pp. 333–379.

Morales-Front, A. (2006). Acquisition of Syllable Structure in Spanish. In F. Martínez-Gil and S. Colina (eds.), *Optimality-Theoretic Studies in Spanish Phonology*. Amsterdam: John Benjamins, pp. 497–524.

Morris, R. (2005). Attraction to the Unmarked in Old Spanish Leveling. In D. Eddington (ed.), *Selected Proceedings of the 7th Hispanic Linguistics Symposium*. Somerville, MA: Cascadilla, pp. 180–191.

Patin, C., Feldhausen, I., and Delais-Roussarie, E. (2017). Structure prosodique et dislocation à gauche dans les langues romanes et bantu: vers une approche typologique unifiée en OT. In A. Lemaréchal, P. Koch, and P. Swiggers (eds.), *Actes du XXVIIe Congrès international de linguistique et de philologie romanes (Nancy, 15–20 juillet 2013), Section 1 : Linguistique générale/linguistique romane*. Nancy ATILF, pp. 107–119. Available from www.atilf.fr/cilpr2013/actes/section-1.html (last access October 13, 2017).

Piñeros, C. E. (2000a). Prosodic and Segmental Unmarkedness in Spanish Truncation. *Linguistics*, 38 (1), 63–98.

Piñeros, C. E. (2000b). Foot-Sensitive Word Minimization in Spanish. *Probus*, 12 (2), 291–324.

Piñeros, C.E. (2006). The Phonology of Nasal Consonants in Five Spanish Dialects. In F. Martínez-Gil and S. Colina (eds.), *Optimality Theoretic Studies in Spanish Phonology*. Amsterdam: John Benjamins, pp. 146–171.

Prince, A. and Smolensky, P. (1993/2004). Optimality Theory: Constraint Interaction in Generative Grammar. *Rutgers University and University of Colorado at Boulder*. Revised version published Malden, MA/Oxford: Wiley-Blackwell.

Roca, I. and Felíu, E. (2003). Morphology in Truncation: The Role of the Spanish Desinence. In G. Booij and J. van Maarle (eds.), *Yearbook of Morphology 2002*. Dordrecht: Kluwer Academic, pp. 187–243.

Saltarelli, (2006). A Paradigm Account of Spanish Number. In F. Martínez-Gil and S. Colina (eds.), *Optimality-Theoretic Studies in Spanish Phonology*. Amsterdam: John Benjamins, pp. 339–357.

Sanz, J. (2015). The Phonology and Morphology of Spanish Hypocoristics (Master's thesis). The Arctic University of Norway.

Smith, J. A. (2011). Subcategorization and Optimality Theory: The Case of Spanish Diminutives (Doctoral dissertation). University of California, Davis.

Smolensky, P., Goldrick, M., and Mathis, D. (2014). Optimization and Quantization in Gradient Symbol Systems: A Framework for Integrating the Continuous and the Discrete in Cognition. *Cognitive Science*, 38 (6), 1102–1138.

Tesar, B. and Smolensky, P. (2000). *Learnability in Optimality Theory*. Cambridge, MA: MIT Press.

Trommer, J. (2001). Distributed Optimality (Doctoral dissertation). University of Potsdam.

Wiltshire, C. (2006). Prefix Boundaries in Spanish Varieties: A Non-Derivational OT Account. In F. Martínez-Gil and S. Colina (eds.), *Optimality Theoretic Studies in Spanish Phonology*. Amsterdam: John Benjamins, pp. 358–377.

Wolf, M. (2008). Optimal Interleaving: Serial Phonology–Morphology Interaction in a Constraint-Based Model (Doctoral dissertation). University of Massachusetts at Amherst.

Xu, Z. (2016). The Role of Morphology in Optimality Theory. In A. Hippisley and G. T. Stump (eds.), *Cambridge Handbook of Morphology*. Cambridge: Cambridge University Press, pp. 550–587.

Xu, Z. and Aronoff, M. (2011a). A Realization Optimality Theory Approach to Blocking and Extended Morphological Exponence. *Journal of Linguistics*, 47 (3), 673–707.

Xu, Z. and Aronoff, M. (2011b). A Realization Optimality Theory Approach to Full and Partial Identity of Forms. In M. Maiden, J. Charles Smith, M. Goldbach, and M. O. Hinzelin (eds.), *Morphological Autonomy: Perspectives from Romance Inflectional Morphology*. Oxford: Oxford University Press, pp. 257–286.

Zubizarreta, M. L. (1998). *Prosody, Focus, and Word Order*. Cambridge, MA: MIT Press.

3

Usage-Based Approaches to Spanish Linguistics

Esther L. Brown

3.1 Introduction

Any linguistic approach that holds the language user's experience with language as central to the analysis is usage-based. Thus, usage-based approaches are evident within all linguistic disciplines (phonology, morphology, syntax, etc.) and encompass a vast array of research questions, illuminating details within the domains of language practice, processing, typology, and change. The variation and gradience evident in linguistic forms takes center stage, and, at the core of usage-based approaches, it is understood that use directly shapes language and that language structure emerges from the usage patterns (Bybee 1985, 2010; Goldberg 2006; Langacker 1987; Tomasello 2003).

Usage-based approaches strive to provide cognitively plausible models of language comprehension and production and, in Spanish, usage-based works have covered a variety of topics vast enough to fill whole volumes. In this chapter, usage-based studies of Spanish /s/ variation will preponderate in order to narrow the breadth of the topic. This approach is chosen for two reasons. First, a seminal usage-based work, without doubt, is Bybee (2001), in which this theoretical and methodological approach to language use is clearly outlined with examples from phonology. In this vein, this chapter will privilege studies of sound variation in Spanish.

Second, variable realizations of Spanish /s/ have been the object of intense academic scrutiny over the years. Academic interest in the variable pronunciations arises for many reasons. Variable patterns of pronunciation clearly demarcate regional varieties of Spanish (e.g. Lipski 2011), social groups and styles (Carvalho 2006a; Lynch 2009; Lewis and Boomershine 2015), and the sibilant serves as a salient feature for analyses of Spanish in contact with different languages (Carvalho 2006b; Brown and

Harper 2009; Waltermire 2011) and dialects (Aaron and Hernández 2007; O'Rourke and Potowski 2016). Further, /s/ forms part of both nominal as well as verbal systems (plural marking, second-person singular marking), and as such deletion could imply a loss of morphological information. One line of research sought evidence as to whether semantically relevant (morphological) information would yield lower rates of /s/ deletion in Spanish, per the functional hypothesis (e.g. Poplack 1980; Hochberg 1986; Ranson 1991; Cameron 1993). These studies, and many more, render /s/ variation as one of the most widely studied variables in Hispanic linguistics. Not surprisingly, therefore, scores of studies have been conducted on /s/ variation from a usage-based approach. As such, this phone serves an instructive purpose: it is both familiar to many readers as well as present in multiple studies engaging in usage-based research.

This chapter presents a brief overview of key constructs central to usage-based approaches (henceforth UB). Special attention is afforded to studies of Spanish that have informed UB theory and methods, as well as to the ways in which UB approaches applied to Spanish data have provided additional perspectives on recalcitrant problems in Hispanic linguistics. After a brief discussion of precursors to UB approaches, data and methods are summarized, along with effects of experience (token, type, and discourse context frequencies) and the role of the lexicon (exemplar model of lexical representation). In each case, examples of studies of Spanish /s/ articulations illustrate the UB theory and methods.

3.2 Background

The term "usage-based linguistics" was coined relatively recently (Langacker 1987), yet the approach builds upon decades of research in linguistics and continues long-standing lines of inquiry. Many central hypotheses examined within this framework have dominated linguistic inquiry for years. For instance, lexical frequency has long been a linguistic variable implicated in phonological variation and change with significant differences observed between low- and high-frequency words (Schuchardt 1885; Zipf 1929).

Although the approach has taken shape over the last decades, UB researchers ask questions that have concerned linguists for centuries, such as the nature and mechanisms of sound change ("Neogrammarian controversy"). This Neogrammarian controversy, according to Labov (1981:268), is "perhaps the most clearly stated issue in our history." The large body of literature is highlighted by Labov (1994:441), who refers to a "long list of articles that have vigorously argued for or against the Neogrammarian principles," the copious ink devoted to the debate, and, on both sides of the argument, "commentators too numerous to mention." The controversy has arisen over how best to answer the following question: "In the evolution of sound systems, is the basic unit of change the word or the sound?" (Labov 1981:268).

In brief, the Neogrammarian stance is that "sound change is phonetically gradual, proceeding by imperceptible increments, but lexically abrupt, affecting all relevant words simultaneously" (Labov 1981:270). For Spanish /s/, for instance, Labov (1981:302) finds that "the sizeable literature on the aspiration and deletion of /s/ shows no evidence of lexical conditioning in the many detailed quantitative investigations of Spanish ... and of Portuguese ..." However, opponents to the regularity hypothesis assert that it is possible for certain words to change while others, in the same phonological environment, do not. The major difference in this opposing viewpoint is not the end result of change (being regular or not), but rather the mechanism of change – that change occurs in the word and not the phoneme. Sound change, it is argued, proceeds in a phonetically abrupt and lexically gradual manner, a concept referred to as "lexical diffusion." Lexical diffusion is apparent for /s/ in a Dravidian language studied by Krishnamurti (1998). The phonetically gradual and lexically abrupt type of change (i.e. Neogrammarian) Labov reports for Spanish /s/ aspiration and deletion does not hold in Gondi. Krishnamurti (1998) reports that the s > h > Ø change proceeds from word to word (or from one word class to another), rather than affecting the sound in all words where the phonetic conditions for change are met.

With regard to the bipartite classification of types of change, however, UB approaches reveal that sound change and variation need not by necessity fall into one of two types of change: Neogrammarian or lexically diffused (Phillips 2006). Bybee (2000:67), using data from t/d deletion in English, illustrates that "sound change can be *both* lexically gradual and phonetically gradual" (emphasis mine). In fact, UB researchers do not concede a clear boundary between phonology and lexicon, which is a fundamental construct underpinning the Neogrammarian controversy (Phillips 2006:17–18). Instead, a non-modular conceptualization of language knowledge is proposed whereby the phonological system itself emerges from generalizations built up from specific instances of sounds existing within words and phrases (Phillips 2006:2–3).

Early on, UB publications were framed in patent opposition to more mainstream formal, structuralist approaches, in some measure to argue for the validity of the UB approach. UB theories and methods, although still relatively new, have been independently corroborated by a substantial body of scientific research (Beckner *et al.* 2009). As such, UB publications stand in their own right today, no longer drawing explicit contrasts and connections with non-UB linguistic approaches, and are valid alternatives to linguistic theories whose origins predate UB. Indeed, the application of UB theory and methods is now embraced in disciplines historically reserved for formal approaches (e.g. Child Language Acquisition, Second Language Acquisition, Language Contact, Typological Studies), yielding innovative results in Spanish (e.g. Amengual 2012; Travis and Torres Cacoullos 2012; Linford and Shin 2013; Rivas 2013; Wilson and Dumont 2015; Shin 2016).

3.3 Data and Methods

UB approaches do not eschew evidence of variation to embrace analyses of linguistic idealizations. The patterns of use and linguistic variability are not peripheral to the theory, but rather are of central theoretical concern (Docherty and Foulkes 2014). We know that discrepancies exist between what is grammatically permissible and what speakers say in actuality (Pierrehumbert 2006). What's more, discrepancies have been found between what a linguist finds acceptable and what a non-linguist (naïve speaker) might find acceptable (Dąbrowska 2010). Thus, data representing natural use and usage patterns are typically privileged in UB analyses over methodological reliance on native-speaker intuition or acceptability judgments for data.

In order, therefore, to conduct systematic analysis of the details of variation evident in use, many UB studies are based upon corpora of spoken language. Corpora themselves, though not theory specific, can provide raw data of how language is actually used and serve as empirical evidence for the existence (or absence) of any linguistic phenomenon. Widely cited corpora in Spanish include the *Corpus del español* (Davies 2002–) and the *Proyecto para el estudio sociolingüístico del español de España y de América* (PRESEEA 2014–), as well as projects highlighting varieties within the United States such as the *Corpus of Mexican Spanish in Salinas, California* (Brown 2016), *The Spanish in Texas Corpus* (Bullock and Toribio 2013), *Corpus del español en el sur de Arizona* (Carvalho 2012–), and the bilingual corpus *New Mexico Spanish–English Codeswitching* (Torres Cacoullos and Travis, in preparation).

As Ernestus and Baayen (2011) highlight, corpora reflecting actual usage patterns allow for the identification of the distributions and frequencies of linguistic forms that constitute the core of linguistic experience. Such patterns of use may be immune to linguistic idealizations since often "the most regular and firmly entrenched patterns of variation lie so far below the level of consciousness that they cannot be intuited" by linguists or native speakers (Poplack and Torres Cacoullos 2015:272). As such, UB approaches often include Variationist methodologies (Poplack and Tagliamonte 2001) to ensure systematicity. When subjected to empirical scrutiny and testing – commonplace in UB approaches – long-held and oft-cited assumptions may be accounted for differently.

3.3.1 Spanish /s/ Realization

The use of corpora reflecting naturalistic speech as applied to Spanish allows for the testing of untested notions. As Eddington (2004:58) notes, "many linguistic processes that are thought to occur in Spanish have been based on impressionistic observations. However, once empirical observations are brought to bear on these phenomena a very different picture often emerges." This assessment is aptly illustrated for what has been called the "intrusive -s" in Caribbean varieties of Spanish, notably in Dominican.

Based upon a paucity of examples and reports, Dominican speakers are characterized as "s-less" speakers whose phonology has been restructured such that historical /s/ is lacking underlyingly in coda position. These speakers are said to then "randomly" insert /s/ through hypercorrection. Nevertheless, through careful examination of approximately 3,500 /s/ realizations in words historically containing syllable-final /s/, Bullock *et al.* (2014:21) note their empirical analyses reveal "intrusive-s evades the characterization that it has to date received." Lexical /s/ has not been lost in this variety of Spanish, and insertion of /s/ is not random but rather context driven. The authors conclude that "semiliterate Dominicans know where s belongs, but choose to express it variably for reasons of identity and covert prestige" (p. 33). Their careful analysis of actual use and usage patterns in a corpus of rural Dominican Spanish provides a more complete, as well as empirically falsifiable, understanding of the intrusive -s.

3.4 Experience

UB theory assumes that language structure emerges from use and is not born out of language-specific structures. As such, UB models assume a great deal of learning happens during acquisition (Clark 2012:56), and factors of experience such as frequency and context (Ellis 2012:7) shape representation throughout the lifespan. Bybee (2006:711) argues that "grammar is the cognitive organization of one's experience with language" and it is "domain-general" in that our experience with language shapes linguistic form in the same way that experience shapes other human cognitive functions. Section 3.4.1 presents a summary of three important components of experience from which grammar and linguistic structure are shaped: token frequency, type frequency, and discourse context frequency. Each of these components of speaker experience will be illustrated with studies from Spanish and applied to Spanish /s/ variation.

3.4.1 Token Frequency

Token frequency, defined as the number of occurrences of a linguistic unit (most typically a word) in language usage, attempts to gauge how often linguistic forms are experienced by speakers in production and perception. As psychological research makes evident, the more often we experience something, "the stronger our memory for it, and the more fluently it is accessed" (Ellis 2012:7). Three effects of high token frequency include the "reducing effect," whereby frequent words and phrases undergo phonetic reduction more readily and at a faster rate than lower-frequency counterparts, the "conserving effect," whereby high-frequency forms resist analogical leveling more than do low-frequency forms, and "autonomy," whereby the internal structure of highly frequent morphologically complex forms becomes less analyzable, which weakens ties to etymologically related forms and promotes autonomy within historically associated forms (Bybee 2006:714–715).

Many studies of Spanish provide compelling evidence in support of these lexical frequency effects (Díaz-Campos 2005; Díaz-Campos and Gradoville 2011; Díaz-Campos and Ruiz-Sánchez 2008; Lamy 2015), where significant differences in phonetic realizations are found to correlate with word frequency. Similarly, multiple studies of Spanish /s/ realizations incorporate token frequency into the analyses, as discussed in the following section.

Token Frequency and Spanish /s/ Realization

As Bybee 2001 argues, each time a word is used it is exposed to the articulatory pressures of speaking. The automization arising from practice leads to decreases in the magnitude or in the timing of gestures (Browman and Goldstein 1992). For instance, an increase in overlap or changes in the phasing of articulatory gestures can effectively hide sounds acoustically (and perceptually). Decreases in magnitudes of gestures can also yield variant forms in cases of target undershoot whereby, for example, a stop ([d]) can be variably realized in a word as a fricative or an approximant ([ð]) (Browman and Goldstein 1992:173). In this way, words that are used more often reduce at higher rates than words used infrequently. For instance, high-frequency words in many varieties of Spanish – e.g. Chihuahua, Mexico (Brown and Torres Cacoullos 2002, 2003), Rivera, Uruguay (Waltermire 2011), New Mexico (Brown 2005), Mérida, Venezuela (Brown 2009b) – evidence increased rates of /s/ reduction compared to lower-frequency words in support of UB theory.

Some studies find a word frequency effect, while others, at times examining an identical linguistic variable, fail to find an effect of word frequency. Such discrepancies between the studies which corroborate and those which contradict the proposed UB effect of token frequency attract scrutiny, given their ramifications for theories of lexical representation (discussed in Section 3.5.1), language variation (Labov 1981), and language change (Phillips 2006). One source of methodological disagreement possibly giving rise to these discrepancies is how frequency is measured. The studies of /s/ reduction cited previously discretize the data into frequency bins (analogous to *low, medium,* and *high*). File-Muriel (2010), however, contends that the cut-off points may seem "arbitrary". Instead, he makes an argument for considering frequency as a continuous variable. He employs a reading task to capture a more representative sample of the range of frequencies found in the lexicon (as opposed to the preponderance of high token-frequency items found in analyses of naturalistic speech). His study of 2,805 instances of word-medial, syllable-final /s/ production demonstrates the more frequent the word, the more likely it is to undergo reduction. Importantly, File-Muriel argues that scalar measurements model more precisely the effect that usage frequency exerts on the lexicon. The Colombian Spanish results, therefore, make the case that frequency should be considered a scalar variable in linguistic analyses generally.

The importance of lexical frequency relative to other linguistic variables is also explored in studies on /s/ reduction. File-Muriel (2009), for instance, in a study of Colombian Spanish, finds word frequency to be the most important predictor in models of phonological reduction. Brown (2009a), however, in a study of a different Colombian variety of Spanish, finds that although lexical frequency is a significant predictor of /s/ reduction, other factors are relatively weightier. Brown *et al.* (2014), on the other hand, find word frequency to exert *no* significant effect in Barranquilla Spanish. The authors note that, in addition to methodological and study-design differences which might account for different findings across these studies of Colombian /s/ reduction, token frequency – like any linguistic factor – loses its predictive power when a sound change is nearing completion. The authors contend that the relative importance is thus mitigated by the degree to which a sound change (or phonetic variation) has spread throughout the lexicon.

In addition to substantiating frequency effects, therefore, these studies on Spanish have been pivotal in shaping UB theoretical notions and methodological protocols (similarly to Erker 2012 for sociophonetic variation). Token frequency, however, is not the only important measure of experience with language. Ellis (2012:9) notes that in addition to the statistical knowledge brought about through token frequency, "humans learn more easily and process more fluently 'regular' patterns which are exemplified by many types." Such effects of high type frequency and type frequency's application to studies in Spanish are discussed in Section 3.4.2.

3.4.2 Type Frequency

Bybee (1999) defines type frequency as the number of items participating in a pattern. Productivity, or the likelihood that a change will spread to new words, correlates positively with type frequency. The more lexical items participate in a pattern (i.e. the higher the type frequency), the more available said pattern is to serve as an attractor for new items. Productivity, then, is seen in UB approaches as a result of generalizations across remembered experiences. For instance, in a nonce-probe experiment, Bybee and

Pardo (1981) illustrate that the stem-vowel alternation in Spanish third-person preterits (*dormir* → *durmió, sentir* → *sintió*) is significantly more likely to be applied to new forms in the case of verbal roots with the front vowel (/e/), owing, they argue, to the much higher type frequency of that class compared to the back vowels (/o/).

In addition to productivity, type frequency is "also relevant for determining the relative strength of phonotactic patterns, stress patterns, and other phonological patterns applying at the word level" (Bybee 2001:13). For instance, Díaz-Campos and Gradoville (2011) find that variable deletion of the voiced, dental obstruent /d/ in the Spanish of Caracas, Venezuela, is constrained by type frequency. The highest rates of consonant deletion are in past participles, and in particular in the *-ado* suffix, which has the highest type frequency. In the same vein, based on the assumption that phonotactic knowledge and structure derive from actually occurring words in the lexicon, Brown (2006) proposes that the paucity of Spanish words containing medial, syllable-final labial stop, coupled with the frequently occurring velar stop in that position, motivates the production of forms such as *Pepsi* > *Pe[k]si*. Type frequency has also been incorporated into studies of Spanish /s/, as summarized in the following section.

Type Frequency and Spanish /s/ Realization

Though most studies of Spanish /s/ examine the variable reduction or weakening of the sibilant's articulation, Barnes (2012) probes the role of /s/ in a non-reductive phenomenon: the regularization of second-person singular preterit forms in Spanish through the addition of a non-etymological /s/ on the end of the verb form (*dijiste* → *dijistes*). Using data extracted from online corpora, Barnes moves beyond impressionistic characterizations of the regularization to empirically test the distribution of the competing forms (*-aste*, *-iste* suffix with and without an expressed *-s*) on variable verbs. Results of statistical analyses show low-frequency items to be more susceptible to the change than high-frequency items. Thus, the addition of *-s* to second-person singular preterit forms reflects the analogical extension and productivity driven by the exceptionally high type frequency form (*-s* to mark second-person singular *tú* forms), in line with UB predictions.

3.4.3 Discourse Context Frequency

Word frequencies, as described in Sections 3.4.1 and 3.4.2, are among the most frequently analyzed factors shaping lexical representations in UB studies. Bybee (2002) also proposes another quantifiable aspect of language experience that has received relatively less scrutiny than type and token frequency. She proposes an effect of words' frequency of use in specific (leniting) discourse contexts on variation and change. Bybee

(2002) argues that words' production contexts impact articulation; some contexts promote articulatory reduction, others do not. A word's propensity for use in reducing contexts logically yields more opportunity for reduced articulations of that word. Speakers' experiences with such reduced articulations leave episodic traces of reduced forms in memory, which can become targets for future realizations.

In an analysis of word-final -t/d deletion in English, Bybee (2002) finds a significant effect of context histories on rates of deletion, whereby words used commonly in deleting contexts delete at a higher rate than words used less frequently in such contexts, independent of target production context. In short, therefore, the proposal is that, since phonological context can affect the phonetic shape words take in speech and phonetic variation becomes registered in memory, context of use is crucial to studies of phonological variation and change (Bybee 2002). Words differ significantly in their likelihood of use in contexts (dis)favoring reduction and would thus be predicted to change at significantly different rates.

The measure of the cumulative exposure of words to specific contexts (phonetic environments) that promote reduction is what has been called a word's Frequency of use in a Reducing Context (or FRC). What constitutes a "reducing environment," however, can be a measure of factors beyond phonetic environment (e.g. Raymond *et al.* 2016). The role of discourse-specific factors such as speech rate (e.g. Brown and Raymond 2014), and social and stylistic factors evident in the speech context (Bybee 1999:221) can also be quantified. Multiple studies show that words are produced in line with their context histories, independent, it seems, of the production context. Words frequently used in contexts promoting reduction reduce more readily (or at a higher rate) than words used infrequently in discourse contexts promoting reduction, even when analyzed in identical contexts. This methodological tactic of measuring words' cumulative use in specific discourse contexts, though exemplified here with phonological variables, has been applied straightforwardly to morphosyntactic variation as well (e.g. *haber* regularization in Spanish (Brown and Rivas 2012), Spanish subject pronoun expression (Brown and Raymond, in preparation)), and has been extensively tested with Spanish /s/ data as discussed in the next section.

Frequency of Use in a Reducing Context and Spanish /s/ Realization

Studies demonstrating a significant word frequency effect were highlighted in Section 3.4.1, and it was noted that such effects are not consistently reported, even for cases of Spanish /s/. For instance, in acoustic analyses of intervocalic /s/ realizations in casual Madrid Spanish, Torreira and Ernestus (2012:145) note that for their study "data do not support the hypothesis that highly frequent and predictable words and function words systematically exhibit more reduction than low-frequency." What might cause such discrepancies between studies? In addition to potential methodological differences, Brown and Raymond (2012) contend that measures of discourse context frequency, or FRC, capture more precisely the effects of use. Thus, effects of frequency of use might be present in the variation, but visible only if quantified as a factor of reducing contexts.

How is FRC measured? Raymond and Brown (2012), in an analysis of 2,423 tokens of word-initial /s/ reduction in New Mexican Spanish, quantify for each lexical item its likelihood of occurrence in a context that would promote /s/ reduction. For word-initial /s/ in this variety, a preceding non-high vowel promotes reduction. Thus the reducing context is target word occurrence after a word ending in /a/, /e/, or /o/. Importantly, however, Raymond and Brown (2012) highlight that this measure is not a straightforward count of co-occurrences, but rather a ratio of occurrence (or probability of occurrence) in a reducing context.

Two ostensibly similar words, *señor* and *señora*, illustrate the measure. Both lexical items, logically, are used in discourse contexts that promote reduction (post non-high vowel) as well as contexts that do not promote reduction. In a multi-million word corpus of spoken Spanish, the word *señor* is used more often in the reducing post non-high vowel context (N = 178) than the feminine counterpart *señora* (N = 140). If just a count of the context is considered, *señor* has more opportunity to be realized with a reduced articulation. Yet, considering the overall frequency, the FRC measure provides each word's probability of occurrence in the reducing context (*señor* 178/593 = 0.30 vs. *señora* 140/176 = 0.80). Using logistic regression, Raymond and Brown (2012) demonstrate that words used more often in a discourse context favoring reduction (high FRC) have higher rates of reduction than words used proportionally less in a reducing context, even when factors of the production context are controlled. Thus, all other things being equal, the /s/ of words with a high FRC will reduce more readily than a word with low FRC (*cada señora* vs. *cada señor*). These authors argue that the Exemplar Model predicts such an outcome. This model of lexical representation is discussed next.

3.5 Lexical Representation (Role of Lexicon)

The effects of experience outlined in Section 3.4 are predicated upon another important key construct of UB approaches: the view of a lexicon rich in fine-grained and redundant detail. Evidence of type and token frequency effects, as well as FRC results, suggest a lexicon that is able to track and store vast amounts of information regarding usage (Pierrehumbert 2001). Each time a word is experienced in production and perception, characteristics of that experience (e.g. information about the phonetic realization, as well as grammatical, semantic, pragmatic, contextual, and extralinguistic information) are stored in memory by speakers (Hinskens *et al.* 2014). These episodic traces or remembered tokens are mapped onto similar or identical tokens, forming exemplar clouds. Such experiences leave an imprint on the lexical representation by strengthening existing exemplars as well as by modulating the most frequent member of the exemplar cloud. Each word, then, is stored as a cloud of remembered tokens, which shifts quite gradually to reflect the variability of language experienced by the user (Bybee 2010:9).

In an Exemplar Model, the smallest unit of storage is the word (Bybee 2001:30). Morphologically complex words are stored lexically as one unit, as may be multi-word combinations. Multiple studies from Spanish provide evidence for such complex storage (i.e. multi-word units). For instance, studies of historical development of constructions (e.g. Torres Cacoullos 2001; Wilson 2009; Torres Cacoullos 2015; Aaron 2016) demonstrate how construction meaning emerges from the patterns of use of the word combinations.

Lexical representations are organized in memory. Storage of words and word combinations is structured through the schematic ties (or generalizations) that emerge from associations between forms. The associations are based upon similarities in form and meaning. Those forms that are semantically and orthographically/phonologically similar have stronger interconnectivity than lexical items that share no such overlap. These lexical connections, then, are evident in paradigmatically related forms (Brown 2009a) and give rise to morphological structure (Eddington 2004:135). Accordingly, no modularity of grammar is presumed (with strict separation of phonetic, phonological, morphological, syntactic processes or knowledge), but rather language is seen as multidimensional.

The modified Exemplar Model (Bybee 2001:37–62) substantiated in many UB works of Spanish, therefore, proposes complex storage with redundant, detailed information of use. The lexicon is made up of exemplar clouds reflecting speaker experience with words and constructions, with the strongest and most numerous members of the clouds emerging through use. Schematic ties of varying degrees of strength (determined by extent of form ~ meaning overlap) give rise to structure. Studies of Spanish /s/ provide evidence for units of lexical storage larger than the word and for the impact of schematic ties between forms, discussed in turn in the following two sections.

3.5.1 The Lexicon and Spanish /s/ Realization

Multi-Word Units

Increased string frequency (or the frequency of two words used together) may increase the likelihood that words will be stored together in memory as a chunk (as if they were one lexical "word") (Bush 2001:269; Bybee 2001:162). For instance, Bybee and Sheibman (1999) argue the phrase *I don't know* is stored as a single lexical unit due to its high string frequency.

Table 3.1 *Syllable-initial /s/ reduction in New Mexican Spanish*

/s/ position	N	% reduction	/s/ position	N	% reduction
Word-initial (*señor*)	2,594	16	In word *sé* (excluding cases of *no sé*)	32	6
Word-medial (*casa*)	3,048	30	In bigram *no sé*	116	36

Source: Adapted from Rivas and Brown (2010:70)

Extending this to Spanish data, Rivas and Brown (2010) examine usage patterns of the translation equivalent *no sé* in three dialects of Spanish and find similarly high frequencies of the string of words. In a corpus of New Mexican Spanish, for example, the combination *no sé* occurs with a frequency per million of 1,230, establishing the word combination as a likely combination to be stored as a single automated unit. In 88 percent of its occurrences, the first-person singular *sé* 'I know' is directly preceded by the word *no* (*no sé*). Evidence of lexical status as a chunk is argued to be apparent in the rates of reduction of word-initial /s/ of the word *sé* in the combination *no sé* as compared to /s/ realizations in *sé* outside the dyad (*lo sé, yo sé, qué sé,* etc.). Rates of /s/ reduction in the combination *no sé* more closely align with word-medial rates of reduction as opposed to word-initial, pointing to the combination's lexical status as a chunk (Rivas and Brown 2010:70). This is summarized in Table 3.1.

Status as a lexical chunk also predicts /s/ lenition in other high-frequency two-word strings. For example, in a study of word-final /s/ realizations in different dialects of Spanish, Brown (2009b) reports increased reduction (in pre-voiced consonant contexts) in high-frequency strings (*antes de* 'before') compared to low-frequency strings (*antes di* 'beforehand I gave') in New Mexico, Venezuela, and Colombia (Brown 2009b:189). In line with UB proposals, Brown (2009b:191) finds that "the frequency with which a multi-word segment occurs affects whether it is stored as a single unit or as two separate words," which in turn is evident in rates of reduction.

In addition to string frequencies, Spanish /s/ studies provide evidence in support of probabilistic language effects. Frequent words are more probable given their high prior likelihood of use. Additionally, contextual probabilities (probability of a target word given the context and surrounding words) have been shown to constrain variation (Jurafsky *et al.* 2001:230), suggesting that "probabilistic relations between words must play a role in the mental representation of language." In their study of /s/ variation in New Mexican Spanish, Raymond and Brown (2012) find effects of the predictability of the target s- word from the preceding word unit [$P(w_{s-}|w_{s-\ -1})$], with increased predictability yielding increased rates of initial /s/ reduction. Thus, if the target /s/ word is predictable from the previous word, studies find increased likelihood of /s/ lenition (see also File-Muriel and Brown 2011). These results support the UB notion that

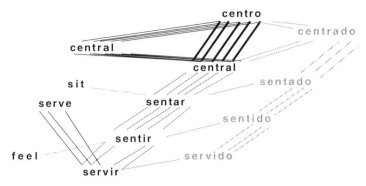

Figure 3.1 Spanish ~ English bilingual lexicon
Source: Adapted from Bybee (2001:24)

speakers are able to track and store information in memory regarding the contextual probabilities of words and word combinations.

Schematic Ties

As outlined in Section 3.5, the Exemplar Model of lexical representation states that the storage of words and frequent phrases, along with the linguistic, nonlinguistic, and contextual information for these units, is organized into a network of connections to "related items that makes storage more efficient" (Bybee 2001:29). These connections in memory vary in strength based upon degrees of (dis)similarity. Extended to a Spanish ~ English lexicon, the schematic ties could be represented as in Figure 3.1.

Brown and Harper (2009) conduct a cross-linguistic analysis to explore the potential impact of these schematic ties between lexical items in two languages. The authors compare 5,569 tokens of word-final /s/ in bilingual speech (New Mexico Spanish) and in the monolingual speech of a historically related variety (Chihuahua, Mexico). The study reveals that in cases where cross-linguistic similarity exists between English and Spanish (such as for a plural -s) rates of reduction are lower in Spanish. This effect is scalar, furthermore, being strongest where more phonological or semantic overlap can be posited (i.e. cognates). Brown and Harper (2009) argue that the gradient impact on rates of reduction mirror schematic ties that vary in strength between exemplar representations in memory.

3.6 Concluding Remarks

The studies summarized in this chapter share the view that language variation and use need to be seen as intrinsic to the grammar and representation of language. Variable forms are not peripheral and are not derived from abstract underlying forms separate from use. Rather, with emphasis on empirical examinations of actually occurring language forms, UB approaches seek to understand how patterns of use and frequent associations of forms and meanings give rise to language structure. Language, then, is directly shaped by the way in which it is used (Bybee 2010). The details of language experience, from which language structure emerges, are often measured through calculations attempting to estimate speakers' experience with linguistic forms in both perception and production. These measures include token frequency, type frequency, and, less commonly, discourse context frequency. Such experiences with language are argued to be captured in a detail-rich lexicon, which enables speakers to track the form ~ meaning associations that arise through use.

UB approaches have been fruitfully applied to a host of phenomena in Spanish in studies too numerous to mention (see also Chapters 4, 6, 20–27, and 32). In turn, studies in Spanish have been integral in the shaping of UB theory and methods in the preceding decades. In this way, Spanish linguistics has benefited from the application of these innovative theories to linguistic problems of the Spanish language and, conversely, UB approaches are strengthened by studies of Spanish, which have tested multiple theories and methods. The privileged position Spanish language data has held, therefore, has been mutually beneficial to Spanish linguistics and UB approaches generally.

References

Aaron, J. E. (2016). The Road Already Traveled: Constructional Analogy in Lexico-Syntactic Change. *Studies in Language*, 40 (1), 26–62.

Aaron, J. E. and Hernández, J. E. (2007). Quantitative Evidence for Contact-Induced Accommodation. In K. Potowski and R. Cameron (eds.), *Spanish in Contact: Policy, Social and Linguistic Inquiries*. Amsterdam and Philadelphia, PA: John Benjamins, pp. 327–341.

Amengual, M. (2012). Interlingual Influence in Bilingual Speech: Cognate Status Effect in a Continuum of Bilingualism. *Bilingualism: Language and Cognition*, 15 (3), 517–530.

Barnes, S. (2012). ¿Qué dijistes?: A Variationist Reanalysis of Non-Standard-s on Second Person Singular Preterit Verb Forms in Spanish. In K. Geeslin and M. Díaz-Campos (eds.), *Selected Proceedings of the 14th Hispanic Linguistics Symposium*. Somerville, MA: Cascadilla, pp. 38–47.

Beckner, C., Blythe, R., Bybee, J., Christiansen, M. H., Croft, W., Ellis, N. C., Holland, J., Ke, J., Larsen-Freeman, D., and Schoenemann, T. (2009). Language is a Complex Adaptive System: Position Paper. *Language Learning*, 59 (s1), 1–26.

Browman, C. P. and Goldstein, L. (1992). Articulatory Phonology: An Overview. *Phonetica*, 49 (3–4), 155–180.

Brown, E. K. (2009a). The Relative Importance of Lexical Frequency in Syllable- and Word-Final /s/ Reduction in Cali, Colombia.

In J. Collentine *et al.* (eds.), *Selected Proceedings of the 11th Hispanic Linguistics Symposium*. Somerville, MA: Cascadilla, pp. 165–178.

Brown, E. K. (2009b). A Usage-Based Account of Syllable- and Word-Final /s/ Reduction in Four Dialects of Spanish. LINCOM Studies in Romance Linguistics, 62. Munich: Lincom.

Brown, E. K. (2016). Corpus of Mexican Spanish in Salinas, California. Available from itcdland.csumb.edu/~eabrown

Brown, E. K., Gradoville, M. S., and File-Muriel, R. J. (2014). The Variable Effect of Form and Lemma Frequencies on Phonetic Variation: Evidence from /s/ Realization in two Varieties of Colombian Spanish. *Corpus Linguistics and Linguistic Theory*, 10 (2), 213–241.

Brown, E. L. (2005). Syllable-Initial /s/ in Traditional New Mexican Spanish: Linguistic Factors Favoring Reduction Ahina. *Southwest Journal of Linguistics*, 24 (1–2), 13–31.

Brown, E. L. (2006). Velarization of Labial, Coda Stops in Spanish: A Frequency Account. *Revista de lingüística teórica y aplicada*, 44 (2), 47–58.

Brown, E. L. and Harper, D. (2009). Phonological Evidence of Interlingual Exemplar Connections. *Studies in Hispanic and Lusophone Linguistics*, 2 (2), 257–274.

Brown, E. L. and Raymond, W. D. (2012). How Discourse Context Shapes the Lexicon: Explaining the Distribution of Spanish f-/h- Words. *Diachronica*, 29 (2), 139–161.

Brown, E. L. and Raymond, W. D. (2014). Contextual Frequency Effects in Spanish Phonology. Paper presented at the Georgetown University Round Table on Languages and Linguistics, Washington, DC, March.

Brown, E. L. and Raymond, W. D. (in preparation). Cumulative Discourse Effects Evidenced in Spanish Subject Pronoun Expression.

Brown, E. L. and Rivas, J. (2012). Grammatical Relation Probability: How Usage Patterns Shape Analogy. *Language Variation and Change*, 24 (3), 317–341.

Brown, E. L. and Torres Cacoullos, R. (2002). ¿Qué le vamoh aher? Taking the Syllable out of Spanish /s/ Reduction. *Penn Working Papers in Linguistics*, 8 (3), 17–31.

Brown, E. L. and Torres Cacoullos, R. (2003). Spanish /s/: A different story from beginning (initial) to end (final). In R. Núñez-Cedeño, L. López, and R. Cameron (eds.), *A Romance Perspective on Language Knowledge and Use: Selected Papers from the 31st Linguistic Symposium on Romance Languages (LRSL), Chicago, 19–22 April 2001*. Amsterdam and Philadelphia, PA: John Benjamins, pp. 21–38.

Bullock, B. E. and Toribio, A. J. (2013). The Spanish in Texas Corpus Project. Center for Open Educational Resources and Language Learning (COERLL), The University of Texas at Austin. Available from spanishintexas.org

Bullock, B. E., Toribio, A. J., and Amengual, M. (2014). The Status of *s* in Dominican Spanish. *Lingua*, 143, 20–35.

Bush, N. (2001). Frequency Effects and Word-Boundary Palatalization in English. In J. Bybee and P. Hopper (eds.), *Frequency and the Emergence of Linguistic Structure*. Amsterdam: John Benjamins, pp. 255–280.

Bybee, J. (1985). *Morphology: A Study of the Relation between Meaning and Form*. Amsterdam and Philadelphia, PA: John Benjamins.

Bybee, J. (1999). Usage-Based Phonology. In Michael Darnell, Edith Moravcsik, Frederick Newmeyer, Michael Noonan, and Kathleen Wheatley (eds.), *Functionalism and Formalism in Linguistics*. Amsterdam: John Benjamins, pp. 211–242.

Bybee, J. (2000). The Phonology of the Lexicon: Evidence from Lexical Diffusion. In Michael Barlow and Suzanne Kemmer (eds.), *Usage Based Models of Language*. Chicago, IL: The University of Chicago Press, pp. 65–85.

Bybee, J. (2001). *Phonology and Language Use*. Cambridge: Cambridge University Press.

Bybee, J. (2002). Word Frequency and Context of Use in the Lexical Diffusion of Phonetically Conditioned Sound Change. *Language Variation and Change*, 14 (3), 261–290.

Bybee, J. L. (2006). From Usage to Grammar: The Mind's Response to Repetition. *Language*, 82 (4), 711–733.

Bybee, J. (2010). *Language, Usage and Cognition*. Cambridge: Cambridge University Press.

Bybee, J. L. and Pardo, E. (1981). On Lexical and Morphological Conditioning of Alternations: A Nonce-Probe Experiment with Spanish Verbs. *Linguistics*, 19 (9–10), 937–968.

Bybee, J. and Scheibman, J. (1999). The Effect of Usage on Degrees of Constituency: The Reduction of Don't in English. *Linguistics*, 37 (4), 575–596.

Cameron, R. (1993). Ambiguous Agreement, Functional Compensation, and Nonspecific *tú* in the Spanish of San Juan, Puerto Rico, and Madrid, Spain. *Language Variation and Change*, 5 (3), 305–334.

Carvalho, A. M. (2006a). Spanish (s) Aspiration as a Prestige Marker on the Uruguayan–Brazilian Border. *Spanish in Context*, 3 (1), 85–114.

Carvalho, A. M. (2006b). Nominal Number Marking in a Variety of Spanish in Contact with Portuguese. In Timothy L. Face and Carol A. Klee (eds.), *Selected Proceedings of the 8th Hispanic Linguistics Symposium*. Somerville, MA: Cascadilla, pp. 154–166.

Carvalho, A. M. (2012–). *Corpus del Español en el Sur de Arizona* (CESA). University of Arizona.

Clark, L. (2012). Dialect Data, Lexical Frequency and the Usage-Based Approach. *The Dialect Laboratory: Dialects as a Testing Ground for Theories of Language Change, Studies in Language Companion Series*, 128, 53–72.

Dąbrowska, E. (2010). Naive v. Expert Intuitions: An Empirical Study of Acceptability Judgments. *The Linguistic Review*, 27 (1), 1–23.

Davies, M. (2002–). Corpus del español; 100 million words, 1200s–1900s. Available from www.corpusdelespanol.org.

Díaz-Campos, M. (2005). The Emergence of Adult-Like Command of Sociolinguistic Variables: A Study of Consonant Weakening in Spanish-Speaking Children. In D. Eddington (ed.), *Selected Proceedings of the 6th Conference on the Acquisition of Spanish and Portuguese as First and Second Languages*. Somerville, MA: Cascadilla, pp. 56–65.

Díaz-Campos, M. and Gradoville, M. (2011). An Analysis of Frequency as a Factor Contributing to the Diffusion of Variable Phenomena: Evidence from Spanish Data. In Luis A. Ortiz-López (ed.), *Selected Proceedings of the 13th Hispanic Linguistics Symposium*. Somerville, MA: Cascadilla, pp. 224–238.

Díaz-Campos, M. and Ruiz-Sánchez, C. (2008). The Value of Frequency as a Linguistic Factor: The Case of Two Dialectal Regions in the Spanish Speaking World. In Maurice Westmoreland and Juan Antonio Thomas (eds.), *Selected Proceedings of the 4th Workshop on Spanish Sociolinguistics*. Somerville, MA: Cascadilla pp. 43–53.

Docherty, G. J. and Foulkes, P. (2014). An Evaluation of Usage-Based Approaches to the Modelling of Sociophonetic Variability. *Lingua*, 142, 42–56.

Eddington, D. (2004). *Spanish Phonology and Morphology*. Amsterdam: John Benjamins.

Ellis, N. C. (2012). What Can we Count in Language, and What Counts in Language Acquisition, Cognition, and Use? In Stefan Th. Gries and Dagmar Divjak (eds.), *Frequency Effects in Language Learning and Processing*, Vol. 1. Berlin: De Gruyter, pp. 7–34.

Erker, D. (2012). Of Categories and Continua: Relating Discrete and Gradient Properties of Sociophonetic Variation. *Penn Working Papers in Linguistics*, 18 (2), 11–20.

Ernestus, M. and Baayen, R. H. (2011). Corpora and Exemplars in Phonology. In John A. Goldsmith, Jason Riggle, and Alan C. L. Yu (eds.), *The Handbook of Phonological Theory* (2nd edn). Chichester: Wiley-Blackwell, pp. 374–400.

File-Muriel, R. J. (2009). The Role of Lexical Frequency in the Weakening of Syllable-Final Lexical /s/ in the Spanish of Barranquilla, Colombia. *Hispania*, 348–360.

File-Muriel, R. J. (2010). Lexical Frequency as a Scalar Variable in Explaining Variation. *The Canadian Journal of Linguistics/La revue canadienne de linguistique*, 55 (1), 1–25.

File-Muriel, R. J. and Brown, E. K. (2011). The Gradient Nature of s-Lenition in Caleño Spanish. *Language Variation and Change*, 23 (2), 223–243.

Goldberg, A. E. (2006). *Constructions at Work: The Nature of Generalization in Language*. Oxford: Oxford University Press.

Hinskens, F., Hermans, B., and van Oostendorp, M. (2014). Grammar or Lexicon. Or: Grammar and Lexicon? Rule-Based and Usage-Based Approaches to Phonological Variation. *Lingua*, 142, 1–26.

Hochberg, J. G. (1986). Functional Compensation for /s/ Deletion in Puerto Rican Spanish. *Language*, 62 (3), 609–621.

Jurafsky, D., Bell, A., Gregory, M., and Raymond, W. D. (2001). Probabilistic Relations between Words: Evidence from Reduction in Lexical Production. *Typological Studies in Language*, 45, 229–254.

Krishnamurti, B. (1998). Regularity of Sound Change through Lexical Diffusion: A Study of s> h> in Gondi Dialects. *Language Variation and Change*, 10 (2), 193–220.

Labov, W. (1981). Resolving the Neogrammarian Controversy. *Language*, 57, 267–308.

Labov, W. (1994). *Principles of Linguistic Change: Internal Factors*. Oxford: Blackwell.

Lamy, D. S. (2015). A Sociophonetic Analysis of Trill Production in Panamanian Spanish. In Rachel Klassen, Juana M. Liceras, and Elena Valenzuela (eds.), *Hispanic Linguistics at the Crossroads: Theoretical Linguistics, Language Acquisition and Language Contact. Proceedings of the Hispanic Linguistics Symposium 2013*. Amsterdam and Philadelphia, PA: John Benjamins, pp. 313–336.

Langacker, R. W. (1987). *Foundations of Cognitive Grammar, Vol. 1, Theoretical Prerequisites*. Stanford, CA: Stanford University Press.

Lewis, G. and Boomershine, A. (2015). The Realization of Word-Final, Preconsonantal /s/ in the Spanish of Mexico City. *Studies in Hispanic and Lusophone Linguistics*, 8 (1), 157–182.

Linford, B. and Shin, N. L. (2013). Lexical Frequency Effects on L2 Spanish Subject Pronoun Expression. In J. Cabrelli Amaro, G. Lord, A. de Prada Pérez, and J. E. Aaron (eds.), *Selected Proceedings of the 16th Hispanic Linguistics Symposium*. Somerville, MA: Cascadilla, pp. 175–189.

Lipski, J. (2011). Socio-Phonological Variation in Latin American Spanish. In Manuel Díaz-Campos (ed.), *The Handbook of Hispanic Sociolinguistics*. Chichester: John Wiley, pp. 72–97.

Lynch, A. (2009). A Sociolinguistic Analysis of Final /s/ in Miami Cuban Spanish. *Language Sciences*, 31 (6), 766–790.

O'Rourke, E. and Potowski, K. (2016). Phonetic Accommodation in a Situation of Spanish Dialect Contact: Coda /s/ and /r/ in Chicago. *Studies in Hispanic and Lusophone Linguistics*, 9 (2), 355–399.

Phillips, B. S. (2006). *Word Frequency and Lexical Diffusion*. New York: Palgrave Macmillan.

Pierrehumbert, J. (2001). Exemplar dynamics: Word Frequency, Lenition and Contrast. In J. Bybee and P. Hopper (eds.), *Frequency and the Emergence of Linguistic Structure*. Amsterdam: John Benjamins, pp. 137–157.

Pierrehumbert, J. (2006). Syllable Structure and Word Structure: A Study of Triconsonantal Clusters in English. In Patricia A. Keating (ed.), *Phonological Structure and Phonetic Form*. Cambridge: Cambridge University Press, pp. 168–188.

Poplack, S. (1980). Deletion and Disambiguation in Puerto Rican Spanish. *Language*, 371–385.

Poplack, S. and Tagliamonte, S. (2001). *African American English in the Diaspora*. Oxford: Blackwell.

Poplack, S. and Torres Cacoullos, R. (2015). Linguistic Emergence on the Ground: A Variationist Paradigm. In Brian MacWhinney and William O'Grady *(eds.)*, *The Handbook of Language Emergence*. Malden, MA: Wiley-Blackwell, pp. 267–291.

PRESEEA (2014–). Corpus del *Proyecto* para el estudio sociolingüístico del español de España y de América. Universidad de Alcalá. preseea.linguas.net.

Ranson, D. L. (1991). Person Marking in the Wake of /s/ Deletion in Andalusian Spanish. *Language Variation and Change*, 3 (2), 133–152.

Raymond, W. D. and Brown, E. L. (2012). Are Effects of Word Frequency Effects of Context of Use? An Analysis of Initial Fricative Reduction in Spanish. In Stefan Th. Gries and Dagmar Divjak (eds.), *Frequency Effects in Language Learning and Processing*, Vol. 1. Berlin: De Gruyter, pp. 35–52.

Raymond, W. D., Brown, E. L., and Healy, A. F. (2016). Cumulative Context Effects and Variant Lexical Representations: Word Use and English Final t/d Deletion. *Language Variation and Change*, 28 (2), 175–202.

Rivas, J. (2013). Variable Subject Position in Main and Subordinate Clauses in Spanish: A Usage-Based Approach. *Moenia. Revista Lucense de Lingüística y Literatura*, 19, 97–113.

Rivas, J. and Brown, E. L. (2010). *Variable Development of Intersubjectivity in Spanish*. In Aquilino Sánchez and Moisés Almela (eds.), *A Mosaic of Corpus Linguistics. Selected Approaches*. Frankfurt and Berlin: Peter Lang, pp. 61–78.

Schuchardt, H. (1885). Über die Lautgesetze: Gegen die Junggrammatiker. Berlin: R. Oppenheim.

Shin, Naomi. (2016). Acquiring Constraints on Morphosyntactic Variation: Children's Spanish Subject Pronoun Expression. *Journal of Child Language*, 43 (4), 914–947.

Tomasello, M. (2003). *Constructing a Language: A Usage-Based Theory of Language Acquisition*. Cambridge, MA: Harvard University Press.

Torreira, F. and Ernestus, M. (2012). Weakening of Intervocalic /s/ in the Nijmegen Corpus of Casual Spanish. *Phonetica*, 69 (3), 124–148.

Torres Cacoullos, R. (2001). From Lexical to Grammatical to Social Meaning. *Language in Society*, 30 (3), 443–478.

Torres Cacoullos, R. (2015). Gradual Loss of Analyzability: Diachronic Priming Effects. In Aria Adli, Marco García García, and Göz Kaufmann (eds.),*Variation in Language: System- and Usage-Based Approaches*. Berlin: De Gruyter, pp. 265–288.

Torres Cacoullos, R. and Travis, C. E. (in preparation). New Mexico Spanish / English Bilingual (NMSEB) corpus. Available from nmcode-switching.la.psu.edu/

Travis, C. E. and Torres Cacoullos, R. (2012). What do Subject Pronouns do in Discourse? Cognitive, Mechanical and Constructional Factors in Variation. *Cognitive Linguistics*, 23 (4), 711–748.

Waltermire, M. (2011). Frequency Effects on the Morphological Conditioning of Syllable-final /s/ Reduction in Border Uruguayan Spanish. *Journal of Language Contact*, 4 (1), 26–55.

Wilson, D. V. (2009). From "Remaining" to "Becoming" in Spanish. The Role of Prefabs in the Development of the Construction *Quedar(se)* + ADJECTIVE. In Roberta Corrigan, Edith A. Moravcsik, Hamid Ouali, and Kathleen Wheatley (eds.), *Formulaic Language,* Vol. 1: *Distribution and Historical Change*. Amsterdam and Philadelphia, PA: John Benjamins, pp. 273–296.

Wilson, D. V. and Dumont, J. (2015). The Emergent Grammar of Bilinguals: The Spanish Verb *hacer* "do" with a Bare English Infinitive. *International Journal of Bilingualism*, 19 (4), 444–458.

Zipf, G. K. (1929). Relative Frequency as a Determinant of Phonetic Change. *Harvard Studies in Classical Philology*, 40, 1–95.

4

Functional-Typological Approaches to Hispanic Linguistics

Rosa Vallejos*

4.1 Introduction

One of the most striking facts about the languages of the world is that they are both similar and unique at the same time. The Functional-Typological approach explains this fact in terms of both the adaptive motivation of languages and their typological diversity. Functionalism starts with the fundamental assumption that languages are the way they are because they have evolved so as to serve their users' demands. Language is a tool for conceptualization, communication, and socialization among human beings. Currently, functionalism includes a range of theoretical models. However, what they have in common is a rejection of the view that grammar is an autonomous and self-contained system. At their core, functional approaches recognize and highlight that communicative factors and general cognitive constraints play a central role in the shape of the linguistic system, and consequently in grammatical theory, description, and methodology.

The functionalist approach naturally enables typological research to be based on functional domains and subdomains coded in particular languages. Typology focuses on recurrent patterns in large numbers of languages which allow generalizations as to what is possible in human languages. It compares the linguistic strategies employed by genetically unrelated languages to encode semantic/pragmatic functions and categorizes linguistic systems into types. On the basis of this categorization, typological studies arrive at implicational universals, which in turn have to be explained in functional or cognitive terms. In this view, universal

---

* My deepest gratitude to Spike Gildea, Keiko Beers, Evelyn Fernández, Haley Patterson, Thomas Goebel-Mahrle, and an anonymous reviewer for comments that helped me to improve the paper. Of course, any remaining errors are fully my own.

functional pressures, iconic principles, processing and learning constraints, and diachronic changes, among others, constitute an explanation for empirically attested cross-linguistic generalizations.

Functional-typological approaches play a prominent role in language change studies. By documenting recurrent patterns, typology informs the hypothesis-building process regarding plausible diachronic pathways. Spanish linguistics is making important contributions to this area of research by focusing not only on the final synchronic outcomes, but also on changes in progress, which have shed light on the mechanisms of change and the circumstances under which universal principles influence emerging structures.

4.2 What is Functionalism?

Functionalism sees languages as dynamic, emergent, and adaptive systems and looks at the context in which language is used to answer a fundamental question: how do speakers achieve communication through linguistic expressions? Functionalism's origins can be traced back to the '60s with the work of Dwight Bolinger (1960, 1961), Simon Dik (1972, 1997), and Michael Halliday (1961). It was Halliday who developed Systemic Functional Linguistics, a model explicitly concerned with the purposes of language use. It focused on the relationship between language and its functions in social settings. Halliday proposes that the resources of language are shaped by how speakers employ them to make meaning. This model brings together purely structural information with overtly social factors in a single integrated framework (Halliday 1985). The guiding questions of this proposal are: what are the speakers trying to accomplish? What linguistic devices are available to them? What motivates their choices?

Functionalism, also known at the beginning as West Coast Functionalism, became generally recognized in the 1970s with the seminal works published by linguists such as Chafe (1970), Comrie (1981), Givón (1979), Hopper (1979), and Hopper and Thompson (1980), among others. Currently, functionalism includes a variety of movements and models, such as Role and Reference Grammar, Cognitive Grammar, Lexical Functional Grammar, Construction Grammar, etc.

Functionalism relies on the following main tenets (cf. Croft 2003; DeLancey 2011; Dik 1997; Dryer 2006; Givón 1995; Payne 1999).

4.2.1 Cognitive Plausibility
Functional linguistics deals with observable patterns, moving away from abstract, deep-derived structures. In this framework, explanations for language are not unique to linguistic behavior. For example, language learning should involve the same cognitive mechanisms as those responsible for

other types of learning. Functionalists believe that explanations for why languages are the way they are rest upon general cognitive and communicative aspects of human behavior. This includes how people attend to, process, understand, and remember information conveyed by others. Therefore hypotheses about language are informed by what we know about human cognition. Some of the cognitive processes related to language include perception, memory, attention, and interpretation.

4.2.2 Cross-Linguistic Validity

A basic assumption in functional linguistics is that languages encode comparable meanings and serve similar functions. However, they may differ with respect to the formal strategies used to code those meanings and functions. In addition, languages may display cross-linguistic dissimilarities due to linguistic idiosyncrasies. This approach allows for a typology based on functional domains, subdomains, and functions coded in individual languages. Patterns that are recurrent across large numbers of languages permit generalizations as to what is possible in human languages, and ultimately contribute to our understanding of what language is.

4.2.3 Grammar-External Explanations

Language does not operate in isolation; thus, linguistic inquiry cannot be reduced to structure alone. Given that languages serve general communicative and social–cultural functions, the explanation for the fact that they display common properties lies outside the linguistic systems themselves. The external factors that determine the shape of languages include "(i) the establishment of high-level communicative relationships between human beings, (ii) the biological and psychological properties of natural language users, (iii) the settings and circumstances in which languages are used for communicative purposes" (Dik 1997:7).

4.2.4 Empirically-Sound Methods

Studies that follow functional approaches are data driven. The patterns to be explained are observed in language use, and the argumentation for the hypotheses put forward relies on those data points. Functionalists seek and rely on data that emerge from actual interaction among members of speech communities, moving away from fabricated examples and grammatical judgments based on personal introspection. Large-scale corpora of naturally occurring language have a central place in functional studies because, in addition to providing quality data, they make replicability possible. This is particularly important when dealing with under-studied languages and language varieties.

Currently, functionalism examines language from a wide range of subfields, including pragmatics, cognitive linguistics, psycholinguistics, sociolinguistics, ethnolinguistics, contact linguistics, historical linguistics, etc. However, the functionalist enterprise represents a unified approach to theory, description, and methodology. In this view, there are several dimensions involved in the use of language. For instance, communicative functions involve the transmission of information, social interactions, speaker–hearer relationships, and discourse context. Cognitive functions entail conceptualization of the world, categorization, recognition, attention, and memory, among others.

Functional approaches to linguistic inquiry have gained more ground over the last two decades with more researchers resorting to functional explanations to account for linguistic patterns, most notably within the subfields of cognitive linguistics and language variation and change.

4.3 What is Typology?

There is a close partnership between functionalism and typology. Linguistic typology aims to both describe and explain similarities and differences among languages. Typology began in the '60s with the pioneering work of Joseph Greenberg on implicational universals of morphology and word order (Greenberg 1966). Since then, it has become a discipline with its own methodologies and research goals that go beyond determining what is plausible in human languages. It went from asking "What's possible?" to "What's where?" and "Why is it there?" (Nichols 2007; Bickel 2007, 2015). This evolution of the discipline entailed not only observing patterns of distribution geographically, but also explaining them in terms of their emergence over time. See, for instance, Greenberg (1966) and Givón (1979), for a call to consider the role of diachrony in the synchronic distribution of linguistic patterns. The major tenets of the typological enterprise are the following.

4.3.1 Implicational Universals

Typology is not committed to "universal grammar" but to probabilities that are born out of observable similarities among language-specific structures. The generalizations put forward by typology are implicational universals, which are the result of cross-linguistic comparisons that demonstrate the connections between two or more features. Implicational universals take the form "if language X has property Y, then it will also have property Z." That is, the presence of one feature implies the presence of another. Take Kennan and Comrie's (1977) accessibility hierarchy to relativization:[1]

SU > DO > IO > OPREP > GEN > OCOMP

---

[1] SU = subject; DO = direct object; IO = indirect object; OPREP = object of preposition; GEN = genitive; OCOMP = object of comparison.

According to this hierarchy, the relativization of direct objects implies the relativization of subjects. As a result, implicational universals restrict logically possible language types, thus limiting linguistic variation (Croft 2003; Givón 1995, 2001).

4.3.2 Competing Motivations

A basic assumption in typology is that there are a number of internal and external factors that shape grammar. Thus, competing motivations can explain the choice between equivalent morphosyntactic patterns for the same functional domain. These may include processing demands, economy, iconicity, harmony, etc.[2] Competing motivation models can account for both variation in language types and also frequency of language types across the world. They provide explanations for both typological variation and constraints on that variation.

4.3.3 Cross-Linguistic Variation

Typology proceeds from the recognition that languages display highly diverse linguistic strategies. Typology aims to explain the variation of structural patterns, the preference for certain patterns over other competing candidates, the skewed geographic distribution of constructions, the different degrees of complexity of patterns, the paths of linguistic change, etc. These phenomena are examined in light of multiple possible explanations. Like functional linguistics, typology considers the cognitive, areal, cultural, communicative and/or evolutionary constraints on language diversity, disparity, complexity, and change. Historical linguistics, areal linguistics, and contact linguistics account for the documented variation.

4.3.4 Limits to Diversity

A foundational question undertaken by typology is what the limits of language variation are. Different types of coding strategies are sufficiently specific to a particular language that any attempt to compare the strategies cross-linguistically turns out to be impossible. Although structural regularities are not universals, recurrent functions have been identified in language use. Typology assumes that there are more cross-linguistic regularities in terms of function than in terms of form. Thus, the objects of concern for typologists are the functional domains and meanings, not specific structures (Givón 1981). For instance,

---

[2] *Iconicity* is the conceived relationship between form and meaning. For example, formal complexity corresponds to conceptual complexity, conceptual distance tends to match with linguistic distance, and the sequential order of events described is mirrored in the speech chain (Givón 1985). *Harmony* is linked to linguistic markedness. A linguistic structure is termed "marked" when it is relatively complex or in some sense defective. Marked representations have lower harmony and tend to be avoided by the language-processing system (Smolensky 2006).

language is used for predication, modification, and reference purposes, so these are taken as motivations for the formal conventionalization of categories such as *verb, adjective*, and *noun* (Croft 2003). In addition, most linguistic patterns display a skewed geographic distribution. Yet when the history and the social structure of the populations are taken into consideration, this asymmetric distribution turns out to not be accidental.

There is an ongoing debate about the need to separate language description from typological comparison. The discrepancy centers around the relationship, if any, between the descriptive categories employed by linguists describing particular languages, and the comparative concepts used by typologists comparing patterns in different languages. The former rely exclusively on language-internal distribution, while the latter primarily on semantic/functional and formal considerations. Some argue that there is no relationship between descriptive categories and comparative concepts (see, for instance, Croft 2016; Dryer 2016; Haspelmath 2010, 2016). Others dispute that the distinction between what is language-specific and what is cross-linguistic is not absolute (Himmelmann 2016), and that both description and comparison should proceed inductively, "staying true to the facts of the languages as manifested in natural data, and not resort[ing] to abstractions that lead to classifying languages or constructions in a way that ignores the actual facts of the languages" (LaPolla 2016:365). Comparative concepts are defined using formal properties that are consistently applied across languages. The question is, though, how much information is lost when comparing constructions apart from their idiosyncrasies.

From a methodological point of view, typology requires a systematic comparison across languages. Like functional linguistics, typology relies on empirically sound methods of discovery to search for explanations that are cognitively plausible. Typological claims are supported by analyses of, at a minimum, dozens of languages that are selected following specific sampling methods. Typology is the subfield that has benefited the most from advances in technology. This, together with the description of newly documented languages, has allowed the development of important typological databases, most notably *The World Atlas of Language Structures* (Dryer and Haspelmath 2013) and *The Atlas of Pidgin and Creole Language Structures* (Michaelis *et al.* 2013). Typology also incorporates sophisticated statistical methods, such as multivariate scaling methods (e.g. Croft and Poole 2008), phylogenetic methods (e.g. Dunn *et al.* 2005; Donohue *et al.* 2008), the naive Bayes classification (e.g. Michael *et al.* 2014). In order to establish connections, quantitative typology operates with narrowly defined structural variables rather than general typological features.

The diverse array of linguistic strategies documented in the world's languages can be explained in part by the fact that they arose diachronically from different source constructions. However, what motivates the selection of certain patterns over other potential candidates is a matter of current debate. Beyond history, typologists are exploring the interaction of linguistic distributions with other patterns, including cognitive principles, communicative preferences, genetic factors, and social configurations. This places typologists in an optimal position for interdisciplinary research (see, for instance, Dunn *et al.* 2005; Enfield 2002; Evans 2003; Levinson 2003; Nichols 1997; among others).

4.4 Applications to Hispanic Linguistics

Functional-typological approaches have made important contributions to Hispanic linguistics. In the following paragraphs, some grammatical structures of Spanish will be placed in the context of the range of cross-linguistic diversity. The discussion focuses on studies that explicitly or implicitly follow the functional-typological framework. The selected topics include sentence grammar phenomena, such as argument structure, differential object marking, transitivity, copular constructions, verb–object compounds, and insubordination. Studies on discourse phenomena, language contact, language variation, and language change will be briefly highlighted as well.

4.4.1 Argument Structure

From a functional-typological perspective, argument structure refers to the number of arguments a lexical item takes (i.e. the core participants in the events denoted by the verb), their syntactic encoding, and their semantic relation to this lexical item (Comrie 1993; Dryer 2007; Goldberg 1995). The argument Selection Principle proposed by Dowty (1991:576) predicts that "the argument for which the predicate entails the greatest number of Proto-Agent properties will be lexicalized as the subject of the predicate; the argument having the greatest number of Proto-Patient entailments will be lexicalized as the direct object."

In Spanish, as in many other languages, psychological verbs display a particular argument structure. Psychological verbs, also known as mental verbs, express mental states, changes of state or psychological processes, and constitute a clear set, with cross-linguistically identifiable semantic and syntactic properties (Croft 1993). The experiencer and the stimulus involved with verbs like *gustar* 'to like,' *encantar* 'to really like,' *fascinar* 'to fascinate' appear as dative and subject, respectively. For example, in *Me gustan los chocolates*, the experiencer (*me*) appears as dative, while the stimulus (*los chocolates*), the cause of the psychological state or emotion, appears as the syntactic subject. Miglio *et al.* (2013) argue that the coding system with psychological verbs in Spanish is a type of inverse construction. An inverse construction does not exhibit a canonical transitive argument structure, with a nominative subject and an accusative patient, as in English *I like chocolates*.³ In that sense, Spanish behaves like many other languages with respect to psychological verbs. Typologically, inverse constructions have been associated with experiential predicates. They are less transitive and are hence associated with properties such as less volition, less control, less affectedness of the object than events that involve prototypical agents (Croft 1993; Dahl and Fedriani 2012).

Building on Vázquez Rozas (2012), Miglio *et al.* (2013:269) focus on the linguistic expression of the experiencer as either dative oblique (4.1a) or accusative (4.1b):

(4.1) a. Le.EXP/OBL   molestan   los estudiantes
          to-him/her   bother   the students
          'S/he is bothered by the students'
       b. La.EXP/ACC   molestan   los estudiantes
          to-her   bother   the students
          'She is bothered by the students'

The results of a variationist examination suggest that the distribution of dative and accusative clitics can be predicted by several factors, one of the main predictors being the animacy of the stimulus (Miglio *et al.* 2013:272).⁴ When the stimulus is animate, then the accusative forms (*lo, la, los, las*) are more likely to be used, and when it is inanimate, the oblique forms (*le, les*) are more likely to appear. This is one of many areas in which the animacy hierarchy helps to explain Spanish grammar.

4.4.2 Differential Object Marking

Differential object marking (DOM) refers to a phenomenon in which direct objects are classified into subclasses. Each class receives different morphosyntactic treatment. Cross-linguistically, DOM is part of a larger pattern of asymmetrical case marking (Iggesen 2013). The phenomenon of case asymmetry is based on the division of a language's nominals into subclasses sharing common semantic (i.e. animate vs. non-animate entities) or functional characteristics (i.e. pronoun vs. noun phrase). DOM manifests in Spanish with the special accusative case marking *a* for certain direct objects, and the lack of *a* for certain others. Features that are normally sensitive to DOM are animacy, definiteness, and specificity (Aissen 2003, and references within). In Spanish, object marking is affected primarily by animacy and specificity (Pensado 1995), as shown in (4.2). The object in (4.2a) is inanimate and specific, in (4.2b) is animate and specific, and in (4.2c) is animate and non-specific.

---

³ Apart from the non-canonical argument structure, Spanish verbs like *adorar* or *amar* do not exhibit an inverse coding but the canonical form, as in *Yo adoro los chocolates* 'I adore chocolates.'

⁴ Other significant factors are the interaction of genre (academic vs. literature vs. news vs. oral) and tense (imperfect vs. present vs. perfect vs. preterit), and genre and clausal stimulus (i.e. the stimulus is a proposition).

(4.2) a. Encontré Ø/*a tu billetera
          'I found your wallet'
       b. Encontré *Ø/a tu gato
          'I found your cat'
       c. Encontré Ø/*a un gato
          'I found a cat'

However, in some Spanish varieties, DOM seems sensitive to parameters beyond the animacy and specificity of the entities in object position. It includes discourse-pragmatic factors such as topicality, referentiality, definiteness, and discourse prominence. The role of these factors in determining the direct object coding has been amply explored (Laca 2002; Pensado 1995, and references within). Schwenter (2006) examines a related phenomenon, the null expression of objects, and uncovers important parallels with asymmetrical object coding. He finds that direct objects (DOs) that tend to receive the *a* marking display similar semantic properties more than anaphoric DOs that are explicitly encoded; in contrast, DOs that tend to lack special case marking share semantic features with null DOs. Another important observation is that null objects in ditransitive constructions are more frequent than specific null objects in transitive constructions. The generalizations to capture all these patterns in Spanish boil down to general cognitive, functional pressures. Both non-null objects and *a*-coded objects signal typologically marked objects. Schwenter indicates that these are considered "atypical or marked DOs, due to both inherent and contextual features, in a way that signals their special status, both in the ongoing discourse and vis-à-vis DOs with more typical or unmarked referents" (2006:34). Importantly, these observations can also be extended to other patterns in Spanish, such as clitic doubling (Dumitrescu 1997).

4.4.3 Transitivity

In one view, transitivity is a categorical feature defined in terms of the number of core arguments of a clause. Core arguments are understood as the participants required overtly within a particular construction. Intransitive constructions have one core argument, transitives have two core arguments, and ditransitives have three core arguments (Dryer 2007). A verb is understood to combine with argument structure constructions (e.g. "slice" can combine with either a transitive or ditransitive construction). In this view, there are arguments of the verb (participant roles) and arguments of the construction (argument roles). Goldberg (1995:49) states that grammatical relations, such as subject and object, "profile particular roles as being either semantically salient or having some kind of discourse prominence."[5] Grammatical constructions can have transparent or abstract

---

[5] Profiled participant roles are "entities in the frame semantics associated with the verb that are obligatorily accessed and function as focal points within the scene ... [they] are obligatorily brought into perspective, achieving a certain degree of 'salience'" (Goldberg 1995:44).

Table 4.1 *Parameters of transitivity as adapted from Hopper and Thompson (1980)*

	High transitivity	Low transitivity
Participants	2 or more: *Juan comió la manzana*	1 participant: *Juan comió*
Kinesis	Action: *Juan agarró un chocolate*	Non-action: *Juan quiere un chocolate*
Aspect	Telic: *Juan leyó el libro*	Atelic: *Juan está leyendo el libro*
Punctuality	Punctual: *Juan pateó la pelota*	Non-punctual: *Juan trajo la pelota*
Volitionality	Volitional: *Juan saltó del quinto piso*	Non-volitional: *Juan cayó del quinto piso*
Affirmation	Affirmative: *Juan trajo la pelota*	Negative: *Juan no trajo la pelota*
Mode	Realis: *Juan llega hoy*	Irrealis: *Tal vez Juan llegue hoy*
Agency	Potent A: *Ese hombre me asustó*	Non-potent A: *Esa foto me asustó*
Affectedness of O	Affected O: *Juan rompió la carta*	Non-affected O: *Juan dobló la carta*
Individuation of O	Individuated O: *Juan curó al paciente*	Non-individuated O: *Juan curó pacientes*

A = agent; O = object

meanings and functions. For instance, the English ditransitive construction possesses its own semantics, "Transfer of Possession," [X CAUSES Y to RECEIVE Z], and its own form [SUBJ V OBJ$_1$ OBJ$_2$]. This is distinct from the English "Caused Motion to a Location" construction, [X MOVES Y TO Z], whose form is [SUBJ V OBJ OBL]. For an application of this approach to evaluate the alignment system in constructions with two objects in Spanish, see Clements (2006a).

In a different view, transitivity is discourse determined. Hopper and Thompson (1980) suggest going beyond the number of participants to calculate the effectiveness or intensity with which the action is transferred from one participant to another. In this view, transitivity is seen as a gradient phenomenon with clauses assigned different degrees of transitivity. The authors incorporate the semantic and pragmatic parameters shown in Table 4.1 in the calculation of a clause's transitivity (Hopper and Thompson 1980:252).

Clements (2006c) applies Hopper and Thompson's (1980) view of gradual transitivity to study the impact of the reflexive *se* (non-anaphoric *se*) in the interpretation of a clause. He argues that the non-anaphoric *se* can both lower and raise the level of transitivity depending on the circumstances.

(4.3)   a. *Carlos enamoró a Luisa*
          'Carlos courted Luisa'
      b. *Carlos se enamoró*
          'Carlos fell in love'

(4.4)   a. *Marta durmió en casa de su amiga*
          'Marta slept at her friend's house'
      b. *Marta se durmió en casa de su amiga*
          'Marta fell asleep at her friend's house'

(4.5) a. *Él comió manzanas*
       'He ate apples'
    b. *Él se comió las manzanas*
       'He ate up the apples'
    c. **Él se comió manzana*
       'He ate up apple'

(4.6) a. *Caen las hojas en otoño*
       'Leaves fall in the fall'
    b. *Se cayeron las hojas de mi rosal*
       'The leaves of my roses have fallen'

It is clear in (4.3) that *se* lowers the transitivity of a middle construction by reducing an argument. However, the most interesting observations Clements makes is regarding those constructions with *se* that do not involve the reduction of arguments. The event in (4.4a) is durative and atelic, and (4.4b) is punctual and telic. Thus, (4.4b) is higher in the transitivity continuum compared to (4.4a). Example (4.5a) contains an indefinite object, whereas the construction with *se* in (4.5b) requires a definite object. Therefore, (4.5b) is higher in transitivity than (4.5a). Note in (4.5c) that *se* is not allowed with indefinite objects. A parallel phenomenon is shown in (4.6a–b). This time *se* co-occurs with specific leaves (4.6b), as opposed to the generic ones in (4.6a). Based on these facts, Clements (2006c:241) concludes that the presence of *se* co-varies with high transitivity (4.4b, 4.5b, 4.6b), whereas the absence of *se* co-varies with low transitivity (4.4a, 4.5a, 4.6a). Transitivity is, then, a promising concept to account for the distribution of *se* in Spanish.

4.4.4 Copulas

Broadly, a copular clause is one that includes a nonverbal predicate, a subject, and some grammatical element that has the function of marking the relation between the two (for instance, in "That man is a congressman," the copula "is" connects the subject "that man" and the predicate "a congressman"). Cross-linguistically, a copula is best treated as a continuum, as it may share a few or more morphosyntactic properties with lexical verbs (Stassen 1997). Copular clauses are typically used for at least the following two functions: identification of the subject as a unique individual (*Mario Bergoglio es el Papa Francisco* 'Mario Bergoglio is Pope Francis'), and categorization of the subject as belonging to the category defined by the predicate noun (*El Papa Francisco es profesor* 'Pope Francis is a professor'). Copular constructions are also used to locate the subject (*El Papa Francisco está en Roma* 'Pope Francis is in Rome'), and to attribute properties to the subject (*El Papa Francisco es valiente* 'Pope Francis is brave,' or *El Papa Francisco está preocupado* 'Pope Francis is worried').

Spanish has two copulas: *ser* is consistently used for identification and categorization functions, and *estar* for locative functions.[6] However, the fact that both copulas can be used to predicate about the properties of an entity has made copula choice a fruitful field for variationist research. Copula choice across dialects of Spanish is an extensively studied phenomenon. While the type of adjective in the predicate position plays a role in the selection of the copula (Geeslin and Guijaro-Fuentes 2008), it can no longer be sustained that a list of semantic features – particularly time stability – can unilaterally predict the selection of copulas in Spanish. For example, Clements (2006b) explains that it is also necessary to look at the animacy of the subject to determine copula choice. He finds that more animate referents will more likely occur with *ser*, while less animate referents will more likely occur with *estar*. Brown and Cortés-Torres (2012) found innovative uses of [*estar* + adjective] in Puerto Rican Spanish. Speakers use *estar* instead of *ser* for pragmatic purposes, typically to emphasize the speaker's personal experience with a referent. Spanish copulas are then another example that highlights the need for a non-modular approach to grammar.

4.4.5 Auxiliary Constructions

The hypothesis that synonymity does not exist among grammatical constructions is found in Givón (1985), Langacker (1985), Goldberg (1995), and several others. The idea is that a difference in syntactic form always spells a difference in meaning. Different constructions can receive subtle systematic differences in interpretation. An example comes from Spanish auxiliary verb constructions that encode aspectual distinctions (see, for instance, Bybee and Eddington 2006; Dumont 2013). The combinations *estar hablando* 'to be speaking' and *andar buscando* 'to look for' express the same type of aspect: imperfect, unfinished events. However, they differ in the types of verbs involved in the two constructions. Torres Cacoullos (2001) shows that *estar* tends to appear with speech verbs (*hablando* 'talking,' *charlando* 'chatting,' *platicando* 'speaking'), verbs denoting perceptible bodily activities (*llorando* 'crying,' *riendo* 'laughing'), and verbs that denote mental activities (*pensando* 'thinking,' *razonando* 'reasoning'). In contrast, *andar* tends to appear with verbs that denote movement and physical activities (*anda trabajando en el campo* 'is working in the field').

Some Spanish constructions also resist analyses of auxiliary constructions or serial verb constructions, and pose a challenge for non-functional

---

[6] *Ser* is also used for temporal location (i.e. the party in the example below is an event with a clear end point), *estar* for more permanent location:

(i)   *La fiesta es en mi casa*
        'The party is at my house'
        El libro está en mi casa
        'The book is at my house'

views of clause syntax. For instance, the examples in (4.7) are difficult to account for by compositional or verb-centered views of argument structure.

(4.7)   a. *Esto no tiene sentido*   'It makes no sense'
         b. *Tomaré una ducha*   'I'll take a shower'
         c. *Perdió la conciencia*   'He/she lost consciousness'

Construction grammar explains the examples in (4.7) as instances of verb–object compounds, when a light verb (i.e. a verb with a low semantic content used in combination with some other element) is followed by an object to form a unitary predicate. In (4.7a) *tener sentido* is a schema conventionalized and shared by most speakers (Travis and Torres Cacoullos 2012). But this pattern is quite common in the languages of the world, and diachronic studies have found that light verbs have evolved crosslinguistically from lexically rich verbs through semantic bleaching, a process in which the verb loses some or all of its original semantics. These recurrent patterns across languages permit generalizations about language change over time, and the source constructions from which they can arise diachronically.

In addition to special auxiliaries, in Spanish the end point of an event can also be highlighted by adverbs. For instance, González Fernández and Maldonado (2006) propose general cognitive factors as the motivations for the emergence of conceptualizations that highlight the endpoint of an event. The authors demonstrate that adverbs such as *finalmente* 'finally,' *por fin* 'at last,' *al fin* 'in the end,' signal several types of completion that can be explained by bringing together a force-dynamics situation and a high degree of transitivity (telicity and agentivity). According to these authors, these parameters constitute the basis for the emergence of the conceptualizer's view of the event. A fine-grained cognitive analysis shows that, in Spanish, the meanings conveyed by *finalmente, por fin,* and *al fin* include temporal closure of an event sequentially scanned, discourse closure of an ordered enumeration, felicitous results of an expected event, and evaluative conclusions regarding a previous situation (2006:19).

4.4.6 Insubordination

Insubordination is "the conventionalised main-clause use of what, on prima facie grounds, appear to be formally subordinate clauses" (Evans 2007:367, e.g. "if you could just sit here for a while please"). It can be characterized both diachronically and synchronically. Diachronically, it is the emergence of main clause structures from subordinate structures, and synchronically it is the use of constructions that display features of subordinate clauses but that can be used independently of a main clause. Although insubordination has not received the attention it deserves, it has turned out to be a widespread phenomenon (Evans and Watanabe 2016). This phenomenon provides an interesting challenge to language change theory as it does not recruit material from main clauses to generate subordinate clauses, but proceeds in the opposite direction. The grammaticalization process of insubordination involves the following phases: subordination > ellipsis of the main clause > conventionalization of ellipsis > conventionalization of the construction. On the functional side, Evans (2007) argues that insubordinate constructions are employed for indirect interpersonal control, for epistemic and evidential meanings, and to signal presupposed information.

Spanish grammar provides opportunities to test the proposed typologies for insubordination. Spanish can also shed light on a disputed point: whether insubordination in fact reaches a stage of true independence from the main clause, or whether insubordination is context dependent as the elided material remains recoverable. Gras (2016) focuses on insubordinated-*que* constructions. He describes two types of insubordination: *que*-modals express a hortatory function, which are used for mandates and desires, as in (4.8), and *que*-connectives relate what is being said with the previous context (i.e. serve to repeat or quote parts of speech), as in (4.9) (Gras 2016:115).

(4.8)   No no/ hay que decírselo porque si es algo
        'No no/ you have to tell him because if there is something wrong'
        que   lo   arreglen
        that 3SG.OBJ.MASC fix.3PL.PRES.SBJV
        'it must be fixed'

(4.9)   A: Tienes que llamar al banco.
            'You have to call the bank.'
        B: **Que ya   he   llamado.**
            that already have.1SG.PRES.IND called
            'I have already called.'

At the syntactic level, these two types of subordinated-*que* constructions differ with respect to four properties: verbal mode, type of sentence, compatibility with mechanisms of coordination and subordination, and position of the topic. Gras' findings partially support Evans' (2007) typology of insubordination. Gras proposes that "the distinction between modal (i.e. deontic), sentence-type (i.e. imperative) and discourse (i.e. contrast) insubordination can lead to a better understanding of the functional range of insubordination cross-linguistically and the functional domains that insubordinate constructions occupy in individual languages" (2016:140).

Schwenter (2016) examines the insubordination of *si*-clauses. Spanish insubordinated-*si* constructions display clear features that set them apart from subordinated-*si* constructions (2016:95–97). First, the polarity of subordinated *si* is dependent on the main clause; that is, subordinated *si* does not need *no* to express negation, as in (4.10), whereas insubordinated *si* requires it to be grammatical, as shown in (4.11). Second, subordinated *si* can be marked by *si* more than once to link several conditional clauses within the same sentence (4.12), but the insubordinated *si* can be marked with *si* only once at the beginning of a sentence, even if there is more than one insubordinated clause (4.13). Third, subordinated *si* can be used with verbs of cognition or communication (4.14), while insubordinate *si* does not allow the use of these verbs, unless *si* appears fronted (4.15, where "#" indicates that the sentence is pragmatically odd).

(4.10)   **Si** tienes duda alguna, me puedes llamar.
         'If you have any doubt, you can call me.'

(4.11)   A: Tienes dudas sobre mi lealtad, ¿no?
            'You have doubts about my loyalty, right?'
         B: **Si** yo *(no) tengo duda alguna.
            'SI I don't have any doubt.'

(4.12)   **Si** sigues asistiendo a clase y **si** estudias mucho, vas a llegar lejos.
         'If you keep attending class and if you study a lot, you will go far.'

(4.13)   A: Julia no va a aprobar el examen.
            'Julia won't pass the test.'
         B: ¡**Si** ha estudiado mucho y (***si**) lo sabe todo!
            'SI she's studied a lot and she knows it all!'

(4.14)   Juan cree/dice que **si** tenemos dinero compraremos un coche nuevo.
         'Juan thinks/says that if we have money we'll buy a new car.'

(4.15)   A: Vamos a comprar un coche nuevo.
            'Let's buy a new car.'
         B1: #¡Juan cree/dice que **si** no tenemos dinero!
            'Juan thinks/says that SI we don't have money!'
         B2: ¡**Si** Juan dice que no tenemos dinero!
            'SI Juan says that we don't have money!'

Schwenter concludes that insubordinated-*si* constructions have their own features and functions. Given that these patterns are found in dialogic sequences, they link adjacent propositions. A key finding is that insubordinated-*si* constructions participate in interpretational relationships not only with their main clauses, but also with other utterances in the discourse (2016:98). This, together with the cluster of formal features outlined above, constitute evidence for the independence and conventionalization of this construction. Overall, Spanish grammar demonstrates that insubordination occurs in situations where a high degree of intersubjective alignment between speaker and hearer can be presupposed. This finding underscores one of the tenets of functional-typology regarding methodology – in order to account for this type of pattern, we need to examine language used in social interactions.

4.4.7 Discourse Phenomena

Abundant work in Hispanic linguistics has demonstrated that sentence level grammar is contingent on discourse organization and communicative context. Studies in this area fit in naturally with the functionalist assumption that there is not a strict divide between semantics and pragmatics. A grammatical construction can include information regarding focus, topicality, referentiality, etc., or in other words, categories that surpass the scope of the clause.

Travis and Torres Cacoullos (2012) elaborate on important methodological points to explore discourse syntax topics, including what counts as valid data and how it should be collected. These authors emphasize that instances of spontaneous language use are key, especially from conversational situations. Such instances represent one of the most natural contexts, the type of language use that we learn first and without any kind of instruction, and which occurs in real time. For instance, to explain the distribution of determiners in Spanish, we need to resort to categories such as *specificity* and *referentiality* in discourse. While the former relates to the way in which noun phrases identify entities (specific vs. non-specific), the latter relates to tracking participants – talking about an object as an entity with continuous identity over a stretch of discourse (Du Bois 1980).

Spanish also provides abundant examples of the link between discourse usage and the emergence of grammatical constructions. Constructions that are very frequent in discourse are converted into individual automated units that speakers produce and store in their minds as a single unit (Bybee 2006; Travis and Torres Cacoullos 2012). For instance, *yo no sé* 'I do not know' is a construction of very frequent use. The pieces of evidence supporting the claim that it is a well-entrenched unit are its strong tendency to appear by itself (i.e. often *yo no sé* appears in its own intonation unit), and its autonomy from other uses of the verb *saber* (i.e. *yo no sé* does not necessarily indicate lack of knowledge, but is also used as a general attenuating element). Distributional evidence of its unique status includes the high rate of the subject pronominal *yo*. Often *yo no sé* can appear at the beginning or the end of another clause. The convergence of these patterns of use suggest that in fact *yo no sé* is a single unit.

The functional view that sentence grammar is intimately related to components of discourse grammar has been amply demonstrated in several studies. These include discourse studies on particles (i.e. Curnow and Travis 2008; Hennemann 2015; Delbecque and Maldonado 2009; Ocampo 2009; Travis 2005), pronoun realization (Otheguy 2014; Shin 2014), and order of constituents (López Meirama 2006; Olarrea 2012). Another area that has received significant attention is Spanish in contact with English and other languages. Several studies have argued that contact-induced change is mediated by communicative needs, particularly in the areas of loanwords (Otheguy and

Lapidus 2003) and substrate effects (Escobar 2012). Another area of fertile research is language change over time, particularly the functional extensions of existing constructions and the emergence of new constructions when general communicative and cognitive forces conspire to motivate innovations in Spanish grammar (Company Company 2012; Otheguy 2011; Vallejos 2014; Wilson 2013).

4.5 Closing Remarks

In summary, functional-typological approaches have made important contributions to our understanding of language, and have informed research in Hispanic linguistics. Achievements have been made in several subfields. For instance, under language variation and change, these approaches have helped to map out the complex temporal sub-processes by which grammar emerges as frequently-used patterns sediment into conventionalized patterns (Hopper 1987; Bybee 2006; Evans and Levinson 2009; Givón 2008). A central question in linguistics is, what do speakers know about their languages? Functional-typological studies in general, and within Hispanic linguistics in particular, have helped us to understand that this tacit knowledge includes the grammatical constructions themselves, but also their use in social context, their pragmatic force, and their patterned variation.

References

Aissen, Judith. (2003). Differential Object Marking: Iconicity vs. Economy. *Natural Language and Linguistic Theory*, 21, 435–448.

Bickel, Balthasar. (2007). Typology in the 21st Century: Major Current Developments. *Linguistic Typology*, 11, 239–251.

Bickel, Balthasar. (2015). Distributional Typology: Statistical Inquiries into the Dynamics of Linguistic Diversity. In Bernd Heine and Heiko Narrog (eds.), *The Oxford Handbook of Linguistic Analysis* (2nd edn). Oxford: Oxford University Press, 901–923.

Bolinger, Dwight. (1960). Linguistic Science and Linguistic Engineering. *Word*, 16, 374–391.

Bolinger, Dwight. (1961). Syntactic Blends and Other Matters. *Language*, 37: 3, 366–381.

Brown, Esther and Cortés-Torres, Mayra. (2012). Syntactic and Pragmatic Usage of the [estar + Adjective] Construction in Puerto Rican Spanish: ¡Está brutal! In Kimberly Geeslin and Manuel Díaz-Campos (eds.), *Selected Proceedings of the 14th Hispanic Linguistics Symposium*. Somerville, MA: Cascadilla, pp. 61–74.

Bybee, Joan. (2006). From Usage to Grammar: The Mind's Response to Repetition. *Language*, 82 (4), 711–733.

Bybee, Joan and Eddington, David. (2006). A Usage-Based Approach to Spanish Verbs of "Becoming." *Language*, 82 (2), 323–355.

Chafe, Wallace. (1970). *Meaning and the Structure of Language*. Chicago, IL: University of Chicago Press.

Clements, J. C. (2006a). Primary and Secondary Object Marking in Spanish. In J. C. Clements and J. Yoon (eds.), *Functional Approaches to Spanish Syntax: Lexical Semantics, Discourse and Transitivity*. New York: Palgrave Macmillan, pp. 115–133.

Clements, J. C. (2006b). *Ser–estar* in the Predicate Adjective Construction. In J. C. Clements and J. Yoon (eds.), *Functional Approaches to Spanish Syntax: Lexical Semantics, Discourse and Transitivity*. New York: Palgrave Macmillan, pp. 161–202.

Clements, J. C. (2006c). Transitivity and Spanish Non-Anaphoric *se*. In J. C. Clements and J. Yoon (eds.), *Functional Approaches to Spanish Syntax: Lexical Semantics, Discourse and Transitivity*. New York: Palgrave Macmillan, pp. 236–264.

Company Company, C. (2012). Historical Morphosyntax and Grammaticalization. In J. I. Hualde, A. Olarrea, and E. O'Rourke (eds.), *The Handbook of Hispanic Linguistics*. Malden, MA: John Wiley and Sons, pp. 673–692.

Comrie, Bernard. (1981). *Language Universals and Linguistic Typology: Syntax and Morphology*. Chicago, IL: University of Chicago Press.

Comrie, Bernard. (1993). Argument Structure. In Joachim Jacobs, Arnim von Stechow, Wolfgang Sternefeld, and Theo Vennemann (eds.), *Syntax: An International Handbook of Contemporary Research*, Vol. 1. Berlin: De Gruyter, pp. 903–914.

Croft, William. (1993). Case Marking and the Semantics of Mental Verbs. In James Pustejovsky (ed.), *Semantics and the Lexicon*. Boston, MA and London: Kluwer, pp. 55–72.

Croft, William. (2003). *Typology and Universals* (2nd edn). Cambridge: Cambridge University Press.

Croft, William. (2016). Comparative Concepts and Language-Specific Categories: Theory and Practice. *Linguistic Typology*, 20 (2), 377–393. doi:10.1515/lingty-2016-0012.

Croft, William and Poole, K. T. (2008). Inferring Universals from Grammatical Variation: Multidimensional Scaling for Typological Analysis. *Theoretical Linguistics*, 34, 1–37.

Curnow, Timothy and Travis, Catherine. (2008). Locational Adverbs in Non-Spatial Settings: The Case of *ahí* in Colombian Spanish Conversations. In Timothy Jowan Curnow (ed.), *Selected Papers from the 2007 Conference of the Australian Linguistic Society*, pp. 1–15. www.als.asn.au.

Dahl, Eystein and Fedriani, Chiara. (2012). The Argument Structure of Experience: Experiential Constructions in Early Vedic, Homeric Greek, and Early Latin. *Transactions of the Philological Society*, 110 (3), 342–362.

DeLancey, Scott. 2011. Grammaticalization and Syntax: A Functional View. In Bernd Heine and Heiko Narrog (eds.), *The Oxford Handbook of Grammaticalization*. London: Oxford University Press, pp. 365–377.

Delbecque, Nicole and Maldonado, Ricardo. (2009). Ya. Ancla conceptual de una visión programática. In Luisa Puig (ed.), *El discurso y sus espejos*. Mexico City: Siglo XXI, pp. 189–235.

Dik, Simon C. (1972). *Coordination: Its Implications for the Theory of General Linguistics*. Amsterdam: North-Holland.

Dik, Simon C. (1997). *The Theory of Functional Grammar: Part 1. The Structure of the Clause*, ed. Kees Hengeveld. Berlin: De Gruyter.

Donohue, Mark, Wichmann, Søren, and Albu, Mihai. (2008). Typology, Areality, and Diffusion. *Oceanic Linguistics*, 47 (1), 223–232.

Dowty, David R. (1991). Thematic Proto-Roles and Argument Selection. *Language* 67, (3), 547–619. doi: 10.2307/415037.

Dryer, Matthew. (2006). Functionalism and the Metalanguage–Theory Confusion. In Grace Wiebe, Gary Libben, Tom Priestly, Ron Smyth, and Sam Wang (eds.), *Phonology, Morphology, and the Empirical Imperative: Papers in Honour of Bruce Derwing*. Taipei: Crane, pp. 27–59.

Dryer, Matthew. (2007). Clause Types. In Timothy Shopen (ed.), *Language Typology and Syntactic Description*, Vol. 1: *Clause Structure*. Cambridge: Cambridge University Press, pp. 224–275.

Dryer, Matthew S. (2016). Crosslinguistic Categories, Comparative Concepts, and the Walman Diminutive. *Linguistic Typology*, 20 (2), 305–331. doi: 10.1515/lingty-2016-0009.

Dryer, Matthew S. and Haspelmath, Martin (eds.) (2013). *The World Atlas of Language Structures (WALS)*. Leipzig: Max Planck Institute for Evolutionary Anthropology. http://wals.info/.

Du Bois, John W. (1980). Beyond Definiteness: The Trace of Identity in Discourse. In Wallace L. Chafe (ed.), *The Pear Stories: Cognitive, Cultural, and Linguistic Aspects of Narrative Production*. Norwood, NJ: Ablex, pp. 203–274.

Dumitrescu, Domnita. (1997). El parámetro discursivo en la expresión del objeto directo lexical: español madrileño vs. español porteño. *Signo y Seña*, 7, 305–354.

Dumont, Jenny. (2013). Another Look at the Present Perfect in an Andean Variety of Spanish: Grammaticalization and Evidentiality in Quiteño Spanish. In Jennifer Cabrelli Amaro *et al.* (eds.), *Selected Proceedings of the 16th Hispanic Linguistics Symposium*. Somerville, MA: Cascadilla, pp. 279–291.

Dunn, Michael J., Terrill, Angela, Reesink, Ger P., Foley, Robert A., and Levinson, Stephen C. (2005). Structural Phylogenetics and the Reconstruction of Ancient Language History. *Science*, 309, 2072–2075.

Enfield, N. J. (ed.) (2002). *Ethnosyntax: Explorations in Grammar and Culture*. Oxford: Oxford University Press.

Escobar, Anna María. (2012). Spanish in Contact with Amerindian Languages. In José Ignacio Hualde, Antxon Olarrea, and Erin O'Rourke (eds.), *The Handbook of Hispanic Linguistics*. Oxford: Blackwell, pp. 65–88.

Evans, Nicholas. (2003). Context, Culture, and Structuration in the Languages of Australia. *Annual Review of Anthropology*, 32, 13–40.

Evans, Nicholas. (2007). Insubordination and its Uses. In Irina Nikolaeva (ed.), *Finiteness: Theoretical and Empirical Foundations*. Oxford: Oxford University Press, pp. 366–431.

Evans, Nicholas and Levinson, Stephen C. (2009). The Myth of Language Universals: Language Diversity and its Importance for Cognitive Science. *Behavioral and Brain Sciences*, 32, (5), 429–448.

Evans, Nicholas and Watanabe, Honoré. (2016). *Insubordination*. Amsterdam and Philadelphia, PA: John Benjamins.

Geeslin, Kimberly and Guijarro-Fuentes, Pedro. (2008). Variation in Contemporary Spanish: Linguistic Predictors of *estar* in Four Cases of Language Contact. *Bilingualism: Language and Cognition*, 11, (3), 365–380.

Givón, T. (1979). *On Understanding Grammar*. New York: Academic Press.

Givón, T. (1981). Typology and Functional Domains. *Studies in Language*, 5 (1), 163–193.

Givón, T. (1985). Iconicity, Isomorphism and Non-Arbitrary Coding in Language in Syntax. In J. Haiman (ed.), *Iconicity in Syntax*. Amsterdam: John Benjamins, pp. 187–219.

Givón, T. (1995). *Functionalism and Grammar*. Amsterdam: John Benjamins.

Givón, T. (2001). *Syntax: An Introduction*, vols. 1–2. Amsterdam: John Benjamins.

Givón, T. (2008). *The Genesis of Syntactic Complexity: Diachrony, Ontogeny, Neuro-Cognition, Evolution*. Amsterdam: John Benjamins.

Goldberg, Adele E. (1995). *Constructions: A Construction Grammar Approach to Argument Structure*. Chicago, IL: University of Chicago Press.

González Fernández, María and Maldonado, Ricardo. (2006). Syntactic Determinants of Pragmatic Markers of Closure. In Bert Cornillie and Nicole Delbecque (eds.), *Pragmaticalization and Modalization in Language and Discourse. Special Issue of the Belgian Journal of Linguistics*. Amsterdam: Benjamins, pp. 19–44.

Gras, Pedro. (2016). Revisiting the Functional Typology of Insubordination: Insubordinate *que*-Constructions in Spanish. In Nicholas Evans and Honoré Watanabe (eds.), *Insubordination*. Amsterdam: John Benjamins, pp. 113–144.

Greenberg, Joseph H. (ed.) (1966). *Universals of Language* (2nd edn). Cambridge, MA: MIT Press.

Halliday, Michael. (1961). Categories of the Theory of Grammar. *Word*, 17 (3), 241–292.

Halliday, Michael. (1985). *An Introduction to Functional Grammar*. London: Arnold.

Haspelmath, Martin. (2010). Comparative Concepts and Descriptive Categories in Cross-Linguistic Studies. *Language*, 86, 663–687.

Haspelmath, Martin. (2016). The Challenge of Making Language Description and Comparison Mutually Beneficial. *Linguistic Typology*, 20 (2), 299–303. doi:10.1515/lingty-2016–0008.

Hennemann, Anja. (2015). A Constructionist Approach to the Development of the Spanish Topic Marker en cuanto a "in terms of." *Constructions*, 2015 (1), 1–13. www.constructions-journal.com.

Himmelmann, Nikolaus P. (2016). What about Typology Is Useful for Language Documentation? *Linguistic Typology*, 20 (3) 473–478. doi: 10.1515/lingty-2016–0020.

Hopper, Paul (1979). Aspect and Foregrounding in Discourse. In Talmy Givón (ed.), *Discourse and Syntax, Syntax and Semantics*. New York: Academic Press, pp. 213–241.

Hopper, Paul (1987). Emergent Grammar. In Jon Aske, Natasha Beery, Laura Michaelis, and Hana Filip (eds.), *Proceedings of the Thirteenth Annual Meeting of the Berkeley Linguistics Society*. Berkeley, CA: University of California at Berkeley, pp. 139–157.

Hopper, Paul and Thompson, Sandra. (1980). Transitivity in Grammar and Discourse. *Language*, 56 (2), 251–299.

Iggesen, Oliver A. (2013). Asymmetrical Case-Marking. In Matthew S. Dryer and Martin Haspelmath (eds.), *WALS Online*. Leipzig: Max Planck Institute for Evolutionary Anthropology. Available from wals.info/chapter/50 (last access May 19, 2017).

Keenan, Edward L. and Comrie, Bernard. (1977). Noun Phrase Accessibility and Universal Grammar. *Linguistic Inquiry*, 8, 63–99.

Laca, Brenda. (2002). Gramaticalización y variabilidad – propiedades inherentes y factores contextuales en la evolución del acusativo preposicional en español. In Andreas Wesch, Waltraud Weidenbusch, Rolf Kailuweit, and Brenda Laca (eds.), *Sprachgeschichte als Varietätengeschichte/Historia de las variedades lingüísticas*. Tübingen: Stauffenburg, pp. 195–203.

Langacker, R. W. (1985). Observations and Speculations on Subjectivity. In J. Haiman (ed.), *Iconicity in Syntax*. Amsterdam and Philadelphia: John Benjamins, pp. 109–150.

LaPolla, Randy J. (2016). On Categorization: Stick to the Facts of the Languages. *Linguistic Typology*, 20 (2), 365–375. doi:10.1515/lingty-2016–0011.

Levinson, Stephen C. (2003). *Space in Language and Cognition*. Cambridge: Cambridge University Press.

López Meirama, B. (2006). Semantic and Discourse-Pragmatic Factors in Spanish Word Order. In J. C. Clements and J. Yoon (eds.), *Functional Approaches to Spanish Syntax: Lexical Semantics, Discourse and Transitivity*. New York: Palgrave Macmillan, pp. 7–52.

Michael, Lev, Chang, Will, and Stark, Tammy. (2014). Exploring Phonological Areality in the Circum-Andean Region Using a Naive

Bayes Classifier. *Language Dynamics and Change*, 4 (1), 27–86. doi:10.1163/22105832-00401004.

Michaelis, Susanne Maria, Maurer, Philippe, Haspelmath, Martin, and Huber, Magnus (eds.). (2013). *The Atlas of Pidgin and Creole Language Structures (APiCS)*. Leipzig: Max Planck Institute for Evolutionary Anthropology. http://apics-online.info/.

Miglio, Viola, Gries, Stefan Th., Harris, Michael J., Wheeler, Eva M., and Santana-Paixão, Raquel. (2013). Spanish *lo(s)–le(s)* Clitic Alternations in Psych Verbs: A Multifactorial Corpus-Based Analysis. In Jennifer Cabrelli Amaro, Gillian Lord, Ana de Prada Pérez, and Jessi Elana Aaron (eds.), *Selected Proceedings of the 16th Hispanic Linguistics Symposium*. Somerville, MA: Cascadilla, pp. 268–278.

Nichols, Johanna. (1997). Modeling Ancient Population Structures and Population Movement in Linguistics and Archeology. *Annual Review of Anthropology*, 26, 359–384.

Nichols, Johanna. (2007). What, if Anything, is Typology? *Linguistic Typology*, 11, 231–238.

Ocampo, F. (2009). *Mirá*: From Verb to Discourse Particle in Rioplatense Spanish. In J. Collentine *et al.* (eds.), *Selected Proceedings of the 11th Hispanic Linguistics Symposium*. Somerville, MA: Cascadilla, pp. 254–267.

Olarrea, A. (2012). Word Order and Information Structure. In J. I. Hualde, A. Olarrea, and E. O'Rourke (eds.), *The Handbook of Hispanic Linguistics*. Malden, MA: John Wiley and Son, pp. 603–628.

Otheguy, Ricardo. (2011). Functional Adaptation and Conceptual Convergence in the Analysis of Language Contact in the Spanish of Bilingual Communities in New York. In Manuel Antonio Díaz-Campos (ed.), *Handbook of Hispanic Sociolinguistics*. Oxford: Wiley-Blackwell, pp. 504–529.

Otheguy, Ricardo. (2014). Remarks on Pronominal Perseveration and Functional Explanation. In Andrés Enrique-Arias, Manuel Gutiérrez, Alazne Landa, and Francisco Ocampo (eds.), *Perspectives in the Study of Spanish Language Variation*, pp. 373–397. http://dx.doi.org/10.15304/va.2014.701

Otheguy, Ricardo and Lapidus, Naomi. (2003). An Adaptive Approach to Noun Gender in New York Contact Spanish. In Richard Cameron, Luis López and Rafael Núñez-Cedeño (eds.), *A Romance Perspective on Language Knowledge and Use*. Amsterdam and Philadelphia: John Benjamins, pp. 209–229

Payne, Doris L. (1999). What Counts as Explanation? A Functionalist Approach to Word Order. In Michael Darnell, Edith Moravcsik, Frederick Newmeyer, Michael Noonan, and Kathleen Wheatley (eds.), *Functionalism and Formalism in Linguistics*. Amsterdam: John Benjamins, pp. 137–165.

Pensado, Carmen (ed.). (1995). *El complemento directo preposicional*. Madrid: Visor.

Schwenter, Scott. (2006). Null Objects across South America. In T. Face and C. A. Klee (eds.), *Selected Proceedings of the 8th Hispanic Linguistics Symposium* Somerville, MA: Cascadilla, pp. 23–36.

Schwenter, Scott. (2016). Independent *si*-Clauses in Spanish: Functions and Consequences for Insubordination. In Nicholas Evans and Honore Watanabe (eds.), *Insubordination*. Amsterdam: John Benjamins, pp. 89–112.

Shin, Naomi L. (2014). Grammatical Complexification in Spanish in New York: 3sg Pronoun Expression and Verbal Ambiguity. *Language Variation and Change*, 26 (3), 303–330.

Smolensky, P. (2006). Harmony in Linguistic Cognition. *Cognitive Science*, 30, 779–801.

Stassen, Leon. (1997). *Intransitive Predication*. Oxford: Oxford University Press.

Torres Cacoullos, Rena. (2001). From Lexical to Grammatical to Social Meaning. *Language in Society*, 30 (3), 443–478.

Travis, Catherine. (2005). *Discourse Markers in Colombian Spanish: A Study in Polysemy*. Berlin: Mouton de Gruyter.

Travis, Catherine and Torres Cacoullos, Rena. (2012). Discourse Syntax. In J. I. Hualde, A. Olarrea, and E. O'Rourke (eds.), *The Handbook of Hispanic Linguistics*. Malden, MA: John Wiley and Son, pp. 653–672.

Vallejos, Rosa. (2014). Peruvian Amazonian Spanish: Uncovering Variation and Deconstructing Stereotypes. *Spanish in Context*, 11 (3), 425–453.

Vázquez Rozas, Victoria. (2012). Construyendo emociones: sintaxis, frecuencia y función comunicativa. In T. Jiménez, B. López Meirama, V. Vázquez Rozas, and A. Veiga (eds.), *Cum corde et in nova grammatica. Estudios ofrecidos a Guillermo Rojo*. Santiago de Compostela: USC Editor, pp. 841–854.

Wilson, Damián V. (2013). One Construction, Two Source Languages: *hacer* with an English Infinitive in Bilingual Discourse. In A. M. Carvalho and S. Beaudrie (eds.), *Selected Proceedings of the 6th Workshop on Spanish Sociolinguistics*. Somerville, MA: Cascadilla, pp. 123–134.

5

Psycholinguistic Approaches to Hispanic Linguistics

Tania Leal and Christine Shea

5.1 Introduction

In this chapter, we present a brief overview of psycholinguistic approaches to Hispanic linguistics. Psycholinguists investigate the cognitive mechanisms underlying language processing, including the way we perceive and read words, as well how we extract meaning from sentences. By studying a variety of languages and participants, psycholinguists can gain a broad understanding of the cognitive mechanisms related to language processing (Carreiras and Duñabeitia 2012). Spanish, for example, has a rich system of nominal and verbal inflections and a very close correspondence between spelling and phonology, which distinguishes it from highly studied languages such as English.

Because we do not aim to provide an exhaustive review of the literature, the chapter presents a selection of the most recent work in two specific areas of psycholinguistics: *lexical access* and *sentence processing* in Spanish and Spanish bilingual populations. Furthermore, in Appendix 5.A we present a list of resources that are helpful for creating stimuli in lexical access experiments.

5.1.1 Lexical Access

We first present monolingual models that have been proposed to account for lexical access.[1] Then we present models of bilingual lexical access, focusing on studies in which Spanish is involved.[2] Interestingly, given

---

[1] Due to space restrictions, we limit our discussion to the visual and auditory modalities and do not address lexical access in speech production (but see work by Costa *et al.* (2006) for lexical activation in Spanish and Spanish-speaking bilingual production) or in the signed modality.

[2] Weber and Scharenborg (2012) offer an excellent review of lexical access, while Carreiras and Duñabeitia (2012) examine lexical access in the visual modality (Spanish).

the high number of bilingual communities where Spanish is spoken (e.g. Spanish–Catalan), there is an abundance of research on the lexical access of Spanish bilinguals and relatively little on monolingual speakers.[3]

5.1.2 The Process of Lexical Access

When listening to speech, the listener's ultimate goal is to recognize words and the meaning they express. Words are stored with information about *form* (phonology, morphology, and orthography) and *meaning*. Word decoding proceeds by mapping auditory or visual information in the speech input onto stored representations of words in the mental lexicon – the process of lexical access.[4] For highly proficient listeners, this process seems effortless. In fact, however, understanding a spoken word is anything but trivial. In auditory word recognition, listeners experience a continuous, transitory signal that offers no clear delineation between lexical items that must be processed in real time. Besides being continuous and variable, the speech signal makes use of a limited set of language-specific sounds, which results in considerable overlap in sound and spelling across words. This state of affairs can be contrasted with visual word recognition because delineation is clear and readers generally process the entire word at once. In speech comprehension, the temporal characteristics of the signal significantly impact lexical processing. This explains why the temporal nature of the signal features prominently in models of spoken word recognition.

Crucially, lexical access research shows that listeners do not wait until the end of a word before they begin to activate potential candidates.[5] Instead, listeners simultaneously consider multiple word candidates consistent with the incoming signal, a process known as parallel activation.[6] Parallel activation also extends to competition in recognition. Figure 5.1 provides a schematic outline of the cognitive processes involved in lexical access.

Figure 5.1 shows that activation occurs when listeners first encounter a word. Words that share similar characteristics of form or meaning will also be activated, competing with the target. Inhibition (indicated in Figure 5.1 by two-way arrows) occurs among all candidates until the incoming signal leads to the best match stored in the mental lexicon.

---

[3] For bilingual models, see Sunderman and Fancher (2013) and Kroll *et al.* (2012).

[4] Processes related to lexical access in the verbal domain necessarily involve speech perception because failures at the level of speech perception can impede lexical access (or lead to the incorrect encoding of lexical entries – see Cutler *et al.* 2006). Nevertheless, speech perception research does not necessarily address how words are accessed as the outcome of this process (see also Chapter 11, this volume).

[5] As we will discuss later, these findings echo research outcomes in the sentence processing literature, which show that listeners process the signal incrementally (Altmann and Steedman 1988; Arai and Keller 2013; Eberhard *et al.* 1995; Marslen-Wilson 1975; Pickering 1994; Steedman 1989).

[6] Again, research on sentence processing has shown that listeners appear to consider multiple structural interpretations in parallel (see, e.g., McRae and Matsuki 2013).

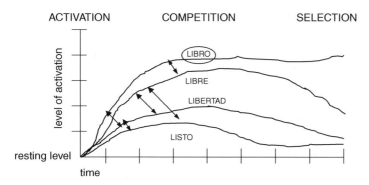

auditory input: LIBRO 'book'

Figure 5.1 Cognitive processes involved in lexical access
Two-way arrows indicate inhibition.

Ease of lexical entry access always depends on its level of activation prior to access.

In fact, multiple word-related factors are known to affect lexical access. Pre-access activation levels depend on lexical items' "resting" level of activation – often a function of frequency and context. For example, listeners access frequent words faster than less frequent words because the higher resting level for frequent words allows them to more swiftly reach the recognition threshold.

Density of a word's lexical neighborhood is another important factor affecting lexical access (e.g. Vitevitch and Rodríguez 2005; Vitevitch et al. 2012). Phonological neighbors are words that differ in one sound only, while orthographic neighbors differ from each other in one letter. Research has shown that words in dense phonological neighborhoods (i.e. words for which there are many similar-sounding words in the lexicon, such as *pay, hay, ray, may*) are harder to access than words in sparse neighborhoods. Furthermore, lexical neighborhood effects interact with frequency such that high-frequency words with low-frequency neighbors are easy to recognize, while low-frequency words with high-frequency neighbors are more difficult to recognize.

Vitevitch and Rodríguez (2005) examined the role of neighborhood density on spoken-word recognition in native speakers (NSs) of Spanish using an auditory lexical decision task in which listeners determined as quickly and accurately as possible whether a word was real or nonce. The authors found that, for Spanish NSs, neighborhood density effects ran counter to those found for English NSs listening to English words: Spanish words with dense neighborhoods elicited swifter, more accurate responses than Spanish words with sparse neighborhoods. These results suggest that similar-sounding Spanish words facilitate lexical access of other words rather than create competition.

Interestingly, neighborhood effects manifest differently in visual-word recognition. Because written words are processed all at once (rather than temporally, as with unfolding spoken speech), words with common combinations of letters are easier to recognize. Thus, larger lexical neighborhoods *facilitate* written word recognition in lexical decision tasks while inhibiting the correct rejection of pseudo-words.[7]

5.1.3 Modeling Lexical Access

Current lexical access models differ in two main ways depending on the abstractness of the units of representation that contact the lexicon and whether models assume a one-way or an interactive flow of information (serial vs. cascading models). Most early word recognition models did capture the notion of competition in lexical access (e.g. Morton 1979), but, being focused on reading, they largely neglected how lexical access unfolds across real time during spoken input (Weber and Scharenborg 2012). Over the past 40 years, models of lexical access have moved from linear, onset-alignment-based activation models (Cohort II, Marslen-Wilson 1990) to connectionist interactive-activation models (TRACE, McClelland and Elman 1986), in which multiple words are activated based upon a match to any part of the speech signal, with feedback occurring in a top-down manner. Other models question the need for feedback (Shortlist B, Norris and McQueen 2008), positing instead that feedback is unnecessary to lexical access.

Current psycholinguistic models of spoken word recognition also differ in whether information from the speech signal flows "up" to higher-level representations in a unidirectional manner (without feedback), or whether higher-level information can indeed feed back and influence lower-level processing (interactive vs. autonomous models).

Finally, we should highlight that current models do coincide, however, on at least three aspects. First, multiple candidates are activated in parallel as words are heard; second, the degree of activation of each word candidate will depend upon the match between the speech signal and stored representations; third, all activated candidates compete for activation in real time (Weber and Scharenborg 2012).

5.1.4 Bilingual Lexical Access

Research on bilingual lexical activation has focused on whether bilinguals activate one lexicon at a time (selective lexical access) or both languages simultaneously (non-selective lexical access). Another focus is whether language activation is context- or task-dependent. A third key question is whether the two languages are integrated. Integration is generally understood as occurring at two levels: form (spelling and phonology) and meaning (semantics). For bilinguals, the central issue is whether representations

---

[7] For research with Spanish NS children, see Duñabeitia and Vidal-Abarca (2008).

take the form of one single, shared lexical form, or distinct representations per language.

Bilingual lexical activation models tend to be either verbal or computationally implemented. Verbal models can be verbally described and their predictions can be tested using behavioral methods (see Revised Hierarchical Model, RHM, below). Computationally-implemented models can be tested behaviorally but also using computational procedures (Li and Zhao 2014).[8] Computationally-implemented models are often connectionist in nature. These models propose that cognition takes the form of parallel processes (simultaneous with multiple information streams) and distributed processes (interactive and not localized in one region of the processing system). Representations emerge as the outcome of many different processing units working simultaneously and interactively (Li and Zhao 2014). Learning occurs through the adjustment of connection weights, either through explicit error feedback (as in supervised learning models; see Bilingual Interactive Activation Plus model, BIA+, below) or implicit feedback (unsupervised learning).

In general, bilingual models of lexical access tend to support non-selective, or parallel, activation of both languages at the initial, form-based stages of processing (Marian and Spivey 2003). Following this, a bottom-up bias for the target language emerges, although both languages are still active. Given the fine-grained nature of phonetic cues, this bias can be established rapidly, as demonstrated for Spanish–English bilinguals (Ju and Luce 2004).

Previous work has shown that bilinguals take longer to access target lexical items than monolinguals do, a result possibly attributable to cross-linguistic interference. Non-selective activation suggests that when bilinguals perform tasks in a given language, they also simultaneously access information from the other language, in a process known as *parallel language activation*. Thus, bilinguals manage lexical competition from a greater number of candidates, which may result in slower and/or weaker access to a given target.[9]

The Revised Hierarchical Model (RHM, Kroll and Stewart 1994) is a "verbal" model that has had significant influence on how researchers conceptualize memory and proficiency effects. The RHM focuses on how bilingual memory is organized – namely, how balanced and unbalanced bilinguals access words that are translational equivalents. The model distinguishes between the lexical level (or form) and the conceptual level of representation. The lexical level is separate across a bilingual's two languages while the conceptual level is shared. For unbalanced bilinguals, L2 (second language) word processing involves meaning to a lesser degree

---

[8] For a recent volume on the topic of memory and bilingual access, see Heredia and Altarribia (2015).
[9] Grosjean's (2001) language mode framework assumes that language-specific lexical access may be possible depending on contextual factors. Green and Abutalebi (2013) consider how this operates in speech production.

than L1 (first language) processing because it is mediated by L1 form. Indeed, asymmetrical translation effects have been shown to exist, whereby L1-to-L2 (forward) translation is slower than L2-to-L1 (backwards) translation (Kroll and Stewart 1994; Kroll and Tokowicz 2005). The RHM can also account for proficiency effects in bilingual memory organization, given that L2 beginners associate L2 words with their L1 translations – only with increased proficiency do links develop between L2 words and conceptual information. Early versions of the RHM did not assume non-selectivity in lexical activation, though it was not explicitly discounted, either. However, more recent versions do allow non-selectivity without assuming integration necessarily occurs at the lexicon level (Kroll *et al.* 2010).

The Bilingual Interactive Activation Plus model, or BIA+ (Dijkstra and van Heuven 2002), is another influential model of bilingual lexical activation. A connectionist model in line with the RHM's newest adaptations (Kroll *et al.* 2010), the BIA+ assumes non-selective access; however, distinct from the RHM, the BIA+ does assume an integrated lexicon. Input from written stimuli activates feature representations in memory, which activate letter representations and, subsequently, lexical representations in both languages. The lexical representations activate language nodes, which then send excitatory feedback to all the lexical nodes in that language, which in turn activate the letters of that particular language. Importantly, language nodes are activated based upon previous input – the L1 node will be more activated if the previous input occurred in that language. This accounts for L2 inhibition while limiting interference across languages. While the initial activation phase is non-selective, language context information serves to suppress lexical representations that are incompatible via top-down inhibitory connections. This is how the BIA+ accounts for cross-language interference. The BIA+ also distinguishes between the lexical access system and a task/decision system. The latter cannot affect processing.[10]

Cognates, Homophones, and Homographs

Cognates, homophones, and homographs share varying degrees of form and semantic overlap. Consequently, research on these has provided insight about the level of integration across bilinguals' languages.

Faster reaction times have been observed across cognates than across non-cognate items. Because cognates overlap in both form and meaning, however, the locus of the cognate effect is not easily determined. For instance, the cognate advantage disappears when phonologically-matched controls are used, suggesting that form overlap could be the source of the advantage (Dijkstra *et al.* 2010). Furthermore, researchers

---

[10] See also the Bilingual Language Interaction Network for Comprehension of Speech (BLINCS, Shook and Marian 2012) for a connectionist model of bilingual processing that uses self-organizing maps to connect across levels (unsupervised learning).

have observed an asymmetry across a bilingual's two languages, whereby L2 words benefit more from being cognates than L1 words do (Gollan et al. 1997). Furthermore, these effects are affected by L2 proficiency (Duñabeitia et al. 2007; van Hell and Dijkstra 2002; see Freeman et al. 2016 for a recent study of how phonotactic constraints operate on cognate activation for Spanish–English bilinguals). Context effects have also been noted for cognates and homographs, although homograph effects are generally weaker in sentence contexts than are the effects observed for cognates. Under highly constraining sentential contexts, cognate effects can be attenuated (Schwartz and Kroll 2006; Gullifer et al. 2013).

Homographs and homophones, on the other hand, share form but not semantic meaning, which allows researchers to discern the relationship between form and meaning in interlingual lexical activation. Macizo et al. (2010) examined how Spanish–English bilinguals performed on a yes/no word similarity task in which semantically related English words were used as written stimuli. Their first experiment asked participants to decide whether word pairs such as "*pie*–toe" were semantically related ("*pie*" is given here in italics because it means "foot" in Spanish; however, for the participants in the task it was not typographically distinguished). These pairs were compared to others without homograph Spanish competitors (e.g. "log–toe") and also to trials where the translational equivalents of the homographs were presented (e.g. "foot–toe," where the Spanish for "foot" is "*pie*," a homograph in English). Participants responded more slowly to homographs presented along with semantically related Spanish words as compared to control words, suggesting that participants activated the two homograph meanings. In selected trials, participants then had to respond to the homograph's irrelevant meaning in the following trial and were slower to respond.

These findings suggest that bilinguals inhibited the irrelevant homograph meaning, which in turn indicates a strong role for orthographic–semantic connections across a bilingual's two languages. These results do not fully align with the BIA+ model's predictions, given the inhibitory effects observed for the language not in use and that the BIA+ model supports a nonselective view of bilingual word recognition whereby only bottom–up stimulus information can influence the activation of semantic representations from the lexicon, regardless of language membership.

Orthographic Transparency

Orthographic transparency also affects bilingual lexical activation. Languages with alphabetic writing systems differ greatly in terms of orthographic transparency; Spanish falls on the more transparent end of this continuum (i.e. letters consistently map to phonemes) while languages such as English and German exhibit considerably less sound–letter transparency.

Researchers have studied these issues in written input by examining the role of language-specific orthography in bilingual lexical activation, in much the same way that low-level phonetic information can activate one language over another in auditory input (van Kesteren et al. 2012). In a recent study, Casaponsa et al. (2014) tested Spanish–Basque balanced and unbalanced bilinguals and a Spanish monolingual control group using a language decision task and a progressive demasking task. Materials included Basque-specific words (e.g. *etxe* 'house,' where *txe* is an illegal orthographic combination in Spanish) and orthographically unmarked words that were possible in Spanish (e.g. *mendi* 'hill'). Critically, balanced and unbalanced bilinguals showed an advantage in recognition speed for L2-marked words when compared to L2-unmarked words. This finding suggests that even tasks where language membership assignment is not required (L2 unmarked words), early detection of the language (through word sub-lexical analysis) aids lexical access. Moreover, results suggest a direct link between sub-lexical information of words and language membership, indicating that lexical access might be guided by the extraction of language-specific orthotactic combinatorial rules.

Both auditory word recognition and word recognition exhibit orthographic neighborhood effects. Orthographic neighbors differ from one another solely by one letter (Carreiras et al. 1997). As on phonological neighbors, research on orthographic neighbors also provides insight into the process of bilingual lexical access because sharing neighborhoods does not imply semantic overlap across the two languages, nor is orthographic form completely overlapping.[11]

Sentential context also affects the activation of cross-linguistic homophones or near-homophones. Schwartz and Arêas da Luz Fontes (2008) investigated the effect of context on between-language mediated form priming and semantic priming. Participants were Spanish–English bilinguals participating in an L2 (English-only) task. Priming was obtained when the prime ("bark") displayed a form-mediated relationship via the L1 (*barco*, Spanish for "boat") to the target ("boat") for isolated words, but not when the words were embedded in sentence contexts (e.g. "The baby woke up every time the dog barked").

To summarize, bilingual lexical activation is generally assumed to be non-selective across both visual and auditory modalities, but this non-selectivity can be influenced by factors such as sentence or discourse contexts, and may not extend to the semantic level under all circumstances.

5.1.5 Bilingual Language Control

Assuming non-selective lexical activation implies that bilinguals activate their two languages at all times – even when only one language is processed. This non-selective activation has led researchers to pose

---

[11] See Müller et al. (2010) for an Event-Related-Potential (ERP) study examining the interaction between orthographic neighborhood density and semantic activation in monolingual Spanish NSs.

a "bilingual advantage" on display in tasks requiring switching between stimuli (Stroop effect) or inhibiting input (see Bialystok *et al.* 2012 for a review). Whether advantages are due to enhanced inhibitory skills or enhanced conflict-monitoring skills (Hernández *et al.* 2010), bilinguals generally outperform monolinguals on these tasks.

The BIA+ model is an inhibitory model positing that language selection in bilinguals proceeds by activation of the target language and suppression of the irrelevant language's representations. The stronger the degree of inhibition required (e.g. suppressing the dominant language requires greater inhibition than suppressing the weaker language), the greater will be the cost when switching between languages. For example, Prior and Gollan (2011) report that Spanish–English bilinguals who used both languages daily exhibited smaller switching costs than monolinguals on a cued-language switching study. Alternatively, other researchers suggest that monitoring and goal maintenance mechanisms might underpin the bilinguals' superior performance in attentional tasks (Colzato *et al.* 2008; Costa *et al.* 2006) whereby monitoring of contextual information cues language selection (Morales *et al.* 2013).

Interestingly, many of the findings reviewed up to this point are echoed in other areas of psycholinguistics, most notably in sentence progressing research. This is in spite of the fact that both areas represent independent, and largely separate, research traditions. In Section 5.2, we address psycholinguistic models of sentence processing, which share certain elements in common with models of lexical access, such as the finding that lexical access and sentence process proceed in an incremental fashion. As ever, our focus will be primarily on Spanish and bilingual processing models.

5.2 Comprehending Word Strings

Analogous to lexical access, sentence processing is a complex – and incremental – process that humans, seemingly without effort, accomplish within the span of a few hundred milliseconds. In addition to the process of word decoding, which involves mapping the information in the speech input onto stored lexical representations (lexical access), sentence processing requires the recognition of syntactic structures to later integrate them with the context in which they occur in order to construct meaning in real time.[12] As noted earlier, although research on lexical access and sentence processing have historically constituted independent traditions operating

---

[12] We should note, however, that several accounts of language processing do not (compulsorily) make use of syntactic information in order to comprehend certain sentences, such as those that are short, frequent or familiar (e.g. the LAST model, Townsend and Bever 2001). Other models also hypothesize that syntactic information is used only when the task demands require it (e.g. Ferreira 2003; Ferreira and Patson 2007).

largely separately, the findings from these strands often echo and complement each other in crucial ways that we hope to highlight here.

For instance, analogously to the findings on lexical access, early sentence processing findings provide ample support for the notion that listeners/comprehenders do not wait until the end of an utterance to start processing it. Instead, there is a wealth of experimental evidence in support of the notion that listeners/comprehenders (both in L1 and L2) process the signal as it unfolds: word by word, activating potential structures in an incremental fashion (Altmann and Steedman 1988; Arai and Keller 2013; Eberhard *et al.* 1995; Marslen-Wilson 1975; Pickering 1994; Steedman 1989). The incrementality of sentence processing allows language comprehenders to compute partial semantic interpretations as the sentence is processed (Dekydtspotter and Renaud 2014). Additionally, however, the incremental nature of processing also contributes to the ambiguities that arise in the interpretation of the partial strings (McRae and Matsuki 2013), a fact that all sentence-processing models must account for and the driving force behind a large part of the research on sentence processing.

Again in parallel with the lexical access research cited above, although perhaps to a lesser degree, research on sentence processing has also focused increasingly on bilingual populations. This research initially sought to address whether bilingual populations process language like native speakers do, including this group with other "atypical" populations such as children and persons with aphasia (see Roberts 2013 and van Gompel 2013). Recently, however, psycholinguistic research has begun to actively investigate bilingual populations in their own right. Kroll and Dussias (2004), for example, make the case that bilinguals can be even *more* representative language users than monolinguals are. In their view, research with bilinguals can address questions beyond those focusing on the organization of language systems in the brain, with research also ideally addressing questions about the nature of the mental representations themselves as well as questions about the learning mechanisms underpinning language comprehension.

Furthermore, in summarizing the relationship between lexical access and sentence processing in bilinguals, Kroll and Dussias (2004) reason that the most important parallel between the findings in these areas (sentence processing and lexical access) is that language systems are "permeable." They argue that this permeability, which is shaped by language acquisition and use, results in three implications. The first is the need for researchers to articulate a theory of inhibitory control. As is evident from code-switching behavior, bilinguals can alternate between languages while also coping with competition between languages; ideally, a theory of control could explain whether particular parsing preferences and selective lexical access follow specific conditions. The second implication is that languages affect each other non-selectively. While it is generally uncontested that the second language is affected by L1 patterns, recent evidence (e.g. Dussias 2004) shows that the second language can also affect L1 parsing. Again, this research echoes findings in bilingual lexical access. Finally, Kroll and Dussias (2004) propose that the findings from both areas indicate that the mechanisms behind the computing of meaning in bilinguals may not be exclusive to a given language (neither the L1 nor the L2).

In what follows, we will briefly elaborate on these notions while attempting to review research on the comprehension of Spanish and other languages that stems from two of the most influential models of sentence processing. Once again, we do not intend to provide an exhaustive review of the literature.[13] Instead, we focus on those findings that have significantly shaped our understanding of online language comprehension, both in monolingual and bilingual populations.

5.2.1 To Restrict the Timing of Information (or not): Garden Path and Constraint Satisfaction

As mentioned earlier, extant models and theories of language processing must account for the fact that language comprehension is a nearly instantaneous process that integrates syntactic, semantic, pragmatic, and prosodic computations with the material and social context in order to arrive at an interpretation. While most accounts of language processing agree that these information sources all influence parsing, there is less agreement with regard to the preeminence of these sources and the timing of their availability to influence processing.

In the context of this discussion, historically, the most contentious debate has centered on the preeminence (or not) of syntactic information in sentence processing. On the one hand, a set of proposals (the most representative of which is the Garden Path Theory) has placed syntax in a privileged position, effectively proposing a set of processing strategies or principles that guide the parsing of a given string (Frazier 1978, 1987; Frazier and Rayner 1982). On the other hand, models such as the Constraint Satisfaction model have proposed that syntax is not privileged; thus, contextual, semantic, and probabilistic information are equally likely to affect processing in parallel, even at the very initial stages of parsing (e.g. MacDonald 1994; MacDonald et al. 1994; McRae et al. 1998; Spivey and Tanenhaus 1998; Tanenhaus and Trueswell 1995; Tabor and Tanenhaus 1999).

The Garden Path Theory, advanced by Frazier and colleagues (see references above), assumes a modular view of language architecture (e.g. Fodor 1983), in which language subsystems have specialized modules with

---

[13] In this brief chapter, we do not engage in a discussion (or even offer a passing description) of the methodologies used to investigate sentence processing and how these have affected research in the area. For an excellent text devoted to the description of the methodologies used in the psycholinguistic study of language (and sentence processing specifically), including self-paced reading, cross-modal priming, event-related potentials, and eye-tracking, we refer readers to the volume edited by Jegerski and VanPatten (2013).

discrete, module-specific combinatorial rules. Within this modular view, the Garden Path Theory proposes that parsing initially privileges category (i.e. syntactic) information. At its core, this model is concerned with reducing cognitive memory loads; in fact, the limits imposed by short-term memory are hypothesized to drive the simplest (and quickest) analysis. Accordingly, early category information immediately and automatically triggers the attachment of specific items into the syntactic derivation (representation). According to Frazier (2013:21), the automaticity of sentence-processing models such as this "fits with a view of the human language ability where the (acquisition and) processing of syntax is assumed to be biologically given to some important extent."

The Garden Path Theory formalized these notions with the articulation of two universal parsing principles: Minimal Attachment and Late Closure. Roughly, Minimal Attachment stipulates that the parser pursues the least complex syntactic structure, where less complex is operationalized as the structure with fewer syntactic nodes. A complement to Minimal Attachment, Late Closure further guides parsing in those cases where two structures have the same number of nodes (i.e. where Minimal Attachment offers no guidance). In this case, Late Closure guides parsing by favoring attachment to the most recently encountered phrase. Thus, by restricting the type of information that is initially considered by the parser, the Garden Path Theory appeals to phrase computation economy.

In order to exemplify Late Closure, let's focus on a Spanish sentence such as that in Example 5.1.

(5.1) Alguien disparó contra el criado de la
someone shoot.PAST.3SG against the.MASC.SG servant.MASC.SG of the
actriz / que estaba en el balcón con su marido.
actress / that was in the balcony with POSS.SG husband.
'Somebody shot the servant (masc.) of the actress who was on the balcony with her husband.'

There are two possible (noun phrase, NP) attachments in (5.1), each leading to a distinct interpretation. One attachment leads to the interpretation that it was the *actress* who was on the balcony with her husband (so-called low attachment or N2 attachment). The other interpretation (so-called high attachment or N1 attachment) indicates that it was the *(male) servant* who was on the balcony with his husband (the Spanish possessive determiner *su* does not mark for gender and can thus be translated as either "her" or "his"). In this case, Late Closure would predict the attachment of the most recently encountered phrase (i.e. *la actriz*) rather than the first NP (i.e. *el criado*). Under this heuristic, the (clearly dated) sentence should have raised no eyebrows due to the gender mismatch. Note that, in this particular case, Minimal Attachment offers no guidance because both attachments involve the same number of syntactic nodes.

In a self-paced reading experiment, Cuetos and Mitchell (1988) employed sentences such as (5.1) to test the Late Closure principle. In this experiment, the authors compared the reading times (RTs) for the last segment in (5.1) with RTs for the last segment in control sentences where the first NP (*el criado*, 'the male servant' in (5.1)) was replaced with a feminine-marked NP (e.g. *la criada*, 'the female servant'). In this last case, either attachment would be equally plausible (i.e. it was the actress who was on the balcony with her husband vs. it was the female servant who was on the balcony with her husband). Against the predictions of Late Closure, however, results showed that Spanish speakers took longer to process the reading requiring low attachment (gender mismatch). This finding led Cuetos and Mitchell to hypothesize that Spanish, unlike English, showed a bias for high attachment (i.e. displaying an Early, as opposed to Late, Closure, unlike that shown by English comprehenders).

These results contrast with other investigations that lend support to Minimal Attachment and Late Closure (e.g. Frazier and Clifton 1989; Pickering and Traxler 2003, for L1 processing; Jegerski 2012, for L2 processing). Additional research developments have led to changes in Garden Path Theory, giving rise to refinements of the theory in the form of additional principles such as the Active Filler Strategy and Construal (Frazier and Clifton 1996). Frazier (2013) notes, for example, that the results obtained by Cuetos and Mitchell could be accounted for by the status of the relative clause itself (being as it is a clausal adjunct, rather than a clausal argument). Noting that relative-clause attachment biases are often weak, Frazier suggests the possibility that structures without strong syntactic biases may allow for other information (prosody in this case) to determine the locus of attachment.

As mentioned earlier, it is uncontested that myriad sources of information influence sentence processing. One assumption that distinguishes accounts such as Constraint Satisfaction is that these models posit no timing restrictions and do not privilege one source of information over others using heuristics or principles. In other words, all sources of information are, in theory, available essentially instantaneously. Moreover, the proposal is that this information can be put to use as soon as it is available (McRae and Matsuki 2013). Another important feature of Constraint Satisfaction models follows on the heels of this notion: given that all sources of information are available (including verb biases, phonological, semantic, pragmatic, and morphological information as well as knowledge of the world), the parser is free and able to pursue multiple interpretations in parallel. These interpretations coexist in competition until there is enough data for the parser to weigh and ultimately settle on an interpretation in a probabilistic fashion. These models can also be considered "rational" in the sense that they use probabilistic information to generate an expectation or prediction with regard to the structural and semantic content of the upcoming signal (e.g. Clark 2013; Elman 1993).

Constraint Satisfaction models have received a great deal of empirical support (e.g. MacDonald *et al.* 1994; McRae *et al.* 1998; Spivey and Tanenhaus 1998; Tanenhaus and Trueswell 1995, for L1 processing; Dussias and Sagarra 2007, for L2 processing), and in this sense the major challenge facing these models has been not empirical but epistemological: namely, given that the models allow for information to be used unrestrictedly, there is a need to delimit specifically how this information is used in order for the models to make accurate predictions. McRae and Matsuki (2013) note that these issues have led to necessary fine-tunings in the models in order to answer questions such as the specification of which are the relevant constraints in a given context, the determination of the comparative strengths of the constraints (the grain size problem), the (*a priori*) identification of the constraints' relative weights in a given context, as well as description of the mechanisms that are responsible for the combination of the constraints themselves.

Although we will not pursue a comparison of these two research traditions, the notion we wish to highlight is that a significant portion of the sentence processing literature has sought to address how the parser deals with ambiguities and whether certain information is, in principle, accessible in a hierarchical fashion or not.[14] These debates have informed questions in a broad range of language disciplines, including language development as well as syntactic theory. Nevertheless, the psycholinguistic study of sentence processing can inform key debates in many other language disciplines. In what follows, we will briefly address how psycholinguistic sentence processing research can weigh in on key debates in the area of second language acquisition.

5.3 Sentence Processing Findings and Second Language Acquisition Research

Among the many issues that have been examined in the psycholinguistic research, we have selected two issues that have had a special impact on L2 acquisition research: the role of (verbal) working memory and the role of the generation of expectations on L2 sentence processing.

5.3.1 Sentence Processing and Verbal Working Memory in Second Language Acquisition

The role of individual verbal working memory variability (where verbal working memory is roughly defined as the capacity to temporarily store

---

[14] We should note that these are not the only extant accounts of sentence processing by any measure; for other influential proposals, see Ferreira 2003; Ferreira and Patson 2007; Townsend and Bever 2001; van Gompel *et al.* 2000, 2001, among others.

linguistic information during processing) on language processing has been investigated since the 70s. Since then, findings have deepened our understanding of how working memory measures interact with sentence processing patterns. In L1 processing research, for example, early findings have uncovered relationships linking individual variability in working memory capacity with processing abilities, as well as links between working memory measures and the processing of complex sentences (Just and Carpenter 1992) or (lexical) access of ambiguous lexical items (Miyake et al. 1994).

In the context of L2 research, Juffs (e.g. 2004, 2005) pioneered research into the effects of working memory on the processing of structures with high processing costs, such as long distance *wh*-dependencies (involving a trace) and reduced relative (subject and object) clauses. More recently, Rodríguez (2008) has explored three additional structures in order to determine the role of different working memory capacities and (online) ambiguity resolution. In these investigations, which used reading span tasks[15] as a measure of working memory, the role of working memory was far from definitive. In fact, none of these studies uncovered the expected relationship between high working memory capacity participants and speedy ambiguity resolution in real time analogous to the findings in the L1 processing literature (e.g. Lim and Christianson 2015). In contrast, other studies using slightly different methods of measuring working memory have found effects of differing working memory capacities. Dussias and Piñar (2010), for instance, investigated the processing of *wh*-filler gap dependencies and found that higher working memory L2 participants, like native speakers, were able to attend to plausibility information when recovering from initial structural misanalyses of subject *wh*-extractions.

Although more research in this area is needed, one important consideration is the effect of the particular (verbal) working memory measure used. Following MacDonald and Christiansen (2002), Farmer et al. (2012) make the case that typical reading span measures, such as the one employed by Just and Carpenter (1992), measure language comprehension skills rather than storage capacities. This conceptualization of working memory measures could prove especially helpful in L2 acquisition in light of evidence linking proficiency/language experience with native-like processing (e.g. Dussias et al. 2013; Hoover and Dwivedi 1998; Hopp 2006; Jackson 2008; Leal et al. 2017; Lim and Christianson 2013). In this regard, the systematic manipulation of linguistic experience could be especially informative.

Another burgeoning area of research in L2 involves prediction and its relationship to acquisition outcomes and sentence processing (Grüter et al.

---

[15] These tasks are designed to gauge working memory (storage and processing functions). Participants are asked to remember words (typically one per sentence) after reading groups of two to six sentences. After each group, participants are asked to utter the words recalled.

2017; Kaan 2014; Leal *et al.* 2017). For this reason, we will devote Section 5.3.2 to addressing the potential this construct has with regard to explaining L2 development.

5.3.2 Sentence Processing and the Generation of Expectations: Prediction in Second Language Acquisition

There is a wealth of evidence in support of the notion that speakers use linguistic and nonlinguistic cues to generate predictions for a variety of aspects of the linguistic input in real-time comprehension (e.g. Arai and Keller 2013; DeLong *et al.* 2005; Dikker *et al.* 2010; Farmer *et al.* 2006; Kamide *et al.* 2003; Levy 2008; Staub and Clifton 2006, among others). This research has also presented evidence that comprehenders can quickly integrate disparate sources of information such as the surrounding visual context (e.g. Altmann and Kamide 1999) or even knowledge of the world (e.g. Kamide *et al.* 2003) to arrive at a semantic interpretation by narrowing potential candidates (Kutas *et al.* 2010).

The investigation of the generation of expectations in L2 processing is a relatively recent yet rapidly expanding area of research, specially in Spanish. In the area of grammatical prediction, L2 research has shown evidence supporting the notion that L2 speakers are indeed able to generate predictions online (e.g. Hopp 2013; Leal *et al.* 2017). However, there is also a body of work showing evidence that L2 expectations can be more variable when compared to those of native speakers (e.g. Dallas *et al.* 2013; Foucart *et al.* 2014; Grüter *et al.* 2012; Martin *et al.* 2013). These findings are not entirely surprising – they echo, in many ways, the L2 acquisition literature using offline methodologies.

Because of the richness of the Spanish inflectional system, research on Spanish morphosyntactic acquisition, in particular, has contributed significantly to our knowledge of prediction in L2 processing. In fact, morphosyntactic agreement in Spanish is one of the best-represented linguistic phenomena in the L2 literature on syntactic predictions. A significant portion of this research has been conducted by tracking eye-movement patterns to objects in a computer display while participants listen to sentences that include linguistic manipulations. Studying eye-tracking patterns allows researchers to understand the representations that listeners activate in comprehension (Tanenhaus *et al.* 1995). Eye-tracking is a particularly germane methodology in this regard because when listeners generate predictions, they launch anticipatory saccades to those objects that are consistent with their expectations. Because these saccades occur before the predicted information is heard (e.g. Altmann and Kamide 1999; Kamide *et al.* 2003), we can be assured that listeners are actively predicting.

The study of anticipated processing of Spanish determiners has played a central role in the research on predictive morphosyntactic agreement (e.g. Lew-Williams and Fernald 2010; Wicha *et al.* 2004). Spanish nouns trigger phi feature agreement with determiners both in gender and number. Gender-marking, which can be either masculine or feminine in Spanish, was investigated by Lew-Williams and Fernald (2010), who examined patterns of anticipatory looks to determine whether L1 and L2 Spanish participants could anticipate the gender of an upcoming noun based on previous exposure to gender-marked determiners. The results from this investigation showed that L1 participants, as expected, anticipated the gender of the noun from the gender-marked determiner. L2 learners, on the other hand, were able to predict gender only with novel nouns (nonce nouns that were introduced in the experiment itself) but not with known nouns. In a follow-up study using eye-tracking again, Grüter *et al.* (2012) showed that advanced learners did generate expectations for the target noun from gender-marked determiners, even if they were less consistent than native speakers.

Dussias and colleagues (2013) also examined the eye-tracking patterns of native Spanish speakers and two groups of Spanish bilinguals: English–Spanish and Italian–Spanish bilinguals. The English–Spanish group was further divided by proficiency (high, low). Results showed that advanced English–Spanish bilinguals, like native Spanish speakers, were able to use gender information predictively while intermediate English–Spanish bilingual learners did not. Italian–Spanish bilinguals used gender predictively on the feminine but not the masculine items.[16] Taken together, these studies suggest that higher proficiency learners can generate expectations that are more native-like in nature even without the benefit of L1 transfer. Dussias and colleagues (2013) also showed that L1–L2 typological similarity can influence linguistic expectations that are generated during processing.

5.4 Concluding Remarks and Future Directions

As mentioned before, although research on lexical access and research on sentence processing have largely occupied separate research spaces, many of the findings in the two areas echo one another, as we have attempted to highlight here. Moreover, in the area of L2 sentence processing, recent hypotheses have sought to link processing difficulties to lexical access. For instance, Hopp's (2014, 2016) Lexical Bottleneck hypothesis predicts that difficulties in lexical access are predictive of structural processing difficulties. Although more research in the area is needed, initial results show that both native speakers and L2 learners show distinctive patterns of processing for words that have less robust representations (e.g. low-frequency

---

[16] The Italian–Spanish group was not divided into proficiency levels, but their L2 proficiency scores were statistically comparable to the lower-proficiency English–Spanish group.

words) than for words that have more robust representations (e.g. high-frequency words). Hopp (2016) argues that these results suggest that lexical access demands have a causal relationship to non-native-like processing patterns. We believe that research that incorporates both psycholinguistic traditions has enormous potential to advance our knowledge of language processing.

The number of psycholinguistic studies using Spanish as at least one of the languages under investigation has increased tremendously over the past decade or so. We expect that future research will continue to explore the nature of bilingual language processing and also the role of contextual knowledge and prediction in the cognitive processes involved. Moreover, psycholinguistic research will need to consider the population of Spanish heritage speakers and how psycholinguistic processing may be different for this group of bilinguals.

Appendix 5.A Resources for Lexical Access Research

There exist many different resources available online to help with the creation of controlled, reliable stimuli for lexical access experiments. For example, the NIM database (Guasch *et al.* 2013) includes English, Spanish, and Catalan words built from the *LEXESP* database (Sebastián-Gallés *et al.* 2000). Crucially, NIM allows researchers to search for words, frequency counts, and orthographic neighbors, among other things.

For researchers interested in controlling for factors such as age of acquisition on lexical items, Davies *et al.* (2013) created a database for Spanish. González-Nosti *et al.* (2014) and Davies *et al.* (2016) carried out a norming study on psycholinguistic variables affecting latencies for 2,765 words in Spanish and English; results are available for consultation. Vitevitch *et al.* (2012) have published an online resource that allows researchers to calculate phonological similarity among Spanish words for L2 Spanish learners.

Finally, to calculate orthographic syllabic frequency for Spanish (and Basque), Duñabeitia *et al.* (2010) created SYLLABARIUM. It is available online for researchers to consult at www.bcbl.eu/syllabarium.

References

Altmann, G. T. and Kamide, Y. (1999). Incremental Interpretation at Verbs: Restricting the Domain of Subsequent Reference. *Cognition*, 73 (3), 247–264.

Altmann, G. and Steedman, M. (1988). Interaction with Context during Human Sentence Processing. *Cognition*, 30 (3), 191–238.

Arai, M. and Keller, F. (2013). The Use of Verb-Specific Information for Prediction in Sentence Processing. *Language and Cognitive Processes*, 28 (4), 525–560.

Bialystok, E., Craik, F. I., and Luk, G. (2012). Bilingualism: Consequences for Mind and Brain. *Trends in Cognitive Sciences*, 16 (4), 240–250.

Carreiras, M. and Duñabeitia, J. A. (2012). Reading Words and Sentences in Spanish. In José Ignacio Hualde, Antxon Olarrea, and Erin O'Rourke (eds.), *The Handbook of Hispanic Linguistics*. New York: Blackwell, pp. 803–818.

Carreiras, M., Perea, M., and Grainger, J. (1997). Effects of the Orthographic Neighborhood in Visual Word Recognition: Cross-Task Comparisons. *Journal of Experimental Psychology: Learning, Memory, and Cognition*, 23 (4), 857–871.

Casaponsa, A., Carreiras, M., and Duñabeitia, J. A. (2014). Discriminating Languages in Bilingual Contexts: The Impact of Orthographic Markedness. *Frontiers in Psychology*, 5 (May), 424. doi: 10.3389/fpsyg.2014.00424

Clark, A. (2013). Whatever Next? Predictive Brains, Situated Agents, and the Future of Cognitive Science. *Behavioral and Brain Sciences*, 36 (03), 181–204.

Colzato, L. S., Bajo, M. T., van den Wildenberg, W., Paolieri, D., Nieuwenhuis, S., La Heij, W., and Hommel, B. (2008). How Does Bilingualism Improve Executive Control? A Comparison of Active and Reactive Inhibition Mechanisms. *Journal of Experimental Psychology: Learning, Memory, and Cognition*, 34, 302–312.

Costa, A., La Heij, W., and Navarrete, E. (2006). The Dynamics of Bilingual Lexical Access. *Bilingualism: Language and Cognition*, 9 (2), 137–151.

Cuetos, F. and Mitchell, D. C. (1988). Cross-Linguistic Differences in Parsing: Restrictions on the Use of the Late Closure Strategy in Spanish. *Cognition*, 30, 73–105.

Cutler, A., Weber, A., and Otake, T. (2006). Asymmetric Mapping from Phonetic to Lexical Representations in Second-Language Listening. *Journal of Phonetics*, 34 (2), 269–284.

Dallas, A. C., DeDe, G., and Nicol, J. (2013). An Event-Related-Potential (ERP) Investigation of Filler-Gap Processing in Native and Second Language Learners. *Language Learning*, 63, 766–799.

Davies, R., Barbón, A., and Cuetos, F. (2013). Lexical and Semantic Age-of-Acquisition Effects on Word Naming in Spanish. *Journal of Memory and Language*, 41 (2), 297–311.

Davies, S. K., Izura, C., Socas, R., and Domínguez, A. (2016). Age of Acquisition and Imageability Norms for Base and Morphologically Complex Words in English and in Spanish. *Behavior Research Methods*, 48 (1), 349–365.

Dekydtspotter, L. and Renaud, C. (2014). On Second Language Processing and Grammatical Development: The Parser in Second Language Acquisition. *Linguistic Approaches to Bilingualism*, 4 (2), 131–165.

DeLong, K. A., Urbach, T. P., and Kutas, M. (2005). Probabilistic Word Pre-Activation during Language Comprehension Inferred from Electrical Brain Activity. *Nature Neuroscience*, 8 (8), 1117–1121.

Dijkstra, T., Miwa, K., Brummelhuis, B., Sappelli, M., and Baayen, H. (2010). How Cross-Language Similarity and Task Demands Affect Cognate Recognition. *Journal of Memory and Language*, 62 (3), 284–301.

Dijkstra, T. and van Heuven, W. J. (2002). Modeling Bilingual Word Recognition: Past, Present and Future. *Bilingualism: Language and Cognition*, 5 (3), 219–224.

Dikker, S., Rabagliati, H., Farmer, T. A., and Pylkkänen, L. (2010). Early Occipital Sensitivity to Syntactic Category is Based on Form Typicality. *Psychological Science*, 21 (5), 629–634.

Duñabeitia, J. A., Cholin, J., Corral, J., Perea, M., and Carreiras, M. (2010). SYLLABARIUM: An Online Application for Deriving Complete Statistics for Basque and Spanish Orthographic Syllables. *Behavior Research Methods*, 42, 118–125.

Duñabeitia, J. A., Perea, M., and Carreiras, M. (2007). Do Transposed-Letter Similarity Effects Occur at a Morpheme Level? Evidence for Morpho-Orthographic Decomposition. *Cognition*, 105 (3), 691–703.

Duñabeitia, J. A. and Vidal-Abarca, E. (2008). Children like Dense Neighborhoods: Orthographic Neighborhood Density Effects In Novel Readers. *The Spanish Journal of Psychology*, 11 (1), 26–35.

Dussias, P. E. (2004). Parsing a First Language like a Second: The Erosion of L1 Parsing Strategies in Spanish–English Bilinguals. *International Journal of Bilingualism*, 8 (3), 355–371.

Dussias, P. E. and Sagarra, N. (2007). The Effect of Exposure on Syntactic Parsing in Spanish–English Bilinguals. *Bilingualism: Language and Cognition*, 10, 101–116.

Dussias, P., Valdés Kroff, J. R., Guzzardo Tamargo, R. E., and Gerfen, C. (2013). When Gender and Looking Go Hand in Hand. *Studies in Second Language Acquisition*, 35, 353–387.

Dussias, P. E. and Piñar, P. (2010). Effects of Reading Span and Plausibility in the Reanalysis of wh-Gaps by Chinese–English Second Language Speakers. *Second Language Research*, 26 (4), 443–472.

Eberhard, K. M., Spivey-Knowlton, M. J., Sedivy, J. C., and Tanenhaus, M. K. (1995). Eye Movements as a Window into Real-Time Spoken Language Comprehension in Natural Contexts. *Journal of Psycholinguistic Research*, 24 (6), 409–436.

Elman, J. L. (1993). Learning and Development in Neural Networks: The Importance of Starting Small. *Cognition*, 48 (1), 71–99.

Farmer, T. A., Christiansen, M. H., and Monaghan, P. (2006). Phonological Typicality Influences On-Line Sentence Comprehension. *Proceedings of the National Academy of Sciences*, 103 (32), 12203–12208.

Farmer, T. A., Misyak, J. B., Christiansen, M. H., Spivey, M., Joannisse, M., and McRae, K. (2012). Individual Differences in Sentence Processing. In M. Sprivey, M. Joanisse, and K. McRae (eds.), *The Cambridge Handbook of Psycholinguistics*. Cambridge and New York: Cambridge University Press, pp. 353–364.

Ferreira, F. (2003). The Misinterpretation of Noncanonical Sentences. *Cognitive Psychology*, 47, 164–203.

Ferreira, F. and Patson, N. D. (2007). The "Good Enough" Approach to Language Comprehension. *Language and Linguistics Compass*, 1, 71–83.

Fodor, J. A. (1983). *The Modularity of Mind: An Essay on Faculty Psychology*. Cambridge, MA: MIT Press.

Foucart, A., Martin, C. D., Moreno, E. M., and Costa, A. (2014). Can Bilinguals See it Coming? Word Anticipation in L2 Sentence Reading. *Journal of Experimental Psychology: Learning, Memory, and Cognition*, 40, pp. 1461–1469.

Frazier, L. (1978). *On Comprehending Sentences: Syntactic Parsing Strategies*. Bloomington, IN: Indiana University Linguistics Club.

Frazier, L. (1987). Sentence Processing: A Tutorial Review. In M. Coltheart (ed.), *The Psychology of Reading. Attention and Performance, Vol. 12*. Hillsdale, NJ: Erlbaum, pp. 559–586.

Frazier, L. (2013). Syntax in Sentence Processing. In R. P. G. van Gompel (ed.), *Sentence Processing*. London: Psychology Press, pp. 21–50.

Frazier, L. and Clifton, C. (1989). Successive Cyclicity in the Grammar and the Parser. *Language and Cognitive Processes*, 4 (2), 93–126.

Frazier, L. and Clifton Jr., C. (1996). *Construal*. Cambridge, MA: MIT Press.

Frazier, L. and Rayner, K. (1982). Making and Correcting Errors during Sentence Comprehension: Eye Movements in the Analysis of Structurally Ambiguous Sentences. *Cognitive Psychology*, 14 (2), 178–210.

Freeman M. R., Blumenfeld H. K., and Marian, V. (2016). Phonotactic Constraints Are Activated across Languages in Bilinguals. *Frontiers in Psychology* 7, 702.

Gollan T. H., Forster, K. I., and Frost, R. (1997). Translation Priming with Different Scripts: Masked Priming with Cognates and Non-Cognates in Hebrew–English Bilinguals. *Journal of Experimental Psychology: Learning, Memory, and Cognition*, 23, 1122–1139.

González-Nosti, M., Barbón, A., Rodríguez-Ferreiro, J., and Cuetos, F. (2014). Effects of the Psycholinguistic Variables on the Lexical Decision Task in Spanish: A Study with 2,765 Words. *Behavior Research Methods*, 46 (2), 517–525.

Green, D. W. and Abutalebi, J. (2013). Language Control in Bilinguals: The Adaptive Control Hypothesis. *Journal of Cognitive Psychology*, 25, 515–530.

Grosjean, F. (2001). The Bilingual's Language Modes. In J. Nicol (ed.), *One Mind, Two Languages: Bilingual Language Processing*. Malden, MA: Blackwell, pp. 1–22. Also in Li Wei (ed.), *The Bilingual Reader* (2nd edn). London: Routledge, 2007, pp. 428–449.

Grüter, T., Lew-Williams, C., and Fernald, A. (2012). Grammatical Gender in L2: A Production or a Real-Time Processing Problem? *Second Language Research*, 28, 191–215.

Grüter, T., Rohde, H., and Shafer, A. (2017). Coreference and Discourse Coherence in L2: The Roles of Grammatical Aspect and Referential Form. *Linguistic Approaches to Bilingualism*, 7 (2), 199–229.

Guasch, M., Boada, R., Ferré, P., and Sánchez-Casas, R. (2013). NIM: A Web-Based Swiss Army Knife to Select Stimuli for Psycholinguistic Studies. *Behavior Research Methods*, 45 (3), 765–771.

Gullifer, J. W., Kroll, J. F., and Dussias, P. E. (2013). When Language Switching has no Apparent Cost: Lexical Access in Sentence Context. *Frontiers in Psychology*, 4, 278.

Heredia, R. R. and Altarriba, J. (eds.). (2013). *Foundations of Bilingual Memory*. New York: Springer Science and Business Media.

Hernández, M., Costa, A., Fuentes, L. J., Vivas, A. B., and Sebastián-Gallés, N. (2010). The Impact of Bilingualism on the Executive Control and Orienting Networks of Attention. *Bilingualism: Language and Cognition*, 13 (3), 315–325.

Hopp, H. (2006). Syntactic Features and Reanalysis in Near-Native Processing. *Second Language Research*, 22 (3), 369–397.

Hoover, M. L. and Dwivedi, V. D. (1998). Syntactic Processing by Skilled Bilinguals. *Language Learning*, 48 (1), 1–29.

Hopp, H. (2013). Grammatical Gender in Adult L2 Acquisition: Relations between Lexical and Syntactic Variability. *Second Language Research*, 29, 33–56.

Hopp, H. (2014). Working Memory Effects on the L2 Processing of Ambiguous Relative Clauses. *Language Acquisition*, 21, 250–278.

Hopp, H. (2016). The Timing of Lexical and Syntactic Processes in Second Language Sentence Comprehension. *Applied Psycholinguistics*, 37 (5), 1253–1280.

Jackson, C. (2008). Proficiency Level and the Interaction of Lexical and Morphosyntactic Information during L2 Sentence Processing. *Language Learning*, 58, 875–909.

Jegerski, J. (2012). The Processing of Subject–Object Ambiguities in Native and Near-Native Mexican Spanish. *Bilingualism: Language and Cognition*, 15 (4), 721–735.

Jegerski, J. and VanPatten, B. (2013). *Research Methods in Second Language Psycholinguistics*. New York: Routledge.

Ju, M. and Luce, P. A. (2004). Falling on Sensitive Ears. *Psychological Science*, 15, 314–318.

Juffs, A. (2004). Representation, Processing and Working Memory in a Second Language. *Transactions of the Philological Society*, 102, 199–225.

Juffs, A. (2005). The Influence of First Language on the Processing of *wh*-Movement in English as a Second Language. *Second Language Research*, 21, 121–151.

Just, M. A. and Carpenter, P. A. (1992). A Capacity Theory of Comprehension: Individual Differences in Working Memory. *Psychological Review*, 99, 122–149.

Kaan, E. (2014). Predictive Sentence Processing in L2 and L1: What is Different? *Linguistic Approaches to Bilingualism*, 4 (2), 257–282.

Kamide, Y., Altmann, G. T., and Haywood, S. L. (2003). The Time-Course of Prediction in Incremental Sentence Processing: Evidence from Anticipatory Eye Movements. *Journal of Memory and Language*, 49, 133–156.

Kroll, J. F., and Dussias, P. E. (2004). The Comprehension of Words and Sentences in Two Languages. In T. K. Bhatia and W. C. Ritchie (eds.), *The Handbook of Bilingualism*. Malden, MA: Wiley, pp. 169–200.

Kroll, J. F., Dussias, P. E., Bogulski, C. A., and Valdés Kroff, J. (2012). Juggling Two Languages in One Mind: What Bilinguals Tell us about Language Processing and its Consequences for Cognition. In B. Ross (ed.), *The Psychology of Learning and Motivation*, Vol. 56. San Diego, CA: Academic Press, pp. 229–262.

Kroll, J. F. and Stewart, E. (1994). Category Interference in Translation and Picture Naming: Evidence for Asymmetric Connections between Bilingual Memory Representations. *Journal of Memory and Language*, 33, 149–174.

Kroll, J. F. and Tokowicz, N. (2005). Models of Bilingual Representation and Processing: Looking Back and to the Future. In J. F. Kroll and A. M. B. de Groot (eds.), *Handbook of Bilingualism: Psycholinguistic Approaches*. New York: Oxford University Press, pp. 531–553.

Kroll, J., van Hell, J. G., Tokowicz, N., and Green, D. W. (2010). The Revised Hierarchical Model: A Critical Review and Assessment. *Bilingualism: Language and Cognition*, 13 (3), 373–381.

Kutas, M., DeLong, K. A., and Smith, N. J. (2011) A Look around at What Lies Ahead: Prediction and Predictability in Language Processing. In M. Bar (ed.). *Predictions in the Brain: Using Our Past to Generate a Future*. New York: Oxford University Press, pp. 190–207.

Leal, T., Slabakova, R., and Farmer, T. A. (2017). The Fine-Tuning of Linguistic Expectations over the Course of L2 Learning. *Studies in Second Language Acquisition*, 39 (3), 493–525.

Levy, R. (2008). Expectation-Based Syntactic Comprehension. *Cognition*, 106 (3), 1126–1177.

Lew-Williams, C. and Fernald, A. (2010). Real-Time Processing of Gender-Marked Articles by Native and Non-Native Spanish Speakers. *Journal of Memory and Language*, 63 (4), 447–464.

Li, P. and Zhao, X. (2014). Connectionist Bilingual Representation. In R. R. Heredia and J. Altarriba (eds.), *Foundations of Bilingual Memory*. New York: Springer, pp. 63–84.

Lim, J. H. and Christianson, K. (2013). Second Language Sentence Processing in Reading for Comprehension and Translation. *Bilingualism: Language and Cognition*, 16, 518–537.

Lim, J. H. and Christianson, K. (2015). Second Language Sensitivity to Agreement Errors: Evidence from Eye Movements during

Comprehension and Translation. *Applied Psycholinguistics*, 36 (6), 1283–1315.

MacDonald, M. C. (1994). Probabilistic Constraints and Syntactic Ambiguity Resolution. *Language and Cognitive Processes*, 9, 157–201.

MacDonald, M. C. and Christiansen, M. H. (2002). Reassessing Working Memory: A Comment on Just and Carpenter (1992) and Waters and Caplan (1996). *Psychological Review*, 109, 35–54.

MacDonald, M. C., Pearlmutter, N. J., and Seidenberg, M. S. (1994). The Lexical Nature of Syntactic Ambiguity Resolution. *Psychological Review*, 101, 676–703.

Macizo, P., Bajo, T., and Cruz Martín, M. (2010). Inhibitory Processes in Bilingual Language Comprehension: Evidence from Spanish–English Interlexical Homographs. *Journal of Memory and Language*, 63 (2), 232–244.

Marian, V. and Spivey, M. J. (2003). Competing Activation in Bilingual Language Processing: Within- and Between-Language Competition. *Bilingualism: Language and Cognition*, 6, 97–115.

Marslen-Wilson, W. D. (1975). Sentence Perception as an Interactive Parallel Process. *Science*, 189 (4198), 226–228.

Marslen-Wilson, W. D. (1990). Activation, Competition and Frequency in Lexical Access. In G. Altman (ed.), *Cognitive Models of Speech Processing: Psycholinguistic and Computational Perspectives*. Cambridge, MA: MIT Press, pp. 148–172.

Martin, C. D., Thierry, G., Kuipers, J. R., Boutonnet, B., Foucart, A., and Costa, A. (2013). Bilinguals Reading in their Second Language do not Predict Upcoming Words as Native Readers do. *Journal of Memory and Language*, 69 (4), 574–588.

McClelland, J. L. and Elman, J. L. (1986). The TRACE Model of Speech Perception. *Cognitive Psychology*, 18, 1–86.

McRae, K. and Matsuki, K. (2013). Constraint-Based Models of Sentence Processing. In R. P. G. van Gompel (ed.), *Sentence Processing*. London: Psychology Press, pp. 51–77.

McRae, K., Spivey-Knowlton, M. J., and Tanenhaus, M. K. (1998). Modeling the Influence of Thematic Fit (and Other Constraints) in On-Line Sentence Comprehension. *Journal of Memory and Language*, 38 (3), 283–312.

Morton, J. (1979). Facilitation in Word Recognition: Experiments Causing Change in the Logogen Model. In P. Kolers, M. E. Wrolstad, and H. Bouma (eds.), *Processing of Visible Language*. New York: Springer, pp. 259–268.

Miyake, A., Carpenter, P., and Just, M. (1994). A Capacity Approach to Syntactic Comprehension Disorders: Making Normal Adults Perform like Aphasic Patients. *Cognitive Neuropsychology*, 11, 671–717.

Morales, J., Gómez-Ariza, C. J., and Bajo, M. T. (2013). Dual Mechanisms of Cognitive Control in Bilinguals and Monolinguals. *Journal of Cognitive Psychology*, 25 (5), 531–546.

Müller, O., Duñabeitia, J. A., and Carreiras, M. (2010). Orthographic and Associative Neighborhood Density Effects: What is Shared, what is Different? *Psychophysiology*, 47 (3), 455–466.

Norris, D. and McQueen, J. M. (2008). Shortlist B: A Bayesian Model of Continuous Speech Recognition. *Psychological Review*, 115, 357–395.

Pickering, M. J. (1994). Processing Local and Unbounded Dependencies: A Unified Account. *Journal of Psycholinguistic Research*, 23 (4), 323–352.

Pickering, M. J. and Traxler, M. J. (2003). Evidence against the Use of Subcategorisation Frequency in the Processing of Unbounded Dependencies. *Language and Cognitive Processes*, 18 (4), 469–503.

Prior, A. and Gollan, T. (2011). Good Language Switchers Are Good Task Switchers: Evidence from Spanish–English and Mandarin–English Bilinguals. *Journal of the International Neuropsychological Society*, 17, 682–691.

Roberts, L. (2013). Sentence Processing in Bilinguals. In R. P. G. van Gompel (ed.), *Sentence Processing*. London: Psychology Press, pp. 221–246.

Rodríguez, G. A. (2008). Second Language Sentence Processing: Is it Fundamentally Different? (Doctoral dissertation). University of Pittsburgh.

Schwartz, A. I. and Arêas da Luz Fontes, A. B. (2008). Cross-Language Mediated Priming: Effects of Context and Lexical Relationship. *Bilingualism: Language and Cognition*, 11, 1–16.

Schwartz, A. I. and Kroll, J. F. (2006). Bilingual Lexical Activation in Sentence Context. *Journal of Memory and Language*, 55 (2), 197–212.

Sebastián Gallés, N., Carreiras, M. F., Cuetos, F., and Martí, M. A. (2000). *LEXESP. Léxico informatizado del español*. Barcelona: Edicions de la Universitat de Barcelona. [CD-ROM]

Shook, A. and Marian, V. (2012). The Bilingual Language Interaction Network for Comprehension of Speech. *Bilingualism: Language and Cognition*, 16 (2), 304–324. doi: 10.1017/S1366728912000466.

Spivey, M. J. and Tanenhaus, M. K. (1998). Syntactic Ambiguity Resolution in Discourse: Modeling the Effects of Referential Context and Lexical Frequency. *Journal of Experimental Psychology: Learning, Memory, and Cognition*, 24 (6), 1521.

Staub, A. and Clifton Jr, C. (2006). Syntactic Prediction in Language Comprehension: Evidence from "either … or." *Journal of Experimental Psychology: Learning, Memory, and Cognition*, 32 (2), 425.

Steedman, M. J. (1989). Grammar, Interpretation, and Processing from the Lexicon. In W. D. Marslen-Wilson (ed.), *Lexical Representation and Process*. Cambridge, MA: MIT Press, pp. 463–504.

Sunderman, G. L. and Fancher, E. (2013). Lexical Access in Bilinguals and Second Language Learners. In J. Schwieter (ed.), *Innovative Research and Practices in Second Language Acquisition and Bilingualism*. Amsterdam and Philadelphia, PA: John Benjamins, pp. 267–286.

Tabor, W. and Tanenhaus, M. K. (1999). Dynamical Models of Sentence Processing. *Cognitive Science*, 23 (4), 491–515.

Tanenhaus, M. K., Spivey-Knowlton, M. J., Eberhard, K. M., and Sedivy, J. C. (1995). Integration of Visual and Linguistic Information in Spoken Language Comprehension. *Science*, 268 (5217), 1632.

Tanenhaus, M. K. and Trueswell, J. C. (1995). Sentence Comprehension. In J. L. Miller and P. D. Eimas (eds.), *Speech, Language, and Communication*. San Diego, CA: Academic Press, pp. 217–262.

Townsend, D. J., and Bever, T. G. (2001). *Sentence Comprehension: The Integration of Habits and Rules*. Cambridge, MA: MIT Press.

van Gompel, R. P. G. (2013). Sentence Processing: An Introduction. In R. P. G. van Gompel (ed.), *Sentence Processing*. London: Psychology Press, pp. 1–20.

van Gompel, R. P. G., Pickering, M. J., and Traxler, M. J. (2000). Unrestricted Race: A New Model of Syntactic Ambiguity Resolution. In A. Kennedy, R. Radach, D. Heller, and J. Pynte (eds.), *Reading as a Perceptual Process*. Oxford: Elsevier, pp. 621–648.

van Gompel, R. P. G., Pickering, M. J., and Traxler, M. J. (2001). Reanalysis in Sentence Processing: Evidence against Current Constraint-Based and Two-Stage Models. *Journal of Memory and Language*, 45 (2), 225–258.

van Hell, J. G. and Dijkstra, T. (2002). Foreign Language Knowledge can Influence Native Language Performance in Exclusively Native Contexts. *Psychonomic Bulletin and Review*, 9 (4), 780–789.

van Kesteren, R., Dijkstra, T., and de Smedt, K. (2012). Markedness Effects in Norwegian–English Bilinguals: Task-Dependent Use of Language-Specific Letters and Bigrams. *Quarterly Journal of Experimental Psychology (Hove)*, 65 (11), 2129–2154. doi: 10.1080/17470218.2012.679946

Vitevitch M. S. and Rodríguez E. (2005). Neighbourhood Density Effects in Spoken Word Recognition in Spanish. *Journal of Multilingual Communication Disorders*, 3, 64–73.

Vitevitch, M. S., Stamer, M. K., and Kieweg, D. (2012). The Beginning Spanish Lexicon: A Web-Based Interface to Calculate Phonological Similarity among Spanish Words in Adults Learning Spanish as a Foreign Language. *Second Language Research*, 28 (1), 103–112. doi:10.1177/0267658311432199

Weber, A. and Scharenborg, O. (2012). Models of Spoken-Word Recognition. *WIREs Cognitive Science*, 3, 387–401. doi: 10.1002/wcs.1178.

Wicha, N. Y., Moreno, E. M., and Kutas, M. (2004). Anticipating Words and their Gender: An Event-Related Brain Potential Study of Semantic Integration, Gender Expectancy, and Gender Agreement in Spanish Sentence Reading. *Journal of Cognitive Neuroscience*, 16 (7), 1272–1288.

6

Corpus Approaches to the Study of Language, Variation, and Change

Manuel Díaz-Campos and Juan Escalona Torres

6.1 Purpose of this Chapter

The main purpose of this chapter is to provide the reader with an introduction to corpus approaches focusing on research into Spanish variable phenomena. The idea is to provide useful information about the area of research and the resources available to interested researchers. We begin with a section defining corpus linguistics and describing what type of research is representative of this field. The next section is concerned with resources available for corpus studies in general and what corpora are available in Spanish. In the last section of the chapter, we have selected the variable expression of the future in Spanish to show how to use available corpora and how to perform an analysis.

6.2 What is Corpus Linguistics?

The word *corpus* (pl. *corpora*) comes from the Latin for "body." In English and other languages, we use the word "corpus" to refer to a collection of things and most particularly to a collection of texts. Corpus linguistics is the study of languages through a collection of texts of different natures in order to make generalizations based on common and divergent patterns. Texts are classified according to topics or genres (e.g. narrative, descriptive, argumentative) depending on particular criteria. Intermediate types of text exist when a discourse or text is written to be delivered orally. Recent developments in technology make it possible to gather language and other sources of data in effective ways. Storage and availability of data have also improved in the last decade, so that these sources for research are more readily available to those interested in the subject. The techniques of corpus linguistics may be used for different goals, from theoretical understanding of language structure based on empirical evidence to more applied purposes such as identification and creation of pedagogical material. Anthony (2013) highlights four key features of corpus linguistics: (i) it is empirical; (ii) it relies on large corpora of the target language; (iii) analyses are based on computer software to identify patterns; and (iv) it uses both qualitative and quantitative techniques to provide an interpretation of findings.

Davies (2008) points out that the idea of collecting large data sets to study language is not new. Structural linguistics and other approaches to the study of language at the beginning of the 19th century relied on corpora for their investigations. Linguists such as Franz Boas (2013) and Edward Sapir (1916), who worked with Native American languages, collected corpora to complement their studies. Later on, the development of generative linguistics, the use of intuitions by native speakers, and the different methodological paradigms that were conceived in the mid-20th century changed the way we approach linguistic research today. However, more recently corpus linguistics has not only gained attention, but has become more sophisticated. The initial critiques attributed to corpus approaches no longer stand, given the evidence presented recently. As Davies (2008) points out, the need for more variable descriptions or implementations of grammar becomes apparent in the modeling of natural language in computer programs. Variability in grammar is of course a central issue to sociolinguistics, given its reliance on the collection of oral and written corpora. Davies (2008) argues that the somewhat misleading use of intuitions from native speakers to identify patterns made it necessary to cross-check with corpora data. The field of digital humanities is another recent development that requires the use of technology for researchers to have access to large corpora. This new field involves interdisciplinary endeavors that can go beyond research to application in collaborative efforts such as publishing and teaching.

The main goal of scholars in corpus linguistics is to create and use corpora for the purpose of analyzing and interpreting generalizable patterns about language. The use and application of corpus linguistic methodology is by nature interdisciplinary and vast. For example, recent studies focus on variable phenomena in English, applied linguistics, and trademark language (e.g. Kilgarriff 2015; Mukherjee and Liu 2012), among many other areas. In the context of this particular chapter, we focus on the study of sociolinguistic phenomena in Spanish by means of corpora. Sociolinguistics is by nature a discipline that aligns with the goals of corpus linguistics because scholars in the area use oral speech samples to analyze language variability in particular communities. As we will discuss in Section 6.3, there are several resources for the study of Spanish, including large-scale projects for the collection of oral samples comprising data from around the Spanish-speaking world (e.g. *Proyecto para el estudio de la norma culta hispánica*; see Samper Padilla *et al.* (1998)). Sociolinguistic research is particularly interested in the study of language in vernacular styles. Study of the vernacular allows us to observe how the use of variable structures reflects the identity of the individual by examining language use in relation to social factors such as gender, age, socioeconomic level, education, ethnicity, etc. By adopting an objective perspective towards language, sociolinguistics makes generalizations using quantitative methods for the analysis of data. Identification of significant effects of linguistic and social factors are used to provide interpretations that are related to current theories in the field. As can be appreciated, while sociolinguistics is considered a separate discipline with its particular goals, it shares features with corpus linguistics. Section 6.2.1 describes some of the current practices in the field and provides connections with sociolinguistic research.

6.2.1 Current Theory and Methods

In their discussion of the current state of the discipline, Arppe *et al.* (2010) describe some of the current challenges that face cognitive corpus linguistics given that the study of language should be based on samples of actual use. For cognitive linguists, language structure (patterns of generalization) is a byproduct of strong tendencies of use. Arppe *et al.* (2010) note that questions about human cognition can be examined using suitable corpora and quantitative research methods. The idea behind approaching language phenomena this way is that in principle an analysis based on corpora and quantitative methodology should be replicable and falsifiable. A set of hypotheses about human cognition can be tested empirically to provide evidence that supports or rejects them. While the focus of sociolinguistic research may not be exclusively associated with a particular discipline (e.g. cognitive linguistics), it coincides with corpus linguistics in the use of samples as a fundamental principle. The use of quantitative research methodology is another principle that makes findings of sociolinguistic research replicable and falsifiable. The corollary is that current methodologies for corpus linguistics depend on observation of natural data (corpus-based data) and quantitative analysis so that scholars can make generalizations. But, as Arppe *et al.* (2010) point out, corpora should not be the only source of data since they represent indirect evidence. In other words, these scholars suggest that off-line evidence is being used to make generalizations about cognition. They indicate the need to check corpus findings against other empirical testing in order to verify and refine hypotheses.

Addressing these issues brings its own challenges, as it would be ideal to have consistent methods across fields in the search for a multidisciplinary approach. Since the idea of combining different methodologies becomes important for testing hypotheses regarding cognition and language use, there should be a process for comparing and understanding different sources of evidence. Arppe *et al.* (2010) explain that there is a distinction between "found data" and "elicited data." *Found data* is corpora data in the form of text which has been included in the corpus according to the relative frequency of a particular pattern based on quantitative methods. *Elicited data* is defined as recorded responses to an experimental test or linguistic responses to obtain samples of specific structures.

More recent studies combine corpus analysis with experimental testing. For example, Arppe and Järvikivi (2007) examine lexical synonymy using corpus data and two psycholinguistic experiments (i.e. a forced-choice and an acceptability rating task). Their paper compares the results of the three sources of evidence to observe how they converge in the explanation of lexical synonymy in Finnish. Synonymy is operationalized in the context of the study as possible "interchangeability" without altering the fundamental meaning of the utterance (e.g. *miettiä* and *pohtia* 'think, reflect,' etc.). According to Arppe and Järvikivi (2007:137), corpus-based studies have shown that the following factors are at play in synonymy selection: (i) style (register, situation); (ii) lexical context; (iii) syntactic argument structure; (iv) semantic classifications of syntactic arguments; and (v) word morphology. Arppe and Järvikivi (2007) hypothesize that *miettiä* and *pohtia* would differ according to agent type. Therefore, *miettiä* would be predicted to be associated with individual human agents, while *pohtia* would be associated with collective human agents. Findings of the study were in general aligned with this hypothesis, but there were fine-grained subtleties as the results of the different tests were compared. The corpus analysis reveals that, in the case of *miettiä*, there was an association with first-person singular agents. However, while an association of *pohtia* with third-person singular agents was documented, the difference was small and not statistically significant. In terms of the findings from the forced-choice test and the acceptability test, there were fundamental similarities in the patterns identified and the patterns found in the corpus analysis. For the forced-choice test, *miettiä* was preferred with first-person singular individual agents, while *pohtia* was more likely to appear with third-person singular collective agents. The acceptability test revealed that there were more subtleties in the findings than expected: *miettiä* was definitely less acceptable with third-person singular collective agents. However, *miettiä* and *pohtia* were equally acceptable with first-person singular individual agents. The authors suggest that the restrictions identified for *miettiä* create the conditions for explaining that *pohtia* is preferred with third-person singular collective agents because *miettiä* cannot be used in those contexts, not because of an inherent semantic trait. The outcome of this research is important because it serves to identify and compare different sources of data, including direct and indirect cognitive evidence.

Sanz (2009), on the other hand, combines the methodological approaches of corpus linguistics, dialectology, and historical linguistics: in this case, with the purpose of examining New Mexican Spanish (NMS). His investigation uses written corpora composed of 216 hand-written samples from three distinct periods. The findings of this investigation question some of the traditional ideas regarding NMS. For instance, NMS shows great similarities with other Latin American varieties that can be explained by taking into account social and linguistic factors. The idea that all features can be traced to the original settlers and linguistic isolation is not enough to describe this variety. Particularly relevant for our corpus linguistic focus is the use of written corpora and its applicability for the analysis of language change.

Arppe *et al.* (2010) outline in their article that a typical corpus linguistics study includes the identification of a form with idiosyncratic properties. Such properties are analyzed and explained according to usage-based patterns identified in the analysis. These scholars argue for an expansion of this particular approach and for connections to be made with other perspectives such as sociolinguistics and the effect of extralinguistic factors: pragmatic, discursive, and historical. These ideas point toward multidisciplinary methods in corpus linguistics and to the diversity of issues that can be explained using available resources.

The use of corpora to study linguistic phenomena serves to answer theoretical questions by adopting a viewpoint based on the scientific methodologies of observation, statistical analysis of the evidence, and presentation of results. With the development of new technologies the collection and accessibility of new corpora has diversified. Furthermore, statistical analyses have become more sophisticated and efficient, which provides researchers with better tools to make stronger generalizations.

6.3 What Resources are Available for Studying Different Sources of Data in Spanish?

The purpose of this section is to give a general idea of the types of resources that have been developed for the study of Spanish. In the last decade several initiatives have been successfully advanced, enriching the types of sources available for researchers. The section is organized into two subparts: (i) corpora and (ii) analytical tools.

6.3.1 Corpora

One of the first organized endeavors to collect oral corpora was the *Coordinated Study of the Educated Linguistic Norm of the Main Cities of Iberoamerica and the Iberian Peninsula* (Lope Blanch 1986; Samper Padilla et al. 1998). The project was proposed by Juan Manuel Lope Blanch at the Second Symposium of the Inter-American Program on Linguistics and the Teaching of Languages held at Indiana University, Bloomington in 1964 (see Díaz-Campos 2011; Lope Blanch 1986). The goal of the project was to collect oral samples of educated speakers in stylistically different situations (careful and less careful speech). The samples include unstructured dialogues, semi-structured dialogues with two participants, concealed recordings, and formal styles such as talks, classes, etc. The participants in these initial corpora were selected according to specific criteria such as origin (born and raised in a particular city), age group (25–35 years, 36–50, and 51 and above), and sex (male, female). There is a sample edition of these materials in electronic format that can be used for research purposes (Samper Padilla *et al.* 1998).

The original projects to collect sample data from different dialects of Spanish have evolved into a multifaceted effort comprising 42 institutions in which linguists record speech samples from several metropolitan areas in the Spanish-speaking world. Under the leadership of the sociolinguist Francisco Moreno-Fernández, this current endeavor, now known as the *Proyecto para el estudio sociolingüístico del español de España y de América* (PRESEEA 2014– : preseea.linguas.net), provides the most recent and diverse samples of speech from different dialectal areas. The advantage of the PRESEEA corpora is that they are collected using similar criteria following sociolinguistic parameters in order that there be equal representation in respect of age, education, and gender. The purpose of the researchers is to create a database of oral samples that is representative of the diversity of the Spanish-speaking world, regionally and socially. The collected samples are available at preseea.linguas.net/Corpus.aspx.

An available source for data analysis online is *Corpus del español* (www.corpusdelespanol.org/). This resource is the product of the invaluable work of Mark Davies and it comprises two sections. The original section, dedicated to historical data, with 100 million words, was created in 2001–2002. The new addition, with the aim of studying contemporary Spanish and containing two billion words, was created in 2015–2016. This new section includes samples from 21 geographical areas of the Spanish-speaking world, making it ideal for the comparison of dialectal varieties. In addition to this specific resource for Spanish research, the page corpus.byu.edu/ offers corpora in English and other languages such as Portuguese.

Well-known databases for the study of Spanish have been developed by the Real Academia Española (Royal Academy of the Spanish Language) which, since the mid-90s, has been digitizing all available resources in different collections:

1 A general archive comprising ten million entries (lexical items): www.rae.es/recursos/banco-de-datos/fichero-general;
2 The *Corpus diacrónico del español* (*Diachronic Corpus of Spanish*, CORDE: http://corpus.rae.es/cordenet.html), which comprises historical texts from the 13th century to 1974. The corpus is composed of over 200 million samples of diverse genres;

3 The *Corpus de referencia del español actual* (*Reference Corpus of Contemporary Spanish*, CREA; http://corpus.rae.es/creanet.html), comprising oral and written texts from 1975 to 2004. This corpus represents a vast array of genres and geographic areas;
4 The *Corpus del nuevo diccionario histórico del español* (*Corpus for the New Historical Dictionary of Spanish*, CDH: http://web.frl.es/CNDHE/view/inicioExterno.view): this resource is described as containing around 53 million entries organized by period;
5 The most recent addition to the set of corpora is the *Corpus del español del siglo XXI* (*Corpus of Twentieth-Century Spanish*, CORPES XXI: http://web.frl.es/CORPES/view/inicioExterno.view). This database comprises 237,678 documents that represent the period between 2001 and now. The initial version had texts from 2001 to 2012.

The *Corpus diacrónico y diatópico del español de América* (*Diachronic and Dialectal American Spanish Corpus*, CORDIAM: www.cordiam.org/) is a source of materials compiled by different scholars and institutions from a variety of countries. It is an important resource for the study of American Spanish and contains texts from 19 Spanish-speaking countries, including the United States. This database covers the period from 1494 to 1905 and the texts therein include non-literary documents, which represent a rich variety of discourse genres. The main goal of this source is to provide historical documents to be used by scholars interested in historical dialectology of the Spanish language in America.

The Linguistic Data Consortium offers a variety of data resources for the study of Spanish: select Spanish from the Languages(s) drop-down menu on its search page (https://catalog.ldc.upenn.edu/search). The Consortium comprises several institutions (universities, libraries, and government institutions) whose aim is to create and distribute language resources. Some relevant examples include oral data from *LATINO-40 Spanish Read News* (https://catalog.ldc.upenn.edu/LDC95S28) – a database providing "a set of recordings for training speaker-independent systems that recognize Latin-American Spanish" – and *CALLHOME* – transcripts (https://catalog.ldc.upenn.edu/LDC96T17) and recordings (https://catalog.ldc.upenn.edu/LDC96S35) of unscripted telephone conversations between Spanish speakers. A final resource that deserves mention is SketchEngine (www.sketchengine.co.uk/), a piece of online concordance software comprising a variety of corpora drawn mainly from web sources. This includes the "esTenTen" corpus, with a diverse array of web texts in Spanish from both Peninsular and Latin American varieties (www.sketchengine.co.uk/esTenTen-spanish-corpus/).

The list of corpora included in this section gives us an idea of the increasing development of oral and written material in Spanish. While not providing an exhaustive list, this section has highlighted some of the more prominent resources available for research in the field. Section 6.3.2 focuses on analytical tools.

6.3.2 Analytical Tools

There has been a recent interest in the analysis of corpora to determine the role of frequency in the creation of grammar patterns (e.g. Bybee and Eddington 2006; Bybee 2006). While the terms "high," "mid" or "low" do not as yet enjoy consistent application or specific definition within the field, the creation of frequency dictionaries has contributed to the testing of predictions of usage-based theories. One of the first Spanish dictionaries of frequencies was written by Julliand and Chang-Rodríguez (1964), used in Diaz-Campos (2004) to examine frequency effects by considering the coefficient of general usage proposed by these scholars. This comprehensive frequency dictionary consists of 5,024 words from five different genres and that provides coefficients of use for lexemes and individual tokens. Another dictionary of frequency for Spanish is the one created by Alameda and Cuetos (1995). This latter resource is more limited in terms of the corpus included and the options available. CREA, mentioned above, also provides information about the lexical frequency of words in the database (corpus.rae.es/lfrecuencias.html). The list is divided into the 1,000, 5,000, and 10,000 most frequent tokens.

Davies (2006) provides a more contemporary version of a Spanish frequency dictionary, with 5,000 lexical entries representing the most common words in Spanish based on a larger sample of 20 million words. The amount of data used for this dictionary is 20 times larger than the corpus employed by Julliand and Chang-Rodríguez (1964). Each entry indicates the part of the speech illustrated, the definition, and the type of discourse it was taken from, and includes an example of its use. This dictionary represents a great resource, drawing as it does on huge updated and diverse corpora, which makes it invaluable for research purposes.

There are also other online resources available that can be used for research purposes. For example, EsPal Frequency (www.bcbl.eu/databases/espal/) is a site that provides ways to analyze properties of words in terms of frequency. This source accesses databases for Peninsular and Latin American Spanish. Zahler and Daidone (2014) use this tool to measure the effect of lexical frequency in trill production (e.g. /pero/ 'dog'). A novel frequency effect included in their research was the calculation of phonological neighbors. They explain that this concept takes into account the similarities and differences of lexical items based on their phonemic structure. These scholars explained that the word *pero* /pero/ 'but' is a phonological neighbor of *perro* /pero/ 'dog' given that they differ in only one phoneme. Furthermore, *erro* /ero/ 'I fail' and *puerro* /pwero/ 'leek' can be considered phonological neighbors of *perro*. The prediction behind this measurement is that words that have more phonological neighbors may need to be phonetically distinguished from related sounding words. These scholars found that the production of a higher number of phonological neighbors favors the production of the canonical trill in order to differentiate the word having the trill from other similar sounding words.

Another tool for analysis is AntConc (www.laurenceanthony.net/software/antconc/), which is free software for text analysis. This tool serves as a search engine that processes corpora and is particularly useful for extracting words and syntactic structures of interest for linguistic research. AntConc is just one example of other tools that have been developed for linguists. The open-source programs R (https://cran.r-project.org/) and R's integrated development environment RStudio (https://www.rstudio.com/) also provide researchers with sophisticated resources to conduct statistical analysis of corpora. R is a very versatile tool providing linear and nonlinear modeling, classical statistical tests, time-series analysis, classification, clustering, and diverse graphical techniques for data analysis. Its popularity has grown due to its multifaceted uses and its free availability. A toolkit developed using R for sociolinguistic analysis is RBRUL (www.danielezrajohnson.com/rbrul.html), which provides a means for performing a variable rule analysis using mixed effects models combining fixed effects and random effects for linguistic data.

Based on R, there is a new application specially designed for linguistic analysis called Language Variation Suite (https://languagevariationsuite.shinyapps.io/Pages/). This is a web application that offers the statistical tools available in R combined with a user-friendly interface. This novel toolkit offers options for the visualization of data, inferential statistics, and applications focusing on sociolinguistic analyses. This new tool promises to be a great boon for corpus-based research.

While limitations of space do not allow us to present a comprehensive list of resources, this section has covered some of the most relevant tools available for linguists.

6.4 Expression of the Future: An Example of how to Perform a Corpus Analysis

6.4.1 The Spanish Future

The following methodological example focuses on the expression of the future in Spanish. In Spanish the periphrastic future (PF), the morphological future (MF), and the futurate present are the most common structures that speakers associate with temporal future expression. In this study, however, we exclude the use of the futurate present because the more productive structure for future expression in our corpora were the PF and the MF. Similarly to English, the periphrastic future in Spanish is composed of the motion verb *ir* 'go' + *a* 'to' + the infinitive form of a verb (see

Example 6.1 below). The morphological future is produced by adding a tensed suffix to the verb (see 6.2 below).

(6.1) pues   ya   te   van   a traer   los   reyes
      well   already   2SG.DAT   go.3PL.PRES   to bring.INF   the   kings
      tus   juguetitos
      your   toys
      'Well then, the Three Wise Men will be bringing you your toys'
                      Source: PRESEEA (2014– , Mexico City, #55)

(6.2) veintidós   años   *cumplir-á*   en   enero
      twenty-two   years   turn.3SG.FUT   in   January
      'S/he will turn twenty-two in January'
                      Source: PRESEEA (2014– , Malaga, #1)

Since both constructions can express futurity in the same or even identical contexts, it is not an easy task to distinguish the use of one from another. In more progressive views of variationist sociolinguistics (cf. Díaz-Campos and Geeslin 2011; Tagliamonte 2011) this contextual overlap can be identified as a variable context. That is, both forms are being used for one function, and, on the surface, adept speakers of the language may have intuitions based on the general tendencies of use. This overlap in function can be observed using a corpus-based analysis. As we will see in Section 6.4.4, different regions reflect varying proportions of use, which may help us locate them on their stage in the well-documented change from MF to PF. The questions we aim to answer in this sample analysis are the following: (i) What are the independent linguistic and social factors that motivate the use of the periphrastic future over the morphological future?; (ii) How do the data sets from Spain and Mexico compare in their use of these forms?

6.4.2 The Corpus

For the purpose of this chapter, we examined two data sets containing sociolinguistic interviews from the PRESEEA 2014– corpus. The data sets pertain to two regions: Mexico City, Mexico and Malaga, Spain. We selected a subset of interviews from each data set to obtain a balanced distribution of social factors (two genders, three socioeconomic levels, and three age groups).

6.4.3 Methodology

The Dependent Variable: Inclusions and Exclusions

The dependent variable for this study was defined according to one function: the temporal expression of futurity. This means that any occurrence of the PF or MF that served a different function was excluded from the analysis. The main exclusions that deserve mention are the discursive functions of both the MF and PF as in (6.3a–b) below, and the epistemic use of the MF exemplified in (6.4) below.

(6.3) a. ¿cómo te diré?
how 2SG.DAT say.1SG.FUT
'How can I say this?'
Source: PRESEEA (2014– , Mexico City, #19)

b. vamos a ver
see.1PL.PRES to see.INF
'Let's see ...'
Source: PRESEEA (2014– , Mexico City, #73)

(6.4) me imagino que tendrá los
1SG.PRON imagine.1SG.PRES that has.3SG.FUT the.PL
estudios básicos
studies basic.PL
'I guess she has the basic knowledge'
Source: PRESEEA (2014– , Malaga, #1)

In (6.3a–b) both structures, MF and PF, are examples of discursive functions where the speakers are thinking aloud and not making reference to the future. In (6.4), the speaker is using *tendrá* 's/he will have' as an epistemic marker showing no evidence of futurity. Instead, the speaker is using it as a modal marker to express uncertainty about the state of affairs of the person under discussion. This function of the MF as a modal expression is an important matter that we will discuss in Section 6.4.4.

All other occurrences of MF and PF that function as temporal future expressions were included in the analysis.

Independent Linguistic Factors

For our analysis, we consider the factors that have been consistently selected as significant predictors of future expression in the literature. The variation between the PF and MF may be said to be born out of their distinct diachronic paths of change. While the PF has been associated with imminence of time and high subjectivity over its development as a future temporal expression, the MF has been associated with distal time and lower degrees of certainty from its inception (cf. Aaron 2010; Claes and Ortiz-López 2011; Kanwit 2017). Not unlike in English, the PF originates from motion-to-a-goal and purposive meaning (cf. Hopper and Traugott 2003), and later it became semanticized as an expression of temporal futurity. This meaning of motion-to-a-goal underlies the modern association with closer proximity of time. Moreover, from its meaning of purpose, various studies have found the PF to have retained high agentive meaning, which has been evidenced by its higher subjectivity in relation to the MF.

Temporal Proximity

The grammaticalization literature (Traugott 1988; Traugott and Dasher 2002) shows that it is common for verbs of movement such as "go" or "come" to acquire temporal meaning and hence become a functional item to express futurity. This phenomenon is evinced cross-linguistically and is considered to be a regularity of natural languages. Based on their evidence using the English periphrastic future "going to," Traugott and Dasher (2002) propose that the plausible first step of the change from spatial movement to temporal movement is a metaphorical association with imminent time. Previous studies on the Spanish expression of temporal futurity have indeed found that the PF is strongly favored in imminent or hodiernal (same day) contexts, while the MF is associated with maximum distance of time (Blas Arroyo 2008; Claes and Ortiz-López 2011; Orozco 2005; Sedano 1994). We therefore identified five temporal distances from closest in time to furthest or indefinite: (i) hodiernal (same day: e.g. *hoy voy a ir* 'today I am going to go'); (ii) attenuated, a distant temporal reference brought closer with the use of a demonstrative or an adverbial (e.g. ***esta** semana que viene vendré* '**this coming** week I'll be coming'); (iii) intermediate (e.g. *la semana que viene lo haré* 'next week I will do it'); (iv) maximal (e.g. *va a ser en dos años* 'it will be in two years'); (v) indefinite (no specification of time; may include hypothetical or conditional).

Subjectivity

Another factor that has been associated with the origin of the PF is subjectivity. Traugott and Dasher (2002) define subjectivity as the relative involvement of the speaker (or writer) with what is said or written, which in turn adds their intention and perspective to the discourse. As Aaron (2006, 2010) points out, using the PF with motion-to-a-goal came with intentionality. This sort of intentionality to achieve a goal came with volition and therefore agency. We would then expect the PF to be associated with higher subjectivity than the MF. To tap into this notion of subjectivity we coded for subject expression and sentence type.

The subject of the sentence can help us identify the speaker's involvement with the proposition as well as its animacy. First and second persons are usually associated with animate subjects while third persons are more of a mixed bag. We therefore expect, as found in previous studies (e.g. Blas Arroyo 2008; Orozco 2005), to see the PF favored by first- and second-person subjects.

Sentence type can also help us identify the degree of subjectivity in a sentence. The literature suggests that certain types of sentences carry inherent involvement of the speaker with the proposition such as exclamatory–exhortatory and direct and indirect interrogative sentences (Aaron 2006; Blas Arroyo 2008). Meanwhile, declarative sentences are considered to be a "default" expression and, unless modified by modal adverbials or pragmatic or discursive markers, are not inherently subjective. Therefore, we would expect the PF to be favored in sentences with higher levels of subjectivity and less so in declaratives.

Clause Type
Similarly, another factor that has been shown to distinguish the two future forms is clause type. Aaron (2010) points out that the MF, from its inception, showed both temporal and epistemic meaning and was used in both matrix clauses as well as subordinate clauses. However, she further adds that in fact the epistemic use of the MF has become more prominent in subordinate clauses, and therefore its temporal use has become more limited to matrix clauses. We thus expect to see the PF to be favored in subordinate clauses, "filling in," as it were, the space the temporal MF has gradually abandoned.

Verb Class
The final linguistic factor relevant to the selection of PF and MF is verb class. In Aaron's (2006, 2010) diachronic analysis, she found that as the PF became generalized as the main form of expressing future events, it gradually lost its favorability for verbs of movement only. That is, it begins to surface with other verb classes. This is seen as a sign that its semanticization to future expression from its original meaning of motion-to-a-goal is at a later stage (see Hopper and Traugott 2003). Blas Arroyo (2008) finds a similar pattern in his synchronic analysis. We expect verb class to have lost predictive strength as the PF has become more generalized as future expression.

Independent Sociolinguistic Factors
Finally, we included four social factors including age, gender, socioeconomic level, and region to identify any patterns of use across social domains. Out of these, only region became a relevant object of analysis in our study.

All factors were entered into RBRUL (see Section 6.3.2 above) to perform a multivariate analysis. This allowed us to look at the contextual probability of the PF as contrasted with the MF.

6.4.4 Results
Table 6.1 displays the distribution of the PF and the MF across the two regional variants of Spanish (Mexico City, Mexico; and Malaga, Spain). The distributional frequencies of the PF and MF in these data sets showcase

Table 6.1 *Distribution of periphrastic future and morphological future across regions*

Region	PF	MF
Mexico City	95% (422/446)	5% (24/446)
Malaga	69% (211/306)	31% (95/306)

Table 6.2 *Distribution of modal MF and temporal MF between regions*

Region	Modal	Temporal
Mexico City	62% (24/63)	38% (24/63)
Malaga	25% (32/127)	75% (95/127)

a clear contrast between the Mexico City (PF 95%, MF 5%) and the Malaga (PF 69%, MF 31%) data. As a first impression, we can begin to see a distinction between the Mexican and Peninsular varieties.

In light of Aaron's (2010) findings, we compared the use of the MF as an epistemic modal expression relative to its use as a future temporal expression (see Table 6.2). Aaron found that the MF is becoming more specialized as an expression of epistemic modality (i.e. to express uncertainty of the speaker), and by means of this, together with the expansion of the PF as a general future expression, the MF has significantly lost ground in the temporal field. As seen in Table 6.2, the Mexican data shows very high use of the MF in its modal expression. The data from Malaga, on the other hand, shows very low percentages of modal use (25 percent). If Aaron's (2010) analysis is correct, it successfully explains the difference in expression of modal use between Mexico and Malaga. As the use of the MF reduces in temporal contexts in Mexico, we see a rise in the use of the modal uses. The opposite is true for the Malaga distribution. Therefore, it is plausible to say that the PF has further advanced in Mexico as the general expression of temporal futurity than it has in Malaga.

The final step of our study involved a variable rule analysis of the factors identified in Section 6.4.3. After several statistical runs, we found that certain factors were consistently being excluded from the model. The factors excluded were polarity, adverbial specification, age, gender, and socioeconomic level. By reducing the number of factors and maintaining the ones that, according to previous studies, have demonstrated consistent predictive power, we were able to strengthen the predictive power of our model. Therefore, the factors inputted in the final model were region, person, clause type, sentence type, verb type, and temporal proximity. Our application value was the PF.

In Table 6.3 we provide the factors that were selected by the variable rule analysis in order from most to least significant. The significant factors included region, person, sentence type, and clause type. Verb type and temporal proximity were not selected as significant. We provide their factor weights in brackets.

The factor to show the highest significant value ($p < 0.000$) was region. The results for region go on a par with the distributional frequencies shown in Tables 6.1 and 6.2. As we can see, the Mexico City data set strongly favors the use of the PF with a factor weight of 0.778. The Malaga data set, on the

Table 6.3 *Contribution of linguistic and extralinguistic factors selected as significant predictor of PF across two data sets*

Factor Group	Probability	% (N)
Region		
Mexico City	0.778	95% (424/446)
Malaga	0.222	69% (211/306)
Range	56	
Person		
1	0.684	91% (293/322)
2	0.468	84% (86/102)
3	0.345	77% (253/328)
Range	34	
Sentence Type		
Exclamatory-interrogative	0.671	88% (106/121)
Indirect interrogative	0.416	83% (35/42)
Declarative or other	0.408	83% (495/589)
Range	26	
Clause Type		
Subordinate	0.604	87% (128/147)
Other	0.396	84% (505/605)
Range	21	
Temporal Proximity		
Hodiernal (same day)	[0.706]	94% (125/133)
Attenuated distance	[0.603]	75% (6/8)
Indefinite distance	[0.492]	84% (470/559)
Intermediate distance	[0.353]	74% (25/34)
Maximum distance	[0.342]	56% (10/18)
Verb Class		
Movement	[0.654]	87% (76/87)
Other	[0.625]	85% (517/608)
Perception	[0.43]	76% (32/42)
Cognition	[0.297]	47% (7/15)
Logarithmic likelihood = −257.428 N = 752 Input = 0.92 R^2 = 0.41		

other hand, shows a highly disfavoring factor weight of 0.222. This factor group displays the greatest magnitude, with a range of 56.

The second factor group selected as significant was person of the subject. The PF is favored in contexts where the subject is in the first person (0.684). Though second person was disfavored in this analysis, it was only slightly so with a borderline factor weight of 0.468. Another point of interest to make is the strong disfavoring of the PF when its subjects are third person (weight of 0.345).

The last two factors selected were sentence type and clause type. With regard to sentence type, exclamatory-interrogative sentences favor the use of PF with a factor weight of 0.671. In terms of clause type, the use of PF is favored in subordinate clauses with a factor weight of 0.604 and is disfavored in matrix and other clauses with a weight of 0.396.

Temporal proximity, though not selected as significant, is worthy of mention given its relative importance in previous studies. The probability of the PF being selected over the MF is higher when the temporal expression involves hodiernal or attenuated time.

Another factor group not selected in the model was verb type; however, as discussed previously, this factor has been important in tracking the grammaticalization of the PF as a temporal structure. Verbs of movement and other (i.e. of state, of volition, of activity) highly favor the use of the PF, with factor weights of 0.654 and 0.625 respectively. In contrast, verbs of perception slightly disfavor the PF, with a weight of 0.43, and verbs of cognition strongly disfavor the use of PF (0.297).

6.4.5 Discussion

Region

Considering the results in order of significance, the regional factor was selected as the more impacting variable in the statistical model and as the only extralinguistic variable. The use of the PF has a strong probability of surfacing in the Mexican data. This result indicates that the PF in the Mexican data set has become much more generalized as the default future expression, while speakers in Malaga maintain a more conservative stance or perhaps follow a slower rate of change. That is, the MF in Malaga still maintains vitality as a future expression, making up 31 percent of the contexts of temporal future expression (cf. Mexico City, MF 5 percent). However, in both varieties (Mexico City 95%, Malaga 69%) the PF is commonly used as a form of future expression.

In addition to this, as explained above, the MF in Malaga is not as limited in contexts of modal expression (25 percent) as it is in the Mexican data (62 percent). It is plausible to say that, at least from our evidence in the Mexican data, the MF has been for the most part reanalyzed (see Harris and Campbell, 1995) as a modal expression, limiting its use to a specialized context and therefore becoming replaced by the PF.

Our findings corroborate those of other studies into Latin American Spanish. Studies of the future expression in the Spanish of Venezuela (Sedano 1994), Colombia (Giraldo 1962), Chile (Silva-Corvalán and Terrell 1989), Mexico (e.g. Lastra and Butragueño 2010), among others, all indicate that the PF is favored as the main expression of futurity. In a contact variety of Spanish in Spain, Castellón Spanish, Blas Arroyo (2008) finds that the MF is more resistant in this region given its strong vitality in Catalan. The results obtained in the present study may reflect a more general trend in the peninsula, where the MF has maintained ground in temporal future expression, and may not necessarily be due solely to influence from Catalan.

Person

The second factor selected was person. First-person subjects favor the use of the PF over the MF, while third persons disfavor the PF with a factor weight of 0.345. These results confirm our hypothesis that if the PF carries more agency and determinacy, it will be favored by first and second persons. Although second persons do not favor the PF in our model, their disfavoring factor is close to neutral with a weight of 0.468. Our assumption of first subjects carrying more agency – which contributes higher subjectivity – is based on the inherent nature of first persons being animate, namely human. On the other hand, the MF, as seen in our results, would be favored in contexts of indeterminacy and less agency. This explains why the MF in our data sets is favored more with third-person subjects, which could be animate or inanimate. These findings go on a par with the literature, which suggest that the PF is associated with higher levels of certainty, determinacy, and agency than is the MF (Orozco 2005).

Sentence Type

As for sentence type, our model shows the PF to be the preferred choice of future temporal expression when in exclamatory-interrogative sentences, which are assumed to be the contexts of higher subjectivity. In line with Aaron (2006) and Blas Arroyo (2008), we postulate that declarative sentences express a "default" proposition and therefore are not inherently subjective in comparison to exclamatory-interrogative. In this sense, our hypothesis is confirmed in that the PF, given its agentive origin, is preferred in contexts of higher subjectivity (i.e. exclamatory-interrogative) than the MF.

Clause Type

Next up is clause type. Clause type turned out to be significant, with the results indicating that the PF is favored in subordinate clauses relative to the MF. This finding is consistent with previous studies (e.g. Aaron 2006, 2010; Blas Arroyo 2008; Tarallo 1989). It goes against Bybee's (2003) proposal that matrix clauses attract innovation. If this were the case we would expect to see the PF more prominent in matrix clauses than the MF. Bybee predicts that grammaticalized uses of subjunctive forms in Spanish tend to be entrenched in subordinate clauses while the prevalent indicative forms will be found in the more common matrix clauses. Nonetheless, Aaron (2006, 2010) highlights that the MF and PF did not share the same modal relationship as the indicative and subjunctive. Rather, the MF expressed modality from its inception as an expression of futurity in the documented cases that she studies in the 13th century, and was used in both matrix and subordinate clauses. Aaron (2006) also notes that, as the PF began to occupy more ground in the futurity reading, it gained dominance over subordinate clauses (i.e. around the 19th century), and consequently the MF lost favorability in this context. While Aaron (2006) tentatively claims that this result could be a consequence of the nature of verbs of motion occurring in subordinate clauses, she does not go further in her explanation.

Temporal Proximity

The loss of distinction in temporal proximity between the PF and MF plausibly indicates that the PF is no longer strongly associated with imminence of time. That is, it predominates across all temporal distances. Given the lack of statistical significance, we can tentatively conclude that the loss of the older purposive reading of the PF has led to a gradual loss of the imminence reading.

We cannot however discard the vestiges of previous trends that the factor weights show in our analysis. For instance, these weights partially confirm previously stated hypotheses regarding the definiteness of the PF and the indefiniteness of the MF. What the literature indicates is that, given that the MF inherently bears an epistemic value that lacks definiteness and certainty, it is expected to be used as an expression of indefinite time or distal time (Claes and Ortiz-López 2011). Our study confirms this notion. After removing the epistemic uses of the MF, the PF still predominates in contexts of immediate and attenuated times, whereas the MF is favored in indefinite and distant times. The MF then, as Orozco (2005) postulates, continues to carry its traditional attribute of indefiniteness (e.g. *Algún día estudiaré* 'I will study one day'). This is not surprising given that it has frequently been observed that, in reanalysis, meaning is not entirely lost, but more often than not is added to over time (Harris and Campbell 1995; Traugott and Dasher 2002).

Verb Class

As with temporal proximity, it is worth discussing the trends found in verb type regardless of its lack of significance. Based on the theory of grammaticalization, we expect to see that as the PF becomes more generalized as the main expression of futurity it would lose its association with trajectory to a goal where it originated from. Aaron (2006, 2010) found that, although the PF gains ground over other types of verbs, it consistently maintains an association with verbs of movement. What we find is that although the PF has expanded its use to other verbs, it is still disfavored with verbs of perception and cognition. This goes in line with Blas Arroyo's (2008) results, which tap into the nature of polysemy. As noted above, in language change meaning is hardly ever lost; rather accretion of meaning is mapped onto a form. Therefore, we can conclude that the PF has not lost its original sense of trajectory to a goal; however, this notion has slowly lost its predictive power, allowing other types of verbs to be used with the PF.

The insignificance of temporal proximity and verb type leads us to tentatively conclude that the original meanings of the PF as motion-to-a-goal and purpose have been gradually lost. Therefore, the PF has indeed become the general expression of temporal futurity and, although it still carries some traces of these meanings, it no longer reads as a single independent verb of motion or as a purposive construction.

6.5 Conclusion

This chapter has presented a general perspective regarding corpus linguistics with a particular emphasis on providing a conceptualization of current practices in the field as well as challenges that this type of research has faced in recent years. While describing current challenges we have established some connections with sociolinguistic research, given that the two disciplines share similarities: both rely on data-driven approaches and empirical analysis. The chapter also offers some introductory information on available corpora in Spanish as well as resources and toolkits for searching and for statistical analyses. We hope our readers find this information useful and that it stimulates further research on this field.

The second part of the chapter was dedicated to illustrating a corpus analysis based on data from Mexico City and Malaga from PRESEEA 2014– . We used future expression as a linguistic variable to determine the linguistic and social constraints predicting the use of PF or MF in oral data. The findings reveal that that the PF in the Mexican data set has become much more generalized as the default future expression, while, in Malaga, speakers maintain a more conservative stance or are perhaps showing a slower rate of change. Furthermore, as the use of the MF is declining in temporal contexts in Mexico City, we see a rise in modal uses. The opposite is true for the Malaga distribution. The variable rule analysis demonstrated that factors predicting the use of PF versus MF were region, person, clause type, and sentence type. In contrast to traditional analysis, the corpus analysis presented in this chapter demonstrates that the distinction between PF and MF is not based on temporal proximity, showing the need to further investigate the linguistic constraints that explain variable structures such as future expression in oral data.

References

Aaron, J. E. (2006). Variation and Change in Spanish Future Temporal Expression (Doctoral dissertation). University of New Mexico.

Aaron, J. E. (2010). Pushing the Envelope: Looking beyond the Variable Context. *Language Variation and Change*, 22 (1), 1–36.

Alameda, J. R. and Cuetos, F. (1995). *Diccionario de frecuencias de las unidades lingüísticas del español*. Oviedo: Servicio de Publicaciones de la Universidad de Oviedo.

Anthony, L. (2013). A Critical Look at Software Tools in Corpus Linguistics. *Linguistic Research*, 30 (2), 141–161.

Arppe, A., Gilquin, G., Glynn, D., Hilpert, M., and Zeschel, A. (2010). Cognitive Corpus Linguistics: Five Points of Debate on Current Theory and Methodology. *Corpora*, 5 (1), 1–27.

Arppe, A. and Järvikivi, J. (2007). Every Method Counts: Combining Corpus-Based and Experimental Evidence in the Study of Synonymy. *Corpus Linguistics and Linguistic Theory*, 3 (2), 131–59.

Blas Arroyo, J. L. (2008). The Variable Expression of Future Tense in Peninsular Spanish: The Present (and Future) of Inflectional Forms in the Spanish Spoken in a Bilingual Region. *Language Variation and Change*, 20 (1), 85–126.

Boas, F. (ed.). (2013). *Handbook of American Indian Languages*. Cambridge University Press. [First published 1911–1922.]

Bybee, J. (2003). Cognitive Processes in Grammaticalization. *The New Psychology of Language: Cognitive and Functional Approaches to Language Structure*, 2, 145–167.

Bybee, J. (2006). *Frequency of Use and the Organization of Language*. Oxford: Oxford University Press.

Bybee, J. L. and Eddington, D. (2006). A Usage-Based Approach to Spanish Verbs of "Becoming." *Language*, 82 (2), 323–355.

Claes, J. and Ortiz-López, L. A. (2011). Restricciones pragmáticas y sociales en la expresión de futuridad en el español de Puerto Rico. *Spanish in Context*, 8 (1), 50–72.

Davies, M. (2006). *A Frequency Dictionary of Spanish: Core Vocabulary for Learners*. London: Routledge.

Davies, M. (2008). New Directions in Spanish and Portuguese Corpus Linguistics. *Studies in Hispanic and Lusophone Linguistics*, 1 (1), 149–186.

Díaz-Campos, Manuel. (2004). Acquisition of Sociolinguistic Variables in Spanish: Do Children Acquire Individual Lexical Forms or Variable Rules? In Timothy Face (ed.), *Laboratory Approaches to Spanish Phonology*. Berlin: De Gruyter, pp. 221–236.

Díaz-Campos, Manuel. (2011). Introduction. In Manuel Díaz-Campos (ed.), *The Handbook of Hispanic Sociolinguistics*. Chichester: John Wiley, pp. 1–7.

Díaz-Campos, M. and Geeslin, K. L. (2011). Copula Use in the Spanish of Venezuela: Is the Pattern Indicative of Stable Variation or an Ongoing Change? *Spanish in Context*, 8 (1), 73–94.

Giraldo, J. J. M. (1962). Sobre la categoría de futuro en el español de Colombia. *Thesaurus*, 1 (3), 527–555.

Harris, A. C. and Campbell, L. (1995). *Historical Syntax in Cross-Linguistic Perspective*. Cambridge: Cambridge University Press.

Hopper, P. J. and Traugott, E. C. (2003). *Grammaticalization*. Cambridge: Cambridge University Press.

Julliand, A. J. and Chang-Rodríguez, E. (1964). *The Spanish Frequency Word Book*. New York: Mouton.

Kanwit, M. (2017). What We Gain by Combining Variationist and Concept-Oriented Approaches: The Case of Acquiring Spanish Future-Time Expression. *Language Learning*. doi: 10.1111/lang.12234

Kilgarriff, A. (2015). Corpus Linguistics in Trademark Cases. *Dictionaries: Journal of the Dictionary Society of North America*, 36 (1), 100–114.

Lastra, Y. and Butragueño, P. (2010). Futuro perifrástico y futuro morfológico en el Corpus Sociolingüístico de la Ciudad de México. *Oralia*, 13, 145–171.

Lope Blanch, J. M. (1986). *El estudio del español hablado culto: historia de un proyecto*. Mexico City: UNAM, Instituto de Investigaciones Filológicas, Centro de Lingüística Hispánica.

Mukherjee, A. and Liu, B. (2012). Aspect Extraction through Semi-Supervised Modeling. In *Proceedings of the 50th Annual Meeting of the Association for Computational Linguistics: Long Papers*, Vol. 1, pp. 339–348. Available from https://aclweb.org/anthology/P/P12/P12-1.pdf (last access October 24, 2017).

Orozco, R. (2005). Distribution of Future Time Forms in Northern Colombian Spanish. In D. Eddington (ed.), *Selected Proceedings of the 7th Hispanic Linguistics Symposium*. Somerville, MA: Cascadilla, pp. 56–65.

PRESEEA (2014–). *Corpus del proyecto para el estudio sociolingüístico del español de España y de América*. Universidad de Alcalá. preseea.linguas.net

Samper Padilla, J. A., Hernández Cabrera, C. E., and Troya Déniz, M. (1998). *Macrocorpus de la norma lingüística culta de las principales ciudades de España y América*. Las Palmas de Gran Canaria: *Universidad de Las Palmas y ALFAL* [CD-ROM].

Sanz, I. (2009). The Diachrony of New Mexican Spanish, 1683–1926: Philology, Corpus Linguistics and Dialect Change (Doctoral dissertation). University of California, Berkeley.

Sapir, Edward (1916). *Time Perspective in Aboriginal American Culture, A Study in Method*. Ottawa: Government Printing Bureau.

Sedano, M. (1994). El futuro morfológico y la expresión *ir a* + infinitivo en el español hablado de Venezuela. Verba, 21, 225–240.

Silva-Corvalán, C. and Terrell, T. (1989). Notas sobre la expresión de futuridad en el español del Caribe. *Hispanic Linguistics*, 2, 191–208.

Tagliamonte, S. (2011). *Variationist Sociolinguistics: Change, Observation, Interpretation*. Malden, MA: Wiley-Blackwell.

Tarallo, F. (1989). Inside and Outside Relative Clauses. In R. Fasold and D. Schiffrin (eds.), *Language Change and Variation*. Washington, DC: Georgetown University Press, pp. 255–274.

Traugott, E. C. (1988). Pragmatic Strengthening and Grammaticalization. *Proceedings of the 14th Annual Meeting of the Berkeley Linguistics Society*, pp. 406–416.

Traugott, E. C. and Dasher, R. B. (2002). *Regularity in Semantic Change*. Cambridge: Cambridge University Press.

Zahler, S. and Daidone, D. (2014). A Variationist Account of Trill /r/ Usage in the Spanish of Málaga. *Indiana University Linguistics Club Working Papers*, 14 (2), 17–42.

Part II

The Spanish Sound System

7

Vowels

Rebecca Ronquest*

7.1 Introduction

The Spanish vowel system is one of the most common systems cross-linguistically (Disner 1984), consisting of five contrastive vowels that are distinguished by three degrees of height and backness. Despite the simplicity of the system, however, considerable research on both monolingual and bilingual Spanish vowel systems has revealed that vowels are highly influenced by a variety of linguistic and extralinguistic factors. This chapter begins with a brief description of the basic articulatory and acoustic properties of Spanish vowels to help familiarize readers with some of the terminology that will be employed throughout. The following two portions of the chapter focus on addressing the influence of linguistic factors on vowel production, namely syllable structure and lexical stress. Subsequent sections describe additional sources of variation, including speech style and speaking rate, dialect, and sociolinguistic factors. A brief description of bilingual vowel systems is presented next, followed by directions for future research. The chapter concludes with some general closing remarks.

7.2 Basic Articulatory and Acoustic Properties of Spanish Vowels

In articulatory terms, the five vowel phonemes of Spanish are categorized based on their height, backness, and the presence or absence of lip rounding (Hualde 2005). The elevation of the tongue body produces three distinct levels of vowel height, such that /i/ and /u/ are classified as *high*, /e/ and /o/ as *mid*, and /a/ as *low*. Vowels are further classified along the front–back

---

* I would like to sincerely thank two anonymous reviewers for their helpful comments and suggestions on this work. All errors are my own.

	front	central	back
high	i		u
mid	e		o
low		a	
	unrounded		rounded

Figure 7.1 Articulatory classification of Spanish vowels

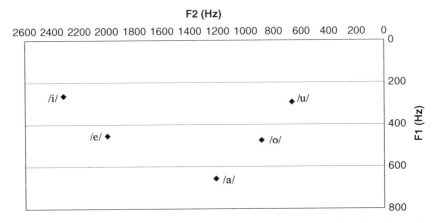

Figure 7.2 Acoustic distribution of Spanish vowels: mean formant values of male speakers of Spanish
Source: Quilis and Esgueva (1983)

dimension based on the proximity of the tongue body to the anterior or posterior portion of the buccal cavity: /i/ and /e/ are *front* vowels, /a/ is a *central* vowel, and /o/ and /u/ are *back* vowels. The back vowels are also considered *rounded* given that they are produced with lip rounding, while the other three phonemes are *unrounded*. Figure 7.1 presents the articulatory classification of the Spanish vowel system (based on Hualde 2005).

The distinct positions of the tongue and lips upon producing the Spanish vowel phonemes result in their being characterized by different vocal tract resonances, or *formants*, which consist of concentrations of energy in certain frequency ranges. The first two formant frequencies (hereafter F1 and F2) are sufficient to distinguish the Spanish vowels (Martínez Celdrán 1995). Figure 7.2 depicts the organization and distribution of the Spanish vowels within the acoustic space based on the F1 and F2 values presented in Quilis and Esgueva (1983), which were obtained from 16 male speakers of Spanish from various parts of Spain and Latin America. Note that the vowels are distributed fairly symmetrically and are relatively equidistant from one another.

The duration of Spanish vowels has not been discussed extensively in the literature, although those studies that do include analyses of duration (e.g. Chládková *et al.* 2011; Marín Gálvez 1995; Ronquest

2012) have revealed intrinsic duration (i.e. high vowels are shorter than low vowels; see, for example, Lehiste 1970). As will be described at various points throughout this chapter, vowel duration is also influenced by factors such as consonantal context, stress, speech style, and gender.

The simplicity and symmetry characteristic of the Spanish vowel system appears to have led to the assumption of little variability in their production, or at least less variation than that observed in the consonantal system. Indeed, Navarro Tomás (1918, sec. 43) noted that the timbre (quality) of Spanish vowels is generally stable throughout their articulation, although he does state that contextual and stylistic factors can result in minor phonetic differences. An examination of some of the earliest studies of Spanish vowels reveals four recurrent claims concerning the (lack of) variability in the Spanish vowel system:

1 The mid vowels have at least two distinct allophones depending on the type of syllable (closed or open) in which they occur.
2 Lexical stress has little impact on vowel quality and duration.
3 Vowels produced in rapid speech and more spontaneous styles tend to be centralized relative to those produced in slower, more controlled speech.
4 The Spanish vowels are relatively stable across dialects.

Each of these points will be discussed in Sections 7.3 through 7.6 by summarizing the impressionistic and acoustic studies related to each topic. The remainder of the chapter is dedicated to describing additional sources of variation and suggesting ways in which they may be addressed in future studies.

7.3 Syllable Structure and Consonantal Context

Navarro Tomás (1918) was one of the first to note distinct quality differences in vowels based on their surrounding consonantal context. He argued that all five vowel phonemes have at least three distinct allophones depending on the nature of the adjacent consonants and/or if the syllable is closed or open. Of greatest interest here are the close and open allophones of the mid vowels, as they have received the most attention in the literature.[1] According to Navarro Tomás, the distribution of the mid vowel allophones – close [e] and [o] and open [ɛ] and [ɔ], respectively – depends not only on if the syllable is closed or open, but also on which consonant closes the syllable. While the close allophones of both vowels are argued to surface in open syllables with primary or secondary stress, [e] is also

---

[1] Further detail concerning phonetic variation of the low and high vowels can be found in Navarro Tomás (1918), sec. 45 through 63.

described as occurring in syllables closed by orthographic *d, m, n, s, z*. The open allophones [ɛ] and [ɔ] occur when preceded or followed by /r/ or preceding /x/, but also in closed syllables, again, depending on the consonantal context: [ɛ] surfaces in syllables closed by consonants other than *d, m, n, s, z*, and [ɔ] in syllables closed by any consonant and in accented position between an /a/ and a following /l/ or /r/. Despite the detailed descriptions of the contexts in which each of these allophones occurs, he argued that the differences between the open, close, and relaxed versions of Spanish vowels are very slight, although the difference between the close and open allophones of the mid vowels are described as more noticeable than the same differences in the high vowels.

Acoustic investigations of the allophonic differences described by Navarro Tomás (1918), however, have generally failed to reveal compelling evidence that the variations in openness are robust enough to warrant distinct allophones. Although in general terms most studies have documented more open vowels in closed syllables and close vowels in open syllables, some investigations did not employ statistical analyses, or, if quantitative methods were applied, the differences failed to reach statistical significance (Martínez Celdrán 1984; Matluck 1952; Morrison 2004; Servín and Rodríguez 2001).[2] The only acoustic investigations that seem to have confirmed the presence of mid vowel allophones were conducted by Skelton (1969) and Jurado and Arenas (2005). Skelton, who analyzed vowels produced by 20 speakers from Spain and Latin America, argued that the overlap of the /e/ in open syllables with the space of /i/ evidenced two distinct allophones for the front mid vowel. Jurado and Arenas concluded that open [ɛ] and [ɔ] occurred only in syllables that were closed by /r/, thus confirming Navarro Tomás' (1918) observations, but their study analyzed the speech of only one male speaker from Argentina.

Given the lack of overwhelming evidence supporting the presence of open and close mid vowel allophones based on syllable structure alone, differences in vowel quality and duration might be better understood taking into consideration consonantal context in addition to syllable structure. Research examining coarticulatory effects between vowels and surrounding consonants in other languages has proven that the place and manner of adjacent segments have a significant impact on vowel quality (Stevens and House 1963) and duration (House and Fairbanks 1953; Peterson and Lehiste 1960). With specific reference to the Spanish language, Chládková *et al.* (2011) reported that some of the differences between Iberian and Peruvian Spanish vowels stemmed from the articulatory and acoustic properties of a following /s/. Bradlow's (2002) analysis of the high vowels in the context of /bV/ and /dV/ revealed considerable

---

[2] In acoustic terms, the open allophones [ɛ] and [ɔ] are characterized by higher F1 values (i.e. lower in the acoustic space) and are slightly more centralized along the F2 dimension.

lowering of F2 of /u/ in the context of /b/ relative to /d/, although the same trend was not observed for /i/. Recasens (1987) also described that, for some CVC sequences in Spanish and Catalan, the magnitude of coarticulatory effects depended on the degree of articulatory constraint.

Analyses of vowel duration have also revealed a complex interplay of syllable structure and consonantal context. Quilis and Esgueva (1983), for example, found that vowels were shortest in the context of /p/, longer when adjacent to /m/, and longest in contact with /b/. Additionally, Chládková et al. (2011) noted that, in the context of /f/ and /s/, the non-back vowels produced by women were longer than those produced by men. Furthermore, Marín Gálvez (1995) reported that vowels followed by fricatives in closed syllables were longer than vowels followed by fricatives in open syllables, but that the opposite pattern was observed for vowels that occurred in contact with nasal and liquid consonants.

Combined research focusing on syllable structure and consonantal context confirms that the acoustic properties of the Spanish vowels are influenced by the phonetic environment in which they are produced. The fine-grained phonetic differences based on the surrounding consonantal context described in previous studies, however, may very well reflect a cross-linguistic tendency, suggesting that coarticulation with adjacent segments may play an equally important (or perhaps larger) role in influencing Spanish vowel quality and quantity (duration) than does syllable structure alone.

7.4 Stress

Despite the observation in Navarro Tomás (1918) that unstressed (atonic) vowels tend to be more "relaxed" than stressed (tonic) vowels, especially in rapid speech, the general assumption is that unstressed vowels in Spanish are not characterized by the same magnitude of reduction typical in English and other languages. While Delattre's (1969) acoustic examination of stressed and unstressed vowels in English, German, French, and Spanish confirmed less reduction in Spanish than in English, additional research does reveal the presence of fine-grained phonetic and durational differences. Quilis and Esgueva (1983) noted slight quality differences between tonic and atonic vowels produced by both male and female speakers, describing a tendency for tonic vowels to be more open than their atonic counterparts. Sadowsky (2012) reported similar tendencies in his analysis of Chilean Spanish, also describing that atonic vowels tended to be slightly more centralized along the F2 dimension, but the trend was not consistent for all vowels within the system and differed depending on if the unstressed vowel was pre- or post-tonic. Willis (2008) noted substantial centralization of unstressed vowels in Dominican Spanish semi-spontaneous speech, although individual speakers varied in terms of the magnitude and direction of the effects. Nadeu's (2014) investigation of Catalan and Spanish vowel systems revealed that, while Catalan speakers showed consistent trends of unstressed vowel reduction, Spanish speakers' productions were highly variable and no clear or consistent pattern could be observed. Finally, durational differences between stressed and unstressed vowels in Peninsular Spanish were reported by Marín Gálvez (1995), who found that, with the exception of /u/, unstressed vowels were always shorter than their stressed counterparts. In conjunction, investigations of the impact of lexical stress on vowels produced by monolingual speakers of Spanish do reveal some minor quality and durational differences, although none suggest the presence of a schwa-like vowel that is characteristic of English. As will be discussed in Section 7.8, however, bilingual speakers of Spanish often exhibit larger stress-induced quality and quantity differences than those described for monolinguals.

7.5 Speech Style and Speaking Rate

Unlike syllable type and stress, the influence of speech style and speaking rate on Spanish vowels has not been addressed extensively in the literature. Even though (or perhaps because) Navarro Tomás (1918) mentioned that vowels produced in slow, emphatic speech are characterized by more stable and consistent timbre than those produced in rapid speech, much of the initial research on Spanish vowel systems has entailed analyses of vowels produced in isolated CVCV (nonce) words or within words embedded in a carrier phrase (Bradlow 1995; Godínez 1978; Martínez Celdrán 1995; Morrison and Escudero 2007; Quilis and Esgueva 1983, among others). Harmegnies and Poch-Olivé's (1992) acoustic investigation was one of the first to directly examine the impact of speech style (i.e. controlled versus (semi-) spontaneous) on vowel quality in Castilian Spanish.[3] Although their study analyzed the speech of only one male informant, they found that vowels produced in the semi-directed interview (spontaneous style) were more centralized in the acoustic space relative to those produced in the word list. Subsequent investigations of stylistic variation in other dialects confirm a general trend of vowel space expansion in controlled speech in both monolingual (Martín Butragueño 2014; Poch-Olivé *et al.* 2008; Willis 2008) and bilingual (Alvord and Rogers 2014; Bradlow 2002; Ronquest 2016; Willis 2005) varieties.[4] Nadeu (2014) reported similar effects in her examination of speaking rate, in which vowels produced in the fast condition were centralized relative to those that were produced at a normal speaking rate. Style- and speaking rate-

---

[3] In studies examining stylistic effects on Spanish vowels, different tasks often serve as a proxy for different styles: Interviews and narratives are generally employed to elicit the least controlled, most spontaneous style, while isolated words or word lists represent the most careful, controlled style.

[4] Dialects investigated in these studies include Mexican, Dominican, and Cuban.

induced variability in Spanish is not surprising, given that vowel space expansion in controlled speech has been documented in other languages and likely represents a cross-linguistic tendency (see, for example, Ferguson and Kewley-Port 2007; Moon and Lindblom 1994; Smiljanić and Bradlow 2005, among others).

7.6 Dialectal Variation

As mentioned in Section 7.2, the Spanish vowel system is traditionally described as both simple and symmetrical – a characterization that has, perhaps, contributed to the notion that vowels are produced relatively similarly throughout the Spanish-speaking world. According to Hualde (2005:128), "[v]owel qualities are remarkably stable among Spanish dialects. There is nothing in Spanish like the differences in vowel quality we find across geographical and social varieties of English." Although certainly true in comparative terms, impressionistic and acoustic research has revealed at least *some* regional variation in vowel production. This section of the chapter includes a summary of several cross-dialectal comparisons of the vowel system as a whole, followed by a description of some region-specific pronunciations of certain vowels.

Acoustic investigations of cross-dialectal variation have revealed some notable differences in terms of both vowel quality and quantity, although the effects are often limited to specific vowels and are not systematic. A comparison of Mexican, Argentine, and Peninsular vowels presented in Godínez (1978), for example, revealed a more condensed vowel space in Peninsular Spanish relative to the other two varieties. In addition, he reported a higher position of /e/ and /i/ in the Argentine variety compared to the Mexican and Peninsular varieties, with /e/ in Argentine Spanish higher than /e/ in Mexican Spanish and /i/ in Argentine Spanish higher than /i/ in Peninsular Spanish. Quilis and Esgueva (1983) analyzed vowels produced by male and female speakers from Mexico, Ecuador, Chile, and various regions throughout Spain. They noted distributional differences across speakers from different regions, but no clear pattern emerged. With respect to duration, however, they found that, on average, the vowels produced by Latin American speakers were slightly longer than those produced by Spaniards. Willis (2008) also described differences in distribution between Dominican Spanish vowels and those presented in Quilis and Esgueva, although he acknowledges that the vowels analyzed in his study were obtained from a different type of speech (semi-spontaneous). O'Rourke (2010) offers a comparison of Spanish vowels produced in Lima and Cuzco, Peru, reporting a more condensed vowel space for the Lima speakers relative to those from Cuzco. She hypothesizes that the differences in distribution could stem from language contact with Quechua. Finally, Sadowsky (2012) compared vowels produced by the Chilean speakers in his study to nearly all of the formant values obtained from previous works. A visual comparison of the vowel spaces suggests that no two dialects of Spanish are characterized by the exact same distribution and formant values, although, again, the type of speech in which vowels were produced and the gender, age, and social class of the speakers vary across studies.

Two additional investigations conducted by Morrison and Escudero (2007) and Chládková *et al.* (2011) compared the vowel systems of speakers from Lima, Peru, and Madrid, Spain, taking into consideration both vowel quality and quantity. The results of Morrison and Escudero's analyses revealed that Peruvian vowels were characterized by longer duration and higher fundamental frequency (F0).[5] Comparisons of individual vowel quality, however, revealed that only /o/ differed across the two varieties, as it was characterized by a lower F2 (i.e. more retracted) in Peruvian Spanish. A larger-scale study carried out by Chládková *et al.* confirmed Morrison and Escudero's initial finding of lengthened duration in Peruvian Spanish compared to Iberian Spanish, attributing the durational variation to differences in speaking rate. Cross-system comparisons revealed additional quality differences and a general trend for more peripheral vowels in Peruvian Spanish relative to Iberian Spanish. A closer examination of coarticulatory effects based on the surrounding consonantal context revealed that the cross-dialectal differences were particularly robust in the context of /s/, in which Peruvian Spanish /o/ and /u/ were produced further back and /i/ further front than their Iberian counterparts. The tendency for Iberian Spanish vowels to centralize in the /s/ context was attributed to articulatory and acoustic differences concerning the production of /s/ itself: Iberian Spanish /s/, which is concave and apico-alveolar in north-central varieties, was characterized by a lower center of gravity than the dental /s/ of Peruvian, ultimately resulting in the observed differences in F2. Taken together, the results indicate that the acoustic properties of Spanish vowels are fairly similar across dialects, although differences in speaking rate and variation in the pronunciation of the *consonants* may actually influence the phonetic properties of the Spanish vowels.

Despite the relative similarity of vowels across dialects of Spanish, a number of vowel-related dialectal phenomena, such as quality differences in final mid vowels and subsequent vowel harmony, raising of unstressed final vowels, and unstressed vowel reduction or devoicing, have been documented in various regions throughout Spain and Latin America. In the eastern portions of Andalusia, for example, where word-final /s/ is often deleted, the mid and low vowels (i.e. /e/, /o/, and /a/) can vary in quality as a means to signal the morphological difference between singular and plural. As impressionistically described by Alvar (1991), the mid

---

[5] For readers unfamiliar with the concept, F0 can be defined as "the number of repetitions or cycles of a periodic wave per unit of time..." (Hualde 2005:60).

vowels are produced with the more open allophones [ɛ] and [ɔ] in plural forms as compared to singular forms (cf. *pobre* 'poor' [poβre] vs. *pobres* 'poor.PL.' [poβrɛ]; *niño* 'boy' [niɲo] vs. *niños* 'boys' [niɲɔ]). The low vowel /a/ is also affected, and typically produced with a more fronted articulation in the plural. The final vowel in the plural noun *niñas* 'girls,' for example, is more advanced, and can even approximate a very open form of *–e* (Alvar 1991:235) which Hualde (2005:130) approximates with English /æ/. Vowel harmony, in which the quality of the final vowel may also spread to other vowels within the word, is also common in this region, resulting in pronunciations such as [lɔβɔ] for *lobos* 'wolves' (Hualde 2005:130 and references therein).[6]

Several impressionistic and acoustic studies have described the raising of unstressed final mid vowels (e.g. *leche* 'milk' [letʃe] produced as [letʃi]) in parts of Spain, Puerto Rico, and Mexico (Barajas 2014; Holmquist 1985, 1998, 2005; Oliver Rajan 2007). Holmquist (1985) documented raising of final /o/ to [u] in northwestern Spain, and Holmquist (1998, 2005) and Oliver Rajan (2007) reported the raising of both mid vowels in Puerto Rico, although final /o/ was raised somewhat more frequently than /e/. Holmquist's (1998, 2005) investigations also revealed a greater likelihood of raising when the vowel was in contact with a preceding palatal and/or a following high tonic vowel. Barajas' (2014) extensive acoustic study in Michoacán, Mexico, confirmed many of the findings reported in earlier, impressionistic work.[7] She found that target vowels that were situated in pronouns, in words in utterance-final position, and in words with penultimate stress, and vowels that were preceded or followed by a palatal consonant, were characterized by the most raising. In addition, the length of the word (number of syllables) influenced vowel raising differently: while raising of /e/ was more frequent in shorter words, longer words promoted raising of /o/. In contrast to previous studies, however, Barajas reported that /e/ was raised more frequently than /o/, and the number of independent variables found to influence raising differed for each vowel. Analysis of vowel formants indicated that the raised variants of both /e/ and /o/ were fronted along the F2 dimension, resulting in the raised /e/ converging on the acoustic space of /i/, but the raised /o/ moving away from /u/. Combined, the results of this large-scale study revealed that the influence of linguistic and extralinguistic factors on mid vowel raising in the Mexican community was not necessarily identical for both vowel phonemes. As will be described in the next section of this chapter, a variety of social factors was found to influence the presence and frequency of mid vowel raising in all of the studies described above.

An additional dialectal phenomenon concerns the reduction of unstressed mid vowels in word-internal position, which has been

---

[6] Vowel harmony and metaphony are also documented in Asturias and Cantabria, but will not be discussed here. For additional review and references, see Hualde (2005).

[7] Although Holmquist's (1985, 1998, 2005) studies are impressionistic, Oliver Rajan (2007) does include some acoustic analysis of vowel formants.

documented in parts of central Mexico and the Andean region. Henríquez Ureña (1938) was the first to comment that the atonic vowels in Mexican Spanish were very short in duration, "reduced," and often deleted in certain contexts. Further exploration of this topic has revealed that reduction and/or deletion of the unstressed mid vowels is most common in the context of voiceless consonants, and more specifically, when preceding /s/ (Lope Blanch 1963; Matluck 1952). Matluck argued that the position of the vowel within the word influenced the frequency of reduction, with word-final vowels reducing and deleting more than word-medial vowels. He also observed reduction in word-initial position, which often resulted in a lengthened following consonant (e.g. *enero* 'January' as [n:ero]). Conversely, Lope Blanch (1963) argued that consonantal context was more influential than word position, reporting the most reduction in the context of a preceding voiceless stop (i.e. /ptk/) and a following /s/. Cases of true deletion were primarily limited to two lexical items, namely *pues* 'well' and *entonces* 'then.'

Delforge's (2008) acoustic examination of the same phenomenon in Andean Spanish confirmed many of the details presented in earlier, impressionistic work, among them the gradient nature of reduction and the greater likelihood (in general) of reduction in word-final position. In contrast, however, Delforge reported that unstressed vowel "reduction" might be better described as devoicing, in that more than half of the unstressed vowel tokens analyzed exhibited varying degrees of devoicing as opposed to actual quality (i.e. F1 and F2) differences. In addition, she noted that /e/, /i/, and /u/ were the vowels most likely to undergo some form of devoicing, and that contact with consonants such as assibilated /r/ and affricates, as well as /s/, promoted devoicing.

In summary, although the Spanish vowel system is simple in nature, considerable research has documented at least some minor differences in formant values and duration across dialects. Impressionistic and acoustic analyses of region-specific characteristics indicate that, like the consonantal system, the pronunciation of the Spanish vowels does vary geographically.

7.7 Sociolinguistic Factors

Research on Spanish vowels has also established a connection between vowel production and sociolinguistic factors such as gender, sexual orientation, social class, age, and social networks. Investigations of vowels produced by male and female speakers of various dialects have revealed lengthened duration and a generally larger vowel space (i.e. higher frequencies) for women compared to men (Chládková *et al.* 2011; Quilis and Esgueva 1983, among others). These findings are expected given the physiological differences (i.e. vocal tract length) between men and women, and such trends are well documented in other languages (see, for example, Hillenbrand, Getty, Clark, and Wheeler 1995). The impact of sexual orientation on vowel quality in Puerto Rican and Peninsular Spanish has also been investigated by Mack (2009) and Osle Ezquerra (2015), respectively. Mack reported that higher F2 values of /e/ correlated with a greater likelihood of a speaker being perceived as gay, whereas Osle Ezquerra described that the height (F1) of the back vowels differed among gay and straight males. Thus, while the impact of gender on vowel quality is well understood, the relationship between the acoustic properties of Spanish vowels and sexual orientation has yet to be fully explored.

Soto-Barba (2007) and Sadowsky (2012) noted that the acoustic distribution of vowels varied considerably based on social class. Soto-Barba's examination of vowels produced by speakers of three different social classes (urban upper class, urban lower class, and rural lower class) in the province of Ñuble, Chile, revealed that rural speakers produced vowels more peripherally than the other two groups, and especially the urban upper class, whose vowels were the most centralized in the acoustic space. The author attributes the greater dispersion of the rural speakers' vowels to lengthened duration, which permits additional stability in formants. Sadowsky (2012) also reported that the vowel systems of men and women residing in Concepción, Chile, contain multiple allophones that are socially stratified. In contrast to Soto-Barba, however, he found that vowels produced by women of the elite class were the most peripheral, and that allophonic differences in women's speech were more numerous than those in men's speech. As the women of the lower-middle and middle class exhibited the greatest number of allophonic variations, he concluded that the vowel system of Concepción is undergoing restructuring, with middle-class women leading a change in progress.

Returning to some of the dialectal phenomena discussed in Section 7.6, unstressed vowel raising has also been found to correlate with multiple social factors (Barajas 2014; Holmquist 1985, 1998, 2005; Oliver Rajan 2007). Despite the different locations and populations described in each of these studies, several general trends emerge. Vowel raising tended to be most common among older speakers, those with lower levels of education, those with less mobility (i.e. spend more time in the community), and among members of dense social networks. Holmquist (1985) reported greater frequency of vowel raising among male speakers in Spain, although his subsequent investigations of men and women in Puerto Rico (1998, 2005, respectively) revealed similar tendencies across genders.

Although brief, the literature survey above confirms that sociolinguistic factors play an important role in shaping the Spanish vowel system. As will be discussed in greater detail in Section 7.9, future studies may consider exploring these relationships further.

7.8 Vowel Systems of Bilingual Spanish Speakers

Investigations of bilingual speech have revealed a number of important differences and similarities between the vowel systems of monolingual and bilingual speakers of Spanish and other languages. As a complete review of all of the bilingual literature will not be possible here given space limitations, this section will focus on summarizing some of the major trends observed in Spanish vowels produced by English learners of Spanish, Spanish–English balanced bilinguals, and heritage speakers of Spanish.[8] When relevant, reference to other bilingual populations will be presented.[9]

A recurring observation across studies of bilingual Spanish vowel systems concerns differences in acoustic organization and distribution. Generally speaking, the vowel systems of most learners and bilinguals tend to be less symmetrical, and vowels are often not distributed as equidistantly as they are traditionally depicted, especially among lower-level learners and less-proficient bilinguals (Boomershine 2012; Cobb and Simonet 2015; Menke and Face 2010; Ronquest 2012; Willis 2005). All of the aforementioned studies, as well as Grijalva *et al.* (2013), have noted that /u/ is more fronted in learner and bilingual speech when compared to monolingual norms. Boomershine (2012) and Ronquest (2012) reported a raised and backed /e/ and a more greatly dispersed front vowel space relative to the back vowel space. Cobb and Simonet (2015) also found variation in the production of /e/, but, as will be discussed below, differences across groups were significant only when taking into consideration the presence or absence of lexical stress. In addition to a more fronted /u/, Willis (2005) also observed that the bilingual speakers' /a/ was fronted relative to monolingual /a/ (based on values presented in Quilis and Esgueva 1983) and that it approached the location of English /æ/. Distributional differences have also been reported for bilingual speakers of Spanish and Quechua. As pointed out by O'Rourke (2010), Quechua–Spanish bilinguals produced /a/ and /u/ similarly to the native monolingual speakers of Spanish, but their /e/ more closely approximated that produced by the Spanish learners, resulting in a hybrid system for the bilinguals.

Bilinguals, and especially English learners of Spanish at low and intermediate levels, have also been shown to reduce unstressed vowels more than monolingual controls, although not all vowels are affected equally (Bland 2016; Cobb and Simonet 2015; Menke and Face 2010). Bland (2016), for example, found that unstressed vowels were shorter and more centralized along the F2 dimension in the speech of L2 learners at three different

---

[8] A *heritage speaker* can be defined as a bilingual who was "raised in a home where a non-English language is spoken. The [individual] may speak or merely understand the heritage language and be, to some degree, bilingual in English and the heritage language" (Valdés 2005:412).

[9] Research examining vowels produced by Catalan–Spanish bilinguals is notably absent from this section. Much of this research, however, focuses on bilingual speakers' production of Catalan vowels as opposed to their production of Spanish vowels. For further information, consult Amengual (2011, 2016), Mora *et al.* (2015), and Simonet (2011).

levels. Cobb and Simonet (2015) reported that stress differences manifested only in the intermediate learners' productions of /e/, in that tonic /e/ was situated higher in the acoustic space than atonic /e/. All three groups of bilingual speakers (first-, second-, and third-generation immigrants of Cuban descent) described in Alvord and Rogers' (2014) investigation exhibited at least some differences in stressed and unstressed vowel quality, although the patterns were not consistent across groups and dimensions. Most unstressed vowels exhibited a slight movement toward the center along the F2 dimension, but were actually higher (lower F1) in the acoustic space and therefore not centralized in the direction of schwa (with the exception of /a/). Ronquest's (2013) investigation of Spanish vowels produced by heritage speakers revealed similar trends with respect to quality, as well as a proportionally larger durational difference between tonic and atonic vowels than has been reported for monolinguals: heritage speakers' atonic vowels were approximately 30 percent shorter than tonic vowels, whereas Marín Gálvez (1995) reported a 20 percent decrease in monolingual speech. When taken together, the influence of stress on bilingual vowel systems reflects some general tendencies observed in monolingual varieties (e.g. inconsistency across the system, centralization along the front–back dimension, shorter atonic vowels), but also differs with respect to the magnitude of the effects.

Despite the differences mentioned above, the impact of speech style appears to have a similar influence on bilingual and learner systems as it does in monolingual varieties. Bland's (2016) comparisons of mid vowels produced in a narrative and a picture task revealed that native speakers and learners alike produced vowels more peripherally in controlled speech (i.e. picture task). Alvord and Rogers (2014) found that vowels produced in the word list (i.e. most controlled task) were more peripheral than those produced in the interview. Ronquest (2016) confirmed the same pattern for heritage speakers, also reporting minor differences in duration for some vowels: /a/ and /o/ were significantly shorter in the most spontaneous task (i.e. narrative) compared to the more controlled picture and carrier phrase tasks.

The brief overview of the bilingual literature presented above describes some of the ways in which bilingual Spanish vowel systems differ from, or are similar to, those of monolingual native speakers. While some bilingual populations exhibit the same trends as those observed in monolingual groups, the effects are, at times, less consistent and/or magnified. Age of onset of bilingualism (or age of onset of learning) has a strong influence on the pronunciation of vowels, as the overall vowel space tends to shift toward monolingual norms as proficiency or experience with Spanish increase (Bland 2016; Cobb and Simonet 2015; Menke and Face 2010). Still, like those of monolingual native speakers, bilingual vowel systems are characterized by considerable variation that merits further investigation.

7.9 Future Directions in Vowel Research

Returning to the four main assumptions this chapter set out to address, the conjunct of research summarized herein suggests that (i) open and close mid vowel allophones are likely the result of both syllable structure *and* coarticulatory effects; (ii) lexical stress *does* influence vowel quality and duration in Spanish, but the influence manifests itself differently in Spanish as compared to languages with phonological reduction such as English and Catalan; (iii) vowels have a tendency to centralize in rapid speech and less controlled styles; and (iv) dialectal differences in the vowel system *do* exist, although they may not be as numerous as in other languages. Combined with the results of studies examining sociolinguistic factors and bilingual vowel systems, these findings indicate that even the simple vowel system of Spanish is rich with variation. Nevertheless, there is still much to be explored, as will be outlined below.

In light of the influence of language-internal and -external factors described throughout this chapter, future investigations should be cautious in directly comparing raw formant values and duration across studies, as contextual, stylistic, and sociolinguistic factors likely vary across works. Comparisons of patterns, however, may still prove insightful, so long as researchers acknowledge that distinct methodologies and analyses may produce distinct results. On a related note, future investigations focusing on dialectal and/or social variation in particular might consider assessing the acoustic properties not only of the vowels themselves, but also of the surrounding consonants. As pointed out by Chládková *et al.* (2011), some of the variation in vowel production may be due, in part, to cross-dialectal differences in the pronunciation of certain consonants. Examining characteristics such as speaking rate and style are also of vital importance. The differences in distribution (i.e. more or less peripheral vowels) in some dialects versus others may very well be a consequence of speaking rate, as vowels produced at faster rates are more likely to centralize (Nadeu 2014).

Additional suggestions concerning methodology and analysis entail further assessment of the interaction between variables, examination of the dynamic properties of vowels in addition to the static, and a movement away from comparisons of aggregate patterns. As described throughout this chapter, much of the research on Spanish vowels has focused on linguistic factors such as stress and syllable type. Fewer investigations have examined the influence of extralinguistic and social factors, and even fewer have investigated the interaction between multiple factors (however, see Barajas 2014; Chládková *et al.* 2011; Ronquest 2012; Sadowsky 2012). The inclusion of multiple variables in future studies, as well as a thorough exploration of how they interact, will facilitate our understanding of the complexity of the Spanish vowel system.

Analyses of the dynamic properties of vowels in conjunction with static measures of F1 and F2 are also important to consider in future vowel research. While their study primarily focused on English vowels, Konopka and Pierrehumbert (2010), for example, reported that although many of the static characteristics of vowels were similar across groups, the differences were rooted in the dynamic properties, such as vowel-inherent spectral change and duration ratios between stressed and unstressed vowels. Spanish vowel research will also benefit from the inclusion of such variables, as well as further investigation of vowel duration in general, which has received considerably less attention in the literature in comparison to vowel quality.

Much of the acoustic vowel research conducted within the past few decades consists of comparisons of mean formant values and aggregate patterns. Future studies of Spanish vowels may consider the analysis of median values as opposed to means, as done by Escudero *et al.* (2009) in their investigation of Brazilian and European Portuguese vowels. They argue that such an approach may help reduce the impact of potential errors in measurement. Additionally, as pointed out by Nadeu (2014), when individual speakers exhibit distinct or opposite patterns of variation, aggregate reporting can, in a sense, "cancel out" the effects, therefore obscuring important individual behaviors. Such variation may be key to understanding cross-linguistic and cross-speaker differences, and is therefore an important avenue to pursue.

Of additional importance, in reviewing the literature presented in this chapter, it is clear that many of the studies of Spanish vowels consist of descriptive, acoustic characterizations. While such descriptions serve as an important first step in understanding the vowel system as a whole, notably absent (from my own work as well) are studies which situate their research questions, predictions, and results within specific theoretical frameworks. Important exceptions include Bradlow (1995), who calls upon the basic tenets of quantal theory, dispersion theory, and language-specific base of articulation when describing differences between the (semi-) analogous vowels of Spanish and English, and Nadeu (2014), who references localized hyperarticulation in her comparison of stress and speaking rate effects on Spanish and Catalan vowels. Future research incorporating specific phonetic and phonological theories, or a stronger theoretical grounding, are the next step beyond the descriptive phase in vowel research.

On a final note, while this chapter has provided a comprehensive review of studies examining vowel production, additional insight into the Spanish vowel system can be gained via analyses of vowel perception. Perceptual models such as the Speech Learning Model (SLM; Flege 1995), the Perceptual Assimilation Model (PAM; Best 1995), and the Second Language Linguistic Perception Model (L2LP; Escudero 2005) are particularly relevant when investigating bilingual speakers and L2 learners, in that each provides mechanisms for both predicting and understanding the patterns observed in production. As a complete description of the models and review of vowel perception literature will not be possible here, interested readers may consult Chapter 11 in this volume for a more complete overview.

7.10 Conclusions

To conclude, the findings of research on Spanish vowels presented in this chapter offer important insight into how distinct linguistic and extralinguistic variables influence their acoustic properties. Advances in technology, methodology, and statistics have facilitated larger-scale studies and complex analyses, all of which have permitted researchers to move beyond basic impressionistic accounts of vowels to more in-depth, acoustic examinations of the systems of different speaker populations. Future research in the field focusing on topics such as regional, social, and individual variation will no doubt offer more insight into the variable nature of the Spanish vowel system.

References

Alvar, M. (1991). *Estudios de geografía lingüística*. Madrid: Paraninfo.

Alvord, S. and Rogers, B. (2014). Miami-Cuban Spanish Vowels in Contact. *Sociolinguistic Studies*, 8 (1), 139–170.

Amengual, M. (2011). Spanish and Catalan in Majorca: Are There Contact-Induced Changes in the Catalan Vowel System? In L. A. Ortiz-López (ed.), *Selected Proceedings of the 13th Hispanic Linguistics Symposium*. Somerville, MA: Cascadilla, pp. 214–223.

Amengual, M. (2016). The Perception and Production of Language-Specific Mid-Vowel Contrasts: Shifting the Focus to the Bilingual Individual in Early Language Input Conditions. *International Journal of Bilingualism*, 20 (2), 133–152.

Barajas, J. (2014). A Sociophonetic Investigation of Unstressed Vowel Raising in the Spanish of a Rural Mexican Community (Doctoral dissertation). The Ohio State University. Available from https://etd.ohiolink.edu/

Best, C. T. (1995). A Direct Realist View of Cross-Language Speech Perception. In W. Strange (ed.), *Speech Perception and Linguistic Experience : Issues in Cross-Language Research*. Timonium, MD: York Press, pp. 171–206.

Bland, J. (2016). Speech Style, Syllable Stress, and the Second-Language Acquisition of Spanish /e/ and /o/ (Master's thesis). Virginia Polytechnic Institute and State University.

Boomershine, A. (2012). What We Know about the Sound System(s) of Heritage Speakers of Spanish: Results of a Production Study of Spanish and English Bilingual and Heritage Speakers. Paper presented at the Hispanic Linguistics Symposium 2012. University of Florida, Gainesville, FL.

Bradlow, A. (1995). A Comparative Acoustic Study of English and Spanish Vowels. *JASA*, 97 (3), 1916–1924.

Bradlow, A. (2002). Confluent Talker- and Listener-Related Forces in Clear Speech Production. In C. Gussenhoven and N. Warner (eds.), *Laboratory Phonology 7*. Berlin and New York: De Gruyter, pp. 241–273.

Chládková, K., Escudero, P., and Boersma, P. (2011). Context-Specific Acoustic Differences between Peruvian and Iberian Spanish Vowels. *JASA*, 130 (1), 416–428.

Cobb, K. and Simonet, M. (2015). Adult Second Language Learning of Spanish Vowels. *Hispania*, 98 (1), 47–60.

Delattre, P. (1969). An Acoustic and Articulatory Study of Vowel Reduction in Four Languages. *International Review of Applied Linguistics in Language Teaching*, 7 (4), 295–325.

Delforge, A. (2008). Unstressed Vowel Reduction in Andean Spanish. In L. Colantoni and J. Steele (eds.), *Selected Proceedings of the 3rd Conference on Laboratory Approaches to Spanish Phonology*. Somerville, MA: Cascadilla, pp. 107–124.

Disner, S. (1984). Insights on Vowel Spacing. In I. Maddieson (ed.), *Patterns of Sounds*. Cambridge: Cambridge University Press, pp. 136–155.

Escudero, P. (2005). Linguistic Perception and Second Language Acquisition: Explaining the Attainment of Optimal Phonological Categorization (Doctoral dissertation). LOT Dissertation Series 113, Utrecht University.

Escudero, P., Boersma, P., Rauber, A., and Bion, R. (2009). A Cross-Dialect Acoustic Description of Vowels: Brazilian versus European Portuguese, *JASA*, 126 (3), 1379–1393.

Ferguson, S. and Kewley-Port, D. (2007). Talker Differences in Clear and Conversational Speech: Acoustic Characteristics of Vowels. *Journal of Speech, Language, and Hearing Research*, 50, 1241–1255.

Flege, J. E. (1995). Second Language Speech Learning: Theory, Findings, and Problems. In W. Strange (ed.), *Speech Perception and Linguistic Experience: Issues in Cross-Language Research*. Timonium, MD: York Press, pp. 233–277.

Godínez, M. (1978). A Comparative Study of Some Romance Vowels. *UCLA Working Papers in Phonetics*, 41, 3–19.

Grijalva, C., Piccinini, P., and Arvaniti, A. (2013). The Vowel Spaces of Southern Californian English and Mexican Spanish as Produced by Monolinguals and Bilinguals. *Proceedings of Meetings on Acoustics*, 19. Retrieved from scitation.aip.org/content/asa/journal/poma/19/1/10.1121/1.4800752

Harmegnies, B. and Poch-Olivé, D. (1992). A Study of Style-Induced Vowel Variability: Laboratory versus Spontaneous Speech in Spanish. *Speech Communication*, 11 (4–5), 429–437.

Henríquez Ureña, P. (1938). *El español en Méjico, los Estados Unidos y la América Central*. Buenos Aires: Biblioteca de Dialectología Hispanoamericana.

Hillenbrand, J., Getty, L. A., Clark, M. J., and Wheeler, K. (1995). Acoustic Characteristics of American English Vowels. *JASA*, 97, 3099–3111.

Holmquist, J. (1985). Social Correlates of a Linguistic Variable: A Study in a Spanish Village. *Language in Society*, 14, 191–203.

Holmquist, J. (1998). High Lands – High Vowels: A Sample of Men's Speech in Rural Puerto Rico. In C. Paradis, D. Vincent, D. Deshaies, and M. LaForest (eds.), *Papers in Sociolinguistics: NWAVE-26 à l'Université Laval*. Quebec: Université Laval, pp. 73–79.

Holmquist, J. (2005). Social Stratification in Women's Speech in Rural Puerto Rico: A Study of Five Phonological Features. In L. Sayahi (ed.), *Selected Proceedings of the 1st Workshop in Spanish Sociolinguistics*. Somerville, MA: Cascadilla, pp. 109–119.

House, A. S. and Fairbanks, G. (1953). The Influence of Consonant Environment upon the Secondary Acoustical Characteristics of Vowels. *JASA*, 25, 105–113.

Hualde, J. I. (2005). *The Sounds of Spanish*. Cambridge: Cambridge University Press.

Jurado, M. and Arenas, M. (2005). *La fonética del español: Análisis e investigación de los sonidos del habla*. Buenos Aires: Editorial Quorum.

Konopka, K. and Pierrehumbert J. B. (2010). Vowel dynamics of Mexican Heritage English: Language Contact and Phonetic Change in a Chicago Community. *Proceedings of the Annual Meeting of the Chicago Linguistic Society*, 46 (2), 127–141. Retrieved from www.phon.ox.ac.uk/jpierrehumbert/publications/CLS_2010_MHE_dynamics.pdf

Lehiste, I. (1970). *Suprasegmentals*. Cambridge, MA: MIT Press.

Lope Blanch, J. (1963). En torno a las vocales caedizas del español mexicano. *Nueva Revista de Filología Hispánica*, 17, 1–19.

Mack, S. (2009) Socially Stratified Phonetic Variation and Perceived Identity in Puerto Rican Spanish (Doctoral dissertation). University of Minnesota.

Marín Gálvez, R. (1995). La duración vocálica en español. *ELUA*, 10, 213–226.

Martín Butragueño, P. (2014). Vocales en contexto. In E. Herrera and R. Barriga (eds.), *Homenaje a Thomas C. Smith-Stark*. Mexico City: El Colegio de México, pp. 971–992.

Martínez Celdrán, E. (1984). *Fonética*. Barcelona: Teide.

Martínez Celdrán, E. (1995). En torno a las vocales del español: Análisis y reconocimiento. *Estudios de Fonética Experimental*, 7, 195–218.

Matluck, J. (1952). La pronunciación del español en el valle de México. *Nueva Revista de Filología Hispánica*, 6 (2), 109–120.

Menke, M. and Face, T. (2010). Second Language Spanish Vowel Production: An Acoustic Analysis. *Studies in Hispanic and Lusophone Linguistics*, 3 (1), 181–214.

Moon, S.-J. and Lindblom, B. (1994). Interaction between Duration, Context, and Speaking Style in English Stressed Vowels. *JASA*, 96, 40–55.

Mora, J. C., Keidel, J., and Flege, J. (2015). Effects of Spanish Use on the Production of Catalan Vowels by Early Spanish–Catalan Bilinguals. In J. Romero and M. Riera (eds.), *The Phonetics–Phonology Interface: Representations and Methodologies*. Amsterdam: John Benjamins, pp. 33–54.

Morrison, G. (2004). An Acoustic and Statistical Analysis of Spanish Mid-Vowel Allophones. *Estudios de Fonética Experimental*, 13, 11–37.

Morrison, G. and Escudero, P. (2007). A Cross-Dialect Comparison of Peninsular- and Peruvian-Spanish Vowels. *Proceedings of the 16th International Congress of Phonetic Sciences: Saarbrücken 2007*. Retrieved from http://www.icphs2007.de/conference/Papers/1006/1006.pdf (last access November 1, 2017).

Nadeu, M. (2014). Stress- and Speech Rate-Induced Vowel Quality Variation in Catalan and Spanish. *Journal of Phonetics*, 46, 1–22.

Navarro Tomás, T. (1918). *Manual de pronunciación española* (12th edn). Madrid: CSIC.

Oliver Rajan, J. (2007). Mobility and its Effects on Vowel Raising in the Coffee Zone of Puerto Rico. In J. Holmquist, A. Lorenzino, and L. Sayahi (eds.), *Selected Proceedings of the 3rd Workshop on Spanish Sociolinguistics*. Somerville, MA: Cascadilla, pp. 44–52.

O'Rourke, E. (2010). Dialect Differences and the Bilingual Vowel Space in Peruvian Spanish. In O. Ortega-Llebaria (ed.), *Selected Proceedings of the 4th Conference on Laboratory Approaches to Spanish Phonology*. Somerville, MA: Cascadilla, pp. 20–30.

Osle Ezquerra, A. (2015). The Impact of Sexual Orientation on the Pronunciation of Stressed Vowels in Peninsular Spanish: An Acoustic Analysis. *Sociolinguistic Studies*, 9 (1), 137–150.

Peterson, G. E. and Lehiste, I. (1960). Duration of Syllable Nuclei in English. *JASA*, 32, 693–703.

Poch-Olivé, D., Harmegnies, B., and Butragueño, P. (2008). Influencia del estilo de habla sobre las características de las realizaciones vocálicas en el español de la ciudad de México. *Actas del XV Congreso Internacional de la Asociación de Lingüística y Filología de América Latina (ALFAL), Montevideo, Uruguay, 18–21 de agosto de 2008*, CD 6–7.

Quilis, A. and Esgueva, M. (1983). Realización de los fonemas vocálicos españoles en posición fonética normal. In M. Esgueva and M. Cantarero (eds.), *Estudios de fonética*. Madrid: CSIC, pp. 159–251.

Recasens, D. (1987). An Acoustic Analysis of V-to-C and V-to-V Coarticulatory Effects in Catalan and Spanish VCV Sequences. *Journal of Phonetics*, 15, 299–312.

Ronquest, R. (2012). An Acoustic Analysis of Heritage Spanish Vowels (Doctoral dissertation). Indiana University.

Ronquest, R. (2013). An Acoustic Examination of Unstressed Vowel Reduction in Heritage Spanish. In C. Howe, S. Blackwell, and M.

Lubbers Quesada (eds.), *Selected Proceedings of the 15th Hispanic Linguistics Symposium*. Somerville, MA: Cascadilla, pp. 151–171.

Ronquest, R. (2016). Stylistic Variation in Heritage Spanish Vowel Production. *Heritage Language Journal*, 13 (2), 275–297.

Sadowsky, S. (2012). Sociolinguistic Stratification and Phonetic Description of the Vowel Allophones of Chilean Spanish (Doctoral dissertation). Universidad de Concepción.

Servín, E. and Rodríguez, M. (2001). Estructura formántica de las vocales del español de la ciudad de México. In E. Herrera (ed.), *Temas de fonética instrumental*. Mexico City: El Colegio de México, Centro de Estudios Lingüísticos y Literarios, pp. 39–58.

Simonet, M. (2011). Production of a Catalan-Specific Vowel Contrast by Early Spanish–Catalan Bilinguals. *Phonetica*, 68 (1–2), 88–110.

Skelton, R. B. (1969). The Pattern of Spanish Vowel Sounds. *International Review of Applied Linguistics in Language Teaching*, 7, 231–237.

Smiljanić, R. and Bradlow, A. (2005). Production and Perception of Clear Speech in Croatian and English. *JASA*, 118, 1677–1688.

Soto-Barba, J. (2007). Variación del F1 y del F2 en las vocales del español urbano y rural de la provincia de Ñuble. *RLA*, 45 (2), 143–165.

Stevens, K. N. and House, A. S. (1963). Perturbation of Vowel Articulations by Consonantal Context: An Acoustics Study. *Journal of Speech Hearing Research*, 6, 111–128.

Valdés, G. (2005). Bilingualism, Heritage Language Learners, and SLA Research: Opportunities Lost or Seized? *The Modern Language Journal*, 89 (3), 410–426.

Willis, E. (2005). An Initial Examination of Southwest Spanish Vowels. *Southwest Journal of Linguistics*, 24 (1/2), 185–198.

Willis, E. (2008). No se comen, pero sí se mascan: Variación de las vocales plenas en la República Dominicana. *Actas del XV Congreso Internacional de la Asociación de Lingüística y Filología de América Latina (ALFAL), Montevideo, Uruguay, 18–21 de agosto de 2008*, CD 6–7.

8

Consonants

Rebeka Campos-Astorkiza

8.1 Introduction

This chapter offers an overview of the consonants of Spanish, focusing on the main phonemes, both in terms of the dialectal variation and the phonological processes that affect them. The topic of Spanish consonants is vast and has given rise to many studies from different perspectives, from generative phonology to Optimality Theory (OT) approaches (see also Chapters 1 and 2, this volume). Due to space limitations, I focus only on some of the main issues that have been explored in the literature. In what follows, I will introduce the reader to the most prominent topics, give relevant references for further exploration and point out some of the current developments. My approach is to focus on phenomena that have received recent attention and benefited from methodological developments, mainly the use of instrumental techniques and the concentration on phonological variation. In revising previous assumptions and accounts of phonological processes in Spanish, I will emphasize the fact that phonological variation is at the core of many recent studies and advances in phonology, and the role it plays in building our assumptions and advancing phonological theory. After giving a general classification of the Spanish consonants, I will discuss them in natural classes according to their manner of articulation.

8.2 Phonemic Consonant Classification

Consonant sounds are defined as being produced with some degree of constriction in the vocal tract, which differentiates them from vowel or vocoid sounds (see also Chapter 7, this volume). Spanish consonants are classified by three articulatory parameters: place of articulation, manner of articulation, and voicing (see Ladefoged and Johnson 2014 for more on articulatory descriptions). Table 8.1 includes the main consonant

Table 8.1 *Main Spanish consonant phonemes*
Sounds on the left-hand side of any given cell are voiceless and those on the right are voiced.

	bilabial	labiodental	interdental	dental†	alveolar	alveopalatal	palatal	velar
Stop	p b			t̪ d̪			ɟ	k g
Fricative		f	(θ)		s			x
Affricate						tʃ		
Nasal		m			n		ɲ	
Lateral					l		(ʎ)	
Tap					ɾ			
Trill					r			

† I omit the dental diacritic from /t, d/ in the rest of the chapter, following other authors' practice (e.g. Hualde 2005).

phonemes of the language according to their articulatory features, taking into account classifications by Quilis (1993), Martínez-Celdrán et al. (2003), Hualde (2005), and Morgan (2010), among others. It should be noted that there is dialectal variation in the Spanish consonantal phonemic inventory, and the parentheses around some of the consonants in Table 8.1 (/θ, ʎ/) denote that they are present only in some dialects, as discussed in later sections. In some cases, the classification of certain sounds is the subject of debate in the literature, most notably the palatal obstruent /ɟ/, which is discussed in Section 8.3.

8.3 Stops

Oral stops are produced with a complete interruption of the airflow as a result of a full closure of the vocal tract. Spanish includes a series of unaspirated voiceless stops /p, t, k/, and another of voiced ones /b, d, g/. Stops may be found in onset position and, with a more limited distribution, in coda position. After continuant sounds, Spanish voiced stops are produced with an approximation of the articulators, rather than with a full closure, resulting in a continuant production with varying degrees of constriction (Martínez-Celdrán 2013). These approximant allophones are represented as [β, ð, ɣ].[1] This contextually-defined alternation between voiced stops and approximants is called *spirantization*, and it has attracted a considerable amount of attention from a myriad of perspectives. The examples in (8.1) illustrate the distribution of the two allophones: voiced stops occur at the beginning of an utterance, sometimes referred to as a post-pausal environment (8.1a), and after a homorganic nasal or lateral consonant (8.1b); the approximant allophones are produced elsewhere, more precisely after a vowel (8.1c) and any consonant that is not an homorganic nasal or lateral (8.1d).

[1] For simplicity I do not include the diacritic [̞] to mark the approximants in the rest of my discussion, following other authors' practice (e.g. Hualde 2005).

(8.1) Distribution of stop and approximant allophones[2]
    a. [ˈbenga] *venga* 'let's go'   [ˈdiselo] *díselo* 'say it to her/him'
       [gaˈnaron] *ganaron* 'they won'
    b. [ˈsamba] *samba* 'samba'   [ˈsenda] *senda* 'path'
       [ˈpoŋgo] *pongo* 'I put'   [ˈsaldo] *saldo* 'balance'
    c. [ˈkaβa] *cava* 'sparkling wine'   [ˈaða] *hada* 'fairy'
       [ˈlweɣo] *luego* 'later'
    d. [ˈselβa] *selva* 'jungle'   [ˈalɣo] *algo* 'something'
       [ˈbarβa] *barba* 'beard'   [ˈarðe] *arde* 'it burns'
       [ˈlarɣo] *largo* 'long'   [ezˈβoso] *esbozo* 'sketch'
       [dezˈðen] *desdén* 'disdain'   [ˈmuzɣo] *musgo* 'moss'

The analysis of Spanish spirantization has been a fruitful avenue of inquiry for formal phonological analyses, and has helped to advance different theoretical approaches. Formal analyses of spirantization differ in their understanding of the process as weakening or fortition. Several authors view spirantization as an instance of weakening, where voiced stops weaken to continuant sounds, lacking a complete closure (e.g. Harris 1984a). On the other hand, spirantization has also been viewed as a case of fortition by which obstruents strengthen to stops when they follow non-continuant consonants and after a pause (e.g. Baković 1997). However, most authors agree that spirantization is an assimilatory process with respect to the continuancy of the preceding phonological context. Another aspect that differentiates formal analyses of spirantization is the nature of the underlying representation, i.e. whether voiced obstruents are fully or partially specified with respect to the feature [continuant]. Many derivational accounts of Spanish spirantization couched within generative phonology assume underspecification of [continuant] and, consequently, the occurrence of one allophone or the other depends on a series of ordered rules that determine their surface specification as either [+continuant] or [–continuant] (Lozano 1979; Harris 1984a; Mascaró 1991; Hualde 1989a). According to these analyses, the surface representation of voiced obstruents is totally conditioned by the phonological context where they occur and these sounds do not contrast with respect to their continuancy.

More recent formal analyses of spirantization have been couched within OT (see also Chapter 2, this volume), where the focus shifts from the underlying representation of the consonants to the ranking of constraints that account for the surface allophonic alternation. Consequently, these analyses do not make use of underspecification but rather propose ranked constraints to explain the process. Those that view spirantization as a weakening phenomenon posit a constraint that bans the occurrence of stops after vowels and continuant consonants, which is in conflict with another constraint that penalizes changes with respect to continuancy (Martínez-Gil 2003; González 2006). These analyses do not posit any

---

[2] Unless otherwise stated, the sample data sets are my own.

restrictions on the underlying representation, which can be fully or partially specified (but see Baković 1997 for a fortition analysis within OT).

All of the formal analyses discussed so far assume that the alternation between voiced stops and approximants is a binary, categorical process, oftentimes represented by the use of [±continuant]. However, instrumental studies on the alternation have presented acoustic and articulatory data showing that there is a great degree of variation in the precise realization of the allophones. The degree of constriction for the continuant allophones is gradient and depends on factors such as stress, vocalic context, speech style and rate, and dialect (Cole *et al.* 1999; Ortega-Llebaria 2004; Eddington 2011; Carrasco *et al.* 2012). These facts have fueled formal analyses that attempt at capturing this variation. Most notably, some authors have argued that spirantization takes place in order to reduce articulatory effort in post-continuant contexts (Piñeros 2002). Within OT, these analyses posit phonetically-grounded constraints, Lazy or "minimize articulatory effort," that penalize articulatory effort, which can be quantified taking into account the context where the sound in question occurs. In the case of Spanish spirantization, the articulatory effort incurred by a continuant consonant in intervocalic position is less than that of a stop in the same context. These effort-based analyses, where phonetic information plays a crucial role, are capable of capturing the gradient nature of the continuant allophones and the fact that the process is conditioned by factors such as stress and speech rate. Colina (2016) offers a different approach to explaining phonetic variation within a formal analysis of spirantization by making use of output or surface underspecification (Keating 1988). According to Colina, Spanish obstruents are produced without a target for continuancy after continuant sounds, and, as a result, the exact production of this feature is conditioned by the phonological context and other factors that affect speech production. Spanish spirantization is an example of how phonological variation unmasked through instrumental techniques and phonological theory have advanced hand in hand.

Several dialects have been described as having a more restricted distribution of approximant allophones, where voiced stops are produced in contexts in which approximants are expected. This pattern of limited spirantization has been observed in central America, Colombia, and Mexico (Canfield 1981; Quilis 1993; Moreno-Fernández 2009). Recent quantitative studies have revealed two dialectal patterns of limited spirantization. In some varieties, we find approximant realizations only after a vowel, while, in other contexts, i.e. after any consonant, stop-like productions are more common, for example [ˈselba], [ˈarde], [ˈmuzgo], etc. (cf. Example 8.1d above). Costa Rican Spanish displays this behavior as described in the acoustic study of Carrasco *et al.* (2012). Other varieties, such as Yucatan Spanish, seem to show a split between stops and approximants after vowels and also consonants, showing a similar distribution of allophones in both environments (Michnowicz 2011). It is worth noting that some of the recent work on limited spirantization has focused on contact varieties of Spanish, such as Peruvian Amazonian Spanish and Yucatan Spanish, and the production of voiced stops and their allophones is helping advance our understanding of the nature of bilingual phonological inventories and tease apart effects of language contact and incomplete second language acquisition (Michnowicz 2009, 2011; O'Rourke and Fafulas 2015).

Spanish voiceless stops may undergo voicing in certain dialects, namely Cuban Spanish, Canary Islands Spanish, and some Peninsular varieties (Quilis 1993; Lewis 2001). This voicing occurs when the stop is next to a voiced sound, especially in intervocalic position. Recent acoustic studies have shown that this voicing process is gradient, and the resulting sound may present partial voicing, fully voicing or be lenited to an approximant (e.g. [taˈkon] ~ [taˈgon] ~ [taˈɣon] 'heel'; Martínez Celdrán 2009; Torreira and Ernestus 2011). Within the dialects that present voicing, there is a considerable amount of interspeaker variation, although recent studies have identified gender and speech rate as two factors that may account for some of this individual variation (Nadeu and Hualde 2015). This voicing phenomenon has been interpreted as a type of weakening and placed within a broader phenomenon of Spanish obstruent weakening, together with voiced stops and their spirantization (Hualde et al. 2011).

The voicing contrast among stops is neutralized in coda position, where only differences in place of articulation are usually maintained (Navarro Tomás 1977; Hualde 2005). These sounds present great variability in this context and their realization in coda ranges from a voiceless stop to a voiced approximant, with other intermediate realizations. Different degrees of obstruction and voicing are possible depending on stylistic factors and the phonetic environment (Navarro Tomás 1977; Hualde 2005:146). The examples in Table 8.2 illustrate the range of possible productions for voiced and voiceless stops in coda position. The crucial observation is that voiced and voiceless stops are not systematically differentiated in this syllabic context.

Table 8.2 *Neutralization of stop voicing contrast in coda position*

Variable productions	Orthography	Gloss
[ˈkapto ~ ˈkab̥to ~ ˈkabto ~ ˈkaβto]	*capto*	'I capture'
[opsoˈleto ~ ob̥soˈleto ~ obsoˈleto ~ oβso ˈleto]	*obsoleto*	'obsolete'
[ˈetnja ~ ˈed̥nja ~ ˈednja ~ ˈeðnja]	*etnia*	'ethnic group'
[atkiˈɾiɾ ~ at̥kiˈɾiɾ ~ adkiˈɾiɾ ~ aðkiˈɾiɾ]	*adquirir*	'purchase'
[ˈakto ~ ˈag̥to ~ ˈagto ~ ˈaɣto]	*acto*	'act'
[akˈnostiko ~ ag̥ˈnostiko ~ agˈnostiko ~ aɣˈnostiko]	*agnóstico*	'agnostic'

Voicing neutralization in coda has been taken as one piece of evidence for the existence of the three archiphonemes /B, D, G/ for Spanish stops in coda position (e.g. Alarcos Llorach 1965; Quilis 1993:205). An archiphoneme is a formal phonological unit that is used to represent the result of a contextually-conditioned neutralization, and it includes the features common to the phonemes involved in the neutralization. Thus, /B, D, G/ include only those features shared by the voiced–voiceless pairs and leave out the voicing feature since it is not contrastive. As a result, these sounds have variable production of their voicing, which can be conditioned by different factors. This formal analysis resembles an underspecification account, according to which the sounds resulting from the neutralization do not have a specification for voicing, resulting in variable voicing production. This last approach relies on output underspecification in a very similar vein to Colina's (2016) analysis of Spanish voiced stops.

The basic neutralization facts regarding coda stops discussed above present dialectal differences. In northern-central Peninsular dialects, voiced stops in coda position tend to undergo devoicing and fricativization, resulting in voiceless fricative productions. This is especially true for coda /g/, that is pronounced as [x] (e.g. [ˈdoxma] *dogma* 'dogma') and coda /d/, that is realized as [θ] (e.g. [seθ] *sed* 'thirst') (González 2002; see below for more on Castilian /θ/). Chilean Spanish presents vocalization of coda voiced and voiceless stops, resulting also in neutralization. More precisely, /p, b/ are vocalized to [w], /t, d/ to [j], and /k, g/ to [w] or [j] depending on the dialect (e.g. /apto/ [ˈawto] 'apt,' /etniko/ [ˈejniko] 'ethnic'; Lenz 1940; Oroz 1966). Caribbean dialects display an extreme case of coda stop neutralization, where these sounds lose their contrast not only in voicing but also in place of articulation. The resulting sound is usually a velar consonant or a glottal stop (e.g. [aɣmiˈtiɾ] *admitir* 'admit,' [ˈeʔniko] *étnico* 'ethnic'; Guitart 1976:23). Finally, coda stop deletion is widespread in Peninsular Spanish and it is also present, although to a lesser extent, in Latin American Spanish (e.g. [eˈsamen] ~ [eɣˈsamen] *examen* 'exam'; Hualde 2005:147). It is important to notice that all of these phenomena that affect coda stops in different dialects may also affect other sounds in this syllabic context. This has been taken as evidence to propose that coda position is an unstable context, where consonants tend to undergo weakening, and in fact the behavior of stops has been analyzed in tandem with that of other consonants, such as fricatives, in this context (e.g. Gerfen 2002).

Orthographic *y, ll*, and *hi* followed by a non-high vowel correspond with a voiced palatal obstruent, which we represent as /ʝ/ here. This sound, which occurs only in onset position, displays much variation in terms of its degree of constriction, which has been found to depend on a number of factors including phonological environment, style, speech rate, and dialect (Aguilar 1997). Its production ranges from a stop [ɟ] or an affricate [ɟʝ] to a very open approximant [j]. In general, we observe an alternation between a continuant and a non-continuant allophone following a similar distribution to that of the voiced stop/approximant alternation resulting from spirantization. More precisely, the voiced palatal continuant [ʝ] tends to occur after a vowel or a continuant consonant (e.g. [ˈkaʝe] *calle* 'street,' [ˈmaʝo] *mayo* 'May,' [laˈʝena] *la hiena* 'the hyena'), and the non-continuant allophone, which may be realized as a stop [ɟ] or an affricate [ɟʝ], occurs after a nasal, a lateral or a pause (e.g. [ˈkonʲɟuxe] *cónyuge* 'spouse,' [elʲɟaˈβero] *el llavero* 'the keychain'). As in the case of voiced stops, this alternation presents some dialectal differences (Jiménez Sabater 1975; Martín Butragueño 2013). Given the similar distribution of the palatal obstruent and voiced stops, we classify this palatal sound as a stop /ɟ/, i.e. the non-continuant obstruent is taken as the phonemic representation emphasizing the parallel behavior with voiced stops (see also Morgan 2010). Other authors also adopt a non-continuant obstruent as the phonemic representation but as an affricate /ɟʝ/ (Martínez Celdrán et al. 2003). On the other hand, some authors classify this obstruent as /ʝ/ (e.g. Quilis 1993; Hualde 2005), taking the continuant palatal as the phonemic representation. In addition, the phonemic status of [ɟ ~ ʝ] has been amply debated in the phonological literature (e.g. Harris 1969, 1983; Cressey 1978; Whitley 1995; Hualde 1997, 2004). One approach is to view this sound as an allophone of the vowel /i/ that results from fortition in word initial position. On the other hand, this palatal sound can be analyzed as an independent consonantal phoneme (see Hualde 2004 for further discussion).

Some dialects, mainly those spoken in the Rioplatense region of Argentina and Uruguay, present a different pronunciation of [ɟ ~ ʝ] (see references below). In these varieties, we find a voiced or voiceless pre-palatal fricative [ʒ ~ ʃ] in contexts where the palatal obstruent is used in other dialects (e.g. [ˈkaʒe] *calle* 'street,' [ˈmaʒo] *mayo* 'May,' [laˈʒena] *la hiena* 'the hyena'). This phenomenon is called *žeísmo* (or *rehilamiento*). Orthographic *hi* has been traditionally claimed to not be part of this development and to present a production similar to other dialects. However, recent studies have shown that this grapheme can also be realized as a prepalatal fricative (e.g. [ˈʒelo] *hielo* 'ice'; Colantoni 2001). *Žeísmo* is reported as far back as the end of the 18th century (Fontanella de Weinberg 1995). The sound was originally voiced and the process of devoicing emerged at the end of the 1940s (Wolf and Jiménez 1979). The devoicing of the prepalatal has been widely explored as a sound change in progress, both impressionistically and with instrumental techniques. The focus has been the social distribution of the devoicing in an effort to draw conclusions regarding the extent of the change. Recent studies present acoustic data that suggests that the change is complete for young speakers born after 1975, while older speakers present variability between voiced and voiceless productions (Chang 2008, Rohena-Madrazo 2011). These studies, and King (2009), also conclude that variation between [ʒ] and [ʃ] is phonetically, socially, and stylistically conditioned. In general, devoicing of *žeísmo* has been a fruitful avenue for exploring methodologies to study sound changes in progress. As with many other sound processes and changes, devoicing is gradient, and this, together with the fact that a phonemic contrast is not involved, poses a challenge for determining the status of the allophone and of the change, more generally. Instrumental techniques have proven crucial in overcoming this challenge. For instance, Rohena-Madrazo (2015) develops a system-internal criterion to establish the degree of [ʒ] devoicing. More precisely, he establishes a baseline for this devoicing by using the amount of voicing of [s] in between vowels, a sound that does not present socially-conditioned allophonic voicing in this context. Based on this methodology and also the phonological patterning of the prepalatal allophones, the author concludes that the change is complete for younger middle-class speakers, and he proposes that the underlying representation for this group is /ʃ/ (see Harris and Kaisse 1999 for a formal analysis of *žeísmo* and a different approach to the underlying representation).

8.4 Fricatives and Affricates

Fricative consonants are produced with a narrowing of the vocal tract, through which the airflow passes uninterrupted, resulting in frication noise. Spanish fricatives include /f, θ, s, x/ although the precise inventory and production of these sounds is subject to dialectal variation. The labiodental fricative /f/ is found only in onset position (e.g. [ˈfoka] *foca* 'seal,' [kaˈfe] *café* 'coffee'), although it might be found in coda in some borrowings (e.g. *afgano* 'afgan'). The alveolar fricative /s/ occurs in onset and coda position and has two main types of articulation depending on the dialect. This sound presents an apico-alveolar production [s̺] in northern-central Peninsular Spanish and a pre-dorso- or lamino-alveolar realization [s̻] in the rest of the dialects. Furthermore, the phenomenon known as /s/ weakening is prevalent in many dialects of Spanish and results in a wide range of reduced productions, from debuccalization – i.e. [h], also known as aspiration – to deletion. This weakening, which is variable, has attracted a lot of attention in the literature (see studies cited below and, among many others, Terrell 1979; Alba 1982; Lipski 1985; Amastae 1989; Carvalho 2006; Erker 2010), and it is a clear example of how instrumental data has helped explore the nature of the phenomenon and its patterning.

The phenomenon of /s/ weakening is found in southern and central Peninsular varieties, the Canary Islands, and in many parts of Latin America, with the exceptions of Mexico, Guatemala, central Costa Rica, and the Andean region (Lipski 1994; Hualde 2005:161). The degree and frequency of the weakening and its resulting production vary across dialects. Furthermore, much of this variation is conditioned by linguistic and social factors, which show certain commonalities across varieties. Socioeconomic status and style have been shown to influence the degree of weakening in many dialects, with higher rates of reduction among less educated speakers and in more casual styles (Alba 2004). However, it should be noted that in many varieties /s/ weakening is the *de facto* norm and there is no apparent social stigma attached to it, although the precise realization, whether for example aspiration or deletion, might present a socially-conditioned distribution (Chappell 2013). The phonological context also has an effect on /s/ weakening. Pre-consonantal contexts result in the highest degrees of weakening (e.g. [ˈkahpa] *caspa* 'dandruff'), followed by prepausal environments (e.g. [ˈbamoh] *vamos* 'let's go'). For this reason, the phenomenon is usually described as affecting syllable-final /s/. However, /s/ may also weaken before a vowel (e.g. [lah ˈalah] *las alas* 'the wings,' [la he ˈmana] *la semana* 'the week'). Although this phonological context usually presents the lowest rates of weakening, there are some dialects where prevocalic /s/ shows the highest degree of /s/ reduction (e.g. New Mexico Spanish; Brown and Torres Cacoullos 2002). Lexical frequency has also been found to influence /s/ weakening with high-frequency words displaying higher rates of reduction and lower-frequency words favoring unreduced productions (Brown 2005; File-Muriel 2009). In fact, this phenomenon has been used as a testing ground for usage-based approaches to phonological patterns, and the role of factors related to use such as frequency on weakening has been taken as evidence for these kinds of models (see e.g. Bybee 2001)

The outcome of /s/ weakening varies from dialect to dialect. High rates of deletion are found in the most extreme dialects, such as Caribbean varieties, where there are reports of hypercorrection, i.e. cases of /s/ insertion in words where there is no etymological fricative (e.g. *fisno* instead of *fino*; Morgan 1998). This behavior has led some authors to argue that /s/ is not present in the underlying representation of these innovative varieties (Terrell 1986 for Dominican Spanish; Chappell 2014 for Nicaraguan Spanish). In some Andalusian varieties, /s/ deletion is accompanied by lengthening or gemination of the following consonant (e.g. [ˈbokke] *bosque* 'forest,' [ˈmimmo] *mismo* 'same'), with possible pre-aspiration of the lengthened consonants in some cases (Gerfen 2002). Merging of /s/ and the following consonant has also been documented in Andalusian Spanish, resulting in a long (or sometimes short) sound that combines features from both consonants (e.g. [reffaˈlaɾ] *resbalar* 'to slide,' [loθeˈβaneh] *los desvanes* 'the attics'; Penny 2000; see Martínez-Gil 2012 for a survey of formal analyses to these two patterns of /s/ weakening). In western Andalusian Spanish, we find yet another type of outcome for /s/ weakening before a voiceless stop. In this environment, a post-aspirated stop or an affricate surfaces as the result of /s/ reduction (e.g. [ˈpet^{h}e ~ ˈpetse] *peste* 'plague,' [ˈet^{h}a ~ ˈetsa] *esta* 'this'; Parrell 2012; Torreira 2012). These types of productions have been analyzed within Articulatory Phonology (Browman and Goldstein 1989) as a change in the timing of the articulatory gestures involved in the /s/ + consonant sequence after the oral gesture for the fricative is lost due to the weakening (Torreira 2012). In Nicaraguan Spanish, word-final /s/ before a vowel may be realized as a glottal stop (e.g. [loʔ ˈotɾo] *los otros* 'the others'), which has been analyzed as a strategy to resolve a hiatus (Chappell 2013). Beyond production, recent studies have explored the perception of /s/ weakening by native speakers, especially how this phenomenon can convey sociophonetic information (Boomershine 2006; Schmidt 2013) and how it is processed by L2 learners of Spanish (Schmidt 2011; see also Chapters 11 and 30, this volume).

In /s/-retaining dialects, this fricative undergoes voicing assimilation to a following voiced consonant, both within and across words (e.g. [ˈmuzɣo] *musgo* 'moss,' [lozˈβaɾkos] *los barcos* 'the ships').[3] Recent instrumental studies have shown that this assimilation is in fact gradient and oftentimes incomplete (Schmidt and Willis 2011; Campos-Astorkiza 2014, 2015).[4] These findings challenge formal phonological accounts of the phenomenon that analyze it as a change in the featural specification of /s/ depending on the following consonant (Hualde 1989b; Martínez-Gil 1991). More recent analyses, couched within Optimality Theory, argue that /s/ is unspecified for voicing in coda position and, consequently, its voicing realization is dependent upon that of the surrounding consonants (Bradley 2005; Bradley and Delforge 2006). However, this approach fails to capture cases that instrumental studies have found where there is no /s/ voicing before a voiced consonant (Campos-Astorkiza 2014, 2015). This pattern, as well as the effects that stress and manner of articulation of the following consonant have on the degree of voicing, have led some authors to analyze /s/ voicing assimilation as an instance of gestural blending within Articulatory Phonology (Campos-Astorkiza 2014, 2015).

The interdental fricative /θ/ is found in northern and central Peninsular dialects, where we observe a phonemic contrast between /s/ and /θ/ (e.g. [ˈmasa] *masa* 'mass' vs. [ˈmaθa] *maza* 'sledgehammer'). The presence of this contrast is known as *distinción* in the Hispanic linguistics literature (Hualde 2005:153). In the majority of dialects, including most of Latin America, Andalusia, and the Canary Islands, this contrast is not present, and we find only the alveolar fricative /s/ (e.g. [ˈmasa] *masa* 'mass' vs. [ˈmasa] *maza* 'sledgehammer'). This phenomenon is called *seseo* (Hualde 2005:153). This lack of contrast has yet another manifestation which is what we encounter in a few dialects that have only a dental fricative, very similar to /θ/. This is called *ceceo* and can be found mainly in eastern Andalusia and some parts of central America (Hualde 2005:153–154; Quesada Pacheco 2010). However, this three-

---

[3] In addition, in some dialects, /s/ voicing also takes place in intervocalic position, especially in word-final position (e.g. [laz ˈolas] *las olas* 'the waves'). This has been documented in Ecuadorian and Peninsular Spanish (Torreira and Ernestus 2012; García 2015).

[4] The voicing assimilation process targeting /s/ can be seen as part of a broader assimilatory phenomenon that affects all coda obstruents in Spanish, according to authors such as Martínez-Gil (2012). However, given the limited occurrence of other obstruents in coda position and the lack of instrumental studies analyzing those other obstruents, their behavior with respect to voicing assimilation is less clearly understood.

way dialectal division is not as clear-cut in Andalusia, where speakers may present variation between *ceceo, seseo,* and *distinción*. More precisely, speakers of certain Andalusian regions alternate their production between an alveolar and an interdental resulting in productions such as [masa ~ maθa] for both *masa* and *maza*. Recent studies have explored this variable phenomenon, focusing on regions that have been traditionally been described as *ceceantes.* What they have found is that younger speakers and women tend to prefer *seseo* or *distinción* over *ceceo,* leading some authors to suggest that *ceceo* is leaving the phonological system of these regions, which are becoming more similar to prestigious varieties that display only *seseo* or *distinción* (Dalbor 1980; Hernández-Campoy and Villena Ponsoda 2009).

The velar fricative /x/, which occurs in syllabic onset position but rarely in coda position, presents the following main realizations [x, χ, h, ç] depending on the dialect. Velar productions are found mainly in Mexico and most of South America (Hualde 2005:155). In northern-central Peninsular Spanish, the production of this phoneme is more retracted and it is usually realized as a uvular fricative [χ], especially before a back vowel (e.g. [ˈχuŋgla] *jungla* 'jungle,' [ˈtaχo] *Tajo* 'Tagus'). In the Caribbean, central America, Andalusia, and the Canary Islands, we find glottal productions [h] (e.g. [haˈβon] *jabón* 'soap,' [ˈaho] *ajo* 'garlic'). In Chilean Spanish, /x/ before a front vocoid [e, i, j] has an anterior articulation and is produced as a palatal fricative [ç] (e.g. [çeneˈral] *general* 'general,' [ˈaçil] *ágil* 'agile' vs. [kaˈxon] *cajón* 'drawer'; Lipski 1994:201; Hualde 2005:155). In fact, this alternation is part of a broader phenomenon called velar fronting that affects all velar consonants /k, g, x/ in Chilean Spanish, and results in palatal productions of these sounds when preceding a front vocoid (e.g. [ˈcema] *quema* 'it burns,' [iˈjeɾa] *higuera* 'fig tree'; examples taken from González 2014, who offers an OT analysis of the process).

Affricates present two phases in their production: they start with a complete closure, followed by a narrow opening of the vocal tract. Acoustically, they are characterized by a period without energy followed by frication. Spanish has one affricate phoneme /tʃ/, a voiceless alveopalatal which occurs only in onset position (e.g. [ˈkatʃo] *cacho* 'piece,' [ˈtʃaɾko] *charco* 'puddle'). In some dialects, the affricate weakens to a voiceless prepalatal fricative [ʃ] (e.g. [ˈkaʃo] *cacho* 'piece'), where the closure phase is lost. These productions can be found most notably in Andalusia, Chile, and the Caribbean (Hualde 2005:22–24).

8.5 Nasals

Nasal consonants are produced with a complete oral closure and an opening of the passage to the nasal cavity, so that the airflow passes through the nose. Spanish has three nasal consonant phonemes /m, n, ɲ/ that are contrastive in their place of articulation only in onset position within the word (e.g. /kama/ *cama* 'bed,' /kana/ *cana* 'gray hair,' /kaɲa/ *caña* 'cane'). In word-initial position, we may find a contrast between /m, n/ but the palatal /ɲ/ is very rare in this context. In coda position, nasals undergo place assimilation and adopt the place feature of the following consonant, both within and across words (8.2a). Before a following vowel or a pause, the nasal is usually alveolar [n] (8.2b), except in velarizing dialects, where it is produced as a velar [ŋ] (8.2c). Velarization is common in the Caribbean, the Pacific coast of South America, the Canary Islands, and several regions in Spain including Asturias, León, Galicia, and Andalusia (Quilis 1993: 239–242; Piñeros 2006). In some varieties of Colombia, and in Yucatan Spanish, a final non-assimilated nasal can be produced as a bilabial [m] (Michnowicz 2008).

(8.2) Distribution of nasal allophones
    a. [ˈkampo]   *campo*   'field'
       [emfaˈðaðo]   *enfadado*   'angry'
       [ˈsen̪da]   *senda*   'path'
       [ˈdenso]   *denso*   'dense'
       [ˈkonʲtʃa]   *concha*   'shell'
       [ˈaŋgulo]   *ángulo*   'angle'
    b. [salˈmon]   *salmón*   'salmon'   [kon ˈeβa]   *con Eva*   'with Eve'
    c. [salˈmoŋ]   *salmón*   'salmon'   [koŋ ˈeβa]   *con Eva*   'with Eve'

Within an autosegmental phonological framework, nasal place assimilation results from the spreading of the place of articulation (PA) features from a following consonant to the preceding nasal, which does not have any PA feature specification due to coda neutralization. Those nasals in coda position that are not followed by a consonant with which to share PA features get assigned a default alveolar value (Goldsmith 1981; Harris 1984b; for earlier generative analyses see Harris 1969; Cressey 1978, and for structuralist accounts using the concept of a nasal archiphoneme see Alarcos Llorach 1965; Quilis 1993:228). In the case of velarizing dialects, one would have to assume that the default value is velar. Within Optimality Theory, nasal place assimilation has been analyzed by making use of a constraint that requires that adjacent sounds have the same place of articulation specification, AGREE(PA) (Baković 2000; Piñeros 2006). Another important element in the OT analysis is the constraint, IDENT (PA), with which AGREE(PA) conflicts and calls for identity between the input and the output, i.e. it penalizes changes in PA. AGREE(PA) dominates this identity constraint, since there is assimilation. However, it affects only nasals in coda position. This is the result of a highly-ranked constraint, IDENTONSET(PA) that protects onsets from any PA featural changes. Beyond the specific OT details, this kind of analysis capitalizes on the difference between onsets and codas, and singles out the latter as a context more prone to phonological changes, along the lines of what was discussed in relation to coda stop neutralization in Section 8.3.

Some recent studies have focused on exploring the phonetic details of nasal place assimilation in Spanish and on the characterization of the process as either categorical or variable (Martínez Celdrán and Fernández Planas 2007; Kochetov and Colantoni 2011; Ramsammy 2011). Ramsammy (2011), based on acoustic data from Peninsular Spanish, finds no difference in the production of a nasal assimilated to alveolar from that assimilated to velar. The author concludes that this assimilatory process is not categorical and argues that pre-consonantal nasals are underspecified for place of articulation in the surface (see above for output underspecification), resulting in high levels of coarticulation with the surrounding sounds. On the other hand, Kochetov and Colantoni (2011) present articulatory data indicating that the assimilation is almost complete and categorical, except before fricative consonants, where nasals present more variation in their production. The authors compare Argentine and Cuban Spanish and conclude that both dialects present the phonological process of assimilation but the actual implementation differs from one dialect to the other. These recent instrumental findings, although reaching different conclusions, offer an innovative way to explore nasal assimilation in Spanish and open the door to adopting similar techniques for dialectal and second language acquisition studies.

Velarization of coda nasals in several Spanish dialects (see Example 8.2c above) has attracted much attention from the phonological literature, especially within the framework of Optimality Theory. The puzzle that velarization poses for formal phonological accounts is that alveolar (i.e. coronal) is argued to be the unmarked place of articulation and, thus, we expect this place of articulation in neutralizing environments where no assimilation takes place. The fact that some dialects present a velar production is unexpected given what is considered as a phonological tenet. Baković (2000) approaches the issue by arguing that, in fact, velar productions are placeless nasals, a kind of output underspecification that auditorily resembles velar consonants. However, Ramsammy (2013) presents electropalatography data that refutes Baković's claim. More precisely, Ramsammy analyzes articulatory data from speakers of a Peninsular velarizing dialect and finds that their production presents a velar closure for the nasals, leading the author to conclude that velar nasals are not placeless but rather have a clear velar specification. Piñeros (2006) also moves away from the underspecification analysis, and instead argues that velarization is an instance of consonant weakening. The author offers a detailed account of dialectal differences within velarizing varieties, and explains that nasal velarization is frequently accompanied by nasalization of the preceding vowel, resulting in complete nasal absorption by the vowel in many cases. Piñeros claims that nasal velarization and absorption are in fact two manifestations of the same phonological force, namely the weakening of consonants in coda position, which affects other consonants in these velarizing dialects. Based on some descriptions of the phenomenon, the author further notes that nasal velarization and absorption are not categorical, but rather variable and gradient within a continuum of consonant weakening. Piñeros argues that this situation can be interpreted as a change in progress from a full coda nasal consonant to a nasalized vowel. This claim makes certain predictions based on what we know about sound change, and opens the door for cross-dialectal sociophonetic analyses of Spanish nasals as a way to test them.

8.6 Liquids: Laterals and Rhotics

Lateral and rhotic sounds are usually grouped together under the phonological class of liquids due to their similar patterning cross-linguistically (Quilis 1993; Ladefoged and Maddieson 1996). In Spanish, these two types of sounds share some similarities in their distribution since these are the only consonants that can be the second member of a complex onset. Furthermore, the process of liquid neutralization, or *trueque de líquidas*, that takes place in coda position is presented as evidence for the connection between rhotics and laterals.

Laterals are produced with a complete closure in the central part of the oral cavity, while the sides of the tongue are open and the air escapes through that opening. Most dialects of Spanish only have one lateral phoneme /l/, which may occur in onset or coda position (e.g. [ˈlaɣo] *lago* 'lake,' [pasˈtel] *pastel* 'cake'). In coda position, the lateral assimilates in place of articulation to a following coronal consonant, i.e. a following (inter)dental, alveolar or palatal, both within and across words (see Example 8.3a for assimilation within words). Before a non-coronal consonant, a vowel or a pause, the lateral is produced as the alveolar [l] (8.3b). Generally, lateral and nasal place assimilation have been analyzed as the same phenomenon (Cressey 1978; Piñeros 2006). According to this unified account, lateral and nasals share the features [+sonorant, +continuant] and they constitute the class of sounds that is affected by place assimilation in Spanish. The fact that laterals do not assimilate to non-coronal consonants is captured by the markedness of laterals that are not coronals.

(8.3) Distribution of lateral allophones
   a. [ˈsal̪to]   *salto*   'jump'
      [ˈbol̪sa]   *bolsa*   'bag'
      [kolʲˈtʃon] *colchón* 'mattress'
   b. [ˈkalβo]   *calvo*   'bald'
      [delˈfin] *delfín* 'dolphin'
      [ˈalɣo]   *algo*   'something'
      [el ˈotɾo] *el otro* 'the other'
      [sol]   *sol*   'sun'

There is another lateral phoneme, a palatal lateral /ʎ/, that can be found in some dialects, especially in northern Argentina, Paraguay, the Andean region, and north and central Spain, although many of these areas show very limited use of this lateral sound (Zampaulo 2013). This palatal sound corresponds with orthographic *ll* and stands in contrast with the palatal obstruent /ʝ/ (see Section 8.3). This situation, where there are two contrasting palatal phonemes, is called *lleísmo* (e.g. [kaˈʎo] *calló* 'became quiet' vs. [kaˈjo] *cayó* 'fell'; see Zampaulo 2013, who refers to this situation as "distinction" and discusses other dialectal variants of the palatal sound). The lack of such a contrast is referred to as *yeísmo* and it is the most common situation across the Spanish-speaking world. Even in regions where the palatal lateral has been documented, there is a move towards *yeísmo* among younger speakers (Gómez and Molina-Martos 2013; Zampaulo 2013).

Spanish has two rhotics, a tap /ɾ/ and a trill /r/. Both are canonically produced with a brief, complete closure; one in the case of the tap and two or more for the trill (Martínez Celdrán and Fernández Planas 2007). The two Spanish rhotics are contrastive only in intervocalic position within a word (8.4a). Word-initially and after a heterosyllabic consonant, only the trill occurs (8.4b), and, in complex onsets, only the tap is possible (8.4c). In coda position before a consonant, there is stylistic variation between a tap and a trill with the trill preferred in emphatic contexts (8.4d, Hualde 2005:182). When a coda rhotic resyllabifies with a following word-initial vowel, we find only the tap (8.4e).

(8.4) Distribution of the tap and trill
    a. [ˈpeɾo] *pero* 'but'   [ˈpero] *perro* 'dog'
    b. [ˈrosa] *rosa* 'rose'   [sonˈrisa] *sonrisa* 'smile'
    c. [ˈtiɣɾe] *tigre* 'tiger'   [tɾes] *tres* 'three'
    d. [ˈnoɾte ~ ˈnorte] *norte* 'north'   [poɾ faβoɾ ~ por faβor] *por favor* 'please'
    e. [maɾ aˈsul] *mar azul* 'blue sea'

The tap and trill may be produced without a complete closure resulting in continuant realizations ranging from fricatives to approximants (Blecua 2001). Furthermore, rhotics display a wide range of productions across and within dialects of Spanish. This variation has been documented extensively, from impressionistic dialectological studies to instrumental production and perception studies. Assibilation of rhotics is a feature of several varieties including those of the Andean region, parts of Mexico and central America, Paraguay, and northern Argentina (Lipski 1994; Moreno de Alba 1994; Bradley 2004). These assibilated productions are characterized by strident frication noise and can be found in different contexts depending on the dialect. For instance, assibilated rhotics are widely reported in coda position in Mexico (e.g. [ˈkařta][5] *carta* 'letter') and

---

[5] [ř] is the symbol for the assibilated rhotic traditionally used in the Hispanic linguistics literature (Face 2008).

in onset position where we would expect a trill in Andean Spanish (e.g. [ˈpeřo] *perro* 'dog'), although Bradley (2004) presents acoustic data showing assibilation also in coda position in Ecuadorian Spanish. Assibilation also affects complex onsets, especially *tr*, in Chile, Costa Rica, Ecuador, and La Rioja, Spain. In this case, the resulting production is a voiceless affricate [tř̥] (Quilis 1993:352–354). Bradley (1999, 2004) has analyzed rhotic assibilation as the result of gestural reduction and extreme coarticulation, taking into account the distribution and variation of these assibilated productions. Dorsal rhotics, where a trill would be expected, can be found in several Caribbean dialects, especially in Puerto Rican Spanish, and they range from velar fricatives [x] to uvular rhotics [ʀ] (Quilis 1993:350–351, Delgado-Díaz and Galarza 2015). These dorsal productions occur in place of the trill both word-initially and medially (e.g. [ˈxoho] *rojo* 'red,' [ˈpexo] *perro* 'dog'). In other Caribbean varieties, we can find pre-aspirated realizations of trills. Instrumental studies have revealed that these productions in fact involve pre-breathy voice followed by an alveolar tap [ɦɾ] or a trill [ɦr] (Willis 2007).

The study of Spanish rhotic variation has been especially fruitful in contexts of language contact, where the phonemic contrast between the tap and trill may be lost, or reinterpreted as a contrast between other rhotics, due to the sociolinguistic situation. Lipski (1985) reports that the intervocalic tap–trill contrast has been lost in Equatorial Guinea Spanish, possibly due to the contact between this variety of Spanish and local languages that do not have this rhotic contrast or a trill in their inventory. O'Brien (2013) instrumentally confirms Lipski's observation and shows that Guinean speakers do not maintain a rhotic contrast based on manner of articulation or duration differences. The author concurs with Lipski and concludes that this dialect presents neutralization of the rhotic contrast. On the other hand, Balam (2013) analyzes rhotic production in Orange Walk, Belize, where Spanish is in contact with English, and finds that the contrast is maintained but realized as a distinction between a tap and a retroflex approximant rhotic [ɻ], rather than a trill. A similar situation is observed in the Spanish of Puerto Ricans in Lorain, Ohio, by Ramos-Pellicia (2007). More precisely the contrast is maintained but the author finds a high number of retroflex rhotics especially among second- and third-generation speakers. Exploring other contexts of contact between Spanish and English, Lopez Alonzo (2016) quantitatively analyzes rhotic production in Bluefields, Nicaragua, a multilingual community where Spanish, English Kriol, and several indigenous languages are spoken. The author acoustically identifies several distinct rhotic productions and concludes that the contrast is maintained, although the linguistic background of the speakers has an impact on possible cases of neutralization. All in all, these studies argue that rhotic variation presents a high degree of correlation with sociolinguistic features in language-contact situations and suggest that these sounds might be perceived differently depending on the context and community.

Neutralization of the liquid contrast in coda position, known as *trueque de líquidas*, can be found in several dialects, where there is reportedly no difference between lexical items such as /maɾ/ *mar* 'sea' and /mal/ *mal* 'bad.' The resulting sound depends on the dialect (Hualde 2005:188). Rhotacism involves the production of coda /l/ as a rhotic, similar to a tap, and it is most commonly found in Andalusia, the Canary Islands, and some Caribbean regions. Lambdacism refers to the production of a coda rhotic as a lateral and is prevalent in the Caribbean varieties.[6] Impressionistic descriptions of lambdacism suggest that the resulting sound is a mix between a rhotic and a lateral (Navarro Tomás 1948; López Morales 1983). In fact, recent studies focusing on Puerto Rican Spanish have shown that the neutralization is usually incomplete both in production and in perception (Simonet et al. 2008; Beaton 2015), and that the resulting sound is different from an underlying lateral. An interesting finding of these studies is that listeners from varieties that do not have *trueque de líquidas* perceive the result of lambdacism and a lateral as the same, meaning that they perceive the sounds as neutralized. On the other hand, listeners from the Puerto Rican dialect can perceive the production differences and distinguish between the two intended sounds. Despite these advances in our understanding of liquid neutralization, the precise articulation of these "mixed sounds" is still not clear and this issue would greatly benefit from the analysis of articulatory data.

8.7 Conclusion

This chapter has provided an overview of the consonants of Spanish, including the main phonemes, dialectal variation, and phonological processes that affect this type of sounds. Given the breadth of the topic, I have offered only a brief survey of the topics that have been more widely discussed in the literature, focusing on recent advances and contributions to these discussions from studies employing instrumental methodologies. The aim has been to bring to the forefront the impact that phonetically-informed approaches to sound variation and change have had on phonological representations and models. Traditional assumptions, especially regarding the categoricity and systematicity of certain phenomena, have been challenged by findings that uncover the gradiency and variability of consonant production in Spanish. Different authors have adopted and developed new approaches to account for the newly-uncovered patterns,

---

[6] Liquids in coda position in these dialects present other realizations that may also result in neutralization: vocalization (e.g. in El Cibao, Dominican Republic) or deletion with or without gemination of the following consonant (e.g. Alba 1990).

including surface or output underspecification, Articulatory Phonology, usage-based models, etc. At the same time, this chapter has identified new avenues for further research, including the status of voicing among stops, especially the incipient voicing of voiceless stops and its implications for sound change; the articulation of nasal and lateral place assimilation as either two faces of the same phenomenon or indeed two distinct processes; and the status of consonantal neutralization processes in Spanish varieties.

References

Aguilar, L. (1997). *De la vocal a la consonante*. Santiago de Compostela: Universidad de Santiago de Compostela.

Alarcos Llorach, E. (1965). *Fonología española*. Madrid: Gredos.

Alba, O. (1982). Función del acento en el proceso de elisión de la /s/ en la República Dominicana. In O. Alba (ed.), *El español del Caribe: Ponencias del VI Simposio de Dialectología*. Santiago: Pontificia Universidad Católica Madre y Maestra, pp. 17–26.

Alba, O. (1990). *Variación fonética y diversidad social en el español dominicano de Santiago*. Santiago: Pontificia Universidad Católica Madre y Maestra.

Alba, O. (2004). *Cómo hablamos los dominicanos: Un enfoque sociolingüístico*. Santo Domingo: Grupo León Jimenes.

Amastae, J. (1989). The Intersection of s-Aspiration/Deletion and Spirantization in Honduran Spanish. *Language Variation and Change*, 1, 169–183.

Baković, E. (1997). Strong Onsets and Spanish Fortition. In C. Giordano and D. Ardron (eds.), *Proceedings of the 6th Student Conference in Linguistics*. Cambridge, MA: MIT Working Papers in Linguistics, pp. 21–39.

Baković, E. (2000). Nasal Place Neutralization in Spanish. In M. Minnic Fox, A. Williams, and E. Kaiser (eds.), *Proceedings of the 24th Annual Penn Linguistics Colloquium*. Philadelphia, PA: University of Pennsylvania, pp. 1–12.

Balam, O. (2013). Overt Language Attitudes and Linguistic Identities among Multilingual Speakers in Northern Belize. *Studies in Hispanic and Lusophone Linguistics*, 6 (2), 247–277.

Beaton, M. (2015). Coda Liquid Production and Perception in Puerto Rican Spanish (Doctoral dissertation). The Ohio State University.

Blecua, B. (2001). Las vibrantes del español: Manifestaciones acústicas y procesos fonéticos (Doctoral dissertation). Universitat Autònoma de Barcelona.

Boomershine, A. (2006). Perceiving and Processing Dialectal Variation in Spanish: An Exemplar Theory Approach. In C. Klee and T. Face (eds.), *Selected Proceedings of the 8th Hispanic Linguistics Symposium*. Somerville, MA: Cascadilla, pp. 58–72.

Bradley, T. G. (1999). Assibilation in Ecuadorian Spanish: A Phonology-Phonetics Account. In M. Authier, B. Bullock, and L. Reed (eds.), *Formal Perspectives on Romance Linguistics*. Amsterdam and Philadelphia, PA: John Benjamins, pp. 57–71.

Bradley, T. G. (2004). Gestural Timing and Rhotic Variation in Spanish Codas. In T. Face (ed.), *Laboratory Approaches to Spanish Phonology*. Berlin: De Gruyter, pp. 197–224.

Bradley, T. G. (2005). Sibilant Voicing in Highland Ecuadorian Spanish. *Lingua(gem)*, 2, 9–42.

Bradley, T. G. and Delforge, A. M. (2006). Systemic Contrast and the Diachrony of Spanish Sibilant Voicing. In R. Gess and D. Arteaga (eds.), *Historical Romance Linguistics: Retrospective and Perspectives*. Amsterdam and Philadelphia, PA: John Benjamins, pp. 19–52.

Browman, C. and Goldstein, L. (1989). Articulatory Gestures as Phonological Units. *Phonology*, 6, 201–252.

Brown, E. (2005). New Mexican Spanish: Insight into the Variable Reduction of "la ehe inihial" (/s-/). *Hispania*, 88, 813–824.

Brown, E. L. and Torres Cacoullos, R. (2002). ¿Qué le vamoh aher?: Taking the Syllable out of Spanish /s/ Reduction. *Penn Working Papers in Linguistics: Papers from NWAV 30*, 8 (3), 17–32.

Bybee, J. (2001). *Phonology and Language Use*. Cambridge: Cambridge University Press.

Campos-Astorkiza, R. (2014). Sibilant Voicing Assimilation in Peninsular Spanish as Gestural Blending. In M. H. Côte and E. Mathieu (eds.), *Variation within and across Romance Languages*. Amsterdam and Philadelphia, PA: John Benjamins, pp. 17–38.

Campos-Astorkiza, R. (2015). Segmental and Prosodic Conditionings on Gradient Voicing Assimilation in Spanish. In R. Klassen, J. Liceras, and E. Valenzuela (eds.), *Hispanic Linguistics at the Crossroads: Theoretical Linguistics, Language Acquisition and Language Contact*. Amsterdam and Philadelphia, PA: John Benjamins, pp. 127–144.

Canfield, D. Lincoln. (1981). *Spanish Pronunciation in the Americas*. Chicago, IL: University of Chicago Press.

Carrasco P., Hualde J. I., and Simonet, M. (2012). Dialectal Differences in Spanish Voiced Obstruent Allophony: Costa Rican versus Iberian Spanish. *Phonetica*, 69, 149–179.

Carvalho, A. M. (2006). Spanish (s) Aspiration as a Prestige Marker on the Uruguayan– Brazilian Border. *Spanish in Context*, 3, 85–114.

Chang, C. B. (2008). Variation in Palatal Production in Buenos Aires Spanish. In M. Westmoreland and J. A. Thomas (eds.), *Selected Proceedings of the 4th Workshop on Spanish Sociolinguistics*. Somerville, MA: Cascadilla, pp. 54–63.

Chappell, W. (2013). Social and Linguistic Factors Conditioning the Glottal Stop in Nicaraguan Spanish (Doctoral dissertation). The Ohio State University.

Chappell, W. (2014). Reanalyses and Hypercorrection among Extreme /s/-Reducers. *Penn Working Papers in Linguistics*, 20 (2), Article 5.

Colantoni, L. (2001). Mergers, Chain Shifts and Dissimilatory Processes: Palatals and Rhotics in Argentine Spanish (Doctoral dissertation). University of Minnesota.

Cole, J., Hualde, J. I., and Iskarous, K. (1999). Effects of Prosodic Context on /g/ Lenition in Spanish. In O. Fujimura, B. D. Joseph, and B. Palek (eds.), *Proceedings of the 4th International Linguistics and Phonetics Conference*. Prague: The Karolinium Press, pp. 575–589.

Colina, S. (2016). On Onset Clusters in Spanish: Voiced Obstruent Underspecification and /f/. In R. A. Núñez Cedeño (ed.), *The Syllable and Stress: Studies in Honor of James W. Harris*. Boston: De Gruyter, pp. 107–137.

Cressey, W. (1978). *Spanish Phonology: A Generative Approach*. Washington, DC: Georgetown University Press.

Dalbor, J. B. (1980). Observations on Present Day ceceo and seseo in Southern Spain. *Hispania*, 63 (1), 5–19.

Delgado-Díaz, G. and I. Galarza. (2015). ¿Que comiste [x]amón? A Closer Look at the Neutralization of /h/ and Posterior /r/ in Puerto Rican Spanish. In E. W. Willis, P. Martín Butragueño, and E. Herrera Zendejas (eds.), *Selected Proceedings of the 6th Conference of Laboratory Approaches to Romance Phonology*. Somerville, MA: Cascadilla, pp. 70–82.

Eddington, D. (2011). What are the Contextual Phonetic Variants of /β ð ɣ/ in Colloquial Spanish? *Probus*, 23, 1–19.

Erker, D. (2010). A Subsegmental Approach to Coda /s/ Weakening in Dominican Spanish. *International Journal of the Sociology of Language*, 203, 9–26.

Face, T. (2008). *Guide to the Phonetic Symbols of Spanish*. Somerville, MA: Cascadilla.

File-Muriel, R. (2009). The Role of Lexical Frequency in the Weakening of Syllable-Final Lexical /s/ in the Spanish of Barranquilla, Colombia. *Hispania*, 92, 348–360.

Fontanella de Weinberg, M. B. (1995). El rehilamiento bonaerense del siglo XIX, nuevamente considerado. *Nueva Revista de Filología Hispánica*, 43 (1), 1–15.

García, C. (2015). Production and Perception of Intervocalic Sibilant Voicing in Highland Ecuadorian Spanish (Doctoral dissertation). The Ohio State University.

Gerfen, C. (2002). Andalusian Codas. *Probus*, 14 (2), 303–333.

Goldsmith, J. (1981). Subsegmentals in Spanish Phonology: An Autosegmental Approach. In D. Napoli (ed.), *Linguistic Symposium on Romance Languages*. Washington, DC: Georgetown University Press, pp. 1–16.

Gómez, R. and Molina-Martos, I. (2013). *Variación yeísta en el mundo hispánico*. Madrid: Iberoamericana.

González, C. (2002). Phonetic Variation in Voiced Obstruents in North–Central Peninsular Spanish. *Journal of the International Phonetic Association*, 32, 17–31.

González, C. (2006). Efecto de la posición en la oración y la frecuencia léxica en /d/ final en español del País Vasco. In T. Face and C. Klee (eds.), *Selected Proceedings of the 8th Hispanic Linguistics Symposium*. Somerville, MA: Cascadilla, pp. 89–102.

Gonzalez, C. (2014). Prevocalic Fronting in Chilean and Proto-Romance. In M. H. Côte and E. Mathieu (eds.), *Variation within and across Romance Languages*. Amsterdam and Philadelphia, PA: John Benjamins, pp. 277–295.

Guitart, J. M. (1976). *Markedness in a Cuban Dialect of Spanish*. Washington, DC: Georgetown University Press.

Harris, J. W. (1969). *Spanish Phonology*. Cambridge, MA: MIT Press.

Harris, J. W. (1983). *Syllable Structure and Stress in Spanish*. Cambridge, MA: MIT Press.

Harris, J. W. (1984a). La espirantización en castellano y la representación fonológica autosegmental. In Departament de Filologia Hispànica (ed.), *Estudis Gramaticals 1. Working Papers in Linguistics*. Barcelona: Universitat Autònoma de Barcelona, pp. 149–167.

Harris, J. W. (1984b). Autosegmental Phonology, Lexical Phonology, and Spanish Nasals. In M. Aronoff and Oehrle, R. (eds.), *Language Sound Structure*. Cambridge, MA: MIT Press, pp. 67–82.

Harris, J. W. and Kaisse, E. (1999). Palatal Vowels, Glides and Obstruents in Argentinian Spanish. *Phonology*, 16, 117–190.

Hernández-Campoy, J. M. and Villena Ponsoda, J. A. (2009). Standardness and Nonstandardness in Spain: Dialect Attrition and Revitalization of Regional Dialects of Spanish. *International Journal of the Sociology of Language*, 196–197, 181–214.

Hualde, J. I. (1989a). Procesos consonánticos y estructuras geométricas en español. *Lingüística ALFAL*, 1, 7–44.

Hualde, J. I. 1989b. Delinking Processes in Romance. In C. Kirschner and J. A. DeCesaris (eds.), *Studies in Romance Linguistics: Selected Proceedings from the 17th Linguistic Symposium on Romance Languages*. Amsterdam and Philadelphia, PA: John Benjamins, pp. 177–193.

Hualde, J. I. 1997. Spanish /i/ and Related Sounds: An Exercise in Phonemic Analysis. *Studies in the Linguistic Sciences*, 27 (2), 61–79.

Hualde, J. I. (2004). Quasi-Phonemic Contrasts in Spanish. In V. Chand, A. Kelleher, A. Rodríguez, and B. Schmeiser (eds.), *Proceedings of the 23rd West Coast Conference on Formal Linguistics*. Somerville, MA: Cascadilla, pp. 374–398.

Hualde, J. I. (2005). *The Sounds of Spanish*. Cambridge: Cambridge University Press.

Hualde, J. I., Simonet, M., and Nadeu, M. (2011). Consonant Lenition and Phonological Recategorization. *Laboratory Phonology*, 2 (2), 301–329.

Jiménez Sabater, M. (1975). *Más datos sobre el español en la República Dominicana*. Santo Domingo: Ediciones Intec.

Keating, P. (1988). Underspecification in Phonetics. *Phonology*, 5, 275–292.

King, C. (2009). Language Attitudes toward Devoicing among Young Adults in Buenos Aires (Honors thesis). The Ohio State University.

Kochetov, A. and Colantoni, L. (2011). Spanish Nasal Assimilation Revisited: A Cross-Dialect Electropalatographic Study. *Laboratory Phonology*, 2, 487–523.

Ladefoged, P. and K. Johnson. (2014). *A Course in Phonetics* (7th edn). Belmont, CA: Cengage Learning.

Ladefoged, P. and I. Maddieson. (1996). *The Sounds of the World's Languages*. Oxford: Wiley-Blackwell.

Lenz, R. (1940). *El español en Chile*. Buenos Aires: Imprenta de la Universidad de Buenos Aires.

Lewis, A. M. (2001). Weakening of Intervocalic /p,t,k/ in Two Spanish Dialects: Toward the Quantification of Lenition Processes (Doctoral dissertation). University of Illinois at Urbana-Champaign.

Lipski, J. (1985). *The Spanish of Equatorial Guinea: The Dialect of Malabo and its Implications for Spanish Dialectology*. Tübingen: M. Niemeyer.

Lipski, J. (1994). *Latin American Spanish*. London: Longman.

Lopez Alonzo, K. (2016). La producción de las róticas en el español de Bluefields, Nicaragua, una comunidad multilingüe en situación de contacto (Doctoral dissertation). The Ohio State University.

López Morales, H. (1983). Lateralización de /-r/ en el español de Puerto Rico. In *Philologia Hispanensia in honorem Manuel Alvar*. Madrid: Gredos, pp. 387–398.

Lozano, M. C. (1979). Stop and Spirant Alternations: Fortition and Spirantization Processes in Spanish Phonology (Doctoral dissertation). Indiana University.

Martín Butragueño, P. (2013). Estructura del yeísmo en la geografía fónica de México. In R. Gómez and I. Molina-Martos (eds.), *Variación yeísta en el mundo hispánico*. Madrid: Iberoamericana, pp. 168–206.

Martínez Celdrán, E. (2009). Sonorización de las oclusivas sordas de una hablante murciana: Problemas que plantea. *Estudios de Fonética Experimental*, 28, 253–271.

Martínez Celdrán, E. (2013). Caracterización acústica de las aproximantes espirantes en español. *Estudios de Fonética Experimental*, 32, 11–35.

Martínez Celdrán, E. and Fernández Planas, A. M. (2007). *Manual de fonética española*. Barcelona: Ariel Lingüística.

Martínez-Celdrán, E., Fernández-Planas, A. M., and Carrera-Sabaté, J. (2003). Spanish. *Journal of the International Phonetic Association*, 33 (2), 255–260.

Martínez-Gil, F. (1991). The Insert/Delete Parameter, Redundancy Rules, and Neutralization Processes in Spanish. In H. Campos and F. Martínez-Gil (eds.), *Current Studies in Spanish Linguistics*. Washington, DC: Georgetown University Press, pp. 495–571.

Martínez-Gil, F. (2003). Resolving Rule-Ordering Paradoxes of Serial Derivations: An Optimality Theoretical Account of the Interaction of Spirantization and Voicing Assimilation in Peninsular Spanish. In P. Kempchinsky and C. E. Piñeros (eds.), *Theory, Practice and Acquisition*. Somerville, MA: Cascadilla, pp. 40–67.

Martínez-Gil, F. (2012). Main Phonological Processes. In J. I. Hualde, A. Olarrea, and E. O'Rourke (eds.), *The Handbook of Spanish Linguistics*. Oxford: Blackwell, pp. 111–132.

Mascaró, J. (1991). Iberian Spirantization and Continuant Spreading. *Catalan Working Papers in Linguistics*, 1, 167–179.

Michnowicz, J. (2008). Final Nasal Variation in Merida, Yucatan. *Spanish in Context*, 5 (2), 278–303.

Michnowicz, J. (2009). Intervocalic Voiced Stops in Yucatan Spanish: A Case of Contact Induced Language Change? In M. Lacorte and J. Leeman (eds.), *Español en Estados Unidos y en otros contextos de contacto: Sociolingüística, ideología y pedagogía*. Madrid: Iberoamericana, pp. 67–84.

Michnowicz, J. (2011). Dialect Standardization in Merida, Yucatan: The Case of /bdg/. *Revista Internacional de Lingüística Iberoamericana*, 18, 191–212.

Moreno de Alba, J. G. (1994). *La pronunciación del español en México*. Mexico City: El Colegio de México, Serie de Estudios de Dialectología Mexicana.

Moreno-Fernández, F. (2009). *La lengua española en sus geografías*. Madrid: Arco/Libros.

Morgan, T. A. (1998). The Linguistic Parameters of /s/-Insertion in Dominican Spanish: A Case Study in Qualitative Hypercorrection. In J. Gutierrez-Rexach and J. del Valle (eds.), *Proceedings of the 1st Hispanic Linguistics Colloquium*. Columbus, OH: The Ohio State University, pp. 79–96.

Morgan, T. (2010). *Sonidos en contexto*. New Haven, CT: Yale University Press.

Nadeu, M. and Hualde, J. I. (2015). Biomechanically-Conditioned Variation at the Origin of Diachronic Intervocalic Voicing. *Language and Speech*, 58 (3), 351–370.

Navarro Tomás, T. (1948). *El español en Puerto Rico*. San Juan: Editorial de la Universidad de Puerto Rico.

Navarro Tomás, T. (1977). *Manual de pronunciación española* (19th edn). Madrid: CSIC, Instituto "Miguel de Cervantes."

O'Brien, V. (2013). Rhotic Production and Contrast in Equatorian Guinean Spanish (M.A. paper). The Ohio State University

O'Rourke, E. and Fafulas, S. (2015). Spanish in Contact in the Peruvian Amazon: An Examination of Intervocalic Voiced Stops. In E. Willis *et al.* (eds.), *Selected Proceedings of the 6th Conference on Laboratory Approaches to Romance Phonology*. Somerville, MA: Cascadilla, pp. 145–162.

Oroz, R. (1966). *La lengua castellana en Chile*. Santiago de Chile: Imprenta de la Universidad de Chile.

Ortega-Llebaria, M. (2004). Interplay between Phonetic and Inventory Constraints in the Degree of Spirantization of Voiced Stops: Comparing Intervocalic /b/ and Intervocalic /g/ in Spanish and English. In T. Face (ed.), *Laboratory Approaches to Spanish Phonology*. Berlin and New York: De Gruyter, pp. 237–253.

Parrell, B. (2012). The Role of Gestural Phasing in Western Andalusian Spanish Aspiration. *Journal of Phonetics*, 40 (1), 37–45.

Penny, R. (2000). *Variation and Change in Spanish*. Cambridge: Cambridge University Press.

Piñeros, C. E. (2002). Markedness and Laziness in Spanish Obstruents. *Lingua*, 112, 379–413.

Piñeros, C. E. (2006). The Phonology of Nasal Consonants in Five Spanish Dialects. In F. Martínez-Gil and S. Colina (eds.), *Optimality-Theoretic Studies in Spanish Phonology*. Amsterdam: John Benjamins, pp. 146–171.

Quesado Pacheco, M. A. (ed.) (2010). *El español hablado en América Central*. Madrid: Iberoamericana.

Quilis, A. (1993). *Tratado de fonología y fonética españolas*. Madrid: Gredos.

Ramos-Pellicia, M. F. (2007). Lorain Puerto Rican Spanish and "r" in Three Generations. In J. Holmquist, A. Lorenzino, and L. Sayahi (eds.), *Selected Proceedings of the 3rd Workshop on Spanish Sociolinguistics*. Somerville, MA: Cascadilla, pp. 53–60.

Ramsammy, M. (2011). An Acoustic Investigation of Nasal Place Neutralisation in Spanish: Default Place Assignment and Phonetic Underspecification. In J. Herschensohn (ed.), *Romance Linguistics 2010*. Amsterdam: John Benjamins, pp. 33–48.

Ramsammy, M. (2013). Word-Final Nasal Velarisation in Spanish. *Journal of Linguistics*, 49, 215–255.

Rohena-Madrazo, M. (2011). Sociophonetic Variation in the Production and Perception of Obstruent Voicing in Buenos Aires Spanish (Doctoral dissertation). New York University.

Rohena-Madrazo, M. (2015). Diagnosing the Completion of a Sound Change: Phonetic and Phonological Evidence for /ʃ/ in Buenos Aires Spanish. *Language Variation and Change*, 27, 287–317.

Schmidt, L. B. (2011). Acquisition of Dialectal Variation in a Second Language: L2 Perception of Aspiration of Spanish /s/ (Doctoral dissertation). Indiana University.

Schmidt, L. B. (2013). Regional Variation in the Perception of Sociophonetic Variants of Spanish /s/. In S. Beaudrie and A. Carvalho (eds.), *Selected Proceedings of the 6th International Workshop on Spanish Sociolinguistics*. Somerville, MA: Cascadilla, pp. 189–202.

Schmidt, L. B. and Willis, E. (2011). Voicing Assimilation of Spanish /s/ in Mexico City. In S. Alvord (ed.), *Selected Proceedings of the 5th Conference on Laboratory Approaches to Romance Phonology*. Somerville, MA: Cascadilla, pp. 1–20.

Simonet, M., Rohena-Madrazo, M., and Paz, M. (2008). Preliminary Evidence of Incomplete Neutralization of Coda Liquids in Puerto Rican Spanish. In L. Colantoni and J. Steele (eds.), *Laboratory Approaches to Spanish Phonology III*. Somerville, MA: Cascadilla, pp. 72–86.

Terrell, T. D. (1979). Final /s/ in Cuban Spanish. *Hispania*, 62, 599–612.

Terrell, T. (1986). La desaparición de /s/ posnuclear a nivel léxico en el habla dominicana. In R. Núñez Cedeño, I. Páez Urdaneta, and J. Guitart (eds.), *Estudios sobre la fonología del español del Caribe*. Caracas: La Casa de Bello, pp. 117–134.

Torreira, F. (2012). Investigating the Nature of Aspirated Stops in Western Andalusian Spanish. *Journal of the International Phonetic Association*, 42, 49–63.

Torreira, F. and Ernestus, M. (2011). Realization of Voiceless Stops and Vowels in Conversational French and Spanish. *Laboratory Phonology*, 2 (2), 331–353.

Torreira, F. and Ernestus, M. (2012). Weakening of Intervocalic /s/ in the Nijmegen Corpus of Casual Spanish. *Phonetica*, 69, 124–148.

Whitley, M. S. (1995). Spanish Glides, Hiatus, and Conjunction Lowering. *Hispanic Linguistics*, 6/7, 355–385.

Willis, E. (2007). An Acoustic Study of the "Pre-Aspirated Trill" in Narrative Cibaeño Dominican Spanish. *Journal of the International Phonetic Association*, 37, 33–49.

Wolf, C. and Jiménez, E. (1979). El ensordecimiento del yeísmo porteño. In A. M. Barrenechea, (ed.), *Estudios lingüísticos y dialectológicos*. Buenos Aires: Hachette, pp. 115–145.

Zampaulo, A. (2013). When Synchrony Meets Diachrony: (Alveolo)palatal Sound Patterns in Spanish and other Romance Languages (Doctoral dissertation). The Ohio State University.

9

The Syllable

Alfonso Morales-Front

9.1 Introduction

> Syllable: From Gr. συλλαβή *syllabḗ m*eaning "what is taken together."

As its etymology suggests, a syllable is a group of segments articulated as a unit. It is normally defined as a set of segments grouped around a sonority peak, but it is also a prosodic unit that imposes structure on top of segmental strings. The syllable plays an important role in speech planning, word-form encoding, and lexical access.

The existence of Sumerian tablets with syllabic writings dating back to 2800 BCE is a good indication that the syllable is not a modern construct. However, we had to wait until the end of the 19th century to arrive at definitions of the syllable as a linguistic unit (Whitney 1873; Sievers 1885). From the outset, the syllable has been a unit subject to dispute mostly because it has no single acoustic or articulatory correlate; and the intuition that it is generated by chest pulses, cycles of the jaw or breath groups, has not been corroborated by phonetic studies. Still, this should not be problematic for a phonological unit. The lack of constant physical correlates does not negate the existence or relevance of the syllable. To be clear, there is plenty of evidence for the syllable. Language games often consist of inserting, deleting or moving syllables around. In speech errors, syllables can be omitted or misplaced and when consonants are misplaced from an onset they normally land on another onset. Aphasics may not recall a word but still be aware of the number of syllables in the word. Similarly, in tip-of-the-tongue phenomena we may have a sense of the syllables without being able to access their phonemic content. Multiple studies of lexical access suggest that the syllable plays an important role, and they provide empirical support for syllabic constituents. Finally, phonological processes that have the syllable as its domain (e.g. emphatic spreading in Arabic); morphological reduplication; stress assignment; and a plethora of phonological alternations that take place in specific syllabic positions – all provide a solid motivation for positing this prosodic constituent at the center of the phonological enterprise.

For a short period, though, many linguists in the generative framework were not convinced. Syllables cannot be phonetically measured (Ladefoged 1967; Ladefoged and Maddieson 1996) and syllabic generalizations can often be expressed at the segmental level (e.g. coda can be formalized as before consonant or word-finally). Following Occam's razor, classic generative phonology did not include the syllable as a linguistic unit. By the end of the 70s this restrictive position had been eroded thanks to researchers such as Joan Hopper and Daniel Kahn. By the 80s, the syllable and prosodic structure were argued to be a central part of phonological representations (Harris 1983; Selkirk 1984; Ito 1986). Still, there is some opposition to the idea that the syllable is organized into peaks and valleys of sonority. Ohala and Kawasaki-Fukumori (1997), for instance, are quick to point out that sonority itself is not a solid concept and that it should not be the foundation of the syllabic building. In more recent years the syllable has come to occupy a central space in phonological explanation due to the insights that Optimality Theory can offer through constraints on syllabic structures and universal markedness.

9.2 The Syllable as a Prosodic Constituent

The syllable is a prosodic unit at the base of the prosodic hierarchy (see Liberman and Prince 1977; Selkirk 1978, 1986; Nespor and Vogel 1986; Beckman and Pierrehumbert 1986). Selkirk (1986:384) depicts the hierarchy as in Figure 9.1. This structure is built on top of the segmental string and the assumption is that all utterances can be parsed exhaustively into these units. The Strict Layer Hypothesis (Selkirk 1984) posits that prosodic units are ordered hierarchically into layers as in Figure 9.1 and that prosodic units cannot dominate units of the same level (i.e. each unit is properly contained in a unit of the next higher level).

9.2.1 Structural Constraints

The syllable is a prosodic unit composed of smaller constituents. Syllabic constituents are assumed to be maximally branching and only syllable >

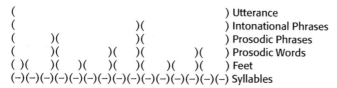

Figure 9.1 Depiction of prosodic hierarchy in Selkirk (1986)

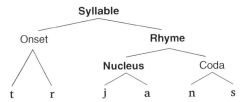

Figure 9.2 Model of syllabic structure
Bold indicates non-optional constituents.

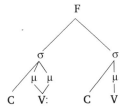

F = foot, σ = syllable, μ = mora, C = consonant, V = vowel

Figure 9.3 Moraic view of the syllable

rhyme > nucleus are obligatory. Figure 9.2 illustrates the maximal syllable allowed by this model. The evidence for syllabic constituents comes from speech errors, language games, experimental blending tasks, etc., but most importantly from phonological processes that have syllabic constituents as their domain. Spanish /s/ aspiration, for instance, takes place when the sound is in a coda. The constituent with weaker support is the rhyme (see Davis 1988). Other than rhyming in poetry there are not many phonological processes or restrictions that crucially require the rhyme. One exception could be the limit of three segments proposed for the Spanish rhyme by Harris (1983).

The template in Figure 9.2 illustrates the most common syllable structure, but there are other proposals in the literature. For Kahn (1976) and Clements and Keyser (1983) the syllabic node directly dominates segments. Pike (1947), Hocket (1955), and Davis (1988) assume three constituents at the same level. Duanmu (2009) assumes that the maximal syllable has the form CVX and examples exceeding this template are considered morphological appendices or coarticulated segments. McCarthy (1979), Kubozono (1989), and Yi (1999) posit a body node dominating onset and nucleus. Codas attach directly under the syllabic node. This position is compatible with the moraic view which posits that the syllable dominates up to two morae and the onset attaches to the syllable node. Moraic theory has been often presented as incompatible with syllabic constituents because both morae and syllabic constituents compete for the space above the segmental tier. Compare Figure 9.3 with Figure 9.2. In fact, cross-linguistic phonological data seems to support both the mora (to account for weight, rhythm, and timing) and syllabic constituents (to account for alternations

The Syllable

Figure 9.4 Moraic view of short and long vowels

Figure 9.5 Example representations of moraic structure

CCVVCC CCVVC CCVCC CVVCC CVVC CCVC CVCC CVC CV VC V

Figure 9.6 Structure of intermediate templates

restricted to sub-syllabic domains). The moraic approach provides optimal representations for encoding weight. The basic tenet is that a short vowel is monomoraic and that a long vowel is bimoraic, as illustrated in Figure 9.4; example representations of moraic structure are provided in Figure 9.5.

Consonant weight is parametric and languages can be classified as quantity-sensitive (Latin, Turkish, Menomini, Lardil, etc.) or quantity-insensitive (Japanese, Icelandic, Warao, etc.). A typical quantity-sensitive language, such as Latin, would have syllable types as in Figure 9.5. For other languages only long vowels, or only long vowels and sonorants, contribute extra weight. Reaching a clear conclusion on the weight status of Spanish codas is not an easy matter. There is no lack of data pointing in the direction of syllabic weight in the Spanish stress system. However, this evidence can be attributed to the fact that Latin, not necessarily Spanish, was a quantity-sensitive language. The phonemic length of Classical Latin had already been lost in Vulgar Latin before 200 CE (Lehmann 2005) and has not been preserved in the Romance Languages. It is not typical for systems lacking contrastive length to have moraic consonants. See Piñeros (2016) for recent arguments regarding the lack of moraicity of Spanish codas.

The structure in Figure 9.2 depicts a maximal CCVVCC template. Given the optionality of codas and onsets, the minimal template has a simple nucleus. The intermediate templates in Figure 9.6 are derived from the logical permutations of optional constituents and the branching parameter.

Not all templates are equally frequent. Cross-linguistic frequencies mostly reflect universal markedness. Being marked entails a degree of disfavor for some structural options or cross-linguistic unusualness. Markedness correlates with complexity, articulatory effort, perceptual difficulty, repair strategies, and delayed acquisition. The unmarked syllable par excellence has a CV template, and this means that it does not go against universal constraints; that it is expected to be present in all languages; and that it will be the first syllable acquired by children. As we move up from the CV syllable in Figure 9.6, complexity increases, and with it markedness. We expect then to find these templates with increasingly lower frequency in cross-linguistic sampling. To the right, VC and V do not add structural complexity, but go against the universal constraint that requires syllables to have an onset. The onset is an important part of the sonority contrast in that it maximizes the movement that takes articulation from a low valley to the peak. The coda, instead, is just a prolongation of the peak. It is not essential and its presence increases complexity and articulatory effort. The fact that markedness is at the base of syllable typology explains why a theory that essentially frames phonology as a conflict between faithfulness and markedness (Optimality) is especially suited to account for syllable typology and syllabic processes (e.g. Colina 2009).

There are at least three types of languages: those with simple syllables such as Senufu (about 13 percent of the languages covered in the World Atlas of Language Structure: Dryer and Haspelmath 2013); those that also allow CVC or CCV syllables such as Hungarian (56 percent); and languages such as English that allow the more complex templates (31 percent). This can be modeled as the result of universal parameters or, as in Optimality Theory, variation in the ranking of syllable-markedness constraints with respect to faithfulness.

The complexity of the Spanish syllable lies somewhere in between Senefu and English. Moreno Sandoval *et al.* (2006) and Guerra (1983) have calculated the percentages shown in Table 9.1. These percentages clearly show that complex codas are very infrequent. This is in sharp contrast to traditional descriptions and accounts of the Spanish syllable that give undue prominence to complex constituents in general, and especially to complex codas. The Spanish syllable does not belong in the simple syllable group with Senefu, but it is actually farther away from languages in the third group like English.

Table 9.1 *Complexity of the Spanish syllable*

	Moreno Sandoval *et al.* 2006	Guerra 1983
CV	51.35	55.81
CVC	18.03	21.61
V	10.75	9.91
VC	8.60	8.39
CVV	3.37	N/A
CVVC	3.31	N/A
CCV	2.96	3.14
CCVC	0.88	0.98
VCC	N/A	0.13
CVCC	N/A	0.02
CCVCC	N/A	0.01

9.2.2 Sequential Constraints: Sonority

If you were to take out random tiles from a Scrabble box and arrange them following the structure in Figure 9.2, the chances of forming a well-formed syllable in any language are exceedingly low. This is because languages impose sequential restrictions on what sounds can combine to form well-formed syllables. Speech sounds must follow a sonority profile such that the most sonorous element occupies the central part while less sonorous segments are peripheral. Sonority is the relative loudness, intensity, or energy of a sound. When we want to be heard at a distance or call for help we will probably utter a vocalic sound. There is a high correlation between sonority and degree of aperture. A number of linguists going back more than a century (Sievers, Jespersen, Saussure, Grammont, Hooper, Kiparsky, Steriade, Selkirk, Clements, among many others) have recognized the importance of the Sonority Sequencing Principle (SSP). This principle states that every syllable has one sonority peak that forms the nucleus and then the syllable margins show a sonority slope that rises toward the nucleus. The syllable [plan] is well-formed according to the SSP, but *[lpan] is not (Figure 9.7).

The SSP can account for the typically attested combinations of two segments in complex onsets (pr, *rp), complex nuclei (je, *oe), and complex codas (ns, *sn). Although the Spanish syllable is eminently consistent with the SSP, many other languages seem to tolerate some sonority reversals. For instance, the Swedish word *skælmsk* 'roguishly' is a well formed monosyllable. As is often the case with exceptions, a good number of formal devices such as non-exhaustive parsing, extrasyllabicity, adjunction, semisyllables, and empty nuclei have been posited to explain cases that seem to question the universal validity of the SSP (see Cho and King 2003 for a review). Sonority conceived as a relative term gives origin to sonority scales. Although there are many different scales that have been proposed over the years, most differences have to do with the number of levels posited, rather than with the relative sonority of each natural class. See Figure 9.8 for a typical sonority scale.

	[P l a n]	*[l p a n]
Sonority level 3	x	x
Sonority level 2	x x	x x
Sonority level 1	x	x

Figure 9.7 Examples of sonority sequencing

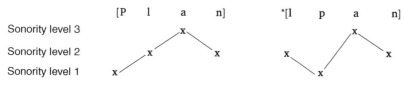

plosives | fricatives | nasals | laterals | rhotics | glides | high vowels | mid vowels | low vowels

Figure 9.8 Depiction of typical sonority scale

The SSP rules out most non-attested combinations such as [lkotn] or [tganl] but would still allow some sequences such as [psi] or [pne] that, while found in some languages (e.g. classical Greek), are not allowed in Spanish. To account for these parametric differences, we need to introduce the notion of sonority distance within syllable constituents and posit that while in Greek the minimal sonority distance of a complex onset is one degree (assuming the scale in Figure 9.8), for Spanish it must be at least three degrees.

9.2.3 Constraints on Syllabic Constituents

While sonority explains many limitations on the possibilities of the syllable there are some gaps that are not directly related to sonority sequencing and tend to be interpreted as restrictions on syllabic constituents.

Onset

All Spanish consonants are possible in an onset – though [ɾ] and [ɲ] are restricted word-initially. Complex onsets are mainly governed by the SSP, which predicts that sequences of an obstruent followed by a liquid such as /bɾ/, /bl/, /pɾ/, /pl/, /fɾ/, /fl/, /tɾ/, /dɾ/, /gɾ/, /gl/, /kɾ/, /kl/ are all well formed. */tl/, */dl/, */sɾ/, */θɾ/, */sl/, */xɾ/, and */xl/ have also a positive sonority slope, but are not found in Spanish.

In Mexico /tl/ can appear word-initially in borrowings from Nahuatl. We have words such as *tlapalería* 'hardware store' and names of a handful of towns such as *Tlalnepantla* or *Tlascala*. Word-internally this sequence tends to be parsed heterosyllabically as in *at.las* or *at.lán.tico*, but in most areas of Latin America and in some Peninsular varieties *a.tlas* is fine. On the other hand, /dl/ is a non-attested type of onset.

The absence, or avoidance, of /tl/, /dl/ is typically analyzed as a result of a lack of alternation at the feature level and disallowed by the Obligatory Contour Principle (OCP) (Leben 1973; Goldsmith 1976). /t/ and /l/ share a coronal node and a [–cont] feature, but the degree of similarity (see Frisch *et al.* 2004) is less than what obtains for /dl/ because in this case the feature [+voice] is also shared.

To account for the absence of fricative+liquid (when the fricative is not /f/) we need to posit that there is a minimum distance requirement between the members of the complex onset such that the fricative+liquid sequence falls below the minimal threshold. Once the sequence fricative+liquid is ruled out, something needs to be done to account for the well-formedness of /fɾ/, /fl/. Martínez-Gil (2001) argues that /f/ is unspecified for [cont] and behaves as a stop; even if well motivated, this seems a fairly *ad hoc* solution.

In a rule-based approach, the SSP does not have a clear place in the grammar. The same is true of other principles such as the OCP or even markedness. These inadequacies motivated to a great extent the innovations in Optimality Theory. OT is a theory of constraint interaction, and both markedness and sonority are in essence constraints. This is in itself an improvement, but an OT account (since it operates with output constraints), introduces a new problem for the Spanish syllable that so far has escaped the gaze of most researchers. The issue is how to account for well-formed outputs that contain two approximants in the onset (e.g. *abrir* [a.'βɾiɾ] 'to open') while at the same time ruling out fricative+liquid sequences that in terms of sonority would be better.

Another issue that will need to be addressed in future research is that the well-formedness of onset sequences is not a binary choice. We have seen that /tl/ seems to enjoy a higher degree of acceptance than /dl/. Similarly, /sɾ/ is better than /θɾ/ and /xɾ/ is better than /xl/. At the base of these gradations we have phonetic factors that have to do with which gestures can be coarticulated; which are in conflict; and which combinations face aerodynamic or motor control difficulties.

Sounds with higher than approximant sonority cannot be onsets in Spanish. This correctly implies that prenuclear glides will not adjoin to the onset and normally belong to the nucleus. However, in those few cases where they are better parsed in the onset their sonority must decrease. This is what we normally call glide fortition.

The alveolar trill is not possible in a complex onset. There are accounts that see the trill as a sequence of two underlying taps (Harris 1983). Under this assumption, it makes sense that [r] cannot occupy the second slot of an onset. Even if [r] is not assumed to be structurally complex it is at least clear that it is stronger (in terms of tension and duration) than the typical short and quick transition that this position favors.

Malmberg (1965) pointed out that onset clusters may have a svarabatic vowel breaking up the sequence of two consonants (e.g. *preciosa* [pᵉɾe.'θjo.sa] 'beautiful'). When the second consonant is lateral the svarabatic vowel is less common. The intrusive vowel has a very short duration and the same quality as the following vowel and, importantly, does not affect stress assignment or judgments about number of syllables. This final characteristic is problematic for an OT account because in the output the svarabatic vowel should be a peak. Future research will need to continue studying the interactions between the phonological and phonetic components.

Nucleus

The nuclear node has its own restrictions. In Spanish only vocoids are allowed in the nucleus. All vowels can appear under a simple nucleus and a complex nucleus has an initial glide. Other languages impose different sonority restrictions for the nucleus. Languages such as Kabardian set the minimum sonority at the level of mid vowels. Nahuatl admits vowels and excludes glides and consonants. In Sanskrit a rhotic can be the peak, while in English the set is expanded to include liquids and nasals. Nuclear fricatives (Hoard 1978) and even obstruents (Dell and Elmedlaoui 1985) have been reported.

Diphthongs can have rising sonority (*Venecia* 'Venice') or falling sonority (*jaula* 'cage'). Triphthongs have rising and falling sonority: *buey* [ˈβwej] 'ox.' A priori, it is not clear which of these vocalic sequences can form a complex nucleus. Hualde (1991) argues – on the basis of language games, hypocoristics, rhyme restrictions, and vowel harmony – that only glide+vowel form a complex nucleus. Accordingly, postvocalic glides are in the coda. Sequences such as [ji], [wu], [wo] go against the Obligatory Contour Principle.

Coda

Word-finally, only coronals are frequent: *más* [ˈmas] 'more,' *arroz* [a.ˈroθ] 'rice,' *sed* [ˈseð] 'thirst,' *dolor* [do.ˈloɾ] 'pain,' *canción* [kan̪.ˈθjon] 'song,' *papel* [pa.ˈpel] 'paper,' *rey* [ˈrej] 'king.' The palatal /tʃ/ is not possible because it is an obstruent with a complex structure. Similar complexity claims have been made for /ɲ/, /ʎ/ (see Carreira 1988). *Reloj* [re.ˈlox] 'watch' is unexpected but a very frequent lexical token. Although it is a word of Greek origin it is likely a modern borrowing from Catalan. There are some 15 other words that can be found in dictionaries that end with orthographic <j>, but only two – *carcaj* [kaɾ.ˈkax] 'quiver' and *boj* [ˈbox] 'boxwood' – can reasonably be expected to be part of the lexicon of an educated native speaker. The former is of Persian origin and the latter again comes from Catalan. Obstruent coronals are far from frequent and tend to be lenited. When an obstruent such as /d/ *sed* appears in final position it undergoes fricativization [ˈseð], and devoicing [ˈseθ] or deletion [ˈse]. The broad generalization for the Spanish final coda is that it optimally licenses one sonorant coronal.

Word-internally, it is common to read that all consonants, with the exception of the palatals /ɲ/ and /ʎ/ and the velar /x/, can close a syllable. Indeed, it is not difficult to find examples with obstruents (*obtuso* [ob̥.ˈtu.so] 'obtuse,' *admirar* [ad.mi.ˈɾaɾ] 'to admire,' *Magdalena* [maɣ.ða.ˈle.na] 'female proper name,' *tacto* [ˈtak.to] 'touch,' *atlas* [ˈat.las], etc.). However, a quick count reveals that these codas are far from common. In fact, word-internal codas also prefer sonorant coronals ({/ɾ,l,n/}), glides ({[j,w]}) or the coronal fricatives ({/s,θ/}). The other consonants have very low frequencies and have been preserved in formal varieties by normative efforts and orthographic conventions. In spontaneous and informal speech, these less-common codas are lenited.

Since in Latin most consonants were allowed in codas (only /f, g, h/ were restricted), the preference for coronal sonorants is a relatively modern development. The loss of contrastive length and with it moraic codas can explain lenition tendencies and the narrowing of the sonority threshold; markedness can also be a factor in the preference for coronals.

Many descriptions state that Spanish allows complex codas of the form /-Cs/ where C is normally {/ɾ, l, n/} or {[w, j]} with a few examples of {/b, d/}. These complex codas again have exceedingly low frequencies and arise mostly from combinations of consonant initial stems with prefixes such as *ad-, ab-, ex-, per-, trans-, sub-*. Another source is medical terms such as *toraks* or *biceps*. Finally, many often-cited examples come from loanwords, but since loanwords often have their own adaptation constraints that may not coincide with native patterns (Ito and Mester 1995), it is better to study them separately.

Interestingly the set of allowed consonants in C_1 of a complex coda exactly corresponds to the set of consonants allowed in single codas. Since /s/ cross-linguistically has exceptional sonority and Spanish prefixes are an independent syllabification domain (Hualde 1991; Wiltshire 2006; Colina 2009), it makes sense to conclude that the Spanish coda cannot be complex and that /s/ is actually an appendix. Again, future research should take into account these observations.

9.3 Syllabification

In most languages syllabic structure is predictable and non-contrastive. Moreover, morphemes typically do not conform to syllabic constraints. Since redundant information is assumed to be absent from the lexicon, syllable structure needs to be derived.

One possibility is to posit a set of ordered rules (see Hualde 1991). In OT, syllables are built by the GENERATOR and it is the role of the EVALUATOR to select outputs. The EVALUATOR uses a language-specific ranking of universal constraints. The two central syllabification constraints, ONSET and *CODA, follow from the observation that all languages have onsets, but not all have codas. Regardless of ranking, the asymmetrical definition of these two constraints correctly predicts that in all languages a string *tata* will be syllabified [ta.ta], and not [tat.a] (Figure 9.9). In a rule-based approach this result is derived by ordering the onset rule before the coda rule.

9.3.1 Resyllabification

In Spanish maximum onset applies both word-internally and postlexically (Example 9.1).

	/tata/	ONSET	*CODA
a. ☞ [ta.ta]			
b. [tat.a]		*!	*!

Figure 9.9 Maximum Onset Principle (Kahn 1976)

(9.1) *a dos adas*   [a.ðo.sa.ðas]   'to two fairies'
       adosadas   [a.ðo.sa.ðas]   'adjoined fem.'
       las alas   [la.sa.las]   'the wings'
       la salas   [la.sa.las]   'you salt it fem.'
       un ido   [u.**ni**.ðo]   'a crazy person'
       unido   [u.ni.ðo]   'united'

However, onset maximization has some well-known exceptions (Example 9.2).

(9.2) *sub+liminal* [suβ.li.mi.ˈnal]   *sublime* [su.ˈβli.me]
       sub+rayar   [suβ.ra.ˈjar]   'underline'   *sobrar*   [so.ˈβrar]   'have left'
       club lindo   [ˈkluβ.ˈlin̪.do] 'nice club'   *cable*   [ˈka.βle]
       des+hielo   [des.ˈje.lo]   'thaw'   *desierto* [de.ˈsjer.to] 'desert'

A similar pattern of exceptionality can be seen in cases of /s/ aspiration that happen in spite of the target segment not being in coda position in the surface (Example 9.3):

(9.3) a. *mes*   [ˈmeh]   'month'
          dos   [ˈdoh]   'two'
       b. *mes anterior* [ˈme.han̪.te.ˈrjor] 'prior month'
          dos amigos   [ˈdo.ha.ˈmi.ɣo]   'two friends'
          deshacer   [de.ha.ˈθer]   'undo'

Hualde (1991) argues that the syllabification domain in Spanish excludes prefixes. To account for (9.2) syllabification must apply a second time postlexically but without the complex onset rule. Since OT is non-derivational, ordering aspiration between syllabifications is not possible. In OT the typical account of (9.2) posits an alignment constraint requiring that the edges of words coincide with the edge of a syllable. For the data in (9.3) an Output-to-output (O-O) constraint of morpheme identity can do the trick (see Colina 2002).

9.3.2 Vocalic Sequences

Vocalic sequences can occur word-internally (*leal* [le.ˈal] 'loyal') or across words (*esta encuesta* [ˈes.ta.en.ˈkwes.ta] 'this survey'). In general, sequences of two nonhigh vowels (VV) are heterosyllabic while sequences containing a high vowel (iV, uV, Vi, Vu) form a diphthong. In guarded speech *esta encuesta* can be pronounced maintaining the V.V sequence, but in spontaneous speech the two syllables have a strong tendency to be reduced and coalesce. The reduction can be the result of fusion (a + a → a), diphthongization (e + u → ew), deletion of one of the vowels (a + o → o) or a number of phonetically intermediate realizations. Chicano Spanish has a consistent system for V.V resolution: it deletes or glides the first vowel. In other varieties the solution typically depends on a number of factors such as stress, vowel quality, content vs. functional word, open vs. closed syllable, or even word frequency.

From an OT perspective, in words such as *teatro* 'theater,' *peor* 'worst,' *roedor* 'rodent,' and *meollo* 'core,' faithfulness is the force behind hiatus preservation. Between words there is the potential of additional pressure from alignment constraints between the edge of the prosodic word and the syllable. In Spanish neither faithfulness to vocalic aperture nor syllable–word alignment seem to have a high ranking. In opposition to faithfulness and alignment, we have markedness constraints that are behind the universal antihiatic tendency. These constraints are the SSP and *STRUC (Prince and Smolensky 2004, Zoll 1996). Structural economy favors syneresis (merging the two vowels in a single syllable), and the SSP requires a sonority slope for the merged syllable.

Word-internally, sequences of decreasing sonority are realized as falling diphthongs [Vj, Vw] (e.g. *boina* 'beret,' *reina* 'queen'). Sequences of rising sonority normally form diphthongs but for a number of lexical entries a hiatus is possible. Factors such as origin, word-initial position, morphological boundaries, and analogical pressure are at play, but none of these factors has a consistent correlation with the contrast. For many speakers the words in Example 9.4a have diphthongs while the words in (9.4b) allow at least two realizations.

(9.4) a. *piedra*   ['pje.ðra]   'stone'
       hueso   ['we.so]   'bone'
       liebre   ['lje.βre]   'hare'
       ambiente [am.'bjen̪.te] 'environment'
       guardián [gwaɾ.'ðjan] 'guardian'
       asiduo   [a.'si.ðwo] 'regular'
       Daniel   [da.'njel]
       cuatro   ['kwa.tro]   'four'

    b. *miope*   [mi.'o.pe] ~ ['mjo.pe]   'short sighted'
       jesuita   [xe.su.'i.ta] ~ [xe.'swi.ta] 'Jesuit'
       piano   [pi.'a.no] ~ ['pja.no]   'piano'
       diadema   [di.a.'ðe.ma] ~ [dja.'ðe.ma] 'diadem'
       biela   [bi.'e.la] ~ ['bje.la]   'rod'
       violento [bi.o.'len̪.to] ~ [bjo.'len̪.to] 'violent'
       mutua   ['mu.tu.a] ~ ['mu.twa]   'mutual'

There are examples of minimal pairs (*pie* ['pje] 'foot' vs. *pié* [pi.'e] 'I chirped') but they have different morphology. Considering quasi-minimal pairs, we can have examples that do not involve morphology:

pliegue pl[je]gue 'fold' vs. *cliente* cl[i.e]nte 'client'
duelo d[we]lo 'mourning' vs. *dueto* d[u.e]to 'duet'
siendo s[je]ndo 'being' vs. *riendo* r[i.e]ndo 'laughing'

Source: Cabré and Prieto (2004)

Still, to avoid redundant underlying representations most researchers assume that glides are not phonemic. Devices such as underspecification and prespecification can encode an underlying contrast between /i/ and /j/

(Padgett 2008). Given that there are no language-specific restrictions on the input ("Richness of the Base"), it is even harder to justify that no syllabic information is present in the underlying representation. Assuming that the difference between Examples 9.4a and 9.4b is encoded in the lexical entry, we just need to account for syneresis. This is not problematic in an OT account that manipulates the ranking of markedness and faithfulness. On the other hand, if there is no underlying contrast then the goal is to account for the blocking of antihiatic tendencies (markedness) but without the help of faithfulness – in OT this is, at best, tricky.

Hualde and Chitoran (2003) note that, while Latin allowed heterosyllabic i.V, u.V sequences, the Romance languages show a range of hiatus avoidance that has Portuguese at one extreme and French at the other. Where French consistently has diphthongs Portuguese preserves the Latin hiatus. Spanish is in between the two extremes. This idea of an incomplete evolution is consistent with the attested dialectal and individual variability.

9.4 The Syllable as a Source of Phonological Alternations

Many phonological alternations can be described as processes that affect specific syllable constituents. In English /l/ velarization happens only in a coda. In Dutch a labiodental approximant becomes labial in the same context. In many varieties of Spanish /n/ is velarized and /s/ is aspirated, again in the same context.

As mentioned above the Spanish coda is a constituent with many restrictions and the language is abundant in lenition processes that are triggered to enforce them. At the other end of the syllable the onset calls for strong variants, and fortition processes are triggered to satisfy this need. The syllable is a movement of the articulators: a transition from a sonority valley to a sonority peak. In physical movements, the maximal energy is normally applied at the onset of movement. After reaching a peak, dampening sets in, and the motion initiates a descent. With repeated movements, a renewed push of energy creates cycles. Understanding the coda as an attempt to prolong the peak resisting the natural tendency to descend, we can grasp the source of the forces in conflict that account for the different processes we find at different points of the syllable.

9.4.1 Onset Processes

A pair such as *viviendo* [bi.ˈβjen̪.do] 'living' and *yendo* [ˈɟjen̪.do] 'going' illustrates onset fortition. Since the glide is in both cases the first segment of the same morpheme, the different output must be a matter of syllabification. In the first example the root provides an onset and the glide is better parsed in a complex nucleus. In the second example the glide is optimally parsed in the onset. Since the onset requires low sonority, it is the tension between avoiding a complex nucleus, the need to have an onset, and the SSP that determines the consonantization of the glide. In some dialects it can be an approximant [jen̪.do], in others a fricative ([ʝen̪.do], [ʃen̪.do], [ʒen̪.do]), and in others a plosive [ɟen̪.do]. With the back glide, the situation is a bit different (*huevo* /uebo/ → [gwe.βo]~[we.βo] 'egg'). Here, the glide remains in the nucleus, and instead of consonantization there is epenthesis of a velar consonant. Since [w] is labiovelar, it makes sense to see the velar as an extension of the glide. Epenthesis is preferred in this case because consonantization of [w] would generate marked outputs in Spanish. While the consonantization of the front glide is a standard process in all Spanish varieties the back counterpart remains circumscribed to very informal registers. Fortition also takes place between words (*una y una* ['u.na.'ʝu.na] 'one plus one' vs. *una y dos* ['u.naj.'ðos] 'one plus two'), but this does not apply to the back glide (*uno u otro* [u.no.wo.tro] 'one or the other').

One alternation that clearly correlates with syllable position is the distribution of rhotics. Trills appear in strong syllable positons and taps in weak ones. The fact that under emphasis the trill can appear in places where we would normally find a tap further supports the view that this alternation has to do with fortition and lenition.

Epenthesis is often presented as a repair strategy for sC onsets (*esprin* < *sprint*). This kind of epenthesis is a hallmark feature of Spanish speakers pronouncing English ([es.'tan.daɾ], [es.'pot], [es.'tejk]) or other languages that have appendices or syllabic consonants. Importantly, we never have *[se.'teik]. In OT the locus of the epenthetic vowel is normally determined by the imperative not to break an underlyingly contiguous string. As Lipski (2016) rightly notes, at the right edge of the word contiguity does not seem to matter, so the Arabic name Sadr is repaired as ['sa.ðeɾ] not *['sa.ðɾe] and the Austrian surname Krankl as ['kraŋ.kel] not *['kraŋ.kle]. Interestingly enough, this pattern of final epenthesis also runs against the most basic syllabification constraints: ONSET and *CODA. In these cases, however, the offending consonant is parsed in a coda, in spite of codas being marked. Other cases often considered epenthetic (e.g. the /e/ in the plural allomorph /-es/ or in the diminutive /-ecito/) are better analyzed as historical processes or lexicalized allomorphs.

9.4.2 Nuclear Processes

Spanish vowels are remarkably stable. They can be nasalized when there is a nasal in the coda (*aman* /'aman/ → ['a.mãn] 'they love'). The fact that this is uncommon when the nasal is in an onset points to a syllabic process. Many traditional descriptions also note that mid vowels can be lowered, shortened, and relaxed in closed syllables as in e.g. *Vélez* ['be.le̞θ] 'surname'; *gordo* ['go̞ɾ.ðo] 'fat.' Both nasalization and shortening have the effect of limiting the overall duration of the rhyme.

9.4.3 Coda Processes

The Spanish coda is weak and favors lenition. Obstruents lack enough sonority to be in the coda and peripheral articulations (labial or velar) are also out because they require extra effort. The repair strategies conspire to narrow the range of articulatory movement of the tongue body in coda consonants to the sweet spot surrounding the resting position (coronal sonorants). In its extreme version, this tendency ends up eliminating the coda.

/s/ aspiration (e.g. *dos* [ˈdoh] 'two,' *vienes* [ˈbje.neh] 'you are coming') is the most common and better-studied repair. Aspiration is often seen as the first step in a chain of weakening processes that ends with the deletion of the coda. Lipski (1985) sees these processes as "merely numerical, gradations of a single process." The alternative term "debuccalization" captures the fact that the oral features of /s/ are lost and what remains is the laryngeal specification. The process is arguably triggered by minimization of articulatory effort (after all, /s/ is an obstruent). As for the other fricatives, /x/ in the word *reloj* [re.ˈloh] 'watch' is also aspirated. In fact, any coda can be aspirated (e.g. *acto* [ˈah.to] 'act', *Magda* [ˈmah.ða] 'female proper name'). In terms of feature geometry, aspiration can be analyzed as the delinking of the supralaryngeal node. However, according to Widdison (1995), aspiration would be better understood as a case of devoicing timing (reverse image of VOT). Aspiration is a partial devoicing that takes place when the vocal cords start opening during the vocalic articulation in anticipation of the upcoming /s/. Even in non-aspirating dialects there is a degree of devoicing in the vowel before /s/. Aspirating dialects are those that have extended this breathy phonation and have lost the buccal features of the /s/. Although this view gives us a better understanding of the nature of the process it is still the case that the coda consonant needs to be lenited for the breathy phonation to be extended into the timing unit in the coda. The fact that in more advanced dialects aspiration results in elision suggests that the coda weakening is for the most part independent of aspiration.

Aspiration is an old process that can be traced to the Peninsular Andalusian dialect and was extended to Latin America through colonization. It can now be found in southern Spain, the Canary Islands, the Caribbean, and all of the Pacific coast from Mexico to Chile. In Argentina, Uruguay, Paraguay, and parts of Bolivia it is also common. In the varieties where the process is more advanced (Andalusian or the Caribbean varieties) word-internal codas favor aspiration and word-final ones, elision.

In areas of El Salvador, Honduras, and New Mexico, /s/ can be aspirated word-initially (e.g. *la semana* [la.he.ˈma.na] 'the week'). This seems to contradict the claim that this is a coda process. However, these data should be interpreted against the background of the resyllabification examples mentioned above (e.g. *los amos* [lo.ˈha.moh] 'the owners'). Cases of word-initial aspiration are not instances of resyllabification but can be seen as the result of analogical extension, or morphological uniformity, from cases in which the aspirated /s/ surfaces word-initially after resyllabification (e.g. *las semanas* [la.he.'ma.nah] 'the weeks'). In central Spain /s/ can be lenited to / ɾ/ (e.g. *los nietos* [loɾ.'nje.to] 'the grandsons'). This is a way of avoiding an obstruent at the end of the syllable. The tap requires only a quick and short articulation with a flip of the tip that leaves the tongue body mostly unaffected.

Rhotacism (/l/ → /ɾ/) and lambdacism (/ɾ/ → /l/) are two salient processes that are associated with the Spanish coda (e.g. *amor* [a.'moɾ]~ [a.'mol] 'love,' *malvado* [mal.'βa.ðo]~[maɾ.'βaǫ] 'evil'). Rhotacism is spread all over southern Spain, the Canary Islands and to a lesser extent can be found in Puerto Rico and the Dominican Republic (Quilis 1993). Lambdacism can be found sporadically in southern Spain, but is characteristic of Caribbean varieties (especially Puerto Rico). This distribution suggests that rhotacism was the initial repair and lambdacism may be seen as ensuing confusion or hypercorrection. Since Navarro Tomás (1948) the neutralized Puerto Rican liquid has been described as an articulation in between the tap and the lateral. However, Simonet *et al.* (2008) show that Puerto Rican speakers can actually tell them apart – it is the speakers of other dialects that do not perceive the difference when Puerto Ricans are speaking.

Gliding of coda liquids is a related process that is characteristic of the Cibao region in the Dominican Republic (Jiménez Sabater 1975). In this variety, coda liquids are lenited by making them palatal glides (e.g. *revólver* [re.'boj.bej]; *celda* 'cell' and *cerda* 'bristle' are both ['sej.ða] – see Guitart (1997).

Rhotacism, lambdacism, and gliding are all part of a lenition continuum that leads to deletion. Indeed, phrase-finally, where the linking with a following consonant does not help, elision of the liquid is quite common. The range of possibilities that may affect a liquid coda is broad. The proper name *Encarna* can be pronounced [eŋ.'kaɾ.na] (careful speech), but also [eŋ.'kar.na] (under emphasis), [eŋ.'kal.na] (lambdacism), [eŋ.'kan.na] (gemination), [eŋ.'kaŋ.ŋa] (velarization with gemination), [eŋ.'kaɳ.ɳa] (retroflexion and gemination), [eŋ.'kah.na] (aspiration), [eŋ.'ka.na] (deletion), etc. There is a hilarious sketch available online (Empanadilla de Móstoles by Martes y trece) that illustrates quite well some of these alternations.

Since /ɾ/ and /l/ are already [+son] and [cor] one may wonder why they are affected by coda weakening. They should be fine in a coda and indeed they are for most dialects, except the radical ones. The same varieties that have rampant elision of codas also tend to mix the liquids. From an articulatory effort point of view the tap has a slight advantage with respect to /l/ – obviously not enough to set a clear direction for the process, but perhaps enough to set it in motion. Finally, the fact that acoustically /ɾ/ and /l/ are not sufficiently different makes this a notoriously marked contrast, cross-linguistically.

N velarization (e.g. *melón* [me.loŋ], *jamón* [xa.moŋ] 'ham'), is attested before a pause in most of the same areas as aspiration and in northern Spain. Word internally n velarization is not common because place assimilation takes precedence. Between words some dialects have velarization after resyllabification, but this is not as common as with aspiration. Before consonant-initial words place assimilation again gets in the way. The fact that velarization also affects other consonants (e.g. *étnico* ['eg.ni.ko] 'ethnic,' *concepto* [koṇ.'θek.to] 'concept,' *himno* ['iŋ.no] 'hymn,' *pepsi* ['pek.si]) suggests that this is the same general coda weakening rather than a property of nasals. According to Trigo (1988), the final velar nasal reported in many studies sounds, and is typically transcribed as, a dorsal because the lowering of the velum necessary to articulate the nasal is perceived as a dorsal articulation. She interprets the lenited coda as a debuccalized nasal glide that lacks an oral place of articulation. This account is in line with the kind of coda lenition that we have been reviewing in this section. When an oral consonant is debuccalized what remains is the laryngeal features but when the nasal is debuccalized what remains is the nasality and the segment is perceived as a velar nasal.

Voice is not a feature licensed by the coda. Coda sonorants are spontaneously voiced. The few cases with voiced obstruents tend to be devoiced word-finally (*sed* [sed̥]~[seθ]). Voiced counterparts arise only before voiced consonants (*admitir* [ad.mi.'tiɾ]~[að.mi.'tiɾ] 'to admit'). The only obstruent that appears frequently in the coda, /s/, assimilates to a following voiced consonant (*mismo* ['miz.mo] 'same') and this can also happen with other obstruents (*juzgar* [xuð̬.'ɣaɾ] 'to judge,' *hipnosis* [ib.'no.sis] 'hypnosis.' This voicing is licensed by the following consonant, not the coda.

The coda does not license its own point of articulation either. This explains the preference for default coronals and predicts that all consonants in coda position will try to assimilate in point of articulation to a following consonant. Nasals and laterals do assimilate whenever the result is phonetically possible (e.g. lateral labials are not possible). /s/ and /ɾ/ do not assimilate in place arguably because of the Principle of Structure preservation (see Kiparsky 1982) but they do participate in total assimilation.

Gemination (*mismo* ['mimmo]~['miʰm.mo] 'same,' *carta* ['kat.ta]~['kaʰt.ta] 'card') is a process that seems to contradict the claim of a general coda weakening as it generates surface coda obstruents. Importantly, in the chain of lenition processes aspiration precedes gemination, and it is only after debuccalization that, by compensatory lengthening, the onset spreads to the available space in the coda. Cross-linguistically, geminates display inalterability and fail to be affected by lenition, allowing coda consonants that otherwise are not possible. These exceptional consonants are licensed by the onset, not the coda.

9.5 Conclusion

In spite of some past controversies, the syllable occupies nowadays a privileged position among phonological units. Thanks to the syllable we can explain the connection between many tendencies that would otherwise be seen as independent processes. The syllable is governed by sonority, and since sonority is a universal tendency we can say that the Spanish syllable is shaped by the same macro currents as those that are active in other languages. It just happens that those currents are not manifested the same way in different contexts because there are local factors at play. OT is particularly good at implementing constraints for those macro currents and factors and for modeling their contribution in different contexts. Besides sonority the other strong current that has been especially highlighted in this chapter is the tendency to have a strong start followed by dampening after reaching a peak. The constraints ONSET and *CODA are important members of this current, but the move towards strong segments in the onset and weak ones in the coda goes beyond these constraints. We have seen that the Spanish onsets and nuclei license all phonemic contrasts and can be complex. The coda, on the other hand, is not complex, does not license voicing contrasts, and disfavors labial and dorsal points of articulation. In Spanish multiple processes of lenition and fortition conspire to enforce these preferences. All languages tend to prefer weak codas, but in Spanish this tendency is particularly strong. Besides the major forces there are a number of local factors and details that may sometimes obfuscate the general picture. These details have to do with lexicalization, phonologization, analogy, language change, language contact, the phonology–phonetics–morphology interface, etc. In this chapter we have tried to provide a balanced review of the macro currents while paying attention to the rich and variegated details of the phonological processes associated with the Spanish syllable.

References

Beckman, M. and Pierrehumbert, J. (1986). Intonational Structure in Japanese and English. *Phonology*, 3, 255–309.
Cabré, T. and Prieto, P. (2004). Prosodic and Analogical Effects in Lexical Glide Formation in Catalan. *Probus*, 16 (2), 113–150.
Carreira, M. (1988). The Structure of Palatal Consonants in Spanish. *Chicago Linguistic Society*, 24 (1), 73–87.
Cho, Y. Y. and King, T. H. (2003). Semi-Syllables and Universal Syllabification. In C. Féry and R. van de Vijver (eds.), *The Syllable in Optimality Theory*. Cambridge: Cambridge University Press, pp. 183–212.
Clements, G. N. and Keyser, S. J. (1983). *CV Phonology. A Generative Theory of the Syllable*. Cambridge, MA: MIT Press.

Colina, S. (2002). Interdialectal Variation in Spanish /s/ Aspiration: The Role of Prosodic Structure and Output-to-Output Constraints. In J. F. Lee, K. L. Geeslin, and J. C. Clements (eds.), *Structure, Meaning and Acquisition in Spanish: Papers from the 4th Hispanic Linguistics Symposium*. Somerville, MA: Cascadilla, pp. 230–243.

Colina, S. (2009). *Spanish Phonology: A Syllabic Perspective*. Washington, DC: Georgetown University Press.

Davis, S. (1988). *Topics in Syllable Geometry*. New York: Garland Press.

Dell, F. and Elmedlaoui, M. (1985). Syllabic Consonants and Syllabification in Imdlawn Tashlhiyt Berber. *Journal of African Languages and Linguistics*, 7 (2), 105–30.

Dryer, Matthew S. and Haspelmath, Martin (eds.) (2013). *The World Atlas of Language Structures Online*. Munich: Max Planck Digital Library. Available from http://wals.info (last access December 29, 2017).

Duanmu, S. (2009). *Syllable Structure: The Limits of Variation*. London: Oxford University Press.

Frisch, S., Pierrehumbert, J., and Broe, M. (2004). Similarity Avoidance and the OCP. *Natural Language and Linguistic Theory*, 22, 179–228.

Goldsmith, J. (1976). Autosegmental Phonology (dissertation). MIT.

Guerra, R. (1983). Estudio estadístico de la sílaba en español. In M. Esgueva and M. Cantarero (eds.), *Estudios de fonética I*. Madrid: CSIC, pp. 9–112.

Guitart, J. M. (1997). Variability, Multilectalism, and the Organization of Phonology in Caribbean Spanish Dialects. In F. Martínez-Gil and A. Morales-Front (eds.), *Issues in the Phonology and Morphology of the Major Iberian Languages*. Washington, DC: Georgetown University Press, pp. 515–536.

Harris, J. W. (1983). *Syllable Structure and Stress in Spanish: A Nonlinear Analysis*. Cambridge, MA: MIT Press.

Hoard, J. (1978). Syllabication in Northwest Indian Languages, with Remarks on the Nature of Syllabic Stops and Affricates. In A. Bell and J. Hooper (eds.), *Syllables and Segments*. Amsterdam: North-Holland, pp. 59–72.

Hockett, C. F. (1955). *A Manual of Phonology*. Baltimore, MD: Waverly Press.

Hualde, J. I. (1991). On Spanish Syllabification. In H. Campos and F. Martinez-Gil (eds.), *Current Studies in Spanish Linguistics*. Washington, DC: Georgetown University Press, pp. 475–493.

Hualde, J. I. and Chitoran, I. (2003). Explaining the Distribution of Hiatus in Spanish and Romanian. In M. J. Solé, D. Recasens, and J. Romero (eds.), *Proceeding of the 15th International Congress on Phonetic Sciences*. Barcelona: Universitat Autónoma de Barcelona, pp. 67–70.

Ito, J. (1986). Syllable Theory in Prosodic Phonology (dissertation). University of Massachusetts.

Ito, J. and Mester, R. A. (1995). Japanese Phonology. In J. Goldsmith (ed.), *The Handbook of Phonological Theory*. Oxford: Blackwell.

Jiménez Sabater, M. A. (1975). *Más datos sobre el español de la República Dominicana*. Santo Domingo: Ediciones INTEC.

Kahn, D. (1976). Syllable-Based Generalizations in English Phonology (dissertation). MIT.

Kiparsky, P. (1982). From Cyclic Phonology to Lexical Phonology. In H. van der Hulst and N. Smit (eds.), *The Structure of Phonological Representations (I)*. Dordrecht: Foris, pp. 131–175.

Kubozono, H. (1989). The Mora and Syllable Structure in Japanese: Evidence from Speech Errors. *Language and Speech*, 32, 249–278.

Ladefoged, P. (1967). *Three Areas of Experimental Phonetics*. London: Oxford University Press.

Ladefoged, P. and Maddieson, I. (1996). *The Sounds of the World's Languages*. Oxford: Blackwell.

Leben, W. (1973). Suprasegmental Phonology (dissertation). MIT.

Lehmann, C. (2005). Latin Syllable Structure in Typological Perspective. *Journal of Latin Linguistics*, 9 (1), 127–148.

Liberman, M. and Prince, A. S. (1977). On Stress and Linguistic Rhythm. *Linguistic Inquiry*, 8, 249–336.

Lipski, J. (1985). /s/ in Central American Spanish. *Hispania*, 68, 143–149.

Lipski, J. (2016). Spanish Vocalic Epenthesis: The Phonetics of Sonority and the Mora. In N. A. Núñez-Cedeño (ed.), *The Syllable and Stress*. Berlin and Boston: De Gruyter, pp. 245–270.

Malmberg, B. (1965). *Estudios de fonética hispánica*. Madrid: CSIC.

Martínez-Gil, F. (2001). Sonority as a Primitive Phonological Feature: Evidence from Spanish Complex Onset Phonotactics. In J. Herschensohn, E. Mallen, and K. Zagona (eds.), *Features and Interfaces in Romance: Essays in Honor of Heles Contreras*. Amsterdam and Philadelphia, PA: John Benjamins, pp. 203–22.

McCarthy, J. (1979). On Stress and Syllabification. *Linguistic Inquiry*, 10, 443–466.

Moreno Sandoval, A., Torre, D., Curto, N., and Torre, R. (2006). Inventario de frecuencias fonémicas y silábicas del castellano espontáneo y escrito. In L. Buera, E. Lleida, A. Miguel, and A. Ortegae (eds.), *IV Jornadas en Tecnología del Habla*. Zaragoza: Universidad de Zaragoza, pp. 77–81.

Navarro Tomás, T. (1948). *El español en Puerto Rico*. San Juan: Editorial de la Universidad de Puerto Rico.

Nespor, M. and Vogel, I. (1986). *Prosodic Phonology*. Dordrecht: Foris.

Ohala, J. and Kawasaki-Fukumori, H. (1997). Alternatives to the Sonority Hierarchy for Explaining Segmental Sequential Constraints. In S. Eliasson and E. H. Jahr (eds.), *Language and its Ecology*. Berlin and New York: De Gruyter, pp. 343–366.

Padgett, Jaye (2008). Glides, Vowels, and Features. *Lingua*, 118 (12), 1937–1955. doi: 10.1016/j.lingua.2007.10.002.

Pike, K. L. (1947). *Phonemics: A Technique for Reducing Languages to Writing*. Ann Arbor, MI: University of Michigan Press.

Piñeros, C. E. (2016). The Phonological Weight of Spanish Syllables. In N. A. Núñez-Cedeño (ed.), *The Syllable and Stress*. Berlin and Boston, MA: De Gruyter, pp. 271–314.

Prince, A., and Smolensky, P. (2004). Optimality Theory: Constraint Interaction in Generative Grammar. In J. J. McCarthy (ed.), *Optimality Theory in Phonology*. Oxford: Blackwell, pp. 1–71.

Quilis, A. (1993). *Tratado de fonología y fonética españolas*. Madrid: Gredos.

Selkirk, E. (1978). On Prosodic Structure and its Relation to Syntactic Structure. In T. Fretheim (ed.), *Nordic Prosody II*. Trondheim: Tapir, pp. 111–40.

Selkirk, E. (1984). *Phonology and syntax. The relation between Sound and Structure*. Cambridge, MA: MIT Press.

Selkirk, E. (1986). On Derived Domains in Sentence Phonology. *Phonology Yearbook*, 3, 371–405.

Sievers, E. (1885). *An Old English Grammar* (translated by A. Cook). Boston, MA: Ginn Heath.

Simonet, M., Rohena-Madrazo, M., and Paz, M. (2008). Preliminary Evidence for Incomplete Neutralization of Coda Liquids in Puerto Rican Spanish. In L. Colantoni and J. Steele (eds.), *Selected Proceedings of the 3rd Conference on Laboratory Approaches to Spanish Phonology*. Somerville, MA: Cascadilla, pp. 72–86.

Trigo, R. L. (1988). The Phonological Derivation and Behavior of Nasal Glides (dissertation). MIT.

Whitney, W. D. (1873). *Oriental and Linguistic Studies*. New York: Scribner, Armstrong.

Widdison, K. (1995). An Acoustic and Perceptual Study of the Spanish Sound Changes s > h. *Rivista di Linguistica*, 7, 175–90.

Wiltshire, C. (2006). Prefix Boundaries in Spanish Varieties: A Non-Derivational OT Account. In S. Colina and F. Martínez-Gil (eds.), *OT Advances in Phonology*. Amsterdam: John Benjamins, pp. 358–377.

Yi, K. (1999). The Internal Structure of Korean Syllables: Rhyme or body? *Korean Journal of Experimental and Cognitive Psychology*, 10, 67–83.

Zoll, C. (1996). Parsing below the Segment in a Constraint Based Framework (dissertation). University of California, Berkeley.

10

Prosody: Stress, Rhythm, and Intonation

Pilar Prieto and Paolo Roseano

10.1 Introduction

Linguistic prosody has traditionally been referred to as "the music of speech." The acoustic correlates of prosody include the actual melody of speech (the so-called intonation), plus the rhythmic and durational patterns which typically characterize a given linguistic variety, as well as its intensity patterns. In addition to uniquely characterizing a given linguistic dialect or sociolect, prosodic patterns in speech provide it with a set of important linguistic and communicative functions. From a typological point of view, Spanish – like all Romance languages – belongs to the group of so-called intonation languages, that is, languages that use intonation not to distinguish lexical items (as do tonal languages), but rather to express a range of discourse meanings that often affect the interpretation of sentences in discourse. It is well known that pitch contours (together with other prosodic features) in a language like Spanish are key contributors to the semantico-pragmatic interpretation of sentences. Prosody conveys various communicative meanings that range from speech act marking (assertion, question, request, etc.), information status (focus, given vs. new information), belief status (or epistemic position of the speaker with respect to the information exchange), and politeness and affective states, to indexical functions such as gender, age, and the sociolectal and dialectal status of the speaker (see Prieto 2015). For example, depending on how a speaker of Spanish utters the sentence *Tiene frío* '(S)he is cold,' it can convey a variety of non-propositional meanings such as "Can you please close the window?," "He is surprisingly cold," "He is cold, and I am contradicting you," "I am not sure whether he is cold or not," "He is cold, I believe you should know," and "He is uncomfortably cold," among others.[1]

Another important function of prosody is that of marking prosodic phrasing (also called prosodic grouping), where speakers use prosody to group constituents into spoken chunks of information in order to give the

---

[1] Please also note that one does not necessarily need a specific pitch contour to get the implicature of the utterance *Please close the window.*

listener key information about syntactic groupings. Prosodic phrasing is necessary in Spanish (as well as in many other languages) to disambiguate utterances. Consider, for example, the sentence *Fueron con la madre de Helena y María*. If a speaker places a prosodic boundary after *Helena*, the hearer will probably interpret the sentence as meaning that "They went out with Helena's mother and María." Conversely, if no phrase boundary is placed between *Helena* and *María*, then the hearer will probably understand that "They went out with Helena and María's mother." English is another language that uses prosody to mark prosodic phrasing, as illustrated by the well-known apocryphal book dedication "To my parents, Ayn Rand and God," which is syntactically ambiguous. This ambiguity can be resolved through the use of intonation. If the speaker places a phrase boundary after "parents" and "Ayn Rand," he/she is dedicating the book to his/her parents as well as to Ayn Rand and God. If the speaker does not place a phrase boundary after "parents," he/she is claiming to be the lucky offspring of Ayn Rand and God (Nielsen Hayden 1994).

In addition to the marking of syntactic groupings, intonation plays an important role as an acoustic correlate of information structure. Information structure is commonly thought to be related with the management of common ground information in discourse and involves certain basic concepts like focus, givenness, and topic (see Krifka 2008 for a review). In English, information that has just been given in the immediate context is usually realized with prosodic reduction and lack of accentuation (typically by means of (very) compressed pitch movements associated with the stressed syllable). By contrast, focalized information is realized through strong pitch accentuation (typically by means of expanded pitch movements associated with the stressed syllable). In Spanish, focalization can be achieved by means of different strategies, either syntactic or intonational, which may vary according to the dialect and other factors (such as the type of focus and the syntactic function of the focalized element) (see Vanrell and Fernández-Soriano 2017). In "Narrow Focus Statements" (in Section 10.5.2 below) we will deal briefly with the intonational strategies of focusing used in Spanish.

Despite the importance of prosody in the linguistic system of languages, and specifically Spanish, its study has been relatively neglected in traditional grammars, which have typically concentrated on the description of syntactic and morphological patterns of the language, as well as the study of sounds. The first detailed description of Spanish prosody (based on central Peninsular Spanish read speech) was put forward by Navarro Tomás in his *Manual de pronunciación española* (1918), which included long sections dedicated to stress, rhythm, and intonation. This was followed up by his detailed *Manual de entonación española* (1944), still one of the most comprehensive books on Spanish intonation and prosody. Decades later, Quilis (1981, 1987, 1993) carried out phonetic comparisons of intonational contours of several dialectal varieties of Spanish, including those of Madrid, Mexico City, and Puerto Rico.

In the last two decades, the Autosegmental-Metrical framework of intonation (henceforth AM framework: Pierrehumbert 1980; Pierrehumbert and Beckman 1988; Gussenhoven 2004; Ladd 2008) has been established as one of the standard and most influential models of intonation, leading to an ample consensus among prosody researchers that intonation has a phonological status in natural languages. The AM framework has provided the basis for developing a diverse set of Tones and Break Indices (ToBI) annotation conventions for a large set of typologically diverse languages, all of which have closely followed the tenets of the AM model (see Jun 2005, 2014 for a review). The AM model describes intonational pitch contours as sequences of two main types of phonologically distinctive tonal units, namely pitch accents and edge tones. Pitch accents are intonational movements that associate with stressed syllables, rendering them intonationally prominent or accented. Edge tones (which can be separated into phrase accents and boundary tones) are also fundamental frequency movements that associate with the ends of prosodic phrases. These units are represented in terms of H(igh) and L(ow) targets. By convention, for pitch accents an asterisk "*" indicates association with stressed syllables (e.g. H*, L*, L+H*, and H+L*), and for edge tones "%" indicates association with the final edges of utterances (L%, H%, and LH%, among other possibilities) whereas "-" indicates association with utterance-internal phrase boundaries (L- and H-, among other possibilities). This phonological representation of tones is mapped onto a phonetic representation through language-specific implementation rules (see Gussenhoven 2004; Ladd 2008, for a review).

Within the AM model, Sosa (1999) offered the first integrated analysis of basic intonational contours in a large number of Spanish varieties, from both the Iberian peninsula (based on the speech of informants from Seville, Barcelona, Pamplona, and Madrid) and Latin America (Buenos Aires, Bogotá, Mexico City, San Juan de Puerto Rico, Caracas, Havana, and Lima). The first Spanish ToBI model was proposed by Beckman and colleagues in 2002 (Beckman et al. 2002) and has been revised several times since then (see Prieto and Roseano 2010, and Hualde and Prieto 2015 for a review). Most recently, the work of several groups of researchers investigating ten different geographical varieties of Spanish – namely Castilian, Cantabrian, Canarian, Dominican, Puerto Rican, Venezuelan Andean, Ecuadorian Andean, Chilean, Argentine, and Mexican – was compiled in Prieto and Roseano (2010), which offers a fully integrated ToBI analysis of these varieties and thus represents a key reference for any dialectal comparison of prosody in Spanish. Finally, Hualde and Prieto (2015) sum up this knowledge in a general and cross-dialectal overview of work-related Spanish prosody.

Typically, the study of Spanish prosody has been separated into four main topics, each the focus of independent study, namely, stress, rhythm, prosodic phrasing, and intonation. This chapter will accordingly address the stress patterns (Section 10.2), rhythmic patterns (Section 10.3), phrasing (Section 10.4), and intonation patterns (Section 10.5) of Spanish.

Importantly, Section 10.4 explains the basics of how to transcribe Spanish intonation and phrasing patterns following the most recent version of the Spanish ToBI labeling system (Sp_ToBI) (for an in-depth hands-on transcription of Spanish prosody, see *Spanish Training Materials*, Aguilar *et al.* 2009).

Though in this chapter we will note the systematic prosodic differences that exist across Spanish dialectal varieties, for purely practical reasons many of the examples given will be based on Peninsular Spanish. For more information on dialectal variation, we invite the reader to access specific dialectal monographs and also listen to the recordings available via the online *Interactive Atlas of Spanish Intonation* (Prieto and Roseano 2009–2013), which at present contains audio examples of 18 different sentence types from 23 locales across the Spanish-speaking world (as well as a video interview and other interactive recordings), and/or AMPER-ESP, the Spanish section of the *Atlas Multimédia de la Prosodie de l'Espace Roman* (Martínez Celdrán and Fernández Planas 2003–2016), which currently offers audio examples of two sentence types from 36 Spanish-speaking locales.

10.2 Stress

Like most Romance languages, Spanish has lexical stress (also called word stress). Lexically stressed syllables are typically one of the last three syllables of the word, except for a few verbs with final enclitics (e.g. mi**rán**domelo 'looking at it.me,' where boldface indicates the stressed syllable). Though Spanish has a few minimal triplets contrasting in lexical stress position (e.g. *cé*lebre 'famous' vs. *ce*lebre 'celebrate.3SG.SBJV' vs. *celebré* 'I celebrated'), there are clear tendencies in stress placement which work differently for the nominal and verbal paradigms. Nouns ending in a vowel in the singular typically have penultimate stress (*ca*sa 'house'), with some marked antepenultimate stress patterns (*bo*lígrafo 'pen') and some exceptional cases of final stress (*dominó* 'domino'). By contrast, nouns ending in a consonant in the singular tend to have final stress[2] (e.g. ca**mión** 'truck'), whereas penultimate stress is less common (**lá**piz 'pencil'), and antepenultimate stress is exceptional (a**ná**lisis 'analysis'). In quantitative terms, more than 95 percent of all nouns, adjectives, and adverbs follow the unmarked patterns (Morales-Front 1999:211). In the verbal paradigm, stress is either penultimate or final in the present tense (ca**mi**no 'I walk,' cami**na**mos 'we walk,' cami**náis** 'you walk') and morphologically triggered in other tenses, with stress falling either on the syllable which contains that conjugation or theme vowel (cami**na**ba 'I was walking,' cami**ná**bamos 'we were walking') or on the tense morpheme (cami**naré** 'I will walk,' camina**re**mos 'we will walk'). Function words are typically

---

[2] As is well known, this is for historical reasons. For a detailed description of how Vulgar Latin words ending in VC lost the VC in question, see Lapesa (1984).

unstressed (e.g. *mi **ca**sa* 'my house,' *su **ca**sa* 'his/her house') with some exceptions (e.g. **u**na ***ca**sa* 'a house,' *es*ta ***ca**sa* 'this house') (for further details on stressed and unstressed functional words, see Quilis 1993:390–395 and Hualde 2005:233). The unstressed–stressed distinction can give rise to phrasal minimal pairs, as in *para los ca**ba**llos* 'for the horses' vs. ***pa**ra los ca**ba**llos* 's/he stops the horses/stop the horses!' or *bajo la **me**sa* 'under the table' vs. ***ba**jo la **me**sa* 'I lower the table' (Hualde 2005:233–235).

Lexically-stressed syllables have been reported to have clear acoustic correlates, namely longer durations,[3] higher fundamental frequency, and higher intensity than unstressed syllables (see Pamies Bertrán 1993 for a review of acoustic correlates of stress in Spanish and other languages). However, it is important to note that the pitch correlates of stress (that is, whether the stressed syllable is associated with a high or low tone) will depend mainly on the intonational pattern of the sentence in question (see Section 10.5). For example, while the final stressed syllable of a rising intonation contour such as *¿Tienen mandarinas?* 'Do you have any tangerines?' bears the lowest levels of pitch within the word *mandarinas* (see Figure 10.9 in Section 10.5.3), the contrary is true in a sentence like *¡Tienen mandarinas!* 'They have tangerines!' in which this same syllable bears the highest pitch level. The position of the target word within the sentence will also play a role in pitch levels. On the other hand, the duration correlates of stress are mainly dependent on the phrasal level of prominence that stressed syllables attain. Cross-linguistic evidence has demonstrated that increased duration is an important acoustic correlate of prosodic heads (or prominent units) and edges of prosodic phrases (see Prieto *et al.* 2012 for a review). First, in Spanish, as in other Romance languages, nuclear stress (or main phrasal stress) is the most prominent stress in the sentence and typically falls on the last content word of the sentence, except for very marked cases of emphatic or contrastive focus (Zubizarreta and Nava 2011; see "Narrow Focus Statements" in Section 10.5.2 below). In comparison with English, which exhibits a greater flexibility in the location of nuclear stress, Romance languages usually show greater flexibility in word order and a more consistent tendency to place nuclear stress at the end of an utterance, e.g. English *JOHN bought them* vs. Spanish *Las compró JUAN* (Ladd 2008; Zubizarreta and Nava 2011). Thus, in Spanish, nuclear stressed syllables exhibit the most prominent stress within the sentence and are one of the longest syllables in the sentence, together with phrase-final syllables.

Similarly to nuclear stressed syllables, non-nuclear stressed syllables (also called prenuclear stressed syllables) quite systematically serve as the anchoring site for pitch accents, giving rise to a high pitch accent

---

[3] The *cordobés* variety of Spanish, spoken in central Argentina, is an interesting exception to the tendency according to which stressed syllables are longer than unstressed syllables. In fact, pretonic syllables have been reported to be considerably longer than stressed syllables in this variety of Spanish (Lang-Rigal 2014).

density. Pitch accents are realized as visible pitch excursions and/or characterized by expanded duration. This one-to-one correspondence between stressed syllables and pitch accents is a feature that contrasts with English pronunciation, which has many more cases of stressed syllables with no associated pitch accent (e.g. Spanish *Vino por detrás de Juliana* vs. English *He came after Juliana*). However, the common one-to-one association between stress and pitch accentuation sometimes breaks down. First, in rhetorical, didactic, or emphatic speech, lexically unstressed (and pretonic) syllables often receive a pitch accent (e.g. **im***portante* vs. *im***por***tante* 'important'; see Hualde 2007, 2009; Hualde and Nadeu 2014). Second, it is also possible for stressed syllables to surface as unaccented. A contextual prosodic factor leading to de-accentuation is stress clash. For example, an utterance like *detrás suyo* 'after him/her' is typically produced with one pitch accent over the last stressed syllable (in other words, the pitch accent we would typically expect on *detrás* is not realized due to clash). Although the prominence of the stressed syllable in such cases tends to be conveyed by duration in the absence of a pitch excursion, complete de-accentuation is also possible (see examples in Hualde and Prieto 2015).

10.3 Rhythm

Rhythm refers to the organization of timing in speech, and it has been shown to be different across languages (see Ramus *et al.* 1999 for a review). Spanish, together with languages such as Italian, has been classified as a syllable-timed language, as opposed to stress-timed languages like English or Dutch. In stress-timed languages stressed syllables are significantly longer than unstressed syllables, creating the sensation of a Morse-type rhythmic effect; by contrast, syllable-timed languages like Spanish create a stronger perception of equal prosodic saliency across syllables.

Work on linguistic rhythm has strongly correlated the differences in rhythmic percept found between languages with a set of language-specific phonetic and phonological properties, of which the two most often cited are syllabic structure and vowel reduction. While stress-timed languages like English have a greater range of syllable structure types, allowing for more complex codas and onsets, and also exhibit vowel reduction, syllable-timed languages like Spanish, by contrast, tend to have a significant proportion of open syllables and no vowel reduction. It has been suggested that the coexistence of these sets of phonological properties is responsible for promoting either a strong saliency of stressed syllables in relation to other syllables – yielding the "stress-timed" effect – or the percept of equal salience between syllables – yielding the "syllable-timed" effect.

Apart from this tendency, cross-linguistic studies on speech rhythm have investigated the timing (or duration patterns) of speech and have found differences in overall timing patterns across languages, as well as what has been called "rhythm metrics" (see Prieto *et al.* 2012 for a review). In a recent study, Prieto *et al.* (2012) showed that when syllable structure properties are controlled for, timing patterns for Spanish and English can be traced back to the duration measures of prominent positions (e.g. accented, nuclear accented, and stressed syllables) and edge positions (e.g. distances to phrase-final positions).

10.4 Intonation and Phrasing

Intonation is what we call in daily language "the melody of an utterance." In more technical terms, it is the linguistic use of the modulation of F0 (or fundamental frequency, which is the lowest harmonic in voiced parts of speech). As noted in the Introduction, intonation has two main linguistic functions: (i) to mark phrasing (see "Levels of Prosodic Phrasing" in Section 10.4.1), and (ii) to encode speech act distinctions, sentence modality, focus (see Section 10.5.2), and belief state (see "Statements of the Obvious" and "Uncertainty Statements," also in Section 10.5.2). We will start this section by explaining the basics of prosodic transcription in Spanish using the Sp_ToBI conventions (see Section 10.4.1). As we do so, however, it is important to bear in mind that dialectal variation (also called diatopic or geographic variation) affects all aspects of Spanish, including intonation.

10.4.1 Transcription of Spanish Prosody Using the Sp_ToBI System

As mentioned, the most common system used at present to transcribe the intonation of Spanish relies on the premises of the Autosegmental-Metrical model and is known by the acronym Sp_ToBI (see the Introduction, Section 10.1). Since its inception nearly two decades ago (Beckman *et al.* 2002) Sp_ToBI has been periodically updated (Hualde 2003, Face and Prieto 2007, Estebas Vilaplana and Prieto 2008, Prieto and Roseano 2010, Hualde and Prieto 2015), so that it can now be used to transcribe the intonation of virtually all dialects of Spanish. The existence of a common transcription system allows for easy comparison of the intonation and phrasing patterns of the different geographic varieties of the language.

An example of Sp_ToBI transcription can be seen in Figure 10.1 for the imperative question ¿*Callaréis?* 'Will you be quiet?' as uttered by a speaker of southern Peninsular Spanish (Henriksen and García-Amaya 2012). The three labeling tiers below the acoustic plot contain an orthographic (or phonetic) transcription of the sentence (top tier), followed by the prosodic annotation in two tiers, namely the Break Indices tier (second tier) and the Tones tier (third tier). The content of the Break Indices and Tones tiers is explained in the following sections ("Levels of Prosodic Phrasing" and "Pitch Accents and Boundary Tones").

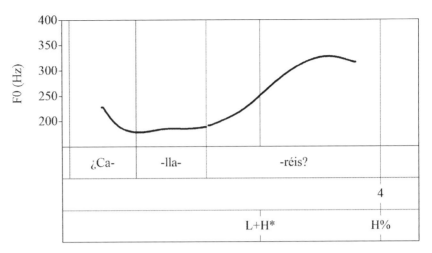

Figure 10.1 Prosodic features of the imperative question ¿*Callaréis?* 'Will you be quiet?' as uttered by a speaker of southern Peninsular Spanish

Levels of Prosodic Phrasing

Two levels of prosodic structure are relevant in the Sp_ToBI notation system: the Intonation Phrase (IP) and the intermediate phrase (ip). The IP is the domain of the minimal tune, and consists of at least one pitch accent followed by a boundary tone. The ip is a minor domain located below the IP which usually corresponds to different types of syntactic elements such as a clause, a dislocated element, a parenthetic element, the subject of the utterance, each element of an enumeration, and so on. In every ip there may be one or more prosodic words (or PW). A PW, in its turn, is made up of one accented word and the adjacent unstressed elements, like articles, prepositions, and so on.

When transcribing the prosody of an utterance according to the Sp_ToBI system, the prosodic phrasing is reflected in the Break Indices or "BI tier," which contains information about the edges of prosodic units. A 4 in this tier marks the end of an IP, while a 3 marks the end of a non-final ip. A 1 marks the end of a PW and 0 can be used (optionally) to mark the end of an unstressed element. Finally, according to the *Sp_ToBI Training Materials* (Aguilar *et al.* 2009), a level 2 break index is supposed to mark two different types of breaks that are less common, namely a perceived disjuncture with no intonation effect, or an apparent intonational boundary that lacks slowing or other break cues.

Pitch Accents and Boundary Tones

Sp_ToBI makes use of two different sets of symbols for tonal events. On the one hand, there are pitch accents (henceforth PA), which are the tonal events anchored to a stressed syllable. On the other, there are boundary tones (henceforth BT), which are the tonal events anchored to phrase-final edges. PAs can appear in either nuclear or prenuclear position (see the Introduction, Section 10.1). The combination of the last PA of an utterance and the following BT is called the nuclear configuration. In Romance languages, the nuclear configuration usually contains the most important

Table 10.1 *Schematic representation, Sp_ToBI labels, and phonetic descriptions of the most common pitch accents in Spanish*

		Monotonal pitch accents
	L*	This pitch accent is phonetically realized as a low plateau at the minimum of the speaker's pitch range.
	H*	This accent is phonetically realized as a high plateau with no preceding F0 valley.
	¡H*	This accent is phonetically realized as a rise from a high plateau to an extra-high level.
		Bitonal pitch accents
	L+H*	This accent is phonetically realized as a rising pitch movement during the stressed syllable with the F0 peak located at the end of this syllable.
	L+¡H*	This pitch accent is phonetically realized as rise to a very high peak located in the accented syllable. It contrasts with L+H* in F0 scaling.
	L+<H*	This accent is phonetically realized as a rising pitch movement in the stressed syllable with the F0 peak in the post-accentual syllables.
	L*+H	This accent is phonetically realized as a F0 valley on the stressed syllable with a subsequent rise on the post-accentual syllable.
	H+L*	This accent is phonetically realized as a F0 fall from a high level within the stressed syllable.
		Tritonal pitch accent
	L+H*+L	This pitch accent displays a rising–falling pattern within the stressed syllable.

Note: In the schematic representations, white rectangles represent unstressed syllables and gray rectangles represent stressed syllables.

information transmitted by intonation (see Section 10.5 for some examples of how different nuclear configurations encode sentence modality). Although the main difference between two pitch contours typically lies in the nuclear configuration, the prenuclear part can also differ.

Table 10.1 contains a description of the most frequent PAs found in Spanish ToBI systems, which may be grouped into four families: flat, rising, falling, and rising–falling (based on Prieto and Roseano 2010, Hualde and Prieto 2015). Some of these PAs are used in all dialects (like L+H*), while others seem to have a very specific geographic distribution (like L+H*+L, which appears only in Argentine dialects). Most pitch accents may appear in either nuclear position (i.e. associated with the last stressed syllable) or prenuclear position (i.e. associated with any stressed syllable except the last). A few pitch accents (like L+<H*), on the other hand, do not appear in nuclear position. Figures 10.2–10.16 offer different examples of the various PA types.

In general, Spanish displays quite a rich inventory of boundary tones, which are the tones associated with the right edge of either an IP (in this case they are marked with a % symbol) or an ip (in this case a - symbol is used). Nonetheless, not all Spanish dialects are equally rich in BTs: while some, like Castilian Spanish, have up to six boundary tones, other varieties like Dominican Spanish – which has only four BTs – make use of a more limited set (Willis 2010).

Boundary tones may have different degrees of complexity, being either monotonal or bitonal. Table 10.2 contains a schematic representation and detailed description of the most frequent BTs found in Spanish (based on Aguilar *et al.* 2009, Prieto and Roseano 2010, Hualde and Prieto 2015).

Table 10.2 *Schematic representation, Sp_ToBI labels, and phonetic descriptions of the most common boundary tones in Spanish*

	Label	Description
Monotonal boundary tones		
	L%	This boundary tone is phonetically realized as a low or falling tone at the baseline of the speaker.
	!H%	This boundary tone is phonetically realized as a rising or falling movement to a target mid point.
	H%	This boundary tone is phonetically realized as a rising pitch movement coming from a low or rising pitch accent.
Bitonal boundary tones		
	LH%	This boundary tone is phonetically realized as a F0 valley followed by a rise.
	L!H%	This boundary tone is phonetically realized as a F0 valley followed by a rise into a mid pitch.
	HL%	This boundary tone is phonetically realized as a F0 peak followed by a fall.

Note: In the schematic representations, white rectangles represent stressed syllables and gray rectangles represent final unstressed syllables.

The intonation contours illustrated in the following section will be analyzed as a series of Sp_ToBI pitch accents and boundary tones.

10.5 Main Intonation Contours

As we have observed (see the Introduction, Section 10.1), one of the main functions of intonation in Spanish is to mark speech act information, in other words, to indicate whether we intend a sentence to be interpreted as an assertion, a question, a request, etc. Within these speech acts, intonation can also mark information status (focus, given vs. new information), as well as belief status (epistemic position of the speaker with respect to the information exchange). In this section, we will exemplify the most common intonation contours characterizing assertions (Sections 10.5.1 and 10.5.2), yes–no questions (Sections 10.5.3 and 10.5.4), *wh*-questions (Section 10.5.5), imperatives (Section 10.5.6), and vocatives/calls (Section 10.5.7).

A comprehensive description of the intonation contours of the most important sentence-types in the major Spanish dialects would require a few hundred pages (Prieto and Roseano 2010 being a case in point). For this reason, in the following pages we will focus on the intonation patterns of a few sentence types found in Castilian Spanish (also known as central Peninsular Spanish) and limit ourselves to noting only the most salient differences between Castilian and other Spanish dialects. The reason why Castilian Spanish has been chosen is that it is one of the varieties that has been described most extensively from a prosodic point of view. The reader will find the actual sound files as well as more complete acoustic representations of those files and dialectal recordings of similar sentences online in the *Interactive Atlas of Spanish Intonation* (Prieto and Roseano 2009–2013).

10.5.1 Broad Focus Statements

A broad focus statement is a sentence that typically communicates a piece of information that is new to the hearer. The information is given neutrally, without any further added nuance (like surprise, doubt, and so on). For example, imagine that a parent calls home to find out what his/her children, named María and Juan, are doing. Juan's answer illustrated in (10.1) is usually realized as a broad focus statement.

(10.1) SPEAKER A (PARENT): What are you guys up to?
SPEAKER B (JUAN): María's drinking her lemonade.

In most dialects of Spanish, broad focus statements display a pitch contour that is similar to that represented in Figure 10.2. It is characterized by a pitch rise associated with the first stressed syllable (a L+ < H*

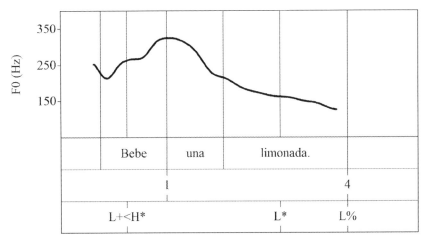

Figure 10.2 F0 contour, spectrogram, orthographic transcription, and prosodic annotation of the broad focus statement *Bebe una limonada* 'He/she's drinking a [his/her] lemonade' in Castilian Spanish

pitch accent in the example below) followed by a set of optional rising pitch accents. The sentence ends in a nuclear stress (or main phrasal stress), which is the most prominent stress in the sentence and is typically realized with a low or falling pitch movement L* followed by a low final boundary tone L%.

One notable exception to the general tendency of Spanish dialects to have a falling pitch movement at the end of assertions is the so-called *entonación circunfleja* ("circumflex intonation") seen in some American varieties like Mexican and Chilean Spanish. Note, however, that in these two dialects the circumflex pattern applied to broad focus statements is an alternative to but does not completely replace the falling contour (Ortiz et al. 2010; Martín Butragueño and Mendoza 2017). This circumflex pattern, characterized by a rise associated with the last stressed syllable (L+H*) and a final fall to a low level (L%), is represented in Figure 10.3, adapted from Martín Butragueño and Mendoza (2017).

In addition, other dialects diverge in the choice of prenuclear pitch accents. For example, varieties like Puerto Rican Spanish use L*+H instead of L+ <H* (Armstrong 2010).

10.5.2 Biased Statements

As mentioned above, two of the main functions of intonation are to mark information structure and belief status (e.g. the epistemic position of the speaker with respect to the information exchange). In this section we describe the typical intonation patterns found for narrow focus statements, statements of the obvious, and uncertainty statements.

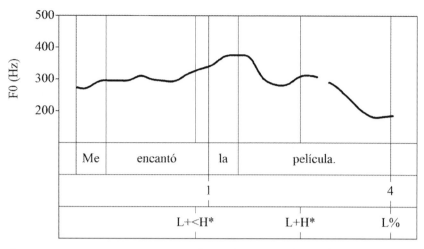

Figure 10.3 F0 contour, spectrogram, orthographic transcription, and prosodic annotation of the broad focus statement *Me encantó la película* 'I loved the film' as uttered by a speaker of Mexican Spanish

Narrow Focus Statements

Whereas in broad focus statements all information is new for the listener, in narrow focus statements only part of the information is in focus. For example, the question–answer test in (10.2) shows that the focused material in the response sentence corresponds to the constituent *mi hermana*, while the information that precedes it (i.e. *Las ha comprado*) is mutually assumed by the two interlocutors.

(10.2)   SPEAKER A: *¿Quién ha comprado manzanas?*
            SPEAKER B: *Las ha comprado mi hermana.*

In Spanish focus marking can alter the canonical SVO order (see Chapter 17, this volume, for an overview). In the example in (10.2), the subject has moved to final position, where it receives main stress in a nuclear stress (or main phrasal stress), which is the most prominent stress in the sentence and is typically realized with a low or falling pitch accent L* followed by a low final boundary tone L%. The intonation of informative narrow focus statements in Spanish is usually the same as that of broad focus statements (Section 10.5.1).

There are two main kinds of narrow focus statement, informative and corrective/contrastive. While the response in (10.2) constitutes an example of informative narrow statement, the examples in (10.3a) and (10.3b) exemplify two types of corrective or contrastive narrow focused statements which challenge and replace information given previously in the discourse. The contrastively focused element may either appear in its canonical position (like in 10.3a) or be displaced (as in 10.3b) (Vanrell et al. 2013).

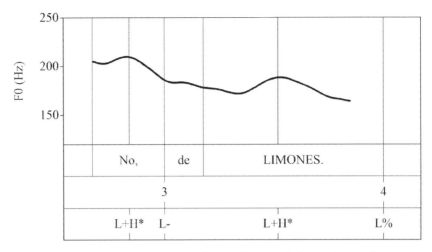

Figure 10.4 F0 contour, spectrogram, orthographic transcription, and prosodic annotation of the narrow focus statement *No, de LIMONES* 'No, [I want a kilo] of LEMONS' as uttered by a speaker of Castilian Spanish

(10.3)   Speaker A: *Quiero un quilo de limones.*
        Speaker B: *¿Qué has dicho, que quieres mandarinas?*

a. Speaker A: *No.*   *Quiero*   LIMONES.
                     No.   want.1sg   LEMONS.

b. Speaker A: *No.*   LIMONES,   *quiero.*
                     No.   lemons   want.1sg

Independently from its position within the sentence, many Spanish dialects signal this corrective focused element through a salient F0 movement, typically a pitch rise, which allows the listener to easily identify it. In all the Spanish dialects documented, this contour is different from that seen in broad focus statements. Although there are differences among dialects, the focal pitch accent is mostly either high or rising. In Castilian Spanish, for example, the focused element is characterized by a rising L + H* accent and a final low boundary tone (L%), as can be seen in Figure 10.4.

Although the strategy described above is very common, it is not the only one. More details on the different focus marking strategies in Spanish may be found in Face (2002) and Vanrell and Fernández-Soriano (in press), among others.

Statements of the Obvious

By using a statement of the obvious, a speaker expresses his/her opinion that the listener should already know the information. Imagine, for example, that two friends are speaking about a mutual long-term acquaintance, María, as in (10.4). They both know that she has been dating her boyfriend, Guillermo, since they were very young. Speaker A tells B that María is now pregnant and B asks who the father is. Speaker A tells her it is Guillermo, astonished that Speaker B should not have drawn the obvious conclusion.

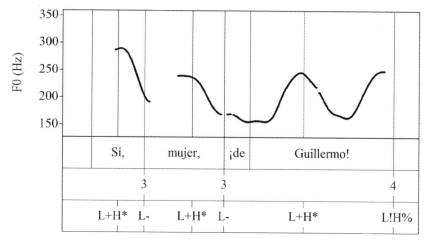

Figure 10.5 F0 contour, spectrogram, orthographic transcription, and prosodic annotation of the statement of the obvious *Sí, mujer, ¡de Guillermo!* '[It's] Guillermo's [of course]!' as uttered by a speaker of Castilian Spanish

(10.4) SPEAKER A: María's pregnant.
        SPEAKER B: Whose baby is it?
        SPEAKER A: It's Guillermo's, of course!

While some languages mark obviousness with a lexical item (like "of course" in English), some dialects of Spanish employ a specific intonational pattern to convey the same meaning. The pattern used to express obviousness in many Peninsular Spanish dialects (like Castilian, Cantabrian, and Canarian Spanish) and some Latin American varieties (like Puerto Rican and Mexican Spanish) is a complex rise-fall-rise pitch movement (L+H* L!H% in Sp_ToBI terms). The F0 contour in Figure 10.5 illustrates this rise-fall-rise pitch contour on the word *Guillermo*.

Other Latin American Spanish varieties like Dominican, Venezuelan Andean, Ecuadorian Andean, Chilean, and Argentine Spanish tend to express obviousness using the same intonation pattern as that seen in narrow focus statements (discussed above).

Uncertainty Statements

Uncertainty statements are used by speakers to convey a lack of commitment to the truth-content of the proposition being expressed. The conversational exchange in (10.5) illustrates a context for low commitment statement, where A asks B whether he/she has bought a gift for C, a person that A does not know very well. B answers positively, but adds that he/she is not sure whether C will like the gift or not.

(10.5) SPEAKER A: Have you bought a gift for C?
        SPEAKER B: Yes, I have. But she may not like it.

While some languages mark uncertainty with a set of lexical items (such as modal verbs like "might" or epistemic adverbs like "possibly"), some Spanish

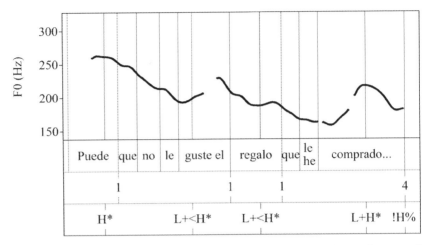

Figure 10.6 F0 contour, spectrogram, orthographic transcription, and prosodic annotation of the uncertainty statement *Puede que no le guste el regalo que le he comprado* ... 'S/he may not like the gift I have bought him/her' as uttered by a speaker of Castilian Spanish

dialects can also employ specific intonational patterns to convey this meaning. For example, Castilian Spanish expresses uncertainty by means of a final rising–falling movement that does not fall to the baseline of the speaker's range (L + H* !H% in Sp_ToBI terms), as illustrated in Figure 10.6.

10.5.3 Information-Seeking Yes–No Questions

Information-seeking yes–no questions are used to ask for a piece of information, with no expectation about the possible answer. Research has shown that the intonation of information-seeking yes–no questions can differ sharply among the different dialects of Spanish (Navarro Tomás 1944; Quilis 1993; Sosa 1999; Prieto and Roseano 2010). In very broad terms, interrogative pitch contours can be classified into rising and falling contours. Central and southern Peninsular Spanish, Ecuadorian Andean, Chilean, and Mexican Spanish all use a pitch contour characterized by a final low-rise. On the other hand, a second dialect cluster including Canarian, Argentine, Venezuelan Andean, and several Caribbean varieties (like Cuban, Dominican, and Puerto Rican) use a pitch contour with a final falling pattern. Figure 10.7 illustrates a rising pattern (the one used in Castilian Spanish), while Figures 10.8 and 10.9 offer examples of falling patterns from, respectively, Puerto Rican (Armstrong 2015) and Argentine Spanish (Kaisse 2001; Gabriel *et al.* 2010). The rise–fall pitch contour seen in Argentine Spanish has a very characteristic final long fall.

10.5.4 Biased Yes–No Questions

Biased yes–no questions are a rather heterogeneous group that includes several kinds of polar questions that a speaker asks when his/her intention

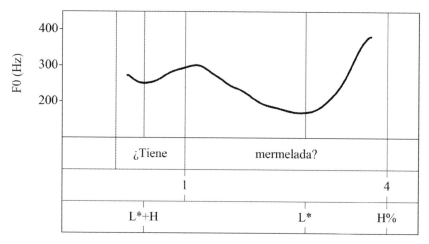

Figure 10.7 F0 contour, spectrogram, orthographic transcription, and prosodic annotation of the information-seeking yes–no question ¿*Tiene mermelada?* 'Do you have any jam?' as uttered by a speaker of Castilian Spanish

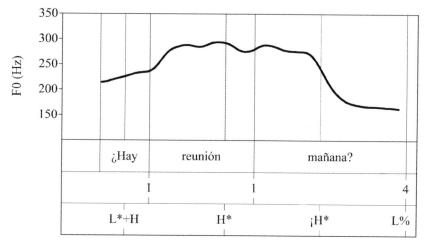

Figure 10.8 F0 contour, spectrogram, orthographic transcription, and prosodic annotation of the information-seeking yes–no question ¿*Hay reunión mañana?* 'Is there a meeting tomorrow?' as uttered by a speaker of Puerto Rican Spanish

is not simply to ask for a piece of information about which he/she has no expectation. Among them, confirmation questions, imperative questions, and echo questions are the most common.

Confirmation-Seeking Questions

When someone asks a confirmation question, he/she has some kind of expectation about the answer. Some languages, like English, usually encode this expectation by means of a tag question, which means that the speaker utters a statement followed by a confirmation tag like "isn't it?" This can happen in Spanish too, where the most common confirmation tags are ¿*no*?

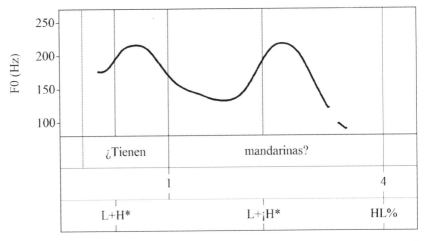

Figure 10.9 F0 contour, spectrogram, orthographic transcription, and prosodic annotation of the information-seeking yes–no question ¿Tienen mandarinas? 'Do you have any tangerines?' as uttered by a speaker of Argentine Spanish

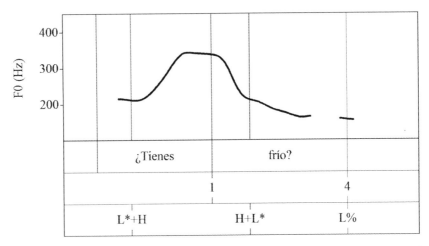

Figure 10.10 F0 contour, spectrogram, orthographic transcription, and prosodic annotation of the confirmation question ¿Tienes frío? 'Are you cold?' as uttered by a speaker of Castilian Spanish

and ¿verdad? '[isn't that the] truth?' In addition to this lexical marking of confirmation-seeking, several varieties of Spanish have specific contours that appear in confirmation-seeking yes–no questions.[4] Speakers of Castilian Spanish, for example, may use the falling pattern exemplified in Figure 10.10 (transcribed as H+L* L% in Sp_ToBI terms), which is radically different from the rising contour of information-seeking yes–no questions that we saw in Section 10.5.3 (Figure 10.7).

[4] "Confirmation-seeking question" is the traditional interpretation/label of the pragmatic function of this contour. Recent research suggests that "confirmation-seeking questions" can be better understood in terms of belief/epistemic states (Armstrong 2015; Henriksen et al. 2016).

Echo Questions

An echo question is a question that repeats more or less verbatim an element that precedes it in the exchange, as illustrated by Speaker A's final "It's nine o'clock?" in (10.6). Echo questions may indicate that a person is not sure he/she has understood what an interlocutor has said, as in (10.6), but they may also be used to show that the speaker has understood the preceding utterance but is surprised or even astonished by it, as in (10.7).

(10.6) SPEAKER A: What time is it?
        SPEAKER B (whispering): It's nine o'clock.
        SPEAKER A: What? It's nine o'clock?

(10.7) SPEAKER A: Have you heard anything about Tracy lately?
        SPEAKER B: She's marrying Sam.
        SPEAKER A: She's marrying Sam?! Wow!

Echo questions show considerable interdialectal variation in Spanish. One of the most common nuclear configurations used for echo questions is the rise–fall tune, which is characterized by a rise to an extra-high level in the last stressed syllable followed by a fall (L+¡H* L% in ToBI transcription). This contour is found in, among other dialects, Canarian and Castilian (Figure 10.11). The more incredulous echo questions like that exemplified in (10.7) are realized either with the contour described above but with an expanded pitch range, or with a specific incredulity pitch contour (see a description of the incredulity interrogative contour L* HL% in Armstrong 2015).

10.5.5 Information-Seeking *wh*-Questions

Information-seeking *wh*-questions are used when speakers ask for a specific piece of information without any further pragmatic intention.

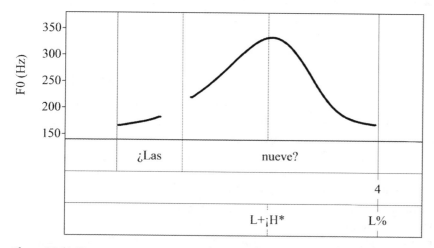

Figure 10.11 F0 contour, spectrogram, orthographic transcription, and prosodic annotation of the echo question *¿Las nueve?* 'Nine o'clock?' as uttered by a speaker of Castilian Spanish

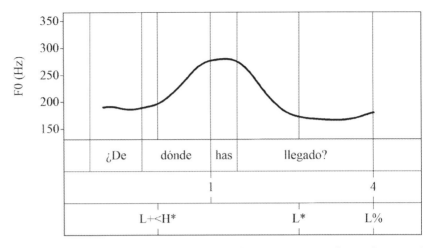

Figure 10.12 F0 contour, spectrogram, orthographic transcription, and prosodic annotation of the information-seeking *wh*-question *¿De dónde has llegado?* 'Where have you arrived from?' as uttered by a speaker of Castilian Spanish

The pitch contour of this sentence type displays as much dialectal variation as that seen in yes–no questions. Nevertheless, the general tendency is for *wh*-questions to end with a low tone, as illustrated in Figure 10.12.

10.5.6 Commands and Requests

Imperatives are linguistic expressions which communicate either an order or a request, depending on the intonation used. For example, the intonation of "Come here!" as spoken by a dog owner to his/her errant dog will reflect the full authority the speaker feels relative to the animal. By contrast, the intonation of "Come on, man!" as spoken by someone trying to cajole a friend into forgetting their work obligations and accompanying him/her to the cinema will reflect a much more peer-to-peer kind of relationship.

In most dialects of Spanish, intonational pitch contours used for orders typically show a final fall or a rise–fall. In other words, they tend to use either the same pitch contour as that used for broad focus statements (Venezuelan Andean, Ecuadorian Andean, and Argentine Spanish) or the pitch contour used for narrow focus statements (Castilian, Canarian, Chilean, and Mexican Spanish). Figure 10.13 provides an example of an imperative in Castilian Spanish, where orders are expressed by means of a rising–falling final movement (L+H* L% in Sp_ToBI terms).

Though imperative requests in Spanish are typically also encoded by means of lexical items like *va* 'come on' or *por favor* 'please,' intonation (as well as a much slower speech rate) plays a key role in conveying this intention. Most dialects use a configuration that is different from that used for orders. In the case of Castilian Spanish, for example, the

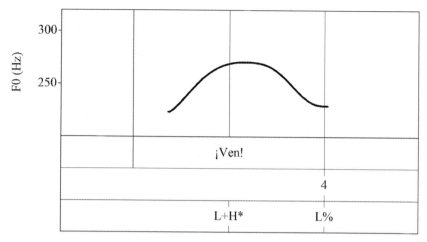

Figure 10.13 F0 contour, spectrogram, orthographic transcription, and prosodic annotation of the command ¡Ven! 'Come here!' as uttered by a speaker of Castilian Spanish

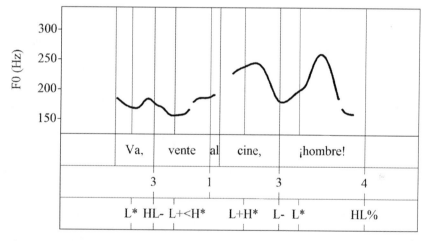

Figure 10.14 F0 contour, spectrogram, orthographic transcription, and prosodic annotation of the cajoling imperative request Va, vente al cine, ¡hombre! 'Come on, come to the cinema, man!' as uttered by a speaker of Castilian Spanish

imperative request contour is characterized by a complex fall–rise–fall pitch contour (L* HL%). While the low part of the nuclear configuration (L*) is temporally associated with the final stressed syllable, the final rise–fall boundary tone (HL%) is associated with the post-tonic syllables. This intonation contour is exemplified in Figure 10.14.

10.5.7 Calls

Vocatives are used to call someone's attention, with different degrees of insistence and/or imperativeness. In several intonational languages calls

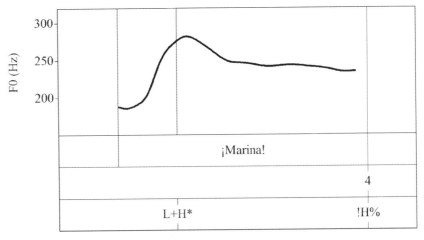

Figure 10.15 F0 contour, spectrogram, orthographic transcription, and prosodic annotation of the call *¡Marina!* 'Marina!' uttered with the common calling contour

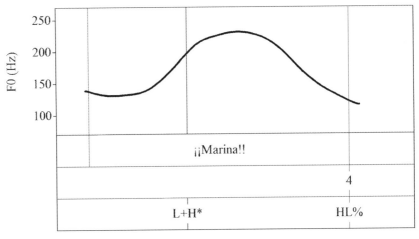

Figure 10.16 F0 contour, spectrogram, orthographic transcription, and prosodic annotation of the insistent call *¡¡Marina!!* 'Marina!!'

are characterized by a chanted intonation (L+H* !H% in Sp_ToBI terms). This contour, which is found in most Spanish dialects, shows an F0 rise in the stressed syllable, followed by a fall to a mid level in the following unstressed syllables (which are usually considerably lengthened), like what we see in Figure 10.15.

A slightly different pitch contour, which seems to convey a more insistent or imperative nuance in several varieties of Spanish, is characterized by a rise in the stressed syllable that ends in the post-tonic stretch and a final fall to the baseline of the speaker's range (L+H* HL% in Sp_ToBI labels). Figure 10.16 offers an example of this contour.

10.6 Summary and Conclusion

This chapter has presented a brief overview of the main features of Spanish prosody and intonation. From a typological perspective, Spanish is a prominence-final language which tends to assign nuclear prominence (or nuclear stress) to the last stressed syllable of the intonational phrase. This contrasts with English, which has a more flexible placement of nuclear stress within the intonational phrase (see Section 10.2). With regard to rhythm, Spanish is a syllable-timed language and therefore does not exhibit a sharp durational difference between stressed and unstressed syllables, unlike stress-timed languages like English (see Section 10.3). Another difference concerns pitch accent density: while Spanish has a tendency to show a one-to-one correspondence between stressed syllables and pitch accents, this is not the case for languages like English.

From an intonational point of view, Spanish is an intonational language which uses melodic modulations for a wide set of pragmatic functions, including speech act marking, epistemic marking, and information structure marking. The present chapter has presented the most common melodic contours used to mark these distinctions (see Sections 10.4 and 10.5). Though most of the examples are drawn from the Peninsular Spanish varieties, we have also illustrated some clear differences between dialects, such as the so-called Mexican declarative circumflex contour (Sosa 1999; Martín Butragueño and Mendoza 2017) or the long fall of Argentine interrogatives (see Kaisse 2001; Gabriel *et al.* 2010). For readers interested in these interdialectal differences in Spanish intonation, we recommend accessing the audio and video recordings of nine dialects of Spanish available at the *Interactive Atlas of Spanish Intonation* website (Prieto and Roseano 2009–2013).

Finally, throughout the chapter we have made use of the most recent version of Sp_ToBI, a consensus prosody transcription system based on the Autosegmental-Metrical model (see Section 10.4.1). Importantly, the fact that full Sp_ToBI descriptions of many of the dialectal varieties of Spanish are now available has meant that cross-dialectal comparisons of Spanish prosody can now be very easily made.

References

Aguilar, L., De-la-Mota, C., and Prieto, P. (eds.) (2009). *Sp_ToBI Training Materials*. Available from prosodia.upf.edu/sp_tobi/.

Armstrong, M. E. (2010). Puerto Rican Spanish Intonation. In P. Prieto and P. Roseano (eds.), *Transcription of Intonation of the Spanish Language*. Munich: Lincom Europa, pp. 155–189.

Armstrong, M. E. (2015). Accounting for Intonational Form and Function in Puerto Rican Spanish Polar Questions. *Probus*. doi: 10.1515/probus-2014-0016.

Beckman, M., Díaz-Campos, M., McGory, J. T., and Morgan, T. A. (2002). Intonation across Spanish, in the Tones and Break Indices Framework. *Probus*, 14, 9–36.

Estebas Vilaplana, E. and Prieto, P. (2008). La notación prosódica en español. Una revisión del Sp_ToBI. *Estudios de Fonética Experimental*, 17, 263–283.

Face, T. L. (2002). Local Intonational Marking of Contrastive Focus. *Probus*, 14 (1), 71–92.

Face, T. L. and Prieto, P. (2007). Rising Accents in Castilian Spanish: A Revision of Sp_ToBI. *Journal of Portuguese Linguistics*, 6 (1), 117–146.

Gabriel, C., Feldhausen, I., Pešková, A., Colantoni, L., Lee, S.-A., Arana, V., and Labastía, L. (2010). Argentinian Spanish Intonation. In P. Prieto and P. Roseano (eds.), *Transcription of Intonation of the Spanish Language*. Munich: Lincom, pp. 285–317.

Gussenhoven, C. (2004). *The Phonology of Tone and Intonation*. Cambridge: Cambridge University Press.

Henriksen, N., Armstrong, M. E., and García-Amaya, L. J. (2016). The Intonational Meaning of Polar Questions in Manchego Spanish Spontaneous Speech. In M. E. Armstrong, N. Henriksen, and M. D. M. Vanrell (eds.), *Intonational Grammar in Ibero-Romance: Approaches across Linguistic Subfields*. Amsterdam: John Benjamins, pp. 181–206.

Henriksen, N. and García-Amaya, L. J. (2012). Transcription of Intonation of Jerezano Andalusian Spanish. *Estudios de Fonética Experimental*, 21, 109–162.

Hualde, J. I. (2003). El modelo métrico-autosegmental. In P. Prieto (ed.), *Teorías de la entonación*. Barcelona: Ariel, pp. 155–84.

Hualde, J. I. (2005). *The Sounds of Spanish*. Cambridge: Cambridge University Press.

Hualde, J. I. (2007). Stress Removal and Stress Addition in Spanish. *Journal of Portuguese Linguistics*, 5 (6), 59–89.

Hualde, J. I. (2009). Unstressed Words in Spanish. *Language Sciences*, 31, 199–212.

Hualde, J. I. and Nadeu, M. (2014). Rhetorical Stress in Spanish. In H. van der Hulst (ed.), *Word Stress: Theoretical and Typological Issues*. Cambridge: Cambridge University Press, pp. 228–52.

Hualde, J. I. and Prieto, P. (2015). Intonational Variation in Spanish: European and American Varieties. In S. Frota and P. Prieto (eds.), *Intonation in Romance*. Oxford: Oxford University Press, pp. 350–391.

Jun, S.-A. (ed.) (2005). *Prosodic Typology: The Phonology of Intonation and Phrasing*. Oxford: Oxford University Press.

Jun, S.-A. (ed.) (2014). *Prosodic Typology 2: The Phonology of Intonation and Phrasing*. Oxford: Oxford University Press.

Kaisse, E. (2001). The Long Fall: An Intonational Melody of Argentinian Spanish. In J. Herschensohn, E. Mallen, and K. Zagona (eds.), *Features and Interfaces in Romance*. Amsterdam: John Benjamins, pp. 148–160.

Krifka, M. (2008). Basic Notions of Information Structure. *Acta Linguistica Hungarica*, 55 (3–4): 243–276.

Ladd, D. R. (2008). *Intonational Phonology* (2nd edn). Cambridge: Cambridge University Press.

Lang-Rigal, J. (2014). A Perceptual and Experimental Phonetic Approach to Dialect Stereotypes: The *tonada cordobesa* of Argentina (Doctoral dissertation). University of Texas at Austin.

Lapesa, R. (1984). *Historia de la lengua española*. Madrid: Gredos.

Martín Butragueño, P. and Mendoza, É. (2017, in press). Prosodic Nuclear Patterns in Narrow and Broad Focus Utterances: Pragmatic and Social Factors in Central Mexican Spanish. In M. García and M. Uth (eds.), *Focus Realization and Interpretation in Romance and Beyond*. Amsterdam: John Benjamins.

Martínez Celdrán, E. and Fernández Planas, A. M. (eds.). (2003–2016). *Atlas Multimédia de la Prosodie de l'Espace Roman*. Available from stel.ub.edu/labfon/amper/.

Morales-Front, A. (1999). El acento. In R. Núñez-Cedeño and A. Morales-Front (eds.), *Fonología generativa de la lengua española*. Washington, DC: Georgetown University Press, pp. 203–230.

Navarro Tomás, T. (1918). *Manual de pronunciación española*. Madrid: Centro de Estudios Históricos.

Navarro Tomás, T. (1944). *Manual de entonación española*. New York: Spanish Institute in the United States.

Nielsen Hayden, T. (1994). *Making Book*. Framingham, MA: NESFA Press.

Ortiz, H., Fuentes, M., and Astruc, L. (2010). Chilean Spanish Intonation. In P. Prieto and P. Roseano, P. (eds.), *Transcription of Intonation of the Spanish Language*. Munich: Lincom, pp. 255–283.

Pamies Bertrán, A. (1993). Acento, ritmo y lenguaje. Elementos de prosodia general y comparada (Doctoral dissertation). Universidad de Granada.

Pierrehumbert, J. B. (1980). The Phonetics and Phonology of English Intonation (Doctoral dissertation). MIT.

Pierrehumbert, J. and Beckman, M. (1988). *Japanese Tone Structure*. Cambridge, MA: MIT Press.

Prieto, P. (2015). Intonational meaning. *WIRES Cognitive Science*, 6, 371–381.

Prieto, P. and Roseano, P. (eds.) (2009–2013). *Atlas interactivo de la entonación del español*. Available from prosodia.upf.edu/atlasentonacion/.

Prieto, P. and Roseano, P. (eds.) (2010). *Transcription of Intonation of the Spanish Language*. Munich: Lincom.

Prieto, P., Vanrell, M. M., Astruc, L., Payne, E., and Post, B. (2012). Phonotactic and Phrasal Properties of Speech Rhythm. Evidence from Catalan, English, and Spanish. *Speech Communication*, 54 (6), 681–702.

Quilis, A. (1981). *Fonética acústica de la lengua española*. Madrid: Gredos.

Quilis, A. (1987). Entonación dialectal hispánica. In H. López Morales and M. Vaquero (eds.), *Actas del I Congreso Internacional sobre el Español de*

América. San Juan, Puerto Rico: Academia Puertorriqueña de la Lengua Española, pp. 117–163.

Quilis, A. (1993). *Tratado de fonología y fonética españolas*. Madrid: Gredos.

Ramus, F., Nespor, M., and Mehler, J. (1999). Correlates of Linguistic Rhythm in the Speech Signal. *Cognition*, 73, 265–292.

Sosa, J. M. (1999). *La entonación del español*. Madrid: Cátedra.

Vanrell, M. M. and Fernández-Soriano, O. (in press). Language Variation at the Prosody–Syntax Interface: Focus in European Spanish. In M. García and M. Uth (eds.), *Focus Realization and Interpretation in Romance and Beyond*. Amsterdam: John Benjamins.

Vanrell, M. M., Stella, A., Gili-Fivela, B., and Prieto, P. (2013). Prosodic Manifestations of the Effort Code in Catalan, Italian and Spanish Contrastive Focus. *Journal of the International Phonetic Association*, 43 (2), 195–220.

Willis, E. W. (2010). Dominican Spanish Intonation. In P. Prieto and P. Roseano (eds.), *Transcription of Intonation of the Spanish Language*. Munich: Lincom, pp. 123–153.

Zubizarreta, M. L. and Nava, E. (2011). Encoding Discourse-Based Meaning: Prosody vs. Syntax. Implications for Second Language Acquisition. *Lingua*, 121, 652–669.

11

Speech Perception

Amanda Boomershine and Ji Young Kim

11.1 Introduction

Speech perception is the process by which sounds are heard, mapped from speech signal to mental representation, and understood. Because languages differ in their sound inventories, second/foreign language learners may have difficulty distinguishing speech sounds in a non-native language. For example, monolingual Spanish speakers can struggle to perceive (and produce) a difference in word-final nasals in English, given that Spanish nasals undergo a process of neutralization in certain word-final contexts (Morgan 2010). Because in much of the Spanish-speaking world two or more languages are in contact (Spanish–English, Spanish–Portuguese, Spanish–Quechua, Spanish–Catalan, etc.), Spanish speakers' sound systems are affected by this contact. In addition, there is often quite a bit of variation within a given language, and speech perception studies allow us to understand how listeners hear and process sounds in other dialects and varieties of their first or second language(s). In order for communication to occur, listeners must be able to understand the speech that talkers use, and understanding how listeners process speech is important to better understand how and why speakers produce speech the way they do. In general, speech perception and production have been investigated separately, as each field poses its own challenges and methodologies.

11.1.1 Models of Speech Perception

When speech is perceived, there are several processes that occur. The listener must first detect the acoustic signal, the lexicon is then activated, and then language comprehension occurs (Johnson and Mullennix 1997; Pisoni 1993). Studies have found that listeners retain in long-term memory non-linguistic information about the speaker's gender, dialect, speaking rate, and emotional state, and that these properties influence the initial perceptual encoding and retention of spoken words (Pisoni 1993). There are also varying approaches to the nature of perceptual representations, including abstract representations, exemplar-based representations (Johnson and Mullennix 1997; Werker and Tees 1984), and how these representations are formed (Kuhl *et al.* 2008).

There are several models of second language (L2) speech perception, but the two most widely used are the Perceptual Assimilation Model (PAM) (Best 1995) and the Speech Learning Model (SLM) (Flege 1995). Best's PAM, based on articulatory phonetics, provides possible cross-language category assimilation patterns and predicts their consequences. This model assumes that, from birth, listeners perceive everything in the speech signal with great detail, but, as we receive more exposure to our native language, we become more attuned to differences that are important in discriminating sounds in that language. This means that listeners, even in their first year, conceive sounds as groups of gestures that connect to produce distinctive sounds, improving processing speed and efficiency in our first language (L1). This model predicts, then, that sounds that are distinct in a listener's L1 will be more easily perceived in the L2. Those sounds that are not contrastive in the L1 are more difficult to perceive in the L2. Best's model predicts that three things can happen when hearing a non-native sound: (i) it is assimilated to an existing L1 category, (ii) it is heard as a non-native sound, or (iii) it is heard as a non-speech sound.

Flege's SLM is based on the premise that a listener's system for categorizing sounds develops throughout their life, maintaining contrasts that are important to the languages they use. His model posits that listeners must be able to hear some of the acoustic differences between sounds in order to be able to perceive them as different. If the sounds are not acoustically different enough, the listener will not perceive them as unique sounds. On the other hand, if they are acoustically different, even if neither sound is present in the listener's L1, the listener will be able to distinguish them based on phonetic cues. The SLM also suggests that bilingual speakers store phones from all of the languages they speak in one space, allowing there to be more of a role for phonetic cues rather than simply phonemic processing.

11.1.2 Techniques Used in Speech Perception

The three most commonly used experimental techniques for measuring speech perception are perceptual similarity rating, speeded discrimination, and identification tasks (Boomershine *et al.* 2008; Johnson and Babel 2010; Logan and Pruitt 1995). In a perceptual similarity rating task, listeners are presented with two stimulus items and are asked to rate how similar or different they sound to and from each other using a scale. Previous research (Boomershine *et al.* 2008; Huang 2004) has shown that the perceptual similarity rating task can reveal cross-linguistic differences that relate to phonological differences between languages. In a speeded discrimination task, on the other hand, listeners are presented with stimulus items and are asked to determine if they are the same or different. The stimuli can be presented in pairs or in groups of three. With three stimuli, the listener is asked to determine either if the third token was similar to the first or the second (ABX discrimination) or if the middle token was similar to the first or the third token (AXB discrimination). Both ABX and AXB tasks have found that listeners are often biased to respond that X=B or X=A, respectively (Gerrits and Schouten 2004). To avoid this bias, researchers often use just two stimuli for an AX discrimination task, where listeners are to decide if the stimuli are the same or different. This technique, however, often leads listeners to only respond 'different' if the stimuli are very different; otherwise, the listeners label most items as being the same (Gerrits and Schouten 2004). Finally, identification tasks are those that present listeners with stimulus items, one at a time, and ask them to identify the sound or word they hear. Identification tasks, because they usually force listeners to associate sounds to written items, are often greatly impacted by the amount of academic exposure listeners have had in the language being studied. Therefore, identification tasks tend to tell researchers more about a listener's literacy level and orthographic accuracy than their ability to perceive sounds (Johnson and Babel 2010). The remainder of this chapter will look at what we know about how a listener's first language is processed (Section 11.2) and how listeners perceive sounds in bilingual speech (Section 11.3). We will end by discussing challenges faced within the field of speech perception and opportunities for future research.

11.2 First Language Speech Perception

11.2.1 Infant Studies

Infants have unlimited potential to acquire speech sounds of any human language. Studies have found that infants as young as six months of age are able to distinguish speech sounds that do not exist in their mother tongue (Werker and Tees 1984). It is still debatable whether infants are born equipped with a linguistic blueprint with language-general phonetic boundaries that help them process speech sounds (Eimas 1975; Hoonhorst et al. 2009) or whether statistical learning of phonetic categories takes place after infants' initial exposure to language (Kuhl et al. 2008). However, there is no doubt that native language has a large effect on the way infants process speech sounds and that this effect occurs early in life. At birth, infants hear differences among all the sounds that exist in human languages, but this language-general ability of speech perception transforms into a language-specific one during the first year of life (Kuhl and Iverson 1995). This section provides evidence from various empirical studies that shows infants' perceptual reorganization at different stages during the first year of life.

Consonants

Most research on Spanish-learning infants' perception of consonants has been done on stop voicing contrasts (e.g. /b/ vs. /p/). One of the strongest acoustic cues that separate them is voice onset time (VOT). In Spanish, there is a two-way contrast with a 0 ms VOT boundary that separates voiced /b, d, g/ (< 0 ms) from voiceless /p, t, k/ (0~30 ms) stops. Lasky et al. (1975) examined whether 4–6.5 month-old Spanish-learning infants are able to distinguish bilabial stop pairs of different VOT boundaries. Results showed that the infants distinguished the –60/–20 and the +20/+60 ms pairs, but not the –20/+20 ms pairs. This is an unexpected outcome, given that the –20/+20 ms pair is the one with the VOT boundary that separates Spanish voiced and voiceless stops. The authors argued that there may be two language-general VOT boundaries that distinguish stops, one between –60 and –20 ms and another between +20 and +60 ms, to which infants, regardless of their native language, are innately predisposed.

Language-specific VOT boundaries are acquired at the second half of the first year. Eilers *et al.* (1979) examined the perception of bilabial voicing contrasts by Spanish- and English-learning infants at six to eight months of age and found that, while Spanish-learning infants were able to separate +10/–20 and +10/+40 ms pairs, English-learning infants were only able to distinguish the +10/+40 ms pairs. This, together with the findings of Lasky *et al.* (1975), imply that, while the English-like VOT boundary is an acoustically salient boundary that is unaffected by linguistic environment, the Spanish-like VOT boundary may need to be acquired through exposure to a language with stop voicing contrasts at this phonetic boundary.

Vowels

Perceptual reorganization has also been observed in Spanish-learning infants' perception of vowels. For instance, Bosch and Sebastián-Gallés (2003) examined the perception of /e/–/ɛ/ contrast by four- and eight-month-old Spanish monolingual, Catalan monolingual, and Catalan–Spanish bilingual infants. This vowel distinction is phonological in Catalan, while it is not in Spanish. Previous studies on adult Catalan–Spanish bilinguals have shown that Spanish-dominant bilinguals tend to have difficulties distinguishing this contrast (Sebastián-Gallés and Soto-Faraco 1999). With respect to infants, Bosch and Sebastián-Gallés (2003) found that, while all infants distinguished the /e/–/ɛ/ contrast at four months of age, at eight months only the Catalan monolinguals were able to do so; such sensitivity declined for Spanish monolingual and Catalan–Spanish bilingual infants regardless of language dominance. While Spanish monolinguals' difficulty in /e/–/ɛ/ discrimination is an expected outcome, as this contrast does not exist in Spanish, it is interesting that the same was observed with the bilingual infants who were exposed to both Catalan and Spanish.

Interestingly, the discrimination ability that was once thought to be lost was regained for 12-month-old bilingual infants, presenting a U-shaped pattern. Moreover, this ability can last throughout the second year of life, although factors such as increased experience with cross-language cognates and input variability (for example, Spanish-accented Catalan) may eventually lead to difficulties in perceiving the contrast (Ramon-Casas et al. 2016).

U-shaped patterns are also observed in Catalan–Spanish bilinguals' perception of vowel contrasts that exist in both languages. Sebastián-Gallés and Bosch (2009) found that, when perceiving the /o/–/u/ contrast, only bilingual infants showed a U-shaped pattern, while monolingual infants were successful in distinguishing the contrast at all ages. This indicates that bilingual infants may undergo a developmental process that is different from that of monolingual infants.

Prosody

From early on, infants are able to extract global rhythmic properties from utterances and detect a switch of utterances spoken in languages of different rhythmic classes (stress-timed, syllable-timed, and mora-timed) (Mehler et al. 1988). During the first six months, infants' sensitivity to speech input becomes more fine-tuned to their native language, to the point that they can distinguish languages or dialects of the same rhythmic class as their native language. Bosch and Sebastián-Gallés (1997, 2001) found that, at four months, Spanish- and Catalan-learning monolingual infants, as well as Catalan–Spanish bilingual infants, were able to tell Spanish and Catalan apart, even though they are both syllable-timed languages. Although this finding suggests that even at four months infants are sensitive to fine-grained rhythmic properties of their native language(s), further research needs to be conducted to corroborate this, as research on infant-directed speech has shown that vowel spectral information is a stronger cue than fine-grained rhythmic properties in distinguishing dialects of the same rhythmic class (Ortega-Llebaria and Bosch 2016).

There have also been studies regarding the perception of stress. Using disyllabic pseudo-words with stress on the first (trochee) and last syllable (iamb), Skoruppa et al. (2009) examined whether nine-month-old infants learning Spanish and French are able to discriminate the two stress patterns. The nature of stress is different in the two languages, in that, while Spanish is a language with lexical stress, which means that stress is phonologically contrastive (*número* 'number' vs. *numero* 'I number' vs. *numeró* 'numbered.3SG') (Hualde 2005), stress in French is fixed to the last syllable of each phrase. Results showed that, while both groups distinguished trochaic and iambic stimuli when the only difference between the two was the location of stress (/ˈpima/ vs. /piˈma/), with segmental variability (/ˈlapi/ vs. /kiˈbu/), only the Spanish-learning infants perceived the difference in stress pattern. However, when testing six-month-old infants, Skoruppa *et al.* (2013) found that neither Spanish- nor French-learning infants succeeded in distinguishing the two stress patterns when there was segmental variability. This suggests that infants are able to perceive acoustic correlates of stress (longer duration, higher pitch, and higher intensity), while only those whose native language has lexical stress learn to process stress in an abstract, phonological way between six and nine months of age.

Apart from the discrimination of stress patterns, Pons and Bosch (2010) further examined whether Spanish-learning infants have trochaic bias (Allen and Hawkins 1978), which has been observed in English-learning infants (Jusczyk *et al.* 1993). However, recent research on infants learning languages of different rhythmic properties found that infants do not show any preference toward a particular stress pattern (Hochbert 1988). Pons and Bosch (2010) support this view in their study with nine-month-old Spanish-learning infants. They found that Spanish-learning infants did not show any stress pattern bias when listening to disyllabic pseudo-words with open syllables (CV.CV). However, when one of the two syllables was closed, they seemed to prefer stress on that syllable (trochaic for CVC.CV and iambic for CV.CVC), suggesting that syllable weight may play a larger role in infants' initial stress assignment.

11.2.2 Adult Native Speakers

Perceptual reorganization during infancy is a necessary process for an effective processing of native speech sounds. However, as the reorganization process reaches stability, the sensitivity to perceive phonological contrasts that do not exist in the native language declines. Thus, difficulties in distinguishing non-native speech sounds are clearly attested in adult listeners.

Consonants

Most research on the perception of consonants has been carried out regarding stop consonants. As mentioned previously in the section on "Consonants" in infant studies, Spanish has a two-way stop voicing contrast, the main distinction of which is VOT. Although VOT is one of the most salient acoustic cues that separate Spanish voiced from voiceless stops, this contrast can also be distinguished by other acoustic properties, such as closure duration. Spanish voiceless stops are generally produced with longer closure duration than voiced stops (Green *et al.* 1997). Zampini *et al.* (2002) examined whether Spanish listeners are sensitive to this cue when perceiving stop voicing contrast. Using nonce words with initial stops preceded by various degrees of closure duration, they found that Spanish listeners' VOT boundaries decreased as the closure duration increased, which indicates that the listeners perceived the stimuli as voiceless stops more often when the closure duration was longer.

There is more evidence that VOT is not the only cue to which Spanish listeners attend when perceiving stop voicing contrast. By removing the prevoicing portion of Spanish voiced stops, Williams (1977) examined whether Spanish listeners are able to identify voiced stops without this critical information. Although the percent of voiced responses decreased when the prevoicing portion was edited out, the Spanish listeners still judged voiced stops as such significantly more than voiceless stops. Williams (1977) suggested two possible acoustic correlates for voicing in Spanish stops: presence of a strong burst and presence of low-frequency periodic energy at articulatory release. He found that when there was a strong burst or high-frequency periodic energy at the moment of release, listeners tended to perceive the stimuli as voiceless.

Native language phonology can also influence listeners' perceived distance between sounds. Boomershine *et al.* (2008) examined Spanish listeners' perceptual distinction among [d], [ð], and [ɾ] and compared their behavior to that of English listeners. The three phones exist in both Spanish and English, but the phonological relationship among them differs in the two languages. While [d] and [ð] are contrastive in English (/d/ vs. /ð/), in Spanish they are allophones of the same phoneme /d/ (stop [d] vs. approximant [ð]). Moreover, [d] and [ɾ] in Spanish are from two different phonemes (/d/ vs. /r/), while in English they are in an allophonic relationship. Concerning [ð] and [ɾ], they are contrastive in both languages, but they belong to different phonemes: the two phones are from /d/ and /r/ in Spanish and /ð/ and /d/ in English. Results showed that Spanish listeners perceived the [d]–[ð] contrast more similarly and the [d]–[ɾ] contrast more differently, compared to English listeners. This suggests that sound pairs that are allophonic in the native language ([d]–[ð]) are perceived as more similar than those that contrast phonologically ([d]–[ɾ]).

Apart from perceptual distance, stop–approximant allophony also has an effect on Spanish listeners' perception of stress location. Using resynthesized disyllabic stimuli /baba/ with varying stop [b, d, g] and approximant [β, ð, ɣ] locations, Shea and Curtin (2010) found that Spanish native listeners perceived [b]-initial syllables as stressed more frequently than [β]-initial syllables, regardless of whether this sound was followed by a stressed vowel (['baβa], [βa'ba]) or an unstressed vowel ([ba'βa], ['βaba]), and showed illusory stress perception even when the first and the second vowels were held steady.

Vowels
With regard to vowels, Escudero and colleagues (Elvin *et al.* 2014; Escudero and Williams 2012) examined Spanish listeners' perception of vowel

contrasts of languages whose vowel inventory is larger than Spanish. They found that Spanish listeners generally have less sensitivity in distinguishing the vowel contrasts, compared to listeners whose native language vowel system contains more vowels than Spanish (Dutch, Australian English, Brazilian Portuguese). However, although vowel inventory size is a good predictor of the discrimination ability of non-native vowel contrasts, it may not be the only one. Elvin *et al.* (2014) found that Spanish listeners outperformed Australian English listeners when distinguishing Brazilian Portuguese vowels, even though Australian English has a much larger vowel inventory (12 monophthongs) than Spanish (five monophthongs). Given that the spectral information of Spanish vowels is more similar to those of Brazilian Portuguese than of Australian English, the authors suggested that acoustic properties may be a stronger predictor of non-native vowel discrimination ability than vowel inventory size.

The importance of acoustic properties is also shown when comparing listeners of different varieties of Spanish. For instance, Escudero and Williams (2012) compared Iberian Spanish (IS) and Peruvian Spanish (PS) listeners' perception of Dutch vowel contrasts. They found differences in the perception of the two dialectal groups, which may be explained by the dialect-specific differences in the spectral properties of IS and PS vowels. Specifically, even though Dutch /a/–/ɑ/ contrast does not exist in Spanish, as IS /a/ and /o/ have first formant (F1) values closer to Dutch /a/ and /ɑ/, compared to PS /a/ and /o/, IS listeners were better at distinguishing the Dutch vowel contrast.

Prosody

Concerning L1 Spanish prosody, Soto-Faraco *et al.* (2001) investigated whether Spanish listeners attend to suprasegmental cues for lexical processing, using a cross-modal fragment priming paradigm, in which fragments of real word pairs that differed only in the position of lexical stress (PRINCI... from *principio* 'beginning' or *príncipe* 'prince') were auditorily presented as primes, followed by a visual target word (*principio* or *príncipe*). Results showed that, compared to the control condition, in which there was no segmental or suprasegmental overlap between the prime and the target, the response time was faster when the stress pattern of the prime matched that of the target, whereas it slowed down when they did not match. This suggests that Spanish listeners use both segmental and suprasegmental cues for lexical processing. Moreover, using an ABX discrimination task, Dupoux *et al.* (1997) compared Spanish and French listeners' perception of nonce word triplets in three conditions: phoneme-only (*fidape–lidape–fidape*), stress-only (*fidape–fidápe–fidape*), and phoneme and stress (*fidape–lidápe–fidape*). They found that Spanish listeners' reaction time was fastest in the redundant condition and equally slow in the other two conditions, while the reaction time of the French listeners was the slowest in the stress-only condition and equally fast in the other two conditions. This finding indicates that Spanish listeners use both segmental and suprasegmental information at low-level phonetic perception.

Overall, the findings of L1 speech perception studies provide empirical evidence that native speakers undergo a language-general to language-specific reorganization process during infancy, which later on helps them attend to fine-grained acoustic properties that are necessary for successful processing of native speech sounds.

11.3 Bilingual Speech Perception

11.3.1 Simultaneous Bilinguals

This section emphasizes the perception by those speakers who were exposed to two languages (primarily Spanish–Catalan) from birth ("simultaneous bilinguals").

Vowels

Spanish and Catalan are in contact in eastern Spain, and both are official languages in the Spanish autonomous communities of Catalonia, the Balearic Islands, and Valencia. This unique situation of contact in which both languages are valued by the speakers and the government allows for a rich research environment on the simultaneous acquisition of two languages. Multiple studies have been conducted on the perception of Catalan vowel contrasts by simultaneous bilingual speakers of Catalan and Spanish.

In their study, Navarra *et al.* (2005) used an implicit method for measuring the L1 effects on the perception of L2 sounds. They asked Catalan–Spanish simultaneous bilinguals who had grown up either in Spanish-speaking homes or in Catalan-speaking homes to categorize the first syllable of bisyllabic stimuli. The only difference in the stimulus items was the vowel in the second syllable – it could contain a Catalan contrastive variation (/ɛ/–/e/) or no variation. Catalan dominants responded more slowly in lists where the second syllable varied from trial to trial, suggesting an indirect effect of the /ɛ/–/e/ discrimination. Spanish dominants did not suffer this interference, performing indistinguishably from Spanish monolinguals. A similar study was conducted by Sebastián-Gallés *et al.* (2005). They investigated how simultaneous and early sequential Catalan–Spanish bilinguals in Barcelona perceived the mid-vowel contrast found in Catalan. The results of their lexical decision task demonstrated that L1 Spanish, L2 Catalan bilinguals had difficulty distinguishing stimuli whose only difference was a contrast found in Catalan, but not Spanish. They also found that the simultaneous bilinguals tended to have a dominant language which affected their perception of Catalan contrasts.

Mora *et al.* (2010) investigated the perception of mid (/e/–/ɛ/, /o/–/ɔ/) and high-mid (/i/–/e/, /u/–/o/) vowel continua by Spanish–Catalan simultaneous bilinguals. The researchers found that all Spanish–Catalan bilinguals perceived the high-mid vowel contrasts more categorically than the mid-mid vowel contrasts, with the size of the difference being affected by how frequently Catalan was used. Notably, this study underscores the importance of understanding language dominance and use by bilingual speakers in perception studies. Sounds that are not contrastive in the dominant language are less easily distinguished than those that are contrastive in both languages. A similar study was conducted by Mora and Nadeu (2012) into the effects of an L2 (Spanish) on the perception of L1 (Catalan) contrastive sounds. They found that all participants performed at near ceiling levels in the tasks, but the reaction time for those participants who had more exposure to Spanish than Catalan was slower than for the Catalan-dominant speakers. The findings suggest that extensive L2 use of/exposure to Spanish and Spanish-accented Catalan in a bilingual language contact setting may modify Catalan natives' phonetic categories.

Prosody

In addition to studying how simultaneous bilinguals perceive segmental features, researchers have also conducted studies on their perception of suprasegmental features. As with the perception of segments, there are few studies on the perception of suprasegmentals by simultaneous bilinguals (compared to sequential bilinguals or L2 learners). Dupoux *et al.* (2010) investigated the perception of Spanish stress by simultaneous French–Spanish bilinguals. Spanish, unlike French, has word-level lexical stress as part of the phonological system. The researchers studied the perception of lexical stress as a means to better understand how simultaneous bilingual speakers process suprasegmental features. Their participants were raised in bilingual French–Spanish homes, with some participants being raised by a Spanish-speaking mother and others a French-speaking mother. They found that the simultaneous bilinguals performed at a level that was intermediate to L1 French speakers of Spanish and L1 Spanish speakers. They also found that the performance of the simultaneous bilinguals showed a bimodal distribution – depending on the dominant language of each participant. In other words, each speaker has only one language that processes speech sounds and segments in a native-like way. More research needs to be conducted on how simultaneous bilinguals process input as adults so that this population's perception can be better understood.

11.3.2 Second Language Speakers

Research related to the acquisition of L2 sounds by language learners has traditionally focused on the production of those sounds, but, due to the link between perception and production, more researchers are turning their attention to the perception of L2 sounds by learners. This section will focus on the perception of Spanish sounds by L1 English speakers who are learning Spanish after adolescence, but attention will also be given to the perception of Spanish sounds by L1 speakers of other languages, as well as to the perception of English sounds by L1 Spanish speakers.

Consonants

Unlike children acquiring their native language (Section 11.2.1) or early bilingual speakers (Section 11.3.1), second language learners often exhibit difficulty perceiving L2 sounds that are non-contrastive in their native language. In the Boomershine et al. (2008) study described above, participants tapped into their L1 phonology when rating the contrastive and allophonic pairs. The researchers found that speakers of a language in which a particular pair of sounds is contrastive at a phonemic level perceive that pair as being more perceptually distinct than do speakers of a language in which the pair is not phonemically contrastive.

Shea and Renaud (2014) also studied the perception of consonants, with a focus on the effects of task type on perception. L1 and L2 speakers of Spanish participated in a similarity rating study in which they heard pairs of stimuli containing [ɟʝ] (affricate) and [ʝ] (fricative). They were asked to rate how similar the stimulus items were, using a scale of 1 (very similar) to 5 (very different). The results indicated that the L2 speakers of Spanish rated these sounds as being very different on average, while the L1 Spanish speakers rated them as both different (62 percent) and similar (29 percent). In other words, the L1 Spanish ratings were not uniform, unlike the L2 listeners'. Shea and Renaud also conducted a speeded AX discrimination task with L1 and L2 Spanish speakers. They found that, unlike the L1 speakers, the L2 speakers' reaction times were significantly different only for the medial position, not word-initially. The results point towards a native-language effect even at low-level phonetic perception.

Vowels

The perception of L2 vowels has also been studied. Most notably, Morrison (2006) investigated the perception of the English /i, ɪ, e, ɛ/ and Spanish vowels /i, e, ei/ by L1 English speakers of Spanish and L1 Spanish speakers of English. In his study, the participants were asked to listen to words in a carrier phrase and indicate how good a representation the target word was to the words on the screen. He found that L1 Spanish speakers of English had difficulty distinguishing English /i/ and /ɪ/. With increased exposure to English, he found that they distinguished English /i/ and /ɪ/ via a category–goodness–difference assimilation, using duration cues, along with spectral cues, to help distinguish the two English vowels. Because Spanish does not distinguish /i/ and /ɪ/, or /e/ and /ɛ/, at the phonemic level (or even allophonic level for most varieties), L1 Spanish speakers learning English must use a variety of perceptual cues to be able to distinguish these contrastive sounds in English.

Studies have also found the target dialect being learned affects the speaker's perception of L2 sounds. Escudero and Boersma (2004) conducted a study into the perception of Scottish and Southern British English vowels (/i, ɪ/) by L1 Spanish speakers. In a forced identification task, the listeners heard two tokens and were asked to indicate whether the sound they heard was the same as the one in *sheep* (/i/) or the one in *ship* (/ɪ/). This identification task differed from others in that they were shown images of the targets, rather than written words, in order to avoid any orthographic association between sounds and letters. The researchers found that the listener's experience and exposure to specific target dialects affected which cues they used when completing the task. Those participants who had more experience with Southern British English tended to use duration as a cue when perceiving the stimuli, but the participants who were more accustomed to Scottish English used spectral cues.

Other studies looked at the amount and type of exposure to the L2 and how that affects speech perception. Flege *et al.*'s study (1997) assessed the effect of English-language experience on non-native speakers' perception of English vowels. L1 Spanish speakers were presented with stimuli on the /i/–/ɪ/ and /ɛ/–/æ/ continua, one at a time, and were asked to indicate if the vowel they heard occurred in *beat, bit, bet,* or *bat*. They found that the L1 Spanish speakers who had greater experience with English used spectral cues more when perceiving these English vowels than the Spanish speakers with limited experience with English. The authors noted, however, that there was probably orthographic interference during the study, as both /i/ and /ɪ/ more closely approximate the Spanish sound represented by Spanish <i>, and thus listeners with limited experience with written English may have been more likely to select *bit* over *beat* due to orthographic similarity.

Prosody

Linguists have also studied the perception of suprasegmental features in Spanish by L2 speakers. In his study, Face (2005) presented listeners with nonce words with equal stress on all syllables, and asked them to indicate which syllable they perceived as being the stressed syllable. The participants were divided into three groups based on Spanish level – beginner, intermediate, and advanced. He found that as students progressed through their Spanish studies, they were more likely to perceive stress according to the unmarked stress patterns in Spanish (as paroxytones).

Ortega-Llebaria *et al.* (2013) also conducted a study on the perception of Spanish stress by L1 English speakers of Spanish. In their identification task, listeners were presented with stimuli containing the word mam<u>á</u> or <u>ma</u>ma with final and penultimate stress. The stimuli were manipulated for duration, intensity, and pitch. The participants were asked to indicate whether they heard a word with final stress or penultimate stress.

The findings demonstrate that L2 Spanish speakers did not perceive variations of duration and f0 in relation to stress in the same manner as L1 Spanish speakers, causing difficulties for the L2 Spanish speakers when perceiving stress in Spanish. The study also found that no one acoustic cue aids or hinders stress perception in Spanish – but rather a cluster of cues are needed to accurately perceive stress placement in Spanish.

Improving Second Language Perception

In addition to investigating how L2 speakers perceive non-native sounds, there are also studies that determine what practices can improve L2 speech perception. Kissling (2015) conducted a study in which L1 English speakers who were enrolled in Spanish courses of various levels participated in an AX discrimination task at various times throughout the course of a semester. The participants were divided into two groups – one which received explicit phonetics instruction and the other which did not. The results of the study demonstrate that the group that received explicit phonetics instruction was able to more accurately discriminate the target phones when compared to the group that did not receive phonetics instruction. While the improvement throughout the semester did not occur immediately following the instruction in all cases, the author posits that the listeners used the information gained from the phonetics instruction to become more attuned to the phonetic cues that distinguish these sounds, allowing them to more accurately perceive relevant differences across phones.

Another study that focused on improving L2 perception is Zampini's study of the perception of varying VOT in Spanish and English stops. Zampini (1998) conducted a study in which L1 English speakers learning Spanish were presented with stimuli containing a bilabial stop, with the VOT ranging from 40 to 56 ms, and were asked to indicate if the token started with a /p/ or a /b/. They participated in the study three times during the semester. She found that, initially, their perceptual boundaries for Spanish /p/ and /b/ were similar to monolingual English speakers, but, over the course of the semester, their boundaries shifted to those of bilingual Spanish–English speakers.

11.3.3 Heritage Speakers

Apart from L2 speakers and simultaneous bilinguals, another type of bilinguals merits attention. We are referring to heritage speakers – descendants of immigrants who grow up speaking an ethnic minority language in a society where a different language is spoken as the majority language. Heritage speakers are linguistically a unique population, because, although they generally acquire the heritage language first, a shift to the majority language is often observed among them as they grow up, given that their first language is a minority language. With regard to heritage speakers of Spanish, because Spanish is the most spoken non-English language in the US (González-Barrera and Lopez 2013), research on this population has been done mainly in this context, and this section will therefore focus on US Spanish heritage speakers.

Consonants

A number of studies have shown that Spanish heritage speakers produce certain sounds differently from Spanish monolinguals, possibly due to influence from English (Amengual 2012; Au *et al.* 2008; Rao 2015; Henriksen 2015). However, little is known about their perception. Regarding the perception of Spanish consonants, Mazzaro *et al.* (2016) investigated Spanish heritage speakers' ability to distinguish Spanish stop voicing contrasts, and compared their behavior to that of Hispanic immigrants who had lived in the US for a long period of time and of Spanish native controls who had recently moved to the US. Results showed that the heritage speakers performed similarly to the control group when distinguishing Spanish stop voicing contrast, even better than the long-term immigrants.

Similarly, in a perception study using cross-spliced stimuli, Kim (2011) found that Spanish heritage speakers perceive Spanish stops in a similar manner to Spanish native controls. That is, when listening to stimuli with contrasting acoustic information in the consonant portion and the vowel portion (/b/ from /be/ + /e/ from /pe/), both the heritage speakers and the native controls attended to the consonant portion more than the vowel portion, such as the VOT, closure duration, and presence of burst/low-frequency amplitude at the articulatory release (Williams 1977; Zampini *et al.* 2002). Although further investigation should be conducted for the generalizability of the results, due to the study's small sample size, it supports Mazzaro *et al.*'s (2016) findings in that early exposure to the heritage language has long-lasting effects on heritage speakers' ability to distinguish heritage language phonological contrasts.

Vowels

Little is known about how heritage speakers perceive Spanish vowels: to our knowledge, the only study that has investigated this topic is Mazzaro *et al.* (2016), mentioned above. Mazzaro *et al.* (2016) examined whether heritage speakers are able to distinguish Spanish front (/e/–/i/) and back vowel contrasts (/o/–/u/). Similarly to the results of stop voicing contrasts, the authors found that the heritage speakers performed more similarly to the control group than did the long-term immigrants. This is an interesting finding, because the long-term immigrants were more dominant in Spanish than were the heritage speakers. Although further investigation is needed, due to the study's small sample size, the findings imply that continued exposure to a L2 may affect the perception of native speech sounds.

The studies above, as well as the studies on simultaneous bilinguals, suggest that the age of L2 acquisition has an effect on listeners' perception of L1 and L2 speech sounds. That is, early exposure to two languages is advantageous in maintaining phonological contrasts in both L1 and L2 (Chang *et al.* 2011). However, with regard to heritage speakers, there may be lasting effects of sequential learning. Casillas and Simonet (2016) found that, when presented with English /æ/–/ɑ/ continua, Spanish heritage speakers did not perceive the two low vowels categorically, as English monolinguals did. Rather, similarly to L1 Spanish speakers of English, heritage speakers processed these vowels as one category, possibly because they assimilated them to Spanish low vowel /a/. This finding suggests that, although heritage speakers behave similarly to Spanish native controls, they do not behave the same way as English controls, despite English being the more dominant language. However, as the authors noted, further research should be carried out in heritage speakers' linguistic input; as heritage speakers generally live in a bilingual environment, it is likely that they are exposed to both Spanish and Spanish-accented English.

Prosody

Heritage speakers' advantage in the perception of heritage language speech sounds also applies to prosody. Kim (2015) examined Spanish heritage speakers' perception of lexical stress in Spanish using stress minimal pairs (*canto* 'I sing' vs. *cantó* 'he/she/you (formal) sang'). Studies in L2 phonology have shown that English L2 speakers of Spanish experience great difficulties identifying the location of lexical stress in Spanish (Saalfeld 2009), because, unlike English in which both segmental and suprasegmental information provides cues to lexical stress, suprasegmental information plays a larger role in the identification of lexical stress in Spanish. Results showed that heritage speakers, as well as Spanish monolinguals, were able to distinguish paroxytones (*canto*) and oxytones (*cantó*), unlike L2 learners who, showed bias toward paroxytones.

With regard to intonation, Zárate-Sández (2015) examined Spanish heritage speakers' perception of peak alignment. In Spanish, pitch contour varies depending on the context in which a word is located. In phrase-final position of a declarative sentence (*La nena lloraba*. 'The girl was crying.'), pitch (f0) peak is aligned with the stressed syllable, while it is generally displaced to a following syllable when the word is located in a non-phrase final position (*La nena lloraba*.) (Prieto *et al.* 1995). However, early f0 alignment can also occur if the word in the non-phrase final position carries emphatic information. Using resynthesized stimuli with f0 peak in various locations, Zárate-Sández (2015) found that Spanish heritage speakers, as well as Spanish monolinguals, perceived f0 peak alignment categorically as either emphatic or non-emphatic, based on whether the f0 peak was positioned before or after stressed vowel offset. However, for L2 English speakers and English monolinguals, a significantly earlier threshold was found within the stressed vowel.

The findings of heritage speakers' perception studies converge, in that heritage speakers, despite shift of language dominance to English, seem to be resistant to influence from English; they are able to maintain their L1 sound categories like Spanish monolinguals. This is different from the findings of production studies that have shown differences in heritage speakers' behaviors from those of Spanish monolinguals. Although more research is needed for the generalizability of the findings, the results of the perceptual studies indicate that investigating heritage speakers' perception or production alone will provide only a one-sided view of their phonological system. Therefore, further research should be conducted into both heritage speakers' perception and production.

11.4 Conclusions and Future Directions

As discussed in this chapter, the field of speech perception is one that is growing within Hispanic linguistics. Perception studies have advanced our understanding of how infants acquire language and process speech, how an adult's phonological system is affected by their experiences in life, and how L2 (or late bilingual) speakers perceive and process sounds in their first and second languages in comparison to heritage speakers and early bilingual speakers. We have also seen that there are limited studies on how explicitly working to improve L2 speech perception can improve accuracy and acquisition overall. The field could benefit from further studies into speech perception in Spanish, especially with regard to the perception of variable input in the L1 and L2. Also needed are studies that investigate the perception of simultaneous bilingual speakers of Spanish, including studies that investigate the perception of Spanish sounds by simultaneous bilingual speakers of indigenous languages in Latin America.

References

Allen, G. and Hawkins, S. (1978). The Development of Phonological Rhythm. In A. Bell and J. Hooper (eds.), *Syllables and Segments*. Amsterdam: North-Holland, pp. 173–185.

Amengual, M. (2012). Interlingual Influence in Bilingual Speech: Cognate Status Effect in a Continuum of Bilingualism. *Bilingualism: Language and Cognition*, 15 (3), 517–530.

Au, T., Oh, J., Knightly, L., Jun, S., and Romo, L. (2008). Salvaging a Childhood Language. *Journal of Memory and Language*, 58 (4), 998–1011.

Best, C. (1995). A Direct Realist View of Cross-Language Speech Perception: New Directions in Research and Theory. In W. Strange (ed.), *Speech*

Perception and Linguistic Experience: Theoretical and Methodological Issues. Baltimore, MD: York Press, pp. 171–204.

Boomershine, A., Hall, K., Hume, E., and Johnson, K. (2008). The Impact of Allophony versus Contrast on Speech Perception. In P. Avery, E. Dresher, and K. Rice (eds.), *Contrast in Phonology*. Berlin: Mouton, pp. 143–172.

Bosch, L. and Sebastián-Gallés, N. (1997). Native-Language Recognition Abilities in Four-Month-Old Infants from Monolingual and Bilingual Environments. *Cognition*, 65, 33–69.

Bosch, L. and Sebastián-Gallés, N. (2001). Evidence of Early Language Discrimination Abilities in Infants from Bilingual Environments. *Infancy*, 2, 29–49.

Bosch, L. and Sebastián-Gallés, N. (2003). Simultaneous Bilingualism and the Perception of a Language-Specific Vowel Contrast in the First Year of Life. *Language and Speech*, 46, 217–243.

Casillas, J. and Simonet, M. (2016). Production and Perception of the English /æ/–/ɑ/ Contrast in Switched-Dominance Speakers. *Second Language Research*, 32 (2), 171–195.

Chang, C., Yao, Y., Haynes, E., and Rhodes, R. (2011). Production of Phonetic and Phonological Contrast by Heritage Speakers of Mandarin. *Journal of Acoustical Society of America*, 129 (6), 3964–3980.

Dupoux, E., Pallier, C., Sebastián-Gallés, N., and Mehler, J. (1997). A Destressing "Deafness" in French? *Journal of Memory and Language*, 36, 406–421.

Dupoux, E., Peperkamp, S., and Sebastián-Gallés, N. (2010). Limits on Bilingualism Revisited: Stress "Deafness" in Simultaneous French–Spanish Bilinguals. *Cognition*, 114, 266–275.

Eilers, R., Gavin, W., and Wilson, W. (1979). Linguistic Experience and Phonemic Perception in Infancy: A Crosslinguistic Study. *Child Development*, 50, 14–18.

Eimas, P. (1975). Auditory and Phonetic Coding of the Cues for Speech: Discrimination of the [r–l] Distinction by Young Infants. *Perception and Psychophysics*, 18, 341–347.

Elvin, J., Escudero, P., and Vasiliev, P. (2014). Spanish is Better than English for Discriminating Portuguese Vowels: Acoustic Similarity versus Vowel Inventory Size. *Frontiers in Psychology*, 5, 1–8.

Escudero, P. and Boersma, P. (2004). Bridging the Gap between L2 Speech Perception Research and Phonological Theory. *Studies in Second Language Acquisition*, 26 (4), 551–585.

Escudero, P. and Williams, D. (2012). Native Dialect Influences Second-Language Vowel Perception: Peruvian versus Iberian Spanish Learners of Dutch. *The Journal of the Acoustical Society of America*, 131 (5), EL406–EL412.

Face, T. (2005). Syllable Weight and the Perception of Spanish Stress Placement by Second Language Learners. *Journal of Language and Learning*, 3 (1), 90–103.

Flege, J. (1995). Second Language Speech Learning: Theory, Findings and problems. In W. Strange (ed.). *Speech Perception and Linguistic Experience: Theoretical and Methodological Issue*). Baltimore, MD: York Press, pp. 233–277.

Flege, J., Bohn, O., and Jang, S. (1997). Effects of Experience on Non-Native Speakers' Production and Perception of English Vowels. *Journal of Phonetics*, 25 (4), 437–470.

Gerrits, E. and Schouten, M. (2004). Categorical Perception Depends on the Discrimination Task. *Perception and Psychophysics*, 66 (3), 363–376.

González-Barrera, A. and Lopez, M. (2013). *Spanish is the Most Spoken Non-English Language in US Homes, even among Non-Hispanics*. Washington, DC: Pew Hispanic Center.

Green, K., Zampini, M., and Magloire, J. (1997). An Examination of Word–Initial-Stop Closure Interval in English, Spanish, and Spanish–English Bilinguals. *Journal of Acoustical Society of America*, 102, 3136.

Henriksen, N. (2015). Acoustic Analysis of the Rhotic Contrast in Chicagoland Spanish: An Intergenerational Study. *Linguistic Approaches to Bilingualism*, 5 (3), 285–321.

Hochbert, J. (1988). First Steps in the Acquisition of Spanish Stress. *Journal of Child Language*, 15, 273–292.

Hoonhorst, I., Colin, C., Markessis, E., Radeau, M., Deltenre, P., and Serniclaes, W. (2009). French Native Speakers in the Making: From Language-General to Language-Specific Voicing Boundaries. *Journal of Experimental Child Psychology*, 104, 353–366.

Hualde, J. (2005). *The Sounds of Spanish*. Cambridge: Cambridge University Press.

Huang, T. (2004). Language-Specificity In Auditory Perception of Chinese Tones (Doctoral dissertation). The Ohio State University.

Johnson, K. and Babel, M. (2010). On the Perceptual Basis of Distinctive Features: Evidence from the Perception of Fricatives by Dutch and English Speakers. *Journal of Phonetics*, 38 (1), 127–136.

Johnson, K. and Mullennix, J. (1997). *Talker Variability in Speech Processing*. San Francisco: Morgan Kaufmann Publishers Inc.

Jusczyk, P., Friederici, A., and Wessels, J. (1993). Infants' Sensitivity to the Sound Pattern of Native Language Words. *Journal of Memory and Language*, 32, 402–420.

Kim, J. (2011). Discrepancy between Perception and Production of Stop Consonants by Spanish Heritage Speakers in the United States (Master's thesis). Korea University.

Kim, J. (2015). Perception and Production of Spanish Lexical Stress by Spanish Heritage Speakers and English L2 Learners of Spanish. In E. Willis, P. Martín Butragueño, and E. Herrera Zendejas (eds.), *Proceedings of the 6th Conference on Laboratory Approaches to Romance Phonology*. Somerville, MA: Cascadilla, pp. 106–128.

Kissling, Elizabeth. (2015). Phonetics Instruction Improves Learners' Perception of L2 Sounds. *Language Teaching Research*, 19 (3) 254–275.

Kuhl, P. and Iverson, P. (1995). Linguistic Experience and the "Perceptual Magnetic Effect." In W. Strange (ed.), *Speech Perception and Linguistic Experience: Issues in Cross-Language Research*. Timodium, MD: York Press, pp. 121–154.

Kuhl, P., Conboy, B., Coffey-Corina, S., Padden, D., Rivera-Gaxiola, M., and Nelson, T. (2008). Phonetic Learning as a Pathway to Language: New Data and Native Language Magnet Theory Expanded (NLM-e). *Philosophical Transactions of the Royal Society of London. Series B, Biological Sciences*, 363 (1493), 979–1000.

Lasky, R., Syrdal-Lasky, A., and Klein, R. (1975). VOT Discrimination by Four to Six and a Half Month Old Infants from Spanish Environments. *Journal of Experimental Child Psychology*, 20, 215–225.

Logan, J. and Pruitt, J. (1995). Methodological Issues in Training Listeners to Perceive Non-Native Phonemes. In W. Strange (ed.), *Speech Perception and Linguistic Experience: Issues in Cross-Language Research*. Timonium, MD: York Press, pp. 351–378.

Mazzaro, N., Cuza, A., and Colatoni, L. (2016). Age Effects and the Discrimination of Consonantal and Vocalic Contrasts in Heritage and Native Spanish. In C. Tortora, M. den Dikken, I. Montoya, and T. O'Neill (eds.), *Romance Linguistics 2013: Selected Papers from the 43rd Linguistic Symposium on Romance Languages*. Amsterdam: John Benjamins, pp. 277–300.

Mehler, J., Jusczyk, P., Lambertz, G., Halsted, N., Bertoncini, J., and Amiel-Tison, C., 1988. A Precursor of Language Acquisition in Young Infants. *Cognition*, 29, 143–178.

Mora, J., Keidel, J., and Flege, J. (2010). Why Are the Catalan Contrasts between /e/–/ɛ/ and /o/–/ɔ/ So Difficult for Even Early Spanish–Catalan Bilinguals to Perceive? *Achievements and Perspectives in the Acquisition of Second Language Speech: New Sounds*, 2, 183–193.

Mora, J. and Nadeu, M. (2012). L2 Effects on the Perception and Production of a Native Vowel Contrast in Early Bilinguals. *International Journal of Bilingualism*, 16 (4), 484–500.

Morgan, T. (2010). *Sonidos en contexto: Una introducción a la fonética del español con especial referencia a la vida real*. New Haven, CT: Yale University Press.

Morrison, G. (2006). L1 and L2 Production and Perception of English and Spanish Vowels: A Statistical Modelling Approach (Doctoral dissertation). University of Alberta.

Navarra, J., Sebastián-Gallés, N., and Soto-Faraco, S. (2005). The Perception of Second Language Sounds in Early Bilinguals: New Evidence from an Implicit Measure. *Journal of Experimental Psychology: Human Perception and Performance*, 31 (5), 912–918.

Ortega-Llebaria, M. and Bosch, L. (2016). Cues to Dialectal Discrimination in Early Infancy: A Look at Prosodic, Rhythmic and Segmental Properties in Utterances from Two Catalan Dialects. In Joaquín Romero and M. Riera (eds.), *The Phonetics–Phonology Interface: Representations and Methodologies*. Amsterdam and Philadelphia, PA: John Benjamins, pp. 55–70.

Ortega-Llebaria, M., Gu, H., and Fan, J. (2013). English Speakers' Perception of Spanish Lexical Stress: Context-Driven L2 Stress Perception. *Journal of Phonetics*, 41 (3), 186–197.

Pisoni, D. (1993). Long-Term Memory in Speech Perception: Some New Findings on Talker Variability, Speaking Rate and Perceptual Learning. *Speech Communication*, 13 (1), 109–125.

Pons, F. and Bosch, L. (2010). Stress Pattern Preference in Spanish-Learning Infants: The Role of Syllable Weight. *Infancy*, 15 (3), 223–245.

Prieto, P., van Santen, J., and Hirschberg, J. (1995). Tonal Alignment Patterns in Spanish. *Journal of Phonetics*, 23, 429–451.

Ramon-Casas, M., Fennel, C., and Bosch, L. (2016). Minimal-Pair Word Learning by Bilingual Toddlers: The Catalan /e/–/ɛ/ Contrast Revisited. *Bilingualism: Language and Cognition*, 1–8. doi: 10.1017/S1366728916001115.

Rao, R. (2015). Manifestations of /bdg/ in heritage speakers of Spanish. *Heritage Language Journal*, 12 (1), 48–74.

Saalfeld, A. (2009). *Stress in the Beginning Spanish Classroom: An Instructional Study* (Doctoral dissertation). University of Illinois at Urbana-Champaign.

Sebastián-Gallés, N. and Bosch, L. (2009). Developmental Shift in the Discrimination of Vowel Contrasts in Bilingual Infants: Is the Distribution Account All There Is To It? *Developmental Science*, 12 (6), 874–887.

Sebastián-Gallés, N., Echeverría, S., and Bosch, L. (2005). The Influence of Initial Exposure on Lexical Representation: Comparing Early and Simultaneous Bilinguals. *Journal of Memory and Language*, 52 (2), 240–255.

Sebastián-Gallés, N and Soto-Faraco, S. (1999). Online Processing of Native and Non-Native Phonemic Contrasts in Early Bilinguals. *Cognition*, 72 (2), 111–123.

Shea, C. and Curtin, S. (2010). Discovering the Relationship between Context and Allophones in a Second Language: Evidence for Distribution-Based Learning. *Studies in Second Language Acquisition*, 32, 582–606.

Shea, C. and Renaud, J. (2014). L2 Perception of Spanish Palatal Variants across Different Tasks. *Bilingualism: Language and Cognition*, 17 (1), 203–221.

Skoruppa, K., Pons, F., Bosch, L., Christophe, A., Cabrol, D., and Pepperkamp, S. (2013). The Development of Word Stress Processing in French and Spanish Infants. *Language Learning and Development*, 9 (1), 88–104.

Skoruppa, K., Pons, F., Christophe, A., Bosch, L., Dupoux, E., Sebastián-Gallés, N., Limissuri, R. A., and Pepperkamp, S. (2009).

Language Specific Stress Perception by 9-Month-Old French and Spanish Infants. *Developmental Science*, 12, 914–919.

Soto-Faraco, S., Sebastián-Gallés, N., and Cutler, A. (2001). Segmental and Suprasegmental Mismatch in Lexical Access. *Journal of Memory and Language*, 45, 412–432.

Werker, J. and Tees, J. (1984). Cross-Language Speech Perception: Evidence for Perceptual Reorganization during the First Year of Life. *Infant Behavior and Development*, 7 (1), 49–63.

Williams, L. (1977). The Voicing Contrast in Spanish. *Journal of Phonetics*, 5, 169–184.

Zampini, M. (1998). The Relationship between the Production and Perception of L2 Spanish Stops. *Texas Papers in Foreign Language Education*, 3 (3), 85–100.

Zampini, M., Clarke, C., and Norrix, L. (2002). *Sensitivity to Voiceless Closure in the Perception of Spanish and English Stop Consonants*. Paper presented at the Conference of the Acoustical Society of America, Cancún, Mexico, December 2–6.

Zárate-Sández, G. (2015). *Perception and Production of Intonation among English–Spanish Bilingual Speakers at Different Proficiency Levels* (Doctoral dissertation). Georgetown University.

Part III

Spanish Morphosyntax and Meaning

12

Word Phenomena: Category Definition and Word Formation

Antonio Fábregas

12.1 Introduction: Overview

The goal of this chapter is to present the main facts about the internal structure of words in Spanish, and to discuss the analytical and theoretical consequences of these facts both for understanding the principles restricting Spanish morphology and for comparing Spanish and other languages. Obviously, the literature on the topic is too abundant to cover in these few pages. For this reason, the discussion is restricted to a few phenomena and facts that have been highlighted in the literature as central problems for Spanish morphology. The reader will notice that there are some issues that run as common threads through the different sections of this chapter: in particular, the fact that Spanish has category class markers that define an intermediate level between root and word contrasts this language with, for instance, English, and raises questions about (among other things) the size of the units stored in the lexicon (Section 12.2.2), the treatment of gender (Section 12.3.2) and their relation to the absence of recursivity in Spanish compounding (Section 12.5.2).

This chapter is structured as follows. In Section 12.2 we introduce the three levels that have been differentiated in the analysis of Spanish words, and discuss whether the smallest elements stored in the lexicon are roots or stems. Section 12.3 overviews how lexical category distinctions are instantiated in Spanish, and highlights some open questions in this area; Section 12.4 concentrates on general properties of inflection, and Section 12.5 discusses word formation (derivation and compounding), focusing particularly on the nature of appreciative morphology and the restrictions on Spanish compounds.

12.2 Words in Spanish: Main Properties and Structure

Traditionally, three morphological levels are distinguished in the analysis of Spanish word formation (see Pena 1999; Bermúdez-Otero 2007a, 2013): root, stem, and word.[1]

Let us illustrate these three levels with the word *cantan* 'sing.3PL' as an example.

(12.1)   *cantan*
        a. root level: *cant-*
        b. stem level: *cant-a*
        c. word level: *cant-a-n*

The root (12.1a) is typically defined as what is left of the word once all affixes, derivational or inflectional, are segmented. There is a debate with respect to whether roots are themselves assigned to a lexical category (thus, *cant-*$_V$)[2] or are category-neutral (thus, $\sqrt{cant}$-) and receive a category only at the stem level (see for instance Oltra-Massuet 1999; Fábregas 2005; Borer 2013 for overviews of the issue).

The stem level (12.1b) is defined as the root plus a morpheme that marks (or defines) the word class ascription of the root, excluding inflectional affixes for tense, person or number. A relevant property of Spanish, to which we will shortly return, is that these category markers define distinct conjugations and nominal classes which are not predictable from the semantic, phonological or syntactic properties of the root. Finally, the whole word, with its relevant inflectional affixes, defines the word level (12.1c).

Inflectional processes, by definition, take stems as their base in order to produce words. This is illustrated in (12.2) for verbal inflection (12.2a, 12.2b), nominal inflection (12.2c) and adjectival inflection (12.2d).

(12.2)   a. [beb-í]-a-mos
           drink.THV.IMPFV.PAST.1PL.AGR
           'we drank [imperfective]'
       b. [corr-e]-ré-is
           run.THV.FUT.2PL.AGR
           'you will run'
       c. [mes-a]-s
           table.NM.PL
           'tables'
       d. [alegr-e]-s
           happy.AM.PL
           'happy [plural]'

---

[1] As is well known, finding a unified definition of "word" is extremely hard, to the point that many authors have argued against the existence of words as morphosyntactic units of analysis, although they all accept a notion of prosodic wordhood (which does not correspond with semantic or syntactic atomicity). See DiSciullo and Williams (1987), Marantz (2000), Julien (2007), Haspelmath (2011), and Fábregas (2014).

[2] Abbreviations are defined at the beginning of the volume.

Different word-formation processes target roots, stems or inflected words. Roots are used as bases in some compounding and derivational processes (12.3).

(12.3)   a. confes-or
confess-er
'confessor'
b. pern-i-quebr-a-r
leg.LE.break.ThV.INF
'to break a leg'

Stems are used as bases in many other types of compounding and most derivational processes. Note that (12.4a), in contrast with (12.3a), contains the verb marker -e- (ascribing the verb to the second conjugation).

(12.4)   a. corr-e-dor
run.ThV.er
'runner'
b. sord-o-mud-a-s
deaf.NM.mute.FEM.PL
'deaf-mute [feminine plural]'

The underlined constituent in (12.4b) does not exhibit gender or number inflection, even though the whole compound does (as a word). It is not easy to find processes where whole words are taken as bases, but there are some cases. In the compound in (12.5a), the second member is inflected for number – the first is, at least on the surface, a stem – even though that marking is not relevant for the whole word, which can be singular. Adjectives appear with feminine inflection inside the productive class of adverbs built with -*mente*, whose analysis has been highly debated in the literature (12.5b; cf. Torner 2003 and Alexeyenko 2015 for recent overviews).

(12.5)   a. abr-e-cart-a-s
open.ThV.letter.NM.PL
b. rápid-a-mente
fast.FEM.ly
'quickly'
c. cual-es-quiera
which.PL.want
'whichever [plural]'

12.2.1 The Stem Level: Main Facts

As we have stated, Spanish has the property that roots are normally marked with affixes that ascribe them to different lexical classes. Traditionally, these markers receive the name of *vocales temáticas* 'theme vowels' for verbs, and *desinencias* 'desinences' for nouns and adjectives. Theme vowels organize the set of Spanish verbs in three conjugation classes, a distinction relevant for the choice of inflectional allomorphs, such as those that express the imperfective past (-ba- for 1st conjugation, -ía- for 2nd and 3rd).

(12.6) a. cant-a
sing.ThV^{I}
b. ten-e
have.ThV^{II}
c. viv-i
live.ThV^{III}

In the case of nouns and adjectives, there are reasons to think that the final affixes in (12.7) are noun and adjective class markers, even though Spanish does not divide nouns and adjectives into distinct declensions (as, for instance, Latin did). We will return to this issue in Section 12.3.2.

(12.7) a. man-o
hand.NM
b. poet-a
poet.NM
c. trist-e
sad.AM

Noun and adjective markers in Spanish have the property that diminutive affixes appear between the root and the affix (12.8). This leads to the conclusion that at least some adverbs also carry class markers, given their similar properties (12.9).

(12.8) a. man-it-o [Latin American Spanish excluding Mexican]
hand.DIM.NM
b. poet-it-a
poet.DIM.NM

(12.9) a. lej-os   >   lej-it-os
far.AdvM   far.DIM.AdvM
c. cerc-a   >   cerqu-it-a
close.AdvM   close-DIM.AdvM

We can show that the choice of the class marker is an idiosyncratic, lexical property by concentrating on verbs. There is no way to predict whether a given root will take the theme vowel of one of the three conjugations. Roots with identical phonological shapes can take different markers (12.10).

(12.10) a. vend-e-r
sell.ThV^{II}.INF
b. vend-a-r
bandage.ThV^{I}.INF

The lexical–semantic content of the root does not determine the choice either; cf. for instance the restricted class of inherently directional verbs:

(12.11) a. baj-a-r
go down.THV^I.INF
b. ascend-e-r
ascend.THV^{II}.INF
c. sub-i-r
go up.THV^{III}.INF

Syntactically, there are stems of the three conjugations in both transitive and intransitive verbs.

(12.12) a. devor-a   ten-e   repart-i
devour.THV^I have.THV^{II} distribute.THV^{III}
b. lleg-a   crec-e   mor-i
arrive.THV^I grow.THV^{II} die.THV^{III}

It is safe to say that, if there is any kind of rule to assign theme vowels to roots, this rule has not been identified, and listing at some level seems inescapable. The debate is about how this listing proceeds, as we will now see.

12.2.2 Storage of Roots vs. Storage of Stems

The existence of a distinct stem level in Spanish has given rise to a debate with respect to the minimal units that are lexically listed in Spanish. Two options suggest themselves: (i) roots are listed, (ii) stems are listed. In favor of (i) we have the fact that roots seem to be segmentable units; if something bigger than roots is what one lists in the Spanish lexicon, we need redundancy rules or morphophonological processes deleting the final vowel to relate the two bases in (12.13). In favor of (ii), we have the fact that class markers are unpredictable, and in any event one needs to list which one goes with which root. This problem is solved automatically if the minimal items listed are already stems, with a root and a class marker of a particular type.

(12.13) a. cant-a
sing.THV 'sing [V]'
b. cant-o
sing.NM 'song [N]'

The two options have recently been discussed in a debate between Neil Myler and Ricardo Bermúdez-Otero (see Myler 2015; Bermúdez-Otero 2013, 2016). An underlying theoretical issue in this debate is whether the insertion of morphemes is in principle restricted to one exponent per syntactic head (*pace* additional operations that fuse two heads together, Halle and Marantz 1993) or whether exponents can spell out sequences of heads forming one syntactic constituent (as in spanning, Ramchand 2008; Svenonius 2016; or phrasal spell-out, Caha 2009). For Myler, following Halle and Marantz (1993) and Embick (2010), Spanish stores roots, as everything that is segmentable in morphology must correspond to one distinct syntactic head; for Bermúdez-Otero, Spanish stores stems. We will now consider his line of argument.

Bermúdez-Otero (2013), who embraces a stratal approach to the relation between morphology and phonology, notes that, if roots were the minimal units stored, we would expect a phonological cycle to apply as soon as the root is merged with a class marker. However, this assumption produces the wrong empirical results, in what Bermúdez-Otero labels "The Problem of the Missing Cycle." Let us see how.

Assume roots are stored, for the sake of the argument. A root like (12.14) has the property that it alternates between a single vowel /o/ and a diphthong /ue/ depending on the position of the stress.

(12.14) cont- 'tell'
c/ué/ntas 'you tell'
c/o/nt/á/mos 'we tell'

Now compare the two forms in (12.15): the noun corresponding to 'tale' (12.15a) and the noun corresponding to 'teller':

(12.15) a. c/ué/nto
b. c/o/nt-a-dor
tell.ThV.er

The problem is that if roots are stored, we should expect diphthongization in both cases. Both words go through a stage where the root is combined with a class marker to produce a stem (abstractly, *[[√cOnt-] F]*). The phonological cycle that applies to (12.15a), assigning stress to the first syllable (12.16a), should also apply to (12.15b), yielding the unattested form *cuentador* 'teller' (12.16b).

(12.16) a. [[cónt]o] → cuento
b. [[cónt]a](dor) → *cuenta(dor)

(12.16b) is unattested, so – Bermúdez-Otero argues – roots are not stored. Instead, Spanish stores two (allomorphic) stems for the verb (12.17). When stress is assigned in that cycle, if it falls on the root, the diphthongized version is chosen; otherwise, the non-diphthongized allomorph is chosen (12.18).

(12.17) a. /kuent-a/
b. /kont-a/

(12.18) a. {/kuént-a/–/kónt-a/}-s → /kuént-a-s/
b. {/kuent-a/–/kont-a/}-dór → /kont-a-dór/

Myler (2015) proposes a different solution to the Problem of the Missing Cycle that does not involve giving up the idea that roots are stored: in Spanish, class assignment to verbs does not trigger a phonological cycle, while nouns and adjectives do. If this is so, the paradox dissolves. The diphthong is triggered in (12.15a), for it is a noun and stress is assigned; however, in (12.15b), when the theme vowel is added, no cycle is run, and thus the vowel does not diphthongize. At the point where the nominalizer -*dor* '-er' is introduced, a cycle is run, but in that cycle the root vowel does not receive stress. Thus, diphthongization is avoided, because at no point in the derivation does stress fall onto the relevant vowel. Schematically:

(12.19) a. /kuénto/ b. /kontadór/
        a. i. √cont-+N   b. i. √cont+V
        a. ii. Run a cycle   b. ii. No cycle is run
        a. iii. /kónt-o/   b. iii. cont-a + N
        a. iv. Apply diphthongization   b. iv. Run a cycle
        a. v. /kuénto/   b. v. /kont-a-dór/

Myler (2015) notes that there is independent evidence that in Spanish class assignment to verbs does not trigger a cycle. Consider the contrast in (12.20): in (12.20a), there is hiatus between the root-final /i/ and the theme vowel; (12.20b) exhibits a diphthong.

(12.20)   a. te.le.gra.fi.á.mos
           b. pro.nun.cjá.mos

Bermúdez-Otero (2013) had argued that the contrast shows that verb stems undergo a phonological cycle: starting from the underlying representations in (12.21a), at the stem level (12.21b) stress is assigned to /i/ in the first, but not in the second word. Once inflectional morphology is added (12.21c), a second cycle is run (at the word level), where an unstressed high vowel undergoes gliding and stress is reassigned. Gliding, because of (12.21b), applies to (12.20b), but not to (12.20a).

(12.21)   te.le.gra.fi.á.mos   pro.nun.cjá.mos
        a. i. te.le.gra.(fi.a)   ii. pro.(nun.cia)   *Foot formation*
        b. i. te.le.gra.(fi.a)   ii. pro.(nún.cia)   *Stress assignment*
        c. i. te.le.gra.fi.á.mos   ii. pro.nun.cjá.mos   *Gliding*

Myler (2015) proposes that what is actually going on here is that the gliding rule applies to nouns but not to verbs, irrespective of the position of stress, because verbs do not trigger a cycle. Starting from the same assumption as Bermúdez-Otero (that the underlying representations of 12.20a and 12.20b are crucially different), this is how the distinction is derived:

(12.22)   te.le.gra.fi.á.mos   pro.nun.cjá.mos
        a. i. te.le.gra.**fi.** + a$_V$ ii. pro.nun.cj + a$_V$
        b. i. No gliding applies   ii. –
        c. i. te.le.gra.fi.a + mos   ii. pro.nun.cja + mos

If a verb like (12.20a) is further derived as noun or adjective – because by the time the nominal or adjectival affix is added the high vowel is already protected inside the previous cycle – no gliding occurs: cf. [[*te.le.gra.fi.a.*]$_V$ *ble*]$_A$ 'telegraph-able.'

The crucial prediction of Myler is, however, that if a base with hiatus is derived as a noun or adjective without first going through the verb stage, gliding should occur, because adjectives and nouns do trigger a cycle. This is what Cabré and Prieto (2007) argue for Spanish. The formations in (12.23) reflect Cabré and Prieto's judgments.

(12.23) a. na.ví.o 'ship'   → [[navi]ero]$_N$,   nav[jé]ro 'shipping'
         b. ma.ní.a 'mania'   → [[mania]tico]$_A$, man[já]tico 'maniac'
         c. po.li.cí.a 'police' → [[polici]al]$_A$ polic[já]l 'police-related'

However, in his response Bermúdez-Otero (2016) casts doubt on the claim that gliding is excluded in verbal environments, and shows that the data in (12.23) are not unproblematic (2016:410–412). His reasoning goes as follows: in Myler's proposal one would expect that forms like those in (12.24) should be attested in Spanish:

(12.24) *de.te.ri.o.rá.mos 'we deteriorate' (cf. *de.te.rjo.rá.mos*)

The absolute absence of such forms is a lexical accident in Myler's story, as all it would take to produce them would be that the lexical entry of the verb define /i/ as syllabic. However, in the account of Bermúdez-Otero, the absolute absence of such forms is expected even if /i/ is lexically defined as syllabic:

(12.25) a. de.te.ri.o.ra (underlying representation)
         b. de.te.ri.(ó.ra) (stress assignment)
         c. de.te.rjo.ra(mos) (gliding)

Myler (p.c.) acknowledges that the evidence that he brought up in his 2015 article is not as solid as he thought, but still believes that the theoretical problems associated with the listing of roots (non-locality of lexical insertion, existence of segmentable units that are however not listed, etc.) should encourage researchers to look for other analytical options. All in all, it seems that the jury is still out on this matter.

12.3 Grammatical Categories and Inflection

Spanish, as is well known, is a synthetic, richly inflectional language. Among lexical categories, a few generalizations can be made:

1. Verbs, nouns, and adjectives are inflected for several properties
2. Verbs, adjectives, and determiners display agreement with nouns
3. Nouns never agree

12.3.1 Morphological Marking of the Main Lexical Classes

We will follow Booij's (1996) distinction between inherent and contextual inflection, where the latter corresponds roughly to agreement and the former involves cases where the inflection is chosen by the semantics conveyed by the affix. Within this distinction, verbs are inherently inflected for tense (past, present, future), aspect (perfect, imperfective, perfective), and mood (indicative, subjunctive, imperative); contextually, for person (first, second, third) and number (singular, plural).

(12.26) cant-a-   ra-   s
       sing.ThV¹   PAST.IMPFV.SBJV   2SG

Nouns do not display agreement and are inherently inflected for gender and number, although most noun stems do not show gender alternations.

(12.27) niñ-   a- -s
        young   F   PL
        'girls'

Adjectives agree in gender and number with nouns, and display some restricted degree of morphology, in the form of a superlative suffix (12.28). Determiners and quantifiers inflect like adjectives, except that they reject degree morphology (12.29).

(12.28) guap-   ísim-   a-   -s
        pretty   SPRLT   FEM   PL
        'very pretty.FEM.PL'

(12.29) est-   (*ísim-) a-   -s
        this   SPRLT   FEM   PL
        'these.FEM.PL'

In contrast, prepositions and conjunctions are invariable. Some adverbs allow degree morphology, subject to some dialectal variation.

(12.30) lent-   ísim-   o
        slow   SPRLT   AM
        'very slowly'

12.3.2 Class Markers and Gender in Nominal Inflection

The existence of class markers, defining the stem level, has given rise to several debates in the field. We will highlight one of those, related to whether the final vowel of nouns and adjectives expresses gender or is better viewed as a class marker on a par with, for instance, the markers of the Latin declensions from which they evolved (-a for first declension, -u for second, -e for third, etc.). On the surface, the idea that the final vowel of nouns and adjectives expresses gender seems intuitively right; most nouns ending in -o trigger masculine agreement, and most nouns ending in -a are feminine (12.31).

(12.31) a. el   { perr-o / abrig-o / corr-o   / hoy-o   ...}
           the.MASC   dog   / coat   / ring   / hole
        b. la   { cas-a   / cost-a   / piedr-a / huell-a ...}
           the.FEM   house   / coast   / stone   / trace

However, Harris (1991) argued that the final vowels are actually class markers that might be associated to typical gender values, but are distinct from them. Part of the evidence is that (i) there are masculine nouns ending in -*a*, (ii) there are feminine nouns ending in -*o*, and (iii) nouns ending in -*e* or consonant (perhaps, with a -Ø marker) can be of either gender.

(12.32) a. *problema* 'problem,' *profeta* 'prophet,' *programa* 'program,' *cometa* 'comet' …
b. *mano* 'hand,' *foto* 'photo,' *nao* 'ship,' *soprano* 'soprano' …
c. *puente* 'bridge.MASC,' *fuente* 'fountain.FEM,' *pez* 'fish.MASC,' *red* 'net.FEM' …

The theory is not without problems. One complication is that in adjectives the final vowel (which is surface-identical to the final vowel of nouns) correlates with gender in all cases (with the exception of some invariable adjectives, which are the plausible result of truncation: *porno* 'pornographic' and *tecno* 'techno').[3]

(12.33) a. izquierd-o   izquierd-a
              left-O   left-A
        b. la mano   izquierd-a
              the.FEM hand   left.FEM
        c. el programa   izquierd-o
              the.MASC program   left.MASC

It is counterintuitive to claim that -*o*/-*a* correlate with gender in adjectives, but with class markers in nouns. Two solutions are conceivable: the first is to argue that in adjectives, as in nouns, the final vowel is a class marker defining the stem (not the inflected word), and gender-variable adjectives are associated to two distinct stems (*izquierd-a* and *izquierd-o*) whose distribution depends on the gender of the NP they modify. The alternative, to treat -*o* and -*a* as gender markers, involves explaining why there is no apparent correlation in (12.32a) and (12.32b). One could claim that in those apparent counterexamples the final vowel actually belongs to the root, and gender is assigned by a zero morpheme (alternatively, by the usual vowel, that gets erased following a morphophonological process). The counterexamples, then, are due to an ambiguity with the segmentation of final vowels: some are gender markers, some are part of the root.

(12.34) [[√mano] Ø]$_{FEM}$

This proposal is supported by other facts: *radio* 'radio' and *foto* 'photo,' two among a handful of nouns that display final /o/ and are feminine, are truncations of longer, gender-regular words (*radiotransmisión* and *fotografía*), so in their case it is plausible to associate the final /o/ to the

---

[3] Other invariable adjectives, such as *rosa* 'pink,' are nouns that have yet to be grammaticalized as adjectives.

root. However, diminutive affixes linearize to the left of the final vowel also in these cases.

(12.35) a. *fot-it-o* 'little photo'
b. *sopran-it-o* 'little soprano'
c. *man-it-{o/a}* 'little hand'

This is the same behavior as that displayed by segmentable final vowels (12.36). If /o/ belonged to the root, these would be instances of infixation where the affix breaks the linear adjacency of the root. We know that this is very uncommon in Spanish, essentially restricted to consonant-final paroxytone nouns (12.37).

(12.36) a. *cas-it-a* 'little house.FEM'
b. *hoy-it-o* 'little hole.MASC'

(12.37) a. *Víctor* > *Vict-it-or*
'Victor' 'little Victor'
b. *azúcar* > *azuqu-it-ar*
'sugar' 'little sugar'

The nature of final vowels in nouns and adjectives is another open problem in Spanish morphology.

12.4 Inflection: Agreement and its Identification

Spanish is a language where inflectional categories show an intricate interaction between morphosyntactic features, morphophonological realization and linearization. For these reasons, Spanish paradigms have been frequently used to argue for Word-and-Paradigm approaches to morphology (Stump 2001; see Ambadiang and Camus Bergareche 2000, for instance), where morphemes are not segmentable units of morphological analysis, or realizational accounts, where exponents do not match sets of morphosyntactic features in a one-to-one fashion (see Bonet 1991; Oltra-Massuet and Arregi 2005, among others).

12.4.1 Morpheme-Based and Word-Based Morphology

In Spanish, all kinds of mismatches between form and meaning at the morphological level are easy to attest (see Matthews 1972 and Stump 1998 for exhaustive treatments).

Morphological theories based on the (traditional) morpheme expect, *ceteris paribus*, that there is a correlation between the form of a morpheme (its morphophonological realization) and its meaning or function (the set of morphosyntactic features that the exponent spells out). Mismatches can occur in several ways, and we will illustrate them for Spanish:

1 **Cumulative exponence**: This is the situation where an alleged morpheme contains information about two or more distinct morphosyntactic categories. For instance, the morphemes -ra/-se are associated with three categories: mood (subjunctive), aspect (imperfective), and tense (past).

(12.38)   cant-a   -se
            sing.ThV[1] PAST.IMPFV.SBJV

2 **Extended exponence**: In such cases, two or more morphemes that appear in the same word express the same morphosyntactic distinction. For instance, this is the case in the second-person plural perfective (12.39a). Note that by comparison with any other second-person plural forms (e.g. 12.39b) the two suffixes, -ste- and -is, should be segmented. However, -ste appears in the second-person singular form also (12.39c), which suggests it is an exponent for the second person in the perfective. Therefore, there seem to be here two exponents associated to the second person, and both of them are necessary in the second-person plural perfective.

(12.39) a.   cant-a-ste-is   'you.PL sang'
               sing.ThV.PFCV.2PL
         b.   cant-a-ré-is   'you.PL will sing'
               sing.ThV.FUT.2PL
         c.   cant-a-ste   'you.SG sang'
               sing.ThV.PFCV.2SG

3 **Syncretism**: Situations of syncretism are cases where two distinct sets of morphosyntactic features that are otherwise spelled out differently receive the same spell-out in particular contexts. For instance, we know that the distinction between the first person singular and the third person singular is relevant in the grammar of Spanish (e.g. for subject agreement), and moreover that it is differentiated in the verbal paradigm (12.40). However, in all past imperfective forms the two persons are spelled out identically (see 12.41 for imperfective indicative; the same syncretism takes place in the conditional and the two imperfective subjunctives).

(12.40)   cant-o 'I sing' / cant-a '(s)he sings'

(12.41)   cant-a-ba 'sang.IMPFV.1/3SG'

The literature that has discussed facts like these to support a word-based approach to inflection or has proposed technical solutions to make them compatible with a morpheme-based approach is too abundant to review here. We refer the reader to Elvira (1998), Burdette (2005), Eddington (2005), and Oltra-Massuet and Arregi (2005) for different approaches.

12.4.2 Object Agreement in Spanish?

To end this section, we will discuss another open issue in Spanish inflection which illustrates that sometimes it is not straightforward to determine whether or not a morpheme spells out agreement features: object clitics such as those in (12.42).

(12.42) a. Le   di   un   libro a   María.
           her.DAT I-gave   a   book   to   María
           'I gave a book to María.'
       b. El   libro, lo   leí.
           the book,   it.ACC I-read
           'The book, I read it.'

Since the 70s there has been a debate as to whether Spanish clitics are object agreement markers or manifestations of (reduced) determiner phrase (DP) arguments. Kayne (1975) argued for the latter approach, and this analysis was assumed for Spanish until Jaeggli (1986). Part of Kayne's reasoning was that object clitics are arguments because they are incompatible with an overt realization of a DP unless the DP is topicalized as a peripheral element (cf. 12.42b, in contrast to 12.43, where "%" indicates that the utterance is acceptable to some speakers as a completely grammatical sentence, while it is rejected by others).

(12.43) % Lo   leí   el   libro.
            it.ACC I-read the book
            'I read the book.'

While the complementary distribution between object clitics and DP objects largely applies to French, Jaeggli (1986) noted that it does not apply to Spanish. Note, first, that dative clitics are always compatible with the overt prepositional phrase (PP) realization of the indirect object (12.42a); second, in River Plate Spanish and other American areas (such as regions in Cochabamba, Bolivia) (12.43) is grammatical without any kind of right-dislocation.

This observation prompted analyses in which object clitics are agreement markers; in both (12.42b) and (12.43) the accusative clitic would agree with a DP argument, which in (12.42b) would be a silent pronoun and in (12.43) would be an overt DP. Dialectal variation would reduce to the conditions under which the agreement marker is spelled out depending on the referential and phonological properties of the argument (see Fernández Soriano 1993; Sportiche 1996). An immediate argument for treating clitics as agreement markers would be that they must be adjacent to the verbal stem (12.44), as "prefixes" or "suffixes."

(12.44) a. {No   lo / *lo   no}   leí
           not   it   it   not   read
       b. Puedes   no   leer-(*bien)-lo.
          you-can   not   read-well-it
          Intended: 'You might not read it well.'

Another frequently noted argument for considering clitics (specifically, dative clitics) as verbal agreement markers is the fact that doublings like (12.42a) are possible with all kinds of datives, and in some cases even compulsory (12.45a; see Cuervo 2003). Beyond this (cf. Company Company 1998), the dative clitic does not need to agree in number with the PP indirect object in many varieties (e.g. Mexican, Peninsular colloquial Spanish . . .), so perhaps it is becoming a grammatical marker of ditransitivity, an applicative morpheme of sorts (12.45b).

(12.45) a. *(Le) hice una tarta a María.
her.DAT made a cake to María
'I made María a cake.'
b. Le-(s) conté la historia a mis padres.
dat.PL told the story to my parents
'I told my parents the story.'

Another supporting piece of evidence is that subject agreement morphemes and (enclitic) object clitics interact morphophonologically in several ways (cf. Harris and Halle 2005). In some varieties object clitics are more internal to the word than is subject agreement (12.46a) and in varieties that use the form *vosotros*[4] the shape of the subject agreement marker is influenced by the presence of a reflexive clitic (12.46b).

(12.46) a. díga-me-lo-n (cf. *díga-n-me-lo*)
say.IMP me.DAT it.ACC 3PL
'Tell.2PL me it!'
b. calla-d > calla-Ø-os (cf. *calla-d-os*)
shut up.2PL.IMP shut up.2PL.IMP.yourselves
'Shut up!' 'Shut up!'

However, it has been noted that an analysis of all object clitics as agreement markers is not problem-free for Spanish. Significantly, accusative object clitics (but not datives) display gender contrasts:

(12.47) a. La manzana, la he tirado.
the.FEM apple.FEM it.ACC.FEM I-have thrown
b. El plátano, lo he tirado.
the.MASC banana.MASC it.ACC.MASC I-have thrown

If object clitics are agreement markers, then they would be inflectional categories of verbs. However, accusative object clitics would be the only type of verbal agreement that in Spanish exhibits gender. Subject agreement morphemes never display gender distinctions (cf. {*Él* / *Ella*} *comió* 'He/She ate'). Finally, the main problem for a theory where object clitics are arguments (namely, the co-occurrence of clitics with overt DPs) has been addressed through other analytical devices: for instance, Uriagereka's

---

[4] Most varieties of Spanish lack the form *vosotros* and use *ustedes*, with its associated agreement.

(1995) "Big DP" proposal. Uriagereka argues that in a clitic-doubling context, the base argument is not a simple DP (12.48a), but a complex DP constituent containing the clitic (12.48b and 12.48c, depending on the realization of the lower layer). In doubling contexts, the clitic abandons the big DP to move to a high clausal functional position; variation internal to Spanish depends on whether different kinds of D can act as arguments without the help of the clitic double.

(12.48)   a. [DP la [NP mesa]] 'the table'
          b. [DP [la] la [NP mesa]] 'it.FEM the table'
          c. [DP [la] D° [NP *pro*]] 'it.FEM'

There are, currently, three options for understanding clitics in Spanish: (i) they are arguments, and doubling occurs with some version of the big-DP structure; (ii) they are agreement markers, and (iii) a non-unitary account where dative clitics are agreement markers while accusative clitics are arguments (Ormazábal and Romero 2013). We refer the reader to Ordóñez (2012) for discussion of these approaches.

12.5 Word Formation: Main Issues

The literature on word formation in Spanish is simply too abundant to review here exhaustively, and we refer the reader to Lang (1992), Rainer (1993), Bosque and Demonte (1999: Chs. 69–78), and RAE and ASALE (2009: Chs. 5–11) for detailed descriptions of the empirical facts. Here we will concentrate on two issues that have contributed to theoretical debates beyond Spanish: the status of appreciative morphology, and the properties of compounding in Spanish.

But first let us review the main facts about Spanish word formation. We can divide the processes into two classes: (i) operations that produce new words where sequences that in some theories correspond to morphemes can be segmented and (ii) operations that produce new words where distinct morphemes are impossible to segment: significantly, truncation and blendings. The first class can be divided into two: (ia) processes that change the grammatical category and frequently the semantics of the base and (ib) processes that alter the semantics of the base, but not its lexical distribution.

In the first subclass we find the processes of nominalization (creation of nouns from verbs, adjectives, and occasionally other classes); adjectivalization (creation of adjectives from other classes), and verbalization (creation of verbs from other classes). It is controversial whether adverbialization exists in Spanish as a productive process: *-mente* adverbs built from adjectives (*claro* 'clear' > *claramente* 'clearly') have been analyzed as compounds or even syntactic phrases in several works (see Zagona 1990). As can be seen in Table 12.1, all productive category-changing processes involve suffixes.

Table 12.1 *Word formation processes with category change (sample)*

Base category	Output category	Example
Noun	Verb	*clase* 'class' > *clas-ificar* 'to class-ify'
Noun	Adjective	*lluvia* 'rain' > *lluvi-oso* 'rain-y'
Adjective	Noun	*claro* 'clear' > *clar-idad* 'clar-ity'
Adjective	Verb	*amarillo* 'yellow' > *amarill-ear* 'to become yellow'
Verb	Noun	*pintar* 'to paint' > *pint-ura* 'painting'
Verb	Adjective	*huir* 'to flee' > *hui-dizo* 'fleeting'
Preposition (restricted)	Adjective	*tras* 'behind' > *trasero* 'rear'
Preposition (restricted)	Verb	*tras* 'behind' > *a-tras-ar* 'to delay'
Adjective	Adverb	*inteligente* 'intelligent' > *inteligente-mente* 'intelligently'
Noun	Adverb	*cima* 'summit' > *en-cima* 'above'

Spanish also forms new words through conversion (Bauer and Valera 2005): conversion is the process whereby a word changes its grammatical category without the addition of other overt morphemes, prefixes or suffixes. In Spanish, given the existence of stems, conversion can in some cases involve a change in the class marking of the root, but no addition of affixes beyond the class marker: for instance, *cost-ar*$_{ThV}$ 'to cost' > *cost-e*$_{AM}$ 'cost (N).'

With respect to (ib), processes that combine morphemes but do not change the grammatical category, there are many distinct cases. Productive prefixation processes fall into this class,[5] and compounding also tends to fall here, to the extent that the category of the whole compound tends to correspond to the category of the head member of the compound. However, some cases of compounding in Spanish have been classified as exocentric, a term used to describe situations where none of the two members seems to act as the categorial and semantic head of the compound (e.g. *limpia-botas* 'lit. clean-boots, shoe-shine,' where neither the verb nor the plural noun is an uncontroversial head in the structure; cf. Rainer and Varela 1992). In Table 12.2, when compounds are illustrated, the head member is underlined.

With respect to (ii), processes where morphemes are impossible or very difficult to segment, we have a number of semi-productive processes that do not change the grammatical category of the base. Truncation is a morphophonological process that takes a word longer than two syllables, normally a noun (12.49a) or adjective (12.49b), and reduces it to a trochee (two syllables, the first of which carries stress). Sometimes truncation comes accompanied by a change in the final vowel or even consonantal

---

[5] The claim that prefixes are unable to change the grammatical category in Spanish is challenged in some works, however. The prefixes *anti-* and *pro-* make it possible for nominal bases to modify other nouns and receive degree adverbs, as in the example below. See Martín García (2001) and references therein for this debate.

(i) Juan es muy *(anti-)aborto.
'Juan is very (anti-)abortion.'

Table 12.2 *Word formation processes involving semantic change, but no category change (sample)*

Base	Semantic notion	Example
Noun	Location	*sala* 'room' > *ante-sala* 'anteroom'
Noun	Time	*guerra* 'war' > *pre-guerra* 'pre-war'
Noun	Quantity	*motor* 'motor' > *bi-motor* 'with two motors'
Adjective	Degree	*guapo* 'pretty' > *super-guapo* 'extra-pretty'
Noun	Activity related to N	*reloj* 'watch' > *reloj-ero* 'watch-maker'
Verb	Irregular action related to V	*bes-ar* 'to kiss' > *bes-uqu-ear* 'to smooch'
Verb	Reflexive	*critic-ar* 'to criticize' > *auto-criticar* 'to criticize oneself'
Noun + Adjective	To have a N with property A	*pelo* 'hair,' *rojo* 'red' > *pel-i-rrojo* 'red-haired'
Adjective + Adjective	To be both A and A	*agrio* 'sour,' *dulce* 'sweet' > *agri-<u>dulce</u>* 'sweet-sour'
Noun + Deverbal Adjective	To take part in a situation V involving N	*radio* 'radio,' *aficionado* 'enthusiast' > *radio-<u>aficionado</u>* 'ham radio-enthusiast'

Underlining marks the head member of compounds.

segments, including expressive palatalization (12.49c) (cf. Felíu and Roca 2003; Sanz 2015). Truncation never changes the meaning of the base, but the truncated word is associated to colloquial, sometimes familiar, contexts.

(12.49) a. *universidad* 'university' > uni
   b. *pornográfico* 'pornographic' > porno
   c. *Concepción* 'female proper name' > Con<u>chi</u>

Blending is an operation that is reminiscent of compounding, but with the twist that the elements combined overlap in such a way that it becomes impossible to cleanly segment them; obviously, such formations require that the two elements combined share segmental or suprasegmental phonological properties. Blending is normally associated to a humorous or stylistically charged interpretation. In (12.50), the area of the word where the overlap takes place is underlined.

(12.50) a. *analfabeto* 'illiterate' + *bestia* 'beast, dimwit' = *anal<u>fa</u>bestia*
   b. *sucio* 'dirty' + *socialista* 'socialist' = *s<u>u</u>cialista*
   c. *manifestación* 'demonstration,' *fiesta* 'party,' *acción* 'action' = *mani-<u>fiesta</u>-<u>acción</u>*

12.5.1 Appreciative Morphology: Between Inflection and Derivation

Appreciative affixes in Spanish are typically suffixes that appear between the root and the class marker (with some phonological twists, studied in Colina 2003 and Bermúdez-Otero 2007a, 2007b). They are normally divided into three classes: diminutives (12.51a), augmentatives (12.51b), and pejoratives (12.51c), of which the first class is by far the most studied. What they have in common is that (i) they do not change the grammatical category of the base, (ii) they do not change the denotation of the base, but add some emotional value to it, and (iii), with the exception of some augmentatives, they do not change gender of the base if it is a noun (cf. 12.51b with 12.51a, 12.51c).

(12.51) a. *bols-a* 'bag.FEM' > *bols-it-a* 'bag.FEM [affectionate]'
b. *piv-a* 'attractive girl.FEM' > *piv-ón* 'attractive girl [mirative].MASC'
c. *profesor* 'teacher.MASC' > *profesor-uch-o* 'teacher.MASC [scornful]'

The interest of diminutives for morphological theory is that they do not display the prototypical properties of word formation processes, and lie in a gray area between derivation and inflection. Here are the reasons:

1 Diminutives never change the grammatical category of the base. In all cases, the category of the diminutivized word is identical to that of the base. In this they resemble prototypical inflection.
2 Like inflection, diminutives are almost completely productive with nouns. There are very few nouns which do not allow them naturally (such as *sed* 'thirst' > ??*sed(ec)ita* 'a bit of thirst'); gradable adjectives always allow them, also.
3 It is a well-known fact that inflectional morphology, which is relevant for syntax, is external with respect to word-formation processes. Thus, a linear order *[[[Base]Inflection]Derivation]* is expected to be ungrammatical. And yet, there are cases where diminutives follow inflectional items, as in (12.52):

(12.52) Está   corr-ie-nd-ito.
         is.3SG   run.ThV.ing.DIM
         'He is running [without much speed].'

4 However, other properties point to diminutive formation as a derivational process. Inflection cannot be iterated: number marking or subject agreement are restricted to just one morpheme per word (**reloj-es-es* 'watch.PL.PL'). However, diminutive marking can appear more than once with the same stem: *chica* 'girl' > *chiqu-ita* 'girl.DIM' > *chiqu-it-ita* 'girl.DIM.DIM.'
5 Finally, inflectional morphology is relevant for syntactic processes: it is copied in agreement or it restricts the syntactic distribution of a word, if not both (cf. case marking, tense marking in sequence of tense contexts, etc.). Diminutive morphology is not copied in agreement and the distribution of a diminutive noun is identical to the distribution of the noun without the diminutive.

These facts have given rise to two different kinds of analyses. The first has been to deny that inflection and derivation are opposed in a strict way, or even that there is a grammatically relevant sense in which they are distinct kinds of processes (cf. Serrano Dolader 2010; Haspelmath 2002). The second has been to treat diminutives as derivational, and account for their marked distribution and properties among derivational affixes by arguing that they are underlyingly prefixes that check a gender feature of the base noun (cf. Eguren 2002; Fábregas 2013): prefixes, as was noted before, never change the grammatical category of the base and can be iterated (*anti-anti-abortion*). However, this does not clearly explain the combination of diminutives with verbal forms like (12.52).

12.5.2 Compounding in Spanish: Why so Restricted?

There are two senses in which compounding in Spanish (and other Romance languages) is more restricted than what one finds in Germanic languages, and both facts have been used to make claims about word-formation processes in Spanish and their consequences for cross-linguistic variation.[6]

First, combinations of two forms into a compound are freer in for instance English than in Spanish, a fact that is most clear in compounds combining two nouns. Compare (12.53a) with (12.53b). We note, in passing, that in Spanish the head of a compound (underlined) is normally the leftmost member, while in English it tends to be the rightmost member.

(12.53) a. bicycle <u>girl</u>
        b. ?<u>chica</u> bicicleta
           girl bicycle

In English (see for instance Downing 1977), (12.53a) can be used to express virtually any relation between the girl and the bicycle: the girl that owns the bicycle, the girl that wears biker clothing, the girl that stands next to a bicycle, etc. In Spanish, to the extent that (12.53b) is acceptable, the meaning seems to be restricted to an attributive interpretation of the second member of the compound (in Scalise and Bisetto's 2009 sense): it denotes a girl who is characterized by some property shared with prototypical 'bicycles' (whatever that amounts to), as in *corbata mariposa* 'tie butterfly, bowtie,' where the tie has some property of butterflies (the shape) and in *azul cielo* 'blue sky, light-blue,' where the shade of blue resembles the sky.

The second sense in which compounding is severely restricted in Spanish is with respect to recursivity. English and German can create compounds of a virtually unlimited number of members (12.54); Spanish compounds are much more restricted in this sense (12.55).

---

[6] An additional complication in the study of compounding is defining the boundary between compound structures and phrasal constituents. In theories that assume an independent word-formation component this is a crucial problem. For different proposals and criteria, see Bustos Gisbert (1986), Piera and Varela (1999), Ruiz Gurillo (2002), and Buenafuentes de la Mata (2007).

(12.54) a. book <u>club</u>
b. student [book <u>club</u>]
c. Harvard [student [book <u>club</u>]]
d. ...

(12.55) a. <u>perro</u> policía
dog police 'dog with properties of a policeman' = 'police dog'
b. *<u>niño</u> [perro policía]
child dog police 'child with properties of a police dog' = 'police dog child'

There are two main approaches to why Spanish compounding is so restricted: a structural one and a semantic one. One example of the first is Piera (1995). Piera's proposal is that there is a simple explanation as to why Spanish compounds are not recursive and why they have the head to the left: Spanish has class markers for grammatical categories (the stem level discussed in Section 12.2). Piera's proposal goes as follows. He argues (1995:306) that the principle in (12.56) restricts adjunction of a morphological word to another in order to build a compound:

(12.56) A double bracket at the end of a word blocks adjunction of a word.

Spanish nouns (12.57a), as opposed to English ones (12.57b), have a double bracket to their left, because of the class marker:

(12.57) a. [[perr]o]
b. [dog]

Consequently, the second member must be attached to the right of the head (12.58a); left-attachment (12.58b) violates (12.56), as there are two brackets to the left of the head.

(12.58) a. [[perr]o] [[polic í]a]
b. *[[polic í]a] [[perr]o] (by 12.56)

The same principle restricts compounds to just two members; once (12.58a) is turned into one single constituent, a second bracket is introduced to its right. Now both edges have multiple brackets, so a third member could never attach to the head.

(12.59) [[[perr]o]^N [[polic í]a]^N]^N

See Moina (2011) for a different analysis, also in structural terms.

The second family of approaches to productivity restrictions in Spanish compounding is semantic in nature. Snyder (1995, 2012), whom we take as illustrative, has proposed the so-called "Compounding Parameter." This is a semantic parameter that determines how flexible modification is in a given language. Specifically, the Compounding Parameter dictates whether the language allows Generalized Modification (12.60); languages which set it positively (English) are able to interpret as modification virtually any combination of two lexical categories, while languages that set it negatively (Spanish) are expected to be much more restrictive.

(12.60) If α and β are syntactic sisters under node γ, where α is the head of γ, and α denotes a kind, then interpret γ semantically as a subtype of α's kind that stands in a pragmatically suitable relation to the denotation of β.

This explanation relates restrictions on compounding not to the existence of stems as a separate level in Spanish or headedness, but to the lack of strong resultative adjectival phrases (APs) such as *Mary shot John dead* and other complex predicates; however, the cross-linguistic accuracy of the Compounding Parameter has been challenged (cf. Son and Svenonius 2008; Mateu and Acedo-Matellán 2015).

12.6 Conclusion: Beyond Spanish Morphology

In this chapter, we have chosen to focus on the fact that Spanish overtly marks stems as combinations of roots with category markers. We hope that the motivation for this decision has become clear to the reader while reading the previous pages: in addition to being one of the most characteristic morphological properties of Spanish, the existence of this intermediate level raises deep questions about foundational issues in morphological theory, which we want to summarize here making explicit their implications for theoretical linguistics beyond research on Spanish and language comparison.

1. **The problem of storage**. The combination of roots with class markers is idiosyncratic: does it mean that stems must be listed, or would it be enough to list roots, together with diacritics that codify in some way the theme vowel or class marker of each root? More generally, does unpredictability amount to lexical storage or could one use rules of restricted application – computation, then – to avoid an explosion in listing?
2. **The problem of the inflection/derivation divide**. The traditional divide between morphology that creates new words and morphology that gives different forms of the same word is challenged by several Spanish phenomena, such as the existence of class markers and the distribution of diminutives. Can the contrast be maintained or should it be treated as mere tendencies differentiating functions of the same kind of processes?
3. **The problem of productivity**. A puzzling fact of morphological theories of any kind is why operations creating words are more restricted in their application than those building up phrases. The problem is quite acute in the realm of Spanish compounding, whose interpretation and recursivity are severely limited. Should the limits in word operations be explained through morphosyntactic properties, through restrictions on semantic interpretation, or perhaps other devices?

The set of facts and problems that we could not refer to in this chapter is too long to allow listing. However, we hope at least to have managed to drive the attention of researchers to a few of these problems, and to encourage other people to make their own contributions to them.

References

Alexeyenko, A. (2015). The Syntax and Semantics of Manner Modification: Adjectives and Adverbs (Doctoral dissertation). University of Osnabrück.

Ambadiang, T. and Camus Bergareche, B. (2000). Morfología verbal del español como L2. In María Tadea Díaz Hormigo (ed.), *IV Congreso de Lingüística General, Cádiz, del 3 al 6 de abril 2000*, Vol. 2. Cádiz: Universidad de Cádiz, pp. 89–102.

Bauer, L. and Valera, S. (2005). *Approaches to Conversion / Zero Derivation*. Münster: Waxmann.

Bermúdez-Otero, R. (2007a). Morphological Structure and Phonological Domains in Spanish Denominal Derivation. In F. Martínez-Gil and S. Colina (eds.), *Optimality-Theoretic studies in Spanish Phonology*. Amsterdam: John Benjamins, pp. 278–311.

Bermúdez-Otero, R. (2007b). Spanish Pseudo-Plurals: Phonological Cues in the Acquisition of a Syntax–Morphology Mismatch. In M. Baerman *et al.* (eds.), *Deponency and Morphological Mismatches*. Oxford: Oxford University Press, pp. 231–269.

Bermúdez-Otero, R. (2013). The Spanish Lexicon Stores Stems with Theme Vowels, not Roots with Inflectional Class Features. *Probus*, 25, 3–103.

Bermúdez-Otero, R. (2016). We Do Not Need Structuralist Morphemes, but We Do Need Constituent Structure. In D. Siddiqi and Heidi Harley (eds.), *Morphological Metatheory*. Amsterdam: John Benjamins, pp. 387–429.

Bonet, E. (1991). Morphology after Syntax. Pronominal Clitics in Romance (Doctoral dissertation). MIT.

Booij, G. (1996). Inherent vs. Contextual Inflection and the Split Morphology Hypothesis. In G. Booij and J. van Maarle (eds.), *Yearbook of Morphology 1995*. Dordrecht: Springer, pp. 1–16.

Borer, H. (2013). *Taking Form*. Oxford: Oxford University Press.

Bosque, I. and Demonte, V. (1999). *Gramática descriptiva de la lengua española*. Madrid: Espasa.

Buenafuentes de la Mata, C. (2007). Procesos de gramaticalización y lexicalización en la formación de compuestos en español (Doctoral dissertation). Universitat Autònoma de Barcelona.

Burdette, K. (2005). New Paradigms: A Rule-and-Feature Based Morpholexical Model of the Spanish Verbal System. In D. Eddington (ed.), *Selected Proceedings of the 7th Hispanic Linguistics Symposium*. Somerville, MA: Cascadilla, pp. 158–168.

Bustos Gisbert, E. (1986). *La composición nominal en español*. Salamanca: Universidad de Salamanca.

Cabré, T. and Prieto, P. (2007). Exceptional Hiatuses in Spanish. In F. Martínez-Gil and S. Colina (eds.), *Optimality-Theoretic studies in Spanish Phonology*. Amsterdam: John Benjamins, pp. 205–238.

Caha, P. (2009). The Nanosyntax of Case (Doctoral dissertation). CASTL, University of Tromsø.

Colina, S. (2003). Diminutives in Spanish: A Morphophonological Account. *The Southwest Journal of Linguistics*, 22, 87–107.

Company Company, C. (1998). The Interplay between Form and Meaning in Language Change: Grammaticalization of Cannibalistic Datives in Spanish. *Studies in Language*, 22, 529–566.

Cuervo, M. C. (2003). Datives at Large (Doctoral dissertation). MIT.

DiSciullo, A.-M. and Williams, E. (1987). *On the Definition of Word*. Cambridge, MA: MIT Press.

Downing, P. (1977). On the Creation and Use of English Compound Nouns. *Language*, 53, 810–842.

Eddington, D. (2005). Spanish Verb Inflection: A Single- or Dual-Route System? *Linguistics*, 47, 173–199.

Eguren, L. (2002). Evaluative Suffixation in Spanish and the Syntax of Derivational Processes. In J. Herschensohn et al. (eds.), *Features and Interfaces in Romance*. Amsterdam: John Benjamins, pp. 71–85.

Elvira, J. (1998). *El cambio analógico*. Madrid: Gredos.

Embick, D. (2010). *Localism vs. Globalism in Morphology and Phonology*. Cambridge MA: MIT Press.

Fábregas, A. (2005). La definición de la categoría gramatical en una morfología orientada sintácticamente (Doctoral dissertation). Universidad Autónoma de Madrid.

Fábregas, A. (2013). Diminutives as Heads or Specifiers: The Mapping between Syntax and Phonology. *Iberia*, 5, 1–44.

Fábregas, A. (2014). On a Grammatically Relevant Notion of Word and Why it Belongs to Syntax. In I. Ibarretxe and J. L. Mendívil (eds.), *To Be or Not To Be a Word*. Cambridge: Cambridge Scholars Publishers, pp. 93–131.

Felíu, E. and Roca, I. (2003). Morphology in Truncation: The Role of the Spanish Desinence. In G. Booij and J. van Maarle (eds.), *Yearbook of Morphology 2002*. Dordrecht: Kluwer, pp. 197–218.

Fernández-Soriano, O. (1993). *Los pronombres átonos*. Madrid: Taurus.

Halle, M. and Marantz, A. (1993). Distributed Morphology and the Pieces of Inflection. In K. Hale and S. J. Keyser (eds.), *The View from Building 20: Essays in Linguistics in Honor of Sylvain Bromberger*. Cambridge, MA: MIT Press, pp. 111–176.

Harris, J. W. (1991). The Exponence of Gender in Spanish. *Linguistic Inquiry*, 22, 27–62.

Harris, J. W. and Halle, M. (2005). Unexpected Plural Inflections in Spanish: Reduplication and Metathesis. *Linguistic Inquiry*, 36, 195–222.

Haspelmath, M. (2002). *Understanding Morphology*. London: Arnold.

Haspelmath, M. (2011). The Indeterminacy of Word Segmentation and the Nature of Morphology and Syntax. *Folia Linguistica*, 45, 31–80.

Jaeggli, O. (1986). Three Issues in the Theory of Clitics: Case, Doubled NPs and Extraction. In H. Borer (ed.), *The Syntax of Pronominal Clitics*. New York: Academic, pp. 15–42.

Julien, M. (2007). On the Relation between Morphology and Syntax. In G. Ramchand and C. Reiss (eds.), *The Oxford Handbook of Linguistic Interfaces*. Oxford: Oxford University Press, pp. 209–238.

Kayne, R. (1975). *French Syntax: The Transformational Cycle*. Cambridge, MA: MIT Press.

Lang, M. (1992). *Formación de palabras en español*. Madrid: Cátedra.

Marantz, A. (2000). Words (Unpublished MS). MIT.

Martín García, J. (2001). Construcciones morfológicas y construcciones sintácticas: Los prefijos "anti-" y "pro-". In A. Veiga *et al.* (eds.), *Lengua española y estructuras gramaticales*. Santiago de Compostela: Universidad de Santiago de Compostela, pp. 225–237.

Mateu, J. and Acedo-Matellán, V. (2015). Parameters and Argument Structure I: Motion Predicates and Resultatives. In A. Fábregas *et al.* (eds.), *Contemporary Linguistic Parameters*. London: Bloomsbury, pp. 99–123.

Matthews, P. H. (1972). *Inflectional Morphology, a Theoretical Study Based on Aspects of Latin Verb Conjugation*. Cambridge: Cambridge University Press.

Moina, M. I. (2011). *Compound Words in Spanish: Theory and History*. Amsterdam: John Benjamins.

Myler, N. (2015). Stem Storage? Not Proved: A Reply to Bermúdez-Otero 2013. *Linguistic Inquiry*, 46, 173–186.

Oltra-Massuet, I. (1999). On the Constituent Structure of Catalan Verbs. In K. Arregi *et al.* (eds.), *Papers in Morphology and Syntax, Cycle One*. Cambridge, MA: MIT Press, pp. 279–322.

Oltra-Massuet, I. and Arregi, K. (2005). Stress by Structure in Spanish. *Linguistic Inquiry*, 36, 43–84.

Ordóñez, F. (2012). Clitics in Spanish. In J. I. Hualde *et al.* (eds.), *Handbook of Hispanic Linguistics*. Cambridge: Blackwell, pp. 423–453.

Ormazábal, J. and Romero, J. (2013). Object Clitics, Agreement and Dialectal Variation. *Probus*, 25, 301–344.

Pena, J. (1999). Partes de la morfología: Las unidades del análisis morfológico. In I. Bosque and V. Demonte (eds.), *Gramática descriptiva de la lengua española*. Madrid: Espasa, pp. 4305–4366.

Piera, C. (1995). On Compounding in English and Spanish. In H. Campos and P. Kempchinsky (eds.), *Evolution and Revolution in Linguistic Theory*. Washington, DC: Georgetown University Press, pp. 302–315.

Piera, C. and Varela, S. (1999). Relaciones entre morfología y sintaxis. In I. Bosque and V. Demonte (eds.), *Gramática descriptiva de la lengua española*. Madrid: Espasa, pp. 4367–4422.

RAE and ASALE (2009). *Nueva gramática de la lengua española*. Madrid: Espasa.

Rainer, F. (1993). *Spanische Wortbildungslehre*. Tübingen: Max Niemeyer.

Rainer, F. and Varela, S. (1992). Compounding in Spanish. *Rivista di linguistica*, 4, 117–142.

Ramchand, G. (2008). *First Phase Syntax*. Cambridge: Cambridge University Press.

Ruiz Gurillo, L. (2002). Compuestos, colocaciones, locuciones: Intento de delimitación. In A. Veiga *et al.* (eds.), *Léxico y gramática*. Lugo: Tris Tram, pp. 327–339.

Sanz, J. (2015). The Phonology and Morphology of Spanish Hypocoristics (Master's Thesis). University of Tromsø.

Scalise, S. and Bisetto, A. (2009). The Classification of Compounds. In R. Lieber and P. Stekauer (eds.), *The Oxford Handbook of Compounding*. Oxford: Oxford University Press, pp. 34–54.

Serrano Dolader, D. (2010). El género en los sustantivos: ¿flexión y / o derivación? In J. F. Val Álvaro and M. C. Horno (eds.), *La gramática del sentido*. Zaragoza: Universidad de Zaragoza, pp. 249–269.

Snyder, W. (1995). Language Acquisition and Language Variation (Doctoral dissertation). MIT.

Snyder, W. (2012). Parameter Theory and Motion Predicates. In L. McNally *et al.* (eds.), *Telicity, Change and State*. Oxford: Oxford University Press, pp. 279–300.

Son, M. and Svenonius, P. (2008). Microparameters of Cross-Linguistic Variation. In N. Abner and J. Bishop (eds.), *Proceedings of the 27th West Coast Conference on Formal Linguistics*. Somerville, MA: Cascadilla, pp. 388–396.

Sportiche, D. (1996). Clitic Constructions. In L. Zaring and J. Rooryck (eds.), *Phrase Structure and the Lexicon*. Dordrecht: Kluwer, pp. 213–276.

Stump, G. (1998). Inflection. In A. Zwicky and A. Spencer (eds.), *The Handbook of Morphology*. London: Blackwell, pp. 13–43.

Stump, G. (2001). *Inflectional Morphology*. Cambridge: Cambridge University Press.

Svenonius, P. (2016). Spans and Words. In Daniel Siddiqi and Heidi Harley (eds.), *Morphological Metatheory*. Amsterdam: John Benjamins, pp. 201–222.

Torner, S. (2003). *De los adjetivos calificativos a los adverbios en -mente: Semántica y gramática*. Madrid: Visor.

Uriagereka, J. (1995). Aspects of the Syntax of Clitic Placement in Western Romance. *Linguistic Inquiry*, 26, 79–124.

Zagona, K. (1990). *Mente* Adverbs, Compound Interpretation and the Projection Principle. *Probus*, 2, 1–30.

13

Properties of Pronominal Subjects

Pekka Posio

13.1 Introduction: Variable Expression of Pronominal Subjects

The variable use of subject personal pronouns is among the most widely studied features of Spanish syntax. Pronominal subjects can be expressed by a subject pronoun placed before the verb (Example 13.1a), after the verb (13.1b) or left unexpressed (13.1c).

(13.1)   a. *Y **yo creo** que eso es sano.*
 'And **I think** that it is healthy.'
 b. *No **creo yo** que mañana tengamos reunión.*
 '**I** don't **think** that we have a meeting tomorrow.'
 c. *Pues **creo** que no lo sabía.*
 'Well **I think** that he didn't know it.'

Source: Real Academia Española (n.d.)

This property distinguishes Spanish from English and some other Western European languages like German and French that have obligatory pronominal subjects. Languages resembling Spanish are frequently referred to as "null subject" or "pro-drop" languages. Both terms originate in the Principles and Parameters version of Generative Grammar (see also Chapter 1, this volume) where the term "pro-drop" is used of a cluster of syntactic properties including null subjects and "free" constituent order (Chomsky 1981). These terms are widely used in linguistics, although conceptualizing the lack of independent subject personal pronouns as "dropping" or as "null" arguments has been criticized as linguistic Anglocentrism (Dryer 2011). In more functionally oriented studies, the term "variable subject expression" has been used instead to better account for the complex nature of the phenomenon (see e.g. Otheguy and Zentella 2012; Travis and Torres Cacoullos 2012; Carvalho *et al.* 2015).

Spanish subject pronoun expression is a textbook example of variable syntax, and exploring what factors condition subject pronoun expression has become a popular topic in studies using variationist sociolinguistic methodology. The first task in variationist studies is to determine the envelope of variation, i.e. the contexts where variation may occur. For example, syntactically impersonal verbs such as meteorological verbs (e.g. *llueve* 'it rains') and existential verbs (e.g. *hay* 'there is/are') are excluded from the envelope of variation, as they do not admit pronominal subjects, with the exception of Dominican Spanish where the neuter personal pronoun *ello* may be used as an expletive subject (Toribio 2000). Another restriction in the use of subject personal pronouns concerns the animacy of the referent: personal pronouns are seldom used for non-human referents in most varieties of Spanish, and thus only noun phrases or null subjects are used to refer to them (however, see Elinzaincín 1995; Bullock and Toribio 2007:56 for Uruguayan and Dominican varieties, where subject personal pronouns can be used for non-human referents). On the other hand, there are also non-variable contexts where subjects must be expressed, e.g. if they carry focal information as when answering the question "Who did it?" (see Section 13.3.1), when they are heads of relative clauses, or when they have adverbial modifiers (e.g. *solo yo* 'only me'). Unlike subject personal pronouns, indefinite and interrogative pronouns (e.g. *alguien* 'someone,' *quién* 'who') are generally not omissible. In addition to excluding the generally recognized non-variable contexts, authors of different studies may decide to exclude, e.g. imperatives and formulaic sequences (such as *tú sabes* 'you know'; see Section 13.3.5), depending on how variable subject pronoun expression is in those contexts in the variety being studied.

Table 13.1 summarizes the types of subject expression found in most standard varieties of Spanish, showing what forms of subject expression are possible depending on the grammatical person[1] and the type of subject referent (human, non-human, non-referential).

Table 13.1 *Variation in subject expression*

	+human referent	–human referent	non-referential or expletive subject
1SG/PL, 2SG/PL	pronoun / null	n/a	n/a
3SG/PL	NP / pronoun / null	NP / null	null

---

[1] The term "grammatical person" is used throughout the chapter to refer to the six combinations of person (first, second, third) and number (singular vs. plural) features found in Spanish. For the purposes of the present chapter, it is not meaningful to separate these two features since they always co-occur in Spanish and because all grammatical persons have unique discourse functions. For example, first-person singular is frequently used with mental predicates expressing the speaker's cognitive or epistemic stance, but the same is not true of first-person plural; third-person plural, unlike third-person singular, can be used for vague or indefinite reference; second-person singular, unlike first-person singular, is frequently used in interrogative sentences.

Most corpus-based studies examine only contexts that fall within the envelope of variation, as explained above. It is therefore important to note that non-variable contexts may actually account for a large proportion of data, in particular if all grammatical persons are included. For example, in Peškova's (2015:140) data from Buenos Aires Spanish, 55 percent of the subjects are obligatorily null, and 3 percent are obligatorily expressed. Thus, only the remaining 42 percent of clauses constitute the envelope of variation.

Even if the overall rates of expressed subject pronouns within the envelope of variation differ across dialects, studies show that factors affecting subject expression are essentially the same in all varieties of Spanish. The internal ranking of the significant factor groups is also very similar, although dialectal differences occur. Thus, it can be generalized very broadly that subject personal pronouns are expressed more often in singular than in plural persons, when there is a change in reference with regard to the previous subject, and when the verb is in an imperfective tense as opposed to a perfective one (e.g. Silva-Corvalán 1982; Enríquez 1984; Bentivoglio 1987; Cameron 1992, 1994, 1995; Travis 2007; Torres Cacoullos and Travis 2011; Otheguy and Zentella 2012). Since several factors affect subject expression simultaneously and in interaction with each other, most data-based studies use logistic regression (often by means of the program VARBRUL or GoldVarb) or other statistical modeling in order to check for the significance of each factor, their internal ranking, and interactions between the factors.

The present chapter sets out by looking at Spanish subject expression in a language typological perspective in Section 13.2. Section 13.3 focuses on linguistic factors and Section 13.4 on the extralinguistic factors of subject expression variation. Section 13.5 deals with the diachrony of subject expression and Section 13.6 with postverbal placement of pronominal subjects. Some concluding remarks and future research directions are summarized in Section 13.7.

13.2 Spanish in a Language Typological Perspective

Comparisons between languages like English and Spanish suggest that a language can do without overt subject personal pronouns as long as the subject person is marked on the verb, as is the case in Spanish. However, examining a wider sample of languages reveals that the connection between bound person marking on the verb and null subjects is not universal. There are languages with obligatory double marking of the subject, i.e. requiring bound markers on the verb as well as the use of independent subject pronouns, like German; there are also languages with no person marking on the verb that nevertheless allow null subjects, as is the case in many East-Asian languages.

In a typological perspective, Spanish belongs to the most common language type, where the subject person is normally expressed by affixes on the verb, whereas languages like English with obligatory subject pronoun expression are a minority. While the use of subject personal pronouns is variable in Spanish, the expression of subject person on the verb is not: all finite verbs are obligatorily marked for grammatical person. In Dryer's (2011) typological sample of 711 languages, 437 (i.e. 62 percent) are similar to Spanish whereas only 82 (i.e. 12 percent) are like English with regard to the expression of pronominal subjects. Other subject marking patterns found in the world's languages include having no marking on the verb and optional use of independent subject pronouns, or using different subject marking strategies depending on the grammatical person or verbal tense. These two types are referred to as "radical" or "discourse pro-drop" and "partial pro-drop," respectively, in the formalist terminology (Roberts and Holmberg 2010).

Although both formal and typological classifications of languages with regard to their subject expression properties have been developed, there have been few attempts to compare actual rates of subject expression in different languages (however, see Seo 2001 for Slavic languages). Languages and language varieties having the same grammatical possibilities of subject expression may actually represent very divergent patterns in actual usage. It has nevertheless been suggested that referential continuity and priming are likely candidates for cross-linguistic constraints on subject expression (Torres Cacoullos and Travis 2016:743).

13.3 Linguistic Factors Affecting Subject Pronoun Expression

13.3.1 Traditional Explanations: Contrast and Emphasis

In the traditional, normative grammar of Spanish, pronominal subject use is considered a way to express contrast, emphasis or individuation of the subject person or as a means to disambiguate morphologically ambiguous person marking (e.g. Gili y Gaya 1964). Similar explanations are found in learners' grammars and textbooks of Spanish as well as in reference grammars (e.g. Fernández Soriano 1999). Butt and Benjamin (2004) give the sentences in (13.2) to illustrate contrastive and emphatic uses of subject pronouns.

(13.2)   a. *Tú* eres listo, pero **ella** es genial.
         '**You**'re clever but **she**'s a genius.'
   b. *Tú* haz lo que te dé la gana.
         '**You** do whatever you like (implies 'what do I care?').'
                       Source: Butt and Benjamin (2004:131)

Although the notions of contrast and emphasis may seem intuitively attractive, they have little explanatory power when considering subject pronoun use in actual discourse. Genuinely contrastive contexts are infrequent in authentic spoken data, so that contrasting the subject referent with other potential referents accounts for only a fraction of expressed subject pronouns (Travis and Torres Cacoullos 2012:723) and not all contrastive contexts require expressed subject pronouns (Matos Amaral and Schwenter 2005). In addition, attributing subject pronoun presence to an emphasizing function is circular in the sense that it is difficult to provide an independent definition of emphasis, i.e. a definition that does not rely on the presence of the subject: since an unexpressed subject pronoun cannot be emphasized, all expressed subject pronouns can be claimed to be emphatic due to being expressed.

13.3.2 Structural Factors: Verb Morphology and Grammatical Person

Alongside contrast and emphasis, traditional grammar maintains that subject pronouns are used to avoid ambiguity in those tenses and moods where first- and third-person singular have the same form. This occurs in the imperfect of indicative (*cantaba* 'I/he/she/it sang'), conditional (*cantaría* 'I/he/she/it would sing'), present and imperfect of subjunctive (*cante, cantara/cantase* 'I/he/she/it sing[s]') and compound tenses containing these forms. In addition, in dialects where postnuclear /s/ is omitted, second-person singular forms may be pronounced similarly to first and third person, thus creating a further syncretism between all singular persons. Thus, it would seem well motivated to use subject pronouns with syncretic verb forms in order to disambiguate the grammatical person, as in (13.3) where not expressing the pronoun *yo* could cause a coreferential interpretation of the subject referent of the verbs, as the verb form *estaba* can refer to both first- and third-person singular.

(13.3)   Y **ella** iba a mi lado y **yo** estaba temblando [...]
'And **she** was walking by my side and **I** was shaking [...]'
Source: Silva-Corvalán (2001:155)

Functional compensation for lacking or impoverished person marking morphology has been suggested to account for obligatory subject pronoun expression in French, formerly a null-subject language with distinctive person marking on the verb (however, see Ranson 2009) and for the increasing use of subject pronouns in Brazilian Portuguese (Duarte 2000). Although some studies have found evidence in favor of the functional compensation hypothesis in Spanish (Hochberg 1986), it has not been supported by other studies with different data (Ranson 1991; Cameron 1992, 1994). While subject pronoun expression may be a way to avoid potential referential ambiguity, immediate discourse context and referential continuity often disambiguate the reference in the absence of expressed subject pronouns. In addition, the fact that subject pronouns are also frequently used in tenses and moods with no ambiguous person marking, such as the present indicative, suggests that functional compensation is not among the main functions of subject pronoun expression.

Other structural factor groups that have been studied in connection with subject pronoun expression are clause type, verb type, and grammatical person. It has been found that pronominal subjects are expressed more often in main clauses than in dependent clauses, and least often in coordinate clauses (e.g. Enríquez 1984:256–258; Orozco and Guy 2008:77), although other studies have found no such effect (e.g. Torres Cacoullos and Travis 2011:254). In addition, reflexive verbs tend to have lower rates of expressed subject pronouns than non-reflexive ones (e.g. Otheguy and Zentella 2012:187).

One of the most significant factor groups is grammatical person. Pronominal subjects are more frequently used in the singular and less frequently in the plural persons. For example, in Otheguy et al. (2007), grammatical person is chosen as the single most important factor group in accounting for subject pronoun use. Since the deictic speech act persons and the anaphoric third person are also functionally very different, researchers often focus on only one grammatical person at a time (e.g. Travis and Torres Cacoullos 2012) or analyze each grammatical person separately (e.g. Geeslin and Gudmestad 2016).

Perhaps the most striking difference is found between first-person singular and plural, whose expression rates in Peninsular Spanish data can be as far from each other as 34.6 percent and 4.5 percent, respectively (Posio 2012b:346). High expression rates of the first-person singular pronoun *yo* have been attributed to the egocentric nature of communication (Davidson 1996:553). This does not necessarily mean that people often tend to talk about themselves: rather, a great deal of first-person singular verb forms in discourse are tokens of mental or communicative verbs whose function is to express the speaker's subjective stance, and such verbs may have subject expression patterns that diverge from general tendencies (see Section 13.3.5).

13.3.3 Referential Continuity: Same and Switch Reference

Continuity of reference is another highly significant predictor of subject pronoun expression. Subjects that are coreferential with the previous subject (or another entity, such as a direct object) are less likely to be expressed by pronouns than subjects that are not coreferential with the previous subject (Cameron 1992, 1994, 1995, 1997). The terms "same reference" and "switch reference" are often used instead of "coreferential" and "not coreferential." This effect derives from a more general principle of information structure (see also Chapter 17, this volume): the less accessible a referent is to the addressee, the more distinctive coding is used to refer to it (Givón 1983, Ariel 1994).

An example of switch reference is given in (13.4) where the pronominal subject *usted* 'you' and the following *nosotros* 'we' refer to different entities and thus trigger the expression of subject pronouns (irrespectively of whether the speaker intentionally wishes to contrast or emphasize these persons).

(13.4) A: *Y es la única casa que no tiene luz.*
B: *Sí sí an- ¿anoche el teléfono que **usted** me dio?*
A: *uhhuh*
B: *De esa casa **nosotros** la llamamos.*
'A: And it's the only house that has no electricity.
B: Yes yes, las- last night the number that **you** gave me?
A: uhhuh
B: From that house **we** called it.' Source: Cameron (1994:314)

Travis and Torres Cacoullos (2012) and Torres Cacoullos and Travis (2016) propose a more elaborate account of switch reference effects by looking at the number of intervening semantically compatible human subjects between two mentions of the same subject referent in discourse (see Example 13.5 below). Their findings suggest that intervening human subjects provide a better explanation of variable subject expression in first-person singular than switch reference as such (Travis and Torres Cacoullos 2012:728).

13.3.4 Psycholinguistic Phenomena: Priming and Frequency Effects

Subject expression has been shown to be affected by psycholinguistic phenomena related with the speakers' short- and long-term memory. Several studies have confirmed the existence of a priming or perseverance effect (e.g. Cameron 1992; Cameron and Flores-Ferrán 2004:50–54; Torres Cacoullos and Travis 2011:251–252, 2012; Travis 2007:120–121). Simply put, priming effect accounts for the finding that subject pronouns are more likely to be used when the previous subject has been expressed by a pronoun, whereas null subjects are more likely to be used when the previous subject has been null. Priming is considered as a mechanical and unintentional effect rather than serving any pragmatic purposes (Bock and Griffin 2000:177). Example 13.5 illustrates a possible priming effect between (a) two coreferential expressed subject pronouns and (b) two coreferential null subjects.[2]

(13.5) a. **Yo** *no tenía máquina de lavar.* **Yo** *lavaba con lavadero.*
'**I** didn't have a washing machine. **I** washed with a washboard.'
b. *ya Ø no quería. . . . it was too hard. . . . (1.5 sec pause) pero Ø lo hice.*
'**(I)** didn't want to any more. . . . it was too hard. . . . (1.5 sec pause) but **(I)** did it.' Source: Torres Cacoullos and Travis (2016:739)

---

[2] Note that in (13.5b) there is an intervening subject *it* in the code-switching sequence *it was too hard*; however, since this is not a human subject it does not trigger the use of a subject pronoun with the following verb (Travis and Torres Cacoullos 2012).

Another psycholinguistic effect targeting the speakers' long-term rather than short-term memory has been argued to account for lexical differences found between different verb forms. Erker and Guy (2012) found that while lexical frequency of verb forms (i.e. the rate at which they occur in speech) did not condition subject expression on its own in their data, it had an amplifying effect on the significant factor groups affecting subject expression in their study (morphological regularity, semantic class, and person). These factor groups significantly predicted pronoun usage among the most frequent lexical items (e.g. *creo* 'I think,' *va* 'he/she/it goes') but not for the less frequent ones (e.g. *crezca* 'grow.1/3sG, subjunctive'). Erker and Guy (2012) argue that patterns of subject expression are more entrenched with the frequently occurring verb forms than with the less frequent ones. However, other studies provide conflicting evidence on the effect of frequency. In Bayley *et al.*'s (2013) data, frequency did not have an amplifying effect on the other factor groups, but instead infrequent verbs slightly favored subject expression. Linford *et al.* (2016b), in their study focusing on third-person verb forms and including null, pronominal, and noun phrase subjects, found neither independent nor mediating effects of lexical frequency on subject expression similar to Erker and Guy's results (2012). However, they did find that frequency mediates the effect of specificity of reference in the third person, although in different ways for native vs. non-native speakers (Linford *et al.* 2016b).

In sum, there is contrastive evidence on the effect of lexical frequency of verbs on subject expression. Linford *et al.* (2016b:210) suggest that the discrepant results between different studies may be due to which grammatical persons are analyzed and how the envelope of variation is defined. The choice of grammatical persons and whether they are analyzed separately or merged together, as well as the decision to include or exclude tokens susceptible of being formulaic sequences in a given variety (such as *tú sabes* 'you know,' excluded by Bayley *et al.* 2013 but included by Erker and Guy 2012), may have a strong influence on the results and renders comparisons between individual studies difficult.

13.3.5 Semantic and Pragmatic Factors, and Formulaic Patterns of Subject Expression

Verb semantics has been found to be connected to subject expression, although the mechanism connecting different verb lexemes or verb forms with different subject expression patterns is not always clear. Several studies have found a connection between higher subject expression rates and verbs expressing mental or cognitive processes such as *creer* 'believe' and *pensar* 'think' (among many others, Enríquez 1984; Bentivoglio 1987; Morales 1997; Hurtado 2005; Posio 2011), and some studies also report a lower rate of expressed subjects with verbs of external activity (e.g. Enríquez 1984; Morales 1997). It should also be noted that verb semantics and grammatical person are tightly interrelated: for example, mental verbs favoring subject expression are most frequently used in first-person singular.

Several explanations have been proposed to account for the observed differences. For example, Enríquez (1984:244–245) argues that subject pronouns are most frequently used with those verbs that express subjective or interior activities where the speaker has a need to individuate the subject more than with verbs expressing external actions. Silva-Corvalán (1997:127) proposes that not expressing the subject may serve the purpose of focusing more attention on the action expressed by the verb, which would account for more frequent subject expression in imperfective tenses rather than in perfective tenses that refer to foregrounded actions. A similar principle of attention focusing could account for the differences between verb classes (Posio 2011). However, definitions of verbal categories and which verbs are included in each category vary considerably from one study to another, making comparisons across studies difficult.

What seems to be a category effect may actually be caused by few frequently occurring members within a category. Thus many of the most frequently occurring verb forms within the category of cognitive verbs serve different pragmatic functions such as expressing the speaker's epistemic stance (e.g. *creo* '[I] think,' *no sé* '[I] don't know') and such sequences may be associated with subject expression patterns differing from the general trends (Posio 2015; see also Linford *et al.* 2016a:150). Token-specific tendencies of subject expression may vary across dialects, suggesting that such tendencies are community-based usage patterns rather than tendencies derived directly from verb semantics. For example, in Orozco's (2015) data from Colombian Spanish, the verb form *sé* '(I) know' favors subject expression while, in Posio's (2015) data from Peninsular Spanish, it favors null subjects.

Within the category of cognitive verbs, the verb form *creo* 'I think' is so frequently used in spoken Spanish that it accounts for 15 percent of all occurrences of first-person singular verb forms in the *Corpus del español* (Davies 2002– ; Posio 2014:8). Since the rate of expressed subjects in the sequence *creo que* 'I think that' can be as high as 62 percent (Posio 2015:64), this sequence boosts the frequency of subject pronoun use in first-person singular and in the category of mental verbs. In fact, sequences containing *creo* are currently grammaticalizing into epistemic markers similar to English *I think* (Thompson and Mulac 1991) and therefore should be analyzed separately from more productive verbs (Posio 2015).

As for the pragmatic functions of pronominal subjects in discourse, it has been proposed by Davidson (1996) that they have the general function of adding "pragmatic weight" to an utterance. This notion is intended to subsume different functions ranging from triggering speech act or epistemic readings of communication and mental verbs to taking or handing over the floor in a conversation. However, it is debatable whether such a unitary function can account for all pragmatic uses of subject pronouns with verbs and to what extent pragmatic usage patterns differ between speaker communities or dialects. Another pragmatic account is proposed by Serrano and Aijón Oliva (2011), who argue that the expression of the subject pronoun in either preverbal or postverbal position and its omission represent different construals of subjectivity versus objectivity of the speaker as well as different grades of prominence vs. informativity of the subject referent in discourse.

13.4 Extralinguistic Factors Affecting Subject Pronoun Expression

13.4.1 Sociolinguistic Factors

Although subject expression has been widely studied using quantitative sociolinguistic methodology, there is only scattered and partially contradictory evidence on the influence of social variables such as age, gender, profession or level of education of the speakers on their subject expression tendencies. For example, Otheguy, Zentella, and Livert (2007:778), in their study of Spanish spoken in New York City, found that neither gender, age, education, socioeconomic status nor class had a significant effect on the rates of subject pronoun expression. However, other studies have reported that older speakers produce higher rates of expressed subject pronouns than younger speakers (e.g. Orozco and Guy 2008 for Barranquilla, Colombia; Alfaraz 2015 for Santo Domingo, Dominican Republic; Lastra and Butragueño 2015 for Mexico City; Orozco 2015 for Costeño Colombian Spanish; de Prada Pérez 2015 for Catalan–Spanish bilinguals in Minorca, Spain). It is unclear whether the age-related pattern instantiates language change or age grading. Diachronic evidence from other Romance languages shows that subject pronoun expression tends to increase rather than decrease over time (see Section 13.5). If this is true for Spanish, the increasing frequency of subject pronoun use may be attributable to age grading rather than to ongoing changes.

Speaker gender has also been shown to have a significant effect in some studies, with females slightly favoring subject expression (e.g. Alfaraz 2015:10, Orozco 2015:30). Shin and Otheguy (2013) observe that women lead the ongoing change in the increasing use of subject pronouns in a contact situation between Spanish and English. There is also some evidence to the effect that speakers' age and gender correlate with the choice of grammatical subjects in discourse (Posio 2016), which in turn may have implications for the rates of expressed subject pronouns per speaker. However, in general, age and gender differences are not among the most significant factor groups accounting for subject pronoun use.

13.4.2 Dialectal Differences

The rates of expressed subject pronouns in speech are subject to extensive dialectal variation. The highest frequencies of expressed subject pronouns are found in Caribbean Spanish (e.g. Orozco and Guy 2008; Otheguy and Zentella 2012). In particular, Dominican Spanish shows general expression rates as high as 51 percent (Martínez-Sanz 2011) or even 96 percent in the case of second-person singular (Alba 2004). The lowest rates have been observed in Mexico: according to Lastra and Butragueño (2015:42), the general rate of expressed subjects in Mexico City Spanish is 21.7 percent, while Michnowicz (2015:109) reports a frequency as low as 16 percent for monolingual speakers of Yucatan Spanish. Despite dialectal differences in subject expression rates, so far all studies point at the same probabilistic constraints on subject expression across dialects and discourse types (Cameron 1992, 1994; Travis 2007; Torres Cacoullos and Travis 2016).

It is not completely clear why different Spanish dialects present different rates of subject expression. One of the explanations proposed is that dialects where syllable-final /s/ is frequently deleted would compensate for the loss of distinctions in person marking by means of increased subject pronoun use (e.g. Hochberg 1986). However, this functional compensation effect is not systematic and thus does not account for all dialectal differences (see Section 13.3.2 above). Interestingly, subject expression rates and the proportion of postverbal subjects (see Section 13.6 below) in a dialect seem to correlate negatively with each other (Morales 1989; Cameron 1992; Toribio 2000). This is the case especially in Caribbean Spanish, where subject pronouns are very frequently expressed and are frequently preverbal even in contexts that would require postverbal placement in other dialects (see Example 13.6).

(13.6) ¿Qué **tú** *piensas*? (acceptable in Caribbean Spanish but not in other varieties) vs.
¿*Qué piensas* **tú**? (acceptable in all varieties)
'What do **you** think?' Source: Morales (1989)

The positive correlation between expressed subjects and the prevalence of the subject–verb order may offer evidence in favor of the clustering of null subjects and "free" constituent order within a single paradigm, as proposed in Generative Grammar (Chomsky 1981).

A special case of subject pronoun expression where dialects of Spanish differ considerably from each other is the non-specific, generic or impersonal use of the second-person singular, illustrated by (13.7) (e.g. Cameron 1994; DeMello 2000; Otheguy *et al.* 2007; Kluge 2010; Guirado 2011).

(13.7) *Es difícil entenderles, muchas veces* **tú** *hablas con un costeño y no le entiendes ni una palabra.* (Bogotá)
'It's difficult to understand them, often **you** speak with a *Costeño* and you don't understand a single word.' Source: DeMello (2000:361)

Table 13.2 *Type of reference and subject expression in second-person singular*

	San Juan		Madrid	
Personal	48%	(N = 145)	40%	(N = 58)
Impersonal	69%	(N = 188)	19%	(N = 150)

Source: Cameron (1994:325)

Dialects of Spanish vary regarding the proportion of the impersonal second-person singular vs. other impersonalization strategies like the pronoun *uno* 'one,' possibly depending on the frequency of the second-person singular as an address form in the dialect (Guirado 2011). In those dialects where the second-person singular is used as an impersonalization strategy, the pronoun expression rate may be significantly higher or lower than when the form is used for personal reference, as shown in Table 13.2 for Puerto Rican and Peninsular Spanish data.

DeMello (2000:369) proposes that the differences observed by Cameron (1994) could be attributed to general differences between syntactically innovative and syntactically conservative dialects. However, the connection between innovativeness and pronoun use is far from clear. Interestingly, Geeslin and Gudmestad (2016:70) note that subject expression tendencies of native speakers are sensitive to impersonality vs. specificity of reference whereas non-native speakers are not. It may be the case that dialect-specific tendencies like subject expression in generic second-person singular are acquired late by second language learners.

13.4.3 Language Contact

Since subject personal pronouns have essentially the same meaning in different languages, they offer a convenient point of comparison for testing hypotheses of language change due to contact situations. The most extensively studied contact situation is that between Spanish and English in the United States (for recent studies on contact situation with other languages, see Carvalho, Orozco, and Shin [2015]). The hypothesis that contact with English, a language with nearly obligatory subject pronoun expression, would increase rates of expressed subject pronouns in Spanish had already been put forward by Granda Gutiérrez (1972) and it has been studied by, among many others, Bayley and Pease-Álvarez (1996), Lipski (1996), Lapidus and Otheguy (2005), and Otheguy and Zentella (2012).

Not all studies have found evidence for a decisive effect of contact with English (e.g. Flores-Ferrán 2004; Travis 2007). Otheguy, Zentella, and Livert (2007:786), who do observe a contact effect in New York Spanish, consider that the contradictory findings may be due to differences in sample size and coding. Otheguy, Zentella, and Livert's (2007) data from New York Spanish speakers, consisting of 142 interviews and 63,500 finite clauses, provides robust evidence that speakers born in or brought to New York City before three years of age produce a significantly higher rate of expressed subject pronouns than newcomers, i.e. speakers who had come to New York City at age 17 or older and spent there less than five years. However, the study also shows that contact with speakers of other varieties of Spanish levels the differences between speakers of Mainland USA and Caribbean dialects in terms of constraint hierarchies for the factor group grammatical person. In practice, speakers of Mainland dialects accommodate their use of subject pronouns in different grammatical persons more towards the usage of the Caribbean dialects (Otheguy, Zentella, and Livert 2007:794; Otheguy and Zentella 2012:218).

The influence of language contact has also been studied with a special focus on code-switching contexts. Again, the language pair that has received most attention is Spanish and English. The presence of code-switching with English can be assumed to boost the rates of expressed subject pronouns, given that subject pronouns are nearly obligatory in English. However, Torres Cacoullos and Travis (2011) observe no differences in subject expression between contexts with and without code-switching in New Mexican data. They nevertheless find that although code-switching has no intrinsic effect on subject expression, it does have an influence on the priming effect for expressed subjects, given that presence of English means more expressed subject pronouns.

13.4.4 Language Acquisition in First and Second Language Spanish

Subject expression provides an interesting phenomenon for studies on language acquisition, as it allows examination of differences in the probabilistic grammar of children compared to adults and determination of the developmental stages at which the variability is acquired. In general, children tend to produce fewer pronominal subjects than adults (Shin and Erker 2015; Montrul and Sánchez-Walker 2015). In Shin and Erker's (2015) data, the subject expression rate of adult speakers of Mexican Spanish is 21 percent, while children between six and eight years of age have a pronoun expression rate of only 9 percent. Nevertheless, the predictors of subject pronoun expression and their internal hierarchy are essentially the same for both children and adults. Geeslin *et al.* (2015:204) find that second language learners of Spanish with the highest and lowest proficiency levels selected similar rates of expressed subject pronouns as native speakers in a task, while intermediate-level students selected higher rates. However, only the advanced-level students were sensitive to the same linguistic predictors as the native speakers.

13.5 Diachrony of Subject Expression

Although variable subject expression is found in both spoken and written language, the majority of research has focused on spoken data: variation in the use of pronominal subjects in texts remains less explored. Similarly, the great majority of studies have focused on synchronic data. Spanish and other Romance languages inherited variable subject expression from Latin. Unlike French, where the expression of subject pronouns has become obligatory and Brazilian Portuguese, where there is evidence of a similar development (Duarte 2000), Spanish and most other Romance languages seem to have conserved the variability present in Latin. However, little is known of the diachrony of subject expression in Spanish.

In one of the few studies on the history of subject pronoun usage, Ramos (2016) finds both similarities and differences between literary texts from the 14th, 15th, and 16th century and present-day spoken Spanish. Although overall rates of expressed subject pronouns are lower in the historical corpora than in present-day data, discontinuity of reference and imperfect tense favor subject expression similarly to modern-day spoken Spanish. Differently from present-day spoken data, the semantic class of the verb has no significant effect in the diachronic corpus. In particular, the tokens *creo* 'I think' and *sé* 'I know' are rather infrequent and show no distinct patterns of subject expression (Ramos 2016:120). While these findings may suggest that the development of verb-specific patterns is a recent phenomenon, it is reasonable to ask to what extent literary texts, even those representing dialogue, are comparable with spoken data. There is no reason why literary dialogue or prose should faithfully simulate the tendencies found in spoken discourse. In particular, frequently occurring discourse formulae may be used sparingly in literary dialogues, resulting in divergent rates of subject expression in comparison to spontaneous speech.

13.6 Postverbal Position of Pronominal Subjects

Despite the extensive literature on constituent order and its relation with information structure (see also Chapter 17, this volume), few studies have focused specifically on the position of pronominal subjects with regard to the verb (however, see Serrano and Aijón Oliva 2010, Posio 2012a, Aijón Oliva and Serrano 2012, Serrano 2013).

As a broad generalization, noun phrases (NPs) representing new information are introduced into discourse in the postverbal position, whatever their syntactic function is. This also concerns NP subjects. However, since subject personal pronouns by default refer to known entities (the speaker, the addressee or other human referents accessible to the addressee), postverbal placement seems to serve different functions for pronominal subjects from its function for NP subjects. It is also considerably less common for pronouns than for NPs to be placed postverbally: while 18–40 percent of all NP subjects in Spanish are postverbal (Meyer-Hermann 1990), much lower percentages have been reported for subject pronouns, ranging from 1.5 percent in Spanish spoken in New York City (Otheguy, Zentella, and Livert 2007:771) to 13.2–17.4 percent in Peninsular Spanish (Serrano and Aijón Oliva 2010).

While preverbal subject pronouns may be separated from the verb by several intervening words, there is a strong tendency for postverbal subject pronouns to occur immediately adjacent to the verb (Posio 2012:155). At least in Peninsular Spanish, the postverbal position is most typically associated with verbs of speech or cognition in formulaic sequences (*digo yo* 'I say,' *creo yo* 'I think'), some imperatives with formulaic meanings (*fíjate tú* 'oh, wow,' literally 'pay attention') and contexts where the pronominal subject is not topical but nevertheless is mentioned for pragmatic purposes (Posio 2012a:161–162). This last function, i.e. the backgrounding or defocusing function of the postverbal position, may explain why the formal address pronoun *usted* often occurs postverbally: speakers tend to express it for politeness reasons even though it is not topical in situations where other personal pronouns would be left unexpressed (Fernández Soriano 1999:1235). Serrano and Aijón Oliva (2011:149) also consider postverbal pronominal subjects to be less agentive and salient than preverbal ones.

13.7 Conclusions

Due to the extensive research on subject pronoun use in Spanish, there is consensus on the effect of several factor groups on subject expression: grammatical person, referential continuity, and priming have been shown to have a significant effect in all varieties studied so far, although the rates of expressed subjects vary considerably from one dialect to another. The frequency of verb forms in speech may also affect subject pronoun use through a mechanical entrenching effect, as argued by Erker and Guy (2012). While the general factors affecting subject pronoun expression are well understood and do not seem to differ significantly across dialects, it is less clear why different varieties of Spanish present different rates of subject pronoun expression and different rankings of the factor groups affecting it. Token-specific usage patterns affecting frequently occurring verbs constitute one potential site for cross-dialectal variation (Posio 2015) but do not account for all differences.

An interesting although little studied topic is the prosody of subject pronouns. In Spanish grammar, subject pronouns are considered to be always lexically stressed. Pešková (2015) offers a systematic prosodic analysis of subject pronouns in Buenos Aires Spanish. Her findings show that there is a clear phonological difference between focal and topical subject pronouns, and that although subject pronouns carry lexical stress akin to nouns, they can easily become de-accented, for example in the postverbal final position in afterthoughts and right-dislocation. One might hypothesize that subject pronouns are more prone to loss of stress in dialects with more frequent subject expression rate such as Caribbean Spanish. However, to the best of my knowledge such hypotheses have not been tested in empirical studies.

Another research direction where few studies have been conducted to date is the historical evolution of pronominal subjects in Spanish, with the exception of Ramos (2016). Similarly, the expression of pronominal subjects in written texts has received considerably less attention than spoken discourse. While the existing body of research provides a basis for understanding variable subject expression in speech, the diachronic stages of subject expression require further investigation.

References

Aijón Oliva, Miguel Ángel and Serrano, María José (2012). La posición del sujeto pronominal en las cláusulas no declarativas. *Onomázein*, 26 (2), 131–164.

Alba, Orlando (2004). *Cómo hablamos los dominicanos: Un enfoque sociolingüístico*. Santo Domingo: Grupo León Jiménez.

Alfaraz, Gabriela G. (2015). Variation of Overt and Null Subject Pronouns in the Spanish of Santo Domingo. In Carvalho *et al.* 2015:3–16.

Ariel, Mira (1994). Interpreting Anaphoric Expressions: A Cognitive versus a Pragmatic Approach. *Journal of Linguistics*, 30, 3–42.

Bayley, Robert, Holland, Cory, and Ware, Kristen (2013). Lexical Frequency and Syntactic Variation: A Test of a Linguistic Hypothesis. *Penn Working Papers in Linguistics*, 19 (2), 21–30.

Bayley, Robert and Pease-Álvarez, Lucinda (1996). Null and Expressed Pronoun Variation in Mexican-descent children's Spanish. In Jennifer Arnold, Renee Blake, and Brad Davidson (eds.), *Sociolinguistic Variation: Data, Theory, and Analysis*. Stanford, CA: Center for the Study of Language and Information, pp. 85–99.

Bentivoglio, Paola (1987). *Los sujetos pronominales de primera persona en el habla de Caracas*. Caracas: Universidad Central de Venezuela, Consejo de Desarrollo Científico y Humanístico.

Bock, J. K. and Griffin, Z. M. (2000). The Persistence of Structural Priming: Transient Activation or Implicit Learning? *Journal of Experimental Psychology*, 129, 177–192.

Bullock, Barbara E. and Toribio, Jacqueline Almeida (2007). Reconsidering Dominican Spanish: Data from the Rural Cibao. *Revista Internacional de Lingüística Iberoamericana*, 7 (2), 49–73.

Butt, John and Benjamin, Carmen (2004). *A New Reference Grammar of Modern Spanish*. London: Arnold.

Cameron, Richard (1992). Pronominal and Null Subject Variation in Spanish: Constraints, Dialects, and Functional Compensation (Doctoral dissertation). University of Pennsylvania at Philadelphia.

Cameron, Richard (1994). Ambiguous Agreement, Functional Compensation, and Nonspecific *tú* in the Spanish of San Juan, Puerto Rico, and Madrid, Spain. *Language Variation and Change*, 5 (3), 305–334.

Cameron, Richard (1995). The Scope and Limit of Switch Reference as a Constraint on Pronominal Subject Expression. *Hispanic Linguistics*, 6/7, 1–27.

Cameron, Richard (1997). Accessibility Theory in a Variable Syntax of Spanish. *Journal of Pragmatics*, 28, 29–67.

Cameron, Richard and Flores-Ferrán, Nydia (2004). Preservation of Subject Expression across Regional Dialects of Spanish. *Spanish in Context*, 1 (1), 41–65.

Carvalho, Ana M., Orozco, Rafael, and Lapidus Shin, Naomi (eds.) (2015). *Subject Pronoun Expression in Spanish. A Cross-Dialectal Perspective*. Washington, DC: Georgetown University Press.

Chomsky, Noam (1981). *Lectures on Government and Binding*. Dordrecht: Foris.

Corbett, G. G. (2006). *Agreement*. Cambridge: Cambridge University Press.

Davidson, Brad (1996). "Pragmatic Weight" and Spanish Subject Pronouns: The Pragmatic and Discourse Uses of "tú" and "yo" in Spoken Madrid Spanish. *Journal of Pragmatics*, 26 (4), 543–565.

Davies, M. (2002–). Corpus del español; 100 million words, 1200s–1900s. Available from www.corpusdelespanol.org

DeMello, George (2000). *Tú* impersonal en el habla culta. *Nueva Revista de Filología Hispánica*, 48 (2), 359–372.

de Prada Pérez, Ana (2015). First Person Singular Subject Pronoun Expression in Spanish in Contact with Catalan. In Carvalho *et al.* 2015:121–142.

Dryer, Matthew S. (2011). Expression of Pronominal Subjects. In Matthew S. Dryer and Martin Haspelmath (eds.), *The World Atlas of Language Structures Online*. Munich: Max Planck Digital Library, Chapter 101. Available from wals.info/chapter/101 (last access January 8, 2018).

Duarte Lamoglia, Maria Eugênia (2000). The Loss of the Avoid Pronoun Principle in Brazilian Portuguese. In M. A. Kato and E. V. Negrão (eds.), *Brazilian Portuguese and the Null Subject Parameter*. Frankfurt am Main: Vervuert Verlag, pp. 17–36.

Elinzaincín, Adolfo (1995). Personal Pronouns for Inanimate Entities in Uruguayan Spanish in Contact with Portuguese. In Carmen Silva-Corvalán (ed.), *Spanish in Four Continents: Studies in Language Contact and Bilingualism*. Washington, DC: Georgetown University Press, pp. 117–131.

Enríquez, Emilia V. (1984). *El pronombre personal sujeto en la lengua española hablada en Madrid*. Madrid: Instituto Miguel de Cervantes.

Erker, Daniel and Guy, Gregory (2012). The Role of Lexical Frequency in Syntactic Variability: Variable Subject Personal Pronoun Expression in Spanish. *Language*, 88 (3), 526–557.

Fernández Soriano, Olga (1999). El pronombre personal. Formas y distribuciones. Pronombres átonos y tónicos. In Ignacio Bosque and Violeta Demonte (eds.), *Gramática descriptiva de la lengua española. Volumen 1: Sintaxis básica de las clases de palabras*. Madrid: Espasa Calpe, pp. 1209–1273.

Flores-Ferrán, Nydia (2004). Spanish Subject Personal Pronoun Use in New York City Puerto Ricans: Can we Rest the Case of English Contact? *Language Variation and Change*, 16, 49–73.

Geeslin, Kimberly and Gudmestad, Aarnes (2016). Subject Expression in Spanish. Contrasts between Native and Non-Native Speakers for First- and Second-Person Singular Referents. *Spanish in Context*, 13 (1), 53–79.

Geeslin, Kimberly, Linford, Bret, and Fafulas, Stephen (2015). Variable Subject Expression in Second Language Spanish. In Carvalho *et al.* 2015:191–209.

Gili y Gaya, Samuel (1964). *Curso superior de sintaxis española*. Barcelona: Bibliograf.

Givón, Talmy (1983). *Topic Continuity in Discourse: A Quantitative Cross Language Study. Typological Studies in Language 3*. Amsterdam: John Benjamins.

Granda Gutiérrez, G. de (1972). *Transculturación e interferencia lingüística en el Puerto Rico contemporáneo (1898–1968)*. Puerto Rico: Editorial Edil.

Guirado, Kristel (2011). La alternancia *tú~uno* impersonal en el habla de Caracas. *Revista de Lingüística*, 26, 26–54.

Hochberg, Judith G. (1986). Functional Compensation for /s/ Deletion in Puerto Rican Spanish. *Language*, 62 (3), 609–621.

Hurtado, Luz Marcela (2005). Condicionamientos sintáctico-semánticos de la expresión del sujeto en el español colombiano. *Hispania*, 88 (2), 335–348.

Kluge, Bettina (2010). El uso de formas de tratamiento en las estrategias de generalización. In M. Hummel, B. Kluge, and M. E. Vázquez Laslop (eds.), *Formas y fórmulas de tratamiento en el mundo hispánico*. Mexico City: El Colegio de México, Graz: Karl-Franzens-Universität, pp. 1107–1136.

Lastra, Yolanda and Butragueño, Pedro Martín (2015). Subject Pronoun Expression in Oral Mexican Spanish. In Carvalho *et al.* 2015:39–58.

Lapidus, Naomi and Otheguy, Ricardo (2005). Overt Nonspecific *ellos* in Spanish in New York. *Spanish in Context*, 2, 157–74.

Linford, Bret, Long, Avizia, Solon, Megan, and Geeslin, Kimberly (2016a). Measuring Lexical Frequency: Comparison Groups and Subject Expression in L2 Spanish. In L. Ortega, A. E. Tyler, H. I. Park, and M. Uno (eds.), *The Usage-Based Study of Language Learning and Multilingualism*. Washington, DC: Georgetown University Press, pp. 137–154.

Linford, Bret, Long, Avizia, Solon, Megan, Whatley, Melissa, and Geeslin, Kimberly (2016b). Lexical Frequency and Subject Expression in Native and Non-Native Spanish: A Closer Look at Independent and Mediating Effects. In F. Sessarego and F. Tejedo (eds.), *Spanish Language and Sociolinguistic Analysis. Issues in Hispanic and Lusophone Linguistics, 8*. Philadelphia, PA: John Benjamins, pp. 197–216.

Lipski, John M. (1996). Patterns of Pronominal Evolution in Cuban-American Bilinguals. In Ana Roca and John B. Jensen (eds.), *Spanish in Contact: Issues in Bilingualism*. Somerville, MA: Cascadilla, pp. 159–86.

Martínez-Sanz, Cristina (2011). Null and Overt Subjects in a Variable System: The Case of Dominican Spanish (Doctoral dissertation). University of Ottawa.

Matos Amaral, Patrícia and Schwenter, Scott A. (2005). Contrast and the (Non-)Occurrence of Subject Pronouns. In D. Eddington (ed.), *Selected Proceedings of the 7th Hispanic Linguistics Symposium*. Somerville, MA: Cascadilla, pp. 116–127.

Meyer-Hermann, Reinhard (1990). Sobre algunas condiciones pragmáticas de la posición del sujeto en español. *ELUA Estudios de Lingüística*, 6, 73–88.

Michnowicz, Jim (2015). Subject Pronoun Expression in Contact with Maya in Yucatan Spanish. In Carvalho *et al.* 2015:101–120.

Montrul, Silvina and Sánchez-Walker, Noelia (2015). Subject Expression in Bilingual School-Age Children in the United States. In Carvalho *et al.* 2015:231–247.

Morales, Amparo (1989). Hacia un universal sintáctico del español del Caribe. El orden SVO. *Anuario de Lingüística Hispánica*, 5, 139–152.

Morales, Amparo (1997). La hipótesis funcional y la aparición de sujeto no nominal: El español de Puerto Rico. *Hispania*, 80, 153–165.

Orozco, Rafael (2015). Pronominal Variation in Colombian Costeño Spanish. In Carvalho *et al.* 2015:17–58.

Orozco, Rafael and Guy, Gregory (2008). El uso variable de los pronombres sujetos: ¿Qué pasa en la costa Caribe colombiana? In M. Westmoreland and J. A. Thomas (eds.), *Selected Proceedings of the 4th Workshop on Spanish Sociolinguistics*. Somerville, MA: Cascadilla, pp. 70–80.

Otheguy, Ricardo and Zentella, Ana Celia (2012). *Spanish in New York: Language Contact, Dialect, Levelling, and Structural Continuity*. Oxford: Oxford University Press.

Otheguy, Ricardo, Zentella, Ana Celia, and Livert, David (2007). Language and Dialect Contact in Spanish in New York: Toward the Formation of a Speech Community. *Language*, 83 (4), 770–802.

Pešková, Andrea (2015). *Sujetos pronominales en el español porteño: Implicaciones pragmáticas en la interfaz sintáctico–fonológica*. Berlin: De Gruyter.

Posio, Pekka (2011). Spanish Subject Pronoun Usage and Verb Semantics Revisited: First and Second Person Singular Subject Pronouns and Focusing of Attention in Spoken Peninsular Spanish. *Journal of Pragmatics*, 43 (3), 777–798.

Posio, Pekka (2012a). The Functions of Postverbal Pronominal Subjects in Spoken Peninsular Spanish and European Portuguese. *Studies in Hispanic and Lusophone Linguistics*, 5 (1), 149–190.

Posio, Pekka (2012b). Who are "We" in Spoken Peninsular Spanish and European Portuguese? Expression and Reference of First Person Plural Subject Pronouns. *Language Sciences*, 34, 339–360.

Posio, Pekka (2014). Subject Expression in Grammaticalizing Constructions: The Case of *creo* and *acho* 'I think' in Spanish and Portuguese. *Journal of Pragmatics*, 63, 5–18.

Posio, Pekka (2015). Subject Pronoun Usage in Formulaic Sequences: Evidence from Peninsular Spanish. In Carvalho *et al.* 2015:59–80.

Posio, Pekka (2016). You and We: Impersonal Second Person Singular and other Referential Devices in Spanish Sociolinguistic Interviews. *Journal of Pragmatics*, 99, 1–16.

Ramos, Miguel (2016). Continuity and Change. First Person Singular Subject Pronoun Expression in Earlier Spanish. *Spanish in Context*, 13 (1), 103–127.

Ranson, Diana (1991). Person Marking in the Wake of /s/ Deletion in Andalusian Spanish. *Language Variation and Change*, 3 (2), 133–152.

Ranson, Diana (2009). Variable Subject Expression in Old and Middle French Prose Texts: The Role of Verbal Ambiguity. *Romance Quarterly*, 56 (1), 33–45.

Real Academia Española (n.d.). Banco de datos (CREA) [en línea]. *Corpus de referencia del español actual*. www.rae.es.

Roberts, Ian and Holmberg, Anders (2010). Introduction: Parameters in Minimalist Theory. In T. Biberauer, A. Holmberg, I. Roberts, and M. Sheehan (eds.), *Parametric Variation: Null Subjects in Minimalist Theory*, Cambridge and New York: Cambridge University Press, pp. 1–57.

Sauerland, Uli (2004). A Comprehensive Semantics for Agreement. Paper presented at the Phi-Workshop, McGill University, Montreal, Canada. August 2004. Available from https://publikationen.ub.uni-frankfurt.de/frontdoor/index/index/year/2009/docId/11827 (last access December 30, 2017).

Seo, Seunghyun (2001). The Frequency of Null Subject in Russian, Polish, Czech, Bulgarian and Serbo-Croatian: An Analysis according to Morphosyntactic Environments (Doctoral dissertation). Indiana University.

Serrano, María José (2013). Variación sociosituacional de la colocación del sujeto pronominal en textos conversacionales. *Spanish in Context*, 10 (2), 261–283.

Serrano, María José and Aijón Oliva, Miguel Ángel (2010). La posición variable del sujeto pronominal en relación con la cortesía interactiva. *Pragmalingüística*, 18, 170–204.

Serrano, María José and Aijón Oliva, Miguel Ángel (2011). Syntactic Variation and Communicative Style. *Language Sciences*, 33, 138–153.

Shin, Naomi and Erker, Daniel (2015). The Emergence of Structured Variability in Morphosyntax. In Carvalho *et al.* 2015:169–189.

Shin, Naomi and Otheguy, Ricardo (2013). Social Class and Gender Impacting Change in Bilingual Settings: Spanish Subject Pronoun Use in New York. *Language in Society*, 42, 429–452.

Silva-Corvalán, Carmen (1982). Subject Expression and Placement in Mexican-American Spanish. In J. Amaste and E. Olivares (eds.), *Spanish in the United States: Sociolinguistic Aspects*. New York: Cambridge University Press, pp. 93–120.

Silva-Corvalán, Carmen (1997). Variación sintáctica en el discurso oral: Problemas metodológicos. In F. Moreno-Fernández (ed.), *Trabajos de sociolingüística hispánica*. Alcalá de Henares: University of Alcalá, pp. 115–135.

Silva-Corvalán, Carmen (2001). *Sociolingüística y pragmática del español*. Washington, DC: Georgetown University Press.

Thompson, Sandra A. and Mulac, Anthony (1991). A Quantitative Perspective on the Grammaticalization of Epistemic Parentheticals in English. In Elizabeth Closs Traugott and Bernd Heine (eds.), *Approaches to Grammaticalization*. Amsterdam and Philadelphia, PA: John Benjamins, pp. 313–339.

Toribio, A. Jacqueline. (2000). Setting Parametric Limits on Dialectal Variation in Spanish. *Lingua*, 110, 315–341.

Torres Cacoullos, Rena and Travis, Catherine E. (2011). Using Structural Variability to Evaluate Convergence via Code-Switching. *International Journal of Bilingualism*, 15, 241–267.

Torres Cacoullos, Rena and Travis, Catherine E. (2016). Two Languages, One Effect: Structural Priming in Spontaneous Code-Switching. *Bilingualism: Language and Cognition*, 19 (4), 733–753.

Travis, Catherine E. (2007). Genre Effects on Subject Expression in Spanish: Priming in Narrative and Conversation. *Language Variation and Change*, 19 (2), 101–135.

Travis, Catherine E. and Torres Cacoullos, Rena (2012). What Do Subject Pronouns Do in Discourse? Cognitive, Mechanical and Constructional Factors in Variation. *Cognitive Linguistics*, 23 (4), 711–748.

14

Properties of the Verb Phrase: Argument Structure, Ellipsis, and Negation

Iván Ortega-Santos

14.1 Introduction

Given a definition of a verb phrase as a phrase whose head is a verb, the verb phrase in (14.1) consists of the predicate (within brackets) to the exclusion of the subject:

(14.1) Pedro [come papas].
       Pedro eats potatoes
       'Pedro is eating potatoes.'

Linguistic theory has added a certain degree of terminological complexity: clausal structure is divided into various syntactic projections, e.g. minimally Tense Phrase (TP) and, crucially, Verb Phrase (VP) (though the exact number of projections and their content may vary depending on the stage in the development of the theory); with the advent of the VP-Internal Subject Hypothesis, subjects are included in the VP, as suggested by the distribution of the so-called floating quantifiers (Koopman and Sportiche 1991; see Valmala 2008 and references therein for recent discussion on Spanish). Because of this tension between the various definitions of the verb phrase, this chapter deals with a broad range of phenomena, including verb classes and the lexicon–syntax interface (Section 14.2), clausal ellipsis (Section 14.3.1) and negation (Section 14.3.2). The emphasis will be put on the so-called Chomskyan tradition.

14.2 Verb Classes, Argument Structure, and the Lexicon–Syntax Interface

This section focuses on argument structure and verb classes within current syntactic theory with an emphasis on the so-called Split-VP Hypothesis

(Larson 1988; Hale and Keyser 2002; among others) and various debates on the syntax of Spanish that emerged in the context of that theory and beyond, e.g. the syntax of ditransitive constructions and the encoding of path and motion in the verb in Spanish. Other topics to be discussed include certain features of the dependents of the verb, namely, the locality properties of its arguments and Differential Object Marking (DOM).

14.2.1 Argument Structure: The Lexicon–Syntax Interface

Verbs are traditionally divided into classes depending on their argument structure properties, including but not limited to the following: ditransitive verbs (*dar* 'to give'), monotransitive verbs (*ver* 'to see'), unergatives (intransitive verbs whose single argument receives an agent theta role, *correr* 'to run'), and unaccusative verbs (intransitive verbs whose single argument is not an agent, *llegar* 'to arrive'). Verb classes have been argued to correlate with various aspects of the grammar of Spanish (see Mendikoetxea 1999, among others), for instance, the availability of arbitrary interpretations or lack thereof and the distribution of bare NPs.[1] Specifically, pro_{arb} – the arbitrary null pronominal found in (14.2) – has been argued to be incompatible with unaccusative verbs (Jaeggli 1986). In turn, unmodified bare NPs have been argued to be restricted to the postverbal subject position of unaccusative verbs (where the notion of subject is used in theory-neutral terms) and to the object position of transitive verbs and, thus, may not occur as subjects of unergative verbs or transitive verbs (14.3), even when surfacing postverbally (Contreras 1986; Casielles-Suárez 2004; Torrego 1989; among others; cf. Benedicto 1998; note that bare NPs in Spanish are interpreted existentially, not generically).[2]

(14.2)   a. pro/pro_{arb} Llaman   a   Pedro.   *Monotransitive verb*
                     call.3PL   to   Pedro
              'They are / Somebody is calling Pedro.'

          b. pro/*pro_{arb} Llegan   al   trabajo.   *Unaccusative verb*
                     arrive.3PL to-the work
              'They are/*Somebody is arriving at their workplace.'

(14.3)   a. Llegan   niños   todos los días.   *Unaccusative verb – subject bare NP*
             arrive.3PL children every the days
             'Children arrive every day.'

---

[1] Verb classes are also relevant in determining transfer or spell-out domains, also referred to as *phases* (Chomsky 1998, 2001). Specifically, transitive and unergative verb phrases would correspond to a phase in contrast to unaccusative verb phrases, though this aspect of the theory has been challenged within the field of Romance linguistics and beyond – see, e.g., Kahnemuyipour's (2009) account of sentential stress in Romance; in turn, for a detailed study on the syntax of phases in Spanish focusing on topics other than sentential stress, see Gallego (2007) and subsequent work.

[2] Torrego (1989) claims that in locative inversion contexts certain unergatives may enter the unaccusative verb class (see Alexiadou 2007 for perspective; see also Fernández-Soriano 1999 for related discussion on the syntax of preverbal locatives). The issue is non-trivial since the subject has been argued to originate as the object of the verb in the case of the unaccusatives (see Perlmutter's 1978 Unaccusative Hypothesis), in contrast to the subject of unergative verbs.

b. Los niños leen libros.   *Transitive verb – object bare NP*
the children read.3PL books
'Children read books.'

c. *Nadan *niños* todos los días.   *Unergative verb – subject bare NP*
swim.3PL children every the days
'*Children swim every day.'

The study of argument structure has provided a particularly fruitful area to study the relationship between lexicon and syntax. In particular, studies on transitivity and verb classes tend to emphasize the relevance of semantics or else syntax in determining those classes. Within the former view, the semantics of the verb determine the number of arguments and their theta roles (agent, causer, patient, theme, experiencer, and goal; see Chomsky's 1981 Government and Binding framework) and theoretical constructs such as the Theta Criterion (Chomsky 1981) and the Uniformity of Theta-Assignment Hypothesis (UTAH, Baker 1988, 1997)[3] are in place to ensure convergence at the lexicon–syntax interface and to deal with the "linking problem," namely, the need to capture regularities in the linking of syntactic functions and theta roles (e.g. the tendency for agents to be subjects as opposed to objects found in accusative languages as opposed to ergative languages, Levin 1983). In contrast, within the latter view, the role of the structural relations found in the syntax when determining those features is emphasized (e.g. see Hale and Keyser 2002 for the view that syntactic relations limit the number of theta roles available in natural language). The treatment of argument structure alternations such as passivization varies accordingly. Thus, in the former view, transformations may affect the lexical entry of the verb via a lexical operation.[4] In contrast, within the latter view, those alternations are purely syntactic in nature; hybrid alternatives exist as well; see, e.g., Reinhart and Siloni's (2005) treatment of reflexivization. Among the various word-order alternations that have figured prominently in the literature are the alternation between lexical causatives and their anticausative (inchoative) counterpart (see Schäfer 2009 for an overview) (14.4), the dative/accusative alternation in psychological verbs (see Wilinski-Hodel 2007; her data in (14.5)), various properties of the syntax of ditransitive constructions, and the

---

[3] UTAH states that identical thematic relationships between items are represented by identical structural relationships between those items at the level of D-structure (Baker 1988:46), whereas the Theta Criterion states that each argument bears one and only one theta role and that each theta role is assigned to one and only one argument (Chomsky 1981:35). With the advent of Minimalism, theoretical constructs such as the Theta Criterion and the D-structure became suspect. Hale and Keyser's work helped eliminate those constructs from the theory (see Harley 2011 and references therein for detailed discussion). Research on the validity of UTAH has been particularly relevant to the study of unaccusative verbs (see fn. 2) and to the study of psych-verbs, which fall into different categories depending on their argument structure patterns, e.g. *amar* 'love' vs. *gustar* 'please' (Belletti and Rizzi 1988; see Franco 1992 and Gutiérrez-Bravo 2006, among others, for Spanish).

[4] Still other relevant information which allegedly is part of the lexical entry of the verb and/or our world knowledge is its combinatorial properties or subcategorization frame, e.g. whether a specific verb can take a clause or an NP as an object, or whether the subject has to be an animate entity.

encoding of path and motion in the verb in Spanish (see below for discussion of the last two issues).

(14.4) a. Julia   abrió   la   puerta.
           Julia   opened the   door
           'Julia opened the door.'
        b. La   puerta se   abrió.
           the   door   REFL   opened
           'The door opened.'

(14.5) A   Juan   le   / lo   preocupa el   dinero.
        to   Juan   DAT.CL / ACC.CL   worries   the money
        'Juan is worried about money.'

In what follows, particular attention is paid to the syntactocentric view, as various ongoing debates on Spanish have emerged within that framework. Specifically, minimalist syntax has adopted a highly articulated structure of the verb phrase, the so-called split-vP, based on (i) the view that the syntactic structure of the verbal predicate reflects the semantic event decomposition (Hale and Keyser 2002, among others); (ii) the well-established assumption that all branching must be binary in syntactic structures (Kayne 1981); (iii) the observation that the verb and the object have a stronger link than the verb and the subject (Marantz 1984 and Kratzer 1996).

This highly articulated syntax of the verb phrase can be illustrated with verbs taking multiple complements, such as *poner (los libros en la estantería)* 'to put (the books on the shelf)' (14.6) (see Harley 2011 for detailed discussion of the proposal and its various virtues; note that the preposition has a specifier by virtue of being inherently "birelational" and that the agent is introduced as the specifier of V; for a discussion of clausal structure above the verb phrase, see the section "Differential Object Marking" below and also Chapter 15, this volume).[5]

(14.6)

The syntactocentric approach to word order alternations can be illustrated with denominal verb formation. Hale and Keyser (2002) argued that denominal verb derivations are syntactic in nature, based on the fact

---

[5] Whether this kind of structure is found across verb classes, in particular with non-agentive verbs, depends on the exact role ascribed to the (upper) V head, sometimes referred to as "little v" (see Chomsky 1995, Hale and Keyser 2002 and Marantz 1997 for discussion, among others).

that principles independently known to be active in syntax constrain denominal verb formation, too. In their view, a verb such as *ensillar (el caballo)* 'to saddle (the horse)' in (14.7) would be derived from a structure similar to the one in (14.6).

(14.7) El   vaquero ensilló el   caballo.
        The   cowboy   saddled the horse
        'The cowboy saddled the horse.'

Specifically, conflation – a kind of incorporation (Travis 1984; Baker 1988; see Hale and Keyser 2002 ch. 3 for discussion), whereby the phonological matrix of the head of the complement replaces the matrix of the governing head – plays a relevant role in deriving the surface form of the verbal predicate starting from (14.8) (P conflates with *silla* and the upper verb conflates with the resulting P, thus giving phonological constituency to the verb):

(14.8)

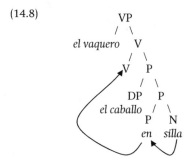

The decomposition of the predicate in the various projections is supported by cross-linguistic facts, e.g. languages where a verb such as *ensillar* shows unincoporated syntax of the kind found in *poner (los libros en la estantería)*. Furthermore, since the subject appears in a projection different from the one hosting the rest of the arguments (see Larson 1988), this helps capture a number of data points related to (iii), including the fact that verb–object idioms (idioms where the verb and the object are fixed, giving rise to a special idiomatic interpretation, e.g. *tocar las narices* 'annoy somebody (lit. touch somebody's nostrils)') are highly frequent across languages, in contrast to subject–verb idioms (Marantz 1984 and Kratzer 1996).

While various aspects of Hale and Keyser's proposal (2002) are subject to debate, the field of Spanish linguistics has paid particular attention to various details of ditransitive constructions and to the syntactic composition of path and motion, to be introduced next.

The Syntax of Ditransitive Constructions

The study of ditransitive constructions in Spanish has received a significant amount of attention. In particular, it has been informed by the so-called dative alternation in English (14.9):

(14.9) a. Carmen sent her professor the book.
b. Carmen sent the book to her professor.

With regard to the technicalities of the analysis of the English facts, two main lines of analysis emerged to capture it: a passive-like transformational analysis that derives (14.9a) from (14.9b) (e.g. Larson 1988), and an approach in terms of alternative projections, where the two orders are generated independently (e.g. Pesetsky 1995 and Harley 2003). Such analyses were meant to capture differences in properties such as the c(onstituent)-command relations among the objects, the behavior of idioms, and the interpretation (possession vs. path); see Rappaport Hovan and Levin (2008) for perspective. The literature on Spanish has attempted to establish whether those very syntactic and semantic properties may also be found in this language. Specifically, clitic-doubled ditransitive constructions in Spanish (14.10a) have been identified with double-object constructions in English (14.9a), whereas non-doubled ones (14.10b) have been identified with prepositional constructions (14.9b) (Masullo 1992; Demonte 1995; Romero 1997; Bleam 2003; Cuervo 2003):

(14.10) a. Carmen le_i envió   el   libro   a   su $profesor_i$.
         Carmen CL   sent.3SG the   book   to   her   professor
       b. Carmen   envió   el   libro   a   su   profesor.
         Carmen   sent.3SG the   book   to   her   professor

Source: Bleam (2003)

For instance, the examples in (14.11), a prepositional construction in English and a non-clitic-doubled construction in Spanish, respectively, have been claimed to be compatible with a caused motion reading in contrast to the examples in (14.12), a double-object construction in English and a clitic-doubled ditransitive construction in Spanish, respectively. The latter can have only a caused possession reading, hence their ungrammaticality (Spanish data from Ormazábal and Romero 2010; see Oehrle 1976 for the English, among others):

(14.11) a. I   sent/gave the book to New York.
        b. Yo   envié   un   libro a   Nueva York.
           I   sent   a   book to New York
           'I sent a book to New York.'

(14.12) a. *I sent/gave New York the book.
        b. *Yo le_i envié un   libro a $Nueva York_i$.
           I   CL   sent   a   book   to New York.

Recently, however, the analysis has been increasingly called into question. For instance, differences in c-command relations among the objects found in the English pairs do not seem to correlate with the presence of the clitic or lack thereof in Spanish (see Pineda 2013; Beavers and Nishida 2010).

On Path and Motion in Spanish

Still another topic that has figured prominently in the literature on Spanish and/or Romance within the context of Hale and Keyser's framework (2002) is the conflation of motion with path, whereby path is encoded (lexically incorporated) into the verb (14.13), as opposed to the conflation of motion with manner typical of English (14.14), (e.g. Mateu 2002; Mateu and Rigau 2002; and Zubizarreta and Oh 2007, among others):

(14.13) La   botella   entró   a   la   cueva   flotando.
         the   bottle   went+*into*   to   the   cave   floating

(14.14) The bottle floated into the cave.

The absence of manner-of-motion verbs in Spanish as opposed to English or Dutch can be seen in the ungrammaticality of the counterpart of (14.14) in Spanish:

(14.15) *La   botella   flotó   a   la   cueva.
          the   bottle   floated+*into*   to   the   cave

This contrast has been blamed on the properties of preposition *a* in Spanish (e.g. its point-locating status in these structures does not give rise to a path reading; see Folli 2001) and on the unavailability of productive compositional compounding of the kind found in Germanic languages, that is to say, lexically unrestricted compounding. In contrast, this phenomenon is restricted to specified combinations of lexical items in Romance. The latter factor can be illustrated with the productivity of novel compounds in the nominal realm in English as opposed to in Spanish, where a paraphrase is necessary (Snyder 2001) (14.16):

(14.16)   a. Apple juice
          b. Jugo   de   fruta
            juice   of   fruit
            'Apple juice'

Arguably, the lexically unrestricted availability of this rule for the semantic composition of compounds is crucial to allow for the conflation of motion and path, hence the data in (14.13)–(14.15) (see Zubizarreta and Oh 2007, following Snyder 2001, among others; see Mateu and Rigau 2002 for an alternative account).

Next, various properties of the dependents of the verb are discussed, namely, their distinct locality properties and DOM.

14.2.2 On the Dependents of the Verb: Locality and Differential Object Marking

Locality within the Verb Phrase

Locality has played a very prominent role in the history of Generative Grammar as it exemplifies the Poverty of the Stimulus (POS) logic: Given the lack of positive (and negative) evidence for locality constraints, their presence, language after language, suggests that they are part of Universal Grammar (UG). Accordingly, their validity and parametrization have been subject to intense research (see Boeckx 2012 for an overview). Lately, the issue has gained further interest as part of the debate on (i) the validity of traditional grammaticality judgments as opposed to experimental methods of gathering data; and (ii) the influence of processing factors on grammaticality judgments, particularly when assessing the grammaticality of island constructions (e.g. Snyder 2000; Sprouse 2007; Sprouse et al. 2013).

While objects show a cross-linguistic tendency to be permeable to extraction, the case of subjects is more controversial. A most prolific literature exists and proposals range from claiming that specifiers (and adjuncts) are opaque to extraction (e.g. see Huang's 1982 Condition on Extraction Domains, CED; see also Chomsky's 1986 Barriers and Uriagereka's 1999 Multiple Spell-Out, MSO, among others) or else that moved elements are (see Stepanov's 2001 Freezing Effects).[6] In the case of Spanish, postverbal subjects, possibly *in situ* in Spec,*v*P (specifier position of *v*P) are transparent for extraction in contrast to preverbal subjects (Gallego and Uriagereka 2007; their data; note that the t(race) marks the place in the structure where the moved phrase originates).

(14.17) a. *¿De qué conferenciantes te parece que las
 of what speakers to-you.SG seems that the
 propuestas t me van a impresionar?
 proposals me go.3PL to impress
 b. ¿De qué conferenciantes te parece que me van
 of what speakers to-you.SG seems that me go.3PL
 a impresionar las propuestas t?
 to impress the proposals
 'The proposals by which speakers do you think will impress me?'

A priori, the data in (14.17) would be consistent with Stepanov's (2001) Freezing Effects as opposed to theories that posit the opacity of specifiers irrespective of whether they are moved (e.g. the CED or MSO), though recent experimental evidence bearing on the issue of the opacity of *in situ* specifiers suggests this might merit further research (see Jurka 2009 and Jiménez-Fernández 2009).

---

[6] Whereas Section 14.2 focuses on the arguments of the verb (that is to say, the core participants in the eventuality denoted by the verb), phrases corresponding to other details of the event are considered to be adjuncts. Their distinct properties, e.g. the said locality properties, provide evidence for the argument–adjunct distinction.

Likewise, there is a cross-linguistic tendency for long-distance object movement to be relatively free of locality restrictions, when compared to subject movement (see the traditional Empty Category Principle, ECP, Chomsky 1986, recently revived in Chomsky 2013 and subsequent work). This contrast is attested, for instance, in English, but not in Spanish:

(14.18) a. Which bones do you wonder if the dog likes t?
         b. *Which dog do you wonder if t likes the bones?

(14.19) a. ¿Qué   huesos no   sabes   si el   perro ama   t?
            what   bones   not know.2sG   if the dog   loves
            'Which bones do you wonder if the dog likes?'
         b. ¿Qué   perro   no   sabes   si t   ama   los huesos?
            what   dog   not know.2sG   if   loves the bones
            'Which dog do you wonder if it likes the bones?'

This contrast has been linked to null subjects (see Rizzi's 1982, 1986 seminal work; see also Chapter 15, this volume), which are a hallmark of Spanish, though the specifics of the analysis within the current framework remain elusive (see Ortega-Santos 2016 for discussion).[7]

Differential Object Marking

Differential Object Marking (DOM), a phenomenon whereby direct objects are marked with the preposition *a* depending on subtle semantic differences, has given rise to much research on Spanish.

---

[7] Still another property of null-subject languages is the absence of that-trace effects. In particular, the extraction of an embedded subject in English is possible only when the complementizer of the embedded clause is absent, hence the following contrast (Chomsky 2013, among others):

(i) a. How many cars did they say that the mechanics fixed t?
     b. How many mechanics did they say (*that) t fixed the cars?

Spanish is not sensitive to this constraint:

(ii) a. ¿Cuántos   coches   dijiste   que   los   mecánicos habían arreglado t?
         how-many   cars   said.2sG   that the   mechanics had   fixed
         'How many cars did you say that the mechanics had fixed?'
      b. ¿Cuántos   mecánicos dijiste   que   t   habían   arreglado los coches?
         how-many   mechanics said.2sG   that   had   fixed   the cars
         'How many mechanics did you say had fixed the cars?'

In turn, null objects are more constrained than null subjects in Spanish (see Armstrong 2016 and references therein for recent discussion, his data):

(iii) María leyó toda la   tarde.
       María read all   the afternoon
       'María read throughout the afternoon.'

An object argument may also go "missing" in the case of clitic climbing under restructuring (a process of clause union of an embedded clause with the matrix clause; see Rizzi 1976, Hernanz 1999, and González López 2008, among others). Specifically, a clitic associated with a nonfinite embedded verb might appear in the main clause as if it were part of the argument structure of the main verb.

In particular, specificity (14.20) and animacy (14.21) have been argued to be the key components to determine this alternation, though telicity, agentivity or verb class have been investigated as relevant factors (see Fábregas 2013 and references therein) to capture further nuances in the data; see e.g. (14.22), where neither specificity nor animacy is relevant:

(14.20) a. Juan ve *(a) los niños.
         Juan sees to the children
         'Juan sees the children.'
       b. Juan ve (*a) niños.
         Juan sees to children
         'Juan sees children.'

(14.21) Juan ve (*a) los juguetes.
        Juan sees to the toys
        'Juan sees the toys.'

(14.22) Los sujetos preceden *(a) los verbos.
        the subjects precede.3PL to the verbs
        'Subjects come before verbs.'   Source: Adapted from Fábregas (2013)

Beyond the debate on the factors that determine the distribution of personal *a*, attention has been paid to the correlates of *a*-marking in the syntax, for instance, (i) the alleged incompatibility of *a*-marking with indirect objects, which are marked with the (homophonous) dative preposition *a* (see Rodríguez Mondoñedo 2007, among others, for detailed discussion) (14.23), and (ii) whether there are asymmetries in subextraction from within *a*-marked objects as opposed to objects without *a*-marking (Torrego 1998; Fábregas 2013; Bassa Vanrell and Romeu 2014) (14.24a). (Note that (14.24b) is included to show that *a*-marking itself is not the problem in the structure with subextraction.)

(14.23) El secuestrador entregó {el niño / ?al niño} a su madre.
        the kidnapper gave   {the child / to-the child} to his mother
        'The kidnapper returned the child to his mother.'

(14.24) a. ¿De qué busca Juan ?(a) un profesor?
           of what looks.for Juan   a teacher
           '*What is Juan looking for a teacher of?'
        b. Juan busca (a) un profesor de Ciencias.
           Juan looks.for a teacher of science
           'Juan is looking for a science teacher.'
                          Source: Bassa Vanrell and Romeu (2014)

Naturally, analyses have emerged in which there is some sort of competition between the *a*-marked direct object and the indirect object in (14.23). For instance, within Rodríguez Mondoñedo's (2007) approach not only indirect objects but also *a*-marked direct objects receive dative case;

this researcher adopts Richards' Distinctness Condition from work that eventually appeared in Richards (2010). This condition, informally speaking, prevents elements of the same type from being linearized too closely together. It forces the drop of *a*-marking in the case of the direct objects, though special provisos have to be added for pronouns and items such as *nadie* 'nobody' or *quién* 'who' which do not allow for *a*-drop irrespective of the syntactic context. Other relevant issues are the exact position of *a*-marked objects in the syntactic structure when compared to non-*a*-marked objects (see Rodríguez Mondoñedo 2007; Torrego 1998; Bassa Vanrell and Romeu 2014; López 2012; among others), the existence of dialectal variation, and the relation between object clitics and *a*-marking (e.g. Ormazábal and Romero 2013; see also Aissen's 2003 optimality theoretic analysis and López's 2012 detailed study of the interpretation of the direct object and its scope, among others; for a state-of-the-art overview on DOM in Spanish, see Fábregas 2013).

14.3 Other Phenomena: Clausal Ellipsis and Negation

As stated in the Introduction to this chapter, there is a mismatch between the traditional definition of the verb phrase and the VP projection used in current syntactic theorizing. In this section, various phenomena involving the verb phrase (though not limited to the VP projection) are discussed, namely (i) clausal ellipsis, loosely understood as a phenomenon whereby a verb phrase goes missing in spite of the fact that the ellipsis remnants are interpreted as if they were part of a whole clause (Section 14.3.1), and (ii) negation (Section 14.3.2).

14.3.1 Clausal Ellipsis

Clausal ellipsis of the kind illustrated in (14.25)–(14.26) involves missing verb phrases (though see fn. 8 for discussion of the exact size of ellipsis):

(14.25) Pedro come algo,   pero no sé   qué.   *Sluicing*
         Pedro eats something but not know.1sG what
         'Pedro is eating something, but I do not know what.'

(14.26) A: ¿Qué come Pedro?   B: Una naranja.   *Fragment answer*
            what eats Pedro   an orange
         'What is Pedro eating?'   'An orange.'

Three main lines of research regarding the exact content of the ellipsis site and its interpretation are being currently explored (see Merchant 2001 and Yoshida *et al.* 2014 for details; see Depiante 2000 and Saab 2008 for discussion on Spanish): A first line of research posits full-fledged syntactic structure at the ellipsis site while relying on the assumption that only syntactic constituents can undergo ellipsis. Under this view, the remnants would move to the left periphery, arguably for independent reasons (e.g. *wh-* or focus-movement) and the clause would be elided (see Merchant 2001). This is illustrated in (14.27) for Fragment Answers (I abstract away from irrelevant details, e.g. whether the embedded subject in TP should be preverbal or postverbal; strikethrough text is used to represent the ellipsis site):[8]

(14.27)   [$_{FocP}$ Una naranja$_x$ [$_{TP}$ ~~Pedro come t$_x$~~]].
          an   orange   Pedro eats

A second line of analysis rejects the assumption that only constituents may undergo deletion. This opens the door to an approach where the remnants are *in situ* (unless they have to undergo fronting for reasons other than ellipsis); see López (2009) and Ott and Struckmeier (2016), among others, for relevant discussion:

(14.28)   [$_{TP}$ ~~Pedro come~~ una naranja].

Inasmuch as these two lines of analysis take for granted the existence of full-fledged structure at the ellipsis site, the interpretation of the ellipsis site is trivial and no new mechanism needs to be added – ellipsis is some sort of Phonetic Form (PF) phenomenon. Connectivity effects (e.g. binding effects or selection requirements) have been argued to provide evidence for this view. For instance, if the remnant is a prepositional phrase, the preposition needs to match the requirements imposed by the verb in the antecedent clause, thus arguing for the view that a verb is also present in the ellipsis site.

Still, a third line of reasoning argues against the idea that there is full-fledged structure in the ellipsis site and attempts to derive such connectivity effects from a parallelism requirement between the antecedent clause and the ellipsis site. Under this kind of account, the ellipsis site in at least a subset of the ellipsis constructions includes a pro-form (e.g. see Hankamer and Sag 1976; see Depiante 2000 and Saab 2008 for relevant discussion for Spanish). Accordingly, the interpretation of the ellipsis is related to the interpretation of pronominals and anaphoras.

Further topics in the study of ellipsis involve the licensing mechanism for ellipsis (see e.g. Merchant 2001 for discussion), the relationship of so-called phases or spell-out domains to the size of ellipsis (Kayne 2006; Gallego 2009; Aelbrecht 2016 and Bošković 2014; among others), and the locality properties of ellipsis structures. The locality facts are particularly important in the debate, as these may vary across the elided and the non-elided counterparts (see (14.29) for Sluicing) or across ellipsis constructions (e.g. sluiced *wh*-phrases are island-insensitive, (14.29a), in contrast to Contrastive Fragment Answers (14.30B) respectively; relative clause islands are used in both cases):

---

[8] It is standardly assumed that V moves out of *v*P / VP into TP in Romance (see Emonds 1978 and Pollock 1989). Given that the ellipsis site includes the verb (arguably hosted in T), it follows that the ellipsis site would have to be, minimally, TP.

(14.29) a. Hoy   Pedro conocerá al   hombre que se   casó   con
           today Pedro will-meet to-the man   who REFL married with
           una chica de   Almería, pero no   recuerdo   con   quién.
           a   girl from Almería but not remember.1SG with whom
           'Today, Pedro will meet the man who married a girl from Almería,
           but I don't remember who he married.'
       b. *¿Con quién conocerá   Pedro al   hombre que se
           with whom   will-meet.3SG Pedro to-the man   who REFL
           casó   t?
           married.3SG
           '*Who will Pedro meet the man who married?'

(14.30) A: ¿Pedro habla   la   misma lengua   romance que
           Pedro   speaks the same language Romance that
           habla   JUAN?⁹
           speaks Juan
           'Does Pedro speak the same Romance language that JUAN speaks?'
       B: *No, Jorge.
           no   Jorge
           '*No, Jorge.'

A priori, under analyses assuming full-fledged syntactic structure at the ellipsis site, the asymmetry in the locality of Sluicing as opposed to overt movement in its non-ellipsis counterpart (14.29) calls for an explanation. In contrast, approaches positing the existence of a pro-form in the ellipsis site predict island effects to be absent under ellipsis – there is no island, after all. For this very reason, the pro-form analysis does not predict the tight locality restrictions found in the case of Contrastive Fragment Answers (14.30B). Various alternatives are being explored to capture these locality facts (see Saab 2008 for Spanish; see Merchant 2004; Nakao 2009 and Griffiths and Lipták 2014 for other languages). While the full-fledged syntax approach combined with movement followed by ellipsis of a full constituent (14.27) has received strong support (see Merchant 2001; cf. Ott and Struckmeier 2016 and references therein), it is an open question whether that analysis is appropriate for each and every single ellipsis construction.

14.3.2 Sentential Negation

The goal of this section is to introduce current theories on the syntax of negation with an emphasis on so-called negative concord, as well as the relevance of the study of negation for our understanding of clausal structure in Spanish.

Basic Properties

For the purposes of this discussion, negation at the sentence level, whether surfacing as a negative particle (*no* 'not'), within the pronominal paradigm (*nadie* 'nobody') or as a determiner (*ningún* X/*ninguna* X 'no X'), is of particular relevance. The negative particle *no* appears in the preverbal position

---

[9] The intonation rise on *Juan* in the yes–no question gives rise to an implicit constituent question where the appropriate *wh*-phrase replaces the accented constituent (Merchant 2004; example adapted from his work).

and only clitics may intervene between it and the verb, a fact that has been interpreted in favor of the clitic status of the negative particle itself:

(14.31) Pedro no te ve.
Pedro not you.2SG see.3SG
'Pedro doesn't see you.'

While the negative particle may license other negative elements (known as n-words following Laka's 1990 work), negation is interpreted only once, a phenomenon known as negative concord:[10]

(14.32) *(No) va a venir nadie.
not goes to come nobody
'Nobody is going to come.'

This property has been widely discussed due to its violation of the principle of compositionality which states that the meaning of an expression is a function of the meanings of its parts and of the way they are syntactically combined (see Ladusaw 1992). In particular, it raises questions about the nature of the n-words, e.g. whether they are inherently negative or not. Matters are complicated further by the fact that n-words may surface preverbally provided that the negative particle is absent (for recent discussion on a variety of fronting mechanisms available in Spanish, including the fronting of n-words, see Jiménez-Fernández 2015 and references therein; note that (14.33) is also relevant in that it provides an argument for the view that the Negative Phrase, NegP, is positioned above TP; see fn. 8 for related discussion):

(14.33) Nadie (*no) va a venir.
nobody not goes to come

This feature has received a number of treatments; for example, Laka (1990) and Bosque (1980) proposed that n-words are negative polarity items with no intrinsic negative meaning, in contrast to Zanuttini (1991) and Haegeman and Zanuttini (1991), who consider n-words to be inherently negative universal quantifiers. Crucially, under both analyses, special provisos need to be added to capture the complexity of the data. In the former case, additional machinery is needed to capture the fact that the n-word *a priori* seems to have negative meaning in (14.33); in turn, under the latter scenario, the absence of double negation in the negative concord case, (14.32), has to be accounted for (see also Herburger's 2001 view that n-words are ambiguous between negative polarity items, which occur in postverbal position, and negative quantifiers, which occur in preverbal position; see Tubau 2008 for a detailed review of the various alternatives

---

[10] See Klima (1964) for discussion of so-called downward entailment contexts where n-words can be licensed in the absence of clausal negation; see Bosque (1980) for Spanish.

found in the literature, including a treatment of n-words as negative indefinites included in Suñer 1995 and Espinal 2000). More recently, Tubau (2008) has related this phenomenon to an anti-locality constraint that would prevent the negative particle and n-words from co-occurring in the same spell-out domain. Within Tubau's framework, postverbal n-words co-occurring with the negative particle do not violate this constraint since they belong to different spell-out units. In contrast, when an n-word surfaces preverbally, it appears in the same spell-out domain as the negative particle and, as a consequence, the negative marker is not given a phonological realization, though it is semantically active.[11] Tubau's proposal is remarkable in that it is linked to broader questions such as similarity-based anti-locality phenomena (cf. Richards' 2010 Distinctness Condition in Section 14.2.2) and the identity of phases/spell-out units in Spanish.[12]

A Note on Negation and its Relevance for the Study of Preverbal Subjects
The fact that *no* may intervene between the subject and the verb (e.g. (14.31)) is relevant for the debate on the syntax of preverbal subjects. In particular, there is an on-going debate as to whether subjects in Spanish are hosted in Spec,TP (14.34a) (see Goodall 2001 and Ortega-Santos 2016, among others), or whether they should be assimilated to topics or instances of Clitic Left Dislocation (CLLD) elements in that they would be hosted above TP, either as base-generated elements or as a result of a movement operation (14.34b) (Alexiadou and Anagnostopoulou 1998; Olarrea 1996; Ordóñez 2000; among others; see Ortega-Santos 2016 and Chapter 15, this volume, for an overview of the debate).

---

[11] For Tubau's proposal to work, she needs to assume the following independently motivated aspects of the syntax of Spanish: (i) Neg-P is merged above TP (see also Laka 1990, among others); (ii) TP is a phase in Spanish as a consequence of V-to-T movement (see Gallego's 2007 Phase Sliding). Furthermore, according to Tubau, n-words have negative morphology at PF, but their uninterpretable polarity features are deleted at Logical Form (LF).

[12] Still another property of the licensing of n-words in Spanish is the fact that the licenser (the negative particle) and the n-word need to appear in the same clause, (i). Nonetheless, this requirement is obviated in embedded subjunctive clauses (Gallego 2015 and references therein), (ii):

(i) No digo que *(no) ves nada.
 not say.1SG that not see.2SG anything
 'I am not saying that you can't see anything.'

(ii) No quiero que veas nada.
 not want.1SG that see.SBJV.2SG anything
 'I don't want you to see anything.'

Within Phase Theory, phases place strict conditions on long-distance phenomena (see Chomsky 1998, 2001) and, thus, such data call for an explanation. Related transparency effects of subjunctive clauses have been found, for instance, in the so-called Subject Disjoint Reference Effect involving Principle B of Binding Theory (see Kempchinsky 2009 for recent discussion). Such phenomena have been interpreted as evidence that embedded subjunctive clauses are not transferred independently of the main clause, in contrast to embedded indicative clauses (see Bobaljik and Wurmbrand 2013 and Gallego 2015).

(14.34) a. [_TP XP T ....]
         b. [_CP XP [_TP T ....]

A priori, the said word order would favor the latter analysis (Bosque 1994 or, more recently Kim 2006), given standard assumptions about verb movement (see fn. 8). Still, such data could receive an explanation compatible with the latter approach under a so-called Split-Infl(ection) Hypothesis (Pollock 1989), whereby Infl, the Inflectional Phrase, is divided into a Subject Agreement Phrase, AgrS, and a TP: If NegP enters the structure between those two projections the relevant word order may result from having the subject hosted in AgrS while either *no* cliticizes onto the verb on its way to AgrS or else the verb remains in TP; preverbal n-words, in turn, would occupy the specifier of NegP (see Belletti 1990 and Bosque and Gutiérrez-Rexach 2009, among others). Minimalism (Chomsky 1995 and subsequent work), however, stresses the need to minimize any theoretical constructs, including the number of projections, thus favoring the abandonment of the Split-Infl Hypothesis. Therefore, other diagnoses are necessary to settle the issue (see Chapter 15, this volume, and references therein for related discussion).

14.4 Conclusion

This chapter has presented an overview of the most relevant issues associated with the verb phrase in Spanish, including but not limited to verb classes, the lexicon–syntax interface, clausal ellipsis, clausal negation, and various properties of the arguments of the verb, e.g. DOM and the locality properties of the argument. Further details on the syntax of the clausal structure of Spanish are provided in Chapter 15, this volume.

References

Aelbrecht, L. (2016). What Ellipsis Can Do for Phases and What it Can't, but not How. *The Linguistic Review*, 33 (2), 453–482.

Aissen, J. (2003). Differential Object Marking: Iconicity vs. Economy. *Natural Language and Linguistic Theory*, 21 (3), 435–483.

Alexiadou, A. (2007). Post-Verbal Nominatives: An Unaccusativity Diagnostic under Scrutiny. Talk at On Linguistic Interfaces (OnLI) Workshop, University of Ulster.

Alexiadou, A. and Anagnostopoulou, E. (1998). Parametrizing AGR: Word Order, V-Movement and EPP Checking. *Natural Language and Linguistic Theory*, 16 (3), 491–539.

Armstrong, G. (2016). Spanish Unspecified Objects as Null Incorporated Nouns. *Probus*, 28 (2), 165–229.

Baker, M. (1988). *Incorporation: A Theory of Grammatical Function Changing*. Chicago, IL: University of Chicago Press.

Baker, M. (1997). Thematic Roles and Syntactic Structure. In L. Haegeman (ed.), *Elements of Grammar*. Dordrecht: Kluwer, pp. 73–137.

Bassa Vanrell, M. del M. and Romeu, J. (2014). A Minimal Cartography of Differential Object Marking in Spanish. *Iberia*, 6, 75–104.

Beavers, J. and Nishida, C. (2010). The Spanish Dative Alternation Revisited. In S. Colina, A. Olarrea, and A. M. Carvalho (eds.), *Romance Linguistics 2009: Selected Papers from the 39th Linguistic Symposium on Romance Languages (LSRL)*. Amsterdam: John Benjamins, pp. 217–230.

Belletti, A. (1990). *Generalized Verb Movement: Aspects of Verb Syntax*. Turin: Rosenberg and Sellier.

Belletti, A. and Rizzi, L. (1988). Psych Verbs and a-Theory. *Natural Language and Linguistic Theory*, 6 (3), 291–352.

Benedicto, E. (1998). Verb Movement and its Effects on Determinerless Plural Subjects. In A. Schwegler, B. Tranel, and M. Uribe-Etxebarria (eds.), *Romance Linguistics: Theoretical Perspectives*. Amsterdam: John Benjamins, pp. 25–39.

Bleam, T. (2003). Properties of the Double Object Construction in Spanish. In R. Núñez-Cedeño, L. López, and R. Cameron (eds.), *A Romance Perspective on Language Knowledge and Use*. Amsterdam: John Benjamins, pp. 233–252.

Bobaljik, J. and Wurmbrand, S. (2013). Suspension across Domains. In O. Matushansky and A. Marantz (eds.), *Distributed Morphology Today – Morphemes for Morris Halle*. Cambridge, MA: MIT Press, pp. 185–198.

Boeckx, C. (2012). *Syntactic Islands*. Cambridge: Cambridge University Press.

Bošković, Ž. (2014). Now I'm a Phase, Now I'm not a Phase: On the Variability of Phases with Extraction and Ellipsis. *Linguistic Inquiry*, 45 (1), 27–89.

Bosque, I. (1980). *Sobre la negación*. Madrid: Cátedra.

Bosque, I. (1994). La negación y el principio de las categorías vacías. In V. Demonte (ed.), *Gramática del español*. Mexico City: El Colegio de México, pp. 167–199.

Bosque, I. and Gutiérrez-Rexach, J. (2009). *Fundamentos de sintaxis formal*. Madrid: Akal.

Casielles-Suárez, E. (2004). *The Syntax–Information Structure Interface*. London: Routledge.

Chomsky, N. (1981). *Lectures on Government and Binding*. Dordrecht: Foris.

Chomsky, N. (1986). *Barriers*. Cambridge, MA: MIT Press.

Chomsky, N. (1995). *The Minimalist Program*. Cambridge, MA: MIT Press.

Chomsky, N. (1998). Minimalist Inquiries: The Framework. *MIT Occasional Papers in Linguistics*, 15.

Chomsky, N. (2001). Derivation by Phase. In M. Kenstowicz (ed.), *Ken Hale: A Life in Language*. Cambridge, MA: MIT Press, pp. 1–52.

Chomsky, N. (2013). Problems of Projection. *Lingua*, 130, 33–49.

Contreras, H. (1986). Spanish Bare NPs and the ECP. In I. Bordelois and K. Zagona (eds.), *Generative Studies in Spanish Syntax*. Dordrecht: Foris, pp. 25–49.

Cuervo, M. C. (2003). Datives at Large (Doctoral dissertation). MIT.

Demonte, V. (1995). Dative Alternation in Spanish. *Probus*, 7, 5–30.

Depiante, M. A. (2000). The Syntax of Deep and Surface Anaphora: A Study of Null Complement Anaphora and Stripping/Bare Argument Ellipsis (Doctoral dissertation). University of Connecticut.

Emonds, J. (1978). The Verbal Complex V'–V in French. *Linguistic Inquiry*, 9 (2), 151–175.

Espinal, M. T. (2000). On the Semantic Status of N-Words in Catalan and Spanish. *Lingua*, 110 (8), 557–580.

Fábregas, A. (2013). Differential Object Marking in Spanish: State of the Art. *Borealis: An International Journal of Hispanic Linguistics*, 2 (2), 1–80.

Fernández-Soriano, O. (1999). Two Types of Impersonal Sentences in Spanish: Locative and Dative Subjects. *Syntax*, 2 (2), 101–140.

Folli, R. (2001). Constructing Telicity in English and Italian (Doctoral dissertation). University of Oxford.

Franco, J. (1992). Towards a Typology of Psych Verbs: Evidence from Spanish. *Anuario del Seminario de Filología Vasca "Julio de Urquijo"*, 27, 119–134.

Gallego, Á. (2007). Phase Theory and Parametric Variation (Doctoral dissertation). Universitat Autònoma de Barcelona.

Gallego, Á. (2009). *Ellipsis by Phase*. Talk at the XIX Colloquium on Generative Grammar, Euskal Herriko Unibertsitatea. Available from http://filcat.uab.cat/clt/membres/professors/gallego/pdf/GAL_vitoria.pdf (last access November 24, 2017).

Gallego, Á. (2015). Subjunctive Dependents in Iberian Romance: A Reprojection Account. *Sintagma*, 27, 25–42.

Gallego, Á. and Uriagereka, J. (2007). Conditions on Sub-Extraction. In L. Eguren and O. Fernández Soriano (eds.), *Coreference, Modality, and Focus*. Amsterdam: John Benjamins, pp. 45–70.

González López, V. (2008). Spanish Clitic Climbing (Doctoral dissertation). Pennsylvania State University.

Goodall, G. (2001). The EPP in Spanish. In W. D. Davies and S. Dubinsky (eds.), *Objects and Other Subjects: Grammatical Functions, Functional Categories and Configurationality*. Dordrecht: Kluwer, pp. 193–223.

Griffiths, J. and Lipták, A. (2014). Contrast and Island Sensitivity in Clausal Ellipsis. *Syntax*, 17 (3), 189–234.

Gutiérrez-Bravo, R. (2006). A Reinterpretation of Quirky Subjects and Related Phenomena in Spanish. In J. P. Montreuil and C. Nishida (eds.), *New Perspectives in Romance Linguistics*. Amsterdam: John Benjamins, pp. 127–142.

Haegeman, L. and Zanuttini, R. (1991). Negative Heads and the Neg Criterion. *The Linguistic Review*, 8 (2–4), 233–251.

Hale, K. L. and Keyser, S. J. (2002). *Prolegomenon to a Theory of Argument Structure*. Cambridge, MA: MIT Press.

Hankamer, J. and Sag, I. (1976). Deep and Surface Anaphora. *Linguistic Inquiry*, 7 (3), 391–426.

Harley, H. (2003). Possession and the Double Object Construction. In P. Pica and J. Rooryck (eds.), *Linguistics Variation Yearbook*. Amsterdam: John Benjamins, pp. 231–270.

Harley, H. (2011). A Minimalist Approach to Argument Structure. In C. Boeckx (ed.), *The Oxford Handbook of Linguistic Minimalism*. Oxford: Oxford University Press, pp. 427–448.

Herburger, E. (2001). The Negative Concord Puzzle Revisited. *Natural Language Semantics*, 9 (3), 289–333.

Hernanz, M. L. (1999). El infinitivo. In I. Bosque and V. Demonte (eds.), *Gramática descriptiva de la lengua española*, Vol. 3. Madrid: Espasa, pp. 2197–2356.

Huang, C.-T. J. (1982). Logical Relations in Chinese and the Theory of Grammar (Doctoral dissertation). MIT.

Jaeggli, O. (1986). Arbitrary Plural Nominals. *Natural Language and Linguistic Theory*, 4 (1), 43–76.

Jiménez-Fernández, Á. (2009). On the Composite Nature of Subject Islands: A Phase-Based Approach. *Sky Journal of Linguistics*, 22, 91–138.

Jiménez-Fernández, Á. (2015). Towards a Typology of Focus: Subject Position and Microvariation at the Discourse–Syntax Interface. *Ampersand: An International Journal of General and Applied Linguistics*, 2, 49–60.

Jurka, J. (2009). Gradient Acceptability and Subject Islands in German (Qualifying Paper). University of Maryland.

Kahnemuyipour, A. (2009). *The Syntax of Sentential Stress*. Oxford: Oxford University Press.

Kayne, R. S. (1981). Unambiguous Paths. In R. May and J. Koster (eds.), *Levels of Syntactic Representation*. Dordrecht: Foris, pp. 143–183.

Kayne, R. S. (2006). On Parameters and on Principles of Pronunciation. In H. Broekhuis, N. Corver, R. Huybregts, U. Kleinhenz, and J. Koster (eds.), *Organizing Grammar. Linguistic Studies in Honor of Henk van Riemsdijk*. Berlin: De Gruyter, pp. 289–299.

Kempchinsky, P. (2009). What Can the Subjunctive Disjoint Reference Effect Tell Us about the Subjunctive? *Lingua*, 119 (12), 1788–1810.

Kim, J.-H. (2006). *La teoría de pro y el sujeto pre / postverbal*. Madrid: Universidad Autónoma de Madrid.

Klima, E. (1964). Negation in English. In J. A. Fodor and J. J. Katz (eds.), *The Structure of Language. Readings in the Philosophy of Language*. Englewood Cliffs, NJ: Prentice Hall, pp. 246–323.

Koopman, H. and Sportiche, D. (1991). The Position of Subjects. *Lingua*, 85 (2–3), 211–258.

Kratzer, A. (1996). Severing the External Argument from its Verb. In J. Rooryck and L. Zaring (eds.), *Phrase Structure and the Lexicon*. Dordrecht: Kluwer, pp. 109–137.

Ladusaw, W. (1992). Expressing Negation. In C. Barker and D. Dowty (eds.), *Proceedings of SALT II*. Columbus, OH: Ohio State University, pp. 237–259.

Laka, I. (1990). Negation in Syntax: On the Nature of Functional Categories and Projections (Doctoral dissertation). MIT.

Larson, R. K. (1988). On the Double Object Construction. *Linguistic Inquiry*, 19 (3), 335–391.

Levin, B. (1983). On the Nature of Ergativity (Doctoral dissertation). MIT.

López, L. (2009). *A Derivational Syntax for Information Structure*. New York: Oxford University Press.

López, L. (2012). *Indefinite Objects. Scrambling, Choice Functions and Differential Marking*. Cambridge, MA: MIT Press.

Marantz, A. (1984). *On the Nature of Grammatical Relations*. Cambridge, MA: MIT Press.

Marantz, A. (1997). No Escape from Syntax: Don't Try Morphological Analysis in the Privacy of Your Own Lexicon. *Penn Working Papers in Linguistics*, 4 (2), 201–225.

Masullo, P. (1992). Incorporation and Case Theory in Spanish. A Cross-Linguistic Perspective (Doctoral dissertation). University of Washington.

Mateu, J. (2002). Argument Structure: Relational Construal at the Syntax–Semantics Interface (Doctoral dissertation). Universitat Autònoma de Barcelona.

Mateu, J. and Rigau, G. (2002). A Minimalist Account of Conflation Processes: Parametric Variation at the Lexicon–Syntax Interface. In A. Alexiadou (ed.), *Theoretical Approaches to Universals*. Amsterdam: John Benjamins, pp. 211–236.

Mendikoetxea, A. (1999). Construcciones inacusativas y pasivas. In I. Bosque and V. Demonte (eds.), *Gramática descriptiva de la lengua española*, Vol. 2. Madrid: Espasa, pp. 1575–1631.

Merchant, J. (2001). *The Syntax of Silence: Sluicing, Islands, and the Theory of Ellipsis*. Oxford: Oxford University Press.

Merchant, J. (2004). Fragments and Ellipsis. *Linguistics and Philosophy*, 27 (6), 661–738.

Nakao, C. (2009). Island Repair and Non-Repair by PF Strategies (Doctoral dissertation). University of Maryland.

Oehrle, R. (1976). The Grammatical Status of the English Dative Alternation (Doctoral dissertation). MIT.

Olarrea, A. (1996). Pre- and Postverbal Subject Positions in Spanish: A Minimalist Account (Doctoral dissertation). University of Washington, Seattle.

Ordóñez, F. (2000). *The Clausal Structure of Spanish: A Comparative Perspective*. New York: Garland.

Ormazábal, J. and Romero, J. (2010). The Derivation of Dative Alternations. In M. Duguine, S. Huidobro, and N. Madariaga (eds.), *Argument Structure and Syntactic Relations: A Cross-Linguistic Perspective*. Amsterdam: John Benjamins, pp. 203–232.

Ormazábal, J. and Romero, J. (2013). Object Clitics, Agreement and Dialectal Variation. *Probus*, 25 (2), 301–344.

Ortega-Santos, I. (2016). *On Focus-Related Operation at the Right Edge in Spanish: Subjects and Ellipsis*. Amsterdam and Philadelphia, PA: John Benjamins.

Ott, D. and Struckmeier, V. (2016). Deletion in Clausal Ellipsis: Remnants in the Middle Field. *Penn Working Papers in Linguistics*, 22 (1), 225–234.

Perlmutter, D. M. (1978). Impersonal Passives and the Unaccusative Hypothesis. In J. J. Jaeger, A. C. Woodbury, F. Ackerman, C. Chiarello, O. D. Gensler, J. Kingston, E. E. Sweetser, H. Thompson, and K. W. Whistler (eds.), *Proceedings of the 4th Annual Meeting of the Berkeley Linguistics Society*. Berkeley, CA: University of California Press, pp. 157–189.

Pesetsky, D. (1995). *Zero Syntax: Experiencers and Cascades*. Cambridge, MA: MIT Press.

Pineda, A. (2013). Romance Double Object Constructions and Transitivity Alternations. In E. Boone, M. Kohlberger, and M. Schulpen (eds.), *Proceedings of ConSOLE XX*. Leiden: Universiteit Leiden, pp. 185–211.

Pollock, J.-Y. (1989). Verb Movement, Universal Grammar, and the Structure of IP. *Linguistic Inquiry*, 20 (3), 365–424.

Rappaport Hovan, M. and Levin, B. (2008). The English Dative Alternation: The Case for Verb Sensitivity. *Journal of Linguistics*, 44 (1), 129–167.

Reinhart, T. and Siloni, T. (2005). The Lexicon–Syntax Parameter: Reflexivization and Other Arity Operations. *Linguistic Inquiry*, 36 (3), 389–436.

Richards, N. (2010). *Uttering Trees*. Cambridge, MA: MIT Press.

Rizzi, L. (1976). Ristrutturazione. *Rivista di Grammatica Generativa*, 1 (1), 1–54.

Rizzi, L. (1982). *Issues in Italian Syntax*. Dordrecht: Foris.

Rizzi, L. (1986). Null Objects in Italian and the Theory of Pro. *Linguistic Inquiry*, 17 (4), 501–557.

Rodríguez Mondoñedo, M. (2007). The Syntax of Objects: Agree and Differential Object Marking (Doctoral dissertation). University of Connecticut.

Romero, J. (1997). Construcciones de doble objeto y gramática universal (Doctoral dissertation). Universidad Autónoma de Madrid.

Saab, A. (2008). Hacia una teoría de la identidad parcial en la elipsis (Doctoral dissertation). Universidad de Buenos Aires.

Schäfer, F. (2009). The Causative Alternation. *Language and Linguistics Compass*, 3 (2), 641–681.

Snyder, W. (2000). An Experimental Investigation of Syntactic Satiation Effects. *Linguistic Inquiry*, 31 (4), 575–582.

Snyder, W. (2001). On the Nature of Syntactic Variation: Evidence from Complex Predicates and Complex Word Formation. *Language*, 77 (2), 324–342.

Sprouse, J. (2007). A Program for Experimental Syntax: Finding the Relationship between Acceptability and Grammatical Knowledge (Doctoral dissertation). University of Maryland.

Sprouse, J., Schütze, C., and Almeida, D. (2013). A Comparison of Informal and Formal Acceptability Judgments using a Random Sample from *Linguistic Inquiry* 2001–2010. *Lingua*, 134, 219–248.

Stepanov, A. (2001). Cyclic Domains in Syntactic Theory (Doctoral dissertation). University of Connecticut.

Suñer, M. (1995). Negative Elements, Island Effects and Resumptive *no*. *The Linguistic Review*, 12 (3), 233–373.

Torrego, E. (1989). Unergative Unaccusative Alternations. *MIT Working Papers in Linguistics*, 10, 253–272.

Torrego, E. (1998). *The Dependencies of Objects*. Cambridge, MA: MIT Press.

Travis, L. (1984). Parameters and Effects of Word Order Variation (Doctoral dissertation). MIT.

Tubau, S. (2008). Negative Concord in English and Romance: Syntax–Morphology Interface Conditions on the Expression of Negation (Doctoral dissertation). Universitat Autònoma de Barcelona.

Uriagereka, J. (1999). Multiple Spell-Out. In S. Epstein and N. Hornstein (eds.), *Working Minimalism*. Cambridge, MA: MIT Press, pp. 251–282.

Valmala, V. (2008). Topic, Focus and Quantifier Float. In X. Artiagoitia Beaskoetxea and J. Lakarra Andrinua (eds.), *Gramatika jaietan: Patxi Goenagaren omenez*. Bilbao: Universidad del País Vasco, pp. 837–857.

Wilinski-Hodel, M. (2007). Comportamiento semántico-pronominal de los verbos psicológicos que presentan la alternancia dativa/acusativa (MA Thesis). University of Georgia.

Yoshida, M., Nakao, C., and Ortega-Santos, I. (2014). Ellipsis. In A. Carnie, Y. Sato, and D. Siddiqi (eds.), *Routledge Handbook of Syntax*. London: Routledge, pp. 192–213.

Zanuttini, R. (1991). Syntactic Properties of Sentential Negation: A Comparative Study of Romance Languages (Doctoral dissertation). University of Pennsylvania.

Zubizarreta, M. L. (1998). *Prosody, Focus, and Word Order*. Cambridge, MA: MIT Press.

Zubizarreta, M. L. and Oh, E. (2007). *On the Syntactic Composition of Manner and Motion*. Cambridge, MA: MIT Press.

15

Properties of the Extended Verb Phrase: Agreement, the Structure of INFL, and Subjects

Julio Villa-García

15.1 Introduction

The Extended Verb Phrase (EVP) refers to those verb-related properties that go beyond the lexical features of verbs: the properties of functional categories above the VP. The following Spanish sentence illustrates major aspects of the EVP:

(15.1) El congreso no le puede haber dado más satisfacción.
 the symposium not CL can have given more satisfaction
 'S/he could not have found the symposium more rewarding.'

First, (15.1) involves a finite, conjugated verb in the indicative mood, *puede*, which is a modal verb. This verb has morphological endings that indicate the tense of the sentence (present) alongside the subject agreement features – person and number features of the subject, *el congreso*. *Puede* is followed by an aspectual auxiliary, *haber*, which marks (grammatical) perfective aspect. (*Haber* in turn is followed by a participle, *dado*, which is the main (i.e. lexical) verb of the sentence, followed by its direct object, *más satisfacción*.) Besides the modal, auxiliary, and main verbs, the (preverbal) subject *el congreso* is also featured in the sentence, along with the negative particle *no* and the third-person singular dative weak pronoun (or clitic) *le*, which precedes the finite verb and performs the indirect object function. In sum, (15.1) discloses several EVP-related pieces of information: the mood of the sentence (indicative), the subject and its agreement relationship with the finite verb in terms of person and number, a pronominal clitic, negation, modality, aspect, and tense. Some of these are manifested morphologically (e.g. mood, tense, person, and number) and some syntactically (e.g. modality, negation). Such EVP properties have attracted a great deal of attention in the history of grammar from different frameworks. In this chapter, I concentrate on the structure of inflection and subject–verb agreement (Section 15.2), as well as subjects in finite contexts in present-day Spanish (Section 15.3). The framework adopted here is Chomsky's generative paradigm.

15.2 Inflection and Approaches to Agreement in the Generative Tradition

Traditionally, verbs have been said to agree in person and number with subjects. In Spanish, subject-agreement features (or phi/φ features) include person and number. Spanish is said to display "rich" agreement and thus to license null subjects – grammatical subjects expressed through morphological suffixes on the verb root. Spanish also allows overt subjects, expressed as a phrase (usually a DP). The two types of subject are illustrated in (15.2), where the overt subject *los chicos* in the first sentence is third-person plural. The null subject is the subject of the second sentence and is also third-person plural, as indicated by the verbal form *estaban*.

(15.2)   Los   chicos   llegaron   a   las   siete.   Estaban   agotados.
         the   guys   arrived   to   the   seven   were   exhausted
         'The guys arrived at seven. They were exhausted.'

A brief historical overview of the development of agreement in the generative paradigm is important for understanding current versions of the theory (see D'Alessandro 2016). The reader should bear in mind that in what follows I do not discuss the morphological structure of Spanish verbal forms – for this topic, see Ambadiang (2016), Pérez Saldanya (2012), and RAE and ASALE (2009:49–93).

15.2.1 Inflection and Agreement in Chomsky's Generative Grammar

The topic of syntactic agreement became prominent in research within Generative Grammar in the Government and Binding/Principles and Parameters (GB/P&P) framework (Chomsky 1981) (on the topic of generative grammar more generally, see also Chapter 1, this volume). For Chomsky (1981), INFL(ection) heralds the sentential projection IP (inflectional phrase), which is the abstract phrase that houses such operations as tense and the agreement relation. The values of INFL could be [±Tense], depending on the (non-)finiteness of the sentence. A finite INFL has "the features person, gender and number; call this complex AGR ('agreement')" (Chomsky 1981:52). Since this point, the issue of agreement has been intimately associated with Case in the syntactic literature, with AGR being the governing element assigning Case in INFL (i.e. on this view, if INFL contains AGR then it governs the subject, thus assigning nominative Case to it via the feature [+INFL]). In the wake of this discussion, "subjects

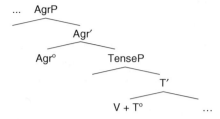

Figure 15.1 V-to-T movement

are nominative when they agree with the matrix verb – technically, with its inflection" (Chomsky 1981:52). Under this analysis, syntactic Case is a structural notion. For instance, nominative Case is associated with the specifier position of INFL (i.e. Spec,INFL), which in turn is linked to the traditional subject function. Note the important role of Spec-Head (i.e. [$_{XP}$ [$_X$]]) agreement relationships under this approach. The theory of empty categories developed within the GB/P&P framework was also crucial for the postulation of the null category *pro*, the non-overt subject of finite sentences in Spanish-style null (or pro-drop) languages. On this view, *pro* is a non-overt element in Spec,INFL, with which AGR agrees.

Pollock (1989) made a proposal to revise the claim that AGR is located in INFL. He contends that INFL is split into two major categories: Tense and Agr(eement). This structural division is partly motivated by the claim that inflected verbs are formed through head movement to collect affixes along the way, in an order primarily determined by the hierarchy of functional projections (cf. Baker's 1985 Mirror Principle). In relation to Spanish, a widely-accepted instantiation of this proposal is that Agr (the host of preverbal subjects under some accounts) dominates Tense, the landing site of verbs, which are standardly assumed to move up to the inflectional domain in the language (i.e. V-to-T (verb-to-tense) movement, as shown schematically in Figure 15.1; the actual height of the verb within INFL remains a controversial issue in the field). As suggested by the order Subject + Negation + (CL+) V (cf. (15.1)), negation can optionally occur in between Agr and Tense in NegP/ΣP (negation/sigma phrase) (Laka 1990; Chapter 14, this volume, among others). An empirical motivation for the claim that AgrP (agreement phrase) is higher than TP (tense phrase) is that agreement morphemes (e.g. *disfrutábamos*) are external with respect to tense morphemes (e.g. *disfrutábamos*) (Bosque and Gutiérrez-Rexach 2009:228).

15.2.2 INFL and Agreement in the Minimalist Program

With the advent of the Minimalist Program for Linguistic Theory (Chomsky 1995 *et seq.*), a geometry of the inflectional domain along the lines of Figure 15.1 was inherited, with specialized AgrSP (agreement subject phrase) and TP projections.

Features

A crucial aspect of the Minimalist Program is the prominent role attributed to *features*, which represent fine-grained grammatical information such as [person], [tense], and [Case]. Since Minimalism puts a premium on economy of derivations and representations, movement operations must be justified: all movement is determined by features. The system distinguishes three types of features: phonetic, semantic, and formal (grammatical/syntactic) (Chomsky 1965; López 2007; among others). The latter type is crucial for driving movement in syntax under early Minimalist approaches. A further distinction within the category of formal features is that of interpretable and uninterpretable features:

1 **Interpretable features**: The inherent features of a nominal (e.g. [person], [number], and [gender]) are interpretable at the LF (Logical Form) component.
2 **Uninterpretable features**: Morphosyntactic features (e.g. the [person] and [number] features of AgrS°) must be checked off against interpretable features before reaching Spell-Out (i.e. the point at which the derivation is handed over to the PF (Phonological Form) and LF components).

According to early versions of Minimalism (Chomsky 1995: Ch. 3), uninterpretable features must be deleted before Spell-Out, in accordance with the *Principle of Full Interpretation* (PFI), which states that every element of LF and PF must receive an appropriate interpretation; thus, unless uninterpretable features are dealt with before the derivation reaches the interfaces, the derivation is said to be non-convergent. This version of Minimalism assumes a strongly lexicalist approach to morphology: lexical items enter the derivation fully inflected; morphemes do not undergo movement or become incorporated in the syntax.

Features as the Locus of Parametric Variation: Verb-to-Tense Movement and the Extended Projection Principle

In the GB/P&P approach, syntactic differences between languages were attributed to differences in the setting of the values of a parameter (e.g. the *Null Subject Parameter*; see Section 15.3.1). An advantage of the feature system is that features constitute the locus of parametric variation, i.e. cross-linguistic variation is restricted to the features of functional heads (cf. *Borer-Chomsky conjecture*; "lexical parameters"). In early Minimalism, uninterpretable features may be *strong features*, which are visible at PF and thus trigger overt movement, or *weak features*, which are invisible at PF and thus trigger non-overt/covert (i.e. LF-only) movement (Bosque and Gutiérrez-Rexach 2009:230–233). The empirical advantages of the strong–weak features distinction include capturing cross-linguistic variation in V-to-I/T (verb-to-inflection/tense) movement as well as the requirement to have a lexical subject in preverbal position – operative in languages like English, but not in Spanish. Consider first the contrast in (15.3).

(15.3)   a. *Linguists read fast those books (cf. Linguists read those books fast)
      b. Los lingüistas leen rápido esos libros
         the linguists read fast those books

In English (cf. (15.3a)), the adverb cannot intervene between the verb and the direct object. This is not the case in Spanish, where that order is perfectly grammatical (see (15.3b)). Since the work of Emonds (1978) and Pollock (1989), the contrast in (15.3) has been taken to indicate that in languages like Spanish, the verb moves past the adverb to a position in the inflectional domain, whereas in English, the lexical verb stays lower. Under the strong–weak features approach, this parametric difference is understood thus: in Spanish, the features of T° are strong, which correlates under some accounts with the "rich" verbal morphology found in Spanish (see Koeneman and Zeijlstra 2014 for discussion of the controversial *Rich Agreement Hypothesis* and arguments for its rehabilitation universally). Thus, strong features cause the verb to move to T° overtly before Spell-Out. In English, on the other hand, due to the impoverished inflectional morphology exhibited by the verb, Tense features are weak, thus causing the verb to move only covertly after Spell-Out, with the result that the overt verb is pronounced in a lower position than in Spanish. Therefore, the strong–weak distinction offered an explanation for this well-known difference between languages such as English and Spanish (though see Camacho and Sánchez 2014 for a recent refinement, Bosque and Gutiérrez-Rexach 2009:233 for discussion of issues arising, and Richards 2016 for much relevant general discussion on what triggers movement in syntax).

The strong–weak feature dichotomy also accounted for a long-noted contrast between English and Spanish. Whereas in English an overt subject must occur preverbally in all clauses, as in (15.4) (with well-documented exceptions such as imperative and diary-drop sentences), word order in Spanish is much freer and subjects may occur postverbally (cf. (15.5b)).

(15.4)   a. My sister has arrived
      b. *Has arrived my sister

(15.5)   a. Mi hermana ha llegado
         my sister has arrived
      b. Ha llegado mi hermana
         has arrived my sister

As noted, the canonical subject position in the generative tradition is Spec,INFL-IP/TenseP (or Spec,AgrSP, assuming the split of INFL). In English, the subject is standardly assumed to occupy this position. Under the early Minimalist approach sketched above, the [person] feature of Tense is strong in this language, consequently requiring overt movement of the subject to the specifier of Tense. However, in Spanish this feature need not be strong, thus allowing the subject to stay in a lower position overtly (cf. (15.5b)).

Operation of Agree

In early late Minimalism (Chomsky 2000, 2001), just as the link between movement and agreement (i.e. Spec-Head configurations) is at least partly abandoned, so is the strength metaphor. The operation of Agree, which Chomsky (2000) defines as the erasure or deletion of the uninterpretable features carried by the probe and the goal, allows for agreement at a distance. This move leads Chomsky (2000) to go beyond the traditional Extended Projection Principle (EPP) – which can informally be defined as the principle ensuring that all sentences have a subject – to postulate phi features alongside [EPP], the feature version of the EPP. More technically, assuming the VP-Internal Subject Hypothesis, which proposes that the subject originates within the VP, the EPP is needed to force movement of the subject to its preverbal position – Spec,TP. For example in the English sentence *Peter arrived at the stadium*, the subject *Peter* starts within the VP and is moved to Spec,TP by the EPP.

Under the Agree system of Chomsky (2000, 2001, 2004, 2008), T° has a set of uninterpretable agreement phi features, which are unvalued.[1] The operation of Agree "establishes a relation (agreement, Case checking) between an LI [lexical item] α and a feature F" (Chomsky 2000:101). These are morphosyntactic features which are not interpretable at LF. Chomsky has also suggested that these features are often not realized visibly at PF, in apparent violation of the aforementioned *Principle of Full Interpretation* (PFI), which posits that the faculty of language operates only with features that are amenable to interpretation at the interfaces (Chomsky 2000). Uninterpretable features (associated with inflectional morphology) must then be deleted in the course of the derivation. On this view, an active probe (i.e. one that contains an uninterpretable feature, e.g. T°) can agree with an active goal (i.e. one comprising an uninterpretable feature, e.g. a noun, whose uninterpretable feature is Case) provided that both probe and goal are *related*, which requires that a *matching* condition be met, with matching being understood as feature identity (Chomsky 2001:4). As Chomsky (2000:39) emphasizes, feature identity should be understood as the choice of features, not the actual value of the feature. Thus, an interpretable feature [3Person] is identical to an uninterpretable/unvalued feature [uPerson]. On the basis of Chomsky's (2000) discussion of interpretable and uninterpretable features of verbs and nouns, the following conclusions can be drawn:

---

[1] In this version of the theory, a conflated TP (missing the AgrSP projection) returns, with TP encoding the relevant tense and agreement features (Bosque and Gutiérrez-Rexach 2009:240; see also Chomsky 1995: Ch. 4). For languages like Spanish, however, the tendency is to assume that both projections are projected (see, e.g., Cardinaletti 2004).

1. Agreement (phi-) features of nominals are interpretable at LF
2. Agreement (phi-) features of verbs are uninterpretable at LF
3. Inherent Case features of nominals are interpretable at LF
4. Structural Case features of nominals are uninterpretable at LF

In this paper I do not explore the issue of Case in any systematic fashion, the focus being on phi features, although both agreement and Case are closely related in the Agree framework. To illustrate the operation of Agree, consider the sentence in (15.6).

(15.6) El   sol   se   pone
        the   sun   CL   sets.3SG
        'The sun sets.'

In this example, when T° – the probe – enters the derivation (i.e. when it is merged), it carries the uninterpretable phi features [uPerson] and [uNumber], making it active for searching and agreeing with a goal. The nominal *el sol*, for its part, contains an unvalued structural Case feature [uCase] (or [uK]), making it active (i.e. searchable by a probe), alongside two interpretable features: [3Person] and [SgNumber].[2] Because the features of the goal match the pertinent features of the probe T°, *el sol* is an appropriate goal. The operation Agree *values* the uninterpretable features of both probe and goal and *deletes* them. One innovation of the Agree system is the concept of feature valuation. For Chomsky, uninterpretable features are unvalued, and they get valued by means of Agree. Uninterpretable features are not just checked, as in previous versions of the theory; they need to acquire a value. This is accompanied by the assumption that such features are then deleted. Thus, Agree for the pair (*el sol*, T°) is represented schematically in (15.7).

(15.7) Agree (el sol,   T°)   = (el sol,   T°)
               [SgNumber]   [uNumber]   [SgNumber]   [SgNumber]
               [3Person]   [uPerson]   [3Person]   [3Person]
               [uCase]   [NomCase]   [NomCase]   [NomCase]

The Agree system exemplified in (15.7) is fully compatible with postverbal subjects (cf. (15.5b)) in languages like Spanish, since this operation does not require a Spec-Head configuration (i.e. the probe searches for a suitable goal that is structurally lower). By way of illustration, in a sentence like (15.8), an agreement relationship is established between the elements T° and *el sol* (i.e. T°, *el sol*), much as in (15.7).

(15.8) Se   pone   el   sol
        CL   sets.3SG   the   sun
        'The sun sets.'

I discuss the non-trivial issue of the EPP in Spanish and the directionality of agreement below.

---

[2] There have been arguments that nominative case is actually not uninterpretable, which challenges the view outlined here. There have also been proposals that nominative case in languages such as Spanish is the default case and is therefore not assigned by INFL/Tense (see Bošković 2007 and the references cited therein).

Recent Developments and Issues for the Agree System
As suggested by the discussion in the preceding sections, the theory of agreement has been the subject of intensive research for several decades. Different versions of the theory proposed to date have been subject to modification, both on empirical (see the following section) and theoretical grounds. A number of questions have been raised, including the suitability of the EPP and whether movement has to be driven by a feature of the moving element, rather than a feature of the target (Bošković 2007 and references therein). The issue of the locality of Agree has also been a point of contention: is Agree impervious to phases? (Bobaljik and Wurmbrand 2005, Bošković 2007). Another question is whether elements that are potential goals can intervene between a probe and a goal (which can be accounted for through Relativized Minimality, as in Rizzi 1990, or through Defective Intervention, as proposed by Chomsky 2000, 2001). Similarly, the link between uninterpretability and valuation has been subject to scrutiny (Pesetsky and Torrego 2001 *et seq.*). The directionality of agreement has also been a matter of controversy, with authors such as Chomsky (2000, 2001) claiming that agreement occurs downwards (probe > goal) and others arguing for upwards agreement (goal > probe) (Zeijlstra 2012) or both (Béjar and Rezac 2009). Research on agreement has also posed the question of what happens when matching failures occur: a crash, finding an alternative (Béjar and Rezac 2009), or fail and carry on (Preminger 2014)? Other questions include whether probes can simultaneously have more than one goal (Hiraiwa 2001, among others). Specifically with regard to null-subject languages like Spanish, Barbosa (2009), drawing on Holmberg (2005), has advocated the hypothesis that the agreement features of $T°$ in Spanish are interpretable (dispensing with the need to postulate the existence of *pro*) (see Section 15.3 for the syntax of subjects).

Non-Canonical Agreement in Spanish

In addition to sentences like (15.6) and (15.8), which exhibit canonical agreement, Spanish – like many of the world's languages – presents some interesting puzzles for theories of agreement. For reasons of space, the list of cases of non-canonically agreeing nominals presented below is by no means exhaustive; instead, I concentrate on some of the most significant discussions here (see Martínez 1999 and RAE and ASALE 2009: 646–652 for data manifesting various agreement patterns in Spanish). For instance, Spanish exhibits discordant subjects (Olarrea 1996; Ordóñez 1997; Saab 2007; Torrego 2014; Torrego and Laka 2015; Villa-García 2010; among others), as in (15.9). Villa-García (2010: fn.2) entertains Corbett's (2006) claim that the DP *los lingüistas* need not be third person. This intuition has been implemented syntactically by Sauerland (2004), who assumes that the DP has a Phi Phrase (PhiP) layer on top of it, responsible for agreeing with $T°$. For Torrego (2014) and Torrego and Laka

(2015), the DP *los lingüistas* is linked to a null subject pronoun with its own, potentially different, set of phi features (see also Saab 2007). According to Torrego (2014) and Villa-García (2010), only null-subject languages license examples such as (15.9).

(15.9)　Los　lingüistas　disfrutan　/disfrutamos/　disfrutáis　con　una　coma
　　　　 the　 linguists　 enjoy.3PL　enjoy.1PL　 enjoy.2PL　with　a　 comma
　　　　 'We/you/Ø linguists enjoy a comma.'

Moreover, in certain dialects of Spanish, such as Argentine Spanish, examples of what have been referred to as comitative agreement constructions can be found, as shown in (15.10). Such configurations involve two participants (akin to coordination cases), although one of them is preceded by the preposition *con* 'with.' However, the verb displays first-person plural agreement. For the properties and current analyses of this construction in Spanish, see Camacho (2000) and Mare (2012).

(15.10)　Vamos　　a　　ir　　con　　Marina　　al　　　　cine
　　　　　go.1PL　　to　　go　　with　　Marina　　to+the　movies
　　　　　'Marina and I are going to the movies.'
　　　　　(cf. standard interpretation: 'We are going to the movies with Marina.')

Furthermore, in Latin American Spanish (and in varieties of Spanish that are in contact with certain Catalan dialects), existential constructions exhibit singular/plural agreement, along the lines of English, as shown by the alternation in (15.11a) and (15.11b). This contrasts with the existential configuration that we find in most Peninsular varieties of Spanish, where the existential verb *haber* is invariably third-person singular regardless of the number of the nominal, as in (15.11c) (see Rodríguez-Mondoñedo 2007 for further exemplification and an Agree-based analysis).

(15.11)　a.　Hubo　　　una　　tormenta
　　　　　　　there-was　a　　　storm
　　　　　　　'There was a storm.'
　　　　　b.　Hubieron　　varias　　tormentas
　　　　　　　there-were　various　storms
　　　　　　　'There were several storms.'
　　　　　c.　Hubo　　　una/varias　tormenta(s)
　　　　　　　there-was　one/several　storm(s)

Finally, as noted by López (2009), interpretable features are assumed in the Agree system to translate directly into the semantics (i.e. LF), but this assumption does not hold for all lexical items, as shown by (15.12). Although the word *gente* 'people' in Spanish is syntactically singular, it is semantically plural (López 2007:81–85). The second clause of (15.12), which features a null subject, contains a verb in the plural, and the referent of *pro* is *mucha gente*, from the previous sentence. In other words, in discourse, López (2009:15) argues, "a pronoun that refers back to *gente* will show up in plural form."

(15.12) Llegó   mucha   gente   al   hotel; *pro* estaban   agotados
        arrived.3SG much people to+the hotel   were.3PL   exhausted.3PL
        'Many people arrived at the hotel; they were exhausted.'

In the following section, I turn to the discussion of the syntax of subjects in Spanish beyond agreement.

15.3 Subjects in Spanish

Our illustrative derivation in (15.7) deliberately leaves out the EPP, since its status in languages like Spanish is far from clear. A long-standing question in the syntax of Spanish is actually whether the EPP (be it a principle or a feature, as in the system outlined in Section 15.2) is active in Spanish. Ortega-Santos (2016) and Ortega-Santos and Villa-García (in preparation) provide relevant discussion. The reader is referred to Bošković (2007) and references therein for the desideratum that the EPP be eliminated from the theory of grammar, given its stipulative nature. In recent work, Richards (2016) advocates a novel account of why Spanish does not display English-like EPP effects. According to his proposal, the Spanish T (tense) affix is reliably preceded by a metrical boundary, as in *cantábamos* 'we sang,' which confirms Oltra-Massuet's (1999, 2000) generalization that stress typically appears on the vowel that precedes the Tense morpheme in Spanish-style languages. Consequently, this avoids movement operations (of elements such as pronouns or expletives) driven by the need to support the T affix, as would be the case in English. Ojea (2017) provides an alternative view of EPP-satisfaction (and word order) in Spanish-type languages that is based on discourse considerations.

As is well known, Spanish subjects may appear in different sentence positions, as shown by the postverbal subject in (15.5b) above. Thus, the question arises as to whether preverbal subjects (cf. (15.5a)/(15.6)) are derived via movement to Spec,TP/Spec,AgrSP, and, if so, whether this movement is EPP-driven, or whether they occur preverbally for other reasons (e.g. topicality) (see Ordóñez 2016). The analysis of the syntactic derivation of null subjects and postverbal subjects is also an active area of research. For these reasons, the account of subjects in paradigmatic null-subject languages like Spanish has spawned much discussion in a vast body of research that spans several decades. This has been particularly so since the beginning of the GB/P&P framework in the early 1980s, and at present remains the object of continuous inquiry.

As has been discussed, Romance languages including Spanish display tacitly implied, null (i.e. phonologically unrealized) subjects in finite clauses (cf. (15.13a, b)). It has been claimed that this property correlates with the availability of preverbal (SV) and postverbal (VS) subjects (Chomsky 1981, among others), illustrated in (15.13c) and (15.13d), respectively.[3] It has been argued that another attending characteristic of null-subject languages is the property of obligatorily null expletives (pro_{expl}), as in (15.13b).

The *Null Subject Parameter* (NSP) (or *Pro-drop Parameter*) was postulated in order to account for the clustering of these syntactic properties. Languages like English are said to be non-pro-drop and languages like Spanish are pro-drop (Barbosa 2009; Chomsky 1981; Rizzi 1982; among others). The reader is referred to Camacho (2013), however, for the view that the link between the properties typically associated with the NSP is not as direct as has traditionally been assumed.

(15.13)   a. Ø   Te   ha   llamado   [Null subject]
               CL   has   called
          'S/he has called you.'
       b. Ø   Está   nevando   [Null "dummy" or expletive]
               is   snowing
          'It's snowing.'
       c. *Luis*   te   ha   llamado   [Preverbal subject]
             Luis   CL   has   called
          'Luis has called you.'
       d. Te   ha   llamado   *Luis*   [Postverbal subject]
           CL   has   called   Luis
          'Luis has called you.'

I discuss below major properties of the three types of subjects found in Spanish: null and overt subjects, with the latter type including preverbal and postverbal subjects.

15.3.1 Null Subjects

Null subjects in Spanish occur in contexts where they are mandatory, such as with atmospheric predicates (cf. (15.13b)), or when the referent of the subject is clear from the preceding discourse, as in (15.14). This example contains a null subject in the second sentence. Here, the subject is associated with third-person singular agreement, is salient, and carries the [–topic shift] pragmatic feature (i.e. it is a case of topic continuity); hence, a null subject (Ø/*pro*) is favored.

(15.14)   Hugo   y   yo   estuvimos   en   Temia.   ¡Ø   Nos   impresionó!
           Hugo   and   I   were   in   Temia.   CL   impressed.3SG
           'Hugo and I were in Temia. It impressed us!'

Subject pronouns in English-type non-null-subject languages perform the grammatical function of representing overt person and number markers. The morphological endings of the verb in pro-drop languages like Spanish seem to perform this function instead. Thus, overt pronominals in [+NSP]

---

[3] Caribbean dialects of Spanish display a higher rate of overt preverbal subjects, suggesting a change in their pro-drop status, an issue which I will not discuss here (see, among many others, Ticio 2004).

languages like Spanish are restricted to focal (i.e. emphatic and contrastive) contexts and to cases where they are needed to identify the referent. It is in this way that overt pronouns in languages like Spanish are not truly optional; they serve a discursive function (see also Chapter 13, this volume).

The syntactic analysis of covert pronominal subjects in null-subject languages has been a major topic of inquiry in the Romance literature for more than three decades. Pioneering work in GB/P&P (Rizzi 1982) underscored the need for the null category *pro* to be both licensed (i.e. legitimized in the structure) and identified (i.e. the referent of *pro* should be determined on the basis of both the discourse context and the person and number agreement markers).

According to Contreras (1991), the subject *pro* occupies Spec,INFL (i.e. Spec,AgrSP/TP) and is, by hypothesis, a preverbal element. One of the questions raised in the literature has been whether *pro* is always present in Spec,INFL/TP, independently of whether the subject is null, postverbal, or preverbal. (Preverbal subjects may occupy a left-peripheral position, under several accounts.) Proposals to dispense with *pro* have been made. On the one hand, authors including Alexiadou and Anagnostopoulou (1998), Ordóñez and Treviño (1999), Taraldsen (1993), and Ticio (2004), among others, have proposed eliminating *pro* altogether by claiming that "rich" subject–verb agreement morphology licenses null subjects and receives Case (and a thematic role, under some accounts). On the other hand, Barbosa (2013), Saab (2009), and Tomioka (2003) have claimed that null subjects in Spanish are subjects under ellipsis – a view that is at least partly challenged by the distinct behavior of non-overt subjects in comparison with their overt counterparts. The reader is referred to Bosque and Gutiérrez-Rexach (2009:344–359), Camacho (2013), and Sheehan (2016) for recent overviews of the existing debates.

15.3.2 Overt Subjects

In addition to null subjects, much controversy has centered on the analysis of (overt) preverbal (cf. (15.13c)) and postverbal (cf. (15.13d)) subjects. In what follows I present the main analyses of overt subjects and the major variants derived from these; the reader is referred to the works cited for arguments in favor of each position.

Preverbal Subjects

The contexts where subjects occur preverbally in Spanish include sentences featuring transitive verbs in neutral, out-of-the-blue contexts with the SVO word order, topic-shift and topic-continuity environments (although the latter tend to favor null subjects, as noted above), and categorical statements in which something is predicated of the subject. Two major approaches have been developed for the analysis of preverbal subjects: the traditional IP/TP-EPP (inflectional phrase, tense phrase-extended projection principle)

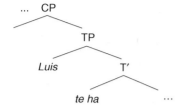

Figure 15.2 Subjects in Spec,AgrSP/TP

account and the CP (complementizer phrase) account. The TP-EPP analysis assumes that overt preverbal subjects in Spanish occupy Spec,AgrSP/TP, in much the same way as subjects in English (cf. Figure 15.2).

This analysis was pioneered by Rizzi (1982) and developed in the work of Cardinaletti (1996), Hill (1991), and Torrego (1984). Recent proponents of this analysis for the Spanish case include Burga (2008), Goodall (2001), Gupton (2014), Ortega-Santos (2006a *et seq.*), and Suñer (2003). Based on the Split-INFL Hypothesis, different TP-related preverbal subject positions have been identified, including Spec,AgrSP and Spec,TP (see, *mutatis mutandis*, Cardinaletti 2004 and Zubizarreta 1999).[4] This approach claims that the syntax of overt subjects in Spanish has much in common with the syntax of subjects in English, although preverbal subjects co-exist with null and postverbal subjects in Spanish. A piece of evidence that has repeatedly been adduced in favor of this proposal is that a *"what-happened"* question tends to be answered with an SVO structure, as in (15.15).

(15.15) A: ¿Qué ha pasado?
          what has happened
          'What happened?'
       B: *Juanito* ha encontrado pareja.
          Juanito has found partner
          'Juanito has found a partner.'

In contrast to the TP proposal, the CP account of preverbal subjects in Spanish argues that overt preverbal subjects are discourse-sensitive Ā-constituents ("A-bar," i.e. constituents in positions other than those reserved for arguments or agreeing/binding elements, such as the landing site of *wh*-movement). On this view, the appearance and distribution of subjects is regulated by discourse notions such as topic and focus (see also Chapter 17, this volume). Under this approach, preverbal subjects are instances of topics or Clitic-Left Dislocated (CLLDed) phrases in a specifier in the CP field (cf. Figure 15.3); assuming Rizzi's (1997) split-CP analysis, such subjects would occupy Spec,TopicP.[5]

---

[4] Ordóñez (2005) argues that Spec,AgrSP is the position reserved for preverbal subjects, with Spec,TP being a position for postverbal subjects with the VSO word order; in this case, the verb would move to AgrS°.

[5] The accounts cited in the text differ from each other as to the precise left-peripheral position occupied by the preverbal subject and its nature (e.g. specifier or adjunct).

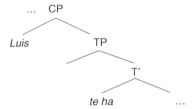

Figure 15.3 Subjects in Spec,CP

This analysis has gained favor since the 1990s and has been adopted by authors including Alexiadou and Anagnostopoulou (1998), Barbosa (2009), Contreras (1991), Holmberg (2005), Olarrea (1996), Ordóñez (1997), Ordóñez and Treviño (1999), and Ticio (2004). This approach typically assumes that Spanish lacks the EPP, or that in Spanish the EPP can be satisfied in an alternative way (e.g. via head movement of the verb and its "rich" agreement morphemes to T°, as argued by Alexiadou and Anagnostopoulou 1998; see Section 15.3.1 for discussion of recent proposals). Under this account, lexical subjects in Spanish do not have to be in Spec,TP, since this position might not be projected, or it might alternatively be occupied by the empty category *pro* (see Section 15.3.1). The aforementioned works develop various lines of argumentation for this position. I provide one piece of evidence here. It is uncontroversial that Spanish subjects may appear in CP-related positions, as shown by the sentences in (15.16). These indicate that overt subjects in Spanish are able to be left-dislocated (López 2009, Villa-García 2015, among others).

(15.16) a. *Susana*, ¿qué compró?
Susana what bought
'As for Susana, what did she buy?'

b. Ya le dije que *yo*, que no voy
already CL said that I that not go
'I have already told him/her/you that I am not going.'
Source: Villa-García (2015:28)

c. A la fiesta, *la niña*, con tu prima no quiere ir
to the party the girl with your cousin not wants go
'The girl doesn't feel like going to the party with your cousin.'

Several authors have pursued accounts alternative to the TP and CP analyses. Authors such as Barbosa (2001), Jiménez-Fernández and Miyagawa (2014), Masullo (1992), and Zubizarreta (1998, 1999) have suggested that Spec,TP in languages like Spanish has Ā-properties and can host Ā-moved elements such as topics and *wh*-items (see Gallego 2007 for discussion). According to Barbosa (2001), this move accounts for the impossibility of subjects' intervening between *wh*-items and verbs in constituent questions: The *wh*-item and the subject would compete for the preverbal slot (i.e. Spec,TP), forcing the subject to stay low, as in (15.17). This would in principle account for their incompatibility in *wh*-questions. This line of analysis remains the object of research (see, e.g., Villa-García 2015: Ch. 3).

(15.17) ¿Cuándo llegan las rebajas?
when arrive the sales
'When do the sales start?'

Within the Spec,TP-as-an-Ā-position approach to preverbal subjects, while some proposals explicitly allow Spec,TP to be occupied by non-subjects such as topics, others argue that Spec,TP is an Ā position that is still reserved for subjects (e.g. Uribe-Etxebarria 1991; for further details, see Villa-García 2015: Ch. 3).

An additional analysis is pursued by authors such as Camacho (2006, 2013), Casielles (2001), López (2009), Richards (2016), and Villa-García (2015), who have argued that preverbal subjects in Spanish may occupy a position in the CP domain or the TP domain, as shown in (15.18). In other words, preverbal subjects in Spanish may be CP- or TP-related elements.

(15.18) a. [CP Subject [C' [TP [T ...]]]]
 b. [CP [C' [TP Subject [T ...]]]]

An argument for this position comes from Casielles (2001) (see also Zubizarreta 1998). As shown by (15.19a), bare nominals are disallowed in Spec,TP – possibly due to a condition to the effect that a nominal in this position must be a full DP in Spanish (cf. (15.19b)). This is a noteworthy – yet poorly understood – contrast with English, where the sentence *Kids were playing on the beach* is grammatical, as shown by the English paraphrase of (15.19a) (see Ojea 2017 for discussion). Nevertheless, preverbal bare NPs are possible as subjects in Spanish provided that they are *bona fide* left dislocated, as in (15.19c), which is a hanging topic construction. The contrast in (15.19) supports the claim that preverbal subjects in Spanish can occupy different preverbal positions – Spec,TP and Spec,CP/TopicP.

(15.19) a. *Niños jugaban en la playa
 kids played in the beach
 'Kids were playing on the beach.'
 b. Los niños jugaban en la playa
 the kids played in the beach
 'The kids were playing on the beach.'
 c. Niños, no creo que jueguen muchos en la playa
 kids not believe that play many in the beach
 'As for children, I don't believe many play on the beach.'

Postverbal Subjects

In parallel fashion to the analysis of preverbal subjects in Spanish, that of postverbal subjects has been rigorously debated. Villa-García and Suárez Palma (2016) provide the following data, which exemplify the major contexts in which postverbal subjects are used in Spanish (see also Ojea 2017 and Ordóñez 2016). These include new-information focus/contrastively focused subjects (Ortega-Santos 2016), as in (15.20a), subjects of unaccusatives, as in (15.20b), subjects of psychological predicates, as in (15.20c), subjects in locative-inversion environments, as in (15.20d), subjects in thetic contexts expressing mere events, as in (15.20e) (as opposed to their categorical counterparts, in which case the subject would be preverbal), subjects that function as sentences, as in (15.20f), subjects in obligatory subject–verb inversion patterns with *wh*-questions, as in (15.20g), and subjects in stylistic-inversion contexts featuring direct quotations, as in (15.20h).

(15.20) a. ¿*Quién*   compró   la   carne?   Me   preguntó   quién   había
          who   bought   the meat   CL   asked   who   had

          comprado   la   carne   y   le   dije   que   la
          bought   the meat   and CL   said   that   CL

          había   comprado   *Juan*
          had   bought   Juan
          'Who bought the meat? S/he asked me who had bought the meat and I told him/her/you that Juan had bought it.'
      b. Llegó   un   *hombre*
         arrived a   man
         'A man got (here).'
      c. Me   gusta   *Ottawa*
         CL   pleases Ottawa
         'I like Ottawa.'
      d. Aquí   anidan   *gavilanes*
         here   nest   sparrowhawks
         'Sparrowhawks nest here.'
      e. Ha   muerto   *Franco*
         has   died   Franco
         'Franco has died.'
      f. Es   bueno   que   se   estudie   *sintaxis*
         is   good   that   CL   studies   syntax
         'It's good that syntax is studied.'
      g. ¿Qué   compró   *Susana*?
         what   bought   Susana
         'What did Susana buy?'
      h. "Nunca   saldremos   de   la   crisis,"   aseguró   *el   presidente*
         never   exit   of   the crisis   assured   the president
         '"Never will we get out of the economic crisis," warned the president.'

Given the diversity of constructions which allow postverbal subjects, it is not surprising that there are multiple analyses of postverbal subjects in the literature (see Ortega-Santos, 2016:84–85, for a detailed discussion of existing accounts).[6] According to several analyses, postverbal subjects are

---

[6] For instance, the postverbal subject of a transitive verb behaves differently from the postverbal subject of an unaccusative verb, whose syntactic behavior mirrors that of the object of a transitive verb (Ordóñez 2016:102–103).

in-situ elements in their base position (e.g. for transitives, Spec,*v*P), with the remaining material moved past the subject (Etxepare and Uribe-Etxebarria 2008; López 2009; Ordóñez 2000; Zubizarreta 1998; among others). For other authors, including Parafita Couto (2005), Torrego (1984), and Zubizarreta (1999), postverbal subjects sit in a rightward specifier/adjunct position. Another strand of research contends that both the postverbal subject and the remaining sentence material undergo complex operations. For instance, the subject may move to a VP or CP focus position, while the rest of the clause rises to a Topic-like position in the periphery (Belletti 1999; Etxepare and Uribe-Etxebarria 2008; Ordóñez 2000; and Ortega-Santos 2016; among others). Alternatively, the subject may actually move to Spec,TP, but assuming the Copy Theory of Movement of Chomsky (1995), a copy is pronounced in a lower position due to PF considerations, such as the generalization that focus in Spanish comes last in the sentence (viz. Sentence Stress Assignment conditions), as argued by Ortega-Santos (2006b), Stjepanović (1999), and Villa-García (2015: Ch. 5). For discussion of the VSO word order found in Spanish, see Ordóñez (2005) and Zubizarreta (1999).

15.4 Conclusion

The EVP, also known as the inflectional domain, can be characterized as a multifaceted workspace where many of the logistic operations underlying a sentence are assumed to occur. This paper has explored the basic structure of INFL/TP in Spanish, with a (historical) focus on existing theories of subject–verb agreement within Chomsky's generative paradigm, as well as V-to-T movement and the lack of English-style EPP effects in Spanish. I then discussed the much-debated analysis of the syntactic derivation of subjects in Spanish. I provided an overview of the contrasting approaches to this issue, which have sought to analyze null, preverbal, and postverbal subjects, whose distribution is contingent on factors that go beyond purely grammatical considerations. These areas constitute central topics in the field of Spanish syntax, and will assuredly remain the topic of intensive research for years to come.

References

Alexiadou, A. and Anagnostopoulou, E. (1998). Parameterizing AGR: Word Order, V-Movement and EPP Checking. *Natural Language and Linguistic Theory*, 16 (3), 491–539.

Ambadiang, T. (2016). Flexión verbal. In J. Gutiérrez-Rexach (ed.), *Enciclopedia de lingüística hispánica*. London: Routledge, pp. 584–594.

Baker, M. (1985). The Mirror Principle and Morphosyntactic Explanation. *Linguistic Inquiry*, 16 (3), 373–415.

Barbosa, P. (2001). On Inversion in *wh*-Questions in Romance. In C. Aafke, J. Hulk, and J.-Y. Pollock (eds.), *Subject Inversion in Romance and the Theory of Universal Grammar*. Oxford: Oxford University Press, pp. 20–59.

Barbosa, P. (2009). Two Kinds of Subject pro. *Studia Linguistica*, 63, 2–58.

Barbosa, P. (2013). Partial Pro-Drop as Null NP Anaphora. In Yelena Fainleib and Nicholas LaCara (eds.), *NELS 41: Proceedings of the 41st Annual Meeting [2010] of the North East Linguistic Society*, Vol. 1. Amherst, MA: GLSA, pp. 71–84.

Béjar, S. and Rezac, M. (2009). Cyclic Agree. *Linguistic Inquiry*, 40, 35–73.

Belletti, A. (1999). 'Inversion' as Focalization and Related Questions. *Catalan Working Papers in Linguistics*, 7, 9–45.

Bobaljik, J. and Wurmbrand, S. (2005). The Domain of Agreement. *Natural Language and Linguistic Theory*, 23, 809–865.

Bošković, Ž. (2007). On the Locality and Motivation of Move and Agree: An Even More Minimal Theory. *Linguistic Inquiry*, 38, 589–644.

Bosque, I. and Gutiérrez-Rexach, J. (2009). *Fundamentos de sintaxis formal*. Madrid: Akal.

Burga, A. (2008). Spanish Subjects (Doctoral dissertation). University of Illinois.

Camacho, J. (2000). Structural Restrictions on Comitative Coordination. *Linguistic Inquiry*, 31 (2), 366–375.

Camacho, J. (2006). Do Subjects Have a Place in Spanish? In J.-P. Montreuil and C. Nishida (eds.), *New Perspectives in Romance Linguistics*. Amsterdam and Philadelphia, PA: John Benjamins, pp. 51–56.

Camacho, J. (2013). *Null Subjects*. Cambridge: Cambridge University Press.

Camacho, J. and Sánchez, L. (2014). Does the Verb Raise to T in Spanish? (MS). Rutgers University. Available from http://www.rci.rutgers.edu/~jcamacho/publications/adverbs-mono.pdf (last access November 25, 2017).

Cardinaletti, A. (1996). Subjects and Clause Structure. *University of Venice Working Papers in Linguistics*, 6, 55–95.

Cardinaletti, A. (2004). Toward a Cartography of Subject Positions. In L. Rizzi (ed.), *The Structure of CP and IP. The Cartography of Syntactic Structures*, Vol. 2. Oxford: Oxford University Press, pp. 115–165.

Casielles, E. (2001). The Syntax and Semantics of Preverbal Topical Phrases in Spanish. In J. Gutiérrez-Rexach and L. Silva-Villar (eds.), *Current Issues in Spanish Syntax and Semantics*. Berlin and New York: De Gruyter, pp. 65–82.

Chomsky, N. (1965). *Aspects of the Theory of Syntax*. Cambridge, MA: MIT Press.

Chomsky, N. (1981). *Lectures on Government and Binding*. Dordrecht: Foris.

Chomsky, N. (1995). *The Minimalist Program*. Cambridge, MA: MIT Press.

Chomsky, N. (2000). Minimalist Inquiries: The Framework. In R. Martin, D. Michaels, and J. Uriagereka (eds.), *Step by Step: Essays on Minimalism in Honor of Howard Lasnik*. Cambridge, MA: MIT Press, pp. 89–155.

Chomsky, N. (2001). Derivation by Phase. In M. Kenstowicz (ed.), *Ken Hale: A Life in Language*. Cambridge, MA: MIT Press, pp. 1–52.

Chomsky, N. (2004). Beyond Explanatory Adequacy. In A. Belletti (ed.), *Structures and Beyond. The Cartography of Syntactic Structures*. Oxford: Oxford University Press, pp. 104–131.

Chomsky, N. (2008). On Phases. In R. Freidin, C. Otero, and M. L. Zubizarreta (eds.), *Foundational Issues in Linguistic Theory: Essays in Honor of Jean-Roger Vergnaud*. Cambridge, MA: MIT Press, pp. 133–166.

Contreras, H. (1991). On the Position of Subjects. *Syntax and Semantics*, 25, 63–79.

D'Alessandro, R. (2016). Syntactic agreement. Course materials, Eastern Generative Grammar (EGG) Summer School. Available from http://www.eggschool.org/earlier-schools/egg-2016-tbilisi-georgia/classes-egg 16/dalessandro-syntactic-agreement/ (last access November 25, 2017).

Emonds, J. (1978). The Verbal Complex V'–V in French. *Linguistic Inquiry*, 9 (2), 151–175.

Etxepare, R. and Uribe-Etxebarria, M. (2008). On Negation and Focus in Spanish and Basque. In X. Artiagoitia Beaskoetxea and J. Lakarra Andrinua (eds.), *Gramatika jaietan: Patxi Goenagaren omenez*. Bilbao: Universidad del País Vasco, pp. 287–310.

Gallego, Á. (2007). Phase Theory and Parametric Variation (Doctoral dissertation). Universitat Autònoma de Barcelona.

Goodall, G. (2001). The EPP in Spanish. In W. D. Davies and S. Dubinsky (eds.), *Objects and Other Subjects: Grammatical Functions, Functional Categories and Configurationality*. Dordrecht: Kluwer, pp. 193–223.

Gupton, T. (2014). Preverbal Subjects in Galician: Experimental Data in the A vs. Ā Debate. *Probus*, 26, 135–175.

Hill, V. (1991). Theoretical Implications of Complementation in Romanian (Doctoral dissertation). Université de Genève.

Hiraiwa, K. (2001). Multiple Agree and the Defective Intervention Constraint in Japanese. In O. Matushansky *et al.* (eds.), *Proceedings of the 1st HUMIT Student Conference in Linguistic Research (HUMIT 2000)*. Cambridge, MA: MITWPL, pp. 67–80.

Holmberg, A. (2005). Is There a Little pro? Evidence from Finnish. *Linguistic Inquiry*, 36, 533–564.

Jiménez-Fernández, Á. and Miyagawa, S. (2014). A Feature-Inheritance Approach to Root Phenomena and Parametric Variation. *Lingua*, 145, 276–302.

Koeneman, O. and Zeijlstra. H. (2014). The Rich Agreement Hypothesis Rehabilitated. *Linguistic Inquiry*, 45 (4), 571–615.

Laka, I. (1990). Negation in Syntax: On the Nature of Functional Categories and Projections (Doctoral dissertation). MIT.

López, L. (2007). *Locality and the Architecture of Syntactic Dependencies*. London: Palgrave Macmillan.

López, L. (2009). *A Derivational Syntax for Information Structure*. Oxford: Oxford University Press.

Mare, M. (2012). *Sobre la naturaleza de la compañía*. Neuquén: EDUCO.

Martínez, J. A. (1999). La concordancia. In I. Bosque and V. Demonte (eds.), *Nueva gramática descriptiva de la lengua española*. Madrid: Espasa Calpe, pp. 2695–2784.

Masullo, P. (1992). Incorporation and Case Theory in Spanish. A Cross-Linguistic Perspective (Doctoral dissertation). University of Washington.

Ojea, A. (2017). Core-Intentional Features in the Syntactic Computation: Deriving the Position of the Subject in Spanish. *Lingua*, 195, 72–92. doi: 10.1016/j.lingua.2017.06.007.

Olarrea, A. (1996). Pre- and Postverbal Subjects in Spanish: A Minimalist Account (Doctoral dissertation). University of Washington.

Oltra-Massuet, I. (1999). On the Constituent Structure of Catalan Verbs. In K. Arregi, B. Bruening, C. Krause, and V. Lin (eds.), *Papers in Morphology and Syntax, Cycle One*. Cambridge, MA: MITWPL, pp. 279–322.

Oltra-Massuet, I. (2000). On the Notion of "Theme Vowel": A New Approach to Catalan Verbal Morphology. *MIT Occasional Papers in Linguistics*, 19.

Ordóñez, F. (1997). Word Order and Clausal Structure of Spanish and Other Romance Languages (Doctoral dissertation). City University of New York.

Ordóñez, F. (2000). *The Clausal Structure of Spanish: A Comparative Perspective*. New York: Garland.

Ordóñez, F. (2005). Two Specs for Postverbal Subjects: Evidence from Spanish and Catalan (MS). SUNY.

Ordóñez, F. (2016). Sujetos. In J. Gutiérrez-Rexach (ed.), *Enciclopedia de lingüística hispánica*. London: Routledge, pp. 101–110.

Ordóñez, F. and Treviño, E. (1999). Left Dislocated Subjects and the Pro-Drop Parameter: A Case Study of Spanish. *Lingua*, 107, 39–68.

Ortega-Santos, I. (2006a). On Locative Inversion and the EPP in Spanish. In Rosa María Ortiz Ciscomani (ed.), *Memoria del VIII Encuentro Internacional de Lingüística en el Noroeste*, Vol. 2. Hermosillo: Unison, pp. 131–150.

Ortega-Santos, I. (2006b). On New Information Focus, Sentence Stress Assignment Conditions and the Copy Theory: A Spanish Conspiracy. *University of Maryland Working Papers in Linguistics*, 14, 188–212.

Ortega-Santos, I. (2016). *Focus-Related Operations at the Right Edge in Spanish: Subjects and Ellipsis*. Amsterdam and Philadelphia, PA: John Benjamins.

Ortega-Santos, I. and Villa-García, J. (in preparation). Evidence for an Active EPP in Spanish (MS). University of Memphis and University of Manchester.

Parafita Couto, M. C. (2005). Focus at the Interface (Doctoral dissertation). University of Kansas.

Pérez Saldanya, M. (2012). Morphological Structure of Verbal Forms. In J. I. Hualde, A. Olarrea, and E. O'Rourke (eds.), *The Handbook of Spanish Linguistics*. Hoboken, NJ: Wiley Blackwell, pp. 227–246.

Pesetsky, D. and Torrego, E. (2001). T-to-C Movement: Causes and Consequences. In M. Kenstowicz (ed.), *Ken Hale: A Life in Language*. Cambridge, MA: MIT Press, pp. 355–426.

Pollock, J.-Y. (1989). Verb Movement, Universal Grammar, and the Structure of IP. *Linguistic Inquiry*, 20 (3), 365–424.

Preminger, O. (2014). *Agreement and Its Failures*. Cambridge, MA: MIT Press.

RAE and ASALE. (2009). *Nueva gramática de la lengua española*. Madrid: Espasa.

Richards, N. (2016). *Contiguity Theory*. Cambridge, MA: MIT Press.

Rizzi, L. (1982). *Issues in Italian Syntax*. Dordrecht: Foris.

Rizzi, L. (1990). *Relativized Minimality*. Cambridge, MA: MIT Press.

Rizzi, L. (1997). The Fine Structure of the Left Periphery. In L. Haegeman (ed.), *Elements of Grammar*. Dordrecht: Kluwer, pp. 281–337.

Rodríguez-Mondoñedo, M. (2007). The Syntax of Objects: Agree and Differential Object Marking (Doctoral dissertation). University of Connecticut.

Saab, A. (2007). Anti-agreement and null subjects in Spanish: A distributed morphology approach. Handout from *IV Encuentro de Gramática Generativa*.

Saab, A. (2009). Hacia una teoría de la identidad parcial en la elipsis (Doctoral dissertation). Universidad de Buenos Aires.

Sheehan, M. (2016). Subjects, Null Subjects and Expletives in Romance. In S. Fischer and C. Gabriel (eds.), *Manual of Grammatical Interfaces in Romance*. Berlin and Boston, MA: De Gruyter, pp. 329–362.

Stjepanović, S. (1999). What do Second Position Cliticization, Scrambling, and Multiple Wh-Fronting Have in Common? (Doctoral dissertation). University of Connecticut.

Suñer, M. (2003). The Lexical Preverbal Subject in a Romance Null Subject Language: Where Art Thou? In R. Núñez-Cedeño et al. (eds.), *A Romance Perspective on Language Knowledge and Use*. Amsterdam and Philadelphia, PA: John Benjamins, pp. 341–357.

Taraldsen, K. (1993). Subject/Verb-Agreement in Celtic and Romance. In Amy J. Schafer (ed.), *Proceedings of the North East Linguistic Society 23, University of Ottawa*, Vol. 1. Amherst, MA: GLSA, pp. 495–504.

Ticio, M. E. (2004). On the Position of Subjects in Puerto Rican Spanish. In M. Rodríguez-Mondoñedo and M. E. Ticio (eds.), *Cranberry Linguistics 2. University of Connecticut Working Papers in Linguistics*, Vol. 12. Cambridge, MA: MITWPL, pp. 77–92.

Tomioka, S. (2003). The Semantics of Japanese Null Pronouns and its Cross-Linguistic Implications. In K. Schwabe and S. Winkler (eds.), *The Interfaces: Deriving and Interpreting Omitted Structures*. Amsterdam and Philadelphia, PA: John Benjamins, pp. 321–340.

Torrego, E. (1984). On Inversion in Spanish and Some of Its Effects. *Linguistic Inquiry*, 15, 103–129.

Torrego, E. (2014). *The Syntax of φ-Features: 1st and 2nd Person Agreement with Plural DPs* (MS). University of Massachusetts

Torrego, E. and Laka, I. (2015). The Syntax of φ-Features: Agreement with Plural DPs in Basque and Spanish. In B. Fernández and P. Salaburu (eds.), *Ibon Sarasola, Gorazarre. Homenatge, Homenaje*. Bilbao: Universidad del País Vasco, pp. 633–646.

Uribe-Etxebarria, M. (1991). On the Structural Positions of the Subjects in Spanish, their Nature and their Consequences for Quantification (MS). University of Connecticut.

Villa-García, J. (2010). To Agree or Not to Agree: Beyond Quintessentially Syntactic Agreement in Spanish. In S. Colina, A. Olarrea, and A. M. Carvalho (eds.), *Romance Linguistics 2009*. Amsterdam and Philadelphia, PA: John Benjamins, pp. 249–266.

Villa-García, J. (2015). *The Syntax of Multiple-que Sentences in Spanish: Along the Left Periphery*. Amsterdam and Philadelphia, PA: John Benjamins.

Villa-García, J. and Suárez-Palma, I. (2016). Early Null and Overt Subjects in the Spanish of Simultaneous English–Spanish Bilinguals and Crosslinguistic Influence. *Revista Española de Lingüística Aplicada/Spanish Journal of Applied Linguistics*, 29 (2), 350–395.

Zeijlstra, H. (2012). There is Only One Way to Agree. *The Linguistic Review*, 29 (3), 491–539.

Zubizarreta, M. L. (1998). *Prosody, Word Order, and Focus*. Cambridge, MA: MIT Press.

Zubizarreta, M. L. (1999). Word Order in Spanish and the Nature of Nominative Case. In K. Johnson and I. Roberts (eds.), *Beyond Principles and Parameters*. Dordrecht: Kluwer, pp. 223–250.

16

Properties of Nominal Expressions

M. Emma Ticio Quesada

16.1 Introduction to Noun Phrases

Traditionally, descriptive grammars have assumed that NPs are syntactic constituents containing minimally an (implicit or explicit) N, and the elements that may surround it. According to this point of view, all underlined constituents in the examples in (16.1) are NPs:

(16.1) a. <u>El   gato   negro   de   María</u>   es   grande.
           the   cat   black   of   María   is   big
           'María's black cat is big.'
        b. Vimos   <u>gatos   negros</u>.
           see.2PL.PAST   cats   black
           'We saw black cats.'
        c. A   Pepe   le   gustan   <u>los   gatos   grandes</u>
           To   Pepe   CL.dat   like.3PL   the   cats   big
           pero   a   Ana   le   gustan   <u>los   (gatos)[1]   pequeños</u>.
           but   to   Ana   CL.dat   like.3PL the   (cats)   small
           'Pepe likes big cats, but Ana likes small ones.'

In other words: the constituents underlined in (16.1) are classified as NPs, independently of the presence or absence of elements such as attributive adjectives (16.1b–c), prepositional phrases (16.1a) or determiners (16.1a and c) within the group of words. This is so because the relevant element for this construction is the (implicit, cf. (16.1c) *los (gatos) pequeños*, or explicit) N *gato* 'cat' in these examples, and any other element present in this syntactic configuration is under the umbrella of the highest projection of that N (i.e. modifies the N).

This traditional way of understanding NPs was challenged in the eighties by some advances in grammatical theory that promoted a different view of

---

[1] Faded Ns in parenthesis, as *(gatos)* in (16.1c), stand for omitted N; that is, these Ns are not pronounced but are understood as part of the Nominal expression. Cf. discussion on nominal ellipsis in Section 16.4.2.

Figure 16.1 Graphic illustration of Determiner Phrase

these expressions. More concretely, the proposal on the existence of clausal functional projections under the generative grammar framework (cf. Chomsky's (1981) C(omplementizer)P and I(nflection)P) and the emphasis of a series of parallelisms between the verb and the noun by authors such as Szabolcsi (1984), among others, were instrumental in launching a line of research that revealed the need for functional projections surrounding the N to account for the language-specific properties of NPs.

These resulting analyses proposed that, similar to verbs (Vs) and verb phrases (VPs), which are embedded within inflectional phrases (see also Chapter 15, this volume), the so-called "noun phrases" (NPs) were actually part of larger structures. Hence, expressions such as *el gato* 'the cat' were assumed to be part of a functional category, the Determiner Phrase (DP), that selects a NP as its complement; Figure 16.1 illustrates graphically this assumption.

Since Abney (1987), this proposal has been called the DP hypothesis, and it assumes that determiners (Ds) perform a role similar to the one performed by inflectional elements with respect to the verb by introducing many of the grammatical properties of the entire structure in the clause and by imposing some of the selectional requirements on the NP. The morphological categories included in this category D contain, among others, the definite/indefinite articles, demonstratives, and personal pronouns (cf. Eguren 1989, Longobardi 1994, and Section 16.3 below for a more detailed explanation).

The DP hypothesis then easily explains the parallelism between Ns and Vs by adopting a uniform approach for the two main types of predicates in languages, and is standardly assumed nowadays in Transformational Grammar, Word Grammar (Hudson 1990), and Lexical Functional Grammar (Bresnan 2001). However, most frameworks outside of generative grammar, such as Head-Driven Phrase Structure grammar, or in general in the so-called "dependency grammars," have not adopted this view and still regard the NP as the highest relevant unit in this syntactic constituent (cf. Gil 2016; Hudson 2004; van Eynde 2006 for recent defenses of the NP), which triggers some confusion when determining the exact scope of the term NP in modern linguistics.

Furthermore, the interest in the DP hypothesis over the last 30 years, in combination with the recent developments in the study of functional categories under the so-called "cartographic approach" (Cinque and Rizzi 2010; Cinque 2010; and previous work), have resulted in a vast number of functional categories proposed to account for the intricacies of nominal constituents cross-linguistically.[2] Some of the functional categories proposed to be host in the highest part of the structure (i.e. left periphery) of the nominal domain, such as the ones related to Case or information structure, are supposed to be placed over (some instantiations of) the DP functional category layer. This fact, along with recent proposals that restrict the presence of DP to some languages (cf. Bošković 2012), have complicated the adoption of a uniform terminology to address the nominal constituent.

To summarize, advances in grammatical theory triggered the postulation of several functional categories associated with the Noun's Extended Projection (cf. Grimshaw 1991), as well as the proposal of NP as the complement of some functional categories. These proposals led not only to important research findings but also to important differences in the terminology used to refer to the constituents containing Ns, depending on the author's assumptions.

Given this last point, in this chapter we reserve the term NP for the inner structure headed by the N, the term DP for the functional category headed by a D, and we use the more general and pre-theoretical term, Nominal expression (Nom$_{exp}$), for the largest structure containing (explicit or implicitly) a N, be it modified or not.

The ensuing sections are a presentation of the main elements that compose the Nom$_{exp}$ in Spanish, and on how their distributions and properties have reinforced recent developments in the architecture of this constituent and core notions on the field, such as the postulation of functional categories and derivational proposals. It is not the goal of this chapter to promote any analysis over another, and different approaches will be introduced without delving into any of them due to space limitations. The remainder of the chapter is structured as follows: two sections that deal with the architecture of Nom$_{exps}$ (Sections 16.2 and 16.3), and a further section that deals with some major relations established within Nom$_{exps}$ (Section 16.4).

16.2 Immediate Internal Structure of the Noun Phrase: The Noun and its Modifiers

This section examines the elements and properties more closely associated with the lexical characteristics of the N heading the Spanish Nom$_{exp}$, to

---

[2] Cf. Alexiadou et al. 2007 for a summary of the different proposals on functional categories. Check also Ihsane (2008) and Durrlemann (2015), among others, for applications of the fine-grained cartographic structure to particular languages adopting structures as elaborated as (i) for the nominal constituent.

(i)   [K(Case)P[DeterminerP [QuantifierP [OrdinalP [CardinalP [NumberP [AP:Subjective.CommentP [SizeP [LengthP [HeightP [SpeedP [WidthP [WeightP [ShapeP [ColorP [Nationality/OriginP [ClassifierP [NounP]]]]]]]]]]]]]]]]]   Source: Durrlemann (2015: 3; her (5))

better understand its structure. To the exclusion of determiners and quantifiers, Nom$_{exps}$ in Spanish can contain prepositional phrases (PPs) and attributive adjectives (As) that directly modify the lexical properties associated with the N heading the Nom$_{exp}$.[3]

16.2.1 Prepositional Phrase Modifiers

The type of modifiers available in a particular Nom$_{exp}$ is defined by the properties of the N in the structure. Consider, to this effect, the behavior of the underlined structures in (16.2):

(16.2) a. Una   fotografía   <u>de</u>   <u>Juan</u>   <u>de</u>   <u>María</u>
      A   picture   of   Juan   of   María
      'Juan's picture of María,' 'María's picture of Juan'
   b. Una   descripción   <u>de</u>   <u>Juan</u>   <u>de</u>   <u>María</u>
      A   description   of   Juan   of   María
      'Juan's description of María,' 'María's description of Juan'
   c. Un   lapicero   <u>de</u>   <u>Juan</u>   (*<u>de</u>   <u>María</u>)
      A   pencil   of   Juan   of   María
   d. Un   profesor   <u>de</u>   <u>Juan</u>   (*<u>de</u>   <u>María</u>)
      A   professor   of   Juan   of   María

In all the Nom$_{exps}$ in the examples in (16.2) the PP *de Juan* 'of Juan' and *de María* 'of María' appear following an N. However, there are important differences regarding the interpretation and properties of these PPs depending on the particular N that linearly precedes them. For instance, in (16.2a), the N *fotografía* 'photograph' is a representational N and the PPs are interpreted as the theme of the photograph (i.e. the represented object), and the possessor (i.e. the owner) or the agent of the photograph (i.e. the photographer). The extralinguistic context will help us to determine which thematic relation each PP establishes with the N. Similarly, some of these notions appear when we use the same PPs with Ns such as *descripción* 'description,' which are representational and have been derived from a V (deverbal N).[4] In (16.2b) the PPs are interpreted as the topic of the description (i.e. a theme) and the agent of the description (i.e. the describer). The situation changes drastically with the N *lapicero* 'pencil' in (16.2c), which allows only one of these PPs with one interpretation of that PP as the

---

[3] Due to space constraints, this chapter does not include any discussion on relative clauses or nominal adpositions, which are also traditionally considered N modifiers. The interested reader can consult Rivero (1991).

[4] Although in the text we offer an example of a deverbal N with two PPs *de* 'of,' the reader should not assume that all deverbal Ns allow two *de* 'of' PPs. As the example in (i) illustrates, the thematic roles can be instantiated in PPs headed by Ps other than *de* 'of':

(i)   a. La destrucción   [de la ciudad]   [por los soldados]
       The destruction   of the city   by the soldiers
     b. *La destrucción   [de la ciudad]   [de los soldados]
       The destruction   of the city   of the soldiers

possessor; likewise, no more than one of these PPs can appear in (16.2d), although the interpretation cannot be a possessive one.

Therefore, it seems that some Ns, i.e. some deverbal (16.2b) and representational Ns (16.2a), require particular interpretations of the PPs that follow them, and that those interpretations are similar to the argumental structure of the verbs they proceed from. This fact led some authors (cf. Grimshaw 1991) to claim that some Ns, mainly those derived from Vs or As, can take argumental PPs, due to the presence of an eventive variable licensing those arguments.[5] In these cases, indicated by (16.2b), the nominalization preserves the verbal or adjectival selection requirements, and the modifier PPs express thematic roles such as 'agent' or 'theme' and receive genitive Case via the preposition *de* 'of' in Spanish, which acts, according to several authors (cf. Ticio 2010, and references therein), as a mere Case marker and does not actually have prepositional character. In contrast, other nouns, cf. (16.2c) or the examples in (16.3), may appear to be accompanied by optional PPs that express additional information (i.e. origin or age (16.3a), type or location (16.3b–c), purpose (16.3d) and type (16.3e)) relative to the noun and create their own separate PP projection that can be headed by other prepositions than *de* 'of.'

(16.3) a. El autobús de Alicante / de 1990
The bus of Alicante / of 1990
'The bus from/to Alicante/of 1990'
b. El reloj sin baterías
The clock without batteries
'The battery-less clock'
c. El robot de cocina
The robot of kitchen
'The food processor'
d. Los vestidos para bailar
The dresses for to-dance
'The dance dresses'
e. La piscina de olas
The pool of waves
'The wave pool'

This division of PPs into argumental and non-argumental has been useful for explaining some of their properties. For instance, it has been claimed that PP arguments are generated in a predetermined structural order that follows the so-called thematic hierarchy[6] (Alexiadou *et al.* 2007; and Ticio 2010, among others). This structural order is largely based on the

---

[5] Cf. Picallo (1991) and Fábregas (2010, 2016) for an in-depth account of nominalizations and the morphological properties of Ns.

[6] The term "thematic hierarchy" stands for some asymmetric relation between thematic roles, according to which some thematic roles are more prominent or higher than others hierarchically. Since Giorgi and Longobardi (1991), it has been assumed that Romance N_{exp} obey a possessor > agent > theme hierarchy as evidenced in the extraction facts discussed in the text.

robust c- (constituent) command and extraction facts out of Nom$_{exps}$, as illustrated in (16.4).

(16.4) a. ¿De quién compramos un libro de lingüística?
          Of whom buy.1PL.PAST a book of linguistics
     b. *¿De qué compramos un libro de Chomsky?
          Of what buy.1PL.PAST a book by Chomsky
     c. ¿De qué compramos un libro?
          Of what buy.1PL.PAST a book

The examples in (16.4) illustrate that Theme PPs can be extracted if no Agent/Experiencer PP nor Possessor PP is present (16.4b–c) and that Agent/Experiencer PPs can be extracted if no Possessor is present (16.4a). Hence, it is standardly assumed that the hierarchy Possessor > Agent > Theme is maintained in the generation order of these argumental PPs, with each type of PP hosted at different functional categories depending on the particular proposal. Adjunct PPs do not intervene in the extraction of argumental PPs and cannot be subject to extraction; cf. (16.5):

(16.5) a. ¿De quién tenemos algunos libros sin cubiertas?
          Of whom have.1PL some books without covers
     b. *¿Sin qué tenemos algunos libros?
          Without what have.1PL some books

The argument/adjunct distinction has traditionally been controversial in the nominal domain. One of the main arguments against the argumental properties of PPs within Nom$_{exps}$ is their apparent optionality. In short: A verbal argument must appear to satisfy the thematic grid of the predicate; on the contrary, the so-called PP arguments within the Nom$_{exp}$ are not mandatory (cf. (16.6) below).

(16.6) a. Escuchamos la descripción de Pedro
          Hear.1PL.PAST the description of Pedro
          'We heard Pedro's description.'
     b. *Pedro describió
          Pedro describe.3SG.PAST

In (16.6b) the lack of the theme, the complement, results in the ungrammaticality of the sentence. However, the lack of the theme in (16.6a) does not produce any ungrammaticality. Albeit there is not a good explanation so far regarding the optionality of nominal arguments, the differences in the categorical status of these PP modifiers trigger abundant differences in their behavior and in the way they interact with the rest of the modifiers in the Nom$_{exps}$.

Putting aside here the discussion about the possible argumental status of the PPs, all PP modifiers must linearly follow the noun in Spanish, and, as illustrated in the examples below, several PPs can co-occur in the Spanish Nom$_{exps}$.

(16.7) a. La   batalla del   Jarama del   ejército sublevado contra la
         The   battle of.the Jarama of.the army   rebel   against the
         II   República española por la   toma   de Madrid durante/en
         2nd   Republic Spanish   for the   capture of Madrid during/in
         la   Guerra Civil española fue extremadamente sangrienta.
         the   Civil   War Spanish was extremely   bloody.
    b. El   ataque a los rebeldes por parte de los soldados fue muy rápido.[7]
       The attack to the rebels   by   the soldiers was very quick

In the examples above there are several PPs that, independently of their status, belong to the Nom_{exp} and must appear as modifiers of N in our structures. Assuming the thematic hierarchy and the properties discussed, some of the PP modifiers must occupy complement or specifier positions where they can interact with the rest of the PP modifiers. On the contrary, some other PP modifiers, the non-argument PPs, which do not interact with the rest of the PPs and often modify the set of N plus argumental PPs, should appear in adjunct positions. The number and variety of PP modifiers within the Spanish Nom_{exp} and their dependency (or not) on the internal lexico-conceptual grid of the N justify the need for multiple structural positions to accommodate all the PPs. Consider in this respect (16.8):

(16.8)   [DP D [PossP $PP_{adjunct}$[PossP PP_{poss} [Poss [NP PP_{agent} [N PP_{theme}]]]]]]

The (simplified) structure in (16.8) displays the position argument and non-argument PPs can occupy. As illustrated, the PP_{agent} and PP_{theme} are generated in the closest position to N, which leaves out of the NP proper any other PP. In order to respect the thematic hierarchy, the PP_{poss} has been placed in the specifier of a functional category (here termed possessive phrase) dominating the NP. After that, non-argument PPs appear attached to the maximal categories present in the structure, and the entire structure is completed with the presence of DP. Note that the linear order predicted by the structure in (16.8) does not match the obligatory linear postnominal position displayed by PP modifiers in Spanish Nom_{exp}. To accommodate the relative word order, the generation structure (16.8) must be altered by displacing some of the elements during the Nom_{exp} derivation, resulting in (16.9).

(16.9)   [DP D [PossP $PP_{adjunct}$[PossP PP_{poss} [Poss+N [NP PP_{agent} [t_N PP_{theme}]]]]]]

The movement of the head N from its original position in (16.8) to its "derived" position in (16.9) produces the desired linear order (i.e. $D>N>PP_{poss}>PP_{agent}>PP_{theme}>PP_{adjunct}$) with all the PPs following the N in the linear string.

To summarize: Spanish Nom_{exps} can have multiple PPs as modifiers. The relationship established between the N and the PP modifier seems to

---

[7] Thanks are due to an anonymous reviewer for suggesting this example.

be largely determined by the types of N present in the syntactic structure, the number of PPs, and the extralinguistic context. Crucially, the possibility of having different (and multiple) types of PPs as N modifiers, and their well-documented different behavior, are relevant for determining the overall architecture and functional categories in the Nom$_{exp}$ discussed. Given that some of these PPs are more dependent than others on the N, their presence shows the need of multiple layers of structure to accommodate their presence and their different properties with respect to the N.

16.2.2 Attributive Adjective Modifiers

Spanish Nom$_{exps}$ can also host some other types of modifiers, such as attributive As. Nevertheless, the type of extraction and domination effects just discussed for PP modifiers cannot be replicated with As given the lack of argumental character of As. Romance attributive As, however, have posed important challenges for grammatical theory since they can appear in different linear positions in the Nom$_{exps}$ (namely, preceding or following the noun) depending on their meaning.[8] Some As can appear in prenominal, some in postnominal positions, and a subset of As can appear in both positions; cf. (16.10).

(16.10) a. Los   estudiantes   interesados   vinieron   a   la   charla
           The   students   interested   came   to   the   talk
           'The interested students came to the talk.'
       b. Los   interesados   estudiantes   vinieron   a   la   charla
           The   interested   students   came   to   the   talk
           'The interested students came to the talk.'

The word order difference in the examples above carries a meaning difference: (16.10a) denotes a subset of students who were interested, implying the existence of a different subset of students who were not interested and did not attend the talk. On the contrary, in (16.10b) all the students were interested and all of them came to the talk.[9] In other words: Spanish attributive As in prenominal position have a non-restrictive character, while postnominal As display a restrictive character.

Traditionally, two main approaches have competed in explaining the A distribution within Romance Nom$_{exps}$. On the one hand, some authors,

---

[8] There are several classifications for attributive As (cf. Demonte, 1999 and references therein). Due to space constraints, the discussion in this chapter will be focused on the linear differences and the restrictive/non-restrictive character of the A discussed.

[9] Some speakers find it easier to see the contrast with a possessive, as in the examples in (i). (Thanks are due to an anonymous reviewer, who drew this issue to my attention and provided the examples.)

(i) a. Hablamos   con   sus   clientes   agradecidos
       talk.2PL.PAST   with   their   customers   grateful
    b. Hablamos   con   sus   agradecidos   clientes.
       talk.2PL.PAST   with   their   grateful   customers
       'We talked to their grateful customers.'

since Cinque (1994), suggest that the different types of As are generated in a unique structural position, which differs depending on the particular instantiation of this line of analysis. Under this approach, the differences found among As are derived from the interaction of other grammatical properties with this unique position, instead of the As' generation site. More concretely, this line of research postulates that the different linear orders are the result of the possibility of having N-movement (i.e. head movement of the N to upper functional categories) in languages such as Spanish. This analysis links a generation structure common to all languages with a derivation affected by the N-movement operation. The sequence can be represented as in (16.11):[10]

(16.11) a. Det – A – N   universal generation
        b. Det – N – A – t_N Romance languages derivation via N-movement

On the other hand, a different line of analyses postulates that the different properties of As are better explained if As are generated in different structural positions. This non-uniform approach to As is the line of research pursued, for instance, by Bernstein (1993, 2001), Demonte (1999), and Valois (1991), among many others, who argue in favor of generating some As in the head position of their own category and other As adjoined to a maximal category within the Nom_{exp} in some of the incarnations of this proposal. In other words, given that the possibility of dual placement is not applicable to all As, this line of research makes use of the syntactic properties of two different structural positions to derive the syntactic and semantic differences of the As within DPs instead of deriving the main properties of As from the existence (or non-existence) of N-movement.

Despite the initial differences between uniform and non-uniform approaches to analyzing As, more recent proposals on the topic have combined aspects of both proposals to achieve a better empirical coverage. This way, in revised uniformity approaches, in addition to the existence of N-movement it is necessary to resort to a layered functional structure within the nominal structure to accommodate the attachment sites of different categories of As. Many authors (cf. Sánchez 1996; Gutiérrez-Rexach and Mallén 2002; and Laenzlinger 2005; among many others) have advanced or followed this line of research within the non-uniformity approach and have proposed that As are specifiers of functional or lexical projections.

More recently, Cinque (2014) has revised previous analyses and assumed that As are merged in two different positions depending on their type of (direct/indirect) modification over the noun. The main difference between direct modifier adjectives (DMAs) and indirect modifier adjectives (IMAs) lies in the predicative properties of the As: namely, DMAs are non-

---

[10] Where "Det" = "determiner" and "t_N"= "trace noun."

predicative, hence they cannot appear as the predicate of a copulative sentence, while IMAs are necessarily predicative and can follow a copulative verb. The examples below illustrate this difference and exemplify the two types of As:

(16.12) a. El   futuro   presidente   *El   presidente   es   futuro
             The   future   president   The president   is   future
         b. El   presidente rubio   El   presidente   es   rubio
             The   president   blonde   The president   is   blonde

Under this approach, DMAs, such as *futuro* 'future,' are merged into the specifier position of dedicated functional heads in the extended projection of the Noun. On the other hand, IMAs, such as *rubio* 'blonde,' are actually reduced relative clauses merged into a particular functional projection hosting only reduced relative clauses. Crucially, some positions in particular languages are specialized in one of the structures (hence, they can host only one type of A, providing only one type of interpretation). For instance, As that occur prenominally in Spanish have only the direct modification source, which helps us to classify As occurring there by the type of interpretive properties and structures associated with that position. In contrast, the postnominal position in Spanish is structurally ambiguous between the two sources.

To achieve the language specific positions from an identical universal generation structure, Cinque's proposal (2014) resorts to the existence of two universal positions for IMAs and DMAs, along with the need to have N-movement in some languages, such as Spanish, to explain the intra- and cross-linguistic differences seen in the word order issues explored above. The derivation for a nominal expression such as *presunto problema serio* 'alleged serious problem' is shown in (16.13):

(16.13) a. serio $_{IMA}$ presunto $_{DMA}$ problema $_N$
            (merge order in all languages)
        b. [presunto $_{DMA(non\text{-}restrictive)}$ problema $_N$]   serio $_{IMA(restrictive)}$ t [DMA (non-restrictive) N]
            (obligatory DMA+N-movement in Romance)

The structure in (16.13a) is universal. The structure in (16.13b) represents the required N-movement in languages such as Spanish, probably due to the need to check number and gender features with the higher Functional Categories, and the optional movement DMAs can undergo as a unit with the N. Thanks to these two movements, the Spanish surface representations always display a restrictive (IMA) in the postnominal position.

To summarize the previous discussion: Research on the properties and types of As occurring in Romance Nom$_{exps}$ has been extensive, and has been the subject of debated proposals based on the existence of N-movement and/or different generation sites for different types of As in languages. Although competing approaches to the analysis of As in

Romance languages initially diverged regarding the possibility of generating As in different structural positions, the most recent research converges in the multiple places of generation for As depending on the type of As involved and in the assumption of the existence of N-movement. In spite of the fact that there is still no accepted analysis for the main properties of Spanish As, there is a link between the presence of functional categories and certain types of adjectives as well as between the presence of certain As in a particular position of the linear string and the availability of some syntactic operations affecting the N.

To conclude: This section has shown that the properties of the different types of modifiers within Nom$_{exps}$ support new developments of linguistic theory, such as the postulation of an extended functional category domain to host these categories, the parallelism between Ns and Vs, and the existence of head movement of the N to account for the different linear orders of Spanish modifiers.

16.3 The Outer Layers of the Noun Phrase: Reference and Quantification

In addition to N modifiers, which restrict or expand the type of properties denoted by the N, Spanish Nom$_{exps}$ can appear with elements that contribute to the individual denotation of the Nom$_{exp}$. These elements are characterized for their mandatory prenominal position in Spanish, and enable us to determine the Nom$_{exp}$'s reference and quantificational properties. Consider (16.14):

(16.14) a. El/Un   elefante   avanzaba   lentamente
           The/An   elephant   approached   slowly
           'The/An elephant approached slowly.'
        b. Varios/Algunos/Bastantes/Cuatro/Muchos elefantes avanzaban lentamente
           Several/Some/Several/Four/Many   elephants approached slowly
           'Several/Some/Several/Four/Many elephants approached slowly.'
        c. Los otros / Los tres   / Todos los elefantes avanzaban lentamente
           The other / The three   / All   the elephants approached slowly
           'The other/The three/All the elephants approached slowly.'
        d. Vimos   __ elefantes / *Elefantes avanzaban   lentamente
           see.2PL.PAST   __ elephants / Elephants approached   slowly
           'We saw elephants/Elephants approached slowly.'

As shown in the examples in (16.14), the elements preceding the N form a heterogeneous group and include, among others, the definite and indefinite articles (16.14a), numerals and quantifiers (16.14b), and combinations of all of these (16.14c). In addition, as (16.14d) shows, these prenominal elements are not always required. Nonetheless, bare Nom$_{exp}$ in Spanish are severely restricted in their distribution, as the ungrammaticality of the second example in (16.14d) manifests.

16.3.1 Bare Noun Phrases

In fact, the limited distribution of bare Nom$_{exps}$ (cf. Bosque 1996; Casielles 2004; Contreras 1996; Espinal 2009; Laca 1996; Leonetti 2013) in some languages and their different interpretation cross-linguistically have been one of the pieces of evidence for the postulation of a DP projection. As shown in the contrast in (16.15), some bare Nom$_{exp}$ cannot take on argumental roles, and are considered an extension of the main predicate without establishing individual denotation.

(16.15)   Tengo coche   /   un coche   /   el coche
          Have.1SG car   /   a car   /   the car
          'I have car/a car/the car.'

The presence/absence of determiners in the examples in (16.15) corresponds to different referential properties. Namely, the bare Nom$_{exp}$ does not denote any individual car, while the other two Nom$_{exps}$ do. To account for related differences, Szabolcsi (1984) proposes that the possibility of establishing reference to individuals is tied exclusively to the presence of the D node. Obviously, the means by which the D node is activated vary cross-linguistically. Taking into consideration that languages differ in the manner in which Ns are mapped into predicates or arguments, Longobardi (1994) proposes the existence of a parameter to analyze the variation between Germanic and Romance languages in this respect. This idea is developed further by Chierchia's (1998) Nominal Mapping Parameter hypothesis, which predicts that languages such as Spanish need articles to turn predicates into arguments.

Under the simplified presentation of these proposals, the prediction is that bare Nom$_{exps}$ should not be argumental in Spanish ever. This is not the case, as the grammatical example in (16.14d) displays. To account for this grammaticality, it has been considered that the plural ending appearing in the bare Nom$_{exp}$ could enable its argumental properties given that it could be the head of a functional category hosting plurality: Number Phrase.

16.3.2 The Higher Functional Structure of Nominal Expressions

Note that the need for a functional category Number Phrase is also supported by the examples in (16.14c). Given that some Ds can co-occur with some other prenominal elements that license the argumental character when appearing as the only element in the Nom$_{exp}$, different structural positions have been postulated for different quantifiers and determiner elements, as is illustrated, for instance, in Figure 16.2.

The structure in Figure 16.2 represents a conservative structure in which elements such as definite articles or demonstratives occupy the head position of the determiner functional category, whereas indefinite articles and quantifiers, such as *un* 'a,' *dos* 'two,' *muchos* 'many' or *alguno* 'some,' are

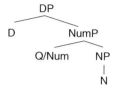

Figure 16.2 Structural positions for different quantifiers and determiners

typically placed in positions that are cross-linguistically lower than the definite article and can co-occur with higher Ds.

However, important differences between bare and indefinite Nom$_{exps}$ invalidate the proposal for a shared position by these two elements. Thus, several authors (cf. Leonetti 2013 and the references therein) have noticed that bare Nom$_{exp}$ must take the narrowest possible scope with respect to any other operators in the same clause, such as negation, intensional predicates, and modals, while indefinite Nom$_{exps}$ can have both narrow and wide scopes. Example 16.16 illustrates the last claim:

(16.16) a. A   la   clase   no   vinieron   algunos   estudiantes
           To   the   class   NEG   come.3PL.PAST   some   students
        b. A   la   clase   no   vinieron   estudiantes
           To   the   class   NEG   come.3PL.PAST   students

The bare Nom$_{exp}$ example above (16.16b) has only the narrow scope reading according to which 'there are no students who came to the class.' In contrast, indefinites (16.16a) may take variable scope and two readings are available; namely, 'there are no students who came to the class' (narrow) and 'there are students such that they didn't came to the class' (wide). These, and some other related facts (cf. Laca 1996; Leonetti 2013; McNally 2004), prevent the treatment of bare Nom$_{exps}$ as a type of indefinite Nom$_{exps}$.

Furthermore, although the existence of DP and NumP seem to accommodate the overall differences between definite article and quantifiers, each of these elements also displays different properties depending on its particular linguistic context. In other words: It is not the case that all Nom$_{exps}$ containing the definite article behave similarly; likewise, indefinite Nom$_{exps}$ do not behave uniformly. As for the definite article, many authors (cf. Torrego 1987; Vergnaud and Zubizarreta 1992) have noticed the diverse nature of the definite article in Spanish. For instance, it seems to behave as a unique operator D (16.17a), or as an expletive D in definite generics cases, such as (16.17b).

(16.17) a. El   león   está sentado bajo   el   árbol   [unique individual lion]
           The   lion   is   seated   under the   tree
        b. El   león   es   un   animal impresionante   [the lion as a kind])
           The   lion   is   an   animal impressive

Similarly, recent research on the properties of indefinite Nom$_{exps}$ (Gutiérrez-Rexach 2003; Martí 2008 and references therein) have focused on the differences between specific and non-specific indefinite Ds. The examples in (16.18) illustrate these notions:

(16.18) a. Busco   a un amigo de Luis [*specific reading, 'a particular friend of Luis'*]
           Look-for.1SG to a friend of Luis
        b. Busco   un amigo de Luis [*non-specific reading, 'any friend of Luis'*]
           Look-for.1SG a friend of Luis

The two sets of examples (16.17) and (16.18) above point to different properties within the elements that have been placed as Ds or Quantifiers (Qs). Recent research has taken the different properties displayed by Ds and Qs as evidence for assuming a greater specialization of functional categories in the highest layers of the Nom_{exp}.[11]

To sum up: The preceding discussion has illustrated that Ns (and their modifiers) appear combined with grammatical items grouped under the category D. Since the study by Abney (1987), most generative grammarians have assumed that the class D is actually the head of the Nom_{exp} and, as such, projects the highest layer in nominal constituents. Over the last several decades, syntactic research has frequently focused on the relevance of the D chosen (definite/indefinite; specific/non-specific, generic/individual, etc.) and has put forward that enlarged structures might be needed to account for the different properties of elements that traditionally fall under the D category.

16.4 Syntactic Relations within the Noun Phrase

Previous sections have shown that Ns can appear with diverse types of elements, which led to proposals containing various functional categories to explain their properties. This section studies a couple of syntactic relationships (namely, agreement relations and information structure representations) established within the boundaries of the Nom_{exp}, which independently support the described architecture for Spanish Nom_{exps}.

16.4.1 Agreement Internal to the Nominal Expression

Starting with the agreement relations, Spanish Nom_{exps} display gender and number endings (cf. Ambadiang 1999 and Harris 1991, among many others) in the N, and in all the agreeing modifiers and Ds (cf. (16.19)).

---

[11] It is not the goal of this section to review all of the proposals regarding the functional category DP and its relationship to the more traditional notions of the category D. The interested reader can consult Bošković (2012) and Ticio (2010) (and the references therein), for an overview of the discussion.

(16.19) a. La   gata   blanca   y   el   gato   negro
           the.   cat.   white.   and   the.   cat.   black.
           FEM.SG   FEM.SG   FEM.SG   MASC.SG MASC.SG MASC.SG
           'The white female cat and the black male cat'
       b. La   mochila   blanca   y   el   cuaderno negro
           the.   backpack.   white.   and   the.   notebook. black.
           FEM.SG FEM.SG   FEM.SG   MASC.SG MASC.SG   MASC.SG
           'the white backpack and the black notebook'
       c. El   mapa   viejo
           the.MASC.SG map.MASC.SG   old.MASC.SG
           'The old map'

The nominal agreement system in Spanish consists of a lexical process inserting the value of the number and gender in the Nom$_{exp}$ (i.e. some lexical items will be introduced in the structure with a value for gender/number), and a syntactic process that occurs within the Nom$_{exp}$, to spread the gender/number value (i.e. a process to guarantee that all elements within the Nom$_{exp}$ display the same value for gender/number).

In Section 16.3, the need for a Number Phrase (NumP) was related to the properties of some types of quantifiers and to the properties of plural Ns in triggering referential status on some occasions. Hence, it is independently attested that Number features are not an inherent property of the N but are hosted in an independent category, which appears in the inflection field between the periphery and the lexical projection in the Nom$_{exp}$. The nature of gender features is still under debate. According to some standard approaches, gender features, which do not reproduce extralinguistic sex and are not completely tied to a particular set of endings, are included in the lexical information to classify Ns. Gender features could then reach the remaining elements in the Spanish Nom$_{exp}$ as a result of N-movement and a series of checking mechanisms. Some other proposals (cf. Picallo 2008) claim the need for an independent functional category for gender, represented as c (i.e. CLASS) in the (simplified) structure below:

(16.20)   [DP[D] [NuP[NU] [c[CLASS] [NP[N[± fem, ± plur]]]]]]

The adoption of a structure similar to (16.20) enables us to unify both gender and number nominal agreement processes within the Nom$_{exp}$ because they both require the presence of a particular functional category and the N's features receive their value via similar syntactic processes. Simplifying the technical details (cf. Picallo 2008 for full details), both gender and number features in the N must establish a local relation with the relevant functional categories (namely, ClassP and NumP). These local relations result then in a valuation of the gender/number features present in the different categories involved. Finally, when the D head is introduced in the structure, its gender and number features are valued locally by the features present in the raised N.

In conclusion: Nominal agreement, one of the fundamental properties of Spanish Nom_{exps}, receives a straightforward account by assuming the existence of additional functional categories and the existence of N-movement. This is a desirable conclusion, as the proposal of the existence of N-movement has been used for analyzing the peculiar properties of As and PP modifiers in Spanish Nom_{exps}.

16.4.2 Nominal Expressions and Information Structure

The last property to be discussed in this section brings us back to the parallelism between Ns and Vs. That is, if the DP layer in the nominal domain parallels the CP layer in the clausal domain, at least to some extent, it should be split into discrete functional projections representing the left periphery of nominals, as is the case in the clausal domain. Section 16.3 suggested the need for some additional functional projections at that level based on D features, such as specificity. This section examines the plausibility an articulated CP internal structure extended to the DP following some recent proposals (for instance, Bernstein 2001 and Eguren 2010; see below) that have argued that Topicalization and Focalization may be represented in the DP.

Consider the meaning contrasts between (16.21a–b) and (16.22a–b):

(16.21) a. Este libro interesante
 this book interesting
 b. el libro interesante este
 the book interesting this

(16.22) a. mi libro de física
 my book of physics
 b. el libro de física mío
 the book of physics mine

The examples above illustrate the different positions of demonstratives and possessive adjectives in Spanish Nom_{exps}: the different positions reflect differences in meaning, with the elements occupying the DP-final position in (16.21)–(16.22) receiving a focus interpretation. Evidence of this focus character is the implicit contrast in the elements occupying the last linear position, which is inexistent in the examples with these elements in the prenominal position. Recent analyses (cf. Bernstein (2001)) of these constructions have capitalized on the fact that the DP-final position of these elements yields a focus interpretation and have linked it to the expression of focus in the Romance CP. Therefore, according to Bernstein (2001), the expression of focus in the Romance DP is the result of a scrambling-type[12] operation (i.e. a leftward movement of a maximal

---

[12] Bernstein's 2001 terminology could be potentially confusing, given that German-type scrambling combines properties of argumental and non-argumental movement. Although Bernstein's 2001 terminology is maintained in the discussion, the reader can interpret it as just "movement" or "optional movement."

projection), similar to the one proposed for the Romance clause (cf. Zubizarreta 1998). The relevant structure is in (16.23):

(16.23)　[$_{DP}$ el [$_{XP}$ libro$_i$ interesante t$_i$]$_k$ este [$_{XP}$ t]$_k$]
　　　　'this interesting book'

Interestingly, this line of analysis suggests that the constituent containing the N and its modifiers, to the exclusion of the D and the demonstrative (i.e. the scrambled constituent), must move to the highest specifier position below DP due to its defocalized character. This movement leaves the demonstrative as the phrase-final element, which confers on it its focus character.

To summarize the discussion so far: Recent research supports the argument that Romance languages may express focus on the right periphery of the DP and has extended proposals originally made for the clausal domain to the nominal domain, postulating the existence of information-based movement and a series of positions that host non-focused elements.

The existence of the information structure relation and of topic–focus relations in the Nom$_{exp}$ has recently revealed itself useful for the analysis of nominal ellipsis. Nominal ellipsis (i.e. the omission of the noun and (some of) its modifiers in Nom$_{exps}$) is a fairly productive construction in Spanish; cf. (16.24)–(16.25). The examples in (16.24) illustrate that Nominal Ellipsis is possible with different types of D and modifiers, while the examples in (16.25) show that it is not possible, for instance, in constructions with unstressed possessives and with the definite article and certain modifiers in Spanish.

(16.24)　a.　María　vendió　varios　libros　de　recetas　y　Ana　compró
　　　　　　María　sold　　several　books　of　recipes　and　Ana　bought
　　　　　　algunos　(libros)　de　terror.
　　　　　　some　　(books)　of　horror
　　　　b.　María vendió varios libros azules y　Pepe compró tres　(libros) rojos.
　　　　　　María sold　several books blue　and Pepe bought three (books) red

(16.25)　a.　*María　vendió　varios　libros　de　lingüística　y　Pepe　compró
　　　　　　María　sold　　several　books　of　linguistics　and　Pepe　bought
　　　　　　mis　(libros)　de　matemáticas.
　　　　　　mine　(books)　of　math
　　　　b.　*María　vendió　varios　libros　con　ilustraciones　y　Pepe
　　　　　　María　sold　　several　books　with　illustrations　and　Pepe
　　　　　　compró　los　(libros)　sin　ilustraciones.
　　　　　　bought　the　(books)　without　illustrations

Traditionally, the distribution of nominal ellipsis has been explained by resorting exclusively to formal conditions. Thus, many authors (cf. Saab 2009, 2010; Ticio 2005, 2010, and references therein) have argued that there is a functional category (either D or some instantiation of agreement) in charge of licensing the elided element or a particular structural configuration that is the only one susceptible to undergoing the operation resulting in nominal ellipsis in Spanish. However, this line of research faces important challenges, which have paved the way to new explanations based on information structure notions. For Spanish, Eguren's (2010) proposal is that there is a contrastive focus condition on the remnant of the ellipsis, which regulates its distribution. More concretely, the proposal is that nominal ellipsis remnants establish a set–subset relation between the items of the same descriptive class denoted by the antecedent, which allows for the content of the elided nominal to be recovered. This proposal successfully explains the lack of nominal ellipsis with some prenominal adjectives or quantifiers that are incompatible with the notion of contrastive focus, and validates again the need to postulate well-defined information structure positions within the DP, similar to the ones justified for the CP.

This section has provided a basic description of two fundamental properties of Spanish Nom$_{exps}$, and shown that the most widely accepted theoretical proposals to analyze them are consistent with the general architecture and operations proposed for Spanish Nom$_{exps}$ on the basis of the different elements allowed in these constituents.

16.5 Conclusion and Further Research

This chapter had a twofold aim: to introduce the most relevant properties of Spanish Nom$_{exp}$ and to explain the basis of recent theoretical proposals tied to these constituents. As for the properties, the chapter has briefly reviewed the main components of the Nom$_{exps}$ (i.e. prenominal elements such as Ds, and modifiers, such as PPs and attributive As), their properties, and the relations they establish (for instance, agreement, information structure, and ellipsis). The brief description of the above-mentioned phenomena led to the discussion of the major theoretical proposals in the nominal domain; namely, the parallelism between Ns and Vs, the different functional categories, and syntactic operations.

Due to space constraints, a full-fledged account of problems and a description of the further research needed in the field is not possible here. Nonetheless, a word is in order regarding a promising line of research that is tying together empirical and theoretical research (cf. Pérez-Leroux et al. 2004; Montrul et al. 2008; and Socarrás 2011; to mention just a few) to refute many of the theoretical proposals discussed in this chapter. This research is greatly advancing our knowledge of Spanish Nom$_{exps}$.

References

Abney, S. P. (1987). The English Noun Phrase in its Sentential Aspect (Doctoral dissertation). MIT.

Alexiadou, A., Stavrou, M., and Haegeman L. (2007). *Noun Phrase in the Generative Perspective*. Berlin and New York: De Gruyter.

Ambadiang, T. (1999). La flexión nominal. Género y número. In I. Bosque and V. Demonte (eds.), *Gramática descriptiva de la lengua española*. Madrid: Espasa, pp. 4843–4913.

Bernstein, J. B. (1993). Topics in the Syntax of Nominal Structure across Languages (Doctoral dissertation). CUNY.

Bernstein, J. B. (2001). Focusing the "Right" Way in Romance Determiner Phrases. *Probus*, 13 (1), 1–29.

Bošković, Ž. (2012). On NPs and Clauses. In G. Grewendorf and T. E. Zimmermann (eds.), *Discourse and Grammar: From Sentence Types to Lexical Categories*. Berlin: De Gruyter, pp. 179–242.

Bosque, I. (ed.). (1996). *El sustantivo sin determinación. La ausencia de determinante en la lengua española*. Madrid: Visor.

Bresnan, J. (2001). *Lexical–Functional Syntax*. Oxford: Blackwell.

Casielles, E. (2004). *The Syntax–Information Structure Interface. Evidence from Spanish and English*. London: Routledge.

Chierchia, G. (1998). Reference to Kinds across Languages. *Natural Language Semantics*, 6, 339–405.

Chomsky, N. (1981). *Lectures on Government and Binding*. Dordrecht: Foris.

Cinque, G. (1994). On the Evidence for Partial N-movement in the Romance DP. In G. Cinque, J. Koster, J.-Y. Pollock, L. Rizzi, and R. Zanuttini (eds.), *Paths Towards Universal Grammar. Studies in Honor of Richard S. Kayne*. Washington, DC: Georgetown University Press, pp. 85–110.

Cinque, G. (2010). *The Syntax of Adjectives: A Comparative Study*. Cambridge, MA: MIT Press.

Cinque, G. (2014). The Semantic Classification of Adjectives. A View from Syntax. *Studies in Chinese Linguistics*, 25 (1), 1–30.

Cinque, G. and Rizzi, L. (2010). The Cartography of Syntactic Structures. In B. Heine and H. Narrog (eds.), *Oxford Handbook of Linguistic Analysis*. Oxford: Oxford University Press, pp. 51–65.

Contreras, H. (1996). Sobre la distribución de los sintagmas nominales no predicativos sin determinante. In Bosque 1996: 141–168.

Demonte, V. (1999). A Minimal Account of Spanish Adjective Position and Interpretation. In J. Franco, A. Landa, and J. Martín (eds.), *Grammatical Analyses in Basque and Romance Linguistics*. Amsterdam: John Benjamins, pp. 45–75.

Durrlemann, S. (2015). Nominal Architecture in Jamaican Creole. *Journal of Pidgin and Creole Languages*, 30 (2) (2015), 265–306.

Eguren, L. (1989). Algunos datos del español en favor de la hipótesis de la frase determinante. *Revista Argentina de Lingüística*, 5 (1/2), 163–209.

Eguren, L. (2010). Contrastive Focus and Nominal Ellipsis in Spanish. *Lingua*, 120 (2), 435–457.

Espinal, M. T. (2009). Bare Nominals in Catalan and Spanish. Their Structure and Meaning. *Lingua*, 120, 984–1009.

Fábregas, A. (2010). A Syntactic Account of Affix Rivalry in Spanish Nominalisations. In A. Alexiadou and M. Rathert (eds.), *The Syntax of*

Nominalizations across Languages and Frameworks. Berlin: De Gruyter, pp. 67–90.

Fábregas, A. (2016) *Las nominalizaciones*. Madrid: Visor.

Gil, J. M. (2016) A Relational Account of the Spanish Noun Phrase. *Australian Journal of Linguistics*, 36 (1), 22–51.

Giorgi, Alessandra and Longobardi, Giuseppe (1991). *The Syntax of Noun Phrases. Configuration, Parameters and Empty Categories*. Cambridge: Cambridge University Press.

Grimshaw, J. (1991). Extended Projection (MS). Brandeis University.

Gutiérrez-Rexach, J. (2003). *La semántica de los indefinidos*. Madrid: Visor.

Gutiérrez-Rexach, J. and Mallén, E. (2002). Toward a Unified Analysis of Prenominal Adjectives. In James F. Lee, Kimberly L. Geeslin, and J. Clancy Clements (eds.), *Structure, Meaning, and Acquisition in Spanish. Papers from the 4th Hispanic Linguistics Symposium*. Somerville, MA: Cascadilla, pp. 178–192.

Harris, J. W. (1991). The Exponence of Gender in Spanish. *Linguistic Inquiry*, 22 (1), 27.

Hudson, R. (1990). *English Word Grammar*. Oxford: Blackwell.

Hudson, R. (2004). Are Determiners Heads? *Functions of Language*, 11 (1), 7–42.

Ihsane T. (2008). *The Layered DP: Form and Meaning of French Indefinites*. Amsterdam: John Benjamins.

Laca, B. (1996). Acerca de la semántica de los plurales escuetos del español. In Bosque 1996: pp. 241–268.

Laenzlinger, C. (2005). French Adjective Ordering: Perspectives on DP-Internal Movement Types. *Lingua*, 115 (5), 645–689.

Leonetti, M. (2013). Information Structure and the Distribution of Spanish Bare Plurals. In J. Kabatek and A. Wall (eds.), *Bare Noun Phrases in Romance: Theory and (Empirical) Data*. Amsterdam: John Benjamins, pp. 121–155.

Longobardi, G. (1994). Reference and Proper Names. *Linguistic Inquiry*, 25 (4), 609–665.

Martí, L. (2008). The Semantics of Plural Indefinite Noun Phrases in Spanish and Portuguese. *Natural Language Semantics*, 16 (1), 1–37.

McNally, L. (2004). Bare Plurals in Spanish are Interpreted as Properties. *Catalan Journal of Linguistics*, 3, 115–133.

Montrul, S., Foote, R., and Perpiñán, S. (2008). Gender Agreement in Adult Second Language Learners and Spanish Heritage Speakers: The Effects of Age and Context of Acquisition. *Language Learning*, 58, 503–553. doi: 10.1111/j.1467–9922.2008.00449.x

Picallo, M. C. (1991). Nominals and Nominalization in Catalan. *Probus*, 3, 279–316.

Picallo, M. C. (2008). Gender and Number in Romance. *Lingue e Linguaggio*, 1, 47–66.

Pérez-Leroux, A na T., Munn, Alan, Schmitt, Cristina, and DeIrish, Michelle. (2004a). Learning Definite Determiners: Genericity and Definiteness in English and Spanish. In Alejna Brugos, Linnea Micciulla, and Christine E. Smith (eds.), *Online Proceedings Supplement of the 28th Boston University Conference on Language Development (BUCLD)*. Somerville, MA: Cascadilla. Available at http://www.bu.edu/bucld/files/2011/05/28-perez-leroux.pdf (accessed February 2, 2018).

Rivero, M. L. (1991). *Las construcciones de relativo*. Madrid: Taurus.

Saab, A. (2009). Hacia una teoría de la identidad parcial en la elipsis (Doctoral dissertation). Universidad de Buenos Aires.

Saab, A. (2010) (Im)possible Deletions in the Spanish DP. *Iberia. An International Journal of Theoretical Linguistics*, 2 (2), 45–83.

Sánchez, L. (1996). Syntactic Structure in Nominals: A Comparative Study of Spanish and Southern Quechua (Doctoral dissertation). University of Southern California.

Socarrás, G. (2011). *First Language Acquisition in Spanish: A Minimalist Approach to Nominal Agreement*. London and New York: Continuum.

Szabolcsi, A. (1984). The Possessor that Ran Away from Home. *The Linguistic Review*, 3, 89–102.

Ticio, M. E. (2005). NP-Ellipsis in Spanish. In D. Eddington (ed.), *Selected Proceedings of the 7th Hispanic Linguistics Colloquium*. Somerville, MA: Cascadilla, pp. 128–141.

Ticio, M. E. (2010). *Locality Domains in the Spanish DPs*. Dordrecht: Springer.

Torrego, E. (1987). On Empty Categories in Nominals (MS). University of Massachusetts.

Valois, Daniel. (1991). The Internal Syntax of DP (Doctoral dissertation). UCLA.

van Eynde, F. (2006). NP-Internal Agreement and the Structure of the Noun Phrase. *Journal of Linguistics*, 42, 139–186.

Vergnaud, J. and Zubizarreta, M. L. (1992). The Definite Determiner and the Inalienable Constructions in French and in English. *Linguistic Inquiry*, 23, 595–652.

Zubizarreta, M. L. (1998). *Prosody, Focus, and Word Order*. Cambridge, MA: MIT Press.

17
Information Structure

Laura Domínguez

17.1 Introduction

This chapter investigates word order in standard Spanish and its relationship to Information Structure (IS) (Chafe 1976; Vallduví 1992),[1] i.e. how new and old information is packed in a sentence. The two main components of IS which account for the felicitousness of sentences (i.e. that they are appropriate in relation to the discourse context) are focus (the information which is new in a sentence), and givenness or presupposed information (the "old" information which is already shared by interlocutors). In order to examine the informational status of sentences, a question–answer test is often applied (see Example 17.1). This test is useful to identify the focus and the presupposition assuming that the focus refers to the *wh*-word in the corresponding question (Rooth 1996).[2]

(17.1) Q: Who stole the picture?
    a. [Focus The <u>thief</u>] [Presupposition stole it] SVO
    b. [Presupposition Lo robó] [Focus el ladrón] OVS
                      it   stole   the   thief
      'The thief stole it.'

Example 17.1 shows that English and Spanish use different mechanisms to mark the focus and the presupposition in this context. Although SVO is

---

[1] Vallduví (1992) does not follow the traditional generative "T model" of the grammar (Chomsky 1993, 1995, 1998), which assumes three levels of representation for the construction of linguistic expressions: a computational system (CS) that generates representations by the application of specific combinatorial rules, and a system of interfaces that connects the CS with the sensori-motor (SM) and conceptual-intentional systems (C-I). CS reaches the two performance systems, C-I and SM, through the two interface levels of representation: Logical Form (LF) and the Phonetic Form (PF). Vallduví proposes IS as an independent module but does not explicitly address how IS and syntax interact (see López-Cortina (2007) for discussion).

[2] Focused phrases appear in square brackets and underlined phrases represent elements which receive nuclear stress. Elements are capitalized if they are contrastively focused.

the canonical word order in both languages, in Spanish the subject appears in sentence-final position when it is narrowly focused.

Existing research on IS in Spanish has generated a solid body of literature from various theoretical backgrounds. One common feature of many of these approaches is that focus is often characterized as a prosodic phenomenon since focused elements receive special intonational or suprasegmental features (length, pitch, duration etc.). That is, the focus phrase is the most prosodically prominent phrase in a sentence (Chomsky 1971; Cinque 1993; Truckenbrodt 1995; Reinhart 2006). Focused elements which receive stress or are accented are considered to be F-marked (Selkirk 1995).[3]

One crucial property of Spanish is that the ordering of elements in a sentence reveals a particular information structure which is unique to that utterance. We can say that focus marking affects the structure of sentences, which often results in the alteration of the canonical SVO order (see Domínguez 2013 for an overview). For instance, the two sentences in Example 17.2 show the same constituents but in different orders. The postverbal subject in (17.2a) is narrowly focused (i.e. it is the only element in the sentence identified as the new information), whereas the preverbal subject in (17.2b) receives a broad focus interpretation.

(17.2)   a. Lo   ha   comprado   [F Marta]   (narrow focus)
              it   has   bought   Marta
              'Marta has bought it.'
        b. [F Marta lo ha comprado]   (broad focus)

The F-marked subject (Marta) is the only element bearing main stress in sentence-final position in Example 17.2a, a position that is unusual for subjects in languages with canonical SVO order (Zubizarreta 1998). This example shows that there is a narrow link between where stress in assigned and where narrowly-focused elements can appear in a sentence in Spanish.

Although the literature often refers to "focus" as a single, unique phenomenon, it is widely assumed that two types of focus can be distinguished: contrastive and informational (Lambrecht 1994).[4] In this respect, É. Kiss (1998) noted that informational or presentational focus (focus which is not quantificational, and stays *in situ*) has different properties from identificational or contrastive focus (see López 2009 for a detailed discussion). Some differences between information and contrastive focus are easily detectable when the question–answer test is applied. For instance, the contrastive focused subject in Example 17.3 does not refer directly to the *wh*-word in a question such as "Who stole the picture?"

---

[3] For analyses of focus in Spanish as a primarily syntactic phenomenon see López (2009), Ordóñez (1997, 2000), and Ortega-Santos (2008, 2016).
[4] See Brunetti (2004) and Buitrago (2013) for a different view.

Instead, Example 17.3 is felicitous as an answer to a question which does not include a *wh*-word, such as "Did the security guard steal the picture?"

(17.3) [F El LADRÓN] lo robó, no el guarda.
'The thief stole it, not the guard.'

The contrastive focus in Example 17.3 is associated with a closed set of possible candidates who are contextually determined. In the framework of "Alternative Semantics" (Rooth 1985, 1992, 1996) a focused sentence presupposes the existence of a set in the discourse environment. This set contains possible alternatives "which potentially contrast with the ordinary semantic value" of a sentence (Rooth 1992:76). Accordingly, each focused sentence asserts its truthfulness among the presupposed alternatives. Likewise, Vallduví and Vilkuna (1998) use the term "kontrast" for a type of focus with similar characteristics. Kontrast assumes that for each "kontrastive" focus a set of alternatives (i.e. the membership set) is generated and determines the semantic interpretation of the variable introduced by the focus:

(17.4) a. Juan presentó [F Carlos] a Marta
'Juan introduced Carlos to Marta.'
b. Membership set M = {Carlos, Marcos, Sonia, etc.}

In this example, any member of the membership test can substitute the contrastively focused *Carlos*. In Spanish, informational and contrastive foci have different prosodic, semantic, and syntactic characteristics. Consider the following pair of sentences, where the subject is narrowly focused but appears in two different positions, in preverbal position (17.5a) and in sentence-final position in (17.5b):

(17.5) a. [F YO]   mando   aquí
I   rule.1SG. here.
'I rule here.'
b. Aquí mando [F yo]
'I rule here.'

Sentence 17.5a, with canonical SVO order, is felicitous if it is assumed that somebody other than the speaker was in charge (a suitable question would be "Which of you two is in charge here?"). Sentence 17.5b would be felicitous in a context where the person asking the same question does not assume that anybody else could be in charge. We can say that these two sentences share the same truth condition, but they have different presuppositions.

There are additional prosodic differences between informational and contrastive focus (see recent experimental evidence in Chung 2012). Previous research has shown that Spanish uses at least two different mechanisms to mark contrastive focus: the element is placed before a phrase boundary to receive some prominence (Sosa 1999), or the peak of the fundamental frequency falls on the stressed syllable, instead of falling on the post-tonic syllable (Beckman *et al.* 2002; Domínguez 2004b;

Face 2002; Fant 1984; Garrido *et al.* 1993; Prieto *et al.* 1995; Sosa 1995, 1999).[5] Zubizarreta (1998) also argues that the so-called "Emphatic/ Contrastive Stress Rule" (ESR) can stress elements which are not sentence-final, and can be used to mark contrastive focus.[6] Informational focus, on the other hand, receives prominence by being aligned with main sentence stress which in Spanish falls in sentence-final position via a different stress assignment mechanism, the Nuclear Stress Rule (NSR), which assigns main stress to the rightmost stressable vowel in a sentence (Chomsky and Halle 1968).

The investigation of Spanish word order has been useful for providing insights into the relationship between different components of the grammar (syntax, prosody, and pragmatics) and how these areas interact with each other. This has been particularly fruitful in generative linguistic theory by investigating the point of contact between the phonological component of the grammar and narrow syntax, the interface level known as PF (Phonetic Form). It is at this level of representation that syntactic structures are assigned a phonetic representation. In the next sections, I will show how word order variation can be accounted for as an operation required by the prosodic (PF) interface, rather than by assuming that word order is altered to fulfill a syntactic requirement. For instance, as the examples in this section have shown, by allowing the subject to appear in postverbal position, a new focus–presupposition configuration arises as the subject can be narrowly focused. This interpretation is not achieved if the subject appears in the canonical SVO order (see Fox 2000; Reinhart 2006; Domínguez 2013).

17.2 Word Order Variation in Standard Spanish

The Extended Projection Principle (EPP) is a condition requiring the subject position (i.e. the specifier of the Inflectional Phrase (IP)) to be filled in all languages (Chomsky 1982, 1995). Since around 70 percent of sentences in standard Spanish have a null subject (Domínguez 2013), the EPP is mainly satisfied by *pro* (a pronoun which is not phonetically realized) in Spanish (see Sheehan 2006; Ortega-Santos 2008). The null pronoun *pro*, as well as other elements, such as a null or expletive pronoun, and a temporal–locative topic, can also satisfy the EPP when overt subjects appear postverbally. This makes it look as if word order in Spanish is rather free (see Contreras 1978, 1980, 1991; Ordóñez 1998; Zubizarreta 1998; Domínguez 2004a for detailed discussion of this phenomenon). Example 17.6 from Domínguez 2013 shows the subject and the object in

---

[5] But see Muntendam and Torreira (2016) for a recent experimental study which shows no clear differences in the phonetic realization of different focus types in Spanish.

[6] Zubizarreta (1998:134) argues that the ESR can, in fact, cancel the Nuclear Stress Rule (NSR) in some contexts.

preverbal (17.6a) as well as postverbal (17.6b, 17.6c, 17.6d) positions. The object too can be preverbal, as shown in (17.6d) and (17.6e):

(17.6)   a. Susana abre el libro.   SVO
'Susana opens the book.'
b. Abre Susana el libro   VSO
c. Abre el libro Susana   VOS
d. El libro abre Susana   OVS
e. El libro, lo abre Susana   O,Cl-VS

It is widely assumed that the verb moves to Tense[7] in all these sentences (Suñer 1994), and that preverbal and postverbal subjects occupy two different positions. The subject is assumed to rise to the specifier of IP when it appears in preverbal SVO position (see Alexiadou and Anagnostopoulou 1998 and Ordóñez and Treviño 1999 for a different analysis), but it stays in its base position, in the specifier of the verbal phrase (VP), when it appears postverbally. *Pro* satisfies the EPP when the subject is not in preverbal position.

There are also interpretative differences between each possible word order. For instance, subjects in SVO configurations have a neutral interpretation, whereas VOS subjects are obligatorily narrowly focused (see Example 17.7c). In contrast, a sentence with an element whose canonical position is final (like the object in Example 17.7b) can have either a narrow (17.7b) or broad focus (17.7a) interpretation. Example 17.7b is an appropriate answer to "Who have the players yelled at?," which requires narrow focus on the object, whereas Example 17.7c is appropriate as an answer to "Who has yelled at the referee?," which requires an answer with a narrow focused subject:

(17.7)   a. [F Los jugadores han gritado al árbitro]   SVO
           the players have yelled at-the referee
'The players have yelled at the referee.'
b. Los jugadores han gritado [F al árbitro]   SVO
c. Han gritado al árbitro [F los jugadores]   VOS

Examples (17.7a) and (17.7b) appear to share the same structure but they are felicitous in different contexts. In Sentence 17.7a all the elements are part of the focus so it is appropriate as an answer to a question in an out-of-the-blue context. In contrast, the object in Sentence 17.7b is the only element in the focus set, i.e. the set of possible candidates that can be part of the focus domain (Reinhart 2006), and it is narrowly focused. Consequently, it can be a felicitous answer to a question such as "Whom have the players yelled at?"

Notice that in order to mark a phrase with narrow focus the rest of the sentence must be presupposed. This is also the case when the subject is focused in VOS configurations (see Example 17.7c) and the sentence

---

[7] The Tense Phrase (TP) is also commonly known as the Inflectional Phrase (IP). TP and IP are interchangeable terms.

answers a question of the type "Who did X?," i.e. "Who yelled at the referee?" In this example, the subject *"los jugadores"* is the only element receiving sentence stress and it is also the only element which is part of the focus set. As for the object, it is no longer the element in final position and does not receive sentence stress.

So far, we have seen how the verb moves overtly to T in Spanish and that movement of the subject to the specifier of IP, the standard subject position, is in fact optional. This optionality cannot be accounted for by a straightforward syntactic requirement, as *pro* can satisfy the EPP in Spanish. The subject appears in postverbal position to satisfy a (syntax–prosody) interface condition: that the narrowly-focused subject is aligned with main stress, which in Spanish falls on the element in sentence-final position.

17.3 Focus–Stress Alignment

One of the basic assumptions of the so-called "stress-based approach of focus" (Cinque 1993; Costa 2000, 2004; Neeleman and Reinhart 1998; Reinhart 1997, 2006; Szendrői 2001, 2003, 2004; Zubizarreta 1998; Büring and Gutiérrez-Bravo 2001; Domínguez 2004a, 2013) is that the focused phrase must contain the main stress of the sentence (Chomsky 1971, Jackendoff 1972).

As already noted (Section 17.1), Chomsky and Halle (1968) first proposed that main stress at the sentence level is assigned by the NSR to the rightmost stressable vowel in a major constituent. Later, Cinque (1993) reformulated the NSR in his "Generalized Stress Rule" to reflect that stress is assigned to the most deeply embedded constituent in a sentence and its application is determined by the head-complement parameter. In Spanish, the most embedded element is always the element in sentence-final position.

Nuclear stress applies in a cyclical manner and its assignment is dependent on the number of syntactic constituents present in a sentence. In Example 17.8 the main stress of the sentence is assigned to the most embedded constituent, which is the object in this sentence:

(17.8) [$_{IP \, cycle}$ La estudiante [$_{VP \, cycle}$ visitó [$_{DP \, cycle}$ al profe**sor**]]]

The assignment of stress (shown in bold type) in this analysis is heavily dependent on the syntactic structure of a clause. Therefore, the position that constituents take in a sentence determines which element receives stress, an important observation for languages with flexible word order. A pre-established default rhythmic pattern determines which constituent is metrically strong, even in cases where two sisters (such as the verb and the object in Example 17.9) are equally embedded. In this example, the last constituent, i.e. the object, will be assigned default prominence in languages like Spanish and English, whose default rhythmic pattern is (w)eak–(s)trong:[8]

(17.9)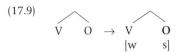

As Example 17.9 shows, the syntactic relationship between the elements in a sentence is crucial for the assignment of default prominence if the NSR applies, as the relative position of phrases is the relevant factor in determining which of the two sisters is going to receive stress.[9] In Example 17.8 the strong prosodic feature is assigned to the rightmost phonological phrase (ϕ) (*al profesor*) in the intonational phrase (IP) (*La estudiante visitó al profesor*). Within the strong phonological phrase, the strong prosodic feature is assigned to the rightmost stressed syllable (i.e. *profesor*).

From an interpretative point of view, the default weak–strong pattern is ambiguous since it is the underlying prosodic structure of sentences with both broad and narrow focus. For instance, Example 17.10 has the same rhythmic pattern when the entire sentence is in focus (it answers the question "What has happened?") and when only the last constituent is narrowly focused (it answers the question "Who has the student visited?"):

(17.10)   [[La estudiante]ϕ   [ha visitado]ϕ   [al pro**fe**sor] ϕ] IP
          [w s]   [w s]   [w **s**]
                               [w   **S**]

In English, a strong–weak configuration always represents a marked pattern. The alteration of the default rhythmic pattern should be sufficient for the listener to perceive that the normal melodic pattern has been modified in order to emphasize an element which otherwise would not be the most prosodically prominent element, as in the case of the verb in Example 17.11:

(17.11)   [[The student]ϕ   [has **vi**sited]ϕ   [the professor] ϕ] I
          [w s]   [w **s**]   [w s]
                             [**S** w]

When a (s–w) rhythmic pattern applies, the focused element is allowed to receive stress in any position in the sentence in English. This is an important property of English, since subjects cannot directly receive

---

[8] This analysis of default stress assignment is subject to parameterization and is determined by the side in which recursion takes place in a language (e.g. OV vs. VO languages). For instance, whilst in English the lower sister is always metrically stronger by default (VO), in Dutch we find the opposite pattern (OV) since the object, although not in final position, is in the recursive side in this language (see Neeleman and Reinhart (1998) for a discussion on this issue). In both languages, the object is the element receiving sentence stress by the NSR.

[9] Büring and Gutiérrez-Bravo (2001) and Domínguez (2004a, 2013) have argued for an alternative analysis of accent placement in Spanish, whereby stress rules apply to prosodic phrases rather than to syntactic phrases (see Selkirk 1986, 1995, 2005). This is in line with similar proposals in other languages (Szendrői 2001, 2004).

sentence stress via the NSR in their sentence-initial position. In these cases, two different elements, the subject in initial position and the element in final position, are both competing to receive stress. In order for the subject to receive prominence an additional operation must then apply, a "stress shift" (Reinhart 1997, 2006), which allows sentence stress to fall on any constituent, even if it is not final:

(17.12)   Stress Shift: Relocate the main stress to a constituent you want to focus on

In the following English example prominence has been shifted from its default (last) position to the initial subject position and as a result the subject is now narrowly focused:

(17.13)   [F My neighbor] is building a desk

Previous studies on the nature of stress shifts (see Cinque 1993, Reinhart 2006, Zubizarreta 1998, Neeleman and Reinhart 1998) have argued that two independent operations are involved in this process, destressing of the element bearing main stress (the object in Example 17.13) and strengthening of an element not included in the focus set (the subject). Destressing is usually linked to cases of "anaphoric destressing," a process that accounts for the fact that elements that refer to entities already mentioned in the discourse tend to lose their prominence. In Example 17.14 the clause-final verb, which is part of the presupposition, is destressed. This allows the subject to be the element carrying the main stress instead (destressed elements appear in curly brackets in the examples).

(17.14)   Q: Who is laughing?
          a. My brother {is laughing}

Reinhart (2006) argues that anaphoric destressing is not a focus-related operation *per se*. She characterizes it as a mechanism that enables anaphora resolution (the process of linking a pronoun with its referent in discourse), and connects elements in a sentence with what has already been mentioned in the discourse. Destressing also applies in certain contexts even if elements are not necessarily anaphoric. In fact, it has long been observed that sentence-final elements do not always necessarily receive stress (see Bolinger 1972; Büring 1997). For instance, constituents which are semantically vacuous are unlikely candidates to be the focus, and therefore tend to not be stressed, even if they are the most embedded element in a sentence. In Example 17.15 "something," the element in a position to receive sentence stress, appears destressed due to its lack of semantic content:

(17.15)   Q: What did you do last night?
          a. I wrote {something}
          b. *I wrote something

The same is observed in the case of pronouns, which are always anaphoric, and therefore tend to be destressed. In the following non-contrastive example, the verb, and not the destressed pronoun, is the element receiving main prominence:

(17.16) a. I haven't <u>seen</u> {her}
\qquad\quad b. *I haven't seen <u>her</u>

These examples show that there is a close relationship between the prosodic characteristics of phrases and their informational status. Accordingly, Neeleman and Reinhart (1998) propose that all anaphoric material (in the sense that it is linked to an entity mentioned in the previous context) has to be destressed – at least in English and Dutch – although this does not seem to be the case in Spanish. Indeed, Zubizarreta (1998) argues that all the phrases in a sentence, regardless of its semantic or pragmatic content, are visible to the NSR in Spanish. Unlike English, destressing of anaphoric or semantically vacuous phrases does not apply. Zubizarreta formalizes this difference as follows:

(17.17) a. Defocalized and anaphoric constituents are metrically invisible for the NSR in English, in German, and in French.
\qquad\quad b. All phonological material is metrically visible for the NSR in Spanish.

Example 17.18, from Zubizarreta (1998), shows that destressing the anaphoric verb to shift the stress to the subject is possible in English, but not in Spanish:[10]

(17.18) Q: Who is crying?
\qquad\quad a. *El <u>bebé</u>   {llora}
\qquad\qquad the baby   cries
\qquad\quad b. The <u>baby</u> {is crying}

As was mentioned in Section 17.1, Zubizarreta (1998) marginally discusses the application of a stress strengthening rule, i.e. the ESR, which can apply freely and without restrictions in order to focus on any element regardless of its position in the sentence. However, for Zubizarreta the ESR can apply only if the focus is contrastive or emphatic, as in Example 17.19 (from Zubizarreta 1998):

(17.19) JUAN llamó por teléfono (no Pedro).
\qquad\quad 'Juan called (not Pedro).'

Crucially, Zubizarreta proposes that Spanish uses word order to resolve the misalignment between (informational, non-contrastive) focus and sentence-final stress, if the focused element is not sentence-final. In Spanish, presupposed elements are moved out of their canonical final position by means of two mechanisms: scrambling and dislocations. These two focus-marking related operations result in an alteration of the canonical SVO order.

---

[10] Although this is commonly assumed in the theoretical literature, some recent empirical studies have shown that SVO is often chosen and used by native Spanish speakers instead of VOS, suggesting that destressing may not be as restricted in Spanish as Zubizarreta argues. See discussion in Section 17.6.

17.4 Scrambling

Focus-induced scrambling allows displacement of a non-focal final element to fulfill a stress-focus requirement. In particular, through scrambling it is ensured that the focus appears in sentence-final position so that it can receive main stress. Zubizarreta (1998) argues that this type of scrambling, unlike other types of movement which are necessary to check a syntactic feature, is motivated by the need to align the focus with main sentence stress. She characterizes it as a type of "Prosodically Motivated Movement," or p-movement.[11] Her analysis of p-movement is also based on the assumption that the focused constituent must contain the rhythmically most prominent element in a sentence, and that prominence is assigned by the NSR. Therefore, for Zubizarreta the NSR is the general rule that allows the focus structure of a sentence to relate to the intonation of that sentence.[12] She furthermore argues that the NSR applies to a pair of sister constituents (e.g. in a head–complement relation). For Zubizarreta, the c-commanding[13] relationship between the two sisters is what determines the assignment of prominence. Zubizarreta (1998) formalizes her notion of the NSR as follows:

(17.20) NSR: Given two nodes C_i and C_j that are symmetrical sisters, the one lower in the asymmetric c-command ordering is more prominent.

When a mismatch between the F-marked structure and the NSR arises (i.e. when the focused element is not in sentence-final position) p-movement can apply. According to Zubizarreta, scrambling is available because all phonological material is metrically visible for the NSR in Spanish (Zubizarreta 1998:76) and stress-shifts are not available. Example 17.21b, from Zubizarreta (1998), shows that the focused subject appears in its non-canonical final position in order to receive prominence; if all the constituents were to be left in their canonical position instead, as in (17.21a), the NSR would assign main stress to the prepositional phrase (PP):

(17.21) a. Los   alumnos   se   enfrentaron   [F con   la   policía]   S-V-PP
           the   students refl.   confronted   with   the   police
           'The students confronted the police.'
        b. Se enfrentaron (con la policía)$_i$ [F los alumnos]   t$_i$ V-PP-S

It needs to be highlighted that VOS as a result of p-movement or scrambling could be regarded as a type of marked word order, in the sense that it is infrequently used, perhaps because all presupposed material remains in

---

[11] Parafita Couto (2009) argues that since p-movement is not a syntactic operation it can displace elements both to the right and to the left of the focus.
[12] See Domínguez (2004a, 2013) for an analysis of p-movement which is not directly linked to the NSR.
[13] Constituent command (c-command) is a basic notion in generative syntax which defines relationships of dominance between elements in a structure. For instance, A c-commands B iff (= if and only if) neither A nor B dominates the other, and the lowest branching node that dominates A also dominates B. This basically means that any node c-commands its sister and everything its sister dominates.

the sentence in this structure. In conversation, it seems more natural to elide the presupposition as this is information which is already known by the interlocutors.

Example 17.22a has an ambiguous interpretation since it can be the answer to three different questions: "What happened?," which requires focus on the entire sentence (IP), "What did the students do?," which requires focus on the verbal phrase (VP) only (17.22b), and "Who did the students confront?," which requires focus on the PP only (17.22c):

(17.22) a. [F-IP Los alumnos se enfrentaron con la policía]
         b. Los alumnos [F-VP se enfrentaron con la policía]
         c. Los alumnos se enfrentaron [F-PP con la policía]

The ambiguity disappears when the subject is in sentence-final position (see Example 17.23a). This sentence can be the answer only to a question such as "Who confronted the police?," which requires an answer with narrow focus on the subject. After scrambling of the object has been applied and the subject appears in final position, the focused subject is the only element left in the focus set (# marks the sentence as infelicitous):

(17.23) a. Se enfrentaron con la policía [F los alumnos]
         b. #Se enfrentaron [F con la policía los alumnos]
         c. #[F Se enfrentaron con la policía los alumnos]

In Example 17.24, from Zubizarreta (1998), scrambling (or p-movement) has been applied. The PP in parentheses has undergone movement from its canonical final position and is left adjoined to the VP.[14] This operation leaves the object, which remains *in situ*, in final position where it can receive stress:

(17.24) Ana   escondió   (debajo de la cama)   [F la muñeca]   S-V-PP-O
         Ana   hid   under of the bed   the doll

Zubizarreta characterizes p-movement as being strictly local (i.e. immediately to the left of the focused phrase) and there is no restriction on what type of elements can undergo this type of scrambling.

17.5 Dislocations

Dislocations[15] are widely attested in Spanish as well as in other Romance languages (see López 2009 for a review). Clitic-left dislocations (CLLD) and

---

[14] In an alternative account, Ordóñez (2000) proposes that in VOS configurations the verb and the object form one single unit which he calls TP. After the focused subject moves to a designated focus projection in the left periphery, TP undergoes remnant movement to a position higher than the focus phrase. More recently, Etxepare and Uribe-Etxebarria (2008) have also argued that remnant movement of non-focal cases allows the focus to appear rightmost. See Ortega-Santos (2013) for a detailed review.

[15] There is a rich inventory of left-dislocation constructions in Spanish which cannot be covered in this chapter. For a recent analysis of the prosodic and syntactic characteristics of hanging-topic left dislocations and left dislocations without a resumptive clitic see Feldhausen (2016).

clitic-right dislocations (CLRD) are both available in Spanish although these two contractions have different syntactic characteristics. In both structures, a phrase which expresses given information is moved and adjoined to either the right or the left of the core clause. The dislocated phrase is coindexed with a resumptive clitic which shares its relevant gender, case and number features as shown in (17.25a) and (17.25b).[16] These examples also illustrate that only CLLDs can function as contrastive topics:

(17.25) Where have you bought this food?
    a. Las manzanas$_i$, *(las)$_i$ he comprado en el mercado
        the apples   them   have-bought   in the market
        'I have bought the apples in the market.'
    b. #Las$_i$ he comprado en el mercado, las manzanas$_i$

Example 17.25b is an example of a CLRD and is not felicitous in this context, as the answer to the question in (17.25) requires the dislocated topic to be in contrast with other items that the person has bought in the market (i.e. "this food" in the immediately preceding question). This is possible only when the dislocated element (las manzanas) is adjoined to the left of the clause.

The use of dislocations to mark the focus was discussed in detail by Vallduví (1992), using Catalan as an example. He links the availability of dislocations to how focus is marked in Catalan, in particular to the fact that by applying dislocations the focus (i.e. el ganivet) can appear in sentence-final position, as in Example 17.26b from Vallduví (1992):

(17.26)   a. [$_F$ Ficarem   el ganivet   al   calaix]   V-O-PP
           will-put   the knife   in-the   drawer
           'We will put the knife in the drawer.'
      b. Hi$_i$ ficarem   [$_F$ el ganivet] t$_i$,   al   calaix$_i$ Cl-V-O, PP
         LOC   will-put   the knife,   in-the   drawer
         'We will put the knife, in the drawer.'

In Vallduví's analysis, dislocations are obligatory to allow the focus to appear in the position where it can receive stress. In Example 17.26b, al calaix, which is not part of the focus, is dislocated and adjoined to the right of the main clause, and the locative clitic, hi, which binds the dislocated element, appears next to the verb. Since the dislocated PP is not part of the core clause in (17.26b), this sentence cannot be a felicitous answer to a question that requires the locative to be part of the focus. In contrast to Catalan, Spanish dislocations are neither obligatory, nor the only option for allowing the focus to receive stress. In fact, right dislocations, although possible in Spanish, are not as frequent as they are in other Romance languages, such as Italian or Catalan, which are languages with a richer inventory of clitic forms, including partitive and locative clitics.

---

[16] Although the dislocated phrase must always be bound by the clitic in CLLD, the clitic is optional in some CLRD.

In Spanish, dislocations also ensure that a focused element appears in sentence-final position so that it can receive sentence stress, as shown in Example 17.27.

(17.27) Q: Who paid the bill?
    a. #[F Susana pagó la cuenta] (non-felicitous)
       'Susana paid the bill.'
    b. *La cuenta*, la pagó [F Susana] (felicitous)
       the bill, it paid Susana

The presupposed object (*la cuenta*) is moved out of its canonical sentence-final position in Example 17.27b so it is not part of the focus set. This operation allows the creation of a new focus domain: this would not be obtainable with the canonical SVO word order (see 17.27a), which is not a felicitous reply to this question.

To summarize, when the focus is not the last element in a sentence, the structure of the clause can be altered by means of different strategies to ensure that information focus appears in a sentence-final position. In Spanish anaphoric/presupposed material cannot be destressed and, consequently, the stress cannot be relocated to fall on the focused element if it is not sentence-final. Both scrambling and dislocations are available options for focus-marking in Spanish because they allow the focus to be aligned with sentence stress in sentence-final position.

17.6 Suggestions for Future Research

This chapter has shown that a rich research agenda investigating Spanish word order and its relationship with information structure has emerged over the last few decades. Significant contributions have been made to different theoretical discussions, in particular to our understanding of the relationship between syntax and pragmatics, as well as between syntax and prosody. In this final section, I highlight some current unresolved issues in this area, and provide some suggestions for future research directions.

First, the classic theoretical models (see, e.g., Zubizarreta's p-movement, 1998) have analyzed Spanish as a uniform grammatical system ignoring the fact that there is a certain level of variation in the realization of subjects across the Spanish-speaking world. For instance, although all varieties of Spanish exhibit both SVO and VOS orders, null and postverbal subjects are realized at lower rates in some varieties, such as those spoken in the Caribbean (Puerto Rico, Cuba, and the Dominican Republic) (see Cabrera-Puche 2008; Martínez-Sanz 2011; Mayol 2012; Ticio 2004; Toribio 2000; Ortiz López 2010). It would be beneficial for future research to acknowledge that infrequent use of VOS in some varieties may mean that scrambling is not a real option as a focus-marking strategy for speakers of those varieties. It would be useful to investigate how narrowly-focused subjects get aligned with sentence stress in these varieties. It may be the case that other strategies are preferred by speakers of Caribbean Spanish where scrambling would be favored by speakers of standard Spanish.

Second, existing theoretical proposals have mainly relied on introspective intuitions as evidence to support their main claims. This is common practice in several frameworks, and in generative linguistic analysis in particular. Due to the complex nature of focus marking in Spanish, however, it is essential that any future proposal combines native speaker intuitions with other types of data (see Gupton and Leal Méndez 2013). This is particularly relevant since some scholars have argued that the requirement that the focus is aligned with main stress, which is the basis of many existing theoretical proposals (including Zubizarreta's (1998) p-movement), is not always observed in Spanish (see e.g. Ordóñez 1997, Casielles-Suárez 2004; Olarrea 2012; Ortega-Santos 2008). Some studies have provided experimental evidence to support this claim. For instance, Muntendam (2009) elicited experimental data from Andean Spanish speakers (from Bolivia and Ecuador) and found that SVO was widely accepted in contexts where the subject was narrowly focused. Similarly, Gabriel (2006, 2010) examined the prosodic realization of different focus structures in various varieties of Argentine Spanish to reach the same conclusion. Recently, Hoot (2012, 2016) has argued that it is not an absolute requirement that stress and focus correspond in Spanish, as narrowly-focused subjects do not need to appear rightmost; instead, he proposes that it is sufficient that stress and focus get aligned as closely as possible. Similarly, Gupton and Leal Méndez (2013) have shown that native speakers of Spanish do not always prefer VOS over SVO in contexts where the subject is narrowly focused. This study reports data from native speakers of Spanish and Galician which were elicited by various contextualized acceptability judgment tasks. The Spanish native speakers were asked about the naturalness of different structures after a context was introduced. Hoot (2016) also reports data elicited by a contextualized acceptability judgment task and argues that native speakers accept a variety of structures, including marking the subject in SVO via stress shifts. I agree with Hoot that speakers may use an array of strategies (scrambling, *in-situ* focus, dislocations) depending on the context. It is important to note, however, that stress-based approaches to focus do not claim that p-movement is the only strategy available to mark the subject with narrow focus (see Domínguez 2013), it is the alignment between the focus and main stress which appears to be obligatory. In this respect, scrambling is one of many strategies available in Spanish to align the focus with stress.

Although there is merit in using data from acceptability tests (which present a predetermined set of possible answers in specific contexts), controlled and naturalistic (corpus) production data may also be useful in order to determine when exactly speakers use each of the strategies available. In an acceptability test, it may be possible that speakers rate VOS structures as less natural with respect to SVO because of the marked nature of VOS (i.e. it is rare and less frequent) even though both structures are equally grammatical. It may also be the case that there is a considerable amount of inter-speaker variation regarding how each of the structures presented in the tests is rated in terms of its naturalness (some speakers may just prefer to use dislocations over scrambling for instance, or the other way around if they are given a choice). This would not be an issue when investigating production data and semi-spontaneous naturalistic data, in particular (see Leal *et al.* (2017) for a study which uses elicited production data).

Finally, the review of these recent studies shows that research in the area of focus marking and its relationship with word order in Spanish faces a methodological challenge. Future research will benefit from developing a methodological approach which combines concrete manipulated tasks with larger-scale datasets of semi-spontaneous data. Researchers in the generative tradition have not exploited the benefits of gaining insights about linguistic knowledge through the use of corpora, perhaps because these types of data are often regarded as evidence of language use, rather than of the grammatical knowledge of speakers (see studies in Penke and Rosenbach 2007). However, the view that corpora (including semi-spontaneous datasets) can be useful for informing formal linguistic debates about grammatical knowledge is rapidly changing (see Armstrong 1994; Newmeyer 2003; Kempchinsky and Gupton 2009). For instance, Sampson (1996) shows how frequency patterns in linguistic corpora are able to reveal that a certain grammatical phenomenon (i.e. central embedding) is possible, even though it had not been acknowledged in theoretical analyses. Wasow (2002) argues that the absoluteness of grammatical judgments may not be the best methodological tool to explore gradience in grammar (which seems to be the case of word order variation in Spanish, as various possible orders are used with different frequency). This is a problem which is not found in corpus data. The combination of multiple experimental methods (see e.g. Cabrera-Puche 2008) can be an appropriate and useful next step in the investigation of the relationship between word order variation and Information Structure in Spanish.

References

Alexiadou, A. and Anagnostopoulou, E. (1998). Parametrizing AGR: Word Order, V-Movement and EPP-Checking. *Natural Language and Linguistic Theory*, 16 (3), 491–539.

Armstrong, S. (1994). *Using Large Corpora*. Cambridge, MA: MIT Press.

Beckman, M. E., Díaz-Campos, M., McGory, J. T., and Morgan, T. A. (2002). Intonation across Spanish in the Tones and Break Indices Framework. *Probus*, 14, 9–36.

Bolinger, D. (1972). Accent is Predictable (If You Are a Mind Reader). *Lingua*, 48, 633–644.

Brunetti, L. (2004). A Unification of Focus (Doctoral dissertation). University of Florence.

Buitrago, N. (2013). Types of Focus in Spanish: Exploring the Connection between Function and Realization (Doctoral dissertation). Cornell University.

Büring, D. (1997). *The Meaning of Topic and Focus: The 59th Street Bridge Accent*. London: Routledge.

Büring, D. and Gutiérrez-Bravo, R. (2001). Focus-Related Word Order Variation without the NSR: A Prosody Based Cross-Linguistic Analysis. In Séamas Mac Bhloscaidh (ed.), *Syntax and Semantics at Santa Cruz*, Vol. 3. Santa Cruz, CA: Linguistics Research Center, University of California, pp. 41–58.

Cabrera-Puche, M. J. (2008). Null Subject Patterns in Language Contact: The Case of Dominican Spanish (Doctoral dissertation). Rutgers University.

Casielles-Suárez, E. (2004). *The Syntax–Information Structure Interface: Evidence from Spanish and English*. New York: Routledge.

Chafe, W. L. (1976). Givenness, Contrastiveness, Definiteness, Subjects, Topics and Point of View In Charles N. Li (ed.), *Subject and Topic*. New York Academic Press, pp. 27–55.

Chomsky, N. (1971). Deep Structure, Surface Structure, and Semantic Interpretation. In D. D. Steinberg and L. A. Jakobovits (eds.), *Semantics: An Interdisciplinary Reader in Philosophy, Linguistics and Psychology*. Cambridge: Cambridge University Press, pp. 183–216.

Chomsky, N. (1982). *Some Concepts and Consequences of Government and Binding Theory*. Cambridge, MA: MIT Press.

Chomsky, N. (1993). A Minimalist Program for Linguistic Theory. In K. Hale and S. J. Keyser (eds.), *The View from Building 20: Essays in Linguistics in Honor of Sylvain Bromberger*. Cambridge, MA: MIT Press, pp. 1–52.

Chomsky, N. (1995). *The Minimalist Program*. Cambridge, MA: MIT Press.

Chomsky, N. (1998). Minimalist Inquiries: The Framework. *MIT Working Papers in Linguistics*, 15, 1–56.

Chomsky, N. and Halle, M. (1968). *The Sound Pattern of English*. New York: Harper.

Chung, H. (2012). Two Types of Focus in Castilian Spanish (Doctoral dissertation). University of Texas at Austin.

Cinque, G. (1993). A Null Theory of Phrase and Compound Stress. *Linguistic Inquiry*, 24, 239–267.

Contreras, H. (1978). *El orden de palabras en español*. Madrid: Cátedra.

Contreras, H. (1980). Sentential Stress, Word Order, and the Notion of Subject in Spanish. In L. R. Waugh and C. H. van Schooneveld (eds.),

The Melody of Language: Intonation and Prosody. Baltimore, MD: University Park Press, pp. 45–53.

Contreras, H. (1991). On the Position of Subjects. In S. Rothstein (ed.), *Perspectives on Phrase Structure: Heads and Licensing*. San Diego, CA and London: Academic Press, pp. 63–79.

Costa, J. (2000). Focus In Situ: Evidence from Portuguese. *Probus*, 12, 187–228.

Costa, J. (2004). *Subject Positions and Interfaces. The Case of European Portuguese*. Berlin: De Gruyter.

Domínguez, L. (2004a). Mapping Focus: The Syntax and Prosody of Focus in Spanish (Doctoral dissertation). Boston University.

Domínguez, L. (2004b). The Effects of Phonological Cues on the Syntax of Focus Constructions in Spanish. In R. Bok-Bennema, B. Hollebrandse, B. Kampers-Manhe, and P. Sleeman (eds.), *Romance Languages and Linguistic Theory 2002*. Amsterdam: John Benjamins, pp. 69–81.

Domínguez, L. (2013). *Understanding Interfaces: Second Language Acquisition and Native Language Attrition of Spanish Subject Realization and Word Order Variation*. Amsterdam: John Benjamins.

É. Kiss, K. (1998). Identificational Focus versus Information Focus. *Language*, 74, 245–273.

Etxepare, R. and Uribe-Etxebarria, M. (2008). On Negation and Focus in Spanish and Basque. In X. Artiagoitia Beaskoetxea and J. Lakarra Andrinua (eds.), *Gramatika jaietan: Patxi Goenagaren omenez*. Bilbao: Universidad del País Vasco, pp. 287–310.

Face, T. (2002). Local Intonational Marking of Spanish Contrastive Focus. *Probus*, 14, 71–92.

Fant, L. (1984). *Estructura informativa en español. Estudio sintáctico y entonativo*. Uppsala: Acta Universitatis Upsaliensis.

Feldhausen, I. (2016). The Relation between Prosody and Syntax: The Case of Different Types of Left-Dislocations in Spanish. In M. E. Armstrong, N. Hendriksen, and M. D. M. Vanrell (eds.), *Intonational Grammar in Ibero-Romance: Approaches across Linguistic Subfields*. Amsterdam: John Benjamins, pp. 153–180.

Fox, D. (2000). *Economy and Semantic Interpretation*. Cambridge, MA: MIT Press.

Gabriel, C. (2006). Focal Pitch Accents and Subject Positions in Spanish: Comparing Close-to-Standard Varieties and Argentinean Porteño. In R. Hoffmann and H. Mixdorff (eds.), *Speech Prosody 2006*. Dresden: TUD Press. Available from http://citeseerx.ist.psu.edu/viewdoc/download?doi=10.1.1.387.6737&rep=rep1&type=pdf (last access January 10, 2018).

Gabriel, C. (2010). On Focus, Prosody, and Word Order in Argentinean Spanish: A Minimalist OT account. *Revista Virtual de Estudos da Linguagem*, 4, 183–222.

Garrido, J. M., Llisterri, J., de la Mota, C., and Ríos, A. (1993). Prosodic Differences in Reading Style: Isolated vs. Contextualized Sentences.

EUROSPEECH' 93, pp. 573–576. Available from www.isca-speech.org/archive/eurospeech_1993/e93_0573.html (last access January 8, 2018).

Gupton, T. and Leal Méndez, T. (2013). Experimental Methodologies: Two Case Studies Investigating the Syntax–Discourse Interface. *Studies in Hispanic and Lusophone Linguistics*, 6 (1), 139–164.

Hoot, B. (2012). Narrow Focus on Pre-Nominal Modifiers in Spanish: An Optimality-Theoretic Analysis. In K. Geeslin and M. Díaz-Campos (eds.), *Selected Proceedings of the 14th Hispanic Linguistics Symposium*. Somerville, MA: Cascadilla, pp. 293–307.

Hoot, B. (2016). Narrow Presentational Focus in Mexican Spanish: Experimental Evidence. *Probus*, 28 (2), 335–365.

Jackendoff, R. S. (1972). *Semantic Interpretation in Generative Grammar*. Cambridge, MA: MIT Press.

Kempchinsky, P. and Gupton, T. (2009). *The Role of Quantitative Data Collection in Theoretical Syntax*. Paper Presented at the 13th Hispanic Linguistics Symposium, Universidad de Puerto Rico.

Lambrecht, K. (1994). *Information Structure and Sentence Form*. Cambridge: Cambridge University Press.

Leal, T., Destruel, E., and Hoot, B. (2017). The Realization of Information Focus in Monolingual and Bilingual Native Spanish. *Linguistic Approaches to Bilingualism*. doi: 10.1075/lab.16009.lea

López, L. (2009). *A Derivational Syntax of Information Structure*. Oxford: Oxford University Press.

López-Cortina, J. (2007). The Spanish Left Periphery: Questions and Answers (Doctoral dissertation). Georgetown University.

Martínez-Sanz, C. (2011). Null and Overt Subjects in a Variable System: The Case of Dominican Spanish (Doctoral dissertation). University of Ottawa.

Mayol, L. (2012). An Account of the Variation in the Rates of Overt Subject Pronouns in Romance. *Spanish in Context*, 9 (3), 420–442.

Muntendam, A. (2009). Linguistic Transfer in Andean Spanish: Syntax or Pragmatics? (Doctoral dissertation). University of Illinois at Urbana-Champaign.

Muntendam, A. and Torreira, F. (2016). Focus and Prosody in Spanish and Quechua: Insights from an Interactive Task. In M. E. Armstrong, N. Hendriksen, and M. D. M. Vanrell (eds.), *Intonational Grammar in Ibero-Romance: Approaches across Linguistic Subfields*. Amsterdam: John Benjamins, pp. 69–90.

Neeleman, A. and Reinhart, T. (1998). Scrambling and the PF Interface. In M. Butt and W. Geuder (eds.), *The Projection of Arguments: Lexical and Compositional Factors*. Stanford, CA: CSLI Publications, pp. 309–353.

Newmeyer, F. J. (2003). Grammar is Grammar and Usage is Usage. *Language*, 79 (4), 682–707.

Olarrea, A. (2012). Word Order and Information Structure. In J. I. Hualde, A. Olarrea, and E. O'Rourke (eds.), *The Handbook of Hispanic Linguistics*. Chichester: Wiley-Blackwell, pp. 603–628.

Ordóñez, F. (1997). Word Order and Clause Structure in Spanish and other Romance Languages (Doctoral dissertation). CUNY.

Ordóñez, F. (1998). Postverbal Asymmetries in Spanish. *Natural Language and Linguistic Theory*, 16 (2), 313–346.

Ordóñez, F. (2000). *The Clausal Structure of Spanish: A Comparative Perspective*. New York: Garland.

Ordóñez, F. and Treviño, E. (1999). Left Dislocated Subjects and the Pro-Drop Parameter: A Case Study of Spanish. *Lingua*, 107 (1), 39–68.

Ortega-Santos, I. (2008). Projecting Subjects in Spanish and English (Doctoral dissertation). University of Maryland.

Ortega-Santos, I. (2013). Corrective Focus at the Right Edge in Spanish. *Lingua*, 131, 112–135.

Ortega-Santos, I. (2016). *Focus-Related Operations at the Right Edge in Spanish: Subjects and Ellipsis*. Amsterdam: John Benjamins.

Ortiz López, L. A. (2010). El español del Caribe: Orden de palabras a la luz de la interfaz léxico-sintáctica y sintácticopragmática. *Revista Internacional de Lingüística Iberoamericana*, 14, 75–93.

Parafita Couto, M. C. (2009). Rightwardho! *Linguistic Analysis*, 35 (1–4), 163–196.

Penke, M. and Rosenbach, A. (2007). *What Counts as Evidence in Linguistics: The Case of Innateness*. Amsterdam: John Benjamins.

Prieto, P., Chilin, S., and Nibert, H. (1995). Pitch Downtrend in Spanish. *Journal of Phonetics*, 24, 445–473.

Reinhart, T. (1997). Interface Economy: Focus and Markedness. In H. M. Gärtner, C. Wilder, and M. Bierwisch (eds.), *The Role of Economy Principles in Linguistic Theory*. Berlin: Akademie Verlag, pp. 146–169.

Reinhart, T. (2006). *Interface Strategies: Reference-Set Computation*. Cambridge, MA: MIT Press.

Rooth, M. (1985). Association with Focus (Doctoral dissertation). University of Massachusetts.

Rooth, M. (1992). A Theory of Focus Interpretation. *Natural Language Semantics*, 1, 75–116.

Rooth, M. (1996). Focus. In S. Lappin (ed.), *The Handbook of Contemporary Semantic Theory*. Oxford: Blackwell, pp. 271–297.

Sampson, G. (1996). From Central Embedding to Empirical Linguistics. In J. Thomas and M. Short (eds.), *Using Corpora for Language Research: Studies in Honor of Geoffrey Leech*. London: Longman, pp. 14–26.

Selkirk, E. (1986). On Derived Domains in Sentence Phonology. *Phonology Yearbook*, 3, 371–405.

Selkirk, E. (1995). Sentence Prosody: Intonation, Stress, and Phrasing. In J. Goldsmith (ed.), *The Handbook of Phonology*. Oxford: Blackwell, pp. 550–569.

Selkirk, E. (2005). Comments on Intonational Phrasing in English. In S. Frota, M. Vigario, and M.-J. Freitas (eds.), *Prosodies*. Berlin: De Gruyter, pp. 11–58.

Sheehan, M. (2006). The EPP and Null Subjects in Romance (Doctoral dissertation). University of Newcastle-upon-Tyne.

Sosa, J. M. (1995). Nuclear and Pre-Nuclear Tonal Inventories and the Phonology of Spanish Declarative Intonation. In K. Elenius and R. Branderand (eds.), *Proceedings of the 13th International Congress of Phonetic Sciences*, Vol. 4. Stockholm: KTH and Stockholm University, pp. 646–649.

Sosa, J. M. (1999). *La entonación del español*. Madrid: Cátedra.

Suñer, M. (1994). V-Movement and the Licensing of Argumental Wh-Phrases in Spanish. *Natural Language and Linguistic Theory*, 12, 335–372.

Szendrői, K. (2001). Focus and the Syntax–Phonology Interface (Doctoral dissertation). University College London.

Szendrői K. (2003). A Stress-Based Approach to the Syntax of Hungarian Focus. *The Linguistic Review*, 20 (1), 37–78.

Szendrői, K. (2004). Focus and the Interaction between Syntax and Pragmatics. *Lingua*, 114, 229–254.

Ticio, M. E. (2004). On the Position of Subjects in Puerto Rican Spanish. In M. Rodríguez-Mondoñedo and M. E. Ticio (eds.), *Cranberry Linguistics 2. University of Connecticut Working Papers in Linguistics*, Vol. 12. Cambridge, MA: MITWPL, pp. 78–92.

Toribio, A. J. (2000). Setting Parametric Limits on Dialectal Variation in Spanish. *Lingua*, 10, 315–341.

Truckenbrodt, H. (1995). Phonological Phrases: Their Relation to Syntax, Focus and Prominence (Doctoral dissertation). MIT.

Vallduví, E. (1992). *The Informational Component*. New York: Garland.

Vallduví, E. and Vilkuna, M. (1998). On Rheme and Kontrast. *Syntax and Semantics*, 29, 79–108.

Wasow, T. (2002). *Postverbal Behavior*. Chicago, IL: University of Chicago Press.

Zubizarreta, M. L. (1998). *Prosody, Focus, and Word Order*. Cambridge, MA: MIT Press.

18

Syntax and its Interfaces

Timothy Gupton*

18.1 Introduction

Informally, interfaces are understood as areas of overlap and interaction between more than one module of the grammar. In practical terms, interfaces imply more than one linguistic subfield in the analysis of a given phenomenon. Although the theoretical underpinnings of this chapter are primarily generative in orientation, I also make selected references to research from other frameworks. This chapter is not intended to be a comprehensive account of syntactic interfaces; such an undertaking goes well beyond the space limitations afforded me by this *Handbook*.

18.2 The Syntax and the Lexicon

Phrase Structure (PS) rules (Chomsky 1957) such as (18.1) represent some of the earliest attempts to capture the mental grammars of human language in formal syntax.[1]

(18.1)   S   → NP VP
         VP → V (NP) (PP)*

Subcategorization frames (Chomsky 1965, Ch. 2) such as those in (18.2) for Spanish represent early attempts to capture the interface of the lexical component with the syntactic component.

(18.2)   dormir: ___
         desayunar: ___ (PP)
         dibujar: ___ (NP)
         poner: ___ NP PP

---

* I would like to thank Kathryn Bove for her assistance in preparing this chapter. I would additionally like to thank my two anonymous reviewers for their insightful and constructive comments, and Kim Geeslin for her guidance in connecting this chapter to the rest of this Handbook.

[1] Abbreviations are defined at the beginning of the volume.

While PS rules could describe categories obligatorily (or optionally) selected by the verb, they could not capture the complex differences between intransitive predicates and other transitive predicates that required one or more phrase-level complements. They were not very effective at distinguishing between purely optional PPs such as *en el centro* and restricted optional PPs such as *con café y pan tostado* as in *Enrique desayunó (con café y pan tostado) (en el centro)*. The fact that there are limits on the lexical items that may felicitously fill a given syntactic position suggests that the interface with the semantic component is also involved. Consider Sentence 18.3 below, translated from Chomsky (1957):

(18.3) Las ideas verdes incoloras duermen furiosamente.

In (18.3), the nominal nucleus of the agent NP is *ideas*.[2] Semantic requirements on categories associated with the verb *dormir* additionally demand that this NP be [+animate], resulting in the generation of a syntactically grammatical, but semantically anomalous sentence.[3] Numerous other semantic mismatches are in evidence in this sentence, given that ideas can be neither green (*verdes*) nor colorless (*incoloras*), and certainly not both simultaneously. The adverb *furiosamente* is also anomalous, given that knowledge of the world tells us that sleep may be peaceful or restless, but not furious. Crucially, the syntactic computation itself does not take into account semantic anomaly, and correctly recognizes (as do speakers of the language) a sentence like (18.3) as a possible sentence of Spanish, however unlikely. This example is a prime example of a modular interface: the "core" syntax has no problem generating and assembling (18.3), but, from there, the syntactic module must interface with the semantic module that assigns meaning to it, and with the pragmatic module that must make sense of it in the real world. Not all interfaces are claimed to take place following the syntactic computation; rather, there have been a number of proposals that seek to account for interface phenomena via functional syntactic projections (e.g. TenseP/TP, AspectP) as part of the core syntactic computation. As one may imagine, there is healthy debate regarding where the division of labor lies, and when the core syntactic component is no longer involved. We examine a number of such interfaces in the following sections.

18.2.1 The Syntax–Lexical Semantics Interface

Studies on the syntax–lexicon interface focus on the division of labor between the lexicon and the computational system. The creation of an utterance involves encoding and semantically interpreting the functions of different constituents within a sentence or phrase. Within a syntactic

---

[2] I use "NP" here for the sake of simplicity, and because the difference for NP and DP is not yet relevant. I discuss the DP hypothesis for Romance and Spanish in Section 18.3.2.

[3] For a more on animacy in DPs with Agent theta roles, see Folli and Harley (2008).

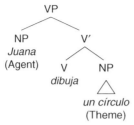

Figure 18.1 VP assignation of Agent theta-role

treatment of thematic roles, or θ-roles, such as (Chomsky 1981), the head of a phrase theta-marks its complement. Theta-role assignment to NPs may be done by different lexical categories, such as a verb (to direct object NPs) or preposition (to indirect object or subcategorized PPs), or VP (to subject NPs). Consider (18.4) with the Spanish verb *dibujar* 'to draw': it is standardly assumed that the verb theta-marks its c-commanding sister node, the NP direct object complement *un círculo* 'a circle,' as a Theme. It is also assumed that the VP assigns an Agent theta role to the external argument *Juana*, as in Figure 18.1.

(18.4)   Juana dibuja un círculo.

Given that (18.5) is also a possible sentence of Spanish, the question arises as to whether the intransitive counterpart of *dibujar* also assigns a (null) Theme role or if the intransitive version of the verb is a separate lexical entry.

(18.5)   Juana dibuja.

The first option is a clear violation of Chomsky's (1981:35) Theta Criterion, as defined in (18.6).

(18.6)   *Theta Criterion*
Each argument bears one and only one theta role, and each theta role is assigned to one and only one argument.

The alternative then appears to be that *dibujar* and *dibujar un círculo* are separate lexical entries. Borer (1994) proposes a third option, arguing for a constructionalist explanation of a verb's lexical entry, such that arguments in the entry are not hierarchically ordered. In this sense, neither internal nor external argument (i.e. subject or objects) may be specified as such. Rather, these functions are derived syntactically via the projection of Aspectual Projections (AspPs) between VP and TP. Consider Figure 18.2 with the verb *dibujar*, which may be specified as event measuring [±EM], and Accusative Case-checking [±Case].

This allows us to capture the semantic difference between *dibujar* and *dibujar un círculo* within the syntactic hierarchy. The projection of AspP in this tree structure is optional, but, if projected, it must be "checked" by movement of an NP to its specifier. The relevant NP in (18.4), *un círculo*, is

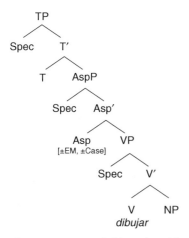

Figure 18.2 Syntactic hierarchy with AspP between VP and TP

crucial in differentiating the unergative atelic predicate *dibujar* in (18.5) from the transitive telic predicate *dibujar un círculo*, and the difference falls out naturally in the syntax. Although this account predates Chomsky's (1995 *et seq.*) Minimalist Program, its elegance is reminiscent of it: the fact that the head of aspect (Asp°) may also check Case prevents instances of overgeneration or improper movement. Borer (1994) additionally proposes that if Asp° is [–EM], an additional AspP projection marked with the feature [+OR] (agentive, causative originator) must be projected, thus correctly predicting that *Juana* is the subject in (18.5). This is reminiscent of Burzio's (1986) Generalization, which observes that a verb can assign a theta role to a constituent in subject position (specifier position in vP (Spec,vP) within a predicate-internal subject approach, as in e.g. Larson 1988) only if it may assign accusative case to an object. Burzio's (1986) approach, however, makes few other stipulations or predictions regarding which roles are assigned to specific syntactic positions.

Baker's (1988) Uniformity of Theta Assignment Hypothesis (UTAH) proposes that certain theta roles are uniquely assigned to particular syntactic positions. Therefore, mapping of theta roles to arguments is largely uniform (Figure 18.3).

Note, however, that *gustar*-type psychological predicates in Spanish pose a problem for this hypothesis, given that the Experiencer theta role may be assigned to the subject in Spec,vP (*mi madre* in 18.7a) or the complement of V (*a mí* in 18.7b).[4]

(18.7)   a. Mi madre detesta las anchoas.
          b. A mí me encantan las anchoas.

This state of affairs is unexpected if theta-role assignment is purely constructionist and determined by the syntax, thus requiring (undesirable) stipulations for violations of UTAH.

---

[4] Baker admits that his proposal does not account for these verbs (1988:489, note 5).

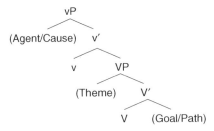

Figure 18.3 Mapping of theta-roles to arguments

Analyzing similar structures in Italian, Belletti and Rizzi (1988) propose that, with psych-predicates like *gustar*, the Theme is the internal argument and the Experiencer is the external argument (Figure 18.4).[5]

Fernández-Soriano (1999) proposes a similar analysis but with the functional projection (EventP) in place of vP, following Harley's (1995) proposal that the specifier of EventP encodes the lexical-conceptual notions CAUSE or BECOME/HAPPEN, with an Experiencer qualifying as the latter.[6] One of the strengths of Fernández-Soriano's analysis lies in that it accounts for the fact that locative inversion (18.8a) and dative fronting (18.8b) constructions appear in complementary distribution (18.8a–c, from Fernández-Soriano 1999:121, ex. 30a–c).

(18.8)   a. Aquí pasa algo.
           b. Me pasa algo.
           c. ??Aquí me pasa algo.

While this approach captures the fact that a locative and a dative clitic may not appear preverbally, it also suggests that it is not the constituent in preverbal position (i.e. the external argument) that agrees with the verb, but rather the internal argument (*las anchoas* in Figure 18.4, *algo* in (18.8)). As we will see in Section 18.3 on the syntax–morphology interface, however, this is not a substantial issue for Belletti and Rizzi's (1988) analysis, since they assume that the dative clitic-doubled DP appears in a preverbal position as a product of movement to a topicalized position to the left of the subject.

Rappaport Hovav and Levin's (1988) analysis of verb meaning examines event structure via lexical-conceptual structures, which bear certain

---

[5] Belletti and Rizzi (1988) do not explicitly assume a split V/v framework. I adapt their analysis for convenience. Additionally, I omit the specific analysis of the dative clitic *le* for reasons of exposition.

[6] Note that the verbal projections VP ("bigVP") and vP ("little vP") are distinct verbal shells in Figure 18.3, with each specializing with respect to a part of a verb's meaning via assignment of its thematic role. The lexical core of the verb is proposed to reside in VP, with V assigning Theme and potentially Goal/Path thematic roles to its specifier and/or complements. The vP shell captures the causative or agentive portion of a verb's meaning, which is expressed overtly in some languages (e.g. Korean *hada*, Japanese *suru*) as "light verbs," roughly translated as 'do/make.' Correspondingly, v assigns the thematic role of Agent/Cause to its specifier. Note also that EventP in Fernández-Soriano (1999) and Harley (1995) corresponds with vP with respect to function and hierarchical syntactic position. This same projection is referred to elsewhere (e.g. Kratzer 1996) as a Voice Projection (VoiceP).

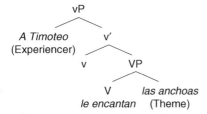

Figure 18.4 Analysis of psychological predicates

similarity to theta roles, but are rooted in lexical aspect. The justification for lexical-conceptual structures (LCSs) lies in the fact that predicates appear to form a number of natural lexical classes, such as manner-of-motion verbs (e.g. *run*) and result verbs (e.g. *break*). From an acquisitional perspective, this is explanatorily desirable, as a child acquiring the language in question has only to acquire the LCS, and, from there, assign newly acquired verbs to one of a number of classes. Manner-of-motion predicates, which are activities, have the LCS event structure representation shown in (18.9). Result verbs may have the representation in (18.10) if they are achievements, or the representation in (18.11) if they are accomplishments.

(18.9)   Melissa corre.   [[x ACT] <MANNER>] (activity)

(18.10) El cristal se rompió.   [BECOME [x <STATE>]] (achievement)

(18.11) Manuel rompió el cristal. [x CAUSE [BECOME [y <STATE>]]] (accomplishment)

Therefore, the LCS provides the building blocks of predicate meaning, including a series of variables (*x, y*) that are central to this meaning. The lexicon of a particular language is responsible for stipulating linking rules between these variables and the arguments of the verb. Within this sort of approach, the linking rules are the interface mapping the aspect template variables *x* and *y* <STATE> to the syntactic constituents *Manuel* and *romper*. It bears mentioning that this approach leaves out a crucial part of the predicate, the direct object *el cristal*, which arguably should be assigned the variable *z* in a structure [x CAUSE [y BECOME [z<STATE>]]. Ritter and Rosen (1998) examine such transitive predicates in greater depth. They challenge the notion that only lexical properties explain the causative alternation by which unergative verbs (18.10) become transitive (18.11), proposing that transitive alternating verbs are delimited in the syntax by the presence of a delimiting DP, such as *el cristal* in (18.10), or *cinco millas* in (18.12).

(18.12)   Melissa corrió cinco millas.

They propose the presence of a specialized, event-related functional projection (FP) in the syntax that may accompany each verbal projection, as in the abbreviated hierarchy in (18.13).

(18.13)   TP > FP-initiation > vP > FP-delimitation > VP

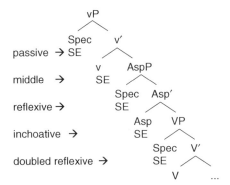

Figure 18.5 Proposed hierarchy for the pronoun SE

By their proposal, the external argument is assigned an initiator event role in Spec,FP-initiation, and the internal argument is assigned the delimiter event role in Spec,FP-delimitation. A criticism of this approach is that event role assignment appears to add an additional step in the computation – unless it piggybacks on Case-checking and theta-role assignment. A logical possibility then is that event-role assignment is a semantic epiphenomenon related to other feature-related processes already assumed in a Minimalist syntax.

Pustejovsky (1991) proposes that event structure consists of a maximum of two subevents, INITIATE (E1) and TRANSITION/RESULT (E2), and Zagona (1999) proposes that they are encoded in the aspectual heads v and Asp, respectively. In a series of articles exploring the syntax of the pronoun SE in Spanish, Kempchinsky (2000, 2004, 2006) builds on Zagona's analysis, proposing that different functions of SE appear in different syntactic projections (Figure 18.5, from Kempchinsky 2006, ex. 6).

Kempchinsky assumes that SE is a clitic, which may be a minimal head (X°) or maximal projection (XP). As a minimal projection, SE is a predicate, and appears in the head of an aspectual projection. As a maximal projection, SE is an argument, and may link to a temporal subevent. Therefore, the combination of these projections can account for states (no subevent), activities (E1), achievements (E2), and accomplishments (E1 and E2). An attractive facet of this analysis is that it explains in part the notion that SE "absorbs" a theta role and perhaps even structurally-assigned Case (see e.g. Burzio 1986 for similar comments on Italian). Therefore, in passive SE sentences (18.14a), in which no external argument or agent typically appears, SE replaces the Agent. A similar phenomenon takes place in reflexive SE sentences (18.14b), in which SE appears to replace the direct object complement.

(18.14) a. Se robó el coche. (passive)
b. Juan se miró al espejo. (reflexive)

Folli and Harley (2005) also take a compositional syntactic approach, but instead differentiate the causes and agents of causative and inchoative verbs within the light verb *little v*, originally proposed by Larson (1988), as we saw in Figure 18.3. These differing "flavors" of v are CAUSE, DO, and BECOME. By this analysis of English, inchoative predicates appear lower in the syntax than in Kempchinsky's (2004) account of Spanish SE inchoative predicates, thus leaving the exact locus of the semantic primitive BECOME rather uncertain.

Future research on the syntax–semantics interface will have to account for cross-linguistic differences related to predicate type and class in order to determine if (i) semantic phenomena can indeed be accounted for in the syntax, and (ii) aspectual projections may be considered syntactic universals or subject to variation among languages. I refer the curious reader to Harley (2011), Ramchand (2013), and Williams (2015) for more up-to-date discussions.

18.3 The Syntax–Morphology Interface

I examine two instances of the syntax–morphology interface in Spanish in this section: subject–verb agreement and noun phrase agreement.

18.3.1 Verb Morphology Agreement

Standard assumptions regarding subject–verb agreement involve the phi features [person] and [number], taking place between the external argument in Spec,vP and the verb in v, while [EPP]-checking and Nominative Case-checking/assignment take place between T and the external argument in Spec,TP. Alexiadou and Anagnostopoulou (1999) propose that [EPP]-checking is parameterized, with non-null-subject languages like English checking [EPP] via movement of the external argument to Spec,TP, while in null-subject languages, [EPP] features are checked by movement of the verb from v° to T°. Ordóñez and Treviño (1999) take a similar approach, assuming (following Taraldsen 1992) that rich person agreement on the verb is a clitic-like "Big DP" in Spanish (Figure 18.6a).

This DP is base-generated in the predicate-internal Spec,VP head, and may merge with or without the doubling DP. The clitic DP is proposed to absorb Case and receive the Agent theta role. Subject–verb agreement occurs via Specifier–head agreement in the VP (Figure 18.6b). Ordóñez and Treviño (1999) follow Uriagereka (1995) in assuming that the verb and pronominal clitics are subsequently attracted to a higher, discourse-related (i.e. syntax–discourse interface) FP.

Following Jaeggli and Safir (1989), verb morphology, in particular strong agreement morphology, licenses the null subject pronoun *pro* in Spec,TP, in the absence of an overt subject. Ordóñez and Treviño (1999), however, observe that preverbal subjects pattern similarly to preverbal direct object and indirect object topics with respect to ellipsis, quantifier extraction, *wh*-extraction, and preverbal quantifier scope. Consider the parallel behavior

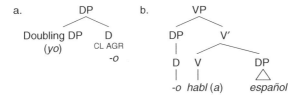

Figure 18.6 "Big DP" proposal for languages with morphologically-rich verb agreement

Figure 18.7 Position of preverbal subjects as Ā constituents

of preverbal subjects (18.15a), preverbal direct objects (18.15b), and preverbal indirect objects (18.15c) under remnant ellipsis (constituents bolded for illustration).

(18.15) a. Él le dio unos libros a Pía y **Pepe** también [le dio unos libros a Pía].
b. **Unos libros** le dio a Pía y **unos cuadros** también [le dio a Pía].
c. **A Pía** le dio unos libros y **a Sara** también [le dio unos libros].

Following their argumentation, if ellipsis targets the TP, the symmetrical behavior of preverbal subjects and topical clitic left-dislocated (CLLD) objects is unexpected. Therefore, as optional, discourse-related, non-argument (i.e. Ā) constituents, preverbal subjects (PVSs) appear in a left-peripheral, topicalized position similar to CLLD constituents (Figure 18.7). Since the phonologically-null pronoun *pro* does not appear in the same distribution as topic XPs, Ordóñez and Treviño (1999) suggest it is not a verbal argument, and perhaps even an unnecessary element.

The analysis of preverbal subjects and *pro* is far from resolved. Goodall (2001) and Suñer (2003) argue convincingly against the unified left-peripheral proposal of Ordóñez and Treviño (1999), maintaining that preverbal subjects are argument (A) constituents. While Barbosa (2000) and Costa (2004) argue the same for European Portuguese based on intuition data, Gupton (2014) argues against a unified analysis of subjects in Galician based on a combination of traditional intuition judgments and experimental data consisting of acceptability and preference judgments. My position is outlined in Gupton and Leal-Méndez (2013), who advocate for adopting quantitative methodologies to inform apparent theoretical stalemates.

18.3.2 Noun Phrase Agreement

While the analysis of the noun phrase in Spanish enjoys a long tradition in traditional grammars, the examination of the Spanish NP within the generative tradition is of great theoretical importance with respect to the syntax–morphology interface, as researchers have grappled with the issue of how much morphological content within the NP is transparent to the syntax. The lexicalist hypothesis (Chomsky 1970) holds that the internal morphological structure of nouns is opaque to the syntax. Important analyses of Spanish data, however, have argued for a non-lexicalist approach, noting that phenomena related to noun derivation (see e.g. Fábregas (2010) in addition to Chapters 12 and 19, this volume) as well as noun–adjective order in Spanish – including associated semantic differences – are accounted for with greater descriptive and explanatory adequacy within an approach that assumes syntactic structure within the word-level domain. If morphological structure is visible to the syntax, the question arises as to whether a syntax–morphology interface truly exists.[7]

In what remains of this section I summarize a non-lexicalist account of noun–adjective order in Spanish.[8] Bernstein (1993) examines agreement processes within the noun phrase including determiners, nouns, and adjectives within an expanded DP structure. She proposes the existence of two morphology-related functional projections between the NP and the DP: a Word Marker Projection (WMP), which checks gender features, and a Number Projection (NumP), which checks number features. I provide an example in Figure 18.8 with noun–adjective order.

In this example, the N *libro* is attracted by the probe on the word-marker head (WM), which needs to check [masc] gender.[9] Since *libro* still has features that require checking, it is available for further operation, the

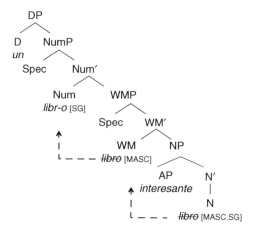

Figure 18.8 Two morphology-related functional projections between the NP and the DP

---

[7] See Picallo (2012) for an overview of many issues in Spanish related to the NP. See Ramchand and Reiss (2007, Chs. 7–12) for a recent examination of the lexicalist debate.
[8] Picallo (2008) takes an approach similar to what follows. See also Demonte (2008) for an alternative DP account.
[9] For the purposes of this chapter, I remain agnostic regarding whether [gender] and [number] are binary or privative features. See Chapter 16, this volume, for further discussion.

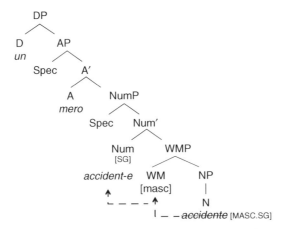

Figure 18.9 Adjective–noun order in *un mero accidente* 'a mere accident'

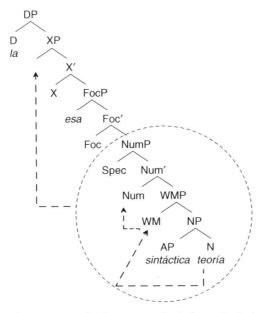

Figure 18.10 Adjective–noun order in *la teoría sintáctica esa* 'that syntactic theory'

next of which involves attraction to the number head (Num), where it checks phi features related to [sing] number. The postnominal AP *interesante* remains adjoined to Spec,NP.

Adjective–noun order in Romance like *un mero accidente* 'a mere accident' is proposed to appear in a slightly different syntactic structure (Figure 18.9). The AP *mero* is a complement of DP generated high in the structure to the left of NumP. The same feature-checking processes in this structure, however, do not lead to any change in word order. Bernstein's (2001) proposal accounts for postnominal demonstratives, which receive focal emphasis, thus invoking the syntax–pragmatics interface. She proposes that focus is encoded via a focus projection (FocP) to the left of NumP (Figure 18.10).

The derivation of focused DPs proceeds as in Figures 18.8 and 18.9, with word marker (gender) and number features checked by head-to-head N-movement. However, following merge of the focus projection (FocP), there is pied-piped movement of NumP to the Specifier of an (unnamed) XP to the left of FocP, thus netting the word order *la teoría sintáctica esa* 'that syntactic theory'. This movement is motivated by the pragmatic interface, ensuring that the (prosodically) emphatic demonstrative *esa* appears at the rightmost edge of the constituent. The operation is similar to Zubizarreta's (1998) *p-movement*, which I discuss in Section 18.5. As we will see, additional challenges remain for the syntactic account of this syntax–pragmatics phenomenon.

18.4 The Syntax–Pragmatics Interface

When examining the syntax–pragmatics interface, there is often overlap between the syntax–information structure interface and the syntax–prosody interface. I attempt to separate these in this section. With respect to the distribution of null and overt subjects in Spanish, the use or non-use of a subject may be related to pragmatic factors, such as disambiguation or switch-reference. Consider the following constructed discourse (18.16):

(18.16)   Enrique y Miguel llegaron por la mañana y (A. #Enrique y Miguel/#ellos/ *pro*) vinieron a la casa, pero (B. Enrique/#él/#*pro*) tuvo que ir a un cajero automático en el centro a sacar dinero. (C. #Él/*pro*) todavía está allí. (D. Miguel/#él/#*pro*) se quedó para echar una siesta.

Following the first mention of *Enrique* and *Miguel*, conjoined R(eferential)-expressions, repeating both names in (18.16A) would not trigger ungrammaticality, nor would using a pronoun, but it would be pragmatically odd (#) in Spanish. However, in the next instance in which a pronoun can be used (18.16B), when talking about only one of the two people involved in the discourse, an R-expression must be used to identify the subject of the singular verb (*tuvo*) since a null or overt pronoun would result in intolerable ambiguity. This is a case of switch reference. In the following Sentence 18.16C, an overt pronoun is unnecessary, given that the topic continues from the previous sentence. In Sentence 18.16D, however, reference shifts to the other R-expression (*Miguel*), thus making use of an overt or null pronoun impossible, since doing so would make reference to the previous R-expression (*Enrique*). Following Chomsky (1982), empty (subject) categories are identified by the governing category AGR. Huang (1984) proposes that null subject and object topics in languages like Chinese, which lack rich agreement, are identified by a free variable. Given the advances of the Minimalist Program (e.g. Chomsky 1995), it remains unclear what theoretical status governing categories currently have. An unresolved issue, to my knowledge, is how the identification of null/overt pronouns may be accounted for in a syntax-based pragmatics account. Variationist studies on subject pronouns in Spanish have shown that, in a number of Spanish varieties, overt pronouns are subject to variation. For example, in switch-reference (e.g. Cameron 1995) and contrastive (e.g. Amaral and Schwenter 2005) contexts, although the prediction is that an overt subject should appear uniformly, pronoun expression is subject to individual variation. There are additional linguistic factors (verb form ambiguity, clause type, verb type, etc.) as well as extra-linguistic factors (dialectal variety, language contact) that may influence subject pronoun expression.[10] These are substantive complications for a descriptively and explanatorily adequate account of subject expression in Spanish.

The expression of corrective contrast in Spanish also involves the syntax–pragmatics interface.[11] Following Zubizarreta (1998:20), sentence 18.17b may not answer a subject narrow-focus question (18.17a). Placing prosodic stress on *Juan* in (18.17b, stress indicated as underscore) is necessarily contrastive, and therefore infelicitous.

(18.17)   a. ¿Quién comió una manzana?
          b. #Juan comió una manzana.

Following López (2009), I assume contrastive readings to be corrective and as simultaneously opening a variable and resolving it. Consider an additional scenario with a direct object: three teenagers (B, C, D) return home from a shopping trip to a department store. The mother of one of the teenagers (A) greets them as they come home with bags full of clothes.

(18.18)   A: ¿Así que comprasteis algo?
          B: Pues sí. Bastante.
          C: Paco compró una bufanda.
          D: UNA CAMISA compró (no una bufanda).

In (18.18) then, teenager D's correction revisits the previous utterance *(Paco) compró X* and immediately resolves the incorrect information in the utterance. Following Rizzi's (1997) analysis of Italian, accounts of Spanish (e.g. Casielles-Suárez 2003) propose that corrective contrastive constituents appear in the Specifier of Focus projection (Spec,FocP), as in Figure 18.11.

This account of corrective contrast is promising with respect to a syntactic account in that pragmatic import has a syntactic reaction. It is important to note, however, that Ortega-Santos (2016) presents data indicating that contrast may also be expressed at the rightmost syntactic

---

[10] See e.g. Carvalho *et al.* (2015) for a number of studies in this vein.
[11] I discuss contrast in this and the following section in relation to focus-related phenomena. Information-structure phenomena are often referred to as pragmatic because related (syntactic) violations result in similar infelicity, not in ungrammaticality.

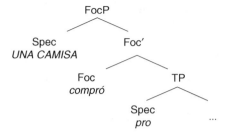

Figure 18.11 Corrective contrast constituents in Spec,FocP

edge. Clearly, Spanish is not monolithic in a number of ways, and more experimental as well as descriptive accounts are necessary for all varieties of Spanish in order to fill in the blanks in our knowledge base.[12]

18.5 The Syntax–Information Structure Interface

While the division of sentences into subject and predicate has a long history, Weil (1879:29) was the first to propose an informational split based upon criteria involving "the ground upon which the two intelligences (speaker and hearer) meet." These are crucial ingredients in the creation of any sentence. The fact that this dynamic should invoke a syntactic interface is clear in Vallduví and Engdahl's (1996:460) definition of information packaging as "structuring of sentences by syntactic, prosodic, or morphological means that arises from the need to meet the communicative demands of a particular context or discourse." There is a vast literature on information structure that cannot be fully reviewed in the space afforded in this volume, but see e.g. Gupton (2014: Ch. 2) for an overview and Chapter 17, this volume. Although much of the literature converges on identifying a less informative portion (topic/theme) of the sentence and the need to differentiate this part from a more informative part of the sentence (focus/rheme), there is a surprising amount of disagreement on where exactly the split occurs. There is also robust disagreement regarding precise definitions of topic/theme and focus/rheme, despite the fact that their universality is frequently taken for granted. The definition I assume for topical/thematic constituents here is based on a common-ground conception of Weil's ideas, and perhaps best summarized by Contreras (1976:16): "elements which are assumed by the speaker to be present in the addressee's consciousness." With respect to focus/rheme, I follow López (2009) in that rheme information resolves a variable created in the formation of a question (18.19).

(18.19) ¿Qué puso María sobre la mesa?

---

[12] It remains an open question whether all pragmatic phenomena have an associated syntactic reflex cross-linguistically. See e.g. Palomäki (2016) for limitations of a syntactic account for the Finnish -han clitic.

Following utterance of (18.19), a variable *x* is opened by the *wh*-word ¿Qué ... ?, creating (18.20).

(18.20)   *x* | María puso *x* sobre la mesa.

While *x* captures the rhematic, or unknown, information, the statement of this equation also captures the common-ground information in the discourse: *María* is the subject, the action in question is *poner*, and the location involved in said placing is *sobre la mesa*. In the reply to this question, one might respond with the answer itself: *un huevo*. However, in considering sentence-length utterances, we can learn more about the clausal position of rheme information – information we are lacking when no constituent appears to either the left or right of the rheme reply. In a sentence-length reply (18.21a), the common-ground subject *María* may be phonologically null, but the PP complement *sobre la mesa* may not be (18.21b) since this would net an entirely different meaning.

(18.21)   a. (María) puso sobre la mesa un huevo.
           b. (María) puso un huevo.

According to Zubizarreta (1998:21–22), the narrow-focused (rheme) information in the reply to (18.19) must appear at the clausal right edge (18.22a), and may not appear *in situ* (18.22b), as this would trigger a contrastive reading (18.22c), which is pragmatically inappropriate in this context.

(18.22)   a. María puso sobre la mesa el libro.
           b. #María puso el libro sobre la mesa.
           c. #María puso el LIBRO sobre la mesa (no la revista).

Narrow-focused information must coincide with prosodic stress, which falls naturally on the rightmost constituent (underlined in (18.22a, b)).[13] Therefore, placing prosodic stress on *el libro* in (18.22c) is incompatible with the object narrow-focus question in (18.19). Zubizarreta (1998) captures rightmost stress prominence in Spanish declaratives with her reformulation of Chomsky and Halle's (1968) Nuclear Stress Rule:

(18.23)   *Spanish and French NSR*
           a. Given two sister nodes C_i and C_j, the one lower in the asymmetric c-command ordering is more prominent.
           b. All phonological material is metrically visible for the NSR in Spanish.

This formalizes why (18.22b) is an unacceptable reply: *sobre la mesa* appears in a structurally lower position than *el libro*. The problem results from *el libro* being marked [+F] and *sobre la mesa* being marked [–F]. Zubizarreta (1998) proposes the Focus Prominence Rule as an additional condition on the Romance Nuclear Stress Rule (RNSR) that must be satisfied in Spanish.

---

[13] See Schwegler *et al.* (2010:318–319) for a description.

(18.24) *Focus Prominence Rule (FPR)*
Given two sister nodes C_i (marked [+F]) and C_j (marked [–F]), C_i is more prominent than C_j.

When focus-marked ([+F]) constituents (i.e. those that are narrow-focused) appear at the rightmost clausal edge, the NSR and the FPR are aligned. However, when conflicts arise between the two, [–F] constituents at the rightmost clausal edge must undergo a type of Last Resort movement, an operation that Zubizarreta (1998) calls prosodically-motivated movement or *p-movement*. This calculus results in (18.22a) being an appropriate reply to (18.19), and also renders (18.22b) unacceptable.

While Chomsky (1971:199–206) sought to link focus to an intonation center, Jackendoff (1972) proposed F-marking as an "artificial construct" to account for focused elements. Horvath (1986) later proposed FOCUS as a formal syntactic feature. However, the existence of this feature has been challenged in the literature. In fact, Zubizarreta (1998:30) herself correctly observes that positing [±F] as a lexical feature is conceptually problematic because it violates Chomsky's (1995:Ch. 4) Inclusiveness Condition (see also Szendrői 2004).[14] Zubizarreta proposes that [F] is not a lexical feature, but rather a derived phrase marker, which remains undefined until after Σ-structure, the point at which all lexical items have been merged and features checked, and prior to Logical Form (LF) (Figure 18.12).

In this model, phrase markers remain inert at the stage in which core syntactic features are checked. It is after Σ-structure (and prior to LF and PF) that Zubizarreta's (1998) proposed operations take place.[15] This proposal is limited by the fact that it has not stood up well to empirical testing, with studies of Argentine (Gabriel 2010), North Mexican (Hoot 2012), and Andalusian (Jiménez-Fernández 2015) Spanish finding that narrow focus need not occur at the clausal rightmost edge in a number of Spanish varieties. Gupton and Leal-Méndez (2013) also discuss particular challenges for the concept of p-movement from Mexican Spanish.

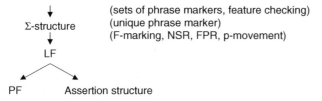

Figure 18.12 [F] as a derived phrase marker

---

[14] Inclusiveness involves the manner in which a given node acquires the Focus discourse feature. Following Chomsky (1995:228), a non-terminal node inherits features from its daughter, while a terminal node may be assigned a feature from the lexicon. Therefore, [+F]-assignment cannot happen once a constituent enters the derivation; consequently, this must take place in the lexicon. Zubizarreta (1998: 33) proposes a relaxation of Inclusiveness.

[15] Note similarities to Reinhart's (2006:158) account of the syntax–focus interface, by which the syntactic component generates a possible focus set, and then interfaces with focus at PF, where stress is calculated and assigned to a member of a given focus set. Selection of the correct candidate is determined by interface requirements.

López's (2009) account of the syntax–information structure interface in Spanish also assumes that rheme/narrow-focus constituents appear at the rightmost clausal edge. Putting this limitation aside, we examine López's proposal because of its elegant account of left-peripheral topics and contrastive focus. According to his proposal, discourse relations are determined by the syntactic configuration in which they appear. In his model of the grammar, a module called *Pragmatics* inspects the syntactic structure at each phase end and assigns pragmatic information structure-related values to constituents that appear at phase edge and within the boundary of the syntactic phase.[16] Once assigned, pragmatic values remain with constituents throughout the derivation. The resulting values dictate the pragmatic interpretation of a constituent.

The pragmatic features assigned are [±a] (anaphoric) and [±c] (contrastive). Simplifying the analysis somewhat, [±a] is assigned at the end of the first phase. An XP in Spec,vP is assigned [+a], and its complement is assigned [–a]. In order to be [+a]-marked, the XP in question must be in an anaphoric dependency with a clitic double; otherwise, it is marked [–a]. At the completion of the second phase (CP), an XP in Spec,CP is assigned [+c]. By this calculus, both contrastive focus-fronted and CLLD topic XPs are marked [+c], but only CLLD topics are [+a, +c]. I summarize these possibilities in (18.25).

(18.25) [–a, –c]   Rheme
        [–a, +c]   Focus Fronted Contrast (FF)
        [+a, –c]   Clitic Right-dislocation (CLRD)
        [+a, +c]   Clitic Left-dislocation (CLLD)

López (2009) proposes a simplified left-peripheral syntax in which neither [Foc] nor [Top] are lexical features.[17] His simplified version of Rizzi's (1997) expanded CP left-peripheral hierarchy (18.26) includes only the functional projections FinitenessP (FinP) and ForceP (FceP), as in Figure 18.13.

(18.26)   ForceP > TopicP > FocusP > TopicP > FinitenessP > TenseP >

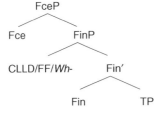

Figure 18.13 Simplified left-peripheral syntax model

---

[16] The phases, vP and CP (Chomsky 2008), are intermediate derivational Spell-Out points at which the syntactic computation may interface with the phonological component, the semantic component, or the pragmatics component (for the latter, see López 2009). See also Uriagereka (1999) and Chomsky (2001) for additional discussion of multiple Spell-Out and phase theory.

[17] He also assumes that CLLD topics are not base-generated XPs, contra Cinque (1990).

This particular approach to the syntax–information structure–pragmatics interface is promising in that it proposes a more economic approach to the left periphery, and is reminiscent of Emonds' (2004) discourse-shell approach to the preverbal field. Future research should consider a number of possible left-peripheral syntactic models, each with associated assumptions, strengths, and weaknesses.

18.6 The Syntax–Prosody Interface

While some syntax-information structure proposals represent a marked departure from the cartographic approach of Rizzi (1997), studies such as Frascarelli and Hinterhölzl (2007) and Bianchi and Frascarelli (2010) have sought to expand it. The former examine interview data in German and Italian following the prosodic marking conventions of the Tones and Break Indices framework (ToBI; see e.g. Beckman *et al.* 2005 and Chapter 10, this volume), by which syllables are described as relatively high (H) or low (L), and a tonic syllable is marked with an asterisk (*). The findings for their data, consisting of six Italian participants and a German radio conversation corpus, are summarized in Table 18.1. Their data suggests a strict correspondence between information structure functions and prosodic contour, thus justifying dividing TopicP into the functional projections A-Topic (Aboutness Topic), C-Topic (Contrastive Topic), and G-Topic (Givenness Topic).

In Spanish, Vanrell and Fernández-Soriano (2013) examine experimental Peninsular Spanish first language (L1) speaker data, finding rising and falling intonation patterns in both *in situ* (18.27a) and fronted narrow (18.27b) focus. With respect to declarative contrastive focus (18.28), only 71 percent of their data exhibited rising prosodic contours.

(18.27) Context: ¿Qué sacó María sin problemas?
  a. María sacó el coche sin problemas.
  b. El coche sacó María sin problemas.

(18.28) No, EL COCHE llevó María a su prima.

The analysis of the data leads them to concur with Face and d'Imperio (2005) that contrastive focus is subject to dialectal variation. Feldhausen (2016a) examines experimental data eliciting CLLD topics (18.29a),

Table 18.1 *Nuclear pitch accent contours for Italian and German by topic type*

	Topic type		
	Aboutness	Contrastive	Familiar/Given
Italian	L*+H	H*	L*
German	L+H*	L*+H	L*

Source: Frascarelli and Hinterhölzl (2007)

hanging-topic left-dislocation (HTLD, 18.29b), and left-dislocation without a resumptive pronoun (LD$_{w/oRP}$, 18.29c) from speakers from Murcia, Spain.

(18.29)   a. El águila la vendió mi hermano.
          b. Pero su águila soñábamos con este monstruo en la juventud.
          c. De los exámenes nadie ha hablado todavía.

His study finds that CLLD is characterized by an L+H* contour in over 80 percent of cases – be it simple CLLD (18.29a) or multiple CLLD (18.30).

(18.30)   El águila a mi abuela se la vendió mi hermano.

His data also suggests that the intonation of CLLD does not significantly differ from those of HTLD or LD$_{w/oRP}$. These findings are not predicted by the expanded cartographic account above. Importantly, his study also finds that pauses are obligatory only for interrogative HTLD utterances (18.31), not for declarative CLLD, HTLD, or LD$_{w/oRP}$.[18]

(18.31)   Tu amiga ¿hablaste con ella por fin?

Future research on Spanish should replicate these methodologies for a multitude of Spanish varieties in order to determine what prosodic profiles obtain for the left periphery.[19] An additional challenge remains regarding what sort of elicitation method offers the greatest insight with respect to the interface of syntax with information structure and suprasegmental phonology-prosody.

References

Alexiadou, A. and Anagnostopoulou, E. (1999). Parametrizing AGR: Word Order, V-Movement and EPP-Checking. *Natural Language and Linguistic Theory*, 16, 491–539.

Amaral, P. and Schwenter, S. (2005). Contrast and the (Non-) Occurrence of Subject Pronouns. In D. Eddington (ed.), *Selected Proceedings of the 7th Hispanic Linguistics Symposium*. Somerville, MA: Cascadilla, pp. 116–127.

Baker, M. (1988). *Incorporation. A Theory of Grammatical Function Changing*. Chicago, IL: University of Chicago Press.

Barbosa, P. (2000). Clitics: A Window into the Null Subject Property. In J. Costa (ed.), *Portuguese Syntax: New Comparative Studies*. New York and Oxford: Oxford University Press, pp. 31–93.

Beckman, M., Hirschberg, J., and Shattuck-Hufnagel, S. (2005). The Original ToBI System and the Evolution of the ToBI Framework. In S.-A. Jun (ed.), *Prosodic Typology: The Phonology of Intonation and Phrasing*. Oxford: Oxford University Press.

---

[18] See e.g. López (2009) for a review of differences between LD, HTLD, and CLLD.
[19] See Feldhausen (2016b) for an Optimality theoretical approach to prosodic variation.

Belletti, A. and Rizzi, L. (1988). Psych Verbs and θ-Theory. *Natural Language and Linguistic Theory*, 6 (3), 291–352.

Bernstein, J. (1993). The Syntactic Role of Word Markers in Null Nominal Constructions. *Probus*, 5, 5–38.

Bernstein, J. (2001). Focusing the "Right" Way in Romance Determiner Phrases. *Probus*, 13, 1–30.

Bianchi, V. and Frascarelli, M. (2010). Is Topic a Root Phenomenon? *Iberia: An International Journal of Theoretical Linguistics*, 2, 43–88.

Borer, H. (1994). The Projection of Arguments. In E. Benedicto and J. Runner (eds.), *Functional Projections, University of Massachusetts Occasional Papers 17*. Amherst, MA: GLSA, pp. 19–47.

Burzio, L. (1986). *Italian Syntax: A Government–Binding Approach*. Boston, MA: D. Reidel.

Cameron, R. (1995). The Scope and Limits of Switch-Reference as a Constraint on Pronominal Subject Expression. *Hispanic Linguistics*, 6/7, 1–27.

Carvalho, A. M., Orozco, R., and Shin, N. L. (2015). *Subject Pronoun Expression in Spanish: A Cross-Dialectal Perspective*. Washington, DC: Georgetown University Press.

Casielles-Suárez, E. (2003). Left-Dislocated Structures in Spanish. *Hispania*, 86 (2). 326–338.

Chomsky, N. (1957). *Syntactic Structures*. The Hague: Mouton.

Chomsky, N. (1965). *Aspects of the Theory of Syntax*. Cambridge, MA: MIT Press.

Chomsky, N. (1970). Remarks on Nominalization. In R. Jacobs and P. Rosenbaum (eds.), *Readings in English Transformational Grammar*. Cambridge, MA: Waltham, pp. 184–221.

Chomsky, N. (1971). Deep Structure, Surface Structure and Semantic Interpretation. In D. Steinberg and L. Jakobovits (eds.), *Semantics*. Cambridge: Cambridge University Press, pp. 183–216.

Chomsky, N. (1981). *Lectures on Government and Binding*. Dordrecht: Foris.

Chomsky, N. (1982). *Some Concepts and Consequences of the Theory of Government and Binding*. Cambridge, MA: MIT Press.

Chomsky, N. (1995). *The Minimalist Program*. Cambridge, MA: MIT Press.

Chomsky, N. (2001). Derivation by Phase. In M. Kenstowicz (ed.), *Ken Hale: A Life in Language*. Cambridge, MA: MIT Press, pp. 1–52.

Chomsky, N. (2008). On Phases. In R. Freidin, C. P. Otero, and M. L. Zubizarreta (eds.), *Foundational Issues in Linguistic Theory. Essays in Honor of Jean-Roger Vergnaud*. Cambridge, MA: MIT Press, pp. 133–166.

Chomsky, N. and Halle, M. (1968). *The Sound Pattern of English*. Cambridge, MA: MIT Press.

Cinque, G. (1990). *Types of Ā dependencies*. Cambridge, MA: MIT Press.

Contreras, H. (1976). *A Theory of Word Order with a Special Reference to Spanish*. Amsterdam: North-Holland.

Costa, J. (2004). *Subject Positions and Interfaces: The Case of European Portuguese*. Berlin and New York: De Gruyter.

Demonte, V. (2008). Meaning-Form Correlations and Adjective Positions in Spanish. In C. Kennedy and L. McNally (eds.), *Adjectives and Adverbs: Syntax, Semantics, and Discourse*. Oxford: Oxford University Press, pp. 71–100.

Emonds, J. (2004). Unspecified Categories as the Key to Root Projections. In D. Adger, C. de Cat, and G. Tsoulas (eds.), *Peripheries: Syntactic Edges and their Effects*. Dordrecht: Kluwer, pp. 75–120.

Fábregas, A. (2010). A Syntactic Account of Affix Rivalry in Spanish Nominalisations. In A. Alexiadou and M. Rathert (eds.), *Nominalisations across Languages and Frameworks*. Berlin: De Gruyter, pp. 59–85.

Face, T. and d'Imperio, M. (2005). Reconsidering a Focal Typology: Evidence from Spanish and Italian. *Italian Journal of Linguistics*, 17, 271–289.

Feldhausen, I. (2016a). The Relation between Prosody and Syntax: The Case of Different Types of Left-Dislocations in Spanish. In M. Armstrong, N. Henriksen, and M. D. M. Vanrell (eds.), *Intonational Grammar in Ibero-Romance: Approaches across Linguistic Subfields*. Amsterdam: John Benjamins, pp. 153–180.

Feldhausen, I. (2016b). Inter-Speaker Variation, Optimality Theory, and the Prosody of Clitic Left-Dislocations in Spanish. *Probus*, 28 (2), 293–333.

Fernández-Soriano, O. (1999). Two Types of Impersonal Sentences in Spanish: Locative and Dative Subjects. *Syntax*, 2 (2), 101–140.

Folli, R. and Harley, H. (2005). Flavors of *v*. In P. Kempchinsky and R. Slabakova (eds.), *Aspectual Inquiries*. Amsterdam: Springer, pp. 95–120.

Folli, R. and Harley, H. (2008). Teleology and Animacy in External Arguments. *Lingua*, 118, 190–202.

Frascarelli, M. and Hinterhölzl, R. (2007). Types of Topics in German and Italian. In S. Winkler and K. Schwabe (eds.), *On Information Structure, Meaning and Form*. Amsterdam and Philadelphia, PA: John Benjamins, pp. 87–116

Gabriel, C. (2010). On Focus, Prosody, and Word Order in Argentinean Spanish: A Minimalist OT Account. *ReVEL*, 4, 183–222.

Goodall, G. (2001). The EPP in Spanish. In W. D. Davies and S. Dubinsky (eds.), *Objects and Other Subjects: Grammatical Functions, Functional Categories, and Configurationality*. Dordrecht: Kluwer, pp. 193–223.

Gupton, T. (2014). *The Syntax-Information Structure Interface: Clausal Word Order and the Left Periphery in Galician*. Berlin: De Gruyter.

Gupton, T. and Leal Méndez, T. (2013). Experimental Methodologies: Two Case Studies Investigating the Syntax-Discourse Interface. *Studies in Hispanic and Lusophone Linguistics*, 6 (1), 139–164.

Harley, H. (1995). Subjects, Events, and Licensing (Doctoral dissertation). MIT.

Harley, H. (2011). A Minimalist Approach to Argument Structure. In C. Boeckx (ed.), *The Oxford Handbook of Linguistic Minimalism*. Oxford: Oxford University Press, pp. 426–447.

Hoot, B. (2012). Presentational Focus in Heritage and Monolingual Spanish (Doctoral dissertation). University of Illinois.

Horvath, J. (1986). *FOCUS in the Theory of Grammar and the Syntax of Hungarian*. Dordrecht: Foris.

Huang, C.-T. J. (1984). On the Distribution and Reference of Empty Pronouns. *Linguistic Inquiry*, 15 (4), 531–574.

Jackendoff, R. (1972). *Semantic Interpretation in Generative Grammar*. Cambridge, MA: MIT Press.

Jaeggli, O. and Safir, K. (1989). The Null Subject Parameter and Parametric Theory. In O. Jaeggli and K. Safir (eds.), *The Null Subject Parameter*. Dordrecht: Kluwer, pp. 1–44.

Jiménez-Fernández, Á. (2015). Towards a Typology of Focus: Subject Position and Microvariation at the Discourse–Syntax Interface. *Ampersand*, 2, 49–60.

Kempchinsky, P. (2000). Aspect Projections and Predicate Type. In H. Campos, E. Herburger, A. Morales-Front, and T. J. Walsh (eds.), *Hispanic Linguistics at the Turn of the Millennium*. Somerville, MA: Cascadilla, pp. 171–187.

Kempchinsky, P. (2004). Romance SE as an Aspectual Element. In J. Auger, J. C. Clements, and B. Vance (eds.), *Contemporary Approaches to Romance Linguistics*. Amsterdam and Philadelphia, PA: John Benjamins, pp. 239–256.

Kempchinsky, P. (2006). Teasing Apart the Middle. In I. Laka and B. Fernández (eds.), *Andolin gogoan/Homenaje a Andolin Eguzkitza*. Bilbao: Universidad del País Vasco, pp. 532–547.

Kratzer, A. (1996). Severing the External Argument from its Verb. In J. Rooryck and L. Zaring (eds.), *Phrase Structure and the Lexicon*. Kluwer: Dordrecht, pp. 109–137.

Larson, R. (1988). On the Double Object Construction. *Linguistic Inquiry*, 19 (3), 335–391.

López, L. (2009). *A Derivational Syntax for Information Structure*. Oxford: Oxford University Press.

Ordóñez, F. and Treviño, E. (1999). Left Dislocated Subjects and the Pro-Drop Parameter: A Case Study of Spanish. *Lingua*, 107, 39–68.

Ortega-Santos, I. (2016). *Focus-Related Operations at the Right Edge in Spanish*. Amsterdam: John Benjamins.

Palomäki, J. (2016). The Pragmatics and Syntax of the Finnish -*han* Particle Clitic (Dissertation). University of Georgia.

Picallo, C. (2008). Gender and Number in Romance. *Lingue e Linguaggio*, 7 (1), 47–66.

Picallo, C. (2012). Structure of the Noun Phrase. In J. I. Hualde, A. Olarrea, and Erin O'Rourke (eds.), *The Handbook of Hispanic Linguistics*. Malden, MA: Wiley, pp. 263–283.

Pustejovsky, J. (1991). The Syntax of Event Structure. *Cognition*, 4, 47–81.

Ramchand, G. (2013). Argument Structure and Argument Structure Alternations. In M. den Dikken (ed.), *Handbook of Generative Syntax*. Cambridge: Cambridge University Press, pp. 265–321.

Ramchand, G. and Reiss, C. (eds.) (2007). *The Oxford Handbook of Linguistic Interfaces*. Oxford: Oxford University Press.

Rappaport Hovav, M. and Levin, B. (1988). What to do with θ-Roles. In W. Wilkins (ed.), *Syntax and Semantics, Vol. 21: Thematic Relations*. San Diego, CA: Academic Press, pp. 7–36.

Reinhart, T. (2006). *Interface Strategies*. Cambridge, MA: MIT Press.

Ritter, E. and Rosen, S. T. (1998). Delimiting Events in Syntax. In M. Butt and W. Geuder (eds.), *The Projections of Arguments: Lexical and Compositional Factors*. Stanford, CA: CSLI Publications, pp. 135–164.

Rizzi, L. (1997). On the Fine Structure of the Left Periphery. In A. Belletti and L. Rizzi (eds.), *Elements of Grammar*. Dordrecht: Kluwer, pp. 281–337.

Schwegler, A., Kempff, J., and Ameal-Guerra, A. (2010). *Fonética y fonología españolas* (4th edn). Hoboken, NJ: Wiley.

Suñer, M. (2003). The Lexical Preverbal Subject in a Romance Null Subject Language. Where Art Thou? In R. Núñez-Cedeño, L. López, and R. Cameron (eds.), *A Romance Perspective on Language Knowledge and Use. Selected Papers from the 31st Linguistic Symposium on Romance Languages (LSRL)*. Amsterdam: John Benjamins, pp. 341–358.

Szendrői, K. (2004). Focus and the Interaction between Syntax and Pragmatics. *Lingua*, 114, 229–254.

Taraldsen, K. (1992). Agreement as Pronoun Incorporation. Paper presented at the 1992 Generative Linguistics in the Old World (GLOW) Colloquium.

Uriagereka, J. (1995). Aspects of the Syntax of Clitic Placement in Western Romance. *Linguistic Inquiry*, 26 (1), 79–123.

Uriagereka, J. (1999). Multiple Spell-Out. In S. Epstein and N. Hornstein (eds.), *Working Minimalism*. Cambridge, MA: MIT Press, pp. 251–282.

Vallduví, E. and Engdahl, E. (1996). The Linguistic Realization of Information Packaging. *Linguistics*, 34, 459–519.

Vanrell, M. and Fernández-Soriano, O. (2013). Variation at the Interfaces in Ibero-Romance. Catalan and Spanish Prosody and Word Order. *Catalan Journal of Linguistics*, 12, 253–282.

Weil, H. (1879) [1844]. *De l'ordre des mots dans les langues anciennes comparées aux langues modernes*. Paris: Joubert. (Translation: C. W. Super, *The Order of Words in the Ancient Languages Compared with that of the Modern Languages*. Philadelphia, PA: John Benjamins, (1978) [1887].)

Williams, A. (2015). *Arguments in Syntax and Semantics*. Cambridge: Cambridge University Press.

Zagona, K. (1999). Voice and Aspect. In J. Franco, A. Landa, and J. Martín (eds.), *Grammatical Analyses in Basque and Romance Linguistics*. Amsterdam and Philadelphia, PA: John Benjamins, pp. 279–293.

Zubizarreta, M. L. (1998). *Prosody, Focus, and Word Order*. Cambridge, MA: MIT Press.

19

Lexis

Grant Armstrong*

19.1 Introduction

Despite the fact that speakers may have an intuitive idea of what a word means in their language, providing precise definitions and/or representations of word meaning, and elucidating how it interacts with grammar, is a difficult and fascinating area of study that encompasses Lexicography, Psychology, and Philosophy as well as the linguistic sub-disciplines of Pragmatics, Lexical Semantics, Morphology, and Syntax. Perhaps the best way to get a basic sense of the kinds of questions commonly posed in research about word meaning is through an example. Consider what a native speaker of Spanish knows intuitively about the verb *comer* 'eat.' For one, she has acquired an intuitive connection between this word and a fairly specific concept, which we might paraphrase as "ingestion of a solid substance, typically by some animate being." Beyond this, however, there is also a fair amount of general, abstract knowledge about *comer* that is part of her linguistic system: (i) it has an agent and theme that are linked to subject and object positions, respectively, (ii) the theme is crucial in determining whether the ingestion event has an endpoint or not, (iii) the theme can be suppressed syntactically while the agent cannot, (iv) the verb routinely appears with the reflexive clitic *se* when the ingestion event has a natural endpoint, (v) it has a metaphorical sense in expressions like *este escritorio se come todo el cuarto* '= this desk takes up the whole room,' and (vi) it forms the base of derived words such as *comedor* '= dining room.' When faced with the apparently simple question "what does *comer* (eat) mean?," how do we go about investigating this and what parts of a native speaker's

---

* I would like to thank the volume's editor, Kimberly Geeslin, for her helpful feedback throughout the writing of this chapter. Two anonymous reviewers provided important commentary on a previous version of this article. While I was unable to incorporate all of the comments due to length restrictions, I am very grateful for their careful reading and helpful suggestions, which have improved the article. I am responsible for any errors or omissions.

knowledge about a verb like *comer* should be included in a theoretical representation of its meaning?

Linguistic research from many different methodological and theoretical perspectives over the past decades has converged on the idea that both specific, idiosyncratic elements of meaning and more general, abstract meaning components like the ones alluded to above are important to our understanding of words and ultimately of grammar. Methods for investigating these issues across different frameworks essentially involve looking at the linguistic contexts in which a particular word can or cannot appear and the interpretation it has in those contexts. When enough words have been scrutinized in enough linguistic contexts, we can begin to discern which aspects of meaning are specific to individual words or a small groups of words, and which ones are shared among large classes of words, and this will ultimately form the raw material for proposing a theoretical representation of the meaning of a word. The main differences between theories of word meaning are concerned with how to distribute the specific/idiosyncratic and general/abstract information extracted from such investigations across different modules of the linguistic system and its interfaces. Broadly speaking, lexicalist/semantic theories are built around the proposal that the mental lexicon or semantic module is where most or all of this information about words, both specific and general, is stored and that it links to syntactic representations through a series of rules (some representative proposals include Dowty 1979; Pinker 1989; Jackendoff 1990; Goldberg 1995; Levin and Rappaport Hovav 1995; Pustejovsky 1995; Wunderlich 1997; Beavers 2010; Asher 2011). On the other hand, syntactically-oriented theories are built around the idea that more general/abstract meaning components of words are part of syntax and that the meaning of a particular word is a product of the specific content of its root component and the meaning of the syntactic construction in which it appears (for some representative proposals see Hale and Keyser 1993, 2002; Marantz 1997, 2013; Mateu 2002; Borer 2005; Ramchand 2008).

There have been a number of recent applications to Spanish of distinct methodologies of investigating word meaning (e.g. introspective elicitation and usage-based corpus approaches) as well as different theoretical proposals for how to represent meaning components in particular groups of words (some representative works on various topics include Bosque and Masullo 1998; Mateu 2002; Cuervo 2003; Bosque 2004; Demonte 2006; de Miguel 2009; Fábregas *et al.* 2012; Espinal *et al.* 2014; Spalek 2014). The main objective of this chapter is to provide a guide of sorts to linking to the theoretical issues at stake the descriptive generalizations that have come out of investigations on topics related to word meaning. I do this by focusing on three important topics in the study of the meaning of nouns, adjectives, and verbs as they pertain to Spanish data. Section 19.2 discusses the mass/count distinction in common nouns, Section 19.3 discusses gradability in adjectives, and Section 19.4 discusses argument and event structure of the widely-studied denominal location and locatum verbs (Hale and Keyser 1993, 2002; Kiparsky 1997; Mateu 2002, among others). As we will see in the next sections, some of these topics have a more universal appeal while others have specific relevance to Spanish. Section 19.5 provides a brief conclusion.

19.2 The Mass/Count Division in Common Nouns

One of the most important topics in the study of word meaning within the nominal domain is the division of common nouns into the categories "mass" and "count." The distinction has received detailed attention in the recent syntactic and semantic literature (Jackendoff 1991; Krifka 1995; Chierchia 1998; Borer 2005; de Belder 2008; Ghomeshi and Massam 2012; Grimm 2012; Acquaviva 2014, among many others).

Let us begin with a short list of mass and count nouns in Spanish (see Bosque 1999; RAE 2009: Ch.12 for a detailed discussion).

(19.1) a. Mass: *leche* 'milk,' *arena* 'sand,' *lodo* 'mud,' *sangre* 'blood,' *madera* 'wood,' *tela* 'cloth'
        b. Count: *libro* 'book,' *perro* 'dog,' *carro* 'car,' *flor* 'flower,' *vela* 'candle,' *casa* 'house'

The difference between the terms in (19.1a and b) is a semantic property that is reflected in their grammatical behavior. In the absence of number inflection, mass nouns have cumulative reference while count nouns do not (see Borer 2005 and references therein for a formal definition). In informal terms, this means that since the term *leche* is mass, adding *leche* to more *leche* can also be described as *leche*. On the other hand, *libro* is a count noun, so adding *libro* and *libro* yields a sum that cannot be described as *libro*. In order to accurately describe the sum of the latter, plural morphology would be required. Based on this difference, mass nouns are often characterized as "unstructured" pluralities while count nouns are characterized as "individuated" or "atomic" units (see Krifka 1995; Chierchia 1998; Grimm 2012).

The signature difference between mass and count nouns in languages like Spanish can be accounted for by claiming that the grammatical notion of number (singular or plural) is possible only for individuated or atomic units. This means that only count nouns can appear with cardinal numbers and be marked with singular/plural morphology as in (19.2).

(19.2) a. **un lodo*   / **dos lodos*   ; **una sangre* / **dos sangres*
            one mud   / two muds   ; one blood   / two bloods
        b. *un libro*   / *dos libros*   ; *una flor*   / *dos flores*
            one book   / two books   ; one flower   / two flowers

At least two additional environments serve to illustrate the grammatical import of the mass/count distinction. First, quantifiers such as *mucho* 'a lot/many' and *poco* 'a little/few' can be thought of as requiring some kind of plurality in the nouns they combine with. With mass nouns, they do not inflect for plurality while with count nouns they do, as shown in (19.3).

(19.3) a. Había   mucha   sangre / poca   sangre en la   camilla
          There-   a-lot-   blood   / a-little- blood   on the stretcher
          was   (of)   / bit-(of)
       b. Había   muchos   libros / pocos   libros
          There-were   many   books   / few   books

This difference can be explained by appealing to the unstructured plurality of mass nouns versus the structured plurality of count nouns. A second environment where the distinction is relevant are those in which bare nouns are permitted, such as in the object position of a verb. In such positions, mass nouns appear in their invariant form while count nouns appear as bare plurals, as shown in (19.4).

(19.4) a. Cargamos   arena   / *arenas[1] hasta el   jardín
          We-carried   sand   / sands   to   the garden
       b. Cargamos   *flor   / flores   hasta el   jardín
          We-carried   flower / flowers   to   the garden

The connection between the semantic properties of mass and count nouns and their syntactic behavior might lead one to think that the difference should be encoded in individual lexical items, perhaps by a feature or by some formal means that captures the difference between cumulative (unstructured pluralities) and non-cumulative (individuated, atomic) reference. Such an idea accounts for a large amount of data and seems like a plausible way to represent the meaning of a given common noun. However, certain questions arise in the wake of such a move. First, there are many instances of words that can be just as naturally used as either mass or count nouns in Spanish, as shown in (19.5).

(19.5) *ajo* 'garlic,' *algodón* 'cotton,' *caramelo* 'candy,' *cristal* 'glass/crystal,' *corcho* 'cork,' *helado* 'ice cream,' *huevo* 'egg,' *madera* 'wood,' *manzana* 'apple,' *pan* 'bread,' *papel* 'paper,' *pelo* 'hair,' *pescado* 'fish,' *piedra* 'rock/stone'

Source: Bosque (1999:18, Ex. 17)

When used in mass contexts, these words describe matter or substance, while, in count contexts, they describe an individuated object (e.g. *piedra*) or have an implicit unit of measurement that enables them to be counted (e.g. *caramelo* = a "piece" of candy). The question is thus: Should these be

---

[1] It is important to note that I am intentionally presenting a naïve view of these tests, assuming that we are talking about normal usage. This sentence does have a completely acceptable interpretation if plural *arenas* is interpreted as different kinds/classes of sand. As is discussed in all of the literature cited above, it is unclear whether any of the asterisked examples in (19.2)–(19.4) is really ungrammatical or simply odd. Nouns can belong to both categories and be coerced into mass and count in different syntactic contexts, which leads to the question of whether it is a lexical property of individual nouns at all, precisely the point I want to highlight here.

represented as two distinct lexical entries, or one with a rule that can derive the other meaning?

In addition to words that have no clear categorization, there are also cases in which a word that has a relatively stable categorization can appear in a context usually reserved for the other class. There are two completely productive processes of mass nouns appearing in count environments. First, consumable liquids can be construed as count nouns in cases where a unit of measurement is understood contextually. Example 19.6a, for example, can be understood as two *glasses* or two *bottles* of milk depending on context. Second, virtually any mass noun *x* can be pluralized and be interpreted as "different kinds of *x*," as shown in (19.6b) (see Bosque 1999 for a detailed discussion).

(19.6) a. Dame dos leches
Give.me two milks
'Give me two (glasses/bottles) of milk'
b. En las playas del Pacífico hay varias arenas:
In the beaches of-the Pacific there-are many sands:
blanca, negra, etc.
white, black, etc.
'On the beaches of the Pacific, there are many kinds of sand: white, black, etc.'

Count nouns can also appear in mass contexts, though the effect is much more salient to the ear of native speakers and is often used as an expressive device in poetry and humor (see Bosque 1999).

(19.7) a. Es demasiado carro para ti
It-is too much car for you
'That is too much car for you (= you have a car that you cannot handle)'
b. Aquí en Homestead hay demasiado hombre soltero
Here in Homestead there's too-much man single
y muy poca mujer
and very little woman
'Here in Homestead, there are too many single men and few women'
Source: RAE (2009:810)

These examples serve to illustrate that it is necessary to have some contextual rules that enable a mass noun to be accommodated in a count context and vice versa. Finally, there are also somewhat arbitrary intra- and cross-linguistic differences that have been noted for certain classes of nouns. Bosque (1999:14) shows that a number of lexical items from the same semantic field in Spanish (particular types of edible fish and vegetables) can be either or mass or count (see Chierchia 1998 and the works in Ghomeshi and Massam 2012 for similar observations in other languages). There is also cross-linguistic variation in terms of how words that describe the same objects/notions in the world are categorized as mass or count. For example, there are differences between English and Spanish that can be observed in the pairs like *furniture*(mass) – *muebles*(count) and *advice*(mass) – *consejos*(count).

With these issues in mind, let us turn to the theoretical question of how to encode or represent the mass/count distinction in the grammar. Current thinking can be partitioned into two different perspectives. One view treats the mass/count distinction as a lexical property of individual nouns. Some have denotations that refer to a homogenized network of matter that has parts but does not specify whether those parts are individuated. These are mass nouns. Count nouns, on the other hand, have denotations that contain a unit size as part of their meaning. In addition to having denotations associated with mass and count respectively, there are other lexical or contextual rules that shift the meaning of mass or count nouns more generally so that cases of apparent ambiguity or coercion like those mentioned above can be accommodated (see Jackendoff 1991, Chierchia 1998, Ghomeshi and Massam 2012, and references therein for different proposals in this regard).

An alternative view has emerged in a number of works that take the division between mass and count nouns to be derived contextually, specifically by syntactic context (Borer 2005; de Belder 2008; Acquaviva 2014, among others). These theories separate the difference between mass and count from individual nouns and derive the relevant interpretations by positing that nouns are composed of a lexical root and various functional heads responsible for introducing different kinds of variables, division into units and quantifiers. In recent work by Acquaviva (2014), for example, it is claimed that nouns are partitioned into at least the four syntactic regions shown in (19.8). The lexical root and Sort are responsible for establishing the conceptual content of the noun and its noun class, and Division partitions this conceptual content into unit sizes (classifiers and other measure phrases are generated here), which are quantified by Quantity (numerals and quantifiers).[2]

(19.8)   [$_{QuantityP}$ Quantity [$_{DivisionP}$ Division [$_{SortP}$ Sort [ROOT]]]]

By decomposing nouns syntactically, and factoring out the grammatically relevant aspects of meaning, approaches like this one lead us to expect widespread flexibility in the distribution of nouns, as was observed in the examples above. A further positive consequence is a transparent linking between abstract meaning components and inflectional morphology such as gender/noun class and number. As Acquaviva (2014) has shown, a theory such as this has much to offer in terms of how morphemes like theme vowels in Romance and plural markers in words like *celos* (jealousy) and

---

[2] Abbreviations are defined at the beginning of the volume.

babas (drool), so-called *pluralia tantum*, spell out different aspects of meaning that determine conceptual content and division into unit size. What needs to be explained is why some nouns seem to be more rigid than others as to the syntactic context in which they may appear. For instance, even though *libro* 'book' may be used as a mass noun, there is a sense that the conceptual information that is packaged into this word involves some kind of unit size. It is the interaction between this conceptual information and grammatical context that ultimately influences our acceptability judgments. The big question is whether unacceptability is due to ungrammaticality or whether it is due to incompatibility between the conceptual content of a lexical root and the grammatical context in which it appears.

The situation just described pinpoints some of the defining empirical and theoretical issues at stake in the study of word meaning. On the empirical side, it is often difficult to define a word rigidly in terms of a set of invariant meaning components. Like the common nouns described above, many, perhaps most, words in human languages are *polysemous* (see Levin and Rappaport Hovav 1995 and Pustejovsky 1995 for detailed discussions), which means they have distinct, related meanings in different contexts. All theories of word meaning take this as something that needs to be accounted for, but they do this in different ways. One way, as discussed above, is to posit meanings for groups of words in terms of the same set of abstract meaning components and enrich the lexicon or compositional semantic component with a series of rules capable of shifting the meaning of words so that they may be interpreted in different contexts with slightly different meanings (see Pinker 1989; Jackendoff 1990, 1991; Levin and Rappaport Hovav 1995; Pustejovsky 1995; Wunderlich 1997). The other way is to eliminate the lexicon as a separate module with its own rules and derive the properties of words from the syntactic structures in which lexical roots appear (Hale and Keyser 1993, 2002; Marantz 1997, 2013; Mateu 2002; Cuervo 2003; Borer 2005; Ramchand 2008).

There are a number of factors that need to be considered when evaluating the merits of each type of approach. For example, it is sometimes taken for granted that a grammar without a lexical module is more theoretically desirable than one with a lexicon since much of the information that is included in the lexicon ends up getting duplicated in the syntactic component. If the syntax, so the story goes, can do what the lexicon can, it is better to eliminate the lexicon and derive its properties by appealing to syntax and its interfaces. This view is typical of the Minimalist (Chomsky 1995 and subsequent work) push to reduce all forms of theoretical machinery that are not needed to explain how grammar works. While this idea is in principle desirable – and evidence has been offered in favor of it to some degree (see the comprehensive discussions in Borer 2005; Ramchand 2008) – it is still contentious whether it will be possible to eliminate the idea of the lexicon and idiosyncratic features of certain words/roots as playing some role in restricting their distribution in syntax (Potts 2008; Bosque 2012; Marantz 2013). As mentioned above, this idea ultimately shifts the focus of the study of word meaning to an area that involves the interaction of grammar with the conceptual knowledge that is activated by or packaged in lexical roots (Borer 2005; Harley 2014). In Sections 19.3 and 19.4 we will see that the same questions arise in the study of adjectives and verbs.

19.3 Gradability in Adjectives

Among the many different semantically-based classifications of adjectives (see Demonte 1999; RAE 2009: Ch. 13 for an overview of Spanish), recent work has dedicated a lot of attention to gradable adjectives, some of which are shown in (19.9).

(19.9)   *alto* 'tall,' *seco* 'dry,' *inteligente* 'smart,' *feliz* 'happy,' *viejo* 'old,' *lleno* 'full'

These contrast with non-gradable ones like *químico* (chemical) and *gubernamental* (governmental) in their ability to combine with degree terms as shown in (19.10).

(19.10) a. una   sustancia   muy   seca   / *química
             a   substance   very   dry   / chemical
         b. un   edificio   bastante alto   / *gubernamental
             a   building   quite   tall   / governmental

Beyond this basic distinction between gradable and non-gradable adjectives, a more fine-grained division among gradable adjectives has been well established in the lexical semantic literature that partitions gradable adjectives according to two criteria: scale structure and standard of comparison (for English see Kennedy and McNally 2005; Kennedy 2007; Toledo and Sassoon 2011; Husband 2012, among many others; for Spanish see Gumiel-Molina and Pérez-Jiménez 2012; Gumiel-Molina et al. 2015 and references therein).

The first sub-dividing criterion, scale structure, is based on the observation that not all gradable adjectives can combine with all degree terms. Proportional degree modifiers like *completamente* 'completely' and *ligeramente* 'slightly' are compatible with only a subset of gradable adjectives as shown in (19.11) (Gumiel-Molina and Pérez-Jiménez 2012; Gumiel-Molina et al. 2015).

(19.11) a. una   puerta   {completamente / ligeramente}   abierta
             a   door   completely   / slightly   open
         b. un   renglón   {completamente / *ligeramente} recto
             a   line   completely   / *slightly   straight
         c. un   palo   {??completamente / ligeramente}   torcido
             a   pole   completely   / slightly   bent
         d. una   cuerda   {*completamente / *ligeramente} larga
             a   (piece of) string completely   / slightly   long

The different patterns in (19.11), according to Kennedy and McNally (2005), are sensitive to whether the scale lexicalized by the adjective has a maximal and/or minimal point. Those scales that have a maximal degree are compatible with *completamente* 'completely' (19.11b) while those that have a minimal degree are compatible with *ligeramente* 'slightly' (19.11c). If a scale has both a maximal and minimal degree, it is compatible with both modifiers (19.11a) and if it lacks maximal and minimal degrees, it is incompatible with all proportional modifiers (19.11d). The maximal and minimal degrees on a scale are said to close that scale on its upper or lower boundary, respectively. The following is a typology of gradable adjectives based on these observations.

(19.12) a. Totally closed scale: *abierto* 'open,' *cerrado* 'closed,' *vacío* 'empty,' *lleno* 'full'
       b. Upper closed scale: *recto* 'straight,' *limpio* 'clean,' *seco* 'dry'
       c. Lower closed scale: *torcido* 'bent,' *húmedo* 'damp,' *cansado* 'tired'
       d. Totally open scale: *alto* 'tall,' *inteligente* 'smart,' *viejo* 'old'

A second criterion that sub-divides gradable adjectives is the standard of comparison that is used to determine the degree to which the property described by the adjective must hold in order to be truthfully applied to its argument. Some adjectives like *inteligente* 'smart' and *alto* 'tall,' called *relative* gradable adjectives in the literature, require a *between-individuals* (Toledo and Sassoon 2011; Gumiel et al. 2015) comparison to properly evaluate the degree argument of the adjective. In (19.13a), we are stating that a girl is tall relative to a standard degree (≈ median height) for children of similar age. A common context for diagnosing whether an adjective is relative are contexts like (19.13b). Such sentences are felicitous since it is possible for one individual to be taller than another but for neither of the two to exceed the standard degree of the entire set of individuals that comprise the relevant comparison class.

(19.13) a. una niña alta
         a girl tall
      b. Mi hija es más alta que tu
         My daughter is more tall than your

         hijo, pero ella no es alta.
         son, but she NEG is tall.
         'My daughter is taller than your son, but she isn't tall.'
         Source: Gumiel-Molina and Pérez-Jiménez (2012:48–49, Exx. (44)–(45))

Other gradable adjectives like *cansado* 'tired' or *lleno* 'full,' labeled *absolute* gradable adjectives, are evaluated based on a *within-individual* (Toledo and Sassoon 2011; Gumiel-Molina et al. 2015) comparison of different stages of the same individual. For example, in (19.14a), a person qualifies as tired if their current stage/physical state surpasses a minimal degree of tiredness with respect to other stages/physical states of the same person. In (19.14b), we see that absolute adjectives display a different type of entailment pattern to that in the comparative contexts alluded to above. Since the property of being tired can be truthfully applied to the argument *Juan* if his current stage/ physical state exceeds a minimum degree of tiredness with respect to other stages of the same individual, it cannot be the case that he is more tired than someone else but that he does not qualify as tired (# marks the usage as pragmatically odd).

(19.14) a. una persona cansada
            a   person   tired
         b. Juan está más cansado que Pedro → Juan (#no) está cansado
            Juan is more tired than Pedro → Juan (#NEG) is tired
            'Juan is more tired than Pedro' → 'Juan is (#not) tired'

The existence of different classes of gradable adjectives described above leads us to the question of whether properties related to scale structure and standard of comparison should be represented as inherent components of the lexical meaning of adjectives or whether these are derived from the syntactic context in which the adjective appears. Lexicalist proposals claim that the properties of gradable adjectives arise from an inherently specified scale structure from which a standard of comparison is derived through a more general interpretative principle (Kennedy and McNally 2005; Kennedy 2007), or the opposite – an inherently specified standard of comparison from which the scalar properties of a given adjective are derived through a more general interpretative principle (Toledo and Sassoon 2011). In these works, it is acknowledged that certain adjectives may be ambiguous depending on the kind of argument that the adjective has. For instance, *seco* 'dry' behaves as a relative adjective with a totally open scale when it describes climate (19.15a) but as an absolute adjective with an upper closed scale when it describes the physical state of an object (19.15b).

(19.15) a. Esta región del país es (??completamente) seca
            This region of.the country is (completely) dry
         b. Mi camisa está completamente seca
            My shirt is completely dry

These data could be handled by proposing that some scalar dimensions (*dryness* in this case) have nuances that are listed in the lexical entry of an individual adjective and activated when the adjective combines with a certain class of nominal arguments.

Syntactic proposals have highlighted cases like (19.15), claiming that they are common enough to motivate the claim that scalar structure and standard of comparison in gradable adjectives are introduced by functional heads in the syntax, independent of individual lexical items (Gumiel-Molina and Pérez-Jiménez 2012; Husband 2012; Gumiel-Molina *et al.* 2015). The evolving work of Gumiel-Molina and Pérez-Jiménez (2012) and Gumiel-Molina *et al.* (2015) has established an intriguing correlation first between scale structure (the 2012 paper) and later between standard of comparison (the 2015 paper) and the *ser/estar* alternation.[3] They observe that most gradable adjectives in Spanish can appear with either the *ser* or the *estar* copula as in (19.16a) and that the difference in copula choice strongly correlates with the relative/absolute division, as it is defined above. *Ser* appears to select for relative gradable adjectives (19.16b) and *estar* for absolute gradable adjectives (19.16c).

(19.16) a. El niño {es/está} alto/bajo
 The child ser/estar tall/short
 b. Mi hija es más alta que tu hijo pero ella no es alta
 My daughter ser more tall than your son but she NEG ser tall
 c. *Mi hija está más alta que tu hijo pero ella no está alta
 My daughter estar more tall than your son but she NEG estar tall
 Source: Gumiel-Molina and Pérez-Jiménez (2012:48–49, Exx. (44)–(45))

They claim that because many adjectives follow this same pattern, a more natural way of accounting for variable behavior, or polysemy, is to divorce standard of comparison from the meaning of individual adjectives and introduce this notion in the syntactic functional structure above the adjective, mainly the degree (Deg) phrase, as in (19.17).

(19.17) [$_{DegP}$ Deg [$_{AP}$ A]]

The locus of the notion of standard of comparison is Deg rather than A. When Deg is merged, it is responsible for binding the degree argument of the adjective and establishing whether that argument is evaluated with respect to a *between-individuals* comparison class or a *within-individual* comparison class. DegP also hosts the PP headed by *para* 'for' that introduces overt comparison class NPs. This, in turn, influences the type of argument that the adjective can combine with as well as whether the entire predicational relation is selected by *ser* or *estar*. The authors also discuss why certain adjectives might resist one of these grammatical contexts based on the incompatibility of their internal meaning components/morphosyntactic structure with either type of comparison class.

As can be observed in this brief discussion, the same kinds of questions that arise in analyzing the mass/count distinction in nouns (Section 19.2) are also relevant for the analysis of gradable adjectives. In this section, components of meaning have been identified that divide gradable adjectives into classes, and it is very much an open question as to whether these should be included as part of the lexical representation of each adjective's meaning or whether they are a product of the structural environment in which a particular adjectival root appears.

[3] Note that this is just one of many possible analyses of what underlies the *ser/estar* distinction, most of which are reviewed in Gumiel-Molina *et al.* (2015). The objective here is not to necessarily advocate this particular view of the *ser/estar* distinction but merely to demonstrate how it has been employed in motivating a syntactic approach to deriving classes of gradable adjectives in Spanish.

19.4 Derivational Morphology, Argument Structure, and Lexical Aspect in Verbs

Verbs are the most widely studied class of words in lexical semantic research. They are typically sub-categorized according to their argument structure (e.g. theta roles) and lexical aspectual properties. We will first consider the descriptive issues at stake in the study of verb meaning by looking at a particular class of well-studied verbs and then linking these to the larger theoretical discussion running through the previous sections.

19.4.1 Descriptive Issues

Let us take as our starting point the sets of verbs in (19.18) and (19.19). These have been labeled denominal *location* and *locatum* verbs in the literature (Hale and Keyser 1993, 2002; Kiparsky 1997; Mateu 2002; Harley 2005, among others).

(19.18) *Location verbs*
    a. El policía encarceló al criminal
       The policeman jailed ACC.the criminal
    b. *almacenar* 'to store,' *archivar* 'to file/archive,' *aterrizar* 'to land/ground,' *embotellar* 'to bottle,' *encarcelar* 'to jail,' *enjaular* 'to cage,' *enlatar* 'to can,' *envainar* 'to sheathe'

(19.19) *Locatum verbs*
    a. El vaquero ensilló el caballo
       The cowboy saddled the horse
    b. *adornar* 'to ornament/decorate,' *cobijar* 'to blanket,' *enharinar* 'to cover with flour,' *empanar* 'to cover/wrap with bread,' *empapelar* 'to paper,' *enmantecar* 'to butter,' *ensillar* 'to saddle,' *vendar* 'to bandage'

Location and locatum verbs have a conspicuous morphological structure that is important in discerning their argument structure and lexical aspectual properties. While not all verbs instantiate the same pattern, it is not a coincidence that the majority of them can be segmented into a root component, which pre-theoretically can be equated with a noun without a theme vowel (*cárcel, jaul(a), mantec(a), adorn(o),* etc.), a locative prefix (*a-, en-*), and verbalizing morphology (*-ar, -izar*).[4] This morphological segmentation aligns in a more or less transparent way with a meaning paraphrase along the lines of "*x* causes *y* to be in/at <root>" or "*x* causes *y* to be with <root>." The root element in this informal description is instantiated by the noun from which the verb is derived. The locative or possessive meaning associated with IN/AT or WITH is mostly instantiated by prefixes,

---

[4] Obviously, things are not as simple as this since these denominal derivations could also be treated as involving a single discontinuous morpheme, so-called "circumfixation" or *parasíntesis* (see Serrano-Dolader 1999). To the extent that separate meaning components can be linked to the prefix and suffix, I leave the idea as is here and refer the reader to work cited and references therein for more details.

and the dynamic element of meaning associated with CAUSE is instantiated by verbalizing morphology.

Let us now turn to the argument structure properties of location and locatum verbs. They have an agent, which initiates the event, and a theme, which is the affected entity that ends up in a new location or with some object or substance as a result of the event's happening. The agent is linked to the external argument position, and theme to the direct internal argument position. Other argument structure characteristics of both location and locatum verbs can be discerned by looking at the types of alternations they exhibit. For instance, location and locatum verbs are limited with respect to the types of intransitive environments in which they can appear. They are generally unacceptable as anticausatives/inchoatives (see Levin and Rappaport Hovav 1995, Mendikoetxea 1999 for details) and with unspecified objects (see Levin 1999; Martí 2011; Armstrong 2016 for details) but are acceptable in the generic middle construction (see Mateu 2002 for details). This is shown in (19.20).

(19.20) a. *El   pájaro se   enjauló (por sí solo)   Anticausative/inchoative
             The   bird   SE   caged   (by itself/on its own)
         b. Este   caballo se   ensilla fácilmente   Generic middle
             This horse   SE   saddles easily
         c. *Archivamos   ayer   Unspecified object
             We-filed   yesterday

Lexical aspect, also called event structure, involves identifying how many subevents a verbal predicate lexicalizes and diagnosing its *aktionsart* (lexical aspect) properties, mainly whether it is dynamic or stative, telic or atelic, and durative or punctual. The number of subevents in a verbal predicate can be diagnosed with certain adverbial expressions such as *otra vez* (again) and *casi* (almost). It has been demonstrated in the literature that these modify subevents (see Dowty 1979; von Stechow 1996; Cuervo 2003; MacDonald 2008, among many others) and give rise to ambiguous interpretations if multiple subevents are present. Consider the examples in (19.21).

(19.21)   a. Embotellamos el vino otra vez
              Repetitive interpretation: We bottled the wine before and we bottled it again
              Restitutive interpretation: The wine was in bottled state before, then was poured out, and we bottled it again
           b. Adornamos el salón otra vez
              Repetitive interpretation: We decorated the room before and we did it again
              Restitutive interpretation: The room was in a decorated state before, then went without decorations, and we decorated it again

In each case, there are two interpretations. One involves a reading in which *otra vez* takes scope over both the agent and result state. This is called the repetitive reading. On the other hand, there is a distinct reading in which *otra vez* takes scope over only over the result state. Here, the agent does not have to be the same one in both the presupposed result state that held before and in the one that is targeted by *otra vez*. This is the restitutive reading. In the case of location and locatum verbs, the ambiguity exhibited by this modifier is taken to be evidence that there is a causing subevent and a result state, either of which can be the target of modification.

Beyond the number of subevents, lexical aspect also encompasses notions such as dynamicity (vs. stativity), telicity (vs. atelicity), and durativity (vs. punctuality). Major subclasses of verb phrases are based on features that they have with respect to these notions. The most common division is the following: *states* (stative), *activities* (dynamic, atelic), *achievements* (dynamic, telic, punctual), and *accomplishments* (dynamic, telic, durative). It is uncontroversial that location and locatum verbs are dynamic (see de Miguel 1999; Marín and McNally 2011 for diagnostic tests of dynamicity in Spanish), so I will focus primarily on telicity and durativity in the remainder of this section.

The test most commonly used to diagnose telicity is the "in/for" test, or *en/durante* test in Spanish. A time frame introduced by the preposition *en* indicates the duration of an event with an inherent boundary while a time frame introduced by *durante* indicates the duration of an event without an inherent boundary. As shown in (19.22), it is the verb and its internal argument that ultimately determine whether an event is telic (19.22a) or atelic (19.22b).

(19.22) a. Escribí   la   carta   {en / *durante} media hora
            I wrote   the   letter   in   / for   half   hour
        b. Escribí   {*en / durante} media hora
            I wrote   in   / for   half   hour

Applying this test to location and locatum verbs yields a result that is superficially similar to the one in (19.22). In (19.23a) below, the internal argument *la colección de libros* describes a specific quantity, or quantized object (see Krifka 1989, Verkuyl 1993 and subsequent work), while, in (19.23b), *libros* describes a non-specific quantity. This appears to be the deciding factor in whether a verb phrase headed by a location or locatum verb will be telic.

(19.23) a. Almacenamos la   colección de libros {en / *durante} una hora
            We-stored   the collection of books in   / for   an   hour
        b. Almacenamos libros {*en / durante} una hora
            We-stored   books   in   / for   an   hour

However, as has been noted in a number of works (Depraetere 1995; de Miguel 1999; MacDonald 2008; Ramchand 2008, among others), there is a slightly different interpretation induced by the time frame headed by *durante* in (19.22b), which has an unspecified object, and (19.23b), which contains a bare plural. The interpretation in (19.22b) is that there is a single writing event construed as a homogeneous totality. In (19.23b), on the other hand, the most natural interpretation involves a sequence of storing events which culminate and iterate successively, something akin to "we stored book after book for an hour." The fact that location and locatum verbs cannot appear with unspecified objects and typically require an iterative interpretation when they combine with *durante* phrases has led some to claim that these verbs are inherently telic even in the presence of a bare plural. In spite of its plausibility, there are some problematic examples for this generalization, as can be seen in (19.24).

(19.24) a. María adornó   la   casa   durante una   hora
           María decorated   the   house   for   an   hour
       b. La niña enmantecó el molde   durante cinco minutos
          The child buttered   the (cake) mold for   five   minutes

In these cases, a locatum verb has a quantized object but it is compatible with the time frame introduced by *durante* on the single-event reading. These data demonstrate that, for the most part, location and locatum verbs are telic, but that there are some examples in which an atelic reading is possible. The source of the atelic reading is not entirely agreed upon (see Mateu 2002; Harley 2005 for some discussion).

Finally, let us consider the notion of durativity. There are a number of ways of diagnosing this (see de Miguel 1999 and Marín and McNally 2011 for careful discussions of how these tests work in Spanish). One of the primary tests involves the interpretation of a verbal predicate in the *seguir* 'continue' + gerund construction. It has been shown that if a verb lexicalizes a durative component of meaning, it will be compatible with this construction on a single-event reading that happens gradually. If it lacks a durative component and is truly punctual, it gives rise to an odd iterative reading. This is shown in (19.25).

(19.25) a. Juan sigue   leyendo   esa   revista
           Juan continues   reading   that   magazine
       b. #La bomba   sigue   explotando
          The bomb   continues   exploding (it explodes again and again)

The results of applying this test to the location and locatum verbs show that these do not behave in a uniform way with respect to durativity. There are verbs in both classes that pattern with durative predicates (19.26) and also with punctual ones (19.27).

(19.27) a. Mi amigo sigue   embotellando la   cerveza
           My friend continues bottling   the beer
           (event started and is still in progress)
       b. Seguimos   empapelando el   salón
          We continue wallpapering the room
          (event started and is still in progress)

(19.27) a. #El piloto sigue   aterrizando el   avión
           The pilot continues landing   the plane
           (event started and is still in progress)
       b. #El vaquero sigue   ensillando el   caballo
          The cowboy continues saddling   the horse
          (event keeps happening over again)

The preliminary conclusion that can be drawn from these data is that location and locatum verbs fall into the accomplishment or achievement classes since they are, for the most part, telic, and can be either durative or punctual.

19.4.2 Theoretical Issues

In dealing with meaning components of any verb class like location and locatum verbs, the theoretical desideratum of any theory is to account, in a principled way, for the sound–meaning correspondence in their morphological make-up as well as for their argument structure and lexical aspectual properties. As discussed in the reviews of Levin and Rappaport Hovav (2005) and Marantz (2013), a consensus has emerged after decades of research into verb meaning to the effect that these elements of meaning generalize over large classes of verbs to the extent that it is undesirable to propose individual representations of the theta roles that a particular verb selects and how a particular verb is interpreted aspectually. Let us contrast two well-known proposals that take different stances on how to account for these issues.

Starting with Hale and Keyser (1993, 2002), there have been a number of syntactically-oriented approaches that attempt to capture the entire range of phenomena treated here by decomposing location verbs into a series of heads in the syntax (Mateu 2002; Harley 2005). The basic proposal is outlined in (19.28).

(19.28) a. El   policía   encarceló   al   criminal
             The   policeman   jailed   ACC.the   criminal
         b. [vP [DP *el policía*] v [PP [DP *el criminal*] en- [Root √*cárcel*]]]

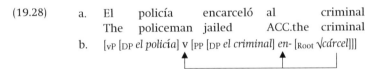

The verb *encarcelar* is composed of a lexical root √*cárcel* (jail), which is embedded under a preposition that is often realized by a prefix (*en-* in this case). This preposition (P) establishes a relation between an entity that is located (a theme or figure), and a space or ground (see Talmy 1985), such that the ground acts as a terminus of some abstract movement of the theme. The prepositional phrase (PP) of terminal coincidence is embedded under a verbal projection that introduces a causing event and licenses the agent in its specifier. It could be argued that verbal theme vowels and other verbalizing suffixes are introduced in this verbal projection.

In this approach, there is a direct link established between the morphological properties of the verb class and its argument structure properties. In essence, the different pieces that make up the verb are responsible for licensing its arguments. There is no need for any type of special linking rules from lexical semantic to syntactic representations since these are one and the same thing. The argument structure properties mentioned in Section 19.4.1 can be accounted for by appealing both to the semantic and structural requirements of *v* (a light verb that introduces a verbal argument) and P, respectively (see Mateu 2002 for discussion). The modification facts can be handled by claiming that either the v projection or the P projection can be targeted by certain classes of modifiers like *otra vez* 'again.' There is less clarity in this general approach as to how the lexical aspectual properties of the syntactic construction in (19.28b) are derived. Mateu (2002) and Harley (2005) claim that the P in (19.28) is of terminal coincidence and this is what makes the verb telic but that atelic readings can arise if the root corresponds to a mass noun such as *manteca* 'lard, butter' as opposed to a count noun like *jaula* 'cage.' The example in (19.24a), an atelic reading with *adornar* 'decorate,' which is derived from the count noun/root *adorn(o)* 'ornament, decoration,' would be a problem for this idea. Durativity is not mentioned at all in these approaches, but there are ways in the systems outlined in MacDonald (2008) and Ramchand (2008) to make subevents invisible to certain syntactic operations or to co-index them in order to derive the punctual interpretations that certain location and locatum verbs have.

There have also been a number of lexicalist proposals for this verb class. Kiparsky (1997) provides the following analysis of location verbs within the frame of Lexical Decomposition Grammar (LDG; see Wunderlich 1997 and references therein). The proposal is that a location verb like *encarcelar* has a semantic representation like that of (19.29b), which is connected to syntax by a set of linking rules.

(19.29) a. El   policía   encarceló   al   criminal
         The   policeman   jailed   ACC.the   criminal
       b. λz.λy.λx [CAUSE (x, (BE-IN (y, z))) & JAIL(z)]

The semantic decomposition of the meaning of *encarcelar* in (19.28b) mirrors the syntactic decomposition in (19.29b), so the explanation of the basic morphological argument structure, and lexical aspectual properties of the verb class rely on very similar mechanisms. However, the point Kiparsky (1997) emphasizes in his analysis echoes the ones mentioned above with respect to how to best account for apparent flexibility in the meaning of nouns and adjectives. Kiparsky's argument can be summarized as follows: Even though it is *possible* to derive certain semantic information about words by appealing solely to syntax and its interfaces, is this empirically and theoretically justifiable? He argues that in the case of location and locatum verbs it is not. First, the approach glosses over the fact that syntax is productive while word-internal syntax exhibits limitations that do not have obvious answers without appealing to some kind of idiosyncratic formal or conceptual semantic notions. For instance, if I put my money in a book to hide it, I might be inclined to say *hoy enlibré* (= *en-* + *libro*) *100 pesos*. Even if my interlocutor could gauge what I meant, it seems that without saying something to the tune of "the root *libr(o)* cannot be integrated into the semantic structure in (19.29b);" or "*libr(o)* has a formal feature that prohibits it from appearing in this position," it is difficult to explain why this is unacceptable (see Pinker 1989 for a discussion along these lines about certain constraints on the double object construction, and Mateu 2002; Borer 2005; Levin and Rappaport Hovav 2005; and Marantz 2013 for different perspectives on how to tackle this problem).

Kiparsky (1997) also notes that if word formation is syntactic, it raises the question of why there are severe limitations on the modification of subcomponents of verbs (although such modification is possible, as shown in Section 19.4.1 – see Bosque 2012 for discussion). For instance, an adjective or an adverb cannot modify the root/noun in the syntactic structure in (19.28b) and then be stranded by head movement as shown in (19.30) (see Mateu 2002; Levinson 2010; Bosque 2012; and Armstrong 2016 for different proposals that attempt to address the limitations of modification of word-internal components).

(19.30) *Lo encarcelamos grande (vs. Lo pusimos en una cárcel grande)
Him we-jailed big
Intended: 'We put him in a big jail.'

In the absence of a constrained theory that accounts for why such limitations exist, claims Kiparsky (1997), it is preferable to adopt a semantic theory that can account for what syntactic decomposition gets right by using decompositions and can also account for what it gets wrong by locating those decompositions in a semantic component of grammar that links to syntax.

19.5 Conclusion

In this chapter I have highlighted a sampling of some of the empirical and theoretical issues involved in the study of word meaning by focusing on a set of semantic components of the core lexical categories – nouns, adjectives, and verbs – and different approaches to representing them. We have seen that, from an empirical standpoint, work on word meaning generally involves investigating the distribution of words in different linguistic contexts and then extracting from those contexts which components of meaning are specific/idiosyncratic and which ones are general/abstract. Though theories differ as to how to represent these meaning components in different modules, there is a consensus to the effect that there is a need to factor out semantic commonalities among groups of words and to allow more general principles to do some work in determining what a word means. Continuing work in this area will no doubt help us sharpen our ideas about what the grammatically-relevant components of meaning are, how they manifest themselves across categories, if/how these may vary among and within languages, and how the conceptual content of words interacts with grammar.

References

Acquaviva, Paolo (2014). The Roots of Nominality, the Nominality of Roots. In A. Alexiadou *et al.* (eds.), *The Syntax of Roots and the Roots of Syntax*. Oxford: Oxford University Press, pp. 33–56.

Armstrong, Grant (2016). Spanish Unspecified Objects as Null Incorporated Nouns. *Probus*, 28, 165–230.

Asher, Nicholas (2011). *Lexical Meaning in Context. A Web of Words*. Cambridge: Cambridge University Press.

Beavers, John (2010). The Structure of Lexical Meaning: Why Semantics Really Matters. *Language*, 86, 821–864.

Borer, Hagit (2005). *Structuring Sense*, Vol. 1: *In Name Only;* Vol. 2: *The Normal Course of Events*. Oxford: Oxford University Press.

Bosque, Ignacio (1999). El nombre común. In I. Bosque and V. Demonte (eds.), *Gramática descriptiva de la lengua española*, Vol. 1. Madrid: Espasa, pp. 3–75.

Bosque, Ignacio (2004). *REDES: Diccionario combinatorio del español contemporáneo*. Madrid: Ediciones SM.

Bosque, Ignacio (2012). On the Lexical Integrity Hypothesis and its (In)accurate Predictions. *Iberia*, 4 (1), 140–173.

Bosque, Ignacio and Masullo, Pascual José (1998). On Verbal Quantification in Spanish. In O. Fullana and F. Roca (eds.), *Studies on the Syntax of Central Romance Languages*. Girona: Universitat de Girona, pp. 9–63.

Chierchia, Gennaro (1998). Plurality of Mass Nouns and the Notion of "Semantic Parameter." In S. Rothstein (ed.), *Events and Grammar*. Dordrecht: Kluwer, pp. 53–104.

Chomsky, Noam (1995). *The Minimalist Program*. Cambridge, MA: MIT Press.

Cuervo, María Cristina (2003). Datives at Large (Doctoral dissertation). MIT.

de Belder, Marijke (2008). Size Matters: Towards a Syntactic Decomposition of Countability. In Natasha Abner and Jason Bishop (eds.), *Proceedings of the 27th West Coast Conference on Formal Linguistics*. Somerville, MA: Cascadilla, pp. 116–122.

de Miguel, Elena (1999). El aspecto léxico. In I. Bosque and V. Demonte (eds.), *Gramática descriptiva de la lengua española*, Vol. 2. Madrid: Espasa, pp. 2977–3060.

de Miguel, Elena (ed.) (2009). *Panorama de la lexicología*. Barcelona: Ariel.

Demonte, Violeta (1999). El adjetivo: Clases y usos. La posición del adjetivo en el sintagma nominal. In I. Bosque and V. Demonte (eds.), *Gramática descriptiva de la lengua española*, Vol. 1. Madrid: Espasa, pp. 129–215.

Demonte, Violeta (2006). Qué es sintáctico y qué es léxico en la interfaz entre sintaxis y léxico-semántica: Hipótesis y conjeturas. *Signo y Seña*, 15, 17–41.

Depraetere, Ilse (1995). On the Necessity of Distinguishing between (Un)boundedness and (A)telicity. *Linguistics and Philosophy*, 18, 1–19.

Dowty, David (1979). *Word Meaning and Montague Grammar*. Dordrecht: Reidel.
Espinal, María Teresa, Macià, Josep, Mateu, Jaume, and Quer, Josep (2014). *Semántica*. Madrid: Akal.
Fábregas, Antonio, Marín, Rafael, and McNally, Louise (2012). From Psych Verbs to Nouns. In V. Demonte and L. McNally (eds.), *Telicity, Change, and State*. Oxford: Oxford University Press, pp. 162–184.
Ghomeshi, Jila and Massam, Diane (eds.). (2012). *Count and Mass across Languages*. Oxford: Oxford University Press.
Goldberg, Adele (1995). *Constructions: A Construction Grammar Approach to Argument Structure*. Chicago, IL: University of Chicago Press.
Grimm, Scott (2012). Number and Individuation (Doctoral dissertation). Stanford University.
Gumiel-Molina, Silvia, Moreno-Quibén, Norberto, and Pérez-Jiménez, Isabel (2015). Comparison Classes and the Relative/Absolute Distinction: A Degree-Based Compositional Account of the *ser/estar* Distinction. *Natural Language and Linguistic Theory*, 33, 955–1001.
Gumiel-Molina, Silvia and Pérez-Jiménez, Isabel (2012). Aspectual Composition in <*ser/estar*+Adjective> Structures: Adjectival Scalarity and Verbal Aspect In Copular Constructions. *Borealis* 1, (1), 33–62.
Hale, Ken and Keyser, Samuel J. (1993). On Argument Structure and the Lexical Expression of Syntactic Relations. In K. Hale and S. J. Keyser (eds.), *The View from Building 20: Essays in Linguistics in Honor of Sylvain Bromberger*. Cambridge, MA: MIT Press, pp. 53–109.
Hale, Ken and Keyser, Samuel J. (2002). *Prolegomenon to a Theory of Argument Structure*. Cambridge, MA: MIT Press.
Harley, Heidi (2005). How do Verbs Get their Names? Denominal Verbs, Manner Incorporation and the Ontology of Verb Roots in English. In N. Erteschik-Shir and T. Rapoport (eds.), *The Syntax of Aspect*. Oxford: Oxford University Press, pp. 42–64.
Harley, Heidi (2014). On the Identity of Roots. *Theoretical Linguistics*, 40, 225–276.
Husband, Matthew (2012). *On the Compositional Nature of States*. Amsterdam and Philadelphia, PA: John Benjamins.
Jackendoff, Ray (1990). *Semantic Structures*. Cambridge, MA: MIT Press.
Jackendoff, Ray (1991). Part and Boundaries. *Cognition*, 41, 9–45.
Kennedy, Christopher (2007). Vagueness and Grammar: The Semantics of Relative and Absolute Gradable Adjectives. *Linguistics and Philosophy*, 30, 1–45.
Kennedy, Christopher and McNally, Louise (2005). Scale Structure, Degree Modification, and the Semantics of Gradable Predicates. *Language*, 81, 345–381.
Kiparsky, Paul (1997). Remarks on Denominal Verbs. In A. Alsina, J. Bresnan, and P. Sells (eds.), *Argument Structure*. Stanford, CA: CSLI Publications, pp. 473–499.

Krifka, Manfred (1989). Nominal Reference, Temporal Constitution and Quantification in Event Semantics. In B. R. Benthem, and P. V. E. Boas (eds.), *Semantics and Contextual Expressions*. Dordrecht: Foris, pp. 75–115.

Krifka, Manfred (1995). Common Nouns: A Contrastive Analysis of Chinese and English. In G. Carlson and J. Pelletier (eds.), *The Generic Book*. Chicago, IL: University of Chicago Press, pp. 398–411.

Levin, Beth (1999). Objecthood: An Event Structure Perspective. In *Proceedings of the Chicago Linguistics Society 35,* Vol. 1: *The Main Session*. Chicago, IL: University of Chicago Press, pp. 223–247.

Levin, Beth and Rappaport Hovav, Malka (1995). *Unaccusativity: At the Syntax–Lexical Semantics Interface*. Cambridge, MA: MIT Press.

Levin, Beth and Rappaport Hovav, Malka (2005). *Argument Realization*. Cambridge: Cambridge University Press.

Levinson, Lisa (2010). Arguments for Pseudo-Resultative Predicates. *Natural Language and Linguistic Theory*, 28, 135–182.

MacDonald, Jonathan (2008). *The Syntax of Inner Aspect*. Amsterdam and Philadelphia, PA: John Benjamins.

Marantz, Alec (1997). No Escape from Syntax: Don't Try Morphological Analysis in the Privacy of Your Own Lexicon. *Penn Working Papers in Linguistics*, 4 (2), 201–225.

Marantz, Alec (2013). Verbal Argument Structure: Events and Participants. *Lingua*, 130, 152–168.

Marín, Rafael and McNally, Louise (2011). Inchoativity, Change of State, and Telicity: Evidence from Spanish Psychological Reflexive Verbs. *Natural Language and Linguistic Theory*, 29, 467–502.

Martí, Luisa (2011). Implicit Indefinite Objects: Grammar, not Pragmatics (MS). Queen Mary, University of London. Available from ling.auf.net/lingbuzz/001317 (last access December 4, 2017).

Mateu, Jaume (2002). Argument Structure: Relational Construal at the Syntax–Semantics Interface (Doctoral dissertation). Universitat Autònoma de Barcelona.

Mendikoetxea, Amaya (1999). Construcciones inacusativas y pasivas. In I. Bosque and V. Demonte (eds.) *Gramática descriptiva de la lengua española*, Vol. 2. Madrid: Espasa, pp. 1575–1629.

Pinker, Steven (1989). *Learnability and Cognition*. Cambridge, MA: MIT Press.

Potts, Christopher (2008). Structuring Sense, Volume I: In Name Only and Structuring Sense, Volume II: The Normal Course of Events (Review). *Language*, 84, 343–369.

Pustejovsky, James (1995). *The Generative Lexicon*. Cambridge, MA: MIT Press.

Ramchand, Gillian (2008). *Verb Meaning and the Lexicon. A First-Phase Syntax*. Cambridge: Cambridge University Press.

Real Academia Española (2009). *Nueva gramática de la lengua española*. Madrid: Espasa.

Serrano-Dolader, David (1999). La derivación verbal y la parasíntesis. In I. Bosque and V. Demonte (eds.), *Gramática descriptiva de la lengua española*, Vol. 3. Madrid: Espasa, pp. 4683–4755.

Spalek, Alexandra (2014). Verb Meaning and Combinatory Semantics: A Corpus-Based Study of Spanish Change of State Verbs (Doctoral dissertation). Universitat Pompeu Fabra.

Stechow, Arnim von (1996). The Different Readings of *Wieder* "Again": A Structural Account. *Journal of Semantics*, 13, 87–138.

Talmy, Leonard (1985). Lexicalization Patterns: Semantic Structure in Lexical Forms. In T. Shopen (ed.), *Language Typology and Syntactic Description*. Cambridge: Cambridge University Press, pp. 57–149.

Toledo, Assaf and Sassoon, Galit (2011). Absolute vs. Relative Adjectives – Variance Within vs. Between Individuals. *Proceedings of SALT*, 21, 135–154.

Verkuyl, Henk (1993). *A Theory of Aspectuality*. Cambridge: Cambridge University Press.

Wunderlich, Dieter (1997). Cause and Structure of Verbs. *Linguistic Inquiry*, 28, 27–68.

20

Pragmatics

Maria Hasler-Barker

20.1 What is Pragmatics?

At its core, pragmatics concerns itself with language in interaction, language users, and the process of making and interpreting meaning. The term "pragmatics" has had a plethora of definitions since Morris' (1938) initial description of the relationship between signs and users. Scholars and philosophers have defined this term in a variety of overlapping and sometimes conflicting ways. Leech (1983:10) refers to pragmatics simply as the "communicative use of language," while Thomas (1995:22) focuses on meaning, which is not "inherent in words alone, nor is it produced by the speaker alone, nor by the hearer alone." Crystal (1997:301) describes pragmatics from the point of view of users, "especially of the choices they make, the constraints they encounter in using language in social interaction and the effect their use of language has on other participants in the act of communication." Escandell-Vidal (2006 [1996]:16) defines pragmatics as the study of extralinguistic factors determining language use in interaction, namely "the conditions that determine the use of particular utterances produced by particular speakers in particular communicative situations, and their interpretation by hearers" (translation mine). Huang's (2007:2) definition emphasizes the inextricable connection between meaning and users, describing pragmatics as "the systematic study of meaning by virtue of, or dependent on, the use of language." These varying definitions contribute to debates about precisely what pragmaticists study.

Since Morris (1938), there have been numerous attempts to define what counts as pragmatics and how to categorize theoretical and functional elements. Bar-Hillel (1971) called pragmatics the "wastebasket" of linguistics because of the wide-ranging collection of components and methods of analysis that have been adopted to define language use in interaction. In fact, for a number of authors, pragmatics is a perspective from which to examine language use in context (e.g. Márquez-Reiter and Placencia

2005; Mey 2001 [1993]; Verschueren 1999). Márquez-Reiter and Placencia (2005:2) characterize pragmatics as "a perspective on communication; more specifically, as the cognitive, social, and cultural study of communication." Verschueren (1999:2) asserts that because pragmatics has no single unit of analysis, it "does not constitute an additional component of a theory of language, but it offers a different *perspective*" (emphasis Verschueren). For these scholars, all aspects of language can potentially be viewed through the lens of pragmatics.

On the other side of the coin are researchers who view pragmatic features as objects of study, on par with other linguistic components (e.g. syntax), rather than examining linguistic components through a pragmatic lens. Levinson (1983) formalized this demarcation when he distinguished the Anglo-American philosophical and linguistic view of pragmatics from a Continental philosophical and linguistic approach. For Levinson, the pragmatic component within linguistic theory is necessary to ground abstract theoretical discussions in everyday, functional language use. At the time that linguistic scholars began discussing contextually-bound uses of language, existing theoretical approaches could not account for certain phenomena without addressing context (Levinson 1983:35–36). Thus, for Levinson, pragmatics must necessarily be an *object* of study, including such context-determined phenomena as deixis, conversational implicature, presupposition, and speech acts.[1]

Scholars have argued against a geographically-bound Anglo-American/Continental contrast, proposing several other types of distinction between different areas of pragmatics. Mey (2001 [1993]) and Huang (2007, 2013) have described the distinction between component and perspective views, as well as between micro- and macropragmatics (e.g. Mey 2001 [1993]; Huang 2007, 2013).[2] Within an overall general theory of pragmatics, Leech (1983) suggested a division between pragmalinguistics and sociopragmatics, while Escandell-Vidal (2004) proposed sociocultural and cognitive perspectives on pragmatics. As shown below, these distinctions are continuous, rather than binary, with significant overlap among the various views of pragmatics.

The component view is roughly analogous to Levinson's (1983:8) Anglo-American view, situating pragmatics as a core constituent of linguistic theory, along with phonetics, phonology, morphology, syntax, and semantics. This view examines the factors that determine the (sometimes radically) different pragmatic effects of forms that have equivalent surface-

---

[1] Levinson (1983) also included conversational structure and discourse in the scope of pragmatics, though this will not be addressed here.

[2] Also found among the schemata for describing pragmatics (e.g. component/perspective and micro-/macropragmatic) is the term "big tent pragmatics" coined by Ariel (2010). She focuses on researchers and categorizes them either as problem-solvers (i.e. those who identify a phenomenon that grammar cannot account for and then find a theory to explain it) or as boundary-seekers (i.e. those who identify a theory and then find a phenomenon to explain). Huang (2013:130, footnote) rejects this analogy primarily because he finds her assertion – that pragmatics contains inferences while grammar contains codes – to be questionable.

level meanings. Unsurprisingly, the perspective view takes pragmatics as "a functional perspective on every aspect of linguistic behavior" (Huang 2007:4). That is, pragmatics is not a separate component of a unified linguistic theory, but it provides a lens through which to examine user choices in phonetics, phonology, morphology, syntax, and semantics. Mey (2001 [1993]) argues that component and perspective approaches should exist side by side, expanding the horizons of pragmatics, rather than limiting its scope. He suggests, "We could either ask how users 'mean what they say,' that is, how they communicate, using language, or how they 'say what they mean,' employing the linguistic devices at their disposal to express themselves" (Mey 2001 [1993]:9). This suggested approach blurs the distinction between component and perspective views and is echoed in the distinction between micro and macro views of pragmatics.

Huang (2013) also mapped micro- and macropragmatics. Central topics in micropragmatics include implicatures, presupposition, speech acts, deixis, and reference. On the other end of the spectrum, Huang divides macropragmatics into three principal areas: (i) cognitively-oriented approaches (e.g. cognitive pragmatics, experimental psychopragmatics, and neuropragmatics); (ii) socially- or culturally-oriented approaches (e.g. sociopragmatics, cross-/intercultural pragmatics, and variational pragmatics); and (iii) a variety of interdisciplinary macropragmatic approaches (e.g. historical pragmatics, legal pragmatics, and literary pragmatics).[3] Teaching of pragmatics and foreign or second language pragmatics is also included in the domain of macropragmatics. While Huang (2013) clearly distinguishes the diverse elements within (and related to) micro- and macropragmatic areas, he too suggests that researchers should employ both complementary views of pragmatics to better understand interaction.

Escandell-Vidal (2004) distinguishes cognitive and sociocultural perspectives in her proposal for a unified theory of pragmatics. She characterizes sociocultural pragmatics as identifying norms that underlie language use. Norms include customs (i.e. habitual behaviors) and conventions (i.e. socially approved behavior patterns), though she acknowledges the difficulty of establishing clear boundaries between customs and conventions. Cognitive pragmatics reflects efforts to establish causal relationships between principles and language use; for example, establishing the outcomes of Grice's (1975 [1967]) Cooperative Principle and Sperber and Wilson's (1995) principles of relevance in real-world language use. Escandell-Vidal (2004) suggests that it is difficult to establish the predictive power of these principles because they are abstracted from communicative context. Ultimately, she proposes that these two seemingly competing ways of looking at language use in context function better together as part of a broader theoretical position.

---

[3] These areas apply philosophical and/or theoretical notions from a specific discipline to pragmatic analysis.

The blurred distinctions in Huang's (2007, 2013), Mey's (2001 [1993]), and Escandell-Vidal's (2006 [1996], 2004) work is mirrored in the definition of pragmatic competence within communicative competence (Canale 1983; Canale and Swain 1980; Hymes 1972). Pragmatic competence has been further subdivided into pragmalinguistic and sociopragmatic competence (Leech 1983; Thomas 1983; Rose and Kasper 2001).[4] Pragmalinguistic competence includes the linguistic resources available for conveying meaning in a language. These include, for example, resources to differentiate directness and indirectness, among other linguistic forms used to convey specific pragmatic meanings and functions. Sociopragmatic competence, on the other hand, refers to social perceptions that underlie performance and interpretation of interaction. For example, rankings of social distance, power, and imposition can differ from communicative context to communicative context, influencing linguistic choices in communication. Furthermore, rankings of sociopragmatic factors are relatively fluid as speaker and hearer negotiate the co-construction of a given interaction.[5] Pragmalinguistic resources are influenced by sociopragmatic factors, while the use of pragmalinguistic resources also influences the sociopragmatic context. As with the above-mentioned dichotomies, the interplay between pragmalinguistic and sociopragmatic competence highlights the interconnected relationship between pragmatic factors.

Given the flexible and interactive nature of the core concepts studied by pragmaticists, it is not surprising that these theoretical frameworks cannot establish clear boundaries between opposing ends of a given spectrum (e.g. Anglo-American vs. Continental, component vs. perspective, micro- vs. macropragmatic, cognitive vs. sociocultural, or sociopragmatic vs. pragmalinguistic). Furthermore, because of the overlap between pragmatics and other disciplines, it is often difficult to establish precisely where pragmatics begins and ends. One thing that is clear, however, is that those who identify themselves as pragmaticists examine language in context. This includes, but is not limited to, examining the linguistic resources available to language users and the influence of a variety of social and contextual factors on the use and perception of those resources. In short, pragmatics seeks to understand the complex, yet systematic, relationship between speaker, hearer, and context, and the choices made throughout interaction.

---

[4] Leech (1983) initially defined these terms, which were subsequently adopted in a model of pragmatic failure (Thomas 1983). Rose and Kasper (2001) clarified these definitions in the context of second language pragmatics, though their definition is equally suited to the present discussion.

[5] Co-construction of interaction refers to the indeterminate and collaborative nature of communication. Though Kecskes (2014) specifically addresses intercultural contexts, his description of co-construction is apt in any context. Co-construction requires finding "commonalities, conventions, common beliefs, shared knowledge, and the like [to] create a core common ground ... on which intention and cooperation-based pragmatics is built." Regardless of cultural or linguistic background, when two (or more) speakers come to the interactive context with preconceived sociocultural notions and pragmalinguistic resources, they must then work together to find core common ground to achieve a given outcome.

Because pragmatics encompasses such a wide range of language features, the remaining discussion is limited primarily to the evolution of speech act theory and politeness theory. Though a comprehensive overview of the entire field of Spanish pragmatics is outside the scope of this chapter, it emphasizes the depth and breadth of research on speech acts and politeness by highlighting current perspectives couched in crucial theoretical underpinnings. Furthermore, the selected topics emphasize the interplay between sociocultural norms and the nature of co-constructing interaction. The remainder of this chapter is organized as follows. First, a general discussion of speech act theory, including debates about its applicability to interaction, is followed by an overview of recent speech act research in Spanish. Next, the notion of universal politeness is addressed, followed by discussions of Hispanic perspectives and their applications in the literature, and of pragmatic variation in Spanish-speaking contexts. Finally, the chapter closes with a brief discussion of several areas that are currently promising for future research.

20.2 Speech Acts and Speech Act Theory

Rooted in Austin's (1975 [1962]) lectures on language philosophy, speech act theory is key in general pragmatics and in work on Spanish pragmatics. Though he was not the first philosopher to question the idea that language's primary function was to convey factual information, Austin's ideas about performative language (i.e. doing things with words) underlie a great deal of the work to date in pragmatics. Austin argued that, rather than being dependent on truth conditions, performative utterances are dependent on felicity conditions, violations of which result in infelicitous or invalid speech acts (see Austin (1975 [1962]) for an in-depth discussion of felicity conditions).

Austin (1975 [1962]) also distinguished locutionary, illocutionary, and perlocutionary acts. Locutionary acts capture the reference and definite meaning of a given utterance, while the illocutionary act captures the force or function of that utterance. A given locutionary act potentially has a variety of forces or illocutionary acts, depending on context and speaker intentions. Conversely, a given illocutionary act may potentially be performed through a variety of locutionary acts. Finally, the perlocutionary act captures the effect of the locutionary and illocutionary acts, though its effects are not speaker-determined but rather hearer-dependent.

Searle (1968, 1969, 1976) elaborated on Austin's (1975 [1962]) work, taking into account Gricean notions of meaning and implicature (Grice 1957). Searle (1968, 1969) defined rules to replace what he saw as an overly simplistic distinction between meaning and force in Austin's (1975 [1962]) work. Searle's (1968) theory instead relies on propositional content, which invokes the referent, as well as preparatory, sincerity, and essential conditions. The preparatory condition refers to circumstances that must be in place prior to performing a speech act. The sincerity of the speaker is captured in the sincerity condition, while the essential condition describes whether the act "counts" as it is intended. These conditions, along with the propositional content, allow for a closer analysis of the illocutionary act, emphasizing both the context and the speaker's state of mind.

As Searle (1969) worked to better define illocutionary intent, he also introduced the concept of the illocutionary force-indicating device. Whereas Austin (1975 [1962]) focused specifically on verbs, Searle recognized that, at least in English, illocutionary force could be conveyed by a number of devices, such as illocutionary verb, intonation, and word order. Searle's (1976) taxonomy of speech acts was centered on illocutionary force, and included representatives (e.g. statement), directives (e.g. command), commissives (e.g. promise), expressives (e.g. thanks), and declaratives (e.g. baptism).

Searle (1975) was one of several philosophers to formalize the notion of indirect speech acts, proposing two types of indirectness: conventional and non-conventional. Conventionally indirect speech acts convey a literal meaning as well as a nonliteral meaning. His classic example of "Can you reach the salt[?]" (1975:61) is conventionally understood as a request in English; meanwhile, its propositional content refers to the hearer's physical ability to reach the salt. In most cases, this utterance is understood as a request and not as a yes/no question about the hearer's abilities. On the other hand, a non-conventionally indirect speech act requires deeper analysis, as its literal meaning may obscure the illocutionary force. An example from Searle (1975:61) highlights this:

(1) Student X: Let's go to the movies tonight.
(2) Student Y: I have to study for an exam.

On the surface, Student Y's declarative is unrelated to Student X's invitation; however, upon further analysis, the intended force is to refuse the invitation. The hearer must rely on pragmatic competence to interpret appropriately such an interaction.

Both Searle (1968, 1969, 1975, 1976) and Austin (1975 [1962]) made great strides in advancing our understanding of language in interaction. Austin provided clear evidence that language users do more than make true or false statements; in fact, we do things with our words. He identified the elements that help speakers and listeners to understand each other. Searle expanded and refined Austin's analysis of speech acts, focusing specifically on the illocutionary force of a given act, whether direct or indirect. He identified the constitutive conditions that create speech acts and proposed broad categories of speech acts that are still in use today. Nevertheless, neither Austin nor Searle conceptualized the role of interaction in determining context in their theories; thus, they are inadequate to account for the collaborative nature of communication.

Haverkate (1979, 1994, 2004) and Edmondson (1981) criticized Austin's (1975 [1962]) and Searle's (1969) substantial theoretical focus on the speaker at the expense of the hearer's role. Haverkate (1979) proposed that the hearer's interpretations could be categorized as a corresponding interpretive act for each component of a speech act (e.g. each illocutionary act has an accompanying illocutionary interpretation act). Edmondson (1981) emphasized that speech acts are not a result of just one utterance, but rather the result of collaboration between speakers. He asserted that illocutionary force might, in fact, be indeterminate and open to negotiation between interlocutors and further suggested that speech acts should be examined in sequences consisting of two or more speech acts that are uttered across two or more turns by the speakers involved. The negotiation of speech act sequences is evident in such speech acts as refusals, which often require multiple turns to be completed. Furthermore, these sequences can consist of more than one canonical speech act. For example, an invitation or other type of directive necessarily precedes a refusal.

An additional criticism of speech act theory is that early philosophers proposed that context consisted of the interlocutors and their physical surroundings (Austin 1975 [1962]), as well as speaker beliefs and/or intentions (Searle 1969). Sbisá (2002) asserts that context is not fully determined prior to an utterance, but rather that context construction continues as interaction develops. According to Félix-Brasdefer (2008a:42), context consists of "shared knowledge between the interlocutors, the social circumstances in which the speech acts are realized and interpreted by a speaker and a hearer, and as a dynamic social entity which is constantly changing according to the speakers' intentions and the interactional needs of the situation." He further specifies that speech act context is characterized by: "[The] social distance and social power between the interlocutors, the speech act in question, the definition of the situation, the sociocultural circumstances during speech act production, and the gender, level of education, social class, and age of the interlocutors." The context of a speech act consists not only of those elements highlighted by early philosophers such as the physical situation and the speakers' beliefs, but also the social context and the co-constructed interactional context. This perspective on contextual factors influencing speech acts blurs the distinction between micropragmatic and macropragmatic perspectives.

Numerous researchers have examined Spanish using the theoretical constructs outlined in this discussion of speech act theory. A wide variety of speech acts and speech act sequences has been investigated, including apologies (e.g. García 2011; González-Cruz 2012; Medina López 2013), blaming (e.g. García 2009), compliments and compliment responses (e.g. García 2012; Hernández Toribio 2017; Placencia 2013), expressions of gratitude (e.g. Dumitrescu 2011), expressions of sympathy (e.g. García 2010, 2011), invitations (e.g. García 2008), refusals (e.g. Félix-Brasdefer 2006, 2008a, 2008b, 2011), requests (e.g. Félix-Brasdefer 2010, 2011;

Ruzickova 2007; Toledo Vega and Toledo Azócar 2014), and wishing (e.g. Dumitrescu 2011). Speech act sequences have also been examined as they unfold throughout interaction. For example, Félix-Brasdefer (2015b) uses speech act sequences as one of his analytical tools in the cross-cultural examination of service encounters in the US and Mexico. His approach emphasizes key cross-cultural differences in this type of interaction, including differences in request–response sequences and the overall organization of the service encounter. This study highlights the interconnectedness of pragmatics research, using speech act and politeness theoretical notions to understand cross-cultural differences as well as intralingual variation in Mexico and the US.

Speech acts are crucial elements of pragmatic competence. In order to successfully communicate in a given language, speakers should have a grasp of both pragmalinguistic resources and sociopragmatic knowledge. Speakers of a given language use appropriate resources to convey illocutionary meaning in socially appropriate situations. These resources are not employed in isolation, but rather in interaction with interlocutors and, therefore, must take into account culturally-bound interactive expectations, as discussed below in the next section.

20.3 Politeness Models

Politeness theory has its roots in Goffman's (1982 [1967]) work in sociology and Grice's (1975 [1967]) philosophical work on conversational behavior. Goffman's (1982 [1967]:5) notion of face refers to " … the positive social value a person effectively claims for himself" as determined by social rules and interactional context. For Goffman, the main purpose of what he calls face-work is to abstain from damaging positive social value by avoiding threats to face and correcting face-threatening situations. Interlocutors can flout face-work, though Goffman claims that most people cooperate in order to preserve their own face and that of others. Watts (2003) clarifies that not only do we work to maintain our face and that of our interlocutors, but our concept of face or self develops within a given interaction as well as across a lifetime of interactions.

Where Goffman (1982 [1967]) was principally concerned with face-work, Grice's primary concern was with (ir)rationality of conversational behavior (Márquez-Reiter and Placencia 2005). Grice's (1975 [1967]) Cooperative Principle assumes that speakers cooperate in conversation in the most efficient way possible by adhering to a series of universal maxims. The Quantity Maxim stipulates that contributions should be precisely as informative as required (not more or less) to move an interaction forward. The Quality Maxim specifies that speakers should be truthful insofar as s/he is aware and not share false or unsubstantiated information.

The Relation Maxim is, simply, "Be relevant,"[6] (Grice 1975 [1967]:46). The Manner Maxim, "Be perspicuous" (Grice 1975 [1967]:46), precludes obscurity and/or ambiguity, and specifies that communication should be brief and orderly. Speakers can violate, opt out, flout or be unable to fulfill a maxim (clash), all of which have interactional consequences such as misleading the hearer or creating an implicatures. While Grice's theory has informed many politeness theoretical models, it is not universal in that non-fulfillment of maxims may be culturally specific and, therefore, expected in interaction (see Leech 1983; Thomas 1998). Grice's theory does not account for indirectness in communication.

Brown and Levinson's (1987 [1978]) universal theory of politeness suggests that indirectness is a result of the preservation of face, as conceived of by Goffman (1982 [1967]). Brown and Levinson (1987 [1978]) assume a norm of cooperation in face-work. Key to their theory are the notions of negative face ("freedom of action and freedom from imposition": 1987 [1978]:61) and positive face ("the desire to be appreciated or approved of": 1987 [1978]:61). The primary face-work of interlocutors, then, is to ensure that face is maintained or enhanced and not undermined by face-threatening acts (FTAs). Brown and Levinson's "pan-cultural" (1987 [1978]:76) features of social distance and power interact to determine the seriousness of FTAs. In this model, social distance is symmetric and established through positive politeness (e.g. demonstrating appreciation). On the other hand, power is asymmetric and is maintained through negative politeness (e.g. deference). They assert that certain acts are intrinsically face-threatening, including directives (e.g. advice-giving), commissives (e.g. promises and offers), and expressives (e.g. compliments and criticisms).

The notion of individual face wants and the emphasis on protection from FTAs is, perhaps, the most criticized aspect of the Brown and Levinson (1987 [1978]) model because it does not account for politeness behaviors in many cultures. Research has shown that the relationships between power, distance, imposition, and perceived politeness are much more variable across cultures than Brown and Levinson's model proposes. Furthermore, researchers have suggested that the distinction between positive and negative face is overly simplistic.

While Spencer-Oatey (2008) also adopts the notion of face, it is balanced with sociality rights to describe rapport management. In this model, "face is associated with personal/social value, and is concerned with people's sense of worth, dignity, honour, reputation, [and] competence," while sociality rights "are concerned with personal/social expectancies, and reflect people's concerns over fairness, consideration, [and] social inclusion/exclusion" (2008:14). Spencer-Oatey contrasts quality face (self-

---

[6] The issue of relevance has since been analyzed and heavily criticized by later theorists (see Sperber and Wilson 1995, for an in-depth discussion of conversational relevance and Relevance Theory).

esteem, positive evaluation of personal qualities) with identity face (perceived public value and competence, support in social roles). She also distinguishes equity rights (individual consideration and fair treatment) from association rights (choosing with whom to affiliate and to what degree). These four components of face and sociality rights offer a finer-grained approach for examining the needs and rights of individuals in interaction. Face reflects the need for positive evaluation and support in social roles, while sociality rights reflect a desire for fairness and individual choice about the level of association developed with others. In this model, the primary concern is not protection from FTAs, but the nuances of personal relationships and rapport management and their effect on interaction.

In contrast with Brown and Levinson's (1987 [1978]) association of power with hierarchical relationships/negative politeness and distance with symmetrical relationships/positive politeness, Scollon et al.'s (2012, revised 3rd edition of Scollon and Scollon 1995) model considers both power (+/–P) and distance (+/–D) in all interactions, in addition to weight of imposition (+/–W) where relevant. These non-binary distinctions allow a social relationship to fall along a continuum between + and – for a given value. The value (+P) reflects hierarchical structures while (–P) reflects egalitarian relationships. The value of distance reflects the closeness of a given relationship with no inherent relationship to power. (–D) is associated with strong interpersonal relationships while (+D) reflects a lack of prior acquaintance.

As these two dimensions interact, their various combinations create three face systems: deference (–P, +D), solidarity (–P, –D), and hierarchical (+P, +/– D). Strategies of involvement and independence,[7] the two sides of face identified by Scollon et al. (2012), are observable in these face systems. In the deference system, participants consider themselves to be equals, but treat each other at a distance. For example, two government officials from different countries will likely use independence strategies in their communication (e.g. use titles and family/surnames). In the solidarity politeness system, participants are on a level playing field in terms of both power and distance. Thus, two close friends are likely to use involvement strategies (e.g. use given names or nicknames). In a hierarchical face system, one participant has social power over another. For example, a department head uses involvement strategies with his/her subordinates (e.g. directness). Meanwhile, subordinates tend to use independence strategies with a manager (e.g. mitigation).

In this model, negotiation of politeness primarily occurs when weight of imposition (+/–W) comes into play. This feature has a powerful impact on

---

[7] Scollon et al. (2012:48) define involvement as "the person's right and need to be considered a normal, contributing, or supporting member of society" and independence as the "right not to be completely dominated by group or social values, and to be free from the impositions of others." They associate involvement with positive face and solidarity politeness, while independence is associated with negative face and deference politeness (terms they have previously used in their descriptions of politeness).

interaction; as imposition increases, so do independence strategies, and, as imposition decreases, involvement strategies increase. Thus, a person asking her friend for a piece of gum (–W) is less likely to be deferential than if she were asking the same friend to act as a gestational surrogate (+W). Scollon et al.'s (2012) disentangling of the notion of power (+/–P) from hierarchical relationships, and social distance (+/–D) from symmetrical relationships, is crucial to in-depth analysis of the way these features, along with weight of imposition (+/–W), affect interactional context. Furthermore, these authors are careful to point out that the notions of power, distance, and weight of imposition are culturally bound and, therefore, the expectations for independence and involvement strategies in interaction vary from culture to culture.

In addition to Scollon et al. (2012), many researchers of Spanish-language politeness have also found the Brown and Levinson (1987 [1978]) model to be an inadequate analytical tool.[8] Fant's (1989:255) contrastive work on Scandinavian and Spanish communication proposes three aspects of face, autonomy, affiliation, and esteem. Autonomy refers to a person's independence and "inviolable territory." Affiliation is a person's belief that s/he is an accepted group member. Esteem reflects a person's belief that s/he is not seen as the lowest person on the social ladder and is worthy of respect. According to Fant, the goal of face-work and politeness in Spain is to build up affiliation and esteem, with less concern for autonomy.

Bravo (1999, 2004, 2008a, 2008b) adopted part of Fant's (1989) terminology, and proposes that *autonomía* (autonomy) and *afiliación* (affiliation) are better able to account for universal human interactional needs than the notions of negative and positive face. Her definition of autonomy refers to the way that people behave in order to be seen by others as having a stand-out role within a group, while affiliation reflects the contrasting desire to be seen as fitting in to the crowd (Bravo 2008b:588). In Bravo's model (1999, 2004, 2008a, 2008b), autonomy and affiliation are empty, open, and dynamic categories (2008b:588). That is, the relationship between individual and group needs are not pre-determined, but rather are filled according to culturally-bound meanings and sociocultural values (Bravo 2004:30). By removing notions of universality, Bravo's model allows for culturally-situated research on the impact of autonomy and affiliation in a given context. Along with the rejection of universal politeness, Bravo (2008a) refutes the idea that a speech act can be intrinsically threatening. She asserts that whether a speech act constitutes a FTA or not is culture-specific and is determined by interlocutors during a given interaction.

---

[8] Escandell-Vidal (2006 [1996]) is a notable exception, arguing that Brown and Levinson's (1987 [1978]) theory adequately addresses the relationship between linguistic forms and sociocultural structures, and suggesting that their model highlights the difficulty of striking a balance between theory and function. For Escandell-Vidal, it is necessary to identify independently motivated functional or social principles. She suggests that the notion of face-saving is just such a universal sociological principle, exerting certain pressures on the linguistic system, regardless of alignment (2006 [1996]:159).

Bravo's model of politeness (1999, 2004, 2008a, 2008b), as well as those of Scollon *et al.* (2012) and Spencer-Oatey (2008), encompass notions of face that are more closely tied to Goffman's initial psycho-social conception. They reflect an individual's perception of him/herself and of his/her relationship with and role within society, rather than the individualistic model proposed by Brown and Levinson (1987 [1978]). Bravo (2008a:567) succinctly summarizes the critical problem: "... it is not enough to analyse the face of individuals, but it is necessary to do the same from the perspective of the social group under analysis." Politeness, from various perspectives, has been a crucial focus in Spanish pragmatics.

Though politeness and face were not the focus of Covarrubias' (2002) ethnographic study of terms of address in Mexican Spanish (i.e. *tú/usted* distinction), she found eleven factors in her study that affected interactions.[9] She proposed that codes of *respeto* and *confianza* can better explain choices about terms of address than can Brown and Levinson's (1987 [1978]) model. *Respeto*, frequently associated with *usted*, conveys respect and deference, while *confianza*, frequently associated with *tú*, conveys familiarity and trust. Covarrubias' research illustrates a clear case of politeness behavior that cannot be accounted for in an Anglo-centric politeness model.

Hernández-Flores (1999) further illustrates the problematic nature of the Anglo-centric model of politeness, this time with respect to the speech act of advice-giving in Spanish. In Brown and Levinson's (1987 [1978]) framework, advice-giving is considered inherently face-threatening. However, Hernández-Flores (1999) finds that this is not the case. In fact, in her evaluation, advice-giving serves to strengthen social links between interlocutors, enhancing *confianza*. Hernández-Flores aligns her definition of *confianza*, a "sense of deep familiarity" (1999:41), with Bravo's (1999, 2004, 2008a, 2008b) notion of affiliation.

Briz's (e.g. 1998, 2004, 2007, 2012) extensive work on politeness has added significantly to our knowledge about Spanish pragmatics. Briz (2012) posits that politeness and mitigation are inextricably intertwined. In fact, he proposes that appropriate mitigation is *the* key to bringing about the social activity of politeness (and that the lack of appropriate mitigation has a negative effect on said social activity). Referring to Brown and Levinson's (1987 [1978]) notion of positive and negative politeness, Briz (2007) suggests that politeness manifests in one of two ways: Either people approach each other with a polite purpose (e.g. responding to a greeting with an appropriate greeting) or they use politeness strategically to achieve a means other than politeness, primarily through mitigation (2007:6–7). Briz posits that Bravo's (1999, 2004, 2008a, 2008b) code of *respeto* is associated with higher

---

[9] Factors identified by Covarrubias (2002): Age; organizational rank/authority; power (unrelated to organizational rank/authority); education; wealth; professional network position; perceived human worth (e.g. political leaders vs. ordinary citizens); levels of acquaintance and interaction; familial or quasi-familial relationship; marital status; and inverted power ("unequal relational alignments created by inverting the hierarchical pyramid" (2002:35)).

levels of mitigation, while the reverse is true for the code of *confianza*. He suggests that mitigation, like politeness, is subject to the factors that affect variation in other aspects of pragmatics.

Not only have researchers of Spanish politeness added to our knowledge of pragmatics in the Spanish-speaking world, their work has made a critical contribution to the ongoing debate about the universality of politeness. As Márquez-Reiter and Placencia (2005) note, Spanish is not universally oriented to negative or positive politeness, nor toward autonomy or affiliation, nor in fact is Spanish universally oriented to either end of any of the continua mentioned previously. Because Spanish politeness has such wide variation, researchers examine pragmatic phenomena in various regional and social contexts, including those that extend beyond "conversations with friends and family and discussions amongst people who know each other (well)" (Márquez-Reiter and Placencia 2005:175).

One of the most prolific sources of research on Hispanic politeness is the EDICE Program (Estudios sobre el Discurso de la Cortesía en Español), housed at Stockholm University. EDICE has published multiple volumes examining variation in politeness phenomena, as well as variation in speech acts. These volumes (e.g. Bravo 2003; Escamilla Morales and Vega 2012; Murillo Medrano 2005; Bernal and Hernández-Flores 2009; Orletti and Mariottini 2010) provide a global perspective on Spanish pragmatics in a variety of regional, cultural, and social contexts. In addition to EDICE's work, scholars have investigated politeness phenomena, including speech acts and speech act sequences, from a politeness perspective throughout the Spanish-speaking world (e.g. Dumitrescu 2011; Félix-Brasdefer 2015a, 2015b; García and Placencia 2011; Placencia and García 2006). The findings of these scholars add to the assertion that politeness is culturally situated and context dependent. While speech act theory and politeness theory do not comprise the entirety of Spanish pragmatics, they provide a lens for examining variation in Spanish pragmatic phenomena.

Though scholars have worked tirelessly to enhance our understanding of Spanish pragmatics, the ever-changing nature of communication requires ongoing research to understand and enhance interaction in Spanish. Several of the most pressing areas of inquiry are highlighted in the following section.

20.4 Future Directions and Remaining Questions

Worldwide proliferation of technology has brought issues of computer-mediated communication (CMC) to the forefront for many linguistics researchers. Spanish pragmatics researchers are no exception, paying particular attention to this burgeoning field of study with work on discourse practices and politeness in digital forums (e.g. Glide 2015; Landone 2012; Pérez-Sabater 2015). Researchers have also made cross-cultural comparisons of electronic personal ads (Zahler 2015), mockery (Maíz-Arévalo 2015), and compliments on Facebook (Maíz-Arévalo 2013), as well as compliments in email (Lorenzo-Dus and Bou-Franch 2013). These forays into digital communication demonstrate that there is a wide open field for further research on pragmatics in CMC contexts.

Issues of pragmatic variation and CMC are also relevant to the intersection of pragmatics and disciplines not traditionally examined within linguistics. For example, institutional discourse work brings pragmatics into contact with a variety of fields, including (but certainly not limited to) education administration, public services, law enforcement, healthcare (both administration and patient care), retail, and other services. Research findings from these types of discourse-focused studies have implications not only for pragmatics, but also for those institutions and service providers. These fields are ripe for interdisciplinary work that can have an impact on a wide range of socioeconomic, cultural, and linguistic contexts.

Finally, interlanguage pragmatics, including effective methods for instruction of pragmatics, is of particular interest in the US, but also throughout the world where Spanish is a second language of choice. In the US, Spanish accounts for 72.1 percent of reported enrollments in primary and secondary school language study programs as of 2007 (ACTFL 2015). Furthermore, more than 50 percent of all language study enrollments in higher education are in Spanish, more than all other languages combined (Goldberg *et al.* 2015). It is abundantly clear that language learners simply do not acquire appropriate pragmatic strategies without specific metapragmatic instruction designed to raise their awareness of cross-cultural differences and to give them choices in their interaction (Bardovi-Harlig and Mahan-Taylor 2003). While research in this area has grown substantially in classroom (e.g. Belpoliti and Pérez 2016; Pablos-Ortega 2011; Gonzales 2013; Sykes 2013) and study abroad (e.g. Bataller 2010; Shively 2011) environments, there is still work to be done. Spanish language teachers and learners often need to be made aware of pragmatic differences between cultures and languages. Furthermore, easily accessible, authentic materials will enhance acquisition of this vital and often neglected part of Spanish foreign/second language instruction.

A substantial body of work on Spanish pragmatics has emerged over the last four decades, expanding well beyond speech acts, contributing to our understanding of Spanish-specific and global politeness phenomena. Research in Spanish pragmatics has broadened our understanding of the rich variety that exists within the Spanish-speaking world. As communication evolves, research in Spanish pragmatics is a field that will surely see significant growth. Scholars will undoubtedly continue to highlight the vibrant variability that exists in Spanish as it is used in interaction in a variety of contexts.

References

ACTFL (2015). *Foreign Language Enrollments in K-12 Public Schools: Are Students Prepared for a Global Society?* Washington, DC: American Council on the Teaching of Foreign Languages. Available from https://www.actfl.org/sites/default/files/pdfs/ReportSummary2011.pdf (last access December 5, 2017).

Ariel, Mira (2010). *Defining Pragmatics*. Cambridge: Cambridge University Press.

Austin, John L. (1975 [1962]). *How to do Things with Words* (2nd edn). Cambridge, MA: Harvard University Press.

Bar-Hillel, Yehoshua (1971). Out of the Pragmatic Wastebasket. *Linguistic Inquiry*, 2 (3), 401–407.

Bardovi-Harlig, Kathleen and Mahan-Taylor, Rebecca (eds.) (2003). *Teaching Pragmatics*. Washington, DC: US Department of State.

Bataller, Rebecca (2010). Making a Request for a Service in Spanish: Pragmatic Development in the Study Abroad Setting. *Foreign Language Annals*, 43 (1), 160–175.

Belpoliti, Flavia and Pérez, María E. (2016). Giving Advice in Medical Spanish: Pragmatic and Intercultural Competence in the Spanish for the Health Professions Curriculum. *Journal of Spanish Language Teaching*, 3 (2), 127–142.

Bernal, María and Hernández-Flores, Nieves (eds.) (2009). *Estudios sobre lengua, sociedad y cultura. Homenaje a Diana Bravo*. Stockholm: EDICE.

Bravo, Diana (1999). ¿Imagen positiva vs. Imagen negativa?: Pragmática sociocultural y componentes de face. *Oralia: Análisis del Discurso Oral*, 2, 155–184.

Bravo, Diana (ed.) (2003). *La perspectiva no etnocentrista de la cortesía: Identidad sociocultural de las comunidades hispanohablantes*. Stockholm: EDICE.

Bravo, Diana (2004). Tensión entre universalidad y relatividad en las teorías de la cortesía. In Diana Bravo and Antonio Briz (eds.), *Pragmática sociocultural: Estudios sobre el discurso de cortesía en español*. Barcelona: Ariel, pp. 15–38.

Bravo, Diana (2008a). (Im)politeness in Spanish-Speaking Socio-Cultural Contexts: Introduction. *Pragmatics*, 18 (4), 563–576.

Bravo, Diana (2008b). The Implications of Studying Politeness in Spanish-Speaking Contexts: A Discussion. *Pragmatics*, 18 (4), 584–603.

Briz, Antonio (1998). *El español coloquial en la conversación. Esbozo de pragmagramática*. Barcelona: Ariel.

Briz, Antonio (2004). Cortesía verbal codificada y cortesía verbal interpretada. In Diana Bravo and Antonio Briz (eds.), *Pragmática sociocultural: Estudios sobre el discurso de cortesía en español*. Barcelona: Ariel, pp. 67–94.

Briz, Antonio (2007). Para un análisis semántico, pragmático y sociopragmático de la cortesía atenuadora en España y América. *LEA: Lingüística Española Actual*, 29 (1), 5–40.

Briz, Antonio (2012). La (no)atenuación y la (des)cortesía, lo lingüístico y lo social: ¿Son pareja? In Julio Escamilla Morales and Grandfield Henry Vega (eds.), *Miradas multidisciplinares a los fenómenos de cortesía y descortesía en el mundo hispánico*. Stockholm: EDICE, pp. 34–75.

Brown, Penelope and Levinson, Stephen C. (1987 [1978]). *Politeness: Some Universals in Language Usage*. Cambridge: Cambridge University Press.

Canale, Michael (1983). From Communicative Competence to Communicative Language Pedagogy. In Jack C. Richards and Richard W. Schmidt (eds.), *Language and Communication*. New York: Longman, pp. 2–27.

Canale, Michael and Swain, Merrill (1980). Theoretical Bases of Communicative Approaches to Second Language Teaching and Testing. *Applied Linguistics*, 1 (1), 1–47.

Covarrubias, Patricia (2002). *Culture, Communication and Cooperation: Interpersonal Relations and Pronominal Address in a Mexican Organization*. Oxford: Rowman and Littlefield.

Crystal, David (ed.) (1997). *The Cambridge Encyclopedia of Language*. Cambridge: Cambridge University Press.

Dumitrescu, Domnita (2011). *Aspects of Spanish Pragmatics*. New York: Peter Lang.

Edmondson, Willis (1981). *Spoken Discourse: A Model for Analysis*. London: Longman.

Escamilla Morales, Julio and Vega, Grandfield Henry (eds.) (2012). *Miradas multidisciplinares a los fenómenos de cortesía y descortesía en el mundo hispánico*. Stockholm: EDICE.

Escandell-Vidal, M. Victoria (2004). Norms and Principles: Putting Social and Cognitive Pragmatics Together. In Rosina Márquez-Reiter and María Elena Placencia (eds.), *Current Trends in the Pragmatics of Spanish*. Amsterdam: John Benjamins, pp. 347–371.

Escandell-Vidal, M. Victoria (2006 [1996]). *Introducción a la pragmática*. Barcelona: Ariel.

Fant, Lars (1989). Cultural Mismatch in Conversation: Spanish and Scandinavian Communicative Behaviour in Negotiation Settings. *HERMES – Journal of Language and Communication in Business*, 2 (3), 247–265.

Félix-Brasdefer, J. César (2006). Linguistic Politeness in Mexico: Refusal Strategies among Male Speakers of Mexican Spanish. *Journal of Pragmatics*, 38 (12), 2158–2187.

Félix-Brasdefer, J. César (2008a). *Politeness in Mexico and the United States: A Contrastive Study of the Realization and Perception of Refusals*. Amsterdam: John Benjamins.

Félix-Brasdefer, J. César (2008b). Sociopragmatic Variation: Dispreferred Responses in Mexican and Dominican Spanish. *Journal of Politeness Research*, 4 (1), 81–110.

Félix-Brasdefer, J. César (2010). Intra-Lingual Pragmatic Variation in Mexico City and San José, Costa Rica: A Focus on Regional Differences in Female Requests. *Journal of Pragmatics*, 42 (11), 2992–3011.

Félix-Brasdefer, J. César (2011). Cortesía, prosodia y variación pragmática en las peticiones de estudiantes universitarios mexicanos y dominicanos. In Carmen García and María Elena Placencia (eds.), *Estudios de variación pragmática en español*. Buenos Aires: Editorial Dunken, pp. 57–86.

Félix-Brasdefer, J. César (ed.) (2015a). Current Issues in Pragmatic Variation. [Special Issue]. *Indiana University Linguistics Club Working Papers*, 15 (1). Available from https://www.indiana.edu/~iulcwp/wp/issue/view/25 (last access December 5, 2017).

Félix-Brasdefer, J. César (2015b). *The Language of Service Encounters*. Cambridge: Cambridge University Press.

García, Carmen (2008). Different Realizations of Solidarity Politeness: Comparing Venezuelan and Argentinean Invitations. *Pragmatics and Beyond* (New series), 178, 269–305.

García, Carmen (2009). The Performance of a Rapport-Challenging Act (Blaming) by Peruvian Spanish Speakers. *Journal of Politeness Research*, 5 (2), 217–241.

García, Carmen (2010). "Cuente conmigo": The Expression of Sympathy by Peruvian Spanish Speakers. *Journal of Pragmatics*, 42 (2), 408–425.

García, Carmen (2011). Variación pragmática situacional de un grupo cultural en la realización de un acto de habla asertivo y un acto de habla expresivo. In Carmen García and María Elena Placencia (eds.), *Estudios de variación pragmática en español*. Buenos Aires: Editorial Dunken, pp. 277–306.

García, Carmen (2012). Complimenting Professional Achievement: A Case Study of Peruvian Spanish Speakers. *Journal of Politeness Research*, 8 (2), 223–244.

García, Carmen and Placencia, María Elena (eds.) (2011). *Estudios de variación pragmática en español*. Buenos Aires: Editorial Dunken.

Glide, Margaret (2015). *¿Cuáles son sus recomendaciones?*: A Comparative Analysis of Discourse Practices Implemented in the Giving and Seeking of Advice on a Mexican Subreddit in both Spanish and English. *Indiana University Linguistics Club Working Papers*, 15 (1), 181–207. Available from https://www.indiana.edu/~iulcwp/wp/article/viewFile/15-07/207 (last access September 15, 2016).

Goffman, Erving (1982 [1967]). *Interaction Ritual: Essays on Face-to-Face Behavior*. New York: Pantheon.

Goldberg, David, Looney, Dennis, and Lusin, Natalia (2015). *Enrollments in Languages Other Than English in United States Institutions of Higher Education, Fall 2013*. New York: Modern Language Association of America. Available from https://www.mla.org/pdf/2013_enrollment_survey.pdf (last access May 4, 2017).

Gonzales, Adrienne (2013). Development of Politeness Strategies in Participatory Online Environments: A Case Study. In Naoko Taguchi and Julie M. Sykes (eds.), *Technology in Interlanguage Pragmatics Research and Teaching*. Amsterdam: John Benjamins, pp. 101–120.

González-Cruz, María-Isabel (2012). A Study of the Strategies Used by University Students in Las Palmas de Gran Canaria. *Pragmatics*, 22 (4), 543–565.

Grice, H. Paul (1957). Meaning. *The Philosophical Review*, 66 (3), 377–388.

Grice, H. Paul (1975 [1967]). Logic and Conversation. In Heimir Geirsson and Michael Losonsky (eds.), *Readings in Language and Mind*. Cambridge, MA: Blackwell, pp. 121–133.

Haverkate, Henk (1979). *Impositive Sentences in Spanish: Theory and Description in Linguistic Pragmatics*. Amsterdam: North Holland.

Haverkate, Henk (1994). *La cortesía verbal: Estudio pragmalingüístico*. Madrid: Gredos.

Haverkate, Henk (2004). El análisis de la cortesía comunicativa: Categorización pragmalingüística de la cultura española. In Diana Bravo and Antonio Briz (eds.), *Pragmática sociocultural: Estudios sobre el discurso de cortesía en español*. Barcelona: Ariel, pp. 55–66.

Hernández-Flores, Nieves (1999). Politeness Ideology in Spanish Colloquial Conversation: The case of Advice. *Pragmatics*, 9 (1), 37–49.

Hernández Toribio, M. (2017). Cumplidos y halagos en el español peninsular: ¿Cuestión de términos? *Onomázein*, 37 (4), 188–210.

Huang, Yan (2007). *Pragmatics*. Oxford: Oxford University Press.

Huang, Yan (2013). Micro- and Macro-Pragmatics: Remapping their Terrains. *International Review of Pragmatics*, 5, 129–162.

Hymes, Dell (1972). On Communicative Competence. In John Bernard Pride and Janet Holmes (eds.), *Sociolinguistics: Selected Readings*. Harmondsworth: Penguin, pp. 53–73.

Kecskes, Istvan (2014). *Intercultural Pragmatics*. Oxford: Oxford University Press.

Landone, Elena (2012). Discourse Markers and Politeness in a Digital Forum in Spanish. *Journal of Pragmatics*, 44 (9), 1799–1820.

Leech, Geoffrey N. (1983). *Principles of Pragmatics*. New York: Longman.

Levinson, Stephen C. (1983). *Pragmatics*. Cambridge: Cambridge University Press.

Lorenzo-Dus, Nuria and Bou-Franch, Patricia (2013). A Cross-Cultural Investigation of Email Communication in Peninsular Spanish and British English: The Role of (In)formality and (In)directness. *Pragmatics and Society*, 4 (1), 1–25.

Maíz-Arévalo, Carmen (2013). "Just Click 'Like'": Computer-Mediated Responses to Spanish Compliments. *Journal of Pragmatics*, 51 (3), 47–67.

Maíz-Arévalo, Carmen (2015). Jocular Mockery in Computer-Mediated Communication: A Contrastive Study of a Spanish and English Facebook Community. *Journal of Politeness Research*, 11 (2), 289–327.

Márquez-Reiter, Rosina and Placencia, María Elena (2005). *Spanish Pragmatics*. New York: Palgrave Macmillan.

Medina López, Javier (2013). Disculpas, cortesía ideológica y restauración de la imagen: A propósito de un real ejemplo a través de la prensa. *Pragmática sociocultural/Sociocultural Pragmatics*, 2 (1), 35–75.

Mey, Jacob (2001 [1993]). *Pragmatics: An Introduction*. Malden, MA: Blackwell.

Morris, Charles (1938). *Foundations of the Theory of Signs. Foundations of the Unity of Science: Towards an International Encyclopedia of Unified Science*, Vol. 1.2. Chicago, IL: University of Chicago Press.

Murillo Medrano, Jorge (ed.) (2005). *Actos de habla y cortesía en distintas variedades del español: Perspectivas teóricas y metodológicas*. Stockholm: EDICE.

Orletti, Franca and Mariottini, Laura (eds.) (2010). *(Des)cortesía en español. Espacios teóricos y metodológicos para su estudio*. Stockholm: EDICE.

Pablos-Ortega, C. de (2011). The Pragmatics of Thanking Reflected in the Textbooks for Teaching Spanish as a Foreign Language. *Journal of Pragmatics*, 43 (9), 2411–2433.

Pérez-Sabater, C. (2015). The Rhetoric of Online Support Groups: A Sociopragmatic Analysis English–Spanish. *Revista Española de Lingüística Aplicada/Spanish Journal of Applied Linguistics*, 28 (2), 465–485.

Placencia, María Elena (2013). Cumplidos de mujeres universitarias en Quito y Sevilla: Un studio de variación pragmática regional. *Pragmática sociocultural/Sociocultural Pragmatics*, 1 (1), 100–134.

Placencia, María Elena and García, Carmen (eds.) (2006). *Research on Politeness in the Spanish-Speaking World*. Mahwah, NJ: Psychology Press, Routledge.

Rose, Kenneth and Kasper, Gabriele (eds.) (2001). *Pragmatics in Language Teaching*. Cambridge: Cambridge University Press.

Ruzickova, Elena (2007). Strong and Mild Requestive Hints and Positive-Face Redress in Cuban Spanish. *Journal of Pragmatics*, 39, 1170–1202.

Sbisà, Marina (2002). Speech Acts in Context. *Language and Communication*, 22 (4), 421–436.

Scollon, Ron and Scollon, Suzanne Wong (1995). *Intercultural Communication*. Oxford: Blackwell.

Scollon, Ron, Scollon, Suzanne Wong, and Jones, Rodney. H. (2012). *Intercultural Communication: A Discourse Approach* (3rd edn). Chichester: Wiley.

Searle, John R. (1968). Austin on Locutionary and Illocutionary Acts. *Philosophical Review*, 77 (4), 405–424.

Searle, John R. (1969). *Speech Acts: An Essay in the Philosophy of Language*. Cambridge: Cambridge University Press.

Searle, John R. (1975). Indirect Speech Acts. In P. Cole and J. Morgan (eds.), *Syntax and Semantics 3: Speech Acts*. New York: Academic Press, pp. 59–82.

Searle, John R. (1976). A Classification of Illocutionary Acts. *Language in Society*, 5 (1), 1–23.

Shively, Rachel (2011). L2 Pragmatic Development in Study Abroad: A Longitudinal Study of Spanish Service Encounters. *Journal of Pragmatics*, 43 (6), 1818–1835.

Spencer-Oatey, Helen (2008). Face, (Im)politeness and Rapport. In Helen Spencer-Oatey (ed.), *Culturally Speaking: Culture, Communication and Politeness Theory*. London: Continuum, pp. 11–47.

Sperber, Deirdre and Wilson, D. (1995). *Relevance: Communication and Cognition*. Malden, MA: Blackwell.

Sykes, Julie M. (2013). Multiuser Virtual Environments: Learner Apologies in Spanish. In Naoko Taguchi and Julie M. Sykes (eds.), *Technology in Interlanguage Pragmatics Research and Teaching*. Amsterdam: John Benjamins, pp. 71–100.

Thomas, Jenny (1983). Cross-Cultural Pragmatic Failure. *Applied Linguistics*, 4 (2), 91–112.

Thomas, Jenny (1995). *Meaning in Interaction*. London: Longman.

Thomas, Jenny (1998). Conversational Maxims. In Jacob Mey (ed.), *Concise Encyclopedia of Pragmatics*. Oxford: Elsevier, pp. 171–175.

Toledo Vega, Gloria and Toledo Azócar, Sonia (2014). Estrategias de cortesía para la petición en hablantes nativos del español de Chile y en hablantes de español como lengua extranjera. *Onomázein*, 29, 47–64.

Verschueren, Jef (1999). Continental European Perspective View. In Yan Huang (ed.), *The Oxford Handbook of Pragmatics*. Oxford: Oxford University Press, pp. 120–131.

Watts, Richard J. (2003). *Politeness*. Cambridge: Cambridge University Press.

Zahler, Sara (2015). Pragmalinguistic Variation in Electronic Personal Ads from Mexico City and London. *Indiana University Linguistics Club Working Papers*, 15 (1), 208–230. Available from https://www.indiana.edu/~iulcwp/wp/article/viewFile/15-08/198 (last access December 5, 2017).

Part IV

Spanish in Social, Geographic, and Historical Contexts

21

Spanish in Contact with Other Languages and Bilingualism across the Spanish-Speaking World

Lotfi Sayahi

21.1 Introduction

Within the field of contact linguistics and bilingualism studies, the Spanish language holds a prominent place. It is spoken in numerous regions across several continents and serves as an official language in 21 countries. It is also used by a number of minority communities, either as a native language or as a heritage language, and is rapidly growing worldwide as an instructed second language. As the field of contact linguistics continues to investigate the role of contact in language change, language maintenance, and language shift, among other key issues, the wide array of situations that involve Spanish have proven to be a valuable laboratory for advancing research into the processes and outcomes of language contact. The different varieties of Spanish existing in the world today offer a wealth of data and opportunities for research in bilingualism and contact linguistics in general. In this chapter, rather than offering a geographical mapping of bilingual communities and contact zones in the Spanish-speaking world, I will follow a thematic division that relies on findings regarding the major issues in contact linguistics that are carried out using Spanish data and the main contact phenomena that obtain across the Spanish-speaking world.

In Section 21.2, I describe the major sources of lexical borrowing into Spanish. The focus is on borrowing from Arabic, the indigenous languages of the Americas, and English. Section 21.3 describes cases of structural convergence in situations of contact between Spanish and other languages at the phonological and morphosyntactic levels. In Section 21.4, I examine the existence of Spanish-based contact varieties, including both creoles and non-creolized varieties. Section 21.5 analyzes the phenomenon of code-switching, with a special focus on English/Spanish code-switching.

Section 21.6 presents two major macro-sociolinguistic issues as they pertain to Spanish: language maintenance and language shift. Finally, Section 21.7 summarizes the status of Spanish as a world language and offers an outlook into the future of bilingualism in the Spanish-speaking world.

21.2 Lexical Borrowing

Lexical borrowing is undoubtedly the most common outcome of language contact. It is a salient phenomenon – of which speakers are themselves often aware – and consists in the incorporation of words from other languages with, although not always, some degree of adaptation into the recipient language.[1] Lexical borrowing is also a reliable tool for assessing the role of language contact in the historical development of a given linguistic variety. In the case of Spanish, contact with other languages is a significant factor in the building of its lexical stock from early on. As the diglossic situation of Classical and Vulgar Latin came to an end in the Middle Ages, Castilian was in contact with other Romance varieties, including Mozarabic, and most notably with Arabic. The latter had been introduced into the Iberian peninsula in 711 CE and was maintained in active use there for over eight centuries. Even with the completion of the Reconquista in 1492, some contact with Arabic continued, as bilingual Arabic speakers did not totally disappear from mainland Spain until the Great Expulsion of the Moriscos that was ordered by Philip III of Spain in 1609. It is known that during the Inquisition some Moriscos, especially women, needed Arabic translators (Galmés de Fuentes 1983:28) and that Christian missionaries attempting to evangelize Moriscos in the mountains around Granada had to rely on Arabic well into the 16th century (Martínez Ruiz 1994:142).

Before the systematic purging of a large part of Arabic loanwords, Spanish in the 15th and 16th centuries counted Arabic as its second lexifying language (Lapesa 1981:133), proof of the high degree of bilingualism that existed among Mozarabs and, later on, among Moriscos. Indeed, Menéndez Pidal (1986:502) states that the most important outcome of the contact of Castilian with Mozarabic was lexical borrowing. The *Diccionario de la lengua española* (*DRAE*; Real Academia Española 2001) indicates that the number of Arabic loanwords in Spanish is around 1,200 words, not counting derivations and toponyms, although Lapesa (1981:133) estimates the total number of all types of Arabisms in Spanish to be around 4,000 items. What is significant about Arabic loanwords in Spanish is not only the number of loans that persist in use today but also

---

[1] See Section 21.5 for a brief discussion of the debate concerning what counts as lexical borrowing and what counts as code-switching.

that some of them are extremely common words with relatively few lexical competitive variants, such as *aceite* 'oil,' *almohada* 'pillow,' and *alcalde* 'mayor.' Also significant is the high number of loans that refer to agriculture, as many of the Moriscos who stayed on after the Reconquista continued to work in this field (e.g. *acequia* 'waterway,' *alberca* 'pond used for irrigation,' and *almazara* 'olive mill'). Finally, an interesting detail about Arabic loans in Spanish is the number of super-loans that spread via Spanish to other European languages including English (e.g. *algebra* 'algebra,' *algoritmo* 'algorithm,' *alcohol* 'alcohol'). There are a few function words, such as *ojalá* 'hopefully' and *hasta* 'until,' that originate from Arabic, as does the derivational suffix *-í*, as in *alfonsí* 'Alfonsine' and *marroquí* 'Moroccan,' but Arabic influence on Spanish outside of lexical borrowing has not been solidly confirmed.

Similarly, Spanish borrowed extensively from indigenous Latin American languages and is responsible for the introduction of a considerable number of Amerindian lexical items into other languages. Indigenous loanwords vary from one variety of Latin American Spanish to another, but usually range from a few hundred to a few thousand words depending on the dialect zone (Lope Blanch 1967:369). Spanish adopted several cultural borrowings that include words such as *canoa* and *cacique* from the Taíno language, *chocolate* and *tomate* from Nahuatl, *choclo* 'corn,' and *carpa* 'tent' from Quechua, among many other examples. Indeed, a significant part of the variation at the lexical level between different Latin American Spanish dialect groups can be attributed to contact with a specific indigenous language as in the case of words used for "corn" and the different products derived from it. Of course, in the other direction, the lexical influence of Spanish on Amerindian languages of Latin America still in use is much more significant and often serves as a reliable indicator of the degree of endangerment of these languages. For example, in the case of the Copala Triqui language of Mexico, Scipione (2011) has shown that there are more than 1,000 Spanish loanwords that cover a wide range of semantic fields and include examples such as *soldado* 'soldier,' *multa* 'ticket,' and *cultura* 'culture.' While earlier loans are fully adapted to Triqui, bilingual speakers increasingly tend to maintain the phonological integrity of the Spanish words and even reanalyze established loans to restore their Spanish form. In the case of Nahuatl, studies have shown that lexical borrowing from Spanish has led to a process of relexification where up to 40 percent of its vocabulary is sourced from Spanish (Hill and Hill 1977:62).

An additional source of lexical influence during the formation of Latin American Spanish has been the African languages, especially visible in the case of Caribbean Spanish varieties, with words such as *guineo* 'banana' and *ñame* 'yam' (Lipski 1987:33). Finally, lexical influence of other European languages is also apparent, mainly in Southern Cone Spanish. For instance, the fact that Lunfardo is recognized as a distinct variety, partly for its

Italian influence, is an indicator of the degree of contact between Spanish and other immigrant languages (Lorenzino 2014).

A third major wave of lexical items entered Spanish through its direct and indirect contact with English. In addition to frequent words such as *fútbol, jersey*, and *detective*, modern age advances in science and technology have contributed English loanwords to Spanish. The *DRAE* now contains items such as *parking, USB*, and *blog*. While the dictionary officially recognizes some 600 words as originating from English, more direct contact has resulted in an even higher number of loans in bilingual communities, especially in US Spanish (Pfaff 1979; Smead 1998; Lipski 2008). Adapted forms of English words such as *high school, truck*, and *roof* are examples that are often mentioned as among the most frequent loanwords used by different Hispanic communities in the United States.

In sum, contact with other languages has led to the incorporation of hundreds of loanwords from other languages into Spanish, reflecting the different situations of bilingualism that the Spanish language has had throughout its history and into the present. Both the need to fill a lexical gap, as in the case of fauna and flora words borrowed from Amerindian languages, and prestige, as in the case of contact with English now or Arabic in Muslim Spain, are factors for lexical incorporation (Weinreich 1963). At the same time, equally important is the fact that Spanish is also the source language for hundreds of loanwords in indigenous languages. The wide-ranging diversity of situations has led to different types of lexical influence and associated phenomena that include lexical borrowing, lexical purging, and relexification.

21.3 Structural Innovation and Convergence

In cases of intense language contact, manifested through high levels of bilingualism and substantial lexical borrowing, it is not uncommon for structural convergence and transfer to occur between the different languages in contact (Thomason and Kaufman 1988). Convergence refers to cases where a certain feature acquires additional functions or increases its frequency as a result of contact (Heath 1984).[2] This process has been described by Silva-Corvalán (1994, 2008) as "indirect transfer" and is different from the importation of features that were previously absent from the recipient language. The latter would be a case of structural borrowing – still a highly debated issue within the field of contact linguistics (Winford 2003). Spanish as used in different bilingual communities offers many

[2] Heath (1984:367–368) offers the following definition of structural convergence, which is the one adopted in this chapter: "*Structural convergence*, also called *pattern transfer* or *calque*, is the rearrangement of inherited material because of diffusional interference. If L1 is the language we are focusing on, convergence takes place when L1 forms (morphemes, words, phrases) undergo rearrangements which appear to make L1 structures more similar to those of a neighboring language L2 (which may or may not itself be converging with L1)" (italics in the original text).

examples of indirect transfer, depending on the degree of bilingualism and the status of the languages involved. For example, in northern Morocco Spanish is acquired as a foreign language, often in a naturalistic setting, and shows in many cases the influence of native Arabic and Berber languages. This is especially evident in phonetic features such as vowel height – mid vowels tend to be raised since in Arabic there is no phonemic differentiation between mid and high vowels (e.g. *tangerino* > tang[i]rino) – and the realization of the palatal nasal as an apico-alveolar nasal plus palatal approximant consonant (*España* > Espa[nj]a), as well as in suprasegmental features including stress shift in cases of vowel reduction (Sayahi 2006, 2011).

In Peninsular Spanish, among the most salient situations that present cases of convergence is that of Spanish in contact with Catalan, both in terms of the number of speakers involved and the historical antecedents that have led to a robust normalization of the use of Catalan in Catalonia, Valencia, and the Balearic Islands. Studies have shown that the influence of Catalan can be observed with regard to several features, for example intervocalic /s/ voicing and the devoicing of final /d/, higher rates of the use of the definite article before proper nouns, and variation in the use of deictic markers including the use of *aquí* for *ahí* and *venir* for *ir* to refer to the interlocutor's location as opposed to the speaker's location (Galindo Solé 2003; Davidson 2015; Stokes 2015). Additionally, Blas Arroyo (2008, 2011) has shown that contact with Catalan is serving another purpose: that of slowing down some changes that are in progress in non-contact varieties. He argues that the maintenance of intervocalic /d/ (e.g. for forms ending with -*ado*: 74 percent for Valencian-dominant bilingual speakers vs. 37 percent for monolingual Spanish speakers) and higher rates of retention of the morphological future could be attributed to contact with Valencian Catalan. In the case of the latter, a rate of use (46 percent) that is much higher than that found elsewhere is attributed by Blas Arroyo (2007) to the use of an analytic form in Catalan to refer to actions in the preterit.[3]

In Latin America, a major contact zone is the Andes region where Spanish is in contact with Quechua, in addition to other languages, and, as a result, shows instances of convergence (Austin *et al.* 2015). Specifically, in the case of clitics, Klee and Caravedo (2005) have discussed the use of *leísmo* and the archmorpheme *lo* for direct object regardless of gender in the speech of first- and second-generation Quechua migrants to Lima. Their results confirm the presence of *leísmo* in the speech of first-generation migrants and its transmission to members of the second generation, given that it is not an overtly stigmatized feature. They also find significantly high rates for the use of the archmorpheme *lo* to refer to

---

[3] See Enrique-Arias (2010) for similar arguments regarding contact with Catalan as a factor in inhibiting change in Spanish in Majorca.

plural masculine direct objects. Rates for the neutralization of the plural by first-generation migrants reach 64 percent while, for second-generation migrants, they reach 57 percent, which is significant especially if compared to speakers who are born in Lima to Limeño parents and who neutralize plural direct objects at the rate of 22 percent. More significant is the neutralization of feminine direct object pronouns: Klee and Caravedo (2005) show that it reaches 76 percent in the case of first-generation migrants and 21 percent in the case of second-generation migrants, while the rate is only 2 percent in the case of native Limeño speakers. In another study, Klee *et al.* (2011) show that indigenous learners of Spanish in Lima use an OV word order more frequently than do L1 Spanish speakers. Both VO and OV are possible in Spanish, but influence from Quechua appears to increase the more marked use of an OV word order by bilingual speakers. Other instances of Quechua influence on Andean Spanish include the use of an evidential function for the present perfect, in contrast with the pluperfect that is used for a reportative function (Escobar 1997, 2011), and the appearance of a double possessive marking in several Andean varieties (Clements 2009).[4]

A well-studied contact situation has been that of Spanish in contact with English in the United States. Although several scholars recognize that there are instances of convergence, the consensus is that US Spanish is not a restructured variety, and the claim that it represents a third stable new variety, popularly denoted Spanglish, is not accurate (Lipski 2008). Silva-Corvalán (1994, 2001) describes several features that represent cases of convergence between Spanish and English including the elimination of the complementizer *que* 'that' in complement clauses, increased prenominal placement of adjectives, and the use of possessive adjectives instead of the definite article with inalienable nouns. Other pervasive features in US Spanish include the erosion of the subjunctive in favor of a more extended use of the indicative mood, and the extended use of the verb *estar*. Silva-Corvalán (2008) nevertheless argues that these features are already present in native vernacular varieties, as opposed to in the Academy-sanctioned standard Spanish, even though they become considerably more prominent in second- and third-generation bilinguals.

The case of the use of subject personal pronouns (SPPs) has in particular attracted a good deal of analysis. The fact that this is a conflict site between Spanish and English, as English generally requires overt pronouns while Spanish is a pro-drop language, has led to suggestions of a possible English influence on the rate of overt SPP use by speakers of Spanish in contact with English. While some scholars have argued that higher rates of overt

---

[4] Due to space considerations, I have chosen to discuss a reduced number of settings both in Spain and in Latin America, principally focusing on cases where larger groups of speakers are involved and on features that better illustrate the phenomena under discussion. But, as argued throughout the chapter, the richness of contact situations of Spanish with other languages is much wider and has been the subject of entire volumes (Roca and Jensen 1996; Silva-Corvalán 1997; Potowski and Cameron 2007; Klee and Lynch 2009).

pronoun use are not the result of influence from English (Cameron 1992; Flores-Ferrán 2004), earlier studies had claimed the opposite (de Granda 1978; Navarro Tomás 1948). More recently, in a larger study, Otheguy *et al.* (2007) and Otheguy and Zentella (2012) have proved that competence in English in fact plays a role in a higher rate of subject pronoun use, as it sets apart New York-born speakers and those with higher levels of competence in English from recent arrivals. Otheguy *et al.* (2007:779) conclude that: "there are, as predicted, positive correlations between rates of overt pronouns and years spent in NYC as well as English skills." But here again, as with other cases discussed above, we have a feature already present in Spanish, and what we see are variable rates of its use as opposed to the incorporation of a totally new feature. It is important to keep in mind, then, that variations in the use of a feature in situations of language contact do not necessarily have as their source the other language. Additionally, Poplack and Levey (2010:394) argue for a distinction between innovation, a possibly transient phenomenon, and change, which usually shows considerable diffusion and acceptability in the community.[5] An example of an item that has achieved diffusion in US Spanish is a form such as *llamar para atrás* 'to call back' (cf. standard Spanish *llamar de vuelta/devolver la llamada* (Otheguy 1993; Lipski 2008)).

21.4 Spanish-Based Contact Varieties

Contact between European languages and indigenous languages in different geographical regions across the globe, principally as a result of the European waves of colonization and slave trade, led to the appearance of several types of contact varieties, ranging from radical vernaculars to pidgins and creole languages. The status of Spanish-based creoles as prototypical creoles has been disputed in the literature with some scholars claiming their non-existence (McWhorter 2000), while others provide significant evidence that Spanish-based creoles show similar grammatical features and processes of formation to other creoles (Clements 2009 and references therein). Overall, studies have shown that there is a wide range of Spanish-based contact varieties, including creoles such as Palenquero and Chabacano, restructured vernaculars including Bozal Spanish and other Afro-Spanish varieties, and even intertwined systems such as Media Lengua.

In the case of creole languages, Palenquero has enjoyed a good deal of attention over the last few decades. Spoken in San Basilio de Palenque in Colombia, it has its origin in the speech of African slaves who escaped from Cartagena in the 17th century and remained isolated for a long

---

[5] See also Silva-Corvalán's (2008) article "The Limits of Language Contact" for an in-depth discussion of what counts as contact-induced change in US Spanish.

period of time. Common creole structural features of Palenquero include a lack of gender marking and definiteness of noun phrases, and, at the verb phrase level, invariant verbs, as Palenquero relies on preverbal markers to express time, mood, and aspect (TMA), a feature common in creole languages. Increased access to Spanish and its use in Palenque is leading to a less natural inter-generational transmission of Palenquero, especially given the low number of its speakers (estimated by Schwegler (2011) to range between 4,000 and 5,000). More recently, an increased awareness of the importance of Palenquero as an ethnic identity marker and its recognition as a valuable cultural product of community, national, and world heritage, has led to its introduction in the school system. Recent studies have shown that younger bilingual speakers present new features that are a result of contact with Spanish, such as the use of verb morphology and definite articles (Lipski 2011).

Another documented Spanish-based creole is Chabacano, spoken principally in and around Zamboanga City, and, less commonly, in other smaller communities in the Philippines. Chabacano emerged as a result of contact between Spanish, introduced in the Philippines as early as the 16th century, and indigenous Filipino languages such as Tagalog. These have had significant influence on the structure of Chabacano, including in its preference for a VSO word order (Lipski 2012). A different case is that of Papiamento, which combines grammatical features that are the result of Afro-Hispanic contact with other lexifying languages including Dutch, English, and Portuguese. Papiamento is spoken in the Caribbean islands of Curaçao, Aruba, and Bonaire; many of the grammatical features of its different varieties are shared with other Iberian-based creoles such as the use of preverbal TMA markers, including the marker *ta* (present in Palenquero and Chabacano (Andersen 1990:67)).

There also exist contact varieties of Spanish that represent the process of L2 acquisition rather than prototypical cases of creole genesis. These include Afro-Hispanic varieties such as the historical pidgin known as Bozal Spanish used by African slaves and possible post-Bozal varieties described by Lipski (2007), Barlovento Spanish in Venezuela (Díaz and Clements 2008), Afro-Boliviano (Lipski 2011), and Chota Valley Spanish (Sessarego 2014). The case of Media Lengua, spoken in the Ecuadorian Andes, is a particularly interesting case from a theoretical standpoint. Media Lengua is a variety formed by the superposition of Spanish lexicon onto Quechua grammar, used by rural migrants and their descendants as an intra-group code. The fact that about 90 percent of the lexicon comes from Spanish while the grammar remains that of Quechua (Muysken 1981; Gómez Rendón 2008) has attracted considerable interest from scholars of mixed languages. In addition, the analysis of Media Lengua has contributed to our understanding of language contact resulting from rapid and massive population movements and the concomitant emergence of new mixed varieties, such as we find with several urban vernaculars in Africa (McLaughlin 2009).

Another example of a contact situation involving Spanish is that of Spanish in contact with Portuguese, whose outcome is generally referred to as Portuñol (Elizaincín 1992). Two Luso-Hispanic contact varieties have attracted interest: Fronterizo and Barranqueño. In the former, different degrees of mixing of Spanish and Portuguese in communities along the border between Brazil and Uruguay have resulted in Fronterizo (or Uruguayan Portuguese) as its major manifestation. Given the structural overlap between Spanish and Portuguese and the variable nature of the different contact systems grouped under Portuñol, no definitive lines have been drawn to account for clear structural distinctive features that could separate the different bilingual communities (Lipski 2006:13). In the second case, the contact is between Spanish and Portuguese on the border between Spain and Portugal in the Iberian peninsula. Barranqueño, which emerged as a variety of Portuguese acquired by Spanish dominant speakers, is spoken by some 2,000 people in Barrancos (Clements et al. 2008). Among the most salient features accounted for as a direct influence of Spanish in Barranqueño, Clements et al. (2011) list the aspiration and deletion of final /-s/ and the deletion of final /-r/, both of which are common in the neighboring regions of Spain, and several phenomena related to the use and placement of pronouns including the doubling of indirect objects with full noun phrases and the preference for proclisis in contexts where Portuguese requires the use of enclisis with third-person indirect object clitics.

Finally, another case of language contact in the Spanish-speaking world is that involving Spanish/Limonese creole speakers in the province of Limón in Costa Rica, where we find an English-based creole in contact with Spanish. Limonese is a variety of the Jamaican creole, and its contact with Spanish is leading to substantial code-switching and influence from Spanish without the appearance of a distinct third variety. Spanish is the source language for frequent lone and multiword insertions in Limonese and for some morphosyntactic claques, including the predominant use of the "have + years" construction to express age as opposed to the "be + years" form (LaBoda 2015).

In sum, the history of Spanish and its large-scale nativization by indigenous and creole populations has led to the creation of varieties that offer a window into different outcomes of intense language contact.

21.5 Code-Switching

Studies of code-switching between Spanish and other languages, especially between English and Spanish, have been among the most influential in the field. Early studies provided an initial description of bilingual speaker use of Spanish and English in the same communicative event (Gingràs 1974; Timm 1975; Pfaff 1979, among others). These studies helped dissipate some of the misunderstandings about code-switching which even today continue to be perceived by non-specialists and users themselves as deviant behavior. They also established that, in bilingual communities, speakers frequently code-switch not randomly but according to a set of social, pragmatic, and grammatical constraints, and that the presence of code-switching may in fact serve as an indicator of the vitality of the languages in contact rather than of their mutual erosion. The occurrence of English/Spanish code-switching has been examined not only in oral conversation but also in other types of discourse, including in written and electronic communication (Callahan 2004; Toribio 2011; Montes Alcalá 2015).

The variationist approach to code-switching introduced by Poplack (1980) has provided proof not only of the quantitatively high frequency of code-switched occurrences in Hispanic communities, but also of the engagement by members of bilingual communities in different types of code-switching which often reflect the richness of their linguistic repertoire. A distinction is made between inter-sentential and intra-sentential code-switching. In the first case, switch points occur across sentence boundaries without major implications for the structure of either of the two languages (21.1).[6] In the second case, code-switching occurs within the same sentence but without violating the grammatical rules of either of the two languages involved (21.2).

(21.1) Está desconectado en este momento. *I have a – I have a local number.* Yo tengo teléfono en mi habitación si eso ayuda.
'It is disconnected at the moment. ... I have a phone in my room if it helps.'

(21.2) En la República Dominicana, *oh it has to be in Spanish.*
'In the Dominican Republic, ...'

Intra-sentential code-switching has been shown to be a good index of the degree of bilingualism: more balanced bilinguals tend to code-switch at the intra-sentential level. Lipski (2014:41) has argued that code-switching also occurs in the speech of low-competency speakers, but that "in the case of low-fluency or semi-fluent bilinguals ... not all language mixing may follow the 'canonical' code-switching trajectory" described above.

In the case of Spanish in contact with English, as with many other contact situations, lone noun insertion remains a very frequent phenomenon (21.3). Debates on how to interpret these – whether as instances of code-switching, of borrowing, or of nonce-borrowing – have been heated.

---

[6] All examples are from Dominican-American bilingual speakers collected as part of the University at Albany Corpus of New York Dominican Spanish.

While Myers-Scotton (2002), for example, argues that non-established noun insertions are cases of code-switching, Poplack and Meechan (1998) have argued that these often behave like instances of borrowing.

(21.3)   Yo trabajé en una fábrica donde hacían *clothes* de *leather* y *jackets* de *leather*. Yo peleaba mucho con el dueño.
'I worked in a factory where they made leather clothes and leather jackets. I argued a lot with the owner.'

A particular focus within code-switching studies has been on the use of English and Spanish discourse markers, which include such frequent particles as "so," "you know," "*entonces*," and "*tú sabes*," among others (Aaron 2004; Lipski 2005). Torres (2002) found that, within the Puerto Rican community in Brentwood (New York), speakers with varying levels of competence in both languages used a high number of English discourse markers when speaking Spanish, albeit to varying degrees and for different discourse functions. The English discourse markers "you know" and "so" are the ones most commonly used by speakers with different levels of bilingual competence, to the degree that Torres considers them to be borrowings integrated into Spanish discourse. At the same time, this does not cause the displacement of Spanish discourse markers, which continue to be used alongside English ones in an overlapping fashion.

In Spain, code-switching between Spanish and Catalan, Basque, and Galician has also been examined, with a special importance given to the emblematic use of minority languages and to the more common discourse functions carried out (Alvarez-Cáccamo 1990; Blas Arroyo 1993). Code-switching is also common in other bilingual communities across the Spanish-speaking world including, to give an example of lesser-known cases, in northern Morocco, Ceuta, and Melilla, where code-switching between Spanish, Arabic, and Berber is frequent, and the British territory of Gibraltar, where, as Moyer (1992) has shown, competence in both English and Spanish again results in frequent code-switching.

21.6 Language Maintenance and Language Shift

The particular ecology of a language contact situation (Mufwene 2001) determines the domains of use of each of the languages involved and leads to the emergence of different phenomena. Contact can lead to language maintenance in cases of balanced bilingualism and a strong ethnolinguistic vitality of both languages, or to language shift in cases of an interruption in the natural transmission of the socially-subordinate language. Spanish as a world language has enjoyed a long history of expansion that in many cases has led to the restricted use of indigenous languages or even to their death.[7] In fact, Spanish is the dominant language in the majority of the cases where it is in contact with other languages. In Latin America, it has advanced quickly at the expense of Amerindian languages, with very few cases of balanced bilingualism such as that which we see in Paraguay (Gynan 2005).

The other side of the coin is when Spanish is a minority language. There are cases where Spanish was not nativized and did not displace an indigenous language, but where it has the status of a foreign language coexisting with a local native language. In North Africa, Equatorial Guinea, and the Philippines, Spanish as a minority language enjoys considerable prestige, leading to its maintenance as a second language. In northern Morocco, about 80 percent of students in the 11 official Spanish education centers which still exist are Moroccan, and the Instituto Cervantes in many Moroccan cities often has long waiting lists for its classes. Spanish is perceived as a language that can provide educational and economic opportunities in addition to access to cultural and audio-visual products. In the disputed territories of the Western Sahara, where Spain was an occupying power until 1975, Spanish has been adopted as one of the official languages of the Sahrawis and is one used for education in the refugee camps. Equatorial Guinea, the only African country where Spanish is an official language, is a typical case of postcolonial language policies, as the colonial language is the language of education and administration, and even the language used for literary production.

In the United States, the status of Spanish as a minority language varies by region and by historical period (Amastae and Olivares 1982; Lipski 2008). In addition to Puerto Rico and the regions with a traditionally heavy Hispanic presence, other areas have seen an increase in the number of Spanish speakers in recent years, including the Midwest (Escobar and Potowski 2015). Moreover, Spanish is among the heritage languages in the US that is best transmitted to the second generation. According to the Pew Research Center (2013), eight out of every ten second-generation Hispanics claim to speak Spanish, which is much higher than is the case with Asian Americans (only four out of ten second-generation Asian Americans claim to speak their heritage language). However, as has been frequently argued, this is not enough to secure Spanish as a fully accepted language in the United States. Misconceptions about the threat of Spanish are abundant, and language shift continues to happen across generations (Potowski 2014; Escobar and Potowski 2015). While new waves of immigration continue to sustain the presence of Spanish in the United States, in traditional communities where Spanish had been maintained in the past – such as in the US Southwest and enclaves like St Bernard Parish in Louisiana – we see Spanish disappearing quickly or being assimilated to other varieties (Bills and Vigil 1999; Torres Cacoullos and Aaron 2003).

---

[7] See Terborg *et al.* (2006) for the situation of the indigenous languages of Mexico, for example.

21.7 Summary

The Spanish language today is used in very diverse settings that range from its status as a native language in Spain and Spanish-speaking Latin America, an official language in Equatorial Guinea, an "unofficial" second language in northern Morocco and the Philippines, and a language with variable status as a heritage language in the United States and other destination countries for Latin American and Spanish immigration. This diversity of situations has promoted the appearance of different language contact phenomena. At the same time, the continued unity of the language, in terms of mutual intelligibility among Spanish speakers regardless of native dialect, is remarkable. Despite its notable lexical and structural variability, Spanish continues to be considered, and rightly so, as a single language. In some 500 years Spanish has become a language used by many types of speakers in very different places: This supports its status as a global language offering a wide range of research opportunities for a better understanding of the nature of bilingualism and the processes and outcomes of language contact.

Moving forward, it appears that – in Spain – a greater recognition and revitalization of minority languages, with a concomitant increase in their normalization and use in a wider set of domains, will lead to increases in language contact. In North Africa, the two autonomous cities of Ceuta and Melilla continue to sustain the use of Spanish in northern Morocco and offer interesting cases of Spanish in contact with Arabic and Berber. In Latin America, as the spread of education and urbanization continues to promote the imposition of Spanish, there are increasing efforts to maintain and teach the indigenous languages. Although these efforts face an uphill battle, given the overwhelming symbolic and socioeconomic power of Spanish, they promise to at least increase awareness at the level of both affected communities and policy makers. Finally, in the United States, demographic changes and the long history of Spanish in the country support a continuing presence of this language well into the future.

In conclusion, a priority of research programs into bilingualism in the Spanish-speaking world and Spanish in contact with other languages should be to provide much-needed data on the many contact situations involving the hitherto far less researched languages with rapidly dwindling numbers of speakers. This can help achieve two things at once: first, to increase awareness about the situation of minority languages in general and to further document the processes of language maintenance and language shift; and, second, to cast additional light on the mechanisms of language variation and language change in situations of bilingualism, which is of interest to the field of linguistics in general given that the majority of people in the world today speak more than one language.

Additionally, massive population movement and migratory trends continue to represent an excellent opportunity for specialists in contact linguistics, including those working on Spanish. Finally, in the age of "big data" and increasingly dominant electronic modes of communication, research on lexical borrowing and contact-induced structural change from and into Spanish should follow suit by becoming even more quantitative and usage-based.

References

Aaron, Jessi Elana (2004). *So* respetamos un tradición del uno al otro. *So* and *entonces* in New Mexican Bilingual Discourse. *Spanish in Context*, 1, 161–179.

Álvarez-Cáccamo, Celso (1990). Rethinking Conversational Code-Switching: Codes, Speech Varieties, and Contextualization. *Annual Meeting of the Berkeley Linguistics Society*, 16 (1), 3–16.

Amastae, Jon and Elías-Olivares, Lucía (1982). *Spanish in the United States: Sociolinguistic Aspects*. Cambridge: Cambridge University Press.

Andersen, Roger W. (1990). Papiamentu Tense-Aspect, with Special Attention to Discourse. In John Victor Singler (ed.), *Pidgin and Creole Tense-Mood-Aspect Systems*. Amsterdam and Philadelphia, PA: John Benjamins, pp. 59–96.

Austin, Jennifer, Blume, María, and Sánchez, Liliana (2015). *Bilingualism in the Spanish-Speaking World: Linguistic and Cognitive Perspectives*. Cambridge and New York: Cambridge University Press.

Bills, Garland D. and Vigil, Neddy A. (1999). Ashes to Ashes: The Historical Basis for Dialect Variation in New Mexican Spanish. *Romance Philology*, 53 (1), 43–68.

Blas Arroyo, José Luis (1993). Perspectiva sociofuncional del cambio de código. Estado de la cuestión y aplicaciones a diversos casos del bilingüismo peninsular. *Contextos*, 11(21–22), 221–263.

Blas Arroyo, José Luis (2007). El contacto de lenguas como factor de retención en procesos de variación y cambio lingüístico: Datos sobre el español en una comunidad bilingüe peninsular. *Spanish in Context*, 4 (2), 263–291.

Blas Arroyo, José Luis (2008). The Variable Expression of Future Tense in Peninsular Spanish: The Present (and Future) of Inflectional Forms in the Spanish Spoken in a Bilingual Region. *Language Variation and Change*, 20 (1), 85–126.

Blas Arroyo, José Luis (2011). Spanish in Contact with Catalan. In Manuel Díaz-Campos (ed.), *The Handbook of Hispanic Sociolinguistics*. Malden, MA: Wiley-Blackwell, pp. 374–394.

Callahan, Laura (2004). *Spanish/English Codeswitching in a Written Corpus*. Amsterdam and Philadelphia, PA: John Benjamins.

Cameron, Richard (1992). Pronominal and Null Subject Variation in Spanish: Constraints, Dialects, and Functional Compensation (Doctoral dissertation). University of Pennsylvania.

Clements, J. Clancy (2009). *The Linguistic Legacy of Spanish and Portuguese: Colonial Expansion and Language Change*. Cambridge: Cambridge University Press.

Clements, J. Clancy, Amaral, Patrícia, and Luís, Ana R. (2008). El Barranqueño: Una lengua de contacto en Iberia. *Estudios Portugueses*, 7, 37–46.

Clements, J. Clancy, Amaral, Patrícia, and Luís, Ana R. (2011). Spanish in Contact with Portuguese: The Case of Barranquenho. In Manuel Díaz-Campos (ed.), *The Handbook of Hispanic Sociolinguistics*. Chichester: John Wiley, pp. 395–417.

Davidson, Justin (2015). Intervocalic Fricative Voicing in the Spanish of Barcelona: Considerations for Contact-Induced Sociophonetic Innovation. In Kim Potowski and Talia Bugel (eds.), *Sociolinguistic Change across the Spanish-Speaking World: Case Studies in Honor of Anna María Escobar*. New York: Peter Lang, pp. 119–146.

de Granda, Germán (1978). *Estudios lingüísticos hispánicos, afrohispánicos y criollos*. Madrid: Gredos.

Díaz-Campos, Manuel and Clancy Clements, J. (2008). A Creole Origin for Barlovento Spanish? A Linguistic and Sociohistorical Inquiry. *Language in Society*, 37, 351–383.

Elizaincín, Adolfo (1992). *Dialectos en contacto: Español y portugués en España y América*. Montevideo: Arca.

Enrique-Arias, Andrés (2010). On Language Contact as an Inhibitor of Language Change: The Spanish of Catalan Bilinguals in Majorca. In Anne Breitbarth, Christopher Lucas, Sheila Watts, and David Willis (eds.), *Continuity and Change in Grammar*. Amsterdam: John Benjamins, pp. 97–118.

Escobar, Anna María (1997). Contrastive and Innovative Uses of the Present Perfect and the Preterite in Spanish in Contact with Quechua. *Hispania*, 80 (4), 859–870.

Escobar, Anna María (2011). Spanish in Contact with Quechua. In Manuel Díaz-Campos (ed.), *The Handbook of Hispanic Sociolinguistics*. Chichester: John Wiley, pp. 321–352.

Escobar, Anna María and Potowski, Kim (2015). *El español de los Estados Unidos*. Cambridge and New York: Cambridge University Press.

Flores-Ferrán, Nydia (2004). Spanish Subject Personal Pronoun Use in New York City Puerto Ricans: Can We Rest the Case of English Contact? *Language Variation and Change*, 16 (1), 49–73.

Galindo Solé, Mireia (2003). Language Contact Phenomena in Catalonia: The Influence of Catalan in Spoken Castilian. In Lotfi Sayahi (ed.), *Selected Proceedings of the 1st Workshop on Spanish Sociolinguistics*. Somerville, MA: Cascadilla, pp. 18–29.

Galmés de Fuentes, Alvaro (1983). *Dialectología mozárabe*. Madrid: Gredos.

Gingràs, Rosario (1974). Problems in the Description of Spanish–English Intrasentential Code-Switching. In G. D. Bills (ed.), *Southwest Areal Linguistics*. San Diego, CA: University of California Institute for Cultural Pluralism, pp. 167–174.

Gómez Rendón, Jorge Arsenio (2008). *Mestizaje lingüístico en los Andes: Génesis y estructura de una lengua mixta*. Quito: Abya-Yala.

Gynan, Shaw N. (2005). Official Bilingualism in Paraguay, 1995–2001: An Analysis of the Impact of Language Policy on Attitudinal Change. In Lotfi Sayahi and Maurice Westmoreland (eds.), *Selected Proceedings of the 2nd Workshop on Spanish Sociolinguistics*. Somerville, MA: Cascadilla, pp. 24–40.

Heath, Jeffery (1984). Language Contact and Language Change. *Annual Review of Anthropology*, 13, 367–384.

Hill, Jane and Hill, Kenneth (1977). Language Death and Relexification in Tlaxcalan Nahuatl. *International Journal of the Sociology of Language*, 12, 55–70.

Klee, Carol A. and Caravedo, Rocío (2005). Contact-Induced Language Change in Lima, Peru: The Case of Clitic Pronouns. In D. Eddington (ed.), *Selected Proceedings of the 7th Hispanic Linguistics Symposium*. Somerville, MA: Cascadilla, pp. 12–21.

Klee, Carol and Lynch, Andrew (2009). *El español en contacto con otras lenguas*. Washington, DC: Georgetown University Press.

Klee, Carol A., Tight, Daniel, and Caravedo, Rocío (2011). Variation and Change in Peruvian Word Order: The Impact of Migration to Lima. *Southwest Journal of Linguistics*, 30, 5–31.

LaBoda, Ashley (2015). A Variationist Approach to Code-Switching and Lexical Borrowing: The Case of Limonese–Spanish bilinguals in Puerto Limón, Costa Rica (Doctoral dissertation). SUNY.

Lapesa, Rafael (1981). *Historia de la lengua española*. Madrid: Gredos.

Lipski, John (1987). African Influence on Hispanic Dialects. In Leonard Studerus (ed.), *Current Trends and Issues in Hispanic Linguistics*. Dallas, TX: Summer Institute of Linguistics, pp. 33–68.

Lipski, John (2005). Code-Switching or Borrowing? *No sé so no puedo decir*, You Know. In Lotfi Sayahi and Maurice Westmoreland (eds.), *Selected Proceedings of the 2nd Workshop on Spanish Sociolinguistics*. Somerville, MA: Cascadilla, pp. 1–15.

Lipski, John (2006). Too Close for Comfort? The Genesis of "Portuñol/Portunhol." In Timothy L. Face and Carol A. Klee (eds.), *Selected Proceedings of the 8th Hispanic Linguistics Symposium*. Somerville, MA: Cascadilla, pp. 1–22.

Lipski, John (2007). Where and How does Bozal Spanish Survive? In Kim Potowski and Richard Cameron (eds.), *Spanish in Contact: Policy, Social and Linguistic Inquiries*. Amsterdam: John Benjamins, pp. 357–373.

Lipski, John (2008). *Varieties of Spanish in the United States*. Washington, DC: Georgetown University Press.

Lipski, John (2011). El "nuevo" palenquero y el español afroboliviano: ¿Es reversible la descriollización? In Luis A. Ortiz-López (ed.), *Selected Proceedings of the 13th Hispanic Linguistics Symposium*. Somerville, MA: Cascadilla, pp. 1–16.

Lipski, John (2012). Características del español filipino y del chabacano. In Isaac Donoso Jiménez (ed.), *Historia cultural de la lengua española en Filipinas: Ayer y hoy*. Madrid: Verbum, pp. 307–323.

Lipski, John (2014). Spanish–English Code-Switching among Low-Fluency Bilinguals: Towards an Expanded Typology. *Sociolinguistic Studies*, 8 (1), 23–55.

Lope Blanch, Juan Manuel (1967). Sobre la influencia de las lenguas indígenas en el léxico del español hablado en México. In Jaime Sánchez Romeralo and Norbert Poulussen (eds.), *Actas del II Congreso Internacional de Hispanistas*. Nijmegen: Instituto Español de la Universidad de Nimega, pp. 395–402.

Lorenzino, Gerardo Augusto (2014). Immigrants' Languages, Lunfardo and Lexical Diffusion in Popular Porteño Spanish. *PAPIA: Revista Brasileira de Estudos do Contato Linguístico*, 24 (2), 357–379.

Martínez Ruiz, Juan (1994). Languages in Contact in Morisco Granada (XVI Century). In Jordi Aguadé, Federico Corriente, and Marina Marugán (eds.), *Actas del Congreso Internacional sobre Interferencias Lingüísticas Árabo-romances y Paralelos Extra-iberos*. Zaragoza: Navarro y Navarro, pp. 141–156.

McLaughlin, Fiona (2009). *The Languages of Urban Africa*. London: Continuum.

McWhorter, John H. (2000). *The Missing Spanish Creoles: Recovering the Birth of Plantation Contact Languages*. Berkeley, CA: University of California Press.

Menéndez Pidal, Ramón (1986). *Orígenes del español: Estado lingüístico de la península ibérica hasta el siglo XI*. Madrid: Espasa Calpe.

Montes Alcalá, Cecilia (2015). iSwitch: Spanish–English Mixing in Computer-Mediated Communication. *Journal of Language Contact*, 9, 19–44.

Moyer, Melissa (1992). Analysis of Code-Switching in Gibraltar (Doctoral dissertation). Universitat Autònoma de Barcelona.

Mufwene, Salikoko (2001). *The Ecology of Language Evolution*. Cambridge and New York: Cambridge University Press.

Muysken, Pieter (1981). Halfway between Quechua and Spanish: The Case for Relexification. In Arnold Highfield and Albert Valdman (eds.), *Historicity and Variation in Creole Studies*. Ann Arbor, MI: Karoma Publishers, pp. 52–78.

Myers-Scotton, Carol (2002). *Contact Linguistics: Bilingual Encounters and Grammatical Outcomes*. Oxford: Oxford University Press.

Navarro Tomás, T. (1948). *El español en Puerto Rico*. Río Piedras: Universidad de Puerto Rico.

Otheguy, Ricardo (1993). A Reconsideration of the Notion of Loan Translation in the Analysis of US Spanish. In Ana Roca and John Lipski (eds.), *Spanish in the United States: Linguistic Contact and Diversity*. Berlin: De Gruyter, pp. 21–45.

Otheguy, Ricardo and Zentella, Ana Celia (2012). *Spanish in New York: Language Contact, Dialectal Leveling, and Structural Continuity*. Oxford: Oxford University Press.

Otheguy, Ricardo, Zentella, Ana Celia, and Livert, David (2007). Language and Dialect Contact in Spanish in New York: Towards the Formation of a Speech Community. *Language*, 83, 770–802.

Pew Research Center (2013). *Second-Generation Americans: A Portrait of the Adult Children of Immigrants*. Washington, DC: Pew Research Center. Available from www.pewsocialtrends.org/2013/02/07/second-generation-americans/ (last access December 8, 2017).

Pfaff, Carol. W. (1979). Constraints on Language Mixing: Intrasentential Code-Switching and Borrowing in Spanish/English. *Language*, 55 (2), 291–318.

Poplack, Shana (1980). Sometimes I'll Start a Sentence in Spanish Y TERMINO EN ESPAÑOL: Toward a Typology of Code-Switching. *Linguistics*, 18 (7/8), 581–618.

Poplack, Shana and Levey, Stephen (2010). Contact-Induced Grammatical Change: A Cautionary Tale. In Peter Auer and Jürgen Erich Schmidt (eds.), *Language and Space: An International Handbook of Linguistic Variation*, Vol. 1. Berlin: De Gruyter, pp. 391–419.

Poplack, Shana and Meechan, Marjory (1998). How Languages Fit Together in Code-Mixing. *International Journal of Bilingualism*, 2 (2), 127–138.

Potowski, Kim (2014). Spanish. In Terrence G. Wiley, Joy Kreeft Peyton, Donna Christian, Sarah Catherine K. Moore, and Na Liu (eds.), *Handbook of Heritage, Community, and Native American Languages in the United States: Research, Policy, and Educational Practice*. New York: Routledge, pp. 90–100.

Potowski, Kim and Cameron, Richard (2007). *Spanish in Contact: Policy, Social and Linguistic Inquiries*. Amsterdam: John Benjamins.

Real Academia Española (2001). *Diccionario de la lengua española (DRAE)*. Madrid: Espasa Calpe.

Roca, Ana and Jensen, John B. (1996). *Spanish in Contact: Issues in Bilingualism*. Somerville, MA: Cascadilla.

Sayahi, Lotfi (2006). Phonetic Features of Northern Moroccan Spanish. *Revista Internacional de Lingüística Iberoamericana*, 8, 167–180.

Sayahi, Lotfi (2011). Spanish in Contact with Arabic. In Manuel Díaz-Campos (ed.), *The Handbook of Hispanic Sociolinguistics*. Chichester: John Wiley, pp. 473–490.

Schwegler, Armin (2011). Palenque (Colombia): Multilingualism in an Extraordinary Social and Historical Context. In Manuel Díaz-Campos (ed.), *The Handbook of Hispanic Sociolinguistics*. Chichester: John Wiley, pp. 446–472.

Scipione, Ruth (2011). Phonetic Adaptations of Spanish Loanwords in Triqui (Doctoral dissertation). SUNY.

Sessarego, Sandro (2014). On the Origins of Chota Valley Spanish: Linguistic and Sociohistorical Evidence. *Journal of Pidgin and Creole Languages*, 29, 86–133.

Silva-Corvalán, Carmen (1994). *Language Contact and Change: Spanish in Los Angeles*. Oxford: Clarendon.

Silva-Corvalán, Carmen (1997). *Spanish in Four Continents: Studies in Language Contact and Bilingualism*. Washington, DC: Georgetown University Press.

Silva-Corvalán, Carmen (2001). *Sociolingüística y pragmática del español*. Washington, DC: Georgetown University Press.

Silva-Corvalán, Carmen (2008). The Limits of Convergence in Language Contact. *Journal of Language Contact*, 2 (1), 213–224.

Stokes, Craig (2015). The Use of Catalan Verbal Periphrases *haver de* and *tenir que* on Twitter. *Sociolinguistic Studies*, 9 (4), 445.

Smead, Robert N. (1998). English Loanwords in Chicano Spanish: Characterization and Rationale. *The Bilingual Review*, 23 (2), 113–123.

Terborg, Roland, García Landa, Laura, and Moore, Pauline (2006). The Language Situation in Mexico. *Current Issues in Language Planning*, 7 (4), 415–518.

Thomason, Sarah G. and Kaufman, Terrence (1988). *Language Contact, Creolization, and Genetic Linguistics*. Berkeley, CA: University of California Press.

Timm, Leonora (1975). Spanish-English Code-Switching: *El porqué y el* How-not-to. *Romance Philology*, 28, 473–482.

Toribio, Almeida Jacqueline (2011). Code-Switching among US Latinos. In Manuel Díaz-Campos (ed.), *The Handbook of Hispanic Sociolinguistics*. Chichester: John Wiley, pp. 530–552.

Torres, Lourdes (2002). Bilingual Discourse Markers in Puerto Rican Spanish. *Language in Society*, 31 (1), 65–83.

Torres Cacoullos, Rena and Aaron, Jessi Elana (2003). Bare English-Origin Nouns in Spanish: Rates, Constraints, and Discourse Functions. *Language Variation and Change*, 15 (3), 289–328.

Weinreich, Uriel (1963). *Languages in Contact: Findings and Problems*. The Hague: Mouton.

Winford, Donald (2003). *An Introduction to Contact Linguistics*. Malden, MA: Blackwell.

22

Spanish as a Heritage Language in the US: Core Issues and Future Directions

Diego Pascual y Cabo

22.1 Introduction

According to most recent reports, the US Hispanic[1] population has now surpassed the 56 million mark and makes up approximately 17 percent of the nation's population. These data represent a net increase of 21 million from 2000 – a growing trend that is expected to continue through the next decades, with some estimates projecting numbers as high as 128 million by 2050 (Pew Research Center 2008). By then, Hispanics will be the largest ethnolinguistic minority group. Such profound changes in the social make-up of the nation necessarily go hand in hand with transformations at different levels (e.g. cultural, political, etc.). Given the scope of the present volume, the focus of this chapter will mainly be on presenting and discussing (some of) the linguistic consequences of such transformations, particularly the acquisition, development, maintenance, and loss of Spanish as a minority language. Attention will also be given to related issues in the field of language education, with emphasis being placed on understanding its pedagogical challenges and on identifying opportunities for improving current practices, particularly those of language retention and revitalization. But before all of this can be meaningfully done, the topic requires definitions of terms such as heritage language (HL) and heritage speaker (HS). It is to an examination of these terms that I turn now.

In the context of the US, the most widely used definition of HS is that put forth by Valdés (2001), who uses the term in reference to someone who is raised in a home where a non-English language is spoken and who is, to

---

[1] In this chapter, the terms "Latino" and "Hispanic" are used interchangeably and without any underlying political, cultural, or linguistic considerations.

some degree, bilingual in English and the HL.[2] In the spirit of developing a more fine-grained distinction, other definitions and considerations have emerged. Particularly useful for this endeavor are Polinsky and Kagan's (2007) efforts in further classifying HSs amongst those who can communicate using the HL (i.e. narrow definition) and those who cannot but who possess an emotional or cultural connection to their heritage (i.e. broad definition). This contrast is clearly illustrative of the heterogeneous nature of heritage speakers as a broad ethnolinguistic group. But even this twofold definition may turn out to be simplistic, particularly when exploring the broad range of characteristics that HSs display. With this in mind, a few general observations related to the significant role that context and community factors play in the acquisition/development of the HL deserve to be pointed out.

22.2 Exploring the Role of Context and its Effects on the Development of Spanish as a Heritage Language

Generally speaking, heritage speakers acquire their home/heritage language from early on, naturalistically, and are therefore to be considered a subset of native speakers of the HL (e.g. Rothman and Treffers-Daller 2014). Not surprisingly, however, HSs tend to differ from monolingual native speakers of the same language, not only in terms of their varying linguistic proficiencies/competencies, but also regarding their attitudes towards the HL language, as well as the extent to which these attitudes affect their overall bilingual/bicultural identity (e.g. Roca 1997, 2000; Colombi and Roca 2003; Beaudrie and Fairclough 2012; Pascual y Cabo 2016; Potowski, forthcoming). The above-mentioned variations can, at least to some extent, be tied to individuals' linguistic experiences during childhood.

Chronologically speaking, acquisition of the HL either precedes acquisition of the main societal language (as is the case for sequential HSs) or is concurrent with it (as is the case for simultaneous bilinguals). While differences in the timing of acquisition can affect their linguistic development (e.g. Müller and Hulk 2001; Montrul 2002, 2008, 2016a; Pascual y Cabo and Gómez Soler 2015), it is not unusual for HSs to exhibit a strong command of the HL during the first few years of life. With time, however, a shift in linguistic dominance that ultimately favors the societal language is generally observed (e.g. Montrul 2008, 2016a). The timing of this shift seems to largely correspond with the onset of schooling, which is normally carried out in the societal language. From that moment on, a number of (extra)linguistic factors related to the newly found academic

---

[2] The reader is referred to Beaudrie and Fairclough (2012); Pascual y Cabo (2016); Potowski (forthcoming) and references therein for more on Spanish heritage speakers in the United States.

and social demands of the HS children's schooling experience contribute to defining distinct developmental paths and outcomes. These include, but are not limited to, a drastic reduction in the amount of HL input they receive, a lack of access to educational resources in the HL, reduced opportunities to be engaged in the use of the HL outside the home/family environment, and generalized negative attitudes towards the HL (e.g. Beaudrie and Fairclough 2012; Pascual y Cabo 2016; Potowski forthcoming). To be sure, all of these factors are interrelated, embedded into one another in such a way as to make it very difficult, if not impossible, to isolate the effects of one without considering the effects of others. To illustrate this, consider the following simplified, yet not unrealistic, scenario: Although a child HS entering school may be able to effectively communicate solely in her HL with perhaps only very basic knowledge of the societal language (or even no knowledge of it at all), by the time she is in second or third grade (third and fourth years of compulsory schooling; aged seven–nine), her linguistic/literacy competence in English has unequivocally become the child's dominant – and most likely preferred – language.[3] The level of complexity and sophistication achieved by child HSs in such a short period of time is remarkable, perhaps even perceptually undistinguishable from that of age-matched monolingual children. Influence of the dominant language on the HL soon becomes noticeable in a variety of properties and domains (i.e. lexicon, phonetics, morphosyntax). With time, the effects of this cross-linguistic influence become much more marked and generally result in increasing variability and innovation patterns, with the most extreme being the partial or complete loss of the HL. Extending beyond the purely linguistic side of things, these outcomes have important implications that carry over into other areas of concern (e.g. HS attitudes and motivations, identity and ideologies, etc.). For example, it is not unusual for HSs to engage in completely normal bilingual behavior (i.e. translingual phenomena such as semantic extensions, borrowings, code-switching) but then to be stigmatized for it by members of society and even in their own homes/families, where they are told they speak "bad Spanish" (e.g. Achugar and Pessoa 2009; Galindo 1995; King 2000). These normative views can not only affect the frequency and the extent to which HSs engage in the use of the HL, particularly in contexts that are outside of their comfort zone, but also unfold negative attitudes towards their own linguistic and cultural identity.

Particularly since 1960s and 70s, in an attempt to better understand these and other observations, the study of HS bilingualism emerged as an important area of inquiry. Currently, given the breadth (and depth) of scope, interest in HS bilingualism has permeated into several sub-fields of

---

[3] This is, more often than not, supported by subtractive bilingual pedagogies (e.g. Bartlett and García 2011) whose goal, simply put, is to help students transition toward acquiring English competency, regardless of the linguistic losses in the heritage language.

study (i.e. formal linguistics, sociolinguistic variation, language contact and change, HL instruction, and many more). The combined efforts and accomplishments of all of these subfields have paved the way to our current understandings, and it is with a survey of these that Section 22.3 is concerned.

22.3 Current Understandings and Research Foci

For the sake of clarity, at the risk of oversimplifying what is a robust body of work and a highly complex set of interrelated interests and perspectives, the present discussion of the core questions and current understandings within the field of HS bilingualism is restricted to two major research approaches: linguistic and pedagogical. Naturally, each of these broad categories can be further broken down into a number of (sub)disciplines (e.g. sociology of language, corpus linguistics, contact linguistics, language assessment, language policy, linguistic landscape, language attitudes, and many more). Unfortunately, space restrictions prevent this here.

22.3.1 Linguistic Approaches

Given the unique conditions under which the HL is acquired, HS research provides insights into long-standing theoretical questions in linguistics such as the necessary and sufficient conditions for language acquisition and the role age of exposure plays in linguistic development and ultimate attainment (e.g. Benmamoun et al. 2013). Our main interest is not only to describe HS linguistic outcomes, but also to explain how the HL is acquired, how it develops, and how it is transmitted inter-generationally. To this end, pioneering work by Silva-Corvalán (1986, 1994) and Montrul (2002, 2004, 2008), among others, has done much to lay the empirical and theoretical base shaping our current understandings of the field.

To date, most findings indicate that HS grammars often differ significantly from those attained by age- and education-matched monolinguals in many, but crucially not all, properties.[4] With regard to the morphosyntactic domain, for example, differences have been documented for the following properties (amongst others):

tense, aspect, and mood (Montrul 2002, 2007, 2009, 2010; Silva-Corvalán 1994; Pascual y Cabo et al. 2012);
gender agreement in nouns (Montrul et al. 2008);
copula selection (Silva-Corvalán 1986; Valenzuela et al. 2015);
null/overt subject pronouns (Montrul 2004; Silva-Corvalán 1994);
object expression (Zapata et al. 2005);

---

[4] For example, HSs have been shown to possess robust knowledge of accusative and object clitics (e.g. Silva-Corvalán 1994; Montrul 2004).

obligatory subject–verb inversion in interrogatives (Cuza 2013);
preposition stranding (Pascual y Cabo and Gómez Soler 2015);
accusative case marking (Montrul 2004; Montrul and Bowles 2009; Montrul and Sánchez-Walker 2013);
dative experiencer verbs (de Prada Pérez and Pascual y Cabo 2011; Pascual y Cabo 2013; Montrul 2016b).

Interestingly, most findings also indicate that HSs exhibit a great deal of variability, whereby, for any given property or domain, both expected "target-like" uses and innovations (i.e. unexpected non "target-like" uses) can be found both within and across individuals. Why this is so has recently become an important topic of research, particularly for theories that aim to explain the nature of the HSs' linguistic mental representation. Although not yet completely understood, what we do know is that this sort of indeterminacy and variability can also be observed in other domains of the HL grammars, such as phonetics, phonology, pragmatics, etc.

Compared to all the advances made in the morphosyntactic domain, relatively little is known about the phonetics/phonology of Spanish HSs. The fact is that, until very recently, most of the literature was quick to indicate, without much evidence, that the phonological systems of HSs were, by and large, monolingual-like and impervious to the kind of cross-linguistic influence/interference witnessed in other areas of linguistic knowledge. These somewhat inaccurate observations were mostly based on the fact that, compared to traditional Second Language (L2) learners, HSs had a clear advantage as they sounded much more like monolingually-raised speakers. Despite there being partial truth to this, particularly regarding the benefits of early exposure to the HL (Oh *et al.* 2003; Au *et al.* 2008), recent empirical and conceptual contributions have provided us with new inroads into HS phonology (for a review on Spanish HS phonetics/phonology, I refer the reader to Rao and Ronquest 2015). Generally speaking, these contributions are consistent with the idea that HS phonology – as is very much the case with what has been reported in the morphosyntax domain – also exhibits differences and higher variability than the monolingual equivalent.[5] For example, in respect of consonants, Spanish HSs have been reported to yield greater voice onset time values than monolingual speakers when producing word-initial voiceless stops (e.g. Amengual 2012) and a more approximant-like pronunciation when producing bilabial voiced stops (Rao 2014). Similarly, cross-generational acoustic analyses of the phonemic tap–trill contrast have revealed instability and variation in HS production of rhotics (Henriksen 2015). Significant differences have also been reported with regard to the Spanish HS vowel system, particularly the duration of, and the tendency to centralize, unstressed vowels (e.g. Alvord and Rogers 2014; Ronquest 2012, 2013;

---

[5] With regard to HS perception data, a series of studies have revealed no significant differences between HSs and native Spanish speakers (e.g. Kim 2015; Colantoni *et al.* 2016).

Willis 2005; but see Kim 2015). HSs' prosodic systems have also been the focus of interest over the last few years. For example, recent analyses of declarative and interrogative tonal configurations have revealed that HSs exhibit a high degree of variation and a reduced inventory of phonological targets, failing to produce what can be considered typical patterns of monolingual speech (Henriksen 2012; Kim 2015; Colantoni *et al.* 2016; Robles-Puente 2014; Rao 2016).[6]

Because the common thread in most of the previous findings is that HL outcomes in adulthood often seem to be divergent from expected monolingual norms, this course of acquisition has been generally referred to as "incomplete" (e.g. Montrul 2002, 2005, 2008, 2011). This notion, adopted from the L2 acquisition literature, has been generally used as an umbrella term to describe HS differences. Despite its influence and continued use in the field, the term "Incomplete Acquisition" has received some criticism in recent years. Some have challenged this label on conceptual as well as terminological grounds, arguing that, despite not being monolingual-like, HS grammars are equally complete and sophisticated (e.g. Pascual y Cabo and Rothman 2012; Putnam and Sánchez 2013; Rothman *et al.* 2016; Kupisch and Rothman 2016). Others have, furthermore, pointed out that using incomplete acquisition as an umbrella term might be imprecise for some specific instances of HS outcomes, as these may result from different processes such as arrested grammatical development, First Language (L1) attrition, and/or qualitative input-induced differences (e.g. Pascual y Cabo and Rothman 2012; Pires and Rothman 2009; Rothman 2007). Teasing these processes apart, however, is a rather complex enterprise, one that can be successfully accomplished only via a longitudinal study. To date, only Silva-Corvalán (2014) has been able to reliably trace the linguistic development, in a situation of language inequality (Los Angeles), of two Spanish–English bilingual children until age six. She found that while the children were able to reach age-appropriate development in the dominant language, they were not so successful in Spanish.

22.3.2 Pedagogical Approaches

From a pedagogical point of view, the main goal has been (and still is) to identify ways to most effectively meet the unique linguistic and socio-affective needs of HL learners. Early on in the pursuit of this goal, at a time when the legitimacy of bilingualism/biliteracy was consistently questioned (if not rejected altogether), researchers and practitioners were charged with the responsibility of challenging unsubstantiated popular assumptions. For example, in the 1950s and early 1960s, it was not unusual for Spanish-speaking students in the Southwest of the US to experience physical/emotional abuse for speaking Spanish in school (e.g.

---

[6] Alternatively, it may be the case that HSs are following community patterns.

MacGregor-Mendoza 2000) or to be considered developmentally disabled (e.g. Light 1971). HSs similarly suffered under "well-intentioned" educators whose goals included eradicating and/or rectifying SHL practices in favor of prestige norms (e.g. Baker 1966; Barker 1971). Much has improved since then due to early work by Valdés (e.g. 1975, 1976, 1978, 1995) and Roca (e.g. 1997), among others. For example, as a result of these early efforts, key developments have taken place in a number of areas, which in turn have helped shape current approaches to HL teaching. Above all, perhaps the most important accomplishment has been the refinement of our understandings regarding (i) the strengths that HSs bring to the classroom (as well as their weaknesses), and (ii) the critical roles that constructs such as identity, attitudes, and motivations play in HL development (e.g. Beaudrie and Ducar 2005; Ducar 2012; Hornberger and Wang 2008; Potowski 2012).

A major positive outcome of this understanding is reflected in the increasing proliferation of courses/programs specifically designed to address the needs of the HS population (e.g. Ingold *et al.* 2002; Beaudrie 2011, 2012). Sara Beaudrie noted that 169 (40 percent) of the 422 university institutions in her (2012) survey offered at least one course for SHL learners. At the time, this amount represented a remarkable increase of over 22 percent from 2002. Given the complexities associated with the HS sociopolitical/sociolinguistic realities, these sorts of programs aim not only to equip HL students with the tools they need to optimize their linguistic skills, but to also aid them in developing knowledge and a critical attitude regarding past, current, and future Hispanic/Latino issues in the context of the US (i.e. social, cultural, historical, etc.). Currently, although the number of such SHL programs continues to increase, it still falls short of meeting the demand of the growing HS population. Reasons for why this is so include, but are not limited to, insufficient administrative support, a generalized shortage of adequate pedagogical resources, and limited opportunities for practitioners to receive theoretically and instructionally sound training (e.g. Beaudrie 2012; Carreira 2014, 2016). A case in point is the repeated observation across the US whereby many HSs end up being (mis)placed in regular classes for L2 learners, where the curriculum and materials used for instruction are, for the most part, inappropriate for the needs of HSs (e.g. Valdés 2005; Carreira 2014). Considering this reality, substantial efforts are being made towards the adaptation of such materials and the development of strategies that will help teachers leverage the complementary skills/needs of HL and L2 learners. For example, Carreira (2016) offers a particularly useful list of strategies to assist students in mixed classes. Whilst the following list is not exhaustive, some of these strategies include the use of "flexible grouping" (i.e. the distribution of group/pair work in a way that fosters differentiated learning depending on the strengths/weaknesses of each student type), the use of "agendas" (i.e. a list of tasks that must be completed over an extended period of time so students can pace themselves depending on their own needs/abilities), or the use of "centers" (i.e. designated physical or virtual areas that contain different materials and activities for students to use depending, for example, on their needs or proficiency levels).[7]

Mindful of the importance of establishing relevance and applicability to the students' lives, identities, and personal interests (e.g. Kember et al. 2008), a number of scholars have also began to explore other ways that can positively affect HSs' development beyond the classroom walls. Fortunately, profiting from the application of interdisciplinary approaches, great work contributing to this vision has been already under way for some years. The emergence of service-learning pedagogies is one such example (e.g. Lowther Pereira 2015, 2016; Pascual y Cabo et al. 2017; Parker-Gwin 1996; Pak 2018). This pedagogical strategy aims to enhance the student's overall learning process via the appropriate integration of the academic curriculum with relevant community engagement. The goal therefore is not to have students do disconnected service/volunteer work, but to enable them to make, through careful planning and implementation in close collaboration with a community partner, explicit connections between what is learnt in the class and what they are asked to do outside of it.[8] Crucially, the desired outcome of this strategy is to benefit the community partner while promoting and underscoring students' continued personal/academic growth via personal reflections (e.g. Parker-Gwin 1996). It is through this kind of reflection that students' experiences become meaningful and can therefore serve as a stepping-stone to reach a higher understanding of the issues and topics discussed in class. As Leeman and colleagues (2011:296) noted, one way to get more out of this strategy is to use it in conjunction with critical pedagogical approaches that not only emphasize the students' active role in the learning process, but that also support and advocate for their "questioning of their own and others' taken-for-granted notions about language." In this sense, students are encouraged to make sense of the intrinsic relationship that exists between language, power, and identity, and to act upon it (e.g. Leeman 2012). It is through this active involvement that they can address (at least some of) the linguistic, socioaffective, and power issues they experience for being speakers of a minority language (e.g. Leeman et al. 2011; Lowther Pereira 2015).

22.4 Future Directions for Research and Practice

This chapter started with a brief report on recent demographic trends in the social make-up of US society, which, unsurprisingly, not only indicated that the number of Hispanics in the US has grown exponentially, but also

---

[7] For a more detailed explanation of these and other concepts/examples, the reader is referred to Carreira (2016).
[8] A few examples of well-planned service learning activities that integrate the above-mentioned conditions include working with an after-school program to develop Spanish HL literacy (Leeman et al. 2011), offering English tutoring services to adult Spanish speakers (Pak 2016), or providing assistance for newly arrived refugees and immigrants (Lowther Pereira 2015).

that in the years to come this trend will not change, at least not substantially. Given this, it is imperative that we continue refining our understandings of the particular social, cultural, and affective characteristics of the HS community as well as the unique experiences they endure. In doing so, we will be better able to make informed decisions regarding a series of important topics such as the acculturation, assimilation, and integration of HS speakers.

At this juncture, with the hope of spurring further developments in the field, I would like to point out a few suggestions for future directions in research and practice. As discussed earlier, from a linguistic perspective, most work done to date has convincingly shown that HSs' grammars, despite being significantly different from that of age-matched monolingual speakers of the same language, reveal a high degree of complexity and sophistication. Much effort has been put into charting and describing the above-mentioned differences, while at the same time hypothesizing about the source(s) of these outcomes. The progress of these efforts is noticeable, yet much remains to be done. Future studies should continue to examine these differences (as well as to replicate previous experimental work) so as to better trace the effects of input, age, literacy, and frequency on HS linguistic outcomes. In understanding these effects, we will be able to refine our knowledge of the nature of HS grammars. Another important observation that has not received enough attention is the inter- as well as the intra-speaker emerging variability that characterizes most HSs. Given our generalized lack of knowledge in this regard, developing explanations that account for this optionality and subsequently testing them seems to be most appropriate.

With regard to HL education, and considering the predicted growth of Spanish HSs for the next several decades, it is of utmost importance that we start (re)considering the goals of the field and the role HSs themselves are going to assume in the shaping of the Spanish teaching profession in the years to come (Torres *et al.* 2017). In this context, a fundamental and as yet underdeveloped line of research is concerned with examining the effectiveness of instruction. To date, only a handful of studies have explored this area directly (e.g. Potowski *et al.* 2009; Montrul and Bowles 2010; Torres 2013), and thus more research is warranted. Some of the questions that drive current research in this area include the following: What areas of HL knowledge does instruction affect? What is the role of explicit information/rule presentation in instructed HL acquisition? What type of knowledge results from instruction (explicit or implicit) and to what extent can it be used in spontaneous production?

Another promising area, which surprisingly has only recently started to receive attention in the SHL field, is that which examines the advantages and challenges of adopting new technologies to meet the students' interests and needs. As Giglio Henshaw (2016) and Torres (2016) note, while fully online and hybrid courses for L2 learners have become increasingly popular, technology-enhanced HL courses remain the exception.

Certainly, preliminary insights into the effectiveness of this method of HL teaching are encouraging (e.g. Giglio Henshaw 2016; Torres 2016), but more effort should be expended to further explore its impact in addressing the students' linguistic as well as socioaffective needs.

Relatedly, one area in which substantial improvement is needed is that of HS-specific instructor training. As Beaudrie and colleagues (2014) note, there is a general misconception among many – particularly among non-linguists – to the effect that any Spanish teacher should automatically be able and qualified to teach SHL courses. To be clear, as many before me have pointed out, this is far from being the case. It is important to bear in mind that instructors who are unfamiliar with the needs and strengths of HS students may come to the HL classroom with the mentality that they are responsible for fixing "a broken system" or even filling their students' linguistic "gaps." Often times, these instructors (inadvertently?) give authority to certain linguistic varieties, usually the standard ones, while delegitimizing others (e.g. García 2009; Showstack 2012). The exclusiveness of these monoglossic language ideologies tends to reinforce ill-informed prescriptive practices and deficit-views of HL bilingualism (e.g. del Valle 2000; García 2009). In turn, such an experience can result in a number of undesirable outcomes, such as HSs' development of negative attitudes towards their HL and culture, low self-esteem, poor academic achievement, etc. Unfortunately, such approaches to HL teaching and negative outcomes are repeatedly observed in schools and institutions of higher education across the country.

Considering all of the above, I join others in highlighting that SHL teachers should undergo specific training.[9] This training should go beyond language and grammar, in the narrowest sense, to also focus on becoming acquainted with both the external and internal factors that affect the acquisition, development, and maintenance of the HL. Central to this initiative, as Carreira and Kagan (2011) have pointed out, instructors need to know their particular student populations as well as the attitudes, goals, and motivations they bring to the classroom. One example that highlights the benefits of this approach to SHL teaching is Vergara Wilson and Ibarra (2015), who found that HL students react very positively to SHL methodology that highlights the value of their culture as well as the norms of their own speech communities, including code switching.

22.5 Concluding Remarks

The goal of this chapter, while modest in its reach, was to provide a general overview and a meaningful discussion of the main issues that are currently at the forefront of research in the field of Spanish as a heritage language,

---

[9] Ideally, novice HL instructors should have the opportunity to receive above-mentioned HS-specific training as well as to shadow/observe more experienced HL instructors before they are charged with the task of teaching their own HL section.

from both a theoretical linguistic and a pedagogical point of view. In doing so, due to the nature of this *Handbook*, the scope of this discussion has necessarily been broad, and, thus, some of its varied and inherent complexities oversimplified. Considering this, those interested in more in-depth discussion of the topics presented here are referred to the following sources (and references listed therein).

Heritage language teaching: Beaudrie *et al.* (2014); Fairclough and Beaudrie (2016), and Potowski (2005).
Critical pedagogies: Leeman (2005, 2012), Correa (2011).
Developing minority language resources: Valdés and colleagues (2006).
Translanguaging practices in the classroom environment: García *et al.* (2017).
Formal linguistic approaches to HL bilingualism: Montrul (2008, 2016a), Benmamoun *et al.* (2013).
Recent edited volumes that focus on a variety of topics within SHL: Beaudrie and Fairclough (2012), Pascual y Cabo (2016), Fairclough and Beaudrie (2016), Potowski (forthcoming).

References

Achugar, M. and Pessoa, S. (2009). Power and Place Language Attitudes towards Spanish in a Bilingual Academic Community in Southwest Texas. *Spanish in Context*, 6 (2), 199–223.
Alvord, S. and Rogers, B. (2014). Miami-Cuban Spanish Vowels in Contact. *Sociolinguistic Studies*, 8 (1), 139–170.
Amengual, M. (2012). Interlingual Influence in Bilingual Speech: Cognate Status Effect in a Continuum of Bilingualism. *Bilingualism: Language and Cognition*, 15 (3), 517–530.
Au, T., Oh, J., Knightly, L., Jun, S., and Romo, L. (2008). Salvaging a Childhood Language. *Journal of Memory and Language*, 58, 998–1011.
Baker, P. (1966). *Español para los hispanos*. Skokie, IL: National Textbook Company.
Barker, G. (1971). *Español para el bilingüe*. Skokie, IL: National Textbook Company.
Bartlett, L. and García, O. (2011). *Additive Schooling in Subtractive Times*. Nashville, TN: Vanderbilt University Press.
Beaudrie, S. (2011). Spanish Heritage Language Programs: A Snapshot of Current Programs in the Southwestern United States. *Foreign Language Annals*, 44 (2), 321–337.
Beaudrie, S. (2012). Research on University-Based Spanish Heritage Language Programs in the United States: The Current State of Affairs. In S. Beaudrie and M. Fairclough (eds.), *Spanish as a Heritage Language in the United States: The State of the Field*. Washington, DC: Georgetown University Press, pp. 203–221.

Beaudrie, S. and Ducar, C. (2005). Beginning Level University Heritage Language Programs: Creating a Space for all Heritage Language Learners. *Heritage Language Journal*, 3, 1–26.

Beaudrie, S., Ducar, C., and Potowski, K. (2014). *Heritage Language Teaching: Research and Practice*. Columbus, OH: McGraw-Hill.

Beaudrie, S. and Fairclough, M. (eds.). (2012). *Spanish as a Heritage Language in the United States: The State of the Field*. Washington, DC: Georgetown University Press.

Benmamoun, E., Montrul, S., and Polinsky, M. (2013). Heritage Languages and their Speakers: Opportunities and Challenges for Linguistics. *Theoretical Linguistics*, 39 (3–4), 129–181.

Carreira, M. (2014). Teaching Heritage Language Learners: A Study of Programme Profiles, Practices and Needs. In Peter Pericles Trifonas and Themistoklis Aravossitas (eds.), *Rethinking Heritage Language Education*. Cambridge: Cambridge University Press, pp. 20–44.

Carreira, M. (2016). A general framework and supporting strategies for teaching mixed classes. In D. Pascual y Cabo (ed.), *Advances in Spanish as a Heritage Language*. Amsterdam: John Benjamins, pp. 159–176.

Carreira, M. and Kagan, O. (2011). The results of the National Heritage Language Survey: Implications for Teaching, Curriculum Design, and Professional Development. *Foreign Language Annals*, 44 (1), 40–64.

Colantoni, L., Cuza, A., and Mazzaro, N. (2016). Task-Related Effects in the Prosody of Spanish Heritage Speakers and Long-Term Immigrants. In Meghan E. Armstrong, Nicholas Henriksen, and Maria del Mar Vanrell (eds.), *Intonational Grammar in Ibero-Romance: Approaches across Linguistic Subfields*. Amsterdam: John Benjamins, pp. 3–24.

Colombi, M. C. and Roca, A. (2003). Insights from Research and Practice in Spanish as a Heritage Language. In Ana Roca and M. Cecilia Colombi (eds.), *Mi lengua: Spanish as a Heritage Language in the United States*. Washington DC: Georgetown University Press, pp. 1–21.

Correa, M. (2011). Advocating for Critical Pedagogical Approaches to Teaching Spanish as a Heritage Language: Some Considerations. *Foreign Language Annals*, 44 (2), 308–320.

Cuza, A. (2013). Crosslinguistic Influence at the Syntax Proper: Interrogative Subject–Verb Inversion in Heritage Spanish. *International Journal of Bilingualism*, 17 (1), 71–96.

de Prada Pérez, A. and Pascual y Cabo, D. (2011). Invariable *gusta* in the Spanish of Heritage Speakers in the US. In Julia Herschensohn and Darren Tanner (eds.), *Proceedings of the 11th Generative Approaches to Second Language Acquisition Conference (GASLA 2011)*. Somerville, MA: Cascadilla, pp. 110–120.

del Valle, José. (2000). Monoglossic Policies for a Heteroglossic Culture: Misinterpreted Multilingualism in Modern Galicia. *Language and Communication*, 20, 105–132.

Ducar, C. (2012). SHL Learners' Attitudes and Motivations: Reconciling Opposing Forces. In S. Beaudrie and M. Fairclough (eds.), *Spanish as a Heritage Language in the United States: The State of the Field*. Washington, DC: Georgetown University Press, pp. 161–178.

Fairclough, M. and Beaudrie, S. (2016). *Innovative Strategies for Heritage Language Teaching: A Practical Guide for the Classroom*. Washington, DC: Georgetown University Press.

Galindo, L. (1995). Language Attitudes toward Spanish and English Varieties: A Chicano Perspective. *Hispanic Journal of Behavioral Sciences*, 17 (1), 77–99.

García, O. (2009). "Livin' and Teachin' *la Lengua Loca*": Localizing US Spanish Ideologies and Practices. In R. Salaberry (ed.), *Language Allegiances and Bilingualism in the US*. Clevedon: Multilingual Matters, pp. 151–171.

García, O., Johnson, S., and Seltzer., K. (2017). *The Translanguaging Classroom. Leveraging Student Bilingualism for Learning*. Philadelphia, PA: Caslon.

Giglio Henshaw, F. (2016). Online Courses for Heritage Learners. In D. Pascual y Cabo (ed.), *Advances in Spanish as a Heritage Language*. Amsterdam: John Benjamins, pp. 281–298.

Henriksen, N. (2012). The Intonation and Signaling of Declarative Questions in Manchego Peninsular Spanish. *Language and Speech*, 55 (4), 543–576.

Henriksen, N. (2015). Acoustic Analysis of the Rhotic Contrast in Chicagoland Spanish: An Intergenerational Study. *Linguistic Approaches to Bilingualism*, 5 (3), 285–321.

Hornberger, N. H. and Wang, S. C. (2008). Who are Our Heritage Language Learners? Identity and Biliteracy in Heritage Language Education in the United States. In D. M. Brinton, O. Kagan, and S. Bauckus (eds.), *Heritage Language Education: A New Field Emerging*. New York: Routledge, pp. 3–35.

Ingold, C. W., Rivers, W., Chavez Tesser, C., and Ashby, E. (2002). Report on the NFLC/AATSP Survey of Spanish Language Programs for Native Speakers. *Hispania*, 85 (2), 324–329.

Kember, D., Ho, A., and Hong, C. (2008). The Importance of Establishing Relevance in Motivating Student Learning. *Active Learning in Higher Education*, 9, 249–263.

Kim, J. Y. (2015). Perception and Production of Spanish Lexical Stress by Spanish Heritage Speakers and English L2 Learners of Spanish. In Erik W. Willis, Pedro Martín Butragueño, and Esther Herrera Zendejas (eds.), *Selected Proceedings of the 6th Conference on Laboratory Approaches to Romance Phonology*. Somerville, MA: Cascadilla, pp. 106–128.

King, K. A. (2000). Language Ideologies and Heritage Language Education. *International Journal of Bilingual Education and Bilingualism*, 3 (3), 167–184.

Kupisch, T. and Rothman, J. (2016). Terminology Matters! Why Difference is not Incompleteness and how Early Child Bilinguals are Heritage

Speakers. *International Journal of Bilingualism.* doi: 10.1177/1367006916654355.

Leeman, J. (2005). Engaging Critical Pedagogy: Spanish for Native Speakers. *Foreign Language Annals,* 38 (1), 35–45.

Leeman, J. (2012). Investigating Language Ideologies in Spanish as a Heritage Language. In S. Beaudrie and M. Fairclough (eds.), *Spanish as a Heritage Language in the United States: The State of the Field.* Washington DC: Georgetown University Press, pp. 43–59.

Leeman, J., Rabin, L., and Román-Mendoza, E. (2011). Critical Pedagogy beyond the Classroom Walls: Community Service-Learning and Spanish Heritage Language Education. *Heritage Language Journal,* 8 (3), 293–314.

Light, R. (1971). The Schools and the Minority Child's Language. *Foreign Language Annals,* 5 (1), 90–94.

Lowther Pereira, K. (2015). Developing Critical Language Awareness via Service-Learning for Spanish Heritage Speakers. *Heritage Language Journal,* 12, 2.

Lowther Pereira, K. (2016). New Directions in Heritage Language Pedagogy: Community Service Learning for Spanish Heritage Speakers. In D. Pascual y Cabo (ed.), *Advances in Spanish as a Heritage Language.* Amsterdam: John Benjamins, pp. 237–258.

MacGregor-Mendoza, P. (2000). *Aquí no se habla español*: Stories of Linguistic Repression in Southwest Schools. *Bilingual Research Journal,* 24 (4), 355–367.

Montrul, S. (2002). Competence and Performance Differences between Monolinguals and 2nd Generation Bilinguals in the Tense/Aspect Domain. In James F. Lee, Kimberly L. Geeslin, and J. Clancy Clements (eds.), *Structure, Meaning, and Acquisition in Spanish: Papers from the 4th Hispanic Linguistics Symposium.* Somerville, MA: Cascadilla, pp. 93–114.

Montrul, S. (2004). Subject and Object Expression in Spanish Heritage Speakers: A Case of Morphosyntactic Convergence. *Bilingualism: Language and Cognition,* 7 (2), 125–142.

Montrul, S. (2005). Second Language Acquisition and First Language Loss in Adult Early Bilinguals: Exploring Some Differences and Similarities. *Second Language Research,* 21 (3), 199–249.

Montrul, S. (2007). Interpreting Mood Distinctions in Spanish as a Heritage Language. In K. Potowski and R. Cameron (eds.), *Spanish in Contact.* Amsterdam: John Benjamins, pp. 23–40.

Montrul, S. (2008). *Incomplete Acquisition in Bilingualism: Re-examining the Age Factor.* Amsterdam: John Benjamins.

Montrul, S. (2009). Knowledge of Tense-Aspect and Mood in Spanish Heritage Speakers. *International Journal of Bilingualism,* 13 (2), 239–269.

Montrul, S. (2010). Dominant Language Transfer in Adult Second Language Learners and Heritage Speakers. *Second Language Research,* 26 (3), 293–327.

Montrul, S. (2011). Interfaces and Incomplete Acquisition. *Lingua*, 121, 591–604.

Montrul S. (2016a). *Heritage Language Acquisition*. Cambridge: Cambridge University Press.

Montrul, S. (2016b). Losing your Case? Dative Experiencers in Mexican Spanish and Heritage Speakers in the United States. In D. Pascual y Cabo (ed.), *Advances in Spanish as a Heritage Language*. Amsterdam: John Benjamins, pp. 99–124.

Montrul, S. and Bowles, M. (2009). Back to Basics: Incomplete Knowledge of Differential Object Marking in Spanish heritage Speakers. *Bilingualism: Language and Cognition*, 12 (3), 363–383.

Montrul, S. and Bowles, M. (2010). Is Grammar Instruction Beneficial for Heritage Language Learners? Dative Case Marking in Spanish. *Heritage Language Journal*, 7 (1), 47–73.

Montrul, S., Foote, R., and Perpiñán, S. (2008). Gender Agreement in Adult Second Language Learners and Spanish Heritage Speakers: The Effects of Age and Context of Acquisition. *Language Learning*, 58 (3), 503–553.

Montrul, S. and Sánchez-Walker, N. (2013). Differential Object Marking in Child and Adult Spanish Heritage Speakers. *Language Acquisition*, 20 (2), 109–132.

Müller, N. and Hulk, A. (2001). Crosslinguistic Influence in Bilingual First Language Acquisition: Italian and French as Recipient Languages. *Bilingualism: Language and Cognition*, 4 (1), 1–21.

Oh, J., Jun, S., Knightly, L., and Au, T. K. (2003). Holding on to Childhood Language Memory. *Cognition*, 86, B53–B64.

Pak, C. S. (2018). Linking Service-Learning with Sense of Belonging: A Culturally Relevant Pedagogy for Heritage Students of Spanish. *Journal of Hispanic Higher Education*, 17 (1), 76–95.

Parker-Gwin, R. (1996). Connecting Service to Learning: How Students and Communities Matter. *Teaching Sociology*, 24 (1), 97–101.

Pascual y Cabo, D. 2013. Agreement Reflexes of Emerging Optionality in Heritage Speaker Spanish (Doctoral dissertation). University of Florida.

Pascual y Cabo, D. (ed.) (2016). *Advances in Spanish as a Heritage Language*. Amsterdam: John Benjamins.

Pascual y Cabo, D. and Gómez Soler, I. (2015). Preposition Stranding in Heritage Speaker Spanish. *Heritage Language Journal*, 12 (2), 186–209.

Pascual y Cabo, D., Lingwall, A., and Rothman, J. (2012). Applying the Interface Hypothesis to Heritage Speaker Acquisition: Evidence from Spanish Mood. In Alia K. Biller, Esther Y. Chung, and Amelia E. Kimball (eds.), *Proceedings of the 36th Annual Boston University Conference on Language Development*. Somerville, MA: Cascadilla, pp. 437–448.

Pascual y Cabo, D., Prada, J., and Lowther Pereira, K. (2017). Effects of Community Service-Learning on Heritage Language Learners' Attitudes toward their Language and Culture. *Foreign Language Annals*, 50 (1), 71–83.

Pascual y Cabo, D. and Rothman, J. (2012). The (Il)logical Problem of Heritage Speaker Bilingualism and Incomplete Acquisition. *Applied Linguistics*, 33 (4), 1–7.

Pew Research Center (2008). *US Population Projections: 2005–2050*. Available from www.pewhispanic.org/2008/02/11/us-population-projections-2005-2050/ (last access December 12, 2017).

Pires, A. and J. Rothman. (2009). Disentangling Sources of Incomplete Acquisition: An Explanation for Competence Divergence across Heritage Grammars. *International Journal of Bilingualism*, 13 (2), 211–238.

Polinsky, M. and Kagan, O. (2007). Heritage Languages: In the "Wild" and in the Classroom. *Language and Linguistics Compass*, 1 (5), 368–395.

Potowski, K. (2005). *Fundamentos de la enseñanza del español a hispanohablantes en los EE.UU.* Madrid: Arco Libros.

Potowski, K. (2012). Identity and Heritage Language Learners: Moving beyond Essentializations. In S. Beaudrie and M. Fairclough (eds.), *Spanish as a Heritage Language in the US: The State of the Field*. Washington, DC: Georgetown University Press, pp. 179–199.

Potowski, K. (forthcoming) *The Routledge Handbook of Spanish as a Heritage/Minority Language*. New York: Routledge.

Potowski, K., Jegerski, J., and Morgan-Short, K. (2009). The Effects of Instruction on Linguistic Development in Spanish Heritage Language Speakers. *Language Learning*, 59 (3), 537–579.

Putnam, M. and Sánchez., L. (2013). What's so Incomplete about Incomplete Acquisition: A Prolegomenon to Modeling Heritage Language Grammars. *Linguistic Approaches to Bilingualism*, 3 (4), 476–506.

Rao, R. (2014). On the Status of the Phoneme /b/ in Heritage Speakers of Spanish. *Sintagma*, 26, 37–54.

Rao, R. (2016). On the Nuclear Intonational Phonology of Heritage Speakers of Spanish. In D. Pascual y Cabo (ed.), *Advances in Spanish as a Heritage Language*. Amsterdam: John Benjamins, pp. 51–80.

Rao, R. and Ronquest, R. (2015). The Heritage Spanish Phonetic/Phonological System: Looking Back and Moving Forward. *Studies in Hispanic and Lusophone Linguistics*, 8 (2), 403–414.

Robles-Puente, S. (2014). Prosody in Contact: Spanish in Los Angeles (Doctoral dissertation). University of Southern California.

Roca, A. (1997). Retrospectives, Advances, and Current Needs in the Teaching of Spanish to United States Hispanic Bilingual Students. *Association of Departments of Foreign Language Bulletin*, 29, 37–43.

Roca, A. (2000). Heritage Learners of Spanish. In Gail Guntermann (ed.), *Teaching Spanish with the Five C's: A Blueprint for Success*. Orlando, FL: Harcourt, pp. 91–106.

Ronquest, R. (2012). An Acoustic Analysis of Heritage Spanish Vowels (Doctoral dissertation). Indiana University.

Ronquest, R. (2013). An Acoustic Examination of Unstressed Vowel Reduction in Heritage Spanish. In Chad Howe *et al.* (eds.), *Selected*

Proceedings of the 15th Hispanic Linguistics Symposium. Somerville, MA: Cascadilla, pp. 157–171.

Rothman, J. (2007). Heritage Speaker Competence Differences, Language Change and Input Type: Inflected Infinitives in Heritage Brazilian Portuguese. *International Journal of Bilingualism*, 11, 359–389.

Rothman, J. and Treffers-Daller, J. (2014). A Prolegomenon to the Construct of the Native Speaker: Heritage Speaker Bilinguals are Natives Too! *Applied Linguistics*, 35 (1), 93–98.

Rothman, J., Tsimpli, M. I., and Pascual y Cabo, D. (2016). Formal Linguistic Approaches to Heritage Language Acquisition: Bridges for Pedagogically Oriented Research. In D. Pascual y Cabo (ed.), *Advances in Spanish as a Heritage Language*. Amsterdam: John Benjamins, pp. 11–26.

Showstack, R. E. (2012). Symbolic Power in the Heritage Language Classroom: How Spanish Heritage Speakers Sustain and Resist Hegemonic Discourses on Language and Cultural Diversity. *Spanish in Context*, 9 (1), 1–26.

Silva-Corvalán, C. (1986). Bilingualism and Language Change: The Extension of *estar* in Los Angeles Spanish. *Language*, 62 (3), 587–608.

Silva-Corvalán, C. (1994). *Language Contact and Change: Spanish in Los Angeles*. New York: Oxford University Press.

Silva-Corvalán, C. (2014). *Bilingual Language Acquisition: Spanish and English in the First Six Years*. Cambridge: Cambridge University Press.

Torres, J. (2013). Heritage and Second Language Learners of Spanish: The Roles of Task Complexity and Inhibitory Control (Doctoral dissertation). Georgetown University.

Torres, J. (2016). Flipping the Classroom. In D. Pascual y Cabo (ed.), *Advances in Spanish as a Heritage Language*. Amsterdam: John Benjamins, pp. 299–324.

Torres, J., Pascual y Cabo, D., and Beusterien, J. (2017). What's Next? Heritage Language Learners Shape New Paths in Spanish Teaching. *Hispania*, 100 (5), 271–276.

Valdés, G. (1995). The Teaching of Minority Languages as Academic Subjects: Pedagogical and Theoretical Challenges. *The Modern Language Journal*, 79 (3), 299–328.

Valdés, G. (2001). *Learning and Not Learning English: Latino Students in American Schools*. New York: Teachers College Press.

Valdés, G. (2005). Bilingualism, Heritage Language Learners, and SLA Research: Opportunities Lost or Seized? *The Modern Language Journal*, 89 (3), 410–426.

Valdés-Fallis, G. (1975). Teaching Spanish to the Spanish-Speaking: Classroom Strategies. *System*, 3 (1), 54–62.

Valdés-Fallis, G. (1976). Language Development versus the Teaching of the Standard Language. *Lektos: Interdisciplinary Working Papers in Language Sciences*, Special Issue, 20–32.

Valdés-Fallis, G. (1978). A Comprehensive Approach to the Teaching of Spanish to Bilingual Spanish-Speaking Students. *Modern Language Journal*, 43 (3), 101–110.

Valdés, G., Fishman, J., Chávez R., and Pérez, W. (2006). *Developing Minority Language Resources. The Case of Spanish in California*. Clevedon: Multilingual Matters.

Valenzuela, E., Iverson, M., Rothman, J., Borg, K., Pascual y Cabo D., and Pinto, M. (2015). Eventive and Stative Passives and Copula Selection in Canadian and American Heritage Speaker Spanish. In I. Pérez-Jiménez, M. Leonetti, and S. Gumiel-Molina (eds.), *New Perspectives on the Study of ser and estar*. Amsterdam: John Benjamins, pp. 267–292.

Vergara Wilson, D. and Ibarra, C. Enrique. (2015). Understanding the Inheritors: The Perception of Beginning-Level Students toward their Spanish as a Heritage Language program. *E-JournALL, EuroAmerican Journal of Applied Linguistics and Languages*, 2 (2), 85–101.

Willis, E. (2005). An Initial Examination of Southwest Spanish Vowels. *Southwest Journal of Linguistics*, 24, 185–198.

Zapata, G., Sánchez, L., and Toribio, A. J. (2005). Contact and Contracting Spanish. *International Journal of Bilingualism*, 9, 377–395.

23

Geographic Varieties of Spanish

Elena Fernández de Molina Ortés
and Juan M. Hernández-Campoy

23.1 Spanish World-Wide

Spanish[1] is used as a mother tongue by more than 472 million speakers from all over the world, according to official data from the Instituto Cervantes (2016). As is shown in Figure 23.1, Spanish is a world-wide international language spoken on four continents and is established as the official language in 22 countries: Spain; Mexico, Colombia, Argentina, Peru, Venezuela, Chile, Ecuador, Cuba, Dominican Republic, Bolivia, El Salvador, Guatemala, Honduras, Paraguay, Nicaragua, Costa Rica, Puerto Rico, Uruguay, and Panama (Latin America); Equatorial Guinea (west Africa); and the Philippines (south-east Asia).

This geographical dispersion of the Spanish language has entailed linguistic diversity within the Spanish-speaking world and the rich proliferation of regional varieties, with pronunciation, grammatical, and/or lexical-semantic variation – although mutual intelligibility still prevails (see also Lipski 2012).

The aim of this chapter is to provide a superficial overview of how Spanish varies across the geographic regions where it is spoken. In a departure from the traditional approach to dialectology, where European Spanish is considered separately from Latin American Spanish, this chapter takes as the starting premise the view that geographic variation is a special case of sociolinguistic variation. This allows both for different regions to be characterized by the combination of features attested in the Spanish spoken there and for the establishment of connections through diagnostic features

---

[1] The terms "Spanish" and "Spanish language" are used here to refer generally to the language spoken in Spain, Latin America and other Spanish-speaking areas all over the world. "Castilian" will be used here to refer to the historic dialect of Spanish spoken in Castile, in the northern geographical areas of Spain.

Figure 23.1 Geographical distribution of Spanish in the world

at dialectal and sociolectal levels. After discussing issues such as standardization, supralocalization, and transplantation in the context of sociolinguistic patterns in international Spanish, the concept of the Pan-Hispanic Norm will be examined, with special emphasis on the prestige and identity that varieties of Spanish have for their native speakers. The different geographic varieties of Spanish will be then described in relation to the contemporary linguistic changes and tendencies that characterize these dialects. Obviously, given the editorial limits on chapter length, coverage of all issues and levels of analysis in all varieties is impossible.

23.2 Standardization, Supralocalization, and Transplantation: Prestige Patterns

The concept of "standard" in language varieties is inevitably associated with extralinguistic practices (see Milroy and Milroy 1985; Trudgill 1998; Milroy 1999, 2000, 2001; Hernández-Campoy 2007; Hernández-Campoy and Villena-Ponsoda 2009, for example). The rise of varieties to the status of national standard normally results from economic, social, political, geographic, and historical circumstances, such as the nationalistic centralization of states. The development and standardization of Castilian Spanish in the Iberian peninsula during Renaissance times was also favored by extralinguistic factors. Nation-building and the creation and perception of a national identity had been a consciously planned project at the level of the state in which language deliberately played a prominent role: "Nationhood was consequently linked to the use of Spanish" (Penny 2000:206). This process of standardization and subsequent supralocalization is termed "Castilianization," i.e. the expansion of Spanish features from Old Castile in north-central Spain from the 10th century on (Molina-Martos 2008:59). The term "Castilian" (*castellano*) comes from *romance castellano*, and refers to the language variety descended from the mixture of Hispano-Romance or Latin-based Spanish dialects originally spoken in the northern areas of the Iberian peninsula during the Middle Ages (Penny 2000:204–205). It is also a superposed variety of language that, having been modified through the centuries by the learned (courtly people, scholars, writers, etc.), came to be regarded as the model for all those who wished to speak and write well (see Menéndez Pidal 1926; López-García 1985; Penny 1991, 2000; Moreno-Fernández 2005, 2007; García Mouton 2006, 2014; Villena-Ponsoda 2006).

Crucial for the expansion of Castilian was the fact that Alfonso X used this variety in his administrative, literary, and scientific writings during the 13th century, rather than other Latin-based Hispano-Romance varieties, Latin, Arabic or Hebrew: "The politically unifying effects of promoting the use of written Castilian in the 13th century are therefore evident" (Penny 2000:205). His aim when sponsoring works written in Castilian Spanish was to produce a linguistic model which could be imitated by other writers, as indeed occurred later during the 15th and 16th centuries. Following the union of the crowns of Castile and Aragon in 1469 – with the marriage of Queen Isabella I of Castile and King Ferdinand II of Aragon, known as "the Catholic Monarchs" – and the discovery of America by Christopher Columbus in 1492, the term *español* ('Spanish') began to be used to refer to the language of the Spanish Empire: Spain, "the Balearic Islands, much of central and southern Italy, Sicily, Sardinia, the Canary Islands, and America (mistakenly thought to be the Indies)" (Penny 2000:205). With Castile established as the dominant power, the Castilian variety of Spanish was used increasingly in situations of prestige and influence (the court, the church, and the army), in legal documents, in the administration of the incipient Spanish state and its empire, and in the prolific literary and artistic output of that period (known as the Spanish "Golden Age," whose writers included Cervantes, Lope de Vega, Calderón, Quevedo, Garcilaso, etc.) (see García Mouton 2006:154). The introduction of the printing press in Spain by Juan Arias Dávila in 1472 – following its invention in Germany in the 1440s by Johannes Gutenberg – was a powerful force in the expansion of the Castilian variety, contributing to (i) ruling out regional variation and the possible effects that the multiplicity of local varieties would have had on the mutual intelligibility of groups and individuals from different areas of the country; and (ii) removing concerns about the effect that the lack of a standard would have had for the preservation and diffusion of texts, which was basically the concern of literary authors at a time when the notion of authorship was making its appearance. The subsequent internationalization of Spanish was directly connected to colonization (see Villa and del Valle 2015).

23.2.1 The Pan-Hispanic Linguistic Norm

Standardization is inherently a process that promotes uniformity and invariance (see Haugen 1966/1972; Trudgill 1998; Milroy 1999, 2001). Most processes of standardization of Castilian Spanish occurred in Spain, with the subsequent prescriptive results being exported to the rest of the Spanish-speaking world during the colonial period (Penny 2000:195). It was during the 18th century, for example, that language policies were established as stages of codification of linguistic norms (corpus planning): the creation in 1713 of the Spanish Royal Academy (Real Academia de la Lengua Española, RAE) to standardize, fix, and create the norms of the national language, with their subsequent publications, such as its first authoritative dictionary (*Diccionario de autoridades*, RAE 1771a), the *Ortografía* for spelling norms (RAE 1741) and the *Gramática de la lengua castellana* (RAE 1771b), as its three main normative pillars. In 1768, Charles III decreed that the Castilian variety was to be used officially throughout the kingdom both in administration and in education (see Mar-Molinero 1997, 2000; Villa and del Valle 2015). For some centuries, American Spanish was considered as deviant from the norm, and its words and uses as "barbarisms," as denounced by Vicente Salvá in his *Nuevo diccionario de la lengua castellana* (1846). This lack of recognition of the American varieties and the old Eurocentric-based linguistic descriptions of Spanish has recently undergone a change in attitude, giving way "to a more global perception of what constitutes 'good' Spanish, as well as to an attempt at establishing a Pan-Hispanic norm obtained from a common ground among different varieties" (Sánchez and Almela 2015:341). Since the second half of the 20th century, when the potential fragmentation of Spanish into unintelligible varieties was perceived to threaten its unity, American Spanish has been taken into account in the development of prescriptive planning of the language (Penny 2000:196). The world-wide range of Spanish, open to substantial variation across geographical areas, with the resulting rich mosaic of dialectal varieties, and the expansion of sociolinguistic approaches to language, has meant an impetus now for the recognition of that Pan-Hispanic dialectal heritage and the development of actions to preserve it. The creation of the ASALE (Asociación de Academias de la Lengua Española) in 1951 was the culmination of the Pan-Hispanic movement, aiming to embrace the pluricentric character of the Spanish language and the promotion of unity and appreciation of linguistic diversity instead of purity and conservatism (Villa and del Valle 2015:574). This new codification of Spanish is more sensitive to language variation and describes varieties of specific geographical areas of varying size (supranational, national, regional) as autonomous entities (Lope Blanch 2001; Demonte 2003), moving from exonormative to endonormative criteria in their linguistic descriptions (Moreno-Fernández 2006:83–90): the 22nd edition of the RAE's *Diccionario* (RAE 2001), the *Diccionario panhispánico de dudas* (RAE and ASALE 2005) and the *Diccionario de americanismos* (ASALE 2010); the *Nueva gramática de la lengua española* (RAE and ASALE 2009) – with the *Manual de la nueva gramática* (RAE and ASALE 2010a) – and the *Nueva gramática básica* (RAE and ASALE 2011); and the 2010 edition of the *Ortografía* (RAE and ASALE 2010b)

23.2.2 Prestige Perceptions and Identity

Together with political, social, cultural, and commercial components, standardization also conveys ideological as well as identificational motivations (see Deyer 2007; Hernández-Campoy 2016:51–62). Standardization has thus traditionally been closely related to processes of nation-building and its subsequent tendencies towards nationalist centralization, as it favors the aims of internal integration and external segregation in terms of symbolism: language becomes a symbol for society. In the past, the view of languages in society was determined by the position occupied by some of the European ones which, since the Renaissance, had been established as national languages in the growing nation-states of Europe. Any other varieties were considered deviations from the standard, inferior or even "primitive" systems, and hence were *inadequate* as a means of communication.

In any process of linguistic standardization, the promotion of one variety to the status of standard triggers the devaluation of the other linguistic varieties present within the boundaries of the multilingual or multidialectal nation-state and impinges upon their domains. This means that the development of the standard may eventually lead to the authoritative extension of a class-based use of language as an example of correctness, inducing a majority of native speakers to believe that their (dialectal) usage is incorrect (see Hope 2000; Trudgill 1975, 2002). Along with a process of prestige norm focusing, there comes the association of the standard with the idea of what is correct, adequate, and aesthetically pleasing, on the one hand, and of the non-standard with what is incorrect, inadequate, and even unattractive, on the other (see Alvar 2012:15; Bizer 2004:246–247; López-Morales 2004:290–291; Hernández-Campoy 2004; Villena-Ponsoda 2005:44; Narbona 2009:26). In fact, as Milroy (2001:531) states, standardization constitutes the imposition of a "legitimized" uniformity upon linguistic variation for (social, economic, political, historical, regional, etc.) prestige reasons.

In studies carried out in both in Spain and America, the cognitively most favorably evaluated Spanish varieties are those of northern Spain, due to the prestige associated with standard Castilian. In Spain, this evaluation has been found both in speakers from Old Castile itself – whose native dialect enjoys overt prestige (see Cestero and Paredes 2015) – and in those from Valencia (Blas Arroyo 1994) and Seville (Santana Marrero 2016) – whose native dialect is not Castilian (see also Moreno-Fernández and

Moreno-Fernández 2002) – for example. Affectively, however, speakers from southern Spain are perceived to be better in the same studies (Blas Arroyo 1994; Santana Marrero 2016). Likewise, although coverage of all situations here is impossible, the Spanish from Spain has been the most positively considered in Chile (Rojas 2012), Costa Rica (Calvo and Castillo 2014), and Mexico (Moreno de Alba 1998; Erdösová 2011), where it is viewed as proper Spanish speech.

23.3 Varieties of Spanish around the World

23.3.1 Contemporary Linguistic Changes and Sociolinguistic Variation

According to Moreno-Fernández and Otero Roth (2008), there are two types of linguistic varieties in Spanish world-wide: (i) *conservative varieties*, which preserve the traditional linguistic features (mostly phonetic) characterizing Standard Spanish and geographically located in Castile, the Mexican interior and the Andes; and (ii) *innovative varieties*, which linguistically diverge from traditional standard features and are found in Andalusia, Extremadura, Murcia, and the Canary Islands in Spain, and in the Caribbean and River Plate regions in America. Diachronically speaking, the formation of these two main types of regional dialects of Spanish may be accounted for with the consideration of some general principles that have been constraining the pronunciation of sounds since the early Middle Ages – mostly affecting syllable structure and phonological inventories (Villena-Ponsoda and Vida-Castro 2004). On the one hand, innovative varieties underwent a set of latent phonological changes, deletion of codas, and simplification of the phonological inventory (Moreno-Fernández 2004) as a consequence of dialect contact and koineization during the period of resettlement of areas conquered by the Christians from the Arabs and the subsequent mélange of people (Penny 2000). As we will see below, since medieval times coda deletion and onset simplification have led to open syllables, as well as to geographically and socially salient mergers such as *ceceo* and *seseo*. These unmarked options produced a series of chain shifts which are responsible for, among others, the contemporary Andalusian dialect (Villena-Ponsoda 2001, 2008). On the other hand, conservative varieties did not undergo the above-mentioned changes, but rather reinforced codas and maintain marked contrasts between dental and alveolar consonants (*ts, dz* vs. *s, z*). The pronunciation of the standard variety remains close to that of the conservative varieties (see Table 23.1), though some differences remain: (i) the contrast /ʎ/–/j/ coexists with merger /j/ ("*yeísmo*": *callo–rayo*), though this last option is more frequent among urban young speakers; (ii) consonant clusters (as [kθ] in *acción* [akˈθjon]) tend to be simplified in conservative varieties through a wide range of realizations; and (iii) elision of /d/ is gaining in frequency among urban speakers in informal styles.

Table 23.1 *Salient features in innovative and conservative varieties of Spanish spoken in Spain*

Standard Castilian	Conservative dialects (north)	Innovative dialects (south)	Gloss
las casas [-s]	[las'kasas] [-s]	[læʰˈkæsæ]/[læˈkæsæ]	*the houses*
caja [-x-]	[ˈkaxa] [-x-]	[ˈkaʰa]/[ˈkaː] [-h-]/Ø	*box*
gente [x-]	[ˈxénte] [x-]	[ˈʰente] [h-]	*people*
coger [-r]	[koxer] [-r]	[koˈʰɛ] Ø	*to take*
piel [-l]	[ˈpjel] [-l]	[ˈpjɛ] Ø	*skin*
luz [-θ]	[ˈluθ] [-θ]	[ˈlu] Ø	*light*
soldado [-l-]	[solˈðaðo] [-l-]	[solˈðaðo]/[sorˈðaðo] [-l-]~[-r-]	*soldier*
casa [-s-]	[ˈkasa] [-s-]	[ˈkasa]–[ˈkaθa] [-s-]~[-θ-]*	*house*
caza [-θ-]	[ˈkaθa] [-θ-]	[ˈkaθa]–[ˈkasa] [-θ-]~[-s-]*	*hunting*
cacho [tʃ]	[ˈkatʃo] [-tʃ-]	[ˈkaʃo] [-ʃ-]	*bit*
lección [-n]	[lekˈθjon] [-n]	[leˈθjõ] Ø	*lesson*
rayo [j]	[ˈrajo] [-j-]	[ˈraʒo] [-ʒ-]	*lightning*
callo [ʎ]	[ˈkaʎo] ~ [ˈkajo] [ʎ] ~ [j]	[ˈkaʒo] [-ʒ-]	*corn*
vosotros tenéis	vosotros tenéis	vosotros tenéis~ustedes tenéis	*you have*

Results of research on linguistic variation have revealed differences in the use and social evaluation of the main innovative and conservative features in World Spanish (see Hernández-Campoy and Jiménez Cano 2003; Villena-Ponsoda and Vida-Castro 2004 or Hernández-Campoy and Villena-Ponsoda 2009, for example, for European Spanish; and Chang 2008; Díaz-Campos and Gradoville 2011; Schmidt and Willis 2011; or Willis *et al.* 2015, among others, for Latin-American Spanish). Certain innovating variants are widespread and fully accepted by urban educated speakers, whereas others are strenuously rejected as rural or coarse. Andalusian dialects, as well as Canarian and Caribbean varieties, are the most salient innovating varieties of Spanish (see also Clements 2009).

Yeísmo vs. Palatal /j/–/ʎ/ Distinction

The contrast between the voiced palatal lateral /ʎ/ (as in *pollo*) and the voiced palatal fricative /j/ (as in *poyo*) has traditionally characterized Castilian Spanish. However, the merger of the two consonants into /j/, known as *yeísmo*, is spreading from southern non-standard varieties (mostly western Andalusia) to the north (Molina-Martos 2013, in press), and more frequently among urban young speakers, in a process that began roughly in the 16th century (Penny 2000:121).

(23.1) $\dfrac{/j/}{/ʎ/} > /j/$

Along with northern varieties of European Spanish, the palatal /j/–/ʎ/ distinction is retained only in the Andes areas (highlands of Bolivia, Peru, Ecuador, Colombia, Chile, and Paraguay; see Hualde 2005:180) of American Spanish. The realization as /ʒ/ (known as "*rehilamiento*" or "*ʒeísmo*") is usual in the River Plate region and Chile in South American

Spanish and in some parts of Extremadura and Andalusia in European Spanish.

Intervocalic /ð/ Deletion vs. Maintenance in European and Latin-American Spanishes

D-dropping consists in the gradual elimination of intervocalic <d> in pronunciation (/ð/), which, however, is maintained in orthography (see also Penny 2000:4; or Simonet *et al.* 2012). The variable deletion of intervocalic /ð/ usually occurs in words ending with the sequences *-ado/ada* and *-ido/ida*. This variation in use provides us with two possibilities for words like *comido* 'eaten.'

(23.2)   Variant /ð/:   Standard Castilian pronunciation   [koˈmiðo]
          Variant Ø: Non-standard pronunciation   [koˈmio]

According to Narbona *et al.* (1998:176), D-dropping is becoming a widespread phenomenon in the casual speech of European Spanish. This traditionally salient feature of non-standard southern Spanish varieties is currently a phenomenon in expansion in apparently standard Castilian Spanish-speaking areas in the northern regions of Spain. It was studied by Williams (1987) in Valladolid, a city in Old Castile, where she found that it is subject to both social and stylistic variation, with a conscious use of the standard Castilian variant in formal contexts (see Penny 1991 and 2000). Similar patterns have been found in Toledo and Madrid (Molina-Martos 1991, 1998, 2001), Alcalá de Henares (Blanco 2004), Getafe (Martín Butragueño 1991), and Barcelona (Turell 1996). In southern areas, such as Murcia and Andalusia, D-dropping is also a marker, though it is both stylistically and socially more widespread (see Narbona *et al.* 1998:176–181; and Hernández-Campoy and Jiménez-Cano 2003:339–340): the non-standard variant is consistently much more frequently found in formal situations and upper social classes in the Spanish of Murcia than in that of Old Castile. Similar patterns have been found in Las Palmas (Samper 1990; Samper and Pérez 1998), Córdoba (Uruburu 1996), coastal Granada (García Marcos 1990), Almería (García Marcos and Fuentes González 1996), La Jara (Paredes-García 1996), Málaga (Bedinghaus and Sedó 2014), and Mérida (Fernández de Molina 2014). A similar situation of indexicalized variability in the use of intervocalic /ð/ is found in American Spanish, as is shown in Table 23.2, with predominance of /ð/ maintenance (see also Díaz-Campos and Gradoville 2011).

Seseo, Ceceo and /s/–/θ/ Distinction

Since the 13th century, coda deletion and onset simplification have resulted in open syllables, as well as to mergers between old Castilian dental (*ç, z*, as in *caça* 'hunting' and *pozo* 'pit, well') and alveolar (*s, ss*, as in *casa* 'house,' *poso* 'dregs'; cf. *oso* 'bear' and *osso* 'I dare') consonants, which can be understood as southern *ceceo* and *seseo* in embryonic form. In both cases there is an ongoing process of neutralization of the contrast between

Table 23.2 *Realization of intervocalic /ð/ in European and American Spanishes*

Area	/ð/ maintenance	/ð/ dropping
Toledo (Molina-Martos 1998)	80%	20%
Valladolid (Williams 1987)	10%	90%
Córdoba (Uruburu 1996)	66%	33%
Madrid (barrio de Salamanca) (Molina-Martos 2006)	78%	21%
Getafe (Martín Butragueño 1991)	68%	32%
Bilbao (Etxebarria 1985)	64%	19%
Valencia (Gómez Molina 2010)	89.93%	10.07%
Jaén (Moya-Corral 1979)	35.3%	64.7%
Granada (Moya-Corral 2008)	73.3%	23.1%
Melilla (Ruiz Domínguez 1997)	52%	48%
Mérida (Fernández de Molina 2014)	42.5%	57.5%
Linares (Jaén) (Gómez Serrano 1994)	22%	78%
Málaga (Villena-Ponsoda 2008)	24%	71%
Las Palmas de Gran Canaria (Samper-Padilla 1990)	62.32%	37.68%
Puerto Rico (López Morales 1983)	79%	21%
Panama (Cedergren 1973)	68%	20%
Caracas (D'Introno and Sosa 1986)	67.8%	11.5%
Venezuela (Puerto Cabello) (Navarro 1995)	72%	28%
Lima (Caravedo 1990)	79%	16%

the voiceless fricative alveolar /s/ (as in *casa* 'house') and the voiceless fricative interdental /θ/ (as in *caza* 'hunt') through merger, having as outcome *ceceo* (when /s/ becomes /θ/: *casa* ['kasa] > ['kaθa]) or, otherwise, *seseo* (when /θ/ becomes /s/: *caza* ['kaθa] > ['kasa]):

(23.3) *ceceo*: $\frac{/\theta/}{/s/} > /\theta/$

 seseo: $\frac{/\theta/}{/s/} > /s/$

Seseo probably had its origins in late medieval Seville, whereas *ceceo* seems to have developed during the 17th century in coastal regions of Andalusia (Penny 2000:119–120). Both cases are currently salient features in Andalusian Spanish (see Figure 23.2), as is *seseo* in American Spanish. The most striking feature of Andalusian Spanish is the social prestige associated with the /s/–/θ/ distinction, which enhances the split of the early merger of old Castilian fricatives. This merger existed as the unique variant among some of the eastern and central Andalusian varieties until recently. The acquisition, therefore, of the standard Castilian prestigious distinction is an ongoing change from above led by young urban educated speakers in Andalusia. This change probably started around the middle of the 20th century (see Moya-Corral and Wiedemann 1995; Villena-Ponsoda 1996, 2001), and the use of the Castilian form increases with the speaker's educational level and decreases with his or her age. Urban university graduates have accepted the convergent inventory, and educated speakers born after 1970 use the /s/–/θ/ distinction pattern consistently. The *seseo*

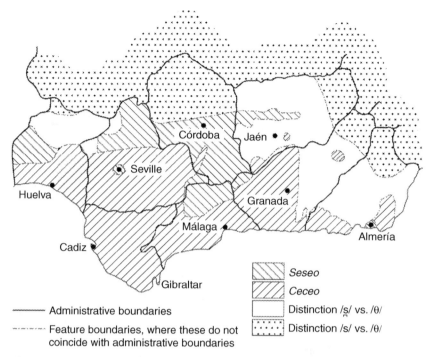

Figure 23.2 Geographical distribution of *seseo* and *ceceo* in Andalusia
Source: Penny (2000:120; Figure 4.1)

phenomenon was also formerly a salient feature in the coastal and inland areas of Murcia and Alicante (see Grandal-López 1999 and Abad-Merino 2004) and Extremadura (Fernández de Molina 2012, 2015b).

Aspiration Phenomena or Maintenance in Velar Sounds

The uvular pronunciation [χ] of the velar fricative /x/ (as in *caja* [ˈkaχa] 'box') used in the northern areas of Spain and in standard Castilian undergoes a process of aspiration (see Table 23.1) in the southwest and central south (most of Andalusia, New Castile, and Extremadura, but not in Murcia): [ˈkaʰa]. But even in those areas the realization of /x/ as aspirated or standard is also socially indexical, conditioned by age and social background (Villena-Ponsoda 2001). In Latin American Spanish the general tendency is the aspirated production and no alternation with the velar fricative /x/ realization, as in Caribbean Spanish, where this categorical use implies no social value for this variable (see Willis *et al.* 2015; also Hualde 2005 and Aleza and Enguita 2010).

A similar outcome of aspiration occurs in the case of postvocalic /s/. There is a weakening of /s/ in syllable-final postvocalic position, as in *estos* (> [ˈeʰtoʰ]), tending to a kind of glottalization or aspiration; this is a change that started during the late medieval period, gaining ground in Andalusia. Its extension to America was not as universal as in the case of *seseo* or *yeísmo* (see Penny 2000:122–125; see Table 23.3), but it has a gradual

Table 23.3 Realization of postvocalic /s/ in European and American Spanishes

Area	Word-medial				Word-final			
	S3	S2	S1	S0	S3	S2	S1	S0
	maintenance	aspiration	assimilation	dropping	maintenance	aspiration	assimilation	dropping
Alcalá de Henares (Blanco 2004)	1.1%	77.4%	5.3%	8.4%	64%	30%	4%	2%
Getafe (Martín Butragueño 1995)	62.38%	34.94%	–	0.94%	47.88%	34.83%	–	9.34%
Toledo (Calero 1993)	64.5%	23.2%	8%	4%	52%	32%	3%	12%
Toledo (Molina-Martos 1998)	56%	39%	4%	2%	48.5%	17.6%	16.6%	17.2%
Las Palmas de Gran Canaria (Samper-Padilla 1990)	5%	94%	–	2.6%	3.6%	45.7%	7.9%	42.6%
Málaga (Vida-Castro 2005)	0.3%	89.7%	0.4%	9.6%	1.8%	14.7%	–	83.4%
Mérida (Fernández de Molina 2014)	5.66%	94.21%	–	0.02%	13.46%	31.49%	0.24%	54.79%
Puerto Rico (López Morales 1983)	7.4%	80.8%	–	11.6%	9.6%	43.8%	–	46.5%
Panama (Cerdegren 1973)	2%	57%	–	41%	14%	36%	–	50%
Cuba (Terrell 1979)	–	–	–	–	3%	97%	–	0%
Buenos Aires (Terrell 1978)	12%	80%	–	8%	46%	40%	–	14%

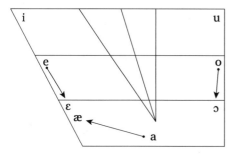

Figure 23.3 Southern European Spanish eight-vowel system

nature (see also Erker 2010; Schmidt and Willis 2011; File-Muriel and Brown 2011; Torreira and Ernestus 2011, 2012).

Vowel Changes in Spanish

Southern varieties of European Spanish, such as Murcian and Andalusian, have a distinctive eight-vowel system (see Figure 23.3). The vowels /ɛ/, /ɔ/ and /æ/ are the result of the historic loss of word-final consonants (see "Consonant Loss," below) after /e/, /o/ and /a/, respectively (with the exception of /a/ preceding deleted /d/, as in the pronunciation of *verdad* 'truth' as [berˈða]), and also of assimilation of consonant clusters word-internally (see Hernández-Campoy and Trudgill 2002).

Some important current morphosyntactic distinctions, such as plurality and person, are marked with vowel quality, not with *-s* endings, in these varieties of Spanish, because of postvocalic consonant loss (Hernández-Campoy 2003, 2011; Monroy-Casas and Hernández-Campoy 2015).

There is also vowel harmony with /ɛ/, /ɔ/ and /æ/, and the occurrence of these vowels at any point in a word prohibits /e/, /o/, and /a/, respectively, in any preceding syllable, with the exception of closed vowels /i, u/ (Hernández-Campoy and Trudgill 2002). In this way, a plural word with these vowel ingredients, such as *mañanas*, is pronounced as [mæˈɲænæ] rather than [maˈɲanas].

Third-Person Pronoun Reference: *Leísmo, Laísmo* and *Loísmo*

A salient feature differentiating Old Castile Spanish from the rest of European Spanish is third–person pronoun reference. The older case-determined system of reference distinguishes the use of *le(s)*: generic indirect object pronoun(s) used for direct object, or *leísmo* (*le quiero* 'I love him/her'); *lo(s)*: generic direct object pronoun(s) used for indirect object, or *loísmo* (*el presidente los mintió* 'the president lied to them'); and *la(s)*: feminine direct object pronoun(s) used for indirect object, or *laísmo* (*la conté mi historia* 'I told her my story'). Whereas most dialectal varieties of Spanish (including American) use only *leísmo* – which is the pattern adopted in standard – Old Castile Spanish areas, nevertheless, still has the older case-determined system of reference, using *lo(s)* just for masculine indirect pronouns and *la(s)* for feminine ones (see Martínez-Martín 1984; Moreno-

Table 23.4 *Examples of neutralization of distinction between liquid consonants*

l > r			
algo > *argo* 'something'	*alta* > *arta* 'high'	*baldosa* > *bardosa* 'floor tile'	*faltar* > *fartar* 'to be missing'
r > l			
comer > *comel* 'to eat'	*olor* > *olol* 'smell'	*amor* > *amol* 'love'	*mujer* > *mujel* 'woman'

Fernández et al. 1988; Fernández-Ordóñez 1999; Ruiz 2003; Blanco 2004; Paredes-García 2006).

Merger of Liquid Consonants: /l/ – /r/

The distinction between liquid consonants /l/ and /r/ is neutralized (or even switched) in coda position in the pronunciation of some non-standard varieties, which is stigmatized as vulgar Spanish and associated with uneducated speakers – although it was attested in the 15th and 17th centuries expanding from medieval northern Spain (León and Galicia). Whereas the change of /l/ into /r/ mostly occurs in word-medial position, the opposite process (r > l) takes place in word-final position (Table 23.4). According to Penny (2000:127), this feature was transported to America as part of the speech of early Spanish colonists, though currently it is only found in the working-class or rural speech of places such as Santiago de Chile, as well as in the islands and coastal areas of the Caribbean and the Pacific coast, especially in Cuba, the Dominican Republic, and Puerto Rico (see Simonet et al. 2008).

Consonant Assimilation

A feature characterizing originally non-standard southern varieties of European Spanish is the process of regressive assimilation in consonant clusters in word-medial position, such as *-ds-* (*adscribir* 'to ascribe'), *-bs-* (*substracción* 'subtraction'/'theft'), *-ks-* (*exponente* 'exponent'/'indicator'), *-rs-* (*intersticio* 'interstice'), *-ns-* (*constar* 'to state'), *-st-* (*canasta* 'basket'), *-sk-* (*esquimal* 'Eskimo'), *-rn-* (*carne* 'meat'), *-rl-* (*Carlos* 'Charles'), *-kt-* (*contacto* 'contact'), *-dk-* (*adquirir* 'to acquire'), and *-gd-* (*Magdalena* 'Madeleine'). Some instances of this assimilation are shown in Table 23.5.

As we will see below, similar consonant clusters in word-final postvocalic position, such as *-ts* (*chalets* 'houses,' *hábitats* 'habitats'), *-ps* (*bíceps* 'biceps,' *tríceps* 'triceps,' *pubs, stops*), *-ks* (*tórax* 'thorax,' *coñacs* 'brandies,' *anoraks*), *-nk* (*cinc* 'zinc'), *-lz* (*selz* 'Selz, = sparkling water'), *-gs* (*zigzags*), and *-ms* (*álbums* 'albums'), etc., are not assimilated, but rather are dropped (cf. Hernández-Campoy and Trudgill 2002).

In European Spanish, according to Martínez Martín (1983), the process of regressive assimilation of consonantal clusters, a salient feature of non-

Table 23.5 *Examples of regressive assimilation in consonant clusters in word-medial position*

carnet 'card/license'	standard Castilian Spanish:	[kaɾˈnet]
	non-standard Spanish:	[kaˈnnɛ]
tacto 'tact/sense'	standard Castilian Spanish:	[ˈtakto]
	non-standard Spanish:	[ˈtatto]
adquirir 'buy/acquire'	standard Castilian Spanish:	[aðkiˈɾiɾ]
	non-standard Spanish:	[akkiˈɾi]
magdalena 'fairy cake'	standard Castilian Spanish:	[magðaˈlena]
	non-standard Spanish:	[maððaˈlena]

Table 23.6 *Phonotactics of southern varieties of European Spanish in word-final position*

	Example	
Codas	singular	plural
(-p), (-b)	sto**p**, pu**b**	sto**p**s, pu**b**s
(-t), (-d), (-s)	hábita**t**, ciuda**d**, diabete**s**	hábita**t**s, ciuda**d**es, diabetes
(-k), (-g), (-x)	coña**c**/anora**k**, zigza**g**, relo**j**	coña**c**s/anora**k**s, zigza**g**s, relo**j**es
(-θ)	fero**z**	fero**c**es
(-m), (-n), (-l), (-r)	álbum, examen, canal, amor	álbumes, exámenes, canales, amores
(-ps)	bícep**s**, trícep**s**	bícep**s**, trícep**s**
(-ks)	tóra**x**	tóra**x**
(-nk)	ci**nc**	ci**nc**
(-lz)	se**lz**	se**lz**

Bold type indicates loss of sound.
Source: Monroy-Casas (1980:60)

standard southern Spanish varieties, is described as a phenomenon also in expansion in apparently standard Castilian Spanish-speaking areas in the northern regions of Spain. In Latin American Spanish, consonant assimilation is a much more generalized feature, as shown for Cuba (Terrell 1975; Dohotaru 2002, 2007) and Venezuela (Obediente 1986; Freites 2008). See also Appendix 23.A.

Consonant Loss

A prominent feature of southern varieties of European Spanish, such as Murcian and most eastern Andalusian, is the loss of postvocalic consonants (except for *-m* and *-n: álbum* and *camión*) in word-final position (see Table 23.6).

This consonant loss dramatically affects postvocalic /s/, which is the marker in Spanish of some important current morphosyntactic distinctions, such as number in nouns and person in verbs (see Hernández-Campoy and Trudgill 2002 and Hernández-Campoy and Jiménez-Cano 2003). In southern non-standard varieties of European Spanish such distinctions are marked with vowel quality, rather than with the *-s* ending (see

Table 23.7 *Word-final /s/ in person marking*

	Simple present tense	
1st person sing.	*(yo)* **com-o**	'I eat'
2nd person sing.	*(tú)* **com-es**	'you (fam.) eat'
	(usted) **com-e**	'you (pol.) eat'
3rd person sing.	*(él/ella)* **com-e**	'he/she eats'
	Simple past tense (imperfective)	
1st person sing.	*(yo)* **com-ía**	'I was eating'
2nd person sing.	*(tú)* **com-ías**	'you (fam.) were eating'
	(usted) **com-ía**	'you (pol.) were eating'
3rd person sing.	*(él/ella)* **com-ía**	'he/she was eating'

"Vowel Changes in Spanish," above). This is true for noun phrases, where /s/ is the plural marker on articles, adjectives and nouns (23.4):

(23.4)   La/una/otra casa bonita   Las/unas/otras casas bonitas
         'The/a/another nice house'   'The/some/other nice houses'

And it is equally true of verb forms, where word-final /s/ is heavily involved in person marking (Table 23.7).

As with Murcian Spanish, eastern varieties of Andalusian exhibit patterns of variation in the realization of the number and person morpheme ending (presence/absence) which is consistently expressed by final /s/ in the standard Castilian variety. But, given that the morphology of the verbal paradigm of eastern varieties is the same as that of the standard – except that they drop final /-s/ as part of the diachronic process of word-final consonant loss – they tend to compensatorily open vowels before the deleted /s/ and even undergo metaphony with the preceding stressed vowel ([kɔmɛ, kɔmɛmɔ] for *comes* and *comemos*); in this way, second- and third-person forms (*comes/come* 'you eat/she, he, it eats') are distinctively opposed by this difference ([ˈkɔmɛ/ˈkome]). This is due to the fact that, diachronically speaking, the loss of any consonant (except *–m* and *–n*) in word-final position had dramatic consequences for the eastern Andalusian and Murcian vowel systems: historical word-final /eC, oC, aC/ have become /ɛ, ɔ, æ/, and the same vocalic developments have occurred word-internally in the case of vowels before assimilated consonants (see Hernández-Campoy and Trudgill 2002).

Although deletion is the most common variant, educated speakers in formal speech are more likely to retain the coda. Closing of syllables by [h] before stops (lah·tapa, *las tapas*) is also a frequent realization more commonly in Andalusia and New Castile, particularly because aspiration tends to be pronounced in the next syllable as an aspirated [th] or even as a dental affricate [ts] (lah·tapa, la·thapa, la·tsapa, *las tapas*) (see Colina 1997; Vida-Castro 2005:49–86; Torreira 2006; Moya-Corral 2008; Ruch 2006; Fernández de Molina 2015a).

Second-Person Address: *Voseo* and *Tuteo*

In second-person singular address, *tuteo* refers to the use of the second-person singular form *tú* (followed by verb in second-person singular: *tú quieres*), and *voseo* to the use of the second-person plural form *vos* (followed by verb in second-person plural/singular: *vos queréis/quieres*). Until the 14th century, like the *tu–vous* distinction in French, the plural *vos* form expressed deference or distance between addresser and addressee, while the singular *tú* form expressed solidarity or closeness. *Voseo* has been lost in European Spanish, except in the Canary Islands, but is a salient feature in Latin America, as with *vos querés* in Buenos Aires (see also Álvarez and Barros 2001; Woods and Rivera-Mills 2010, 2012; and Rivera-Mills 2011, among others).

23.3.2 Geographic Varieties of Spanish

European Spanish

The current rich mosaic of dialectal varieties in European Spanish is a reflection of what at a given moment constituted a confluence of traditional Hispano-Romance dialects (especially Castilian, Aragonese, and Leonese), of languages from other, earlier, civilizations (Iberian, Carthaginian, Phoenician, Greek, Roman, Visigothic, and Jewish), and of the then-existent varieties during the re-conquest of Spain from Arab rule with the subsequent processes of Castilianization. Every regional dialect of Spanish, therefore, derives from Spain's *common language* (Coseriu 1970), i.e. 14th- and 15th-century Castilian Spanish (see Figures 23.4–23.6 and

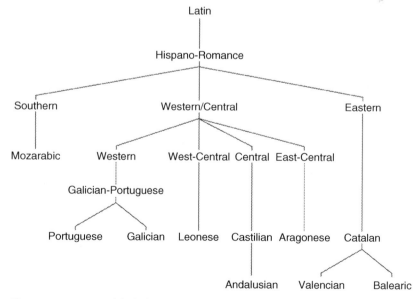

Figure 23.4 Tree model of Hispano-Romance varieties
Source: Adapted from Penny (2000:21)

Figure 23.5 Main dialect/**language** areas in Spain

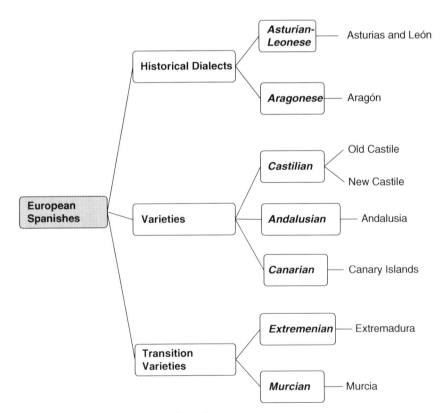

Figure 23.6 European varieties of Spanish

Appendix 23.A). The standard Castilian variety is thus based on northern dialects, which have remained close to the medieval phonological system, whereas the southern varieties are still undergoing innovating changes:

> In the language of Castile, northern dialects are distinguished from transitional and southern dialects. The north represents the most conservative and original stage while the varieties of the center and south, which were developed as a consequence of the *Reconquista*, show more innovative features. Old Castile is attached to the northern area, whereas Madrid and New Castile are considered as transitional dialects, mid-way between the openly innovative southern dialects and the conservative ones of the north. (Molina-Martos 2008: 61)

In her study, Molina-Martos (2008) found a general tendency in the dialects of the central areas of Castile to converge with the peripheral ones in a process "which is becoming more marked among higher sociocultural levels, but also affects lower strata" in that "dialectical variations lose the prestige that is gained by the cities" (Molina-Martos 2008:72).

According to Hernández-Campoy and Villena-Ponsoda (2009), there are two opposing processes currently taking place in central and southern dialects in Spain: The first is a convergent trend toward the standard variety (Castilian Spanish) which affects transitional varieties (such as Murcian and Extremenian) and eastern Andalusian regional dialects (from Almería, Granada, and Jaén) and whose result is the formation of a leveled koine of varieties (*español común* 'common Spanish': Hernández-Campoy and Villena-Ponsoda 2009; Hernández-Campoy 2011) containing prominent features from these areas (see Figures 23.5 and 23.7). The second refers to the diachronically innovative divergence of western Andalusian (*sevillano* 'Sevillian') which is reinforcing its salient features and gaining prestige. As a result of these two processes, three different spoken varieties can now be differentiated in these areas: (i) the traditional

Figure 23.7 Geographical varieties in Andalusian Spanish

Table 23.8 *Usage rates (percent) of the subjunctive past perfect forms in Spanish*

Country	-ra	-se	Total
Spain	565 (77%)	170 (23%)	735
Argentina	398 (82%)	86 (18%)	484
Colombia	450 (91%)	45 (9%)	495
Cuba	382 (90%)	44 (10%)	426
Mexico	472 (89.5%)	55 (10.5%)	527
Venezuela	409 (90%)	46 (10%)	455
Total	2676 (86%)	446 (14%)	3122

Source: Nowikov (1984)

Castilian Spanish national standard (*español estándar*), (ii) the regional spoken standard (*sevillano*), and (iii) the emerging inter-dialectal spoken variety (*español común*) corresponding, respectively, to three different historical domains: Castile, Seville, and Granada/Murcia.

At a grammatical level, the alternation of the morphological endings -*ra* and -*se* for the subjunctive past perfect forms, whose uses are functionally and semantically identical in both European and South American Spanish (see Gili Gaya 1961; Ridruejo 1983; Zamora Munné and Guitart 1982; Alarcos 1984, 1994; Lapesa 1988; Lunn 1989, 1995), is disappearing to the detriment of the form -*se* (23.5):

(23.5)   Si la carta **llegara** mañana, todavía podríamos hacerlo.
Si la carta **llegase** mañana, todavía podríamos hacerlo.

Nowikov's (1984) quantitative study of the presence of both subjunctive past perfect endings in Spanish and Latin American journalistic texts (see Table 23.8) showed that the use of the morphological form -*se* is being abandoned (used in only 14 percent of cases).

Similar results for the -*ra*/-*se* variance have been found in descriptive as well as dialectological studies (see Tavernier 1979; Marín 1980; Alvar and Pottier 1983), and in the sociolinguistic analyses carried out in urban speech communities such as Seville (Lamíquiz 1985), Burgos (Martínez-Martín 1983), Castellón (Blas Arroyo and Porcar 1994), and La Laguna in Tenerife (Serrano 1996).

Latin American Spanish Varieties

Different divisions of American Spanish have been drawn up (see Henríquez Ureña 1921; Canfield 1962; Rona 1962; Resnick 1976; Cahuzac 1980). Moreno-Fernández and Otero Roth (2008) divide the Spanish spoken in Latin America into five areas (Figures 23.8–23.9 and Appendix 23.A): (i) *Caribbean region*, embracing Cuba, Puerto Rico, the Dominican Republic, and the north of Venezuela and Colombia; (ii) *Mexico and central America*, with Mexico, Honduras, Nicaragua, Guatemala, Costa Rica, and Panama; (iii) *Andean region*, including Colombia, Ecuador, Peru, Bolivia, and northern

Figure 23.8 Spanish-speaking areas in America

Chile; (iv) *River Plate region*, with Paraguay, Argentina, and Uruguay; and (v) *Chilean region*, embracing the central and southern areas of Chile.

African and Asian Spanish Varieties

On the African continent, in addition to Ceuta and Melilla – Spanish exclaves on the Mediterranean coast of Morocco – Spanish is also spoken in Equatorial Guinea (see Nistal Rosique 2007). In south-eastern Asia, Spanish is used in the Philippines (see Moreno-Fernández and Otero Roth 2008) (see Figure 23.10 and Appendix 23.A).

23.4 Conclusion

The geographical dispersion of the Spanish language beyond the Iberian peninsula has entailed an array of geolinguistic and sociolinguist

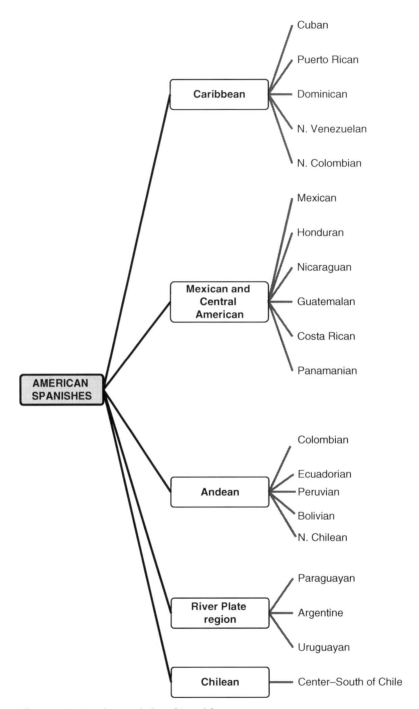

Figure 23.9 American varieties of Spanish

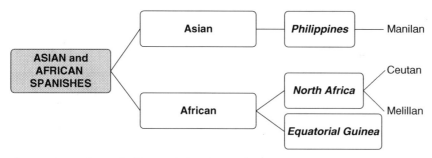

Figure 23.10 Asian and African varieties of Spanish

manifestations within the Spanish-speaking world since medieval times. Variation at the levels of pronunciation (*seseo, ceceo, yeísmo, ʒeísmo*, postvocalic consonant loss/aspiration, assimilation of consonant clusters, merger of liquid consonants, etc.), grammar (*leísmo, laísmo, loísmo, voseo, tuteo*, etc.), and/or lexicon (Peninsularisms/Americanisms) characterizes the rich mosaic of varieties of Spanish worldwide: European, Latin American, African, and Asian Spanish dialects. In turn, the processes of standardization and supralocalization of Castilian Spanish and the subsequent prescriptivism have given way to prestige and ideology patterns and the development of attitudes towards these different dialect and accent varieties and their respective identity values. But languages are continuously changing, and Spanish is as much subject to linguistic evolution as any other language due to both endogenous and exogenous factors: "the natural drift of languages over time, contact with other languages, internal population migrations, language propagation through missionary activities, the rise of cities, and the consequent rural–urban sociolinguistic divisions, educational systems, community literacy, mass communication media, and official language policies" (Lipski 2012:1). These linguistic and extralinguistic factors determine speakers' awareness of linguistic diversity, both standard and non-standard, and of the role of national standards, minority languages, and vernaculars – and their decisions as to when to use which variety.

Appendix 23.A Summary of Spanish Linguistic Patterns

Variety	Yeísmo vs palatal /ʝ/–/ʎ/ distinction			Intervocalic /d/ dropping		s/z phenomena			Velar sound /x/		Vowel changes	Liquid consonant merger	Consonant assimilation	Final consonant loss	
	Palatal distinction	yeísmo	ʒeísmo	-/ð/-	Ø	seseo	ceceo	Distinction	[x]	[h]				Maintenance	Deletion
European Varieties of Spanish															
Aragonese	+	+	–	+	–	–	–	+	+	–	–	–	–	+	–
Leonese	–	+	–	+	–	–	–	+	+	–	+	–	–	+	–
Castilian (Old Castile)	+	+	–	+	–	–	–	+	+	–	–	–	–	+	–
Castilian (New Castile)	+	+	–	+	–	–	–	+	+	–	–	–	–	+	–
Andalusian	–	+	+	+	+	+	+	–	–	+	+	+	+	–	+
Extremenian	–	+	+	+	+	–	–	+	+	+	+	+	–	–	+
Murcian	–	+	–	+	+	–	–	+	–	–	+	+	–	–	+
Canarian	–	+	–	+	+	+	–	–	+	+	+	+	+	–	+
American Varieties of Spanish															
Caribbean	+	+	–	+	–	+	–	–	+	+	–	+	+	–	+
Mexican and central American	–	+	–	+	–	+	–	–	+	+	–	+	–	+	+
Andean	+	+	–	+	–	+	–	–	+	+	+	+	+	–	+
River Plate	+	+	+	+	–	+	–	–	+	+	–	–	+	–	+
Chilean	+	+	+	+	–	+	–	–	–	–	–	+	+	–	+
African and Asian Spanish															
African Spanish (Equatorial Guinea)	–	+	–	+	+	+	–	–	+	+	–	–	+/–	+	+
Philippines	+	–	–	–	+	+	–	–	+	–	–	–	–	+	–

References

Abad-Merino, M. (2004). Apuntes históricos y nuevas perspectivas en torno al seseo de Cartagena. Las Ordenanzas de 1738. *Tonos Digital*, 8, 167–183.

Alarcos, E. (1984). *Estudios de gramática funcional del español*. Madrid: Gredos.

Alarcos, E. (1994). *Gramática de la lengua española*. Madrid: Espasa Calpe.

Aleza, M. and Enguita, J. M. (2010). *La lengua española en América: Normas y usos actuales*. Universidad de Valencia. Available from www.uv.es/aleza/esp.am.pdf (last access December 12, 2017).

Alvar, M. (2012). *Manual de dialectología hispánica. El español de España* (8th edn). Barcelona: Ariel [1996].

Alvar, Manuel and Pottier, Bernard (1983). *Morfología histórica del español*. Madrid: Gredos.

Álvarez, Alexandra and Barros, Ximena (2001). Sistemas en conflicto: Las formas de tratamiento en la ciudad de Mérida, Venezuela. *Lengua y Habla*, 6, 9–32.

ASALE (2010). *Diccionario de americanismos*. Madrid: Santillana.

Bedinghaus, R. and Sedó, B. (2014). Intervocalic /d/ Deletion in Málaga: Frequency Effects and Linguistic Factors. *Indiana University Linguistics Club Working Papers in Linguistics*, 14, 62–79.

Bizer, G. (2004). Attitudes. In Ch. Spielberg (ed.), *Encyclopedia of Applied Psychology*, Vol. 1. London: Elsevier, pp. 245–249.

Blanco, M. (2004). *Estudio sociolingüístico de Alcalá de Henares*. Alcalá de Henares: Universidad de Alcalá.

Blas Arroyo, J. L. (1994). Valenciano y castellano: Actitudes lingüísticas en la sociedad valenciana. *Hispania*, 77 (1), 143–156.

Blas Arroyo, J. L. and Porcar, M. (1994). El empleo de las formas *ra* y *se* en las comunidades de habla castellonenses. Aproximación sociolingüística. *Español Actual*, 62, 73–98.

Cahuzac, P. (1980). La división del español de América en zonas dialectales. Solución etnolingüística o semántico-dialectal. *Lingüística Española Actual*, 2, 385–461.

Calero, M. A. (1993). *Estudio sociológico del habla de Toledo*. Lleida: Pagés.

Calvo, A. and Castillo, J. (2014). Opiniones de los costarricenses acerca del español general, la corrección lingüística, el español en los medios de comunicación y en la educación. *Revista de Filología y Lingüística de la Universidad de Costa Rica*, 30 (2), 167–180.

Canfield, D. L. (1962). *La pronunciación del español de América*. Bogotá: Instituto Caro y Cuervo.

Caravedo, R. (1990). *Sociolingüística del español de Lima*. Lima: Fondo Editorial de la Pontificia Universidad Católica de Perú.

Cedergren, H. (1973). The Interplay of Social and Linguistic Factors in Panama (Doctoral dissertation). Cornell University.

Cestero, A. M. and Paredes, F. (2015). Creencias y actitudes hacia las variedades normativas del español actual. Primeros resultados del Proyecto PRECAVES-XXI. *Spanish in Context*, 12 (2), 255–279.

Chang, Charles. (2008). Variation in Palatal Production in Buenos Aires Spanish. In M. Westmoreland and J. A. Thomas (eds.), *Selected Proceedings of the 4th Workshop on Spanish Sociolinguistics*. Somerville, MA: Cascadilla, pp. 54–63.

Clements, J. C. (2009). *The Linguistic Legacy of Spanish and Portuguese: Colonial Expansion and Language Change*. Cambridge: Cambridge University Press.

Colina, S. (1997). Identity Constraints and Spanish Resyllabification. *Lingua*, 103, 1–23.

Coseriu, E. (1970). "Historische Sprache" und "Dialekt." In J. Göschel, P. Ivic, and K. Kehr (eds.), *Dialekt und Dialektologie. (Zeitschrift für Dialektologie und Linguistik*, 26). Wiesbaden: Steiner, pp. 106–122.

Demonte, V. (2003). Lengua estándar, norma y normas de difusión actual de la lengua española. *Circunstancia*, 1 (1). Available from www.ortegaygasset.edu/publicaciones/circunstancia/ano-i—numero-1—abril-2003/estados-de-la-cuestion/lengua-estandar–norma-y-normas-en-la-difusion-actual-de-la-lengua-espanola (last access January 3, 2018).

Dohotaru, P. (2007). El segmento fonológico -/R/ en el habla popular de la ciudad de La Habana. In M. Domínguez (ed.), *La lengua en Cuba. Estudios*. Santiago de Compostela: Universidad de Santiago de Compostela, pp. 101–145.

Díaz-Campos, Manuel and Gradoville, Michael (2011). An Analysis of Frequency as a Factor Contributing to the Diffusion of Variable Phenomena. Evidence from Spanish Data. In Luis A. Ortiz-López (ed.), *Selected Proceedings of the 13th Hispanic Linguistics Symposium*. Somerville, MA: Cascadilla, pp. 224–238.

D'Introno, F. and J. M. Sosa (1986). Elisión de la /d/ en el español de Caracas: Aspectos sociolingüísticos e implicaciones. In R. Núñez (ed.), *Estudios sobre la fonología del español del Caribe*. Caracas: La Casa de Bello, pp. 135–163.

Deyer, Y. (2007). Language and Identity. In C. Llamas, L. Mullani, and P. Stockwell (eds.), *The Routledge Companion to Sociolinguistics*. Abingdon and New York: Routledge, pp. 101–108.

Dohotaru, P. (2002). La variación de -/l/ en el habla espontánea de habaneros universitarios. In Milagros Aleza Izquierdo (ed.), *Estudios lingüísticos cubanos*, Vol. 2. Valencia: Universidad de Valencia, pp. 62–85.

Erdösová, M. Z. (2011). El español de México en los ojos de sus hablantes. Un estudio desde la sociolingüística y la dialectología perceptiva. *Lengua y Voz*, 1 (1), 57–81.

Erker, D. (2010). A Subsegmental Approach to Coda /s/ Weakening in Dominican Spanish. *International Journal of the Sociology of Language*, 203, 9–26.

Etxebarria Arostegui, M. (1985). *Sociolingüística urbana: El habla de Bilbao*. Salamanca: Universidad de Salamanca.

Fernández de Molina, E. (2012). Una aproximación al seseo en Fuente del Maestre (Badajoz). *Revista de Estudios Extremeños*, 68, 129–159.

Fernández de Molina, E. (2014). El habla de Mérida (Doctoral dissertation). Universidad de Extremadura.

Fernández de Molina, E. (2015a). El nivel social como indicador de la variación de -/s/ en el habla de Mérida. *Dialectología*, 16, 149–279.

Fernández de Molina, E. (2015b). El seseo en Fuente del Maestre: Un estudio sociolingüístico. In Y. Congosto Martín *et al.* (eds.), *Fonética experimental, educación superior e investigación*. Madrid: Arco Libros.

Fernández-Ordóñez, I. (1999). Leísmo, laísmo y loísmo. In V. Demonte and I. Bosque (eds.), *Gramática descriptiva de la lengua española*, Vol. 1. Madrid: Espasa Calpe, pp. 1317–1398.

File-Muriel, Richard and Brown, Earl (2011). The Gradient Nature of s-Deletion in Caleño Spanish. *Language Variation and Change*, 23, 223–243.

Freites, F. (2008). *De hablantes, gravedad y péndulos. Identidad andina fronteriza y uso lingüístico*. Caracas: Academia Venezolana de la Lengua.

García Marcos, F. J. (1990). *Estratificación social del español de la costa granadina*. Almería: Departamento de Lingüística General y Teoría Literaria.

García Marcos, F. J. and Fuentes González, A. D. (1996). *Estratificación social del español de Almería. Fuentes de prestigio y repercusión sociolingüística*. Almería: Grusta.

García Mouton, P. (2006). El castellano hoy: Sus principales rasgos lingüísticos. In E. de Miguel (ed.), *Las lenguas del español: Un enfoque filológico*. Madrid: Ministerio de Educación, Ciencia y Tecnología, pp. 151–174.

García Mouton, P. (2014). *Lenguas y dialectos de España* (6th edn). Madrid: Arco Libros [1994].

Gili-Gaya, S. (1961). *Curso superior de sintaxis*. Barcelona: Vox.

Gómez Molina, J. R. (2010). Mantenimiento y elisión de la /d/ intervocálica en el español de Valencia. *Verba*, 37, 89–122.

Gómez Serrano, A. (1994). Aspectos sociolingüísticos del habla de Linares (Jaén) (Doctoral dissertation). Universidad de Málaga.

Grandal-López, A. (1999). Sobre el origen del seseo cartagenero. *Estudios de Lingüística de la Universidad de Alicante*, 13, 269–279.

Haugen, E. (1966/1972). Dialect, Language, Nation. *American Anthropologist* 68, 922–935. Also in J. B. Pride and J. Holmes (eds.), Sociolinguistics: Selected Readings. Harmondsworth: Penguin, 1972, pp. 97–111.

Henríquez Ureña, P. (1921). Observaciones sobre el español de América. *Revista de Filología Española*, 8, 357–390.

Hernández-Campoy, J. M. (2003). Exposure to Contact and the Geographical Adoption of Standard Features: Two Complementary Approaches. *Language in Society*, 32 (2), 227–255.

Hernández-Campoy, J. M. (2004). El fenómeno de las actitudes y su medición en Sociolingüística. *Tonos Digital*, 8, 29–56.

Hernández-Campoy, J. M. (2007). The Fight of Non-Standardness under Standard Pressures. In A. Papapavlou and P. Pavlou (eds.), *Sociolinguistic and Pedagogical Dimensions of Dialect in Education*. Cambridge: Cambridge Scholars Publishing, pp. 50–77.

Hernández-Campoy, J. M. (2011). Variation and Identity in Spain. In M. Díaz-Campos (ed.), *The Handbook of Hispanic Sociolinguistics*. Chichester: John Wiley, pp. 704–746.

Hernández-Campoy, J. M. (2016). *Sociolinguistic Styles*. Malden, MA: Wiley-Blackwell.

Hernández-Campoy, J. M. and Jiménez Cano, J. M. (2003). Broadcasting Standardisation: An Analysis of the Linguistic Normalisation Process in Murcia. *Journal of Sociolinguistics*, 7 (3), 321–347.

Hernández-Campoy, J. M. and Trudgill, P. J. (2002). Functional Compensation and Southern Peninsular Spanish /s/ Loss. *Folia Linguistica Historica*, 22, 31–57.

Hernández-Campoy, J. M. and Villena-Ponsoda, J. M. (2009). Standardness and Nonstandardness in Spain: Dialect Attrition and Revitalization of Regional Dialects of Spanish. *International Journal of the Sociology of Language*, 196/197, 181–214.

Hope, J. (2000). Rats, Bats, Sparrows and Dogs: Biology, Linguistics and the Nature of Standard English. In J. Hope and L. Wright (eds.), *The Development of Standard English, 1300–1800. Theories, Descriptions, Conflicts*. Cambridge: Cambridge University Press, pp. 49–56.

Hualde, J. I. (2005). *The Sounds of Spanish*. Cambridge: Cambridge University Press.

Instituto Cervantes (2016). El español en cifras. In *El español: Una lengua viva. Informe 2016*. Available from https://cvc.cervantes.es/lengua/espanol_lengua_viva/pdf/espanol_lengua_viva_2016.pdf (last access December 12, 2017).

Lamíquiz, V. (1985). El sistema verbal idealizado y su comportamiento discursivo. In V. Lamíquiz and P. Carbonero (eds.), *Sociolingüística Andaluza*, Vol. 3. Sevilla: Universidad de Sevilla, pp. 113–120

Lapesa, R. (1988). *Historia de la lengua española* (9th edn). Madrid: Gredos.

Lipski, J. (2012). Geographical and Social Varieties of Spanish: An Overview. In J. I. Hualde, A. Olarrea, and Erin O'Rourke (eds.), *The Handbook of Hispanic Linguistics*. Malden, MA: Wiley, pp. 2–26.

Lope Blanch, J. M. (2001). La norma lingüística hispánica. Address to *II Congreso Internacional de la Lengua Española. El Español en la Sociedad de la Información*. Available from http://congresosdelalengua.es/valladolid/ponencias/unidad_diversidad_del_espanol/1_la_norma_hispanica/lope_j.htm (last access December 12, 2017).

López-García, A. (1985). *El rumor de los desarraigados. Conflicto de lenguas en la península ibérica*. Madrid: Anagrama.

López Morales, H. (1983). *Estratificación social del español de San Juan de Puerto Rico*. México: Universidad Autónoma de México.

López Morales, H. (2004). *Sociolingüística* (3rd edn). Madrid: Gredos. [1989].

Lunn, P. (1989). Spanish Mood and the Prototype of Assertability. *Linguistics*, 27 (4), 687–702.
Lunn, P. (1995). The Evaluative Function of the Spanish Subjunctive. In J. Bybee and S. Fleischman (eds.), *Modality in Grammar and Discourse*. Amsterdam: John Benjamins, pp. 429–449.
Marín, D. (1980). El uso moderno de las formas RA y SE del subjuntivo. *Boletín de la Real Academia Española*, 60, 197–230.
Mar-Molinero, C. (1997). *The Spanish-Speaking World. A Practical Introduction to Sociolinguistic Issues*. London: Routledge.
Mar-Molinero, C. (2000) *The Politics of Language in the Spanish-Speaking World*. London and New York: Routledge.
Martín Butragueño, P. (1991). Desarrollos sociolingüísticos en una comunidad de habla (Doctoral dissertation). Universidad Complutense de Madrid.
Martín Butragueño, P. (1995). La variable (s) en el sur de Madrid. Contribución al estudio de la frontera de las hablas meridionales del español. *Anuario de Letras*, 33, 5–57.
Martínez-Martín, M. (1983). *Fonética y sociolingüística en la ciudad de Burgos*. Madrid: CSIC.
Martínez-Martín, M. (1984). Datos sobre el leísmo y laísmo de persona en el habla de la ciudad de Burgos. *Epos*, 1, 158–176.
Menéndez Pidal, R. (1926). *Orígenes del español. Estado lingüístico de la Península Ibérica hasta el siglo XI*. Madrid: Gredos.
Milroy, J. (1999). The Consequences of Standardisation in Descriptive Linguistics. In T. Benx and R. J. Watts (eds.), *Standard English: The Widening Debate*. London: Routledge, pp. 16–39.
Milroy, J. (2000). Historical Description and the Ideology of the Standard Language. In L. Wright, *The Development of Standard English*. Cambridge: Cambridge University Press, pp. 11–28.
Milroy, J. (2001). Language Ideologies and the Consequences of Standardization. *Journal of Sociolinguistics*, 5 (4), 530–555.
Milroy, J. and Milroy, L. (1985). *Authority in Language: Investigating Language Prescription and Standardisation*. London and New York: Routledge and Kegan Paul.
Molina-Martos, I. (1991). *Estudio sociolingüístico de la ciudad de Toledo*. Madrid: Universidad Complutense.
Molina-Martos, I. (1998). *La fonética de Toledo. Contexto geográfico y social*. Alcalá de Henares: Universidad de Alcalá.
Molina-Martos, I. (2001). Geografía y estratificación social de un cambio fonético: La -d- en español peninsular. *Verba*, 28, 81–99.
Molina-Martos, I. (2006). Innovación y difusión del cambio lingüístico en Madrid. *Revista de Filología Española*, 86 (1), 127–149.
Molina-Martos, I. (2008). The Sociolinguistics of Castilian Dialects. *International Journal of the Sociology of Language*, 193, 57–78.

Molina-Martos, I. (2013). Yeísmo madrileño y convergencia dialectal campo/ciudad. In R. Gómez and I. Molina (eds.), *Variación yeísta en el mundo hispánico*. Madrid: Iberoamericana Verbuert, pp. 93–112.

Molina-Martos, I. (in press). Laterales: Variación geográfica y social. In J. Gil and Joaquim Llisterri (eds.), *Fonética y fonología descriptiva de la lengua española*. Madrid: CSIC.

Monroy-Casas, R. (1980). *Aspectos fonéticos de las vocales españolas* (2nd edn). Madrid: SGEL and Buenos Aires: LibrosEnRed.

Monroy-Casas, R. and Hernández-Campoy, J. M. (2015). Illustrations of the IPA: Murcian Spanish. *Journal of the International Phonetic Association*, 45 (2), 229–240.

Moreno de Alba, J. G. (1998). Actitudes de los mexicanos con respecto a la corrección lingüística y a la relación de la lengua española con la identidad nacional. In E. Forastieri *et al.* (eds.), *Estudios de lingüística hispánica: Homenaje a María Vaquero*. Puerto Rico: Editorial de la Universidad de Puerto Rico, pp. 472–382.

Moreno-Fernández, F. (2004). Cambios vivos en el plano fónico del español. Variación dialectal y sociolingüística. In R. Cano (ed.), *Historia de la lengua Española*. Barcelona: Ariel, pp. 973–1009.

Moreno-Fernández, F. (2005). *Historia social de las lenguas de España*. Barcelona: Ariel.

Moreno-Fernández, F. (2006). Los modelos de lengua. Del castellano al panhispanismo. In A. M. Cestero (ed.), *X aniversario del máster de enseñanza de español para extranjeros*. Alcalá de Henares: Universidad de Alcalá, pp. 75–94.

Moreno-Fernández, F. (2007). Social Remarks on the History of Spanish. *International Journal of the Sociology of Language*, 184, 7–20.

Moreno-Fernández, F., Amorós, M., Bercial, J., Corrales, F., and Rubio, M. de los A. (1988). Anotaciones sobre el leísmo, el laísmo y el loísmo en la provincia de Madrid. *Epos*, 4, 101–122.

Moreno-Fernández, J. and Moreno-Fernández, F. (2002). Madrid Perceptions of Regional Varieties in Spain. In D. Long and D. R. Preston (eds.), *Handbook of Perceptual Dialectology*, Vol. 2. Amsterdam and Philadelphia, PA: John Benjamins, pp. 295–320.

Moreno-Fernández, F. and Otero Roth, J. (2008). *Atlas de la lengua española en el mundo* (2nd edn). Madrid: Fundación Telefónica and Ariel.

Moya-Corral, J. A. (1979). *La pronunciación del español de Jaén*. Granada: Universidad de Granada.

Moya-Corral, J. A. (2008). *Datos del estudio sociolingüístico del español de Granada*. Lleida: Reunión de Coordinación Científica.

Moya-Corral, J. A. and Wiedemann, E. (1995). *El habla de Granada y sus barrios*. Granada: Universidad de Granada.

Narbona, A. (2009). *La identidad lingüística de Andalucía*. Sevilla: Centro de Estudios Andaluces. Consejería de la presidencia.

Narbona, A., Cano, R., and Morillo-Velarde, R. (1998). *El español hablado en Andalucía*. Barcelona: Ariel.

Navarro, M. (1995). *El español hablado en Puerto Cabello*. Valencia, Venezuela: Universidad de Carabobo.

Nistal Rosique, G. (2007). El caso del español en Guinea Ecuatorial. In *Enciclopedia del español en el mundo. Anuario del Instituto Cervantes 2006–2007*. Madrid: Instituto Cervantes, pp. 375–380.

Nowikov, N. (1984). El valor doble de la forma -SE en el español peninsular y americano. *Iberoamericana Pragensia*, 18, 61–66.

Obediente, E. (1986). *Las nasales en el español venezolano*. Mérida: Universidad de Los Andes.

Paredes-García, F. (1996). *Estudio sociolingüístico del habla de La Jara*. Alcalá de Henares: Universidad de Alcalá.

Paredes-García, F. (2006). Leísmo, laísmo y loísmo en la lengua hablada en Madrid (barrio de Salamanca). *Lingüística Española Actual*, 28 (2), 191–220.

Penny, R. (1991). *A History of the Spanish Language*. Cambridge: Cambridge University Press.

Penny, R. (2000).*Variation and Change in Spanish*. Cambridge: Cambridge University Press.

RAE (1741). *Orthographía española*. Madrid: Imprenta de la Real Academia Española.

RAE (1771a). *Diccionario de autoridades*. Facsimile edn. Madrid: Gredos [1980].

RAE (1771b). *Gramática de la lengua castellana*. Madrid: Ibarra.

RAE (2001). *Diccionario de la lengua española* (22nd edn). Madrid: Espasa.

RAE and ASALE (2005). *Diccionario panhispánico de dudas*. Madrid: Santillana.

RAE and ASALE (2009). *Nueva gramática de la lengua española. Morfología y sintaxis*. Madrid: Espasa.

RAE and ASALE (2010a). *Nueva gramática de la lengua española. Manual*. Madrid: Espasa.

RAE and ASALE (2010b). *Ortografía de la lengua española*. Madrid: Espasa.

RAE and ASALE (2011). *Nueva gramática básica de la lengua española*. Barcelona: Espasa.

Resnick, M. C. (1976). Algunos aspectos histórico-geográficos de la dialectología hispanoamericana. *Orbis*, 25, 264–276.

Ridruejo, E. (1983). La forma verbal en -ra en español del siglo XIII (oraciones independientes). In F. Marcos Marín (ed.), *Introducción plural a la gramática histórica*. Madrid: Cincel, pp. 170–185.

Rivera-Mills, S. V. (2011). Use of *voseo* and Latino Identity: An Intergenerational Study of Hondurans and Salvadorans in the Western Region of the US. In Luis A. Ortiz-López (ed.), *Selected Proceedings of the 13th Hispanic Linguistics Symposium*. Somerville, MA: Cascadilla, pp. 94–106.

Rojas, D. (2012). Actitudes lingüísticas de hispanohablantes de Santiago de Chile: Creencias sobre la corrección idiomática. *Onomázein*, 26 (2), 69–93.

Rona, J. P. (1962). El problema de la división del español americano en zonas dialectales. In *Actas de la Asamblea de Filología del I Congreso de Instituciones Hispánicas*. Madrid: Ediciones Cultura Hispánica, pp. 215–226.

Ruch, A. (2006). *El fenómeno de la africada [ts] < /-st-/ en el andaluz: Aspectos fonéticos y sociolingüísticos*. Zürich: Universität Zürich Seminararbeit.

Ruiz, A. M. (2003). Leísmo, laísmo y loísmo en el nordeste madrileño. In M. Á. Álvarez and M. S. Villarubia (eds.), *Actas del Congreso Internacional de la Asociación Coreana de Hispanistas*. Alcalá: Servicio de publicaciones de la Universidad de Alcalá, pp. 129–141.

Ruiz Domínguez, M. M. (1997). *Estudio sociolingüístico del habla de Melilla*. Almería: Universidad de Almería.

Salvá, V. (1846). *Nuevo diccionario de la lengua castellana*. Paris: Librería de Don Vicente Salvá.

Samper, J. A. and Pérez, A. M. (1998). La pérdida de la -/d/- en dos modalidades del español canario. *Philologica canariensia*, 4–5, 393–412.

Samper-Padilla, J. A. (1990). *Estudio lingüístico del español de las Palmas de Gran Canaria*. Las Palmas: Caja de Canarias.

Sánchez, A. and Almela, M. (2015). Spanish Lexicography. In Manel Lacorte (ed.), *The Routledge Handbook of Hispanic Applied Linguistics*. New York and Oxford: Routledge, pp. 332–349.

Santana Marrero, J. (2016). Percepción de las variedades del español por parte de los hablantes de Sevilla: Datos del proyecto PRECAVES-XXI. Paper presented at *Sociolinguistic Symposium 21*, Murcia 2016. Available from https://www.researchgate.net/profile/Saeed_Rezaei3/publication/309636325_e-Book_of_Abstracts_SS21_Murcia2016/links/581b01fd08aed2439387e168/e-Book-of-Abstracts-SS21-Murcia2016.pdf?origin=publication_list (last access December 26, 2017).

Schmidt, L. and Willis, E. (2011). Systematic Investigation of Voicing Assimilation of Spanish /s/ in Mexico City. In S. M. Alvord (ed.), *Selected Proceedings of the 5th Conference on Laboratory Approaches to Romance Phonology*. Somerville, MA: Cascadilla, pp. 1–20.

Serrano, M. J. (1996). El subjuntivo *ra* y *se* en oraciones condicionales. *Estudios Filológicos*, 31, 129–140.

Simonet, M., Hualde, J. I., and Nadeu, M. (2012). Lenition of /d/ in Spontaneous Spanish and Catalan. In *Proceedings of InterSpeech 2012*. Available from http://www.isca-speech.org/archive/interspeech_2012/i12_1416.html (last access December 26, 2017).

Simonet, Miguel, Rohena-Madrazo, Marcos, and Paz, Mercedes (2008). Preliminary Evidence for Incomplete Neutralization of Coda Liquids in Puerto Rican Spanish. In Laura Colantoni and Jeffrey Steele (eds.), *Selected Proceedings of the 3rd Conference on Laboratory Approaches to Spanish Phonology*. Somerville, MA: Cascadilla, pp. 72–86.

Tavernier, M. (1979). La frecuencia relativa de las formas verbales en -ra y –se. *Español Actual* 35–36, 1–12.

Terrell, T. (1975). La nasal implosiva y final en el español de Cuba. *Anuario de Letras. Lingüística y Filología*, 13, 257–271.

Terrell, T. (1978). La aspiración y elisión de /s/ en el español porteño. *Anuario de Letras de México*, 16, 41–66.

Terrell, T. (1979). Final /s/ in Cuban Spanish. *Hispania*, 62 (4), 599–612.

Torreira, F. (2006). Coarticulation between Aspirated-s and Voiceless Stops in Spanish: An Interdialectal Comparison. In Nuria Sagarra and J. T. Almeida (eds.), *Selected Proceedings of the Ninth Hispanic Linguistics Symposium*. Somerville, MA: Cascadilla, pp. 113–120.

Torreira, F. and Ernestus, M. (2011). Realization of Voiceless Stops and Vowels in Conversational French and Spanish. *Laboratory Phonology*, 2 (2), 331–353.

Torreira, F. and Ernestus, M. (2012). Weakening of Intervocalic /s/ in the Nijmegen Corpus of Casual Spanish. *Phonetica*, 69, 124–148.

Trudgill, P. (1975). *Accent, Dialect and the School*. London: Arnold.

Trudgill, P. (1998). Standard English: What It Isn't. *The European English Messenger*, 7 (1), 35–39.

Trudgill, P. (2002). *Sociolinguistic Variation and Change*. Edinburgh: Edinburgh University Press.

Turell, M. L. (1996). El contexto de la variación lingüística y su aplicación al studio del morfema español -ADO. In F. Gutiérrez (ed.), *El español, lengua internacional*. Murcia: Compobell, pp. 639–654.

Uruburu, A. (1996). La lengua española hablada en Córdoba (España). *Revista Española de Lingüística Aplicada*, 11, 225–250.

Vida-Castro, M. (2005). *Estudio sociofonológico del español hablado en la ciudad de Málaga. Condicionamientos sobre la variación de /-s/ en la distensión silábica*. Alicante: Universidad de Alicante.

Villa, L. and del Valle, J. (2015). The Politics of Spanish in the World. In Manel Lacorte (ed.), *The Routledge Handbook of Hispanic Applied Linguistics*. New York and Oxford: Routledge, pp. 571–587.

Villena-Ponsoda, J. A. (1996). Convergence and Divergence in a Standard-Dialect Continuum: Networks and Individuals in Malaga. *Sociolingüística*, 10, 112–137.

Villena-Ponsoda, J. A. (2001). *La continuidad del cambio lingüístico: Tendencias conservadores e innovadoras en la fonología del español a la luz de la investigación sociolingüística urbana*. Granada: Universidad de Granada.

Villena-Ponsoda, J. A. (2005). Efectos fonológicos de la coexistencia de modelos ideales en la comunidad de habla y en el individuo para la representación de la variación fonológica del español de Andalucía. *Interlingüística*, 16 (1), 43–70.

Villena-Ponsoda, J. A. (2006). The Iberian Peninsula. In Ulrich Ammon *et al.* (eds.), *Soziolinguistik/ Sociolinguistics. An International Handbook of the Science of Language and Society* (2nd edn), Vol. 3. Berlin and New York: De Gruyter, pp. 1802–1810.

Villena-Ponsoda, J. A. (2008). Sociolinguistic Patterns of Andalusian Spanish. *International Journal of the Sociology of Language*, 193, 139–160.

Villena-Ponsoda, J. A. and Vida-Castro, M. (2004). The Effect of Social Prestige on Reversing Phonological Changes: Universal Constraints on Speech Variation in Southern Spanish. In M. Thelander *et al.* (eds.), *Language Variation in Europe. Papers from ICLAVE 2. Papers from the 2nd International Conference on Language Variation and Change in Europe*. Uppsala: Uppsala University, pp. 432–444.

Williams, L. (1987). *Aspectos sociolingüísticos del habla de la ciudad de Valladolid*. Valladolid: Universidad de Valladolid and Exeter University.

Willis, Erik, Delgado-Díaz, Gibran, and Galarza, Iraida (2015). Allophonic Variation of the Velar Fricative /h/ in Puerto Rican Spanish. In Erik W. Willis, Pedro Martín-Butragueño, and Esther Herrera (eds.), *Selected Proceedings of the 6th Conference on Laboratory Approaches to Romance Phonology*. Somerville, MA: Cascadilla, pp. 52–69.

Woods, Michael R. and Rivera-Mills, Susana V. (2010). Transnacionalismo del voseante: salvadoreños y hondureños en los Estados Unidos. *Lengua y Migración*, 2(1), 97–112.

Woods, Michael R. and Rivera-Mills, Susana V. (2012). El tú como un "mask": *Voseo* and Salvadoran and Honduran Identity in the United States. *Studies in Hispanic and Lusophone Linguistics*, 5(1), 191–216.

Zamora Munné, J. and Guitart, J. (1982). *Dialectología hispanoamericana*. Salamanca: Almar.

24

Sociolinguistic Approaches to Dialectal, Sociolectal, and Idiolectal Variation in the Hispanophone World

Daniel Erker

24.1 Introduction

All of us are many things at once. In a single person we may encounter a mother, a daughter, a lawyer, an African American, a Christian, a liberal, a Latina, and a New Yorker. In another individual, we may find a fisherman, a grandfather, a retiree, an atheist, a Cuban, a painter, etc. The goal of this chapter is to highlight the ways in which the many dimensions of individual human identity have served to illuminate language use within the Hispanophone world. To consider language this way, that is, to focus on the link between characteristics of people and patterns of linguistic behavior, is to take a *sociolinguistic* perspective. From this perspective two attributes of language use are of central importance; namely, its inherent variability and its social nature. The first of these refers to the fact that when people use language, whether through speech, through writing, or some other medium, they do so in ways that vary. For instance, to inquire about the geographic origin of a new acquaintance, one person may ask ¿De dónde eres? 'Where are you from?' while another may say ¿De dónde sos vos? 'Where are you from?' Furthermore, this second individual may, in another context with a different interlocutor, ask ¿y usted, de dónde es? 'and you, where are you from?' This kind of variation – as well as that found at other levels of linguistic structure – is not only pervasive in the use of language, it is also socially constrained. As suggested by this simple example, speakers may, depending on the context in which they find themselves, request similar information in different ways. In other words, the choice to use a particular linguistic form or forms is partially influenced by a person's knowledge of the social signaling potential that such forms have when embedded in a specific interactional context.

These interconnected attributes of language use, its systematic variability and intrinsic sociality, are hallmarks of linguistic interaction not only in Spanish-speaking communities, but wherever language and society intersect. Several fields of study take a central theoretical interest in understanding this intersection, including the sociology of language (Fishman 1971; Bernstein 2003), linguistic anthropology (Ochs 1992; Eckert 2000; Bucholtz and Hall 2004), and variationist sociolinguistics (Labov 1963, 1966, and 2001, among others). While scholars in these fields ask different research questions and use different methods to answer them, they are unified by their view of language as a multifaceted instrument for communication, one that has the capacity to transmit social, as well as linguistic, meanings and messages. That is, a sociolinguistic perspective sees language as both a means of information exchange and a medium through which speakers relate themselves to others in the world around them. The present chapter adopts this perspective and aims to provide a general sociolinguistic account of language use in the Hispanophone world, principally by focusing on the relationship between dimensions of social organization and patterns of linguistic variation.

A first step towards doing so is to address the nature of the relationship between familiar identity categories and linguistic behavior. The frequency with which we encounter many such categories – age, sex, occupation, nationality, social class, ethnicity, sexual orientation, religious affiliation, place of residence, native speaker, etc. – can create the impression that they are natural and given by the world itself. This, in turn, can lead to the view that the linguistic behavior of particular persons is the product of the various identity category values that describe them at a certain point in their lives. However, there are several problems with this perspective. The first is that it runs the risk of accepting named identity categories without acknowledging their abstract, socially constructed, and frequently contested nature. Even a personal attribute as seemingly natural and objective as age is, in fact, subject to wide-ranging cultural variation in interpretation. For instance, in her investigation of age as a sociolinguistic variable, Eckert 1997 (citing Fortes 1984) remarks that

> In industrial society chronological age, measured as an accumulation of years since birth, serves as an official measure of the individual's place in the life course and in society, by reference to a societal dating system ... This can be reversed in societies that do not traditionally use chronological age. Fortes (1984:110), for example, observed the Ashanti assigning a chronological age of 16 to females at the time of their nubility ceremonies, even though their actual birth dates were unknown. (Eckert 1997:156)

Similar issues arise with respect to more obviously socially constructed identity categories such as gender, ethnicity, nationality, and class. With respect to the last of these, for instance, Guy (1988) recounts various debates on the definition of social class, not only in linguistics, but also within sociology, political science, and history. He notes that conceptions of class that are common in Western industrialized societies – which are often based upon attributes of individual experience such as income, occupation, education level, and place of residence – make little sense in other parts of the world. For example, citing Rickford's (1986) research in Guyana, Guy (1988:47) reports that

> if applied unaltered [such a conception of class] would probably put everyone together in one of the lowest categories. But this does not mean that local class distinctions do not exist. On the contrary, Rickford demonstrates that people in Canewalk [Guyana] have a lively awareness of class distinctions.

The locally defined, socially constructed, and contested nature of this and other identity categories is a topic of considerable attention within linguistic inquiry. This research includes, but is far from limited to, discussions of the relationship between language and nationality (Gal and Irvine 1995; del Valle 2013), gender (Cameron 1992; Holmes and Meyerhoff 2003), race (Chun 2001; Bucholtz 2011), and sexual orientation (Gaudio 2001; Zimman 2013).

Another problem with what might be described as a deterministic perspective on sociolinguistic variation – that is, the view that linguistic behavior is merely the probabilistically conditioned output of a particular combination of identity category values – is that it has the relationship between language and identity in the wrong order. It is not our identities that determine the way we use language. Rather, it is partly through linguistic behavior that we make our identities. That is, identity *emerges* through linguistically mediated interaction; it is neither given, granted, nor static, but is instead constructed, negotiated, and reproduced dynamically. In other words, identity is not the source but rather a product of linguistic practice (Bucholtz and Hall 2010:19). To acknowledge this is to see language users as active participants in the ongoing construction of their identities and to see language as a tool over which they have a substantial degree of individual agency.

It may seem that the preceding considerations conflict with the stated aim of the present chapter, i.e. surveying patterns of sociolinguistic variation in the Spanish- speaking world. Indeed, might not the socially constructed nature of named identity categories invalidate or at least seriously limit them as tools for linguistic inquiry? Will applying them to a certain person or group of people as way of framing their linguistic behavior amount to putting the cart before the horse, misunderstanding the dynamic and emergent nature of identity as well as the agency of language users? The answer to these questions is "No." Recognizing identity categories as social constructions does not deny them meaning or dismiss their capacity to shape human behavior. Rather, it properly locates the source of their meaning and influence, which is within human ideologies that impose (sometimes rather arbitrary) divisions between people in societies and inform attitudes and expectations about how their members should behave. Furthermore, when we describe someone in terms of familiar identity categories – e.g. *a young African American Latina* or *a retired Cuban fisherman* – we are not requiring that they behave in any particular way. To the extent that such descriptions allow patterns of linguistic behavior to emerge, they do so as the result of linguistic choices made by individual language users, not from a lock-step relationship between identity category values and linguistic output. Indeed, as will be seen in some of the research literature reviewed below, within many groups there are often individuals who diverge from or represent exceptions to general patterns – a fact that is sometimes indicative of incipient language change in a community (Labov 2001).

With these considerations in mind, let us take, as an organizing principle, the following observation of Bucholtz and Hall (2010:21): "Identities encompass (a) macro-level demographic categories; (b) local, ethnographically specific cultural positions; and (c) temporary and interactionally specific stances and participant roles." Bucholtz and Hall refer to this as the *Positionality Principle*, and it suggests that the multifaceted nature of individual identity emerges, and therefore can be profitably explored, across numerous levels of social organization and positions within linguistic interaction, i.e. from the broadly demographic identity category to the in-the-moment context of spontaneous conversation. Since the goal of this chapter is to provide an overview of sociolinguistic variation in the Spanish-speaking world, the focus will be on large-scale demographic categories and ethnographically specific cultural positions. These categories and positions will serve as windows into the three primary ways in which variation in the use of Spanish has been investigated. These are dialectal, sociolectal, and idiolectal approaches to variation, respectively.

The first of these, *dialectal variation*, refers to patterns of language use delimited in terms of physical space. Research on dialectal variation typically utilizes the terminology and categories of geography as well as those of international and municipal politics to circumscribe groups of speakers. Such terms and categories, like the physical spaces they are meant to delimit, vary in size, ranging from the global to the hyper-local in scope. For example, the same group of individuals may be described as Latin Americans, Caribbeans, Colombians, residents of Cartagena, and/or occupants of a specific apartment building within the colonial zone of that particular city. Another group might be variously described as Europeans, Iberians, Spaniards, Madrileños, and/or residents of a given block in that city's La Latina neighborhood. *Sociolectal variation*, by comparison, refers to patterns of linguistic behavior that emerge along social vectors between and within specific locales, where groups are frequently delimited in terms of census-style categories such as age, sex, class, rurality–urbanity, and ethnicity as well as in terms of attitudinal, political, ideological, or lifestyle categories, e.g. liberal, conservative, feminist, Catholic, vegetarian, socialist, jock, nerd, etc. Finally, variation at the *idiolectal level* refers to differences in linguistic behavior both between and within particular individuals: Two speakers may overlap or differ in their use of a given linguistic form or feature, and the linguistic behavior of any single individual will vary across social and interactional contexts. These three approaches to sociolinguistic variation are, of course, necessarily interconnected, as they share a common source: individual speakers, who construct and reproduce their multidimensional identities through linguistic practice. So, while dialectal, sociolectal, and idiolectal variation will first be outlined in separate sections below, the chapter culminates with a series of case studies that highlight their intersection.

24.2 Dialectal Variation

Physical space represents an important dimension of variation for all groups of language users, as physical proximity has, at least for the vast majority of human history, been a prerequisite for linguistic interaction. Even in the digital age, the people we talk to the most and talk the most like are those with whom we share physical space. This was also the case during the five centuries that encompass the geographic expansion of Spanish. During this period, what were once the linguistic practices of a relatively small group of people living in the central northern part of a peninsula in western Europe spread to a community of language users that today spans the globe. This expansion occurred through face-to-face interaction, as Castilians first encountered other Iberians, and then, over the long course of the rise and fall of the Spanish empire, as they interacted with people in the Americas, Africa, and Asia. As the linguistic practices of Castilians spread, they changed, and these changes are presently reflected in geographically constrained patterns of variation within the Hispanophone world. For instance, one is likely to eat a *palta* 'avocado' in the Andes, but an *aguacate* 'avocado' in Mexico. Gratitude is likely to be expressed with gra[θ]ia[s̪] 'thanks' in Madrid but with gra[s]ia[h/Ø] in Puerto Rico. In Buenos Aires, a speaker will refer to herself with [ʒo] or [ʃo], but in the Caribbean, "I" is [jo] or [dʒo]. If the speakers around you are using *vosotros* to address groups of familiars, you are assuredly not in Latin America. And if someone remarks that *Tengo que pagar mis taxes* 'I have to pay my taxes,' it is a good bet that he or she has lived in the United States.

The sources of such dialectal variation, which is lexically, phonologically, and morphosyntactically ubiquitous, are numerous. A primary cause is to be found in the interaction between language change and the physical proximity of speakers. A linguistic innovation that arises within one group of speakers is likelier to spread to another that is nearby than to one that is far away (Mufwene 2008). Furthermore, even among groups that are not separated by sheer mileage, linguistic interaction (and therefore the transmission of linguistic innovations) may be impeded by natural barriers, e.g. rivers, jungles, mountain ranges, etc. The impediment to interaction that such physical obstacles represent can and was overcome as the Spanish empire expanded, but contact between the European seat of power and colonial settlements was uneven, geographically speaking (Lipski 2014; Mufwene 2014).

Such considerations play a central role in accounting for the present-day distribution of a number of linguistic features, particularly those that represent innovations that occurred within Spain itself over the course of colonial development. For instance, consider *voseo*, which was alluded to in Section 24.1: In the 16th century, the use of *vos* as a second-person singular pronoun began to fade in the Iberian peninsula (for a discussion of factors that contributed to this change see Kany 1969 and Benavides 2003). This trend made its way across the Atlantic in a geographically variable fashion, such that the Peninsular shift away from *voseo* towards *tuteo* was directly transmitted to areas that were administrative, economic, and cultural centers of colonial activity, e.g. the viceroyalties that were established in Mexico, Peru, and the Caribbean. By contrast, in areas that were both physically distant from and characterized by more infrequent contact with new arrivals from Europe, Iberian shifts in pronominal behavior failed to take root, e.g. in central America, parts of Colombia, and the River Plate region of South America.

A related factor that has had a relatively more recent impact on dialectal variation in the Hispanophone world is the emergence of modern urban centers in the Americas (for discussion of dialectal diversification outside of the Americas, see Quilis 1992; Sayahi 2004, Clements 2009; and Lipski 2012). As American cities came into being, their increasing populations helped to establish and reinforce local linguistic norms and also mute the influence of linguistic innovation in Spain:

> Once cities reached a critical mass of several tens of thousands (which usually occurred during the late eighteenth or early nineteenth century), these speech communities effectively resisted full incorporation of language changes that occurred in Spain and arrived with new settlers.
> (Lipski 2014: 44)

That is, the large populations and increased autonomy achieved in urban centers of Hispanic America shifted the sociolinguistic center of gravity, diminishing the impact of European linguistic norms and amplifying the significance of those that were locally emergent.

Yet another factor that shaped the historical emergence of dialectal variation in the Hispanophone world is what modern linguistics refers to as *language contact* (Weinreich 1953; Thomason and Kaufman 1988; Silva-Corvalán 1994; Winford 2005; Poplack and Levey 2010; Mufwene 2014; amongst others). The many different European, Amerindian, African, and Asian peoples that Castilians encountered had their own well-established linguistic traditions. Because the settlements of such groups – the Taíno, Inca, Yoruba, Catalan, Aymara, Kimbundu, Chiquitano, etc. – were themselves variably distributed across areas of Spanish imperial expansion, the influence of their respective linguistic practices within the Hispanophone world is geographically constrained. For instance, a range of features that have been interpreted as arising from contact with speakers of Quechua (e.g. the presence of third-person possessive markers accompanying nouns in genitive phrases: *su casa de Juan* 'Juan's his house,' the use of diminutive affixes to express modesty and deference *ellita* 'she,' etc.) is concentrated in the Andean region of South America (see Escobar 2012 for a broad survey of the linguistic outcomes of contact between Iberians and Amerindians). Another phenomenon that has been analyzed as a potential outcome of language contact is coda consonant lenition (e.g. weakening and deletion of coda /s, n, l, d, r/). High rates of coda consonant lenition are routinely observed in Caribbean and coastal communities of Hispanic America as well as in Lusophone America, a distribution that Guy (2014:445) attributes to contact with Africans:

> Brazil and the Hispanic Caribbean were two of the major destinations of the Atlantic slave trade, but few Africans were ever taken to the highland regions of South America or Mesoamerica. Typologically, this account is also well-motivated: the great majority of Africans taken to the Americas spoke West African languages which favored open, CV syllable structures, and in many cases, prohibited coda consonants entirely.

An additional, and more recent, instance of contact-induced dialectal variation can be found in Argentina, which was a major destination of European, and especially Italian, immigrants from the mid-1800s until the onset of World War II. Various intonational, lexical, and morphophonological features typical in the speech of some Argentines have been attributed, in part, to an Italian substrate (e.g. a circumflex intonational contour; deletion rather than aspiration of coda /s/ in first-person plural verb morphology such that *-amos* is produced as [amo] in parallel with the Italian cognate *-iamo*, Lipski 1994:167).

Intertwined with the question of causation – that is, determining what factors gave rise to and continue to shape geographically constrained differences in the linguistic behavior of Spanish speakers – is the more descriptive (and onerous) task of delimiting the boundaries of dialectal variation. This topic represents a major site of inquiry within Hispanic linguistics (Henríquez Ureña 1921, 1930, 1931; Navarro Tomás 1942; Rona 1964; Zamora Vicente 1970; Resnick 1980; Canfield 1981; Zamora Munné and Guitart 1982, Alba 1992; Lipski 1994; Penny 2000; among others). Of central interest in this literature is the linguistic relationship between Spain and its colonial territories (particularly those in the Americas), as well as the linguistic zonification of these territories. Among the earliest proposals for the dialectal zones of Latin America is that of Henríquez Ureña, whose three works titled *Observaciones sobre el español de América* (1921, 1930, 1931) emphasize both the heterogeneity of linguistic behavior in Spanish America and the limitation inherent to the enterprise of dialectal zonification; namely, that any zone will be further divisible into yet smaller zones:

> Provisionally I would distinguish in Spanish-speaking America five main zones: first, the zone that includes the bilingual regions of southern and southwestern United States, Mexico and the central American republics; second, the three Spanish Antilles (Cuba, Puerto Rico and the Dominican Republic, the old Spanish part of Santo Domingo), the coast and plains of Venezuela and probably the northern region of Colombia; third, the Andean region of Venezuela, the interior and western coast of Colombia, Ecuador, Peru, the larger part of Bolivia and perhaps northern Chile; fourth, the larger part of Chile; fifth, Argentina, Uruguay, Paraguay and perhaps part of southeastern Bolivia ... Inside of each zone, there are then subdivisions. (1921: 360; my translation)

In the decades following this proposal, several scholars took seriously Henríquez Ureña's remark about subdivision, substantially expanding upon his five dialectal zones. Rona (1964), for instance, subdivided Henríquez Ureña's five-zoned system – (i) north/central American, (ii) Caribbean, (iii) Andean, (iv) Chilean, and (v) River Plate zones – and expanded it into a system of 16 dialectal regions. Three features served as the linguistic basis for these zones: *zh-/sheísmo, yeísmo,* and *voseo*. These refer, respectively, to (i) the production of the initial sound of words like *yo* and *llamar* as a post-alveolar fricative, (ii) the merger of the palatal approximant /j/ and the palatal lateral approximant /ʎ/, through which words like *haya* 'she/he/it has (auxiliary).SBJV' and *halla* 'she/he/it finds' become homophonous, and (iii) the use of the second-person singular pronoun *vos*. For instance, in Rona's scheme, speakers in the *zona ultraserrana del Uruguay* are mirror images of those in the *zona andina de Colombia*, in that the former are *yeístas* and *zheístas* but not *voseantes* while the latter maintain a contrast between *calló* 'she/he/it silenced' and *cayó* 'she/he/it fell,' say [jo] rather than [ʒo], and routinely use *vos*. Resnick (1980) proposed an even more granular system based on eight binarily variable phonological features, which has the potential to delimit 256 distinct dialectal zones. The features included: (i) *yeísmo*; (ii) the neutralization of liquids, e.g. *mal* 'badly/poorly' and *mar* 'sea' are homophonous; (iii) the weakening of /s/ in syllable coda position; (iv) a glottalized realization of /x/; (v) the spirantization of /b/ after /l/; (vi) the velarization of coda /n/; (vii), an assibilated production of /r/; and (viii) the devoicing of vowels.

Our understanding of regionally defined dialectal zones in Hispanic America has been further enriched by scholars who have utilized geopolitical boundaries as convenient heuristics for illuminating variation. Canfield (1981), for example, provides a country-by-country analysis of phonological variation in the Americas. In this work, consonantal weakening figures prominently as a unifying theme and leads Canfield to make a broad areal distinction, contrasting "highland conservatism" (i.e. lower rates of consonantal weakening) with the "relaxed trends of much of coastal Spanish America" (1981:52). Another country-level analysis can be found in Lipski's monumental 1994 work. In *Latin American Spanish*, Lipski surveys not only phonological variation, but also morphological, lexical, and syntactic behavior at the national level, providing an historical overview of each country as well as a description of extra-Hispanic influences on the linguistic behavior of its residents. What ultimately connects the work of pioneering dialectologists, such as Henríquez Ureña, to the more sociolinguistically sophisticated research of scholars like Canfield, Lipski, and Penny is a shared recognition of the central role that physical space plays in shaping linguistic variation. Indeed, the regional and national origins of speakers have come to be widely acknowledged as key components in any characterization of linguistic variation in the Hispanophone world. Furthermore, an accurate account of geographically constrained norms is a prerequisite for properly understanding variation within a given community, as such norms help establish baseline expectations for the linguistic behavior of its members. It is to this level of analysis, that of sociolectal variation, that we now turn.

24.3 Sociolectal Variation

While scholars of dialectal variation principally aim to describe and explain patterns of language use that correlate with the distribution of communities across physical space, those interested in sociolectal variation often seek to understand linguistic behavior *within*, as well as between, these communities. An iconic and seminal exemplar of such research is Labov's (1966) investigation of variability in the production of post-vocalic /ɹ/ among English-speaking employees of three New York City department stores. In this study, Labov identifies the *social stratification* of communities as a central force that shapes linguistic behavior within them. According to Labov, social stratification is

> the product of social differentiation and social evaluation. The use of this term does not imply any specific type of class or caste, but simply that the normal workings of society have produced systematic differences between certain institutions or people, and that these differentiated forms have been ranked in status or prestige by general agreement.

He goes on to specify how this view informs the guiding hypothesis of his study: "If any two subgroups of New York City speakers are ranked in a scale of social stratification, then they will be ranked in the same order by their differential use of /ɹ/" (1966:44). In his department store study, Labov found abundant evidence in support of this hypothesis, observing, among other things, the highest rates of *r-lessness* among workers at S. Klein, a discount department store, and the lowest rates among workers at Saks, a luxury goods store.

This and other early work of Labov's (1963, 1968; Weinreich, Labov, and Herzog 1968) helped to establish the research paradigm of *variationist sociolinguistics*, which seeks to understand language variation and change through quantitative modeling of sociolinguistic variables (Cedergren and Sankoff 1974; Bayley 2002; Tagliamonte 2006; among others). The central assumption underlying such models is that variability in a given linguistic feature – be it a speech sound, morpheme, lexical item, etc. – is sensitive to the influence of sets of linguistic and social factors. The former consist of factors internal to the workings of linguistic systems *per se*, e.g. the phonetic context in which a sound occurs, the frequency of use of a lexical item, the grammatical category of some morpheme, the tense-mood-aspect and/or person and number of a verb, etc. The second set, the external constraints, consists of factors that describe characteristics of language users in a speech community, e.g. social class, sex, age, ethnicity, etc.

Among the first social categories to be extensively examined from this perspective were class and sex. Emblematic of such work is that of Trudgill (1972, 1974), whose investigations in Norwich, UK, contributed to the explicit formulation of the concepts of *overt* and *covert linguistic prestige*, or the social value associated with *standard* and *non-standard* (or *vernacular*) language forms, respectively. Standard forms are those features and ways of speaking which are sanctioned as correct or proper by institutions that wield social, political, and economic power in a particular community. Non-standard forms fail to conform to such prescriptions. Trudgill observed systematic differences in the use of standard features across levels of social class and sex: Speakers of higher social class, defined in terms of their level of education and occupation, tended to use standard forms at higher rates than speakers of lower social class. He also observed that women tend to produce standard features at higher rates than men, even within a given social class. For instance, in Trudgill's Norwich study, lower working-class males' rates of *-ing* reduction, that is, their production of a word like *working* as work[n], were substantially higher than those of women in the same social class.

Trudgill suggests that class- and sex-based differences in language use depend on speakers' varying orientations towards overtly and covertly prestigious behavior. It is not that lower working-class males are *unaware* of overtly prestigious forms. Rather, it is that their linguistic choices reflect their orientation towards the social value that is covertly ascribed to non-standard forms, which are themselves frequently linked to connotations of masculinity and toughness that are supposedly characteristic of working-class life. More recent research has refined these interpretations, resulting in a clearer understanding of the role of sex in sociolectal variation as well as its interaction with age, class, and linguistic innovation (Eckert 1989, 1997, 2008; Labov 1990). Eckert, for instance, has challenged the notion of *female conservatism* in linguistic variation by showing that in cases of language change, in contrast to cases of *stable variation*, women (and young women in particular) are often linguistic innovators, a phenomenon that has been dubbed "the Gender Paradox" (Labov 2001:292–293). Eckert's work has also helped broaden conceptions of the social meaning of linguistic forms, allowing language scholars to move beyond questions of linguistic prestige. Instead, she and others have focused on the *indexicality* of linguistic forms, that is, the ability of a sound, word, or construction to dynamically communicate a speaker's attitude(s) toward his or her interlocutors and to point to attributes of their identity, including their membership in certain social groups, e.g. jocks, burnouts, nerds, etc.

Both the variationist paradigm and the insights of linguistic anthropology have been brought to bear on the study of sociolectal variation in the Hispanophone world. It is not possible to mention all of the relevant research here (see Díaz-Campos 2011 for a handbook-length treatment of this topic). Suffice it to say that nearly every variable feature that has been systematically studied has revealed differentiation along social and linguistic dimensions. For instance, investigations of variation in coda /s/ have found that it is more likely to be weakened by men than by women (Fontanella de Weinberg 1974; Cepeda 1995; among others), by younger rather than older speakers (Poplack 1979; Guillén Sutil 1992), and by working-class speakers (Alba 1990; Cepeda 1995). Other features for which class, sex, and/or age differentiation have been reported include (but are not limited to) the lenition of /tʃ/, deletion of intervocalic /d/, voicing of post-alveolar fricatives, *ceceo, voseo, leísmo*, lexical borrowing, and code-switching.

In her 1987 study of /tʃ/, in Panama, Cedergren found that rates of deaffrication (i.e. *mucho* realized as [muʃo]) were significantly higher among younger speakers overall, and among young women in particular. Cameron's 2005 investigation of intervocalic /d/ deletion in the speech of Puerto Ricans in San Juan observed that differences between men and women waxed and waned with age (for detailed discussion of this study see Section 24.5 below). Rohena-Madrazo's 2015 study of *zh-/sheísmo* (also detailed in Section 24.5) found that a shift towards devoiced fricatives in Buenos Aires was being led by younger, working-class speakers. In a 2008 study conducted in Jerez de la Frontera, Spain, García-Amaya observed that women were more sensitive than men to the social signaling potential of the use of [s] vs. [θ] in cases of orthographic *ci, ce, s*, and *z*. Both Quintanilla

Aguilar (2009) and Michnowicz and Place (2010) examined attitudes towards *voseo* in central America. These studies affirm the complex indexicality of this form, highlighting a tension between the generally non-standard, historically stigmatized status of *voseo* in central America and the possibility that an expansion of the use of *vos* is being led by younger, more educated speakers. In her 1979 study of clitic pronouns (discussed further in Section 24.5), Klein identifies an interaction between class and region. While *leísmo* is observed in the speech of residents of three provinces in Rioja, Spain, its frequency of use and sensitivity to social class differences varies widely across the provinces. Varra's 2013 investigation of lexical borrowing among Spanish-speaking New Yorkers identifies social class as a key determinant of borrowing frequency. Among first-generation immigrants, the most frequent borrowers of English-origin lexical items into Spanish discourse were individuals with more education. Finally, Poplack's (1980) study of code-switching among Puerto Ricans in New York City revealed significant differences along lines of sex (women produced intra-sentential switches at a significantly higher rate than men) and age of acquisition of Spanish and English (those who learned these languages in early childhood were the most frequent intra-sentential code-switchers). What these and many other studies illustrate is that the notions of social stratification, linguistic prestige, and the indexical field generalize to Spanish-speaking (and very likely all linguistic) communities, and that social dimensions are rich and regular vectors of linguistic variation within them.

24.4 Idiolectal Variation

If sociolinguistics is a field that puts language variation under a microscope, then the study of idiolectal variation is sociolinguistics at its highest level of resolution. For at this level, we zoom in to focus on single individuals. That is, while dialectal and sociolectal patterns reveal how language use varies between and within communities, idiolectal variation illuminates differences between and within particular individuals. Differences between language users are unsurprising for two reasons. First, inter-speaker variation is the underlying basis of sociolectal variation, as generalizations about groups of people – e.g. younger speakers, men, working-class women, etc. – depend on differences in the behavior of individuals who fit these descriptions. Second, while the cognitive and biological basis of the human language faculty may be uniform across our species, the life experiences that shape its expression are unique to individual language users. This all but guarantees, for example, that one individual will accept a certain construction as grammatical while another in the same community will not, and that one person may use a particular feature at a significantly different rate from another.

Perhaps less immediately apparent than differences between individuals is the presence of structured linguistic variation within the behavior a single person. However, when we consider that the entirety of individual linguistic competence is never brought to bear in any single linguistic interaction, and that linguistic forms have social as well as referential meanings, then variation within the individual also becomes unsurprising. Indeed, in the same way that a professional singer may know jazz standards, gospel numbers, and pop songs, each of us possesses a rich *linguistic repertoire*. Just as the singer knows when a pop tune is appropriate and when it is time to sing the blues, a language user knows which linguistic features to deploy, given the social context and interpersonal dynamics that characterize a particular linguistically-mediated interaction. A language user may draw from very different parts of her repertoire, choosing between entire linguistic systems, or speaker-internal variation may manifest as fine-grained modulation in the production of a single speech sound.

Such variation has been central to the sociolinguistic perspective from the outset. In the foundational research mentioned in the preceding paragraph, intra-speaker variation is frequently discussed in the context of *stylistic variation*. In Trudgill's work (1974), for instance, lower working-class women varied substantially in their production of -*ing* depending on whether they were reading a word list or making casual conversation. In her 1982 study Cheshire found that young boys' rates of non-standard features varied significantly in relation to context, namely, depending on whether they were in the classroom or out on the playground. The notion that speakers shift across formal and informal styles has also featured prominently in Labov's work (1990, 2001). Similar patterns of stylistic variation have been observed throughout the Spanish-speaking world. For example, Alba (2004) reports on stylistic variation in the speech of Dominicans across numerous levels of linguistic structure. With regard to phonological variation, for instance, Alba observes that raising of /e/ to /i/ (e.g. *pasear* 'to go for a walk' realized as *pasiar*) as well as deletion of coda /s/ and intervocalic /d/ (e.g. *dedo* produced as *deo*, *hablado* realized as *hablao*) increase in frequency as situational formality decreases. With respect to morphosyntax, he notes more frequent use of diminutive suffixes (e.g. *cafecito* 'coffee,' *tempranito* 'early' vs. *café*, *temprano*) in informal settings. At the lexical level he identifies pairs of synonyms that are characterized by their varying likelihood of use in formal and informal settings, respectively (e.g. *centavo* 'cent' vs. *chele*, *borrachera* 'drunkenness' vs. *jumo*, *poco* 'little' vs. *chin*, etc.)

In addition to stylistic considerations, another dimension of idiolectal variation is temporal in nature. That is, the content of our linguistic repertoires, as well as our use of them, changes across our lifetimes. This is most obvious in early life, when children come to acquire the linguistic norms of their communities. However, there is a growing body of research that reveals linguistic change across the lifespan of individuals (Zentella 1997; Harrington *et al.* 2000; Sankoff and Blondeau 2007; Bowie 2010; Baxter and Croft 2016). Of particular relevance is the work of Zentella (1997), whose longitudinal study of bilingualism in *El Barrio* directly bears on variation across the lifetime and also offers a segue into the final section of this chapter, which highlights the intersection of dialectal, sociolectal, and idiolectal variation. Zentella's study focuses on five girls of Puerto Rican origin who lived on the same block in New York City's East Harlem neighborhood. Zentella first examined the girls' behavior when they were children (ranging in age from six to eleven years old) and then again when they were young adults (ages 19–24). While all of the adult women continued to self-identify as bilingual and retained the ability to use Spanish in locally sensitive and sociolinguistically sophisticated ways – a capacity Zentella calls *communicative competence* – differences emerged in their use of Spanish verbal inflectional morphology. Some of the women were able to hit prescriptive targets across a wide range of tense, mood, and aspectual combinations (e.g. they demonstrated standard usage of the *pluperfect subjunctive, conditional perfect*, etc.). Others among the women were more restricted in this regard and instead relied heavily on the *present, preterit*, and *imperfect* at the expense of other tenses. Remarking on the source of these differences, Zentella writes that "individual differences were rooted in the life experiences which weakened their participation in Spanish-dominant networks and immersed them in English-only settings to greater or less degrees" (1997:211). Zentella's study highlights the ways in which patterns of dialectal, sociolectal, and idiolectal variation flow in and out of one another, finding their confluence in individual language users whose identities encompass each of these dimensions at once, i.e. speakers' identities simultaneously include their geographic origin, place of residence, level of education, sex, age, social network, linguistic repertoire, etc. The final section of the chapter surveys a selection of studies that highlight the ways in which these various dimensions intersect, working in tandem to reveal patterns of linguistic behavior.

24.5 Dialectal, Sociolectal, and Idiolectal Variation in Interaction

The studies that are discussed below were selected because together they highlight Spanish speakers across a broad geographic range, including the Iberian peninsula, Latin America, and the United States. In addition, they illustrate variation across different levels of linguistic and social organization, examining phonological, morphological, and morphosyntactic phenomena along dimensions of region, sex, class, and age. They also bear on the outcomes of linguistic contact, both between speakers of Spanish with differing regional origins as well between speakers of Spanish and English. Finally these studies highlight group-level trends as well as individual variation within particular groups. They include an investigation of (i) *le/laísmo* in Castilla la Vieja (Klein 1979; Section 24.5.1), (ii) *consonantal lenition* in Puerto Rico (Cameron 2005; Section 24.5.2), (iii) *devoicing* of /ʒ/ in Buenos Aires (Rohena-Madrazo 2015; Section 24.5.3), (iv) *subject pronouns* in New York City (Otheguy and Zentella 2012; Section 24.5.4), and (v) *coda /s/ weakening* in New York City (Erker and Otheguy 2016; Section 24.5.5).

24.5.1 *Le/Laísmo* in Castilla la Vieja

Klein's study (1979), which highlights the intersection of dialectal and sociolectal variation, examines the variable use of *le, la,* and *lo* in interviews with residents of three provinces in the Castilla la Vieja region of Spain: Valladolid, Soria, and Logroño (now known as La Rioja). Speakers in this region are well known for using these clitic pronouns in a way that distinguishes them from much of the rest of the Hispanophone world. Instead of being distributed in terms of structural case, *le, la,* and *lo* are used, in Klein's terms, *referentially* by these speakers. The referential uses of these forms are commonly referred to as *leísmo, laísmo,* and *loísmo,* respectively. The first of these, which refers to the use of the clitic *le* as a direct object, is sometimes subdivided into *leísmo animado* (in which the referent is animate, e.g. **Le** *vi a Marco* 'I saw Mark') and *leísmo inanimado* (in which the referent is inanimate, e.g. **Le** *leímos en la escuela* 'we read it in school'). *Laísmo* and *loísmo,* refer, respectively, to the use of **la** and **lo** as indirect objects in examples like *Su novio* **la/lo** *dio una sortija* 'His/her boyfriend gave him/her a ring.'

Klein's data reveal a number of relevant trends, the first of which is that across the three provinces, each of which belongs to the larger region of Castilla la Vieja, speakers vary substantially, echoing Henríquez Ureña's remark on the dialectal zones of Latin America that "Inside of each zone, there are then subdivisions" (1921:360; my translation). Consider Figure 24.1a, which displays percentages of *referential* as opposed to *case-based* use of *le* and *la* across the three provinces (Klein's data for *loísmo* is relatively restricted and will not be discussed in detail). The figure reveals similarities as well as differences between the provinces. Speakers in all three demonstrate referential uses of *le* and *la,* and *leísmo animado* is the most frequent type observed. At the same time, geographically constrained differences emerge, with speakers in Logroño and Soria producing referential *le* and *la* at much lower rates than speakers in Valladolid. In addition to a pattern of substantial *inter*-provincial variation, Klein's data also illustrate *intra*-provincial variation along lines of social class (see Figure 24.1b).

In Valladolid, referential use of *le* for animates does not vary along lines of social class (which Klein defines largely in terms of place of residence and rurality vs. urbanity). That is, rates of *leísmo animado* are similarly high

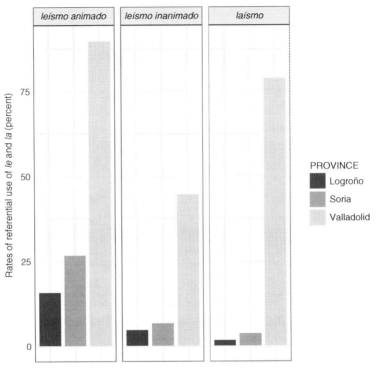

Figure 24.1a Rates of referential use of *le* and *la* across three provinces in Castilla la Vieja
Source: Klein (1979)

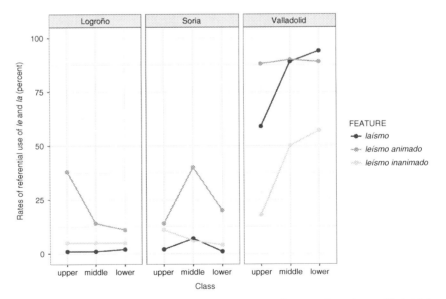

Figure 24.1b Rates of referential use of *le* and *la* across three provinces in Castilla la Vieja: *intra*-provincial variation along lines of social class
Source: Klein (1979)

across speakers whose social class Klein categorized as *alta* 'upper,' *media* 'middle,' or *baja* 'lower.' Evidence of class-based variation in Valladolid *does* appear, however, with respect to *leísmo inanimado* and *laísmo*: as class shifts from upper, to middle, and then to lower, rates for these features increase. This, in turn, contrasts with the data from Soria, where overall rates of referential usage are much lower, and where there *is* evidence of class-based differences in the distribution of *leísmo animado*: In Soria, middle-class speakers have higher rates of *leísmo animado* than both the upper and lower classes. Remarking on the results from Soria, Klein writes:

> It suggests that this zone – even being predominantly "case-based" in its use of clitics and in this sense more similar to the Spanish-speaking world *outside* of Castile itself – nevertheless shows evidence of positively valuing the typical uses of clitics from Castile in that the middle class tends to adopt them. (1979:59; my translation)

Finally, results from Logroño show referential usage in this province to be very infrequent:

> Therefore, with respect to clitic use we could say that, of the three provinces examined, Logroño is the least "Castilian" in the synchronic and geographic sense of the word. (1979: 59; my translation).

That being said, even within the Logroño data set there is evidence of two things: (i) the broad regional preference for *leísmo animado* over other referential uses and (ii) differentiation by class. For instance, among Logroño males, it is the upper-class speakers who have the highest rates of *leísmo animado*. This contrasts with Valladolid, where use of this feature was not sensitive to class differences, and is also different from Soria, where the class effect amounted to the middle class preferring *leísmo animado* more than the upper- and lower-class speakers. Klein's study provides a valuable demonstration of the complex relationship between physical space, social stratification, and linguistic variation. Though all three provinces are part of a single larger region, clear inter-provincial differences emerge. Of particular importance is that the geographically-constrained differences are not limited to variation in rates of use but that they also arise with respect to the social distribution of patterned variation. Indeed, the same social dimension, class, is not equivalently predictive of differences in speakers' behavior in each province, reflecting the influence of independent and local community norms.

24.5.2 Consonantal Lenition in Puerto Rico

Among the patterns of dialectal variation mentioned above, few have received as much attention as consonantal lenition in the Caribbean. However, while it is true that higher rates of consonantal weakening are typically reported among speakers in this region than among those who

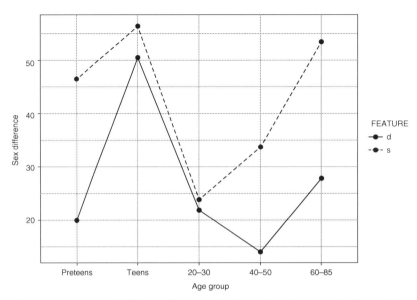

Figure 24.2 Degrees of difference between females and males across the lifespan for word-final /s/ and intervocalic /d/
Source: Cameron (2005)

reside in the interior and highland regions of Latin America, there is clear evidence of sociolectal variation within Caribbean communities. In his 2005 study Cameron investigates two dimensions of such variation, focusing on the intersection of sex and age. Data were collected from 62 speakers in Puerto Rico, ranging from five to 85 years old. Guiding Cameron's analysis is the notion that sex segregation varies across the lifespan, with male and female segregation peaking in teenage years, dropping when adults enter the work force, and then increasing again as adults grow old. Cameron links these trends to patterns of linguistic variation, showing that greater sex segregation correlates with greater sex differences in linguistic behavior. The linguistic features under investigation are lenition of word-final /s/ and intervocalic /d/. Figure 24.2 summarizes Cameron's main results, plotting the degrees of difference (as measured by weights assigned by the VARBRUL statistical analysis program) between sexes across different age groups. The dashed line corresponds to sex differences for /s/ lenition and the solid line corresponds to sex differences in the production of intervocalic /d/. Cameron interprets the trends as follows:

> During the working years of the middle age groups, age separation and, consequently, gender separation are relaxed. Thus, the reduction in degree of difference stems from increased cross-age and cross-gender interaction. With increased cross-gender interaction comes convergence between female and male speakers. This convergence, in quantitative terms, is revealed in the decreased degree of difference between females and males of the middle age groups. (2005: 40)

Cameron's study is valuable for several reasons. First, it serves as another reminder that sociolectal variation is a regular feature of language use in geographically circumscribed communities – i.e. all of his participants are Puerto Ricans from San Juan, and they vary widely in their treatment of the variables under analysis. This study is also important in that it shows sex differences in language use to be dynamic, varying across the lifespan in relation to factors in the external world, i.e. the ebb and flow of sex segregation.

24.5.3 Devoicing of /ʒ/ in Buenos Aires

The central aim of Rohena-Madrazo's (2015) study is to assess the potential completion of a sound change among speakers in Buenos Aires, Argentina; namely a shift from a voiced to a voiceless post-alveolar fricative (/ʒ/ → /ʃ/) in the first sound of words like *yo* and *llamar*. Of relevance to the present discussion are the patterns of sociolectal and idiolectal variation that Rohena-Madrazo identifies in his analysis. Earlier work on the possible shift from the voiced to devoiced variant suggested that the change was being led by younger females (Wolf and Jiménez 1979; Fontanella de Weinberg 1983). In more recent work, Chang (2008), also working in Buenos Aires, observed an age difference effect such that speakers born before 1945 were *voicers* while those born after 1975 were *devoicers*. To investigate the possible completion of the change, Rohena-Madrazo compared rates of voicing – defined as the percentage of a given fricative that shows evidence of vocal fold vibration – in alveolar as well as post-alveolar fricatives. The former category of sounds was used to establish a baseline rate of voicing that emerges during frication, largely as a result of coarticulatory effects. That is, when phonologically voiceless fricatives occur between/adjacent to voiced segments, they are naturally likely to evince some coarticulatory voicing, especially at the onset and offset of frication. Rohena-Madrazo's logic is that if a speaker has a higher rate of percentage voicing for post-alveolar than alveolar fricatives, then s/he remains a *voicer*. However, if a speaker's percentage of voicing is comparable across alveolar and post-alveolar fricatives, then s/he has completed the change, i.e. s/he is a *devoicer*.

Rohena-Madrazo's (2015) study included 16 participants stratified by sex, age, and class. There were eight men and eight women, eight younger (18–29 years of age) and eight older speakers (55 and up), as well as eight upper- and eight middle-class speakers (defined in terms of place of residence, i.e. residents of northern Buenos Aires were considered upper class while residents of the southern part of the city were grouped into the middle class). Data were collected from production tasks, including a word list and a sentence list, with the first designed to elicit more careful speech than the second. When divided by class and age, the older upper-class speakers showed the highest amount of percentage voicing in their post-alveolar fricatives (M = 53.2 percent). Younger upper-class and older middle-class speakers showed comparable percentage voicing (M = 29 percent and 34.8 percent, respectively), and younger middle-class speakers had a mean percentage voicing of 18.6 percent. Rohena-Madrazo then compared these rates to the amount of voicing that occurs in these speakers' production of /s/, which, we should recall, is phonologically voiceless but variably phonetically voiced. The mean percentage voicing rates of /s/ for the older–upper-, younger–upper-, older–middle-, and younger–middle-class groups were 13, 18, 12, and 20 percent, respectively. On the basis of these comparisons Rohena-Madrazo concludes that for the younger middle-class speakers, the change has been completed, as their post-alveolar fricatives are no more voiced than are their productions of /s/. Figure 24.3a illustrates the results with a series of boxplots.

An additional feature of this study is its analysis of individual speakers, which reveals group-internal differences. For instance, while all four speakers classified as younger middle class fit the overall pattern of the group – i.e. there is no significant difference in percentage voicing between their alveolar and postalveolar fricatives – there is substantial internal variation among the other groups: One older upper-class speaker is actually a *devoicer*, only one younger upper-class speaker turns out to be a *voicer*, and the older middle-class speakers are split, with two *voicers* and one *devoicer*. These results, illustrated in Figure 24.3b, highlight not only the potential for idiolectal variation to emerge within any socially defined group of speakers, but they also serve as a reminder that the relatively extreme behavior of a single individual can distort group-level behavior. Indeed, the quantitative evidence supporting the conclusion that younger upper-class speakers are *voicers* is largely based on the behavior of Speaker 21.

In addition to providing an innovative way for assessing the dynamics of a sound change that manifests at the subsegmental level, this study also highlights the complex relationship between groups and individuals. Only one group defined by the study's social parameters (age and class) is internally homogenous with respect to participation in the change under investigation (i.e. the younger middle class). Internal variation among the other groups is non-trivial. Indeed, in each of the other three groups there is at least one individual who differs from his or her age-class cohort in terms of (non-)participation in the sound change.

24.5.4 Subject Pronouns in New York City

Otheguy and Zentella's 2012 study of Spanish in New York City is based on sociolinguistic interviews with 140 speakers with origins in one of two regions in Latin America; 72 of the speakers were either born in or have family roots in the Caribbean (represented in the study by Puerto Ricans, Dominicans, and Cubans), and 68 speakers have family backgrounds in the Latin America mainland (in Mexico, Colombia, or Ecuador). Speakers in the study also vary across several social dimensions, including age, sex,

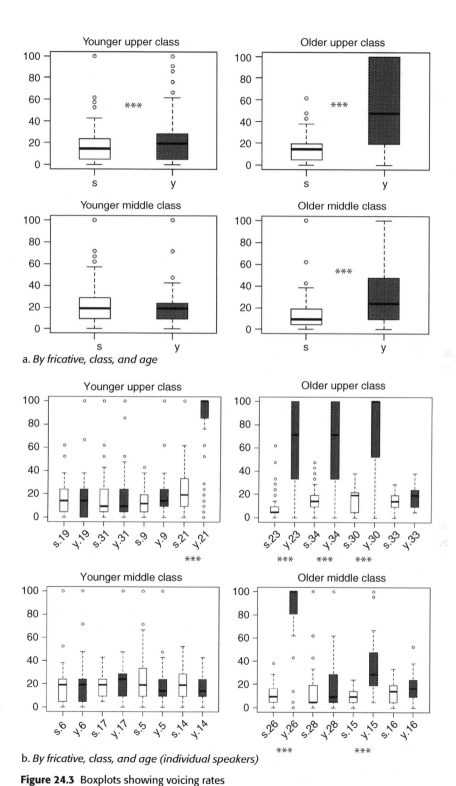

Figure 24.3 Boxplots showing voicing rates
The white and black rectangles show the 2nd and 3rd quartiles of the data distribution for the variable on the y-axis, which is Percentage Voicing. The white rectangles refer to the alveolar fricative and the black rectangles refer to the post-alveolar fricative. "y" represents postalveolar fricatives. Asterisks indicate a significant difference (*** = $p < 0.001$). The number to the right of "s" or "y" in Figure 24.3b indicates the subject identification number.
Source: Rohena-Madrazo (2015)

and socioeconomic status, as well as in terms of age of arrival in and time spent living in New York City. Otheguy and Zentella's analysis of this corpus focuses primarily on the variable use of subject personal pronouns, e.g. *(yo) canto* 'I sing,' *(ella) canta* 'she sings,' etc. Variation in this feature has been the subject of extensive investigation in Hispanic linguistics (Guitart 1982; Silva-Corvalán 1982; Cameron 1993; Bayley and Pease-Alvarez 1996; Flores-Ferrán 2004; Orozco and Guy 2008; Torres Cacoullos and Travis 2010; Claes 2011; Holmquist 2012; Shin 2014; Shin and Montes Alcalá 2014; Michnowicz 2015; Carvalho *et al.* 2015). Two aspects of this research are relevant to the topic at hand. The first is that rates of pronoun use in variable contexts, or simply *pronoun rates*, observed in Caribbean communities are typically higher than those reported among communities located in the Latin American mainland. In addition, subject pronouns represent a site of cross-linguistic difference, i.e. pronoun rates among Spanish speakers are considerably lower than those of English speakers, who have been shown to use subject pronouns at rates upwards of 90 percent (Shin and Montes Alcalá 2014). In New York City, then, pronominal variation can function as a diagnostic for potential outcomes of contact between (i) Spanish speakers with different regional origins and (ii) speakers of Spanish and English.

Otheguy and Zentella's (2012) analysis centers on comparisons of groups defined by speakers' ages of arrival and years spent living in NYC, proposing the groups *Newcomers, Established immigrants,* and *New York raised* (Table 24.1).

The authors interpret the higher pronoun rates of the *Established immigrants* and *New York raised* as evidence of the influence of English pronominal norms upon members of these groups. Though Otheguy and Zentella do not focus on idiolectal variation in their analyses, they do provide, for each speaker in their study, a listing of pronoun rates, ages of arrival in, and years spent living in New York City (Otheguy and Zentella (2012:77–80). These data make it possible to address an issue of interest to the present chapter, namely the relationship between group-level trends and individual behavior (Figure 24.4a). Each dot in this figure represents an individual in Otheguy and Zentella's study. The x-axis corresponds to the

Table 24.1 *Pronoun rates (percent) for three generational groups in New York City*

	Age of arrival	Years in USA	Pronoun rate (%)
Newcomers (N = 39)	≤ 17	≤ 5	29
Established immigrants (N = 73)	≥ 13	≥ 11	33
New York raised (N = 28)	< 3 or NYC born	–	38

$F(2, 137) = 4.4; p < 0.01$
Source: Otheguy and Zentella (2012)

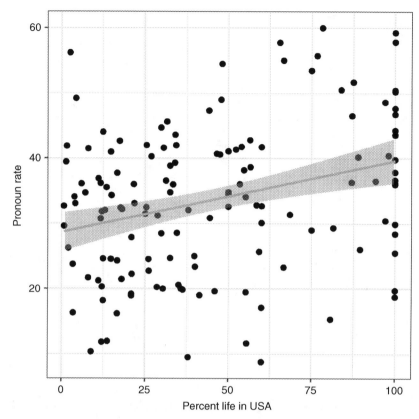

Figure 24.4a Subject pronoun rates of 140 speakers in New York City
Source: Otheguy and Zentella (2012)

percentage of a person's life that has been lived in the United States, which is calculated by dividing the numbers of years that s/he has lived in the US by overall age; e.g. a 40-year-old who has lived in the US for 20 years has a *percent life in USA* (PLUS) of 50; for a person born and raised in the USA, the value of this variable is 100. As the regression line illustrates, speakers with a greater proportion of life experience in the US tend to have higher pronoun rates: $r(138) = 0.3$, $p < 0.001$. It is also clear, both from the relatively modest correlation coefficient and from the distribution of individuals across the figure, that not every speaker in the study participates in the overall trend. That is, the group-level pattern coexists with wide-ranging variation at the speaker level. The extent to which a particular individual might diverge from a group-level pattern can be extreme. Consider Figure 24.4b, which differs from Figure 24.4a in that a separate regression line has been calculated for each regional group in the data. Two speakers are also highlighted, *Dario* and *Denisa*. The overall trend in the data – that is, higher pronoun rates with increased PLUS – emerges within each regional group of speakers. The region-specific correlations between these two parameters are, for Caribbeans ($r(70) = 0.39$, $p < 0.001$),

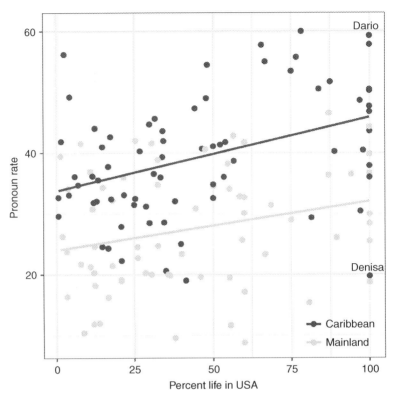

Figure 24.4b Subject pronoun rates of 140 speakers in New York City – Caribbeans and Mainlanders
Source: Otheguy and Zentella (2012)

and, for Mainlanders (r(66) = 0.26, p < 0.03). Additionally, results of a linear regression indicate that both *Region* (B = 0.5, p < 0.001) and *PLUS* (B = 0.28, p < 0.001) are significant predictors of pronoun rates. There is no statistical evidence of an interaction between them, however. In other words, there is evidence supporting the interpretation that contact with English is driving pronoun rates higher for both regional groups, but there is, at least in the aggregate, no statistical evidence to suggest that contact between Caribbeans and Mainlanders is leading to the leveling of regional differences in pronoun rates. (NB: Otheguy and Zentella do report evidence of leveling in relation to linguistic constraint hierarchies that condition pronoun use.)

A speaker like Dario, with a *PLUS* of 100 and a pronoun rate of 59.2, helps drive these trends. Dario is a 25-year-old of Dominican origin who was born in the Bronx. He reports speaking English *excellently* and Spanish *very well*. A speaker like Denisa, however, is an exception to the group-level analyses in two ways. She is an 18-year-old of Dominican heritage with a *PLUS* of 100 and a pronoun rate of 19.7. Not only is her behavior inconsistent with the interpretation that the contact setting promotes structural convergence with English pronominal norms; it is also hard to square with her regional origin. Even more intriguing is that despite having lived in the NYC area her entire life, Denisa reports being a *less than excellent* English speaker and remarks that she likes speaking Spanish more than English. She can read and write in both languages, and while she reports speaking mostly English with her father, siblings, and friends, she speaks Spanish with her mother. Speakers like Dario and Denisa highlight the fact that patterns of linguistic variation are not deterministic but rather probabilistic in nature, and that any given individual may participate in or diverge widely from a group-level trend. These results also highlight the well-recognized methodological challenges presented by the task of relating groups and individuals in a speech community (Guy 1980; Bayley et al. 2012). For quantitative variationist sociolinguistics at least, the focus on individuals often results in a problematic reduction of statistical power. At this level of analysis, the ability to confidently characterize structured variability is greatly limited: "To subdivide the data too finely – by limiting the scope to individuals and multiplying the number of environments – is inherently self-defeating" (Guy 1980:13). Overcoming this challenge can be difficult, as reliable tests of the relationship between individual and group behavior require large amounts of data.

24.5.5 Coda /s/ in New York City

Another feature examined using Otheguy and Zentella's (2012) data is variation in the production of coda /s/, a feature that has received tremendous attention within Hispanic linguistics. Of relevance here are well-established dialectal and sociolectal trends: Higher rates of /s/ weakening are routinely observed among communities located in the Caribbean and in coastal areas of Latin American; within specific locales, males tend to reduce /s/ at higher rates than women (see Lynch 2009 for a survey of dialectal and sociolectal patterns in /s/ production). In their 2016 study, Erker and Otheguy examine the acoustic properties of /s/ in the speech of 20 speakers, ten of Caribbean and ten of Mainland origin. Nine speakers fit Otheguy and Zentella's (2012) criteria for *Newcomers*, having arrived in New York after their 17th birthdays and having spent five years or less in the city at the time of their interview. The other 11 speakers are treated as *Longtime residents*. On average, members of this latter group arrived in New York City at the age of 12 and have spent 22 years in the city. 200 tokens of coda /s/ were collected for each speaker and were measured using two acoustic parameters, (i) *duration* in milliseconds and (ii) *center of gravity* (COG) in Hertz. COG is a weighted average calculated with equation (24.1):

(24.1) $COG = \sum fI / \sum I$

where I is the amplitude in decibels and f the frequency in Hertz of the spectral components. Consider Figure 24.5a, which plots duration on the *x*-axis and COG on the *y*-axis. Each dot in the plot represents the mean

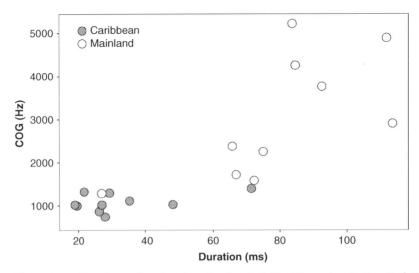

Figure 24.5a Duration and center of gravity of coda /s/ for 20 speakers in New York City
Source: Erker and Otheguy (2016)

duration and COG of coda /s/ for each speaker in the study. Speakers' region of origin is indicated by shade.

As expected in light of the research literature, most Caribbean speakers are clustered towards the lower left corner of the plot, indicating that for them /s/ is typically shorter in duration and lower in COG than it is in the speech of Mainlanders, who mostly populate the upper right quadrant of the plot. However, despite the general regional clustering observed in Figure 24.5a, there are also several speakers whose behavior locates them on the regional fringes or, in some cases, distinguishes them entirely from their regional counterparts. Figure 24.5b, which replicates the immediately preceding scatterplot, but treats *Newcomers* and *Longtime residents* separately, shows that regionally atypical behavior is restricted to speakers who belong to the latter group. When compared simultaneously in terms of duration and COG (through multiple analysis of variance, MANOVA), a significant regional difference emerges among *Newcomers*: $F = 40.79$, $p < 0.001$. However, region of origin fails to significantly predict differences in the speech of *Longtime residents*: $F = 2.94$, $p < 0.11$. The statistical attenuation of a regional difference among *Longtime residents* is largely the result of the behavior of three speakers, *Eduardo, Paula,* and *Delfina*, who are Ecuadorian, Puerto Rican, and Dominican, respectively. Their behavior suggests that diminished regional differences among *Longtime residents* is the result of different kinds of shifts among men and women. Eduardo, a Mainland male, produces /s/ in a way that is closer to Caribbean norms, while Paula and Delfina have approximated Mainland norms. A possible interpretation of their behavior is that the contact setting has redefined targets for what constitutes the prestige standard with respect to /s/. Consider, for instance, the case of Caribbean women, and in particular those recently arrived in New York City. While

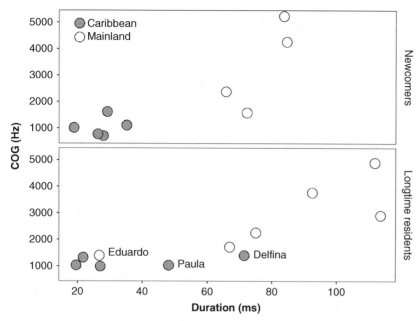

Figure 24.5b Duration and center of gravity of coda /s/ for 20 speakers in New York City – *Newcomers* compared to *Longtime residents*
Source: Erker and Otheguy (2016)

their speech may meet the standard for locally prestigious behavior outside of the US setting, it may fail to do so relative to the norms of their new home. Indeed, within the context of New York City, the behavior of Caribbean women is not only further from the standard when compared to Mainland women, but their /s/ production, locally defined, is likely to be more non-standard than that of Mainland men as well. Conversely, for Mainland men, what might represent covertly prestigious behavior in Latin America may fall short of doing so in New York City. This study, along with Otheguy and Zentella's (2012) analysis of pronominal variation in New York City, highlights the intersection of dialectal and sociolectal variation, and the two works demonstrate that contact-induced change is dependent on the innovative linguistic behavior of particular individuals.

24.6 Conclusion

This chapter began with the observation that each human being has a rich and multifaceted identity. Let us conclude by reaffirming that these many facets represent spaces in which the inherent variability and intrinsic sociality of language use may be circumscribed, described, and (ideally) explained. Patterns of dialectal, sociolectal, and idiolectal variation remind us that variability in language use is organized, predictable, and systematic. At the same time, the non-random nature of linguistic variation does not make us linguistic automatons. Indeed, the studies reviewed here emphasize that the systematicity of variation in language use is probabilistic rather than deterministic in nature. Patterns of variability that characterize how Spanish is used across the world, within communities, and between individuals are the result of choices that individuals make in linguistic interaction. These choices are not the product of our identities, but rather help bring our identities into being. In the years to come, sociolinguists will likely strive to continue refining our understanding of the relationship between individuals and the communities to which they belong. While the obstacles to such an understanding are significant, recent trends in quantitative analysis, along with related advances in sociolinguistic theory, have offered new pathways in the exploration of individuals and groups. For instance, the emergence of mixed-effects statistical models as the norm in quantitative analysis reflects the field's growing sophistication in accounting for the unique contribution of individuals to aggregated sets of linguistic data (Johnson 2009). Furthermore, innovative use of principal components analysis (Torres Cacoullos and Berry, forthcoming) suggests a method for "reverse-engineering" the relationship between social organization and linguistic behavior. Instead of categorizing speakers according to a set of *a priori* social dimensions and then examining variation across these categories, this approach relies on patterns of language use to establish social groups, thus building sociolinguistic analysis upon a more richly empirical foundation.

References

Alba, Orlando (1990). *Variación fonética y diversidad social en el español dominicano de Santiago.* Santiago: Pontificia Universidad Católica Madre y Maestra.

Alba, Orlando (1992). Zonificación dialectal del español en América. In César Hernández Alonso (ed.), *Historia y presente del español de América.* Valladolid: Pabecal, pp. 63–84.

Alba, Orlando (2004). Cómo hablamos los dominicanos: Un enfoque sociolingüístico (MS). Brigham Young University. Available from https://scholarsarchive.byu.edu/books/3/ (last access December 26, 2017).

Baxter, Gareth and Croft, William (2016). Modeling Language Change across the Lifespan: Individual Trajectories in Community Change. *Language Variation and Change*, 28, 129–173.

Bayley, Robert (2002). The Quantitative Paradigm. In J. K. Chambers, Peter Trudgill, and Natalie Schilling (eds.), *The Handbook of Language Variation and Change.* Malden, MA: Blackwell, pp. 117–141.

Bayley, Robert, Cárdenas, Norma L., Treviño Schouten, Belinda, and Vélez Salas, Carlos Martin (2012). Spanish Dialect Contact in San Antonio, Texas: An Exploratory Study. In K. Geeslin and M. Díaz-Campos (eds.),

Selected Proceedings of the 14th Hispanic Linguistics Symposium. Somerville, MA: Cascadilla, pp. 48–60.

Bayley, Robert and Pease-Alvarez, Lucinda (1996). Null and Expressed Pronoun Variation in Mexican-Descent Children's Spanish. In Jennifer Arnold, Renee Blake, and Brad Davidson (eds.), *Sociolinguistic Variation: Data, Theory, and Analysis*. Stanford, CA: Center for the Study of Language and Information, pp. 85–99.

Benavides, Carlos. (2003). La distribución del voseo en Hispanoamérica. *Hispania*, 86 (3), 612–623.

Bernstein, B. B. (2003). *Class, Codes and Control: Applied Studies towards a Sociology of Language*, Vol. 2. London: Routledge.

Bowie, David. (2010). The Ageing Voice: Changing Identity over Time. In Carmen Llamas and Dominic Watt (eds.), *Language and Identities*. Edinburgh: Edinburgh University Press, pp. 55–66.

Bucholtz, M. (2011). Race and the Re-Embodied Voice in American Film. *Language and Communication*, 31, 255–265.

Bucholtz, M. and Hall, K. (2004). Language and Identity. In Alessandro Duranti (ed.), *A Companion to Linguistic Anthropology*. Oxford: Blackwell, pp. 369–394.

Bucholtz, M. and Hall, K. (2010). Locating Identity in Language. In Carmen Llamas and Dominic Watt (eds.), *Language and Identities*. Edinburgh: Edinburgh University Press, pp. 18–28.

Cameron, Deborah (1992). *Feminism and Linguistic Theory* (2nd edn). New York: St. Martin's.

Cameron, Richard (1993). Ambiguous Agreement, Functional Compensation, and Nonspecific *tú* in the Spanish of San Juan, Puerto Rico, and Madrid, Spain. *Language Variation and Change*, 5, 305–334.

Cameron, Richard (2005). Aging and Gendering. *Language in Society*, 34, 23–61.

Canfield, D. Lincoln (1981). *Spanish Pronunciation in the Americas*. Chicago, IL: University of Chicago Press.

Carvalho, Ana M., Orozco, Rafael, and Lapidus Shin, Naomi (eds.) (2015). *Subject Pronoun Expression in Spanish: A Cross-Dialectal Perspective*. Washington, DC: Georgetown University Press.

Cedergren, Henrietta. (1987). The Spread of Language Change: Verifying Inferences of Linguistic Diffusion. In P. H. Lowenberg (ed.), *GURT '87. Language Spread and Language Policy: Issues, Implications, and Case Studies*. Washington, DC: Georgetown University Press, pp. 45–60.

Cedergren, H. J. and Sankoff, D. (1974). Variable Rules: Performance as a Statistical Reflection of Competence. *Language*, 50, 333–355.

Cepeda, G. (1995). Retention and Deletion of Word-Final /s/ in Valdivian Spanish (Chile). *Hispanic Linguist*, 6–7, 329–353.

Chang, Charles. (2008). Variation in Palatal Production in Buenos Aires Spanish. In M. Westmoreland and J. A. Thomas (eds.), *Selected proceedings of the 4th Workshop on Spanish Sociolinguistics*. Somerville, MA: Cascadilla, pp. 54–63.

Cheshire, J. (1982). *Variation in an English Dialect: A Sociolinguistic Study*. Cambridge: Cambridge University Press.

Chun, Elaine. (2001). The Construction of White, Black, and Korean American Identities through African American Vernacular English. *Journal of Linguistic Anthropology* 11, 52–64.

Claes, Jeroen (2011). ¿Constituyen las Antillas y el Caribe continental una sola zona dialectal? Datos de la variable expresión del sujeto pronominal en San Juan de Puerto Rico y Barranquilla, Colombia. *Spanish in Context*, 8 (2), 191–212.

Clements, Clancy J. (2009). *The Linguistic Legacy of Spanish and Portuguese: Colonial Expansion and Language Change*. Cambridge: Cambridge University Press.

del Valle, J. ed. (2013). *A Political History of Spanish: The Making of a Language*. Cambridge: Cambridge University Press.

Díaz-Campos, M. (ed.) (2011). *The Handbook of Hispanic Sociolinguistics*. Hoboken, NJ: John Wiley.

Eckert, P. (1989). *Jocks and Burnouts: Social Categories and Identity in the High School*. New York: Teachers College Press.

Eckert, P. (1997. Age as a Sociolinguistic Variable. In Florian Coulmas (ed.), *The Handbook of Sociolinguistics*. Oxford: Blackwell, pp. 151–167.

Eckert, P. (2000). *Linguistic Variation as Social Practice: The Linguistic Construction of Identity in Belten High*. Oxford: Blackwell.

Eckert, P. (2008). Variation and the Indexical Field. *Journal of Sociolinguistics*, 12 (4), 453–476.

Erker, Daniel and Otheguy, Ricardo (2016). Contact and Coherence: Dialect Leveling and Structural Convergence in NYC Spanish. *Lingua*, 172–173, (131–146).

Escobar, Anna María (2012). Spanish in Contact with Amerindian Languages. In José Ignacio Hualde, Antxon Olarrea, and Erin O'Rourke (eds.), *The Handbook of Hispanic Linguistics*. Hoboken, NJ: Blackwell, pp. 65–88.

Fishman, Joshua (1971). *Advances in the Sociology of Language*. The Hague: Mouton.

Flores-Ferrán, Nydia (2004). Spanish Subject Personal Pronoun Use in New York City Puerto Ricans: Can We Rest the Case for English Contact? *Language Variation and Change*, 16, 49–73.

Fontanella de Weinberg, M. B. (1974). Aspectos sociolingüísticos del uso de -s en el español bonaerense. *Orbis*, 23, 85–98.

Fontanella de Weinberg, M. B. (1983). Variación y cambio lingüístico en el español bonaerense. *Lingüística Española Actual*, 27, 215–247.

Fortes, M. (1984). Age, Generation, and Social Structure. In D. I. Kertzer and J. Keith (eds.), *Age and Anthropological Theory*. Ithaca, NY: Cornell University Press, pp. 99–122.

Gal, Susan and Irvine, Judith T. (1995). The Boundaries of Languages and Disciplines: How Ideologies Construct Difference. *Social Research*, 62 (4), 967–1001.

García-Amaya, L. J. (2008). Variable Norms in the Production of /θ/ in Jerez de la Frontera, Spain. In J. F. Siegel, T. C. Nagle, A. Lorente-Lapole, and J. Auger (eds.), *Indiana University Linguistics Club Working Papers 7: Gender in Language: Classic Questions, New Contexts*. Bloomington, IN: Indiana University Linguistics Club Publications, pp. 49–71.

Gaudio, Rudolf P. (2001). White Men do it too: Racialized (Homo)sexualities in Postcolonial Hausaland. *Journal of Linguistic Anthropology*, 11, 36–51.

Guillén Sutil, R. (1992). Una cuestión de fonosintaxis: Realización en andaluz de la /s/ final de palabra seguida de vocal. *Anuario de Estudios Filológicos*, 15, 135–153.

Guitart, Jorge M. (1982). Conservative versus Radical Dialects in Spanish: Implications for Language Instruction. In Joshua A. Fishman and Gary D. Keller (eds.), *Bilingual Education for Hispanic Students in the United States*. New York: Teachers College Press, pp. 167–177.

Guy, Gregory (1980). Variation in the Group and the Individual: The Case of Final Stop Deletion. In W. Labov (ed.), *Language in Time and Space*. New York: Academic Press, pp. 1–36.

Guy, Gregory (1988). Language and Social Class. In F. Newmeyer (ed.), *Linguistics: The Cambridge Survey*, Vol. 4: *Language: The Sociocultural Context*. Cambridge: Cambridge University Press, pp. 37–63.

Guy, Gregory (2014). Variation and Change in Latin American Spanish and Portuguese. In P. Amaral and Ana M. Carvalho (eds.), *Portuguese–Spanish Interfaces: Diachrony, Synchrony, and Contact*. Amsterdam: John Benjamins, pp. 443–464.

Harrington, J., Palethorpe, S., and Watson, C. (2000). Monophthongal Vowel Changes in Received Pronunciation: An Acoustic Analysis of the Queen's Christmas Broadcasts. *Journal of the International Phonetic Association*, 30 (1–2), 63–78.

Henríquez Ureña, Pedro. (1921). Observaciones sobre el español de América. *Revista de Filología Española*, 8, pp. 357–390.

Henríquez Ureña, Pedro. (1930). Observaciones sobre el español de América. *Revista de Filología Española*, 17, pp. 277–284.

Henríquez Ureña, Pedro. (1931). Observaciones sobre el español de América. *Revista de Filología Española*, 18, pp. 120–148.

Holmes, Janet, and Meyerhoff, Miriam (eds.) (2003). *The Handbook of Language and Gender*. Oxford: Blackwell.

Holmquist, Jonathan. (2012). Frequency Rates and Constraints on Subject Personal Pronoun Expression: Findings from the Puerto Rican Highlands. *Language Variation and Change*, 24, 203–220.

Johnson, D. E. (2009). Getting off the GoldVarb Standard: Introducing Rbrul for Mixed-Effects Variable Rule Analysis. *Language and Linguistics Compass*, 3 (1), 359–383.

Kany, Charles E. (1969). *Sintaxis hispanoamericana*. Madrid: Gredos.

Klein, Flora. (1979). Factores sociales en algunas diferencias lingüísticas en Castilla La Vieja. *Revista de Sociología*, 11, 45–64

Labov, W. (1963). The Social Motivation of a Sound Change. *Word*, 19, 273–309.

Labov, W. (1966). The Linguistic Stratification of "r" in New York City Department Stores. In W. Labov (ed.), *Sociolinguistic patterns*, Pennsylvania University Press, *Philadelphia*, pp. 43–69.

Labov, W. (1968). *The Social Stratification of English in New York City*. Washington DC: Center for Applied Linguistics.

Labov, W. (1990). The Intersection of Sex and Social Class in the Course of Linguistic Change. *Language Variation and Change*, 2, 205–254.

Labov, W. (2001). *Principles of Linguistic Change, Vol. 2: Social Factors*. Oxford: Blackwell.

Lipski, J. (1994). *Latin American Spanish*. London: Longman.

Lipski, J. (2012). Características del español filipino y del chabacano. In Isaac Donoso Jiménez (ed.), *Historia cultural de la lengua española en Filipinas: Ayer y hoy*. Madrid: Editorial Verbum, pp. 307–323.

Lipski, J. (2014). The Many Facets of Spanish Dialect Diversification in Latin America. In S. S. Mufwene (ed.), *Iberian Imperialism and Language Evolution in Latin America*. Chicago, IL: University of Chicago Press, pp. 38–75.

Lynch, Andrew (2009). A Sociolinguistic Analysis of Final /s/ in Miami Cuban Spanish. *Language Sciences*, 31 (6), 766–790.

Michnowicz, Jim (2015). Subject Pronoun Expression in Contact with Maya in Yucatan Spanish. In Ana Carvalho, Rafael Orozco, and Naomi L. Shin (eds.), *Subject Pronoun Expression in Spanish: A Cross-Dialectal Perspective*. Washington, DC: Georgetown University Press, pp. 101–119.

Michnowicz, Jim and Place, Soraya (2010). Perceptions of Second Person Singular Pronoun Use in San Salvador, El Salvador. *Studies in Hispanic and Lusophone Linguistics*, 3 (2), 353–377.

Mufwene, Salikoko. (2008). *Language Evolution: Contact, Competition and Change*. London and New York: Continuum.

Mufwene, Salikoko S. (2014). Latin America: A linguistic curiosity from the point of view of colonization and the ensuing language contacts. In S. S. Mufwene (ed.), *Iberian Imperialism and Language Evolution in Latin America*. Chicago, IL: University of Chicago Press, pp. 1–37.

Navarro Tomás, Tomás. (1942). The Linguistic Atlas of Spain and the Spanish of America. *Bulletin of the American Council of Learned Societies*, 34, 68–74.

Ochs, Elinor. (1992). Indexing gender. In Alessandro Duranti and Charles Goodwin (eds.), *Rethinking Context: Language as an Interactive Phenomenon*. New York: Cambridge University Press, pp. 335–358.

Orozco, Rafael and Guy, Gregory R. (2008). El uso variable de los pronombres sujetos: ¿Qué pasa en la costa Caribe colombiana? In Maurice

Westmoreland and Juan Antonio Thomas (eds.), *Selected Proceedings of the 4th Workshop on Spanish Sociolinguistics*. Somerville, MA: Cascadilla, pp. 70–80.

Otheguy, Ricardo and Zentella, Ana Celia (2012). *Spanish in New York: Language Contact, Dialect Leveling and Structural Continuity*. Oxford: Oxford University Press.

Penny, Ralph. (2000). *Variation and Change in Spanish*. Cambridge: Cambridge University Press.

Poplack, Shana (1979). Function and Process in a Variable Phonology (Doctoral dissertation). University of Pennsylvania.

Poplack, Shana (1980). Sometimes I'll Start a Sentence in Spanish Y TERMINO EN ESPAÑOL: Toward a Typology of Code-Switching. *Linguistics*, 18 (7/8), 581–618.

Poplack, Shana and Levey, Stephen (2010). Contact-Induced Grammatical Change: A Cautionary Tale. In Peter Auer and Jürgen Erich Schmidt (eds.), *Language and Space: An International Handbook of Linguistic Variation*, Vol. 1: *Theories and Methods*. Berlin: De Gruyter, pp. 391–419.

Quilis, Antonio. (1992). *La lengua española en cuatro mundos*. Madrid: Mapfre.

Quintanilla Aguilar, J. R. A. (2009). Actitudes de los hablantes de San Salvador hacia el tuteo y el voseo. *Hispania*, 92 (2), 361–373.

Resnick, Melvyn C. (1980). *Phonological Variants and Dialect Identification in Latin American Spanish*. Munich: De Gruyter.

Rickford, J. R. (1986). The Need for New Approaches to Social Class Analysis in Sociolinguistics. *Language and Communication*, 6 (3), 215–221.

Rohena-Madrazo, M. (2015). Diagnosing the Completion of a Sound Change: Phonetic and Phonological Evidence for /ʃ/ in Buenos Aires Spanish. *Language Variation and Change*, 27, 287–317.

Rona, José Pedro (1964). El problema de la división del español Americano en zonas dialectales. *Presente y Futuro de la Lengua Española*, 1, 215–226.

Sankoff, G. and Blondeau, H. (2007). Language Change across the Lifespan: /r/ in Montreal French. *Language*, 83 (3), 560–588.

Sayahi, L. (2004). The Spanish Language Presence in Tangier, Morocco: A Sociolinguistic Perspective. *Afro-Hispanic Review*, 23 (1), 54–61.

Shin, N. L. (2014). Grammatical Complexification in Spanish in New York: 3sg Pronoun Expression and Verbal Ambiguity. *Language Variation and Change*, 26, 303–330.

Shin, N. L. and Montes-Alcalá, C. (2014). El uso contextual del pronombre sujeto como factor predictivo de la influencia del inglés en el español de Nueva York. *Sociolinguistic Studies*, 8 (1), 85–110.

Silva-Corvalán, Carmen. (1982). Subject Expression and Placement in Mexican-American Spanish. In J. Amastae and L. Elías-Olivares (eds.), *Spanish in the United States: Sociolinguistic Aspects*. New York: Cambridge University Press, pp. 93–120.

Silva-Corvalán, Carmen. (1994). *Language Contact and Change: Spanish in Los Angeles*. Oxford: Oxford University Press.

Tagliamonte, S. A. (2006). *Analysing Sociolinguistic Variation*. Cambridge: Cambridge University Press.

Thomason, S. G. and Kaufman, T. (1988). *Language Contact, Creolization and Genetic Linguistics*. Berkeley, CA: University of California Press.

Torres Cacoullos, Rena and Berry, Grant M. (forthcoming). Language Variation in US Spanish: Social Factors. In K. Potowski (ed.), *Handbook of Spanish as a Minority/Heritage Language*. London and New York: Routledge.

Torres Cacoullos, Rena and Travis, Catherine E. (2010). Variable *yo* expression in New Mexico: English influence? In Susana Rivera-Mills and Daniel Villa Crésap (eds.), *Spanish of the US Southwest: A Language in Transition*. Madrid: Iberoamericana/Vervuert, pp. 189–210.

Trudgill, P. (1972). Sex, Covert Prestige and Linguistic Change in the Urban British English of Norwich. *Language in Society*, 1 (2), 179–195.

Trudgill, P. (1974). *The Social Differentiation of English in Norwich*. Cambridge: Cambridge University Press.

Varra, Rachel M. (2013). The Social Correlates of Lexical Borrowing in Spanish in New York City (Doctoral dissertation). CUNY.

Weinreich, Uriel. (1953 [1967]). *Languages in Contact*. The Hague: Mouton.

Weinreich, Uriel, Labov, William, and Herzog, Marvin (1968). Empirical Foundations for a Theory of Language Change. In Winfred P. Lehmann and Yakov Malkiel (eds.), *Directions for Historical Linguistics*. Austin, TX: University of Texas Press, pp. 95–195.

Winford, Donald. (2005). Contact-Induced Changes: Classification and Types of Processes. *Diachronica*, 22 (2), 373–427.

Wolf, C. and Jiménez, E. (1979). *El ensordecimiento del yeísmo porteño, un cambio fonológico en marcha*. In A. M. Barrenechea, M. de Rosetti, M. L. Freyre, E. Jiménez, T. Orecchia, and C. Wolf (eds.), *Estudios lingüísticos y dialectológicos*. Buenos Aires: Hachette, pp. 115–145.

Zamora Munné, J. C. and Guitart, Jorge M. (1982). *Dialectología hispanoamericana: Teoría, descripción, historia*. Salamanca: Colegio de España.

Zamora Vicente, Alonso (1970). *Dialectología española*. Madrid: Gredos.

Zentella, Ana Celia (1997). *Growing Up Bilingual: Puerto Rican Children in New York*. Malden, MA: Wiley-Blackwell.

Zimman, Lal (2013). Hegemonic Masculinity and the Variability of Gay-Sounding Speech: The Perceived Sexuality of Transgender Men. *Journal of Language and Sexuality*, 2 (1), 1–39.

25

National and Diasporic Spanish Varieties as Evidence of Ethnic Affiliations

Almeida Jacqueline Toribio

25.1 Introduction

Since the latter half of the 20th century, the United States has witnessed a shift towards greater ethnic and racial diversity; the presence of Hispanic immigrants and their native-born children has figured centrally in this reconfiguration and is projected to continue to contribute to increasing diversity for the coming decades.[1] The academic literature in the social sciences indicates that many Hispanics embrace views of identity that are often at odds with the social classifications they encounter in the receiving US society. As one example, the 2014 National Survey of Latinos (Pew Hispanic Center 2015) records that US-born Hispanics variously identify themselves with terms that refer to their family's country of origin (e.g. *Dominican*) or with a pan-ethnic descriptor such as *Latino*, in addition to the label *American*. Further defying US classifications, a full one-fourth identify themselves as racially "other" and volunteer "Hispanic" as their race (Pew Hispanic Center 2015), perhaps attempting to find expression for a multiracial *mulatto* and *mestizo* ancestry.[2] As a consequence, many Hispanics experience heightened attention to issues of distinctiveness and belonging, concepts that are closely linked with language practices. In an analysis of a Pew Hispanic Center survey (2015), Spanish was reported to be spoken by nearly three-fourths of Hispanics aged five and older, and a full 95 percent said that it was important for future

---

[1] Although Hispanic immigration has declined since 2000, rapid growth in the number of Hispanic births means the population will continue to increase (Source: Pew Research Center tabulations of the 2006–2012 American Community Survey). The terms "Hispanic" and "Latino" are used interchangeably in this chapter. The US government uses the label "Hispanic" to categorize Americans who trace their roots to Spanish-speaking countries.

[2] The term *mestizo* describes people of mixed white European and indigenous background; *mulatto* refers to a mixed-race ancestry that includes white European and black African roots.

generations to speak Spanish, suggesting that Spanish may follow a path different from the pattern of decline of other non-English languages in the US (López 2016).

For Hispanics, then, the maintenance of Spanish and specific features of the vernaculars of the country of origin and of diasporic enclaves may come to serve as emblems of affiliation with given home and host communities, whereas adoption of other vernaculars or affinity or shift towards English may signal a transition towards a more collective association or towards assimilation with American customs and values. Thus, language variation and language choice may be fruitfully employed as a lens through which to examine identity in Hispanic populations. In the present contribution we focus specifically on the linguistic practices of immigrant and US-born groups with roots in the Hispanophone nations of the Greater Antilles – Puerto Rico, Cuba, and the Dominican Republic – as they navigate conventional classifications that circulate in the US and eschew fixed categories and attendant terminology, among these, the binary descriptors of black vs. white, American vs. national origin, and Spanish-speaker vs. English-speaker. As will be appreciated in the following discussion, the notions of ethnicity and race that shape beliefs about language and language use are altered with movement from the Caribbean to US metropolises, particularly among Afro-Hispanics, an adjustment that must be acknowledged in interpreting their linguistic behaviors in diasporic settings.[3] Envisioned in this way, inquiry into the language practices of immigrants from the Spanish-speaking Caribbean necessitates an interdisciplinary approach that draws on methods and findings from multiple sub-disciplines, including demography, sociology, history, cultural anthropology, and social psychology, in addition to our point of interest: linguistics. We begin in Section 25.2 with a sketch of the Hispanophone Caribbean nations and the migration histories, settlement patterns, and broad characteristics of the three groups under study.

25.2 Persons with Origins in the Hispanophone Nations of the Greater Antilles: A Thumbnail Portrait

Hispanophone Antillean groups have origins in regions with shared colonial histories, imprinted in racial compositions and cultural traditions that resulted from the admixture of Taíno, Spanish, and African peoples. As a variety of Spanish, the Caribbean vernaculars are labeled "radical" and contrasted with the more conservative Latin American dialects of capital centers such as Bogotá, Mexico City, and Lima (Lipski 1994).

---

[3] The National Survey of Latinos conducted in 2014 by the Pew Research Center shows that one quarter of Hispanic adults self-identify as Afro-Latino, Afro-Caribbean or of African descent with roots in Latin America (López and González-Barrera 2016).

In evaluating the phonology of Caribbean Spanish, academics and laypersons point to what has been called the "tyranny" of coda /s/ deletion (Zentella 2004) and to the uncertain fate of coda liquids, as in the pronunciation of *cartas* 'letters,' which may be rendered as [kartah]/[karta], [kaltah]/[kalta], [kajtah]/[kajta], and [kattah]/[katta] across regions of Puerto Rico, Cuba, and the Dominican Republic. The lexicon, too, readily reflects characteristics of its past; there are indigenisms and Africanisms such as *zafacón* 'waste basket' and *gandul/guandul* 'pigeon pea,' alongside Canarian *guagua* 'bus.' At the level of morphosyntax, Caribbean Spanish varieties exhibit an increased incidence of expressed pre-verbal pronominal subjects, in finite and nonfinite clauses and even in interrogatives, as in *Es difícil para uno pronunciar las cosas*, 'It's difficult for one to pronounce things' and *¿Qué tú quieres?*, 'What do you want?,' where more conventional dialects demonstrate a marked preference for the prescribed null and/or postverbal forms. Of course, other regional and social lects of Spanish are shown to present many of the same linguistic attributes that are thought to distinguish Caribbean Spanish, although perhaps not with the same clustering or frequency. To be sure, what renders Caribbean Spanish distinct is not solely linguistic, but social: Caribbean Spanish is commonly racialized – i.e. imbued with racial connotations, a subject we return to below.

As noted at the outset, Hispanic immigrants and their offspring have transformed the US landscape in the latter half of the 20th century. Census data record that, as of 2013, Hispanics constituted 17.1 percent of the nation's total population and one of the nation's largest ethnic or racial minority groups, of which Hispanics with roots in the Caribbean accounted for 16.5 percent (López and Patten 2015). In these Caribbean countries, populations with African ancestry are larger, and, indeed, in the Pew National Survey of Latinos as reported by López and Barrera (2015), respondents with origins in the Caribbean are more likely to identify as Afro-Latino or Afro-Caribbean than those with roots elsewhere. Moreover, those who identify as Afro-Caribbean are more concentrated in metropolitan areas on the east coast and in the south: Puerto Ricans, who comprise 9.5 percent of the total Hispanic population, reside in the northeast (51 percent) and the southeast (31 percent); those of Cuban origin, totaling 3.7 percent of the total Hispanic population, are largely clustered in the southeast, with 68 percent living in Florida; and those of Dominican origin, comprising 3.3 percent of the total Hispanic population, have traditionally settled in the northeast (79 percent). Table 25.1 highlights some characteristics of each of these groups; the data are compiled from the resources in López and Patten's (2015) Pew Research Center report, which is derived from the 2013 American Community Survey.

While affording a convenient overview of the characteristics of the populations of interest, the figures in the above schema obscure important cross- and within-group disparities. Taylor *et al.* (2012) report that Hispanics in the US say that they represent many different cultures rather

Table 25.1 *Characteristics of Hispanics with origins in Puerto Rico, Cuba, and the Dominican Republic*

	Puerto Rican (5.12 million)	Cuban (1.98 million)	Dominican (1.78 million)
Immigration status	29% island-born 100% US citizens	57% foreign-born 59% US citizens	55% foreign-born 50% US citizens
Age	Median: 29	Median: 40	Median: 28
Educational attainment	18% Bachelor's degree	25% Bachelor's degree	17% Bachelor's degree
Identify as "white"	53.1%	85.4%	29.6%
Terms of identity	55% Puerto Rican 28% American 14% Hispanic/Latino	63% Cuban 19% American 11% Hispanic/Latino	66% Dominican 16% American 16% Hispanic/Latino
English proficiency	83% speak English proficiently	60% speak English proficiently	57% speak English proficiently
Spanish at home	61% speak Spanish at home	79% speak Spanish at home	88% speak Spanish at home
Language dominance[a]	42% English-dominant 36% bilingual 16% Spanish-dominant	13% English-dominant 36% bilingual 51% Spanish-dominant	10% English-dominant 43% bilingual 48% Spanish-dominant

[a] In the Pew Research Center surveys, respondents are classified as English dominant if they say they speak and read English very well or pretty well, but their ratings of Spanish on both categories are lower.

Source: Compiled from López and Patten (2015)

than a common culture, by a ratio of two to one (69 percent vs. 29 percent). For populations with origins in Spanish-speaking Caribbean nations, these perceived differences are based on the unique political projects of their homelands and on the specific periods and contexts of their incorporation into US society.

The influx of members of Cuba's elite classes and the reunification of families that followed (1959–1962 and 1965–1973, respectively) were supported by the US government and by the larger citizenry, which welcomed the surges of immigrants as political exiles of the Castro regime. Absent transnational ties and investments in the home country, this privileged group established itself firmly in Miami-Dade County, Florida, and gave rise to a robust Cuban-American community. As displayed in Table 25.1, 63 percent of persons with origins in Cuba identify as "Cuban"; however, these figures include second- and third-generation US residents who maintain only symbolic forms of Cuban culture and possess only receptive abilities in Spanish. In contrast to the influx of white, upper-class Cuban migrants incited by Castro's ascent, it was working-class, darker-skinned Puerto Ricans who were attracted by New York's garment industry post WWII. They settled into tall tenement buildings, toiled in factories, and forged affiliations with other minority groups, particularly African Americans. Although the racial tensions of the 1970s provoked a return to the Island, the more recent decline in the Puerto Rican economy has instigated new migratory paths to the mainland, though with notable modifications in settlement patterns and social characteristics. Note that, unlike other immigrants, Puerto Ricans are US citizens, facilitating their circular migration. Moreover, Puerto Rican immigrants are familiar with English; as a commonwealth territory of the US, Puerto Rico recognizes Spanish and English as co-official, though Spanish remains the primary language of business and education and the dominant language of the populace. This balance of languages is reversed stateside, as anticipated: a mere 16 percent are Spanish-dominant and only 61 percent speak Spanish at home. While this figure rises to 36 percent for those Puerto Ricans born on the Island, the number remains well below that of US- and foreign-born Cuban and Dominican groups. The latter group – Dominicans – present the highest rates of Spanish language in the home and the highest rates of bilingualism among the three groups depicted, a characteristic that may be correlated with ethnic pride and with racial self-identification, as members of this community struggle to cross racial borders in national *and* in diasporic contexts. Language maintenance among Dominicans in the diaspora reflects the nature and extent of their social and emotional ties to the cultural and social institutions of the homeland. Often sharing in phenotype with Haitians and with African Americans, many Dominicans find recourse in the performative function of language in marking themselves as "Dominican."

As should be evident, only through delving into facets of specific historical episodes and contemporary societies can we begin to understand the linguistic behaviors of immigrants. In Section 25.3, we examine language socialization in home and host contexts; this discussion is supported by published findings on the linguistic situation of Puerto Ricans in New York and central Florida enclaves, as well as by findings on the political and racial ideologies of Cuban immigrants, whose endurance is illustrated in the language attitudes conveyed by members of the Miami enclave. Section 25.4 elucidates the circumstances of Dominicans and Dominican-Americans, who straddle African and Hispanic classifications, in the Dominican Republic and in the US, by referring to research on the "acts of identity" performed via language by Dominicans in the country of origin and in the established migration and settlement destinations of New York, Providence (Rhode Island), and Reading (Pennsylvania).

25.3 Spanish Varieties in Home and Host Contexts

The presence of Puerto Ricans once defined the US Latino experience in the northeast (Zentella 2003, 2004). In the Spanish Harlem of the 1970s, Puerto Ricans established alliances with African American and other minoritized populations; this yielded common cultural and linguistic practices (as well as social struggles) that were recognized as *Nuyorican*. Successive decades of migration have given way to a new Puerto Rican enclave, in the Orlando metropolitan area of Florida, with a socioeconomic and cultural predominance that is far more favorable and has allowed this community to foster an identity that is based in Island traditions and vernacular. Unlike Nuyoricans, who prefer to speak English, Orlando Ricans prefer to speak Puerto Rican Spanish (Duany 2010; Lamboy 2011).

Belying the reported statistical facts concerning "Spanish" and "English" is the diversity of speakers' repertoires, diversity that can be uncovered only through ethnographic study. In their seminal works, Zentella (1997) and Urciuoli (1985, 1991) unearthed processes of socialization to and through bilingual and multidialectal varieties of Spanish and English. Espousing the methods of Hymes (1974), these authors offered informed portraits of two New York City Puerto Rican neighborhoods. In Zentella's study of the 20 families in the enclave of *el bloque* 'the block,' five varieties of Spanish and English were discerned, with the selection of particular codes dictated by age-, gender-, space-, and culture-related factors. For instance, younger males preferred African American Vernacular English, and children and teens primarily used Hispanicized and New York City English, but young women increasingly preferred popular Puerto Rican Spanish as they assumed adult roles and relationships that were inexorably tied to the preservation of Puerto Rican culture (e.g. motherhood and *padrinazgo* 'godfathership'). Notably, all members of *el bloque* had access to multiple languages and varieties and deployed them in normative ways. In the excerpted exchange in (25.1), two girls (Doris and Blanca) assist another (Isabel) in fixing her microphone (attached to the recorder in a knapsack) and are interrupted by José, an elderly alcoholic. As another example, parents were observed to reprimand children's use of English, as in (25.2).

(25.1)   *Doris:*   Hol' your head up.
       Blanca: Cuando hablas tienes que hablar you know, regular. No vire[h] la cabeza pa(-ra a-)llá y eso. OK? Remember, don' put your mou[f] in the en el micrófono.
                   'When you speak you have to speak ... Don't turn your head that way and stuff. ... in the microphone'
       Doris to all: Blanca be actin' big an' baad.
       José: Tú eres la más fea que hay.
                   'You're the ugliest there is.'
       Isabel: No.
                   'No.'
       José: No estoy hablando contigo. Y no me toque[-].
                   'I'm not talking with you. And don't touch me.'

Source: Zentella (1997:33)

(25.2) ¡Mira, no me hables así en inglés; soy tu madre y me debes respeto!
'Look, don't talk to me in English like that; I'm your mother and you owe me respect.' Source: Urciuoli (1991:298)

Urciuoli (1985) similarly pointed to the interweaving of Spanish and English in the everyday interactions of seven Puerto Rican families (and one African American family) in New York City's Lower East Side. Speakers' utterances combined Spanish and English at all linguistic levels, e.g. in blended pronunciations, in parallel morphosyntactic structures, and in a unified lexicon, producing a "continuity of code" that the author described as "confounded." She noted, for example, that contact forms such as loan translations occurred alongside more standard monolingual phrases, e.g. *make a party, hacer fiesta,* and *throw a party* were equivalently deployed, and fused phonologies often mediated between identifiably Spanish and English segments of discourse, as in (25.3).

(25.3) kʷiðáo kõ éso ke ɪ fol daʊŋ wai ɪz hi kɹajən
Cuidado con eso, que it fall down. Why is he crying?
'Careful with that, that ... ' Source: Urciuoli (1985:382)

In both of the New York Puerto Rican neighborhoods studied by Zentella and Urciuoli, residents considered the mixing of languages to be emblematic of a decidedly local, "Nuyorican" identity, distinct from the identity of Puerto Ricans on the Island, and, thus, a measure of covert prestige was accorded to the blurring and erasure of linguistic boundaries. Nevertheless, community members recognized that they were targeted by their Island compatriots and by US institutions for not speaking Spanish or English well, whether separately or in conjunction, a convergence of negative attitudes that inspired linguistic insecurity.[4] Many expressed significant apprehension about how their non-standard speech varieties (Puerto Rican Spanish, African American Vernacular English, and "Spanglish") would be evaluated in employment and educational settings and they were unequivocal in identifying the appropriate limits of their speech practices to "just around here."

Since the 1980s, there has emerged a visible Puerto Rican presence – the second-largest concentration of Puerto Ricans on the mainland – in Orlando, Florida. In this new enclave, Puerto Ricans challenge the depiction of mainland Puerto Ricans projected by the older New York communities. The analyses of Duany and Matos-Rodríguez (2006), based on census statistics, returned a portrayal of a privileged group with elevated

---

[4] A compelling reflection of the linguistic insecurity experienced by Puerto Ricans is found in the work of renowned Nuyorican poet Tato Laviera, whose collections of poetry include *La Carreta Made a U-Turn* (1979), *AmeRícan* (1985), and *Mixturado and Other Poems* (2008), titles that directly reflect the nature and content of his writings. The poem "My Graduate Speech" depicts the anxiety of a graduate who lacks in confidence about and is disapproving of his abilities in Spanish, English, and Spanglish and who ultimately abandons the notion that he can speak at all: ... *hablo lo inglés matao / hablo lo español matao /no sé leer ninguno bien / so it is, Spanglish to matao/ what i digo / iay virgen, yo no sé hablar!* 'I speak slaughtered English / I speak slaughtered Spanish / I don't know how to read either one well / so it is, Spanglish all slaughtered / what am I saying / my God, I can't speak!' (Laviera 1979:17).

socioeconomic, occupational, and educational levels, sustained transnational connections with persons and current events on the Island, and a preference for identifying itself as white and as Puerto Rican (rather than Latino or Hispanic). Duany's (2010) follow-up study drew on in-depth interviews with 16 community leaders yielding qualitative data that further illuminated the situation of Orlando Puerto Ricans. Their middle-class backgrounds and their light skin color shielded them from the prejudice experienced by the lower-class, dark-skinned Puerto Ricans of the northeast, and, as an insular and predominantly Island-born group, its members measured the "authenticity" of Puerto Rican identity by how well one maintained Puerto Rican traditions such as cuisine (e.g. *arroz con gandules*) and activities (e.g. playing dominoes or dancing to salsa music) and how conversant one was in the Island's vernacular and issues. Based on these benchmarks, Nuyoricans were evaluated by one informant as having failed: "Puerto Ricans in New York already had their struggle [to survive] ... and they didn't triumph" (Duany 2010:108).

In Lamboy's (2011) study, too, the 45 Central Florida Puerto Ricans surveyed went to great lengths to distinguish themselves from Nuyoricans, especially on dimensions of language and race; the excerpts in (25.4) are representative of the views expressed:

(25.4)   a. Allá [...] hablan español por todas partes, pero es un español como [...] diferente. Lo mezclan más con el inglés y como que no usan bien la gramática. Acá se habla más parecido al español de Puerto Rico.
'There they speak Spanish everywhere, but it's a Spanish that is sort of different. They mix it more with English and they sort of don't use grammar well. Here they speak Spanish more like in Puerto Rico.'
  b. Aquí no hay tantos de esos [puertorriqueños] que se creen que son morenos con las cadenas y los pantalones por acá abajo, y con ese hablar de la calle. Y hablan así en español y en inglés.
'Here there aren't so many of those Puerto Ricans who think they are black with their chain necklaces and pants down to here and with that street talk. And they talk like that in Spanish and English.'
  c. A mí a cada rato me dicen "¿de dónde tú eres?" Porque la imagen que tienen es del puertorriqueño de Nueva York que no sabe hablar bien. Y yo rápido le digo que yo vine de Puerto Rico, no de Nueva York.
'People often ask me "Where are you from?" Because the image they have is of the New York Puerto Rican who doesn't speak well. And I quickly tell them that I came from Puerto Rico, not from New York.'
Source: Lamboy (2011:74–76)

As can be gleaned from these comments, Lamboy's interviewees rejected the multilingual, multidialectal, multicultural, and multiracial behaviors associated with the Nuyorican *barrios*. Especially noteworthy is the Florida Puerto Ricans' belief that their own Spanish casts a more faithful – and *better* – model of the variety spoken in Puerto Rico and the insistence that their linguistic and social practices are immune to the effects of African American culture.

In marked contrast to Puerto Ricans in New York, Cubans in Miami-Dade County, Florida are exempt from condemnation for their diaspora Spanish variety; and unlike the Orlando Ricans, Miami Cubans reject the Spanish spoken in their country of origin. Recall that the 1959 Cuban Revolution triggered large waves of Cuban immigration that continued through 2005, and the vast majority have settled in Miami. Today, Cubans constitute 53 percent of the population of Miami and the second largest Cuban population in the world. Miami is also host to a large number of Spanish-speaking immigrants and internal migrants with origins in other countries and regions, contributing to the widespread and "normative" public presence of Spanish. Thus, residents with established roots and newcomers are socialized in a context in which US Cuban Spanish finds prestige, in its ubiquity and vitality and in the status accorded to its speakers; in Miami-Dade, this prestige appears to be rooted in political and racial ideology.

In a series of sociolinguistic studies, Alfaraz (2002, 2014) examined the perceptions of 148 demographically diverse Cubans residing in Miami-Dade County regarding 21 regional dialects of Spanish, including those of 19 nations and the two varieties spoken in Cuba pre- and post-Castro. The studies adopted the approach of perceptual dialectology, which aims to discern the beliefs and attitudes of everyday people towards language varieties and their speakers (Niedzielski and Preston 2000). In the first study, the evaluative responses elicited yielded statistically significant correlations between measures of race and ratings of correctness: The varieties assessed most positively were those from predominantly "white" countries (Spain, Argentina, pre-Revolution Cuba), and those assessed most negatively were from predominantly "black" regions of the Caribbean (particularly the Dominican Republic). Interestingly, pre- and post-Revolution Cuban Spanish lects were perceived as distinct, with respondents asserting that the more correct version was exported with the exiles, and describing post-Revolution Cuban Spanish as a "black" variety endorsed by Castro, as in (25.5). The exchange with the author (Gabriela) reproduced in (25.6) further sustains the respondent's consideration that Cuban Spanish is a stigmatized Afro-Cuban variety.

(25.5) Es que la cantidad de negros que hay en La Habana es extraordinaria. En Cuba entera ... hablan muy anegrado.
'It's that the number of blacks in Havana is extraordinary. In all of Cuba ... they talk very black-like.' Source: Alfaraz (2002:6)

(25.6) Gabriela: Tú dices que en Cuba hablan muy anegrado, ¿cómo es eso?
'You say that in Cuba they speak very black-like, how is that?'
Manuela: Sí, anegrado en el sentido de las expresiones. [...] de lo chabacano.
'Yes, black like in terms of the expressions. [...] of the sloppiness.'

Gabriel:	Pero no la pronunciación.
	'But not the pronunciation.'
Manuela:	Sí, sí, todo, todo. La pronunciación, la tonalidad de la voz.
	'Yes, yes, everything, everything. Pronunciation, tone of voice.'
Gabriela:	¿De qué vendrá eso? ¿Qué raíces tiene?
	'Where do you think that comes from? What roots does it have?'
Manuela:	Las raíces que tiene son africanas. Africanas. Porque en Cuba actualmente, o cuando yo salí, había una tendencia a lo africano.
	'The roots it has are African. African. Because in Cuba now, or when I left, there was a tendency towards the African.'

Source: Alfaraz (2002:7)

The follow-up study, conducted 12 years later (Alfaraz 2014), validated the general findings: perceptions of the Miami Cuban dialect and of non-Cuban regional dialects remained relatively stable, i.e. pre-Castro Spanish held its place, behind Spain, as the second most correct variety. Significantly, however, perceptions of the Cuban Spanish spoken on the Island were downgraded, reflecting respondents' beliefs about the racial make-up of Cuba. Alfaraz interprets this dramatic decline – the largest change from the findings in the first study – as indicative of the strengthening of the ideological boundary that separates Miami Cubans from their compatriots in the homeland and that separates established Cubans from Cuban newcomers with whom they do not align politically or racially.

The real-time study of the perceptions of Miami Cubans also allows us to speculate on the future of the Cuban diaspora variety of Spanish. While the strong presence of Spanish speakers from throughout Latin America augurs well for the maintenance of Spanish, the linguistic capital accorded the Cuban diaspora variety suggests that Cubans will not accommodate to the growing populations of speakers of other Spanish varieties. Instead, newcomers (from Cuba and elsewhere) will likely move towards the local diaspora Cuban dialect, a US Spanish variety that comprises English. In fact, some of the newcomers interviewed by Alfaraz joked that they needed to learn to speak *Spanglish* in Miami. In this respect, members of the Miami Cuban enclave may be said to be less strict in their attitudes towards Spanish than members of the Orlando Puerto Rican community. For Cubans, Spanish interacts with English, for example in borrowings (e.g. *overtime* pronounced [oβeɾtajŋ]), calques (e.g. *corriendo para alcalde* 'running for mayor'), and code-switching (Otheguy *et al.* 2000; Carter and Lynch 2015). In contraposition, the Orlando Ricans sampled by Duany (2010) observed a "clash in mentality" between their preference for "authentic" Island Spanish and the linguistic behaviors of third- and fourth-generation Cubans whom they considered to be assimilated and "American."

The foregoing explorations of the socialization of immigrant groups with origins in Puerto Rico and Cuba in diverse contexts of reception foreground significant differences in how they define themselves and each other linguistically, as they engage with (trans)national agendas. In the subsequent paragraphs, we consider the situation of Dominican immigrants and their children in the US, for whom language attitudes can be shown to serve as a proxy for racial attitudes, and language ideologies as a proxy for socio-political ideologies, which are imported as part and parcel of Dominican consciousness and which may be reinforced in the US context. Many entered the US as transient immigrants in the 1960s in the wake of the turmoil occasioned by dictator Rafael Trujillo; as they stayed on and families (re)united, these *dominicanos ausentes* 'absentee Dominicans' forged ethnic communities that replicated the institutions of the home country. In New York neighborhoods in the south Bronx and upper Manhattan's Washington Heights, inhabitants could become transnationals, maintaining *un pie aquí y el otro allá* 'one foot here and the other there,' or simply remain Dominican (Grasmuck and Pessar 1991; Torres-Saillant and Hernández 1998; Duany 2008).

25.4 The Role of Spanish in Reconciling African(-American) and Hispanic Classifications

In the Dominican Republic, people self-identify as "European" or as of mixed European-indigenous heritage, variously emphasizing their Spanish and Taíno ancestral roots, while rejecting the contributions of African peoples.[5] In fact, questionnaires collected throughout the country show that, of the many labels for identification (e.g. *blanco, mestizo, mulatto, trigueño, indio claro, indio oscuro,* ...), *negro* and *prieto* are most commonly reserved for residents of the border, who most typically present darker profiles and often have Haitian lineage (Wheeler 2015).[6] As discussed in the literature emerging from Dominican studies projects (e.g. Torres Saillant 2010), "black" has been erased from the Dominican racial vocabulary; it is associated with otherness, epitomized by Haitians with whom they share their Caribbean island. The nationalist vision authored by Trujillo and his intellectual elites constructed Haiti as a black nation from whose influence the Dominican Republic should be spared. The effects of this campaign were especially strongly felt along the border, where, prior to 1937, residents shared a common currency (*gourde*), intermarriage and concubinage, religious practices (*voudou*), contraband economy, schooling (in the towns of Dabajón or Ouanaminthe), and languages (Spanish and Creole) (Paulino 2005). Three-quarters of a century later, Dominicans and Haitians in the region continue to share beliefs and

---

[5] Estimates of Afro-descendants in the Dominican Republic range from about a quarter to nearly 90 percent, depending on whether these include individuals who identify as "indio," which includes non-whites and mixed-race persons with African ancestry (López and González-Barrera 2016).

[6] Concepts of multiracial identity have been present since colonial times, as the Spanish caste system specified the ways in which European colonists should mix with other peoples.

practices that are shunned by the elite, the plight of poverty and lack of resources, and a single language: Spanish. As documented through qualitative analysis of in-depth interviews conducted by Bullock and Toribio (2014) with 90 children and adolescents in the contested border region, the residue of 75 years of anti-Haitian rhetoric has left an enduring legacy in the Dominican psyche: a fear of being fully "Haitianized" through language and a consequent disinclination to learn Creole (25.7):

(25.7) a. [No quiero hablar Creole] porque después se lo llevan para Haití. [Male, age 11]
'[I don't want to learn Creole] because then they'll take you to Haiti.'
Source: Bullock and Toribio (2014:95)

b. A mí no me gustaría hablar haitiano no. Ay y después y si me ponen a hablar haitiano a mí y la policía me agarra como si yo soy haitiana... [Female, age 15]
'I would not like to learn Haitian Creole, no way. What if then they make me speak Haitian and the police catch me as if I am Haitian.'
Source: Bullock and Toribio (2014:96)

So deeply ingrained is the othering of Haitians that many Dominicans continue to believe that Haitians are the only blacks on the island. But, once stateside, Dominicans encounter a black/white dichotomy that disregards nuances or gradations between people of color. In (25.8a), this state of affairs is lamented by an adult male, and the extract in (25.8b) illustrates that children, too, wrestle to locate themselves in this dualistic racial design.

(25.8) a. El blanco no distingue entre claros y el negro, sino todo lo conceptúa en el mismo marco.
'The white person doesn't distinguish between the light and the black, instead s/he conceptualizes it all in the same frame.' [Male 60+]
Source: Toribio (2000:1149)

b. White people don't consider us white, we're like peach. And the black people consider them [Dominicans] brown, so Dominicans are between black, brown, and peach. [Male, age 11]
Source: Toribio (2006:136)

One means of engaging with a US system that would classify them as black is to identify racially as Dominican, Hispanic, or Latino, as was reported in the sociological treatment of Jensen *et al.* (2006), which examined the characteristics of 65 Dominican-origin adults in the enclave of Reading, Pennsylvania. As another strategy, Dominicans may identify as "Spanish" because they speak Spanish, as was attested among Dominican adolescents in Bailey's (2000a, 2000b) cultural-anthropological study of a Dominican enclave in Providence, Rhode Island, and in Toribio's sociolinguistic studies of Dominicans in New York (2003).

Hence, while there is no overt prestige ascribed to the Dominican vernacular (see the discussion of Alfaraz's perceptual dialectology studies above, Bullock and Toribio 2009; and Toribio 2000, 2003), there is covert prestige attached to the national variety as an expression of *dominicanidad*, and it is recognized and exploited in conveying information about the speaker's identity. Via the Dominican vernacular, then, Dominicans make themselves distinct.

In a series of articles, Toribio and colleagues (Toribio 2000, 2003, 2006; Bullock and Toribio 2009) corroborated the central role of the Spanish language as a "shibboleth" of identity among Dominicans; the publications are based on interviews with adults and children carried out over many years and across geographical locations in the Dominican Republic and in established Dominican neighborhoods in New York. In the anecdote shared in (25.9) by a Dominican male, it is the ill-fated Haitian's inability to emulate the Dominican Spanish vernacular pronunciation that betrays his identity and guarantees his repatriation.

(25.9) El tío tuyo Otilio andaba en Dajabón recogiendo a los haitianos, para la inmigración. Entonces, el camión ya estaba lleno, en camino para Haiti para llevarlos, y cuando iban para la frontera, había un morenito sentado en el parque. Otilio dijo, "Déjame ver, déjame chequear a este morenito a ver." Se desmontó Otilio y le dijo, "Ven acá, ¿tú eres dominicano?" Y dice el haitiano, "¡Sí!" Dice Otilio, "Si tú eres dominicano, tú vas a repetir lo que yo te diga." Dice el haitiano, "Tá bien." Dice Otilio, "Repíteme ahí: El Generalísimo Rafael Leónidas Trujillo, benefactor de la patria nueva, nació en San Cristóbal, el pueblo del perejil." Dice el haitiano, "Mejor dime que me suba a la camiona."

[Male, age 45]

'Your uncle Otilio was in Dajabón, picking up Haitians for immigration. Then, the truck was full, en route to take them to Haiti, and when they were going towards the border, there was a dark man sitting in the park. Otilio says, "Let me see, let me check that dark man, to see." Otilio got out and says to him, "Come here. Are you Dominican?" And the Haitian says, "Yes!" Otilio said, "If you are Dominican, you will repeat what I tell you." The Haitian says, "Alright." Otilio says, "Repeat this: General Rafael Leónidas Trujillo, benefactor of the new motherland, born in San Cristóbal, the town of *perejil* [parsley]." The Haitian says, "Why not just tell me to get in the truck?"'

Source: Toribio (2006:131)

The socio-cultural context of the US similarly demands evidence of ethnic and/or racial affiliations, and language and specific linguistic traits again fulfill this purpose. Dominicans are united in accrediting an essential role to the vernacular in symbolizing their own *dominicanidad*, and the informant in (25.10) argues that language should be isomorphic with ethnicity for all immigrants. In (25.11), we observe an older adult who volunteers negative evidence of her identity in providing the linguistic verification that would preclude her misidentification as African American.[7]

(25.10) I said, "Well, what do you categorize yourself as?" Like, "Italian?" and I said, "Well do you speak Italian?" He said no. I said, "Well I'm Spanish: ¿Cómo tú estás? Yo me siento muy bien. Mi nombre es Felipe." He got so pissed. ... You know, he's got a little nice Infinity [automobile], he's got some nice rims, he's got a nice little Italian sticker on the car, Italian things inside the car. [But] You don't know Italian! I got my Dominican flag in there, I'm Dominican. I know Spanish. [Male, age 32]   Source: Toribio (2003:8)

(25.11) *Mara*: Buenos días. (To two Anglo passers-by)
'Good morning.'
Interv: ¡Ellos no hablan español!
'They don't speak Spanish!'
Mara: Yo les dije así para que no fueran a creer que yo soy de esa gente negra de aquí.
'I said that to them so they wouldn't think that I am one of those [black] people from here.' [Female, age 60+]
Source: Toribio (2006:143–144)

But it is in comparing the linguistic behaviors of "white" versus "black" Dominicans in New York that we most readily comprehend the work that speakers accomplish through language in responding to the racial ideologies imposed by the US context. Toribio (2003) reported on a "black" Dominican parent who seeks to alleviate the perceived burden of the African American labeling by securing linguistic training to correct the African American English vernacular features of her daughter's speech. In that same study, first- and second-generation Dominican children are observed to provide evidence of a non-African American identity by demonstrating Spanish-language abilities or accessing other cultural referents, as in (25.12).

(25.12) a. Sometimes African Americans are, like, brown colored. And there are people in [the] Dominican Republic who are brown colored. But some African Americans don't talk Spanish. So, you could tell if that person talks a lot, a lot of Spanish, you can tell that they're not African American. [I have a friend] But he says that his mom is from [the] Dominican [Republic], and I was like, "Give me some words in Spanish," and he was like "Hola." And he says some stuff and he looks like an African American, but then he showed me a picture from the Dominican [Republic] and I was like, "Oh." [Male, age 11]
Source: Toribio (2003:9)
b. People, like, ask me if you know English and Spanish ... I say, like, "Yeah," and then, like, one of the Spanish kids come, and then, like,

---

[7] In a Pew Research Center survey of 1,555 multiracial adults, 21% said they had attempted to influence how others saw their race, most by the way they talked (Morin 2015).

> I have to talk Spanish. [...] They always find out [I'm not African American] because they ask me weird questions, like, how old am I [in Spanish]. I get very confused and I forget everything.
> [Male, age 8] Source: Toribio (2003:6)

Similar findings can be documented in examining the sociolinguistic dimensions of Dominican identity in other US cities where Dominicans have settled, such as Reading, a small industrial city in southwestern Pennsylvania. In the decade between 1990 and 2000, Dominican (im)migration to Reading increased by nearly 800 percent, as Dominicans bypassed traditional gateway cities. For sociologists, such redistribution of immigrants and internal migrants allows for the new lines of research on questions about the context of reception and immigrant outcomes. Via an in-depth ethno-survey of open-ended and fixed-response items administered to 65 Dominican-origin adults, Jensen *et al.* (2006) found that Reading Dominicans have availed themselves of social and economic opportunities that they could ill afford in New York, and, relative to other Hispanic groups, they present the hallmarks (e.g. business- and home-ownership) of having made significant strides. Moreover, Dominicans in Reading were found to construct their identities in two ways: Many identify simply as Dominican, whereas others, particularly those who have spent more years in the US and those with lighter self-assessed skin tone, choose pan-ethnic terms. Interestingly, their conceptualizations were tied to their use of Spanish; two-thirds of the respondents identified with the Spanish term "Hispano/a" (rather than Hispanic or Latino). Subsequent analyses of the interviews (Toribio 2009) revealed Reading Dominicans' attachment to the Spanish language, considered part of the Dominican cultural patrimony that must be preserved:

(25.13) [Mis hijos] son hispanos, de descendientes hispanos; no quiero que nieguen la raza. [El español] es una forma de que se acepten ellos mismos.
'My children are Hispanic, of Hispanic descendants; I don't want them to deny their race. Spanish is a way for them to accept themselves.' Source: Toribio (2009:37)

Furthermore, the vast majority (83 percent) of Reading Dominicans reported that Spanish is easy to retain in this context, a belief that was supported by findings of patterns of reactions towards Spanish and those who use it, or language attitudes (Garrett 2010). In a telephone survey administered by Toribio (2009), 114 Hispanic and non-Hispanic respondents credited Hispanics with having revitalized and strengthened the city and all were in complete agreement that Spanish–English bilingualism is advantageous in Reading. Accordingly, the presence of Spanish may be less problematic in Reading than might be the case in other destination communities, promoting its maintenance.

In all of these settings, language is shown to serve a dual unifying and separatist function, binding Dominicans to their Hispanic past and isolating them from their African and African American neighbors. Couched within the interpretive paradigms of researchers in sociolinguistics and social psychology (Le Page and Tabouret-Keller 1985; Bucholtz and Hall 2005), these findings may be interpreted as illustrating Dominicans' expression of ethnolinguistic and racio-linguistic identities in host (and home) contexts, as individuals perform and accentuate their heritage through Spanish. In immigrant enclaves, Dominicans demonstrate loyalty to their Spanish variety; although stigmatized, they abandon their vernacular neither in favor of higher-prestige or more conservative pan-American norms through leveling nor in favor of the dominant English language through rapid language shift (although, like the other groups discussed here, they alternate between varieties and languages). It remains to be known whether the Dominican vernacular is an invariable factor in the display of a national or ethnic identity or whether it is reprised as a facet of cultural endowment in the immigration context. In either case, historical memory and contemporary concerns portend the maintenance of Dominican Spanish in US immigrant enclaves.

It cannot go unremarked that the factors that promote Spanish-language usage among members of the Dominican communities considered here differ in significant respects from those that motivate Spanish-language maintenance in the contemporary Puerto Rican enclave in Orlando discussed above. For the former, language is intimately linked with race; as regularly recounted and enacted by adults and children, a Dominican who does not speak Spanish may be unwittingly identified as an African American. But for the latter, language is tied to cultural legacy; Orlando Ricans hold tightly to their Spanish vernacular in laying claim to an "authentic" Puerto Rican identity, distinct from that of others with Island origins who have suffered language loss.

25.5 Conclusion

To recapitulate, Hispanics with origins in the Caribbean nations of Cuba, Puerto Rico, and the Dominican Republic have been shown to deploy their distinctive Spanish vernaculars in anticipating and serving identity and social outcomes. Navigating their ambiguous status within US hierarchies, immigrants from the Spanish-speaking Caribbean and their children construct ethnic and racial identities that are dynamic and formed through engagement and interaction. For this reason, their identities are dictated by the multiple meanings that can be performed and inferred from linguistic behaviors at any given moment, in the country of origin, in the larger US social sphere, and in the specific receiving communities. As Hispanophone Caribbeans broaden their migration trajectories and settle into new host societies, different narratives of the multiple dimensions of identity will unfold; the story of Spanish within these remains to be written.

References

Alfaraz, G. (2002). Miami Cuban Perceptions of Varieties of Spanish. In D. Long and D Preston (eds.), *Handbook of Perceptual Dialectology*, Vol. 2. Amsterdam: John Benjamins, pp. 1–11.

Alfaraz, G. (2014). Dialect Perceptions in Real Time: A Restudy of Miami-Cuban Perceptions. *Journal of Linguistic Geography*, 2, 74–86.

Bailey, B. (2000a). Language and Negotiation of Ethnic/Racial Identity among Dominican Americans. *Language in Society*, 29, 555–582.

Bailey, B. (2000b). Language and Ethnic/Racial Identities of Dominican American High School Students in Providence, Rhode Island (Doctoral dissertation). UCLA.

Bucholtz, M. and Hall, K. (2005). Identity and Interaction: A Sociocultural Linguistic Approach. *Discourse Studies*, 7 (4–5), 585–614.

Bullock, B. E. and Toribio, A. J. (2009). Reconsidering Dominican Spanish: Data from the Rural Cibao. *Revista Internacional de Lingüística Iberoamericana*, 2 (14), 46–74.

Bullock, B. E. and Toribio, A. J. (2014). From Trujillo to the *terremoto*: The Effect of Language Ideologies on the Language Attitudes and Behaviors of the Rural Youth of the Northern Dominican Border. *International Journal of the Sociology of Language*, 227, 83–100.

Carter, P. and Lynch, A. (2015). Multilingual Miami: Current Trends in Sociolinguistic Research. *Language and Linguistics Compass*, 9, 369–385.

Duany, J. (2008). *Quisqueya on the Hudson: The Transnational Identity of Dominicans in Washington Heights*. New York: CUNY Dominican Studies Institute. Available from academicworks.cuny.edu/cgi/viewcontent.cgi?article=1000&context=dsi_pubs (last access December 26, 2017).

Duany, J. (2010). The Orlando Ricans: Overlapping Identity Discourses among Middle-Class Puerto Rican Immigrants. *CENTRO: Journal of the Center for Puerto Rican Studies*, 22, 84–116.

Duany, J. and Matos Rodríguez, F. V. (2006). *Puerto Ricans in Orlando and Central Florida*. New York: Centro de Estudios Puertorriqueños.

Garrett, P. (2010). *Attitudes to Language*. Cambridge: Cambridge University Press.

Grasmuck, S. and Pessar, P. (1991). *Between Two Islands: Dominican International Migration*. Oakland, CA: University of California Press.

Hymes, D. (1974). *Foundations in Sociolinguistics: An Ethnographic Approach*. Philadelphia, PA: University of Pennsylvania Press.

Jensen, L., Cohen, J., Toribio, A. J., DeJong, G., and Rodríguez, L. (2006). Ethnic Identities, Language and Economic Outcomes among Dominicans in a New Destination. *Social Science Quarterly*, 87, 1088–1099.

Lamboy, E. (2011). Language and Identity Construction: Can We Talk about a *New* Puerto Rican in the United States? In L. Ortiz-López (ed.), *Selected Proceedings of the 13th Hispanic Linguistics Symposium*. Somerville, MA: Cascadilla, pp. 70–80.

Laviera, T. (1979). *La Carreta Made a U-Turn*. Houston, TX: Arte Público Press.

Laviera, T. (1985). *AmeRícan*. Houston, TX: Arte Público Press.

Laviera, T. (2008). *Mixturado and Other Poems*. Houston, TX: Arte Público Press.

Le Page, R. B. and Tabouret-Keller, A. (1985). *Acts of Identity: Creole-Based Approaches to Ethnicity and Language*. Cambridge: Cambridge University Press.

Lipski, J. (1994). *Latin American Spanish*. London and New York: Longman.

López, M. H. (2016). Is Speaking Spanish Necessary to be Hispanic? Most Hispanics Say No. Pew Research Center. Available from http://www.pewresearch.org/fact-tank/2016/02/19/is-speaking-spanish-necessary-to-be-hispanic-most-hispanics-say-no/ (last access January 5, 2018).

López, G. and González-Barrera, A. (2016). Afro-Latino: A Deeply Rooted Identity among US Hispanics. Pew Research Center. Available from http://www.pewresearch.org/fact-tank/2016/03/01/afro-latino-a-deeply-rooted-identity-among-u-s-hispanics/ (last access January 5, 2018).

López, G. and Patten, E. (2015). *The Impact of Slowing Immigration: Foreign-Born Share Falls among 14 Largest US Hispanic Groups*. Pew Research Center. Available from http://www.pewhispanic.org/2015/09/15/the-impact-of-slowing-immigration-foreign-born-share-falls-among-14-largest-us-hispanic-origin-groups/ (last access January 5, 2018).

Morin, R. (2015). *Among Multiracial Adults, Racial Identity can be Fluid*. Pew Research Center. Available from http://www.pewresearch.org/fact-tank/2015/06/16/among-multiracial-adults-racial-identity-can-be-fluid/ (last access January 5, 2018).

Niedzielski, N. A. and Preston, D. R. (2000). *Folk Linguistics*. Berlin: De Gruyter.

Otheguy, R., García, O., and Roca, A. (2000). Speaking in Cuban: The Language of Cuban Americans. In S. L. McKay and S.-L. C. Wong (eds.), *New Immigrants in the United States*. Cambridge: Cambridge University Press, pp. 165–188.

Paulino, E. (2005). Erasing the Kreyol from the Margins of the Dominican Republic: The Pre- and Post-Nationalization Project of the Border, 1930–1945. *Wadabagei: A Journal of the Caribbean and Its Diaspora*, 8, 39–75.

Pew Hispanic Center (2015). Multiracial in America: Proud, Diverse and Growing in Numbers. Available from http://www.pewsocialtrends.org/2015/06/11/chapter-7-the-many-dimensions-of-hispanic-racial-identity/ (last access January 5, 2018).

Taylor, P., López, M. H., Martínez, J., and Velasco, G. (2012). When Labels don't Fit: Hispanics and their Views on Identity. Pew Research Center.

Available from http://www.pewhispanic.org/files/2012/04/PHC-Hispanic-Identity.pdf (last access January 5, 2018).

Toribio, A. J. (2000). Language Variation and the Linguistic Enactment of Identity among Dominicans. *Linguistics: An Interdisciplinary Journal of the Language Sciences*, 38, 1133–1159.

Toribio, A. J. (2003). The Social Significance of Language Loyalty among Black and White Dominicans in New York. *The Bilingual Review/La Revista Bilingüe*, 27, 3–11.

Toribio, A. J. (2006). Linguistic Displays of Identity among Dominicans in National and Diasporic Settlements. In C. E. Davies and J. Brutt-Grifler (eds.), *English and Ethnicity*. New York: Palgrave, pp. 131–155.

Toribio, A. J. (2009). Language Attitudes and Linguistic Outcomes in Reading, PA. In M. Rafael Salaberry (ed.), *Language Allegiances and Bilingualism in the US*. Clevedon: Multilingual Matters, pp. 24–41.

Torres-Saillant, S. (2010). Introduction to Dominican blackness (Research monograph). Dominican Studies Institute, CUNY. Available from https://www.ccny.cuny.edu/sites/default/files/dsi/upload/Introduction_to_Dominican_Blackness_Web.pdf (last access December 14, 2017).

Torres-Saillant, S. and Hernández, R. (1998). *The Dominican Americans*. Westport, CT: Greenwood Press.

Urciuoli, B. (1985). Bilingualism as Code and Bilingualism as Practice. *Anthropological Linguistics*, 27, 363–386.

Urciuoli, B. (1991). The Political Topography of Spanish and English: The View from a New York Puerto Rican Neighborhood. *American Ethnologist*, 18, 295–310.

Wheeler, E. M. (2015). (Re)framing *raza*: Language as a Lens for Examining Race and Skin Color Categories in the Dominican Republic (Doctoral dissertation). UCSB.

Zentella, A. C. (1997). *Growing Up Bilingual: Puerto Rican Children in New York*. Malden, MA: Wiley-Blackwell.

Zentella, A. C. (2003). José, Can You See? In D. Sommer (ed.), *Bilingual Games. Some Literary Investigations*. New York: Palgrave Macmillan, pp. 51–66.

Zentella, A. C. (2004). Spanish in the Northeast. In E. Finegan and J. Rickford (eds.), *Language in the USA: Themes for the 21st Century*. Cambridge: Cambridge University Press, pp. 182–204.

26

Current Perspectives on Historical Linguistics

Patrícia Amaral

26.1 Introduction

This chapter offers a critical overview of recent research on syntactic and semantic change in Spanish, from both formal and functional perspectives. It aims to show how current work on the history of Spanish bears on debates of ongoing interest in historical linguistics. While some topics from the history of Spanish are classic textbook examples for historical linguists (e.g. the formation of the synthetic future and the present perfect), others have not been fully explored with respect to their theoretical implications. The chapter focuses on the theoretical contribution of studies on Spanish with respect to four topics: (i) mechanisms of syntactic and semantic change (i.e. reanalysis, analogy, bleaching, pragmatic inferencing), (ii) the relation between syntactic change and information structure, (iii) the identification of units of change (e.g. constructions, collocations), and (iv) the relation between language change and cognitive processes in language production. This chapter does not aim to provide an exhaustive overview of historical research on Spanish, but rather to situate studies on Spanish within the broader endeavors of historical linguistics. Contact-induced change will not be discussed.

Three fundamental differences between formal and functional approaches to language change reflect diverging conceptions of language: (i) different conceptions of *what changes* – in the formal approach, the internalized grammar or *competence*, and, in the functional approach, language use in communicative situations (in other words, an abstract change in the system vs. change as constrained by concrete speakers' experience with language, involving variable input), (ii) conceptions of the *locus* of change (do children acquire a grammar with specific parameter settings or do adult users change language?), and (iii) conceptions of *how* change happens at the level of the grammar: abruptly (from the grammar of one generation to the next, through parameter setting) vs. gradually, along clines or "paths."[1]

26.2 Mechanisms of Syntactic and Semantic Change

This section presents studies that bear on current discussions on syntactic and semantic change,[2] specifically the debate about the role and nature of reanalysis and analogy (Harris and Campbell 1995; Hopper and Traugott 2003; Roberts and Roussou 2003; Fischer 2007; Eckardt 2006; Lightfoot and Westergaard 2007; de Smet 2016; for a focus on Spanish, see Company Company 2010 and Elvira 2015). I discuss syntactic change first.

Reanalysis has been the main mechanism used to explain syntactic change; it alters "the underlying structure of a syntactic pattern and ... does not involve any immediate or intrinsic modification of its surface manifestation" (Harris and Campbell 1995:61). Reanalysis affects constituency and hierarchical structure, grammatical relations, and cohesion of a linguistic sequence, yet it can be perceived only when there is extension of the reanalyzed structure to new syntactic contexts, i.e. when actualization has occurred. The motivations for reanalysis are much debated; while some have argued for ambiguity as the main cause (Timberlake 1977), others have explored a combination of semantic and pragmatic factors (cf. "exploratory expressions," Harris and Campbell 1995:72–75).

Analogy is a mechanism with a long tradition in historical linguistics, particularly in morphology, receiving recent attention as a general principle of cognition and learning, pervasive in both language change and language acquisition (Fischer 2007, Itkonen 2005). It consists in the generalization of a pattern based on similarity ("a process whereby one form of a language becomes more like another with which it is somehow associated," Arlotto 1972:130 *apud* Campbell 2013:91). It operates at the paradigmatic level. Although analogy is traditionally considered irregular since it seems to happen randomly, recent research has shown that it is governed by cognitive principles that are sensitive to different dimensions of similarity, whether of form, meaning, or grammatical function (see Elvira 1998; Wanner 2006; and Section 26.5 below).

In the debate about mechanisms of syntactic change, some authors have questioned the abrupt nature of reanalysis and its dependence on ambiguity. De Smet (2009) proposes to decompose reanalysis into gradual steps

---

[1] At the level of output both formal and functional approaches agree that change is gradual and that evidence for rules that correspond to different stages of a change may be found at any given time in actual productions. Hence, the distinction made here pertains to the level of the grammar itself. For a thorough comparison of the theoretical assumptions and methods of both types of approaches to morphosyntactic change, see Fischer (2007).

[2] In the discussion of semantic change I leave aside lexical change. Change in this domain has been considered irregular, i.e. not subject to systematic principles, and highly dependent on historical and cultural facts (for Spanish, see Penny 2002; Dworkin 2012).

consisting of successive analogical changes. However, this proposal does not explain how innovation, i.e. a "leap into the unconventional" (de Smet 2016:100), comes about. While Hopper and Traugott (2003) see reanalysis as primary and analogy (understood as extension or rule generalization) as secondary, Fischer (2007, 2013) argues for the primacy of analogy: "It is the superficial similarity (analogy) that a language user perceives between two structures and between two communicative uses of them that causes a reanalysis in one of them, so as to bring it in line with the other" (Fischer 2007:123–4). The focus on analogy has also revealed that multiple sources may play a role in a particular change (Fischer 2013; Aaron 2016 for a Spanish example). Section 26.2.1 presents studies on Spanish that use reanalysis or analogy as explanatory tools and hence contribute to this ongoing debate.

Although syntactic change is closely intertwined with semantic and pragmatic factors, the role of meaning in syntactic change has proved elusive. Eckardt (2006, 2012) builds on research on syntactic change to propose the term "semantic reanalysis," which is programmatic in defining semantic change as change in the semantic compositionality of an expression, as a response to "pragmatic overload" imposed on the hearer. Eckardt eventually comes to rely on the two mechanisms of semantic change proposed in the literature: bleaching (loss of meaning) and pragmatic enrichment (or strengthening). The former goes back to Meillet's seminal generalization that change happens from lexical to grammatical (Meillet 1912); in language change, specific lexical meanings are lost and meanings become increasingly abstract, e.g. the verb *vivir* 'to live' becomes an aspectual marker in the verbal periphrasis *vive lloviendo* 'it keeps raining,' which is found in several American varieties of Spanish, and the noun meaning 'man' becomes the indefinite pronoun *omne* in medieval Spanish. This is a robust tendency across languages, but the concept of *bleaching* presupposes that function words have little or no meaning, which is problematic (see von Fintel 1995 for discussion). Additionally, bleaching does not explain the motivation of change or the relation between original and final meanings.

This is precisely what research on pragmatic enrichment seeks to explain: semantic change is assumed to be regular, i.e. predictable, because it is driven by general pragmatic mechanisms of language use. In this view the agent of change is the adult language user, who draws systematic inferences in conversation; what begins life as an inference may eventually become part of the coded meaning of a word (Traugott and Dasher 2002). The idea that semantic change results from the conventionalization of inferences triggered in specific contexts is widely accepted in research from both functional and formal approaches (Gianollo et al. 2015). Both explore the role of bridging or "onset" contexts (Diewald 2002; Traugott 2012), in which structural ambiguity and pragmatic inferencing favor language change. As semantic change takes place, meanings tend to express the speaker/writer's perspective explicitly (a process known as "subjectification,"

Traugott 1995).[3] An example of the achievements and challenges of studies on semantic change is presented in Section 26.2.2.

26.2.1 The Creation of New Subordination Patterns

The creation of subordinating patterns and complementizers in Spanish and other Romance languages has a long tradition in diachronic studies (Tarr 1922; Herman 1963; Serradilla 1997; Barra Jover 2002). Of particular interest has been the evolution of prepositional finite clauses in Spanish. Before the 16th century the common pattern is the lack of a preposition with argumental finite clauses, as in (26.1), while after the 16th century sentences like (26.2) become grammatical (despite some earlier attested examples; see Serradilla 1997):

(26.1) ayudándole **que** faga sienpre tales cosas
        helping-him **that** does.3SG always such things
        Source: Alfonso X, *Siete partidas*; example and gloss from Delicado Cantero (2013:282)

(26.2) Y el ser él tan principal y gentil hombre ...
        ayudó **a** **que** el demonio ...
        helped PREP **that** the devil ...
        tuviese bastante leña ...[4]
        Source: Cervantes (1614: fol. 126r) (*Don Quijote*)

The debate has focused on the mechanisms responsible for this change, specifically on the role of reanalysis vs. analogy. In his seminal work, Herman (1963) proposed an explanation based on analogy. He argues that the Romance languages built their subordinating system through the analogical extension of a pattern consisting either of a pronoun (often preceded by a preposition) or an adverb + the conjunction *que* (e.g. *por eso que, ya que*). This Romance innovation would provide the template for a broader pattern largely attested in Spanish, underlying the emergence of finite clauses selected by verbs, nouns or adjectives followed by a preposition, as exemplified in (26.2). Explanations based on analogy are also found in Bogard and Company Company (1989) and Serradilla (1997).

On the other hand, Barra Jover (2002) argues for an account based on reanalysis (i.e. an abrupt structural change), according to which in the 16th century subordinate clauses acquired a nominal feature. By this token, clauses could be complements of prepositions, hence creating clausal complementation in Spanish. However, both the existence of early examples showing the pattern in (26.2) and other sources of evidence for the nominal nature of clausal complements support an

---

[3] For a proposal to operationalize the notion of subjectification based on Spanish historical data, see Torres Cacoullos and Schwenter (2006).

[4] Glosses and translations of examples are mine unless otherwise indicated. In the glosses, PREP stands for "preposition," SBJV for "subjunctive," and 3SG for "third-person singular."

explanation based on analogy rather than reanalysis (see Delicado Cantero 2013). An account based on analogy may also lend itself to quantitative investigation, e.g. by tracing the extension of the new complementation pattern within different categories (specific classes of verbs, nouns, etc.).

26.2.2 Creation of Concessive Markers

This topic has sparked interest in the history of Spanish due to the variety of expressive resources and the tendency for forms to be renewed and innovated in this domain, both in Spanish and in Romance (Rivarola 1976; Garachana Camarero 1997; Márquez Guerrero 2006; Pérez Saldanya and Salvador 2014). This cyclic tendency, which has parallels in other areas such as Jespersen's (1917) Cycle of Negation, sheds light on the role of pragmatic inferences in semantic change.

From a syntactic perspective, concessive connectives are classic examples of reanalysis and recategorization. For example, *maguer* instantiates a stage-divided process of change: from a vocative to an interjection, to a conditional concessive and finally to a concessive conjunction 'although' (Pérez Saldanya and Salvador 2014:3728). From a semantic perspective, the creation of concessive markers shows that bleaching is insufficient and inappropriate; concessive connectives introduce complex argumentative relations and hence do not result from the "fading" of content. For instance, the use of *maguer* as 'although' cannot be explained by mere loss of the meaning of a desiderative interjection ('hopefully').

The source domains of concessive subordinators reflect the semantic connections among causal, conditional, and adversative relations found across languages (König 1988). Concessive connectives presuppose a causal or conditional link between propositions, and build on the negation of this link, initially as an inferential process that comes at a "pragmatic cost" (Pérez Saldanya and Hualde in press). Pérez Saldanya and Salvador (2014) argue that *aunque* 'although' has its origin in the focus adverb *aun* 'even' as a modifier of subordinate clauses headed by *que* (cf. Elvira 2003). Starting with a conditional value in clauses with the subjunctive from the 13th century, as in (26.3), the adverb introduces a maximum value on a scale of possibilities, hence conveying high informativity because all the lower values on the scale are entailed:

(26.3)   E allí fallaron un campo tan llano e tan bueno e tan grand que estando en medio d'él ... semejóles que allí cabrién todos, e **aun si** más fuessen
   'And there they found a field so flat, and so good, and so big, that, standing in the middle ... it seemed to them that they would all fit there, and *even if* there were more of them'
   Source: *General estoria*, 1.74 [1270–1280], example and translation from Pérez Saldanya and Hualde (in press)

Several classes of words are reanalyzed as concessive subordinators: aspectual adverbs (meaning 'already', 'still'); focus particles (meaning 'even'); and conditional and desiderative expressions. In argumentative texts, these words are used to contrast points of view, creating an implicit dialogue, and trigger scalar inferences that eventually become conventionalized (see Elvira 2003 on *por mucho que*). Studies on concessives, which constitute prime examples of inference-based accounts of semantic change, also demonstrate the difficulty of operationalizing and testing for the notion of *pragmatic cost* or *pragmatic overload*.

The creation of concessive connectives, by which originally complex syntagmatic strings lose their internal structure and are recategorized as units, is viewed as evidence of the crucial role constructions play in syntactic and semantic change. For example, Torres Cacoullos (2006) explains the creation of the concessive connective *a pesar de* 'although' through decategorization of the noun *pesar* in specific collocations; *a pesar de* becomes an unanalyzable unit over time, with increasing fixedness. But recent research suggests that this view of constructions as being indivisible may need to be nuanced. In a study on the diachrony of *sin embargo de que* 'despite,' Amaral and Delicado Cantero show that the subcategorization properties of the noun *embargo* – the selection of the preposition *de* and later *de que* – are relevant to the development of the concessive connective. In fact, the chronology of the selection of nominal and clausal complements by *sin embargo de* coincides with the chronology of patterns of prepositional complementation in Spanish (see Section 26.2.1), showing that constructions may retain properties of their elements and hence display some compositionality (Amaral and Delicado Cantero 2018).[5] This study makes it apparent that an essential question in diachronic research concerns the nature of units of change and their combinatorial properties, the topic of Section 26.4.

26.3 Syntactic Change and Information Structure

The two studies surveyed in this section, Batllori and Hernanz (2008) and Pensado (1995b), relate syntactic change with information structure, albeit in different ways. The first adopts a minimalist approach to grammaticalization (see also Chapter 27, this volume) assuming a rich left periphery, as in Rizzi (1997) and subsequent work, in which information structure is modeled according to specific assumptions about syntactic structure (Section 26.3.1). The second, not based on this theoretical framework,

---

[5] It may be argued that the analyzability of constructions is a matter of degree and that change takes the form of gradual alterations in analyzability. However, at least for the development of *sin embargo* and *a pesar*, a focus on the concept of construction leads us to analyze the individual changes as gradual expansions of contexts of use as part of recategorization, rather than as the predictable development of clause-taking elements in Spanish, which can be traced to the properties of the nouns involved (*embargo* and *pesar*).

sees information structure constraints as motivation for the creation of a new syntactic pattern from Latin to Spanish (Section 26.3.2).

26.3.1 The Diachrony of Polarity Items

Under a minimalist approach to grammaticalization, syntactic change consists of change from a lexical to a functional category and relies on reanalysis; an item comes to be generated at a hierarchically higher position rather than being lower generated with a subsequent Move operation (Roberts and Roussou 2003; Roberts 2007). The motivation for change is economy (similar to the notion of transparency or "avoid structural complexity" from Lightfoot 1979, 1991); loss of movement is less costly for the language learner and hence is replaced by Merge. The semantic counterpart of reanalysis is bleaching, usually presented as a by-product of syntactic change; syntax is considered autonomous. Grammaticalization cycles may differ for lexical items in different languages, allowing for microvariation within a more general (and universal, in this view) grammar (UG). Hence, comparative studies in this approach aim to uncover individual changes in a given language within systematic principles of diachronic syntax that reflect the general architecture of UG.

In this framework, Batllori and Hernanz (2008) analyze the creation of polarity markers *bien* 'well' and *poco* 'little' in Spanish in comparison with Catalan[6] as a result of focalization of adverbs that were originally manner adverbs (verb phrase (VP) adverbs, i.e. modifiers occupying a structurally low position). The original postverbal position is exemplified in (26.4):[7]

(26.4) Et yo sabía **bien** tu malvestad et tu loçanía
'And I knew well the wickedness of your exuberance'
Source: *Calila e Dimna*

The fronting of *bien* to a preverbal position due to focalization, as in (26.5) and (26.6), leads to the eventual loss of the manner interpretation. As the adverb loses its bond to the predicate and increases its scope by having scope over the whole sentence, it comes to mark the positive polarity of the sentence (the expression of the speaker's commitment to the truth of a proposition, called "emphasis" by the authors). While (26.5) retains ambiguity between the manner and the polar readings, in (26.6) the topicalization is made apparent by the co-occurrence with a pronoun (*lo*), presumably with a clearer polar interpretation:

(26.5) **Bien** sepa el abbat que buen galardón dello pendra
'The abbot must know very well that he will be rewarded for it'

---

[6] Due to space limitations I focus here on the development of Spanish *bien*. For comparison with polarity markers in Catalan, see Batllori and Hernanz (2008, 2013). Martins (2014) and Delicado Cantero (2014) also build on comparison with other languages (specifically, Portuguese) in order to unveil principles of historical syntax.
[7] Examples (26.4)–(26.7) and their translations are from Batllori and Hernanz (2008).

(26.6)   **Bien** lo sabemos que el algo gaño
'Well/indeed we know that he won something'

The reanalysis to an emphatic polarity marker can be identified when there has been actualization, i.e. when we find examples of *bien* co-occurring in pre-verbal position with predicates that could not be modified by a manner adverb, as in (26.7):

(26.7)   Con tantas lágrimas acompañaba la enamorada pastora las palabras que decía, que **bien** tuviera corazón de acero quien de ellas no se doliera.
'The words spoken by the enamoured shepherdess were accompanied by so many tears that anyone who did not feel distress on hearing them would be hard-hearted indeed.'   Source: Cervantes, *La Galatea*

According to the authors, this change is due to "upward" and "leftward" movement leading to reanalysis and eventual recategorization of the original manner adverb and is an instance of a systematic process of grammaticalization involving functional categories at the left periphery (specifically, FocusP and PolarityP). Hence, focalization is seen as a source for the creation of emphatic polarity markers across languages.

In this framework, the interface with information structure is modeled within the syntactic architecture of the grammar. But information structure is also present within other frameworks that emphasize the role of pragmatic factors as motivation for language change, as shown in the next section.

26.3.2   The Origin of Differential Object Marking ("*a* personal") in Spanish

Spanish marks certain direct objects with the preposition *a*, as exemplified by the contrast between (26.8) and (26.9); examples from Pensado (1995a: 11):

(26.8)   Veo **a** la madre de Juan.
'I see Juan's mother.'

(26.9)   Veo la casa de Juan.
'I see Juan's house.'

The absence of *a* in (26.8) and its presence in (26.9) would be ungrammatical in modern Spanish. This pattern was not always found in the history of Spanish; both medieval and classical Spanish allowed for a great deal of variation in this respect (Lapesa 2000).

According to Laca (2006), three explanations for the origin of Differential Object Marking (DOM) have been proposed in the literature: (i) the need to distinguish between direct and indirect objects, (ii) the need to formally mark the distinction between subject and object after the demise of the Latin case system, and (iii) a combination of semantic and pragmatic factors. The account presented here, which connects the creation of this syntactic pattern to information structure, belongs to the third group. Pensado (1995b) explains the origin of DOM through the topicalization of tonic personal pronouns introduced by a preposition to express a topic change.

Several studies mention a functional competition in late Latin between the dative and the sequence AD + accusative (e.g. MIHI, AD ME 'to me,' and even a combination of the two, AD MIHI). Additionally, in Latin the preposition AD was also used with an NP to introduce a topic "as for X," typically with left dislocation of the constituent, as in (26.10):

(26.10) **ad Dolabellam**, ut scribis, ita puto faciendum
'As for Dolabella, as you write, I believe that things should be done as follows'
Source: Cicero, *Letters to Atticus*, 13, 10, 2; example from Pensado (1995b: 201)

For Pensado, when this topicalization strategy is used with pronouns referring to human and animate entities, the conditions are created for the grammaticalization of the preposition *a* as a marker of direct object with an animate referent. This would have favored the conflation of the morphological expression of direct and indirect objects.

Melis (1995) and Laca (2006) also note that in corpus data, left-dislocated direct objects tend to occur with the preposition *a* and with clitic doubling, as in (26.11):[8]

(26.11) **A** las sus fijas enbraço **las** prendia
PREP the his daughters in-arm **them** held.3sG
Source: *Cid*, 275–276; example from Laca (2006:455)

This factor, combined with the semantic properties of the object (Laca's "local factors"), would lead to a gradual extension of *a*-marking from human and definite referents to non-human and in some cases indefinite referents. Von Heusinger (2008) confirms the role of semantic and discourse-pragmatic properties of the direct objects (definiteness, specificity, and topicality) and shows the importance of the lexical semantics of transitive verbs in the origin of DOM.

26.4 Units of Change

Syntactic and semantic change does not usually happen to words in isolation, but rather to syntagmatic strings. The nature of such units has been explored by functional approaches focusing on patterns that can be documented in language use. Of particular interest is the notion of construction – a form–function mapping that can range from lexical item to

---

[8] Ledgeway (2012:288) notes the same coincidence of prepositional accusative and clitic-doubling in other Romance varieties.

pattern (Goldberg 2003; Traugott and Trousdale 2014). The frequency of constructions in speech, the linguistic expressions they collocate with[9] and the way in which they are stored by native speakers, through fixation and schematization, are considered major factors in change (Bybee and Torres Cacoullos 2009; Torres Cacoullos and Walker 2011; Bybee 2015).

Although compositionality is generally treated as relevant for synchronic studies, its role is crucial in understanding mechanisms of change (Vincent 2014). Studies on Spanish show a tension between those who argue for the primacy of constructions, seen as unanalyzable units, and those who adopt a compositional view and focus on syntactic reanalysis. Much current work on Spanish adopts the former, usage-based perspective, and explores quantitative methods to study change in constructions; for example, Bauman (2016) uses a variationist methodology to track changes in the collocations of *tener que* 'to have to' in order to investigate changes in the internal structure of modal categories.

A theoretically-informed discussion of units of change is important because it may reveal relations between individual changes and broader changes in subsystems of the language, as shown in the sections below.

26.4.1 New Indefinite Pronouns

An early phenomenon in the history of Spanish is the creation of complex indefinite pronouns (e.g. *quienquiera, cualquiera*) from the reanalysis of a sequence containing a relative pronoun (*quien, cual*) and a form of the verb *quaero* 'I seek, want.'[10] Company Company and Pozas Loyo (2009) present this formation as a typical case of grammaticalization; both the nominal and the verbal elements lost syntactic and semantic autonomy as they became parts of a new word now integrated in the paradigm of indefinites, the verbal element (*-quier*) was restricted to an invariable form, losing the potential to be inflected, and the whole form underwent phonetic reduction through the apocopated form *cualquier* (Company Company and Pozas Loyo 2009:1085, Pérez Saldanya and Salvador 2014). While these changes are uncontroversial, the mechanisms behind the formation of the new pronominal forms and the status of the new unit raise questions with theoretical implications. Are these forms a calque of the Latin pronouns with a similar structure, e.g. *quivis, quilibet* 'whoever, whatever you want/please' (Lenz 1920; Menéndez Pidal 1926; among

---

[9] In corpus studies the term "collocation" is generally understood in empirical terms; a collocation is a combination of words that occurs with higher frequency than would be expected from two randomly selected words. When a sizable corpus is available and hence it is possible to rely on such frequency measures, a change in collocations can be seen as an output manifestation of syntactic and semantic change (see Bartsch 2004 for discussion). Some authors also use "collocation" to denote a sequence of words with semi-compositional meaning (a definition that has the disadvantage of being more difficult to operationalize).

[10] It is subject to discussion whether *se* was part of this construction (i.e. *cual N se quier(a)* 'which *N se* want'); see Company Company and Pozas Loyo (2009), Rivero (1988).

others) or have they independently evolved from a relative clause (Cuervo *et al.* 1886–1994; Penny 2002; Rivero 1988)? The explanation according to which the pronoun evolved from a subordinate clause relies on corpus data supporting an evolution as in (26.12), from Company Company and Pozas Loyo (2009:1116):

(26.12)   haga   en   él   **cual**   castigo
         do.SBJV.3SG   in   him   **which**   punishment

considere/pareciere/quiera   >
consider/seem-right/want.SBJV.3SG   >

haga   en   él   **cual**   castigo   **quiera**   >
do.SBJV.3SG   in   him   **which**   punishment   **want.SBJV.3SG**   >

haga   en   él   **cual**   **quiera**   castigo   >
do.SBJV.3SG   in   him   **which**   **want.SBJV.3SG**   punishment   >

haga   en   él   **cualquier(a)**   castigo
do.SBJV.3SG   in   him   **any**   punishment

Rivero (1988) details the structural ambiguity underlying this change by showing that in medieval Spanish *cual* and related elements were both quantifiers and relative pronouns, and occurred in sequences of relative clauses that could have either an explicit or a null lexical antecedent.[11] In this process of reanalysis, the verb of the subordinate clause loses its predicative properties, e.g. its ability to select arguments, and both *cual* and *quiera* undergo recategorization; the sequence becomes a cohesive unit and it now occurs as a modifier of a noun. Company Company and Pozas Loyo (2009) point out that the two theories accounting for this change are not incompatible; the existence of a similar structure in Latin could have provided a model for the reanalysis of similar elements in Romance. Although the connection with semantic change is not mentioned in these studies, the parallel between the Latin forms and the Romance creations may be seen as the expression of a semantic universal tendency; the creation of free-choice items through pragmatic enrichment of a quantifier has parallels across languages (for the diachrony of free-choice and epistemic indefinites cross-linguistically, see Aguilar-Guevara *et al.* (2011)).

This topic reveals the complexity of the debate on units of change: while the recategorization of a syntagmatic sequence as a word may be seen as evidence for a construction-based approach, the properties of the pronouns and the interpretation of verb mood demonstrate the need to explain the contribution of the parts in the creation of the new complex pronoun.

---

[11] For Rivero, this is part of a broader change in the properties of *wh*-elements in Spanish, by which they lose their double nature. According to the author, this change affecting the paradigm of *wh*-words is complete by the 16th century: "The compound ones become (syntactic) quantifiers, and the ones that are not compound, like *qual*, are relative pronouns, independently of the semantic properties of the clauses in which they occur" (Rivero 1988:70, my translation).

26.4.2 Existential *Haber*

The creation of the existential meaning of the verb *haber* (from Latin HABĒRE 'to have') in Spanish instantiates the cross-linguistic connection between possession, location, and existence (Lyons 1967; Heine 1997). It also raises questions as to the motivation for reanalysis, which bears on the identification of the unit of change.

The replacement of *haber* by *tener* as verb of possession takes place in medieval Spanish; during the 13th–15th centuries there is variation between the two verbs as verbs of possession, sometimes even in the same text, but after the 16th century there are practically no instances of *haber* with possessive meaning (Hernández Díaz 2006). Hernández Díaz notes that the stative verb *haber* enters the grammar of Spanish in a variety of uses associated with possession (alienable and inalienable), in which its transitivity is low. It occurs with subjects and objects lacking prototypical properties of agent and patient, and appears in light verb constructions, e.g. *aver menester* 'to need,' *aver duda* 'to doubt.'

In corpus examples either there is no explicit subject or the subject is difficult to retrieve (for example, because its referent is not mentioned in the same or the previous clause). Since the verb is in third-person singular, there is ambiguity between a possessive and an existential interpretation (26.13):

(26.13) Et **él** assí ... tornóse a la mesa, jurando que si **mil cavallos et omnes et mugeres oviesse en casa** quel saliessen de mandado, que todos serían muertos[12]
'And he, in this manner ... returned to the table, swearing that if (he) had/there were at home one thousand horses and men and women that would appear, all would end up dead'
Source: *Libro de los enxiemplos del Conde Lucanor et de Patronio*

In yet other cases, the referent of the subject of *haber* is expressed through an oblique,[13] as in (26.14), and is not a prototypical agent since it is an inanimate entity:

(26.14) Agua es cosa húmida e **ha en ssí dos cosas que ssemeian contrarias**. La una es pesadumbre, et la otra es de liuiandat
'Water is something humid and has/there are in it two things that seem opposite. One is weight and the other is lightness'
Source: Alfonso X, *Setenario*

---

[12] Examples (26.13) and (26.14) are from Hernández Díaz (2006: Exx. (39) and (65), respectively).

[13] This demotion of the subject eventually facilitated the reinterpretation of the direct object of the transitive verb as a subject, triggering pluralization of the verb. This process, repeated synchronically in varieties of Spanish like Rioplatense, though normatively proscribed, assigns to *haber* the syntax of intransitives. Fontanella de Weinberg (1992:44) summarizes this connection between the synchronic and diachronic variation as follows: "We can say that the variation that exists nowadays between existential-impersonal *haber* and existential-intransitive *haber* is the result of a large change that we can observe in five centuries of American Spanish, but that in fact begins 2,000 years earlier and involves the multiple uses of *haber* as a main verb and as an auxiliary verb, developing from its original possessive value" (my translation). For a recent study of the different developments of *haber*, see de Benito Moreno and Octavio de Toledo y Huerta (2016).

The connection between the existential meaning and the locative domain is apparent in Spanish, in the form *hay* 'there is.' First, the locative pronoun *y* (< Latin *ibi* 'there, in that place') was reanalyzed as part of existential *haber* in the third person singular of the present (for the morphologization of this sequence, see García 1991). Second, in (26.14) the logical subject of the verb is expressed through a prepositional phrase (PP); this entity has the role of a locative.

The fate of *haber* in Spanish as it becomes an existential verb reflects a phenomenon with potential theoretical implications: the fact that verbs like *haber* (cf. *ter* in Portuguese; see Viotti 1998) systematically undergo this change shows a reanalysis of their argument structure, involving both semantic and syntactic factors. As Fontanella de Weinberg points out, verbs like *haber* have a tendency to undergo changes in argument structure (1992:44–45). The subject of such verbs lacks the properties of an agent and often resembles a locative, and its direct object lacks the properties of a prototypical patient. This creates the conditions for a verbal alternation, with arguments being locative and theme, rather than agent and patient, respectively, eventually leading to syntactic change. The role of argument structure in this change points to the need to further explore the verb complex (i.e. its syntactic and semantic restrictions) as a unit of change.[14]

26.5 Language Change and Cognitive Principles of Language Production

Recent research on Spanish connects insights from historical linguistics, psycholinguistics, and information theory, in what can be seen as a new interpretation of the Uniformitarian Principle (Labov 1972) according to which "[t]he general processes and principles which can be noticed in observable history are applicable in all stages of language history" (Hock 1991:630). Hence, cognitive mechanisms operating in language production and processing in the present should be relevant in explaining the past (Fischer 2007; Jäger and Rosenbach 2008). These approaches stem from usage-based and cognitive backgrounds; they see grammar as a dynamic system emerging from general cognitive processes and from patterns created in discourse. For example, it is known that high lexical frequency has a conserving effect in language change; it has been shown that as the Spanish perfect formed with *haber* underwent extension in the grammar, high-frequency intransitive verbs like *morir* 'to die' or *venir* 'to come' were among the last to retain the perfect formed with *ser*, and low-frequency verbs underwent the change more rapidly (Rosemeyer 2014). The two topics surveyed in this section exemplify this approach, investigating how constraints on variation that can be identified in corpora may shed light on mechanisms of change.

---

[14] Another example is the change undergone by psychological verbs in Spanish (see Elvira 2015, among others).

Although analogy has traditionally been described as unpredictable and irregular, recent work on morphosyntactic change suggests that it does not proceed in a "blind" manner. Brown and Rivas (2012) analyze the pluralization of *haber* in Puerto Rican Spanish as an instance of analogical change. In their view (building on Montes de Oca-Sicilia 1994), impersonal *haber* is regularized by analogy with other verbs with a similar meaning, like *ser* and *existir*, and becomes gradually integrated in the larger paradigm of intransitive verbs in Spanish. Brown and Rivas analyze the sequence [*haber* + noun phrase (NP)] with person/number agreement between the verb and its NP argument as a construction, and investigate whether the properties of the noun in this construction play a role in the analogical process. Specifically, they show that nouns that more frequently occur with subject function favor the pluralization of the verb over nouns that are less typical subjects, thus contributing to the analogical regularization of *haber*. Moreover, this probabilistic measurement is context-independent, i.e. pluralization of *haber* is favored by the overall likelihood that a noun be used as subject in Spanish, not just the likelihood of being a subject in the construction allowing for variation. Hence, knowledge of noun usage patterns in general plays a role in the pluralization of *haber*, and if this is an instance of change in progress (see references in Brown and Rivas 2012), then analogical change is affected by predictive probabilities that reflect patterns of use. These findings reinforce the need to better understand the cognitive and empirical foundations of analogy as a regularizing mechanism. The perception that analogy is unpredictable and proceeds randomly may have been due to the fact that the factors governing it, like probability measures and frequency, have not been systematically studied until recently.

Although most research on language change focuses on *why change occurs*, a related and pertinent question is why it does *not occur*, i.e. why a certain form or construction, often alternating with another variant, fails to disappear from a language. Rosemeyer and Schwenter (2017) set out to answer this question with respect to the variation between -*se* and -*ra* past subjunctive forms in Spanish (e.g. *comiese* vs. *comiera*), the former gradually disappearing from the language since the 13th century. Although previous studies claim that there were semantic-pragmatic differences between the two forms, Rosemeyer and Schwenter (2017) show that neither morphosyntactic factors (e.g. negation, subordination) nor semantic-pragmatic factors predict the selection of one of the variants over the other in the corpus data. Rather, the presence of a -*se* token in a recent context is the most statistically significant predictor of the distribution of a -*se* form by favoring its production. This is not only true for specific -*se* forms, but also for the whole -*se* construction in Spanish; the occurrence of an obsolescing form, which is less predictable and hence more surprising for the speaker, primes the use of the whole pattern and eventually contributes to its survival over time. In other words, persistence or structural priming proves to be highly relevant to the maintenance of morphosyntactic alternations.

Psycholinguistically-informed studies of language change in Spanish, like this one, make a theoretical contribution by connecting disciplines that traditionally have not communicated: psycholinguistics and historical linguistics. This connection is promising as it sheds light on the grammatical units that speakers know and store, and provides insight into the cognitive processes behind language change.

26.6 Conclusion

The studies presented in this chapter address foundational questions in historical linguistics from different perspectives. The overview shows that certain theoretical issues should be further explored in diachronic studies on Spanish: (i) the motivations behind reanalysis and analogical change, (ii) how to best model semantic change, and (iii) the role of compositionality in language change. Additionally, it would be enriching to consider the role of dialectal and register differences in diachronic research as well as in textual genres[15] in the corpora used to study instances of language change in Spanish. Such issues have traditionally been addressed by philological studies and have not been sufficiently incorporated into current approaches. Also rarely addressed is the contribution of diachronic research on Spanish to theoretical semantics (but see Amaral 2016), though it is found in theoretical syntax (cf. Batllori and Hernanz 2008, Delicado Cantero 2013).

Finally, given the growing number of quantitative diachronic studies of Spanish, it is important to assess the contribution of these methods to historical research. The availability of large electronic corpora that can be analyzed with quantitative methods not only improves the empirical coverage of diachronic studies; it also transforms our knowledge of mechanisms of change: large corpora have the potential to change the research questions asked in historical linguistics. What do collocations reveal about the knowledge a speaker has of his/her language and, consequently, what can we infer from an attested change in collocations of a word? How can we integrate findings from research into production and processing in diachronic studies? Cross-pollination with disciplines like sociolinguistics and psycholinguistics is desirable, but this also requires reflection on these new questions and on how they relate to theories in the field. Additionally, although these methods have proved promising for morphosyntactic change, their contributions to the study of semantic change are still unclear.

---

[15] For recent work that addresses this issue, see Kabatek (2005, 2008).

References

Aaron, Jesse (2016). The Road Already Traveled. Constructional Analogy in Lexico-Syntactic Change. *Studies in Language*, 40 (1), 26–62.

Aguilar-Guevara, Ana *et al.* (2011). Semantics and Pragmatics of Indefinites: Methodology for a Synchronic and Diachronic Corpus Study. In Stefanie Dipper and Heike Zinsmeister (eds.), *Beyond Semantics: Corpus-Based Investigations of Pragmatic and Discourse Phenomena. Proceedings of the Deutsche Gesellschaft für Sprachwissenschaft (DGfS) Workshop, Göttingen, February 23–25, 2011*. Bochum: University of Bochum, pp. 1–16.

Amaral, Patrícia (2016). When *something* Becomes *a bit*. *Diachronica*, 33 (2), 151–186.

Amaral, Patrícia and Delicado Cantero, Manuel (2018). Subcategorization and Change: A Diachronic Analysis of *sin embargo (de que)*. In Jonathan E. MacDonald (ed.), *Contemporary Trends in Hispanic and Lusophone Linguistics: Selected Papers from the Hispanic Linguistic Symposium 2015*. Amsterdam: John Benjamins, pp. 31–47.

Arlotto, Anthony (1972). *Introduction to Historical Linguistics*. Lanham, MD: Houghton Mifflin.

Barra Jover, M. (2002). *Propiedades léxicas y evolución sintáctica. El desarrollo de los mecanismos de subordinación en español*. La Coruña: Toxosoutos.

Bartsch, Sabine (2004). *Structural and Functional Properties of Collocations in English*. Tübingen: Narr.

Batllori, Montserrat and Hernanz, Maria-Lluïsa (2008). La polaridad negativa enfática en español: Un estudio diacrónico y comparativo. In José Moreno de Alba (ed.), *Actas del VII Congreso Internacional de Historia de la Lengua Española. Mérida (Yucatán), México, 4–8 de septiembre de 2006*, Vol. 2. Madrid: Arco Libros, pp. 1183–1200.

Batllori, Montserrat and Hernanz, Maria-Lluïsa (2013). Emphatic Polarity Particles in Spanish and Catalan. *Lingua*, 128, 9–30.

Bauman, Joseph (2016). From Possession to Obligation via Shifting Distributions and Particular Constructions. *Diachronica*, 33 (3), 297–329.

Bogard, Sergio and Company Company, Concepción (1989). Estructura y evolución de las oraciones completivas de sustantivo en el español. *Romance Philology*, 43, 258–273.

Brown, Esther and Rivas, Javier (2012). Grammatical Relation Probability: How Usage Patterns Shape Analogy. *Language Variation and Change*, 24, 317–341.

Bybee, Joan (2015). *Language Change*. Cambridge: Cambridge University Press.

Bybee, Joan L. and Torres Cacoullos, Rena (2009). The Role of Prefabs in Grammaticalization: How the Particular and the General Interact in Language Change. In Robert Corrigan, Edith A. Moravcsik, Hamid Ouali, and Kathleen M. Wheatley (eds.), *Formulaic Language*, Vol. 1: *Distribution and Historical Change*. Amsterdam: John Benjamins, pp. 187–217.

Campbell, Lyle (2013). *Historical Linguistics. An Introduction*. Cambridge, MA: MIT Press.

Cervantes, Miguel de (1614). *Segundo tomo del ingenioso hidalgo Don Quijote de la Mancha, que contiene su tercera salida y es la quinta parte de sus aventuras*. Tarragona: Felipe Roberto. Virtual edition consulted at http://www.cervantesvirtual.com/obra-visor/segundo-tomo-del-ingenioso-hidalgo-don-quixote-de-la-mancha-que-contiene-su-tercera-salida-y-es-la-quinta-parte-de-sus-auenturas–0/html/ (last access December 16, 2017).

Company Company, C. (2010). Reanálisis, ¿mecanismo necesario de la gramaticalización? Una propuesta desde la diacronía del objeto indirecto en español. *Revista de Historia de la Lengua Española*, 5, 35–66.

Company Company, C. and Pozas Loyo, Julia (2009). Los indefinidos compuestos y los pronombres genérico-impersonales *omne* y *uno*. In C. Company Company (ed.), *Sintaxis histórica de la lengua española. Segunda parte: La frase nominal*. Mexico City: FCE/UNAM, pp. 1075–1219.

Cuervo, Rufino *et al.* (1886–1994). *Diccionario de construcción y régimen de la lengua castellana*. Bogotá: Instituto Caro y Cuervo.

de Benito Moreno, Carlota and Octavio de Toledo y Huerta, Álvaro (eds.) (2016). *En torno a "haber." Construcciones, usos y variación desde el latín hasta la actualidad*. Frankfurt: Peter Lang.

de Smet, Henrik (2009). Analyzing Reanalysis. *Lingua*, 119, 1728–1755.

de Smet, Henrik (2016). How Gradual Change Progresses: The Interaction between Convention and Innovation. *Language Variation and Change*, 28, 83–102.

Delicado Cantero, Manuel (2013). *Prepositional Clauses in Spanish. A Diachronic and Comparative Syntactic Study*. Berlin: De Gruyter.

Delicado Cantero, Manuel (2014). *Dequeísmo* and *queísmo* in Portuguese and Spanish. In P. Amaral and Ana M. Carvalho (eds.), *Portuguese–Spanish Interfaces: Diachrony, Synchrony, and Contact*. Amsterdam: John Benjamins, pp. 95–120.

Diewald, Gabriele (2002). A Model for Relevant Types of Contexts in Grammaticalization. In Ilse Wischer and G. Diewald (eds.), *New Reflections on Grammaticalization*. Amsterdam: John Benjamins, pp. 103–120.

Dworkin, Steven (2012). *A History of the Spanish Lexicon. A Linguistic Perspective*. Oxford: Oxford University Press.

Eckardt, Regine (2006). *Meaning Change in Grammaticalization: An Enquiry into Semantic Reanalysis*. Oxford: Oxford University Press.

Eckardt, Regine (2012). Grammaticalization and Semantic Reanalysis. In Claudia Maienborn, Klaus von Heusinger, and Paul Portner (eds.), *Semantics: An International Handbook of Natural Language Meaning*, Vol. 3. Berlin: De Gruyter, pp. 2675–2701.

Elvira, Javier (1998). *El cambio analógico*. Madrid: Gredos.

Elvira, Javier (2003). Sobre el origen de la locución concesiva *por mucho que* y similares. In José Luis Girón Alconchel *et al.* (eds.), *Estudios ofrecidos al*

profesor José Jesús de Bustos Tovar. Madrid: Editorial Complutense, Vol. 1, 217–231.
Elvira, Javier (2015). *Lingüística histórica y cambio gramatical*. Madrid: Síntesis.
Fischer, Olga (2007). *Morphosyntactic Change: Functional and Formal Perspectives*. Oxford: Oxford University Press.
Fischer, Olga (2013). An Inquiry into Unidirectionality as a Foundational Element of Grammaticalization. *Studies in Language*, 37 (3), 515–533.
Fontanella de Weinberg, María Beatriz (1992). Variación sincrónica y diacrónica en las construcciones con *haber* en el español americano. *Boletín de Filología*, 33, 35–46.
Garachana Camarero, Mar (1997). Los procesos de gramaticalización. Una aplicación a los conectores contraargumentativos (Doctoral dissertation). Universidad de Barcelona.
García, Érica (1991). Morphologization: A Case of Reversible Markedness? *Probus*, 3 (1), 23–54.
Gianollo, Chiara *et al.* (eds.) (2015). *Language Change at the Syntax–Semantics Interface*. Berlin: De Gruyter.
Goldberg, Adele (2003). Constructions: A New Theoretical Approach to Language. *TRENDS in Cognitive Sciences*, 7 (5), 219–224.
Harris, Alice and Campbell, Lyle (1995). *Historical Syntax in Cross-Linguistic Perspective*. Cambridge: Cambridge University Press.
Heine, Bernd (1997). *Possession. Cognitive Sources, Forces and Grammaticalization*. Cambridge: Cambridge University Press.
Herman, József (1963). *La formation du système roman des conjonctions de subordination*. Berlin: Akademie Verlag.
Hernández Díaz, Axel (2006). Posesión y existencia. La competencia de *haber* y *tener* en la posesión y *haber* existencial. In C. Company Company (ed.), *Sintaxis histórica del español. Primera parte: La frase verbal*, Vol. 2. Mexico City: FCE/UNAM, pp. 1053–1160.
Hock, Hans Heinrich (1991). *Principles of Historical Linguistics*. Berlin: De Gruyter.
Hopper, Paul and Traugott, Elizabeth (2003). *Grammaticalization*. Cambridge: Cambridge University Press.
Itkonen, Esa (2005). *Analogy as Structure and Process*. Amsterdam: John Benjamins.
Jäger, Gerhard and Rosenbach, Anette (2008). Priming and Unidirectional Language Change. *Theoretical Linguistics*, 34 (2), 85–113.
Jespersen, Otto (1917). *Negation in English and Other Languages*. Copenhagen: A. F. Høst.
Kabatek, J. (2005). Tradiciones discursivas y cambio lingüístico. *Lexis*, 29, 151–177.
Kabatek, J. (ed.) (2008). *Sintaxis histórica del español y cambio lingüístico: Nuevas perspectivas desde las tradiciones discursivas*. Madrid and Frankfurt: Iberoamericana/Vervuert.

König, E. (1988). Concessive Connectives and Concessive Sentences. Cross-Linguistic Regularities and Pragmatic Principles. In J. A. Hawkins (ed.), *Explaining Language Universals*. Oxford: Blackwell, pp. 145–166.

Labov, William (1972). *Sociolinguistic Patterns*. Philadelphia, PA: University of Pennsylvania Press.

Laca, Brenda (2006). El objeto directo. La marcación preposicional. In C. Company Company (ed.), *Sintaxis histórica de la lengua española, Primera parte, La frase verbal*, Vol. 1. Mexico City: FCE/UNAM, pp. 423–478.

Lapesa, R. (2000) Los casos latinos: Restos sintácticos y sustitutos en español. In R. Lapesa (ed.), *Estudios de morfosintaxis histórica del español*. Madrid: Gredos, pp. 73–122.

Ledgeway, Adam (2012). *From Latin to Romance: Morphosyntactic Typology and Change*. Oxford: Oxford University Press.

Lenz, Rodolfo (1920). *La oración y sus partes*. Madrid: Junta para la Ampliación de Estudios e Investigaciones Científicas.

Lightfoot, David (1979). *Principles of Diachronic Syntax*. Cambridge: Cambridge University Press.

Lightfoot, David (1991). *How to Set Parameters: Arguments from Language Change*. Cambridge: Cambridge University Press.

Lightfoot, David and Westergaard, Marit (2007). Language Acquisition and Language Change: Interrelationships. *Language and Linguistics Compass*, 1 (5), 396–416.

Lyons, John (1967). A Note on Possessive, Existential and Locative Sentences. *Foundations of Language*, 3, 390–396.

Márquez Guerrero, María (2006). *Todavía*: Valores y usos en textos de los siglos XII–XVI. In J. J. de Bustos Tovar and J. L. Girón Alconchel (eds.), *Actas del VI Congreso Internacional de Historia de la Lengua Española*. Madrid: Arco Libros, pp. 879–897.

Martins, Ana M. (2014). Syntactic Change in Portuguese and Spanish. Divergent and Parallel Patterns of Linguistic Splitting. In P. Amaral and Ana M. Carvalho (eds.), *Portuguese–Spanish Interfaces: Diachrony, Synchrony, and Contact*. Amsterdam: John Benjamins, pp. 35–64.

Meillet, A. (1912). L'évolution des formes grammaticales. *Scientia (Rivista di Scienza)*, 12 (6), 384–400. Reprinted in A. Meillet (ed.), *Linguistique historique et linguistique générale*. Paris: Champion [1965], pp. 130–148.

Melis, Chantal (1995). El objeto directo personal en el *Cantar de mio Cid*. Estudio sintáctico-pragmático. In C. Pensado (ed.), *El complemento directo preposicional*. Madrid: Visor, pp. 133–163.

Menéndez Pidal, Ramón (1926). *Orígenes del español. Estado lingüístico de la Península Ibérica hasta el siglo XI*. Madrid: Espasa Calpe.

Montes de Oca-Sicilia, M. del Pilar (1994). La concordancia con *haber* impersonal. *Anuario de Letras*, 32, 7–35.

Penny, Ralph (2002). *A History of the Spanish Language*. Cambridge: Cambridge University Press.

Pensado, Carmen (1995a). El complemento directo preposicional: Estado de la cuestión y bibliografía comentada. In C. Pensado (ed.), *El complemento directo preposicional*. Madrid: Visor, 11–91.

Pensado, Carmen (1995b). La creación del complemento directo preposicional y la flexión de los pronombres personales en las lenguas románicas. In C. Pensado (ed.), *El complemento directo preposicional*. Madrid: Visor, pp. 179–233.

Pérez Saldanya, M. and Hualde, J. I. (in press). Recurrent Processes in the Evolution of Concessive Subordinators in Spanish and Catalan. In Miriam Bouzouita, Ioanna Sitaridou, and Enrique Pato (eds.), *Studies in Historical Ibero-Romance Morpho-Syntax*. Amsterdam: John Benjamins, pp. 223–248.

Pérez Saldanya, M. and Salvador, V. (2014). Oraciones subordinadas concesivas. In C. Company Company (ed.), *Sintaxis histórica de la lengua española. Tercera parte: Preposiciones, adverbios y conjunciones. Relaciones interoracionales*. Mexico City: FCE/UNAM, pp. 3699–3839.

Rivarola, J. L. (1976): *Las conjunciones concesivas en español medieval y clásico*. Tübingen: M. Niemeyer.

Rivero, María Luísa (1988). La sintaxis de *qual quiere* y sus variantes en el español antiguo. *Nueva Revista de Filología Hispánica*, 36 (1), 47–73.

Rizzi, Luigi (1997). The Fine Structure of the Left Periphery. In L. Haegeman (ed.), *Elements of Grammar. Handbook in Generative Syntax*. Dordrecht: Kluwer, pp. 281–337.

Roberts, Ian (2007). *Diachronic Syntax*. Oxford: Oxford University Press.

Roberts, Ian and Roussou, Anna (2003). *Syntactic Change. A Minimalist Approach to Grammaticalization*. Cambridge: Cambridge University Press.

Rosemeyer, Malte (2014). *Auxiliary Selection in Spanish: Gradience, Gradualness, and Conservation*. Amsterdam: John Benjamins.

Rosemeyer, Malte and Schwenter, Scott (2017). Entrenchment and Persistence in Language Change: The Spanish Past Subjunctive. *Corpus Linguistics and Linguistic Theory*. doi: 10.1515/cllt-2016-0047.

Serradilla, Ana (1997). *El régimen de los verbos de entendimiento y lengua en español medieval*. Madrid: Universidad Autónoma de Madrid.

Tarr, Frederick C. (1922). Prepositional Complementary Clauses in Spanish with Special Reference to the works of Pérez Galdós. *Revue Hispanique*, 56, 1–264.

Timberlake, Alan (1977). Reanalysis and Actualization in Syntactic Change. In C. N. Li (ed.), *Mechanisms of Syntactic Change*. Austin, TX: University of Texas Press, pp. 141–177.

Torres Cacoullos, Rena (2006). Relative Frequency in the Grammaticization of Collocations: Nominal to Concessive *a pesar de*. In Timothy L. Face and Carol A. Klee (eds.), *Selected Proceedings of the 8th Hispanic Linguistics Symposium*. Somerville, MA: Cascadilla, pp. 37–49.

Torres Cacoullos, Rena and Schwenter, Scott (2006). Towards an Operational Notion of Subjectification. In Rebecca Cover and Yuni Kim (eds.), *Proceedings of the 31st Annual Meeting of the BLS*. Berkeley, CA: BLS, pp. 347–358.

Torres Cacoullos, Rena and Walker, James A. (2011): Collocations in Grammaticalization and Variation. In Bernd Heine and Heiko Narrog (eds.), *Handbook of Grammaticalization*. Oxford: Oxford University Press, pp. 225–238.

Traugott, Elizabeth (1995). Subjectification in Grammaticalisation. In Dieter Stein and Susan Wright (eds.), *Subjectivity and Subjectivisation: Linguistic Perspectives*. Cambridge: Cambridge University Press, pp. 31–54.

Traugott, Elizabeth (2012). The Status of Onset Contexts in Analysis of Micro-Changes. In Merja Kytö (ed.), *English Corpus Linguistics: Crossing Paths*. Amsterdam: Rodopi, pp. 221–255.

Traugott, Elizabeth and Dasher, Richard (2002). *Regularity in Semantic Change*. Oxford: Oxford University Press.

Traugott, Elizabeth and Trousdale, Graeme (2014). *Constructionalization and Constructional Changes*. Oxford: Oxford University Press.

Vincent, Nigel (2014). Compositionality and Change. In Claire Bowern and Bethwyn Evans (eds.), *The Routledge Handbook of Historical Linguistics*. London: Routledge, pp. 103–123.

Viotti, Evani (1998). Uma história sobre *ter* e *haver*. *Cadernos de Estudos Lingüísticos*, 34, 41–50.

von Fintel, Kai (1995). The Formal Semantics of Grammaticalization. In Jill N. Beckman (ed.), *Proceedings of the North East Linguistic Society 25*, Vol. 2. Amherst, MA: Graduate Linguistic Student Association, pp. 175–198.

von Heusinger, K. (2008). Verbal Semantics and the Diachronic Development of DOM in Spanish. *Probus*, 20 (1), 1–31.

Wanner, Dieter (2006). *The Power of Analogy: An Essay on Historical Linguistics*. Berlin: De Gruyter.

27

Grammaticalization

Chad Howe

27.1 Grammaticalization as Grammar Creation

Grammaticalization concerns linguistic change, both as a diachronic phenomenon requiring time and space, and as a synchronic one with structural and semantic shift being played out at the level of frequency. Following Meillet's (1912) coinage of the term, Kuryłowicz provides one of the earliest explanations of grammaticalization, noting that it "consists in the increase of the range of a morpheme advancing from a lexical to a grammatical or from a less grammatical to a more grammatical status, e.g. from a derivative formant to an inflectional one" (1965:69). Perhaps the most widely cited definition of grammaticalization is that provided by Hopper and Traugott, who observe the following:

> Grammaticalization ... is the process whereby lexical items and constructions come in certain linguistic contexts to serve grammatical functions, and, once grammaticalized, continue to develop new grammatical functions ... whereby the properties that distinguish sentences from vocabulary come into being diachronically or are organized synchronically. (2003:xv)

Included in this definition are several important observations related to the understanding of grammaticalization as grammar creation (Croft 2006). First, the grammaticalization view[1] of language change encodes, at its core, the change from lexicon to grammar. In Romance, this shift is manifested in a variety of constructions, perhaps most well studied among these being the inflectional future, which evolved from a periphrastic construction in Latin illustrated in (27.1) below.[2] The main verb, HABEŌ,

---

[1] Throughout this chapter, I will refrain from referring to grammaticalization as a theory proper, since, at least in my view, it is better understood as an overarching perspective on the evolution of grammar.
[2] See Ewert (1961) and, more recently, Graham (2015) for a discussion of the evolution of the inflectional future in Spanish.

undergoes a pattern of phonological and semantic reduction resulting in the full-fledged inflectional paradigm attested across modern varieties of Romance Languages. What remains of HABEŌ in this construction are morphological reflexes, now represented in the grammar as bound morphology, with the lexical item *haber* also attested in the language as a free lexical item. This pattern is characteristic of what is sometimes referred to as primary grammaticalization (Givón 1991:305). Secondary grammaticalization, thus, involves the development of "new grammatical functions" such as the use of the inflectional future as an epistemic or modal marker shown in Example 27.2.

(27.1)   CANTĀRE HABEŌ (Latin) > cantaré (modern Spanish)

(27.2)   – ¿Y Paquito y María dónde están ahora?
'And Paquito and María, where are they now?'
– No lo sé si **estarán** con sus abuelos o **estarán** en Valencia dónde **andarán**.
'I don't know if they might be with their grandparents or they might be in Valencia where they might be.'   Source: Aaron (2014:219)

What links together the study of the development of CANTĀRE HABEŌ in Spanish, and indeed in Romance, with that of forms of future reference in other languages is the observation that processes of grammaticalization tend to follow predetermined "pathways" (also known as "gradients" or "clines") of development (Bybee *et al.* 1994). The latter, and later Heine and Kuteva (2002), have provided typological evidence of how these grammaticalization pathways are manifested cross-linguistically, with striking parallels between typologically distinct languages in the development of, for instance, auxiliaries, temporal adverbs, and indefinite pronouns. Explaining the pragmatic and cognitive motivations for these changes has also been the target of a wide body of literature focused on understanding the role of metaphor and metonymy, not to mention analogy, in the evolution of grammatical categories. The modern grammaticalization enterprise is comprised of studies that attempt to reconcile the typological generality of language change observed in this approach with the details gleaned from language-specific analyses of structural and semantic change. Studies across a variety of Spanish dialects, consequently, have been central to this endeavor, offering qualitative and quantitative perspectives on the development of new grammatical structures and on the emergence of new grammatical functions.

These and other issues related to the study of grammaticalization in Spanish will serve as the basis for the remainder of this chapter, beginning with an overview in Section 27.2 of several basic concepts that have been proposed to explain the changes observed both in primary and secondary grammaticalization. In Section 27.3, several related processes, often viewed through the lens of grammaticalization studies, are surveyed, including cases of pragmaticalization and lexicalization observed in Spanish. Section 27.4 provides a summary of different approaches that have been used to explain structural and semantic change in Spanish across a variety of different phenomena that range from language use in digital contexts to situations of language contact. The final section offers an overview of current trends in this field, noting specifically those that assume a Construction Grammar perspective, and concludes with a few general remarks regarding the contribution of studies concerning Spanish to the broader grammaticalization enterprise.

27.2 Basic Concepts in Grammaticalization Studies

The form–function pairing constitutes an important focus for grammaticalization studies in that it lies at the core of how structures evolve, come to compete with, and potentially replace, other structures. Hopper and Traugott (2003) characterize this process schematically as A > A/B (> B), where A and B are understood to be forms that enter into a state of structural and/or semantic overlap. This competition can, but, as Hopper and Traugott rightly observe, does not necessarily result in a switch in preference (viewed often as a question of frequency of use) from form A to form B. According to Howe, "[a]s competing forms emerge, there is considerable interaction between these and older forms, creating an ongoing tension that can result in the gradual loss of the older structure" (2009:153). The nature of the form–function pairing is such that change is cyclical, with new forms and thus new competition being introduced at various diachronic stages. In the evolution of future expression in Spanish, the loss of the original Latin future was followed by the emergence of a periphrastic form with the verb *ir* 'to go,' giving rise to another stage of structural overlap depicted in (27.3).

(27.3) | **Stage 1** | | **Stage 2** | | **Stage 3** |
| --- | --- | --- | --- | --- |
| CANTĀRE HABEŌ | > | CANTĀRE HABEŌ | > | cantaré |
| | > | cantaré | | voy a cantar |

As this process unfolds, a variety of structural and semantic correlates can be observed. Lehmann (1995) has referred to these correlates as parameters of grammaticalization, developmental benchmarks that often coincide with the transition from lexicon to grammar and, similarly, with the development of a wider range of grammatical functions. Of the four parameters outlined by Lehmann, and discussed and extended by numerous other authors, decategorialization (loss of morphosyntactic properties), erosion (loss of phonetic substance), and desemanticization (loss or generalization of meaning)[3] can be observed in the shift illustrated in (27.3) between Stage 1 and Stage 2, where the Latin verb HABEŌ undergoes a series of changes that result in (i) a shift from main verb to auxiliary verb and then to bound morphology, (ii) phonological reduction from HABEŌ to -*é*, and (iii) loss of the original lexical meaning of HABEŌ, meaning 'I have.' These changes, characteristic of primary grammaticalization, occur in tandem as a form develops from an erstwhile lexical source into a new construction, related to the original via the pathway of development but distinct in that it is used in new contexts. This facet of development – i.e. the "rise of new grammatical meanings when linguistic expressions are extended into new contexts" (Heine and Narrog 2010:405) – constitutes Lehmann's fourth parameter, extension, and is, according to Heine and Narrog, the first step in the grammaticalization process and more generally characterizes the types of changes associated with secondary grammaticalization.[4]

Principal among the overarching notions regarding the study of change from a grammaticalization perspective is the claim that these processes are unidirectional – i.e. they are hypothesized to occur as a specific series of changes that do not, and for some authors cannot, occur in the opposition direction. This notion is reflected in Givón's (1979:209) description of syntactic change, exemplified in the cline *discourse > syntax > morphology > morphononemics > zero*, and reiterated by other authors, including Traugott and Hopper (2003:8), who offer the more general cline of *content word > function word > clitic > affix > zero*. Unidirectionality predicts that, for instance, clitics will not develop into content words and that bound morphemes will not become "unbound." Grammaticalization skeptics have pointed to possible cases of reversal of grammatical development as evidence that grammaticalization and, consequently, its entrenched assumption of unidirectionality, are epiphenomenal in that they merely represent more general processes involved in language change, such as reanalysis and analogy (Janda 2001; Joseph 2001; Newmeyer 2001). The evidence for what some have referred to as degrammaticalization notwithstanding, the assumption that grammatical evolution follows a non-reversible path is widely accepted in the literature.

One path that has been the subject of considerable scrutiny in Spanish is the evolution of the periphrastic past (present perfect, PP) and its opposition vis-à-vis the simple past (preterit). According to Bybee *et al.* (1994:105), the resultative-to-anterior pathway can be characterized as in (27.4) and exemplified in Spanish with (27.5).

---

[3] In the grammaticalization literature, the loss of semantic meaning is commonly referred to as (semantic) bleaching.
[4] According to Heine and Narrog, grammaticalization "tends to start out with extension, which triggers desemanticization, and subsequently decategorialization and erosion" (2010:405).

Table 27.1 *Development of the periphrastic and simple past in Romance languages*

Stage	Simple past	Periphrastic past	Languages
1	All past perfectives	Present states resulting from past actions	Calabrés, Sicilian
2	Most past perfectives	Durative and iterative situations still ongoing at utterance time	Portuguese, Mexican Spanish
3	Past situations without current relevance	Past situations with current relevance	Catalan, Peninsular Spanish
4	Used only in formal registers; written language	All past situations	French, northern Italian

Source: Adapted from Fleischman (1983:195) and Schwenter and Torres Cacoullos (2008:7)

(27.4) 'be' / 'have' > Resultative > Anterior > Perfective/Simple Past

(27.5) Esta es una cátedra que **he desempeñado** durante largos años y, como fruto de mis investigaciones, de mis estudios y de mi labor docente, **he publicado** un libro que se **editó** *(Preterit)* en España en mil novecientos setenta y nueve.
'I **have filled** this position for many years and, as a product of my research, of my studies, and of my teaching, I **have published** a book that **was produced** in Spain in 1979.'

Source: Marrone (1992:68); translation mine

Studies of the opposition between periphrastic forms such as *he desempeñado* and *he publicado*, on the one hand, and preterit forms like *editó*, on the other, have focused on those factors that characterize the use of the periphrastic form across Spanish dialects – such as compatibility with definite past adverbials and use in sequenced narratives – as well as the behavior of this form in comparison to other Romance languages (Harris 1982; Fleischman 1983). This development, shown in Table 27.1, is indicative of the type of extension, in Lehmann's (1995) terms, attested in early stages of grammaticalization.

In Romance languages, the periphrastic past with HABĒRE (*haber* in Spanish) begins as a resultative construction and, following the pathway proposed by Bybee *et al.* (1994), it has been observed to develop the functions of an anterior (as in Spanish) and then of a perfective past (as in French). The interplay between forms as new meanings develop, often replacing older ones, is referred to as "layering" (Hopper 1991:22). The use of the periphrastic past to indicate a sequence of events, attested of some varieties of Peninsular Spanish and exemplified in (27.6), is an obvious case of layering. The terms "retention" and "persistence" (Bybee and Paglicua 1987; Hopper 1991) refer to the maintenance of features inherited from source constructions – e.g. the use of the periphrastic past in Spanish to refer to resultant states, as in *Yo he abierto la ventana* 'I have opened the window (... and it is still open)' to refer to a window that is open at the time of utterance.

(27.6) Bueno pues **me (he) levantado** a las ocho de la mañana y **he desayunado** mi café mis galletas etcétera etcétera. [...] Después cuando **me (he) levantado** y **me he vestido** a las nueve y media de la mañana [...] Luego **me (he) vuelto** a la biblioteca y **he estado estudiando** también la lingüística. Y después me **han** ... **han venido** unas compañeras y **me han dicho** de salir al colegio de Málaga.
'Well, I **woke up** at 8:00 in the morning and I **had** my coffee, my cookies, etc. [...] Afterwards when I **got up** and **got dressed** at 9:30 in the morning [...] Later I **returned** to the library and I **was** also **studying** linguistics. And afterwards some friends **came** to me and **told** me to leave for Málaga College.'[5]

Although the literature on grammaticalization represents contributions from a variety of different theoretical perspectives, including those from generative syntax (Roberts and Roussou 1999, 2003) and formal semantics (Eckardt 2006), the dominant view is certainly functionalist and, more specifically, usage-based (see Chapter 3, this volume). It has long been recognized that one of the hallmarks of grammaticalizing forms is an increase in overall frequency. In fact, as Bybee notes, "our understanding of usage effects on grammar has been greatly informed by research on grammaticalization" (2011:68). In Copple's study of the early development of the periphrastic past in Peninsular Spanish, she observes that, between the 15th and 20th centuries, this form shifted from 26 percent in comparison to the Preterit to 54 percent (2011:171). This increase in overall frequency is paralleled by analogous extensions into other perfective contexts, such as hodiernal and irrelevant past reference, an issue that will be addressed later in the chapter. From Copple's study, and those of many other like-minded researchers, it is easy to see that there has been a natural affinity between grammaticalization approaches and usage-based perspectives, which, in general, have assumed that "language structure is created as language is used" (Bybee 2011:69).

The flipside of the debate surrounding unidirectionality concerns the possibility that otherwise bound grammar would, through some sequence of developments, become free of its host and be used in a way that would suggest status as a free lexical item or that a particular process that has already undergone the change from lexical to grammatical would be reversed. This possibility, referred to most generally as "degrammaticalization," has long been criticized by grammaticalization authors who, like Lehmann, view these purported counter-examples to unidirectionality as "statistically insignificant" or "the result of an inadequate

---

[5] This example was extracted from sociolinguistic interviews conducted in Alcalá de Henares, Spain, in 2009 (Howe 2013).

analysis" (1995:16). Nevertheless, proponents who view unidirectionality not as a driving force but rather as a largely epiphenomenal result of the nature of language change (see, for example, Janda 2001) have explored processes of "degrammaticalization" and argue that these instances, though uncommon, constitute a type of marked directionality in which changes do not follow the typical patterns attested in grammaticalization (Norde 2009:89). Among the cases of degrammaticalization that have been discussed for Spanish, Janda (1995:122) has proposed the New Mexican Spanish first-person plural verbal ending -*mos*, which, according to him, has been reanalyzed as the first-person plural enclitic pronoun =*nos*. Norde (2009:118) has pointed out that this change occurs when "a highly grammaticalized item (typically an inflectional affix) [i.e. -*mos*] is replaced by a (near-) homophonous, less grammatical item [i.e. *nos*]."[6] Another possible instance of degrammaticalization in Spanish might be observed with the use of the (re)iterative prefix *re*- in some varieties of Argentine and Uruguayan Spanish. In these cases, the prefix *re*-, which developed from Latin and was used originally to modify verbs and, to a lesser degree, adjectives, and has expanded its scope in modern Spanish to occur with nouns (*un reamigo* 'a very close friend'), interjections (*recojones* 'Damn!'), and adverbs (*relejos* 'very far') (Pharies 2009). For some, *re*- can also have scope over an entire verb phrase, as in **re** *está para hacer algo hoy* '[s/he] is very ready to do something today' (from Twitter), suggesting an expansion beyond its origin as a bound morpheme.

27.3 Related Processes

Research in grammaticalization covers a wide swath of distinct developments, addressing issues related to the evolution of lexical into grammatical forms and to the development of "a less grammatical to a more grammatical status," as pointed out by Kuryłowicz (1965:69). The distinction between these two stages of development is captured in the terms "primary" and "secondary" grammaticalization coined by Givón (1991:305) and used to characterize, respectively, initial and later stages. The evolution of the periphrastic past in Spanish again provides an excellent vantage point from which to observe these concepts. The Latin resultative source construction, shown in (27.7), is inherited by early Romance and continues to develop with primary grammaticalization reflected in (i) the change of word order, specifically with respect to the fixation of the participle in postverbal position, (ii) the lack of agreement between the participle and noun (MANUM LEVATAM), and (iii) the reduction of the verb

---

[6] To be clear, Norde does not consider this case of -*mos* ~ =*nos* as an instance of degrammaticalization since "the affixes do not degrammaticalize 'on their own'" but instead they are "confused with a similar, less grammatical item, which eventually comes to occupy the morphosyntactic position of the erstwhile affix" (2009:118–119).

HABĒRE (HABEŌ > *he*). The result of these changes produces the structure in Example 27.8, which, at least initially, expressed a meaning similar to that expressed by its Latin predecessor. Subsequent developments have seen the periphrastic past extend beyond its resultative meaning to express increasingly past and, in some varieties of Spanish, perfective meanings. These later developments are characteristic of secondary grammaticalization. Interestingly, modern Spanish also has a resultative structure with the verb *tener* (< Latin TENĒRE), as in Example 27.9, which echoes the semantic and morphosyntactic properties of the Latin LEVATAM HABEŌ construction. This construction with *tener*, referred to by Detges (2000) as a "Resultative II structure," "exists in many languages as a conventionalized structure" and, according to him, these structures serve as "the direct precursors to perfects" (2000:350). Though it is debatable that the TENĒRE + participle construction can be said to have produced perfects across different Romance Languages,[7] it is nonetheless likely that the development in Spanish of the *tener* and *haber* constructions has, in tandem, played a significant role in the evolution of the features observed in the modern grammar.

(27.7) MANUM   LEVATAM   HABEŌ
       hand.ACC   raised.ACC   have.1SG
       'I have my hand raised.'
                                   Source: Roca Pons (1958:108); my translation

(27.8) He levantado la mano.
       'I have raised my hand.'

(27.9) Tengo la mano levantada.
       'I have my hand raised.'

Properly characterizing "phases" in the grammaticalization of a structure has also been a prominent topic of discussion in this area of research. One such line of inquiry has invested considerable attention in the development of discourse markers and modal particles, which, for many, appear to display the types of semantic changes characteristic of forms undergoing grammaticalization, but eschew the typical structural tendencies that produce greater degrees of morphological or structural fixation. Instead, discourse markers and modal particles are often presented as cases of pragmaticalization, distinguished by Aijmer from grammaticalization in that the former are processes that involve a "speaker's attitude to the hearer" (1997:2) or, as described by Wischer (2000) and others, movement towards discourse. It is this notion of pragmatic change that Ocampo adopts in his analysis of the Spanish discourse marker *claro*. In Example 27.10, *claro* 'clearly' is used as a tool for "self-selection" by

---

[7] See Amaral and Howe (2010) for a discussion of the *Pretérito Perfeito Composto* in Portuguese. For Spanish, Chamorro has discussed the use of *tener* with participles in the Spanish of Galicia to indicate pluractional meaning, as in *Tengo salido poco porque trabajo hasta tarde* 'I haven't been going out much because I work until late' (2012:97).

speaker L to secure his turn in the conversation (2006:314). Ocampo argues that the evolution of *claro*, and by extension other discourse markers, should be considered a distinct phenomenon from grammaticalization in that these structures represent "movement outside of syntax and towards discourse" rather than the type of paradigmaticization and fixation proposed as hallmarks in grammaticalization processes.[8]

(27.10)   M: Le paga p[ara] siempre para ayudarlas a ellas que ... que tanto le habían hecho por él cuando vino de Italia.
'He always pays the guy to ... to help them who had done so much [because of] him when he came from Italy.'
L: **Claro**, porque ellas a él lo han criado, se puede decir.
'**Claro**, because they had practically raised him.'
Source: Ocampo (2006:314); translation adapted

Wrapped up in the distinction drawn by Ocampo and others is the notion that a complete theory of semantic change should involve some notion of subjectification, which describes the process by which "forms and constructions that at first express primarily concrete, lexical, and objective meanings come through repeated use in local syntactic contexts to serve increasingly abstract, pragmatic, interpersonal, and speaker-based functions" (Traugott 1995:32). In his analysis of the (semi-)auxiliaries *parecer* and *resultar*, Cornillie (2008:70) observes that various structural changes – e.g. number agreement between the subject and the verb – correlate with the attrition of the original meanings of these verbs. With *resultar*, for example, he argues that "the first step in the attenuation of the resultative reading of the *resultar* + infinitive pattern [as in Example 27.11] is found in the *resultar* + adjective construction [Example 27.12], which conveys a subjective, evaluative meaning" (2008:70).

(27.11)   La escuela laica que escogimos para Philip **resulta** estar llena.
'The secular school that we chose for Philip **turns out** to be full.'
Source: Cornillie (2008:57)

(27.12)   Según tengo entendido, **resulta difícil** el regreso para los científicos españoles que trabajan fuera, por ejemplo en Estados Unidos.
'According to what I've understood, the return of the Spanish scientists who work abroad, say in the US, **turns out to be difficult**.'
Source: Davies (2002–)

One common critique of studies involving subjectification as a pattern in semantic change is the difficulty in providing clear criteria for determining how these processes are to be recognized and analyzed in the data. This problematic issue is addressed in an analysis by Torres Cacoullos and Schwenter (2005), who provide an operational notion of subjectification, attempting to discern greater and lesser degrees of subjectivity with the

---

[8] The terms "paradigmaticization" and "fixation" are in fact two of the six parameters of grammaticalization proposed in Lehmann (1995), the others being "attrition," "obligatorification," "condensation," and "coalescence."

development of Spanish *a pesar de* 'in spite of,' which developed from the noun *pesar* 'sorrow' to the concessive connective meaning 'in spite of.' They propose three measures that are argued to correlate with greater subjectification – subject coreferentiality, subjunctive verb forms with *a pesar de*, and preposing of the *a pesar de* clause with respect to the main verb. The results of their quantitative analysis reveal that subjectification can indeed be viewed empirically as a gradual and increasing phenomenon in the case of *a pesar de*. The approach that seeks to verify grammaticalization principles and phenomena via the quantitative analysis of natural data has become a hallmark in the study of semantic and structural change in Spanish.

One final notion frequently discussed in tandem with or in contrast to grammaticalization studies is lexicalization, viewed by some as a distinct development from those processes that produce, for example, bound morphology from a full lexical item. Brinton and Traugott (2005) explain that lexicalization is "the change whereby in certain linguistic contexts speakers use a syntactic construction or word formation as a new contentful form with formal and semantic properties that are not completely derivable or predictable from the constituents of the construction or the word formation pattern" (2005:96). The analysis of discourse markers in Spanish is commonly couched in some notion of lexicalization, given that the output of such development is "semantically contentful" (2005:98). Viewed in this way, the cases of *claro* and *a pesar de* discussed above could be considered as instances of lexicalization, due to the discursive nature of their uses and the sense in which their meanings cannot necessarily be discerned from their constituent parts.

27.4 Approaches to Grammaticalization

Studies in grammaticalization have been rooted strongly in the presentation of case studies, observing single constructions or groups of constructions that are argued to be undergoing some common set of changes. These studies are also typically historical, in either the deep or shallow sense of the word, relying on diachronic corpus data to discern pathways and mechanisms of change. In the work by Verveckken (2012) on binominal constructions, these techniques are in full display as a means of explaining how elements like *un montón de*, used in the 13th century as in (27.13) to describe a physical collection of material, develop into quantifiers capable of taking abstract complements not attested in the earliest instances of this structure. Thus, in Example 27.14 from modern Spanish, *montón de* is used with a temporal complement, showing a clear extension from its original usage with complements denoting physical quantities, such as *tierra*. Verveckken's analysis, based on data from the CREA corpus (Real Academia Española n.d.), makes the case that *montón de* serves as a prototype for other low-frequency binominal quantifiers, like *barbaridad de* 'barbarity of,' *hatajo de* 'herd of,' and *litanía de* 'litany of' (2012:425). The hallmark of many grammaticalization studies is the proposal of a pathway of development, typically based on the analysis of individually analyzed tokens extracted from a corpus. Following this approach, Verveckken proposes a four-stage development of *montón de* with the first step representing the effects of quantity implicatures that arise in the use of examples like (27.13) and the final steps reflecting syntactic reanalysis and schematic extension (2012:458).

(27.13) E aquel castiello. / estaua en un otero que / non era muy alto and semeiaua / que era **un monton** / **de** tierra fecho por mano / de omne. (1293)
'And that castle / was on a hill / that was not very high and it seemed / as if it was **a heap** / **of** earth handmade / by men.'
Source: Verveckken (2012:439)

(27.14) Silvia y François se habían conocido en un café de París hacía un **montón de** años.
'Silvia and François got to know each other in a bar in Paris (lit.) **a lot of** years ago.'
Source: Verveckken (2012:424)

Moving beyond this traditional approach to tracking the development of a grammaticalizing structure, Verveckken and Cornillie (2012) apply a decidedly more quantitative approach to binominal quantifiers that focuses on patterns of agreement between verbs and the nominal elements in these constructions. The prescriptive take on these constructions, as might be expected by their diachrony, is that any verbal agreement should occur with the noun phrase NP1 of a NP1 + *de* + NP2 construction. Nevertheless, agreement patterns of the type illustrated in Example 27.15 are common, both in spoken and written Spanish, reflecting, as argued by Verveckken and Cornillie, the shift of the NP1 as the head of the binominal phrase to the NP2. The authors provide quantitative evidence for this claim and observe that, in addition to overall changes in the frequency of individual binominal structures and rates of NP2/Verb agreement, a number of other factors can be viewed as reflecting this shift, including (i) the type of determiner with the NP1, (ii) the "distance" between the binominal structure and the verb, and (iii) position of the binominal phrase with respect to the verb (i.e. pre- vs. postposition). The resulting analysis seemingly demonstrates that a constellation of factors should be considered in understanding how the verbal agreement of NP1 + *de* + NP2 structures reflects "the conceptual intentions of the speaker" (2012:249; translation mine).

(27.15) **Un aluvión de enfermos**, la mayoría personas mayores con infecciones respiratorias de carácter vírico, han sobrecargado los servicios de Urgencias y han llenado los hospitales de Gipuzkoa.
'**A flood of sick people**, the majority older people with viral respiratory infections, have overwhelmed the Emergency Services and have filled the hospitals of Gipuzkoa.'
Source: Verveckken and Cornillie (2012:220); translation mine

Beyond the use of canonical written and spoken corpora in the study of grammaticalization, there have been attempts to show that language change occurs via other means of linguistic interaction.

In her study of loan-word adaptation and neologisms in computer-mediated language, Morin (2014) observes that "[t]he Internet gives us an unprecedented opportunity to observe language change that is occurring at a very accelerated rate" and that "it is the Internet that in large part is fueling this language change" (2014:358). Following up on this claim, Howe (2016) explores the meaning and properties of *pedazo de* using data extracted from the micro-blogging platform Twitter. The construction *un pedazo de* + NP2, which can express admirative meaning in many varieties of Spanish (e.g. *un pedazo de jugador* 'a hell of a player'), displays a variety of non-canonical morphosyntactic patterns that suggest a loss of syntactic headedness analogous to that observed by Verveckken and Cornillie (2012), including a high rate of bare NPs, as in (27.16), and determiners that do not reflect the gender and/or number of *pedazo* (singular/masculine), as in (27.17). The preponderance of cases like (27.17) in the Twitter data and the fact that these irregular patterns do not reflect other attested types of gender/number transfer issues (e.g. with bilinguals who frequently overgeneralize the masculine forms) strongly suggests that *pedazo de* has grammaticalized along the same lines as other binominal elements. Moreover, it is precisely the type of data represented by Twitter and other forms of digital communication that, according to Howe (2016), gives access to incipient structural change, perhaps further offering a window into the elusive "onset contexts," as presented by Eckardt (2006:42), that offer the "right kind of structural and semantic ambiguity plus additional instigating factors" required for grammaticalization and semantic change.[9]

(27.16) un muy mal amigo pocho, **pedazo de** snap me mand[ó]
'a very bad friend *pocho*, **hell of a** snap[chat] that you sent to me'
Source: *Twitter*

(27.17) Tenéis que ver **las pedazo de** ganas que tengo de llegar a casa … para hacer un comentario de texto
'You guys have to see **the tremendous** desire that I have to get back home … to make a text comment'
Source: *Twitter*

The quantitative, and largely variationist, paradigm has allowed grammaticalization research to move beyond simple frequency as a metric for discerning language change. Of this method, Torres Cacoullos (2011) observes the following:

---

[9] Various other terms have been proposed as similar explanation for what Eckardt refers to as "onset contexts," including "critical contexts" (Diewald 2002) and "bridging contexts" (Heine 2002).

> The empirical study of language change is not based on unverifiable intuitions about meaning differences or example-by-example ascriptions of speaker intentions ..., since speaker motivations in the choice of one form over another cannot be directly ascertained in a replicable manner.
>
> (2011:151)

This provocative statement summarizes an approach that assumes that change should be understood via the analysis of "linguistic sub-contexts" or factors (2011:151) rather than through comparison of rates of overall frequency. From a diachronic view, this perspective has been important, since a shift in overall frequency does not serve as a reliable index for structural or semantic change. Returning to the development of the Spanish periphrastic past, Copple (2011:171) provides a comparison of this form vis-à-vis the simple past, observing that in her data there is a steady increase of the periphrastic form between the 15th and the 20th centuries, which, as observed above, increases from 26 percent to 54 percent. This increase in relative frequency, while informative, gives at best only a partial indication of the trajectory of the proposed perfectivization of the periphrastic past in Peninsular Spanish. The most revealing aspect of Copple's analysis is provided in her factors (i.e. "linguistic sub-contexts") observed with each token. Following the seminal analysis by Schwenter and Torres Cacoullos (2008) of the PP/Preterit distinction, using corpora from two varieties of Spanish (Peninsular and Mexican), Copple (2011) observes the evolution of the constraint hierarchies underlying the usage of the PP. One factor in particular, temporal reference, emerged in Schwenter and Torres Cacoullos' data as having the most sizable effect (as indicated by the range measure) in both the Peninsular and Mexican samples, with the PP being used in different contexts that are suggestive of perfective meaning – e.g. hodiernal reference. Not surprisingly, such cases were practically non-existent in the Mexican sample while in the Peninsular data the use of the PP in contexts of hodiernal reference was almost categorical (see also Example 27.6). Copple's approach takes this and other factors and applies them diachronically to show that a proper understanding of the PP to perfective development should also include an analysis of shifting constraint hierarchies. Thus, as shown in Table 27.2, adapted from Copple (2011), there is a preference for the PP in hodiernal contexts, represented in the changes in factor weights from 0.20 (dispreferred) to 0.54 (slightly preferred), a point made even more striking by the fact that the PP in Schwenter and Torres Cacoullos' (2008) Peninsular data was preferred with a factor weight of 0.93 in these same contexts. Viewed in this light, the locus of the shift from perfect to perfective with the PP in Peninsular Spanish should be understood as largely associated with the factor temporal reference, with some

Table 27.2 *Factor weights for temporal reference of present perfect across three centuries (Peninsular Spanish)*

	Century		
Temporal Reference	**15th**	**17th**	**19th**
Very recent	0.61	0.74	0.75
Irrelevant	0.54	0.83	0.83
Indeterminate	0.47	0.61	0.64
Hodiernal ("today")	0.20	0.42	0.54
Prehodiernal ("before today")	[0]	0.02	0.09
Range	41	81	74

Source: Adapted from Copple (2011:177)

contexts, such as irrelevant, indeterminate, and hodiernal reference, serving as specific contexts of expansion:[10] this facet of development is not easily discernible if one considers only relative frequency as a metric for linguistic change.

The use of multivariate and corpus analyses to further the agenda of grammaticalization studies has proven critical in elucidating a number of micro- and macro-level developments in Spanish, both across dialects and in diachrony. Similarly, these methods and others have been crucial in exploring how possible grammaticalization phenomena are motivated or shaped by language contact (see Chapter 21, this volume). Matras concisely summarizes the relationship between grammaticalization and language contact:

> Language contact and bilingualism are potential triggers of language change at various levels. These include changes that are internal to the language under scrutiny, in the sense that they involve an adaptation to the function, meaning, or distribution of an inherited structure. At the same time, they are triggered by replication of a model that is external to the language under scrutiny, one that is found in a contact language.
>
> (2011:279)

From these comments, it should be understood that language change attested in multilingual contexts can be viewed as involving internal and/or external factors, not the least of which is the role of understanding the possibilities of a change that may arise from structural propensities inherent in the language. By way of illustration, the indefinite article + possessive structure in (27.18) – i.e. *unos sus hijos* – has been observed by Pato Maldonado (2002) and others in varieties of Spanish spoken in contact with different Latin American indigenous languages expressing an emphatic or discursive meaning. The claim is that this structure in Spanish arises

---

[10] Howe and Rodríguez Louro (2013) argue for a concomitant process of contextual retraction in the development of the PP. Specifically, they maintain that "the opposition of the PP with the [Present Tense] is a *Peripheral Context*, one that, in the process of change from perfect to perfective, is subject to considerable recession" (2013:50).

as a result of contact with languages like Tzutujil or Quechua, languages in which both the possessor and the possessum are marked morphologically. Pato Maldonado's claim, then, would fall in line with Matras' description of change occurring as "replication of a model," invoking the chance-as-contact-induced argument common in the literature. Nevertheless, Company Company (2005) reconsiders the development of this structure and maintains that "it has acquired no new meanings, but rather has activated values that were already latent in Old Spanish." In her analysis, the evolution of the indefinite article + possessive construction in these contact varieties is the result of "natural internal change, without it being necessary to having to propose language contact or linguistic interference" (2005:143, translation mine).

(27.18) Jorge me dijo que si yo le encontraba **unos sus hijos**, me daba libre el viernes
'Jorge told me that if I found his children for him, he'd give me Friday off'
Source: Pato Maldonado (2002:144); translation mine

A similar line of argumentation is employed by Dumont and Wilson (2016), who employ a variationist approach to explore the hypothesis that, in contact with English, the synthetic simple present and imperfect forms in Spanish have receded in the face of the extension of the present and past progressive forms. To understand this claim they analyzed corpus data from monolingual speakers from Quito, Ecuador, and Spanish–English bilinguals from New Mexican Spanish, and found that there was little evidence to suggest that New Mexican Spanish was changing as a result of linguistic convergence. The general grammaticalization enterprise – at least insomuch as it concerns the relationship between internally-motivated change and externally-motivated (possibly contact-induced) change – is advanced by these and other studies of Spanish because (i) both historical and contemporary corpora are widely available for Spanish and (ii) researchers from across a wide range of methodological and theoretical perspectives have contributed to the analysis of Spanish phenomena.

27.5 Current Issues in the Grammaticalization of Spanish

To conclude, there are numerous issues that continue to be discussed in the grammaticalization literature and for which the study of Spanish phenomena have been key. As mentioned above, language contact as a source of grammatical innovation continues to be a topic of some controversy, with the current research on different phenomena in Spanish suggesting that an explanation based solely or primarily on language contact may not be tenable (see e.g. Ocón Gamarra 2015 for an extended discussion of *pues* 'well' in Andean Spanish). Other researchers have applied quantitative methods in the study of structures that have largely disappeared from the language. For instance, Blas Arroyo and Vellón Lahoz (2015) utilize a comparative variationist method to explore the use of the modal periphrasis *haber de* 'to have to' + infinitive. They find that as other competing variants emerge (e.g. *tener que*), the *haber de* periphrasis is relegated to very specific contexts, such as indicative future, and moreover that the somewhat dramatic decrease in frequency of this construction is accompanied by changes in the constraint hierarchies across time (2015:107).

In the past decade, the focus on constructions in the grammaticalization literature has become widespread (see Traugott and Trousdale 2013). Howe (2011) discusses the use of *hacer* + TIME 'TIME + ago' in Spanish and proposes that it has undergone a process of neutralization resulting in a hybrid structure in which the erstwhile verbal element *hacer* displays largely adjunct-like (and perhaps even preposition-like) behavior. Examples such as (27.19), in which a past perfect (*había muerto* 'had died') is used with a "present"-tense form of the verb *hacer*, are taken as evidence for the constructionalization of *hacer* + TIME which, at least in this context, does not display the morphosyntactic properties typical of verbal elements – e.g. sequence of tense phenomena.

(27.19) [La Señora X] había muerto **hace mucho tiempo**
'[Mrs. X] had died **long before**' Source: Howe (2011:261)

Similarly, Claes (2015) develops an analysis of the pluralization of *haber* (as in Example 27.20) using data from Dominican Spanish and assuming a Cognitive Construction Grammar approach (e.g. Goldberg 1995, 2006). Claes argues that "the pluralization of presentational *haber* corresponds to a slowly progressing language change from below during which the argument–structure construction <**AdvP** *haber* **Subj**> is replacing the <**AdvP** *haber* **Obj**> pattern" (2015:26). Within this framework, Claes is able to address both internal (grammatical) as well external (sociolinguistic) issues related to the *haber* construction.

(27.20) Y, e, **han habido** ciertos cambios en, en la sociedad
'And, [um], **there have** been.PL certain changes in, in society.'
Source: Claes (2015:2)

Finally, one overarching consideration, raised by Norde (2009), relates to the fact that the analysis of grammaticalization phenomena, especially in well-studied languages such as Spanish, is often based on what are considered to be analogous changes in related languages – e.g. the development of the *passé composé* in French – rather than on "a detailed examination of the change itself" (2009:33). In other words, Norde's observation is intended as a bit of cautionary advice about how to avoid letting the "pathway" metaphor, ubiquitous in the grammaticalization literature, dictate the results of an analysis. And though the literature on Spanish is replete with analyses that display precisely this analytical pitfall, the cumulative contribution of the research into Spanish, in terms of both theoretical and methodological innovations, to the broader grammaticalization endeavor cannot be overstated.

References

Aaron, J. E. (2014). A Certain Future: Epistemicity, Prediction, and Assertion in Iberian Spanish Future Expression. *Studies in Hispanic and Lusophone Linguistics*, 7 (2), 215–240.

Aijmer, K. (1997). *I Think*: An English Modal Particle. In T. Swan and O. J. Westvik (eds.), *Modality in Germanic Languages: Historical and Comparative Perspectives*. Berlin: De Gruyter, pp. 1–47.

Amaral, P. and Howe, C. (2010). Detours along the Perfect Path. In S. Colina, A. Olarrea, and A. M. Carvalho (eds.), *Romance Linguistics 2009*. Amsterdam and Philadelphia, PA: John Benjamins, pp. 387–404.

Blas Arroyo, J. L. and Vellón Lahoz, J. (2015). The Refuge of a Dying Variant within the Grammar: Patterns of Change and Continuity in the Spanish Verbal Periphrasis *haber de* + infinitive over the Past Two Centuries. *Language Variation and Change*, 27 (1), 86–116.

Brinton, L. J. and Traugott, E. C. (2005). *Lexicalization and Language Change*. Cambridge: Cambridge University Press.

Bybee, J. L. (2011). Usage-Based Theory and Grammaticalization. In H. Narrog and B. Heine (eds.), *The Oxford Handbook of Grammaticalization*. Oxford: Oxford University Press, pp. 69–78.

Bybee, J. L. and Pagliuca, W. (1987). The Evolution of Future Meaning. In A. G. Ramat, O. Carruba, and G. Bernini (eds.), *Papers from the 7th International Conference on Historical Linguistics*, Amsterdam: John Benjamins, pp. 109–122.

Bybee, J. L., Perkins, R., and Pagliuca, W. (1994). *The Evolution of Grammar: Tense, Aspect, and Modality in the Languages of the World*. Chicago, IL: University of Chicago Press.

Chamorro, P. (2012). Pluractionality and Aspectual Structure in the Galician Spanish *tener*-Perfect (Doctoral dissertation). The Ohio State University.

Claes, J. (2015). Competing Constructions: The Pluralization of Presentational *haber* in Dominican Spanish. *Cognitive Linguistics*, 26 (1), 1–30.

Company Company, C. (2005). Frecuencia de uso y contacto lingüístico en sintaxis: Artículo indefinido + posesivo en el español americano. *Spanish in Context*, 2 (2), 131–156.

Copple, M. T. (2011). Tracking the Constraints on a Grammaticalizing Perfect(ive). *Language Variation and Change*, 23, 163–191.

Cornillie, B. (2008). On the Grammaticalization and (Inter)subjectivity of Evidential (Semi-) auxiliaries in Spanish. In E. Seoane and M. J. López-Couso (eds.), *Theoretical and Empirical Issues in Grammaticalization*. Amsterdam and Philadelphia, PA: John Benjamins, pp. 55–76.

Croft, W. (2006). The Relevance of an Evolutionary Model to Historical Linguistics. In O. N. Thomsen (ed.), *Different Models of Linguistic Change*. Amsterdam: John Benjamins, pp. 91–132.

Davies, M. (2002–). Corpus del español; 100 million words, 1200s–1900s. Available from www.corpusdelespanol.org.

Detges, U. (2000). Time and Truth: The Grammaticalization of Resultatives and Perfects within a Theory of Subjectification. *Studies in Language*, 24 (2), 345–377.

Diewald, G. (2002). A Model for Relevant Types of Contexts in Grammaticalization. In I. Wischer and G. Diewald (eds.), *New Reflections on Grammaticalization*. Amsterdam: John Benjamins, pp. 103–120.

Dumont, J. and Wilson, D. V. (2016). Using the Variationist Comparative Method to Examine the Role of Language Contact in Synthetic and Periphrastic Verbs in Spanish. *Spanish in Context*, 13 (3), 394–419.

Eckardt, R. (2006). *Meaning Change in Grammaticalization: An Enquiry into Semantic Reanalysis*. Oxford: Oxford University Press.

Ewert, A. (1961). *The French Language* (2nd edn). Cambridge: Cambridge University Press.

Fleischman, S. (1983). From Pragmatics to Grammar: Diachronic Reflections on Complex Pasts and Futures in Romance. *Lingua*, 60, 183–214.

Givón, T. (1979). *On Understanding Grammar*. New York: Academic Press.

Givón, T. (1991). The Evolution of Dependent Clause Morpho-Syntax in Biblical Hebrew. In E. C. Traugott and B. Heine (eds.), *Approaches to Grammaticalization*, Vol. 1. Amsterdam: John Benjamins, pp. 257–310.

Goldberg, A. E. (1995). *Constructions: A Construction Grammar Approach to Argument Structure*. Chicago, IL: Chicago University Press.

Goldberg, A. E. (2006). *Constructions at Work: The Nature of Generalizations in Language*. Oxford: Oxford University Press.

Graham, L. (2015). The History of the Future: Morphophonology, Syntax, and Grammaticalization (Doctoral dissertation). University of Georgia.

Harris, M. (1982). The "Past Simple" and "Present Perfect" in Romance. In M. Harris and N. Vincent (eds.), *Studies in the Romance Verb*. London: Croom Helm, pp. 42–70.

Heine, B. (2002). On the Role of Context in Grammaticalization. In I. Wischer and G. Diewald (eds.), *New Reflections on Grammaticalization*. Amsterdam: John Benjamins, pp. 83–101.

Heine, B. and Kuteva, T. (2002). *World Lexicon of Grammaticalization*. Cambridge: Cambridge University Press.

Heine, B. and Narrog, H. (2010). Grammaticalization in Linguistic Analysis. In B. Heine and H. Narrog (eds.), *The Oxford Handbook of Linguistic Analysis*. Oxford: Oxford University Press, pp. 401–424.

Hopper, P. J. (1991). On some Principles of Grammaticalization. In E. C. Traugott and B. Heine (eds.), *Approaches to Grammaticalization*, Vol. 1. Amsterdam: John Benjamins, pp. 17–35.

Hopper, P. J. and Traugott, E. C. (2003). *Grammaticalization* (2nd edn). Cambridge: Cambridge University Press.

Howe, C. (2009). Revisiting Perfect Pathways: Trends in the Grammaticalization of Periphrastic Pasts. In P. Epps and A. Arkhipov (eds.), *New Challenges in Typology: Transcending the Borders and Refining the Distinctions*. Berlin and New York: De Gruyter, pp. 151–174.

Howe, C. (2011). Structural Autonomy in Grammaticalization: Leveling and Retention with Spanish *hacer* + TIME. *Probus*, 23, 247–282.

Howe, C. (2013). *The Spanish Perfects: Pathways of Emergent Meaning*. Basingstoke and New York: Palgrave Macmillan.

Howe, C. (2016). Tracking Language Change in Social Media: Non-Canonical Agreement with Spanish *pedazo de*. Paper presented at the 8th International Workshop on Spanish Sociolinguistics, San Juan, Puerto Rico.

Howe, C. and Rodríguez Louro, C. (2013). Peripheral Envelopes: Spanish Perfects in the Variable Context. In A. M. Carvalho and S. Beaudrie (eds.), *Selected Proceedings of the 6th Workshop on Spanish Sociolinguistics*. Somerville, MA: Cascadilla, pp. 41–52.

Janda, R. D. (1995). From Agreement Affix to Subject "Clitic" – and Bound Root: *-mos* > *-nos* vs. (-)*nos*(-) and *nos-otros* in New Mexican and Other Regional Spanish Dialects. In Audra Dainora, Rachel Hemphill, and Barbara Need (eds.), *Papers from the Parasession on Clitics*. Chicago, IL: Chicago Linguistic Society, pp. 118–139.

Janda, R. D. (2001). Beyond "Pathways" and "Unidirectionality": On the Discontinuity of Language Transmission and the Counterability of Grammaticalization. *Language Sciences*, 23 (2–3), 265–340.

Joseph, B. D. (2001). Is there such a Thing as Grammaticalization? *Language Sciences*, 23 (2–3), 163–186.

Kuryłowicz, J. (1965). The Evolution of Grammatical Categories. *Diogenes*, 13 (51), 55–71. doi: 10.1177/039219216501305105.

Lehmann, C. (1995). *Thoughts on Grammaticalization*. Munich and Newcastle: Lincom.

Marrone, N. (1992). *El habla de la ciudad de La Paz. Materiales para su estudio*. La Paz: Signo.

Matras, Y. (2011). Grammaticalization and Language Contact. In H. Narrog and B. Heine (eds.), *The Oxford Handbook of Grammaticalization*. Oxford: Oxford University Press, pp. 279–290.

Meillet, A. (1912). L'évolution des formes grammaticales. *Scientia (Rivista di Scienza)*, 12 (6), 384–400. Reprinted in A. Meillet (ed.), *Linguistique historique et linguistique générale*. Paris: Champion [1965], pp. 130–148.

Morin, R. (2014). Linguistic Integration of Computer and Internet Related Anglicisms in Spanish Language Web Pages. *Studies in Hispanic and Lusophone Linguistics*, 7 (2), 328–367.

Newmeyer, F. (2001). Deconstruction Grammaticalization. *Language Sciences*, 23 (2–3), 187–229.

Norde, M. (2009). *Degrammaticalization*. Cambridge: Cambridge University Press.

Ocampo, F. (2006). Movement towards Discourse is not Grammaticalization: The Evolution of *claro* from Adjective to Discourse Particle in Spoken Spanish. In N. Sagarra and A. J. Toribio (eds.), *Selected Proceedings of the 9th Hispanic Linguistics Symposium*. Somerville, MA: Cascadilla, pp. 308–319.

Ocón Gamarra, M. (2015). Non-Contact versus Contact Induced Language Change: The Case of Andean *pues* (Doctoral dissertation). University of Georgia.

Pato Maldonado, E. (2002) La estructura posesiva "una mi amiga" en el español de Guatemala. In A. Palacios and I. García Tesoro (eds.), *El indigenismo americano III*. Valencia: Universitat de Valencia, pp. 121–155.

Pharies, D. (2009). *Rebién, retebién, requetebién*: Allomorphy of the Spanish Prefix *re-*. *Romance Quarterly*, 56 (1), 13–20.

Real Academia Española (n.d.). Banco de datos (CREA) [en línea]. *Corpus de referencia del español actual*. www.rae.es.

Roberts, I. and Roussou, A. (1999). A Formal Approach to "Grammaticalization." *Linguistics*, 37, 1011–1041.

Roberts, I. and Roussou, A. (2003). *Syntactic Change. A Minimalist Approach to Grammaticalization*. Cambridge: Cambridge University Press.

Roca Pons, J. (1958). *Estudios sobre perífrasis verbales del español*. Madrid: CSIC.

Schwenter, S. A. and Torres Cacoullos, R. (2008). Defaults and Indeterminacy in Temporal Grammaticalization: The "Perfect" Road to Perfective. *Language Variation and Change*, 20 (1), 1–39.

Torres Cacoullos, R. (2001). Variation and Grammaticalization. In M. Díaz-Campos (ed.), *The Handbook of Hispanic Sociolinguistics*. Chichester: John Wiley, pp. 148–167.

Torres Cacoullos, R. and Schwenter, S. A. (2005). Towards an Operational Notion of Subjectification. *Proceedings of the 31st Annual Meeting of the Berkeley Linguistics Society*, 31, 347–358.

Traugott, E. C. (1995). Subjectification in Grammaticalization. In D. Stein and S. Wright (eds.), *Subjectivity and Subjectivisation: Linguistic Perspectives*. Cambridge: Cambridge University Press, pp. 31–54.

Traugott, E. C. and Trousdale, G. (2013). *Constructionalization and Constructional Change*. Oxford: Oxford University Press.

Verveckken, K. and Cornillie, B. (2012). Un análisis cognitivo-funcional de la concordancia verbal con construcciones (pseudo)partitivas del tipo [N1 + *de* + N2]. *Revue Romane*, 47 (2), 219–257.

Wischer, I. (2000). Grammaticalization vs. Lexicalization. "Methinks" there is Some Confusion. In O. Fischer, A. Rosenbach, and D. Stein (eds.), *Pathways of Change. Grammaticalization in English*. Amsterdam and Philadelphia, PA: John Benjamins, pp. 355–370.

Verveckken, K. (2012). Towards a Constructional Account of High and Low Frequency Binominal Quantifiers in Spanish. *Cognitive Linguistics*, 23 (2), 421–478.

Part V

The Acquisition of Spanish

28

Child Language Acquisition

Anna Gavarró*

28.1 Introduction

Language acquisition is the process by which children get attuned to and get to master the language(s) of their environment. By and large, this follows the same trajectory in all languages: children first utter a few words, then that repertory of words enlarges and they proceed to the production of short syntactic sequences (the two-word stage), then these syntactic sequences become longer and more complex constructions are attested. If one looked at the Earth from a distance it would appear that children from all over the planet are acquiring the one same system – to put it in Pinker's terms, acquiring human language (Searchinger 1995). On closer inspection, children acquire different languages, with variation in the lexicon, the phonological system, and (perhaps derived from variation in the functional lexicon, as assumed in minimalist work) the syntax. This variation justifies the study of the acquisition of languages as different systems: because some present more morphological complexity than others, some have a more complex syllabic structure, and so on, we can observe language acquisition from different viewpoints by focusing on different languages. In this chapter we deal in particular with the acquisition of Spanish (with reference when necessary to other, related, languages).

The chapter is organized as follows. Section 28.2 provides evidence for early setting of basic parameters: agreement and the null subject parameter. Section 28.3 deals with one construction of the Romance languages, that of pronominal clitics, which has received some attention in the literature, and the inferences about acquisition we can draw from it. Section 28.4 is devoted to two long-distance phenomena, *wh*-questions and relative clauses, which have raised several interesting questions in the literature on acquisition in

---

* I would like to thank the editor of this volume for her help and support throughout, as well as two anonymous reviewers, who provided insightful observations and suggestions. Any remaining errors are my own.

many languages. Within each of these sections a chronological perspective is taken. The last section presents topics that have received less attention but promise to be of much interest in future research.

28.2 Early Morphosyntactic Awareness

Much work on early grammar is based on the spontaneous productions of children and their caretakers; CHILDES (MacWhinney 1995) is the main database in which such productions can be found. Torrens (1995, 2002) was one of the first authors to examine the early speech of several Spanish- (and Catalan-) speaking children. He looked at subject–verb agreement, which is obligatory in Spanish, and found that children complied with person and number in their productions, as illustrated in (28.1). Errors were computed; they amounted to 3 percent for the first period, ending at age 2;2.

(28.1) a. Falta   un   coche.   (M, 2;3,24)
            miss.3SG   a   car
            'There is a car missing.'
        b. ¿Me   das   uno?   (M, 2;2,11)
            CL.1SG   give.2SG   one
            'Can you give me one?'
        c. Te   pillo.   (M, 2;2,11)
            CL.2SG   catch.1SG
            'I'm going to catch you.'

Source: Torrens (2002); translations mine

Needless to say, given the very young age of the children, their productions may have consisted of only one or two words, but they still conformed to subject–verb agreement as in adult Spanish. The fact that these children resorted to a high number of verbs and to the three verbal conjugations (or: verbal classes) of Spanish is clear indication that they were not merely repeating what they had heard.[1] The percentage of error is similar to that found for Italian (Pizzuto and Caselli 1992, Guasti 1993–1994).[2]

---

[1] See, for more details on the acquisition of verbal morphology, including the subjunctive mood, Montrul (2004). Further evidence for the acquisition of morphology in child grammar is provided by examples of overregularization, which quite clearly are not mere imitations of adult speech. These were attested for English long ago; for Spanish, see the results in Pérez-Pereira (1989) and Clahsen et al. (2002).

[2] Despite this consistently target-like performance, the comprehension literature has revealed that children may ignore number marking in a third-person verb when the subject is null. Therefore they miscomprehend sentences such as (i) in a sentence–picture matching task.

(i) Nadan   en   el   charco.   Nada   en   el   charco.
     swim.3PL   in   the   pond   swim.3SG   in   the   pond

These results can be found in Pérez-Leroux (2005) and, more cautiously, in Legendre et al. (2014), who found an effect of number marking in the plural, but not in the singular. It is not clear how to reconcile these comprehension results with the production data.

In the case of one-word utterances, the subject is null, and that takes us to a second property of Spanish, the licensing of null subjects. It was noted many years ago that sentences without an overt subject have language-specific properties from early on: Valian (1991) examined the early productions of English-speaking and Italian-speaking children and discovered that the null subjects of the Italian-speaking children had features of adult Italian, while those of the English-speaking children did not (see Wexler 2011 for a review). Spanish-speaking children also perform in an adult-like manner with respect to null subjects; see (28.2). Evidence for the early setting of the null subject parameter comes from the percentage of null subjects, which is the same in child and adult production – 32.7 percent in Bel's 2003 analysis of overt subjects in child Spanish (based on the corpora of three Spanish-speaking children).

(28.2)   a. E(s)tudia.   (Irene, 1;8,9)
study.3sg
'He is studying.'

b. Pue(d)e Irene.   (Irene, 1;8,9)
can.3sg Irene
'Irene can.'

If we turn to a closely related language, Catalan, Gavarró and Cabré-Sans (2009) examined the speech of three children from the CHILDES database. The children's production were divided into two periods according to their mean length of utterance (MLU), MLU < 2.5 and MLU > 2.5 (up to 3.4, 2.6, and 2.5 for each child). Gavarró and Cabré-Sans found that the percentage of null subjects was the same as the adults' in the second period. At that point the position of subjects (postverbal vs. preverbal) varied as a function of verb class (transitive, unergative, unaccusative); up until then, subjects were mostly postverbal (a grammatical option in Catalan as well as in Spanish). After MLU 2.5 subjects of transitives and unergatives were preferably preverbal, as they were in child-directed speech. This means that shortly after MLU 2.5 children differentiate verb classes and place subjects depending on verb class, as do adults (see also Bel 2003, where a Spanish-speaking child's productions are analyzed and the same conclusion is reached). It follows that basic word order is also an early acquisition.

Grinstead (2004) was the first to study subjects in Spanish (and Catalan). He claimed that early productions lack subjects entirely. This holds true for one-word utterances, of course, since to have an overt subject there must be a verb as well, and thus a two-word sentence. However, past this one-word stage, I see no evidence to argue that only null subjects are found. The percentage of overt subjects reported by Bel (2003) in her study of early subjects is the aggregate mean over a period of time, which might obscure an early period with no overt subjects, but Bel provides percentages by age for a Spanish-speaking child, María, as well as for a Catalan-speaking child, and there is no stage without overt subjects. (The same claim is made in Aguado-Orea and Pine 2002.) Rather, there is alternation of null and overt subjects.

The results for Spanish, therefore, are the same as those attested for the null-subject Romance languages (see Lorusso *et al.* 2005 for Italian, for example). It is generally considered that in these languages children attain adult subject–verb agreement from very early on and, unlike what we see in the non-null-subject languages, there are no optional infinitives as main verbs (see Wexler 1994, Rizzi 1993–1994 for a characterization of optional or root infinitives). Bel (2001) quantified finite and non-finite clauses in three Spanish-speaking children and, out of 1,956, 1,588, and 345 clauses, the three children produced only 50, two, and seven optional infinitives respectively.

Again, some authors have argued that verbs akin to root infinitives are found in the null-subject languages. Salustri and Hyams (2003), in their study of verbal inflection in Italian (close to Spanish in this respect), found that children overused imperatives (by 15 percent) when compared to adults. These putative tenseless forms have *irrealis* meaning, just as do optional infinitives in the non-null-subject languages. However, *irrealis* meaning is a feature of the (adult) imperative, and so child production was not deviant as it would be in the non-null subject-languages. Therefore, this analysis of child Italian imperatives as optional infinitive analogues is supported only by their rate of production and I do not extend it to Spanish.

Pratt and Grinstead (2007), on the other hand, considered Spanish third-person singular forms (which lack overt person/number agreement markers) to be analogous to optional infinitives. Again, as in Salustri and Hyams' (2003) proposal, it is difficult to see why, in their production study, third-person present tense verbs should be classed as deviant rather than target-like. The number of unambiguously erroneous examples is very small and often involves irregular verbs. Pratt and Grinstead also ran grammaticality judgment tasks and asked five-year-old children to judge sentences with an infinitival as main verb; these ill-formed sentences were accepted 27 percent of the time (and otherwise rejected). Contrary to the conclusions of Pratt and Grinstead, their results are indicative of knowledge of the ungrammaticality of the sentences and, even though rejection was not at ceiling (at only 73 percent), this can be expected from the kind of task employed. Note as well that Pratt and Grinstead regard five-year-olds as belonging to the optional infinitive stage, when they are past the optional infinitive stage so clearly attested in the non-null-subject languages (Guasti 2002). All in all, the evidence for a period when non-finite forms are produced by Spanish-speaking children appears to be weak at best.[3]

---

[3] Readers are referred to Grinstead *et al.* (2014) for further, later references and discussion of the contention that Spanish presents an optional infinitive stage.

28.3 A Romance Construction: Pronominal Clitics

Pronominal clitics, exemplified in (28.3), are one of the constructions characteristic of the Romance languages, and one of the most extensively researched, in early and adult grammar. As we shall see, their study has shed light on acquisition well beyond Romance.

(28.3) a. Te   ayudo.   (M, 2;5,5)
          CL.2SG   help.1SG
          'I'll help you.'
       b. ¿Me   compras   e(l)   tambor?   (M, 2;5,5)
          CL.1SG   buy.2SG   the   drum
          'Will you buy me the drum?'
       c. ¡No   lo   guardamos!   (M, 2;5,5)
          NEG   CL.3SG   keep.1PL
          'We didn't put it away!'

Source: CHILDES database

On the issue of the interpretation of pronouns, Chien and Wexler (1992) observed that English-speaking children can interpret a pronoun as coreferential with the subject (i.e. as if it were a reflexive) if the subject is not a quantifier:

(28.4) Mama Bear$_i$ touches her$_{*i/j}$

This is known in the literature as delay of Principle B effect (or DPBE), as Principle B of the binding theory regulates the distribution of pronouns (Chomsky 1981). McKee (1992) found that such DPBE did not occur in the Italian equivalent of (28.4), which involves a clitic pronoun, in contrast with English, in which the sentence involves a strong pronoun. Baauw et al. (1997) ran an experiment on the comprehension of sentences such as those in (28.5) and found that Spanish-speaking children side with Italian-speaking children: that is, comprehension of reflexives was at ceiling and pronominal clitics were interpreted in an adult-like manner at a rate of 90 percent at a mean age of 5;6.

(28.5) La   niña   la   señala.
        the   girl   CL.3.FEM.SG   point-to.3SG
        'The girl points at her.'

They found, however, that a DPBE could also be identified in Spanish, if one looked at exceptional case marking (ECM) sentences, exemplified in (28.6).

(28.6) La   niña$_i$ la$_{*i/j}$ ve   saltar.
        the   girl   CL.3.FEM.SG   see.3SG   jump
        'The girl sees her jump.'

In cases like (28.6), children interpreted *la* randomly between an adult pronoun with disjoint reference with the subject and a non-adult pronoun coreferential with the subject. This shows that the Spanish DPBE is attested in a subset of cases of the English DPBE (subsequent work shows the same phenomenon at work in Catalan, at a mean age of 4;4; see Escobar and Gavarró 2000).

Clitic interpretation illustrates how child grammar can inform adult grammar (and a theory of grammar in general): child Spanish compared to child English reveals that clitics are referentially different from strong pronouns. The ECM sentences, if the argument is pursued, should involve a (silent) element with the referential properties of a strong pronoun and hence induce DPBEs.

The study of Spanish pronominal clitics has also been crucial to our understanding of clitic production in child grammar. The first experimental studies for the elicitation of pronominal clitics, carried out by Jakubowicz *et al.* (1996) in French and Schaeffer (2000) in Italian, indicated high rates of clitic omission at age three (and to a lesser degree at age four). An experiment first reported in Wexler *et al.* (2004) showed that omission was found in early Catalan, but not in early Spanish. The contexts in which the clitics were elicited followed Schaeffer's (2000) method, given in (28.7), the best method developed so far to elicit pronominal clitics.

(28.7) Experimenter 1: Here we have Little Red Riding-hood. The king finds her and thinks: "Look what a mess her hair is!" And since he has a comb, look what he does.
Experimenter 2: I know what he does: he washes Little Red Riding-hood.
Experimenter 1: No! You tell her: What is the king doing to Little Red Riding-hood?
Expected response: La peina.
CL.FEM comb.3SG
'He is combing her hair.'
Source: Wexler *et al.* (2004)

Spanish clitic omission, in this study, ranged from 0 percent (present tense) to 17 percent (present perfect) at age two, in clear contrast with Catalan, for which omission was 74 percent and 81 percent respectively at age two and 25 percent and 19 percent at age three. The performance of Spanish-speaking children was crucial in establishing that clitic omission is not a universal phenomenon in early grammar, but rather subject to cross-linguistic variation. Later investigations revealed that Spanish is not an isolated case: Romanian, Greek, and Albanian were other languages in which clitic omission was negligible (see Gavarró *et al.* 2010 and references therein).

On the other hand, studies on clitic production in other Spanish varieties were inconsistent with those of Wexler *et al.* (2004) and Gavarró *et al.*

(2010). Castilla *et al.* (2008) ran an experiment on Colombian Spanish-speaking children: they omitted 35 percent of pronominal third-person clitics at age three, and 15 percent at ages four and five. Gavarró *et al.* (2010) argued that this followed from the characteristics of Colombian Spanish, in particular from the availability of third-person, specific null pronouns, unavailable in Peninsular Spanish and exemplified in (28.8), where "[e]" stands for a phonetically empty pronominal.

(28.8) Machaque las cebollas y ponga [e] a hervir en agua.

'Crush the onions and put to boil in water.'

This remained controversial until recently, when Elliot and Pirvulescu (2016) tested Peninsular Spanish-speaking children with the methods previously employed by Castilla *et al.* (2008), and found very little omission at age three. This settled a controversy that has rumbled on for over ten years. This result also confirms the relevance of the variety of language that children are exposed to when acquisition is considered. As is common in the generative tradition, varieties of Spanish (and any other language) may differ substantially and, therefore, speakers may produce quite different grammaticality judgments. The path of acquisition of these varieties (in the case at hand, Peninsular Spanish and Colombian Spanish) may not be homogeneous. When we refer to "the acquisition of Spanish" we are therefore referring to the acquisition of several different grammars.

The observations reported on the acquisition of Spanish pronominal clitics (in fact, third-person object clitics) have had an impact on our understanding of the acquisition of clitics beyond Spanish. To begin with, in the first study of early target behavior, Wexler *et al.*'s (2004) study showed that pronominal clitics are not inherently difficult for children. It had been already established that children place clitics as adults do, and as illustrated in (28.9; my examples); this was first reported, for Spanish, in Hernández Pina's (1984) study of spontaneous production.

(28.9) a. La   compro.   a'. *Compro   la.
            CL.FEM   buy.1SG   buy.1SG   CL.FEM
            'I'll buy it.'

        b. No   quiere   comprarla.   b'. *No   quiere   la   comprar.
            NEG   want.3SG   buy.CL.3FEM   NEG   want.3SG   CL.3FEM   buy
            'He/she doesn't want to buy it.'

In the second place, clitics form complex structures, in which the clitic co-occurs with the full argument it is coreferential with (so-called clitic doubling); Spanish children have knowledge of this construction (see Torrens and Wexler 2000 for the analysis of María's spontaneous productions, where she avoids ungrammatical doubling, and produces doubling in all obligatory contexts except for one). Third, it was known that children who omit clitics in, for example French (Jakubowicz *et al.* 1996) do not always omit them, so that omission is optional. This implies that clitics in themselves have been acquired (children have identified their form, grammatical features, and meaning). Several hypotheses put forward in the literature that state that pronominal clitics are inherently difficult (Jakubowicz *et al.* 1996; Jakubowicz and Nash forthcoming) can be dismissed because they make erroneous predictions for Spanish. Other hypotheses that place the source of clitic omission in a general availability of null objects in child grammar and (lack of) lexical knowledge of verb transitivity (Pérez-Leroux *et al.* 2008, 2012) are also not supported by the facts of child (Peninsular) Spanish.[4]

An additional property of third-person object clitics in most Romance languages is that they are homophonous with definite articles (compare *la* in (28.9a) above and in *la niña* 'the.FEM girl'). In the child languages with pronominal clitic omission, such as Catalan, French, and Italian, articles attain adult levels of production earlier than pronominal clitics. In Peninsular Spanish, since there is virtually no pronominal clitic omission, articles are not early in comparison. In general, Romance determiners are acquired earlier than their Germanic counterparts. Two kinds of explanation have been given for this instance of cross-linguistic variation.

Lleó and Demuth (1999) were the first to point out the contrast between Spanish and German, with Spanish children acquiring articles before (by six months) their German peers (within the age range of 1;4 and 2;3). They attributed the contrast to prosodic differences between the two languages: while the vocabulary of Spanish contains more trisyllabic words than German vocabulary, Germanic syllables are more complex than the Spanish ones (in having more complex rhymes, etc.). Lleó and Demuth argue that the sequence of an article preceding a bisyllabic word is prosodically identical to a trisyllabic word, common in the Spanish input. In this way, Spanish allows for articles (and protoarticles) to be integrated prosodically even at early stages; see the examples in (28.10).

(28.10) a. [haveva:] la vaca 'the cow' (Miguel, 1;4,5)
b. [hekuwo] el cubo 'the bucket' (María, 1;6,3)
Source: Lleó and Demuth (1999)

This need not mean that determiners are absent from early German, only that German prosody weakens their phonological realization. The prosodic and syllabic characteristics of Spanish do, of course, shape children's production as well. So, for example, when we consider third-person object clitic production in two- and three-year-olds, children in Gavarró *et al.*'s (2010) experiment produced non-target sequences *la* and [l] for *las*. Because, as noted by Lleó and Demuth (1999) and Saceda (2005),

---

[4] Mateu (2015) tests the interpretation that children acquiring Spanish assign to intransitive sentences with verbs that also allow a transitive reading; she shows that they do not assign them transitive interpretations (as one would expect if a null object had been projected).

the syllabic structure of Spanish is of comparatively low complexity, we take examples such as these to be phonologically non-adult but syntactically adult-like.

Work by Guasti and Gavarró (2003) examined languages such as Catalan, with prosodic features closer to those of German (presence of monosyllabic words in the vocabulary, etc.) and did not find the expected lower production of determiners. This undermined Lleó and Demuth's (1999) proposal and led to another hypothesis, based on Chierchia *et al.* (1999). Guasti *et al.* (2008) put forward the idea that the fundamental divide in the acquisition of articles was between Romance and Germanic. These constitute two language types in Chierchia's (1998) nominal mapping parameter, which also includes another language type, namely Chinese. These language types differ in the way a nominal may become an argument in a predicative structure. In Chinese a noun phrase (NP) maps onto an argument and so a determiner (D) is not required. In Romance, in sharp contrast, NPs require D to act as arguments, and so D is generally mandatory. In Germanic, NPs map onto predicates and arguments, and as a consequence there may be arguments without an article (*Russian novels are unforgettable*) although with a subset of Ns an article is indispensable (*I read *(a) Russian novel*). Guasti *et al.* (2008) contended that the Romance setting of the nominal mapping parameter boosts article production, while the Germanic setting leads the child to a period of oscillation, resulting in higher D omission rates. Their study was based on spontaneous production (like Lleó and Demuth's (1999)) but the languages examined were Catalan, Italian, and Dutch. Article omission decreased faster in Catalan and Italian than in Dutch, although first use of (proto)articles was the same in the three languages. This approach is not incompatible with prosodic considerations, which, nevertheless, cannot in themselves account for the cross-linguistic variation encountered.

To summarize, in this section we have looked at two homophonous grammatical elements: definite articles and third-person pronominal clitics. While their phonology is identical, their syntactic nature is not. By considering their developmental paths it becomes clear that acquisition is driven by phonological properties together with other grammatical properties. Syntactic features and properties of the semantic mapping of syntactic categories have an impact on the acquisition of articles and pronominal clitics. In Spanish both definite articles and third-person pronominal clitics are early acquisitions, but this is not so universally. We need turn only to Catalan to argue that pronominal clitics are not produced in an adult-like manner at the same age (they are later than in Spanish, as are French and Italian pronominal clitics).

28.4 Long-Distance Phenomena

In this section we focus on a topic to which much research is being devoted: long-distance phenomena. (We leave aside A(rgument)-movement, since there is little done in this area other than Pierce's (1992) early work on passive comprehension; her experiment reported passive delay in Spanish, as attested in many languages of the world.) The two long-distance phenomena we examine are *wh*-questions and relative clauses, which have inspired grammatical and processing analyses. *Wh*-questions in Spanish involve *wh*-movement of the interrogative phrase to the left periphery and obligatory so-called subject inversion.[5] These are exemplified with the child productions seen in (28.11) from the CHILDES database: *dónde* 'where' appears in initial position and the subject *e lapicito* 'the little pencil' appears after the verb *(es)tá*, so that *dónde* and the verb are adjacent.

(28.11)   ¿Dónde (es)tá e   lapicito?   (Koki, 1;11)
          where   is   the pencil.DIM

Pérez-Leroux and Dalious (1998) examined the *wh*-questions spontaneously produced by six Spanish-speaking children (age range 1;7–4;11); all without exception followed the pattern of adult *wh*-questions, with *wh*-fronting and subject inversion. (An informal observation to the same effect had been previously made by Hernández-Pina 1984 and López-Ornat 1994.) Likewise, word order constraints in *wh*-interrogatives are complied with in both Italian (Guasti 1996) and Catalan (Gavarró and Cabré-Sans 2009).

So far the evidence is for early convergence to the adult grammar. Gutiérrez Mangado (2006) unraveled some cases of long-distance *wh*-questions in which children are deviant with respect to adult Spanish. Her study was inspired by Thornton (1990), where similar phenomena were discovered for English. The data for Spanish come from the study of M, a girl aged 4;9 at the beginning of the experimental sessions, and the experiments replicate those of Thornton. The elicitation method is illustrated in (28.12).

(28.12)   Experimenter: Here we have a man and two cars. You choose which car the man bought. [Experimenter places a folder between herself and the child so as not to see what the child chooses. The child chooses a car and places it next to the representation of the man.]

---

[5] It should be noted that Caribbean Spanish does not present obligatory subject inversion and does not invert subject pronouns at all (see Toribio 2000).

Experimenter:	Pregúntame	qué	coche	creo
	ask.me	which	car	think.1SG
	que	compró.		
	that	bought.3SG		
	'Ask me which car I think he bought.'			
Expected response:	¿Qué	coche	crees	que	compró?
	which	car	think.2SG	that	bought.3SG
	'Which car do you think he bought?'				

Source: Gutiérrez Mangado (2006)

The questions produced by the child (in the period 4;9–6;2) were subject, object, and adjunct *wh*-questions, and only 15.6 percent were fully adult-like; of the remainder, the most common non-adult productions were partial questions, exemplified in (28.13), and 8.7 percent were copying *wh*-questions, exemplified in (28.14).

(28.13) ¿Tu crees dónde fue el niño? (M, 4;10)
you believe.2SG where went the child
'Where do you think the child went?'

(28.14) ¿Dónde crees dónde ha ido el niño?
where believe.2SG where has gone the child
'Where do you think the child has gone?'

In (28.13) the *wh*-word *dónde* 'where' has moved to the left periphery of the embedded clause, and remained there instead of moving to the left periphery of the main clause, as in adult Spanish. In (28.14) the *wh*-word is overtly produced where silent copies would be found in adult Spanish (*¿Dónde crees que ha ido el niño?*). These two constructions have also been reported in other languages: English, Basque, and Dutch (see Gutiérrez Mangado 2006 and references therein), besides the languages in which copying or partial movement are an option in the adult grammar. Gutiérrez Mangado found another construction unattested so far in other languages – see (28.15).

(28.15) ¿Tu qué crees que quién ha hecho el pastel?
you what believe.2SG that who has made the cake
Intended meaning: 'Who do you believe baked the cake?'

Source (Examples 28.13–28.15): Gutiérrez Mangado (2006); translations mine

The presence of the complementizer *que* demonstrates that what follows the verb is an embedded clause. The order *que* followed by *wh*-phrase is colloquial in Spanish; the fact that the child uses it can be taken as evidence for the full array of complementizer (C) and focus (Foc) functional projections (if *wh*-words move to FocP, as in Rizzi 1997, Belletti 2004). In the child's productions partial movement appears early on (4;10–5;5) followed by adult questions and then a period when partial movement and adult questions coexist with *wh*-copying. Gutiérrez Mangado (2006) concludes that long distance *wh*-questions conform to natural language patterns in child Spanish, albeit with constructions that disappear in adult Spanish (and remain just as well formed in other languages). With respect to the construction of grammatical theory, the behavior of Spanish-speaking children can be adduced as an argument for the movement operation, and for long-distance movement as a step-by-step composition of more local movements.

Relative clauses are another case of long-distance movement in which children opt for constructions that are not necessarily available in the input, but an option in universal grammar. Pérez-Leroux (1995) elicited relative clauses with a task in which children were asked to describe one of two characters. The experiment was run with children aged 3;5 to 6;8. Adult-like subject relative clauses were produced by all the children, but object and oblique/locative relative clause elicitation gave rise to non-target-like constructions: relatives with resumptive pronouns (28.16) and resumptive full determiner phrases (DPs) (28.17), together with target gapped relative clauses.

(28.16) el que *lo* (es)tán montando
the that CL.3SG are riding
'the one they are riding'

(28.17) el que la nena no lleva *al* perro a pasear
the that the girl not take to-the dog to walk
'the one that the girl does not take (the dog) for a walk'

Source (Examples 28.16–28.17): Pérez-Leroux (1993)

In a further comprehension task, children were given interrogative and relative clauses with a pronoun; they interpreted it as resumptive in a way banned in adult Spanish. Resumptive pronouns like those seen in (28.16) are marginal in adult speech, and resumptive DPs are ill-formed and never produced by adults. This is one case that illustrates the widely attested asymmetry between subject and object relative clauses. In many languages, subject relative clauses are produced and understood earlier than object relatives (within Romance, this is attested for Catalan, Italian, and Portuguese, for example). In Friedmann *et al.* (2009) it is proposed that this subject/object asymmetry is derived from relativized minimality effects (Rizzi 1990), whereby a structurally intervening DP leads to miscomprehension, as it is interpreted as the antecedent of a moved element:

(28.18)   +A, +B … +A … <+A, +B>

In adult grammar, intervention effects occur only when A in (28.18) shares all relevant grammatical features with the displaced element. In child grammar, by hypothesis, if the intervener and the moved element are in a subset–superset relation (+A, +B in (28.18)), A still acts as an intervener. This analysis is contested by authors who attribute the asymmetry to similarity-based interference effects (Choe and Deen 2015; Omaki and Lidz 2015); these processing approaches can capture the fact that the same asymmetry is found in adult performance under certain conditions, when clearly adult performance is not immature. On the other hand, structural factors are at play in the miscomprehension of object relative clauses, as witnessed by the results from Chinese (Hu 2014), a language with prenominal relative clauses: there intervention holds only structurally, not linearly. Deciding which analysis is best is beyond the scope of this chapter, but it should nevertheless be pointed out that Spanish belongs to the long list of languages for which asymmetry holds in relative-clause production and comprehension (see Friedmann *et al.* 2009 and references therein).

28.5 New Topics and Future Research

The study of language acquisition began in the late 1960s and has developed steadily since. Our knowledge of the path of acquisition in many languages of the world is considerable, especially in the core domain of morphosyntax. In this last section I consider two fields that started developing only later – or even very recently.

The first of these domains is that of semantics, by which I refer to meaning that is conveyed by specific lexical items and not syntactic structure, e.g. quantifiers. To this we can add the pragmatics of those same lexical items.

In Section 28.3 the acquisition of articles was touched on, but in the studies reported nothing was said about whether those articles were specific or non-specific, whether their use allows the speaker to make certain pragmatic inferences, and so on. There is some research addressing these often subtle distinctions. We illustrate this with three studies on Spanish.

Vargas-Tokuda *et al.* (2009) looked at two determiners in Spanish, *unos* and *algunos* 'some.' Based on Gutiérrez-Rexach (2001) they observe that, although both are indefinite, *unos* is non-D(iscourse)-linked and is not a "collectivizer," while *algunos* is D-linked and is a group determiner (i.e. it is used in collective and group predication). In one of the experiments they detailed, they tested the comprehension of sentences such as those in (28.19) by 20 five-year-olds (age range: 4;9–6;7).

(28.19) a. Algunos X saltaron sobre A.
            some   X jumped   over   A

         b. Unos   X saltaron sobre A.
            some   X jumped   over   A

Source: Vargas-Tokuda *et al.* (2009)

Judging by their answers, children distinguished between *unos* and *algunos* exactly as adults would and were furthermore able to compute the implicature that *algunos* X 'some X' is not felicitous when "all X" holds true. The authors concluded that pragmatics of implicature, in this case at least, is not delayed with respect to semantics, contrary to the claims of others (see Noveck 2001 for scalar implicatures). Some recent work by Katsos *et al.* (2016) considers the semantics and pragmatics of quantifiers in several languages, and in this case Spanish-speaking five-year-olds indeed performed better with truth conditional semantics than with their pragmatics (i.e. children were better at rejecting false statements involving *algunos* than underinformative ones, in sentences such as *Algunas manzanas están en las cajas* 'Some apples are in the baskets,' analogous to (28.19a)).

In a related domain, that of genericity and definiteness, Pérez-Leroux *et al.* (2004) explored the comprehension of sentence pairs like (28.20).

(28.20) a. ¿Los   tigres   comen   carne/zanahorias?
            the   tigers   eat   meat/carrots
            'Do tigers eat meat/carrots?'
         b. ¿Esos   tigres   comen   carne/zanahorias?
            those   tigers   eat   meat/carrots
            'Do those tigers eat meat/carrots?'

The subjects exemplified in (28.20a), with a definite article, can have a generic or a specific interpretation, while subjects with a demonstrative, as in (28.20b), can be interpreted only as specific. The method used in Pérez-Leroux *et al.*'s (2004) experiment consisted of a short story about atypical members of a species (e.g. vegetarian tigers). Children in the age range of 3;5–5;3 distinguished definite from demonstrative subjects; they overwhelmingly assigned specific interpretations to demonstrative subjects, and chose the generic reading for subjects with definite articles (although specific readings are also possible in Spanish) – thus showing a generic bias. Generic reference is encountered with present tense; when a clause is in the past tense, genericity is less likely, unless the speaker is referring to an extinct species, as in (28.21).

(28.21) Los dodos tenían plumas.
         the dodos had   feathers
         'Dodos had feathers.'

The same subjects of the first experiment were tested in a new experiment manipulating tense, and they ascribed both specific and generic readings to sentences like (28.21) once the past tense was used. This result corroborates that the co-occurrence of tense and genericity is well established between ages three and five. The paper also offered results for English (comparing generic *Do zebras have stripes?* to specific *Do the zebras have stripes?*); in that language, children mastered specificity later than in Spanish, so that a cross-linguistic contrast was found – as we saw in determiner use at an earlier age.

Pérez-Leroux *et al.* (2004) showed an effect of tense (present vs. past) in the interpretation of genericity. Now we turn to more recent studies focusing on aspectual distinctions. Spanish aspect resides in part in the functional domain (thus, there are perfect and imperfect markers in the tense phrase (TP) field), in part in the verb itself (some predicates are telic, some atelic). Therefore, an accomplishment can be expressed by the conjunction of a functional category in tense (T) and a verb, as in (28.22); # marks the clause as pragmatically odd.

(28.22) El   payaso   construyó un   puente   #pero no
        the   clown   built   a   bridge   but   NEG
        terminó.
        finished
        'The clown built a bridge #but didn't finish.'

Source: García del Real (2015)

Hodgson (2010) was one of the first to explore the acquisition of telicity in the Romance languages. She investigated the interpretation of sentences with simple telic predicates (28.23a) and with locatum predicates (28.23b).

(28.23) a. El   niño   cubrió   el   piano.
           the   boy   covered   the   piano
        b. El   mantel   cubrió   la   mesa.
           the   tablecloth covered the   table

Source: Hodgson (2010)

Both sentences in (28.23) are interpreted by adults as describing complete events; Hodgson tested children in the age range of 3;6 to 7;11 and found that incomplete events were accepted as corresponding to sentences like (28.23a) more often than sentences like (28.23b); in fact, even the youngest children rejected incomplete events for (28.23b) 73 percent of the time, so that, at least with the group of locatum predicates, which by hypothesis present a derived subject, the entailment of completion is understood from early on. Such early understanding of telicity had not been attested in child learners of any other language before.

Recently, García del Real (2015) inquired into the acquisition of aspect by means of a series of experiments. She designed a truth-conditional task with sentences such as those in (28.24) with five-year-old Spanish-speaking children and found that they were adult-like in grasping that the action had reached its end-point, as marked in the perfective form of the verb.

(28.24) Mientras sonaba   la   música ...
         while   sounded   the   music
         'While the music was playing ... '
         ¿el   payaso   apagó   la   vela?
         the   clown   blew-out the   candle
         'Did the clown blow out the candle?'

In contrast to the adult-like performance with change-of-state predicates (*apagar* 'blow out'), she uncovered non-target performance when the verb was an incremental-theme predicate, as in (28.25).

(28.25) ¿el payaso dibujó una estrella?
         the clown drew   a   star
         'Did the clown draw a star?'

Here children were more willing to accept the action having reached an end-point when it had not. The source of this delay in comprehension remains unclear – but see van Hout *et al.* (2017) on Spanish three-year-olds and also performance in other, unrelated languages.

The work reported so far bears testimony to the development of research methods in language acquisition. With few exceptions, work in the 70s and the 80s was based on spontaneous production corpora – and that was certainly the case for the acquisition of Spanish. Experimental methods were introduced, and, if we were now to anticipate which kind of research will gain ground in the future, we could argue that it would be based on increasingly sophisticated methods.

The acquisition of phonological systems, with methods that allow testing from the first week of life, has already shown evidence of such a development. There is a temporal gap between the segmentation of speech and the discrimination of phonological features on the one hand, and the production of sentences at the two-word stage on the other. With the seminal work of Hirsh-Pasek and Golinkoff (1996) a new line of inquiry was initiated: that of syntax prior to production. Their experiment introduced the preferential looking paradigm: the experimenter infers what interpretation the subject gives to a sentence by presenting a representation of the sentence and a distractor and measuring fixation time against each image. The underlying assumption is that speakers, upon hearing a sentence, direct their gaze to the graphic representation that matches it. By this method Hirsh-Pasek and Golinkoff demonstrated that English-speaking 17-month-old children are sensitive to word order and can parse reversible subject–verb–object (SVO) sentences. Work has been carried out into the acquisition of inflection in Spanish using this experimental paradigm (see, for example, Lew-Williams and Fernald 2007; Arias-Trejo *et al.* 2014) but, to my knowledge, none on the acquisition of word order; for this reason I mention incipient work in some related languages.

For French, Franck *et al.* (2011) combined the preferential looking paradigm with the use of pseudoverbs in their experimental items, as well as grammatical and ungrammatical sequences (target French SVO and ungrammatical SOV). Their purpose was to see if children at 19 months behave differently when confronted with well-formed and ill-formed sentences, in particular in connection with word order. Children interpreted SVO as adults do, but had chance performance with ungrammatical SOV, everything else remaining constant. The conclusion that can be drawn from this experiment is that the syntactic properties of French (in particular, it being a head-initial language) have been acquired at 19 months at the latest, and this is observable even when pseudoverbs are used (*contra* the claim that children at that age have no access to abstract syntax, Dittmar *et al.* 2008 amongst others). Lassotta *et al.* (2014), building on Franck *et al.*'s experiment, tested French children of the same age on non-canonical word orders, including (28.26), an instance of clitic left-dislocation (CLLD).

(28.26) Le garçon, la fille le dase.
 the boy the girl CL.3SG V
 'The boy, the girl V.SG.'

Again, children understood these sentence types, judging by their time of fixation on the target video representation. No such work has been carried out for Spanish, but one would expect similar behavior from 19-month-old children exposed to Spanish. As a null-subject language, Spanish displays a wider array of word orders than French; future research should tell us about infants' ability to parse different sentence structures at 19 months of age and before. These developments open out new and exciting prospects in the field of language acquisition.

References

Aguado-Orea, J. and Pine, J. M. (2002). There is no Evidence for a "No Overt Subject" Stage in Early Child Spanish: A Note on Grinstead (2000). *Journal of Child Language*, 29, 865–874.

Arias-Trejo, N., Cantrell, L. M., Smith L. B., and Alva Canto, E. A. (2014). Early Comprehension of the Spanish Plural. *Journal of Child Language*, 41, 1356–1372.

Baauw, S., Escobar, M. A., and Philip, W. (1997). A Delay of Principle B Effect in Spanish Speaking Children: The Role of Lexical Feature Acquisition. In A. Sorace, C. Heycock, and R. Shillcock (eds.), *Proceedings of the GALA '97 Conference on Language Acquisition*. Edinburgh: Edinburgh University Press, pp. 16–21.

Bel, A. (2001). *Teoria lingüística i adquisició del llenguatge. Anàlisi comparada dels trets morfològics en català i en castellà*. Barcelona: Institut d'Estudis Catalans.

Bel, A. (2003). The Syntax of Subjects in the Acquisition of Spanish and Catalan. *Probus*, 15, 150–177.

Belletti, A. (ed.) (2004). *Structures and Beyond – The Cartography of Syntactic Structures*, Vol. 3. Oxford: Oxford University Press.

Castilla, A., Pérez-Leroux, A.-T., and Eriks-Brophy, A. (2008). Omissions and Substitutions in Early Spanish Clitics. In A. Gavarró and M. J. Freitas (eds.), *Language Acquisition and Development. Proceedings of GALA 2007*. Newcastle: Cambridge Scholars Press, pp. 112–122.

Chien, Y. C. and Wexler, K. (1992). Children's Knowledge of Locality Conditions in Binding as Evidence for the Modularity of Syntax and Pragmatics. *Language Acquisition*, 1, 225–295.

Chierchia, G. (1998). Reference to Kinds across Languages. *Natural Language Semantics*, 6, 339–405.

Chierchia, G., Guasti, M. T., and Gualmini, A. (1999). Nouns and Articles in Child Grammar and the Syntax/Semantics Map. Paper presented at Generative Approaches to Language Acquisition, Potsdam.

Choe, J. and Deen, K. (2015). Children's Difficulty with Raising: A Performance Account. *Language Acquisition*, 23 (2), 112–141.

Chomsky, N. (1981). *Lectures on Government and Binding*. Dordrecht: Foris.

Clahsen, H., Aveledo, F., and Roca, I. (2002). The Development of Regular and Irregular Verb Inflection in Spanish Child Language. *Journal of Child Language*, 29, 591–622.

Dittmar, M., Abbot-Smith, K., Lieven, E., and Tomasello, M. (2008). Young German Children's Early Syntactic Competence: A Preferential Looking Study. *Developmental Science*, 11 (4), 575–582.

Elliot, M. and Pirvulescu, M. (2016). Very Early Object Clitic Omission: How Early is too Early? Paper presented at the Romance Turn 8, Bellaterra. Available from http://filcat.uab.cat/theromanceturn/wp-content/uploads/2016/01/Elliott_et_alii.pdf (last access January 6, 2018).

Escobar, L. and Gavarró, A. (2000). The Acquisition of Clitics and Strong Pronouns in Catalan. In B. Gerlach and J. Grijzenhout (eds.), *Clitics in Phonology, Morphology and Syntax*. Amsterdam and Philadelphia, PA: John Benjamins, pp. 161–180.

Franck, J., Millotte, S., Posada, A., and Rizzi, L. (2011). Abstract Knowledge of Word Order by 19 Months: An Eye-Tracking Study. *Applied Psycholinguistics*, 34 (2), 323–336.

Friedmann, N., Belletti, A., and Rizzi, L. (2009). Relativized Relatives: Types of Intervention in the Acquisition of A-Bar Dependencies. *Lingua*, 119, 331–344.

García del Real, I. (2015). The Acquisition of Tense and Aspect in Spanish (Doctoral dissertation). UPV/EHU.

Gavarró, A. and Cabré-Sans, Y. (2009). Subjects, Verb Classes and Word Order in Child Catalan. In J. Grinstead (ed.), *Hispanic Child Languages. Typical and Impaired Development*. Amsterdam and Philadelphia, PA: John Benjamins, pp. 175–194.

Gavarró, A., Torrens, V., and Wexler, K. (2010). Object Clitic Omission: Two Language Types. *Language Acquisition*, 17 (4), 192–219.

Grinstead, J. (2004). Subjects and Interface Delay in Child Spanish and Catalan. *Language*, 80 (1), 40–72.

Grinstead, J., Lintz, P., Vega-Mendoza, M., de la Mora, J., Cantú-Sánchez, M., and Flores-Avalos, B. (2014). Evidence of Optional Infinitive Verbs in the Spontaneous Speech of Spanish-Speaking Children with SLI. *Lingua*, 140, 52–66.

Guasti, M. T. (1993–1994). Verb Syntax in Italian Child Grammar: Finite and Non-Finite Verbs. *Language Acquisition*, 3, 1–40.

Guasti, M. T. (1996). Acquisition of Italian Interrogatives. In H. Clahsen (ed.), *Generative Perspectives on Language Acquisition*. Amsterdam: John Benjamins, pp. 241–269.

Guasti, M. T. (2002). *Language Acquisition. The Growth of Grammar*. Cambridge, MA: MIT Press.

Guasti, M. T. and Gavarró, A. (2003). Catalan as a Test for Hypotheses Concerning Article Omission. In B. Beachley, A. Brown, and F. Colin (eds.), *Proceedings of the 27th Annual Boston University Conference on Language Development*. Somerville, MA: Cascadilla, pp. 288–298.

Guasti, M. T., Gavarró, A., de Lange, J., and Caprin, C. (2008). Article Omission across Child Languages. *Language Acquisition*, 15 (2), 89–119.

Gutiérrez Mangado, M. J. (2006). Acquiring Long-Distance *wh*-Questions in L1 Spanish. In V. Torrens and L. Escobar (eds.), *The Acquisition of Syntax in Romance Languages*. Amsterdam and Philadelphia, PA: John Benjamins, pp. 251–287.

Gutiérrez-Rexach, J. (2001). The Semantics of Spanish Plural Existential Determiners. *Probus*, 13, 113–154.

Hernández-Pina, F. (1984). *Teorías psicolingüísticas y su aplicación a la adquisición del español*. Madrid: Siglo XXI.

Hirsh-Pasek, K. R. and Golinkoff, R. M. (1996). *The Origins of Grammar*. Cambridge, MA: MIT Press.

Hodgson, M. (2010). Locatum Structures and the Acquisition of Telicity. *Language Acquisition*, 17 (3), 155–182.

Hu, S. (2014). Intervention Effects and the Acquisition of Relativization and Topicalization in Chinese (Doctoral dissertation). Universitat Autònoma de Barcelona/Università degli Studi di Milano-Bicocca.

Jakubowicz, C., Müller, N., Kang, O.-K., Biemer, B., and Rigaut, C. (1996). On the Acquisition of the Pronominal System in French and German. In A. Stringfellow, D. Cahana-Amitay, E. Hughes, and A. Zukowski (eds.), *Proceedings of the 20th Annual Boston University Conference on Language Development*. Somerville, MA: Cascadilla, pp. 374–385.

Jakubowicz, C. and Nash, L. (forthcoming). Why Accusative Clitics are Avoided in Normal and Impaired Language Development. In C. Jakubowicz, L. Nash, and K. Wexler (eds.), *Essays in Syntax, Morphology and Phonology of SLI*. Cambridge, MA: MIT Press.

Katsos, N., Cummins, C., Ezeizabarrena, M.-J., Gavarró, A., Kuvač Kraljević, J., *et al.* (2016). Cross-linguistic patterns in the acquisition of quantifiers. *Proceedings of the National Academy of Science*, 113 (33), 9244–9249. doi: 10.1073/pnas.1601341113.

Lassotta, R., Omaki, A., and Franck, J. (2014). Abstract Knowledge of Non-Canonical Word Order by Age 2. Paper presented at the 39th Boston University Conference on Language Development. Abstract available from www.bu.edu/bucld/files/2015/03/BUCLD-39-Handbook.pdf (last access January 6, 2018).

Legendre, G., Culberston, J., Zaroukian, E., Hsin, L., Barrière, I., and Nazzi, T. (2014). Is Children's Comprehension of Subject–Verb Agreement Universally Late? Comparative Evidence from French, English, and Spanish. *Lingua*, 144, 21–39.

Lew-Williams, C. and Fernald, A. (2007). Young Children Learning Spanish Make Rapid Use of Grammatical Gender in Spoken Word Recognition. *Psychological Science*, 18 (3), 193–198.

Lleó, C. and Demuth, K. (1999). Prosodic Constraints on the Emergence of Grammatical Morphemes: Crosslinguistic Evidence from Germanic and Romance Languages. In A. Greenhill, H. Littlefield, and C. Tano (eds.), *Proceedings of the 23rd Annual Boston University Conference on Language Development*. Somerville, MA: Cascadilla, pp. 407–418.

López-Ornat, S. (1994). La adquisición del lenguaje: Talón de Aquiles y poción mágica de la teoría cognitiva. *Cognitiva*, 6 (2), 213–239.

Lorusso, P., Caprin, C., and Guasti, M. T. (2005). Overt Subject Distribution in Early Italian Children. In A. Brugos, M. R. Clark-Cotton, and S. Ha (eds.), *BUCLD 29 Online Proceedings Supplement*. Somerville, MA: Cascadilla. Available from http://www.bu.edu/bucld/files/2011/05/29-LorussoBUCLD 2004.pdf (last access December 27, 2017).

MacWhinney, B. (1995). *The CHILDES Project: Tools for Analyzing Talk* (2nd edn). Hillsdale, NJ: Lawrence Erlbaum.

Mateu, V. E. (2015). Object Clitic Omission in Child Spanish: Evaluating Representational and Processing Accounts. *Language Acquisition*, 22 (3), 240–284.

McKee, C. (1992). A Comparison of Pronouns and Anaphors in Italian and English Acquisition. *Language Acquisition*, 2, 21–54.

Montrul, S. (2004). *The Acquisition of Spanish*. Amsterdam and Philadelphia, PA: John Benjamins.

Noveck, I. (2001). When Children are More Logical than Adults: Experimental Investigations of Scalar Implicature. *Cognition*, 78 (2), 165–188.

Omaki, A. and J. Lidz (2015). Linking Parser Development to Acquisition of Syntactic Knowledge. *Language Acquisition*, 22 (2), 158–192.

Pérez-Leroux, A. T. (1993). Empty Categories and the Acquisition of wh-Movement (Doctoral dissertation). University of Massachusetts–Amherst.

Pérez-Leroux, A. T. (1995). Resumptives in the Acquisition of Relative Clauses, *Language Acquisition*, 4, 105–138.

Pérez-Leroux, A. T. (2005). Number Problems in Children. In C. Guski (ed.), *Proceedings of the 2005 Canadian Linguistics Association Annual Conference*. Published online at http://cla-acl.ca/actes-2005-proceedings/.

Pérez-Leroux, A. T., Castilla, A. P., and Brunner, J. (2012). General and Specific Effects of Lexicon in Grammar: Determiner and Object Pronoun Omissions in Child Spanish. *Journal of Speech, Language, and Hearing Research*, 55 (2), 313–327.

Pérez-Leroux, A.-T. and Dalious, J. (1998). The Acquisition of Spanish Interrogative Inversion. *Hispanic Linguistics*, 10, 84–114.

Pérez-Leroux, A.-T., Munn, A., Schmitt, C., and de Irish, M. (2004). Learning Definite Determiners: Genericity and Definiteness in English and Spanish. In Alejna Brugos, Linnea Micciulla, and Christine E. Smith (eds.), *BUCLD 28 Online Proceedings Supplement*. Somerville, MA: Cascadilla. Available from http://www.bu.edu/bucld/files/2011/05/28-perez-leroux.pdf (last access December 27, 2017).

Pérez-Leroux, A.-T., Pirvulescu, M. and Roberge, Y. (2008). Null Objects in Child Language: Syntax and the Lexicon. *Lingua*, 118 (3), 370–398.

Pérez-Pereira, M. (1989). The Acquisition of Morphemes: Some Evidence from Spanish. *Journal of Pyscholinguistic Research*, 18 (3), 289–312.

Pierce, A. (1992). The Acquisition of Passives in Spanish and the Question of A-Chain Maturation. *Language Acquisition*, 2, 55–81.

Pizzuto, E. and Caselli, M. C. (1992). The Acquisition of Italian Morphology: Implications for Models of Language Development. *Journal of Child Language*, 19, 491–557.

Pratt, A. and Grinstead, J. (2007). Optional Infinitives in Child Spanish. In A. Belikova, L. Meroni, and M. Umeda (eds.), *Proceedings of the 2nd Conference on Generative Approaches to Language Acquisition North America (GALANA)*. Somerville, MA: Cascadilla, pp. 351–362.

Rizzi, L. (1990). *Relativized Minimality*, Cambridge, MA: MIT Press.

Rizzi, L. (1993–1994). Some Remarks on Linguistic Theory and Language Development. *Language Acquisition*, 3, 371–393.

Rizzi, L. (1997). The Fine Structure of the Left Periphery. In L. Haegeman (ed.), *Elements of Grammar*. Dordrecht: Kluwer, pp. 281–337.

Saceda, M. (2005). Adquisición prosódica en español peninsular septentrional: La sílaba y la palabra prosódica (MA thesis). Universitat Autònoma de Barcelona.

Salustri, M. and Hyams, N. (2003). Is there an Analogue to the RI Stage in the Null Subject Languages? In B. Beachley, A. Brown, and F. Colin (eds.), *Proceedings of the 27th Boston University Conference on Language Development*. Somerville, MA: Cascadilla, pp. 692–703.

Schaeffer, J. (2000). *The Acquisition of Direct Object Scrambling and Clitic Placement*. Amsterdam: John Benjamins.

Searchinger, Gene (dir.) (1995). *Acquiring the Human Language, Part 2: Playing the Language Game*. New York: Equinox Films/Ways of Knowing.

Thornton, R. (1990). Adventures in Long-Distance Moving: The Acquisition of Complex *wh*-Questions (Doctoral dissertation). University of Connecticut.

Toribio, J. (2000). Setting Parametric Limits on Dialectal Variation in Spanish. *Lingua*, 110, 315–341.

Torrens, V. (1995). The Acquisition of Inflection in Spanish and Catalan. In C. Schütze, J. Ganger, and K. Broihier (eds.), *Papers on Language Processing and Acquisition*. Boston, MA: MITWPL, pp. 451–472.

Torrens, V. (2002). *La adquisición del tiempo y la concordancia*, Madrid: UNED.

Torrens, V. and Wexler, K. (2000). The Acquisition of Clitic Doubling in Spanish. In S. Powers and C. Hamann (eds.), *The Acquisition of Scrambling and Cliticization*. Dordrecht: Kluwer, pp. 279–297.

van Hout, A., Arche, M., Demirdache, H., García del Real, I., García Sanz, A., Gavarró, A., Gómez Marzo, L., Hommes, S., Kazanina, N., Liu, J., Lungu, O., Martin, F., and Strangmann, I. (2017). Agent Control and the Acquisition of Event Culmination in Basque, Dutch, English, Spanish, and Mandarin. In Maria LaMendola and Jennifer Scott (eds.), *Proceedings of the 41st Boston University Conference on Language Development*. Somerville, MA: Cascadilla, pp. 323–332.

Valian, V. (1991). Syntactic Subjects in the Early Speech of American and Italian Children. *Cognition*, 40, 21–81.

Vargas-Tokuda, M., Gutiérrez-Rexach, J., and Grinstead, J. (2009). Context and the Scalar Implicatures of Indefinites in Child Spanish. In J. Grinstead (ed.), *Hispanic Child Languages: Typical and Impaired Development*. Amsterdam: John Benjamins, pp. 93–116.

Wexler, K. (1994). Optional Infinitives, Head Movement and the Economy of Derivations. In D. Lightfoot and N. Hornstein (eds.), *Verb Movement*. Cambridge: Cambridge University Press, pp. 305–350.

Wexler, K. (2011) Grammatical Computation in the Optional Infinitive Stage. In J. de Villiers and T. Roeper (eds.), *Handbook of Generative Approaches to Language Acquisition*. Dordrecht: Springer, pp. 53–118.

Wexler, K., Gavarró, A., and Torrens, V. (2004). Feature Checking and Object Clitic Omission in Child Catalan. In R. Bok-Bennema, B. Hollebrandse, B. Kampers-Mahne, and P. Sleeman (eds.), *Romance Languages and Linguistic Theory 2002*. Amsterdam and Philadelphia, PA: John Benjamins, pp. 253–268.

29

Theories of Second Language Acquisition

Bill VanPatten

29.1 Introduction

The quest for theory in second language acquisition (SLA) has been filled with debate. From the first instance of a theory of second language acquisition (e.g. Krashen 1982), to discussions of what is needed for a theory (e.g. Gregg 1989; Jordan 2004; Long 1990), to current overviews of theoretical approaches (e.g. VanPatten and Williams 2015), the field of second language acquisition has been unable to unify around a particular theory. Currently, various theoretical approaches vie for the attention of scholars, including generative theory, functional approaches, emergentism and usage-based approaches, sociocultural theory, skill theory, dynamic systems, the Declarative/Procedural Model (D/PM), processability theory – all in seemingly contradictory positions of how best to research and explain second language acquisition. If we consider that the study of acquisition of language is a scientific endeavor (i.e. is part of the language sciences), it is a bit disconcerting to think that unlike some of the disciplines in the natural sciences, second language acquisitionists do not seem to coalesce around some central ideas. To what do we owe this state of affairs?

As I see it, the problem lies in two conflating factors. The first is the nature of language and what acquisitionists claim or assume to be the focus of acquisition. The second has to do with instruction. We will start with the nature of language. Historically, only generative and functional approaches have begun the quest to understand acquisition with a construct of language at the center of their enterprise (e.g. Bardovi-Harlig 2000; Gregg 1989; Slabakova 2016; White 2003). One might also consider Processability Theory to fall into this same camp, given its adoption of Lexical Functional Grammar (e.g. Pienemann 1998). Other approaches have typically begun their quests without the construct of language defined and only recently have some of them adopted a position about the nature of language (e.g. some usage-based approaches adopting construction grammar; see, for example, Ellis and Wulff 2015). In short, the quest for theory has used three different avenues in its enterprise:

- language defined first then acquisition studied (e.g. generative, functional, processability);
- acquisition studied first then language defined (e.g. some usage-based approaches);
- acquisition studied but no definition of language (e.g. skill theory, sociocultural theory).

The end result is discordant approaches to the study of acquisition and "squabbles for turf" because of different approaches (or lack of approaches) to the nature of language. As more than one scholar has put it, it is the "L" of SLA that is the problem. This situation stands in stark contrast to first language acquisition research, in which the phenomenon of language and what it means to acquire language are more clearly staked out (e.g. Berko Gleason and Bernstein Ratner 2016; Lust 2006; Rowland 2014).

The second factor underlying the inability for the field to unify around a singular theory has to do with the extent to which the researcher-theorist is concerned with instructional issues. Second language acquisition occurs both in classroom and non-classroom contexts, and often occurs in mixed environments. But there has been an underlying concern among some researchers – often unstated – for linking theory to instruction. Thus, on the one hand, we have theories such as sociocultural theory and skill acquisition theory that have their roots in the domain of education, while other theories, such as generative theory and functional approaches, do not (see, for example, the collection in VanPatten and Williams 2015). So, another issue underlying the discordant nature of theory development is the extent to which researchers want to "apply" theory to instructional issues. (See Whong *et al.* 2013, for recent attempts to apply generative theory to instructional concerns. And, to be sure, Processability Theory has treated the issue of instruction but from the construct of "constraints on the effects of instruction." See Pienemann 1987.)

With this background in mind, the purpose of this chapter is to discuss three broad questions. These questions are not necessarily new, but it is important for the field to revisit issues from time to time (see, for example, the opening chapters in VanPatten and Williams 2015). The questions are these.

1. What is a theory and what is it supposed to do?
2. What second language phenomena are in need of explanation?
3. Is a single theory possible?

Because the present volume is a volume on Spanish linguistics, I will necessarily focus on the acquisition of Spanish and I will pull toward explaining the acquisition of language. I begin with the first question.

29.2 What is a Theory and What is it Supposed to Do?

In science, a theory is a set of laws or statements set out to explain observed natural phenomena (e.g. Kuhn 1996). As such, the central purpose of a theory is to explain things we see around us. In the theory of evolution, for example, the phenomena in need of explanation are, essentially, two. The first is why species vary within a given related group. Why are some canaries completely yellow but some yellow and black? Why does human skin color vary among various ethnic groups? Why do some people have blue eyes, others brown, and still others green? The second thing evolution attempts to explain is inter-species differentiation. For example, dolphins and humpback whales are both mammalian, live in the oceans and breathe through blowholes, but they are not of the same species. What makes them different and how did they get that way? Evolutionary theory is an attempt to explain things we see in the natural world.

Another related purpose of theories is to provide testable hypotheses. That is, a theory must offer hypotheses that can be researched. These testable hypotheses are critical for evaluation of the theory itself. If the hypothesis is supported by research, then the theory is supported. If sufficient evidence runs counter to the hypothesis, then the theory is questioned and may be refined or replaced. Returning to evolution, two of the fundamental laws of the theory are (i) mutation occurs by chance (at the genetic level) and (ii) natural selection encourages mutations that increase the possibility of reproduction. So, from these two laws we can create a hypothesis that says, "Over successive generations of a species, a particular change that increases survival which in turn increases chances of reproduction (passing along the genetic trait responsible for the mutation) will spread through the population." Traditionally, this hypothesis was "tested" through fossil record and reconstruction. But a decade or so ago the hypothesis was experimentally tested in a study on leg length in lizards. Losos et al. (2006) report the findings of a study in which a new predatory species of lizard, *Leiocephalus carinatus*, was introduced into six Bahamian islands. The prediction was that the introduction of this lizard would force a smaller terrestrial lizard, *Anolis sagrei*, to become arboreal in order to escape predation. As it became arboreal, *A. sagrei*'s legs would become shorter in order to better accommodate its movement along rough tree limbs and branches. One year after the introduction of the new predatory lizard, the researchers compared hind leg lengths on *A. sagrei* to those of a control population on other islands where the predatory lizard was not introduced. As predicted, the lizards moved into tree habitats and after twelve months the researchers found a significant change in hind leg length. The legs indeed became shorter. The results, then, support the hypothesis that in turn adds evidence for the tenets of the theory.

This scientific orientation toward theory contrasts with how the term is often used in popular culture. In many everyday conversations, "theory" is used interchangeably with "hypothesis" or even "guess" or "good idea." In an Agatha Christie novel, Hercule Poirot might say, "I have a theory about the murder." What Poirot means is that he has a good idea or hypothesis about what happened, not a set of laws from which he can conduct an experiment to see if the theory is right. We might hear someone speculating about the actions of another at a faculty meeting and say "I have a theory about that guy." Again, what this colleague means is that she has a good idea about that person's motivation, a possible hypothesis about the cause of his actions. The point here is that hypotheses or "good ideas" are not theories. Hypotheses may be derived from theories (as stated above) but hypotheses in and of themselves are not theories. This is important because some "frameworks" used in second language research are equated with theories when they shouldn't be (e.g. the Noticing Hypothesis, the Interaction Hypothesis). And this discussion brings us to the role of theories in second language research.

In second language acquisition, a theory should do the same as it does in other scientific endeavors. It should (i) provide a set of laws or statements with (ii) the purpose of explaining observed phenomena. And it should provide means by which to test the theory itself through empirical research on hypotheses derived from the theory. We now turn our attention to what needs to be explained in second language research.

29.3 What Second Language Phenomena are in Need of Explanation?

As stated at the outset, one's perspective about what needs to be explained is colored by one's orientation (e.g. linguistic, psychological, educational, social). Because this volume's focus is linguistics, I will take a linguistic orientation, meaning that the phenomena in need of explanation involve the acquisition and use of *formal properties* of language. The reader's attention is drawn to *acquisition* and *use*. Clearly, language acquisition involves both the development of an underlying system and the development of mechanisms that put that system to use in communicative contexts. For the purposes of the present chapter, I will focus on the acquisition of underlying competence or what I have called in other publications *mental representation* (e.g. VanPatten 2013, 2014; VanPatten and Rothman 2014). Mental representation is the implicit, abstract, and complex linguistic system that underlies all language use. I take *use* to mean the *processing of language* that occurs in both comprehension and production. Like its counterpart "mental representation," processing is largely implicit and involves abstract and complex notions.

For illustrative purposes I am going to focus on two well-studied phenomena in Spanish second language acquisition: (i) staged development in the acquisition of the verbs *ser* and *estar*; (ii) acquisition of the null-subject parameter. I will begin with *ser* and *estar*.

29.3.1 *Ser* and *Estar*

Spanish has two verbs roughly equivalent to English 'be': *ser* and *estar*. Most readers of this chapter know that these two verbs are in complementary distribution (e.g. only *ser* can be used to link nominatives with other nominatives as in *Bill es/*está profesor* 'Bill is a professor' and only *estar* can be used as an auxiliary to form progressives as in *Bill está/*es escribiendo* 'Bill is writing'). With adjectives and adjectives derived from past participles, the verbs are not always in complementary distribution (e.g. *Bill es/está gordito* 'Bill is chubby' but *Bill está/*es muerto* 'Bill is dead').

Extensive research has been conducted on the staged development of the acquisition of *ser* and *estar*. First documented in VanPatten (1985, 1987) and then continued by research from others (e.g. Bruhn de Garavito and Valenzuela 2008; Finnemann 1990; Geeslin 2000; Geeslin and Guijarro-Fuentes 2005; Guntermann 1992; Ryan and Lafford 1992), the empirical evidence supports the following broadly-sketched staged development:

Stage 1. No verbs (e.g. *El chico alto* 'The boy tall' = 'The boy is tall'; *El chico triste* 'The boy sad' = 'The boy is sad')

Stage 2. Appearance and "overgeneralization" of *ser* (e.g. *El chico es alto* 'The boy is tall' but *El chico es triste* 'The boy is sad,' *El chico es en la clase* 'The boy is in the classroom,' and *El chico es jugar* 'The boy is playing')

Stage 3. Appearance and acquisition[1] of *estar* with progressive (e.g. *El chico está jugando* 'The boy is playing')

Stage 4. Appearance and acquisition of *estar* with locatives and adjectives (e.g. *El chico está en su cuarto* 'The boy is in his room,' *El chico está perplejo* 'The boy is puzzled')

What we have here is a set of observations about how, overall, the acquisition by second language learners of these verbs in Spanish proceeds over time. The task of theory is to explain these stages, if not also explain why stages would exist to begin with. What theory can do this?

---

[1] I use *acquisition* in this context in juxtaposition to *appearance*. By *appearance* I mean that something is clearly emerging in the learner's system but is far from being under control or having a robust representation in the system. By *acquisition*, I mean that something is largely under control and seems to be robustly represented in the system.

It is not clear to me that a social theory can explain these stages (e.g. Atkinson 2011). Social theories focus on factors such as identity, power relationships, and attitudes, among others, and how these factors affect interactions. When related to acquisition, such theories are useful for understanding the quantity (and perhaps quality) of input that learners receive over time – and possibly how learners respond to that input. There is nothing in the theories that could explain why Stage 3, for example, appears before Stage 4 in the acquisition of *ser* and *estar*. The reason for the inability of social theories to explain these ordered stages goes back to an earlier discussion: social theories tend not to be concerned with the nature of language and with what winds up in learners' heads. In making this observation, I am not saying there is no role for social theories in second language acquisition. My observation is only that such theories can't explain staged development of language itself, and, in the present case, the staged development we see with the acquisition of *ser* and *estar*.

Moving from the social to the neuro-psychological, it is also not clear to me how something like the D/PM explains such stages (e.g. Ullman 2015). The purpose of the D/PM is to account for the roles that declarative memory and procedural memory might play in the acquisition of language. Specifically, declarative memory is predicted to underlie the acquisition of "idiosyncratic" aspects of a language (Ullman 2015:140). These aspects would encompass vocabulary including the phonological shape of words, their meanings, and subcategorization information (e.g. *eat* requires an agent, *die* requires an experiencer). Irregularities in morphology (e.g. *eat* → *ate* and not *eated*) would also be learned through declarative memory. Procedural memory, on the other hand, would underlie the acquisition of "sequences" and "rules" (Ullman 2015:141) and would result in slow and gradual learning. This system is particularly responsive to statistical frequencies and underlies implicit learning. Given these broad parameters, how would the D/PM account for the acquisition of *ser* and *estar*? Ullman himself sidesteps its application to accounting for staged development, and in his list of the observed phenomena from SLA (VanPatten and Williams 2015:9–11), such development does not appear. In short, there is nothing about the distinction between declarative and procedural memory that would help explain the staged acquisition of *ser* and *estar*. At best, the D/PM would say that the acquisition of the "rules" of these verbs' use would occur through procedural memory.

Processability theory is largely a theory about feature unification using Lexical Functional Grammar. Under this theory there is staged development for the emergence of various properties of a given language based on whether or not feature unification is required (e.g. subjects and verbs agreeing, adjectives and nouns agreeing) and syntactic distance (i.e. whether unification happens within or across syntactic phrases and, in the latter case, how many phrases). To my knowledge, processability theory has never been applied to the staged development of *ser* and *estar* and I do not see how it can account for what we have seen in the literature to date. This may surprise some readers familiar with the theory as it has been successful in accounting for a wide range of developmental sequences in a number of languages. As I see it, processability may not be able to account for the staged development of *ser* and *estar* because the stages do not represent the typical problems associated with feature unification and syntactic distance.

Cutting to the chase and avoiding a complete review of all theories and types of theories, it seems that acquisitionists must look to linguistic, psycholinguistic, or cognitive theories to explain staged development. In 2010 I explored how linguistic theory might account for staged development (VanPatten 2010). To understand the explanation, we need to back up for a moment and re-examine the observed stages. Stripped away of the specifics, we see that *ser* is acquired easily (and overused) and that the real acquisition problem for learners is that of *estar* and its properties. The sole exception to problems with *estar* is the not too difficult acquisition of its use in progressive constructions. So, what we have is the early acquisition of *ser* as the main if not sole copular verb but then the acquisition of *estar* as the sole auxiliary verb with progressives. To understand what was happening here I examined current linguistic theory and its account of the nature of the two verbs.[2] In various analyses, *ser* and *estar* have been tied to the aspect feature. Schmitt (2005) has argued that *ser* is a true copula and thus featureless. That is, it does not encode for any aspectual distinctions and has no features related to aspect that must get checked in the syntax. On the other hand, Schmitt claims, *estar* encodes [+perfective], making it more marked and having a functional feature that must get checked somewhere in the syntax. At the same time, it is argued that predicates themselves (adjectives in this case) are also marked for [± perfective]. If an adjective is marked for [–perfective], then it must be used with a copular verb that is unmarked for aspect or marked for [–perfective] as well. If an adjective is marked for [+perfective], then it must be used with a copular verb that is also marked for [+perfective]. In short, the predicates must get their features checked with the copular verbs. *Ser* presents no problem for learners because, under Schmitt's analysis, it has no features that enter into any kind of relationship with another lexical item.

In terms of acquisition, featureless and/or unmarked aspects of language are always easier to acquire than those that encode features and/or are more marked. Masculine gender (unmarked) is always easier than feminine gender (marked); subject relative clauses (unmarked) are always easier than object relative clauses (more marked); and phonological contrasts in syllable initial position (unmarked) are easier than the same contrasts in final position (marked). Thus, *ser* is "easier" than *estar* because the former is featureless and unmarked when it comes to aspect. *Estar*

---

[2] These paragraphs are slightly reworked arguments from VanPatten (2010), especially pp. 34–35.

carries a feature that *ser* does not, thus presenting more of a challenge to learners. It has more linguistic "baggage" than *ser*.

Under a different analysis, Roby (2007) assumes that *ser* is [–perfective] and *estar* is [+perfective]. Both verbs contain aspectual features but their values are different. Under this scenario, *ser* appears earlier than *estar* because of first language (L1) transfer. The English copular verb *be* is featureless (as it is in French, German, and other languages); that is, it carries no aspectual information. Second language (L2) learners of Spanish with an L1 having only one copular verb impute *ser* with the featureless values of their L1 copular verb; that is, they make *ser* behave the way Schmitt claims it behaves because that is the way *be* behaves in English, French, German, and so on. It is only later, when the perfective nature of *estar* is encoded in the grammar, that the grammar also encodes *ser* as [–perfective]. To be sure, it could be the case that for learners' grammars *ser* remains featureless – that the verb is never encoded as [–perfective]. The acquisition results (stages) would still be the same; early acquisition of *ser* with adjectives and its overextension to domains where native speakers would use *estar*.

So, we have one explanation for why learners acquire *ser* before *estar* with adjectives. What about *estar* in progressive structures? Why would learners acquire this use of *estar* before its use with adjectives? Different from its use with adjectives, *estar* with *-ndo* does not represent a copular function. Here, *estar* is an auxiliary and does not compete with *ser* in this function. In short, what the stages of acquisition for these verbs suggest is that learners acquire *ser* as copular verb followed by *estar* as a (featureless) auxiliary. In linguistic theory, copular verbs and auxiliaries are categorically different, and this shows up repeatedly in the acquisition literature. For example, in L1 and L2 morpheme studies (e.g. Brown 1973; Dulay and Burt 1974; Bailey *et al.* 1974), copular *be* is systematically acquired before auxiliary *be*. One explanation for this is that copulas originate in the verb phrase (VP) whereas auxiliaries must be inserted into a tense phrase (TP) (e.g. Hawkins 2001). If learners begin acquisition with the simplest phrase structures possible, then the copular verb would be acquired to carry tense features in languages like English and Spanish before any auxiliary would. In addition, because there are no new features associated with *estar* as auxiliary, the system does not add any complicating feature checks. For this reason, the auxiliary function of *estar* is acquired before its copular function.

In my 2010 essay, I suggested that the stages in the acquisition of the two verbs can be restated as the following to reflect how linguistic theory might account for their acquisition (VanPatten 2010:35):

Stage 1. No copular/auxiliary verb
Stage 2. Acquisition of copular verb (*ser*) to carry tense and agreement features (probably featureless in terms of aspect)

Stage 3. Acquisition of auxiliary verb (*estar*)
Stage 4. Acquisition of aspect as new copula feature

In short, under current theory, staged development of *ser* and *estar* is ultimately tied to associating verbs with particular features and categories (i.e. copular/auxiliary). However, we cannot ignore some statistical facts about *ser* and *estar* that push us to examine the role of usage-based theories in their acquisition.[3] The first is that *ser* is far more frequent in the input than *estar* (VanPatten 1987). This fact might lead us to consider this as a major factor in why *ser* is chosen as a copular verb first. What is not clear is that *estar* used as an auxiliary in progressive structures is more frequent than its use as a copular verb – but let's assume this is true. Then usage-based accounts could account for two major stages of acquisition of *ser* and *estar* in Spanish. (I am ignoring here individual frequencies for very particular uses of *ser* and *estar* that might shape the stages at the micro-level.) For usage-based theories to account for all of the stages we see in the acquisition of these verbs, we would have to demonstrate that *ser* is more frequent with adjectives than *estar*. This is certainly possible, and if it is true, then which approach offers a better explanation for acquisition? The only way to answer this question is to examine the acquisition of a variety of phenomena other than *ser* and *estar* to see which account holds up best. I now turn my attention to null subject phenomena.

29.3.2 Null and Overt Subjects

As the reader likely knows, Spanish licenses null subjects in simple declarative sentences.[4]

(29.1) ¿Escribe Bill mucho? Sí, cuando *pro* puede.
'Does Bill write a lot? Yes, when he can.'

(29.2) ¿Por qué *pro* quieres leer esto?
'Why do you want to read this?'

At the same time, null subjects are required when there is no antecedent.

(29.3) Está nevando/*Ello está nevando.[5]
'It's snowing.'

(29.4) Es la una/*Ello es la una.
'It's one o'clock.'

---

[3] I do not wish to reduce usage-based accounts to mere statistical tallying. However, such tallying is a fundamental component of usage-based accounts, which is why I focus on frequency here (e.g. Ellis and Wulff 2015).

[4] I am basing these paragraphs on another publication of mine (VanPatten 2014). For discussion of the various properties related to null subjects and the null subject parameter, in addition to the citations in this section see Liceras et al. (1998); Rothman and Iverson (2007); Holmberg (2010); among others.

[5] I am excluding here certain Caribbean dialects of Spanish, principally located in the Dominican Republic, which are showing signs of movement toward non-null subject status (see Toribio 2000).

(29.5)   Es probable que ... /*Ello es probable que ...
         'It's probable that ... '

(29.6)   ¿Hay razón para esto? ¿*Allí hay razón para esto?
         'Is there a reason for this?'

(29.7)   ¡Me robaron!/*¡Ellos me robaron!
         'I was robbed!/They robbed me!' ("they" refers to an unknown person or persons)

In addition, because of the Overt Pronoun Constraint (OPC), overt subject pronouns cannot take quantified and negative antecedents (e.g. Montalbetti 1984).

(29.8)   a. Cada profesor$_i$ piensa que $pro_{i/j}$ es muy inteligente.
         b. Cada profesor$_i$ piensa que él$_{*i/j}$ es muy inteligente.
            'Each professor thinks he is very intelligent.'
         c. El profesor$_i$ piensa que $pro_{i/j}$ es muy inteligente.
         d. El profesor$_i$ piensa que él $_{i/j}$ es muy inteligente.
            'The professor thinks he is very intelligent.'

Tied to null subjects is verbal morphology. Spanish has rich person-number morphology; that is, there are unique verbal inflections for all combinations of person and number allowing for the semantic information contained in subject pronouns to be recovered by verbal inflections when these pronouns are null. The exception occurs with first-person singular and third-person singular in limited situations (e.g. imperfect morphology, subjunctive morphology). These facts have led some theorists to posit a relationship between underlying knowledge of null subjects and knowledge of person-number inflections on verbs.

So far, we have described only the purely syntactic aspects of null and overt subjects. In terms of use, the distribution of null and overt subjects is governed by discourse factors, namely topic shift. While both null and overt subject pronouns are syntactically licit in (29.9), the overt subject sounds odd as there is no topic shift.

(29.9)   ¿Qué escribió Bill? pro/Él escribió este capítulo.
         'What did Bill write? He wrote this chapter.'

Finally, there is evidence that speakers of Spanish prefer the subject of a previous clause as the antecedent for a null subject while not having a strong preference of antecedence for overt subjects.

(29.10) Juan vio a Carlos mientras pro/él caminaba en la playa.
         'Juan saw Carlos while he was walking on the beach.'

In our research (Jegerski et al. 2011), for example, when we asked native speakers, "Who was walking on the beach, Juan or Carlos?" they demonstrated about a 70 percent response rate selecting Juan when the second clause contained a pro. However, the response rate was at around 50 percent with overt subject pronouns (see also Alonso Ovalle et al. 2002).

Given the above description of null and overt subjects in Spanish, what follows is a brief summary of their acquisition (see also White 2016).

1. Learners do not have problems grasping the null-subjectness of Spanish. Very early on they accept sentences with null subjects (e.g. Liceras 1989; Rothman and Iverson 2007). They also tend to reject sentences with overt subject pronouns where null subjects are required (e.g. Liceras 1989).
2. Once learners have determined that Spanish is a null-subject language, they show evidence of knowledge of the OPC (e.g. Pérez-Leroux and Glass 1999).
3. L2 learners of Spanish often violate the discourse and pragmatic conventions governing the distribution of subject pronouns in both production and non-production tasks (e.g. Liceras 1989; Lubbers Quesada and Blackwell 2009).
4. There appears to be very late acquisition – and, for some learners, no acquisition – of native-like interpretation strategies for Sentence 29.10. Very advanced L2 learners of Spanish may overwhelmingly link both null and overt subject pronouns with the subject of the previous clause, behaving distinctly from how native speakers link null and overt subject pronouns to previous antecedents (e.g. Jegerski et al. 2011).
5. L2 learners of Spanish seem to have null subject grammars even when their productive abilities with verbal inflections for person-number is far from under control (e.g. Liceras et al. 1998). Indeed, the building up in the mental lexicon of person-number as part of verbal structure may lag far behind the syntax associated with such inflections (e.g. VanPatten et al. 2012).

How do we account for the observed phenomena listed in 1–5 above? Again, social and socio-cultural theories cannot explain these observations for the same reasons they cannot explain the staged development of *ser* and *estar*. Likewise, something like the Declarative/Procedural Model cannot explain the facts surrounding the acquisition of null-subject related aspects of Spanish. The model does not have constructs that deal specifically with language. We can also rule out Processability Theory accounting for the observations. It is difficult to see how feature unification and syntactic distance account for something like why learners quickly reject overt subjects where they should be rejected or how learners come to demonstrate OPC effects.

As the reader may guess, current linguistic theory offers greater explanatory capacity with the acquisition of the phenomena described above. Under the theory, universal grammar (UG) permits null subjects as an option. Thus, the acquisition of *pro* as an underlying option should not be problematic for the learner. What is more, null subject sentences are abundant in the input. (However, as we will see, linguistic theory has little to say about input processing.) In addition, an approach to acquisition guided by linguistic theory would also claim that the learner's internal grammar is constrained by UG. A consequence is that, once the L2 grammar has been set as null-subject, the OPC is instantiated – constraining the co-indexing of overt subjects. Also, once the internal mechanisms have determined that Spanish is a null-subject language, the derived property that requires null subjects when there is no antecedent is triggered (i.e. learners would reject sentences with an overt subject pronoun where one is barred). That is, learners do not have to learn this aspect of the grammar because it follows from the nature of null versus overt subject pronouns as governed by UG.

In spite of these explanations, linguistic theory has little or nothing to say about how learners actually come to know that Spanish is a null-subject language. It is one thing to have UG license null subjects in an L2 grammar, but it is another to explain how learners process null subjects in the input so that UG can inform the grammar that Spanish is null subject. What is needed is a theory of input processing that can mediate between "input out there" and the "internal mechanisms" that push the organization of language in particular directions. In the case of null subjects, what is required is a parser that somehow "notes" a subjectless verb and under what circumstances. This information is then delivered to the internal mechanisms that subsequently use the data to determine whether the language being learned is null-subject or not. Currently, work on L2 parsing related to acquisition is minimal and no theory of L2 parsing exists (note that input processing is not a full theory of parsing – see VanPatten 2015 – nor is the Shallow Structure Hypothesis as advanced by Clahsen and Felser 2006). Such a theory would have to link parsing to theta grids of verbs and the Extended Projection Principle, for example, such that learners would have expectations about some kind of nominal having to occupy Spec,TP (specifier position of TP) in a sentence for it to be licit. The parser would have to deliver a null position in Spec,TP as part of its computation, which would then be "calculated" by the internal mechanism as evidence that the language being parsed is null subject.

But what of the distribution of null and overt subject pronouns and its relationship to topic shift? Because the discourse/pragmatic aspects of null and overt subject alternation fall outside of the scope of the syntax proper, generative theory cannot address the difficulty learners face in acquiring these aspects of usage. The reader will recall that the preference of native speakers to link null subjects with previous syntactic subjects but not with overt subjects is just that: a preference. It is not a hard and fast constraint or rule (i.e. the rate of preference is about 70 percent). In addition, the use of overt subjects with topic shifting is also not such a hard and fast "rule" (i.e. the rate of preference is about 50 percent). Thus, it would appear that non-OPC antecedent preference might be related to something like frequency. That is, the more learners have success with interpreting null subjects as referring to previous subjects, and overt subjects as not doing so, will increase the likelihood of the kind of interpretation behaviors we see in the research. This sounds very much like a usage-based explanation. So, it could be that, in SLA, some aspects of acquisition are best accounted for by linguistic theory while others are accounted for by usage-based approaches.

29.4 Is a Single Theory Possible?

The preceding discussion suggests that a single theory to account for SLA may not be possible and that the proliferation of theories may be reflective of (again) scholars simply being interested in different things. When it comes to formal properties of language, some things are best accounted for by generative theory – especially those aspects of the grammar that could not be learned through input. Here I am referring to the well-known Poverty of the Stimulus (POS) situation. We saw this with null subjects. At least two aspects of null subject grammars are grasped by learners early on: (i) the OPC and (ii) the requirement that overt pronouns have antecedents – which is why they are barred in Examples 29.3 through 29.7 above. This information is not available in the input and thus cannot be accounted for by usage-based theories. On the other hand, both null and overt subjects as well as their distributional properties are evidenced in the input and do not present a POS situation. Not only is something like UG not necessary for the learner to pick up the null-subjectness of a language (i.e. subjectless sentences are readily available in the input), it is not a mechanism that can account for the distributional properties of subject pronouns in the language. Thus, some kind of usage-based theory is needed for us to understand the full range of "behaviors" of the learner's null subject grammar. In short, theories that have historically been seen as competitive for explanatory power may not be mutually exclusive, a point underscored in Rothman and VanPatten (2013).

So far, I have painted a somewhat rosy picture of second language acquisition as though every L2 learner creates and uses a grammar resembling that of a native speaker. We know this not to be true; non-nativeness is the norm and learners fall on a continuum of how non-native they are. Some parts of the grammar seem to be more difficult to acquire than others (e.g. distributional properties of null and overt subjects, the complete range of uses of *estar* with adjectives). There is argument about the "why" of non-nativeness. From my perspective, something like the critical period hypothesis is suspect as having explanatory power for a variety of reasons explored by others (e.g. Herschensohn 2007). More promising is the L1 and how it interacts with processing. Although almost all theories used in L2 research discuss the role of the L1 in some way (e.g. VanPatten and Williams 2015), only usage-based accounts seem to incorporate the L1 directly into a learning device. The L1 may inhibit the accurate processing of surface features in the input, in a mechanism called "blocking." If such surface features are not processed adequately or correctly, then the internal mechanisms responsible for creating the grammar receive "faulty" data. In contrast, linguistic theory is not a theory of learning and thus the role of the L1 is always *ad hoc* to the theory itself. Other theories discount a role for the L1 (e.g. Processability Theory). This does not mean, however, that usage-based theories alone can account for non-nativeness, as such theories cannot predict which parts of the grammar will prove to be difficult and which will not due to the role of the L1. It seems, again, that more than one theory is needed to fully articulate the role of the L1 in second language acquisition and to make testable predictions about which parts of language are susceptible to non-nativeness.

Just to be sure, I add here that non-linguistic theories will be necessary for a complete picture of SLA because linguistic and cognitively oriented theories do not attempt to explain such things as individual differences, access to input, how interaction occurs, and other factors affecting development. I have limited my discussion in this chapter to specific formal properties of language to narrow the discussion, given the focus of the present volume. However, it is fair to ask whether second language acquisition is a strictly linguistic phenomenon. Likewise it is fair to ask if it is a psychological-cognitive phenomenon, or an educational phenomenon, or a social phenomenon. In a sense, to fully account for second language acquisition is like trying to fully account for disease. In the case of medical research, disease is nutritional, it is environmental, it is genetic-cellular, and it is behavioral. That is, all of these factors come to bear in trying to understand how diseases originate, spread, and are cured. It is possible that second language acquisition is linguistic, psychological-cognitive, social, and educational all at once. Yet, the researcher has to focus on something. Regarding diseases, one medical expert may focus on nutrition. Another may have a specialty in genetics. Another in environmental factors. So it is in second language acquisition. One may focus on the linguistics of acquisition. One may focus on the cognitive-psychological. And so on. In this chapter I chose to focus on the linguistic. In a volume on the social context of language, a scholar might focus on something different.

29.5 Conclusion

In this chapter, I began with the difficulty for L2 research to coalesce around a singular theory. I argued that much of this has to do with the way scholars define language (or ignore its definition) and what perspectives color their approach to acquisition: linguistic, cognitive, educational, social. I also outlined what theories are supposed to do: namely, explain observed phenomena. For the purpose of the present volume, I chose some well-documented observed acquisitional sequences in Spanish L2 to examine how a theory might account for them. Finally, I touched upon the idea that, in the end, multiple theories may be necessary to account for the sequences observed in this chapter. In addition, multiple theories might be necessary to account for the totality of things observed in second language acquisition.

This brings us to a point we made in the preface to our book on theories (VanPatten and Williams 2015:ix–x). The point concerns the old story (parable) about the four blind Brahmin who chance upon an elephant for the first time. One grabs the elephant's tail and, because he can't see, says, "Oh. The elephant is like a rope!" Another grabs hold of the elephant's trunk and likewise sightless says, "Oh. The elephant is like a snake!" The third puts his arms around the mighty leg of the pachyderm and says, "Oh. The elephant is like a tree!" And the fourth, groping along the massive side of the elephant says, "Oh. The elephant is like a wall!" The point of the story is that SLA is, in some respects, an elephant, and different theories grab on to different parts in an attempt to explain that particular part. The problem is that if the researcher tries to extend his or her explanation beyond that part, the effort is doomed to fail. The generative linguist can no more explain the role of frequency than the usage-based person can explain the POS situation. The processability person can no more explain interaction and the impact of identity on interaction than the social-identity person can explain staged behavior in the acquisition of negation. But we are not blind as researchers. We can see beyond what our own hands can touch. Rather than argue that one theory is right and one theory is wrong, we need to simply say, "This, and only this, is what I can explain for now."

References

Alonso Ovalle, L., Fernández-Solera, S., Frazier, L., and Clifton, C. (2002). Null vs. Overt Pronouns and the Topic-Focus Articulation in Spanish. *Rivista di Linguistica*, 14 (2), 151–169.

Atkinson, D. (ed.). (2011). *Alternative Approaches to Second Language Acquisition*. New York: Routledge.

Bailey, N., Madden, C., and Krashen, S. D. (1974). Is There a "Natural Sequence" in Adult Second Language Learning? *Language Learning*, 4 (2), 235–243.

Bardovi-Harlig, K. (2000). *Tense and Aspect in Second Language Acquisition: Form, Meaning, and Use*. Oxford: Blackwell.

Berko Gleason, J. and Bernstein Ratner, N. (2016). *The Development of Language* (9th edn). Boston, MA: Pearson.

Brown, R. (1973). *A First Language: The Early Stages*. Cambridge, MA: Harvard University Press.

Bruhn de Garavito, J. and Valenzuela, E. (2008). Eventive and Stative Passives in Spanish: A Matter of Aspect. *Bilingualism: Language and Cognition*, 11 (3), 323–36.

Clahsen, H. and Felser, C. (2006). Grammatical Processing in Language Learners. *Applied Psycholinguistics*, 27 (1), 3–42.

Dulay, H. and Burt, M. (1974). Natural Sequences in Child Second Language Acquisition. *Language Learning*, 24 (1), 37–53.

Ellis, N. C. and Wulff, S. (2015). Usaged-Based Approaches to SLA. In B. VanPatten and J. Williams (eds.), *Theories in Second Language Acquisition* (2nd edn). New York: Routledge, pp. 75–93.

Finnemann, M. D. (1990). Markedness and Learner Strategy: Form- and Meaning-Oriented Learners in the Foreign Language Context. *The Modern Language Journal*, 74 (2), 176–187.

Geeslin, K. L. (2000). A New Approach to the Second Language Acquisition of Copula Choice in Spanish. In R. P. Leow and C. Sanz (eds.), *Spanish Applied Linguistics at the Turn of the Millennium: Papers from the 1999 Conference on the L1 and L2 Acquisition of Spanish and Portuguese*. Somerville, MA: Cascadilla, pp. 50–66.

Geeslin, K. L. and Guijarro-Fuentes, P. (2005). The Acquisition of Copula Choice in Instructed Spanish: The Role of Individual Characteristics. In D. Eddington (ed.), *Selected Proceedings of the 6th Conference on the Acquisition of Spanish and Portuguese as First and Second Languages*. Somerville, MA: Cascadilla, pp. 66–77.

Gregg, K. R. (1989). Second Language Acquisition Theory: The Case for a Generative Perspective. In S. M. Gass and J. Schachter (eds.), *Linguistic Perspectives on Second Language Acquisition*. Cambridge: Cambridge University Press, pp. 15–40.

Guntermann, G. (1992). An Analysis of Interlanguage Development over Time: Part II, *ser* and *estar*. *Hispania*, 75 (5), 1294–1303.

Hawkins, R. (2001). *Second Language Syntax: A Generative Introduction*. Oxford: Blackwell.

Herschensohn, J. (2007). *Language Development and Age*. Cambridge: Cambridge University Press.

Holmberg, A. (2010). Null Subject Parameters. In T. Biberauer, A. Holmberg, I. Roberts, and M. Sheehan (eds.), *Parametric Variation*. Cambridge: Cambridge University Press, pp. 88–124.

Jegerski, J., VanPatten, B., and Keating, G. D. (2011). Who Was Walking on the Beach? Anaphora Resolution in Spanish Heritage Speakers and Adult Second Language Learners. *Studies in Second Language Acquisition*, 33 (2), 193–221.

Jordan, G. (2004). *Theory Construction in Second Language Acquisition*. Amsterdam: John Benjamins.

Krashen, S. D. (1982). *Principles and Practice in Second Language Acquisition*. New York: Pergamon.

Kuhn, T. S. (1996). *The Structure of Scientific Revolutions*. Chicago: The University of Chicago Press.

Liceras, J. M. (1989). On Some Properties of the "Pro-Drop" Parameter: Looking for Missing Subjects in Non-Native Spanish. In S. M. Gass and J. Schachter (eds.), *Linguistic Perspectives on Second Language Acquisition*. Cambridge: Cambridge University Press, pp. 109–133.

Liceras, J. M., Díaz, L., and Mawell, D. (1998). Null Arguments in Non-Native Grammars: The Spanish L2 of Chinese, English, French, German, Japanese and Korean Speakers. In E. Klein and G. Martohardjono (eds.), *The Development of Second Language Grammar: A Generative Approach*. Amsterdam: John Benjamins, pp. 113–149.

Long, M. H. (1990). The Least a Second Language Acquisition Theory Needs to Explain. *TESOL Quarterly*, 24 (4), 649–666.

Losos, J. B., Schoener, T. W., Langerhans, B., and Spiller, D. A. (2006). Rapid Temporal Reversal in Predator-Driven Natural Selection. *Science*, 314 (Nov.), 1111.

Lubbers Quesada, M. and Blackwell, S. E. (2009). The L2 Acquisition of Null and Overt Spanish Subject Pronouns: A Pragmatic Approach. In J. Collentine, M. García, B. Lafford, and F. Marcos Marín (eds.), *Selected Proceedings of the 11th Hispanic Linguistics Symposium*. Somerville, MA: Cascadilla, pp. 117–130.

Lust, B. (2006). *Child Language: Acquisition and Growth*. Cambridge: Cambridge University Press.

Montalbetti, Mario, M. (1984). After Binding. On the Interpretation of Pronouns (Doctoral dissertation). MIT.

Pérez-Leroux, A. T. and Glass, W. R. (1999). Null Anaphora in Spanish Second Language Acquisition: Probabilistic versus Generative Approaches. *Second Language Research*, 15 (2), 220–249.

Pienemann, M. (1987). Psychological Constraints on the Teachability of Languages. In C. Pfaff (ed.), *First and Second Language Acquisition Processes*. Rowley, MA: Newbury House, pp. 143–168.

Pienemann, M. (1998). *Language Processing and Second Language Development: Processability Theory*. Amsterdam: John Benjamins.

Roby, D. B. (2007). Aspect and the Categorization of States: The Case of ser and estar in Spanish (Doctoral dissertation). University of Texas at Austin.

Rothman, J. and Iverson, M. (2007). On Parameter Clustering and Resetting the Null-Subject Parameter in L2 Spanish: Implications and Observations. *Hispania*, 90 (2), 328–341.

Rothman, J. and VanPatten, B. (2013). On Multiplicity and Mutual Exclusivity: The Case for Different SLA Theories. In M. del P. García-Mayo, M. Junkal Gutiérrez-Mangado, and M. Martínez Adrián (eds.), *Contemporary Approaches to Second Language Acquisition*. Amsterdam: John Benjamins, pp. 243–256.

Rowland, C. (2014). *Understanding Child Language Acquisition*. New York: Routledge.

Ryan, J. and Lafford, B. (1992). The Acquisition of Lexical Meaning in a Study Abroad Environment. *Hispania*, 75 (3), 714–22.

Schmitt, C. (2005). Semi-Copulas: Event and Aspectual Composition. In P. Kempchinsky and R. Slabakova (eds.), *Syntax, Semantics and the Acquisition of Aspect*. New York: Springer, pp. 121–145.

Slabakova, R. (2016). *Second Language Acquisition*. Oxford: Oxford University Press.

Toribio, J. (2000). Setting Parametric Limits on Dialectal Variation in Spanish. *Lingua*, 10, 315–341.

Ullman, M. T. (2015). The Declarative/Procedural Model: A Neurobiologically Motivated Theory for First and Second Language. In B. VanPatten and J. Williams (eds.), *Theories in Second Language Acquisition* (2nd edn). New York: Routledge, pp. 135–158.

VanPatten, B. (1987). Classroom Learners' Acquisition of *ser* and *estar*: Accounting for the Data. In B. VanPatten, T. R. Dvorak, and J. F. Lee (eds.), *Foreign Language Learning: A Research Perspective*. Cambridge, MA: Newbury House, pp. 61–76.

VanPatten, B. (2010). Some Verbs are More Perfect than Others: Why Learners have Difficulty with *ser* and *estar* and What it Means for Instruction. *Hispania*, 93 (1), 29–38.

VanPatten, B. (2013). Mental Representation and Skill in Instructed SLA. In J. Schwieter (ed.), *Innovations in SLA, Bilingualism, and Cognition: Research and Practice*. Amsterdam: John Benjamins, pp. 3–22.

VanPatten, B. (2014). On the Limits of instruction: 40 Years after "Interlanguage." In Z.-H. Han and E. Tarone (eds.), *Interlanguage: 40 Years Later*. Amsterdam: John Benjamins, pp. 105–126.

VanPatten, B. (2015). Input Processing in Adult SLA. In B. VanPatten and J. Williams (eds.), *Theories in Second Language Acquisition* (2nd edn). New York: Routledge, pp. 111–134.

VanPatten, Bill. (1985). The Acquisition of *ser* and *estar* by Adult Learners of Spanish: A Preliminary Investigation of Transitional Stages of Competence. *Hispania*, 68 (2), 399–406.

VanPatten, B., Keating, G. D., and Leeser, M. J. (2012). Missing Verbal Inflections as a Representational Problem: Evidence from Self-Paced Reading. *Linguistic Approaches to Bilingualism*, 2 (2), 109–140.

VanPatten, B. and Rothman, J. (2014). Against "Rules." In A. Benati, C. Laval, and M. J. Arche (eds.), *The Grammar Dimension in Instructed Second Language Acquisition: Theory, Research, and Practice*. London: Bloomsbury, pp. 15–35.

VanPatten, B. and Williams, J. (eds.). (2015). *Theories in Second Language Acquisition* (2nd edn). New York: Routledge.

White, L. (2003). *Second Language Acquisition and Universal Grammar*. Cambridge: Cambridge University Press.

White, L. (2016). Prodrop then and now: Changing Perspectives on Null Subjects in Second Language Acquisition. In A. Alba de la Fuente, E. Valenzuela, and C. Martínez-Sanz (eds.), *Language Acquisition beyond Parameters: Studies in Honour of Juana M. Liceras*. Amsterdam: John Benjamins, pp. 17–35.

Whong, M., Gil, K-H., and Marsden, H. (2013). *Universal Grammar and the Second Language Classroom*. Dordrecht: Springer.

30

The Acquisition of Second Language Spanish Sounds

Megan Solon

30.1 Introduction

As a field or area of empirical interest, the second language (L2) acquisition of sounds has garnered relatively less attention than research on the acquisition of other aspects of the L2 linguistic system, such as morphosyntax. Nevertheless, a "conspicuous growth of interest in L2 phonology" (Ellis 2008:103) has been witnessed in recent decades. Today, primarily guided by models such as the Perceptual Assimilation Model (PAM, Best 1995), the PAM-L2 (Best and Tyler 2007), and the Speech Learning Model (SLM, Flege 1995), empirical efforts to account for the acquisition of L2 sounds are aimed at testing hypotheses regarding learners' perceptual and productive capacities based on the existence and similarity of categories in the first and new language, how these abilities and systems may develop over time or with greater experience, and how this development may be influenced by various linguistic and extralinguistic factors. Nevertheless, as will be illustrated occasionally in what follows, these models do not model all aspects of L2 sound acquisition, as they cannot fully account for phenomena such as the acquisition of allophones and phonetic detail, suprasegmental acquisition, or the acquisition of variable features. Although our knowledge of the acquisition process of L2 Spanish phonetics and phonology has increased greatly in recent years, there remains much work to be done. The following sections assess some of the key constructs, issues, and debates guiding current research (Section 30.2) and review some central empirical findings within this subfield (Section 30.3) before discussing important future directions for research into the acquisition of Spanish sounds (Section 30.4).

30.2 Key Constructs, Debates, Issues, and Assumptions

Research on the acquisition of sounds must contend with and define what it means to "know" or "acquire" a sound and how that knowledge or acquisition can be measured. For instance, research on L2 speech perception can test learners' ability to discriminate particular sounds or can examine how learners categorize sounds they hear. Whereas the former provides information about whether learners can hear a particular distinction, the latter involves categorical distinctions and whether learners map variable sounds to the same or different phonemes. Both types of information are important in discovering and describing L2 sound systems, but their distinction is also very important, methodologically and empirically, as they describe and account for different types of abilities and are of distinct systematic import. Research into the L2 production of Spanish sounds has generally operationalized development as the production of L2 phones with characteristics that (increasingly) approximate the properties of the same phones as produced by native speakers of the target language. For instance, the production of word-initial voiceless stops /p t k / has most frequently been measured in relation to voice onset time (VOT) or the time between the burst at the release of the occlusion of the stop and the onset of voicing of the following vowel. Thus, acquisition of these phones has been operationalized as producing /p t k/ with VOT values within or closer to native speaker ranges. These types of analyses and operationalizations have their strengths in the fact that production and development can be precisely quantified, tracked, and subsequently analyzed statistically in relation to learner characteristics and contextual factors and in comparison to native speakers. These methods, though, are not without their limitations. First, they define accurate production in a restricted fashion – as, for example, VOT measures – without taking into account other potentially relevant production characteristics. Additionally, and perhaps more problematic, they generally impose native speaker values as the assumed target (and judge acquisition in terms of nativelikeness or targetlikeness) without considering whether to sound like *x* native speaker is actually the goal of the group of learners examined (an issue we will return to in the final section of this chapter).

Another important consideration for production studies, however, is that of the listener. Derwing and Munro (2015) argue that research using listener ratings is essential to understanding how learner speech is perceived; although research using acoustic measures can tell us about specific and precise modifications to production patterns, without incorporating listener-raters, we lack information about how those modifications are perceived during communication. Research on the acquisition of Spanish sounds would do well to incorporate more consideration of central listener-oriented components of pronunciation such as comprehensibility (or a listener's difficulty in understanding), intelligibility (or the degree of agreement between the intended message and what the listener understood), and foreign accent (i.e. pronunciation patterns perceived to indicate a speaker's belonging to a different speech community) (Derwing and Munro 2015). As we will see in the following sections, exciting new research has begun to combine precise acoustic-phonetic measurement techniques with listener ratings in innovative ways that allow us to begin to understand which phonetic changes affect how learner speech is perceived, which of these changes learners themselves perceive, and whether or not different types of listeners (e.g. native speakers vs. learners) perceive such changes in the same way. In the following section, we review recent scholarly research on the acquisition of L2 Spanish sounds to gain a glimpse of what is known about the acquisition process and what remains to be learned.

30.3 Recent Findings and Current Scholarly Research

This section focuses on research that has investigated the acquisition of Spanish sounds by adult learners of Spanish. This review focuses primarily on native English-speaking classroom learners in the United States, although it should be noted that research on the acquisition of Spanish sounds by learners from other first language (L1) groups (e.g. Escudero and Boersma 2002, for L1 Dutch learners of Spanish; Carranza 2008, for L1 Japanese; and Long 2016, for L1 Korean, to name just a few) and in other contexts also exists.

30.3.1 Acquisition of Spanish Vowels

Spanish possesses a five-vowel system comprised of pure monophthongs /i e a o u/ (Hualde 2005). General American English, in contrast, is often described as having 11–14 vowels (e.g. Bradlow 1995; Ladefoged 2006). Although several of the vocalic phonemes that comprise the Spanish system are also present in the English system (i.e. /i e o u/), none of the Spanish vowels is exactly like any of the English vowels (Hualde 2005). English speakers learning Spanish, then, have to reorganize their vowel systems, learning to make fewer distinctions in their L2 than in their L1. Additionally, targetlike production of Spanish vowels by L1 English learners requires the adjustment of the phonetic properties of phonemes they already possess (e.g. producing the Spanishlike higher /i/ or more posterior /u/) and the elimination of Englishlike diphthongs. Research on the production of Spanish vowels by English-speaking learners has primarily focused on vowel quality, typically measured acoustically via formants. The first formant (F1) has been used to index vowel height, whereas the second formant (F2) provides information on the position of the vowel production along a horizontal (i.e. front–back) dimension. Research has also examined duration, given that, in comparison to English vowels, Spanish vowels are typically shorter and have less tendency to diphthongize. Additionally, research has employed both of these cues (formants and duration) to examine the role of stress in L2 Spanish vowel production, given that Spanish is not thought to exhibit unstressed vowel reduction and centralization as does English.

Menke and Face (2010), for instance, found that their 60 native English-speaking learners of Spanish produced vowels with more targetlike formant values as learner level increased. Specifically, whereas fourth-semester learners' vowel productions differed significantly from those of native Spanish speakers on most measures for most vowels, graduating majors (final-year undergraduates) and Ph.D. students produced vowels that were largely similar to those of native speakers, although some differences did persist even at these advanced levels (e.g. /o/ with significantly lower F1s indicating productions were higher in the oral cavity and /u/ with significantly higher F2 values indicating a more fronted /u/). Menke and Face also examined the influence of stress on L2 vowel production, exploring whether L2 learners exhibited centralization of unstressed vowels as compared to stressed vowels. Interestingly, they found that even their six native Spanish speakers exhibited some (minimal) centralization. All three learner groups exhibited greater and more widespread centralization in unstressed than in stressed vowels, with significant differences being found between stressed and unstressed /e/, /a/, and /u/ along the F2 (front–back) dimension for all three groups and additionally for /i/ for the graduating majors and Ph.D. students.

Cobb and Simonet (2015) further explored the question of the role of stress in their cross-sectional study of five intermediate and five advanced learners of Spanish, along with five native speakers. Although they found differences in vowel production between vowels and participant groups, the case of /u/ was "clearly different" from the other vowels: Along the F1 (height) dimension, unstressed /u/ had a significantly higher value – that is, was produced lower in the vowel space – than stressed /u/ across speaker groups. Along the F2 dimension, all three groups produced a significantly more fronted /u/ in unstressed position than in stressed position. Nevertheless, overall, whereas the intermediate learners produced very fronted /u/, advanced learners and native speakers produced back /u/s (with the advanced learners' /u/s being even further back than the native speakers').

Finally, Díaz and Simonet (2015) examined the acquisition of the Spanish pronunciation contrast between /e/, as in *pena* 'pity,' and /ei/, as in *peina* 'comb.3sg.' The L2 Spanish of native English speakers was expected to exhibit some differences from native Spanish in the realization of these two sounds, especially given differences between native English and Spanish mid front vowels: The English phonological system includes the mid front phoneme /ɛ/ (e.g. *let*) as well as the mid to high front diphthong /eɪ/ (e.g. *late*), both of which are similar to but differ from Spanish /e/ and /ei/. Using a delayed repetition technique (to avoid possible effects of orthography) and F1 and F2 measurements taken at three time points during the production of the vowel (25, 50, and 75 percent), these authors quantified vowel production as it unfolds over time. Results suggested that, whereas productions of Spanish /e/ were similar for both learner groups and Spanish native speakers, productions of /ei/ differed: Native speakers and advanced learners' formant movements suggested highly diphthongal productions; intermediate learners' productions exhibited less movement. Thus, phonetic development is seen in early acquisition of the monophthongal quality of /e/ and, later, the ability to produce the formant movement necessary for the diphthong /ei/. This innovative approach to quantifying vowel production as it unfolds in time allows for the investigation of complex contrasts and relationships in the L2 phonetic/phonological system.

Research has also explored the role of factors such as context of learning in the development of L2 Spanish vowel pronunciation. Stevens (2011), for example, found that learners who spent four weeks abroad produced vowels with significantly shorter (i.e. more nativelike) durations at the end (Time 2) than at the beginning (Time 1) of the program. A comparable group of learners who studied during the same semester in the at-home environment and produced statistically equivalent vowel durations at Time 1 showed no change in vowel duration patterns. Menke (2010) explored vowel productions of first-, third-, fifth-, and seventh-grade[1] L2 learners of Spanish enrolled in one of two types of immersion groups: one-way (i.e. foreign language) or two-way (i.e. bilingual). She found that vowel productions of the two-way immersion learners became more nativelike as grade level increased, whereas the vowel productions of the one-way immersion learners did not. She attributed at least some of this difference to the context of learning and to the fact that the primary difference between the programs was the amount of contact with native Spanish speakers.

Less research has been performed on the perception of Spanish vowels by L2 learners than on L2 vowel production; nevertheless, studies in this vein have pointed to relatively high accuracy in identification and categorization. For example, García Bayonas (2007) showed that English-speaking L2 learners of Spanish identified Spanish vowels with greater accuracy than L2 learners of English identified English vowels. Gordon (2008) examined the role of the L1 (English) vowel inventory in the perception of L2 (Spanish) vowels and found that learner participants at all levels (beginning, intermediate, and advanced) mapped single L2 vowel categories to more than one L1 vowel category, suggesting influence of English's larger

---

[1] In the US, first grade corresponds roughly to age 6–7, third grade to age 8–9, fifth grade to age 10–11, and seventh grade to age 12–13.

inventory. As previously mentioned, research also exists on the perception of Spanish vowels by Dutch learners; Escudero and Boersma (2002) showed that, although Dutch learners (whose L1, like English, has a larger vowel inventory than Spanish) experienced few difficulties in perceiving Spanish vowels, they had more challenges identifying Spanish /i/ and /e/ than Spanish /u/ and /o/, due perhaps to the fact that Dutch has three vowels that occupy the same mid front space as Spanish /i/ and /e/, but only two in the same space as /o/ and /u/. Thus, overall, a wide-ranging and growing body of research on L2 Spanish vowels has contributed to our understanding of the production and perception of these segments by L2 learners as well as the many factors that influence their acquisition.

30.3.2 Acquisition of Spanish Consonants

Research on the acquisition of Spanish consonants has adopted various categorization techniques and acoustic measures to account for L2 realizations and development. In the following subsections, we will review research on several groups of phones such as word-initial and intervocalic stops, rhotics, and laterals as well as phonological processes involving consonants.

/p t k/

Perhaps the most studied of L2 Spanish sounds, the production and perception of voiceless stops /p t k/ has garnered major attention in research into the L2 acquisition of Spanish phonetics and phonology. As previously mentioned, research on the production of these phones has generally employed VOT as the object of study. English voiceless stops are typically considered to be long lag: Their VOTs generally exceed 30–35 ms. Spanish voiceless stops, on the other hand, are considered to be short lag, rarely exceeding 35 ms (Lisker and Abramson 1964; Zampini and Green 2001). Numerous studies have examined VOT values in the production of L2 learners of Spanish from a variety of proficiency levels (e.g. González-Bueno 1997; Lord 2005; Zampini 1998) as well as in relation to various extralinguistic and/or experiential factors, such as the impact of study abroad (e.g. Bongiovanni et al. 2015; Díaz-Campos 2004; Díaz-Campos and Lazar 2003) or phonetic training (e.g. González-Bueno 1997; Lord 2005). In general, research has found that learners produce Spanish /p t k/ with longer VOT values than those produced by native Spanish speakers. Nevertheless, most learners – and especially as proficiency level or time learning Spanish increases – reduce their VOT values toward more targetlike Spanish values. Despite general targetlike reductions in overall VOT durations, however, several studies have shown that even advanced learners of Spanish tend to exhibit "intermediate" or "compromise" VOT values in their L2 Spanish (e.g. Díaz-Campos and Lazar 2003; Zampini 1998) – that is, values that are shorter than those the learners produce in their own L1s but longer than those produced by native speakers of the target language (although see Amengual 2012 for an exception).

Voice onset time, however, is not the only relevant acoustic cue for voiceless stop production. The duration of the voiceless closure preceding the release of the stop – or voiceless closure interval – has also been shown to productively distinguish between Spanish voiceless and voiced stops in native perception (Martínez Celdrán 1993) and production (Green et al. 1997). Zampini, Clark, and Green (2000) showed that learners, too, pick up on this cue (which is not used in the same way for English stops) and use it, along with VOT, to make perceptual categorical decisions in L2 Spanish.

Finally, innovative research on the impact of voiceless stop production – and specifically VOT duration – on foreign accent perception has shown that VOT is indeed a cue that contributes significantly to foreign accent, not only as perceived by native speakers of the target language but also by learners of Spanish. Schoonmaker-Gates (2012) showed that both native and L2 Spanish listeners rated speech with longer VOT values (modified to be 200 and 300 percent longer than original values in native and nonnative speech) as less nativelike. Additionally, learners enrolled in higher-level Spanish language classes, learners with more exposure to native Spanish-speaking instructors, and learners who had received more pronunciation instruction during their language learning were more sensitive to adjustments in VOT. Such findings contribute to our understanding of learners' perceptions of learner speech and of the acoustic correlates of foreign accent, and open the door to research that connects learners' perceptions with their production patterns.

/b d g/

A substantial amount of attention has also been dedicated to the acquisition of Spanish voiced stops /b d g/, with most research examining whether learners of Spanish acquire the stop–approximant alternation of these phones (i.e. using a stop after a pause, after a nasal consonant, and, for /d/, after /l/ and using an approximant allophone in all other contexts). Most research exploring this topic has examined learner production and defined /b d g/ realization categorically (e.g. as a stop or as an approximant: Alvord and Christiansen 2012; Díaz-Campos 2004; Face and Menke 2009; González Bueno 1995; Lord 2005, 2010; Zampini 1994). These studies have investigated whether learners progress toward more nativelike rates of approximant production in the appropriate contexts over time, as learner level increases, and/or as a result of some sort of intervention or experience and, in general, have shown that learners produce more spirantized variants with training (Lord 2005, 2010) and increased exposure or greater proficiency (Alvord and Christiansen 2012; Face and Menke 2009; Lord 2010; although see Zampini 1994).

Two recent studies have employed intensity differences measures (i.e. the intensity of /b d g/ at its lowest point subtracted from the intensity of the following vowel at its highest point) to examine development in the pronunciation of the reduced variants of these phones. Rogers and Alvord (2014) compared the pronunciation of [β ð ɣ] by two groups of L2 learners – one that had taken four semesters of university Spanish and one that had spent two years abroad in a Spanish-speaking country – to that of a group of native speakers. They found that the university learners group exhibited median intensity difference measures more than four times as high (indicating consonant realizations with greater degrees of occlusion or closure) as the native comparison group; the abroad learner group exhibited intensity difference measures closer to (although still twice as high as) the native Spanish speakers. Bongiovanni et al. (2015) also employed intensity difference measures in their comparison of pronunciation by an at-home and a study abroad group. They showed that learners studying abroad in the Dominican Republic demonstrated greater gains in producing forms of /d/ with greater degrees of spirantization (i.e. smaller intensity differences) after the four-week sojourn abroad than did the at-home comparison group, but no differences were observed in the production of /b/ or /g/ over time.

Thus, research has documented both categorical and gradient development in the production of these variants. In Section 30.3.4, we will briefly discuss a recent study (Solon et al. forthcoming) that combined these techniques and utilized them within a variationist approach to explore the production of intervocalic approximants (specifically /d/) by advanced non-native speakers of Spanish through the lens of (the acquisition of) sociophonetic variation.

Rhotics

Spanish rhotics present a notable challenge to English-speaking L2 learners for several reasons. Spanish contains two rhotic phonemes – the tap /ɾ/ and the trill /r/. Whereas [ɾ] in Spanish corresponds to the phoneme /ɾ/ and the grapheme "r," in General American English [ɾ] corresponds to the phonemes /t/ and /d/ and the graphemes "t," "tt," "d," and/or "dd" (e.g. the sound in *later, latter, lady, ladder*). The trill, on the other hand, is a sound that does not exist in English and, though readily perceptible, presents significant articulatory and production challenges for the native English-speaking L2 learner. Thus, several studies have examined learners' abilities to produce and perceive these phones in Spanish. Face (2006), for instance, found that his fourth-semester Spanish learners produced the tap accurately (defined as "when a brief closure was evidenced in the waveform or spectrogram as a result of the tongue tapping the alveolar ridge," 2006:51) 48.5 percent of the time and the trill accurately (defined as "when voiced airflow was interrupted by a series of brief obstructions resulting from the vibrating tongue approaching the alveolar ridge multiple times) 5.1 percent of the time. His more advanced group – Spanish majors or minors enrolled in upper-division (i.e. two levels beyond fourth-semester) elective Spanish courses – produced the tap accurately 78.7 percent of the time and the trill accurately 26.6 percent of the time. It should be noted that Face's group of five native speakers, recorded for comparison purposes, did not always produce accurate taps and trills using these definitions; rather, they produced the target tap 92 percent of the time and the target trill 86 percent of the time. Such a finding emphasizes, especially for phonetic (and thus, inherently variable) targets, the importance both of clearly defining "accuracy" for coding purposes (as Face did) and of including a native speaker comparison group (as opposed to assuming 100 percent native accuracy). Another important aspect of Face's study was that all rhotic productions were not just coded as accurate and inaccurate but were additionally labeled according to their production properties. This methodological innovation revealed that, whereas 92 percent of the fourth-semester learners' nontarget taps were produced as Englishlike voiced alveolar approximants, advanced majors and minors began to shift away from Englishlike realizations. This "type" still constituted the largest percentage of nontargetlike realizations (73 percent) produced by the majors and minors but these more advanced learners' rhotic repertoire also included non-Englishlike voiced alveolar approximants (a realization not observed at the fourth-semester level). Thus, in addition to allowing the observation of changes in accuracy rates, this approach permitted the examination of patterns in production that indicated other types of developmental modifications.

Rose (2010a) similarly developed categories for the rhotic realizations observed in her study of 21 learners of Spanish at four institutional levels and six native speakers of Spanish. Coding rhotic productions for duration, number of occlusions, presence of frication, formant structure, and intensity, she developed seven categories, which she then used to describe and quantify rhotic production by her participants. She found clear evidence of development as learner level increased: For phonemic taps, the lowest level learners produced phonetic taps in 22 percent of cases and alveolar approximants (Englishlike realizations) in 40 percent of cases, whereas the highest level learners produced phonetic taps in 50 percent of cases and alveolar approximants in 18 percent of cases. For phonemic trills, the percentage production of phonetic trills gradually increased from 5 percent at the third-semester level, to 23 percent at the fifth-semester level, then (surprisingly) falling to 2 percent at the eighth-semester level, and finally rising again to 67 percent at the doctoral level. It should be noted that, at the eighth-semester level, where only 2 percent of trills were targetlike, learners did not realize any trills as alveolar approximants. Instead, their realizations included taps (56 percent of productions) or tap+s (i.e. taps followed by frication or an approximant realization; 27 percent of productions), suggesting more Spanishlike realizations even though not target trills. It should also be noted that, as in Face (2006), Rose's native speakers did not categorically produce phonetic taps and trills as described in the literature. In fact, phonemic taps were realized as phonetic taps only 72 percent of the time by native speakers and phonemic trills as phonetic trills 65 percent of the time.

Rose (2010b) further examined rhotics in L2 Spanish by exploring learners' abilities to discriminate between various phonemic and allophonic contrasts involving intervocalic rhotics. Specifically, 60 native English-speaking learners of Spanish, 15 native speakers of English who had never studied Spanish, and 15 native speakers of Spanish participated in an AXB discrimination task that tested participants' discrimination of the following contrasts: /ɾ/–/r/, /ɾ/–[ɾʃ], [r]–[ɾʃ], /ɾ/–/t/, and /ɾ/–/d/. For the native speakers, all *phonemic* contrasts and the /ɾ/–[ɾʃ] contrast were discriminated at a rate above 97 percent, but [ɾʃ] (the tap+) was not consistently distinguished from the trill [r] (discrimination rate 45 percent). Learners showed similar patterns, but with lower discrimination rates that increased for some contrasts as level increased. However, the learner groups most clearly differ from the native Spanish speakers in their low rates of discrimination of /ɾ/–/d/. Learners at the first three proficiency levels exhibited discrimination rates below 70 percent, whereas the highest level learners discriminated these Spanish phonemes at a rate of 82.5 percent. Thus, despite lingering challenges, development is seen with an increase in learner experience or proficiency level. Rose also showed that even English speakers who had never studied Spanish were able to distinguish between several of these Spanish sounds: For this group, all contrasts were discriminated above 70 percent except /r/–[ɾʃ], which, quite similar to the Spanish native speakers, had a discrimination rate of 42.5 percent.

Finally, in order to help explain the patterns of difficulty in production observed in previous studies, Daidone and Darcy (2014) explored whether lexical encoding abilities could explain difficulties (and ease) in discrimination of Spanish rhotic phones. They hypothesized that if discrimination ability predicts L2 lexical encoding, then words that comprise minimal pairs containing /r/ and /ɾ/ (e.g. *caro* 'expensive' and *carro* 'car') would be "more likely to be differentiated in lexical representations than minimal pairs containing /ɾ/ and /d/" (e.g. *miro* 'look.1sg' and *mido* 'measure.1sg'), given that the discrimination of /ɾ/ and /d/ has been shown to be more difficult/less accurate (2014:41). Intermediate and advanced learners of Spanish as well as native Spanish speakers performed two tasks: a lexical decision task and an ABX discrimination task. The results of the ABX task indicated that, as expected, although learners were able to discriminate between /ɾ–d/, /ɾ–r/, and /r–d/ at above-chance levels, it was the /ɾ–d/ contrast that presented the most difficulty (mirroring Rose's 2010b results). Nevertheless, the results of the lexical decision task indicated that learners had the most difficulty distinguishing between words and nonwords with the /ɾ–r/ contrast (and less difficulty with words with the /ɾ–d/ contrast).

The authors suggest that this finding indicates that learners "do not appear to be differentiating between the tap and trill in lexical representations, despite their ability to distinguish these phones" (2014:48). Thus, as they write, in contrast to what is predicted by the PAM-L2 (Best and Tyler 2007), "an ability to discriminate two L2 sounds does not guarantee that separate phonological categories will be created for two phonemes" (2014:48). They suggest various explanations for their finding, including the low functional load of this contrast as well as the fact that a common realization for the phoneme /r/ is [ɾ] even in native Spanish. In fact, even the native speakers in their study tended to accept nonwords containing a rhotic as real words in 29 percent of cases. Thus, the authors conclude that learners' difficulties in distinguishing between the tap and trill in production (as found in previous studies) may stem not just from the articulatory challenge of the trill but also from the way in which words are encoded in the L2 lexicon, and that this encoding is not strictly determined by a learners' perceptual discrimination abilities.

Although not reviewed in detail here, additional research on L2 Spanish rhotics exists that explores in more depth the linguistic and sociolinguistic factors influencing rhotic acquisition in L2 Spanish (Hurtado and Estrada 2010) as well as the role of L1 articulatory patterns in L2 rhotic pronunciation (Olsen 2012).

Laterals

Perhaps given the existence of the /l/ phoneme in both English and Spanish and the relative similarity in its production in the two languages, very little research has explored the acquisition of Spanish laterals by L2 learners. Nevertheless, lateral realization does differ between English and Spanish: Spanish /l/s are, overall, "lighter" or produced in a more fronted position in the oral cavity than are English laterals. Additionally, in many varieties of English, /l/ realization varies on the basis of syllable position, with a lighter variant [l] produced in onset positions and a darker variant [ɫ] produced in coda positions (e.g. Olive *et al.* 1993). Using the second formant (F2) as an index for lateral frontness–backness (or lightness–darkness), Solon (2017) explored the acquisition of the phonetic details of Spanish /l/s by 85 English-speaking learners from various levels of study and also examined development in the (lack of) conditioning by syllable position. Her results indicated that, generally, as learner level increased, learners produced lighter /l/s overall (i.e. /l/s with higher F2 values, indicating more fronted realizations). Nevertheless, even the most advanced learners (i.e. graduate students) produced /l/s that were darker than those produced by native Spanish speakers. With regard to allophonic patterns, whereas lower-level learners (i.e. those in their first, second, or third year of university study of Spanish) produced /l/s with significantly different formant values in onset versus coda position (a pattern that reflects Englishlike allophony), higher-level learners (fourth-year and graduate students of Spanish) made no statistical distinctions between onset and coda laterals, a result that approximated findings for a comparable group of Spanish native speakers. This research paves the way for future examinations of the acquisition of L2 sounds that may exist in a learner's L1 inventory but differ in phonetic details or allophonic patterns in the L2.

Phonological Processes

Finally, an important line of recent research has begun to explore the acquisition of phonological processes in L2 Spanish. For instance, Schmidt (2014) examined the realization of regressive voicing assimilation (e.g. *mismo* /mismo/ ['miz.mo] 'same') in advanced L2 Spanish, recognizing that this process is a (variable) feature of native Spanish speech that may present a challenge to English-speaking learners because of, for example, the differences in the phonemic status of [s] and [z] in English and Spanish and the contexts of voicing assimilation processes in the two languages. Noting that voicing does not necessarily occur throughout the production of an entire phone, she established a cutoff whereby 60 percent of a particular phone had to exhibit voicing for the realization to be considered voiced. She compared learners' realizations and voicing patterns during a picture-description task to those of a group of monolingual native Mexican Spanish speakers. She found that, when /s/ preceded a voiced consonant, the native speaker group voiced 63.3 percent of /s/s, whereas the learner group realized only 5.6 percent as the voiced allophone. Nevertheless, an examination of individual learner results indicated that, in fact, four of the 14 learners did exhibit a greater percentage of voicing before a voiced consonant, thus suggesting a contextual voicing effect for these learners. Schmidt encouraged further work to investigate the role of linguistic (e.g. speech rate, continuity of speech) and learner (e.g. linguistic experience, pronunciation training) factors on the realization of this and other L2 phonological processes.

30.3.3 Acquisition of Stress and Intonation

In general, as compared to development in segmental phonology, much less is known about the acquisition of suprasegmental aspects of the L2 Spanish sound system. This review will focus on those studies that have explored the acquisition of stress and intonation.

Lord (2007) and Face (2005) explored the role of syllable weight in the production and perception of stress in L2 Spanish, respectively. Recognizing that, descriptively, Spanish stress patterns favor stress on "heavy" syllables (i.e. those containing a final diphthong or consonant), Lord set out to test whether such patterns influence L2 stress placement during production. Participants (learners plus a native speaker control group) read 120 sentences – 60 containing real-word target tokens and 60 containing invented words chosen/created based on syllabic properties.

Lord's results indicated that accuracy in expected stress production was significantly related to proficiency: The beginning learners produced accurate or expected stress patterns 62.5 percent (real word) and 64.4 percent (invented word) of the time, whereas the intermediate group produced accurate patterns 79.0 percent (real word) and 69.8 percent (invented words) of the time. The advanced learner group did not significantly differ from the native speaker group, who produced accurate or expected stress patterns above 90 percent of the time.

Face (2005) examined whether L2 learners make use of syllable weight in the perception of stress placement in Spanish – something he showed to be a characteristic of native Spanish speakers' perceptual systems in Face (2000). Thirty learners of Spanish from three levels listened to 100 nonce Spanish words. Sixty of them were bi- and trisyllabic words comprised of each of the 12 possible combinations of heavy and light syllables. In these words, stress was neutralized in the sense that the acoustic correlates of stress (i.e. pitch and duration of vowels) had equal values across all syllables of a word. In the other 40 words, the acoustic correlates of stress were manipulated so that each word contained a stressed syllable. Participants listened to the 100 stimuli and indicated the syllable of the word they perceived as stressed. Results indicated that perception of the expected (i.e. unmarked) stress pattern across the board increased as learner level increased, and that the unmarked pattern was always perceived much more often in words with light final syllables – the same as the patterns found for native speakers in Face (2000).

With regard to the L2 acquisition of intonation, Nibert (2005) explored the perception and judgments by L2 learners and native speakers of syntactically ambiguous phrases that represented potential semantic contrasts; these syntactically identical phrases differed minimally (i.e. in the sense of a minimal pair or group) in their fundamental frequency (F0) contours. For example, the phrase *lilas y lirios amarillos* could be interpreted syntactically as "lilacs and yellow irises" or as "yellow lilacs and [yellow] irises." The interpretation of such sentences could be disambiguated via intonation in various ways, such as the presence/absence and position of a phrase accent, the presence of H- versus L- (i.e. high versus low monotonal intermediate phrase accents, respectively), and the presence of H- or L- in combination with a high or low boundary tone (i.e. H% or L%). She found that advanced L2 learners made judgments in a manner that was more similar to the native speaker group than to the beginning learner group – a finding that suggested development in the L2 perception of intonation.

Henriksen *et al.* (2010) and Trimble (2013) extended the study of the L2 acquisition of intonation to the study-abroad context. Both studies explored the intonation production patterns of their learners at the beginning and the end of their respective programs (i.e. a seven-week program in León, Spain, in Henriksen *et al.* 2010 and a semester-long program in Mérida, Venezuela, in Trimble 2013). Both studies described the most frequent strategies employed by individual learners, the frequency with which each strategy was used, and whether patterns changed over the time of the sojourn abroad. Henriksen *et al.* (2010) found great variability in results between their four learners, with the most consistent results occurring with absolute interrogatives and the least consistent findings for pronominal interrogatives. These authors stress that a key finding of their study is the variability between learners, which they suggest may in part be due to interlanguage development but may also be influenced by variation found in native Spanish intonation patterns. Trimble (2013) describes three main trends in intonational pattern changes for his nine learners. First, several learners had adopted a new preferred intonation pattern for broad focus declaratives and absolute interrogatives by the end of the program. Second, several learners showed an increase in consistency in pattern use by Time 2. Third, in some cases, learners exhibited an expanded pitch range at Time 2 as compared to Time 1. Trimble also observed an increase in the use of targetlike intonational features (e.g. prenuclear rising pitch accents and circumflex boundary movements) by the end of study abroad and a decrease in L1 (English)-like features such as high initial tones, falling prenuclear F0, and final slight rises in declaratives. Methodologically, both studies also take important steps in paving the way for future technically-principled examinations of L2 Spanish intonation development.

30.3.4 Acquisition of Variable Features

Finally, recent, innovative research is looking at the acquisition of sociophonetic variation in L2 Spanish from various perspectives and in both perception and production. In production, for example, a small group of studies has examined the use of a regional dialectal phonetic feature – the Spanish /θ/ – either by a large pool of L2 learners from various levels (Geeslin and Gudmestad 2011) or after a sojourn abroad in a particular region whose dialect exhibits that feature (George 2014; Knouse 2012; Ringer-Hilfinger 2012). In general, these studies have shown that learners rarely produce [θ] and that production patterns are influenced by a range of individual learner factors as well as linguistic context.

Also investigating the acquisition of variation, Solon *et al.* (forthcoming) revisited the well-researched topic of the production of intervocalic /d/ by native and advanced non-native speakers of Spanish and used a variationist approach to examine the occurrence and factors conditioning both the degree of reduction of /d/ as well as its deletion – a sociolinguistic phenomenon common in native Spanish. These authors found that, whereas native speakers' realizations of deleted and reduced forms were largely conditioned by the same linguistic factors, such as surrounding phonetic context, stress, and lexical frequency, for the advanced learners the two processes appeared to operate separately. For the learner group, deletion was most strongly conditioned by the frequency of the lexical item containing /d/ – that is, /d/ in more frequent lexical items was deleted more often than /d/ in less frequent words; the degree of reduction of /d/ for learners was conditioned only by two contextual/articulatory factors: stress and preceding vowel. These findings suggested that, whereas for native speakers deletion may represent the end stage of the spirantization or reduction process, for learners these two phenomena (deletion and reduction/spirantization) may represent distinct processes governed by different factors.

Fascinating research now also exists into learners' perception of dialectal variants and how this perception may change as learner experience changes. Schmidt (2011) examined the identification of aspirated /s/, a variant specific to particular geographic regions and dialects and subject to social and stylistic variation. Two-hundred and fifteen learners and 45 native speakers listened to nonce words and were asked to identify the word heard from among seven possible choices. Target stimuli included a word-internal aspirated coda. After hearing a stimulus, participants then had to choose from possible identification options that differed only in the coda consonant: "s," "r," "l," "f," "n," and "V" (in addition to a "none" option). Control stimuli contained each of these syllable-final codas. Schmidt found evidence of stages of development in the perception of this dialectal feature, with learners at the intermediate level just starting to identify syllable-final aspiration as /s/ and the most advanced learners patterning like native speakers. She also found evidence for the influence of learner study-abroad experience, with learners who had studied in regions where /s/ aspiration is common exhibiting greater identification of aspiration as a possible variant of /s/. Thus, methodological and analytical techniques previously used to capture development in the production and perception of isolated phones with specific, prescriptive targets, are now being adapted and extended to the exploration of variable processes and features, undoubtedly an important step in expanding our understanding of the L2 Spanish sound system and its development.

30.4 Future Directions

As the previous sections have elucidated, our knowledge and understanding of the L2 Spanish sound system and how it develops has grown immensely in recent years. Nevertheless, much remains to be explored. In this conclusion, three possible avenues for such future research are described although by no means do they represent the only directions for this growing subfield.

First, research on the role of study abroad in the acquisition of Spanish sounds has garnered growing attention in recent years. Although many reviews on the issue assert that study-abroad literature on phonetics and phonology has lagged behind research into other linguistic realms, a recent systematic review (Solon and Long 2016) has shown that numerous studies on the topic exist. In fact, limiting their review to studies that measured L2 pronunciation (i.e. production) quantitatively and using a pre- and post-test design (i.e. before and after study), these authors found 19 studies that specifically explore the L2 acquisition of Spanish pronunciation abroad. Nevertheless, this systematic review (which included studies of other L2s as well) also found that drawing conclusions from this body of research is difficult given differences in data types, measurement and analytical techniques, and participant and program characteristics. Thus, additional research on the development of L2 Spanish sounds during study abroad that replicates methods and measurement techniques as well as research that advances methods for systematically accounting for the myriad of factors that influence experience abroad will further our ability to make conclusions regarding this often important component of foreign-language study.

Also needed is greater attention given to the acquisition of phonetic variation. As reviewed in the previous section, several studies have explored the use of regional dialectal features during study abroad, and at least one has examined the use and conditioning factors of a sociophonetic variable among advanced learners of Spanish. Nevertheless, additional research is warranted on this topic, and is especially needed regarding the influence of social factors (e.g. age, sex/gender, dialect exposure, etc.) in the use of sociolinguistic variables and on the *development* of sociophonetic variation – that is, not just the use and factors conditioning the use of particular variants but also how these patterns change over time or with greater experience. Future research is also warranted into the potential existence of phonetic variation in interlanguages that may not approximate or replicate native variation but is systematic and meaningful to learners.

Finally, as the studies on learners' use of dialectal variants (e.g. Geeslin and Gudmestad 2011; Knouse 2012; Ringer-Hilfinger 2012) have made clear, the choice to adopt a particular phonetic variant in production depends on many factors. Yet, given the inherently variable nature of phonetics, we must assume that the same holds true for all L2 sounds (and L1 sounds for that matter). Thus, moving forward, studies of L2 Spanish sounds (especially in production) should attempt to also consider learners' individual autonomy (Moyer 2017) in representing who they are in their L2 and what their L2 means. Future studies on L2 Spanish phonetics and phonology should take steps to account for the role of learners' decisions in the patterns observed in L2 speech and speech perception. This is a challenge, but an exciting one, and one that will allow us to move the field forward to further connect L2 sound acquisition to larger issues in second language acquisition.

References

Alvord, S. M. and Christiansen, D. E. (2012). Factors Influencing the Acquisition of Spanish Voiced Stop Spirantization during an Extended Stay Abroad. *Studies in Hispanic and Lusophone Linguistics*, 5, 239–276.

Amengual, M. (2012). Interlingual Influence in Bilingual Speech: Cognate Status Effect in a Continuum of Bilingualism. *Bilingualism: Language and Cognition*, 15, 517–530.

Best, C. (1995). A Direct Realist View of Cross-Language Speech Perception. In W. Strange (ed.), *Speech Perception and Linguistic Experience: Issues in Cross-Language Research*. Timonium, MD: York Press, pp. 171–206.

Best, C. T. and Tyler, M. D. (2007). Nonnative and Second-Language Speech Perception: Commonalities and Complementarities. In O.-S. Bohn and M. J. Munro (eds.), *Language Experience in Second Language Speech Learning: In Honor of James Emil Flege*. Amsterdam: John Benjamins, pp. 13–34.

Bongiovanni, S., Long, A. Y., Solon, M., and Willis, E. W. (2015). The Effect of Short-Term Study Abroad on Second Language Spanish Phonetic Development. *Studies in Hispanic and Lusophone Linguistics*, 8, 243–283.

Bradlow, A. R. (1995). A Comparative Acoustic Study of English and Spanish Vowels. *Journal of the Acoustical Society of America*, 97, 1916–1924.

Carranza, M. (2008). Fenómenos de interferencia fónica relacionados con la vocal /u/ en la interlingua de estudiantes de español como lengua extranjera. *Estudios Lingüísticos Hispánicos*, 23, 1–21.

Cobb, K. and Simonet, M. (2015). Adult Second Language Learning of Spanish Vowels. *Hispania*, 98, 47–60.

Daidone, D. and Darcy, I. (2014). *Quierro comprar una guitara*: Lexical Encoding of the Tap and Trill by L2 Learners of Spanish. In R. T. Miller et al. (eds.), *Selected Proceedings of the 2012 Second Language Research Forum*. Somerville, MA: Cascadilla, pp. 39–50.

Derwing, T. M. and Munro, M. J. (2015). *Pronunciation Fundamentals: Evidence-Based Perspectives for L2 Teaching and Research*. Amsterdam: John Benjamins.

Díaz, M. and Simonet, M. (2015). Second Language Acquisition of Spanish /e/ and /ei/ by Native English Speakers. *Hispania*, 98, 750–761.

Díaz-Campos, M. (2004). Context of Learning in the Acquisition of Spanish Second Language Phonology. *Studies in Second Language Acquisition*, 26, 249–273.

Díaz-Campos, M. and Lazar, N. (2003). Acoustic Analysis of Voiceless Initial Stops in the Speech of Study Abroad and Regular Class Students: Context of Learning as a Variable in Spanish Second Language Acquisition. In P. Kempchinsky and C.-E. Piñeros (eds.), *Theory, Practice, and Acquisition. Papers from the 6th Hispanic Linguistics Symposium and the 5th Conference on the Acquisition of Spanish and Portuguese*. Somerville, MA: Cascadilla, pp. 352–370.

Ellis, R. (2008). *The Study of Second Language Acquisition* (2nd edn). Oxford: Oxford University Press.

Escudero, P. and Boersma, P. (2002). The Subset Problem in L2 Perceptual Development: Multiple-Category Assimilation by Dutch Learners of Spanish. In B. Skarabela, S. Fish and A. Do (eds.), *Proceedings of the 26th Boston University Conference on Language Development*. Somerville, MA: Cascadilla, pp. 208–219.

Face, T. L. (2000). The Role of Syllable Weight in the Perception of Spanish Stress. In H. Campos, E. Herburger, A. Morales-Front, and T. J. Walsh (eds.), *Hispanic Linguistics at the Turn of the Millennium*. Somerville, MA: Cascadilla, pp. 1–13.

Face, T. L. (2005). Syllable Weight and the Perception of Spanish Stress Placement by Second Language Learners. *Journal of Language and Learning*, 3, 90–103.

Face, T. L. (2006). Intervocalic Rhotic Pronunciation by Adult Learners of Spanish as a Second Language. In C. A. Klee and T. L. Face (eds.), *Selected Proceedings of the 7th Conference on the Acquisition of Spanish and Portuguese as First and Second Languages*. Somerville, MA: Cascadilla, pp. 47–58.

Face, T. and Menke, M. (2009). Acquisition of the Spanish Voiced Spirants by Second Language Learners. In J. Collentine (ed.), *Selected proceedings of the 11th Hispanic Linguistics Symposium*. Somerville, MA: Cascadilla, pp. 39–52.

Flege, J. E. (1995) Second Language Speech Learning: Theory, Findings, and Problems. In W. Strange (ed.), *Speech Perception and Linguistic Experience: Issues in Cross-Language Research*. Timonium, MD: York Press, pp. 233–277.

García Bayonas, M. (2007). *The Acquisition of Vowels in Spanish and English as Second Language*. Munich: Lincom.

Geeslin, K. and Gudmestad, A. (2011). The Acquisition of Variation in Second-Language Spanish: An Agenda for Integrating Studies of the L2 Sound System. *Journal of Applied Linguistics*, 5, 137–157.

George, A. (2014). Study Abroad in Central Spain: The Development of Regional Phonological Features. *Foreign Language Annals*, 47, 97–114.

González-Bueno, M. (1995). Adquisición de los alófonos fricativos de las oclusivas sonoras españolas por aprendices de español como segunda lengua. *Estudios de Lingüística Aplicada*, 13, 64–79.

González-Bueno, M. (1997). The Effects of Formal Instruction on the Acquisition of Spanish Phonology. In W. R. Glass and A. T. Pérez-Leroux (eds.), *Contemporary Perspectives on the Acquisition of Spanish*. Somerville, MA: Cascadilla, pp. 57–75.

Gordon, L. S. (2008). Factors Affecting English Speakers' Perception of L2 Spanish Vowels (Doctoral dissertation). Georgetown University.

Green, K. P., Zampini, M. L., and Magliore, J. (1997). An Examination of Word-Initial-Stop Closure Interval in English, Spanish, and Spanish-English Bilinguals. *Journal of the Acoustical Society of America*, 102, 3136.

Henriksen, N. C., Geeslin, K. L., and Willis, E. W. (2010). The Development of L2 Spanish Intonation during a Study Abroad Immersion Program in León, Spain: Global Contours and Final Boundary Movements. *Studies in Hispanic and Lusophone Linguistics*, 3, 113–162.

Hualde, J. I. (2005). *The Sounds of Spanish*. Cambridge: Cambridge University Press.

Hurtado, L. M. and Estrada, C. (2010). Factors Influencing the Second Language Acquisition of Spanish Vibrants. *Modern Language Journal*, 94, 74–86.

Knouse, S. K. (2012). The Acquisition of Dialectal Phonemes in a Study Abroad Context: The Case of the Castilian Theta. *Foreign Language Annals*, 45, 512–542.

Ladefoged, P. (2006). *A Course in Phonetics* (5th edn). Boston, MA: Thomson.

Lisker, L. and Abramson, A. S. (1964). A Cross-Language Study of Voicing in Initial Stops: Acoustical Measurements. *Word*, 20, 384–422.

Long, A. Y. (2016). The Acquisition of Sociolinguistic Competence by Korean Learners of Spanish: Development and Use of the Copula, Subject Expression, and Intervocalic Stops (Doctoral dissertation). Indiana University.

Lord, G. (2005). (How) Can we Teach Foreign Language Pronunciation? On the Effects of a Spanish Phonetics Course. *Hispania*, 88, 557–567.

Lord, G. (2007). The Role of the Lexicon in Learning Second Language Stress Patterns. *Applied Language Learning*, 17 (1–2), 1–14.

Lord, G. (2010). The Combined Effects of Instruction and Immersion on Second Language Pronunciation. *Foreign Language Annals*, 43, 488–503.

Martínez Celdrán, E. (1993). La percepción categorial de /b-p/ en español basada en las diferencias de duración. *Estudios de Fonética Experimental*, 5, 223–239.

Menke, M. R. (2010). The Acquisition of Spanish Vowels by Native English-Speaking Students in Spanish Immersion Programs (Doctoral dissertation). University of Minnesota.

Menke, M. R. and Face, T. L. (2010). Second Language Spanish Vowel Production: An Acoustic Analysis. *Studies in Hispanic and Lusophone Linguistics*, 3, 181–214.

Moyer, A. (2017). Autonomy in Second Language Phonology: Choice vs. Limits. *Language Teaching*, 50 (3), 395–411. doi: 10.1017/S0261444815000191. Published online May 19, 2015.

Nibert, H. J. (2005). The Acquisition of the Phrase Accent by Intermediate and Advanced Adult Learners of Spanish as a Second Language. In D. Eddington (ed.), *Selected Proceedings of the 6th Conference on the Acquisition of Spanish and Portuguese as First and Second Languages*. Somerville, MA: Cascadilla, pp. 108–122.

Olive, J. P., Greenwood, A., and Coleman, J. (1993). *Acoustics of American English Speech: A Dynamic Approach*. New York: Springer.

Olsen, M. K. (2012). The L2 Acquisition of Spanish Rhotics by L2 English Speakers: The Effect of L1 Articulatory Routines and Phonetic Context for Allophonic Variation. *Hispania*, 95, 65–82.

Ringer-Hilfinger, K. (2012). Learner Acquisition of Dialect Variation in a Study Abroad Context: The Case of the Spanish [θ]. *Foreign Language Annals*, 45, 430–446.

Rogers, B. M. A. and Alvord, S. M. (2014). The Gradience of Spirantization: Factors Affecting L2 Production of Intervocalic Spanish [β, ð, ɣ]. *Spanish in Context*, 11, 402–424.

Rose, M. (2010a). Intervocalic Tap and Trill Production in the Acquisition of Spanish as a Second Language. *Studies in Hispanic and Lusophone Linguistics*, 3, 379–419.

Rose, M. (2010b). Differences in Discriminating L2 Consonants: A Comparison of Spanish Taps and Trills. In M. T. Prior, Y. Watanabe, and S.-K. Lee (eds.), *Selected Proceedings of the 2008 2nd Language Research Forum*. Somerville, MA: Cascadilla, pp. 181–196.

Schmidt, L. B. (2011). Acquisition of Dialectal Variation in Second Language: L2 Perception of Aspiration of Spanish /s/ (Doctoral dissertation). Indiana University.

Schmidt, L. B. (2014). Contextual Variation in L2 Spanish: Voicing Assimilation in Advanced Learner Speech. *Studies in Hispanic and Lusophone Linguistics*, 7, 79–113.

Schoonmaker-Gates, E. (2012). Foreign Accent Perception in L2 Spanish: The Role of Proficiency and L2 Experience. In J. Levis and K. LeVelle (eds.), *Social Factors in Pronunciation Acquisition: Proceedings of the 3rd Pronunciation in Second Language Learning and Teaching Conference*. Ames, IA: Iowa State University, pp. 84–92.

Solon, M. (2017). Do Learners Lighten Up? Phonetic and Allophonic Acquisition of Spanish /l/ by English-Speaking Learners. *Studies in Second Language Acquisition*, 39 (4), 801–832.

Solon, M., Linford, B., and Geeslin, K. L. (forthcoming). Acquisition of Sociophonetic Variation: Intervocalic /d/ Reduction in Native and Nonnative Spanish. *Revista Española de Lingüística Aplicada*.

Solon, M. and Long, A. Y. (2016). Context of Learning and the Development of Pronunciation: A Systematic Narrative Review. Paper presented at the Second Language Research Forum, Columbia Teachers' College, New York.

Stevens, J. J. (2011). Vowel Duration in Second Language Spanish Vowels: Study Abroad versus At-Home Learners. *Arizona Working Papers in SLA and Teaching*, 18, 77–104.

Trimble, J. C. (2013). Acquiring Variable L2 Spanish Intonation in a Study Abroad Context (Doctoral dissertation). University of Minnesota.

Zampini, M. L. (1994). The Role of Native Language Transfer and Task Formality in the Acquisition of Spanish Spirantization. *Hispania*, 77, 470–481.

Zampini, M. L. (1998). The Relationship between the Production and Perception of L2 Spanish Stops. *Texas Papers in Foreign Language Education*, 3, 85–100.

Zampini, M. L., Clarke, C. M., and Green, K. P. (2000). Language Experience and the Perception of Stop Consonant Voicing in Spanish: The Case of Late English-Spanish Bilinguals. In R. P. Leow and C. Sanz (eds.), *Spanish Applied Linguistics at the Turn of the Millennium: Papers from the 1999 Conference on the L1 and L2 Acquisition of Spanish and Portuguese*. Somerville, MA: Cascadilla, pp. 194–209.

Zampini, M. L. and Green, K. P. (2001). The Voicing Contrast in English and Spanish: The Relationship between Perception and Production. In J. Nicol (ed.), *One Mind, Two Languages: Bilingual Language Processing*. Malden, MA: Blackwell, pp. 23–48.

31

The Acquisition of Second Language Spanish Morphosyntax

Jason Rothman, Jorge González Alonso, and David Miller

31.1 Introduction

The increasing importance of Spanish as a global language over the past few decades has ushered in both an impressive influx of non-native speakers learning it in adulthood as well as a dramatic upswing in second language (L2) acquisition and processing studies focusing on this language. The proliferation is relatively new: despite having an established record of nearly four decades, by the late 90s research into L2 Spanish was still comparatively rare within the field of Second Language Acquisition (SLA) (Montrul and Bruhn de Garavito 1999), which at the time was – and still is – dominated by L2 English studies. And yet, doing even descriptive justice to what in 2018 can be viewed as an extensive literature on L2 Spanish greatly exceeds the possibilities of a chapter like this one. Although this is perhaps unusual, we will start, then, by stating what this chapter cannot (and *should not*) be: an exhaustive survey of the field, one that discusses the nature and state-of-the-art knowledge of most linguistic properties investigated to date, and one that tells the reader all there is to know about the L2 acquisition of Spanish morphosyntax from the perspective of as many competing L2 theories as possible. While such a text would undoubtedly be useful for many, trying to provide one such here would be to invite self-inflicted failure from the start, as a meaningful summary of this type could be done well only in a text of monograph length. Instead, we have aimed to offer you here a broad, authoritative index; an approachable and hopefully intriguing access point to a field that has grown rapidly in scope and methodological and theoretical approaches, especially in the past two decades.

Our task, then, is to give the reader a sense of the amount and the nature of studies that have dealt with the L2 acquisition of Spanish morphosyntax, providing as many useful references as possible to a plethora of domains of grammar investigated over the years. At the same time, we would be neglecting our duty as curators if we did not expand on our coverage of some specific points. The domains of grammar we cover in greater detail are meant to serve as examples of what could equally be written for all the other domains of L2 Spanish morphosyntax that we touch upon more in passing. What we give up in detail for most domains we hope to make up for in broader coverage overall, so that those wishing to delve further into any given topic on L2 Spanish morphosyntax will have access in this overview chapter to the citation of as much primary research as possible to get them started properly.

This chapter is structured into two main sections, which bring together work focusing on properties associated with the verbal and nominal domains respectively,[1] painting the overall picture of L2 Spanish morphosyntax studies with broad, medium, and narrow strokes. Within each of these sections, we provide a cursory overview of the range of linguistic properties that have been investigated (the broad strokes), which readers can follow up on through the cited studies and reviews. Next, we isolate one specific property in more detail (the medium strokes), and finish by describing a key study which has investigated that property (the narrow strokes). Although a different approach to our task might do the job just as well or better, we believe that the one outlined above is the best way to confront the embarrassment of riches – the sheer quantity of grammatical properties and the sheer number of high-quality studies that could be reviewed in this chapter. We hope that, by adjusting the granularity of our survey in this manner, we will have achieved a fair balance between the sharpness and the breadth that are simultaneously expected from a chapter of this type.

Despite a bias in the number of studies from a formal linguistic perspective that have traditionally populated the literature on L2 Spanish morphosyntax – especially when considering the last 40 years as opposed to the last decade or so – there are indeed many theories and frameworks of L2 acquisition (see, e.g., Herschensohn and Young-Scholten 2013, and Geeslin 2014a, as applied specifically to Spanish), all of which we hope to represent here. The beauty of working on acquisition is that we can afford, when appropriate, to put important paradigmatic discussions aside and deal primarily with the byproduct of well-designed studies: the data

---

[1] For ease of exposition, we will present structures in one or the other section as if they were purely related to the "topic," e.g. a property of the verbal domain. Of course, most properties do not sit so neatly in one given "topic." For example, clitics can be viewed as part of the verbal domain because they are the overt expression of the argument structure of a verb, that is, its required accusative or dative complement; but they can also be viewed as part of the nominal domain because they are themselves determiner or noun phrases (DPs/NPs) and are subject to nominal agreement. We are aware of this oversimplification, but put it aside while noting it for the purpose of greater explanatory clarity. Moreover, although this chapter is primarily concerned with morphosyntax, many, if not most, of the structures we refer to relate to interfaces – by the very nature of language, this is unavoidable – with other modules such as semantics, pragmatics, and phonology. We will, however, discuss primarily the morphosyntactic exponents of these properties.

themselves. Data that are well collected can sit neutrally at the periphery of both theory-internal and cross-theoretical debates, precisely because they can be treated descriptively and constitute the basis of evidence that all theories must ultimately account for. With this in mind, two general questions, which all cognitive theories of L2 acquisition are concerned with, underlie our discussion: (i) whether or not child and adult acquisition are destined to be fundamentally different in development and outcome; and (ii) how previous linguistic experience constrains, if at all, the progress and ultimate success of the L2 learning task.

31.2 Acquisition of Properties Related to the Verbal Domain

We begin this section by summarizing key findings about one of the most widely studied properties of Spanish: the Spanish copula (*ser* vs. *estar*) (e.g. Brown and Cortés-Torres 2012; Bruhn de Garavito 2009; Bruhn de Garavito and Valenzuela 2008; Camacho 2012; Collentine and Asención-Delaney 2010; Dorado 2011; Geeslin 2003, 2014b; Geeslin and Guijarro-Fuentes 2006, 2008; Roby 2009; VanPatten 1985, 1987; Woolsey 2008; Zyzik and Gass 2008). Most of this work shows that L2 learners, especially when their L1 does not have a two-way copula distinction, have difficulty converging on the distributional patterns throughout development. However, some studies also show that at later stages of acquisition this contrast can be fully mastered. This is an interesting property to study in part because the *ser* vs. *estar* distinction is a variable property across dialects of Spanish and the difference seems to be a moving target, that is, *ser* vs. *estar* seem to be in a continuous synchronic process of change, especially and differentially across particular native dialects (Sánchez-Alonso et al. 2016). The sociolinguistic side of SLA theories has rightly taken this factor into consideration (see, e.g., Geeslin 2003).

Additionally, the study of verbal arguments, be they subjects or objects, has been a source of great insight into the underpinnings of SLA theories more generally, as well as into the study of Spanish more specifically. The acquisition and distribution of the subject arguments of the verb in Spanish have been topics of particular focus, in part because a minimal requirement of all verbs (in use) is the associated subject. That is, a verb must project a subject position (whether morphophonologically present or not), whereas object arguments are – depending on the argument structure of the verb – optional. Subjects are, therefore, one of the most frequent syntactic structures in any language. As is well known, languages can vary syntactically with regard to whether they require an overtly expressed subject (e.g. English, French, German) or allow for the optionally overt expression of subjects (e.g. Spanish, Arabic, Italian) (see Alexiadou and Anagnostopoulou 1998). In the case of so called null-subject languages, the distribution of overt and null subjects is typically constrained by discourse pragmatic factors. Spanish is relatively straightforward in that the null pronoun is the default and thus tends to be used unless there is a discourse reason not to do so. Overt pronouns are pragmatically conditioned, typically indicating a shift in topic, contrastive focus or other discourse marking. The literature on L2 Spanish has examined both the syntactic and the syntax/discourse sides of subjects. Details aside, there is relative agreement that L2 learners of Spanish, irrespective of whether their L1 is or is not a null-subject language, eventually acquire the syntactic properties of subjects, that is, that there are null expletive (e.g. __ *Llueve* 'It rains'; obligatory) and null referential (e.g. *Él/__ vino ayer* '(He) came yesterday'; optional) pronouns (e.g. Liceras 1989; Liceras and Díaz 1999; Lozano 2002a; Montrul and Rodríguez Louro 2006; Pérez-Leroux and Glass 1997, 1999; Rothman 2007, 2009; Geeslin and Gudmestad 2008, 2011). However, the literature that has also examined the syntax-discourse knowledge regarding the distribution of overt and null subjects reveals that the syntactic properties are acquired much earlier than the discourse-dependent ones, if the latter are acquired to native-likeness at all (e.g. Lozano 2002b; Montrul and Rodríguez Louro 2006; Rothman 2007, 2009).

Object arguments, especially clitic pronouns (*me/nos, te/os, la/s, le/s, lo/s*, and so on), are much like subjects. Thus they can be treated either as the exponents of verbs (e.g. related to syntactic case) or, because they are themselves DPs/NPs, particular properties related to them such as morphosyntactic agreement in gender and number can be treated as part of the nominal domain. What makes clitics interesting is that for English native speakers – the majority of L2 learners tested – their L1 lacks this syntactic category entirely.[2] Concerning the licensing of clitic object pronouns, their appropriateness for case assignment, and their collocational distributions (where they are placed with respect to finite and nonfinite verbal forms), research shows that clitics can be acquired (including sociolinguistic variation such as *leísmo* in study-abroad contexts) even when the L1 lacks this syntactic category, despite developmental errors in apparent surface case forms (e.g. dative used for accusative and vice versa) and related word order issues (e.g. Bruhn de Garavito and Montrul 1996; Geeslin *et al.* 2010; Halloran and Rothman 2015; Lee 2003; Liceras 1985; Liceras *et al.* 1997; Malovrh 2008; Malovrh and Lee 2010; Montrul 2010a, 2010b; Perales and Liceras 2010; VanPatten 1990; Zyzik 2004, 2006; among others). Additionally, Spanish allows for some objects to be null (based on semantic factors such as specificity), crucially those outside of syntactic islands. Recent studies have examined whether or not L2 learners of Spanish can acquire such restrictions (e.g. Bruhn de Garavito and Guijarro Fuentes 2002; Zyzik 2008; Rothman and Iverson 2013; Cuza *et al.* 2013b). This is an interesting topic since it has not been so

---

[2] We are putting aside the question of whether reduced pronominal forms in English can be taken as a type of clitic, for example, whether '(e)m in a sentence such as *I see '(e)m* vs. *I see them* is a proper syntactic clitic.

exhaustively examined and because available data exists from a multitude of L1s learning Spanish as an L2. In this domain, results are mixed regarding the ultimate level of success of each learner group relative to the complexity of the L2 learning task, which, in turn, is conditioned by how learnability follows from L1 transfer (see Iverson and Rothman 2015).

31.2.1 Preterit/Imperfect Distinction

The general linguistic domain of verbal morphology is a vulnerable one during all types of language acquisition, as well as one that can be affected by attrition or language loss (see, e.g., Brown 1973; Montrul 2002; Prévost and White 2000; Wexler 1994; among others). It is no surprise, then, that a large body of research has focused on the preterit vs. imperfect distinction or grammatical (viewpoint) aspect given its persistent difficulty for many learners of Spanish, especially those whose L1 does not signal aspect in the same way Spanish does (see, e.g., Bardovi-Harlig 1999; Domínguez et al. 2013; Montrul 2002; Montrul and Slabakova 2003; Slabakova and Montrul 2003, 2007; Rothman 2008; Long and Rothman 2013; Salaberry 1999, 2003, 2011; Geeslin et al. 2012; among others). Grammatical aspect, in the case of the preterit vs. imperfect distinction, refers to the morphological encoding of perfectivity. Perfective aspect (preterit) relates to the notion of boundedness or completion of an event from the viewpoint of the speaker. In other words, the choice of the preterit indicates that an action/event has a fixed start and completed endpoint in the past (e.g. *Juan vino anoche*, 'Juan came.PRET last night'), whereas the imperfect makes no commitment with regard to the start or ultimate completion of an event (e.g. *Juan venía en coche*, 'Juan came.IMPF by car'). When imperfect morphology is chosen, the focus is on the (unbounded) duration of an event and, as such, one knows only that an event took place in the past – whether or not it was completed is unknown. All languages have the ability to express the meanings encoded in the preterit and imperfect morphology; however, crucially, languages such as English do not grammaticalize this with dedicated morphology.

A significant part of research into the preterit–imperfect distinction in Spanish has been carried out by analyzing distinctive distributions of specific verb forms, such as preterit and/or imperfect, across categories of verbs that differ semantically in terms of their lexical aspectual properties (see Cadierno 2000; Camps 2002; Comajoan and Pérez Saldanya 2005; Liskin-Gasparro 2000). Some interesting trends follow neatly from research in this domain, such as the finding that tense-aspectual morphology among L2 learners emerges systematically (Bardovi-Harlig 2000; Dietrich et al. 1995; Salaberry 2008) and in three main stages in the progression of how L2 tense-aspect marking is acquired (see Comajoan 2014 for further details). In brief, the first stage is one in which learners tend to rely primarily on lexico-pragmatics, such as the context of language production and/or the interaction between speakers or expressions that may be transferable from the L1. The second stage is one in which the use of time adverbials, but crucially not verbal morphology, marks temporal and aspectual information (e.g. *Juan viene anoche, 'Juan comes last night'). The third and final stage is one in which verbal morphology emerges. Perfective past marking appears first and is initially used with achievement and accomplishment verbs, extending later to stative and activity verbs. The imperfective past emerges later: first with statives, then with activities and accomplishments, and finally with achievements (as is the case for child L1 acquisition). In general, verbal forms are acquired before verbal uses, such that forms are said to precede meanings (Bardovi-Harlig 2000; Comajoan 2014; Dietrich et al. 1995; Montrul 2004; Salaberry 2008). Moreover, it has been shown that while L2ers of Spanish may be able to produce both preterit and imperfect verbal forms, they do not always use them in contextually appropriate ways (Hasbún 1995; Ramsay 1990; Salaberry 2008) and that the imperfect forms are semantically more varied than the preterit ones, potentially making them inherently more difficult to acquire (Bardovi-Harlig 2000; Comajoan 2014; Dietrich et al. 1995; Montrul 2004; Salaberry 2008). This is particularly relevant to Spanish and other Romance languages because the imperfect has more pragmatic or non-prototypical uses than the preterit, which may affect the time it takes learners to detect prototypical instantiations of the imperfect in the input and incorporate them into their interlanguage grammar (Comajoan 2014; Salaberry 2005). In general, however, it is not the case that one single variable can account for the patterns observed in the acquisition of tense/aspect and at the same time be comprehensively explanatory (e.g. Wulff et al. 2009; Bardovi-Harlig and Comajoan 2008; Comajoan 2014; Salaberry 2008). While there are many variables discussed in the literature (e.g. individual needs of the learners, identity, and context of learning/instruction), the most commonly cited explanatory factors are the input that learners receive and the L1 from which they begin the process of L2 acquisition.

An exemplar proposal aimed at explaining the patterns of use of tense and aspect morphology, specifically among L2ers, is the Lexical Aspect Hypothesis (LAH) (Andersen and Shirai 1994). This hypothesis posits that inherent aspectual properties of a verb play a deterministic role in the acquisition of tense and aspect morphology. More specifically, it suggests that there is a correlation between certain morphological forms and aspectual properties of verbs that are given preference in interlanguage grammars. Following from the above-mentioned patterns of emergence of preterit/imperfect morphology, then, such morphology is claimed to appear in distinct stages as determined by specific verbal properties. On the one hand, perfective forms are said to surface with achievements and accomplishments (i.e. telic verbs, verbs whose lexical meaning entails an inherent endpoint), followed by activities and states, and on the other hand imperfective forms are said to surface with states first, followed by activities, accomplishments, and achievements (Andersen 1986). The LAH further claims that input, specifically the way in which the distinct distributional pattern of morphological forms is presented, also plays a crucial role in the acquisition of tense/aspect morphology. This claim, as highlighted by Domínguez et al. (2013), is based on the idea that learners acquire the most stand-out morphological forms first (the "Relevance Principle"; see Bybee 1985) and that they will likely make an association between features that are semantically compatible, such as telicity and perfectivity (the "Congruence Principle"; see Andersen and Shirai 1994). Finally, the LAH posits that, following Prototype Theory (Rosch 1973), there is a link between grammatical marking(s) and lexical class such that any given category will contain both its most prototypical exemplars and other non-prototypical exemplars that are featurally less similar to the prototypical members.

Domínguez et al. (2013) is a representative example of research that tests the LAH by examining grammatical aspect in L2 Spanish. The aim of the study was to verify the development observed in previous research showing that learners use present morphology in past-tense contexts (at least initially), which is succeeded by a stage where the preterit is the sole past-tense morphological marker produced, though it is used for telic predicates only and, finally, that the imperfect emerges later than the preterit and is first used with state and activity verbs. The authors examined "[d]ata elicited through one comprehension and three oral tasks" (distinct types of narratives) given to 60 learners of L2 Spanish divided into three separate groups based on proficiency (beginner, intermediate, and advanced).

The first narrative was designed to elicit past-tense forms through the retelling of a short story. After looking at a series of pictures, participants were asked to tell the story to the experimenter. This task included habitual/imperfective contexts, as well as a non-iterative perfective context. The second was an impersonal controlled narrative designed to test learners' use of infrequent *form-to-meaning associations*. There were four contexts involving prototypical pairings of discourse grounding and lexical class while another four contexts were designed to elicit non-prototypical pairings. The third was a personal narrative that gave learners the chance to talk freely about memories from their childhood and their upbringing. The comprehension task examined whether learners knew that the use of past-tense forms was influenced by context, and whether state (imperfect) and event (preterit) associations guided learners' choices.

The overall results demonstrated that learners' use of preterit forms did not coincide more often with telic than atelic predicates. Instead, the learners' pattern of responses revealed an association between state (imperfect) and event (preterit) forms. In other words, although lexical aspect played a role in this case, dynamicity – and not telicity as predicted by the LAH – affected learners' choices to use either imperfect or perfect forms. Furthermore, the use of imperfect and preterit forms did not spread across lexical classes. This is an important study since it showed that L2 learners of Spanish do diverge from natives in expected use of grammatical aspect; however, such differences did not neatly align with the LAH. And so, while there is a clear pattern to their use that can be explained in formal linguistic terms, L2 learners seem to differ from the developmental sequence of child L1 Spanish speakers, who appear to converge progressively on the adult grammatical aspect system via lexical aspectual biases. Domínguez *et al.*'s (2013) study dovetails nicely with other formal linguistic studies on grammatical aspect that have shown that, at least at an advanced level of proficiency, L2 learners have the complete representations of grammatical aspect in their interlanguage grammars (e.g. Montrul and Slabakova 2003; Slabakova and Montrul 2003, 2007).

31.3 Acquisition of Properties Related to the Nominal Domain

We start our discussion here with L2 Spanish research into articles. Certain nominal semantic features (e.g. definiteness, specificity) regulate the use of articles (definites vs. indefinites) and demonstratives, creating an area of difficulty for learners that might be compounded by the fact that articles and demonstratives also reflect morphosyntactic agreement for gender and number (see Section 31.3.1 below for details). To date, article use in L2 Spanish has received a modest amount of attention in the literature (e.g. Cuza *et al.* 2013a; Ionin *et al.* 2013; Montrul and Ionin 2012). Typically, English-speaking learners of Spanish and other Romance languages such as Italian (see Slabakova 2006) are charged with the task of unlearning the one-to-one mapping of definiteness vs. genericity expressed in English through definite plurals (e.g. *The elephants seem nervous*) and bare plurals (e.g. *Elephants have trunks*), respectively, since Spanish uses definite plurals in both cases. Furthermore, L1 English learners have to reconfigure the semantics of bare plurals in L2 Spanish, since these can have an existential reading (e.g. *Animales de todo tipo salían de las jaulas del zoo*, 'Animals of all kinds came out of the zoo's cages') but not a generic one (**Animales son seres vivos*, 'Animals are living beings,' where the article *los* would be obligatory). Research into this topic has shown that, by advanced stages of proficiency, L1 English–L2 Spanish learners appear to have native-like knowledge of the distribution of plural subject expressions in Spanish, despite the asymmetry between their native and their second language (e.g. Cuza *et al.* 2013a).

Certain determiners (e.g. articles, quantifiers, numerals, etc.) give rise to pragmatically calculated inferences that extend beyond the purely semantic meaning of the lexical items themselves. These pragmatic inferences are known as implicatures (e.g. Grice 1975). A sub-type of these inferences, scalar implicatures (SI), is said to be derived from determiners which form part of a scale in which each term is ordered according to its informativity, such as the English quantifiers <some, most, all>, where the stronger terms naturally entail the weaker ones but not vice versa (Horn 1972). Strictly speaking, *some* means 'at least one.' In this sense, it can refer to both a fraction as well as the entirety of a given set. This contrasts with *all*, which can denote only the entire set. Tacit principles of communication assume that, when an interlocutor uses the informationally weaker term *some*, the stronger term *all* does not apply, hence the pragmatically-based interpretation of *some* as meaning 'not all.' While some studies have found that adult L2ers are indeed able to process SIs just as native speakers do – at times being even more pragmatic than natives, as in Slabakova (2010) – others have found that SIs are a property that challenges even the most advanced L2 learners (Miller et al. 2016). Spanish is particularly interesting, at least from the perspective of L1 English learners, because it has two plural indefinites (*algunos* and *unos*) that roughly translate to 'some' but that have inherently different semantic and pragmatic distributions (e.g. Gutiérrez-Rexach 2001). While *algunos* is, in most cases, partitive, *unos* maps more faithfully to 'some' in English. Miller et al. (2016) showed that, though at times approximating a native-like distribution of *algunos* and *unos*, advanced L1 English–L2 Spanish learners did not reliably distinguish between them, even when the context would have supported one reading over the other. In line with Papafragou and Musolino (2003) and Guasti et al. (2005), Miller and colleagues (2016) suggest that SI calculation can be task dependent, and that more specialized methodologies might be needed to determine whether SIs can be acquired to native-like levels.

Spanish also presents a typologically rare structure in the nominal domain (see López 2012) called Differential Object Marking (DOM), whereby direct objects are signaled, under certain conditions, by the insertion of the overt accusative case marker *a* 'to' immediately preceding the object noun phrase (e.g. *Marcos visitó a Juan*, 'Marcos visited (a) Juan'; *Todos los días veo a tu novia en el autobús*, 'Every day I see (a) your girlfriend on the bus'). For Spanish L2 learners who are native speakers of languages with no DOM, the learning task involves acquiring the insertion of *a* in limited contexts, for example, before direct objects that are both animate and specific (e.g. *Laura vio a Carlos*, 'Laura saw a.DOM Carlos' vs. *Laura vio (a) una mujer*, 'Laura saw a woman'). The complete distribution of DOM – that is, the exact semantic, syntactic, and pragmatic conditions regulating when DOM is licensed beyond the canonical case of animate, specific accusative objects in Spanish – is definitely complex and potentially varies across native dialects (see Torrego 1998; López 2012). The acquisition of DOM in L2 Spanish speakers has received increasing attention in the literature (e.g. Guijarro-Fuentes and Marinis 2007; Guijarro Fuentes 2012; Bowles and Montrul 2009; Farley and McCollam 2004; Montrul 2010a, 2010b, 2011; Montrul and Gürel 2015). On the whole, research has shown that L2 learners can acquire DOM, especially in the canonical contexts; however, the complete distribution is acquired gradually throughout development, if indeed it is completely acquired at all.

A further difference between English and Spanish – and, indeed, Romance in general – relevant to the nominal domain is the order in which nouns and (attributive) adjectives (can) appear within the noun phrase. While in English and other Germanic languages (as well as in unrelated language families such as Chinese) the adjective almost invariably precedes the noun (e.g. *a red car*), Spanish attributive adjectives are canonically postnominal (e.g. *un coche rojo*, 'a red car'), although they can optionally appear in prenominal position. When the adjective appears prenominally it may: (i) convey an entirely different meaning of the adjective, as in *un hombre pobre*, 'a poor man' vs. *un pobre hombre* 'a pitiful man'; (ii) not change the adjectival meaning at all but the position correlates to whether the adjective describes a set reading (*las mujeres bonitas*, 'the beautiful women,' where the phrase refers to a subset of women who happen to be beautiful) or a kind-denoting reading (*las bonitas mujeres*, 'the beautiful women,' where being a woman means one is beautiful); or (iii) be a member of a limited class of adjectives that appear only prenominally – most frequently, qualitative non-restrictive adjectives such as *mero* in *el mero problema* 'the mere problem' (see Demonte 1999, 2008, for more in-depth analyses and description). Research carried out in this domain has benefited from a considerable variety in learners' L1 backgrounds, examining native speakers of Chinese (Guijarro-Fuentes 2014), French (Bruhn de Garavito and White 2002), Italian and German (Rothman *et al.* 2009), and English (e.g. Guijarro-Fuentes *et al.* 2009; Judy *et al.* 2008; Rothman *et al.* 2010). Importantly, the learning task for any of these groups involves acquiring the appropriate distribution of pre- and postnominal adjectives in the face of ambiguous evidence in the input. While L1 effects seem to obtain at lower and intermediate levels of proficiency (e.g. Bruhn de Garavito and White 2002; Rothman *et al.* 2010), most if not all of these studies report convergence on native-like adjective placement by advanced stages of proficiency (see Guijarro-Fuentes 2014 for discussion). This means that irrespective of any advantage L1 transfer might provide if the syntax is the same, as it was for the Italians in Rothman *et al.* (2009), the fact that all learners converge on the Spanish properties entails that new morphosyntactic structure is acquirable in adulthood.

31.3.1 Gender and Number Agreement

Research on the L2 acquisition and processing of properties related to the nominal domain in Spanish has been largely dominated by the study of gender and number agreement in the interlanguage of L2 learners, as well as properties that follow from grammatical gender, such as nominal ellipsis (noun-drop) (e.g. Alarcón 2011; Alemán Bañón *et al.* 2014; Bruhn de Garavito and White 2002; Fernández-García 1999; Franceschina 2002, 2005; Gabriele et al. 2013; Grüter et al. 2012; Hawkins and Franceschina 2004; Iverson 2009, 2010; Keating 2009, 2010; Lew-Williams and Fernald 2010; Liceras et al. 2000, 2008; Montrul 2011; Montrul et al. 2008, 2013; Sagarra and Herschensohn 2010, 2011, 2013; see Alarcón 2014 for review). Such a trend follows naturally from the bias in the literature towards L1 English learners of Spanish as an L2: grammatical gender is absent in English (see Example 31.1), and therefore constitutes a particular challenge for native speakers of this language when present in the L2. Number, a grammatical feature triggering comparable agreement inflection in associated words (articles and adjectives), is partially realized similarly in both languages – i.e. English displays number agreement between demonstratives and nouns, but not between nouns and adjectives and articles and nouns – and therefore provides a baseline to which the L2 acquisition of gender assignment and gender agreement can be compared within the same domain (Examples 31.2a and b). It is important to note, however, that number agreement is present beyond the nominal domain (e.g. subject verb agreement) in Spanish (and English), while gender is restricted to the nominal domain.

(31.1) La   casa   roja   tiene los   suelos
        The.FEM.SG house.FEM.SG red.FEM.SG has   the.MASC.PL floors.MASC.PL
        desgastados.
        worn-out.MASC.PL
        'The red house has worn-out floors.'

(31.2) a. This house is red. / These houses are red. / The house/houses are red.
        b. Esta casa es roja. / Estas casas son rojas. / La casa es roja. / Las casas son rojas.

White et al. (2004) report the findings of a comprehensive study on gender and number agreement in L2 Spanish by native speakers of French and English. Importantly, the study included both production and comprehension measures and examined learners at three levels of proficiency. In considering potential linguistic transfer from the L1, French- and English-speaking learners differ in several important aspects when it comes to the acquisition of gender and number agreement in Spanish, since these features are realized similarly in French but are either only partially present (number) or absent (gender) in English. Oral production of noun phrases was elicited through a picture-description task and a guessing game, whereas comprehension was tested using a picture-identification task making use of null nominals (noun-drop). All groups, irrespective of proficiency and L1, displayed comparatively higher scores in both production and comprehension of number relative to gender agreement. Furthermore, being a native speaker of an L1 that instantiates gender did not seem to determine whether this feature could be acquired in Spanish, nor did it appear to have notable consequences for development: both L1 groups seemed to find gender agreement equally problematic at first, but all showed signs of having acquired it by intermediate stages of proficiency – so much so, in fact, that the authors found no significant differences between intermediate and advanced learners and a control group of native speakers.

The comprehension task in this study is of particular methodological importance, since it involves the recovery of the appropriate referent noun based solely on the gender and number features instantiated in the article and the adjective, as these nouns were "dropped" or elided (e.g. *ponlas ahí, cerca de la __ roja*, 'put them there, close to the.FEM.SG __ red.FEM.SG'). Successful completion of this task thus demonstrates knowledge of the morphological reflexes of the noun's gender specification, a knowledge that might be obscured by morphophonological matching when a noun with canonical word marking (*-a* for feminine, *-o* for masculine) is present. Indeed, as with other kinds of ellipsis, noun drop in Spanish is intimately related to the expression of agreement features in associated elements, in this case gender and number (although see Snyder *et al.* 2001). As a result, it has been typically examined in studies examining gender and number agreement in L2 populations, both in children (e.g. Liceras *et al.* 2000) and in adults (e.g. Iverson 2009, 2010; Grüter *et al.* 2012; Montrul *et al.* 2008).

One notable result in White *et al.*'s (2004) study is that learners seemed to have fewer problems with masculine than with feminine nouns. A closer inspection of the data revealed that, indeed, masculine agreement morphology was used with feminine nouns in some cases, whereas the opposite did not hold. White and colleagues advance an account in terms of markedness, arguing that masculine morphology seems to be the default (or unmarked) form to which these learners resort when the mechanisms of gender agreement fail or when the gender specification of a certain noun has not been fully acquired (see also Bruhn de Garavito and White 2002; Fernández-García 1999; Liceras *et al.* 2008; McCarthy 2008; among others). Markedness effects have been investigated in the processing literature, which has shown that native speakers are sensitive to asymmetries between the unmarked and the marked specifications of features such as gender and number (e.g. Alemán Bañón and Rothman 2016). Beyond the role of markedness, online measures of linguistic processing have been widely used to investigate gender agreement resolution in L2 learners of Spanish. Within the eye-tracking literature, for example, researchers have often probed non-native speakers' abilities to use gender cues in order to predict an upcoming noun, in the same way that native speakers of Spanish have been shown to do from as young as three to four years of age (Lew-Williams and Fernald 2007). Dussias *et al.* (2013; cf. Lew-Williams and Fernald 2010) found that only at advanced levels of proficiency did L1 English–L2 Spanish learners display a gender-based anticipatory effect, and that lower–intermediate L1 Italian learners did so only for feminine nouns – suggesting a markedness effect similar to the one discussed above. Similar studies employing both predictive processing and agreement violation paradigms suggest that traditionally reported learner difficulties in gender agreement do not necessarily mean that this is unacquirable in adulthood (e.g. Alarcón 2009; Keating 2009, 2010; Sagarra and Herschensohn 2010, 2011, 2013; cf. Franceschina 2005), although processing problems may extend beyond production (e.g. Gillon Dowens *et al.* 2010; Grüter *et al.* 2012).

While the literature on L1 English learners of L2 Spanish has consistently addressed the issue of gender agreement on the basis of differences between these languages and the subsequent difficulty for L1 English learners, there is still no widespread agreement on whether the presence of a grammatical gender system in the L1 facilitates – or indeed impacts in any way – the acquisition and processing of gender agreement in L2 Spanish (e.g. White *et al.* 2004; Dussias *et al.* 2013). This is not to say that studies have found no influence of the L1. Indeed, despite behavioral findings of successful ultimate attainment by L1 English speakers (e.g. White *et al.* 2004), evidence in the processing literature is mixed. Gillon Dowens *et al.* (2010) report evidence from an electroencephalography/event-related potential (EEG/ERP) paradigm of persistent effects of what could be interpreted as L1 transfer even in advanced learners, who display native-like electrophysiological responses to violations of number agreement, but subtly different responses to violations of gender agreement. Crucially, a further study with L1 Chinese learners (Gillon Dowens *et al.* 2011) confirmed that the L1 English learners' native-like sensitivity to number agreement violations might be explained by the presence of number in the English inflectional system: Chinese learners, who do not have experience with gender or number agreement in their L1, showed similar responses to both types of violations which were, in turn, similar to the L1 English learners' response to gender agreement violations in Gillon Dowens *et al.* (2010). On the other hand, more recent EEG/ERP studies focusing on the acquisition and processing of gender agreement in L2 Spanish have found, both cross-sectionally (Gabriele *et al.* 2013) and longitudinally (Alemán Bañón *et al.* 2014), that native English speakers show native-like processing of (both number and) gender agreement violations at advanced stages of proficiency, irrespective of potential markedness effects (Alemán Bañón *et al.* 2017). Furthermore, these studies have found that advanced L2 learners, like native speakers, can establish agreement dependencies beyond the noun phrase (e.g. with an intervening verb) and are sensitive to various degrees of structural distance (cf. Keating 2009). Beyond the potential influence of the L1 in the acquisition and processing of the L2, a number of studies have provided evidence that other factors, pertaining both to the semantics of the head noun (e.g. animacy: Alarcón 2009; Sagarra and Herschensohn 2011, 2013) and to L2 processing more generally (e.g. working memory capacity: Sagarra and Herschensohn

2010), may be crucial in predicting non-native performance in gender and number agreement.

Taken together, studies on the acquisition and processing of properties within the Spanish nominal domain suggest that, while linguistic phenomena such as adjective placement or gender assignment and agreement – in addition to (or compounded with) target-like use and distribution of articles – may be initially challenging for learners, all properties of the nominal system can eventually be acquired, even by learners who do not have previous experience with some of these features. However, while maturational constraints do not seem to be in place (for this domain at least), effects of this lack of experience – or, potentially, of experience with a grammatical system encoding similar properties in a different way – may linger well into advanced stages of proficiency, at least in what pertains to online language processing. In the absence of widespread agreement within the processing literature, it is at present difficult to ascertain whether these effects may by themselves explain the kind of non-targetlike behavior at near-native levels of proficiency that some authors have attributed to maturational constraints on linguistic representation (e.g. DeKeyser 2000; Franceschina 2005; Hawkins and Chan 1997; Tsimpli and Dimitrakopoulou 2007).

31.4 Conclusions and Future Directions

Our aim in the present chapter has been to offer the reader an overview of the research carried out on the L2 acquisition of Spanish by speakers of different L1s and, in so doing, to highlight some of the insights that might be gleaned from a collective consideration of these results. We hope that, by adjusting our exposition to different levels of granularity for different linguistic properties, the chapter can be both a window onto the variety and depth of the literature and a useful analytical tool that enables a wider perspective on what the available data tell us about the acquisition of Spanish in non-native contexts, and L2 acquisition more generally.

The studies reviewed in these pages have examined the acquisition of different properties of Spanish with a common methodological concern: making sure that the linguistic property under investigation was not present in some of the learners' L1s (in those studies that compare different L1 groups) or, alternatively, that two linguistic properties were tested within the same domain, with only one of them being present in the L1 (as is the case with some of the studies with L1 English speakers). By manipulating these two-way distinctions, researchers have been able to comment on the ultimate acquirability of properties that are new to L2 learners (i.e. not instantiated in the

L1), especially with regard to how L1 transfer might condition the learning task (see, e.g., Ellis *et al.* 2016; Eubank 1993; Gass 1996; Lardiere 2009; Long 2007; Ortega 2009, 2013; Schwartz and Sprouse 1996; Tsimpli and Dimitrakopoulou 2007 for different perspectives on this issue). Across domains, most of the available evidence seems to suggest that learners can acquire native-like expression and distribution of most linguistic properties, including those not present in the L1. However, a mismatch between the learner's native language and L2 Spanish will often result in a developmental path that diverges from that of learners with L1s that are similarly configured for a given property. In short, then, a large portion of the literature on L2 Spanish suggests that L1/L2 (mis)matches condition the learnability of particular linguistic properties and thus constrain interlanguage development, but crucially they are not deterministic to the ultimate attainment of those properties, at least under conditions that could reasonably give rise to native-like ultimate attainment in the first place. It is important to note that, taken together, these studies offer a level of description and modeling of the developmental sequence that allow us to predict not only that L1 transfer/cross-linguistic influence *will* impact learner interlanguage, but also *how* this may happen.

There is no question that the significant and impressive spike of the past 20 years in L2 Spanish studies has contributed to correcting, at least in part, the bias present in SLA towards English as an L2. However, our field is still similarly biased towards L2 learners of Spanish whose L1 is English. So, while we can confidently say that at present we have a good idea of how Spanish is acquired as an L2, we should perhaps qualify this and state more accurately that we have a better idea of how Spanish is acquired as an L2 when English is the L1. Of course, (some) important generalizations that pertain to L2 acquisition proper can be and have been made from this literature, but well-established L1-specific developmental variation in L2 acquisition should encourage us to be measured with generalized claims that stem primarily from one language pairing. One strength of the literature examining English as an L2 comes from the combined power of patterns that emerge irrespective of the language pairing itself – i.e. irrespective of the L1. In such cases, we can deduce that universal effects reflect either a byproduct of bilingualism proper or an age effect on acquisition/processing. Conversely and by comparison, when cross-linguistic patterns do not obtain, one can appreciate more clearly where and why the L1 imposes an influence on L2 development and ultimate attainment. We believe that a significant part of the work ahead for the field will inevitably be related to diversifying our knowledge base in this manner. Fortunately, some attention has been dedicated in recent years to L2 Spanish studies that use non-English L1 speakers (see Judy and Perpiñán 2015, and the works therein), alongside meta-analyses of research into L2 Spanish that compare and contrast results for the same properties by speakers of different L1s (see, e.g., Iverson and Rothman 2015).[3]

It should be clear from the treatment of research in this chapter that the acquisition and processing of Spanish as a non-native language is an expanding field that has much to offer to linguistic theory and application. Although paradigmatic differences between researchers delineate, to some extent, not only the types of properties examined but also the methodologies used and the interpretation of available data, it is clear that, irrespective of theoretical differences, there is a common bond bringing us together that decisively hovers around the Spanish language itself. We are not just linguists; we are Hispanic linguists.

References

Alarcón, I. (2009). The Processing of Gender Agreement in L1 and L2 Spanish: Evidence from Reaction Time Data. *Hispania*, 92 (4), 814–828.

Alarcón, I. (2011). Spanish Grammatical Gender under Complete and Incomplete Acquisition: Early and Late Bilinguals' Linguistic Behavior within the Noun Phrase. *Bilingualism: Language and Cognition*, 14 (3), 332–350.

Alarcón, I. (2014). Grammatical Gender in Second Language Spanish. In K. L. Geeslin (ed.), *The Handbook of Spanish Second Language Acquisition*. Oxford: Blackwell, pp. 202–218.

Alemán Bañón, J., Fiorentino, R., and Gabriele, A. (2014). Morphosyntactic Processing in Advanced Second Language (L2) Learners: An Event-Related Potential Investigation of the Effects of L1–L2 Similarity and Structural Distance. *Second Language Research*, 30 (3), 275–306.

Alemán Bañón, J., Miller, D., and Rothman, J. (2017). Examining Morphological Variability in the Online Comprehension and Production of Number and Gender Agreement in L2 Spanish: An ERP Study. *Journal of Experimental Psychology: Learning, Memory and Cognition*, 43 (10), 1509–1536. doi: 10.1037/xlm0000394.

Alemán Bañón, J. and Rothman, J. (2016). The role of Morphological Markedness in the Processing of Number and Gender Agreement in Spanish: An Event-Related Potential Investigation. *Language, Cognition and Neuroscience*, 31 (10), 1272–1298. doi: 10.1080/23273798.2016.1218032. Published online August 12, 2016.

---

[3] Iverson and Rothman (2015) present a meta-analysis of the type we are advocating. They examine together the results of three independent studies (Bruhn de Garavito and Guijarro-Fuentes 2002; Rothman and Iverson 2013; Cuza *et al.* 2013b) into the same domain of grammar (null objects) in L2 Spanish with speakers of various L1s: English, European Portuguese, Brazilian Portuguese, and Mandarin. They discuss the similar patterns and explain, on the basis of distinctions in the L1 baseline, why the differences across the groups are likely to have obtained.

Alexiadou, A. and Anagnostopoulou, E. (1998). Parameterizing Agr: Word Order, V-Movement and EPP-Checking. *Natural Language and Linguistic Theory*, 16 (3), 491–539.

Andersen, R. (1986). El desarrollo de la morfología verbal en el español como segundo idioma. In J. M. Meisel (ed.), *Adquisición de lenguaje/Aquisição da linguagem*. Frankfurt: Vervuert, pp. 115–138.

Andersen, R. W. and Shirai, Y. (1994). Discourse Motivations for Some Cognitive Acquisition Principles. *Studies in Second Language Acquisition*, 16 (2), 133–156.

Bardovi-Harlig, K. (1999). Exploring the Interlanguage of Interlanguage Pragmatics: A Research Agenda for Acquisitional Pragmatics. *Language Learning*, 49 (4), 677–713.

Bardovi-Harlig, K. (2000). *Tense and Aspect in Second Language Acquisition: Form, Meaning, and Use*. Hoboken, NJ: Wiley-Blackwell.

Bardovi-Harlig, K. and Comajoan, L. (2008). Order of Acquisition and Developmental Readiness. In B. Spolsky and F. M. Hult (eds.), *The Handbook of Educational Linguistics*. Oxford: Blackwell, pp. 383–397.

Borgonovo, C., Bruhn de Garavito, J., and Prévost, P. (2005). Acquisition of Mood Distinctions in L2 Spanish. In A. Brugos, M. R. Clark-Cotton, and S. Ha (eds.), *BUCLD 29: Proceedings of the 29th Boston University Conference on Language Development*. Somerville, MA: Cascadilla, pp. 97–108.

Bowles, M. and Montrul, S. (2009). Instructed L2 Acquisition of Differential Object Marking in Spanish. In R. Leow, H. Campos, and D. Lardiere (eds.), *Little Words. Their History, Phonology, Syntax, Semantics, Pragmatics and Acquisition*. Washington, DC: Georgetown University Press, pp. 199–210.

Brown, R. (1973). *A First Language*. Cambridge, MA: Harvard University Press.

Brown, E. and Cortés-Torres, M. (2012). Syntactic and Pragmatic Usage of the [estar + adjective] Construction in Puerto Rican Spanish: *¡Está brutal!* In K. L. Geeslin and M. Díaz-Campos (eds.), *Selected Proceedings of the 14th Hispanic Linguistics Symposium*. Somerville, MA: Cascadilla, pp. 61–74.

Bruhn de Garavito, J. (2009). Eventive and Stative Passives: The Role of Transfer in the Acquisition of *ser* and *estar* by German and English L1 Speakers. In J. Collentine, M. García, B. A. Lafford, and F. Marcos Marín (eds.), *Selected Proceedings of the 11th Hispanic Linguistics Symposium*. Somerville, MA: Cascadilla, pp. 27–38.

Bruhn de Garavito, J. and Guijarro-Fuentes, P. (2002). L2 Acquisition of Indefinite Object Drop. In J. Costa and M. J. Freitas (eds.), *GALA 2001 Proceedings*. Lisbon, Portugal: Associação Portuguesa de Linguística, pp. 60–67.

Bruhn de Garavito, J. and Montrul, S. (1996). Verb Movement and Clitic Placement in French and Spanish as a Second Language. In A. Stringfellow, D. Cahana-Amitay, E. Hughes, and A. Zukowski (eds.), *Proceedings of the 20th Annual Boston University Conference on Language Development*, Vol. 1. Somerville, MA: Cascadilla, pp. 111–122.

Bruhn de Garavito, J. and Valenzuela, E. (2008). Eventive and Stative Passives in Spanish L2 Acquisition: A Matter of Aspect. *Bilingualism: Language and Cognition*, 11 (3), 323–336.

Bruhn de Garavito, J. and White, L. (2002). L2 Acquisition of Spanish DPs: The Status of Grammatical Features. In A. T. Pérez-Leroux and J. M. Liceras (eds.), *The Acquisition of Spanish Morphosyntax: The L1/L2 Connection*. Dordrecht: Kluwer, pp. 153–178.

Bybee, J. (1985). *Morphology*. Amsterdam and Philadelphia, PA: John Benjamins.

Cadierno, T. (2000). The Acquisition of Spanish Grammatical Aspect by Danish Advanced Language Learners. *Spanish Applied Linguistics*, 4 (1), 1–53.

Camacho, J. (2012). Ser and Estar: The Individual/Stage-level Distinction and Aspectual Predication. In J. I. Hualde, A. Olarrea, and E. O'Rourke (eds.), *The Handbook of Hispanic Linguistics*. Malden, MA: Wiley-Blackwell, pp. 453–475.

Camps, J. (2002). Aspectual Distinctions in Spanish as a Foreign Language: The Early Stages of Oral Production. *International Review of Applied Linguistics in Language Teaching*, 40 (3), 179–210.

Collentine, J. and Asención-Delaney, Y. (2010). A Corpus-Based Analysis of the Discourse Functions of *Ser/Estar* + Adjective in Three Levels of Spanish as FL Learners. *Language Learning*, 60 (2), 409–445.

Comajoan, L. (2014). Tense and Aspect in Second Language Spanish. In K. L. Geeslin (ed.), *The Handbook of Spanish Second Language Acquisition*. Oxford: Blackwell, pp. 235–252.

Comajoan, L. and Pérez Saldanya, M. (2005). Grammaticalization and Language Acquisition: Interaction of Lexical Aspect and Discourse. In D. Eddington (ed.), *Selected Proceedings of the 6th Conference on the Acquisition of Spanish and Portuguese as First and Second Languages*. Somerville, MA: Cascadilla, pp. 44–55.

Cuza, A., Guijarro-Fuentes, P., Pires, A., and Rothman, J. (2013a). The Syntax-Semantics of Bare and Definite Plural Subjects in the L2 Spanish of English Natives. *International Journal of Bilingualism*, 17 (5), 634–652.

Cuza, A., Pérez-Leroux, A. T., and Sánchez, L. (2013b). The Role of Semantic Transfer in Clitic-Drop among Chinese L1–Spanish L2 Bilinguals. *Studies in Second Language Acquisition*, 35 (1), 93–125.

DeKeyser, R. M. (2000). The Robustness of Critical Period Effects in Second Language Acquisition. *Studies in Second Language Acquisition*, 22 (4), 499–533.

Demonte, V. (1999). A Minimal Account of Spanish Adjective Position and Interpretation. In J. Franco, A. Landa, and J. Martín (eds.), *Grammatical Analyses in Basque and Romance Linguistics: Papers in Honor of Mario Saltarelli*. Amsterdam and Philadelphia, PA: John Benjamins, pp. 45–76.

Demonte, V. (2008). Meaning-Form Correlations and Adjective Position in Spanish. In C. Kennedy and L. McNally (eds.), *The Semantics of Adjectives and Adverbs*. Oxford: Oxford University Press, pp. 71–100.

Dietrich, R., Klein, W., and Noyau, C. (1995). *The Acquisition of Temporality in a Second Language*. Amsterdam: John Benjamins.

Domínguez, L., Tracy-Ventura, N., Arche, M. J., Mitchell, R., and Myles, F. (2013). The Role of Dynamic Contrasts in the L2 Acquisition of Spanish Past Tense Morphology. *Bilingualism: Language and Cognition*, 16 (3), 558–577.

Dorado, D. (2011). Second Language Variation of Ser and Estar: A Comparative Analysis of Advanced Second Language Learners (Doctoral dissertation). University of Florida.

Dussias, P. E., Valdés Kroff, J. R., Guzzardo Tamargo, R. E., and Gerfen, C. (2013). When Gender and Looking Go Hand in Hand. *Studies in Second Language Acquisition*, 35 (2), 353–387.

Eubank, L. (1993). On the Transfer of Parametric Values in L2 Development. *Language Acquisition*, 3 (3), 182–208.

Ellis, N. C., Römer, U., and O'Donnell, M. B. (2016). *Usage-Based Approaches to Language Acquisition and Processing: Cognitive and Corpus Investigations of Construction Grammar*. Hoboken, NJ: Wiley-Blackwell.

Farley, A. P. and McCollam, K. (2004). Learner Readiness and L2 Production in Spanish: Processability Theory on Trial. *Estudios de Lingüística Aplicada*, 22, 47–69.

Fernández-García, M. (1999). Patterns of Gender Agreement in the Speech of Second Language Learners. In J. Gutiérrez-Rexach and F. Martínez-Gil (eds.), *Advances in Hispanic Linguistics: Papers from the 2nd Hispanic Linguistics Symposium*. Somerville, MA: Cascadilla Press, pp. 3–15.

Franceschina, F. (2002). Case and Φ-Feature Agreement in Advanced L2 Spanish Grammars. *EUROSLA Yearbook*, 2, 71–86.

Franceschina, F. (2005). *Fossilized Second Language Grammars: The Acquisition of Grammatical Gender*. Amsterdam: John Benjamins.

Gabriele, A., Fiorentino, R., and Alemán Bañón, J. (2013). Examining Second Language Development Using Event-Related Potentials: A Cross-Sectional Study on the Processing of Gender and Number Agreement. *Linguistic Approaches to Bilingualism*, 3 (2), 213–232.

Gass, S. M. (1996). Second Language Acquisition and Linguistic Theory: The Role of Language Transfer. In W. C. Ritchie and T. K. Bhatia (eds.), *Handbook of Second Language Acquisition*. London: Academic Press, pp. 317–348.

Geeslin, K. L. (2003). A Comparison of Copula Choice: Native Spanish Speakers and Advanced Learners. *Language Learning*, 53 (4), 703–764.

Geeslin, K. L. (ed.) (2014a). *The Handbook of Spanish Second Language Acquisition*. Oxford: Blackwell.

Geeslin, K. L. (2014b). The Acquisition of the Copula Contrast in Second Language Spanish. In K. L. Geeslin (ed.), *The Handbook of Spanish Second Language Acquisition*. Oxford: Blackwell, pp. 219–234.

Geeslin, K. L., García-Amaya, L. J., Hasler-Barker, M., Henriksen, N., and Killam, J. (2010). The SLA of Direct Object Pronouns in a Study Abroad Immersion Environment where Use is Variable. In C. Borgonovo, M. Español-Echevarría, and P. Prévost (eds.), *Selected Proceedings of the 12th Hispanic Linguistics Symposium*. Somerville, MA: Cascadilla, pp. 246–259.

Geeslin, K. L., García-Amaya, L. J., Hasler-Barker, M., Henriksen, N., and Killam, J. (2012). The L2 Acquisition of Variable Perfective Past Time Reference in Spanish in an Overseas Immersion Setting. In K. L. Geeslin and M. Díaz-Campos (eds.), *Selected Proceedings of the 14th Hispanic Linguistics Symposium*. Somerville, MA: Cascadilla, pp. 197–213.

Geeslin, K. L. and Gudmestad, A. (2008). Variable Subject Expression in Second-Language Spanish: A Comparison of Native and Non-Native Speakers. In M. Bowles, R. Foote, S. Perpiñán, and R. Bhatt, *Selected Proceedings of the 2007 Second Language Research Forum*. Somerville, MA: Cascadilla, pp. 69–85.

Geeslin, K. L. and Gudmestad, A. (2011). Using Sociolinguistic Analyses of Discourse-Level Features to Expand Research on L2 Variation in Forms of Spanish Subject Expression. In L. Plonsky and M. Schierloh (eds.), *Selected Proceedings of the 2009 Second Language Research Forum: Diverse Contributions to SLA*. Somerville, MA: Cascadilla, pp. 16–30.

Geeslin, K. L. and Guijarro-Fuentes, P. (2006). A Longitudinal Study of Copula Choice: Following Development in Variable Structures. In N. Sagarra and A. J. Toribio (eds.), *Selected Proceedings of the 9th Hispanic Linguistics Symposium*. Somerville, MA: Cascadilla, pp. 144–156.

Geeslin, K. L. and Guijarro-Fuentes, P. (2008). Variation in Contemporary Spanish: Linguistic Predictors of *estar* in Four Cases of Language Contact. *Bilingualism: Language and Cognition*, 11 (3), 365–380.

Gillon Dowens, M., Guo, T., Guo, J., Barber, H. A., and Carreiras, M. (2011). Gender and Number Processing in Chinese Learners of Spanish – Evidence from Event Related Potentials. *Neuropsychologia*, 49 (7), 1651–1659.

Gillon Dowens, M., Vergara, M., Barber, H. A., and Carreiras, M. (2010). Morphosyntactic Processing in Late Second-Language Learners. *Journal of Cognitive Neuroscience*, 22 (8), 1870–1887.

Grice, P. (1975). Logic and Conversation. In P. Cole and J. L. Morgan (eds.), *Syntax and Semantics III: Speech Acts*. New York: Academic Press, pp. 41–58.

Grüter, T., Lew-Williams, C., and Fernald, A. (2012). Grammatical Gender in L2: A Production or a Real-Time Processing Problem? *Second Language Research*, 28 (2), 191–215.

Guasti, M., Chierchia, G., Crain, S., Foppolo, F., Gualmini, A., and Meroni, L. (2005). Why Children and Adults Sometimes (but not Always) Compute Implicatures. *Language and Cognitive Processes*, 20 (5), 667–696.

Gudmestad, A. (2012). Acquiring a Variable Structure: An Interlanguage Analysis of Second-Language Mood Use in Spanish. *Language Learning*, 62 (2), 373–402.

Guijarro-Fuentes, P. (2012). The Acquisition of Interpretable Features in L2 Spanish: Personal *a*. *Bilingualism: Language and Cognition*, 15 (4), 701–720.

Guijarro-Fuentes, P. (2014). Adjectival Modification in L2 Spanish Noun Phrases. *EUROSLA Yearbook*, 14, 143–172.

Guijarro-Fuentes, P., Judy, T., and Rothman, J. (2009). On Transfer, Proficiency and Cross-Individual/Aggregate SLA Differences: Examining Adjectival Semantics in L2 Spanish. In A. Benati (ed.), *Issues in Second Language Proficiency*. London: Continuum, pp. 233–253.

Guijarro-Fuentes, P. and Marinis, T. (2007). Acquiring Phenomena at the Syntax/Semantics Interface in L2 Spanish. *EUROSLA Yearbook*, 7, 67–87.

Gutiérrez-Rexach, J. (2001). The Semantics of Spanish Plural Existential Determiners and the Dynamics of Judgment Types. *Probus*, 13 (1), 113–154.

Halloran, B. and Rothman, J. (2015). The Acquisition of Clitics in L2 Spanish. In J. Smith and T. Ihsane (eds.), *Romance Linguistics 2012: Selected Papers from the 42nd Linguistic Symposium on Romance Languages*. Amsterdam: John Benjamins, pp. 3–16.

Hasbún, L. M. (1995). The Role of Lexical Aspect in the Acquisition of the Tense/Aspect System in L2 Spanish (Doctoral dissertation). Indiana University.

Hawkins, R. and Chan, C. Y.-H. (1997). The Partial Availability of Universal Grammar in Second Language Acquisition: The "Failed Functional Features Hypothesis." *Second Language Research*, 13, 187–226.

Hawkins, R. and Franceschina, F. (2004). Explaining the Acquisition and Non-Acquisition of Determiner–Noun Gender Concord in French and Spanish. In P. Prévost and J. Paradis (eds.), *The Acquisition of French in Different Contexts*. Amsterdam: John Benjamins, pp. 175–205.

Hengeveld, K. (2004). Illocution, Mood and Modality. In G. Booij, C. Lehmann, and J. Mugdan (eds.), *Morphology: An International Handbook on Inflection and Word-Formation*, Vol. 2. Berlin: De Gruyter, pp. 1190–1201.

Herschensohn, J. and Young-Scholten, M. (eds.) (2013). *The Cambridge Handbook of Second Language Acquisition*. Cambridge and New York: Cambridge University Press.

Horn, L. R. (1972). On the Semantic Properties of Logical Operators in English (Doctoral dissertation). UCLA.

Ionin, T., Montrul, S., and Crivos, M. (2013). A Bidirectional Study on the Acquisition of Plural Noun Phrase Interpretation in English and Spanish. *Applied Psycholinguistics*, 34 (3), 483–518.

Iverson, M. (2009). N-Drop at the Initial State of L3 Portuguese: Comparing Simultaneous and Additive Bilinguals of English/Spanish. In A. Pires and J. Rothman (eds.), *Minimalist Inquiries into Child and Adult Language Acquisition: Case Studies across Portuguese*. Berlin: De Gruyter, pp. 221–244.

Iverson, M. (2010). Informing the Age of Acquisition Debate: L3 as a Litmus Test. *International Review of Applied Linguistics in Language Teaching*, 48 (2–3), 221–243.

Iverson, M. and Rothman, J. (2015). Object Drop in L2 Spanish, (Complex) Feature Reassembly and L1 Pre-emption: Comparing English, Chinese, European and Brazilian Portuguese Learners. In T. Judy and S. Perpiñán (eds.), *The Acquisition of Spanish in Understudied Language Pairings*. Amsterdam: John Benjamins, pp. 255–280.

Judy, T., Guijarro-Fuentes, P., and Rothman, J. (2008). Adult Accessibility to L2 Representational Features: Evidence from the Spanish DP. In M. Bowles, R. Foote, S. Perpiñán, and R. Bhatt (eds.), *Selected Proceedings of the 2nd Language Research Forum 2007*. Somerville, MA: Cascadilla, pp. 1–21.

Judy, T. and Perpiñán, S. (eds.) (2015). *The Acquisition of Spanish in Understudied Language Pairings*. Amsterdam: John Benjamins.

Keating, G. D. (2009). Sensitivity to Violation of Gender Agreement in Native and Nonnative Spanish. *Language Learning*, 59 (3), 503–535.

Keating, G. D. (2010). The Effects of Linear Distance and Working Memory on the Processing of Gender Agreement in Spanish. In B. VanPatten and J. Jegersky (eds.), *Research in Second Language Processing and Parsing*. Amsterdam: John Benjamins, pp. 113–134.

Lardiere, D. (2009). Some Thoughts on the Contrastive Analysis of Features in Second Language Acquisition. *Second Language Research*, 25 (2), 173–227.

Lee, F. (2003). Anaphoric R-Expressions as Bound Variables. *Syntax*, 6 (1), 84–114.

Lew-Williams, C. and Fernald, A. (2007). Young Children Learning Spanish Make Rapid Use of Grammatical Gender in Spoken Word Recognition. *Psychological Science*, 18 (3), 193–198.

Lew-Williams, C. and Fernald, A. (2010). Real-Time Processing of Gender-Marked Articles by Native and Non-Native Spanish Speakers. *Journal of Memory and Language*, 63 (4), 447–464.

Liceras, J. M. (1985). The Value of Clitics in Non-Native Spanish. *Second Language Research*, 1 (2), 151–168.

Liceras, J. M. (1989). On Some Properties of the "Pro-Drop" Parameter: Looking for Missing Subjects in Non-Native Spanish. In S. Gass and J. Schachter (eds.), *Linguistic Perspectives on Second Language Acquisition*. Cambridge: Cambridge University Press, pp. 109–133.

Liceras, J. M. and Díaz, L. (1999). Topic-Drop versus Pro-Drop: Null Subjects and Pronominal Subjects in the Spanish L2 of Chinese, English, French, German and Japanese Speakers. *Second Language Research*, 15 (1), 1–40.

Liceras, J. M., Díaz, L., and Mongeon, C. (2000). N-Drop and Determiners in Native and Non-Native Spanish: More on the Role of Morphology in the Acquisition of Syntactic Knowledge. In R. P. Leow and C. Sanz (eds.), *Spanish Applied Linguistics at the Turn of the Millennium: Papers from the 1999 Conference on the L1 and L2 Acquisition of Spanish and Portuguese*. Somerville, MA: Cascadilla, pp. 67–96.

Liceras, J. M., Fernández-Fuertes, R., Perales, S., Pérez-Tattam, R., and Spradlin, K. T. (2008). Gender and Gender Agreement in Bilingual Native and Non-Native Grammars: A View from Child and Adult Functional-Lexical Mixings. *Lingua*, 118 (6), 827–851.

Liceras, J. M., Maxwell, D., Laguardia, B., Fernández, Z., Fernández, R., and Díaz, L. (1997). A Longitudinal Study of Spanish Non-Native Grammars: Beyond Parameters. In A. T. Pérez-Leroux and W. R. Glass (eds.), *Contemporary Perspectives on the Acquisition of Spanish*, Vol. 1. Somerville, MA: Cascadilla, pp. 99–132.

Liskin-Gasparro, J. (2000). The Use of Tense-Aspect Morphology in Spanish Oral Narratives: Exploring the Perceptions of Advanced Learners. *Hispania*, 83 (4), 830–844.

Long, D. and Rothman, J. (2013). Generative Approaches and the Competing Systems Hypothesis: Formal Acquisition to Practical Application. In. J. Schweiter (ed.), *Theoretical and Pedagogical Innovations in SLA and Bilingualism*. Amsterdam: John Benjamins, pp. 63–83.

Long, M. (2007). *Problems in SLA*. Mahwah, NJ: Erlbaum.

Lopez, L. (2012). *Indefinite Objects. Scrambling, Choice Functions and Differential Marking*. Cambridge, MA: MIT Press.

Lozano, C. (2002a). Knowledge of Expletive and Pronominal Subjects by Learners of Spanish. *ITL Review of Applied Linguistics*, 135, 37–60.

Lozano, C. (2002b). The Interpretation of Overt and Null Pronouns in Non-Native Spanish. *Durham Working Papers in Linguistics*, 8, 53–66.

Malovrh, P. A. (2008). A Multifaceted Analysis of the Interlanguage Development of Spanish Direct-Object Clitic Pronouns Observed in L2-Learner Production (Doctoral dissertation). Indiana University.

Malovrh, P. A. and Lee, J. F. (2010). Connections between Processing, Production and Placement. In B. VanPatten and J. Jegersky (eds.), *Research in Second Language Processing and Parsing*. Amsterdam: John Benjamins, pp. 231–256.

McCarthy, C. (2008). Morphological Variability in the Comprehension of Agreement: An Argument for Representation over Computation. *Second Language Research*, 24 (4), 459–486.

Miller, D., Giancaspro, D., Iverson, M., Rothman, J., and Slabakova, R. (2016). Not Just *algunos*, but indeed *unos* L2ers Can Acquire Scalar Implicatures in L2 Spanish. In A. Alba de la Fuente, E. Valenzuela, and C. Martínez-Sanz (eds.), *Language Acquisition beyond Parameters: Studies in Honour of Juana M. Liceras*. Amsterdam: John Benjamins, pp. 125–145.

Montrul, S. (2002). Incomplete Acquisition and Attrition of Spanish Tense/Aspect Distinctions in Adult Bilinguals. *Bilingualism: Language and Cognition*, 5 (1), 39–68.

Montrul, S. (2004). Psycholinguistic Evidence for Split Intransitivity in Spanish L2. *Applied Psycholinguistics*, 25 (2), 239–267.

Montrul, S. (2010a). How Similar are L2 Learners and Heritage Speakers? Spanish Clitics and Word Order. *Applied Psycholinguistics*, 31 (1), 167–207.

Montrul, S. (2010b). Dominant Language Transfer in Spanish L2 Learners and Heritage Speakers. *Second Language Research*, 26 (3), 293–327.

Montrul, S. (2011). Morphological Errors in Spanish Second Language Learners and Heritage Speakers. *Studies in Second Language Acquisition*, 33 (2), 155–161.

Montrul, S. and Bruhn de Garavito, J. (1999). The L2 Acquisition of Spanish: Generative Perspectives. *Second Language Research*, 15 (2), 111–114.

Montrul, S., de la Fuente, I., Davidson, J., and Foote, R. (2013). The Role of Experience in the Acquisition and Production of Diminutives and Gender in Spanish: Evidence from L2 Learners and Heritage Speakers. *Second Language Research*, 29, (1), 87–118.

Montrul, S., Foote, R., and Perpiñán, S. (2008). Gender Agreement in Adult Second Language Learners and Spanish Heritage Speakers: The Effects of Age and Context of Acquisition. *Language Learning*, 58 (3), 503–553.

Montrul, S. and Gürel, A. (2015). The Acquisition of Differential Object Marking in Spanish by Turkish speakers. In T. Judy and S. Perpiñán (eds.), *The Acquisition of Spanish in Understudied Language Pairings*. Amsterdam: John Benjamins, pp. 281–308.

Montrul, S. and Ionin, T. (2012). Dominant Language Transfer in Spanish Heritage Speakers and L2 Learners in the Interpretation of Definite Articles. *The Modern Language Journal*, 96 (1), 70–94.

Montrul, S. and Rodríguez Louro, C. (2006). Beyond the Syntax of the Null Subject Parameter. In V. Torrens and L. Escobar (eds.), *The Acquisition of Syntax in Romance Languages*. Amsterdam: John Benjamins, pp. 401–418.

Montrul, S. and Slabakova, R. (2003). Competence Similarities between Native and Nearnative Speakers: An Investigation of the Preterite/Imperfect Contrast in Spanish. *Studies in Second Language Acquisition*, 25 (3), 351–398.

Ortega, L. (2009). *Understanding Second Language Acquisition*. London: Hodder.

Ortega, L. (2013). SLA for the 21st Century: Disciplinary Progress, Transdisciplinary Relevance, and the Bi/Multilingual Turn. *Language Learning*, 63 (Supplement 1), 1–24.

Papafragou, A., and Musolino, J. (2003). Scalar Implicatures: Experiments at the Semantics–Pragmatics Interface. *Cognition*, 86, 253–282.

Perales, S. and Liceras, J. M. (2010). Looking for Universals in the Acquisition of L2 Spanish Object Clitics. In P. Guijarro-Fuertes and L. Domínguez (eds.), *New Directions in Language Acquisition: Romance Languages in the Generative Perspective*. Newcastle upon Tyne: Cambridge Scholars Publishing, pp. 323–355.

Pérez-Leroux, A. T. and Glass, W. R. (1997). OPC Effects on the L2 Acquisition of Spanish. In A. T. Pérez-Leroux and W. R. Glass (eds.), *Contemporary Perspectives on the Acquisition of Spanish*, Vol. 1. Somerville, MA: Cascadilla, pp. 149–165.

Pérez-Leroux, A. T. and Glass, W. R. (1999). Null Anaphora in Spanish Second Language Acquisition: Probabilistic versus Generative Approaches. *Second Language Research*, 15 (2), 220–249.

Prévost, P. and White, L. (2000). Accounting for Morphological Variation in L2 Acquisition: Truncation or Missing Inflection? In M. A. Friedemann and L. Rizzi (eds.), *The Acquisition of Syntax: Issues in Comparative Developmental Linguistics*. London: Longman, pp. 232–235.

Ramsay, V. (1990). Developmental Stages in the Acquisition of the Perfective and the Imperfective Aspects by Classroom L2 Learners of Spanish (Doctoral dissertation). University of Oregon.

Roby, D. B. (2009). *Aspect and the Categorization of States: The Case of ser and estar in Spanish*. Amsterdam: John Benjamins.

Rosch, E. H. (1973). Natural Categories. *Cognitive Psychology*, 4, 328–350.

Rothman, J. (2007). Pragmatic Solutions for Syntactic Problems: Understanding Some L2 Syntactic Errors in Terms of Pragmatic Deficits. In S. Baauw, F. Dirjkoningen, and M. Pinto (eds.), *Romance Languages and Linguistic Theory 2005*. Amsterdam: John Benjamins, pp. 299–320.

Rothman, J. (2008). Aspect Selection in Adult L2 Spanish and the Competing Systems Hypothesis: When Pedagogical and Linguistic Rules Conflict. *Languages in Contrast*, 8 (1), 74–106.

Rothman, J. (2009). Pragmatic Deficits with Syntactic Consequences?: L2 Pronominal Subjects and the Syntax–Pragmatics Interface. *Journal of Pragmatics*, 41 (5), 951–973.

Rothman, J., Guijarro-Fuentes, P., Iverson, M., and Judy, T. (2009). Noun-Raising and Adjectival Interpretative Reflexes in the L2 Spanish of Germanic and Italian Learners. In J. Chandlee, M. Franchini, S. Lord, and G.-M. Rheiner (eds.), *Proceedings of the 33rd Annual Boston University Conference on Language Development*. Somerville, MA: Cascadilla, pp. 444–455.

Rothman, J. and Iverson, M. (2013). Islands and Objects in L2 Spanish. *Studies in Second Language Acquisition*, 35 (4), 589–618.

Rothman, J., Judy, T., Guijarro-Fuentes, P., and Pires, A. (2010). On the (Un)-Ambiguity of Adjectival Interpretations in L2 Spanish: Informing Debates on the Mental Representations of L2 Syntax. *Studies in Second Language Acquisition*, 32, 47–77.

Sagarra, N. and Herschensohn, J. (2010). The Role of Proficiency and Working Memory in Gender and Number Agreement Processing in L1 and L2 Spanish. *Lingua*, 120 (8), 2022–2039.

Sagarra, N. and Herschensohn, J. (2011). Proficiency and Animacy Effects on L2 Gender Agreement Processes during Comprehension. *Language Learning*, 61 (1), 80–116.

Sagarra, N. and Herschensohn, J. (2013). Processing of Gender and Number Agreement in Late Spanish Bilinguals. *International Journal of Bilingualism*, 17 (5), 607–627.

Salaberry, R. (1999). The Development of Past Tense Verbal Morphology in Classroom L2 Spanish. *Applied Linguistics*, 20 (2), 151–178.

Salaberry, R. (2003). Tense Aspect in Verbal Morphology. *Hispania*, 86 (3), 559–573.

Salaberry, R. (2005). Evidence for Transfer of Knowledge about Aspect from L2 Spanish to L3 Portuguese. In D. Ayoun and M. R. Salaberry (eds.), *Tense and Aspect in the Romance Languages: Theoretical and Applied Perspectives*. Amsterdam and Philadelphia, PA: John Benjamins, pp. 179–210.

Salaberry, R. (2008). *Marking Past Tense in Second Language Acquisition: A Theoretical Model*. London: Continuum.

Salaberry, R. (2011). Assessing the Effect of Lexical Aspect and Grounding on the Acquisition of L2 Spanish Past Tense Morphology among L1 English Speakers. *Bilingualism: Language and Cognition*, 14 (2), 184–202.

Sánchez-Alonso, S., Deo, A., and Piñango, M. (2016). Copular Variation in Spanish: Implications for the Study of Heritage Speaker Spanish. Paper presented at the Workshop on Heritage Language Acquisition, UiT–The Arctic University of Norway.

Schwartz, B. and Sprouse, R. (1996). L2 Cognitive States and the Full Transfer/Full Access Model. *Second Language Research*, 12 (1), 40–72.

Slabakova, R. (2006). Learnability in the Second Language Acquisition of Semantics: A Bidirectional Study of a Semantic Parameter. *Second Language Research*, 22 (4), 498–523.

Slabakova, R. (2010). Scalar Implicatures in Second Language Acquisition. *Lingua*, 120 (10), 2444–2462.

Slabakova, R. and Montrul, S. (2003). Genericity and Aspect in L2 Acquisition. *Language Acquisition*, 11 (3), 165–196.

Slabakova, R. and Montrul, S. (2007). L2 Acquisition at the Grammar–Discourse Interface: Aspectual Shifts in L2 Spanish. In J. Liceras, H. Zobl, and H. Goodluck (eds.), *The Role of Formal Features in Second Language Acquisition*. Mahwah, NJ: Erlbaum, pp. 452–483.

Snyder, W., Senghas, A., and Inman, K. (2001). Agreement Morphology and the Acquisition of N-Drop in Spanish. *Language Acquisition*, 9, 157–173.

Torrego, E. (1998). *The Dependencies of Objects*. Cambridge, MA: MIT Press.

Tsimpli, I. M. and Dimitrakopoulou, M. (2007). The Interpretability Hypothesis: Evidence from *wh*-Interrogatives in Second Language Acquisition. *Second Language Research*, 23 (2), 215–242.

VanPatten, B. (1985). The Acquisition of *ser* and *estar* by Adult Learners of Spanish: A Preliminary Investigation of Transitional Stages Of Competence. *Hispania*, 68 (2), 399–406.

VanPatten, B. (1987). Classroom Learners' Acquisition of *ser* and *estar*: Accounting for Developmental Patterns. In B. VanPatten, T. Dvorak, and J. F. Lee (eds.), *Foreign Language Learning: A Research Perspective*. Cambridge. MA: Newbury House, pp. 61–75.

VanPatten, B. (1990). Attending to Form and Content in the Input. *Studies in Second Language Acquisition*, 12 (3), 287–301.

Wexler, K. (1994). Optional Infinitives, Head Movement and the Economy of Derivations. In D. Lightfoot and N. Hornstein (eds.), *Verb Movement*. Cambridge: Cambridge University Press, pp. 305–350.

White, L., Valenzuela, E., Kozlowska-Macgregor, M., and Leung, Y. K.-I. (2004). Gender and Number Agreement in Nonnative Spanish. *Applied Psycholinguistics*, 25 (1), 105–133.

Woolsey, D. (2008). From Theory to Research: Contextual Predictors of "*estar* + adjective" and the Study of the SLA of Spanish Copula Choice. *Bilingualism: Language and Cognition*, 11 (3), 277–295.

Wulff, S., Ellis, N. C., Römer, U., Bardovi-Harlig, K., and LeBlanc, C. J. (2009). The Acquisition of Tense-Aspect: Converging Evidence from Corpora and Telicity Ratings. *The Modern Language Journal*, 93 (3), 354–369.

Zyzik, E. (2004). Encoding Meaning with Polyfunctional Forms: The Acquisition of Clitics in L2 Spanish (Doctoral dissertation). University of California at Davis.

Zyzik, E. (2006). Learners' Overgeneralization of Dative Clitics to Accusative Contexts: Evidence for Prototype Effects in SLA. In C. A. Klee and T. L. Face (eds.), *Selected Proceedings of the 7th Conference on the Acquisition of Spanish and Portuguese as First and Second Languages*. Somerville, MA: Cascadilla, pp. 122–134.

Zyzik, E. (2008). Null Objects in Second Language Acquisition: Grammatical vs. Performance Models. *Second Language Research*, 24 (1), 65–110.

Zyzik, E. and Gass, S. (2008). Epilogue: A Tale of Two Copulas. *Bilingualism: Language and Cognition*, 11 (3), 383–385.

32

Variation in Second Language Spanish

Matthew Kanwit

32.1 Early Work on Second Language Variation, Relevant Constructs, and Issues

In the past few decades, the focus of research in second language (L2) acquisition has often moved away from error analyses and toward reporting what learners produce and select regardless of prescriptive accuracy. Whereas early work in L2 acquisition isolated supplied and obligatory contexts, later work acknowledged that interlanguage systems were detectable in spite of output that might not be target-like (Corder 1967; Selinker 1972). That is to say, what were previously viewed as errors were then re-conceptualized as evidence of an underlying, rule-governed system that is dynamic, changing over time. In earlier stages of acquisition, such a system does not reflect the sorts of rules that govern adult, native-like speech. In other words, the manner in which a lower-level learner varies in expressing the same function in more than one way is typically evidence of Type I (Rehner 2002), or vertical (Adamson and Regan 1991), variation. As can be inferred from the term "vertical," such variability reflects development and movement toward some next stage. For example, a learner might vary between use of a regularized, non-target-like preterit *hací and the target-like, irregular *hice* 'I did.' On the other hand, more proficient learners may demonstrate a rule-based system in which they use one form in a certain linguistic or social context and another variant in a different context. This form of variability is known as Type II, or horizontal, variation. To use a similar example, at a later stage in development the same learner might demonstrate aspectual variation between preterit *hice* and imperfect *hacía* 'I was doing' in a linguistically-conditioned manner, utilizing the former more often to describe completed actions and the latter more frequently with actions that were in progress.

One body of research in this vein is that of L2 variationism. Early L2 variationist analyses often focused on the acquisition of English or

French (e.g. Adamson and Regan 1991; Bayley and Langman 2004; Canale and Swain 1980; Preston 1993, 2000; Regan 1995, 2004; Rehner et al. 2003; Tarone 1983), but investigations of Spanish soon followed and have been robust in the past two decades (e.g. Fafulas 2012; Geeslin 2000, 2003; Geeslin and Gudmestad 2008a, 2010; Geeslin and Guijarro-Fuentes 2006; Geeslin and Long 2015; Gudmestad 2006, 2012; Kanwit 2017; Kanwit and Geeslin 2014; Linford and Shin 2013; Malovrh 2006, 2014). This work followed the lead of first language (L1) work on variationist sociolinguistics (Labov 1966), which investigated not only the overall rates of use of the variants of a dependent variable, but also the independent predictors of such use (see Chambers 2008; Díaz-Campos 2011; and Walker 2010 for comprehensive overviews of empirical research in sociolinguistics). In other words, in addition to having concern for learners' overall rates of use of given variants, L2 variationists are also interested in what factors constrain the use of each variant. Let us initially consider the first half of that statement. If a researcher is interested in future-time expression, she might note that the periphrastic future (PF, e.g. *voy a comer* 'I am going to eat') occurs more frequently than the morphological future (MF, e.g. *comeré* 'I will eat') in numerous dialects across the Spanish-speaking world, including regions of Argentina, Chile, Colombia, the Dominican Republic, Ecuador, Mexico, Peru, Puerto Rico, central Spain, the southwestern United States, Venezuela, and in that of Puerto Rican residents of New York (Escobar 1997b; Gutiérrez 1995; Kanwit and Solon 2013; Lope Blanch 1972; Montes Giraldo 1962; Orozco 2005; Sedano 1994; Silva-Corvalán and Terrell 1989; Zentella 1997). Accordingly, L2 variationists will report learners' overall rates of use of each variant, and might note to what extent learners approximate or fail to approximate this tendency. Nevertheless, simply because a learner matches a native-like pattern of using the PF more than the MF does not mean that the forms are used in target-like contexts. That is to say, the linguistic and social contexts that favor one form over others for the learner may or may not be consistent with how native speakers (NSs) use the variants. For instance, across numerous dialects, for NSs the MF is favored by distant temporality and the presence of temporal adverbial modification (Aaron 2006; Blas Arroyo 2008; Gudmestad and Geeslin 2011; Kanwit and Solon 2013; Orozco 2005). An L2 variationist might then note to what extent this claim applies to learner data. Are temporal distance and the presence of temporal adverbs also significant for learners? If they are significant, do they have the same directions of effect as they do for NSs? Answering such questions enables the researcher to report, for example, not only that an advanced learner group uses the MF at rates that are not significantly different from NSs, but also that the learner group uses MF forms in similar contexts as NSs, such as with distant temporality, in the presence of temporal adverbs, after having spent an extended period of time in Spain, etc.

The preceding paragraph has demonstrated that L2 variationists often seek to answer at least three questions: (i) What is the overall rate of use/selection of the given variants of a dependent linguistic variable? (ii) What independent linguistic and extralinguistic (i.e. social and stylistic) factors predict the occurrence of the variants? and (iii) How does development proceed in terms of rates and predictors of use/selection as learners gain proficiency? Since research in this vein frequently borrows from techniques of variationist sociolinguistics, independent variables are often chosen based on the variables that are known to condition native-speaker variation (e.g. temporal distance in future-time expression, as coded in Gudmestad and Geeslin 2013), although acquisitionists might also choose to code variables that do not affect NS expression of the structure but that do affect learner language more generally. For example, let us consider (32.1) and (32.2):

(32.1)   Cuando venga María, iremos a la fiesta.
'When María arrives, we will go to the party.'

(32.2)   Iremos a la fiesta cuando venga María.
'We will go to the party when María arrives.'

Although adverbial clauses may precede or succeed main clauses as in (32.1) and (32.2), respectively, since early stages of acquisition are marked by pragmatic strategies such as interpreting information as being relayed in chronological order (e.g. Bardovi-Harlig 2004; Dietrich *et al.* 1995; Meisel 1987), Kanwit and Geeslin (2014), in their variationist study, also manipulated clause order and found, sure enough, that it significantly affected lower-level learner interpretation of such sentences.

32.2 Common Methods Used by Second Language Variationists

Now that we have seen some of the underlying principles at the heart of L2 variationist research, we turn to a number of common methods used within the approach. As with L1 variationist studies, this work typically involves amassing large data sets for which all tokens of the dependent variable are coded for a range of independent linguistic and social factors that are thought to constrain potential variation. Such coding of each token enables the researcher subsequently to perform multivariate analyses to determine which independent variables, in which order of significance, form the predictive model that best explains the occurrence of one variant of the dependent variable over others for a particular participant group. For example, Kanwit and Geeslin (2014) found that adverbial clause interpretation was most constrained by the mood of the verb in the adverbial clause for NSs and a group of highly advanced learners (but that which adverb was used also played a role for NSs), whereas mood was not significant for lower-level learners. Here, the need for large data sets is important in order to avoid small cells, which prevent a researcher from performing statistical tests such as chi-square comparisons or regression analyses. Small cells occur when there are fewer than five tokens of one of the variants of the dependent variable for a particular category of an independent variable (e.g. if there are three uses of the MF in the absence of temporal adverbs). In the last few years, researchers have been encouraged to report not only where differences are statistically significant (e.g. p-values of < 0.05 in null hypothesis significance testing) but also the effect sizes which indicate the magnitude of such differences (Larson-Hall and Plonsky 2015).

Borrowing from methods of L1 variationist sociolinguistics, earlier work in L2 variationism focused on exactly two variants of a dependent variable, and binomial regressions were performed, often using the program GoldVarb (Sankoff et al. 2005). Despite its popularity within the sociolinguistic research community, GoldVarb was later criticized because of its difficulty in accounting for possible interactions among independent variables and the general assumption of the binomial regression that each data point is independent, coming from a different individual, even though this was rarely, if ever, the case in studies that used the program (Johnson 2009; Tagliamonte 2012). More recent work has generally implemented other forms of predictive statistics. As the program R has gained popularity in recent years, researchers have used it to perform a number of statistical tests, including general linear mixed models (i.e. mixed-effects models), random forests, and conditional inference trees (Gries 2009; Tagliamonte 2012). Mixed-effects models offer the benefit of allowing the researcher to enter the individual participant as a random effect, which helps identify to what extent variability in the data might be indicative of variability across individuals; similarly, individual lexical items can be entered as a random effect in order to determine to what extent variation might be affected at the word level. For a set of factor groups, random forests indicate which of the variants is most probable, thereby illustrating which factor groups are useful predictors (Breiman 2001; Tagliamonte 2012). A large number of conditional inference trees form the random forest, and those inference trees depict interactions in the data in a hierarchical fashion, indicating how the factors work together (Baayen 2008; Tagliamonte 2012). Furthermore, as researchers have considered dependent variables that have more than two variants, the need to consider tests that account for three or more variants has arisen. Accordingly, recent work using the program SPSS has included analyses based on multinomial regressions, which include the comparison of one variant to the other variants, all performed in the same predictive model. This model provides information as to the contexts which increase the odds of selection of one variant over another based on 95 percent confidence interval values of lower and upper limits that are both larger than 1, or which decrease the odds of selection of the variant when both values are smaller than 1. Values that include 1 do not significantly affect the odds of selection of one variant over another (Gudmestad and Geeslin 2013).

Another common method in studies of L2 variation is the analysis of group, as opposed to individual, data. In the early stages of research, influential L2 variationist studies found that the linguistic behavior of learner groups was quite reflective of the individuals within those groups (Bayley and Langman 2004; Regan 2004). Since that time, researchers have followed this example, and L2 variationists typically report group rates of use/selection rather than the rates of use of individuals (e.g. Fafulas 2012; Geeslin 2003; Geeslin and Gudmestad 2008a; Kanwit and Solon 2013; Malovrh 2006; Woolsey 2008). Nevertheless, some recent work has presented, for example, the range of rates of selection for learners at a particular proficiency level (e.g. ranges of rates of variable subject expression in Geeslin et al. 2013b; see Chapter 24, this volume, for more on the role of the individual in variation).

Depending on the theoretical orientation of a particular approach, it is not uncommon for a certain type of task to be highly popular within a specific vein of research. For example, since generative acquisitionists are primarily interested in the competence (rather than performance) of a learner as evidence of an underlying grammar, generative L2 studies often make use of grammaticality judgement tasks (e.g. Borgonovo et al. 2005; Bruhn de Garavito and Valenzuela 2006; Español-Echevarría and Prévost 2004; see Chapter 1, this volume, for an overview of generative theory). To the extent that L2 variationism shares a theoretical orientation with L1 variationism, the sociolinguistic interview is one popular elicitation tool on the L2 side. If the researcher is interested in a particular linguistic structure prior to conducting the interviews, she may create specific questions thought to elicit potential contexts of use (e.g. questions about childhood in research of past-time expression). In addition to sociolinguistic interviews, other methodologies that target learner production, be it oral or written, have also been implemented, including the use of oral contextualized elicitation tasks and oral discourse completion tasks (e.g. Gudmestad 2012), oral personal prompt response tasks (e.g. Kanwit 2017), written letter tasks and oral information gap tasks utilizing story squares (e.g. Moses 2002; Solon and Kanwit 2014), silent film retells or simultaneous narrations (e.g. Fafulas 2015; Malovrh 2014), and computer-mediated electronic chats between learners and NSs (e.g. González-Lloret 2011; Kanwit in press). In addition to a variety of production tasks, selection instruments have also been quite popular, including the contextualized preference task, sometimes referred to as a written contextualized task (WCT, e.g. Geeslin 2003). The WCT is thought to offer many benefits. Firstly, due to differences in the cognitive demands of production as opposed to selection (e.g. Ellis 2005), lower-level learners may not yet be able to produce a particular form, but they might understand and select it. Development in selection as opposed to production also applies to independent variables, as learners may demonstrate conditioning according to linguistic constraints in the selection of variants earlier than when use demonstrates such constraints. For example, Kanwit (2014) found that clause type was a significant predictor of future-time expression in WCT data for his third through fifth levels of learners (i.e. fifth-semester, fourth-year, and graduate students), whereas it was not a significant predictor for any of the learner groups in production data.[1] WCTs enable us to monitor how the effects of linguistic factors develop across proficiency levels because researchers construct the tasks by systematically manipulating certain independent variables. Such practices also ensure that there will be a sufficient number of tokens for each category of an independent variable, which again helps to avoid small cells. For example, in Fafulas' (2012) analysis of progressive expression, he manipulates the variables lexical aspectual class and adverb type. It is also common that WCTs do not force a particular response, instead giving the participant the option to indicate that multiple options are equally acceptable (e.g. Geeslin 2003; Gudmestad 2006). Consider (32.3) from Fafulas (2012), which would be coded as an achievement (for lexical aspectual type, as in *despertarse* 'to wake up') and as not containing an adverb (for adverb type, since this item lacks a frequentative or immediate adverbial such as *frecuentemente* 'frequently' or *ahora* 'now,' respectively):

(32.3) La mujer lo mira con cara de irritación y le responde:
A. Nada. Es que Emilia se está despertando después de un sueño profundo.
B. Nada. Es que Emilia se despierta después de un sueño profundo.
___ Prefiero A. ___ Prefiero B. ___ Ambos.
'The woman looks at him with an irritated expression and responds to him:
A. Nothing. It's just that Emilia is waking up after a deep sleep.
B. Nothing. It's just that Emilia wakes up after a deep sleep.
___ I prefer A. ___ I prefer B. ___ Both.'

In addition to production tasks and written contextualized tasks, in recent years L2 variationists have increasingly utilized interpretation tasks. In an interpretation task, rather than requiring a learner to create language or select a preferred variant in a given context, a learner simply indicates how he interprets a given item. For example, in a recent study, Kanwit and Geeslin (2014) provided learners with decontextualized sentences and then had participants indicate how they interpreted those sentences. One such item can be seen in (32.4):

(32.4) Cuando Marta tiene tiempo libre, Julio la visita.
'When Marta has free time, Julio visits her.'
a. Marta regularly has free time.

---

[1] In addition to revealing cases where target-like selection might precede production, comparison across tasks may also reveal differences according to mode and register.

b. Marta has not yet had free time.
c. Both interpretations are possible.

The authors were interested in how participants interpreted mood in adverbial clauses. In (32.4), since the indicative (*tiene* 'has') is used in the adverbial clause, NSs typically interpret such actions as having already occurred, since there is a meaning-bearing contrast for adverbs such as *cuando* 'when' with the subjunctive in such contexts, with subjunctive indicating that the action has not yet occurred. By testing how learners interpreted sentences like (32.4), Kanwit and Geeslin (2014) were able to determine to what extent mood played a role in how learners read adverbial clauses and to what extent learner interpretation might be constrained by other factors (e.g. clause order and verbal morphological regularity). Given the popularity of multinomial analyses, researchers who include WCTs that do not force one response (i.e. that allow a response that two forms are equally acceptable for a particular item) are now able to run statistical tests in which they determine whether the "both" response behaves differently from the other two variants of the dependent variable, whereas in the past they were forced to combine the "both" response with one of the other two variants in order to perform a binomial regression, or to exclude the "both" responses from higher-level statistical analyses.

32.3 Second Language Variationist Research of Spanish Structures

Among the variable structures that have been analyzed in L2 Spanish are the copula contrast, subject pronouns, the mood contrast, past-perfective expression, future-time expression, and the present progressive. Such work is motivated by prior investigations of L1 variation across languages, as researchers consider relevant independent variables based on factors known to constrain the L1 use of a given variant, in addition to considering factors which may be of particular relevance for L2 learners, based on what are perceived to be universal processes. The body of work cited in the current section centers on development in learners in classroom-based, also known as at-home (AH), environments.

Research on the contrast between the copulas *ser* and *estar* was among the first to be considered from an L2 variationist perspective (Geeslin 2000). L1 research has revealed that NS copula choice is not categorical, and is instead constrained by independent linguistic and social factors that may be semantic, pragmatic, or syntactic (e.g. Díaz-Campos and Geeslin 2011; Gutiérrez 1992; Kanwit *et al.* 2015; Ortiz-López 2000; Silva-Corvalán 1994). L2 variationist research has demonstrated that learner copula selection is predicted by factors similar to those operating for NSs (Geeslin

2000, 2003; Geeslin and Guijarro-Fuentes 2006; Kanwit *et al.* 2015; Woolsey 2008), although, for example, pragmatic extensions of a copula are possible for learners in instances where NSs may have a syntactic or semantic restriction (e.g. learners' selection of *estar* to indicate a change in co-occurrence with adjectives with which NSs prefer *ser*: Geeslin and Guijarro-Fuentes 2006). Research on copula variation now extends to Spanish learners of different L1 backgrounds (e.g. the L1 Korean learners in Geeslin and Long 2015) and to study-abroad contexts (e.g. the learners studying in Spain and Mexico in Kanwit *et al.* 2015).

Because Spanish is a pro-drop language (i.e. it allows null, or non-overt, subjects), research on variation between overt and null-subject pronominal expression has received great interest, beginning with work on L1 variation (e.g. Bayley and Pease-Álvarez 1997; Cameron 1995; Flores-Ferrán 2002; Otheguy and Zentella 2012; Ranson 1991; Shin and Otheguy 2013). Following the fruitfulness of the topic in the L1 setting, and since English offers the distinction of not being a pro-drop language, research on variable subject expression by L1 learners of English has subsequently gained popularity (e.g. Geeslin and Gudmestad 2008b; Linford and Shin 2013; Quesada and Blackwell 2009). Research in this vein has also uncovered that learners use and select null subjects to a greater extent as they gain proficiency; that they often overshoot NS targets, which may mean creating contexts that have ambiguous subject referents; and that they gradually add independent linguistic variables to their predictive models as proficiency increases (e.g. Geeslin and Gudmestad 2008b; Linford and Shin 2013). Recent research on L2 variable subject expression has also considered the role of frequency and its effect on pronominalization (Linford *et al.* 2016; Linford and Shin 2013).

The variable mood contrast in Spanish is another well-researched topic. For over two decades, we have had empirical accounts for the erosion of the subjunctive, which has given way to the indicative in contexts that traditionally favored the subjunctive (Silva-Corvalán 1994). Research on the acquisition of the variable mood contrast is diverse, including the production of subjunctive mood forms across linguistic contexts (e.g. Collentine 1995), contexts of learning (e.g. Quesada 1998), and levels of proficiency (e.g. Gudmestad 2012). For English-speaking learners of Spanish, we know that the subjunctive mood is late-acquired (Collentine 1995; Geeslin and Gudmestad 2008a; Gudmestad 2006; Quesada 1998). Furthermore, patterns of use and selection are variable across learners, tasks, and linguistic contexts (Gudmestad 2012). The complexity of the mood contrast is augmented by the aforementioned variability present for NSs (Silva-Corvalán 1994). Nevertheless, for the mood contrast in nominal clauses, learners have been shown to connect the subjunctive with the presence of independent variables such as futurity, morphological irregularity, and the semantic notions of desire and emotion (Collentine 1995; Gudmestad 2012; Quesada 1998). Although the subjunctive in nominal clauses received early attention in L2 research on the mood contrast, recent work has shifted the focus to the adverbial-clause context and to interpretation, rather than production or selection, of mood (Kanwit and Geeslin 2014, 2017).

The variable contrast between the present indicative and present progressive forms for actions in progress has received recent attention in L2 research, following earlier work on NS variability that demonstrated selectional constraints according to lexical aspect, co-occurring adverbs, clause type, polarity, animacy, and the temporal aspect of the sentence (Fafulas 2012; Fafulas and Díaz-Campos 2010; Mayberry 2011; Torres Cacoullos 2000). More specifically, for actions that are ongoing at speech time, the cited body of research indicates that the progressive tends to be favored over the present indicative in co-occurrence with a moment adverbial (e.g. *ahora* 'now'), activity verb, or animate subject. Recent L2 work on the topic also considers the range of progressive periphrases that speakers use. For example, learners use more *estar* + V-*ndo* progressive forms with stative verbs than NSs, and fewer auxiliary + V-*ndo* canonical progressive types (i.e. *andar, ir, venir*, and *seguir* + V-*ndo*) than NSs (Fafulas 2015; Geeslin and Fafulas 2012).

32.4 Acquiring Variation in Study-Abroad Contexts

In addition to an analysis of at-home learning contexts, since regional variation across the Spanish-speaking world can be quite robust (see Chapter 23, this volume), researchers have turned their attention to comparing learners in a study-abroad (SA) context who are immersed in a region where one variant is particularly common with those who study in regions which demonstrate differing preferences. To the extent that varieties of Peninsular Spanish often exhibit differences when compared to the diverse varieties across Latin America, and since many US institutions have popular SA programs in Spain and numerous Latin American nations, the SA context has proven to be a rich testing ground for comparative research on the acquisition of regional variation. Among the variable structures that have received recent consideration are object pronoun expression, past-perfective expression, and future-time expression. The studies outlined below also mark a notable change in research on acquisition in SA contexts. After many early studies reported minimal improvement with respect to grammatical structures following a period of stay in an SA context, authors began to call for new methods that were more sensitive to the types of gains that are made when learners are immersed in contexts with naturalistic input (e.g. Freed 1990; Lafford and Uscinski 2013). Heeding the call for methodological changes to gauge more accurately the augmentation of sociolinguistic competence abroad (Canale and

Swain 1980), researchers drew upon methods that had gained popularity in the study of the acquisition of variation in the AH environment, such as contextualized preference tasks and production tasks that targeted structures for which NSs had demonstrated the ability to vary between two or more forms.

Based on differences in the object pronominal systems across the Iberian peninsula and Latin America, variable object expression has received great attention in the L1 and L2 literature. L1 studies have considered *leísmo, laísmo,* and *loísmo,* in addition to object drop in South America, and have demonstrated, for example, that definite, countable, animate nouns are most likely to be marked as overt (as opposed to null) objects and that use of *le* as an accusative (i.e. direct object) pronoun occurs frequently in parts of north-central Spain and Latin America, with *laísmo* and *loísmo* (or the use of the feminine or masculine accusative pronouns, respectively, in dative contexts) occurring across parts of north-central Spain and Latin America as well (e.g. Fernández Ordóñez 1999; Klee and Lynch 2009; Klein-Andreu 1999; Schwenter 2006). Given the complexity of the object pronoun systems across regions, recent research has compared learners studying in areas of the Iberian peninsula in which objects are marked differently. In one of the first investigations of Spanish to compare the acquisition of a variable structure in two different regions of SA, Salgado-Robles (2014b) reported that learners in the *leísta* zone of Valladolid moved toward the regional norm by increasing use of *le,* whereas learners in Seville moved toward the local, case-system norm (e.g. *lo/la* as accusative pronouns) by decreasing use of *le* during their period abroad.

Past-perfective expression is another popular topic in the study of variability in Spanish given the general vitality of the preterit in most of Latin America and of the present perfect in Spain and parts of south America (e.g. regions of Argentina and Ecuador) (Dumont 2013; Escobar 1997a; Howe and Schwenter 2003; Rodríguez Louro 2009; Schwenter and Torres Cacoullos 2008). Accordingly, recent work has compared learners studying in a present perfect-favoring region of Spain (i.e. Valencia) with learners studying in a preterit-favoring region of Mexico (i.e. San Luis Potosí), and has demonstrated that learners moved toward the NS targets in each region (Kanwit *et al.* 2015). Specifically, the study reported learner and NS similarities not only regarding greater selection of the preterit in Mexico than in Spain, but also based on the effect of temporal reference, with hodiernal (i.e. same day) contexts favoring the present perfect in Spain, but disfavoring it in Mexico.

In recent years, variable future-time expression has been investigated for both NS and learner populations. The L1 sociolinguistic research generally indicates that the periphrastic future (PF) is the most popular variant of future-time expression across the majority of dialects of the Spanish-speaking world, but that there are portions of Spain, especially in bilingual

Spanish–Catalan[2] zones, in which the morphological future (MF) is used more frequently than it is across most of Latin America (Aaron 2006; Blas Arroyo 2008; Escobar 1997b; Gutiérrez 1995; Orozco 2005; Sedano 1994; Silva-Corvalán and Terrell 1989). Given these purported differences in the viability of the MF across dialects, Kanwit and Solon (2013) compared learners studying in the Spanish–Catalan bilingual region of Valencia with learners studying in Mérida, Mexico. The study found that the learner groups did not differ significantly in their rates of selection of the MF at the start of their stay abroad, but that, following six weeks of immersion, learners in Valencia selected the form significantly more than learners in Mérida, which matched the significant difference present for NS participants in the two regions.

As researchers continue to uncover regional differences for variable structures across zones of the Spanish-speaking world, subsequent research will again draw on learners studying abroad in order to determine to what extent immersion may affect use of and preference for the relevant variants. Furthermore, many of the summarized studies above compare groups of learners studying in two regions but also note the shortcoming of failing to include an at-home comparison group, which would enable them to tease apart more accurately longitudinal changes that are the result of a general process (e.g. restructuring, U-shaped development (i.e. high rates of use or accuracy with a given form that decrease before increasing again), the integration of a new form into the grammar) as opposed to a change that might be fomented based on input that is especially representative of a particular region.

32.5 Future Directions and Remaining Questions

As the number of researchers working within L2 variationist perspectives continues to grow, there are many avenues for future investigations. Given similarities with usage-based approaches (e.g. Ellis and Wulff 2015; Goldberg 2006; Gries and Wulff 2005; Tomasello 2003; see also Chapter 3, this volume) and functional, concept-oriented approaches (e.g. Andersen 1984; Bardovi-Harlig 2004, 2015; Dietrich *et al.* 1995; Shirai 1995; von Stutterheim and Klein 1987), and the fact that L2 variationism is itself an interdisciplinary combination of variationist sociolinguistics and L2 acquisition, empirical research which combines approaches will likely expand over the coming years. In fact, recent work specifically notes the compatibility of variationism with concept-oriented approaches (Bardovi-Harlig 2015; Kanwit 2014, 2017), and future studies will do well to implement the strengths of multiple approaches. Research that integrates

---

[2] This body of research differs in its terminology, with the majority of studies using an umbrella term of "Catalan," and other studies differentiating among Catalan, Valencian, Majorcan, and Menorcan varieties, among others.

usage-based and concept-oriented approaches will help to answer lingering questions about how learners express form–function mappings as they produce variable structures in an L2.

Additionally, independent *linguistic* variables have received great attention thus far, and researchers will likely explore *social* variables with greater interest in the coming years. Along with macro-level extralinguistic variables commonly studied in the L1 sociolinguistic body (e.g. gender, age, socioeconomic level, geographic region; Eckert 2012), individual variables such as motivation, language anxiety, intercultural competence, and other indices of individual differences will gain additional interest in the study of L2 acquisition and will merit inclusion in predictive models, as researchers continue to tease apart which variables constrain linguistic variation (Allen 2010; Bennett 2004; DeKeyser 2010; Pellegrino Aveni 2005; Young 2013).

Given the current boom in study-abroad research and the popularity of US programs in Spanish-speaking countries, comparing AH to SA groups will likely expand, as a stated limitation of much of the SA research to date has been the lack of an AH control group (Geeslin *et al.* 2013a; Kanwit and Solon 2013; Salgado-Robles 2014b). Such task designs will enable researchers to better differentiate universal processes of acquisition from the effect of region-specific linguistic input. Furthermore, interest in immersion settings beyond relatively traditional SA programs will likely expand, as seen in recent work on international service-learning programs, in which students sojourn abroad to perform volunteer work (Cubillos 2013; Salgado-Robles 2014a).

As L1 English is vastly overrepresented in our study of the L2 acquisition of Spanish, future work will undoubtedly consider additional L1s (Geeslin and Long 2015; Judy and Perpiñán 2015). Promising work in this vein will help disentangle which aspects of the acquisition of Spanish are universal and which demonstrate specific effects for L1 English.

Since L2 variationists are particularly concerned with how learners gain sociolinguistic competence (Canale and Swain 1980), it is not surprising that pragmatic variation in L2 Spanish is a growing field of investigation (e.g. Cohen and Shively 2007; Félix-Brasdefer and Hasler Barker 2015; Félix-Brasdefer and Koike 2014; Shively 2015). Studies that analyze pragmatic variation in an L2, both in domestic and study-abroad settings, will likely increase in the coming years (for more on pragmatics and the role of discourse, see Chapter 20, this volume).

In sum, multidisciplinary approaches which combine the fields of variationist sociolinguistics and second language acquisition have shed great light on both the factors that constrain native-speaker variation and the extent to which learners diverge from and follow native-speaker constraints, and future research will continue to uncover how both learners and native speakers express similar concepts in more than one way.

References

Aaron, J. (2006). *Me voy a tener que ir yendo*: A Corpus-Based Study of the Grammaticalization of the *ir a* + INF Construction in Spanish. In N. Sagarra and A. J. Toribio (eds.), *Selected Proceedings of the 9th Hispanic Linguistics Symposium*. Somerville, MA: Cascadilla, pp. 263–272.

Adamson, H. D. and Regan, V. (1991). The Acquisition of Community Speech Norms by Asian Immigrants Learning English as a Second Language. *Studies in Second Language Acquisition*, 13, 1–22.

Allen, H. (2010). Language-Learning Motivation during Short-Term Study Abroad: An Activity Theory Perspective. *Foreign Language Annals*, 43, 27–49.

Andersen, R. W. (1984). The One-to-One Principle of Interlanguage Construction. *Language Learning*, 34, 77–95.

Baayen, H. (2008). *Analyzing Linguistic Data: A Practical Introduction to Statistics*. Cambridge: Cambridge University Press.

Bardovi-Harlig, K. (2004). The Emergence of Grammaticalized Future Expression in Longitudinal Production Data. In M. Overstreet, S. Rott, B. VanPatten, and J. Williams (eds.), *Form and Meaning in Second Language Acquisition*. Mahwah, NJ: Erlbaum, pp. 115–137.

Bardovi-Harlig, K. (2015). *One Functional Approach to SLA: The Concept-Oriented Approach*. In B. VanPatten and J. Williams (eds.), *Theories in Second Language Acquisition: An Introduction* (2nd edn). New York: Routledge, pp. 54–74.

Bayley, R. and Langman, J. (2004). Variation in the Group and the Individual: Evidence from Second Language Acquisition. *International Review of Applied Linguistics in Language Teaching*, 42 (4), 303–318.

Bayley, R. and Pease-Álvarez, L. (1997). Null Pronoun Variation in Mexican-Descent Children's Narrative Discourse. *Language Variation and Change* 9 (3), 349–371.

Bennett, M. (2004). Becoming Interculturally Competent. In J. Wurzel (ed.), *Toward Multiculturalism: A Reader in Multicultural Education* (2nd edn). Newton, MA: Intercultural Resource, pp. 62–77.

Blas Arroyo, J. L. (2008). The Variable Expression of Future Tense in Peninsular Spanish: The Present (and Future) of Inflectional Forms in the Spanish Spoken in a Bilingual Region. *Language Variation and Change*, 20, 85–126.

Borgonovo, C., Bruhn de Garavito, J., and Prévost, P. (2005). Acquisition of Mood Distinctions in L2 Spanish. In A. Burgos, M. R. Clark-Cotton, and S. Ha (eds.), *Proceedings of the 29th Boston University Conference on Language Development*. Somerville, MA: Cascadilla, pp. 97–108.

Breiman, L. (2001). Random Forests. *Machine Learning*, 45, 5–32.

Bruhn de Garavito, J. and Valenzuela, E. (2006). The Status of *ser* and *estar* in Late and Early Bilingual L2 Spanish. In C. A. Klee and T. L. Face (eds.),

Selected Proceedings of the 7th Conference on the Acquisition of Spanish and Portuguese as First and Second Languages. Somerville, MA: Cascadilla, pp. 100–109.

Cameron, R. (1995). The Scope and Limits of Switch Reference as a Constraint on Pronominal Subject Expression. *Hispanic Linguistics*, 6/7, 1–28.

Canale, M. and Swain, M. (1980). Theoretical Bases of Communicative Approaches to Second Language Teaching and Testing. *Applied Linguistics*, 1, 1–47.

Chambers, J. K. (2008). *Sociolinguistic Theory* (3rd edn). Oxford: Blackwell.

Cohen, A. D. and Shively, R. L. (2007). Acquisition of Requests and Apologies in Spanish and French: Impact of Study Abroad and Strategy-Building Intervention. *Modern Language Journal*, 91 (2), 189–212.

Collentine, J. (1995). The Development of Complex Syntax and Mood Selection Abilities by Intermediate Level Learners of Spanish. *Hispania*, 78, 122–135.

Corder, P. (1967). The Significance of Learners' Errors. *International Review of Applied Linguistics*, 5 (4), 161–170.

Cubillos, J. (2013). Community Engagement and Proficiency Gains in Short Term Study Abroad Programs. *Northeast Conference on the Teaching of Foreign Languages Review*, 71, 17–36.

DeKeyser, R. (2010). Monitoring Processes in Spanish as a Second Language during a Study Abroad Program. *Foreign Language Annals*, 43, 80–92.

Díaz-Campos, M. (ed.) (2011). *The Handbook of Hispanic Sociolinguistics.* Chichester: John Wiley.

Díaz-Campos, M. and Geeslin, K. L. (2011). Copula Use in the Spanish of Venezuela: Social and Linguistic Sources of Variation in Spanish. *Spanish in Context*, 8, 73–94.

Dietrich, R., Klein, W., and Noyau, C. (1995). *The Acquisition of Temporality in a Second Language.* Amsterdam: John Benjamins.

Dumont, J. (2013). Another Look at the Present Perfect in an Andean Variety of Spanish: Grammaticalization and Evidentiality in Quiteño Spanish. In J. Cabrelli Amaro, G. Lord, A. de Prada Pérez, and J. E. Aaron (eds.), *Selected Proceedings of the 16th Hispanic Linguistics Symposium.* Somerville, MA: Cascadilla, pp. 279–291.

Eckert, P. (2012). Three Waves of Variation Study: The Emergence of Meaning in the Study of Sociolinguistic Variation. *The Annual Review of Anthropology*, 41, 87–100.

Ellis, N. C., and Wulff, S. (2015). Usage-Based Approaches to SLA. In B. VanPatten and J. Williams (eds.), *Theories in Second Language Acquisition: An Introduction* (2nd edn). New York: Routledge, pp. 75–93.

Ellis, R. (2005). Planning and Task-Based Research: Theory and Research. In R. Ellis (ed.), *Planning and Task-Performance in a Second Language.* Amsterdam: John Benjamins, pp. 3–34.

Escobar, A. M. (1997a). Contrastive and Innovative Uses of the Present Perfect and the Preterite in Spanish in Contact with Quechua. *Hispania*, 80, 859–870.

Escobar, A. M. (1997b). From Time to Modality in Spanish in Contact with Quechua. *Hispanic Linguistics*, 9 (1), 64–99.

Español-Echevarría, M. and Prévost, P. (2004). Acquiring Number Specification on L2 Spanish Quantifiers: Evidence against the Rich Agreement Hypothesis. In J. van Kampen and S. Baauw (eds.), *Proceedings of the 2003 Conference on Generative Approaches to Language Acquisition*. Utrecht: LOT, pp. 151–162.

Fafulas, S. (2012). Nuevas perspectivas sobre la variación de las formas presente simple y presente progresivo en español y en inglés. *Spanish in Context*, 9, 58–87.

Fafulas, S. (2015). Progressive Constructions in Native-Speaker and Adult-Acquired Spanish. *Studies in Hispanic and Lusophone Linguistics*, 8 (1), 85–133.

Fafulas, S., and Díaz-Campos, M. (2010). Variación morfosintáctica y lenguas en contacto: Las formas analíticas y sintéticas del presente progresivo en el español monolingüe y bilingüe. *Boletín de Filología*, 45 (2), 71–89.

Félix-Brasdefer, J. C. and Hasler Barker, M. (2015). Complimenting in Spanish in a Short-Term Study Abroad Context. *System*, 48, 75–85.

Félix-Brasdefer, J. C. and Koike, D. (2014). Perspectives on Spanish SLA from Pragmatics and Discourse. In M. Lacorte (ed.), *Handbook of Hispanic Applied Linguistics*. New York: Routledge, pp. 25–43.

Fernández Ordóñez, I. (1999). Leísmo, laísmo y loísmo. In I. Bosque and V. Demonte (eds.), *Gramática descriptiva de la lengua española*. Madrid: Espasa Calpe, pp. 1317–1398.

Flores-Ferrán, N. (2002). *A Sociolinguistic Perspective on the Use of Subject Personal Pronouns in Spanish Narratives of Puerto Ricans in New York City*. Munich: Lincom.

Freed, B. (1990). Language Learning in a Study Abroad Context: The Effects of Interactive and Non-Interactive Out-of-Class Contact on Grammatical Achievement and Oral Proficiency. In J. Alatis (ed.), *Linguistics, Language Teaching and Language Acquisition: The Interdependence of Theory, Practice and Research*. Washington, DC: Georgetown University Press, pp. 459–477.

Geeslin, K. L. (2000). A New Approach to the Second Language Acquisition of Copula Choice in Spanish. In R. Leow and C. Sanz (eds.), *Spanish Applied Linguistics at the Turn of the Millennium: Papers from the 1999 Conference on the L1 and L2 Acquisition of Spanish and Portuguese*. Somerville, MA: Cascadilla, pp. 50–66.

Geeslin, K. L. (2003). A Comparison of Copula Choice in Advanced and Native Spanish. *Language Learning*, 53, 703–764.

Geeslin, K. L. and Fafulas, S. (2012). Variation of the Simple Present and Present Progressive Forms: A Comparison of Native and Non-Native

Speakers. In K. Geeslin and M. Diaz-Campos (eds.), *Selected Proceedings of the 14th Hispanic Linguistics Symposium*. Somerville, MA: Cascadilla, pp. 179–196.

Geeslin, K. L., Fafulas, S., and Kanwit, M. (2013a). Acquiring Geographically-Variable Norms of Use: The Case of the Present Perfect in Mexico and Spain. In C. Howe, S. Blackwell, and M. Quesada (eds.), *Selected Proceedings of the 15th Hispanic Linguistics Symposium*. Somerville, MA: Cascadilla, pp. 205–220.

Geeslin, K. L. and Gudmestad, A. (2008a). Comparing Interview and Written Elicitation Tasks in Native and Non-Native Data: Do Speakers Do what we Think they Do? In J. Bruhn de Garavito and E. Valenzuela (eds.), *Selected Proceedings of the 10th Hispanic Linguistics Symposium*. Somerville, MA: Cascadilla, pp. 64–77.

Geeslin, K. L. and Gudmestad, A. (2008b). Variable Subject Expression in Second-Language Spanish: A Comparison of Native and Non-Native Speakers. In M. Bowles, R. Foote, S. Perpiñán, and R. Bhatt (eds.), *Selected Proceedings of the 2007 Second Language Research Forum*. Somerville, MA: Cascadilla, pp. 69–85.

Geeslin, K. L. and Gudmestad, A. (2010). An Exploration of the Range and Frequency of Occurrence of Forms in Potentially-Variable Structures in Second Language Spanish. *Studies in Second Language Acquisition*, 32, 433–463.

Geeslin, K. L. and Guijarro-Fuentes, P. (2006). Second Language Acquisition of Variable Structures in Spanish by Portuguese Speakers. *Language Learning*, 51, 53–107.

Geeslin, K. L., Linford, B., Fafulas, S., Long, A. Y., and Díaz-Campos, M. (2013b). The L2 Development of Subject Form Variation in Spanish: The Individual vs. the Group. In J. Cabrelli Amaro, G. Lord, A. de Prada Pérez, and J. E. Aaron (eds.), *Selected Proceedings of the 16th Hispanic Linguistics Symposium*. Somerville, MA: Cascadilla, pp. 156–174.

Geeslin, K. L. and Long, A. Y. (2015). The Development and Use of the Spanish Copula with Adjectives by Korean-Speaking Learners. In I. Pérez-Jiménez, M. Leonetti, and S. Gumiel Molina (eds.), *New Perspectives on the Study of ser and estar*. Amsterdam: John Benjamins, pp. 293–323,

Goldberg, A. E. (2006). *Constructions at Work: The Nature of Generalization in Language*. Oxford: Oxford University Press.

González-Lloret, M. (2011). Conversation Analysis of Computer-mediated Communication. *CALICO Journal*, 28 (2), 308–325.

Gries, S. T. (2009). *Statistics for Linguistics with R*. New York: De Gruyter.

Gries, S. T. and Wulff, S. (2005). Do Foreign Language Learners also Have Constructions? Evidence from Priming, Sorting, and Corpora. *Annual Review of Cognitive Linguistics*, 3, 182–200.

Gudmestad, A. (2006). L2 Variation and the Spanish Subjunctive: Linguistic Features Predicting Mood Selection. In T. L. Face and C. L. Klee (eds.), *Selected Proceedings of the 7th Conference on the Acquisition of Spanish and*

Portuguese as First and Second Languages. Somerville, MA: Cascadilla, pp. 170–184.

Gudmestad, A. (2012). Acquiring a Variable Structure: An Interlanguage Analysis of Second Language Mood Use in Spanish. *Language Learning*, 62, 373–402.

Gudmestad, A. and Geeslin, K. (2011). Assessing the Use of Multiple Forms in Variable Contexts: The Relationship between Linguistic Factors and Future-Time Reference in Spanish. *Studies in Hispanic and Lusophone Linguistics*, 4, 3–33.

Gudmestad, A. and Geeslin, K. (2013). Second-Language Development of Variable Forms of Future-Time Expression in Spanish. In A. M. Carvalho and S. Beaudrie (eds.), *Selected Proceedings of the 6th Workshop on Spanish Sociolinguistics*. Somerville, MA: Cascadilla, pp. 63–75.

Gutiérrez, M. (1992). The Extension of *estar*: A Linguistic Change in Progress in the Spanish of Morelia, Mexico. *Hispanic Linguistics*, 5, 109–141.

Gutiérrez, M. (1995). On the Future of the Future Tense in the Spanish of the Southwest. In C. Silva-Corvalán (ed.), *Spanish in Four Continents: Studies in Language Contact and Bilingualism*. Washington, DC: Georgetown University Press, pp. 214–223.

Howe, C. and Schwenter, S. (2003). Present Perfect for Preterit across Spanish Dialects. *Penn Working Papers in Linguistics*, 9, 61–75.

Johnson, D. E. (2009). Getting off the GoldVarb Standard: Introducing Rbrul for Mixed Effects Variable Rule Analysis. *Language and Linguistics Compass*, 3 (1), 359–383.

Judy, T. and Perpiñán, S. (eds.) (2015). *The Acquisition of Spanish in Understudied Language Pairings*. Amsterdam: John Benjamins.

Kanwit, M. (2014). The Acquisition of Future Expression in L2 Spanish (Doctoral dissertation). Indiana University.

Kanwit, M. (2017). What we Gain by Combining Variationist and Concept-Oriented Approaches: The Case of Acquiring Spanish Future-Time Expression. *Language Learning*, 67 (2), 461–498.

Kanwit, M. (in press). Encantado de conocerte virtualmente: Native/Non-Native Speaker Electronic Chats in Spanish. *International Journal of the Linguistic Association of the Southwest*, 33 (2).

Kanwit, M. and Geeslin, K. L. (2014). The Interpretation of Spanish Subjunctive and Indicative Forms in Adverbial Clauses. *Studies in Second Language Acquisition*, 36, 487–533.

Kanwit, M. and Geeslin, K. L. (2017). Exploring Lexical Effects in Second Language Interpretation: The Case of Mood in Spanish Adverbial Clauses. *Studies in Second Language Acquisition, FirstView*, 1–25.

Kanwit, M., Geeslin, K. L., and Fafulas, S. (2015). Study Abroad and the SLA of Variable Structures: A Look at the Present Perfect, the Copula Contrast, and the Present Progressive in Mexico and Spain. *Probus*, 27 (2), 307–348.

Kanwit, M. and Solon, M. (2013). Acquiring Variation in Future-Time Expression Abroad in Valencia, Spain and Mérida, Mexico. In J. Cabrelli Amaro, G. Lord, A. de Prada Pérez, and J. E. Aaron (eds.), *Selected Proceedings of the 16th Hispanic Linguistics Symposium*. Somerville, MA: Cascadilla, pp. 206–221.

Klee, C. A. and Lynch, J. (2009). *El español en contacto con otras lenguas*. Washington, DC: Georgetown University Press.

Klein-Andreu, F. (1999). Variación actual y reinterpretación histórica: le/s, la/s, lo/s en Castilla. In M. J. Serrano (ed.), *Estudios de variación sintáctica*. Frankfurt and Madrid: Vervuert, pp. 197–220.

Labov, W. (1966). *The Social Stratification of English in New York City*. Washington, DC: Center for Applied Linguistics.

Lafford, B. A. and Uscinski, I. (2013). Study Abroad and Second Language Spanish. In K. L. Geeslin (ed.), *The Handbook of Spanish Second Language Acquisition*. Oxford: Blackwell, pp. 386–403.

Larson-Hall, J. and Plonsky, L. (2015). Reporting and Interpreting Quantitative Research Findings: What Gets Reported and Recommendations for the Field. *Language Learning*, 65, Supp. 1, 127–159.

Linford, B. and Shin, N. L. (2013). Lexical Frequency Effects on L2 Spanish Subject Pronoun Expression. In J. Cabrelli Amaro, G. Lord, A. de Prada Pérez, and J. E. Aaron (eds.), *Selected Proceedings of the 16th Hispanic Linguistics Symposium*. Somerville, MA: Cascadilla, pp. 175–189.

Linford, B., Solon, M., Long, A. Y., Whatley, M., and Geeslin, K. (2016). Lexical Frequency and Subject Expression in Native and Non-Native Spanish: A Closer Look at Independent and Mediating Effects. In S. Sessarego and F. Tejedo-Herrero (eds.), *Spanish Language and Sociolinguistic Analysis*. Amsterdam: John Benjamins, pp. 197–216.

Lope Blanch, J. M. (1972). *Estudios sobre el español de México*. Mexico City: UNAM.

Malovrh, P. (2006). L2 Sentence Processing of Spanish OVS Word Order and Direct Object Pronouns: An Analysis of Contextual Constraints. In N. Sagarra and A. Toribio (eds.), *Selected Proceedings of the 9th Hispanic Linguistics Symposium*. Somerville, MA: Cascadilla, pp. 169–179.

Malovrh, P. (2014). Variability and Systematicity in Interlanguage Development: An Analysis of Mode and its Effect on L2 Spanish Morphology. *Studies in Hispanic and Lusophone Linguistics*, 7 (1), 43–78.

Mayberry, M. (2011). Synchronous Narratives in Spanish: The Simple Present/Present Progressive Aspectual Contrast. *Hispania*, 94, 462–482.

Meisel, J. M. (1987). Reference to Past Events and Actions in the Development of Natural Language Acquisition. In C. W. Pfaff (ed.), *First and Second Language Acquisition Processes*. Cambridge, MA: Newbury House, pp. 206–224.

Montes Giraldo, J. (1962). Sobre la categoría de futuro en el español de Colombia. *Boletín del Instituto Caro y Cuervo*, 16, 527–555.

Moses, J. (2002). The Expression of Futurity by English-Speaking Learners of French (Doctoral dissertation). Indiana University.

Orozco, R. (2005). Distribution of Future Tense Forms in Northern Colombian Spanish. In D. Eddington (ed.), *Selected Proceedings of the 7th Hispanic Linguistics Symposium*. Somerville, MA: Cascadilla, pp. 56–65.

Ortiz-López, L. A. (2000). Extensión de *estar* en contextos de *ser* en el español de Puerto Rico: ¿Evolución interna o contacto de lenguas? *Boletín de la Academia Puertorriqueña de la Lengua Española*, 98–118.

Otheguy, R. and Zentella, A. C. (2012). *Spanish in New York: Language Contact, Dialectal Leveling, and Structural Continuity*. New York: Oxford University Press.

Pellegrino Aveni, V. (2005). *Study Abroad and Second Language Use*. Cambridge: Cambridge University Press.

Preston, D. (1993). Variationist Linguistics and Second Language Acquisition. *Second Language Research*, 9, 153–172.

Preston, D. (2000). Three Kinds of Sociolinguistics and SLA: A Psycholinguistic Perspective. In B. Swierzbin *et al.* (eds.), *Social and Cognitive Factors in SLA*. Somerville, MA: Cascadilla, pp. 3–30.

Quesada, M. L. (1998). L2 Acquisition of the Spanish Subjunctive Mood and Prototype Schema Development. *Spanish Applied Linguistics*, 2, 1–23.

Quesada, M. L. and Blackwell, S. E. (2009). The L2 Acquisition of Null and Overt Spanish Subject Pronouns: A Pragmatic Approach. In J. Collentine, M. García, B. Lafford, and F. Marcos Martín (eds.), *Selected Proceedings of the 11th Hispanic Linguistics Symposium*. Somerville, MA: Cascadilla, pp. 117–130.

Ranson, D. L. (1991). Person Marking in the Wake of /s/ Deletion in Andalusian Spanish. *Language Variation and Change*, 3, 133–152.

Regan, V. (1995). The Acquisition of Sociolinguistic Native Speech Norms. In B. Freed (ed.). *Second Language Acquisition in a Study Abroad Context*. Amsterdam: John Benjamins, pp. 245–267.

Regan, V. (2004). The Relationship between the Group and the Individual and the Acquisition of Native Speaker Variation Patterns: A Preliminary Study. *International Review of Applied Linguistics in Language Teaching*, 42 (4), 335–348.

Rehner, K. (2002). The Development of Aspects of Linguistic and Discourse Competence by Advanced Second Language Learners of French (Doctoral dissertation). University of Toronto.

Rehner, K., Mougeon, R., and Nadasdi, T. (2003). The Learning of Sociolinguistic Variation by Advanced FSL Learners. *Studies in Second Language Acquisition*, 25, 127–156.

Rodríguez Louro, C. (2009). Perfect Evolution and Change: A Study of Preterit and Present Perfect Usage in Contemporary and Earlier Argentina (Doctoral dissertation). University of Melbourne.

Salgado-Robles, F. (2014a). Desarrollo de la competencia estratégica oral en español como segunda lengua mediante el Aprendizaje-Servicio en el Bluegrass de Mexington. *Estudios de Lingüística Aplicada*, 59, 125–149.

Salgado-Robles, F. (2014b). Variación dialectal por aprendientes de español en un contexto de inmersión en el extranjero: Un análisis cuantitativo del uso leísta en el discurso oral y escrito. *Lenguas Modernas*, 43, 97–112.

Sankoff, D., Tagliamonte, S., and Smith E. (2005). GoldVarb X: A Variable Rule Application for Macintosh and Windows. Available from http://individual.utoronto.ca/tagliamonte/goldvarb.html (last access December 24, 2017).

Schwenter, S. A. (2006). Null Objects across South America. In T. L. Face and C. A. Klee (eds.), *Selected Proceedings of the 8th Hispanic Linguistics Symposium*. Somerville, MA: Cascadilla, pp. 23–36.

Schwenter, S. A. and Torres Cacoullos, R. (2008). Defaults and Indeterminacy in Temporal Grammaticalization: The "Perfect" Road to Perfective. *Language Variation and Change*, 20, 1–39.

Sedano, M. (1994). El futuro morfológico y la expresión *ir a* + infinitivo en el español hablado de Venezuela. *Verba: Anuario Galego de Filoloxia*, 21, 225–240.

Selinker, L. (1972). Interlanguage. *International Review of Applied Linguistics*, 10, 209–231.

Shin, N. L. and Otheguy, R. (2013). Social Class and Gender Impacting Change in Bilingual Settings: Spanish Subject Pronoun Use in New York. *Language in Society*, 42, 429–452.

Shirai, Y. (1995). Tense-Aspect Marking by L2 Learners of Japanese. In D. MacLaughlin and S. McEwen (eds.), *Proceedings of 19th Annual Boston University Conference in Language Development*. Somerville, MA: Cascadilla, pp. 575–586.

Shively, R. L. (2015). Developing Interactional Competence during Study Abroad: Listener Responses in L2 Spanish. *System*, 48, 86–98.

Silva-Corvalán, C. (1994). *Language Contact and Change: Spanish in Los Angeles*. Oxford: Oxford University Press.

Silva-Corvalán, C. and Terrell, T. (1989). Notas sobre la expresión de futuridad en el español del Caribe. *Hispanic Linguistics*, 2, 191–208.

Solon, M. and Kanwit, M. (2014). The Emergence of Future Verbal Morphology in Spanish as a Foreign Language. *Studies in Hispanic and Lusophone Linguistics*, 7 (1), 115–148.

Tagliamonte, S. (2012). *Variationist Sociolinguistics: Change, Observation, Interpretation*. Malden, MA: Wiley-Blackwell.

Tarone, E. (1983). On the Variability of Interlanguage Systems. *Applied Linguistics*, 4 (2), 142–163.

Tomasello, M. (2003). *Constructing a Language*. Boston, MA: Harvard University Press.

Torres Cacoullos, R. (2000). *Grammaticization, Synchronic Variation, and Language Contact: A Study of Spanish Progressive -ndo Constructions*. Philadelphia, PA: John Benjamins.

von Stutterheim, C. and Klein, W. (1987). A Concept-Oriented Approach to Second Language Studies. In C. W. Pfaff (ed.), *First and Second Language Acquisition Processes*. Cambridge, MA: Newbury House, pp. 191–205.

Walker, J. (2010). *Variation in Linguistic Systems*. New York: Routledge.

Woolsey, D. (2008). From Theory to Research: Contextual Predictors of *estar* + adjective and the Study of SLA of Spanish Copula Choice. *Bilingualism: Language and Cognition*, 11 (3), 277–296.

Young, D. J. (2013). Affective Factors and Second Language Spanish. In K. L. Geeslin (ed.), *The Handbook of Spanish Second Language Acquisition*. Oxford: Blackwell, pp. 369–385.

Zentella, A. C. (1997). *Growing up Bilingual: Puerto Rican Children in New York*. Malden, MA: Blackwell.

33

Third Language Acquisition

Jennifer Cabrelli Amaro and Michael Iverson

33.1 Introduction

Language acquisition research has long made distinctions between first (L1) and second language (L2) acquirers, recognizing the potentially different paths and outcomes and carrying out systematic investigation of these acquisition scenarios. However, only recently – within the past 20 years – has the distinction between second and third language (L3) acquirers been treated with the same fervor. Acknowledging that acquiring a second and third language are different processes is a crucial step for both second and third language research. For L2 research, it means abandoning the tacit assumption that all acquisition beyond the native language is comparable and identifying the possible confound of including multilinguals in an L2 study. For L3 research, it has meant the birth of a new subfield. In this chapter, we give a brief history of L3 research, detail the current state of the field with a focus on the impact of Spanish on the study of L3 acquisition, and provide possible directions for future lines of inquiry.

33.2 Early Studies of Third Language Acquisition

To understand the origin of the lines of inquiry that currently drive L3 acquisition, it is necessary to consider a set of studies which arguably constructed the field's foundation at the end of the 20th century. The research we report on here ranges from early impressionistic diary studies to large-scale quantitative studies, and dates from Vildomec (1963), which to our knowledge was the first systematic treatment of multilingualism. Larger-scale experimental work began later in the 1960s (e.g. Rabinovitch and Parver's data on bilingual children's discrimination of

L3 Russian phonemes, 1966) and 1970s (e.g. Stedje 1977 for lexical transfer), but, as our review will reflect, appearance of these studies was sporadic and an appreciable increase in output did not begin until the 1980s and 1990s. From this body of work, we have pulled out the variables with the most substantial presence, and detail general findings.[1] We then segue into a brief discussion of the limitations of this research before moving on to research from the last 15 years. We note that, while most of the studies mentioned in this section do not involve Spanish, the incorporation of these studies is necessary to establish the early trajectory of this area of investigation.

When considering the L3 research that came out of the last decades of the 20th century, a central theme can be identified, which is that of transfer/cross-linguistic influence (CLI). Herein, we focus on this theme, while acknowledging that this is one of several lines of inquiry in the field of multilingualism. The fundamental questions related to CLI come out of the notion that, unlike L2 acquisition, there are two background languages to contend with. So, what CLI patterns are present at different stages in L3 acquisition, and what are the variables that yield these patterns?

One primary variable proposed to drive L3 acquisition has been language status. Is the source of transfer more likely to be the L1, the L2, or both, and why? Early research suggested that reliance on the L1 as opposed to the L2 depends on the domain of grammar, with research from this period limited primarily to lexical transfer and, to a lesser degree, phonetic/phonological transfer. Several studies showed that lexical transfer comes primarily from the L2 (e.g. Rivers 1979; Stedje 1977; Vogel 1992), although semantic transfer has been posited to originate with the L1 (Ringbom 1987). Regarding phonological transfer, Llisterri and Poch-Olivé (1987) and Ringbom (2001) report evidence of L1 transfer (with Ringbom 2001 showing long-term effects of L1 transfer, particularly for intonation), while Bentahila (1975) and Chumbow (1981) report L2 phonological influence in learner speech.

How might age of acquisition of a language relate to source of transfer? There was a common assumption that L1 transfer occurs due to the entrenched nature of the system and the cumulative experience that a learner has with the language compared to the L2, referred to as the "mother tongue effect" (Chumbow 1981). Some researchers proposed that L2 transfer might be driven by a conscious desire to avoid the L1 in order to sound "non-foreign" (see e.g. Hammarberg 2001 for a discussion of this phenomenon). Other proposals for a "foreign language effect" (e.g. Meisel 1983) focused on similarities in L2 and L3 acquisition processes (cf. Stedje 1977 and Ringbom 1987, who claim that L2 transfer is more likely if

---

[1] We recognize that this overview of L3 research in the 20th century is abbreviated and (necessarily) simplified. For exhaustive reviews of earlier L3 research, we direct the reader to de Angelis (2007) for a general overview, Cabrelli Amaro (2012), Cabrelli Amaro and Wrembel (2016), and Wrembel (2015) for phonology, García-Mayo (2012) for cognitive approaches, and García-Mayo and Rothman (2012) for morphosyntax.

acquired naturalistically), which results in the blocking of L1 transfer (e.g. Dewaele 1998). Still others noted that L2 transfer could be the product of recency, whereby the L2 is transferred because it has most recently been activated (Hammarberg 2001; Vildomec 1963), or that L2 transfer will be more likely in an L2 context (Stedje 1977).

How can we be certain of an L2 effect and explain contradictory findings such as those reported earlier for L3 phonological transfer? Unfortunately, we cannot isolate the role of language status without considering other potential variables in the research design. For example, Stedje's (1977) investigation of L1 Finnish/L2 Swedish L3 German learners' lexical transfer reported L2 transfer, but the learners' L2 also happens to be more similar than is Finnish to German. Therefore, it was not possible to pinpoint whether there was an L2 effect or whether the typological relationship between Swedish and German drove transfer. This confound was present in most early research, which primarily consisted of a single learner or group of learners with similar linguistic backgrounds. Several studies reported (perceived) typological similarity as a catalyst for transfer (e.g. Bild and Swain 1989; Singh and Carroll 1979; Singleton 1987) but none of these could rule out the role of other factors in their design. The few exceptions are studies by Ringbom (1987), Cenoz and Valencia (1994), and Llisterri and Poch-Olivé (1987), all of which employed a design using *mirror-image groups*: they observed two groups of sequential bilinguals that had each acquired the same language pair, but in reverse order; this design made it possible to tease apart language status and similarity. For example, Ringbom (1987) compared two groups of L3 English learners, L1 Finnish/L2 Swedish and L1 Swedish/L2 Finnish, and found that both groups transferred Swedish lexical items independently of whether Swedish was the L1 or L2. These early studies informed methodological issues, and prompted foundational questions of current research, which we review in the following section.

33.3 Research Questions that Drive the Study of Third Language Acquisition and a Review of the Literature

The research discussed in Section 33.2 made clear the value of examining third language acquisition as more than just another instance of L2 acquisition, and established several research questions that have been further refined over the last two decades. Researchers have begun to fill in some of the gaps pointed out by Fouser (1995) in his synthesis of L3 acquisition research, including the lack of investigation of both process and product, production and comprehension, and facilitative and non-facilitative transfer. Within this section, we address the progress that has been made towards what we see as the primary research questions that drive this field: understanding (i) what catalyzes initial transfer to the L3 and (ii) the developmental processes and their effects on the L3 as well as the L1/L2. Throughout this discussion, the substantial role of Spanish in the investigation of L3 acquisition will become clear.

33.3.1 Cross-Linguistic Influence during the Third Language Initial Stages

While L3 acquisition is a distinct area of inquiry, it borrows from insights in the second language acquisition (SLA) literature. L2 research shows that a learner's prior linguistic experience (the L1) can influence L2 development, and that the entire L1 grammar may form the initial state of L2 acquisition (e.g. Schwartz and Sprouse 1996). This is readily acknowledged in L3 research, as is the additional layer of complexity of two potential sources of cross-linguistic influence, the L1 and the L2. The first explicit models of L3 acquisition aimed to predict patterns of linguistic transfer for beginning L3 learners (specifically, morphosyntactic transfer, which was not a focus of the research reported in Section 33.2). However, they vary in their conception of (i) the consistency of transfer – is the source of transfer fixed (always the L1 or L2) or variable (possibly the L1 or L2)? – and (ii) the selectivity of transfer – is it a full grammatical system that is transferred, or only a partial system? – as well as the underlying catalysts for transfer.

One logical possibility in L3 acquisition is that the L1 serves as the L3 initial state and influences behavior in the L3 at the initial stages. This is consistent with models of L2 acquisition in which the L1 serves as the initial state of the L2 (e.g. Full Transfer/Full Access: Schwartz and Sprouse 1996). In such a model, the L1 holds a privileged role as the sole source of transfer, to the exclusion of other factors. This should give rise to two observable consequences. First, behavior at the initial stages of L3 acquisition of (for example) French by a speaker of (for example) L1 Spanish and L2 English should be similar to the behavior of a native speaker of Spanish learning French as an L2, as L2 English won't factor into the initial state of L3 French. Second, acquisition beyond an L3 – L4, L5, etc. – should yield similar results, at least at the outset. In cases where a linguistic property is shared in the L1 and the L3, acquisition will be facilitated (i.e. positive or facilitative transfer); however, in cases where the L1 and L3 do not align, acquisition will be hindered (i.e. negative or non-facilitative transfer).

L1 transfer has been demonstrated. In L1 Moroccan Arabic/L2 French learners of L3 English, L1 influence has been evidenced by placement of negation and adverbs (Hermas 2010), subject–verb inversion in declarative sentences (Hermas 2014), and knowledge of restrictive relative clauses (Hermas 2015), despite the closer typological relation between L2 French and L3 English. Sanz et al. (2015) examined reliance on L1 (English) or L2 (Japanese or Spanish) morphosyntactic cues in the processing and interpretation of transitive sentences in L3 Latin at the initial stages. In English, thematic roles in a transitive sentence are established primarily via rigid

SVO word order; neither case nor subject–verb agreement is consistently marked. In contrast, word order in Japanese and Spanish is flexible, and is therefore not a reliable indicator of an entity's role. The relationship among entities is established through morphology: Case in Japanese and subject–verb agreement in Spanish are (sufficiently) unambiguously marked. Latin, like Japanese and Spanish, exhibits free word order, and also marks both case and agreement. Despite the possibility of using a morphological cue as in L2 Japanese or Spanish, L3 learners of Latin relied on word order for interpretation – consistent with transfer from L1 English.

Another logical possibility is that the L2 always serves as the L3 initial state. This has been formalized as the L2 Status Factor (e.g. Bardel and Falk 2007; Falk and Bardel 2011). In this model, the L2 serves as the source of transfer because of its status as a non-native language, a characteristic which it shares with the L3 and all subsequently acquired languages. This distinction has roots in Paradis' (2004) Procedural/Declarative model, in which native and non-native languages are stored in fundamentally different ways, and therefore rely on different types of knowledge. Native languages are stored in procedural memory, while non-native languages (learned in adulthood) are learned skills that utilize declarative memory. One consequence of such a model is that the initial state of L3 acquisition should be the same for learners who share an L2, regardless of L1.

Seminal work by Bardel and Falk (2007) tested the placement of negation in L3 Swedish or Dutch by two groups of speakers of Germanic L1s and L2s. Both Swedish and Dutch are classified as verb-second (V2) languages, in which the verb must be the second element in main clauses. Placement of negation is considered to be a property related to V2. In this study, one group had an L1 without V2, but spoke an L2 with V2, and the other group had an L1 with V2, but spoke an L2 without V2. The group who spoke an L2 with V2 showed no difficulty with the placement of negation, outperforming the non-V2 L2 group. Given these results, the nature of the L2 seemed to be the decisive factor in L3 performance. This study was followed by an examination of L1 French/L2 English and L1 English/L2 French learners of L3 German. In German, object pronouns are post-verbal in matrix clauses, patterning with English, and preverbal in subordinate clauses, patterning with French. Both groups showed non-facilitative influence from their respective L2s, failing to reject ungrammatical sentences in German if the word order was grammatical in the L2. The L2 status factor has also been posited to explain L3 Spanish phonological transfer of voiceless stops by mirror-image groups of English–French bilinguals (Llama et al. 2010); both groups were shown to produce L2-like voice onset time (VOT) in Spanish. To our knowledge, this is the only mirror-image study involving Spanish to show an L2 effect for phonology.

The scenarios mentioned above assume that transfer is non-selective – an entire grammatical system is transferred – and that transfer is fixed – it is always the L1 or always the L2 that is transferred. However, the empirical evidence supporting both L1 and L2 transfer calls this assumption into question, and suggests that transfer into an L3 may be variable. Unlike models in which the source of transfer is fixed, models in which the L1 or the L2 may be transferred require some sort of trigger for transfer, tipping the proverbial scale to one grammar or the other.

One such model is Rothman's Typological Primacy Model (TPM) (2011, 2013, 2015). In this model, structural similarity serves as the trigger for the transfer of the L1 or L2 into the L3. Early conceptualizations of this model claimed that it was the learner's perception of overall typological similarity, in the vein of Kellerman's (1983, 1986) psychotypology, which drives transfer. If a learner (unconsciously) deemed the L3 more globally similar to their native language, the L1 would be transferred. In cases where the L2 was determined to be more similar, the L2 would be transferred. Because this is a model which envisions the transfer of an entire grammatical system, transfer can be both facilitative and non-facilitative.

Later instantiations of this model (Rothman 2013, 2015) detailed how selection of the source of transfer might happen. As learners are confronted with L3 input, they make use of the most salient cues across linguistic domains. Rothman (2015:185) states that the following factors impact the source of transfer, with decreasing influence: lexicon, phonological/phonotactic cues, functional morphology, syntactic structure. The lexicon is the first point of comparison. In the case that the learner is able to parse individual lexical items in the L3 *and* a sufficient number are similar to those in a previously acquired language, that language will serve as the source of transfer. If, on the other hand, both the L1 and the L2 lexicons are comparably similar to the L3 lexicon, or neither the L1 nor the L2 lexicon aligns with the L3 lexicon, or individual lexical items in the L3 are not able to be parsed (and cues from the L3 lexicon are therefore unavailable), the learner will make use of the next set of cues – phonological and phonetic cues. If these cues are unusable, or result in a tie of sorts, the learner moves on to the next set of cues, and so on. In this model, typological/structural similarity must be assessed in a global sense, and independently of the linguistic property under investigation. Furthermore, because the source of transfer must be determined early, the learner makes this assessment with extremely limited L3 data, and any claims as to whether the L1 or L2 grammar will be transferred should take this into consideration.

Although the expected source of transfer is not always easy to determine, much of the work on the TPM, including the foundational research, has avoided potential confounds in gauging the more similar language pair by exploiting the close historical, typological, and linguistic ties between Spanish and other Romance languages. Rothman and Cabrelli

Amaro (2010) tested L1 English/L2 Spanish learners of L3 Italian or L3 French on properties related to the availability of null subjects. Because Italian and French are both Romance languages, L3 learners are expected to transfer Spanish. However, Spanish and Italian are null-subject languages, while French and English are not, so transfer of Spanish would facilitate acquisition of only Italian, while transfer of English would facilitate acquisition of only French. L3 learners showed behavior consistent with transfer of Spanish, treating both Italian and French like null-subject languages. This is also consistent with the L2 Status Factor, leading Rothman to incorporate mirror-image groups in subsequent studies.

Many studies evaluating the TPM have examined the acquisition of L3 (Brazilian) Portuguese (BP), often using mirror-image groups of L1 English/L2 Spanish and L1 Spanish/L2 English speakers. The grammars of Spanish and Portuguese are similar in many respects, and an L1 or L2 speaker of Spanish is expected to use the Spanish grammar at the initial stages of L3 Portuguese. Knowledge of Spanish as an L1 or an L2 has been shown to facilitate acquisition of a range of properties in L3 Portuguese, including adjective placement and interpretation of prenominal and postnominal adjectives (Rothman 2010), and gender/number marking and noun-drop (Iverson 2009). For properties in which Spanish and Portuguese diverge, non-facilitative transfer is predicted. This has obtained for a range of morphosyntactic properties, including relative clause attachment and word order (Rothman 2011), Differential Object Marking (DOM) (Giancaspro et al. 2015), verb raising across dative experiencers (Cabrelli Amaro et al. 2015), and object expression (Montrul et al. 2011). Recent data from Cabrelli Amaro and Pichan (unpublished) also indicate that L3 BP vowel and intervocalic underlying stop production patterns with learners' Spanish productions. Considering the entire body of work on English/Spanish/L3 Portuguese, it seems evident that transfer may be non-facilitative. It is also notable that Spanish, whether it is the L1 or L2, is transferred for each property that has been tested – consistent with the transfer of an entire grammar.

The models mentioned so far all assume transfer of an entire grammatical system. However, this is not the only logical possibility, and there are models in which transfer is assumed to happen on a property-by-property basis. The Cumulative Enhancement Model (CEM) (Flynn et al. 2004) claims that third language acquisition is both a cumulative and a non-redundant process. Transfer is not wholesale, but rather structures or properties from any previous language are equally available to an individual L3 learner. Additionally, transfer into the L3 will happen only in cases in which the transfer is facilitative, which distinguishes this model from the rest. The basis of this model is data from L1 Kazakh/L2 Russian speakers of L3 English. While Kazakh is a head-final language (i.e. complements precede heads), both Russian and English are head-initial languages. These learners' production of L3 English relative clauses was head-initial, suggesting influence from L2 Russian and contradicting a claim of any privileged status for the L1. These results were corroborated by data from L1 German (head-final in embedded clauses) and L1 German/L2 Hungarian (head-initial) learners acquiring L2 or L3 English (Berkes and Flynn 2012). L3 learners showed influence from L2 Hungarian, facilitating the acquisition of relative clause structure as compared to L2 English learners.

More recent models of L3 acquisition are similar to the CEM in that they question wholesale transfer. The Linguistic Proximity Model (LPM) (Mykhaylyk et al. 2015; Westergaard et al. 2017) claims that transfer into the L3 happens on a property-by-property basis, and can be sourced from all previously acquired languages. Transfer is conditioned by abstract linguistic structure. In cases where a target L3 property is structurally similar to a property from a previously acquired language, transfer into the L3 will be facilitative. If, however, the L3 input is misanalyzed, resulting transfer may be non-facilitative. This process is active at any stage of L3 acquisition, not just the beginning stages: L3 development does not only compare initial hypotheses about the L3 grammar to the L3 input and make subsequent adjustments to the L3 linguistic system. Learners entertain their initial hypotheses, the L3 input, but also continue to access any previously acquired linguistic structures (and perhaps recruit them based on the L3 input), even at later stages of the acquisition process. Slabakova's (2017) Scalpel Model also stipulates transfer on a property-by-property basis, and allows for facilitative and non-facilitative transfer. In contrast with the LPM, however, transfer is conditioned by other factors in addition to structural similarity, such as frequency and misleading input. Low-frequency constructions and those that would require negative evidence for acquisition (with respect to the competing property in the L1/L2) are predicted to be susceptible to non-facilitative transfer.

33.3.2 Third Language Development

Transfer at the initial stages is (literally) just the beginning in terms of the questions we can explore at different stages of L3 acquisition and how these questions can inform linguistic theory more generally. In this section, we focus on two questions related to the nature of cross-linguistic influence throughout acquisition: What are the roles of the L1 and L2 after initial transfer, and what effects does the development of an L3 have on the L1 and L2? A small but growing body of work indicates that the roles of the L1 and L2 may change substantially.

Ringbom (2001) put forth the logical notion that the L1 and L2 exert the heaviest amount of influence on the L3 at the earlier stages of L3 acquisition, and that, as L3 proficiency increases, L1 and L2 influence decreases. Early research suggested that the influence of the L1 and L2 might change throughout development. Specifically, analysis of production data from case studies by Vogel (1992) and Williams and Hammarberg (1998) suggests that the learners' reliance on the L2 diminishes earlier than that on the L1. Without controlling for variables such as order of acquisition (via inclusion of a mirror-image learner group) and similarity, however, it was not possible to definitively conclude that these learners overcame non-facilitative transfer from the L2 earlier than that from the L1 because of language status.

As shown in Section 33.3.1, most studies involving Spanish as an L1 or L2 and a Romance L3 find that Spanish transfers regardless of other factors. To tease apart the predictions of the CEM and TPM, the property selected should be a mismatch in its realization between the two similar languages, resulting in non-facilitative transfer of Spanish. The subsequent L3 learning task is for the learners to retreat from initial non-facilitative transfer. Cabrelli Amaro and Rothman (2010) first noted that this task might pose more of a challenge for learners who transfer their L1 than for learners who transfer their L2, citing the entrenched nature of the L1 as a potential source of difficulty. Recently, researchers have begun to examine differences in the rate of L3 morphosyntactic development in cases of initial non-facilitative transfer. Following up on Giancaspro et al. (2015) and using their initial stages DOM data, Cabrelli Amaro et al. (in press) administered the same acceptability judgment task to a pair of mirror-image English/Spanish groups of advanced L3 BP learners. A cross-sectional analysis reveals that the L2 Spanish advanced group patterns with BP native controls and appears to have overcome Spanish transfer of DOM, while the L1 Spanish advanced group continues to pattern with the initial stages groups. Cabrelli Amaro (2015) has replicated this finding with the raising of an embedded subject across a dative experiencer to subject position in the matrix clause (RExp) in L3 BP, a structure which is ungrammatical in Spanish (*Pedro me parece estar triste 'Pedro seems to me to be sad' vs. Me parece que Pedro está triste 'It seems to me that Pedro is sad'; Cabrelli Amaro et al. 2015), but not in English or BP. She took the initial stages data from Cabrelli Amaro et al.'s (2015) study of RExp in L3 BP and compared it with data from the same groups of advanced L3 BP speakers from Cabrelli Amaro et al. (in press). The L1 Spanish advanced group rated grammatical RExp in BP lower than the BP control, although the ratings were significantly higher than the L1 Spanish initial stages group. The L2 Spanish advanced group, on the other hand, rated RExp higher than the L2 Spanish initial stages group and the advanced ratings were not different from those of the BP controls. Therefore, the L2 Spanish group appears to have converged on the L3 target while the L1 Spanish group is still in the process of L3 reconfiguration. The question that follows from this apparent consequence of L1 transfer is whether these learners can eventually converge on the L3 target. Based on his study of L1 Greek/L2 English/L3 Spanish learners, Lozano (2002) states that fossilization will occur when the relevant L1 features do not match the L2 or L3 features, a finding supported by Jin (2009) for L1 Mandarin/L2 English/L3 Norwegian learners.

However, there is evidence from other language triads that L1 transfer can be overcome when the relevant L3 features are available in the background language(s) (Hermas 2014). This finding is supported by Slabakova and García-Mayo (2015) who examine the acquisition of L3 English syntax–discourse interface properties by Spanish–Basque bilinguals who exhibit Spanish transfer. The results show non-facilitative Spanish transfer of topicalization to be persistent even at advanced L3 English proficiency for Spanish-dominant and Basque-dominant speakers alike. However, a subset of learners in both groups exhibit L3 English convergence, and the authors conclude that "trilingual learners are not permanently constrained by the native grammar in this domain" (2015:221). Even if access to linguistic universals is limited in L3 acquisition, the logical prediction is that the L1 Spanish group in this case will eventually converge on the L3 target. Cabrelli Amaro et al. (in press) propose that the asymmetry between the L1 Spanish and L2 Spanish groups is due to probabilistic processes in L3 acquisition, and that feature reconfiguration will eventually obtain for both groups. Specifically, L3 input must reach a certain threshold, at which point the mismatch between the L3 and the Spanish hypothesis will drive reanalysis. They assume that the difference between the L1 and L2 Spanish speakers comes down to cumulative Spanish experience, and that a greater amount of L3 input is necessary for the L1 Spanish speakers to reach the same threshold.

Our discussion up to this point has revolved around progressive transfer, that is, transfer from the L1 and/or L2 to the L3. However, a large body of work has established that cross-linguistic influence is bidirectional and an L2 can affect an L1 (see Schmid 2016 for an annotated bibliography). A logical extension of this is that an L3 can affect previously acquired systems, and researchers have begun to examine a couple of questions via observation of L3 effects on the L1 and/or L2. The first is a new take on the long-standing question of whether L1 and L2 systems are fundamentally different (see e.g. Rothman and Slabakova 2017 for discussion), and the second is whether L3 acquisition can result in facilitative effects on the L2. To understand potential differences in stability between native versus non-native systems when an L3 is acquired, Cabrelli Amaro and Rothman (2010) and Cabrelli Amaro (2013a, 2017a) compare Spanish perception and production by L1 English/L2 Spanish and L1 Spanish/L2 English speakers. Cabrelli Amaro (2013a) did not find any significant differences in effects of L3 BP word-final vowel reduction on L1 versus L2 Spanish perception or production. As a follow-up, Cabrelli Amaro (2017a) reduced the data set to include only L3 BP speakers who patterned with a group of BP controls. She found that, while perception appeared to remain stable for both groups, L2 Spanish vowel production was more BP-like than L1 Spanish vowel production, although productions in both groups showed L3 effects. Sypiańska (2016) found L3 English effects on L1 Polish but not on L2 Danish vowel production, although proficiency was not controlled for in this study. Cabrelli Amaro (2017b) found similar results for morphosyntactic competence in a comparison of initial stages L3 BP data (from Cabrelli Amaro *et al.* 2015) with advanced L3 BP data. As in Cabrelli Amaro (2017a), only the advanced learners who rated RExp in BP within the confidence interval of a BP control group were included. While both learner groups rate RExp higher than a group of Spanish controls, the L1 Spanish speakers rated RExp lower in Spanish than the L2 Spanish speakers and the BP controls. These initial findings from phonology and morphosyntax suggest that there might indeed be a critical period for stability of a linguistic system, but further (longitudinal) research is necessary to confirm these data.

The L3 can also have beneficial effects on a background language(s). Recent research by Hui (2010), Matthews, Cheung, and Tsang (unpublished data), and Tsang (2015) compares an L1 Cantonese/L2 English control group with an L1 Cantonese/L2 English/L3 French or German experimental group. In each case, the French or German property under investigation patterns with English and differently from Cantonese. Results show that the L2 English of the experimental groups exhibits acquisition of properties that the control groups' does not; this is the case for subject relative clauses (Hui 2010), tense/aspect (Matthews *et al.* 2014 found that L3 German morphological tense marking overrode L1 Cantonese transfer in L2 English), and number agreement (Tsang 2015). A similar result comes from Llinàs-Grau and Mayenco (2016), who examined *that*-deletion in L3 English/L4 German learners (early simultaneous bilingual, or 2L1, Catalan/Spanish speakers); they report a higher rate of *that*-deletion in L3 English by the L4 German learners than by a control group of 2L1 Catalan/Spanish speakers of L3 English. This finding is attributed to (facilitative) regressive influence from the L3/L4.

Although cross-sectional studies illustrate the potential impact of developmental data on our understanding of how multiple systems interact across the lifespan, researchers cannot go back in time and confirm what (advanced) L3 learners' L2 looked like prior to L3 acquisition. Subsequent calls have been made for longitudinal research, given the ability to control for variation (e.g. Cabrelli Amaro and Wrembel 2016; Cenoz 2003). Currently we know of only a few longitudinal studies involving Spanish (see e.g. Kopečková 2016 for acquisition of L3 Spanish rhotics; García-Mayo and Villareal Olaizola 2011 and Ruiz de Zarobe 2005, 2008 for L3 English acquisition by Spanish–Basque bilinguals; Sánchez 2015 for L3 German lexical acquisition by Spanish–Catalan bilinguals). By observing learners over time, it is possible to first establish the L3 initial state for each learner, that is, the state of the L1 and L2 prior to L3 exposure. Learners can then be tested in all three languages over time to observe (i) initial stages transfer, (ii) the roles of the learner's background languages during acquisition, and (iii) how the background languages are affected as L3 proficiency increases. Without this research, we cannot confirm whether the existing developmental findings hold up. For example, consider the studies that show regressive transfer: It is not outside the realm of possibility that the L3 groups had already acquired those properties in their L2 (in the case of facilitative transfer) or that their L2 was not native-like at the onset of L3 acquisition (in the case of non-facilitative transfer). If we are unable to test those learners prior to L3 acquisition, however, we simply cannot know.

33.4 Future Directions

As with any line of inquiry, progress in the field of L3 acquisition has given way to new questions (and extensions of existing questions) as well as new ways of addressing these questions. In this section we outline a set of research questions yielded by the existing literature, followed by a brief discussion of some of the novel methods that are being explored.

33.4.1 New and Understudied Research Questions

As with any young field of scientific inquiry, progress is incremental. To date, the primary concerns of the study of multilingual acquisition have overwhelmingly addressed the initial stages of acquisition and the nature of linguistic transfer, and, to a lesser extent, L3 development. While questions in these areas are still being answered, new questions are being asked, and additional lines of investigation are ripe for research. Herein, we consider some (but certainly not all) areas that merit further pursuit.

What Happens with Three Unrelated Languages?

Practical limitations often restrict the scope of research, and studies on L3 acquisition are no exception to this. Researchers use the populations to which they have access, and L3 learners are more difficult to find than L2 learners. For many, language learning in adulthood is a costly endeavor in both time and effort, especially to reach the highest levels of proficiency, and learning a third language compounds this. This immediately restricts the number of L3 learners. The combinations of languages are also generally restricted. A person learning a third language does so for many reasons, but advancing linguistic research is not one of these. The combinations that are found are often the result of geographic and/or educational practicalities, as well as of the status of English as the current lingua franca. Consequently, many L3 studies involve English and a major European language, and what has been very rarely seen are studies involving languages that are truly (typologically) unrelated. We know of only a handful of examples of these to date: L1 Tuvan/L2 Russian/L3 English (Kulundary and Gabriele 2012), L1 Polish/L2 French/L3 English (Wrembel 2014), L1 English/L2 Spanish/L3 Arabic (Goodenkauf and Herschensohn, unpublished data, who found evidence of L2 Spanish transfer of grammatical gender to L3 Arabic), L1 Arabic/L2 French/L3 English (Hermas 2010, 2014, 2015), Basque/Spanish/L3 English (Slabakova and García-Mayo 2015).

The purposeful inclusion of unrelated languages might offer insights that using related languages cannot. For example, some models such as the TPM rely on the L3 learner's sensitivity to typological similarity. These relationships might be obscured in unrelated languages, perhaps to the point where the learner is either severely delayed in identifying similarities, or perhaps completely unable to do so. What happens in such a scenario? It could be the case that the strategy for selecting the L1 or L2 for transfer is variable. If the learner is unable to recognize any similarities between the L3 and L1/L2, perhaps they resort to a default secondary strategy, such as using the L2 as the initial hypothesis about the L3 grammar. Such an insight is available only if we examine unrelated languages.

Is Fourth Language Acquisition (and Beyond) Another Instance of Third Language Acquisition?

To our knowledge, there has not to date been a systematic investigation comparing L3 acquisition and L4 acquisition. At first glance, it may seem like an uninteresting comparison. On the other hand, it may be an entirely new scenario with results that differ from L3 acquisition. Consider the learning task as a speaker progresses from a monolingual to a multilingual. In the case of L2 acquisition, there is one possible source of transfer, and it is the first experience learning an additional language. L3 acquisition is slightly different: The speaker has experience acquiring an additional language, but this is the first experience in which there are multiple possible sources of transfer. For any language beyond the L3, the speaker has already had experience acquiring an additional language and in dealing with multiple possible sources of transfer. Perhaps this could result in further streamlining of the acquisition process.

Do Different Types of Bilinguals Show Similar Patterns in Third Language Acquisition and Development?

A central finding from research on second language acquisition is that there are general differences in path and ultimate attainment among cases of simultaneous bilingualism, childhood second language acquisition, and adult second language acquisition (see Montrul 2004, 2008 for an overview). It is not unreasonable to expect that any differences in the linguistic systems and language experience among these types of bilinguals could influence the acquisition of a third language, warranting a systematic investigation of their L3 acquisition patterns. This line of research would be complementary to the increasingly prominent body of research on heritage speakers, which in general goes beyond treating age of acquisition as a macro-variable, instead seeking a more nuanced look at variables relating to the relationship between the L1 and the L2 (or the two L1s). These variables include effects of age of acquisition, language dominance, metalinguistic knowledge, and relative influence of a native vs. non-native language.

Although the current L3 models do not make explicit predictions for different scenarios of bilingualism, a handful of studies have examined L3 acquisition by heritage speakers. Results from Giancaspro *et al.* (2015) and Cabrelli Amaro *et al.* (in press) showed that both English-speaking heritage speakers of Spanish and sequential bilinguals of English and Spanish incorrectly used Spanish-like DOM at the initial stages of acquisition of L3 BP. At later stages of L3 proficiency, this initial non-facilitative transfer was overcome by L1 English/L2 Spanish speakers. However, errors persisted for native speakers of Spanish, including the English-dominant heritage speakers of Spanish, suggesting dominance was not a deterministic factor in rate of acquisition. It is unclear if this result applies to all areas of the grammar, however, and language dominance may be an explanatory variable for L3 phonology. In fact, English-dominant heritage speakers of French have been found to produce longer English-like VOTs in L3 Spanish, despite the more similar, shorter VOTs found among Romance languages (Llama and López-Morelos 2016). Language dominance has also been shown to influence an L3 accent more globally, as German-dominant heritage speakers of Turkish learning L3 English are perceived to exhibit German-like accents (Lloyd-Smith *et al.* 2017).

33.4.2 New Methodological Considerations

As the questions at the core of third language acquisition research are further developed, a need arises for new methodologies. L3 methodological considerations have been addressed previously for syntax (e.g. García-Mayo and Rothman 2012) and phonology (e.g. Cabrelli Amaro 2013b), and recent applications of methods that have been gaining traction in the field of second language acquisition have the potential to provide new insights into the cognitive organization of multiple linguistic systems.

Although selective transfer has been examined exclusively via behavioral methodology, ranging from grammatical judgments to story retelling to spontaneous production, none have captured online linguistic processing. Rothman *et al.* (2015) suggest using neurological data, such as event-related potentials (ERPs) measured by electroencephalography (EEG), for testing initial stages models and argue that online methods can "strengthen the descriptive and explanatory power of these models or present novel data requiring refinements to them" (2015:11). If learners show evidence of native-like ERP signatures in their L2, the L2 should be a viable source of transfer and these learners can be tested in their L3. Rothman *et al.* (2015) propose a study that examines two ERP signatures associated with gender agreement violations and explain how the initial stages models could be tested in L3 learners of artificial languages (ALs) who are English–Spanish bilinguals. One of the artificial languages is lexically similar to Spanish (mini-Spanish) while the other is similar to English (mini-English), and both languages have number (like English and Spanish) and gender agreement (like Spanish only). The ALs consist of Spanish or English lexical items and word order but instantiate novel number and gender morphology. Since English does not have gender, transfer of English to mini-English would not be facilitative. Transfer of Spanish, however, would be facilitative for both ALs. To carry out the study, a pair of mirror-image groups would be trained on mini-English or mini-Spanish, for a total of four groups. After training, brain activity would be recorded via EEG while the learners completed a grammaticality judgment task in the relevant mini-language. The authors predict that sensitivity to gender violations will reflect Spanish transfer while absence of sensitivity will point to English as the source of transfer. The methodology the authors propose is promising in its ability to tap unconscious processes, and can be extended to other domains.

Rothman et al.'s (2015) use of artificial language learning (ALL) warrants a brief discussion of the benefits of using artificial languages in L3 acquisition research. As alluded to in the previous paragraph, an artificial language is constructed "according to rules and properties (deterministic or probabilistic) that generate language-like sentences using pseudowords" (Onnis 2012:35–36). While these systems are not natural languages, ALL stimuli have been found to elicit similar ERP signatures to those elicited by natural language stimuli (e.g. Friederici et al. 2002, but cf. Christiansen et al. 2012, who found signatures suggestive of domain-general processing). The use of the ALL paradigm gives the researcher control over the input the learner receives, which is especially important in L3 initial stages research, where one of the greatest challenges is finding a sufficient sample of learners who have comparable outside exposure to and prior knowledge of the target language. Another benefit is the control that the researcher has over the experimental design. As outlined in Section 33.3.1, testing all the initial stages models requires the selection of a linguistic phenomenon that patterns in a specific way across the three languages under investigation. In practice, when working with the natural language triplets, the number of properties or phenomena that meet the criteria for initial stages testing is limited. However, with ALL, it is possible to construct a language with the configuration needed to specifically examine the role of the L1 and L2 we are investigating, while controlling for variables that are otherwise uncontrollable when the L3 is a natural language.

33.5 Conclusion

As the field of third language acquisition continues to grow, its contribution to our understanding of language acquisition and linguistic theory more generally becomes increasingly apparent. As seen in this chapter, there are a number of questions related to cross-linguistic influence that currently drive the field. As we get deeper into their examination, new questions arise that have the potential to make their own mark on how we look at the multilingual mind, and the ways in which we approach these questions will evolve.

References

Bardel, C. and Falk, Y. (2007). The Role of the Second Language in Third Language Acquisition: The Case of Germanic Syntax. *Second Language Research*, 23, 459–484.

Bentahila, A. (1975). The Influence of the L2 on the Learning of the L3 (MA thesis). Bangor University.

Berkes, É. and Flynn, S. (2012). Further Evidence in Support of the Cumulative-Enhancement Model: CP Structure Development. In J. Cabrelli Amaro, S. Flynn, and J. Rothman(eds.), *Third Language Acquisition in Adulthood*. Amsterdam: John Benjamins, pp. 143–164.

Bild, E. R. and Swain, M. (1989). Minority Language Students in a French Immersion Programme: Their French Proficiency. *Journal of Multilingual and Multicultural Development*, 10 (3), 255–274.

Cabrelli Amaro, J. (2012). L3 Phonology: An Understudied Domain. In J. Cabrelli Amaro, S. Flynn, and J. Rothman(eds.), *Third Language Acquisition in Adulthood*. Amsterdam: John Benjamins, pp. 33–60.

Cabrelli Amaro, J. (2013a). The Phonological Permeability Hypothesis: Measuring Regressive L3 Influence to Test L1 and L2 Phonological Representations (Doctoral Dissertation). University of Florida.

Cabrelli Amaro, J. (2013b). Methodological Issues in L3 Phonological Acquisition Research. *Studies in Hispanic and Lusophone Linguistics*, 6 (1).

Cabrelli Amaro, J. (2015). Does the Source of Transfer Affect the Rate of L3 Morphosyntactic Development? Paper presented at the Boston University Conference on Language Development, Boston, USA.

Cabrelli Amaro, J. (2017a). Testing the Phonological Permeability Hypothesis: L3 Phonological Effects on L1 versus L2 Systems. *International Journal of Bilingualism*, 21, 698–717. doi: 1367006916637287.

Cabrelli Amaro, J. (2017b). Regressive Transfer in L3 Syntactic Development. In A. Hahn and T. Angelovska (eds.), *L3 Syntactic Transfer: Models, New Developments and Implications*. Amsterdam: John Benjamins, pp. 173–194.

Cabrelli Amaro, J., Amaro, J. F., and Rothman, J. (2015). The Relationship between L3 Transfer and Structural Similarity across Development: Raising across an Experiencer in Brazilian Portuguese. In H. Peukert (ed.), *Transfer Effects in Multilingual Language Development*. Amsterdam: John Benjamins, pp. 21–52.

Cabrelli Amaro, J., Iverson, M., Giancaspro, D., and Halloran González, B. (in press). Implications of L1 versus L2 Transfer in L3 Rate of Acquisition.

In K. Molsing, C. Becker Lopes Perna, and A. M. Tramunto Ibaños (eds.), *Linguistic Approaches to Portuguese as an Additional Language*. Amsterdam: John Benjamins.

Cabrelli Amaro, J. and Rothman, J. (2010). On L3 Acquisition and Phonological Permeability: A New Test Case for Debates on the Mental Representation of Non-Native Phonological Systems. *International Review of Applied Linguistics in Language Teaching*, 48, 275–296.

Cabrelli Amaro, J. and Wrembel, M. (2016). Investigating the Acquisition of Phonology in a Third Language – a State of the Science and an Outlook for the Future. *International Journal of Multilingualism*, 13 (4), 395–409.

Cenoz, J. (2003). The Additive Effect of Bilingualism on Third Language Acquisition: A Review. *International Journal of Bilingualism*, 7 (1), 71–87.

Cenoz, J. and Valencia, J. F. (1994). Additive Trilingualism: Evidence from the Basque Country. *Applied Psycholinguistics*, 15 (2), 195–207.

Christiansen, M. H., Conway, C. M., and Onnis, L. (2012). Similar Neural Correlates for Language and Sequential Learning: Evidence from Event-Related Brain Potentials. *Language and Cognitive Processes*, 27 (2), 231–256.

Chumbow, B. S. (1981). The Mother Tongue Hypothesis in a Multilingual Setting. In J. G. Savard and L. Laforge (eds.), *Proceedings of the 5th Congress of the International Association of Applied Linguistics*. Quebec: Les Presses de l'Université Laval, pp. 367–388.

de Angelis, G. (2007). *Third or Additional Language Acquisition*. Clevedon: Multilingual Matters.

Dewaele, J.-M. (1998). Lexical Inventions: French Interlanguage as L2 versus L3. *Applied Linguistics*, 19 (4), 471–490.

Falk, Y. and Bardel, C. (2011). Object Pronouns in German L3 Syntax: Evidence for the L2 Status Factor. *Second Language Research*, 27, 59–82.

Fouser, R. (1995). Problems and Prospects in Third Language Acquisition Research. *Language Research*, 31 (2), 387–414.

Friederici, A. D., Steinhauer, K., and Pfeifer, E. (2002). Brain Signatures of Artificial Language Processing: Evidence Challenging the Critical Period Hypothesis. *Proceedings of the National Academy of Sciences*, 99 (1), 529–534.

Flynn, S., Foley, C., and Vinnitskaya, I. (2004). The Cumulative-Enhancement Model for Language Acquisition: Comparing Adults' and Children's Patterns of Development in First, Second and Third Language Acquisition of Relative Clauses. *The International Journal of Multilingualism*, 1, 3–16.

García-Mayo, M. del P. (2012). Cognitive Approaches to L3 Acquisition. *International Journal of English Studies*, 12 (1), 129–146.

García-Mayo, M. del P. and Rothman, J. (2012). L3 Morphosyntax in the Generative Tradition: The Initial Stages and beyond. In J. Cabrelli Amaro, S. Flynn, and J. Rothman(eds.), *Third Language Acquisition in Adulthood*. Amsterdam: John Benjamins, pp. 9–32.

García-Mayo, M. del P. and Villarreal Olaizola, I. (2011). The Development of Suppletive and Affixal Tense and Agreement Morphemes in the L3

English of Basque–Spanish Bilinguals. *Second Language Research*, 27 (1), 129–149.

Giancaspro, D., Halloran, B., and Iverson, M. (2015). Transfer at the Initial Stages of L3 Brazilian Portuguese: A Look at Three Groups of English/Spanish Bilinguals. *Bilingualism: Language and Cognition*, 19, 191–207.

Hammarberg, B. (2001). Roles of L1 and L2 in L3 Production and Acquisition. In J. Cenoz, B. Hufeisen, and U. Jessner (eds.), *Cross-Linguistic Influence in Third Language Acquisition: Psycholinguistic Perspectives*. Clevedon: Multilingual Matters, pp. 21–41.

Hermas, A. (2010). Language Acquisition as Computational Resetting: Verb Movement in L3 Initial State. *International Journal of Multilingualism*, 7, 343–362.

Hermas, A. (2014). Multilingual Transfer: L1 Morphosyntax in L3 English. *International Journal of Language Studies*, 8.

Hermas, A. (2015). The Categorization of the Relative Complementizer Phrase in Third-Language English: A Feature Re-Assembly Account. *International Journal of Bilingualism*, 19 (5), 587–607.

Hui, B. (2010). Backward Transfer from L3 French to L2 English Production of Relative Clauses by L1 Cantonese Speakers in Hong Kong. *Hong Kong Journal of Applied Linguistics*, 12 (2), 45–60.

Iverson, M. (2009). N-Drop at the Initial State of L3 Portuguese: Comparing Simultaneous and Additive Bilinguals of English/Spanish. In A. Pires and J. Rothman (eds.), *Minimalist Inquiries into Child and Adult Language Acquisition: Case Studies across Portuguese*. Berlin: De Gruyter, pp. 221–244.

Jin, F. (2009). Third Language Acquisition of Norwegian Objects: Interlanguage Transfer or L1 Influence? In Leung, Y.-K. I. (ed.), *Third Language Acquisition and Universal Grammar*. Clevedon: Multilingual Matters, pp. 144–161.

Kellerman, E. (1983). Now You See It, Now You Don't. In S. Gass and L. Selinker (eds.), *Language Transfer in Language Learning*. Rowley, MA: Newbury House, pp. 112–134.

Kellerman, E. (1986). An Eye for an Eye: Crosslinguistic Constraints on the Development of the L2 Lexicon. In E. Kellerman and M. S. Smith (eds.), *Crosslinguistic Influence in Second Language Acquisition*. New York: Pergamon, pp. 35–48.

Kopečková, R. (2016). The Bilingual Advantage in L3 Learning: A Developmental Study of Rhotic Sounds. *International Journal of Multilingualism*, 13 (4), 410–425.

Kulundary, V. and Gabriele, A. (2012). Examining the Role of L2 Syntactic Development in L3 Acquisition: A Look at Relative Clauses. In J. Cabrelli Amaro, S. Flynn, and J. Rothman (eds.), *Third Language Acquisition in Adulthood*. Amsterdam: John Benjamins, pp. 195–222.

Llama, R., Cardoso, W., and L., C. (2010). The Influence of Language Distance and Language Status on the Acquisition of L3 Phonology. *International Journal of Multilingualism*, 7, 39–57.

Llama, R. and López-Morelos, L. P. (2016). VOT Production by Spanish Heritage Speakers in a Trilingual Context. *International Journal of Multilingualism*, 13 (4), 444–458.

Llinàs-Grau, M. and Mayenco, E. P. (2016). Regressive Transfer from L4 German to L3 English: The Case of *that*-Deletion. In A. Ibarrola-Armendariz and J. Ortiz de Urbina Arruabarrena (eds.), *Glancing Backwards to Build a Future in English Studies*. Bilbao: University of Deusto, pp. 281–288.

Llisterri, J. and Poch-Olivé, D. (1987). Phonetic Interference in Bilingual's Learning of a Third Language. In Tamaz Gamqrelidze *et al.* (eds.), *Proceedings of the 11th International Congress of Phonetic Sciences*. Tallinn: Academy of Sciences of the Estonian SSR, pp. 137–147.

Lloyd-Smith, A., Gyllstad, H., and Kupisch, T. (2017). Transfer into L3 English: Global Accent in German-Dominant Heritage Speakers of Turkish. *Linguistic Approaches to Bilingualism*, 7 (2), 131–162.

Lozano, C. (2002). The Interpretation of Overt and Null Pronouns in Non-Native Spanish. In H. Marsden, S. Pourcel, and M. Whong-Bharr (eds.), *Durham Working Papers in Linguistics*. Somerville, MA: Cascadilla, pp. 53–66.

Matthews, S. J., Cheung, S. C., and Tsang, W. L. (2014). Anti-Transfer Effects in Third Language Acquisition. Paper presented at the 9th International Conference on Third Language Acquisition and Multilingualism, Uppsala, Sweden.

Meisel, J. (1983). Transfer as a Second Language Strategy. *Language and Communication*, 3, 11–46.

Montrul, S., Dias, R., and Santos, H. (2011). Clitics and Object Expression in the L3 Acquisition of Brazilian Portuguese: Structural Similarity Matters for Transfer. *Second Language Research*, 27, 21–58.

Mykhaylyk, R., Mitrofanova, N., Rodina, Y., and Westergaard, M. (2015). The Linguistic Proximity Model: The Case of Verb-Second Revisited. In E. Grillo and K. Jepson (eds.), *Proceedings of the 39th Annual Boston University Conference on Language Development*. Somerville, MA: Cascadilla, pp. 337–349.

Montrul, S. (2004). *The Acquisition of Spanish: Morphosyntactic Development in Monolingual and Bilingual L1 Acquisition and Adult L2 Acquisition*. Amsterdam: John Benjamins.

Montrul, S. A. (2008). *Incomplete Acquisition in Bilingualism: Re-Examining the Age Factor*. Amsterdam: John Benjamins.

Onnis, L. (2012). Artificial Language Learning. In P. J. Binson (ed.), *Routledge Encyclopedia of Second Language Acquisition*. New York: Routledge, pp. 35–41.

Paradis, J. (2004). The Relevance of Specific Language Impairment in Understanding the Role of Transfer in Second Language Acquisition. *Applied Psycholinguistics*, 25, 67–82.

Rabinovitch, M. S. and Parver, L. M. (1966). Auditory Discrimination in Monolinguals and Polyglots. Paper Presented at Meeting of Canadian Psychological Association, Montreal.

Ringbom, H. (1987). *The Role of First Language in Foreign Language Acquisition.* Clevedon: Multilingual Matters.

Ringbom, H. (2001). Lexical Transfer in L3 Production. In J. Cenoz, B. Hufeisen, and U. Jessner (eds.), *Cross-Linguistic Influence in Third Language Acquisition: Psycholinguistic Perspectives.* Clevedon: Multilingual Matters, pp. 59–68.

Rivers, W. M. (1979). Learning a Sixth Language: An Adult Learner's Daily Diary. *Canadian Modern Language Review. La Revue Canadienne des Langues Vivantes*, 36 (1), 67–82.

Rothman, J. (2010). On The Typological Economy of Syntactic Transfer: Word Order and Relative Clause High/Low Attachment Preference in L3 Brazilian Portuguese. *International Review of Applied Linguistics in Teaching*, 48 (2/3), 245–273.

Rothman, J. (2011). L3 Syntactic Transfer Selectivity and Typological Determinacy: The Typological Primacy Model. *Second Language Research*, 27, 107–127.

Rothman, J. (2013). Cognitive Economy, Non-Redundancy and Typological Primacy in L3 Acquisition: Evidence from Initial Stages of L3 Romance. In S. Baauw, F. Dirjkoningen, and M. Pinto (eds.), *Romance Languages and Linguistic Theory 2011.* Amsterdam: John Benjamins, pp. 217–248.

Rothman, J. (2015). Linguistic and Cognitive Motivations for the Typological Primacy Model (TPM) of Third Language (L3) Transfer: Timing of Acquisition and Proficiency Considered. *Bilingualism: Language and Cognition*, 18, 179–190.

Rothman, J., Alemán Bañón, J., and Alonso, J. G. (2015). Neurolinguistic Measures of Typological Effects in Multilingual Transfer: Introducing an ERP Methodology. *Frontiers in Psychology*, 6, 1–14.

Rothman, J. and Cabrelli Amaro, J. (2010). What Variables Condition Syntactic Transfer? A Look at the L3 Initial State. *Second Language Research*, 26, 198–218.

Rothman, J. and Slabakova, R. (2017). The Generative Approach to SLA and its Place in Modern Second Language Studies. *Studies in Second Language Acquisition.* doi: 10.1017/S0272263117000134.

Ruiz de Zarobe, Y. (2005). Age and Third Language Production: A Longitudinal Study. *International Journal of Multilingualism*, 2 (2), 105–112.

Ruiz de Zarobe, Y. (2008). CLIL and Foreign Language Learning: A Longitudinal Study in the Basque Country. *International Content and Language Integrated Learning Research Journal*, 1 (1), 60–73.

Sánchez, L. (2015). L2 Activation and Blending in Third Language Acquisition: Evidence of Crosslinguistic Influence from the L2 in a Longitudinal Study on the Acquisition of L3 English. *Bilingualism: Language and Cognition*, 18 (2), 252–269.

Sanz, C., Park, H. I., and Lado, B. (2015). A Functional Approach to Cross-Linguistic Influence in ab initio L3 Acquisition. *Bilingualism: Language and Cognition*, 18 (2), 236–251.

Schmid, M. S. (2016). First Language Attrition. *Language Teaching*, 49 (2), 186–212.

Schwartz, B. and Sprouse, R. (1996). L2 Cognitive States and the Full Transfer/Full Access Model. *Second Language Research*, 12, 40–72.

Singh, R. and Carroll, S. (1979). L1, L2 and L3. *Indian Journal of Applied Linguistics*, 5, 51–63.

Singleton, D. (1987). Mother and Other Tongue Influence on Learner French. *Studies in Second Language Acquisition*, 9 (3), 327–345.

Slabakova, R. (2017). The Scalpel Model of Third Language Acquisition. *International Journal of Bilingualism*, 21, 651–665. doi: 1367006916655413.

Slabakova, R. and García-Mayo, M. del P. (2015). The L3 Syntax–Discourse Interface. *Bilingualism: Language and Cognition*, 18, 208–226.

Stedje, A. (1977). Tredjespråksinterferens i fritt tal-en jämförande studie. In R. Palmberg and H. Ringbom (eds.), *Papers from the Conference on Contrastive Linguistics and Error Analysis*. Åbo: Åbo Akademi, pp. 141–158.

Sypiańska, J. (2016). Multilingual Acquisition of Vowels in L1 Polish, L2 Danish and L3 English. *International Journal of Multilingualism*, 13 (4), 476–495.

Tsang, W. L. (2015). Acquisition of English Number Agreement: L1 Cantonese–L2 English–L3 French Speakers versus L1 Cantonese–L2 English speakers. *International Journal of Bilingualism*. doi: 1367006915576398.

Vildomec, V. (1963). *Multilingualism: General Linguistics and Psychology of Speech*. Leiden: A. W. Sythoff.

Vogel, T. (1992). "Englisch und Deutsch gibt es immer Krieg": Sprachverarbeitungsprozesse beim Erwerb des Deutschen als Drittsprache. *Zielsprache Deutsch*, 23 (2), 95–99.

Westergaard, M., Mitrofanova, N., Mykhaylyk, R., and Rodina, Y. (2017). Crosslinguistic Influence in the Acquisition of a Third Language: The Linguistic Proximity Model. *International Journal of Bilingualism*, 21, 666–682. doi: 1367006916648859.

Williams, S. and Hammarberg, B. (1998). Language Switches in L3 Production: Implications for a Polyglot Speaking Model. *Applied Linguistics*, 19, 295–333.

Wrembel, M. (2014). VOT Patterns in the Acquisition of L3 Phonology. *Concordia Working Papers in Applied Linguistics*, 5, 750–770.

Wrembel, M. (2015). *In Search of a New Perspective: Cross-linguistic Influence in the Acquisition of Third Language Phonology*. Poznan: Wydawnictwo Naukowe UAM.

Index

ʒeísmo, 518
θ role. *See* thematic role
φ features. *See* phi features

Aaron, J. E., 584
acquisition, 39–42
  first language, 38, 298
  second language, 40, 298, 649–663, 668–683, 689–704
  variation, 681–682
adjectives. *See* attributive adjectives
African American Vernacular, 568, 569
Agree, 16, 334–336
agreement, 110, 269, 273–275, 330–338, 364–366, 399–403, 698–702
Alexiadou, A., 355, 691
alignment, 32, 40
allophonic relationship, 243
Alvord, S., 157, 675
Amaral, P., 587
Anagnostopoulou, E., 691
analogy, 582–596
Andersen, R. W., 694, 695
archiphoneme, 170, 176
argument structure, 78–79, 308–311, 426–432
article, 696–697
  definite, 361–364
  indefinite, 361–364
Articulatory Phonology, 173
aspect, 43, 693–696
aspiration, 505–507
attitudes, language, 38, 480, 573, 577
attributive adjectives, 351
Autosegmental-Metrical (AM) framework, 213

Baker, M., 309
Barbosa, P., 342
Bardovi-Harlig, K., 450
Belletti, 309
Bermúdez-Otero, R., 42, 266
Bernstein, J. B., 359
Bilingual Interactive Activation Plus model (BIA+), 100

bilingualism, 40, 156, 459–472, 478–488
  second language learners, 246–249
  simultaneous bilinguals, 245–246
binding theory, 12
Blas Arroyo, J. L., 463, 500, 514, 618
bleaching, 584–585
blending, 277
Boersma, P., 39, 40, 41, 248, 673
Boomershine, A., 243
Bosch, L., 240, 241, 242
Bosque, I., 18, 26, 320, 322
boundary tone, 213, 218–221
Bradlow, A., 159
Brown, E. L., 61, 595
Bullock, B., 574, 575
Bybee, J., 52, 54, 58, 59, 604, 606, 607, 608, 695

Cabrelli Amaro, J., 40, 743, 745, 746, 750
calques, 572
Cameron, R., 291, 545–547
Carreiras, M., 701
case, 43
Case theory, 12
Casielles-Suárez, E., 362
Castilianization, 497, 511
ceceo, 174, 503–505, 518
Cedergren, H., 539
change
  contact-induced change, 43, 87, 535
  historical change, 36–37, 38
  language change, 534, 539
  semantic change, 582–596
  sound change, 54
  syntactic change, 582–596
Chierchia, G., 362, 635, 697
Chomsky, N., 12, 14, 309, 315, 322, 330, 334, 377
Cinque, G., 353, 359, 360, 377
Clements, J. C., 81, 465, 466, 467
clitics, 22–24, 42, 382–384, 540, 543–545, 692–693, 725
  laísmo, 507–508, 543
  leísmo, 463, 507–508, 543
  loísmo, 507–508, 543
coarticulation, 57, 147–149, 152, 547
coda, 191–194

code-switching, 467–469, 572
cognates, 100–101
Colantoni, L., 177
Colina, S., 33, 34, 194, 200
collocations, 587, 591
Company Company, C., 585, 591, 592
competence
   communicative competence, 542
   pragmalinguistic competence, 440
   sociolinguistic competence, 681–682
   sociopragmatic competence, 440
complex onsets, 196–197
compounding, 279
concessive markers, 586–587
consonant weight, 193
conservatism, female, 539
consonants, 165–182, 673–679
   aspiration, 172, 204, 467, 553–555, 682
   assibilation, 179–180, 536
   assimilation, 37, 167, 174, 176–177, 206, 508–509
   consonant cluster, 178, 180
   debuccalization, 172, 204
   deletion, 503, 509–510
   fortition, 167, 171
   gemination, 173, 206
   gliding, 205
   lambdacism, 205
   limited spirantization, 168
   neutralization, 37, 170–171, 174–175, 178, 181, 536
   neutralization, incomplete, 181
   perception, 240, 242–243
   rhotacism, 205, 508
   sonority, 39, 41, 195, 196–197
   spirantization, 40, 166–169, 171, 463, 503, 536, 541, 674–675
   velarization, 37, 176, 177, 206, 536
   voicing, 169–170, 174, 206, 463, 679
   weakening, 167, 172–174, 177, 198, 204, 205, 535, 536, 541, 545, 553–555
constituent order. *See* word order
Constraint Demotion Algorithm (CDA), 39
constraints, 194
   faithfulness, 32
   markedness, 32
contact. *See* language contact
Contreras, H., 340, 362
control theory, 12
convergence, 462–465
conversion, morphology, 276
Cooperative Principle, 444
copula, *ser* and *estar*, 82, 425, 653–657, 722
corpora, 74
   analytical tools, 128–129
   available corpora, 55, 125–128
   corpus analysis, 121–139
creoles, 465–467
Croft, W., 603
crosslinguistic influence, 480, 482

data
   elicitation, 385
   elicited data, 124
   found data, 124
Declarative/Procedural Model (D/PM), 654, 659
deixis, 438, 463
del Valle, J., 498, 499

Demonte, V., 359, 499
derivation, 42, 263, 275–281, 359, 360, 426–432
derivational morphology. *See* derivation
Determiner Phrase (DP), 366–368
   DP hypothesis, 352
development. *See* acquisition
   phonological development, 41
dialects
   dialectal variation, 36–37, 296–297, 496–515
   dialectology, 124
Díaz-Campos, M., 59, 128, 466, 503
Differential Object Marking (DOM), 79–80, 315–317, 589–590, 697
digital humanities, 122
diglossia, 460
diminutive, 277–279, 541
discourse, 87–88
   discourse context frequency, 59–61
discourse markers, 469
dislocation, 382–384
distinción, 174, 179, 503–505
Domínguez, L., 376, 695
Dryer, M., 289
Dupoux, E., 244, 246
Dussias, P. E., 104, 109, 111, 700

Eckardt, R., 614
Eckert, P., 530
electroencephalography/event-related potential (EEG/ERP) paradigm, 701
electropalatography (EPG), 34, 177
Elvira, J., 583, 587
ellipsis, 317–319, 367–368
epenthesis, 197, 203
Erker, D., 293, 553–555
Escudero, P., 40, 41, 152, 243, 248, 673
estar and *ser*. *See* copula
Evaluator (EVAL), 32, 199
exemplar model, 62, 64
Extended Projection Principle (EPP), 12, 375
Extended Verb Phrase (EVP), 329
eye-tracking, 110, 111

Fábregas, A., 317
face, 444–449
   face-threatening acts, 445
   negative face, 445
   positive face, 445
Face, T., 248, 671, 675, 679, 680
Fafulas, S., 298, 725
features, 331–338. *See also* phi features
   interpretable features, 14, 332
   morphosyntactic features, 271
   pragmatic features, 408
   uninterpretable features, 14, 332
Fernald, A., 700
Fernández de Molina, E., 505
File-Muriel, R., 57
first language acquisition, 298
Flege, J. E., 238, 248
focus, 43, 372–386
   broad focus, 221–222
   focus–stress alignment, 377–380
   narrow focus, 223–224
Focus Prominence Rule (FPR), 406
Fontanella de Weinberg, M. B., 594
formants, 146

forms of address, 448, 511
  voseo, 534, 536, 540
  tuteo, 511, 517, 534
form-to-meaning associations, 695
fortition, 197, 202
Freezing Effects, 314
frequency, 128, 293, 591
  conserving effect, 57
  reducing effect, 57
  token frequency, 56–58
  type frequency, 58–59
  word, 53, 57, 173
functional compensation, 290
functionalism, 53, 649
future, expression of, 129–138, 725

Gabriel, C., 385
Gallego, A., 314
García-Mayo, M. del P., 746
Gavarró, A., 629, 632, 634
Geeslin, K., 297, 298, 681, 718, 722, 725
gender, grammatical, 269–271, 698–702
gender marking, 111
generative linguistics, 9–26, 330–338, 649
  minimalist program, 14–17, 331–338
  principles and parameters, 11–14
Generator (GEN), 31, 199
Givón, T., 73
Goodall, G., 321
Government and Binding (GB), 12
gradience, 52
  syntactic gradience, 81
Gradual Learning Algorithm (GLA), 39, 40, 41
grammaticality judgment, 18
grammaticalization, 132, 582–596, 603–619
Grimshaw, J., 353, 355
Grinstead, J., 629, 630
Guasti, M. T., 635, 697
Gudmestad, A., 297
Gupton, T., 385
Gutiérrez-Rexach, J., 18, 26, 359, 363, 639
Guy, G., 293, 531, 535

Harley, H., 310, 312
Heine, B., 604, 606
Henríquez Ureña, P., 154, 536,
heritage language, 470
  heritage language speakers, 157, 249–252, 478–488
Hernández-Campoy, J. M., 507, 508, 510, 513
historical linguistics, 299, 582–596
Holmquist, J., 153, 155
Holt, E., 38
homographs, 100–101
homophones, 100–101
Hoot, B., 385
Hopper, P. J., 81, 584
Hualde, J. I., 151, 198, 200, 586
hypercorrection, 173

identity, 485, 500–501, 563–579
ideologies, 487, 573–578
illocutionary force, 442
implicational universals, 72, 75–76
imposition, 446–447
indexicality, 539
inflection, 35–36, 110, 262, 268–275, 330–338
Inflectional Phrase (IP), 330

information structure, 212, 222, 366–368, 372–386, 405–409
insubordination, 84
interface, 392
  syntax–lexicon interface, 393–399
  syntax–morphology interface, 42, 399–403
  syntax–pragmatics interface, 41, 403
  syntax–prosody interface, 409–410
interlanguage, 716
intermediate phrase (ip), 218
intonation languages, 211
intonation(al) phrase (IP), 218
island constructions, 314, 319
Iverson, M., 697

Jaeggli, O., 308
Jegerski, J., 658
Jiménez-Fernández, A., 320

Kanwit, M., 718, 722, 725, 726
Kayne, R., 310
Keating, G. D., 658
Kempchinsky, P., 398,
Kim, J. Y., 250, 251
Klee, C., 463
Klein, C., 543–545

Labov, W., 53, 537, 594
LaFond, I. I., 41
language choice, 564
language contact, 180, 297, 459–472, 535,
language maintenance, 469–470, 567, 578
language shift, 469–470
Lapesa, R., 589
learning algorithms, 39
left periphery, xvii, 24, 25, 317, 353, 365, 366, 382, 409, 410, 587, 589, 636, 637
Levin, B., 309, 312
Lew-Williams, C., 700
lexical access, 95–102
lexical aspect, 427, 693–695
Lexical Aspect Hypothesis (LAH), 694–696
lexical borrowing, 460–462, 540, 572
Lexical Decomposition Grammar (LDG), 431
lexical diffusion, 54
lexical encoding, 677
Lexical Functional Grammar (LFG), 649, 654
lexical neighborhood. See neighborhood density
lexical representation, 61–64
lexical stress, 145, 147, 150, 156, 158, 214–216, 241, 242, 244, 246, 251, 300, 301
lexicalization, 612
lexis, 415–432
  lexical access, 95–102
  lexical borrowing, 460–462, 540, 572
Lightfoot, D., 588
Linford, B., 293
linguistic insecurity, 569
linguistics
  cognitive linguistics, 11, 123
  corpus-based linguistics, 121–139
  functionalism, 649
  generative linguistics, 9–26, 330–338, 649
  historical linguistics, 124
  psycholinguistics, 95–112
  structuralism, 54
Lipski, J., 464, 466, 467, 468, 496, 564

lleísmo, 179
Lleó, C., 634
locality, 307–322
Logical Form (LF), 12
Lope Blanch, J. M., 499
López, L., 317, 318, 337, 408, 697
Lord, G., 679

Marantz, A., 310, 311
markedness, 193, 700
Martín Butragueño, P., 503
McCarthy, J. J., 33, 35, 42
McNally, L., 363
Menke, M, 671
Merge, 14
Michnowicz, J., 540
Miller, D., 697, 701
Milroy, J., 499, 500
Minimalist Program, 14–17, 331–338
Molina-Martos, I., 503
Montrul, S., 368, 689
mora, 192–193
Moreno-Fernández, F., 499, 501, 514, 515
morphological future, 463
morphology, 34–36, 42, 261–262
morphophonology, 36
morphosyntactic features
    cumulative exponence, 272
    extended exponence, 272
    syncretism, 272
morphosyntax
    second language morphosyntax, 689–704
movement, 22, 332–334, 359, 360. *See also* wh-movement

Nadeu, M., 150, 158, 159, 246
Navarro Tomás, T., 147, 148, 149, 150, 212
negation, 43, 319–322
neighborhood density, 97
    orthographic neighbors, 102
    phonological neighbors, 97
Neogrammarian controversy, 53
nominal domain, 366–368, 696–702
nominalization, 355
nouns. *See* nominal domain
nuclear stress, 215
Nuclear Stress Rule (NSR), 406
number, 698–702

Obligatory Contour Principle (OCP), 196
operator theory, 12
Optimality Theory (OT), 31–44, 167, 174, 176, 177, 191, 197
Ortega-Llebaria, M., 248
Ortega-Santos, I., 315
Otheguy, R., 291, 295, 465, 548–555
Overt Pronoun Constraint (OPC), 658

pan-Hispanic norm, 499–500
Penny, R., 504, 508, 592
perception, 237–252
    consonants, 677, 682
    second language learners, 672, 677
    vowels, 672
Perceptual Assimilation Model (PAM), 159, 238, 668
Pérez-Leroux, A. T., 368, 628
perfectivity, 693–696

perseverance effect. *See* priming
phi-features, 16, 337
phonemes, 166
phonological neighbors, 128
phonology, 31–44, 52–65
    second language phonology, 40, 668–683
Phrase Structure (PS), 392
pidgins, 465–467
Pierrehumbert, J., 191
pitch accent, 213, 218–221
pitch accent density, 216
pitch contours, 211
pitch range, 229
p-movement, 381, 407
politeness theory, 444–449
Poplack, S., 465, 468, 469, 540
Posio, P., 300
Potowski, K., 470
Poverty of the Stimulus (POS), 314, 661
pragmatic enrichment, 584–585
pragmaticalization, 610
pragmatics, 294, 437–450
    macropragmatics, 438–439, 443
    micropragmatics, 438–439, 443
    pragmalinguistics, 438
    sociopragmatics, 438
    speech act, 441–444, 447, 448
prenuclear stress, 215
prestige, 56, 497–501
    covert prestige, 56, 538
    overt prestige, 538
presupposed information, 372
priming, 292
Prince, A., 31, 33, 191
Principles and Parameters (P&P), 286
processability theory, 649, 654
pro-drop, 286, 339, 464, 657–661, 723
pronouns
    pronominal reference, 657–661
    subject pronouns, 286–301, 339, 404, 464, 543, 548–553, 636, 657–661, 722
prosodic phrasing, 211, 218
prosody, 40, 43, 241–242, 244–245, 246, 251–252, 483, 679–681
psycholinguistics, 95–112
quantitative approaches, 123, 719

Quilis, A., 146, 149, 151, 212

reanalysis, 582–596
recategorization, 586
reflexive *se*, 81
rehilamiento, 171. *See also* ʒeísmo; sheísmo; žeísmo; zheísmo
Reinhart, T., 309, 376, 379
resyllabification, 179
Revised Hierarchical Model (RHM), 99
rhyme, 191–194
rhythm, 216–217
Rivas, J., 595
Rivero, M. L., 592,
Rizzi, L., 25, 315, 340, 396, 587, 638
Roberts, I., 588
Rodríguez Louro, C., 616
Rogers, B., 157, 675
Rohena-Madrazo, M., 172, 539, 547–548
Romero, J., 312, 317
Ronquest, R., 157,

root, 262, 265–268
Rooth, M., 372
Rothman, J., 700, 701, 742, 745, 746, 750, 751

s insertion, 56, 173
s realization, 52–65, 174, 204, 463, 505–507, 536, 539, 541, 553–555, 679, 682
Saab, A., 318, 319, 367
Sánchez, L., 359
Schmidt, L. B., 679, 682
Schmitt, C., 655
Schwenter, S., 85, 595, 611, 615
scrambling, 381–382
Sebastián-Gallés, N., 240, 241, 245
second language variation, 716
second language acquisition, 108–111, 298, 649–663, 668–683, 689–704
second language learners, 246–249
second language phonetics, 668–683
second language phonology, 40, 668–683
second language production, 40
second language variation, 716–727
semantics
  semantic extension, 603–619
  verbal semantics, 293
ser and *estar*. *See* copula
Serrano, M. J., 514
seseo, 174, 503–505, 518
Shea, C., 243, 247
sheísmo, 536, 539, 547–548
Shin, N. L., 295
Silva-Corvalán, C., 294, 462, 464, 483
Simonet, M., 156, 251, 671,
skill theory, 650
Slabakova, R., 744, 746
Smolensky, P., 31, 39
Snyder, W., 313
sociocultural theory, 650
sociolinguistics, 154–155
  envelope of variation, 287
  female conservatism, 539
  variation, 37–39, 529–556
  variationist sociolinguistics, 287, 538, 716–727
Solon, M., 678, 681, 726
sonority, 39, 41, 195–197, 198, 201
Sonority Sequencing Principle (SSP), 195–196, 201, 203
Sosa, J. M., 213
Soto-Faraco, S., 244
Sp_ToBI (Spanish tones and break indices labeling system), 217
speech acts
  illocutionary, 441
  locutionary, 441
  perlocutionary, 441
Speech Learning Model (SLM), 238. *See also* perception
speech perception, 237–252
  adult speech perception, 242–245
  consonants, 240, 242–243, 247, 250
  infant speech perception, 239–242
  prosody, 241–242, 244–245, 246, 248–249, 251–252
  second language learners, 246–249
  vowels, 240–241, 243–244, 245–246, 247–248, 250–251

spell-out, 16, 321
spirantization, 40, 166–169, 171, 536, 674–675
standardization, 497–501
statistical analysis, 719
stem, 262, 265–268
Stepanov, A., 314
stress, 149–150, 214–216, 671
  lexical stress, 241, 251
stress-timed languages, 216
study abroad, 724–726
subcategorization, 392
subjacency theory, 12
subject pronouns, 548–553
subjects, 286–301, 338–345, 464–465
  null subjects, 41, 286, 339–340, 657–661
  overt subjects, 340–345, 657–661
Suñer, M., 9, 26, 321
svarabatic vowel. *See* epenthesis
syllable, 147–149
  coda, 191–194, 198–199, 204–206
  nucleus, 191–194, 197–198, 203
  onset, 196–197, 202–203
  rhyme, 191–194
syllable weight, 679–680
syllable-timed language, 216
syntax, 42–44, 307–322, 372–386, 392–410. *See also* word order
  left–periphery, 24, 408
  syntax–lexicon interface, 393–399
  syntax–morphology interface, 399–403
  syntax–pragmatics interface, 403–405
  syntax–prosody interface, 409–410
Systemic Functional Linguistics, 73

t/d deletion, 54, 60
thematic hierarchy, 355, 357,
thematic role, 394
theme vowels, 263
Theta Criterion, 394
Ticio, M. E., 367
tonal languages, 211
Tones and Break Indices (ToBI), 213, 217
Toribio, J., 574, 575, 576, 577
Torrens, V., 628, 633
Torres Cacoullos, R., 87, 292, 298, 587, 611, 615
transfer, 463
transitivity, 80–82, 309
Traugott, E., 584, 603, 605, 606, 611
Travis, C., 87, 292, 298
Trudgill, P., 507, 508, 510, 538
truncation, 276
tuteo, 511
typology, 288–289

underspecification, 167, 170, 177, 201
unidirectionality, 606, 608
Uniformity of Theta Assignment Hypothesis (UTAH), 395
Universal Grammar (UG), 17, 659
Uriagereka, J., 314
US Spanish, 249–252
usage-based approaches, 52–65, 650, 662

Valenzuela, E., 699
VanPatten, B., 653, 658
variable rule, 129, 134
variation. *See also* sociolinguistics
  acquisition of variation, 681–682

cross-linguistic variation, 76, 332
diachronic variation, 299
dialectal variation, 36–37, 151–154, 170, 172, 296–297, 496–515, 529–556
envelope of variation, 287
idiolectal variation, 529–556
sociolectal variation, 154–155, 532, 537–540
sociolinguistics, 122
stable variation, 539
stylistic variation, 150–151, 157, 541
verbal domain, 307–322, 329–345, 542, 691–696
   aspect, 43, 693–696
   extended verb phrase, 329
   mood, 723
   tense, 725
   verbal inflection, 268–275
verbs. *See* verbal domain
Villa-García, J., 310, 343
Voice Onset Time (VOT), 240, 242–243, 250, 482, 673–674
voseo, 511, 534, 536, 540
vowels, 145–160, 670–673
   centralization, 149–150, 151, 156
   devoicing, 152, 536
   duration, 672
   nasalization, 177, 203
   perception, 243–244, 245–246
   svarabatic vowel. *See* epenthesis
   unstressed vowel reduction, 149–150, 153, 156, 671
   vocalic sequences, 200–202

vowel duration, 146, 148, 149
vowel harmony, 153, 507
vowel quality, 145, 147, 148, 670–673
vowel raising, 153, 155, 541
vowel reduction, 216
vowel space expansion, 151

Wexler, K., 631, 632,
White, L., 699, 700
wh-movement, 12
wh-questions, 229
Willis, E., 149, 151, 505
Wilson, D. V., 617
word, 261–262
word order, 299, 358, 372–386, 401–403, 464, 698
word phenomena
   derivation, 275–281
   inflection, 110, 268–275
working memory, 108

X′ (X-bar) theory, 12

yeísmo, 179, 502, 518, 536

Zampini, M., 242, 249
žeísmo, 171
Zentella, A. C., 291, 295, 542, 548–553, 565, 567, 568, 569
zheísmo, 536, 539
Zubizarreta, M. L., 363, 367, 375, 380, 381, 382

Printed in the United States
by Baker & Taylor Publisher Services